International Directory of
COMPANY
HISTORIES

International Directory of
COMPANY
HISTORIES

VOLUME 47

Editor

Jay P. Pederson

St J

**ST. JAMES
PRESS**®

THOMSON
GALE

Detroit • New York • San Diego • San Francisco • Cleveland • New Haven, Conn. • Waterville, Maine • London • Munich

THOMSON

GALE

International Directory of Company Histories, Volume 47

Jay P. Pederson, Editor

Project Editor
Miranda H. Ferrara

Editorial
Erin Bealmear, Joann Cerrito, Jim Craddock,
Stephen Cusack, Peter M. Gareffa,
Kristin Hart, Melissa Hill,
Margaret Mazurkiewicz, Carol A. Schwartz,
Christine Tomassini, Michael J. Tyrkus

Imaging and Multimedia
Randy Bassett, Robert Duncan, Lezlie Light

Manufacturing
Rhonda Williams

LIBRARY OF CONGRESS CATALOG NUMBER 89-190943

ISBN: 1-55862-465-1

BRITISH LIBRARY CATALOGUING IN PUBLICATION DATA

International directory of company histories. Vol. 47
I. Jay P. Pederson
33.87409

Printed in the United States of America
10 9 8 7 6 5 4 3 2 1

CONTENTS _____

Company Histories

PREFACE

The St. James Press series *The International Directory of Company Histories (IDCH)* is intended for reference use by students, business people, librarians, historians, economists, investors, job candidates, and others who seek to learn more about the historical development of the world's most important companies. To date, *IDCH* has covered over 5,550 companies in 47 volumes.

Inclusion Criteria

Most companies chosen for inclusion in *IDCH* have achieved a minimum of US$25 million in annual sales and are leading influences in their industries or geographical locations. Companies may be publicly held, private, or nonprofit. State-owned companies that are important in their industries and that may operate much like public or private companies also are included. Wholly owned subsidiaries and divisions are profiled if they meet the requirements for inclusion. Entries on companies that have had major changes since they were last profiled may be selected for updating.

The *IDCH* series highlights 10% private and nonprofit companies, and features updated entries on approximately 45 companies per volume.

Entry Format

Each entry begins with the company's legal name, the address of its headquarters, its telephone, toll-free, and fax numbers, and its web site. A statement of public, private, state, or parent ownership follows. A company with a legal name in both English and the language of its headquarters country is listed by the English name, with the native-language name in parentheses.

The company's founding or earliest incorporation date, the number of employees, and the most recent available sales figures follow. Sales figures are given in local currencies with equivalents in U.S. dollars. For some private companies, sales figures are estimates and indicated by the abbreviation *est.* The entry lists the exchanges on which a company's stock is traded and its ticker symbol, as well as the company's NAIC codes.

Entries generally contain a *Company Perspectives* box which provides a short summary of the company's mission, goals, and ideals, a *Key Dates* box highlighting milestones in the company's history, lists of *Principal Subsidiaries, Principal Divisions, Principal Operating Units, Principal Competitors,* and articles for *Further Reading.*

American spelling is used throughout *IDCH,* and the word "billion" is used in its U.S. sense of one thousand million.

Sources

Entries have been compiled from publicly accessible sources both in print and on the Internet such as general and academic periodicals, books, annual reports, and material supplied by the companies themselves.

Cumulative Indexes

IDCH contains three indexes: the **Index to Companies**, which provides an alphabetical index to companies discussed in the text as well as to companies profiled, the **Index to Industries**, which allows researchers to locate companies by their principal industry, and the **Geographic Index**, which lists companies alphabetically by the country of their headquarters. The indexes are cumulative and specific instructions for using them are found immediately preceding each index.

Suggestions Welcome

Comments and suggestions from users of *IDCH* on any aspect of the product as well as suggestions for companies to be included or updated are cordially invited. Please write:

The Editor
International Directory of Company Histories
St. James Press
27500 Drake Rd.
Farmington Hills, Michigan 48331-3535

ABBREVIATIONS FOR FORMS OF COMPANY INCORPORATION _____

A.B.	Aktiebolaget (Sweden)
A.G.	Aktiengesellschaft (Germany, Switzerland)
A.S.	Aksjeselskap (Denmark, Norway)
A.S.	Atieselskab (Denmark)
A.Ş.	Anomin Şirket (Turkey)
B.V.	Besloten Vennootschap met beperkte, Aansprakelijkheid (The Netherlands)
Co.	Company (United Kingdom, United States)
Corp.	Corporation (United States)
G.I.E.	Groupement d'Intérêt Economique (France)
GmbH	Gesellschaft mit beschränkter Haftung (Germany)
H.B.	Handelsbolaget (Sweden)
Inc.	Incorporated (United States)
KGaA	Kommanditgesellschaft auf Aktien (Germany)
K.K.	Kabushiki Kaisha (Japan)
LLC	Limited Liability Company (Middle East)
Ltd.	Limited (Canada, Japan, United Kingdom, United States)
N.V.	Naamloze Vennootschap (The Netherlands)
OY	Osakeyhtiöt (Finland)
OAO	Otkrytoe Aktsionernoe Obshchestve (Russia)
OOO	Obshchestvo s Ogranichennoi Otvetstvennostiu (Russia)
PLC	Public Limited Company (United Kingdom)
PTY.	Proprietary (Australia, Hong Kong, South Africa)
S.A.	Société Anonyme (Belgium, France, Switzerland)
SpA	Società per Azioni (Italy)
ZAO	Zakrytoe Aktsionernoe Obshchestve (Russia)

ABBREVIATIONS FOR CURRENCY _____

$	United States dollar	KD	Kuwaiti dinar
£	United Kingdom pound	L	Italian lira
¥	Japanese yen	LuxFr	Luxembourgian franc
A$	Australian dollar	M$	Malaysian ringgit
AED	United Arab Emirates dirham	N	Nigerian naira
		Nfl	Netherlands florin
B	Thai baht	NIS	Israeli new shekel
B	Venezuelan bolivar	NKr	Norwegian krone
BFr	Belgian franc	NT$	Taiwanese dollar
C$	Canadian dollar	NZ$	New Zealand dollar
CHF	Switzerland franc	P	Philippine peso
COL	Colombian peso	PLN	Polish zloty
Cr	Brazilian cruzado	PkR	Pakistan Rupee
CZK	Czech Republic koruny	Pta	Spanish peseta
DA	Algerian dinar	R	Brazilian real
Dfl	Netherlands florin	R	South African rand
DKr	Danish krone	RMB	Chinese renminbi
DM	German mark	RO	Omani rial
E£	Egyptian pound	Rp	Indonesian rupiah
Esc	Portuguese escudo	Rs	Indian rupee
EUR	Euro dollars	Ru	Russian ruble
FFr	French franc	S$	Singapore dollar
Fmk	Finnish markka	Sch	Austrian schilling
GRD	Greek drachma	SFr	Swiss franc
HK$	Hong Kong dollar	SKr	Swedish krona
HUF	Hungarian forint	SRls	Saudi Arabian riyal
IR£	Irish pound	W	Korean won
K	Zambian kwacha	W	South Korean won

International Directory of
COMPANY
HISTORIES

Abiomed, Inc.

22 Cherry Hill Drive
Danvers, Massachusetts 09123
U.S.A.
Telephone: (978) 777-5410
Fax: (978) 777-8411
Web site: http://www.abiomed.com

Public Company
Incorporated: 1987
Employees: 264
Sales: $24.9 million (2001)
Stock Exchanges: NASDAQ
Ticker Symbol: ABMD
NAIC: 339112 Surgical and Medical Instrument
   Manufacturing

Abiomed, Inc. gained world recognition in 2001 when its AbioCor artificial heart, the first fully implantable device of its kind, was placed in a human being. The event was the culmination of almost 20 years of effort for the Boston-area company. Through grants, private investments, and conservative management, it has been able to conduct its pursuit of the artificial heart without having to sacrifice its independence, as has been the case with numerous biotechs that have sold themselves piecemeal to the major pharmaceuticals. Although the artificial heart has been the focus of Abiomed, the company is also involved in developing devices to help assist heart patients on a temporary and permanent basis. Abiomed's BVS5000 cardiac support system is used worldwide as a bridge-to-recovery device, essentially performing the functions of a heart to allow patients sufficient time for their natural hearts to rest, heal, and recover normal function, generally following heart surgery.

First Artificial Heart Developed in the 1950s

Heart replacement has been an age-old dream of medicine. However, it was not until the 1950s that Dr. Paul Winchell developed an implantable artificial heart, which he subsequently donated to the University of Utah. There, a group of scientists led by Dutch-born Willem Kolff developed a working model, testing it in animals in 1957. The technology was advanced enough that in 1964 the National Institutes of Health established the Artificial Heart Program Office. Three years later Dr. Christian Bernard performed the first heart transplant in Cape Town, South Africa, which ultimately resulted in a successful method of replacing damaged or diseased hearts. The need for an artificial heart remained, because the number of available donor hearts would always fall short of the need.

In 1969, Denton Cooley of the Texas Heart Institute implanted the first human artificial heart in a patient, serving as a bridge for 64 hours before the 47-year-old patient received a transplant. With scientists in the 1960s making steady progress in landing a man on the moon, it was assumed by many that the development of the artificial heart was very much in reach. It was seen as the Apollo project of the medical field. Progress, however, would prove to be painfully slow.

It was the Jarvik-7 heart, named after Robert Jarvik, who was instrumental in its development at the University of Utah, that truly excited the public imagination about the realistic possibilities of an artificial heart. In 1982, surgeon William DeVries implanted the Jarvik-7 in a retired dentist named Barney Clark, for whom a transplant was not a medical option. He died after 112 days from organ failure not related to the heart device. Several other patients received the Jarvik-7, with one man, William Schroeder, living as long as 620 days. Excitement over the artificial heart, however, was soon replaced by revulsion. The device was a pneumatic pump that connected an external compressor the size of a washing machine to the patient through two six-foot air hoses attached to the chest. Although the patients were kept alive, their quality of life was poor. During his four months on the Jarvik-7, Clark suffered from strokes and infections, and grew so depressed that he begged his doctors to allow him to die. Schroeder lived far longer than Clark, and he too suffered: 70 percent of the time he had a fever, for 366 days he had to be fed through a tube, and he endured four strokes caused by blood clots. The Jarvik-7 was simply too invasive: the tubes leading into the chest were both a breeding ground for infection and a source of stroke-inducing blood clots. After boldly announcing that the age of the artificial heart was dawning, Jarvik ultimately abandoned hope that the idea would ever be fully realized. Nevertheless, he improved the Jarvik-7, helping to develop a smaller model that found use as a bridge to a heart transplant.

A number of companies shared Jarvik's early enthusiasm for inventing the human heart, including the forerunner of Abiomed, Applied Biomedical Corp., which was formed in 1981. The founding scientists, led by Dr. David M. Lederman, were working together for the medical research division of Avco Corp. when they decided to start their own company, taking with them some of Avco's government-funded research and development contracts. Lederman—Abiomed's chairman, president, and CEO—earned a doctorate in Aerospace Engineering from Cornell University before joining Avco in 1972 and becoming chairman of the Medical Research Group. He originated the design of blood pumps and valves that Applied Biomedical exploited in its effort to develop an artificial heart. By the mid-1980s, there more than a dozen other companies with a similar goal, many of which were forging ties with major corporations. Applied Biomedical received some early funding from Eli Lilly & Co. but was careful not to be become too deeply tied to a corporate giant or incur heavy debt.

Applied Biomedical elected to husband its money, relying on NIH research grants and a private investment group, and developing other products to sell while technology advanced far enough to make an implantable artificial heart a reality. After optimism over the Jarvik heart gave way to disenchantment in the mid-1980s, the company resolved to be patient. It developed the Bi-Ventricular Support System 5000 (the BVS5000) and began selling it in Europe in 1987. Not only did the device supply a source of income, it provided a way to test technology that could be used in a complete artificial heart. The company also looked to develop other unrelated, interim products such as advanced dental probes.

Incorporated in 1987

In preparation for a public offering of stock, Abiomed was incorporated in 1987 and Applied Biomedical subsequently merged into it. Abiomed then went public at $11 per share. It also continued to seek out research grants, receiving in 1988 a five-year, $5.6 million NIH contract to develop an artificial heart in collaboration with the Texas Heart Institute. In all, NIH awarded Abiomed four national grants totaling $20 million. However, Dr. Laude Lenfant, director of NIH's National Heart, Lung, and Blood Institute, ultimately announced that after awarding nearly $240 million for two decades the unit was terminating all grants investigating the development of a total artificial heart, maintaining that "the biology didn't work" and preferring instead to focus on heart-assist devices. An advisory panel soon endorsed the funding of artificial heart research, and politicians from states impacted by the loss of the funding also brought pressure to bear, eventually forcing Lenfant to reverse his decision. At the very least, the incident reflected the lessening expectations of success in developing a viable artificial heart.

Abiomed pressed on in its research efforts, electing to pursue a risky strategy of not patenting its technology as much as possible. Because an artificial heart was such a long-term, complicated endeavor, patents taken out on early, but key, developments might easily expire by the time the company had an approved device ready to market. Abiomed preferred to maintain trade secrets and not start the clock on patents, which lasted 20 years, until the last possible moment. In some cases, however, because of grant requirements, the company had to reveal how certain technology worked. In these instances, patent protection was sought. In 1989, Abiomed received its first patent, which covered the hydraulic pumping system key to its concept for an artificial heart.

Efforts at producing secondary products to generate revenues also continued. In 1989, Abiomed also received FDA approval to market the Perio Temp Probe, a microprocessor-based instrument intended to detect gum disease by measuring the minute differences in temperature between normal and inflamed tissues. Later the company developed the Halimeter, which detected bad breath. To consolidate its dental business, a subsidiary named Abiodent was formed in 1990. Also in that year, Abiomed gained FDA approval on a noninvasive device to detect lead content in adults. Two years later, following five years of trials, the FDA approved the BVS5000 for sale in the United States. Because of these interim products, Abiomed generated increasing revenues, which grew from $2 million in 1992 to $16.5 million in 1997. The company was also able to turn an annual net loss of $5.1 million in 1992 to profits of $500,000 in 1996 and $700,000 in 1997. After years of risky research, not only had Abiomed maintained its independence, it was debt free, with millions in the bank to support a final push and get the company through extensive FDA clinical trials for an artificial heart, provided it could actually produce such a device.

In the fall of 1993, Abiomed and its partner, the Texas Heart Institute, were only one of three groups to be awarded contracts by the National Heart, Lung, and Blood Institute to complete the final development of a battery-powered heart. It was clear that whoever was first to reach the market with a product would hold a significant advantage. Abiomed imposed a deadline on itself, intending to begin clinical trials in the year 2000, and began a final push in its research. The company raised the necessary cash by selling a 14 percent stake to Genzyme Corp. for $15 million. Genzyme's chairman, CEO, and president, Henri A. Termeer, was a member of Abiomed's board of directors and therefore familiar with the company's research efforts. In addition, the two companies agreed to work together on the new field of "biosurgery," which combined biotechnology with biomedical engineering. The emphasis would be on minimally invasive cardiac surgery.

To meet the demands of completing its artificial heart, Abiomed added staff, essentially doubling in size by the fall of 1997. It stress-tested components to ensure reliability and suc-

Key Dates:

1981: Applied Biomedical Corp. is formed.
1987: Applied Biomedical is merged into newly formed Abiomed, which is taken public.
1994: The National Institutes of Health (NIH) selects company to receive funding for final stage of artificial heart development.
2000: The Food and Drug Administration (FDA) grants approval to conduct clinical trials on the AbioCor artificial heart.
2001: First patient receives the AbioCor and lives 152 days.

cessfully implanted the devices in calves. Because of the history of the Jarvik-7, the company was very sensitive about the ethical concerns surrounding the use of an artificial heart. In 1999, it enlisted Elizabeth Haavik Morreim of the University of Tennessee's College of Medicine to set up an independent Patient Advocacy Council, which would name a knowledgeable mentor for each patient involved in clinical trials of the device. Other than Morreim, no members of the council were to be revealed to the media, and Abiomed was also not permitted to interfere with the council's work. Moreover, no council members, surgeons, or any other parties connected to the clinical phase were permitted to hold stock in Abiomed. The company also produced a lengthy consent agreement, totaling some 13 pages, detailing 14 potentially fatal risks.

Abiomed's artificial heart, made of titanium and plastic, was originally called PulsaCor, then changed to AbioCor. It incorporated technologies unavailable to the Jarvik-7, using bladder-like liquid pumps instead of a bulky pneumatic system and a microprocessor the size of a videocassette embedded in the abdomen to adjust the blood flow. Improved batteries also eliminated the need for external power, allowing recipients of the AbioCor to leave their beds, unlike the tethered Jarvik patients. To eliminate any tubing or wiring that might break the skin and cause infection, a spiral induction coil located under the skin permitted recharging of the lithium-ion battery cell. Streamlined in comparison to the Jarvik-7, the AbioCor, roughly the size of a grapefruit and weighing two pounds, remained a relatively large unit, only suitable at this stage for use in males.

While pre-clinical work proceeded on the AbioCor, Abiomed elected to discontinue its dental business, which was not performing as hoped. The company suffered a further setback when it had to issue a recall on some of its BVS5000 units. Increased spending on AbioCor also resulted in mounting losses. Nevertheless, Abiomed, thanks to disciplined management of its funds, remained well financed. In September 2000, in fact, the company was able to acquire the exclusive rights to the so-called Penn State Heart and the assets of BeneCor Heart Systems, a company created to commercialize the artificial heart developed by the Pennsylvania State University. The BeneCor applied slightly different techniques, which might prove useful in pursuing the next generation of artificial hearts. Lederman characterized Abiomed's position as having ''both the Mercedes and Rolls-Royce of artificial hearts.''

Although Abiomed did not meet its goal of entering clinical trials in 2000, by the end of that year it sought approval from the FDA to begin testing the AbioCor on humans. A few weeks later the FDA granted permission to implant the device in five patients. Over the ensuing months, the company prepared to take the next crucial steps. Rather than becoming the victim of media hype, Abiomed downplayed expectations and tried to conduct its business in secret. It looked for candidates who had less then 30 days to live and who had no chance for a heart transplant or any other way to survive. The initial goal was to double the patient's life expectancy to 60 days. The company also made it clear that all five patients were certain to die in a relatively short period of time. Moreover, while preparing to conduct the initial implant, Abiomed quietly began to file for a series of patents covering every aspect of the technology involved in the AbioCor. As had been the plan for over a dozen years, the company now started the clock on the 20-year patent period.

AbioCor Implanted in First Patient in 2001

On July 2, 2001, a surgical team led by Dr. Laman A. Gray and Dr. Robert D. Dowling implanted the AbioCor in the chest of an anonymous 59-year-old male patient, ushering in a new era in the development of the artificial heart. Everyone involved with the project was protective of the patient and it was not until 51 days after the operation that his identity was revealed at his own request to head off speculation. He was Robert Tools, a former teacher and telephone worker. To the surprise of most gathered for his first public appearance, he walked into the press conference. In June, when he had first met with the surgical team after reading about the AbioCor in a *Newsweek* article, he barely had enough strength to speak. Tools's condition improved enough in the weeks following his press conference that he was able to take walks with his wife in a nearby park and engage in other activities with his family. Without question, the quality of his life had been significantly improved by the introduction of the AbioCor.

The subsequent recipients of the AbioCor faced much less media attention. The second operation occurred in Louisville on September 13, 2001, just two days after the terrorist attacks on the Pentagon and New York City. Tools eventually suffered a debilitating stroke on November 11 and never recovered, dying later in the month after living 152 days with the world's first fully implanted artificial heart. Nevertheless, the clinical trial showed enough early success that the FDA approved the AbioCor for use with an additional five patients. After another patient suffered a stroke caused by a blood clot, Abiomed decided in early 2002 on a design modification, eliminating a small plastic cuff that had been necessary for use with animal subjects. The company was not certain that the cuff was the cause of the blood clots, but it was a likely suspect, and it served no function in humans. The company also announced that it planned to have a smaller model of the AbioCor, suitable for all adults, ready for testing by 2004. Even though the clinical trials for the original model were far from over, the company began looking forward. Although the company had already achieved a notable success, the result of 20 years of dedicated effort, the future remained uncertain. Should the FDA allow Abiomed to market its artificial heart, there appeared to be a potentially sizeable market for the product, but there also remained a number of uncertainties. Other devices might replace it—not only rival artificial hearts but also cardiac-assisted devices that had the advantage of using a patient's real heart as a backup. Moreover, there was the possibility that scientists might one day ''grow'' organs employing new biotech discoveries. Although such a concept might currently belong to the realm of science fiction, the idea of a human being surviving even five minutes with a portable mechanical heart was once considered equally as fantastic.

Principal Subsidiaries

Abiomed Cardiovascular, Inc.; Abiomed R&D, Inc.; Abiomed B.V.

Principal Competitors

ATS Medical; Arrow International; Boston Scientific Corporation; Edwards Lifesciences; Medtronic, Inc.; St. Jude Medical, Inc.; Thoratec Corp.; Zoll Medical.

Further Reading

Altman, Lawrence K., ''For Heart Surgeons, Many Careful Steps,'' *New York Times,* July 10, 2001, p. F1.

——, ''Self-Contained Mechanical Hearts Throbs for First Time in Human,'' *New York Times,* July 4, 2001, p. A1.

Cook, Gareth, ''Heart Device Faces a Challenge,'' *Boston Globe,* December 15, 2001, p. A1.

Cowley, Geoffrey, and Anne Underwood, ''Next Frontiers: New Heart, New Hope,'' *Newsweek,* June 25, 2001, pp. 42–49.

Hall, Alan, ''Why This May Change Health Care As We Know It,'' *Business Week,* September 24, 2001, p. 64.

Hamilton, Anita, ''Invention of the Year,'' *Time,* November 19, 2001, pp. 74–75.

Johannes, Laura, and Antonio Regalado, ''Milestone Artificial Heart Raises Hopes—and Faces Competition,'' *Wall Street Journal,* July 5, 2001, p. B1.

Knox, Richard A., ''Building a Better (Artificial) Heart,'' *Boston Globe,* April 18, 2000, p. F1.

Krasner, Jeffrey, ''Abiomed Puts Soul into Heart,'' *Boston Globe,* July 11, 2001, p. C1.

——, ''Abiomed's Pulse Is on Its Patents,'' *Boston Globe,* August 1, 2001, p. C1.

McCabe, Kathy, ''To Mend a Broken Heart,'' *Boston Globe,* February 13, 1994, p. 80.

Regalado, Antonio, ''CPR for the Artificial Heart,'' *Technology Review,* May/June 1999, pp. 53–55.

Salemi, Tom, ''Abiomed Stock Shows Heart After Big Investments,'' *Boston Business Journal,* August 25, 1997.

—Ed Dinger

Alvis Plc

34 Grosvenor Gardens
London SW1W 0AL
United Kingdom
Telephone: (+44) 20 7808 8888
Fax: (+44) 20 7808 8877
Web site: http://www.alvis.co.uk

Public Company
Incorporated: 1909 as TG John Ltd.
Employees: 1,600
Sales: £203.5 million ($325.6 million) (2000)
Stock Exchanges: London
Ticker Symbol: ALV
NAIC: 336992 Military Armored Vehicle, Tank, and
   Tank Component Manufacturing

Alvis Plc has weathered the odds to become a candidate for the position as the United Kingdom's sole surviving armored vehicle supplier. After absorbing former rival GKN's armored vehicle division in 1998, Alvis has made public its intention to acquire Vickers Defence Systems, the heavy-armored vehicle component of Rolls-Royce, in 2002. The acquisition would not only place Alvis as the United Kingdom's top armored vehicle maker but also give it a leading place on the European market. Alvis concentrates on designing and manufacturing light armored vehicles, such as the wheeled armored vehicle Scarab, the Supacat all-terrain vehicle, the Warrior infantry fighting vehicle, the Piranha armored vehicle, and the Stormer armored vehicle. Alvis is also a partner in the MRAV (multi-role armored vehicle) being developed by the Artec consortium. The company, headquartered in London, has manufacturing facilities both in the United Kingdom and, through its tracked armored vehicle subsidiary Hägglunds, in Sweden and elsewhere in Scandinavia. Led by CEO and Chairman Nicholas Prest, Alvis has undergone a thorough streamlining since the end of the 1990s, cutting out most of its noncore operations, such as its stake in Singapore's Avimo optical glasses operation, a remote controlled bomb disposal robotics unit, and its Barracuda Technologies camouflage equipment subsidiary.

Automobile Maker in the 1920s

Alvis began operations when T.G. John, an engineer who had designed battleships for Vickers during World War I, founded a business to design and manufacture motor cars. The company, TG John Ltd., was based in Coventry, which had by then become a major British automotive manufacturing center. John's earliest production, however, focused on manufacturing stationary and scooter engines while the company developed its own automotive design.

By 1920, John had found its first automobile, based on designs by French engineer Geoffrey de Freville, who had set up a company producing aluminum pistons in 1914. De Freyville chose the name "Alvis" for his automobile design, in part because it sounded good in a variety of languages. The first Alvis car, called the 10/30, was launched in 1920, and by the following year, the company had changed its name to The Alvis Car & Engineering Co. Ltd.

The launch of the 10/30 was not enough to guarantee the company's survival, and the company began to waver toward bankruptcy. In 1922, the company brought in two new employees. G.T. Smith-Clarke, who had designed cars for Daimler, became chief engineer, and W.M. Dunn was named chief draughtsman. Both were to remain with the company for nearly 30 years and took over the design and engineering of the company's automobiles. T.G. John, meantime, shifted his focus toward the company's administrative and financial operations.

In 1923, Alvis launched its second model, 12/50, which became the company's first successful automobile. By then the company had gone bankrupt and was placed into receivership. Yet the success of the 12/50 enabled the company to climb back onto its feet and by the end of the decade Alvis had built a strong reputation for the quality of its automobiles and for its technical innovation. During the decade, Alvis models came to include such features as front-wheel drive, an all-synchromesh gearbox, and four-wheel independent suspension, which not only helped win the company new orders, but also helped it win a number of races, including the Brookline 200 in 1923, won with a car featuring an engine with four valves per cylinder. By then, the company already had carved out a niche for

7

Company Perspectives:

The strategic aim of Alvis is to achieve above average returns to shareholders through profitable growth in the market for military vehicles and related products. In turn, this requires that we satisfy the aspirations of our customers and employees in a high degree.

In pursuit of this aim Alvis employs a business formula which combines: high quality applications engineering and project management; concentration on ''high-end'' product niches; intense efforts to understand our customer needs and match our product offerings to them; global marketing reach; and a management style which mixes delegation and encouragement of entrepreneurship with simple but effective controls.

itself in the luxury car class, as something of a ''poor man's Bentley.''

The 12/50 was replaced by models including the Speed 20 and the Speed 25 and by the end of the decade the company boasted cars capable of offering a ''genuine'' 100 mph top speed. Yet during the 1930s, Alvis sought to diversify its operations. The company began production of aircraft engines, building a new manufacturing facility next to its existing plant, and then began developing designs for tanks and armored cars. The company continued to produce new automobiles, meanwhile, including the 12/7, introduced in 1938, and the Silver Crest, which also debuted before the end of the 1930s. The development of the company's aircraft and military vehicle components led it to shorten its name, to Alvis Ltd., in 1936.

The outbreak of World War II, however, gave a boost to Alvis's aircraft engine and military vehicle production. The company scored a new success with its Leonides aircraft engine, unveiled in 1939. During the war, Alvis became an important contributor to the United Kingdom's war effort, becoming a primary producer of the Merlin engine for the Lancaster bomber. Although the destruction of much of the company's automotive manufacturing plant during bombing raids in 1940 forced the company to place greater emphasis on its aircraft engine production, the company also began to produce a steadily growing number of light armored vehicles.

Postwar Armored Vehicle Specialist

Alvis faced an uphill struggle rebuilding its automotive business in the postwar period. The company's position in the luxury automobile class exposed it to the high taxes placed on this class of car. Alvis adopted a new policy of producing only one model of car at a time. The first of its postwar cars was the TA 14 of 1946, which remained in production until 1950 when it was replaced by the TA 21. The 1950s saw the company's full-fledged entry into the light-armored vehicle field with the launch of its Saladin and Saracen high-mobility vehicles; as with the company's later products, these were wheeled—rather than tracked—vehicles.

Alvis followed up these two early armored vehicle models with the release of its Scorpion in the mid-1950s. A light-

armored vehicle useful for reconnaissance missions, the Scorpion became the company's most successful vehicle design and was to remain in production into the next century. Alvis continued to make cars, but was finding it increasingly difficult to find suppliers for its car bodies. At the same time, the automobile division was losing money, kept in operation in part for its public relations value as the Alvis brand grew to become one of the most treasured of British classic car enthusiasts. The company produced several new models during the 1950s, including the TC 21/100 (capable of speeds greater than 100 mph) and the TD 21, designed in part by Hermann Graber of Switzerland. Another model, the TE 21 launched in 1964, was to be Alvis's last car. Meanwhile, the company's aircraft engine designs were facing a declining market as the aviation industry switched over to gas turbine engines during the 1960s.

Alvis was acquired by Rover in 1965, which in turn was taken over by British Leyland, then the United Kingdom's largest car-making group, in 1967. Leyland promptly ended production of the Alvis car and also cut out its aircraft engine manufacturing division. Although the company continued to produce parts and components for the aircraft industry, Alvis now began to specialize in its light armored vehicle class, propelled by the continued success of its Scorpion series.

During the recession of the 1970s, Alvis was more or less overlooked by its hard-pressed parent. Finally, in 1981, Alvis was sold off to United Scientific Holdings (USH). That company had originated as a seller of military optical equipment in the 1960s. Through a series of acquisitions as well as through its own organic growth, USH had grown into one of the United Kingdom's leading designers and manufacturers of military sights and other optical equipment. Yet USH ran into difficulties during the mid-1980s after its longtime chief executive left the company for a position with the British defense department. As military spending began to dry up as a result of the end to the Cold War, hard-hit USH cycled through a series of chief executives. By 1989, the company had become a target for a hostile takeover by Meggitt, one of its chief competitors.

Nicholas Prest, who had joined USH as a marketing director in 1982, was appointed chief executive and charged with defending the company against the takeover attempt. Ultimately, however, USH's own dismal performance, as it slipped into losses at the end of the decade, scared Meggitt off. Prest was now faced with the task of rebuilding USH in the midst of the post-Cold War era drop-off in military spending.

Prest began trimming USH's operations at the beginning of the 1990s, selling off a number of its optics subsidiaries. By 1992, the company's focus shifted still closer toward its military vehicle division when the company changed its name to Alvis Holdings Plc. The following year, the company restructured, splitting off its optics division into a 51 percent stake in Singapore-based Avimo, a public company listed on the Singapore stock exchange. The spinoff enabled the company to slash its debt. Meanwhile, Alvis went on a cost-cutting spree in its remaining operations, which included reducing its own manufacturing costs by subcontracting for certain components. These measures helped the company boost its profit margins on its armored vehicle range.

Key Dates:

1919: T.G. John founds company to develop automobile designs in Coventry, England.

1920: The first automobile, the Alvis 10/30, is launched.

1921: The company changes its name to the Alvis Car & Engineering Co. Ltd.

1923: The 12/50, the company's first successful automobile design, is launched.

1936: The company shortens its name to Alvis Ltd. as it diversifies and begins designing and manufacturing aircraft engines and armored vehicles.

1938: The 12/70 automobile is unveiled.

1939: The Leonides aircraft engine is introduced.

1950: Alvis enters the light armored vehicle field with the launch of its Saladin and Saracen high-mobility vehicles.

1955: The Scorpion-class light-armored vehicle becomes the company's market breakthrough.

1964: The TE 21, the last automobile designed by Alvis, is launched.

1965: Alvis is acquired by Rover, which is then acquired by British Leyland in 1967.

1981: The Alvis armored vehicle division is acquired by United Scientific Holdings.

1992: United Scientific Holdings undergoes restructuring, focusing on armored vehicles and changing its name to Alvis Holdings Plc.

1997: Alvis reaches an agreement to acquire Hägglunds Vehicle AB, the largest light-armored vehicle maker in Scandinavia.

1998: Alvis merges with GKN's light-armored vehicle division, creating the United Kingdom's largest armored vehicle manufacturer and one of the largest in Europe.

2001: Alvis sells off its remaining noncore holdings to become a "pure-play" armored vehicle manufacturer.

2002: Alvis indicates its interest in acquiring the heavy armored-vehicle division from Vickers.

European Leader for the 21st Century

By the mid-1990s, Alvis's profits were leading the European armored vehicle market. Yet Alvis was preparing to move to a new level. In 1997, the company surprised the industry when it announced its agreement to acquire Swedish light armored vehicle maker Hägglunds. The purchase, at a cost of £80 million, doubled Alvis in size, allowing it to stand shoulder-to-shoulder with U.K. market leaders GKN and Vickers. Hägglunds also brought Alvis a complementary product range—the Swedish company concentrated on tracked vehicles—as well as complementary geographic scope.

Alvis struck again a year later when it announced that it had reached an agreement to acquire GKN's light armored vehicle division in exchange for a 30 percent stake in Alvis. The deal now placed Alvis in a position of strength from which to prepare for the forecasted consolidation of the European armored vehicle market, which numbered more than 30 major companies competing for a steadily shrinking number of vehicle contracts. The GKN purchase also gave Alvis a stake in the contract for a new class of MRAV vehicles—a contract Alvis had lost out on when it bid in partnership with Vickers.

Following the GKN acquisition, Alvis moved to become a pure-play vehicle manufacturer, shedding a number of its noncore operations, including its Barracuda camouflage equipment division, sold to Saab in 1999, and nearly half of its stake in Avimo, sold to Thales (formerly Thomson-CSF). The following year, Alvis sold off a subsidiary that manufactured robots for bomb disposal units to Northrup Grumman. Then in 2001, Alvis sold off the rest of its share of Avimo to Thales. The company also shut down its historical Coventry facilities, moving its manufacturing operations to Telford.

By the beginning of 2002, Alvis was ready to continue its singlehanded consolidation drive. In February, the company announced that it was in advanced talks with Rolls-Royce to acquire that company's Vickers Defence Systems unit, a specialist in heavy-armored vehicles. Such a move would create a single British armored vehicle manufacturer. At the same time, analysts began suggesting other possible marriage prospects for Alvis, including Germany's Krauss-Maffei Wegmann, and U.S.-based United Defense, owned by Carlyle, creating a U.S.-European armored vehicle giant. Alvis entered the 21st century not merely an unlikely survivor, but a possible leader of the coming consolidation of its market.

Principal Subsidiaries

Alvis Vehicles Ltd.; Hägglunds Vehicle AB; Artec Consortium; Patria Hägglunds OY (50%); Hägglunds Moelv AS.

Principal Competitors

CIC International Ltd.; AM General Corporation; General Dynamics Corporation; GIAT Industries S.A.; Krauss-Maffei Wegmann GmbH & Co; United Defense Industries, Inc.

Further Reading

Deshmukh, Anita, "The Warrior Class," *Birmingham Post,* March 23, 2001, p. 23.

Goldsmith, Belinda, "Britain's Alvis Buying Hägglunds for $121 Million," *Reuters Business Report,* September 25, 1997.

Harrison, Michael, "Alvis Set to Buy Vickers Tank Business," *Independent,* February 11, 2002, p. 15.

Muradia, Valgo, "GKN Merger Makes Alvis UK's Leading Armor Firm," *Defense Daily,* September 18, 1998.

Nicolson, Bryan, "Luxury Cars Give Way to Tanks," *Evening Post,* November 8, 1996, p. 8.

Swann, Christopher, and Andrew Edgecliffe-Johnson, "Turning an Ailing Tank Back on to the Right Tracks," *Financial Times,* September 18, 1998.

"Tank Battle Is Confusing the Field," *Birmingham Post,* February 14, 2002, p. 24.

—M.L. Cohen

Amdocs Ltd.

1390 Timberlake Manor Pkwy
Chesterfield, Missouri 63017
U.S.A.
Telephone: (314) 212-7000
Fax: (314) 212-7500
Web site: http://www.amdocs.com

8 Hapnina St.
Ra'anana 43000
Israel
Telephone: (+972) 9 754-6222

Public Company
Incorporated: 1982 as Aurec Information and Directory
    Systems
Employees: 8,600
Sales: $1.53 billion (2001)
Stock Exchanges: New York
Ticker Symbol: DOX
NAIC: 511210 Software Publishers; 541613 Marketing
    Consulting Services; 541219 Other Accounting
    Services

Amdocs Ltd. is one of the world's leading providers of billing, customer relationship management (CRM), and order management software systems to the telecommunications industry. The company delivers end-to-end software systems and support services that enable telecommunications providers to offer multiple platform, and multiple services billing, ordering, and support to their fixed-line and mobile telephone customers. With the turn of the new century, Amdocs has also begun to provide outsourcing services, taking over the billing, customer care, and customer relationship management services for many of its top customers. The company is one of the only companies in its field providing software systems capable of handling telephone networks ranging from 20 to 40 million subscribers. Since the late 1990s, Amdocs has made a series of key acquisitions, including International Telecommunications Data Systems (ITDS) of the United States in 1999; Canada's Solect Technology Group in 2000; and Clarify, from Nortel Networks, in 2001. The acquisitions have helped the

company to position itself as a full-service provider of turnkey CRM solutions. Originally based in Ra'anana, Israel, where the company continues to maintain the bulk of its research and development activity, as well as nearly half of its 8,600 employees, Amdocs has moved its headquarters to Chesterfield, Missouri. The company is also listed on the New York Stock Exchange, after one of the largest initial public offerings of the late 1990s. SBC Communications, the parent company for Southwestern Bell, was one of the key forces behind the establishment of the company and remains its largest single shareholder, at 14 percent of shares, and largest customer as well. Other prominent customers include Deutsche Telecom, British Telecom, Vodaphone, Bell Canada, and Nextel. The company is led by Chairman and CEO Bruce K. Anderson, and Dov Baharav, president and CEO of Amdocs Management Ltd., the company's management group.

Automating the Yellow Pages in the 1980s

Israel's Avinoam Naor graduated from the University of Tel Aviv with a degree in computer science in the mid-1970s. Naor's interest from the outset was the telecommunications industry, and in the late 1970s he found a niche in which to work: that of automating telephone directory systems. By the early 1980s, Naor had perfected the industry's first computer-based directory assistance system. In 1982, Naor, together with investors including Morris Kahn, launched Aurec Information and Directory Systems, which was brought under Kahn-controlled Aurec Group, one of the leading telecommunications providers in Israel at the time. Another primary partner in Aurec Group was Southwestern Bell, which was to become one of the Naor-led company's major customers.

Aurec continued to develop products geared toward the telephone directory market. In 1984, the company launched a new unit, Automated Directory Systems, as a joint venture with Southwestern Bell. The new company was formed as the commercial and support services arm for a new Aurec product, a software-based publishing system for telephone directories. Southwestern Bell stepped up its participation in that joint venture in 1985, becoming an equal partner.

By the end of the 1980s, Aurec Information had succeeded in gaining the worldwide leadership in its telephone directory

Company Perspectives:

For two decades, we have been helping leading communications providers across the world turn their visions into reality. We lead the communications systems market with outstanding products, carrier-grade scalability and an unparalleled track record of delivery and reliability. We support all lines of business, including mobile and wireline, voice and IP, and prepaid and postpaid. We fully integrate CRM, billing and ordering systems with a unified customer view.

niche market, and had extended its operations to include offices in Israel, the United States, Europe, and elsewhere. In the late 1980s, the company extended its product line again, to include software solutions for advertising sales and placement with telephone directories. Southwestern once again benefited as one of the first users of the Aurec system, which was added in 1988. As one Southwestern Bell Yellow Pages executive told the *St. Louis Post-Dispatch:* "It makes it easier for our sales organization to sell advertising, and it makes it easier for us to actually publish the information in the directory."

Part of Aurec's success was its conservative approach to growth and a commitment to creating systems that worked—from the beginning, the company was able to claim a 100 percent implementation rate. In addition, Aurec Information proved equally adept at keeping its clients, boasting that it had never lost a client to a competing system.

Growing the Business: 1990s

Despite its success in capturing the lead of its core market, Aurec Information remained a modestly sized operation into the 1990s. Yet Naor and his team, which by then included Dov Baharav, appointed as president of the company's U.S. subsidiary in 1991, had identified a new and high-potential market for the company's software systems development. As Naor stated in an interview with the *Wall Street Corporate Reporter:* "In the early 1990s, we realized that telecommunications was going to become a booming industry with huge potential so we began developing products to service this industry."

Aurec Information set out to develop a full-service billing and customer care software system. This package, called Ensemble, was ready for the market in 1995. The advent of Ensemble proved the turning point in the company's transformation from a small-sized niche market player to an industry powerhouse ranked among the world's top 30 software companies. As part of its transformation, Aurec Information was restructured into a new holding company, Amdocs Ltd., which grouped Aurec Information and other Aurec Group assets. Registered as an Isle of Guernsey company, Amdocs featured as major shareholders the investment firm Welsh, Carson, Anderson & Stowe based in New York, which held 29.2 percent; Morris Kahn, through Amdocs International Ltd., with 23.4 percent; and SBC Communications, with 23.4 percent.

While continuing to develop and support its telephone directory business—which had been implemented by nearly all of the telephone services providers in the United States—Amdocs

began asserting itself deeper into the telecommunications industry. SBC remained the company's single largest customer, accounting for more than 40 percent of its sales, while five other major customers made up another nearly 43 percent of the company's sales, which topped $200 million in 1996. Yet the successful rollout of Amdocs' Ensemble customer care software system quickly enabled the company to reduce its reliance on this core customer group.

Part of the appeal of Ensemble and other Amdocs systems was the increasing complexity of the telecommunications industry in general. The mid- to late 1990s were to see the widescale implementation of a variety of new technologies, including the explosive growth of the mobile telephone market. As telecommunications companies were able to offer their customers a growing variety of products, services, and pricing and billing options, these companies found themselves unable to develop billing, customer service, and other CRM systems robust enough to handle the increasingly complex billing and servicing needs. As an early player in the CRM systems market, with a specific focus on the telecommunications industry, Amdocs proved uniquely placed to profit from this trend.

Amdocs began preparations to go public in 1997 when it moved its corporate headquarters to Chesterfield, Missouri. At that time, Bruce Anderson, from Welsh, Carson, Anderson & Stowe, was named Amdoc Ltd.'s chairman and chief executive officer, while Naor maintained the CEO spot with the Amdoc's main operating company, Amdocs Management Ltd. The bulk of the company's research and development operations, including most of its employees, remained at Amdoc's Ra'anana, Israel headquarters.

By 1998, Amdocs was ready to go public, selling 11.7 percent of its stock on the New York Stock Exchange, and raising more than $250 million in an initial public offering that counted as the largest ever made by an Israeli company. The company used that money to pay down debt, then began to look toward expanding its activities, including branching out into the growing Internet telephony market through a cooperation agreement with Vocaltec.

By the end of 1998, Amdocs was riding high on the surging telecommunications industry. Posting revenues of more than $400 million, the company had successfully implemented its Ensemble system into nearly all of the United States' RBOCs (Regional Bell Operating Companies, also known as "Baby Bells"), as well as GTE and Sprint. Amdocs was also making strong headway into the European and South American markets.

A new wave of consolidations within the telecommunications industry, rather than reduce the pool of Amdocs' customers, instead opened up new possibilities as the newer, larger operators, often combining multinational telephone systems and a variety of traditional and cutting-edge services, turned to Amdocs to solve the new complexities of their billing, ordering, and customer service needs.

Amdocs now began to seek to position itself as a full-service solutions provider. While the company continued to target organic growth, it now began to seek to complement its existing operations with a number of key acquisitions. One of the first of these came in March 1999, when Amdocs paid $400 million in

Key Dates:

1982: Avinoam Naor and a group of investors found Aurec Information and Directory Services in order to develop and market directory information services software.

1984: Southwestern Bell acquires 50 percent of Aurec Information and becomes its primary customer.

1988: Aurec Information launches directory advertising sales and publishing software systems.

1995: Aurec Information reorganizes as Amdocs Ltd.

1998: Amdocs goes public on the New York Stock Exchange.

1999: Company acquires Architel, based in Toronto, and International Telecommunications Data Systems Inc., based in Connecticut.

2000: Company acquires Solect Technology Group in $1 billion stock swap.

2001: Amdocs acquires Clarify Inc. for $200 million from Nortel Networks.

2002: Company launches fully integrated CRM billing, customer services, and order management software for the telecommunications industry.

stock to acquire Toronto-based Architel, a provider of an automated service activation system. In November of that same year, Amdocs launched a new acquisition, of International Telecommunications Data Systems Inc. (ITDS), a Stamford, Connecticut-based provider of billing and CRM software and services primarily to the wireless telecommunications market. The ITDS acquisition not only boosted Amdocs' entry into the mobile telephony sector, but also, with its focus on medium-sized telecommunications providers, complemented Amdocs' own focus on large-scale providers.

Telecommunications Services Solutions Provider in the 21st Century

Amdocs continued to put the pieces of its acquisition puzzle in place at the turn of the millennium. In 2000, the company paid $1 billion in shares to acquire Solect Technology Group. Based in Toronto, Solect had established itself as a leading provider of Internet protocol (IP) billing and customer care software, with clients including AT&T Canada, British Telecommunications, GTE, Swiss Online, Sun Microsystems, and Cisco Systems.

In 2001, Amdocs moved to enhance its product offering still further, when it paid Nortel Networks $200 million to acquire Clarify Inc. That company had been founded in 1990 with a focus on customer care services, and particularly on developing customer complaint and product defect tracking software. After going public in 1996, Clarify adapted its software systems to the telecommunications industry, launching the Clarfiy Comm-Center; in 1998 Clarify launched a new product, eFrontOffice,

which enabled web-site based customer care services. In 2000, Clarify was acquired for $2.1 billion by Nortel Networks as part of that company's spending spree—which ended with the tech market slump at the turn of the millennium.

The addition of Clarify enabled Amdocs to complete its own product offering, and by the beginning of 2002 the company launched what it called the industry's first end-to-end fully integrated CRM, billing, and order management system for the communications industry. Meanwhile, Amdocs had moved into a new direction at the end of 2001, when it began offering outsourcing services for its customers. One of the first to take up Amdocs' outsourcing services was Nextel Communications, which turned over its billing functions to Amdocs in a seven-year contract. The idea seemed to catch on quickly, as Amdoc signed a five-year billing services contract with Verizon Communications in early 2002.

By then, Amdocs had grown to a software industry powerhouse, with annual revenues of more than $1.5 billion, placing it among the top 30 of the world's software companies. At the same time, Amdocs maintained its longstanding tradition of perfection, as it continued to boast a 100 percent implementation success rate after 20 years in business.

Principal Subsidiaries

Amdocs operates subsidiaries in the United States, Canada, the United Kingdom, Israel, Cyprus, Ireland, France, Italy, Germany, Australia, Spain, Japan, and Brazil.

Principal Competitors

Accenture Ltd.; ADC Telecommunications, Inc.; ALLTEL Corporation; American Management Systems, Incorporated; Cap Gemini Ernst & Young; Computer Sciences Corporation; Convergys Corporation; DSET Corporation; Electronic Data Systems Corporation; Eyretel plc; International Business Machines Corporation; Lucent Technologies Inc.; MetaSolv, Inc.; Nortel Networks Limited; Portal Software, Inc.; Siebel Systems, Inc.; Telcordia Technologies, Inc.

Further Reading

"Amdocs Eyes More Buys," *Jerusalem Post*, October 4, 2001, p. 12.

Gerstenfeld, Dan, "Amdocs to Buy Solect in $1b. Deal," *Jerusalem Post*, March 1, 2000.

——, "Morris Kahn Sells Amdocs Shares for $440m," *Jerusalem Post*, October 8, 1999.

Holyoke, Larry, "Internet Connection Boosts Investor Interest in Amdocs," *St. Louis Business Journal*, December 3, 1999.

Manning, Margie, "Amdocs Goes Shopping," *St. Louis Business Journal*, June 8, 2001.

Mayoros, Diane, "Amdocs Limited—President and Chief Executive Officer—Interview," *Wall Street Corporate Reporter*, January 4, 2000.

Stub, Zev, "Amdocs Beat Earnings Expectations," *Jerusalem Post*, January 24, 2002, p. 12.

—M.L. Cohen

American International Group, Inc.

70 Pine Street
New York, New York 10270
U.S.A.
Telephone: (212) 770-7000
Fax: (212) 425-3499
Web site: http://www.aig.com

Public Company
Incorporated: 1967
Employees: 81,000
Total Assets: $492.98 billion (2001)
Stock Exchanges: New York London Tokyo Paris Swiss
Ticker Symbol: AIG
NAIC: 523120 Securities Brokerage; 523920 Portfolio
  Management; 524126 Direct Property and Casualty
  Insurance Carriers; 524113 Direct Life Insurance Car-
  riers; 524130 Reinsurance Carriers; 524210 Insurance
  Agencies and Brokerages; 532411 Commercial Air,
  Rail, and Water Transportation Equipment Rental and
  Leasing; 551112 Offices of Other Holding Companies

American International Group, Inc. (AIG) is a holding company for a network of subsidiaries primarily engaged in insurance and insurance-related activities, including property, casualty, life, financial services, retirement savings products, asset management, and aircraft leasing. AIG operates in more than 130 countries and jurisdictions, and its combined revenues make it the largest U.S.-based international insurance organization and one of the largest insurance firms in the world. AIG is the leading underwriter of commercial and industrial insurance in the United States and holds the number two position in the U.S. life insurance sector. The corporation, whose earliest roots were in Asia, has had an active history of mergers, acquisitions, and consolidations, and under the renowned stewardship of Maurice R. "Hank" Greenberg from the late 1960s into the early 21st century the company has grown into a global insurance giant.

Origins As a Chinese Insurance Agency

In 1919 a 27-year-old U.S. businessman, Cornelius Vander Starr, opened a two-room, two-clerk insurance agency in Shanghai, China, and named it American Asiatic Underwriters (AAU). AAU, which later became part of American International Underwriters (AIU), initially served as an underwriter for insurance companies that had established branches in Shanghai. During a trip to New York in 1921 Starr added representation of other U.S. companies to his operations, including the Globe & Rutgers Company. Later that decade Starr brought representation of the Pittsburgh, Pennsylvania, company, National Union Fire Insurance, into his fold.

Starr's next quest was to gain general life insurance agency powers, but he found no U.S. companies willing to assume the risk because there were no life-expectancy statistics available for the Chinese population. In 1921 Starr overcame this obstacle by forming his own company, Asia Life Insurance Company (ALICO). ALICO's most popular product was a 20-year endowment policy, with rates established on the basis of Starr's personal observation that in general Chinese enjoyed longer life expectancies than their Western counterparts.

In 1926 Starr opened a New York office under the name American International Underwriters to serve as an insurance writer on U.S.-owned risks outside of North America. Like its Chinese counterpart, AIU also served as a general agent for U.S. insurers. By the end of the decade Starr's Chinese operations were seeing modest profits, and branch offices for both general and life insurance had been established throughout the Shanghai region. In 1931 Starr joined British and Chinese businessmen in a partnership and established the International Assurance Company (INTASCO).

AIU established a foundation for Latin American business in 1932 when George Moszkowski, who ran the company's New York office, negotiated the purchase of the Central American and Caribbean portfolios of a U.S. insurer withdrawing from foreign operations. AIU's operations in Central America remained modest throughout the decade.

Before, during, and after World War II, AIU was able to capitalize on world economic and political situations. With much of the world on the brink of war, in 1939 Starr moved his headquarters to New York, temporarily closing the Shanghai office. After hostilities broke out, operations of dominant Italian, German, and British agencies were reduced, and AIU ex-

13

panded in Central America. In 1940 AIU established a regional headquarters in Cuba, and a half dozen offices in South America soon followed. AIU's Central American business grew with the local economies of these neutral countries during the war years.

At the end of World War II, the Shanghai office was re-opened under the guidance of K.K. Tse. Several profitable years followed until the late 1940s, when the future of foreign activities in Shanghai grew dim. In 1949 key employees and documents were airlifted out of Shanghai and the regional headquarters moved to Hong Kong. In late 1950 operations in China were closed.

Meanwhile, many surrounding countries were recovering from war. With economic improvement underway, AIU entered Japan and West Germany by selling insurance to occupying U.S. troops. AIU's prewar operations in Europe had been limited to small agencies in France, Belgium, and the Netherlands, but postwar conditions, resulting in tight financing for local insurers, placed AIU in a position to expand its European business. At the same time, expansion of U.S. business abroad created opportunities for AIU's "home-foreign" business.

In 1947 Starr began a reorganization designed to revive war-torn operations and lay the groundwork for future growth. Starr's first move was to announce the incorporation of a Philippine arm of the American Life Insurance Company, the Philippine American Life Insurance Company (Philam Life), in 1947. U.S. businessman Earl Carroll was named to head up the new company, which grew quickly, largely through the sale of endowment policies. These policies provided farmers and small merchants with the means to build their savings in a country with few banks. Sales revenue was frequently reinvested in the local economy.

Started as a partnership, INTASCO, which until this time had maintained a relatively small life insurance business, was reorganized in 1948 when Starr took control of the business. He added "American" to the company's name, changed the company's abbreviated name to AIA, and assigned it the Southeast Asian territories of Malaysia, Singapore, and Thailand and the home-base front of Hong Kong.

That same year Starr began uniting his somewhat fragmented network of insurance companies, beginning with the creation of two Bermuda-based entities. The first, American International Underwriters Overseas, Ltd. (AIUO), became the parent of all established AIU agency companies overseas. The second, American International Reinsurance Company, Inc. (AIRCO), was designed to hold companies dealing primarily in

life insurance. AIRCO also took control of company investment programs and served as a reinsurer for these subsidiaries. The last of Starr's trio of new organizations was American International Underwriters Association (AIUA), established in 1949 to serve as a partnership of U.S. insurance companies that were represented by AIU. AIUA provided for pooled business in stipulated percentages and shared assets that were kept overseas to meet local regulations.

Perhaps the most dramatic reorganization occurred within Starr's oldest life insurance company, ALICO. After lying dormant for a decade, the company was renamed American Life Insurance Company and assigned the Caribbean, Middle East, and some growing African nations. ALICO marketed life insurance to populations previously not attractive to insurers.

Rapid Expansion in the 1950s

The 1950s were a period of rapid expansion for AIU. Branches were established in Western Europe, the Middle East, North Africa, and Australia. By the end of the decade AIU was operating in 75 countries. The 1950s also marked the emergence of Starr's companies in domestic markets.

In 1952 AIRCO acquired a majority interest in the Globe & Rutgers Insurance Company, a medium-sized U.S. fire insurance company once represented by AIU. A Globe & Rutgers subsidiary, the Insurance Company of the State of Pennsylvania, came with the purchase. Founded in 1794, the Pennsylvania subsidiary was the second oldest stock insurance company in the United States. American Home Assurance Company, which was founded in 1853, was also included in the package. Globe & Rutgers was later merged with American Home and took its name.

Starr and his colleagues joined the American Home board but left the company largely under old management. Earnings at the new subsidiary fluctuated greatly for several years. A net loss of $1.4 million was reported in 1957, followed by a net profit of better than $950,000 the following year. In an effort to stabilize earnings, AIRCO sold American Home's agency business to another insurer in 1962. That same year Starr named Maurice R. Greenberg as American Home president, and the company formed the American International Life Assurance Company of New York to specialize in term and group insurance. Greenberg had begun his insurance career ten years earlier with Continental Casualty Company. In 1960 he joined American International and was assigned the task of developing an overseas accident and health business.

In leading American Home, Greenberg focused on broker sales, allowing the company to issue its own policies and maintain underwriting control. The company concentrated on commercial and industrial risks, which involved negotiated rather than state-controlled rates. American Home also developed substantial reinsurance facilities in order to cover large shares of major risks and control insurance ratings. Greenberg initiated new products and services such as personal accident insurance, which emphasized deductibles. Meanwhile, American Home avoided medical insurance. The new sales system caught on, offering brokers the high deductibles that traditional

Key Dates:

1919: Cornelius Vander Starr forms American Asiatic Underwriters, a two-clerk insurance agency in Shanghai, China.

1926: Starr opens a New York office under the name American International Underwriters.

1939: With much of the world on the brink of war, Starr moves his headquarters from Shanghai to New York.

1948: Starr begins uniting his fragmented network of insurance companies by forming two Bermuda-based entities: American International Underwriters Overseas, Ltd. and American International Reinsurance Company, Inc. (AIRCO).

1949: Following the communist takeover of China, Starr moves his regional headquarters to Hong Kong.

1952: AIRCO gains control of American Home Assurance Company.

1960s: Several acquisitions are completed, including National Union Fire Insurance Company of Pittsburgh, Pennsylvania, and New Hampshire Insurance Company.

1967: As part of a major reorganization, American International Group, Inc. (AIG) is formed to become the holding company for the various insurance companies; Maurice R. Greenberg becomes president and CEO of AIG.

1968: Starr dies and Greenberg adds the chairmanship to his duties.

1969: AIG goes public.

1976: AIG is organized into four broad categories: the foreign general insurance division, the brokerage division of domestic general insurance, the agency division of domestic general insurance, and a life insurance division.

1987: The Financial Services Group is formed, consolidating the firm's burgeoning financial services operations.

1999: SunAmerica Inc., a major player in annuities and mutual funds, is acquired for $18.3 billion.

2001: AIG acquires American General Corporation for $23 billion; AIG reports losses of $820 million stemming from the events of September 11.

insurers avoided but that some large corporations sought in order to cut costs.

Late 1960s: Creation of the Modern AIG

During the late 1960s American International's corporate structure began to resemble its present form as it became an important commercial and industrial property and casualty insurer. While a new company organization was being forged through further acquisitions and reorganization, the insurance group began capitalizing on its innovative products and entrance into new markets.

Acquisitions during this period included controlling interests in the National Union Fire Insurance Company of Pitts-

burgh, Pennsylvania, which had been represented by AIU since 1927, and the New Hampshire Insurance Company. The former, which was threatened by high underwriting losses, was transformed much like American Home, and then linked with it in a pooling agreement. Commerce and Industry Insurance Company, a small property insurer specializing in highly protected risks, and Transatlantic Reinsurance Company were also acquired during this period.

The wholly owned American International Group, Inc. was formed by AIRCO in 1967. AIG represented the beginning of a major corporate reorganization, with the company formed to hold shares of other domestic companies, including American Home and New Hampshire. ALICO was soon added to AIG's holdings. Greenberg was elected president and CEO of AIG in 1967. The following year Starr died, having seen only the beginning of a new era for the insurance empire he had created.

In 1969, after going public, AIG acquired majority interests in National Union, New Hampshire, and American Home, paying for its increased stake in the three companies with AIG stock. In 1970 AIU and its agencies and subsidiaries became wholly owned subsidiaries of AIG.

Throughout the 1960s AIU's overseas business grew, despite the loss of its large Cuban business following Fidel Castro's takeover of that country. Since it had entered most major markets a decade earlier, expansion during this time was limited to growth within areas with established territories. In an effort to strengthen AIG's overseas position, an 18-month program was initiated in 1972 creating a regional system of benefits managers for Europe, Africa, Central America, South America, the Middle East, the Far East, and the United States. That same year the AIG subsidiary ALICO became the first foreign-owned company granted a license to sell insurance to Japanese nationals in Japan.

During the early 1970s AIG increased its specialization by forming a number of new groups. Subsidiaries created by AIG during this time included A.I. Credit Corporation to finance general insurance premiums written through both affiliate and nonaffiliate insurers; North American Managers, Inc., to sell insurance in the United States for foreign companies; AIG Oil Rig, Inc., to initiate and manage insurance for offshore oil- and gas-drilling rigs; AIG Risk Management, Inc., to provide worldwide risk management services; AIG Data Center, Inc.; and American International Insurance Company of Ireland, Ltd. During this period AIG also acquired all remaining shares of the New Hampshire and National Union companies.

AIG's profits took off in the 1970s, at a compounded growth rate of roughly 20 percent, with AIG's net income surpassing $50 million by 1975. High premiums in the new market areas of oil rigs and pension-fund management as well as the use of limited partnership insurance for high risks contributed to the growth.

Consolidation and reorganization continued in 1976, when AIU stopped writing policies for insurance companies it did not own. That same year the company was organized into four broad categories: the foreign general insurance division, the brokerage division of domestic general insurance, the agency division of domestic general insurance, and a life insurance division. The following year the subsidiary Transatlantic Reinsurance was reorganized as a major reinsurer, with shares sold to seven other companies. AIG absorbed its parent company, AIRCO, in 1978, completing a nine-year consolidation plan to simplify the corporate structure.

In 1979 AIG entered Eastern Europe and initiated joint ventures with state-owned insurers in Hungary, Poland, and Romania. In succeeding years similar operations were started in China and Yugoslavia. At the end of the 1970s AIG had 20 percent annual growth in revenues and had increased its size nearly tenfold. In 1979 AIG reported over $250 million in net income.

Diversification and Consolidation in the 1980s

During the 1980s AIG ventured into healthcare services, and acquired a variety of financial and investment sources as well as real estate holdings. Acquisitions included United Guaranty Corporation, a residential mortgage insurance company; the Swiss bank Uberseebank A.G.; Ticino Societa d'Assicurazioni Sulla Vita, a Swiss-based life insurer; Southeastern Aviation Underwriters—later renamed AIG Aviation, Inc.—an airlines, aviation, and space program insurer; and Jurgovan & Blair, a health maintenance organization consulting business. In 1981 AIG, in combination with Presidio Oil Company, purchased a majority interest in 109 natural gas wells.

In 1984 the company reported its first decline in profits, largely owing to underwriting losses including those resulting from a major hurricane. Some of AIG's specialty companies, such as AIG Oil Rig, AIG Energy, AIG Entertainment, and AIG Political Risk, which were created during the preceding 15 years, were consolidated in 1984 under the name AIG Specialty Agencies, Inc. That same year AIG special services division was introduced to underwrite risks such as extortion, kidnapping, and ransom demand.

In 1985 AIG's profit margin rebounded, with the company exceeding 1983 earnings and posting a net income of $420 million. In 1987 AIG surpassed $1 billion in net income. That same year AIG was authorized by the South Korean government to begin life insurance operations, ending a 15-year struggle to break into the Korean market. AIG became the second foreign insurance company in South Korea, with its largest international competitor, CIGNA Corporation, given approval earlier in the year.

Two important AIG executives, National Union President Joseph P. DeAlessandro and American Home President Dennis Busti, left AIG in 1987 for other companies. Maurice Greenberg's son, Jeffrey W. Greenberg, was moved over from the presidency of AIU's North American division and named new president of National Union, while Joseph R. Wiedemann was named American Home president. Wiedemann had been president of AIG's Boston-based subsidiary Lexington Insurance Company.

AIG broadened its trading markets in 1987 when it became the first foreign insurance organization on the Tokyo Stock Exchange. The following year AIG was listed on the London International Stock Exchange. Additional listings include Paris and Switzerland, added in 1990.

AIG continued diversification moves in 1988, forming a Hong Kong-based venture to introduce U.S. fast-food franchises into the Asian market. The venture marked the first time a U.S. institutional investor—AIG's Financial Investment Corporation of Asia—moved into an overseas franchise market.

That same year AIG also experienced some difficulty. It was involved in what is believed to be one of the largest insurance-related arbitration awards in history. Enron Corporation was awarded a $162 million claim from insurers for Peruvian properties that had been expropriated, and AIG was forced to pay nearly two-thirds of the judgment.

Throughout the 1980s AIG operated as one of two major sources of environmental-impairment-liability (EIL) insurance. Early in 1989 Greenberg proposed the creation of a hazardous-waste-cleanup tax funded through a 2 percent premium fee assessed on all commercial and casualty and property policies, with insurers matching that amount. Greenberg suggested the tax could help fund cleanup of Environmental Protection Agency Superfund sites and ultimately bring more insurers into EIL writing, but critics charged the plan was self-serving.

Late 1980s to Mid-1990s: Continued Diversification into Financial Services

The late 1980s saw continued consolidation for AIG. The Financial Services Group was formed in 1987 to consolidate specialized financial operations. UNAT, AIG's general insurance company on the European continent, was formed later that year to consolidate operations in Europe and prepare for the elimination of trade barriers among European nations in 1992. Headquartered in Paris, UNAT's expanding territory included France, Belgium, the Netherlands, Sweden, Norway, and Denmark.

In 1989 AIGlobal was formed to provide a single source of comprehensive property and casualty, life, and group insurance, and facilitate corporate financial services for multinational companies. That same year International Healthcare and Jurgovan & Blair were merged to form American International Healthcare, Inc., an international consulting and management company for healthcare services.

From 1987 into the mid-1990s AIG continued its diversification into financial services. In 1987 a joint venture, AIG Financial Products Corp., was established to structure complex financial transactions, including interest rate and currency swaps. In 1988 AIG acquired ownership of 30 percent of A.B. Asesores Bursatiles, a Spanish brokerage, and invested in certain investment management and venture capital operations in the United Kingdom and Hong Kong. AIG Trading Corporation, a joint venture engaging in commodity transactions, was established in early 1990, and later that year AIG acquired International Lease Finance Corporation, which was engaged primarily in the acquisition of new and used commercial jet aircraft and the leasing of such aircraft to domestic and foreign airlines (it later became the leader in such leasing). In 1994 AIG Combined Risks Ltd. was formed as a London-based investment bank providing risk management solutions involving corporate finance, reinsurance, and derivative instruments. All of these companies were placed under the umbrella of AIG's Financial Services Group. By 1994 operating income for the group had climbed to $404.9 million.

During 1990 Transatlantic Holdings, Inc., a holding company formed to hold Transatlantic Reinsurance Company and another reinsurer, Putnam Reinsurance Company, went public in a secondary offering. AIG continued to hold approximately 41 percent of Transatlantic Holdings after the public offering.

In June 1990 AIG agreed to buy Fischbach Corporation for $43 million. Fischbach, a Florida-based contractor, was an AIG performance-bond customer that had begun to experience financial difficulties. If Fischbach had failed, AIG could have been forced to pay hundreds of millions of dollars to companies with which Fischbach had contracted. After the purchase, AIG sold 51 percent of Fischbach to contractor Peter Kiewit Sons' Inc.

In 1992 AIG garnered much bad publicity over a memo written by Jeffrey Greenberg, who by then had become an executive vice-president of AIG. Issued on the day that Hurricane Andrew reached the coast of Florida, the memo, sent to presidents of AIG subsidiary companies, seemed to suggest that AIG underwriters should be encouraged to push for premium increases in the wake of the hurricane: "Begin by calling your underwriters together and explaining the significance of the hurricane. This is an opportunity to get price increases now. We must be the first and it begins by establishing the psychology with our own people. Please get it moving today." When the memo was made public it prompted investigations in both Florida and Louisiana, and denunciations from insurance watchdog groups, as well as consumer activist Ralph Nader who accused AIG of trying to start a cycle of "price gouging." Maurice Greenberg maintained, however, that the contents of the memo were taken out of context and were part of a larger AIG discussion of long-needed rate increases for commercial insurance.

During the early 1990s AIG continued to expand outside the United States, thereby increasing its non-U.S. revenue to 52 percent of the total by 1994. Asia and the states of the former Soviet Union were particular targets during this period. Led by Maurice Greenberg's son Evan, AIG's Asia-Pacific Division reentered the Chinese market in 1992 when it became the first insurer to receive a license there since the Communist revolution in 1949. Two years later AIG also became the first insurer to return to Pakistan when it formed a subsidiary of ALICO to sell life and related types of insurance (the Pakistani government had nationalized all insurance companies in 1972). In early 1995, AIG reached an agreement with the Tata Group of India to jointly operate a life and nonlife insurance business in India once these insurance markets were opened to private and foreign investment. Meanwhile, AIG continued to be the largest foreign insurer in Japan.

To the west, Russia and Uzbekistan were added to the AIG empire in 1994. Through joint ventures with local firms, AIG established commercial insurance and political risk insurance operations in Uzbekistan. Later in 1994 AIG received a license for its joint venture in Russia, the Russian American Insurance Company, which would offer commercial insurance to Russian companies and foreign firms operating in Russia.

During 1994 AIG also branched out into additional insurance lines within the U.S. market. AIG made an initial $216 million investment in 20th Century Industries, a private auto insurer in California that had incurred heavy losses as a result of the Northridge earthquake and was on the brink of insolvency. AIG pledged to invest additional capital if certain conditions were met. AIG also stepped in to rescue Alexander & Alexander Services, Inc. (A&A), a New York-based independent insurance broker. AIG's $200 million investment was intended to allow A&A to reorganize itself and improve profitability.

In the 27 years since Maurice Greenberg had taken over as CEO from the company founder, Greenberg had guided AIG into position as a leader in its field with total assets reaching $114.35 billion in 1994. In an industry that had been rocked by several huge natural disasters in the late 1980s and early 1990s, AIG's return on equity remained remarkably stable throughout the period, ranging from 11.75 percent to 18.83 percent, thanks largely to the geographic and operational diversity engineered by Greenberg.

Major Acquisitions at the Turn of the Millennium

In the late 1990s AIG made a number of significant acquisitions and investments as part of Greenberg's continuing expansion drive. In 1996 the firm spent more than $100 million to acquire SPC Credit Ltd., a medium-size Hong Kong company specializing in consumer and commercial finance. Two years later AIG spent $150 million for a 7 percent stake in the Blackstone Group, a leveraged buyout firm, and also agreed to invest $1.2 billion in future Blackstone buyout funds. Also in 1998 AIG gained majority control of 20th Century Industries and also took control of the company board as its influence at the company increased. Two years later 20th Century changed its name to 21st Century Insurance Group.

Having maintained prominent positions in two key business areas—general insurance and life insurance—over the decades and having more recently built up a significant financial services business, AIG next sought to add a fourth leg to its operations in the area of retirement savings and asset management. The first major move toward this end came at the beginning of 1999 when SunAmerica Inc. was acquired for $18.3 billion. Based in Los Angeles, SunAmerica was a major player in the hot area of variable annuities, a retirement savings product similar to a mutual fund but with insurance features and tax advantages. SunAmerica was also involved in the more traditional area of fixed annuities as well as in managing mutual funds. In 1997 it had $2.1 billion in revenue, $379 million in net income, and $40 billion in assets. The synergies that could be gained through the acquisition were quite apparent: AIG would gain access to SunAmerica's network of more than 9,000 U.S. brokers who could sell AIG life insurance and other products, while SunAmerica's retirement savings products could be sold through AIG's huge life insurance sales force in Asia, Europe, and South America.

In November 2000 AIG acquired HSB Group Inc. for about $1.2 billion. HSB was the parent company of the Hartford Steam Boiler Inspection and Insurance Company, which specialized in insuring steam boilers and other mechanical and electrical equipment. Also in 2000 AIG became the first U.S.

insurance company to receive a license to establish a subsidiary in Vietnam. Early the following year, a bankruptcy court in Japan named AIG to be the exclusive sponsor of the reorganization of the troubled Chiyoda Mutual Life Insurance Company, the 12th largest insurer in Japan. This led later in the year to the acquisition of Chiyoda, which was renamed AIG Star Life Insurance Co., Ltd., a move that further added to AIG's already strong position in Japan.

In August 2001 AIG completed the largest acquisition in its history—in fact, the largest insurance takeover ever—the $23 billion purchase of American General Corporation. This deal was a logical follow-up to the SunAmerica acquisition as Houston-based American General had a strong position in fixed and variable annuities and in mutual funds. But American General, which had total assets in excess of $120 billion, was also a major player in the U.S. life insurance and consumer finance markets, and the acquisition resulted in AIG becoming the number two life insurance firm in the United States, trailing only Prudential Financial, Inc. Life insurance was also now by far AIG's largest business segment, accounting for 48.3 percent of 2001 pretax income, with general insurance contributing 25.5 percent; financial services, 17.1 percent; and retirement savings and asset management, 9.1 percent.

In December 2001, with insurance rates surging in the aftermath of the events of September 11, and with the insurance industry facing in excess of $50 billion in claims—by far the largest insurance event in history—AIG joined with Chubb Corporation, a unit of Goldman, Sachs & Co., and other investors to form Allied World Assurance Company Holdings, Ltd. Based in Bermuda, the new firm was created to provide additional commercial property and casualty insurance and reinsurance capacity to meet the needs of clients with large and complex risks. For insurance companies, joint ventures such as this one—and there were several others formed around this same time—provided a way for the firms to pool risks.

Despite suffering $820 million in losses related to September 11 and taking a special charge of $1.36 billion in connection with the acquisition and integration of American General, AIG still managed to post net income for 2001 of $5.36 billion, which was only a slight decline over the $5.64 billion figure for the preceding year. Revenues increased 9.4 percent for the year, to $62.4 billion, and total assets grew 15.5 percent, to $492.98 billion. Return on equity was 11.9 percent, an uncharacteristically low figure for a company that had reported four straight years of return on equity in excess of 15 percent.

It was clear that AIG was continuing its remarkable period of stellar performance under Maurice Greenberg's leadership, and Greenberg during his more than 30 years in charge had become a legend in the insurance industry. One question that kept recurring year after year in regard to AIG's future was who would succeed Greenberg (he turned 76 in 2001) and become only the third leader in AIG history. Over the years several potential successors had left AIG to head up other firms, not willing to wait for Greenberg to retire. A new and louder round of speculation arose in mid-1995 when Jeffrey Greenberg, who had been widely rumored to be the latest heir apparent, abruptly resigned from the firm. Some observers then raised the possibility that Jeffrey's brother Evan was the new heir apparent, using his recent promotion to executive vice-president to support their theory. Evan remained the assumed heir until September 2000 when he too resigned suddenly. This latest departure led to expressions of concern from certain analysts, but Maurice Greenberg continued to state that he had no plans to retire and that a succession plan was in place—although he refused to provide any details about it.

Principal Subsidiaries

AIG Annuity Insurance Company; AIG Financial Products Corp.; AIG Global Investment Group, Inc.; AIG SunAmerica Life Insurance Company; American General Finance, Inc.; American General Life Companies; American Home Assurance Company; American Life Insurance Company; The Hartford Steam Boiler Inspection and Insurance Company; International Lease Finance Corporation; Lexington Insurance Company; National Union Fire Insurance Company of Pittsburgh, Pa.; New Hampshire Insurance Company; SunAmerica Asset Management Corp.; SunAmerica Life Insurance Company; Transatlantic Reinsurance Company; United Guaranty Residential Insurance Company; The Variable Annuity Life Insurance Company; American International Assurance Company (Bermuda) Limited; American International Reinsurance Company Limited (Bermuda); American International Underwriters Overseas, Ltd. (Bermuda); American International Assurance Company, Limited (Hong Kong); AIG Star Life Insurance Co., Ltd. (Japan); Nan Shan Life Insurance Company, Ltd. (Taiwan).

Principal Competitors

Allianz AG; AXA; ING Groep N.V.; Zurich Financial Services; Prudential Financial, Inc.; Metropolitan Life Insurance Company; State Farm Insurance Companies; The Allstate Corporation; Travelers Property Casualty Corp.

Further Reading

Brady, Diane, "Like Father, Like Sons," *Business Week,* March 1, 1999, pp. 112–13.

Campanella, Frank W., "Global Insurer: American International Group's Heavy Foreign Stake Proves Sound Policy," *Barron's,* September 27, 1982, pp. 50+.

Chen, Kathy, Tom Hamburger, and Christopher Oster, "AIG's Chief Executive Gets His Way in Washington: Greenberg Uses Personal Touch for Airline and Insurance Bills, China Trade," *Wall Street Journal,* December 7, 2001, p. A20.

History of AIG, New York: American International Group, Inc., 1985.

Jennings, John P., "AIG Moves to Make It a Smaller World," *National Underwriter,* June 22, 1987, pp. 15+.

Laing, Jonathan R., "A Father-Son Rift," *Barron's,* September 25, 2000, p. 15.

——, "Mr. Irreplaceable: Hank Greenberg Made AIG a Powerhouse; Could Any Successor Do As Well?," *Barron's,* November 29, 1999, pp. 33–34, 36, 38.

Lipin, Steven, and Deborah Lohse, "AIG to Buy SunAmerica for $18 Billion," *Wall Street Journal,* August 20, 1998, p. A3.

"Local Hero: AIG," *Economist,* July 4, 1992, pp. 71–72.

Lohse, Deborah, "AIG's Deal for SunAmerica Signals Faith in Annuities," *Wall Street Journal,* August 21, 1998, p. A3.

Loomis, Carol J., "AIG: Aggressive. Inscrutable. Greenberg.," *Fortune,* April 27, 1998, pp. 106–08+.

Mack, Toni, "The Vince Lombardi of Insurance," *Forbes,* October 24, 1983, pp. 60+.

McLeod, Douglas, "Heir Apparent Leaves AIG," *Business Insurance,* June 12, 1995, p. 1.

Meakin, Thomas K., "AIG Hits Home Run with 20th Century, Analysts Say," *National Underwriter Property and Casualty-Risk & Benefits,* October 17, 1994, pp. 29–30.

Milligan, John W., "Can Hank Greenberg Keep the Magic Alive at AIG?," *Institutional Investor,* January 1986, pp. 286+.

——, "Maurice Greenberg, Chairman, American International Group," *Institutional Investor,* June 1987, pp. 206+.

"Risky Business," *Chief Executive,* June 1993, pp. 34–37.

Scism, Leslie, and Christopher Oster, "AIG Heir Apparent Abruptly Quits Posts," *Wall Street Journal,* September 20, 2000, p. A3.

Scism, Leslie, and Deborah Lohse, "AIG's Steady Chief at Last Kicks Up Heels with a Deal: SunAmerica Fits with Greenberg's Aim of Making Firm a Household Name," *Wall Street Journal,* August 25, 1998, p. B4.

Treaster, Joseph B., "Warren Buffett Gets All the Attention, but Hank Greenberg Is Posting Better Returns," *New York Times,* July 23, 2000, sec. 3, p. 1.

Wells, Chris, "Insurers Under Siege," *Business Week,* August 21, 1989, pp. 72–79.

—update: David E. Salamie

American Vanguard Corporation

4695 MacArthur Court
Newport Beach, California 92660
U.S.A.
Telephone: (949) 260-1200
Fax: (949) 260-1201
Web site: http://www.amvac-chemical.com

Public Company
Incorporated: 1969
Employees: 180
Sales: $87.0 million (2001)
Stock Exchanges: American
Ticker Symbol: AVD
NAIC: 325320 Pesticide and Other Agricultural Chemical
Manufacturing

American Vanguard Corporation is a southern California holding company, the primary business of which is conducted through its Amvac Chemical Corporation subsidiary. The company manufactures and markets insecticides, fungicides, herbicides, plant-growth regulators, and soil fumigants. In recent years, it has made a specialty of acquiring the rights to niche products that much larger chemical companies have developed but neglected in favor of concentrating their resources on blockbuster products. American Advantage takes acquired brand names and customer lists, then looks for new markets and applications to more fully realize the products' potential. The company does a limited amount of business outside of the United States through operations in Mexico and the United Kingdom. In addition to Amvac, American Vanguard owns GemChem, Inc., a national chemical distributor which also serves as Amvac's domestic sales force, and Environmental Mediation, Inc., which provides a wide range of services regarding environmental issues, including government relations and regulatory strategy.

Incorporated in 1969

American Vanguard was incorporated under the laws of Delaware in January 1969, with Herbert A. Kraft named chairman of the board and chief executive officer. The new holding company then acquired operational subsidiaries in April 1969 by purchasing all of the shares of Absco Distributing, Captive Air, and Manufacturers Mirror and Glass Co. It was Absco that would form the basis of American Vanguard's entry into the chemical business. Absco began business in 1945 supplying a variety of southern California businesses with industrial gases, as well as electrical and gas welding equipment. It purchased liquid oxygen, argon, nitrogen, carbon dioxide, and other specialty gases which it stored in large storage tanks then transferred to smaller cylinders for resale. Absco's customers included construction companies, defense contractors and subcontractors, machine shops, and original equipment manufacturers.

In 1971, American Vanguard entered into another aspect of the chemical industry—pesticides and insecticides—when it acquired Durham Chemical Co. One of Durham's subsidiaries, Alco Chemical Co., was subsequently merged with Durham to form a new entity, Amvac Chemical Corp. It originally acted as a distributor of agricultural chemicals before acquiring the rights to produce some of the products. Through Absco and Amvac, American Vanguard joined the ranks of southern California's many chemical companies. Although better known for film and television, as well as its defense contractors, the area was also home to Dow Chemical, Union Carbide, and scores of smaller chemical companies that made chemicals out of other chemicals, catering to the needs of a wide variety of businesses, such as pharmaceuticals, cosmetics companies, paint manufacturers, and detergent makers. With the proliferation of environmental protection laws in the 1960s and 1970s, however, it became increasingly difficult for these companies to function. Moreover, companies operating in California faced additional safety measures due to the possibility of accidental contamination caused by earthquakes. According to Kraft, American Vanguard recognized that it was entering an era of tighter government control and simply decided that ''in order to continue in the chemical business, anytime they would pass a rule we would comply.'' Over the years, a number of other chemical companies were less responsive and dropped out of the business, allowing Amvac to ''fill the vacuum.'' It was this willingness to adjust product offerings, depending upon industry conditions, that became a signature trait of American Vanguard.

Company Perspectives:

Amvac is proud to be a global partner in the agricultural industry. Our people are dedicated to providing excellent products and services to ensure better harvests through the new millennium. We look forward to serving your needs and helping the efforts to feed a hungry planet.

Moreover, flexibility was essentially a requirement for a company dealing in chemicals in the final decades of the 20th century. Amvac's agricultural chemicals were under constant scrutiny, often the subject of litigation, and in some cases were banned by the government.

Sell-Off of Absco: 1989

Although there was greater risk in the production of agricultural chemicals, it was this sector that offered more long-term promise to American Vanguard. The company enjoyed a string of record results in the 1980s but was held back by its industrial gases business, which was dependent on other industries that endured tough economic conditions during the decade. In September 1989, management decided to end its involvement in industrial gases, selling the assets of Absco, including some real estate, to Phoenix Distributors for $4.5 million. The name of the Absco subsidiary was changed to 2110 Davie Corporation, a real estate venture, the sole function of which was to own the land that Amvac occupied.

Amvac began to develop its strategy of acquiring niche products from larger companies. In 1989, it purchased from DuPont the Phosdrin line of insecticides, a business it was already involved in, having manufactured Phosdrin for the international market since 1985, supplying Shell, American Cyanamid, and BASF. Phosdrin, however, was a risky acquisition. The chemical was already targeted by Cesar Chavez and his United Farm Workers Union, which claimed that the chemical made workers ill. Phosdrin had been in use since 1953, popular with farmers because it could be used close to the time of harvest. Easily decomposing in water and sunlight, Phosdrin needed only 48 hours before workers could enter a field, provided they wore protective clothing. Whether workers who had become ill had taken necessary precautions was a matter of some dispute. Controversy regarding Phosdrin would continue for several more years until in 1994 American Vanguard agreed to discontinue its domestic production, although the product continued to be sold overseas.

In 1991, Amvac acquired the Naphthalene Acetic Acid plant growth regulator chemical product line from Rhone-Poulenc AG Company. The company had already been a major supplier of the necessary chemicals to Rhone-Poulenc. Also in 1991, GemChem, a national chemical distributor, was hired to serve as Amvac's domestic sales force. (By 1994, Amvac's business grew large enough that American Vanguard elected to acquire GemChem, whose president, Eric Wintemute, was already familiar with Amvac's operations, having worked for Amvac from 1977 to 1982. He now became the chief operating officer of American Vanguard.) Moreover, in 1991 American Vanguard instituted "stewardship contracts" with its distributors. Because it relied so heavily on distributors, the company offered greater potential profits but also required regular monthly reports before payments were issued. In the first year, American Vanguard deducted a large amount of stewardship payments, outraging some of its distributors. Ultimately, however, the tough approach worked. Distributors began to supply the information the company needed and both sides prospered.

Picking up the rights to niche chemical lines was a difficult enterprise for American Vanguard in the early 1990s. Major corporations were reluctant to let go of their products until the small company proved itself. In 1992, American Vanguard gained the non-U.S. rights to the Dibrom insecticide line from Chevron. In 1998, it acquired the U.S. Dibrom business of Valent USA Corporation, which had previously acquired the domestic rights from Chevron. Amvac had been producing Dibrom for both Chevron and Valent since 1981. The next major niche product acquired by American Vanguard came in late 1993, when it purchased the rights to Bidrin, an insecticide used on cotton crops, from DuPont Agricultural Products.

As American Vanguard built up its agricultural chemicals business, it faced mounting expenses in complying with government regulations as well as the cost of litigation, sometimes caused by third parties. For instance, in 1991 a train derailment in northern California resulted in a spill of 19,000 gallons of metam sodium (a soil fumigant made by Amvac) into the Shasta River. The company was named in a class-action suit and a year later agreed to pay a settlement. From 1990 to 1994, American Vanguard was sued by more than 20 California municipalities, water districts, and water companies regarding the leaching of some of its products in normal agricultural use into the groundwater. The company ultimately reached a settlement in March 1995. Because of these and other matters, relations became strained between American Vanguard and both the state of California and the federal Environmental Protection Agency. The man who would endeavor to repair that breach was its new president and CEO, Eric Wintemute, who replaced Kraft in 1994. Because of the company's involvement in regulatory issues it was not surprising that American Vanguard became a major investor in Environmental Mediation, Inc., a California company formed in the early 1990s to assist clients on a wide range of issues, including government relations and regulatory strategy. The relationship between the two companies was not made public until 1998, when Environmental Mediation's president, Wayne Nastri, was appointed by California Governor Pete Wilson to serve on the South Coast Air Quality Management District, the so-called smog board. The press then reported that American Vanguard, in fact, owned a majority interest in Environmental Mediation, resulting in some controversy before Nastri's appointment was confirmed. It was not until its 2000 10K filing to the Securities and Exchange Commission (SEC), however, that American Vanguard would begin to include Environmental Mediation as one of its operations.

Wintemute continued the plan to acquire the rights to chemicals that had an annual sales track of $5 million to $15 million, as well as joint marketing ventures. An example of the latter was an agreement with CIBA, which used CIBA's sales force to sell CIBA's Ridomil product packaged with Amvac's PCNB soil fungicide. Under Wintemute, American Vanguard also

---

Key Dates:

1969: American Vanguard Corporation is formed.
1972: Amvac Chemical subsidiary is formed.
1989: Absco Distributing is sold.
1994: GemChem, Inc. is acquired.
2001: Axix, Alabama, manufacturing plant is acquired.

---

began to look overseas. Although some of Amvac's products were sold to some 50 countries through local distributors, export sales accounted for just 10 percent of revenues and offered great promise for future growth. In 1994, the company established an office in the United Kingdom in order to coordinate European sales. American Vanguard also established a subsidiary to sell products in Mexico.

Securing the Rights to Vapam: 1997

After several years having difficulty convincing major corporations to sell them niche product lines, American Vanguard finally gained sufficient credibility that it began to pick up brands at an increasing pace in the late 1990s. In 1997, it gained the rights to Vapam, a soil fumigant used to suppress weeds, manufactured and marketed by Zeneca Inc. The product was a good fit with Amvac because it already manufactured metam sodium, the active ingredient in Vapam. In addition to gaining the U.S. rights to Dibrom in 1998, American Vanguard also purchased the naled pesticide product line from a Valent subsidiary, a substance which Amvac had formulated and manufactured for Valent since 1991.

The year 2000 proved to be American Vanguard's most active year in acquiring mature product lines. In May of that year, the company added its first herbicide, acquiring the world-wide rights to Dacthal from Zeneca. Dacthal was used to control annual grasses and broadleaf weeds in such crops as broccoli, onions, and strawberries. For Zeneca, Dacthal's sales were too small to warrant the necessary support, so that the product had not been effectively marketed for three years, resulting in a loss of 70 percent of its sales. Amvac began to immediately sell Dacthal overseas and several months later began to market it in the United States. Also in 2000, American Vanguard acquired the exclusive U.S. marketing rights to Bayer's Aztec 4.6G, a corn soil insecticide. In addition, Aztec complemented another corn soil insecticide product American Vanguard acquired that year, DuPont's Fortress. In addition to the insecticide, the company gained the "Strong Box" distribution technology, which along with Fortress failed to live up to DuPont's expectations. The closed plastic containers, pre-filled with Fortress, were slotted into a unit towed by a tractor, thereby permitting the safe handling of the insecticide. Aztec and Fortress had competed directly, but now American Vanguard was in a position to also prepackage Aztec in the Strong Box. This meant that farmers, who rotated insecticides, could make fuller use of their investment in the Strong Box system by simply switching off between Fortress and Aztec. In this way, rather than cannibalizing sales, the two products now reinforced one another.

In 2001, American Vanguard again turned to DuPont, this time acquiring a manufacturing facility in Axis, Alabama, which promised to lead to even further growth for its Amvac subsidiary. Not only could the plant double the company's production capacity, it allowed Amvac to branch into a number of other types of chemistries. Moreover, the location offered greater access to markets in the South, Midwest, and East. American Vanguard, as a result, was better positioned to take advantage of current conditions that might free up potentially lucrative product niches. Due to consolidation in the chemical industry, a number of product lines were likely to come on to the market. Moreover, some companies might be reluctant to pay for re-registration of certain products. American Vanguard was also eager to extend the use of Strong Box to new products. Although still generating less than $100 million in annual revenues, the company was consistently profitable and had been trending up for many years. Its program of taking over niche chemicals appeared to be a sound recipe for even greater growth in the future.

Principal Subsidiaries

Amvax Chemical Corporation; GemChem, Inc.; Environmental Mediation, Inc.

Principal Competitors

Aceto Corp.; Crompton Corporation; FMC Corp.

Further Reading

"American Vanguard on Track for Major Growth," *Chemical Market Reporter,* November 19, 2001, p. 18.

Elliott, Alan R., "Rapid Merger Activity Doesn't Bug Pesticide Maker," *Investor's Business Daily,* February 26, 2002, p. 10.

Lee, Samantha, "American Vanguard Finds Growth in Old-Line Products," *Orange County Business Journal,* October 29, 2001.

Plishner, Emily S., "Expanding Horizons for American Vanguard," *Chemical Week,* February 15, 1995, p. 62.

Seewald, Nancy, "Amvac Rakes the Pesticide Fields," *Chemical Week,* May 5, 2001, p. 41.

—Ed Dinger

Amey Plc

Sutton Courtenay
Abingdon
Oxfordshire OX14 4PP
United Kingdom
Telephone: (+44) 1235-848-811
Fax: (+44) 1235-848-822
Web site: http://www.amey.co.uk

Public Company
Incorporated: 1921
Employees: 6,278
Sales: £700.16 million ($1.01 billion) (2000)
Stock Exchanges: London
Ticker Symbol: AMY
NAIC: 561210 Facilities Support Services; 488999 All
    Other Support Activities for Transportation (pt);
    561499 All Other Business Support Services; 541330
    Engineering Services

Amey Plc has tried on a new hat for the 21st century. Formerly one of the United Kingdom's largest public works construction companies, with a specialty in road building, Amey has shifted its focus to the support services sector, including railroad and highway maintenance services, facilities design, maintenance and management services for schools, hospitals, and other public and private structures, as well as infrastructure and support services for the public utilities and telecommunications sectors. The company also boasts a strong information technology component for both public sector and private industry customers. The company maintains a construction and civil engineering component, which does business primarily for its other divisions. In 2001, Amey restructured its operations into four primary divisions: Public Sector Services, Private Sector Services, Transportation Services, and Technology Services. In 2000, Amey posted revenues of more than £700 million ($1.1 billion). The company is led by CEO Brian Staples and Chairman Neil Ashley.

Quarrying Beginning in the 1920s

Amey PLC was initially founded by Ron Amey as a quarrying operation and gravel producer in the Thames Valley region. The company expanded as a general aggregates producer in the years leading up to World War II. By the end of the war, the company had emerged as one of the United Kingdom's leading aggregates producers. The company leveraged this position with a move into road construction, setting up subsidiary Amey Asphalt. The company's timing proved fortuitous, as the postwar reconstruction effort and then a lasting economic boom—which in turn sparked the rise of the automobile in the United Kingdom—created strong demand for road construction in the 1950s.

The company, which listed on the London Stock Exchange in 1963, extended its construction interests into the civil engineering sector during the 1960s. By the early 1970s, however, Amey caught the attention of acquisitive Consolidated Gold Fields. The mining conglomerate had decided to expand its operations into the quarrying of aggregates for the construction industry, as part of an overall diversification program. In 1973, Consolidated Gold Fields acquired Amey, then added the company to two other recently added quarrying operations, Greenfields and Amalgamated Roadstone. The three operations were combined into a single entity, Amey Roadstone Construction, or ARC.

Under Consolidated Gold Fields, ARC became a modernized company that helped to transform the quarrying industry in the United Kingdom. The company also began to expand geographically, adding operations in continental Europe, as well as in Africa and other parts of the world. ARC also continued to build its civil engineering and construction operations, notably through its Amey construction wing. The company's civil engineering and construction work led it into other public service areas, such as railway maintenance and services to various military installations. Emphasizing its expanding construction business, the company took on a new name, ARC Construction, in 1986.

By the end of the 1980s, Consolidated Gold Fields itself had come into the focus of one of the United Kingdom's largest conglomerates, Hanson PLC, which bought the mining giant, including ARC Construction, in 1969. Several months after its acquisition of Consolidated Gold Fields, Hanson agreed to spin off the ARC Construction component in a management buyout led by Neil Ashley, Eddie King, and other Amey directors. The management buyout, at a cost of just £6.2 million, was financed by backer Close Securities. The new company, placed as a

Company Perspectives:

Amey seeks to be a leading provider of outsourced business support services, operating in all segments of the economy, adding value to its many quality clients in the process. Through the delivery of continuous improvement, supported by innovation, technology and investment, Amey will strive to exceed expectations in order to achieve lasting customer satisfaction. By striving for excellence, Amey will provide a challenging and rewarding environment for its employees, which will be the catalyst for the continuing growth of shareholder value.

subsidiary under the newly created Amey Holdings, was renamed Amey Construction Ltd.

Developing Independently: 1990s

Amey's first years as an independent company were hampered by the deep recession of the early 1990s, and particularly the crisis affecting the United Kingdom's construction sector in general. Led by Ashley as chairman and King as chief executive, Amey began making acquisitions, including acquiring a mechanical and electrical engineering business in 1990 and taking over the construction contracts, placed under the name Amey Building, from two failed construction companies that same year. Amey was unable to make a breakthrough with its new mechanical and electrical engineering wing, however, and, after posting losses, the unit was discontinued in 1993. Meanwhile, the company's house building unit, hard hit by the economic downturn, was also struggling.

Yet, Amey remained primarily a road building company—that division, which built roads for the Department of Transport as well as for the Ministry of Defense and also provided road and related construction for the United Kingdom's civil airports, contributed more than 80 percent of its profits and the largest share of its sales. By the mid-1990s, the company was ranked sixth in the United Kingdom's road building sector.

By 1994, Amey had recovered from its financial difficulties enough to go public with a listing on the London exchange. While road construction continued to play a prominent role in the company's operations, especially with government plans to spend as much as £2.3 billion on road construction and maintenance in the mid-1990s, Amey increasingly turned its attention to expanding its facilities management and support services operations, a market it had first entered in 1991. An important moment in Amey's facilities management and support services operations came when the company won a management contract with the city of Portsmouth in 1995.

Amey continued building up its construction and road work operations in the mid-1990s, including winning resurfacing contracts for Manchester Airport. Yet road building by then accounted for only about one-third of Amey's total business. Instead, the company's interest was turning more and more to facilities management and support services. In 1996, the company paid £15 million to acquire majority control of Western Infrastructure Maintenance Company (WIMC), which had been part of the newly privatized British Rail (renamed Railtrack).

The purchase was described by Ashley as representing a ''quantum leap'' in the company's facilities management and maintenance operations, and raised the portion of the company's profits generated by the sector to more than 75 percent of its total profits. Soon after that, the WIMC acquisition, Amey, together with partner Sir Robert McAlpine, was awarded a £175 million contract to build the Croydon Tramlink, a 28-kilometer light rail network. By the end of 1996, the company's sales had grown past £312 million.

Brian Staples took over as chief executive after Edward King retired in 1997. Staples now stepped up Amey's transformation into a facilities management and support services group, boasting a war chest of some £100 million that the company intended to put toward acquisitions. The company's repositioning had been achieved just as the United Kingdom's support services sector promised to enter a new era of growth. In the mid-1990s, the British government had announced the creation of a so-called Private Finance Initiative (PFI) as it sought to turn over the management and maintenance of many formerly government-run services to the private sector. The new program was expected to provide a strong increase to the numbers of contracts turned over to non-government businesses, and Amey had placed itself in line as a strong contender for PFI contracts.

Meanwhile, the company continued adding to its road and rail operations, joining the Autolink Concessionaires consortium, with partners Sir Robert McAlpine and Taylor Woodrow Construction, to win a £370 million contract to build a highway linking Carlisle and Glasgow in 1997. The company also won a £40 million management and maintenance contract for roads spanning Buckinghamshire, Berkshire, Essex, Hertfordshire, and Oxfordshire. Then, at the beginning of 1998, Amey and French partner SECO/DEF won a rail replacement contract worth £140 million.

Amey sold off its homebuilding division in September 1998, to Try Homes for £4.8 million, as it turned its focus toward facilities management. The company also began petitioning the London stock exchange to change its listing from the construction and homebuilding category to the support services sector. Toward this aim, the company restructured these operations, placing its civil engineering and construction operations into a single division.

Support Services Company for the 21st Century

The year 1999 was to provide the breakthrough for Amey's conversion into a support services leader. At the beginning of that year, the company won a £65 million contract from Centrica to provide business support services, including security, catering, and postal services, on a national scale. Next, Amey, along with partners Kvaerner and Hyder, won the renovation and maintenance contract for the Ministry of Defence's headquarters at Whitehall. Buoyed by this activity, Amey launched a hostile takeover offer for Servisair, in an attempt to enter the airport ground support services market. Yet Servisair rejected Amey's £82 million offer and agreed to be acquired by Penauille Polyservices, based in France. Thwarted, Amey began to look about for another large-scale acquisition target, announcing its intention to spend up to £90 million in order to complete its shift away from the construction industry.

Key Dates:

1921: Ron Amey begins quarrying and gravel business in Thames Valley.
1948: Company forms Amey Asphalt, dedicated to road construction.
1963: Company goes public on London Stock Exchange.
1973: Amey is acquired by Consolidated Gold Fields, which merges it with Greenfields and Roadstone Construction to form Amey Roadstone Construction (ARC).
1989: Consolidated Gold Fields is acquired by Hanson Plc; ARC is spun off in a management buyout as Amey Construction.
1991: Amey makes first move into facilities management sector.
1994: Amey goes public as Amey Plc.
1999: Amey acquires Comax, a specialist in high-security support services; this acquisition enables Amey to change its stock exchange listing to the support services sector.

After contenting itself with the modest £1.1 million acquisition of Enviresponse, a provider of environmental disaster recovery services, the company finally found a large-sized match. In July 1999 the company agreed to pay £86 million to acquire Comax, a specialist in high-security support services. That company had been created in 1995 as the internal support services division of the British government's Defence Evaluation Research Agency (Dera). The division was then spun off in a management buyout, backed by Cinven, in 1997. The Comax acquisition, described by CEO Staples as "a complete step change in Amey's development," ultimately proved enough to tip the balance and led to the company's reclassification from the underrated construction industry to the more dynamically growing facilities management and support services sector.

Following the Comax purchase, Amey shifted its construction division, which was renamed Amey Asset Services, away from winning outside contracts toward providing construction services for the company's new core operations. An example of the new role was seen when the company won a £155 million contract to construct and modernize facilities for the Northern Birmingham Mental Health Trust in 2000. Upon completion, the project was to be turned over to Amey's support services division, which would then initiate a 35-year facilities management contract.

Meanwhile, Amey continued to reap the rewards of PFI contracts, including winning, as part of the 3ED consortium (with Halifax and Miller Group), a £1.9 billion contract to modernize and manage 29 secondary schools in Glasgow. Another important contract came that same year when Amey was signed on to design, build, and manage a new facility for the

Immigration Service. At the end of 2000, Amey expanded its facilities management operation, entering Ireland through the purchase of a 33 percent stake in Irish Facilities Management. Closing out the year, the company, as part of a consortium including infrastructure specialist Jarvis Plc, was awarded the contract to redevelop a large part of the London Underground. The company's one-third stake in the consortium gave it a prime share of the expected annual value of £400 million to £500 million over some 30 years.

At the beginning of 2001, Amey restructured its operations to reflect its new focus. The company now divided up into four primary divisions: Public Sector Services, Private Sector Services, Transportation Services, and Technology Services. The company continued to show itself an aggressive participant in the race to outsourced government contracts—by the end of 2001, the company claimed to have its bid in on more than 144 contracts, including 38 PFI projects. Amey was clearly on the right road to building a position as a leader in the U.K. support services sector.

Principal Subsidiaries

Amey Building Limited; Amey Business Services Limited; Amey Construction Limited; Amey Fleet Services Limited; Amey Group Services Limited; Amey Highways Limited; Amey Information Services Limited; Amey Projects Limited; Amey Properties Limited; Amey Vectra Limited; Amey Ventures Limited; IT Counsel Limited.

Principal Divisions

Public Sector Services; Private Sector Services; Transportation Services; Technology Services.

Principal Competitors

AMEC PLC; Balfour Beatty PLC; Bechtel PLC; Bouygues SA; Colas SA; Fluor SA; Jarvis PLC; Sodexho SA; Tarmac PLC; WS Atkins PLC.

Further Reading

Batchelor, Charles, "Amey in Focus on PFI Schemes," *Financial Times*, September 11, 2001.
Moreton, Philippa, "Amey Unveils Record Orders, 2000 Profits Up," *Reuters*, March 20, 2001.
Potter, Ben, ed., "Amey Is Still Building, but Turns Its Attention to Maintenance," *Daily Telegraph*, March 24, 1999.
Ridge, Mian, "Amey H1 up, Sees Booming Growth Ahead," *Reuters*, September 11, 2001.
Thackray, Rachelle, "Amey Builds on PFI with £155m Mental Health Trust Deal," *Independent*, August 17, 2000, p. 17.
Yates, Andrew, "Amey Amasses £100m War Chest for Acquisition Spree," *Independent*, September 4, 1997, p. 22.
Young, Andrew, "Amey Boosts Support Services with Buy," *Reuters*, July 1, 1999.

—M.L. Cohen

Anchor Brewing Company

1705 Mariposa Street
San Francisco, California 94107
U.S.A.
Telephone: (415) 863-8350
Fax: (415) 552-7094
Web site: http://www.anchorbrewing.com

Private Company
Founded: 1896
Employees: 50
Sales: $10 million (2000 est.)
NAIC: 312120 Breweries

Anchor Brewing Company has been making unique, traditional beer in San Francisco, California, since the 1860s. Priding itself on its commitment to small-scale production, the company sells about 110,000 barrels a year of its seven brews, distributing them nationwide and exporting them to pubs and retail outlets in Sweden, France, Italy, England, Australia, Japan, and Hong Kong. Along with its flagship beer, Anchor Steam, the company's beers and ales include Anchor Porter, Anchor Small Beer, Anchor Wheat, Liberty Ale, Old Foghorn, and Our Special Ale—a seasonal holiday brew that changes each year. In addition, Anchor also operates a small distillery on its premises, manufacturing limited quantities of Old Potrero whiskey and Junipero gin.

Early Roots: 1860s–1960s

In the mid-1860s, Ernst Baruth and Otto Schinkel began selling beer to a handful of local restaurant and bar owners from a brewing facility in San Francisco, California, on Pacific Avenue between Larkin and Hyde Streets. Named Anchor Brewing in 1896, the brewery sold only steam beer—Anchor Steam—available on tap and made using a higher temperature brewing process developed during the Gold Rush.

"Steam" beer probably described the unique brewing method used by early Gold Rush brewers. Because of the city's climate, brewers were able to avoid using costly ice; the hot liquid produced during the brewing process cooled rapidly when placed in shallow brewing vessels, with steam rising in the open air as the liquid cooled. There was also a burst of steam whenever a keg of the highly carbonated brew was tapped. Equally possible, "Steam was a nickname that meant any primitive beer, not something made in a particular way . . . ," according to Fritz Maytag, the man who bought the company in 1965, in a July 30, 2000 *Boston Herald* article. Although popular with local customers, it was often poorly made with an unreliable, quirky taste.

For the first 100 years of its history, Anchor Brewing was purchased and resold several times. However, its owners changed little except its location. Joe Allen, an employee, purchased Anchor after Prohibition and then sold it to Laurence Steese in 1958, who moved the company to Eighth Street between Bryant and Brannan Streets. But Anchor never turned much of a profit, and by 1965 the company was going bankrupt. Just as the brewery was about to close its doors permanently, the 26-year-old Fritz Maytag stepped in and gave Steese $5,000 to keep Anchor open, buying a 51 percent interest in the company. In a January 1983 article in *Inc.*, Maytag described the reason for his investment: "I was sort of drifting along, the way you do when you get out of graduate school, looking for something to do. . . . [Anchor] needed an angel, someone to come through with a tiny bit of money. [My intention was] to give a little advice and go away." Before he stepped in, the company was in such desperate financial condition that "[Anchor was] selling the old wooden beer kegs on the sidewalk for 50 cents . . . ," according to Maytag in a March 1999 article in the *San Francisco Chronicle*.

Fritz Maytag, born Frederick Louis Maytag III—the first son of the family home-appliance makers whose enterprises include The Maytag Company and Maytag Blue Cheese—had the financial resources that Anchor needed. However, he had no skill in brewing. He had attended prep school in the East and then Stanford University in 1959 where he graduated with a degree in American literature. By 1964, he had dropped out of Stanford's graduate program in Japanese. Shortly after he made his investment in 1965, Maytag left for Chile to start a wine export business.

Company Perspectives:

Our brewers employ no modern short-cuts and each brew is virtually handmade with an all-malt mash, in our handmade copper brewhouse; a veritable museum of the simple, traditional brewhouses of old. While we strive to practice the art of classical brewing, we employ state-of-the-art methods to ensure that our products are clean and clear, pure and fresh. Every bottle and keg of our precious beer is kept under refrigeration at the brewery, and at the warehouse of your local distributor. We know of no brewery in the world that matches our efforts to combine traditional, natural brewing methods with the most careful and modern methods of sanitation, finishing, packaging and transporting.

When Maytag returned to San Francisco in 1969, he found the company near bankruptcy again. "The brewery was a disaster," he said in a January 1983 *Inc.* article. "The equipment was antiquated. The quality of the beer was inconsistent. And some of the bad beer was getting into the trade and making a poor sales situation worse. I finally decided that I had either to get out or get into the business all the way and try to make it a going concern." At this point, Maytag bought out his partners. When he took over, Anchor was producing about 600 barrels (each holding 31 gallons) of beer a year. The company had one employee and no up-to-date machinery or refrigeration. As the new brew master and president, Maytag decided that his mission would be to save Anchor, restore traditional brewing methods, and preserve the art of classical brewing.

A New Owner and a New Tradition: 1969–74

Maytag's first goal was to increase sales by improving the quality of his product. After reading voraciously and seeking advice from brew masters in this country and in Europe, Maytag came to the conclusion that his only ingredients would be barley, hops, yeast, and water. Furthermore, he insisted that his beer would be made only with expensive two-row barley malt (rather than the less flavorful six-row variety) and would not include any adjuncts, such as corn or rice—cheaper grains that replace 30 to 40 percent of the barley in most U.S. brews. Rather than using pellets or extract, he used whole hops in the proportion of one pound per barrel—three or four times the industry average. He also refused to add any of 100 permissible additives and preservatives, such as enzyme papain for clarity, propylene glycol for a stable head, or caramel to darken the color.

To brew his beer, Maytag brought in ultra-modern equipment to supplement the brewery's traditional machinery, which included an antique malt-crushing mill. He implemented strict methods of processing, including a costly, time-consuming fermentation process practiced by few large commercial breweries called *krausening*—a German technique used to develop natural carbonation that produces a creamier, richer, long-lasting head and finer bubbles. In *krausening*, beer is placed in a closed aging tank after fermentation and newly fermenting beer is blended with the already fermenting beer. Once brewed, instead of filtering the beer, Maytag processed it with centrifugation. He avoided tunnel pasteurizing—a method of cooking the beer at high heat for 15 minutes to kill harmful bacteria—because the process risked destroying the flavor. Instead, he flash-pasteurized, using 15 seconds of heat and aseptic bottling. Maytag trademarked this unique process of brewing, making Anchor Brewing the sole extant brewer of "steam" beer. His new version of Anchor Steam beer was distinctive, rich, thick, bitter, and heavily hopped, somewhere between an ale and a lager. Unique among American beers, *Brewers Digest* described Anchor Steam as "a beer for connoisseurs and suds lovers alike."

Marketing and Company Expansion: 1975–95

However, brewing "the perfect beer" was insufficient grounds on which to build a company; so Maytag began a strategy to market his product that was unlike anything previously tried in the industry. Following a family precept to "make better, not more," he decided to sell a small amount of his handmade beer at a high price and let its reputation spread by word of mouth.

To enhance the nostalgic image of quality and create a mystique around Anchor Steam, Maytag began a brewery tour. He also used hand-painted delivery trucks and old-fashioned labels with a legend that read "Made in San Francisco since 1896" across the bottom. Four-packs instead of six-packs in an open-bottomed carton lowered costs as well as distinguished the beer from its competitors.

By 1975, ten years after his initial investment, Maytag was not only making a profit, but his company had achieved a level of notoriety. Anchor Steam beer was winning recognition and prizes and was considered a beer for connoisseurs. In 1977, it was the grand prizewinner of *New West* magazine's taste test, called the "Best Beer in America" by *Quest* magazine, and was labeled the "Rolls Royce" of U.S. beers by Joseph Owades, director of the Center for Brewing Studies. With this kind of popularity, the brewery reached the height of its production power at 12,500 barrels—a staggering increase from the mere 600 barrels that were produced annually in 1965. This same year, sales passed the $1 million mark. Running at full capacity, Anchor was selling to customers in Minnesota, New Jersey, and ten western states. With demand exceeding supply, Maytag decided to build a new brewery to accommodate his expanding business.

To fund the company's expansion, Maytag pledged all of his personal assets, real estate, and stock, stretching both his and his company's funds to the limit. In August 1979, when the former Chase and Sanborn coffee plant on Mariposa Street was finally converted into a brewery, bankruptcy threatened. To make matters worse, the first year the new facility was open, it lost money. However, because the new facility allowed Anchor to expand its supply, soon its sales began to climb and the company reached profitability.

Growth continued, and by 1982 the company was selling 28,500 barrels in 20 different states. In 1983, Anchor had more than $3 million in sales. Although these sales did not amount to much in the $30 billion, 177 million-barrel U.S. brewing industry, competing on a grand scale was never Maytag's intention. Anchor produced less each year than the industry's two giants—

Key Dates:

1896: Anchor Brewing gets its name.
1965: Fritz Maytag saves Anchor from bankruptcy.
1969: Maytag buys out his partners and becomes president.
1971: Previously only sold in kegs, Anchor Steam beer is now bottled.
1975: Anchor turns a profit and begins producing other beers.
1993: Anchor begins limited production of Old Potrero rye whiskey and Junipero gin.
2000: The company sells 110,000 barrels of beer in 49 states, Japan, and Europe.

40.3 million-barrel Miller Brewing Company and 54.3 million barrel Anheuser-Busch Company—produced in a few hours. In keeping with Maytag's goal of modest growth, by1985 the company had 14 full-time employees. By 1988, Anchor brewed about 44,000 barrels annually with sales of $5.3 million.

In 1990, Anchor sold 68,000 barrels—up 16 percent from the 58,500 barrels it sold in 1989. At the beginning of 1991, a new federal beer tax took effect and helped to boost Anchor's sales further. Companies that produced more than two million barrels per year saw their tax doubled to $18 per barrel. However, breweries such as Anchor that produced less than this amount were exempt from paying the increased tax on their first 60,000 barrels. Because Anchor's production was only 8,000 over this limit, the tax helped to narrow the price gap between Anchor's product and its competition's. By 1995, Anchor was producing 100,000 barrels of Anchor Steam, Liberty Ale, a porter, a barley wine, and a wheat beer (which the company believed to be the first of its kind produced in the United States after Prohibition). The company began exporting its products to pubs and retail outlets in Sweden, France, Italy, England, Australia, and some to Japan and Hong Kong. In 1998, its sales were $10 million.

Pioneering an Industry: The Rise of the Microbrewery

As Anchor grew, the brewing industry gradually began to change. Maytag and several other brewers nationwide whose brews were richer and fuller-bodied following traditional brewing techniques had a huge influence on the beer industry. In a January 29, 1991 *San Francisco Chronicle* article, David Edgar, assistant director of the Institute of Brewing Studies, a division of the Association of Brewers, said: "Anchor started it all. It's the granddaddy of the microbreweries."

Although he refused to diversify his beers, Maytag was interested in exploring other traditional beverages, and in 1993, he opened a small distillery in the back of the Potrero Hill brewery. There, he began limited production of a traditional U.S. rye whiskey that dated back to George Washington's day—Old Potrero, the only single-malt rye being produced in the United States in the 1990s. Because whiskey is distilled beer, Maytag regarded Old Potrero as a natural progression of brewing. Old Potrero is pot-distilled from 100 percent rye malt. In the same distillery, Anchor also began to distill a minuscule amount of a premium gin called Junipero.

Maytag's commitment to remaining small caused him to eschew the trend set by many microbreweries, that of focusing on heavily diversifying their products. Anchor prided itself on being slow to change and insisted on only producing seven brews, including a wheat beer and a limited edition holiday brew, launched in 1975, that varied from year to year—Our Special Ale. Maytag's philosophy was the result of his desire to keep his company a hands-on operation. In an August 30, 1990 article in the *Los Angeles Times*, he stated: "The idea isn't to grow big. It's to make good beer consistently." By 2000, Anchor had leveled off its production to 110,000 barrels per year. It sold its beers in 49 states, Japan, and Europe.

Principal Divisions

Anchor Distilling.

Principal Competitors

Boston Beer Company; The Gambrinus Company; Redhook Ale Brewery, Inc.

Further Reading

Berger, Dan, "Anchor Steam: The Giant of Micro-Breweries," *Los Angeles Times,* August 30, 1990, p. 42.

Berling-Manuel, Lynn, "Anchor Finds Smooth Sailing Without Advertising," *Advertising Age,* January 31, 1985, p. 27.

Blair, Ian, "Is There Strength in Diversity: Although Their Ranks Have Dwindled, America's Small Regional Brewers May Be on the Brink of a Renaissance," *Beverage World,* October 1985, p. 26.

Gumpert, David E., "The Joys of Keeping the Company Small," *Harvard Business Review,* July/August 1986, p. 6.

Hartman, Curtis, "The Alchemist of Anchor Steam," *Inc.,* January 1983, p. 31.

Higgins, Kevin T., "Boutique Breweries: Passing Fad or Viable Competitors to Imports?," *Marketing News,* October 25, 1985, p. 10.

McNicol, Tom, "Anchor Aweigh, Full Steam Ahead," *Los Angeles Times Magazine,* March 10, 1996, p. 22.

Romel, Lund, "Technology Coexists with Old-Fashioned Philosophy," *Modern Office Procedures,* December 1981, p. 74.

Shaw, Jan, "Maytag Hops for a Different Brew," *San Francisco Business Times,* September 26, 1988, p. 1.

Tarpey, John P., and Jonathan B. Levine, "Small-Time Brewers Are Putting the Kick Back into Beer," *Business Week,* January 20, 1986, p. 90.

—Carrie Rothburd

Atlantic Southeast Airlines, Inc.

---

100 Hartsfield Centre Parkway, Suite 800
Atlanta, Georgia 30354-1356
U.S.A.
Telephone: (404) 766-1400
Toll Free: (800) 282-3424
Fax: (404) 209-0162
Web site: http://www.asa-air.com

Wholly Owned Subsidiary of Delta Air Lines, Inc.
Incorporated: 1979
Employees: 4,400
Sales: $621.94 million (2000)
NAIC: 481111 Scheduled Passenger Air Transportation

Atlantic Southeast Airlines, Inc. (ASA) is a leading regional airline based in Atlanta, Georgia. A subsidiary of Delta Air Lines, Inc. since 1999, ASA carries more than six million passengers a year, with a large portion of them making connections to mainline Delta flights.

Formation of Company: 1979

Atlantic Southeast Airlines was formed after Southern Airways, a local carrier based in Atlanta, agreed to merge with North Central Airlines in 1978. Three Southern Airways executives—George F. Pickett, Jr., Robert Priddy, and John Beiser—resigned in January 1979 to form their own airline. Atlantic Southeast Airlines was registered on March 12, 1979 and began service on June 26.

Pickett, Priddy, and Beiser believed Republic Airlines—the sum of the Southern/North Central merger—would neglect local routes as it attempted to expand nationally after the merger went into effect in July 1979. They raised $260,000 from investors who shared this belief.

ASA's first scheduled service consisted of daily flights between Atlanta and Columbus, Georgia, via a single, 14-seat Twin Otter aircraft. The airline carried 12,000 passengers its first year. Macon, Georgia, was added in 1980. By 1982, ASA was connecting 16 destinations.

In 1983, ASA acquired Coastal Air Limited, which had been operating as Southeastern Airlines, gaining a new hub in Memphis as well as nine other new markets in Georgia, Florida, Mississippi, and Tennessee. By this time, ASA was trading over-the-counter under the NASDAQ ticker symbol ASAI.

One outstanding feature of ASA's success, wrote R.E.G. Davies and George Haddaway in their book *Commuter Airlines of the United States,* was the airline's ability to keep its break-even load factor in the neighborhood of 33 to 36 percent. The airline only had to fill a third of its available seats to make money; the rest was profit.

Flying with Delta in 1984

Delta Air Lines, the major carrier based in Atlanta, had also been growing since deregulation in the early 1980s. ASA became a "Delta Connection" airline traffic provider on May 1, 1984; its flights were listed in computer reservation systems with Delta's prefix (DL), leading travel agents to route Delta's connecting flights to ASA. ASA's net income tripled to $5 million in the first year of this new association. In May 1986, Delta acquired 20 percent of ASA's voting stock for about $38 million.

On December 14, 1986, ASA opened a new hub at Dallas/Ft. Worth International, which was dominated by American Airlines, not Delta. Within six months, ASA was flying 110 daily flights out of DFW, connecting nine cities. Revenues for the year were $92.3 million, up 22.5 percent from 1985. Net income increased slightly to $10 million. ASA was already known as the most profitable commuter airline in the United States, though price competition was putting new pressure on margins. Delta's merger with Western Airlines, announced in 1987, created even more demand, yet profits soon stalled, noted *Business Week,* due to ASA's investment in its new hubs.

A strike at Eastern Airlines, Delta's main competitor in Atlanta, worked in ASA's favor. The strike cut Eastern's traffic by 60 percent and drove thousands of passengers to Delta and ASA. Revenues increased to $181 million in 1989, making ASA second only to WestAir among U.S. commuter airlines.

One of the three original founders, Robert Priddy, left the company in 1987. After working with Air Midwest and Mesa Airlines, he created another Atlanta-based airline: ValuJet (later called AirTran).

Profits in the 1990s

The 1990s began with disaster for ASA: the April 5, 1991 crash of an Embraer EMB-120 Brasilia turboprop near Brunswick, Georgia, killed 23 people. The fact that former Senator John G. Tower was among the fatalities compounded the media's exposure. The National Transportation Safety Board (NTSB) cited a malfunctioning propeller as the likely cause. Nevertheless, ASA's financial state remained healthy. It posted a record $32.5 million profit in 1991, while its giant partner Delta lost $239.5 million. Other feeder airlines were tending to fare better than the majors, who collectively were losing billions due to the Gulf War and a worldwide economic downturn. ASA's fortunes continued to grow into the mid-1990s, as competing feeder airlines dropped out of certain markets.

Turboprop airliners used by various regional carriers continued to malfunction into the mid-1990s, creating negative publicity for this sector of the airline industry. An ASA aircraft suffered another fatal crash on August 21, 1995, near Carrollton, Georgia. Also attributed to a propeller failure, this was ASA's 12th accident since 1983.

ASA had operated a number of different types of turboprop aircraft since its founding, including the Embraer EMB-110 Bandeirante and EMB-120 Brasilia (for which it was the launch customer in 1985), the de Havilland Dash 7, the Shorts 360, and the ATR 72. Company executives had considered operating small jets for several years but rejected the idea due to fear of alienating their major airline partner. Finally, in late 1995, ASA began leasing five British Aerospace BAe 146 jets configured to seat 88 passengers each. In addition to offering passengers greater perceived comfort and safety, the jets tripled the range of ASA's turboprop-driven planes. This made them perfect for picking up some longer, low-traffic routes that Delta was handed over to ASA. However, the BAe 146 ultimately proved to be rather unreliable, resulting in an embarrassing number of canceled flights just as Atlanta was hosting the 1996 Summer Games.

ASA wagered its fortunes on an even smaller jet, the Canadair Regional Jet built by Bombardier. In 1997, the carrier ordered 30 of these sleek, 50-seat planes and placed options on

60 more, paying about $600 million. (Rival Comair, another Delta feeder airline, had begun flying regional jets in 1991). ASA ordered another 27 regional jets in 1998 (for delivery between 2000 and 2003). In 1998, ASA was operating 85 planes and had annual income of more than $55 million.

From 1,600 employees in 1995, employment at ASA grew to about 2,500 in the late 1990s. Record hiring by the airline industry meant that ASA would soon resort to classified ads to find qualified pilots. Many pilots saw regional airlines such as ASA as a transitional step towards a job with the majors, resulting in a constant need for new flight crews. ASA had 850 pilots in 1999; 200 of them were new hires.

Purchase of ASA by Delta: 1999

ASA Holdings, parent company of Atlantic Southeast Airlines, Inc., agreed to be acquired by Delta in early 1999. Delta had proposed the buyout in late January at the same time it was demanding changes in its relationship with ASA that would certainly cut into the regional's profits, reported the *Atlanta Journal and Constitution*. Passengers connecting from Delta flights accounted for 80 percent of ASA's business. The ASA board agreed to sell the 80 percent of the company that Delta did not already own for about $700 million rather than watch its share values dwindle. ASA became a wholly owned subsidiary of Delta in May 1999.

Delta soon began integrating ASA's Atlanta schedule more closely with its own, an action that allowed the major airline to transfer its larger jets to longer routes. The acquisition of ASA was intended to keep other carriers from making inroads into Delta's strongest areas, the Southeast and Texas. However, with the purchase came a large pay differential between Delta and ASA pilots that threatened to become a contentious bargaining issue, noted the *New York Times*. American Airlines, which had recently acquired Reno Air Inc., faced a similar situation, which resulted in work disruptions.

The remaining two founders, George F. Pickett, Jr., and John Beiser, left ASA after it was acquired by Delta. Skip Barnette, the first head of Delta Express, a low-cost offshoot of Delta, was made ASA's new CEO. His immediate goal was to raise the level of customer service, which had fallen markedly in the past few years, to the standards that its parent company had set.

A $4 million renovation of ASA's Atlanta facilities was launched almost immediately; another $14 million in capital investment from Delta soon followed as well as acquisitions of new aircraft. In contrast to the slow expansion that characterized ASA's first years in business, in 2000 ASA added 22 new markets and 18 new planes, lifting the fleet to 106 aircraft. Employment reached 3,500.

As reported by *Air Transport World*, Delta was using some of ASA's 38 regional jets as a cost-effective way to test new markets. When demand grew sufficiently, as on routes to Manchester, New Hampshire, and Jacksonville, Florida, Delta assigned its own larger planes to them. At the same time, it would replace mainline service with regional jets when demand fell, as in Chattanooga, Tennessee, and Augusta, Georgia.

Principal Competitors

AirTran Holdings, Inc.; AMR American Eagle Holding Corporation; Atlantic Coast Airlines Holdings, Inc.; Comair, Inc.

Further Reading

Arnoult, Sandra, "The Vision Thing," *Air Transport World*, January 2001, pp. 52–53.

"ASA's Goals Achieved Through Slow, Consistent Growth," *Aviation Week & Space Technology*, August 10, 1998, p. 63.

"ASA Shareholders Sue to Block Acquisition of Airline by Delta," *Wall Street Journal*, March 8, 1999, p. B5.

"Atlantic Southeast Airlines: The Regionals Take Off," *Financial World* (New York), June 8, 1993, p. 44.

Brannigan, Martha, "Commuter Pilots at Delta Units Aim to Merge Unions," *Wall Street Journal*, July 19, 2000, p. A10.

Davies, R.E.G., and I.E. Quastler, "George F. Pickett, Jr.: Atlantic Southeast Airlines," *Commuter Airlines of the United States*, Washington and London: Smithsonian Institution Press, 1995.

"Delta Strikes Deal to Acquire Atlantic Southeast," *Airfinance Journal*, March 1999, p. 17.

Fehr, Stephen C., "4 Dead, 25 Hurt in Plane Crash Near Atlanta; Pilot Cited Engine Trouble Before Turboprop Went Down," *Washington Post*, August 22, 1995, p. A3.

"Flight Attendant Hailed As Hero of Georgia Crash; 'She Was Extremely Terrific,' Passenger Says," *Washington Post*, August 24, 1995, p. A3.

Ho, Rodney, "Delta Feeder Line Makes Deal to Lease Jets; ASA to Absorb More Routes, Analyst Predicts," *Atlanta Journal and Constitution*, July 8, 1995, p. 1C.

Lenckus, Dave, and Stacy Shapiro, "Propeller Cited in Crash of ASA Plane," *Business Insurance*, August 28, 1995, pp. 1+.

Moorman, Robert W., "Delta Takes Charge," *Air Transport World*, September 1999, pp. 50–57.

——, "King of the South," *Air Transport World*, December 1995, p. 51.

——, "Raking in the Big Bucks," *Air Transport World*, October 1992, p. 107.

Ott, James, "Regional Jet Pilots Sue ALPA Over Scope," *Aviation Week & Space Technology*, May 14, 2001, p. 82.

——, "Top Airline Competitors Share Growth Strategy," *Aviation Week & Space Technology*, August 10, 1998, p. 53.

Phillips, Edward H., "Blade Failure Focus of NTSB Crash Probe," *Aviation Week & Space Technology*, August 28, 1995, p. 31.

——, "Engines, Propeller System Scrutinized in Atlantic Southeast Airlines Accident," *Aviation Week & Space Technology*, April 15, 1991, p. 32.

Preble, Cecilia, "Atlantic Southeast Expects to Double Service at Dallas/Ft. Worth Hub," *Aviation Week & Space Technology*, May 4, 1987, p. 41.

Thurston, Scott, "ASA Ordering More Small Jets," *Atlanta Journal and Constitution*, September 5, 1998, p. 1E.

——, "Delta Plans to Replace Some Flights with ASA," *Atlanta Journal and Constitution*, April 9, 1999, p. 3E.

——, "Hartsfield City Limits; ASA Thinks Big with New Breed of Small Jet," *Atlanta Journal and Constitution*, September 29, 1997, p. 4E.

——, "SEC Filing: ASA's Options Included Linking with AirTran," *Atlanta Journal and Constitution*, February 26, 1999, p. 1F.

——, "Wanted: Entry-Level Pilots; Small Airlines Hunt Qualified Candidates," *Atlanta Journal and Constitution*, August 5, 1999, p. 1E.

Ticer, Scott, and James E. Ellis, "Small Planes, Tiny Towns, Big Bucks," *Business Week*, August 7, 1989, p. 64.

Wayne, Leslie, "Delta to Buy Rest of Stake in Atlantic," *New York Times*, February 17, 1999.

"World Airline Financial Statistics—2000," *Air Transport World*, World Airline Report, July 2001, http://www.atwonline.com.

—Frederick C. Ingram

Autobytel Inc.

18872 MacArthur Boulevard
Irvine, California 92612-1400
U.S.A.
Telephone: (949) 225-4500
Fax: (949) 225-4541
Web site: http://www.autobytel.com

Public Company
Incorporated: 1995 as Auto-By-Tel LLC
Employees: 276
Sales: $71.1 million (2001)
Stock Exchanges: NASDAQ
Ticker Symbol: ABTL
NAIC: 541519 Other Computer Related Services

Autobytel Inc., an Irvine, California company, bills itself as the world's largest Internet automotive marketing services company that helps dealers sell cars and manufacturers build brands through efficient marketing and customer relationships management tools and programs. Since its inception in 1995 as a referral service, linking prospective car buyers with participating dealers, Autobytel, due to the evolution of online automotive services, has been forced by increased competition from auto manufacturers, dealership web sites, and other third party ventures to adjust its game plan. While many online rivals have gone out of business, Autobytel has been able to take advantage of its brand recognition to remain a viable concern. The company owns and operates four web sites: Autobytel.com, Autoweb.com, CarSmart.com, and AutoSite.com. It has relationships with some 8,800 automobile dealers and 30 international automotive manufacturers. According to company statistics, it is responsible for generating $17 billion in annual sales of new cars in the United States in 2001, or 4 percent of all domestic new vehicle sales. Autobytel also has branded licensed web sites and partners around the world, including Canada, Europe, Asia, and Australia. In addition to its referral service for new cars, Autobytel also provides car insurance services and automotive marketing data and technology, operates a "Pre-Owned CyberStore" for the sale of used cars, and offers a program to help car owners with the maintenance of their vehicles by providing a wealth of online information as well as by emailing service reminders. Moreover, the company's lead management system provides tools to car dealers, allowing them to make better use of the Internet.

Recession of Early 1990s and Bankruptcy of Autobytel's Founder

The man responsible for the creation of Autobytel was California businessman Peter Ellis, whose father had been a car dealer. As soon as he was old enough to drive, Ellis sold his first car, and he owned his first dealership by the age of 24. During the 1980s, he built a southern California and Arizona empire of new and used car dealerships, at one point operating the largest Jeep, Eagle, Chrysler dealership in the country. Ellis also gained a reputation as an innovator, pioneering the concepts of no-haggle selling and the used-car superstore. At his peak, Ellis owned 16 dealerships and related businesses, then a downturn in the economy in the early 1990s proved devastating. One by one, he sold off or closed down his dealerships. By 1994, he was forced to file for personal bankruptcy, in the process losing $15 million, a private prop jet, and houses in Bel Air, Aspen, and Palm Springs. To make ends meet, his wife went to work as a spa consultant, while Ellis stayed at home, searching for a way to forge a comeback in his business career.

Rather than seek a new line of endeavor, however, Ellis looked for a new way to sell cars. He toyed with the idea of selling cars over a television shopping network via a toll-free line, originally coining the business name "Auto-by-Tel" with the telephone in mind. Then Ellis became aware of the Internet, and "telephone" soon evolved into "telecom." At first he was hardly comfortable with a computer, the only one at home belonging to his wife. Nevertheless, he began to investigate cyberspace. "It seemed to me that a lot of people were using the online services and I had to check them out," he told a reporter in a 1996 interview. "What I saw was kind of like the wild, wild West and I thought I saw an opportunity."

Drawing on his many years of selling cars, Ellis looked for a way to improve the car-buying experience for the public, which had been the motivation for his earlier no-haggle price policy. He knew all too well the adversarial relationship that existed between customers and salespeople. Traditionally, automobile manufacturers licensed too many dealerships, over-saturating markets in order to stimulate the sale of cars. After a boom period following World War II, dealerships increasingly fought with one another over a limited number of customers and in turn fought with customers over every dollar. In addition to footing the bill for inventory and shipping, dealers spent a great deal of money on advertising, much of it the bait-and-switch variety, and salespeople tried every possible ploy to sell more expensive models to customers, who in many cases had been lured onto the lot by low-priced cars that were not even in inventory. The buyer was at a further disadvantage because the actual cost of the car to the dealership was withheld from him.

Ellis's plan for Auto-by-Tel was to empower the car buyer while providing dealers with a more efficient sales process. The company would offer the buyer, at no charge, pertinent information, such as the dealer's true cost, and an online request form detailing the car and desired options. A local participating car dealer, which would pay a fee to Auto-by-Tel, would then contact the buyer with a no-haggle price, and offer an opportunity for a test drive. Dealers would benefit because Auto-by-Tel sales were essentially found business. Moreover, these leads would be less expensive than the cost of generating customers through traditional advertising, as well as resulting in a reduction in labor costs. Because advertising and labor account for about 60 percent of most dealers' operating expenses, these savings were large enough that a significant discount could be passed on to the buyer. In theory, Auto-by-Tel was a win-win situation that promised to redress the longstanding animosity between car salespeople and buyers. Ellis saw Auto-by-Tel as a revolutionary concept that might eliminate the commissioned salesperson altogether, replaced instead by a salaried employee who was no longer placed in an adversarial relationship with customers. Furthermore, Internet-channeled business would result in the weeding out of marginal, noncompetitive dealerships.

Birth of Auto-by-Tel: 1995

Needing a partner with money, Ellis teamed with John Bedrosian, cofounder of National Medical Enterprises. Together they officially founded Auto-by-Tel in January 1995. Ellis traveled to New York to meet with executives of Prodigy, an online service, and very quickly convinced them to put Auto-by-Tel to the test. It debuted on Prodigy in March 1995 and, although Ellis projected that at the outset Auto-by-Tel would likely generate 50 purchase requests per week, on the fourth day it received more than 1,300. Three months later, Auto-by-Tel launched its own web site. By the end of the year the company also signed up more than 350 car dealerships to subscribe to the service and received financing from such prominent investors as GE Capital Services, insurer American International Group (AIG), and Michael Fuchs, the former head of HBO and Warner Music Group.

Revenues of just $274,000 in 1995 grew to $5 million in 1996, and Ellis was predicting that number would increase tenfold by the end of the following year. Hardly the only one to view the Internet as a tool for selling cars, he was anxious to gain market share in the new field. In April 1996, Auto-by-Tel entered the Canadian market, and Ellis was already talking about overseas expansion. Although the number of participating auto dealers grew rapidly, most of them were not yet online. Instead of email, at this stage Auto-by-Tel generally relied on the fax machine to communicate with its clients.

Early in 1997, Auto-by-Tel became the first of the new Internet-based companies to advertise on the Super Bowl, paying $1.2 million for a 30-second spot. Although a steep price, Ellis considered it a smart buy because of the surrounding publicity that helped in his efforts to transform Auto-by-Tel into a national brand. A few months after the Super Bowl, the company launched a used-car service through a network of participating dealers, essentially emulating its new car business model. All used vehicles would be subjected to a 135-point certification process and further backed by a 72-hour, money-back guarantee and a three-month/3,000-mile warranty. Also in the early months of 1997, Auto-by-Tel began to offer low-cost car insurance through a partnership with AIG, financing through Chase Manhattan Bank and leasing through GE Capital. To support the growth of Auto-by-Tel, which was heavily dependent on marketing, Ellis planned to take the company public in 1997. When the stock market soured, however, he elected to postpone the offering. Instead, the company raised $13 million in a private placement of preferred stock, the third such sale in little more than a year. Despite Ellis's enthusiasm and bold predictions, Auto-by-Tel was beginning to face some difficult realities. Not only did revenues not reach $50 million for 1997, they totaled just $15.3 million.

Auto-by-Tel launched its first overseas operation in 1998, entering the United Kingdom. It also announced plans to expand into Scandinavia, teaming with Sweden's Bilia AB, which sold Volvo and Renault vehicles in ten European countries. By June 1998, however, Ellis stepped down from his leadership role in the company. He was replaced as president and chief executive officer by Mark Lorimer, the company's chief operating officer. In addition, Michael Fuchs became the chairman of the board, and the company soon changed its name to autobytel.com in order to emphasize its Internet base. The purpose of the personnel changes was to enhance Auto-by-Tel's credibility in the market and take it to the next level. Although the company increased revenues it also saw losses mount. In 1998, the company generated sales of $23.8 million while losing $19.4 million, after having lost $16.8 million in 1997.

Going Public: 1999

Lorimer took the company public in March 1999, netting more than $80 million. The money was earmarked for sales and marketing in order to support efforts to build brand awareness for Autobytel, which was a common goal for dot-com companies at this time. The ability to actually turn a profit seemed of little importance to investors. Nor did they reveal any concern over the changing dynamics in the relationship between car buying and the Internet. Aside from a number of third-party rivals, Autobytel faced increased competition from auto makers

Key Dates:

1995: Auto-By-Tel is founded by Peter Ellis.
1997: Auto-By-Tel becomes first Internet-based company to advertise on the Super Bowl.
1998: Ellis resigns as president and CEO.
1999: The company goes public.
2001: Autoweb.com is acquired and company changes its name to Autobytel Inc.

and car dealers who were both gaining an online presence. A clear advantage Autobytel held was its independence, with most car buyers simply unwilling to trust the web sites of manufacturers and dealers. Although some critics argued that the Autobytel business model would not work long-term, investor demand for the company's stock was so heavy that the price was twice raised, increasing from $16 to $23 per share. It rose as high as $58 during the first day of trading.

In 1999, the company continued to aggressively pursue plans for expansion. It announced an initiative to establish an auction-based program so that dealers could sell used vehicles to one another, with the hope of eventually adding related products such as stereos and auto parts to the mix. The company then acquired rival CarSmart.com in a $32 million cash-and-stock deal, adding a further 1,000 dealerships, although management decided to maintain CarSmart as a separate brand. In addition, the company participated in the creation of Autobytel Japan, launched in October 1999. By the end of the year, Autobytel saw its revenues grow to $40.3 million and losses grow to $23.3 million.

In 2000, Autobytel searched for a more diversified source of revenue. It expanded its referral service in Europe and tried to make its web site more friendly towards women, introducing ''For Her'' features. Less than a quarter of the company's Internet traffic came from women, who were regarded as strong candidates for Autobytel services because they had been traditionally intimidated by car salespeople and on average paid more for a car than men. The auto dot-com sector was also entering a period of consolidation. Because of its high name recognition, Autobytel held an advantage over its competitors. Despite the company's dominant position, however, the price of Autobytel stock fell steadily in 2000. For the year, revenues increased to $66.5 million, while the company posted a $29 million loss. Nevertheless, the company still had more than $80 million in cash and remained better positioned than most of its rivals.

Early in 2001, Lorimer attempted to boost investor confidence by promising that the company was on track to post its first quarterly profit later in the year. Prospects appeared even brighter when in February 2001 General Motors Corporation hired Autobytel to be involved in a 90-day pilot program of an improved system for car shopping on the Internet. Shoppers in the Washington, D.C., area were able to view dealers' available inventory and prices online. The press speculated that if the test program proved successful, GM might take an equity position in Autobytel. In the meantime, Autobytel used $9.4 million in

stock to acquire Autoweb.com, further increasing its network of dealerships. It also elected to change its name from Autobytel.com to Autobytel Inc. to reflect that the company now owned four branded web sites. GM extended the test program with Autobytel from three to six months before ending it. In the end, GM decided to incorporate its e-business unit into the corporate structure. Although both GM and Autobytel characterized the test program as a success, some in the press portrayed its termination as a serious defeat for Autobytel.

In December 2001, Lorimer stepped down as Autobytel's president and chief executive, replaced by Jeffrey Schwartz, who had been Autoweb's president and CEO. By cutting back on marketing and other cost-saving measures, the company was able to post its first operating profit in the fourth quarter of 2001, fulfilling Lorimer's earlier pledge. Early in 2002, Schwartz announced his intention to broaden Autobytel's marketing services to better support car dealerships and manufacturers. On the consumer side, Autobytel faced increased competition from manufacturer and dealer sites. Third party companies such as Autobytel, however, were still preferred because of their independence. Autobytel also had more than $30 million left in the bank and was better positioned than most of the other survivors among the car referral companies. In the ongoing shakeout, there was an excellent chance that Autobytel would be the last one standing, emerging finally as a very profitable business.

Principal Subsidiaries

Autoweb.com; Carsmart.com; Autosite.com.

Principal Competitors

Auto Channel; AutoNation; AutoTrader; CarsDirect.com; Trader.com.

Further Reading

Armstrong, Larry, ''The Hottest Web IPO You Never Saw,'' *Business Week,* April 14, 1997, p. 37.

Borzo, Jeanette, ''Autbytel.com Plans to Increase European Push,'' *Wall Street Journal,* September 27, 1999, p. B9.

Gaw, Jonathan, ''Autobytel.com Gets Off to a Rapid Start,'' *Los Angeles Times,* March 27, 1999, p. 1.

Greenman, Catherine, ''Car Dot-Coms: The Dust Settles,'' *New York Times,* February 10, 2002, p. 1.

Halliday, Jean, ''Shakeout Foreseen for Car-Buying Sites, *Advertising Age,* May 22, 2000, pp. 58–61.

Harris, Donna, ''Dot-Com Deal Expands Autobytel's Reach,'' *Automotive News,* April 16, 2001, p. 1.

Kichen, Steve, ''Cruising the Internet,'' *Forbes,* March 24, 1997, pp. 198–99.

''Make or Break for Autobytel,'' *Business Week,* July 9, 2001, p. 30.

Mayersohm, Norm, ''Wheel Dealer,'' *Chief Executive,* April 2001, p. 20.

Rafter, Michelle V., ''Auto-By-Tel Your On-Line Auto Source,'' *St. Louis Post-Dispatch,* August 21, 1996, p. 5C.

Welles, Edward O., ''Burning Down the House,'' *Inc.,* August 1997, pp. 66–73.

Young, Stanley, ''Hot Wheels,'' *People Weekly,* April 13, 1998, p. 43.

—Ed Dinger

Automatic Data Processing, Inc.

One ADP Boulevard
Roseland, New Jersey 07068-1728
U.S.A.
Telephone: (973) 974-5000
Fax: (973) 974-5495
Web site: http://www.adp.com

Public Company
Incorporated: 1949
Employees: 41,000
Sales: $7.02 billion (2001)
Stock Exchanges: New York Chicago Pacific
    Philadelphia Boston
NAIC: 514210 Data Processing Services; 511210
    Software Publishers; 334611 Software Reproducing;
    541211 Offices of Certified Public Accountants;
    541214 Payroll Services (pt); 541219 Other
    Accounting Services

The undisputed number one paymaster to the nation, Automatic Data Processing, Inc. prepares the paychecks for one out of seven American workers. The company, widely known as ADP, is also a leading supplier of stock quotation systems, handles the back-office processing for many securities brokers, and provides a variety of computerized services to auto dealers as well as claims service support for auto insurers and repairers.

Inventing a Better Way to
Manage Payrolls: 1940s–50s

The multibillion-dollar operation owes its start to the fact that when the bright and innovative Henry Taub graduated from New York University in 1947, he was still shy of his 20th birthday, and thus more than a year away from eligibility for the CPA exam. Consequently, Taub, who had worked part-time for a small Manhattan public accounting firm while a commuter student at NYU, became a full-time employee. The work entailed keeping the books for dozens of small businesses, coupled with lots of handholding.

Taub soon became aware that preparing payrolls and maintaining the necessary supporting data were a major headache for smaller employers. Social security was as yet less than a dozen years old, and income tax withholding had only started during World War II. All in all, payroll accounting was becoming steadily more demanding.

So, in 1949, with the support of two business acquaintances, Taub opened a company to provide that specialized service. He called his new business Automatic Payrolls, Inc. As he readily recalled later, the "Automatic" defined the service only from the point of view of the client, who was spared many burdensome tasks; on the company's side, automation started with little more than an adding machine. Taub also noted the deeper significance of the carefully chosen name. In his hometown of Paterson, New Jersey, an old-line textile center where the automation of looms had long been a major issue, "automatic" carried the connotation of "an advanced form of work."

From a small office in Paterson, Taub solicited accounts in the surrounding area, often utilizing public transportation to pick up time sheets and return the finished payroll. During this time, Taub's company did not handle the clients' money; signing the checks or placing cash in the pay envelopes was left for the employer to do on site. In 1951, Taub's younger brother Joe joined the organization, specializing in administrative functions for the next 25 years.

In 1953 the third member of Automatic Payrolls' longtime guiding trio came aboard. He was Frank R. Lautenberg, the son of a Paterson textile worker. Three years older than Henry, Lautenberg served in Europe during World War II and then earned an economics degree at Columbia University and became a sales trainee for Prudential Insurance. The local Prudential office was in the same Paterson building as Automatic, and he and the Taubs met occasionally at a nearby coffee counter. Since most of Lautenberg's life insurance sales calls took place in the evening, he found time to solicit business for Automatic during the day, and after a while joined the company full-time.

Henry Taub recollected: "We formed an effective trio, with complementary strengths—me in accounting, Joe in organization, and Frank in marketing—and very compatible in personal-

Company Perspectives:

ADP's objectives are sustained growth in shareholder value through ever-improving financial results, World Class Service, and being an employer of choice. We will achieve these objectives by having a total commitment to the highest ethical standards, by treating everyone with honesty, fairness and respect, and by conducting our business with the highest level of integrity. We believe in open, informal communications, hard work, and prudent financial management. These are ADP's core values, the foundation on which our business culture is based.

But a statement of values is not enough. Unless our values are consistently practiced, they become just platitudes. Consistent implementation occurs only when each of us respects the rights of others, when our actions are free from discrimination, and when each associate is accorded full equal opportunity.

As we continue to grow and as our businesses become increasingly complex, a shared, well-communicated Corporate Philosophy is more important than ever. We are not perfect. Our actions will occasionally fall short of our aspirations. Such shortcomings should be viewed as an opportunity to learn and to refocus our efforts to live up to our values and Corporate Philosophy.

ity and business style.'' Eventually, Lautenberg succeeded Henry Taub as chief executive in 1975 and held that job until his election as U.S. senator from New Jersey in 1982. Henry Taub then became the company's honorary chairperson while remaining an active director and chairing the executive committee.

The young company kept adding customers in northern New Jersey and the New York City area, but progress was moderate. By the June 1957 fiscal year, operating revenues had grown to $150,000; profits for the entire year, however, were a mere $964. One factor was the switch that year from manual bookkeeping machines to an early IBM computer. Lautenberg later told *Investor's Reader* magazine that the punch card computer system ''damned near killed us. It wasn't a very good improvement. Then we started developing techniques that enabled us to start working with computers.''

With the new equipment, Automatic Payrolls also branched into some general data processing services such as analytical reports covering sales, costs and inventories, questionnaire tabulation, and even the maintenance of bowling league statistics. In 1959 the Taubs set up a separate company, Automatic Tabulating Services, to handle the general data processing business. Then, in June 1961, in preparation for going public, the payroll and tabulating companies were merged into the newly named Automatic Data Processing. At the time, ADP had about 200 payroll clients, including the cast and crew of the Broadway hit *My Fair Lady* and 30 general processing customers.

Rapid Growth in the 1960s and 1970s

With only a modest $419,000 in revenues and $25,000 in net profits for the June 1961 year, ADP was very much of a ''penny stock'' when the first 100,000 shares were offered to the public in September 1961 at $3 a share. Henry Taub reflected: ''Those first dozen years were our incubation period. We learned how to operate what was essentially a brand-new business.'' When it emerged from the incubator, ADP was set to mature. Starting with its first quarter as a public company, ADP managed an unbroken string of double-digit earnings per share growth—a string that encompassed 128 quarters as of the end of the 1993 fiscal year. Meantime, each share bought for $3 in 1961 had multiplied into 144 shares worth more than $7,000 by 1993.

Just prior to offering its stock publicly, ADP went to Wall Street to drum up business. Encouraged by a couple of brokerage houses that were already payroll clients, ADP opened an office in downtown Manhattan in July 1961 to process ''back office'' data such as customer trade confirmations and related reports—the start of what was to become ADP's second most important line.

Buoyed by strong internal growth after going public, ADP was ready to speed its development through aggressive use of acquisitions by the mid-1960s. Since then, it acquired more than 100 companies or corporate units. Management stressed, however, that these acquisitions should serve as ''catalysts'' and not as ''our main engine of growth.'' As Josh S. Weston, who joined the company in 1970 and became CEO in 1982, explained to security analysts, acquisitions were intended ''to telescope time and risk in helping us pursue a strategic direction that we wanted to pursue anyway.''

The acquisition drive got underway in 1965 when ADP broadened its brokerage business with the addition of Brokerage Processing Center and shortly thereafter expanded its payroll service with Payrolls for Industry of Long Island. Then, in 1967, Miami Beach-based Computer Services of Florida was purchased. This represented a significant geographic breakout, since ADP had effectively been limited to customers that could be served by its local pickup and delivery facilities, except for a handful of payroll clients whose requirements permitted mail communication (computer transmission of payroll data and checks was not yet possible). The Florida beachhead was followed by a flurry of other East Coast acquisitions. Thereafter, the company acquired or established its way into other parts of the nation. By 1972 it operated centers in 20 cities from which it paid more than one million people.

That year ADP acquired CSI Computer Systems of Cincinnati, which helped about 500 car dealers with their paper work. This led ADP into its third major line, which it called Dealer Services. Since then ADP vastly expanded both the concept and scope of these services. By 1993 it served more than 7,000 North American car and truck dealers, while 1,000 European dealers were added with the 1992 acquisition of Germany's Autonom Computer. While Autonom served primarily German GM/Opel dealers, ADP planned to add more European cars and countries.

In North America, ADP clients represented roughly one-third of all dealerships while accounting for more than half of vehicle sales. Many used ADP-supplied computers and programs that eliminated preprinted forms. After blank sheets were inserted into the printer and pertinent data entered, completed invoices emerged. Other programs handled scheduling for the repair shop or kept track of all data on showroom visitors (including their preferences and dislikes) to give sales staff a better shot at closing a deal. Some of the software used to show potential financing and insurance costs came under FTC attack in 1991 for allegedly making financing the car through the dealer seem cheaper than paying cash; ADP, while insisting that the pro-financing claims were "standard industry practice," agreed to remove the challenged segment. Even though, as Chairperson Weston quipped to stockholders in 1992, the U.S. auto industry nowadays "seldom has one good year in a row," ADP steadily increased its dealer business, which accounted for roughly 12 percent of total ADP revenues.

Entering the Information Age: The 1980s and 1990s

With the acquisition of Itel Corp.'s Autadex division in 1980, ADP began developing another auto-related business line, now known as Automotive Claims Services. Through a huge database maintained in Ann Arbor, Michigan, that cataloged the components of virtually every model produced since 1970, adjusters and repair shop operators could instantly obtain detailed repair estimates, including parts and labor. In 1985 ADP added a Vehicle Valuation Service for cars that were stolen or "totaled." It also started a parts service showing price and availability of private brand and salvage yard parts. Moreover, in 1993, ADP undertook a minority investment in National BioSystems, which evaluated medical costs of accident victims.

Claims Service, whose clients included most of the major insurance companies, brought in about 5 percent of ADP revenues in the early 1990s. Since that time, it received less emphasis. In 1993, the "Other" group, which, along with Claims, covered such minor activities as network, general accounting, and wholesale distribution, as well as overseas payroll services (mostly Britain and the Benelux countries), registered 6 percent of revenues as opposed to 9 percent in fiscal 1992. The "Other" contribution may have been somewhat understated, however, because this category was also the domain for certain corporate accounting adjustments.

Strongest growth in the early 1990s was in Brokerage Services, which produced 23 percent of fiscal 1993 revenues. ADP processed more than one-fifth of the trades executed on Wall Street each day. Nevertheless, these back-office functions were eclipsed by ADP's presence in the front office. In 1983 ADP bought GTE's Telenet Information Services, which put it into

stock quote machines, and three years later it acquired the Bunker Ramo quote machine operations. ADP was thus in the forefront of the industry revolution that replaced "dumb terminals" with intelligent work stations that provided each individual broker not only with current stock quotations and market news but instant access to client account records, background data, and analysts' opinions on securities, as well as offering the capability to enter orders electronically. By 1991 ADP was the top provider of such information services. Some infringement disputes with previous industry leader Quotron (which became a Citicorp subsidiary in 1986) were settled in 1993 when, as part of a deal in which ADP bought Quotron's overseas stock quotation business, ADP obtained a permanent license to certain Quotron stock information software.

ADP entered the proxy distribution business in 1989. This segment sent out stockholder reports and proxy statements to investors whose stock was held in "street name" by brokerage houses, and then processed the returned proxy votes. In 1992 ADP acquired another major proxy distribution company, Independent Election Corp. of America. Whereas the ADP service was directed at individual customers of brokerage houses, Independent dealt with large institutional holders. The difference in client groups and operating systems slowed the integration of the two proxy units and, while net results were beneficial, this generated some embarrassing problems during the 1993 proxy season. ADP remained confident, however, that the glitches would be overcome, and the company was set for a smooth 1994 season.

By far the largest ADP business, with 59 percent of total revenues in 1993, remained what is now called Employer Services. The broadened title reflected the fact that, beyond payroll-related work, this sector offered such services as job costing, labor distribution analysis, management reporting, unemployment compensation management, human resources information, and personnel benefit services. In 1993, the core of this operation paid more than 16 million employees of some 275,000 employers and prepared all of the related W-2 forms and other required reports, as well as all sorts of internal personnel reports for the employer. More than 75 percent of the payroll clients also used ADP's tax filing service (started in 1982) in which ADP handled the actual submission of tax payments to all levels of government. During this time, more than 95,000 clients submitted their payroll by computer. ADP also was able to arrange the laser printing of paychecks on site, while an increasing number of payments were electronically deposited directly to the employee's designated bank account.

Although traditional banking institutions were a major competitor for payroll services, ADP gradually acquired such payroll businesses, often arranging for the bank to remain the upfront marketing agent while ADP operated the service. The largest such acquisition (indeed, ADP's largest single acquisition ever) was the takeover of Bank of America's 17,000-client, $110 million revenue payroll business in May 1992. Interestingly, this deal was concluded just one month after Bank of America completed the merger of Security Pacific, another California banking giant whose payroll business had been acquired by ADP eight years earlier.

Although ADP started out "helping those who couldn't help themselves" when it came to payroll automation, and it continued to derive about half its payroll revenues from firms with less than 100 employees, large ''national accounts'' with more than 1,000 employees were increasingly shifting to ADP from in-house installations. Here ADP benefited from the almost universal belt-tightening mode at most major corporations, which became willing to outsource nonstrategic functions. Furthermore, the constant growth and change in regulations on both the federal and local level required unending adjustment in payroll software programs, and many companies found it easier to leave the adjusting to a specialist like ADP. The same logic applied in adjusting a program to fit all the many jurisdictions in which a national company retained employees. Furthermore, ADP offered great flexibility. For instance, it could take in ready stride the requirements of clients like H&R Block, whose payroll, depending on the time of the tax year, fluctuated from 2,000 to 65,000 employees.

For all of its business lines ADP set certain criteria. To realize economies of scale, the company preferred computing services that could be mass marketed and mass produced. ADP stipulated that its services should induce long-term client relationships with repetitive revenues and should require enough specialization and knowhow to raise barriers to entry by competitors and exit by clients.

Josh Weston also looked for what he called ''a silent third force''—a set of conditions that provided a relatively uniform framework within which ADP could design its products. Therefore, the IRS and the wage and hour laws set an overall pattern for wage payments, the SEC and the stock exchanges regulated the handling of securities transactions, and the auto manufacturers informed franchised dealers how to keep their records.

ADP also maintained, ''it is a prime criterion for us in either starting up or later staying in a business that we think we have an excellent chance to be number one in that particular business.'' In September 1993 Weston told security analysts that ADP was assessing potential opportunities in four new data service markets, any one of which, if entry through a suitable acquisition could be arranged, might develop into a fourth major ADP line. The company's presumed target would be volume in the $200 million-plus range, or more than double the Claims Service peak.

Since the mid-1980s, ADP also actively engaged in ''pruning,'' which it defined as having ''sold, shrunken, or milked'' various product lines or businesses that no longer, according to Weston, ''fit our long-term strategic objectives.'' Among others, ADP sold a computerized tax processing business, its electronic funds transfer operation that serviced automatic teller machines, and its interest in a Brazilian payroll company. It also planned to simply shrink some businesses ''where a smaller ongoing operation gives ADP a better return'' than selling it, especially when a unit might continue to generate cash that could build up other operations. While counting on outsourcing by other companies to feed its growth, ADP also used outsourcing when appropriate. Thus in 1990 it arranged for IBM to take over the maintenance of its stock quote terminals.

Throughout its existence, ADP relied upon highly conservative accounting, with a strong cash position, low debt, and quick depreciation, allowing it to move into technologically advanced replacements without incurring big write-offs of the displaced equipment. This operating scheme permitted the longest string of consecutive earnings advances on the New York Stock Exchange, where the company arrived in 1970. ADP crossed the billion-dollar mark in revenues in 1985 and topped $2 billion in fiscal 1993 when earnings reached a record $294 million. Dividends, while fairly conservative, were raised each year since payments started in 1974. Furthermore, the company was convinced that room existed for additional progress. In 1993, ADP noted that it still had only about a 15 percent penetration of the payroll market nationally and even in its New York-New Jersey home area only about 25 percent.

Insisting that ADP push toward continually higher goals, Weston cited the example of the pole vaulter who, even after all competitors have been eliminated, is made to try for ever higher jumps until he fails to clear the bar three times. Only after the inevitable final failure is the vaulter brought to the winner's stand. As Weston sought to inspire his company to ever greater efforts with the pole vault analogy, he concluded: ''Since they're going to be recognized as winners anyway, asking them to jump an inch higher isn't dirty pool.''

New Services for the Information Age: Entering the 21st Century

The rapid evolution of computer technology in the 1990s provided ADP with a golden opportunity to expand many of its core products and services. By mid-decade, the Internet had made it possible for a company to manage all aspects of its finances, from payroll to banking, on a personal computer. The intricacies involved with mastering this new technology, however, combined with the increasing complexity of benefits packages and tax laws, was turning accounting into a major headache for small and mid-sized business owners. Rather than trying to handle the problem on their own, many of these companies began turning to outside firms to handle their bookkeeping needs.

It was in this atmosphere that ADP began developing a host of services designed to help employers integrate these new technologies into their day-to-day operations. The company set the stage for this transition when it acquired a bank charter in 1995. The Interstate Banking and Branching Efficiency Act of 1994 had already removed limitations on interstate banking, and so the charter provided ADP with the opportunity to augment its payroll business with loan processing, bill payment, and investment services. From the point of view of cost, the transition was a relatively easy one: The expense of maintaining a banking web site was negligible and did not require a complete overhaul of the company's infrastructure. The challenge for ADP was to create services unique enough to draw customers away from the traditional bank branches.

One of ADP's first new offerings arose out of its merger with Checkfree Corp. in July 1995. Through this venture, the company introduced its electronic banking service, providing small businesses with a convenient, affordable way to pay bills and balance accounts online. The company built upon this innovation when it formed its Electronic Banking Unit in 1997, which established partnerships with banks and software designers to create a centralized, web-based banking resource center.

By making financial products and services readily available online, the resource center could offer valuable support to business owners looking for a way to cut administrative costs. ADP PayExpert, the industry's first complete payroll processing service, was introduced in 1998, and in 1999 the company created Solution Profiler, a program designed to allow small businesses to customize their payroll service.

This heightened focus on small businesses did not mean ADP was neglecting its larger clients. In 2000 it launched ADP Enterprise Payroll Services, which offered a comprehensive web-based payroll and accounting platform for corporations with more than one location. That same year it launched Accountant Advantage, a referral network that allowed accounting firms to market ADP's payroll products. The company also remained dedicated to global expansion, solidifying its foothold in the burgeoning Asian payroll processing business with the acquisition of the Australian firm PayConnect Solutions, the largest payroll processor in the Asia/Pacific market, in July 2000. Heading into the new century, however, it was clear that the small business sector was the area with the largest potential for growth. With research data indicating that payroll services for small businesses would blossom into a $4 billion industry by 2000, ADP was determined to put itself in position to become the undisputed leader in this promising new market.

Principal Divisions

ADP Employer Services; ADP Brokerage Services; ADP Dealer Services; ADP Claims Services.

Principal Competitors

Administaff, Inc.; Ceridian Corporation; Paychex, Inc.

Further Reading

"Automatic Data Processing Hews to Winning Formula," *Wall Street Journal,* December 24, 1992.

Crone, Richard K., "Notes on the Infobahn: ADP Positioned to Control Funds at Point of Payroll," *American Banker,* January 9, 1995, p. 6A.

Marjanovic, Steven, "Checkfree, ADP to Start PC Payment System Aimed at Small Business," *American Banker,* July 20, 1995, p. 8.

"Payroll Specialist," *Investor's Reader,* July 26, 1972.

"They Make Money Paying Us," *Forbes,* January 4, 1993.

Weston, Josh, "Soft Stuff Matters," *Financial Executive,* July/August 1992.

—Henry R. Hecht
—update: Steve Meyer

Bell Industries, Inc.

1960 East Grand Avenue, Suite 560
El Segundo, California 90245
U.S.A.
Telephone: (310) 563-2355
Fax: (310) 648-7280
Web site: http://www.bellind.com

Public Company
Incorporated: 1952 as Bell Radio Supply
Employees: 670
Sales: $183.62 million (2001)
Stock Exchanges: American Pacific
Ticker Symbol: BI
NAIC: 421690 Other Electronic Parts and Equipment
   Wholesalers; 334111 Electronic Computer
   Manufacturing; 421720 Plumbing and Heating
   Equipment and Supplies (Hydronics) Wholesalers;
   421730 Warm Air Heating and Air-Conditioning
   Equipment and Supplies Wholesalers

Bell Industries, Inc. competes in three business sectors: computer systems integration, distribution of aftermarket products for recreational vehicles, and specialty electronics manufacturing. Bell's systems integration business, operating as Bell Tech.logix, provides integrated technology solutions to more than 5,000 customers. The company's recreational products group distributes replacement parts and accessories for recreational vehicles, mobile homes, snowmobiles, motorcycles, powerboats, and other leisure-time vehicles, serving more than 4,800 dealers and retail stores in the upper Midwest. Bell's electronics manufacturing business, operating as the J.W. Miller Division, produces and distributes more than 5,000 products used in circuitry found in computer, medical, and telecommunications equipment.

Retail Origins

Bell began as Bell Radio Supply, the name of a small retail store in Los Angeles that opened in 1952 to sell component parts to the radio trade and to consumers. Bell did not remain a retailer for long. Within four years, the company was shedding off the last vestiges of its origins as a retail concern and shaping itself into a distributor of electronic components to the industrial market. As a distributor, Bell would earn its place within the national landscape of influential companies, eventually evolving into a nearly $1 billion company. Distribution, however, ultimately proved to be a business ill-suited for the company's long-term survival, forcing management to withdraw from the industry segment that supported its prolific growth and to fashion Bell into a different entity.

Before market conditions dictated Bell's exit from the distribution business, the company thrived as a go-between. By the late 1950s, Bell's annual sales eclipsed the $1 million mark, fueled largely by the growth of the southern California market. Ambition within the company grew along with revenue, prompting management to sell shares in the company's stock as a means to obtain capital that could be used to take advantage of the favorable business conditions. Bell's IPO occurred in 1959, when the company was traded as an over-the-counter stock. In 1962, the growing stature of the Los Angeles firm was reflected in a move of its stock to the more prestigious American Stock Exchange.

Shortly after Bell's stock began trading on the American Stock Exchange, a general corporate trend, sweeping across all industries, became a strategic model Bell management followed. During the mid- to late 1960s, the era of diversification through acquisition began, creating holding companies whose diversity of businesses mitigated the cyclical risks of one particular business or industry, insulating financial performance from capricious fluctuations—a safeguard attractive to company executives and investors alike. Increasingly during this period, companies shaped themselves into conglomerates, trading their narrow business scope for a broad presence in variegated businesses and markets. As the pattern of diversification through acquisition took root during the latter half of the 1960s, Bell's management followed suit, transforming its electronics distribution business into a multifaceted enterprise.

The Development of a Mini-Conglomerate

During the 1960s and 1970s, Bell's acquisitive activity was fast-paced. The company acquired approximately 30 companies during this period, adding to its strength in its core electronics

40

distribution business and expanding its reach into markets related to graphic arts, building products, motor vehicle parts, and recreational products. The company acquired manufacturing operations in industries such as marine, aerospace, electronic components, consumer goods, and computer products. From its sole business of electronics distribution, Bell leapt far afield, enabling it to describe itself variously as a hydraulic aircraft parts manufacturer, a bar stool company, a capacitor manufacturer, a manufacturer of illuminated aerospace displays, and a builder of mini-bikes.

Bell's acquisition and diversification campaign ignited revenue growth, increasing sales more than fivefold in less than a decade. In 1968, the company generated $20 million in sales. In 1977, Bell surged past the $100 million mark, a milestone celebrated by the transfer of its stock listing to the New York Stock Exchange. By the end of this period, Bell had become a "mini-conglomerate," boasting a broad business presence in a number of markets that offset and complemented its primary role as an electronics distributor. The transformation was dramatic, taking the company into a diversified collection of manufacturing and distribution businesses. But Bell's decentralized, multifaceted corporate structure would not last. External forces again dictated a change in Bell's corporate strategy, as companies and industries rethought the merits of aggressive diversification and decentralized corporate structures.

During the 1980s, Bell focused on developing a more centralized corporate structure. Company management selected Bell's businesses in electronics, computers, and graphics as the core to build upon, giving way to a period of divestiture. Bell sold businesses in manufacturing and distribution that were deemed to be non-core assets and used the proceeds to strengthen its presence in its three main business lines. Acquisitions completed during the decade were absorbed into the company's new, more centralized structure, extending its geographic and operational scope.

The 1990s: A Decade of Change and Retreat

Bell recorded impressive growth during the first half of the 1990s, generating the bulk of its revenue from its electronics distribution business—a company mainstay since the late 1950s. During the decade, the distribution industry underwent significant changes, as an era of mega-mergers reshaped the industry and the criteria for future success. Many of the major participants in the industry were seeking to acquire large rival firms in a bid to secure massive gains in market share, creating a scenario in which only the largest distribution firms would survive. Smaller distributors, those companies unable to develop an entrenched, nationwide presence, would likely be crushed, unable to compete against the industry behemoths. For Bell, the 1990s proved to be a crucible: the company either had to increase its stature exponentially or risk losing its business to those who succeeded in the merger frenzy that described the electronics distribution industry in the 1990s.

During the mid-1990s, the electronics distribution industry comprised three tiers of competitors led by industry giants Arrow Electronics Inc. and Avnet, Inc. Arrow and Avnet were by far the biggest electronics distribution firms in the country, generating between $3 billion and $4 billion more in annual sales than their closest rivals, those firms occupying the second tier of the industry. Within this segment, electronics distribution firms were recording between $500 million and $1 billion in annual sales, including companies such as Pioneer-Standard Electronics, Wyle Electronics, and UK-based Farnell. Bell, as the mid-1990s neared, was flirting with promotion into the industry's second-tier, its revenue volume drawing close to the $500 million mark. The company was more rightly grouped into the third tier of the industry, which contained companies whose annual sales totals ranged between $100 million and $500 million.

In a bid to exponentially increase its stature, Bell made an attempt to acquire one of its third-tier brethren. In 1995, the company submitted an offer to buy Sterling Electronics Corp., proposing a $142 million-in-stock deal for the electronics distribution company. In September 1995, Sterling dismissed the offer, declaring the acquisition bid to be "unsolicited," according to an October 2, 1995 article in *Electronic News*. Bell decided against a hostile takeover, but the company had yet to abandon its efforts to acquire a competitor.

1996 Acquisition of Milgray and Its Effects

Bell executives, itching to delve into the acquisition game, did not have to wait long after the scuttled Sterling Electronics deal. In November 1996, the company announced it had signed a merger agreement with Farmingdale, New York-based Milgray Electronics Inc. Discussions about the acquisition had been underway well before the Sterling Electronics deal fell through, beginning in 1994, according to reports in trade periodicals. The $100 million deal was completed in early 1997, coupling Bell with another third-tier electronics distribution company. Milgray, roughly one-half of Bell's size in terms of revenue, gave Bell entry into New York, Kansas City, and Canadian markets, where Milgray had an established presence. Once the deal was concluded, Bell emerged as a nearly $900 million company earning $18 million in annual profits, its position secure in the second tier of the electronics distribution industry, from which the company derived nearly 80 percent of its revenue.

The consummation of the Milgray deal required Bell to restructure itself. As part of the 1997 restructuring program, Gordon Graham was named Bell's president, replacing Bruce Jaffe, who resigned when the merger agreement was announced in November 1996. Graham assumed the responsibility of overseeing all of Bell's electronics and non-electronics distribution businesses, which included the company's graphic arts and auto-

```
┌─────────────────────────────────────────────┐
│                 Key Dates:                   │
│                                              │
│  1952:  Bell Radio Supply opens in Los Angeles. │
│  1959:  Initial public offering of stock is completed. │
│  1978:  Bell's System Integration Group, the precursor to │
│         Bell Tech.logix, is formed.          │
│  1996:  Milgray Electronics is acquired.     │
│  1998:  Bell's graphics business is divested as part of the │
│         company's restructuring plan.        │
│  1999:  Bell's electronics distribution business is sold to │
│         Arrow Electronics.                   │
│  2000:  The company's restructuring is complete, and Bell │
│         operates principally as an integrated technology so- │
│         lutions concern.                     │
└─────────────────────────────────────────────┘
```

motive aftermarket products. Initially, the plan was to consolidate some of the functions of the two companies, but, aside from eliminating some administrative and corporate redundancies, the companies were to be operated as two separate units. Quite quickly, however, the corporate marriage encountered profound difficulties. Bell's bid to join the industry elite was forsaken for a thoroughly revamped version of itself—a company divorced from the distribution business for the first time in 40 years.

In the years leading up to the Milgray acquisition, Bell experienced dramatic growth. In 1996, the company celebrated its fifth consecutive year of increased sales and earnings. The company's consistent financial growth stopped shortly after the Milgray acquisition closed in January 1997, when problems stemming from the combination of the two entities first surfaced. Suppliers of electronics products—Bell's customers—reacted negatively to the union of Bell and Milgray, voicing concern about sharing shelf space with competitors included within the new distribution network of Bell/Milgray. Within a year, Bell lost the business of important vendors such as Analog Devices, Atmel, BI Technologies, Fujitsu, Hitachi, and Kemet. The company's financial health suffered as a result, leading to four consecutive quarters of revenue and net income decline following the Milgray acquisition. In an October 5, 1998 interview with *Electronic Buyers' News,* an analyst with Credit Suisse First Boston offered his assessment: "Milgray squeezed them. It seems like it was a big burden on the company. They did a poor job at integrating the company and never seemed to bounce back after suppliers pulled their business. Also, they didn't have the foresight to realize the entire industry was going into a down cycle when they pursued this deal."

In the wake of the Milgray acquisition, Bell management chose to thoroughly alter the company's business scope. In September 1998, Bell sold its graphics business, which distributed graphics and electronic imaging products to advertising and printing industries located in the upper Midwest and western United States. The graphics business, representing $100 million of Bell's annual revenue volume, was sold to PrimeSource Corporation for roughly $40 million, enabling the company to realize approximately $5 million in cost savings. As the graphics divestiture was being completed, Bell made the stunning announcement it also was selling its electronics distribution group, a contributor of 77 percent of the company's $890

million in sales at the time. In January 1999, the divestiture was completed. Arrow Electronics, the industry leader, acquired Bell's electronics distribution business for $185 million. Bruce Jaffe, who had resigned as Bell's president shortly before the Milgray acquisition, offered a harsh assessment of Bell's decision to retreat from the distribution business. "I was surprised to hear about the deal," he remarked in an October 5, 1998 interview with *Electronic Buyers' News.* "I felt the company should have continued to be an independent entity. It looks like Bell management has thrown in the towel and said, 'You take the problems we can't manage.' "

At the time of the divestiture, the company began formulating a major restructuring plan. At the heart of the reorganization was changing the company's focus from distribution to reselling, with the proceeds from the two divestitures used to pay the company's debt obligations. The company that emerged from sweeping strategic realignment represented the "new" Bell, the Bell of the 21st century.

Bell prepared for the celebration of its 50th anniversary as a roughly $200 million concern, a fraction of the company's size during the 1990s. Its greatest contributor to sales was a company called Bell Tech.logix, formed in 1998 as Bell's Systems Integration Group. A provider of integrated technology (IT) solutions to customers in the Midwest and Atlantic regions, Bell Tech.logix generated $130 million in sales in 2001, down substantially from the $189 million the division produced in 2000. The two smaller divisions constituting the company were the Recreational Products Group and Bell's specialty electronics manufacturing business, J.W. Miller. The Recreational Products Group distributed replacement parts and accessories for recreational vehicles, motorcycles, snowmobiles, and other leisure-time vehicles, accounting for $46 million in sales in 2001. J.W. Miller, a manufacturer of products found in all types of circuitry housed in computer, medical, and telecommunications equipment, generated approximately $7 million in sales in 2001. Owing largely to the decline in sales posted by Bell Tech.logix in 2001, Bell's total sales dropped from $252 million in 2000 to $189 million in 2001, leaving much for the revamped Bell to prove as it prepared for its second half-century of business.

Principal Subsidiaries

Bell Industries, Inc.; J.W. Miller Company; Bell Tech.logix, Inc.; Milgray Ltd.

Principal Divisions

Bell Tech.logix; Recreational Products Group; J.W. Miller Division.

Principal Competitors

Computer Sciences Corporation; Electronic Data Systems Corporation; International Business Machines Corporation.

Further Reading

Baljko, Jennifer L., "Sale Marks End of Bell's Struggle," *Electronic Buyers' News,* October 5, 1998, p. 116.
"Bell Industries Posts Results with Merged Milgray," *Electronic News,* July 21, 1997, p. 46.

''FTC OKs Bell Industries' Acquisition of Milgray,'' *Electronic News,* December 23, 1996, p. 28.

Jastrow, David, ''Keeping Bell Industries on Track—Integration Now Accounts for 70 Percent of Sales at Former Distributor,'' *Computer Reseller News,* August 16, 1999, p. 41.

——, ''Sheds Distribution Roots: Wave of Mergers Validates Decision—Bell Tolls Start of Service-Focused Model,'' *Computer Reseller News,* January 18, 1999, p. 53.

Jorgensen, Barbara, ''Bell Industries 'Resizes,' '' *Electronic Buyers' News,* July 20, 1998, p. 8.

Levine, Bernard, ''Bell Industries Integrates Milgray into Name, Operations,'' *Electronic Buyers' News,* May 19, 1997, p. 4.

——, ''Bell Industries to Buy Milgray,'' *Electronic News,* December 2, 1996, p. 1.

——, ''No Letup Seen in Distributor Mergers,'' *Electronic News,* October 2, 1995, p. 1.

Liotta, Bettyann, ''Bell Industries' Sales Remain Flat,'' *Electronic Buyers' News,* October 20, 1997, p. 3.

——, ''Bell Moves Forward Following Milgray Buy,'' *Electronic Buyers' News,* October 20, 1997, p. 40.

—Jeffrey L. Covell

Benton Oil and Gas Company

15835 Park Ten Place Drive, Suite 11
Houston, Texas 77084
U.S.A.
Telephone: (281) 579-6700
Fax: (805) 566-5610
Web site: http://www.bentonoil.com

Public Company
Incorporated: 1988
Employees: 926
Sales: $140.3 million (2000)
Stock Exchanges: New York
Ticker Symbol: BNO
NAIC: 211111 Crude Petroleum and Natural Gas
Extraction

Benton Oil and Gas Company is engaged in the exploration, development, and production of oil and gas properties, relying on 3-D seismic technology to find leftover oil and gas in fields abandoned by major oil companies. While the company's interests may present little risk geologically, they have been mostly located in politically questionable regions of the world. Benton Oil operates primarily in Venezuela and Russia. It has also drilled in China, Senegal, and Jordan. Following the 1999 resignation of its founder, Alexander Benton, the company has undergone a retrenchment effort that has included moving its headquarters from Carpinteria, California, to Houston, Texas.

Arrival of Alexander Benton in United States: 1950

Alexander Benton, the founder of Benton Oil, was born Alexander Strochenko in 1942 in a Russian village located near the Black and Caspian Seas. Less than a month later, his family fled, fearful of both the Nazis targeting the Caspian oil fields and the Soviet government. As intellectuals, Benton's parents were in danger of becoming victimized by one of Soviet leader Joseph Stalin's periodic purges. During the rest of World War II, the family wandered Europe as refugees, eventually landing in Munich, where they remained after the war because

returning home to Russia would be risking incarceration or possibly execution. Even Russian soldiers who had the misfortune of being taken prisoner by the German Army were, once liberated, sent to the infamous Soviet gulags. Benton's father taught veterinary medicine at the University of Munich, lecturing in the same building where the family once sought shelter from Allied bombings. In 1950, Benton's family was able to immigrate to the United States, sponsored by a Presbyterian church in northern California. They settled in the town of Gilroy in the San Jose area, where Benton's parents scraped together a living by doing menial labor. Benton's father was employed as a janitor by the sponsoring church, and his mother, a bacteriologist by training, cleaned houses and later found work in a garlic and onion factory. Benton would find employment in the factory as well, eventually saving enough money to study geophysics at San Jose State College. Four years older than the average college student, he excelled enough in the classroom to attract the attention of oil giant Amoco, which recruited him during his senior year.

When Benton went to work for Amoco in 1968, its geologists were just becoming involved in bright spot analysis, an advanced technique for detecting oil deposits. Benton proved to be a valuable addition to the company who was instrumental in a number of major finds, and he was ultimately named director of applied geophysical research at Amoco's Tulsa, Oklahoma, think tank. After a decade with Amoco he decided to take advantage of prosperous times in the oil business and joined an independent Houston oil company, TransOcean Oil. When Mobil acquired the company, it kept on Benton as the manager of geophysics at its Dallas affiliate, Mobil Exploration Special Projects. Soon, Benton again opted for employment with a smaller independent, in 1981 going to work for May Petroleum, a Dallas exploration company, where he was named senior vice-president of exploration.

It was at May Petroleum that Benton expanded his knowledge beyond science, gaining a practical business education. Several years later, when May was acquired, he bought out a Ventura, California, district office that he had set up for the company. Financially backed as a subsidiary of Michigan-based Patrick Petroleum, he called the new enterprise Benton Petroleum. In September 1988, he incorporated Benton Oil and Gas Company under Delaware law, then six months later took the new business public, raising $4 million, out of which he paid Patrick $1.2 million to acquire Benton Petroleum and the natural gas assets he had accumulated in the Sacramento Basin. Although he was now an entrepreneur, Benton remained very much a geophysicist. His plan was to buy interests in known but depleted oil fields, then use the new 3-D seismic technology (he became one of the earliest independents to employ it) in order to locate untapped pockets of oil and gas. If promising assets could be acquired at a reasonable cost, Benton Oil stood to make a tidy profit. The concept certainly appeared promising enough to investors, who over the course of the first two years paid $26 million for stock or limited partnerships in the company.

Benton Oil's first major move outside of the Sacramento Basin came in 1989 when the company purchased a small stake in proven reserves (the West Côte Blanche Bay Field) in the Gulf of Mexico, off the shores of Louisiana. The field was originally discovered by Texaco in 1938 and over the course of 50 years produced more than 200 million barrels of oil and 195 billion cubic feet of gas. Benton Oil teamed with Texaco to conduct a 3-D seismic survey of the area's deep gas assets, which now became economically attractive due to higher gas prices. After completing a number of separate transactions, the company acquired over 43 percent of the field by early 1992 at a cost of $23.2 million. In addition to gas, the field also began to produce a considerable amount of oil from its shallower depths. Benton Oil soon employed 3-D seismic technology on other Louisiana fields for which it gained sizeable interests from joint-venture partners, including Belle Isle Field, a salt dome discovered in 1941, as well as the Rabbit Island Field.

Negotiating with the Russians: 1990

Benton Oil was quickly gaining an international reputation as a technically savvy operation. In 1990, the company was approached by the Russian Republic of the Soviet Union to be involved in a joint venture to exploit a newly discovered western Siberia oil field. Benton Oil was recommended to the Russians by a London geological data firm. Because Alexander Benton was able to negotiate in Russian, his mother tongue, it was a good fit. In January 1991, along with several other Benton Oil executives, he returned to the country where he was born, then made the arduous trip to the North Gubkinskoye field, some 2,000 miles north of Moscow, above the Arctic Circle, where he was greeted by temperatures as low as 60 degrees below zero. Benton Oil subsequently agreed to form a joint venture, named Geoilbent, with two Russian ministries as partners. In less than a year, the enterprise was operational. For Benton Oil, with a 34 percent interest, the arrangement was

especially advantageous because seismic studies had already been done and the company was grandfathered so that it did not have to pay an excise tax to export the oil. Essentially the Russians provided the field as well as the bulk of equipment and labor, and Benton Oil provided the funding and expertise.

In addition to Russia, Benton Oil was also asked in 1991 by Venezuela's national oil company, Petroleos de Venezuela, to bid on the right to work nine mature oil fields in that country. A failed coup attempt in February 1992 scared away other companies, and Benton Oil was able to secure oil concessions on very favorable terms. Aside from its technology, Benton Oil was now established as a company willing to work in politically risky areas of the world. In order to fund its ambitions, however, the company had to attract new investors, but its business was a financial high wire act that a number of analysts predicted was destined to fail. Benton Oil attempted a public offering of three million shares in December 1991, hoping to raise $35 million. A drop in oil prices caused the underwriter, PaineWebber, to cancel the offering, and Benton Oil was able to raise only $5 million by selling shares by itself. To concentrate on assets with greater potential and pare down debt, in 1992 the company sold off most of its California interests, as well as interests in some Colorado properties. A year later it raised another $8.2 million by selling off some of its Louisiana interests.

Benton Oil's financial condition was complicated in 1993 when the new Russian government imposed a $5.50 per barrel excise tax on exported oil, only three months after the completion of a pipeline that would connect the Siberian field to the Soviet pipeline, which in turn would connect to refineries in the Czech Republic, Slovakia, and Germany. The tax, which virtually eliminated a profit for Benton Oil, completely violated the promise made to the company when it originally agreed to fund the project. Russian President Boris Yeltsin imposed the tax in order to generate much needed revenues, but mostly to appease political opponents. Because of the tax burden, instead of producing 100,000 barrels a day, the field pumped little more than 3,500 barrels. Yeltsin soon lifted the tax, but considerable time would elapse before entrenched bureaucrats would acknowledge the change. Benton Oil cut back its capital spending on the project and waited for tax relief.

Accepting political complications was simply the price a company like Benton Oil had to be willing to pay in order to gain access to potentially high-yield reserves of oil and gas. It also encountered obstacles in Venezuela when local politicians, whose behavior the company characterized as ''grandstanding,'' called for an investigation of how the oil concession had been granted. Despite such difficulties, Benton Oil increased its commitment to the country, acquiring additional rights in 1994 and 1996. In the meantime, the company sold off most of its domestic interests, including a 1996 sale of its Louisiana operations to Shell Oil for $35.4 million. It subsequently moved into other high-risk areas of the world. Benton Oil entered into a joint venture to exploit an oil field in southeastern Jordan, near the border with Saudi Arabia, then signed an agreement with the state oil company of the West African nation of Senegal to study and develop its 600,000-acre Thies Block. It acquired Creston, a Colorado oil company with interests in the South China Sea that were the subject of territorial claims between the People's Republic of China and Vietnam.

Through an agreement with Shell Exploration Limited, Benton Oil also acquired a 50 percent participation in China's third largest producing oil and gas field. Moreover, the company renewed its interest in California, acquiring a 40 percent working interest in the Molino project, which covered three offshore oil and gas leases spread across more than 12,000 acres.

Collapse in Oil Prices and Revenues: 1998

With Venezuelan interests providing the bulk of the earnings, revenues for Benton Oil totaled $165.1 million in 1996, growing to $179 million in 1997. The company posted net earnings of $28.3 million in 1996 and $18 million in 1997. In 1997, the company borrowed $240 million through junk bonds in order to finance further growth, but a short time later, world crude oil prices collapsed. Coupled with declining revenues, which fell to $112 million in 1998, Benton's was now carrying a heavy debt load. Moreover, the Molino project came up dry. Consequently, Benton Oil was forced to take a one-time write-off of $153 million on properties that failed to live up to projections, resulting in a net loss in 1998 of $183 million.

In early 1999, despite cost-cutting measures and rebounding oil prices, Benton Oil lacked the necessary cash flow to pay its debts and properly exploit its assets. It hired J.P. Morgan & Co. to explore its choices, which included the sale of assets and possibly the entire company. The situation was complicated further by the dire financial condition of Alex Benton, who over the course of the three previous years had borrowed some $7.5 million, secured by company stock that was now worth considerably less than the loans. In August 1999, he filed for personal bankruptcy and two weeks later resigned as chairman, CEO, and president of Benton Oil. He remained a director of the company and a consultant to the Russian operations, while making arrangements through the courts to repay his debt to the company.

Benton's departure reassured the market, and the company's stock, which had been in a free fall, finally stabilized. Replacing Benton on an interim basis were directors Bruce M. McIntyre and Michael B. Wray, who shared the office of chief executive while recruiting a permanent occupant for the post. They settled

on Dr. Peter J. Hill, who boasted 25 years of experience at British Petroleum, where he served as Chief Geologist. After leaving BP in 1994, he went to work for Deminex, Germany's largest oil company. Believing that Benton Oil still controlled a valuable asset base, Hill agreed to become the company's CEO. With Wray staying on as chairman, Hill revamped the board of directors to regain investor confidence in the company. In addition, he hired a new chief financial officer and senior vice-president of exploration and production. Although committed to aggressively exploiting the asset base of Benton Oil, Hill was also mindful of putting the company's financial house in order and studied all the options, which again included the sale of assets or the company in its entirety.

Under Hill's direction, Benton Oil opted to impose cost-cutting measures and to restructure its debt. To lower its general and administrative expenses, the company moved its headquarters in June 2001 from California to Houston, Texas. It received some good news a short time later when one of its Russian ventures struck oil. In February 2002, Benton Oil took a major step in its financial recovery when it sold some of its Russian interests for $190 million. This infusion of cash allowed the company to retire $108 million in debt while allowing it to better exploit its remaining Russian assets and Venezuelan interests. Hill characterized the sale as a landmark transaction that he hoped would convince analysts of the intrinsic value of the Russian market and in turn the inherent value of Benton Oil. He also hoped that by reducing the company's debt load, investors would be willing to take a fresh look at the potential of Benton Oil.

Principal Subsidiaries

Energy International Financial Institution, Ltd.; Benton Offshore China Company; Geoilbent, Ltd.; Arctic Gas Company.

Principal Competitors

Exxon Mobil Corporation; Royal Dutch Petroleum Company; Sibneft.

Further Reading

Apodaca, Patrice, "Benton Oil Seeking Cash to Pump into Drilling Projects," *Los Angeles Times,* January 28, 1992, p. 9A.

"CEO Resigns from Beleaguered Benton Oil & Gas," *Los Angles Times,* September 2, 1999.

Miller, Greg, "Northern Explorers New Soviet Oil Export Tax Keeps Oxnard Firm Waiting for the Rewards of Its Joint Venture," *Los Angeles Times,* August 30, 1994, p. 12.

Morgenson, G., and J. Zweig, "Better Luck This Time," *Forbes,* April 1, 1991, p. 134.

Petruno, Tom, "Big Debate Over a Small Energy Firm's Prospects," *Los Angeles Times,* June 6, 1991, p. 1.

Toai, Brian A., "Benton: The Venturesome Kind," *Oil & Gas Investor,* March 1992, p. 51.

—Ed Dinger

BERNINA®

Bernina Holding AG

Seestrasse
Steckborn
CH-8266
Switzerland
Telephone: +41-52 762 11 11
Fax: +41-52 762 16 11
Web site: http://www.bernina.com

Private Company
Founded: 1893
Employees: 887
Sales: $154.5 million (2000)
NAIC: 335228 Other Major Household Appliance
Manufacturing

Bernina Holding AG is the parent company of Fritz Gegauf AG, one of the world's five largest sewing machine manufacturers. Headquartered in Steckborn, Switzerland, the company has won a reputation for top-of-the-line sewing machines under the Bernina brand name. Bernina's daughter companies include distributors in the United States, Western Europe, Scandinavia, Asia, Australia, and New Zealand. In addition, a worldwide network of close to 70 independent distributors brings Bernina machines to locations across South America, Eastern Europe, Southeast Asia, and the Middle East. Altogether, the company sells about 100,000 sewing, serger, and embroidering machines yearly, as well as machine accessories, software, and patterns. Bernina prides itself on machines that are known for durability and precision, and the company's market share is particularly strong in the high-end sector, with versatile, technologically advanced machines that usually cost more than twice as much as the average machine. Education is a central aspect of Bernina's customer relations strategy. The company offers its dealers regular training seminars and promotes a long-lasting educational relationship with its customers, whether through Internet tutorials or through classes offered at Bernina dealerships. Technology is another hallmark of the company's product line. The newest Bernina machines are highly computerized, operated in large part through a touch screen interface. Bernina's customers can take advantage of such features as digitalized patterns and custom pattern selection software. The company has been privately held throughout its 110-year history and is now headed by Hanspeter Ueltschi, great-grandson of the company founder.

The Gegauf Hemstitching and "Fitz" Machines: 1893–1932

The great-grandfather of Bernina sewing machines, Karl Friedrich Gegauf, moved to Steckborn, Switzerland, in 1890. There, in the Feldbach Convent, he established an embroidery shop and a mechanical workshop for the production of a monogram embroidering machine. Ten mechanics were employed in the machine workshop, while the embroidery shop served both to provide a steady income to the business and as a laboratory for trying out new inventions. Gegauf's goal was to develop a machine that could do hemstitching, which was performed by hand at the time.

Gegauf achieved his goal two years later when he obtained a patent for the world's first hemstitch sewing machine. In 1893 he set up a workshop in the Feldbach Convent for the production of hemstitching machines, which would remain the business's main product for more than 30 years. When a fire destroyed the convent in 1895, a prototype of the hemstitch machine was saved and new, more spacious workshops were established in a barn. Both hemstitch and embroidery machines were produced there.

The hemstitch machine soon garnered widespread attention, and "gegaufen" became a commonly used term for the mechanical production of hemstitching. By 1900, more than 70 people were employed in the Steckborn workshop. Karl Friedrich acted as technical director, while his brother Georg tended to the commercial side of the business. The workshop prospered until the advent of World War I put a brake on the young company's progress. During the war, exports to foreign countries were forbidden, and the Gegauf works had to turn to the manufacture of other items, such as tin-openers, to survive this period. Adding to the hardship, Georg Gegauf died in an accident in 1917.

Karl Friedrich persevered on his own, establishing new workshops in the so-called "Neue Schloss," while his late brother's family oversaw operations in the "Gruene Haus." Karl Friedrich's son Fritz received a patent for a new hemstitch machine in 1919. After the war, old connections were reestablished and the business was back on solid ground for a time. But a new artificial silk factory, started in 1923 on the site of the Feldbach Convent, threatened the prosperity of the Gegauf business, since silk was ill suited for hemstitching. At first, however, Karl Friedrich found a way to turn the new factory to his advantage. On a tour of the silk production facility, he noted that the method used to tie thread up into skeins before dying was inefficient. He came up with a machine that could perform this task, known as "fitzen," mechanically. Karl Friedrich's death in December 1926, however, prevented him from ever seeing an operating fitz machine.

The Gegauf sons, Fritz and Gustav, took over operations and delivered the first fitz machine to the silk factory in July 1927. So many orders came in that the factory in the Neue Schloss could no longer support the production of both fitz and hemstitch machines. As a result, new workshops were built on the edge of town, which would be the location of the Bernina factory into the 21st century. The new facility housed both administrative offices and the manufacturing plant. Presser feet and other attachments were produced alongside the hemstitch machines.

Developing a Name for
Bernina Sewing Machines: 1932–71

By the early 1930s the business, now known as Fritz Gegauf's Sons, was entering another difficult period. A worldwide economic crisis began in October 1929 and, with too little work to do, the workshop was cut back to 35 employees. Furthermore, technological advances in the production of artificial silk made the fitz machine unnecessary. A new product was needed. The Gegauf sons noted that 20,000 sewing machines were being imported annually into Switzerland and saw an opportunity for domestic production. Wilhelm Brutsh, a sewing machine specialist, was recruited to help promote this new sector of the business. In 1932, Model 105 became the first home sewing machine to be made in Switzerland. It was given the brand name "Bernina" after a nearby mountain. The machine established a precedent for quality and durability. It began to sell, but the Depression and the onset of World War II prevented any rapid growth.

Over the next several decades, Fritz Gegauf piloted the company toward world-class status with skillful and creative leadership. The first Bernina sewing machine was exported in 1935, and in 1938 Model 117 became the first zigzag sewing machine produced in Switzerland. The world's first free-arm zigzag sewing machine, Model 125, was developed in Steckborn and unveiled in 1944. In 1947 Gustav Gegauf died, and the firm's name was changed to Fritz Gegauf AG. The regular introduction of new models continued, keeping Bernina on the cutting edge technologically. Model 530 came out in 1954. The machine offered new decorative stitches, a buttonhole device, and the first patented clip-on presser feet. Model 730, which was launched in 1963, was the successor to Model 530. It was the first top-of-the-line machine to include a knee-activated presser foot lifter. Also in 1963, the one millionth Bernina machine was manufactured in Steckborn.

By this time women were beginning to sew less, attracted by the relatively inexpensive, imported clothing that was becoming available. The craft of sewing began to transform from a practical necessity into a creative hobby. The future leadership of the company would have to be sure to promote the creative side of sewing to keep the company viable. The third generation in Bernina leadership was Fritz Gegauf's daughter Odette Ueltschi-Gegauf. She began taking on responsibilities at the company under her father's guidance when Fritz's son died in 1965. Despite a lack of formal business training, Ueltschi-Gegauf was praised for her intuitive business sense and an ability to capitalize on connections with people. Bernina's reach broadened under the joint leadership of father and daughter. Bernina of America was established in Chicago in 1969. By taking over from the independent distributors that had been selling Bernina machines since the early 1960s, it was hoped that the North American location would ensure consistent service to both dealers and consumers.

Technologically Advanced Machines
for the Late 20th Century

In 1971 the first Bernina machine with electronic foot control was introduced. This machine, known as Model 830, remained the top-of-the-line model for 11 years and became the company's all-time best-seller. Meanwhile, control was decisively handed over to the third generation when, in 1975, Fritz Gegauf retired after 50 years at the head of Bernina. Odette Ueltschi-Gegauf assumed primary control and became president in 1979. Under her guidance, Bernina machines entered the computerized realm, developing, for example, the ability to automatically set the appropriate stitch width, length, and needle position based on the stitch selected.

New models were introduced at a rapid pace through the 1980s. Model 930, which came out in 1982, was able to create multi-motion stretch stitches and decorative patterns. The machine came with DC power. Model 1130, introduced in 1986, became the first fully electronic computerized machine, with capabilities such as automatic one-step buttonholes and stitch pattern memory. Model 1230, which appeared in 1989, had

Key Dates:

1893: Karl Friedrich Gegauf obtains a Swiss patent for the world's first hemstitching machine; production begins in Steckborn.

1927: The Gegauf sons begin providing "fitz" machines to the local silk factory.

1932: Model 105 becomes the first sewing machine to be produced in Switzerland; the brand name "Bernina" is taken from a nearby mountain peak.

1944: Model 125, the world's first free-arm zigzag sewing machine, is introduced in Steckborn.

1963: The one millionth Bernina sewing machine is manufactured in Steckborn.

1975: Fritz Gegauf dies; daughter Odette Ueltschi-Gegauf takes over.

1988: Hanspeter Ueltschi replaces his mother as head of Bernina.

1998: The "artista" machine brings computer-controlled sewing to a new level.

expanded memory capabilities that made it more versatile than its predecessor. Altogether, Bernina was producing about 140,000 machines a year and employed approximately 1,100 people worldwide.

In 1988 Hanspeter Ueltschi assumed the leadership role after his mother retired. Odette Ueltschi-Gegauf died in 1992. Her son's tenure at the head of Bernina would see the development of technologically advanced machines, allowing the sewer to produce intricate quilting and embroidery pieces that were formerly done only by hand. During this time, Bernina also began moving some of its production overseas. A factory was established in Thailand in 1990 for the manufacture of sewing machine parts, the Bernina 950 semi-industrial machine, and, later, the simplified "classic" Model 1008. In 1992 the appearance of Model 1530 continued the progression toward computerization. This machine had an LCD display and a command ball mechanism that offered simplified and superior sewing control. The model was upgraded the following year to Model 1630, which offered sewing control on an even more intricate level. The 1630 machine came with more than 400 stitched patterns, five alphabets, eight fully automatic buttonholes, expanded memory, and 12-direction stitching.

These innovative machines were part of an effort to add modern appeal to a traditional craft that was in danger of being lost in the younger generation. Business continued to be good through 1992, when the company announced a profit on net revenues of SFr 225 million. Sales at just the Fritz Gegauf plant in Steckborn rose 4 percent that year. The company, now with 1,160 employees, hoped to hold ground in Switzerland and even increase sales in Japan and Germany. Unfortunately, results for 1993 fell short of that goal as revenues fell 3 percent from the previous year. Although domestic sales were up 10 percent, a poor economic situation in New Zealand, Scandinavia, and Australia led to an overall drop in sales. The downward trend continued in 1994, due in part to the poor showing of the Swiss franc in exchange markets. Exports to Japan had fallen consid-

erably and sales in Switzerland were also down. Bright spots were the German and North American markets, where sales rose. A new president, Martin Favre, had just taken over in the United States.

As a whole, however, the sewing machine market was stagnating, and 200 jobs were cut between 1993 and 1995. More workforce reductions were called for in June 1995, when Bernina announced that 200 more jobs would be cut at the Steckborn factory by 1998. The move was part of a transition to a new production method that entailed buying more pre-made machine parts and manufacturing more components abroad. The number of employees in Steckborn fell to 650 by early 1996, and the company announced worldwide revenues for 1995 that were down 5 percent from the previous year, although revenues at the Steckborn plant had risen slightly.

In 1997 Bernina invested SFr 4 million in the development of machines that were completely computer-operated, hoping that the high-tech machines would effect a turnaround in the company's fortunes. Production costs remained high and the Steckborn plant reduced its staff to the low 500s by the end of the year. Sales in Europe were mediocre, but business in the United States was prospering. The new computer sewing machine came out in 1998 and was dubbed the "artista." The artista was run almost entirely from a touch screen. It could exchange stitches with Bernina Customized Pattern Selection software, accept an embroidery module to become a combination sewing/embroidery machine, and convert computer-scanned, digitized artwork into an embroidery design.

Another step toward computerized sewing freedom was taken in 2000 when the Bernina "Magic Box" hit the market. The device was intended to address the problem of incompatible embroidery card standards among the various sewing software manufacturers. With the Magic Box, a sewer could transfer a design from one card type to another, so that design cards from any manufacturer could be used on any computerized machine. The Magic Box also was able to link with a personal computer and transfer a design file to an embroidery card. Even sewers who did not use Bernina machines could use the Magic Box.

An emphasis on technology seemed to be the best way to attain growth in revenues. High-end computer sewing machines, which could cost up to $5,000, were the fastest-growing segment of the sewing machine market in the late 1990s. Sales of more traditional machines were flat, as discount clothing stores made the money-saving potential of handmade clothing negligible. Bernina, therefore, promoted sewing as a creative activity through its publications and customer education programs, encouraging sewers to produce heirlooms for future generations. Recognizing that the majority of sewers used the Internet regularly, Bernina decided to capture their attention with an enhanced web site. The new site, launched in August 2001, included a Learning Center, streaming video, and live interviews with guest sewers. Visitors could compare machine models, download free projects, and interact with fellow craftspeople in chat rooms. In addition, a new Bernina machine was introduced that would offer avid sewers the latest in computerized control. The activa 145, like its artista predecessor, included an LCD panel and an array of buttons and controls that gave the user precise control. But the activa was promoted as being more compact and easier to use than the artista. With an extensive library of stitches, designs, and alphabets, the new machine made possible the detailed personalization of sewing techniques. By combining the latest technology with a traditional craft, Bernina hoped to hold the interest of a new generation of sewers.

Principal Subsidiaries

Fritz Gegauf AG Näh- und Sticksysteme; BERNINA (Thailand) Co., Ltd.; Crown Technics Ltd.; Bernina Verwaltungs AG; Proxomed Medizintechnik GmbH; BERNINA of America Inc.; BERNINA Australia Pty., Ltd.; BERNINA New Zealand Ltd.; BERNINA Japan, Inc.; BERNINA (Switzerland) AG; BERNINA Europe S.A.; BERNINA Finland Oy; BERNINA Denmark AS.

Principal Competitors

Singer N.V.; Brother International; Electrolux AB.

Further Reading

"Bernina Stellt Abbau von bis zu 200 Arbeitsplätzen in Aussicht," *AP Worldstream,* June 7, 1995.

"Firmennachrichten; Schweiz," *Neue Zuercher Zeitung,* March 6, 1993, p. 34.

"Firmennachrichten; Schweiz," *Neue Zuercher Zeitung,* March 3, 1994, p. 39.

"Firmennachrichten; Schweiz," *Neue Zuercher Zeitung,* March 1, 1995, p. 30.

"Firmennachrichten; Schweiz," *Neue Zuercher Zeitung,* March 22, 1996, p. 28.

"Firmennachrichten; Schweiz," *Neue Zuercher Zeitung,* October 7, 1997, p. 26.

"The History of the Sewing Machine," Steckborn, Switzerland: Fritz Gegauf AG, 1997.

"The Story of Bernina," Aurora, Ill.: BERNINA of America, Inc., 2001.

Wolinsky, Howard, "High-Tech Machines Keep Sewing Fans in Stitches," *Chicago Sun-Times,* August 8, 2000, p. 45.

—Sarah Ruth Lorenz

Berry Petroleum Company

28700 Hovey Hills Road
Taft, California 93268
U.S.A.
Telephone: (661) 769-8811
Fax: (661) 768-8960
Web site: http://www.bry.com

Public Company
Incorporated: 1985
Employees: 115
Sales: $138.5 million (2001)
Stock Exchanges: New York
Ticker Symbol: BRY
NAIC: 211111 Crude Petroleum and Natural Gas
  Extraction

Berry Petroleum Company is a small independent oil producer whose reserves are mostly located in the California counties of Kern, Los Angeles, and Ventura. Virtually all of the company's reserves are heavy crude oil, which must be heated and then pumped to the surface (unless the deposits are located deep in the earth and thereby naturally heated). Berry uses steam in order to facilitate drilling and pumping, then blends with lighter crudes in order to transport the heavy crude through pipelines. Because of its dependence on steam, Berry owns three cogeneration plants that run on natural gas. Not only do these facilities supply 60 percent of the company's steam needs, their turbines produce secondary electricity which is then sold to California utilities. As a result, Berry is able to turn a profit on steam and maintain a low-cost in its drilling operation. Berry also owns its oil-producing properties rather than leasing, freeing the company of royalty payments. In addition, the company owns other aspects of the field operation, including transportation, treating facilities, and storage. By maintaining an ownership position in so many facets of its operation, Berry has been able to remain profitable under difficult economic conditions, unlike many competitors whose financial health is overly dependent on the fluctuating price of oil.

Striking Gold in the Yukon: Clarence J. Berry and the 1890s

The founder of the oil companies that would one day be combined to form Berry Petroleum Company was Clarence J. Berry. He grew up in Fresno, California, the son of a struggling fruit farmer. Anxious to avoid the hardscrabble life of his parents, Berry grew into an ambitious young man who was eager to make his fortune. In 1894, he borrowed money from friends and relatives to travel to Alaska, but not before convincing his childhood sweetheart, Ethel Bush, who lived on a neighboring farm, to wait for him. Although the major gold discovery in the Klondike was still two years away, Alaska had already experienced an influx of prospectors because of the 1886 discovery of gold on the Fortymile River (east of Fairbanks, close to the Canadian border). Berry arrived in Alaska with only a few dollars in his pocket, yet stayed for 18 months before returning home to marry Ethel in March 1896. Along with his younger brother, Fred, the newlyweds caught a boat from Seattle to Skagway, Alaska, where they then trekked north by foot and dog team to the mining town of Fortymile. The area had now been combed over by prospectors for a decade, and Berry had no luck in his attempts to find gold. Instead of continuing to prospect for gold, he went to work as a bartender for a man named Bull McPhee. He was practically broke when news came of the Yukon gold strike upriver, which would prove to be one of the richest discoveries in history. In order to take advantage of a once-in-a-lifetime chance, Berry borrowed money from McPhee to quickly outfit an attempt to strike a claim in the new gold fields. Wasting no time, he dispatched Ethel to hail a boat headed upriver, while he and his brother took only enough time to gather food, bedding, a tent, and essential tools. Because of Berry's quick actions, they were among the first to reach the Yukon and stake a claim on Eldorado Creek, one that soon made them wealthy. (McPhee's help would also be amply rewarded. A decade later when McPhee's Fairbank's establishment burned down, Berry allowed his old boss to draw on his funds in order to rebuild and restock. In addition, he arranged a lifelong pension for McPhee.) After working the claim for a year, the Berry party returned home to California for the winter, taking the steamship *Portland* to Seattle. Once the *Portland*

> ### Company Perspectives:
>
> *Berry Petroleum Company is an independent oil producer with significant experience in heavy crude production.*

arrived in Seattle and word of the Yukon strike became general knowledge, the famous Alaskan gold rush was launched.

Unlike so many other Yukon millionaires, Berry kept both his head and his wealth. In fact, he continued to work hard in Alaska and made even more money. He and his family worked the Yukon claim for the next five years. Interestingly enough, he was credited with introducing the use of steam to the area's mining efforts. Attaching a steam hose to a rifle barrel, he helped develop the steam point, which thawed the hard frozen ground by injecting steam under the surface. After 1902, he and his brothers relocated to the Ester Creek areas near Fairbanks, where he made yet another fortune, followed by a third in Circle, Alaska.

Berry and his wife then returned to live in California, where as early as 1899 he had become involved in starting up oil companies. For decades area tar pits had been drilled for oil, but it was not until the success of hand-dug oil wells in the Kern River field in 1899 that a regional oil boom resulted. By the time Berry left Alaska, Kern River, along with the nearby Midway-Sunset field, had made California into the leading oil producing state in the nation. With the wealth he had accumulated in Alaska, Berry was able to buy up promising tracts of land in Kern County, and soon he began drilling for oil. In 1909, he completed his first successful well in the Midway-Sunset field. To exploit this property he created the Ethel D. Company, named after his wife, which continued to produce oil some 90 years later.

Family Operation Leading to Formation of Berry Petroleum Company: 1900s–80s

Berry, the former farmer turned gold prospector, was now an oilman who relished his new line of endeavor. He formed a wide array of oil companies to exploit his various properties, often forming partnerships with friends and family, who shared in the rewards of such operations, including B & E, BB & O, Berry & Ewing, Tightwad, and Surprise. To manage some of his various business interests, Berry formed Berry Holding Company in 1916. When he died suddenly in 1930, members of his family continued to run the operation until 1983, when professional managers were brought in, led by Harvey L. Bryant. In 1985, in order to streamline the operation, Berry Petroleum Company was incorporated in Delaware. It became the surviving company after merging with Berry Holding and a number of other family enterprises. Also in 1985, Eagle Creek Mining and Drilling Company was created to hold non-oil and gas producing assets, including a well servicing and drilling company. The next step in the transformation of Berry was the December 1986 purchase of an 80 percent stake in the Norris Oil Company from ABEG, Inc. The balance of the company was then acquired in June 1987. Not only did Berry pick up oil and gas properties in the Rincon field in Ventura County, as

well as gas reserves in Colorado, it also, through the Norris purchase, became a publicly traded company, available over the counter on the NASDAQ. In June 1989, the company increased the number of total shares, making more than 1.5 million shares priced at $25.50 available to the public. Berry subsequently moved to the New York Stock Exchange. Nevertheless, the company remained very much a family-controlled business, with at least three-quarters of the company's stock in the hands of Clarence Berry's descendants.

Berry was a small but profitable company through the 1980s. Nevertheless, while it generally enjoyed the benefits of controlling so many aspects of the production process, it was at the mercy of the major oil companies in transporting its Kern County crude to California refineries. The situation improved somewhat with the opening of the All-American pipeline, which allowed crude to be transported to refineries on the Gulf Coast. In addition, the independent Four Corners pipeline opened, transporting product to Los Angeles refineries. Because Four Corners was not heated, however, Berry had to build a blending station in order to mix its heavy crude with lighter grades of oil in order to create a blend capable of being piped. Because of the heavy crude, Berry also invested in cogeneration plants, at first relying on its own fuel to fire the turbines, then moving to natural gas in order to meet state environmental regulations.

Throughout the 1980s the major oil companies invested heavily in Kern County. The price for this crude would be suppressed by the influx of Alaskan oil transported by pipeline into the California market. When the entire world was glutted with oil in the early 1990s following the Gulf War, the result was a price per barrel for California's heavy oil that was less than it cost most companies to produce. While the majors and many independents were forced to shut down their wells, Berry, with its lower cost structure, was still able to turn a profit. Nevertheless, the company needed to initiate some retrenching efforts. Approximately 400 of the company's 1,300 wells were shut down, as was an unprofitable blending plant. The budget for drilling was suspended. Electricity and steam usage was trimmed, as was the well-service fleet (from nine units to just four). Overall, staff was cut by 20 percent; the salaries of those that remained were reduced by 10 percent, and for the first time in a generation there was no Christmas bonus for workers. With zero debt, $35 million in cash, and the ability to make money on California crude in the harshest of economic conditions, Berry was much better situated than its competitors.

Despite this advantage, management felt the need to spread to other regions of the country, in particular south Texas and Louisiana. Such attempts at diversification, however, did not amount to much. Berry remained a California oil company, and once oil prices rebounded in the mid-1990s it renewed its focus on its traditional core oil fields.

Pipeline Rupture: 1993

Berry lost $1.1 million in 1994 after essentially breaking even in 1993. The company would have actually turned a slight profit in 1994 had it not incurred a $1.3 million charge related to an oil spill that occurred in December 1993, an accident that not only resulted in bad publicity but threatened criminal prosecu-

Key Dates:

1909: Clarence Berry first strikes oil in California.
1916: The Berry Holding Company is formed.
1930: Clarence Berry dies.
1985: Berry Holding is merged into newly formed Petroleum Company.
1987: Berry becomes a publicly traded corporation after acquiring Norris Oil.
1993: A major oil spill results from ruptured pipeline.
1997: A civil case resulting from oil spill is settled.

tion of Berry's senior officers. An underground pipeline used by Berry subsidiary Bush Oil Co. began to leak on December 16, then suffered a major rupture five days later and spewed oil for four days before being stopped. All this activity went undetected by workers despite the fact that approximately 84,000 gallons of oil failed to reach a storage tank. Instead, the crude seeped into McGrath Lake, located in the wildlife habitat of McGrath State Park, as well as the ocean near Oxnard. To make matters worse, at least seven area public safety agencies were alerted to the spill by witnesses, but none of them took the trouble to investigate. Thousands of additional gallons continued to pour from the ruptured pipeline before a federal Minerals Management Service worker happened to notice offshore oil slicks from a helicopter while on his way to inspect an offshore oil platform. It was Ventura County's worst oil spill, contaminating miles of beach, dunes, and sensitive wildlife refuges. Cleanup efforts ultimately cost around $15 million, although Berry's insurance covered much of the expense.

In the aftermath of the spill, as cleanup efforts made significant progress, local prosecutors threatened Berry's management with felony charges, although this was more than likely only a plea-bargaining ploy. The facts surrounding the spill certainly left Berry in a vulnerable position. The company had acquired the 40-year-old pipeline from Chevron in 1990 after it had been abandoned for some ten years. The line had been used to transport natural gas, yet Berry began to pump crude oil through it without making any upgrades. Moreover, it was revealed that ten months before the oil spill occurred, a safety valve that might have prevented the leak had broken, and no one supervising the pipeline bothered to repair it. Both Berry and the state negotiated through the press, with Berry countering prosecutors threats with talk of suing the agencies that neglected to investigate witness reports and notify company officials of the leak. Several months later Berry agreed to pay a $600,000 settlement and pleaded no contest to a single misdemeanor charge of failing to report the leak. In addition, the foreman on duty during the spill pleaded no contest to a charge of illegally releasing oil into marine water and was ordered to perform 320 hours of beach cleanup. Although free of criminal charges, Berry still faced a civil case from the state attorney general's office. That matter was not to be settled until January 1992, when the company agreed to a $3.2 million fine.

Berry returned to profitability in 1995 and initiated a five-year growth strategy that resulted in the acquisition of a number of valuable oil properties in the South-Midway-Sunset field as well as three cogeneration facilities. As a result, Berry's reserves increased significantly and the company was well positioned to increase production to take advantage of oil prices that rebounded after a 1998 collapse in the market. Early in 1999, California crude was selling at $7 per barrel. A year later, it sold at $19 per barrel. The company's profit was also enhanced by an improved infrastructure, especially its cogeneration capabilities. Not only did its turbines supply most of the company's need for steam and electricity, Berry also began selling off excess electricity at a profit. Sales of electricity grew from $11.5 million in 1996 to $52.77 million in 2000. Although the cost to operate the facility also rose dramatically, due in large part to the rising cost of natural gas, the company began to turn a profit on electricity by the end of the 1990s. Overall, Berry enjoyed record results in 1999 and 2000, posting net earnings of $18 million and $37.2 million, respectively.

The energy crisis that gripped California in 2000 and 2001 had an adverse effect on Berry. Two of its major customers for electricity, Pacific Gas and Electric Company and Southern California Edison Company, were pushed to the edge of bankruptcy and in early 2001 were unable to pay for the power that Berry had delivered in the previous months. Berry cut back on its production of electricity, shutting down four of its five turbines. Because there was less steam as a result, the company was forced to curtail its 2001 capital development program and took on a modest debt load. Despite these developments, Berry enjoyed another profitable year in 2001, with net earnings of nearly $22 million.

The power situation in California stabilized, and by March 2002 Edison was able to repay Berry $13.5 million, which was earmarked to reduce the company's long-term debt from $25 million to around $12 million. Because of its cogeneration plants, 100 percent ownership of most of its oil-bearing properties, and financial stability, Berry appeared to be well positioned for years of profitable operation.

Principal Competitors

ChevronTexaco Corporation; Key Production; Royal Dutch Petroleum Company.

Further Reading

Jaffe, T., ''Oil Berry,'' *Forbes,* June 25, 1990, p. 298.

Mack, Toni, James R. Norman, Howard Rudnitsky, and Andrew Tanzer, '' 'History Is Full of Giants That Failed to Adapt,' '' *Forbes,* February 28, 1994, p. 73.

McDonald, Jeff, ''Berry Petroleum Pleads No Contest in Oil Spill Penalty,'' *Los Angeles Times,* August 18, 1994, p. 1.

Montano, Alexanger G., ''Berry Petroleum Co.,'' *Oil & Gas Investor,* February 2000, p. 66.

Savitz, Eric J., ''Heavy Trip,'' *Barron's,* November 5, 1990, p. 19.

Steepleton, Scott, ''Record $3.2 million Settlement Ok'd Over Spill,'' *Los Angeles Times,* January 24, 1997, p. 1.

Toal, Brian A., ''Kern County,'' *Oil & Gas Investor,* June 1994, p. 24.

—Ed Dinger

Biovail Corporation

2488 Dunwin Drive
Mississauga, Ontario L5L 1J9
Canada
Telephone: (416) 285-6000
Fax: (416) 285-6499
Web site: http://www.biovail.com

Public Company
Incorporated: 1993 as Biovail Corporation
Employees: 1,200
Sales: $583.30 million (2001)
Stock Exchanges: New York Toronto
Ticker Symbol: BVF
NAIC: 334514 Totalizing Fluid Meter and Counting
Device Manufacturing

Biovail Corporation is a pharmaceutical company that uses its patented controlled-release technology to improve upon drugs already approved by the U.S. Food and Drug Administration. Biovail is involved in the formulation, clinical testing, registration, manufacturing, and marketing of these products throughout North America. Among the company's most important products is Tiazac, a drug used to treat hypertension. Biovail is run by Barbados-based Eugene Melnyk and operates facilities in Canada, the United States, Ireland, and Puerto Rico.

Origins

Biovail began operating in the 1970s, nearly two decades before the company rose from obscurity and dazzled investors and analysts alike. For years, Biovail operated as a small, research and development firm based in the suburban Toronto city of Mississauga, Ontario. As a generic drug maker, the company existed outside the periphery of recognition. Its annual revenue volume was insignificant when compared with the pharmaceutical concerns competing against the company, and its contributions to the pharmaceutical market were unremarkable. Biovail eked out an existence during the first chapter of its history, not reaching $10 million in revenues—a pittance in the multibillion-dollar pharmaceutical industry—until the 1990s began. The company's second era of existence began when it attracted the attention of a young Canadian publisher. Although it would be several years before Biovail began to exude the luster that titillated Wall Street, the relationship between Biovail and Eugene Melnyk, begun in 1989, marked the beginning of the small, Mississauga firm's rise to fame.

The paths of Melnyk and Biovail were connected by Trimel Corp. Melnyk started Trimel Corp. in 1983, when the entrepreneur (later to be one of the richest individuals in Canada) was 24 years old. Trimel Corp. operated as a publisher of medical journals, which introduced Melnyk to an enticing technology in the medical field. During his perusal of medical publications, Melnyk learned of oral controlled-release technology, which regulated a drug's dosage throughout the day, enabling patients to take only one pill a day, rather than several pills. Melnyk was excited about the potential of time-release technology in the pharmaceutical market, prompting him to sell Trimel Corp.'s publishing operations in 1988. A year later, he paid $6.5 million for the little-known Biovail, which was developing drugs using controlled-release technology at the time. Roughly five years later, it appeared as if Melnyk had made a grave error. Before Biovail achieved much applauded success, Melnyk's 1989 purchase teetered on the brink of bankruptcy.

Operating as a generic drug maker, Biovail found itself embattled. The small company was positioned in a highly competitive market fraught with litigious battles. Biovail shared in the fate of nearly all generic drug makers: The company endured frequent lawsuits filed by brand-name pharmaceutical concerns who accused Melnyk's firm of patent infringement, which led to costly legal fights that the small company was ill-equipped to sustain. By 1993, Biovail was nearly destitute, particularly after a failed attempt to secure public financing early in the year blackened hopes for the immediate future. The company could not meet payroll, unable to muster the $100,000 needed to pay its employees. One employee, a future senior vice-president, mortgaged his house to give the company the funds to pay its workers. Stumbling, Biovail managed to keep its balance until Melnyk merged the drug company with Trimel, whose shares traded on the Toronto Stock Exchange, in late

1993. The situation was bleak, but Biovail's salvation was on the horizon.

Tiazac: A Mid-1990s Saviour

In late 1994, Biovail's future quickly brightened. News spread that the company was likely to get approval for Tiazac, its controlled-release formulation of diltiazen, a leading calcium channel blocker that represented a class of drugs widely used in the treatment of hypertension, a condition that accounted for 15 percent of all prescriptions written in the United States. The news caused a measurable and substantial stir among analysts and investors. Expecting Biovail's profits to increase exponentially, the investment community flocked to the unknown Biovail, which generated $16.5 million in revenue in 1994. Shares in the company, trading at $2.75 per share in November 1994, experienced dizzying growth, increasing to $80 per share, after a sustained buying frenzy, in December 1995. Melnyk, through the investor frenzy surrounding Tiazac, was making Biovail a known name in the vast pharmaceutical industry.

In September 1995, the Food and Drug Administration (FDA) officially approved Biovail's request to market Tiazac. That same month, Melnyk supplied perhaps his greatest contribution to the finances of Biovail. Melnyk brokered a 16-year marketing and distribution deal with Forest Laboratories Inc. Under the terms of the agreement, Biovail licensed its angina-fighting drug Tiazac in exchange for 35 percent of the drug's sales and $20 million in cash. The agreement led to the February 1996 launch of Biovail's new product, giving Melnyk's company its first taste of robust financial growth. During the first six months of 1996, Biovail's sales soared to $34.6 million, more than 400 percent higher than the total registered during the same period in 1995. The company's net income during the first half of 1996 rose to $10.4 million, far eclipsing the $1.8 million posted during the first six months of 1995. By the end of 1996, Biovail was a more than $66 million-in-sales company, one year after being unable to generate $20 million in sales. Wall Street watched, and became intrigued.

Not long before Melnyk engineered the pivotal agreement with Forest Laboratories, he handed his responsibilities as Biovail's chief executive officer to Bruce Brydon. Melnyk, who had moved to Barbados in 1990, continued serving as chairman, taking responsibility for legal and financial matters, long-term planning, and part of research and development. Brydon's re-

sponsibility, Melnyk explained in a December 31, 2001 interview with *Canadian Business,* was "to make sure everything's going according to plan." Toward this end, Brydon distinguished himself, orchestrating Biovail's transformation into an influential drug maker.

The Late 1990s Rise of Biovail

The combination of Brydon in Mississauga and Melnyk in Barbados worked well, particularly from 1997 forward, after the pair refined Biovail's agenda. Instead of subjecting themselves to a never-ending barrage of patent infringement lawsuits, Melnyk and Brydon decided to focus on drugs that had already gained regulatory approval. Biovail then would add its patented controlled-release technology and market the products. The strategic alteration gave the company a new, lucrative direction to pursue. "The genius of Biovail," an analyst remarked in a December 31, 2001 *Canadian Business* article, "is that they figured out you don't need to spend $500 million and take ten years to develop a new product. You can take something that's out there on the market, tweak it a little bit, repackage it as a new brand and make just as much money."

As Melnyk charted a new course for Biovail, he gave Brydon a lofty goal to pursue. At Biovail's annual shareholder meeting in 1997, Melnyk promised shareholders that the company would achieve growth of 30 percent each year into the future. To Brydon fell the responsibility of ensuring that the goal was met, a task he accomplished, helping Biovail to record prolific growth as it exited the 1990s and entered the 21st century.

In 1998, Biovail had 13 products on the market. Of the total, 11 products were developed under research sponsored by other pharmaceutical companies. Biovail sold these products under license in 55 countries, with the sales generating royalties that were paid to Biovail. By this point, however, the company was pursuing its declared goal of becoming a leading producer of branded drugs before 2005. Accordingly, the future of the company was represented by Tiazac and a new product, launched in the fall of 1998, Trental, which was used to treat peripheral vascular disease. Tiazac and Trental, in contrast with the company's other 11 products on the market during the year, represented the first two medications that Biovail selected, developed, and navigated through the legal and approval process to bring to market. In the years ahead, the ranks of such branded products within Biovail's portfolio swelled, enabling Melnyk and Brydon to realize their vision.

In 1999, a year in which the company's sales leaped from $112.8 million to $176.5 million, further progress was made in the company's development of branded pharmaceuticals. Much of the revenue growth recorded by Biovail was attributable to the increasing sales of Tiazac, which increased its share of the diltiazen market in the United States to approximately 16 percent. New product introductions also fueled growth, helping Biovail to exceed Melnyk's ambitious growth projections. During the year, Biovail launched a generic version of the calcium channel blocker Vevelan in the United States, which was marketed by the company's U.S. generic product marketing partner, Teva Pharmaceutical Industries Ltd. Also in 1999, Biovail received approval from the FDA for the introduction of generic versions of Cardizem CD and Adalat CC, two leading treat-

Key Dates:

1977: Biovail begins developing its proprietary controlled-release technology.
1989: Eugene Melnyk acquires Biovail.
1993: Melnyk merges Trimel Corp. with Biovail.
1995: The U.S. Food and Drug Administration (FDA) approves Biovail's request to market Tiazac.
1996: Biovail begins marketing Tiazac.
1999: Biovail acquires Fuisz Technologies Ltd.
2000: Biovail acquires DJ Pharma, Inc.
2001: Biovail's sales eclipse the half-billion dollar mark.

ments for hypertension and angina. Adding to Biovail's growing stature was the acquisition of Fuisz Technologies Ltd., announced in July and completed in November. Based in Virginia, Fuisz Technologies was a leading pharmaceutical company specializing in advanced drug delivery technology. The integration of the acquisition formed Biovail Technologies.

In 2000, Biovail exceeded the accomplishments of 1999. Revenue increased 79 percent during the year, reaching an impressive $309 million. Sales of Tiazac continued to lead the way, as its share of the U.S. diltiazen market increased to 22 percent. During the year, the company acquired the exclusive Canadian marketing and distribution rights for Monocor, a cardioselective beta blocker, and Ampligen, used to treat Chronic Fatigue Immune Deficiency Syndrome. The rights to Monocor and Ampligen were acquired in February, the same month Biovail received U.S. marketing approval for its generic version of Voltaren XR, used to treat arthritis, and acquired a 120,000-square-foot manufacturing plant in Dorado, Puerto Rico. The acquisition of this facility promised to increase the company's total manufacturing operations by more than 100 percent. Perhaps the most significant event of 2000 occurred in October, when Biovail acquired San Diego, California-based DJ Pharma, Inc., a leading pharmaceutical sales and marketing concern. The addition of DJ Pharma, which formed Biovail Pharmaceuticals, gave Biovail 300 pharmaceutical sales professionals in the United States and established the company as a full-scale competitor in the U.S. controlled-release drug market, estimated to generate more than $8 billion in revenue annually.

By 2001, Melnyk, residing in a hilltop mansion in Barbados, also sat atop a vast fortune. His net worth was estimated to be $1.8 billion. Biovail's stock, of which Melnyk owned 25 percent, was trading at $90 per share after splitting 12 times during the previous six years. Although he continued to live in Barbados, Melnyk took over the responsibilities of Biovail's chief executive office in early 2002. Brydon, his achievements a record of success, became executive director of Biovail Ventures, the company's venture capital division. Looking to the future, Melnyk plotted a concerted attack on the U.S. pharmaceutical market, the largest market in the world. He planned to increase Biovail's sales staff in the United States from 300 to 800 by June 2002. As he shaped Biovail into a genuine North American powerhouse, Melnyk could rely on the introduction of a handful of new pharmaceutical products in the United States. Biovail's parade of drugs for the immediate future included Cardizem XL, a bronchitis medication named Cedax, a decongestant marketed as Rondec, and a coldsore ointment called Zovirax. Melnyk could also look forward to revenues gleaned from Biovail's new patented technology called FlashDose, which tripled a medication's absorption rate by "melting" in a patient's mouth. The full-scale launch of products using the FlashDose technology was expected to occur by 2003.

Principal Subsidiaries

Biovail Ventures; Biovail Pharmaceuticals; Biovail Technologies; Crystaal.

Principal Competitors

Alkernes, Inc.; Andrx Corporation; ALZA Corporation.

Further Reading

Anderson, Mark, "Bad News for Bears," *Canadian Business,* October 1996, p. 25.
Copple, Brandon, "A Bitter Pill to Swallow?," *Forbes,* March 18, 2002, p. 70.
Fuchs, Pablo, "Power Play: Eugene Melnyk Is Taking Over As CEO of Biovail—Again, But Will He Be Able to Deliver on His Very Big Promises?," *Canadian Business,* December 31, 2001, p. 36.
Schonfeld, Erick, "Drug Deal," *Fortune,* June 26, 1995, p. 168.
Sparks, Debra, "A Tough Pill to Swallow: Why Biovail's Shares Need a Dose of Reality," *Financial World,* November 18, 1996, p. 42.

—Jeffrey L. Covell

Bodum Design Group AG

Weinmarkt 7
CH-6000 Luzern 5
Switzerland
Telephone: (41) 41 418 60 10
Fax: (+41) 41 418 60 11
Web site: http://www.bodum.com

Private Company
Incorporated: 1944
Employees: 500
Sales: CHF 200 million (2001 est.)
NAIC: 335211 Electric Housewares and Household Fan Manufacturing; 332214 Kitchen Utensil, Pot, and Pan Manufacturing; 327215 Glass Product Manufacturing Made of Purchased Glass; 327212 Other Pressed and Blown Glass and Glassware Manufacturing

Bodum Design Group AG is a Switzerland-based manufacturer of household appliances, table service, and utensils featuring Scandinavian design. Led by Jorgen Bodum, who, together with other members of the Bodum family, continues to control 100 percent of the company founded by his father, Peter Bodum, the firm has long been synonymous with its Santos and other vacuum-type coffee makers. Since the early 1980s, however, Bodum has diversified its product range to cover nearly all aspects of table service. The company's products include both vacuum and "French press" coffee makers, tea pots, presses and kettles, silverware, coffee, tea and drink glasses, china, serving and storage items, and kitchen utensils. The company also has its own branded line of teas. Most of Bodum's designs are created by Carsten Jorgensen, Bodum's longtime director of design; the company has also hired outside designers from time to time. In addition to designing and producing its products, Bodum operates an international retail store network, with nearly 20 stores in ten countries. The company's products are also sold through third-party retailer channels. Bodum's sales in 2001 were estimated to be CHF 200 million.

Designing a Good Cup of Coffee in the 1940s

The 20th century saw a number of innovations in coffee brewing. Among these was the so-called "French Press" method, developed in fact by an Italian named Calimani. This type of coffee maker, also called the "presso" or "plunger" maker, separated coffee grounds from the brewed coffee by means of a plunger, which pressed or pushed the grounds down in the beaker. The result was more full-flavored coffee than other common methods.

Yet many coffee purists considered another method as the best method for brewing coffee that tasted as good as it smelled. This method had been originally developed in 1840 by Robert Napier, a marine engineer in Scotland, who devised a means of brewing coffee using a vacuum. Napier's system used two separate glass compartments connected by a tube. As water in the lower compartment was heated, it flowed into the upper compartment containing the coffee grounds. The cooling of the air in the lower compartment then created a vacuum that sucked the coffee back into the lower compartment, from which it could be served.

The "Napierian" method caught on to some extent in the mid-19th century, winning an award in 1856 from the Institution of Mechanical Engineers. Yet despite the method's success, Napier never took out a patent on the device. Its fragility, and other factors—such as a means to prevent the buildup of too much vacuum pressure and the difficulties in filtering out the coffee grounds from the brewed coffee—meant that the vacuum method did not achieve widespread popularity.

The vacuum method might have passed out of use altogether had it not been for Peter Bodum, a merchant based in Denmark. Bodum had founded his business in 1944 with the initial purpose of importing glassware from Eastern Europe. Over the next decade, Bodum's business expanded to include imports from other countries as well.

One of the products Bodum had begun importing during the 1950s was a French-made vacuum type coffee maker. The product proved not only expensive, but also had the same filtration and pressure problems that had long been associated with the Napier design. Yet Bodum was won over by the taste of

Company Perspectives:

"For more than two decades Bodum has aimed to produce articles that are designed and manufactured to the highest level of functionality and quality, making top design available to everyone throughout the world, thanks to affordable prices. Simplicity and functionality are the basic requirements for a Bodum design. Out of this basic concept grows a shape with a unique and simple beauty. Beauty—a quality that is eminently satisfying to our senses and intellect and that enhances our daily life. Often it is the small, scarcely noticed objects that display optimum functionality and design, simply because they were created from pure necessity. The Bodum design team hopes you will enjoy the fruits of our efforts."   —Carsten Jorgensen, Director of Design

Key Dates:

1944: Peter Bodum founds company to import glassware from Eastern Europe to Denmark.
1955: Bodum launches its first coffee maker design, Mocca, based on vacuum-type makers invented by Robert Napier in 1840.
1958: Bodum and architect Kaas Klaeson develop an improved vacuum coffee maker, the Santos, which becomes the company's first strong-selling product.
1960s: Bodum launches variations on the Santos.
1974: Son Jorgen Bodum takes over company and with designer Carsten Jorgensen introduces the French-press coffee maker Bistro.
1979: Bodum moves headquarters and manufacturing facilities to Lucerne, Switzerland.
1981: The company launches the Osiris water kettle as part of a diversification of its product line.
1986: Bodum opens its first retail store in London, which serves as a flagship store for its international retail network.
1996: Bodum now includes stores in nine countries.
2001: Bodum adds new store in Birmingham and new 7,000-square-foot flagship store in New York City.

vacuum-filtered coffee and decided to improve upon the design. Working with Kaas Klaeson, a Danish architect and designer, Bodum began to improve on the vacuum method, launching his first design in the mid-1950s, called "Mocca." Bodum and Klaeson continued to make improvements to the company's vacuum maker design and in 1958 launched Bodum's breakthrough product, the "Santos."

The Santos was to become one of the most popular coffee makers in Scandinavia—to the point where it was said that nearly every household in the region owned one. With the Santos, Bodum was able to solve a number of the problems associated with the vacuum method. The company devised and patented a new type of nylon filter that proved more effective in removing sediment than the cloth and paper filters available at the time, which, unlike the nylon filter, also altered the flavor of coffee. Bodum also solved the pressure problem, patenting a "valve seal" to prevent the Santos from developing too much pressure. The Santos was also one of the first coffee makers that could be used both on the stovetop and on the tabletop—the water chamber was heated with a bunsen type burner and brewing coffee suddenly became a dining spectacle.

Bodum solved another problem with the Santos—that of cost. By mass producing the Santos the company was able to meet its slogan that "design should not be expensive." Through the 1960s, Bodum concentrated on its highly successful coffee maker line, releasing variations on the design, such as the Domingo, a smaller maker for brewing four to six cups, and the Rio, a 12-cup brewer suitable for the restaurant circuit.

Diversified Design Group for the New Century

Peter Bodum's son Jorgen went to work for the company, then took over its leadership in the early 1970s. Joining the younger Bodum was a young designer, Carsten Jorgensen, who became Bodum's director of design and whose designs were to become the driving force behind the company's expansion in the 1980s. Bodum and Jorgensen's partnership got off to a strong start with the 1974 launch of the Bistro coffee maker.

The Bistro was Bodum's first "French press" style coffee maker. Its simple design set a standard for the category and became another perennial strong seller for the company. The

Bistro also continued the company's commitment to affordable, high-quality design. By the end of the 1970s, Bodum began plans to expand beyond coffee makers. In 1979, the company moved its headquarters to Lucerne, Switzerland.

Bodum released a new Jorgensen design in 1980, a line of cutlery based on the Bistro design. A year later, Bodum branched out into a new category, releasing the Osiris water kettle. The following year came a new member of the Bistro design family, a vacuum flask. Toward the mid-1980s, Bodum added other new product lines, including the Teabowl teapot in 1984 and the Chambord family of products, beginning with coffee glasses, that same year.

While Jorgensen became responsible for the company's designs, Jorgen Bodum was making plans to expand the company's business operations. In 1986, Bodum turned to the retail front, opening the first Bodum store in London. Designed by Jorgensen, that store served as the company's flagship as it opened new stores in other major cities, including Paris, Copenhagen, Zurich, Lucerne, Porto, Tokyo, and Lisbon. Meanwhile, Bodum also pursued sales through a series of shop-in-shop boutiques, as well as through traditional retail channels.

In the 1990s, Bodum continued to expand its product lines. The company launched its Shin Cha tea press and teapot line in 1991, which was followed by the Neptun water filter, part of the Bistro family in the same year. The following year saw the debut of an electric water kettle, the Ibis, a new line of tea glasses in the Bistro family, and the Kvadrant series of drinking glasses. In 1993, the company unveiled a new design family, Kenya, which included a French-press type coffee maker and accompanying coffee mugs.

Bodum's design family remained strong into the late 1990s, as the company rolled out its Corona family of china, cups, and other tableware in 1997. The company also debuted an espresso type of coffee maker, the Verona, that used high heat pressure to force water through the ground coffee. At the same time, Bodum extended its product range again, adding serving and storage products, such as the Yohki group of storage jars in 1997, and the Tuscany cutlery caddy in 1998. The company also began offering other kitchen utensils, including the Allium garlic press, tongs, and vegetable peelers.

Preparing for the new millennium, Bodum remained a strong force in tabletop design, releasing such products as the Eileen series of coffee glasses in 1999 and the Piccolo Passione espresso cup and saucer set. The company's retail network meanwhile continued to grow. By the end of 2001, Bodum's retail network included new stores in Birmingham, England, and a new flagship store in New York City. The store, which at 7,000 square feet became the company's largest, featured not only the company's coffeemakers, tabletop and kitchen utensils, and other products, but also designs for the bath and home office, as well as matching the company's Scandinavian designs with a 100-seat café operated by fashionable New York restaurant Aquavit. By now, Bodum had grown to a business with some 500 employees, with annual sales estimated at some CHF 200 million. Nevertheless, the company had not forgotten its origins: the Santos, though updated with a built-in heating element, remained an essential part of Bodum's extensive product line.

Principal Subsidiaries

Bodum (Skandinavien) A/S (Denmark); Bodum (UK) Ltd.; Bodum (France) SA; Peter Bodum GmbH (Germany); Bodum (Italia) Srl (Italy); Bodum Japan Co. Ltd.; Bodum (Benelux) BV (Netherlands); Bodum (Skandinavien) A/S (Norway); Bodum Portuguesa SA (Portugal); Bodum (Espana) SA (Spain); Bodum (Skandinavien) A/S (Sweden); Bodum (Schweiz) AG (Switzerland); Bodum Inc. (U.S.A.).

Principal Competitors

ARC International; Brown-Forman Corporation; Corning Incorporated; Guy Degrenne SA; International Cutlery, Ltd.; Lifetime Hoan Corporation; Mikasa, Inc.; Noritake Co., Limited; Oneida Ltd.; Royal Doulton plc; Swiss Army Brands, Inc.; Taittinger S.A.; Waterford Wedgwood plc; WKI Holding Company, Inc.

Further Reading

"Coffee, Tea and Bodum," *Gifts & Decorative Accessories*, November 1, 2001.

Knoer, Eva Maria, "Ping-Pong zum ausgereiften Design," *Forum Magazin*, July 2001.

—M.L. Cohen

BRAATHENS

Braathens ASA

Oksenoyveien 3
P.O. Box 55
1330 Fornebu
Norway
Telephone: + 47 67 59 70 00
Fax: + 47 67 59 70 10
Web site: http://www.braathens.no

Public Company
Incorporated: 1946 as Braathens South American & Far
    East Airtransport A/S
Employees: 4,000
Sales: NKr 6.74 billion ($768 million) (2000)
Stock Exchanges: Oslo
Ticker Symbol: BRA
NAIC: 481111 Scheduled Passenger Air Transportation;
    481112 Scheduled Freight Air Transportation; 481212
    Nonscheduled Chartered Freight Air Transportation;
    481211 Nonscheduled Chartered Passenger Air
    Transportation

Braathens ASA is Norway's largest airline. Most of its destinations are in Sweden and Norway, though Braathens has been affiliated with the KLM/Northwest global airline alliance. Thanks to the country's fjords and mountains, Norwegians take more plane trips per year per person than any other nationality except U.S. citizens.

Shipping Origins

Ludvig G. Braathen founded one of the largest shipping lines in Norway, Ludv G Braathens Rederi A/S, in 1926. Twenty years later, the airline bearing his name was started. The launch was delayed a decade by government intervention and war.

As Kjell Oskar Granlund details in *Airways,* Braathen had seen the potential of air freight as early as 1936, when he used KLM to deliver a replacement propeller shaft to a ship stranded in Jakarta. In 1937 he made the same pilgrimage as other European aviation pioneers, that of touring aircraft factories and airlines in the United States. He discussed the possibility of launching a transatlantic airline with Bernt Balchen of the prewar Det Norske Luftfartselskap (DNL). The following year (1938), Braathen unsuccessfully applied for rights to fly to the United States. Soon, World War II intervened: unlike Denmark and Sweden, Norway fielded no civil aircraft of its own during its occupation by Nazi Germany.

DNL was reestablished after the war as Norway's preferred scheduled airline. At practically the same time, Braathens South American & Far East Airtransport A/S (Braathens SAFE) was created to provide ad hoc charter services with Douglas war surplus cargo aircraft. It was incorporated on March 26, 1946.

Initially, Braathens found more demand for flights to the East than to the West. The first flight, Oslo-Copenhagen-Paris-Cairo, departed on January 30, 1947. Soon, Braathens SAFE was flying to Hong Kong via Amsterdam, Marseille, Cairo, Basra, Karachi, Calcutta, and Bangkok.

The success of Braathens SAFE was bringing it into contention with Scandinavian Airlines System (SAS). SAS was at the time a regional alliance of the state-sponsored airlines of Norway (DNL), Denmark (Det Danske Luftfartselskap or DDL), and Sweden (Svensk Interkontinental Lufttrafik AB or SILA). Braathens SAFE's license to fly to Hong Kong was suspended in April 1954 to keep it out of competition with the ever expanding SAS, which, notes Kjell Granlund, did not actually fly to Hong Kong until 1992.

In 1952, Braathens forged an alliance of its own with Loftlei'ir Icelandic Airlines, which had licenses to fly to both Europe and the United States. The decade-long cooperation between the two airlines extended to sharing aircrews and planes.

As compensation for losing its Far East routes, Braathens was allowed to begin domestic service between Oslo and Stavanger and between Oslo and Trondheim in August 1952. Braathens added another local destination when it took over an airline based in Bergen in 1958. The airline, Vestlandske Luftfartselskap, had been founded, like Braathens, by shipping interests as a charter company after the war. In subsequent years, Braathens agreed to limit its range to southern Norway, while SAS concentrated on the north.

In 1959, Braathens began flying charters to the island of Spitzbergen for the mining company Store Norske Spitsbergen Kulkompani. The ground at the landing strip was frozen solid enough to support planes during the winter months only, which conveniently coincided with the closing of the fjord to sea traffic. Traffic grew and a proper airport was constructed eventually, but the government awarded the route to SAS during the early 1970s.

Jets in 1969

Braathens began operating Boeing 737 jets in January 1969. Although a few Fokker F28 jets arrived a couple of months later, Braathens would remain loyal to Boeing for decades.

Company founder Ludvig G. Braathen died in 1976 and was succeeded by his son Bjorn. Erik G. Braathen, grandson of the founder, took over in 1989. Braathens had recently standardized the fleet with the Boeing 737. Norway was developing plans to deregulate its air industry along European Union lines (though the country was not itself a member).

During this time it was proposed that SAS should take over Braathens SAFE. The Braathen family opposed this and instead listed the company on the Oslo stock exchange.

Deregulation in 1994

Norway's airline industry was deregulated on April 1, 1994. Braathens seemed to fare well at first, claiming a 51.8 percent market share in Norway in 1996. At the time, Braathens had a fleet of 25 aircraft, all Boeing 737s. The airline was carrying more than five million people a year. Charter traffic accounted for less than 20 percent of operations in the mid-1990s; the company had made a decision to focus on scheduled services ten years earlier.

Both Braathens and SAS recorded their 50th anniversaries in 1996. Both introduced promotional fares to celebrate— Braathens offered roundtrips within Norway for only NKr 500 ($75).

The new environment allowed Braathens to challenge SAS on the Oslo-Stockholm route in 1996. Braathens acquired a controlling interest in Transwede Airways in the same year,

bringing it into the domestic Swedish market. The remaining shares were acquired in 1998, and this unit was renamed Braathens Sverige.

In August 1998, Braathens acquired another Swedish airline, Malmö Aviation, for SKr 600 million ($74 million). Malmö operated a busy route connecting Stockholm with the country's west coast and was Sweden's second largest domestic carrier. It earned pre-tax profits of SKr 400 million ($48.8 million) on turnover of SKr 911 million in 1997 and had 11 BAe 146 jets and 450 employees. The acquisition gave Braathens control of a quarter of the domestic Swedish market.

The Braathens SAFE name was abbreviated to simply Braathens A/S in 1998. A new corporate logo was introduced that featured a stylized wing over an aurora borealis.

Changes and Challenges in the Late 1990s

KLM Royal Dutch Airlines acquired 30 percent of Braathens' stock in 1997 for Fl 200 million (£60 million) and brought the carrier into limited participation in the KLM/Northwest Airlines global alliance. Braathens began making changes to attract more lucrative business class customers. The carrier introduced its first dual class cabins in 1997. At the time, Braathens connected 14 destinations in Norway, seven in Sweden, and another eight in Europe.

Unfortunately, Braathens posted its first loss ever—NOK 23 million ($2.5 million) in 1998. Overcapacity in the domestic market and problems at the new international airport in Gardermoen contributed. The loss exploded to NOK 612 million in 1999.

Upon the retirement of Erik Braathen, the company hired Arne A. Jensen as chief executive in March 1999. Jensen was the first person outside the family to hold this position. Before joining Braathens, he had been chief executive and editor-in-chief of the Norwegian television company TV2. Braathens was not the only one in trouble. SAS was taking losses and Color Air, a domestic Norwegian start-up, stopped flying in September 2000.

Jensen took a number of actions to restore the company's profitability. Money-losing routes were closed. The engine maintenance division was sold off to Pratt & Whitney.

Flying with SAS in 2001

With bankruptcy looming, an agreement was worked out in May 2001 for archrival SAS to take a controlling interest in Braathens, buying out the 38.8 percent held by the Braathen family and the 30 percent held by KLM. Malmö Aviation, the Swedish operation, was not to be included. At NKr 35 ($6.32) a share, the deal was to value the Norwegian operations at NKr 1.13 billion ($124 million). Norwegian officials strongly opposed the takeover on antitrust grounds, yet had few alternatives to offer.

In the middle of this process, Braathens named a new leader—Mr. Vida Meum. Arne Jensen left to head the information technology group Merkantildata. In November 2001 Meum announced plans to cut as many as 800 of 4,000 jobs, eliminate

Key Dates:

1946: Braathens SAFE is formed by shipping magnate Ludvig G. Braathen.
1952: Braathens is awarded domestic routes.
1958: Braathens takes over Vestlandske Luftfartselskap.
1969: Jet service begins.
1976: Second generation assumes the leadership of the company.
1994: The Norwegian air industry is deregulated; Braathens goes public.
1996: Control of Transwede Airways is obtained.
1997: KLM acquires 30 percent of Braathens stock.
1998: Malmö Aviation is acquired.
1999: Arne Jensen becomes first executive outside Braathen family to lead the airline.
2001: SAS agrees to acquire controlling interest in Braathens.

20 percent of flights, and dispose of seven aircraft in order to restore the carrier's profitability.

On November 27, 2001, SAS announced that it was proceeding with its takeover bid, but at a reduced price due to the global downturn in the industry following the September 11 terrorist attacks on the United States. At NKr 27 ($3) per share, the offer valued KLM's 30 percent stake at NKr 34 million ($30 million). SAS also was buying out other principal shareholders.

Principal Subsidiaries

Braathens Holding AB (Sweden); Braathens (Cayman) Leasing Ltd. (Cayman Islands); Braathens (Cayman) Leasing II Ltd. (Cayman Islands); Braathens (Cayman) Leasing III Ltd. (Cayman Islands); Braathens (Cayman) Leasing IV Ltd. (Cayman Islands); Braathens 737-500 1 1990 AS; Smart Norge AS (30%); Spitsbergen Travel AS (16%); Wings Lojalitetsutvikling AS.

Principal Competitors

Wideroes Flyveselskap ASA.

Further Reading

Canning, Rachel, "Spot the Difference," *Airfinance Journal,* June 1995, p. 30.
Cramb, Gordon, and Greg McIvor, "KLM Buys into Nordic Carrier," *Financial Times* (London), Cos. & Markets, August 19, 1997, p. 15.
Criscione, Valeria, and Nicholas George, "SAS-Braathens Deal in Doubt," *Financial Times* (London), Cos. & Finance—Europe, August 21, 2001, p. 22.
Davies, R.E.G., *A History of the World's Airlines,* London: Oxford University Press, 1964.
Doyle, Alister, "Braathens Takes Out Axe: Norway's Airline to Chop 20% of Flights, Up to 800 Workers," *National Post,* November 6, 2001, p. FP13.
Dwyer, Rob, "Just Warming Up," *Airfinance Journal,* January 2000, p. 30.
Feldman, Joan M., "The Nordic Airline War," *Air Transport World,* November 1997, pp. 85–89.
——, "Stirring Scandinavia," *Air Transport World,* December 1997, pp. 77–79.
"Finding the Perfect Fleet Finance Solution," *Airfinance Journal,* September 1996, p. 36.
Granlund, Kjell Oskar, "Against All Odds: Braathens Well Connected with SAS," *Airways,* March 2002, pp. 53–56.
Morrocco, John D., "Malmo Aviation Acquisition Boosts Braathens in Sweden," *Aviation Week & Space Technology,* August 31, 1998, p. 49.
"Norwegian Airline Rivals SAS in Scandinavia," *European Report,* No. 2147, July 10, 1996.
"Ny Sjef Gir Ingen Garantier" ("The New Head of Braathens Offers No Guarantees"), *Dagens Naeringsliv,* abstracted in *Global News Wire,* November 6, 2001, p. 8.
O'Connor, Anthony, "It's a Piece of Cake," *Airfinance Journal,* September 1996, pp. 34–36.
Olley, Margaret, "Witty Ad Campaign Raises Airline's Profile," *Campaign,* July 19, 1996, p. 23.
"SAS Closes JOL But Is Denied Braathens," *Airfinance Journal,* September 2001, p. 12.
"SAS to Acquire Norway's Braathens," *Nordic Business Report,* May 21, 2001.
Skold, Valeria, "Braathens Breaks with Tradition," *Financial Times* (London), March 23, 1999, p. 15.
Skold, Valeria, and Tim Burt, "Braathens to Take Over Malmo Aviation," *Financial Times* (London), August 18, 1998, p. 21.
Sparaco, Pierre, "SAS Opposes Norway's Competition Authority," *Aviation Week & Space Technology,* August 27, 2001, p. 47.
"World Airline Financial Statistics—2000," *Air Transport World,* World Airline Report, July 2001, http://www.atwonline.com.

—Frederick C. Ingram

The First Name in Avocados™

Calavo Growers, Inc.

2520 Red Hill Avenue
Santa Ana, California 92705
U.S.A.
Telephone: (949) 223-1111
Toll Free: (800) 4-Calavo; (800) 422-7286
Fax: (949) 223-1112
Web site: http://www.calavo.com

Public Company
Incorporated: 2001
Employees: 200
Sales: $217.7 million (2001)
Stock Exchanges: OTC
Ticker Symbol: CVGW
NAIC: 311400 Fruit and Vegetable Preserving and
    Specialty Food Manufacturing

Calavo Growers, Inc. is the for-profit corporation that in 2001 supplanted Calavo Growers of California, a cooperative association formed in 1924 to market avocados. Today, Calavo not only sells the avocados of some 1,600 growers, it also manufactures and markets ready-made guacamole for food service sales and 100 private labels through its processed products division, Calavo Foods. The company's Mexican facility also exports avocados to Canada, Europe, and Japan. To ensure that its production facilities and produce customers have year-round access to avocados during California's off-season, Calavo imports from Mexico, Chile, and New Zealand. In addition to avocados, Calavo also markets several varieties of papayas and mangoes.

Introduction of Avocados to
the United States: 19th Century

According to a 1927 issue of the *Calavo News*, a house production of the cooperative, the avocado was introduced to California by travelers and sailors who had become familiar with the fruit in the tropics. They brought samples to friends in Santa Barbara and Los Angeles Counties "who were so pleased with their gift that they planted the seeds and grew trees which bore more delicious fruits." According to other sources, the avocado was likely introduced into the United States when Mexican trees were sent to Florida during the 1830s. Judge R.B. Ord of Santa Barbara supposedly brought Mexican avocado trees to California in 1871. Perhaps the man most responsible for the California avocado industry was Carl Schmidt, who in 1911, at the age of 21, was sent to Mexico by the West Indian Nursery of Alatadena, California, in order to discover the best avocados for sale in the local markets, then secure budwood from the trees of origin. He returned with a large number of prospects, which he subsequently planted. Of the avocados that adapted to California conditions, the one he numbered "15" survived a major frost in 1913, earning it the name of "fuerte," Spanish for vigorous and strong. The Fuerte variety of avocado would prove instrumental in the commercialization of the fruit in the United States.

Schmidt's interest in avocados was shared by a number of California growers and hobbyists, who were continually on the lookout for new fruits or varieties. Many of them were also involved in citrus fruits, the success of which paved the way for the California avocado industry. The gold rush of the 1840s had brought a large number of prospectors to California as well as the scourge of scurvy. Because citrus fruits prevented the disease, coupled with the mild southern California climate, it was natural for lemons and oranges to be introduced to the region. When the railroad made nationwide distribution possible, the California citrus industry took shape, but growers became increasingly frustrated by an ad hoc system that put them at the mercy of middlemen. To coordinate their marketing and maximize profits, groups of southern California growers formed associations. In 1893, the local associations were united into one organization, the Southern California Fruit Exchange, which set the standard for all cooperatives to follow. To stimulate the sales of citrus fruit, the Exchange began advertising in the early 1900s, and in 1908 its ad agency coined the name "Sunkist," which would soon become the brand name printed on stickers placed on the highest grade of lemons and oranges marketed by the organization. Decades later the Exchange would become known by its present-day name, Sunkist Growers.

A number of members of the California Fruit Growers Exchange were also pioneers in the avocado industry. The fruit may have been little known, but by 1915 there was enough interest that the idea of forming an association was in the air. While it came as no surprise when avocado enthusiasts received a mailing that called for a meeting to organize an avocado association, the two men who signed the letter were completely unknown. Some 80 people gathered at the Alexandria Hotel in Los Angeles on May 15, 1915, and heard from one of the signers, who was writing a book on avocado culture. His co-signer of the call was a friend who, if the necessary funds became available, was willing to serve as the official lecturer of the avocado association. Their aspirations were quickly set aside, however, and they were presumably never heard from again, while the growers seized the opportunity to form the California Avocado Association. Although the early years of the association were devoted to cultivation issues, from the start it was also very much interested in the marketing of the fruit, passing a bylaw that called for the cooperative marketing and distribution of the avocado crop when "the development of the industry makes it desirable." The total crop at the time could have fit in a bushel basket, yet the Association continually addressed marketing issues at its regular meetings. As avocado acreage increased, the Association also made efforts to introduce the fruit to area consumers. In October 1921, at a ten-day flower show held at Exposition Park in Los Angeles, the first major public display of avocados reportedly drew more attention than any other exhibit on the grounds.

Birth of the California Avocado Exchange: 1924

By 1923, as the large number of avocado trees that had been planted in earlier years were now reaching maturity and capable of producing a crop large enough to be formally introduced into the local economy, the Association realized that it now faced a serious marketing problem. It decided to form a new organization, the California Avocado Growers' Exchange. Meetings were held throughout the growing districts to allow everyone an ample opportunity to weigh in on how the new cooperative should be structured and run. The incorporators also studied the most successful cooperatives, in particular the California Fruit Growers Exchange, adopting the features that best suited avocados. In addition, they took advantage of a California law passed in 1923 that made it easier to form a stronger marketing association than had been possible under the previous statute. On January 21, 1924, the California Avocado Growers Exchange was incorporated in California and commenced operations a month later.

Relying at first on the American Fruit Growers of Los Angeles as brokers, the Exchange got off to a rough start. Avocado growers had become accustomed to a high price for their specialty fruit, receiving as much as $1.50 per pound. The wholesale price was 50 cents per pound when the Exchange commenced operations, and the price quickly plummeted to as little as 15 cents. The Exchange elected to establish its own packing plant near the Terminal Market of Los Angeles, which allowed wholesalers easier access to the produce and resulted in a higher price. Moreover, the Association established a retail store where avocados could be displayed and samples given out to passers-by. Recipe leaflets, signs, and posters were also printed and distributed to fruit stands. A number of valuable lessons were learned by the Association from this early experience: lower prices did not mean greater consumption of avocados; growers selling their fruit on consignment only hurt themselves as well as the Association; and promotion was paramount.

Even as the Exchange was incorporating, the California Avocado Association was engaged in a major promotional initiative. On January 11, 1924, it announced a contest to coin a trade name to be used in advertising California avocados, just as Sunkist had done with citrus fruit. Some 3,300 replies came in and over the next two years the Association and the Exchange attempted to settle on one of the suggested names. A few were adopted for a brief period of time only to be discarded because they were either previously trademarked by another industry or member growers simply did not like them. Finally, on January 8, 1926, the two organizations settled on "Calavo," formed by joining "California" and "avocado," a name submitted by no less than 16 people, all of whom received a prize of a year-long supply of avocados. In addition, a slogan was created, "The Famous Butterfruit of California," and the words "Calavo" and "butterfruit" were copyrighted and became the property of the Exchange. As had been the case with Sunkist, Calavo became the brand name of the highest grade of approved avocado varieties sold by the Exchange. Each piece was hand stamped with the trademark in yellow letters.

The importance of "Calavo" went beyond the coining of a clever name. The Exchange wanted to create a specific market for Calavos. Mere avocados from Florida, Cuba, and Mexico could be purchased for much less, but Calavos were to be seen as an entirely different commodity. Not only could the Exchange charge a premium price for its product, the Calavo strategy was in many ways a matter of necessity. It was clear that the major markets were in the East. With higher production and shipping costs, the Exchange would be at a significant disadvantage to Florida and Cuban avocados if the issue was merely one of price. In essence, the Exchange had no choice but to sell "Calavos" instead of avocados. As part of this marketing approach, the Exchange decided in May 1927 to change its name to Calavo Growers of California.

In the spring of 1926, a representative of the Exchange traveled to Chicago to establish contacts with eastern brokers. To stimulate consumer interest in avocados and promote the Calavo brand, an advertising campaign was initiated in the fall of 1926. The early efforts focused on the upscale metropolitan market, reached by advertising in such magazines as the *New Yorker* and *Vogue*. A copy of *The New Calavo Hostess Book*, which included numerous recipes, was sent free to anyone returning an enclosed coupon. Calavo advertising also appeared in restaurant trade publications appealing to chefs, with coupons redeemable for booklets containing special restaurant recipes. The belief was that chefs would be more likely to try something

Key Dates:

1915: The California Avocado Association is formed.
1924: The California Avocado Growers Exchange is formed as a cooperative.
1927: The Exchange changes its name to Calavo Growers of California.
1965: Frozen avocado dip is introduced.
1975: A processing plant opens in Santa Paula.
1998: A Mexican packing facility opens.
2001: Calavo converts from a cooperative to a corporation.

new, as would restaurant customers, and that eventually avocado restaurant dishes would make their way to the home. Calavo also capitalized on the rising medium of radio, creating a yearly theme song around which an advertising campaign was formed. Moreover, it took advantage of its proximity to Hollywood to generate numerous newspaper photographs of aspiring starlets posing with a bunch of plump, ripe avocados. The organization, however successful in promoting avocados, never succeeded in making "Calavo" synonymous with the fruit in the mind of consumers. Unable to convince outside avocado growers to share in the expenses of promoting the industry, Calavo held back its marketing efforts. By the early 1960s, consumer advertising for the entire avocado industry was turned over to the California Avocado Advisory Board. Calavo lobbied the state to engage in generic advertising for California avocados and, as a result, in 1977 the Board became the California Avocado Commission.

In the early days of Calavo, there were almost 50 varieties of avocados that its growers produced. The best were stamped with the Calavo name while the rest were sold unmarked and limited to local markets. The emphasis at first was on how well a variety shipped rather than on its eating quality. The hardy Fuerte avocado, therefore, served as the backbone of the industry for many years. In 1935, Robert Haas patented the Haas variety, a pebbly-skinned dark avocado. For decades the Haas would be neglected until it caught on and replaced the Fuerte as the most popular variety. Today Haas is the most profitable variety and accounts for 80 percent of all avocado sales.

Guacamole dip was a major reason for the widespread popularity of avocados, assisted in large measure by the emergence of the Super Bowl as a food holiday. It was estimated that on Super Bowl Sunday of 2002, approximately 26 million avocados were consumed, virtually all of which were used in guacamole recipes. Calavo became involved in producing guacamole when it began selling "Avocado Dip" in one pound refrigerated cans in 1965, the organization's first successful processed consumer product. Sales supported Calavo's Processed Products Division until a frozen avocado pulp product was created in the mid-1970s, resulting in the establishment of a major processing plant in Santa Paula, California. After several years of struggle, Calavo's Processed Products Division found its stride by devoting 2 percent of sales to advertising in trade publications that served the restaurant market. The unit ultimately became Calavo Foods in 1988. By 2002, the plant produced 20 million pounds of guacamole and other avocado-based products per year, for both the food industry and under private labels for retailers.

Aside from processed foods, over the years Calavo became involved in fruits and byproducts other than avocados. As early as 1931, the organization expanded into limes, followed by coconuts, mangos, kiwi fruit, and persimmons. A Calavo label for papaya, Calavo Gold, was introduced in 1949. It was not until 1997, however, that Calavo would make a deep commitment to other fruits. In that year it established papaya and mango programs, forging relationships with Mexican and South American growers to allow for the year-round importation and distribution of mangoes. Calavo also began looking for new sources of papayas to augment already affiliated Hawaiian growers.

The amount of land devoted to avocados in California peaked in 1987–88, totaling 76,307 acres. Urbanization, root rot, the cost of water, and the elimination of marginal groves resulted in a loss of acreage, and California by the early 1990s faced the prospect of cheap Mexican avocados entering the U.S. market after years of being banned because of a seed weevil. Despite an increase in the demand for avocados, growers anticipated a drop in prices. Although Calavo was a growers cooperative, as a marketer of avocados and avocado-based products it required a steady supply of the fruit, especially during California's off-season. To protect its position in the market, Calavo began to look for sources of avocados outside of the United States to ensure year-round availability, ultimately leading to import agreements with Chile and New Zealand. After the ban on Mexican avocados was lifted in 1997, Calavo opened a major packing plant in Mexico in order to process avocados destined for export to the U.S. market and around the world. Soon the facility was handling one-third of Mexico's avocado export.

Converting to For-Profit Status: 2001

In the 1990s, it was becoming clear that the traditional cooperative model of Calavo, one that had worked so well for California growers during the formative years of the avocado industry, was becoming outmoded. In 1998, Calavo initiated a restructuring plan that consolidated processing and packing house operations, combined all sales activities into one department, and established a centralized marketing department to oversee strategic planning. These changes were only a precursor to the decision to convert Calavo from a non-profit cooperative into a for-profit corporation in order to allow Calavo to become more competitive in the increasingly competitive avocado industry. Member growers approved the change in October 2001, and the cooperative was merged into a new corporation, Calavo Growers, Inc., a company that was already generating nearly $220 million in annual revenues. Going forward, management maintained that it would endeavor to strike a balance between the income of growers and maximizing the profitability of Calavo. It also expressed a belief that Calavo would now be in a position to bring into the fold new growers, who had hitherto dismissed the cooperative model as being outdated, and thereby increase market share. Moreover, as a corporation Calavo would have an easier time in raising money through banks and the public markets in order to expand its operations into new agricultural products. Growth through acquisition also became a likely possibility. How such growth would be balanced against the desire to stay true to the Calavo legacy remained to be seen.

Principal Subsidiaries

Calavo Foods; Calavo International.

Principal Competitors

Index Fresh; Olivado; Mission Produce; Sunny Avocado, Ltd.

Further Reading

Alvarez, Fred, "Here's the Scoop on Guacamole," *Los Angeles Times,* December 6, 2001, p. B1.

Brazil, Eric, "Super Bowl Viewers Will Consume About 26 Million Avocados on Game Day," *San Francisco Chronicle,* February 1, 2002, p. B1.

"CEO Glimpses Cooperatives of the Future," *Farmer Cooperatives,* July 1994, p. 12.

Maher, Philip, "From Misunderstood to Cash Crop: A Marketing Success Story," *Business Marketing,* August 1983, p. 52.

—Ed Dinger

Callon Petroleum Company

Callon Building
200 North Canal Street
Natchez, Mississippi 39120
U.S.A.
Telephone: (601) 442-1601
Fax: (601) 446-1410
Web site: http://www.callon.com

Public Company
Incorporated: 1950
Employees: 103
Sales: $61.75 million (2001)
Stock Exchanges: New York
Ticker Symbol: CPE
NAIC: 211111 Crude Petroleum and Natural Gas Extraction

Callon Petroleum Company has been searching the Gulf Coast for oil since 1950. In the late 1980s, the company used seismic mapping technology developed by the major petroleum companies to explore shallow water properties on the continental shelf. In the late 1990s, Callon went in search of deepwater finds in cooperation with other oil companies.

Birth of Company: 1950

John S. Callon founded the company that would become the Callon Petroleum Company in 1950. On July 14, 1952, two of his wells struck oil. In 1954, brother Sim C. Callon was brought into the operation, then known as Callon Oil & Gas Company.

Callon Oil & Gas was renamed Callon Petroleum Company in 1962. The company had two major oil finds in Mississippi in the mid-1960s: Quitman Bayou Field in Adams County in 1963 and Clear Springs Field, Franklin County, in 1965.

Sims Callon was company president from 1972 to 1974, when he took the offices of chairman and CEO. Callon Petroleum was privately held until 1974. It became publicly owned towards the end of the year following a merger with the newly formed Pacific Oil and Gas Development Corporation/Pacific

Energy Corporation. Shares were traded on the NASDAQ exchange. In the same year, Callon and Hughes Aircraft Company formed a joint venture to develop geothermal steam leases at a property in Sonoma County, California.

Callon renovated a former grocery warehouse in Natchez to use as a headquarters in the late 1970s. The site would eventually house a considerable computer operation dedicated to modeling the company's new oil and gas properties.

In 1979, the company organized a new division, Callon Royalty Funds, through which investors could buy landowners' royalties on oil and gas. This division was soon accounting for a quarter of Callon's total revenues, which were $6.6 million in the fiscal year ending May 31, 1980. Earnings were $1.2 million.

Changes in the 1980s

At age 60, John Callon added the position of chairman to his duties as president and CEO upon the January 1981 retirement of his older brother Sim, then 64 years old. Callon formed a joint venture with Amwar Petroleum, led by Texas International Petroleum CEO Alan M. Warren, in November 1981. Callon was providing capital, while Amwar identified and acquired prospects. In 1982, Callon's Lockhart Crossing Wilcox Oil Field in Livingston Parish, Louisiana, was the largest onshore oil discovery in the contiguous United States. At 25 million barrels, it equaled Callon's 1962 Quitman Bayou find.

Fred L. Callon, nephew of the company founder, became president and CEO of Callon Petroleum in 1984. He had worked for the company since 1976 and had visited its rigs as a boy. Before joining Callon Petroleum, he earned an M.B.A. from the Wharton School of the University of Pennsylvania and worked as an accountant for KPMG Peat Marwick.

Callon's revenues were $34.1 million in 1985, producing, after a $29.4 million writedown in oil and gas properties, a $41.1 million loss. Callon had earned $4.7 million the previous year on revenues of $40.3 million. The 1980s and 1990s were not the best of times for independent producers on the Gulf Coast. Foreign oil was cheap again and natural gas prices were low. Still, Callon stood out as the ranks of its peers thinned.

Company Perspectives:

The Company's operations and experience are geographically concentrated in the offshore waters of the Gulf of Mexico—one of the most active and prolific basins in the world. We employ a strategy of drilling a balanced portfolio of exploration and development prospects within the Deepwater and Shelf Regions. In the Deepwater Region, we target reserve deposits in excess of 100 Bcfe ["billion cubic feet equivalent," a measurement whereby one barrel of oil is equivalent to 6,000 cubic feet of natural gas] at well depths up to 25,000 feet. In the Shelf Region, we focus on low to moderate-risk exploration prospects which, if successful, can be brought online in less than a year and provide early cash flow.

The price of oil fell from $40 to $11 per barrel in 1985 and 1986. In 1987, the company sold 90 percent of its producing properties and retired all of its bank debt. In the dozen years after 1975, the business had expanded to 27 limited partnerships, which were merged into the publicly traded Callon Consolidated Partnership, L.P. (CCP) in 1987. The Callon family attained ownership of 100 percent of Callon Petroleum's common stock the next year, and the company was privately owned again.

In the late 1980s, major oil companies like Shell, Exxon, and Mobil began to abandon the Gulf in favor of international deepwater opportunities. Callon grew by acquiring producing properties from them on shore and in shallow water areas. Skillful negotiating was the key to success here; few independents had as much experience operating in the Southeast. Callon spent $213 million acquiring oil and gas properties between 1989 and 1995. A major pension fund, which the company did not reveal, provided three-quarters of the money needed for those acquisitions.

The Black Bay Field, located off the coast of Louisiana in shallow waters, was acquired from Chevron U.S.A. Inc. in 1992. It had been discovered 43 years earlier by Gulf Oil Co. Callon studied the field, reengineered operations, and was able to reduce costs by nearly a third.

In 1993, Callon paid ARCO $31 million for a 94.4 percent working interest in North Dauphin Island Field, located in shallow waters off the coast of Alabama. An advanced, environmentally friendly computerized drilling platform and a 12-mile pipeline were included in the deal.

Public Again in 1994

Callon formed the CN Resources joint venture in 1992 with a group of European companies led by Norway's Fred Olsen shipping and oilfield construction group. In September 1994, Callon Petroleum Holding Company, CCP, and CN Resources were merged into the Callon Petroleum Company, making it a public company again. "Taking the company public simplified and streamlined our business, gave some critical mass to the company, and put us in a position to take much larger interests in the things that we're doing," John S. Callon told the *Mississippi Business Journal.*

In 1994, *Oil & Gas Journal* pronounced Callon Petroleum the country's 146th largest publicly traded oil and gas exploration and production company. The Callon family owned about a third of the company's common stock after the reorganization, while Olsen-controlled companies owned another third.

Going public gave Callon the capital to exploit advances in exploration and production technology while pursuing aggressive policies for expansion. The once prohibitively expensive tools of 2-D and 3-D seismic mapping technology, originally developed by the major oil companies, began to drop considerably in price after 1985. In 1995, contractors were charging $40,000 per square mile for 3-D seismic mapping of onshore sites, and $100,000 in shallow waters, noted the *Mississippi Business Journal.* Callon was applying 3-D seismic mapping to shallow water areas that had never been probed in this way.

In June 1995, Callon agreed to buy oil and gas holdings in southeast Alabama from Scott Paper Co. for $12 million, which included interests in more than two dozen oil and gas fields, as well as ownership of a Scott subsidiary, the Escuhbia Oil Company.

Callon's total reserves were split 60–40 between oil and natural gas. Unusual among its peers, the company was carrying practically no debt after a $30 million public offering of convertible preferred stock in November 1995. Callon acquired its first deepwater leases in the Gulf of Mexico in 1996. Revenues were $43.6 million in 1997, and the company began listing its shares on the New York Stock Exchange in April 1998.

Going Deeper in the Late 1990s

Callon ventured out of its traditional shallow waters in the late 1990s, partnering with Shell Oil and Murphy Exploration & Production Company to probe deeper in the Gulf of Mexico. Its first two prospects, recorded the *Mississippi Business Journal,* turned out to be its largest discoveries to date.

In February 1998, Callon announced a deepwater natural gas find, its second, at the Habanero prospect, located 2,000 feet under the ocean's surface. Callon was only able to venture this far in partnership with major oil companies due to the expense and expertise required. The company also was drilling on the continental shelf, at depths of up to 500 feet, and in shallow ten-foot waters. The payoffs for the risk of drilling in deep water were the greater size of the reserves and the chance to drill in relatively virgin territory.

At the same time as Callon was making this important find, oil and natural gas prices seemed to be rising. However, company officials felt their stock was undervalued. One possible factor was the relatively short lifespans of underwater wells compared to those on land.

The year 1998 ended up being a difficult one for the oil and natural gas industry. Producers like Callon took advantage of lower drilling costs resulting from the slump. In 1999, Callon reduced its drilling budget about 15 percent to $55 million; most of this was targeted at shallow-water prospects. Still, the company boosted proved reserves 100 percent during the year.

<table>
<tr><td colspan="2" align="center">**Key Dates:**</td></tr>
<tr><td>**1950:**</td><td>John S. Callon forms an oil and gas company.</td></tr>
<tr><td>**1952:**</td><td>Two Callon wells strike oil on July 14.</td></tr>
<tr><td>**1954:**</td><td>John Callon's brother Sim C. Callon joins the company.</td></tr>
<tr><td>**1962:**</td><td>The firm is renamed Callon Petroleum Company.</td></tr>
<tr><td>**1974:**</td><td>Callon merges with Pacific Energy and goes public.</td></tr>
<tr><td>**1981:**</td><td>Sim Callon retires.</td></tr>
<tr><td>**1984:**</td><td>Fred Callon succeeds John Callon as CEO.</td></tr>
<tr><td>**1987:**</td><td>Twenty-seven partnerships are merged into Callon Consolidated Partnership.</td></tr>
<tr><td>**1988:**</td><td>The Callon family takes company private again.</td></tr>
<tr><td>**1994:**</td><td>Callon Petroleum merges with partners and goes public.</td></tr>
<tr><td>**1998:**</td><td>Callon stock migrates from the NASDAQ to the New York Stock Exchange.</td></tr>
<tr><td>**2000:**</td><td>Deepwater success produces record earnings.</td></tr>
<tr><td>**2001:**</td><td>A Houston office is opened to house new technical staff.</td></tr>
</table>

Fifty in 2000

The year of Callon's 50th anniversary started out as another difficult one. The company's share price fell 30 percent after three dry holes, two of them in deep water, were discovered in the first quarter. Nevertheless, the company had success with four out of six deepwater wells drilled. Callon's exploration budget for 2000 was $35 million for the continental shelf and $48 million in deepwater. Callon did not operate any of its own deepwater fields. Murphy Oil Corp. operated two, and Shell Oil Co. and Vastar Resources Inc., part of BP plc, operated one each.

Callon ended 2000 with record revenues, net income, and oil and gas reserves. Revenues were up nearly 50 percent to $58.1 million, while net income nearly quadrupled to $12.5 million. The company ended the year with estimated net proved reserves of 334 billion cubic feet of natural gas equivalent (Bcfe), up 28 percent from year-end 1999.

Callon opened an office in Houston in early 2001 to house technical staff dedicated to shelf and deepwater development. Revenues rose to $61.8 million, though net income of $1.8 million was a fraction of the company's 2000 record. The results of two new drilling operations—Medusa, which was scheduled to be online by the end of 2002, and Habanero, which was expected to begin production in the second half of 2003—remained to be seen.

Principal Subsidiaries

Callon Petroleum Operating Company.

Principal Competitors

Apache Corporation; COHO Energy, Inc.; Nuevo Energy; Parker & Parsley; Stone Energy.

Further Reading

"Blowout in Gulf Forces Evacuation of Workers," *Gas Daily,* January 5, 2000.
"Callon Acquires Interest in Five Offshore Blocks, Gas Production Facilities," *Petroleum Finance Week,* June 10, 1996.
"Callon Agrees to Buy Gulf of Mexico OCS Interest from Chevron," *Petroleum Finance Week,* November 10, 1997.
"Callon Buys US Gulf Blocks from Murphy," *Platt's Oilgram News,* June 15, 1999, p. 6.
"Callon Expands Gulf Interests," *Mississippi Business Journal,* November 17, 1997, pp. 6+.
"Callon Gets Additional Working Interest in 'Boomslang'," *Worldwide Energy,* January 2000.
"Callon Petroleum Secures $95 Million Term Loan from Duke Capital Partners," *Petroleum Finance Week,* July 16, 2001.
"Corporate Insight; Callon Petroleum Co.," *Times-Picayune,* Special Report: Louisiana Inc.: The Pelican State's Top 50 Stocks, May 21, 2000, p. I10.
"Fred Olsen Energy to Sell 15 Pct Stake in Callon Petroleum to Bonheur, Ganger," *AFX European Focus,* August 21, 2000.
Gilette, Becky, "Callon's Deep-Water Drilling Program Paying Handsome Dividends; Company Gambled on Going Deep into the Gulf," *Mississippi Business Journal,* August 30, 1999, p. 25.
Haines, Leslie, "Companies Emphasize Strengths, Drilling Ideas at Howard, Weil Conference," *Petroleum Finance Week,* April 19, 1999.
The History of Callon Petroleum Company: 1950–2000, Natchez, Miss.: Callon Petroleum Company, 2000.
"Interest in Producers Rises with Oil Prices," *Los Angeles Times,* February 26, 2000, p. C3.
Montgomery, Shep, "Callon Petroleum Defies Odds to Succeed in Oil and Gas Business," *Mississippi Business Journal,* December 11, 1995.
"Purchase Expands Callon's Ownership in Mobile Area OCS Blocks," *Petroleum Finance Week,* September 22, 1997.
Sloane, Leonard, "Business People; Callon Brother Adds Post," *New York Times,* January 5, 1981, p. D2.
"Small Firms Can Find Deepwater Success," *Hart's Deepwater International,* September 25, 2000.
"Small to Mid-Sized Producers Do Well in Less Glamorous Deepwater Fields," *Petroleum Finance Week,* September 25, 2000.
Tang, Peter, "Callon, Chevron Plan Mobile Bay Natural Gas Pipeline," *Offshore,* April 1995, p. 18.

—Frederick C. Ingram

ChevronTexaco Corporation

575 Market Street
San Francisco, California 94105-2856
U.S.A.
Telephone: (415) 894-7700
Fax: (415) 894-0583
Web site: http://www.chevrontexaco.com

Public Company
Incorporated: 1906 as Standard Oil Company
    (California)
Employees: 53,000
Sales: $104.41 billion (2001)
Stock Exchanges: New York Pacific
Ticker Symbol: CVX
NAIC: 211111 Crude Petroleum and Natural Gas
    Extraction; 324110 Petroleum Refineries; 325110
    Petrochemical Manufacturing; 447110 Gasoline
    Stations with Convenience Stores; 447190 Other
    Gasoline Stations; 486110 Pipeline Transportation of
    Crude Oil; 486210 Pipeline Transportation of Natural
    Gas; 486910 Pipeline Transportation of Refined
    Petroleum Products

ChevronTexaco Corporation is the creation of the 2001 merger of California-based Chevron Corporation, one of the many progeny of the Standard Oil Trust, and Texaco Inc., a company whose history traces back to the early boom years of the Texas oil industry. The two firms' histories previously began to intertwine in the 1930s with the formation of the Caltex and Aramco ventures in the Middle East. Chevron-Texaco began its existence as the number two U.S.-based integrated oil company (behind Exxon Mobil Corporation) and number four in the world, behind Exxon Mobil, BP p.l.c., and Royal Dutch/Shell Group. The company had some 11.5 billion barrels of oil and gas reserves and had daily production of 2.7 million barrels. Major producing areas included the Gulf of Mexico, California, Texas, Canada, Kazakhstan, Argentina, Angola, Nigeria, Republic of Congo, Venezuela, Australia, Indonesia, Thailand, China, Papua New Guinea, the North Sea,

and the Middle East. On the downstream side, ChevronTexaco operated 22 refineries around the world and more than 25,000 service stations on six continents under such brands as Chevron, Texaco, Caltex, Delo, and Havoline. Within the United States, the company's marketing operations were strongest in the western, southwestern, and southern regions of the country. Among the company's other operations and interests were a 50 percent interest in Chevron Phillips Chemical Company LLC, a major petrochemical manufacturer (the other 50 percent was held by Phillips Petroleum Corporation); equity interests in 47 power projects worldwide; and a 27 percent stake in Dynegy, Inc., a marketer and trader of energy products, including electricity, natural gas, and coal.

The Chevron side of the corporation grew from its modest California origins in the late 19th century to become a major power in the international oil market. Its dramatic discoveries in Saudi Arabia gave Chevron a strong position in the world's largest oil region and helped fuel 20 years of record earnings in the postwar era. The rise of the Organization of Petroleum Exporting Countries (OPEC) in the early 1970s deprived Chevron of its comfortable Middle East position, causing considerable anxiety and a determined search for new domestic oil resources at a company long dependent on foreign supplies. The firm's 1984 purchase of Gulf Corporation—at $13.2 billion, the largest industrial transaction to that date—more than doubled Chevron's oil and gas reserves but failed to bring its profit record back to pre-1973 levels of performance. By the mid-to-late 1990s, however, Chevron was posting strong earnings, a result of higher gasoline prices and the company's restructuring and cost-cutting efforts.

Company Origins

Chevron's oldest direct ancestor is the Pacific Coast Oil Company, founded in 1879 by Frederick Taylor and a group of investors. Several years before, Taylor, like many other Californians, had begun prospecting for oil in the rugged canyons north of Los Angeles; unlike most prospectors, Taylor found what he was looking for, and his Pico Well #4 was soon the state's most productive. Following its incorporation, Pacific Coast developed a method for refining the heavy California oil into an acceptable grade of kerosene, then the most popular lighting source, and the company's fortunes prospered. By the turn of the century Pacific had assembled a team of producing wells in the area of Newhall, California, and built a refinery at Alameda Point across the San Francisco Bay from San Francisco. It also owned both railroad tank cars and the *George Loomis,* an oceangoing tanker, to transport its crude from the field to the refinery.

One of Pacific Coast's best customers was Standard Oil Company of Iowa, a marketing subsidiary of the New Jersey-headquartered Standard Oil Trust. Iowa Standard had been active in northern California since 1885, selling both Standard's own eastern oil and also large quantities of kerosene purchased from Pacific Coast and the other local oil companies. The West Coast was important to Standard Oil Company of New Jersey not only as a market in itself but also as a source of crude for sale to its Asian subsidiaries. Jersey Standard thus became increasingly attracted to the area and in the late 1890s tried to buy Union Oil Company, the state leader. The attempt failed, but in 1900 Pacific Coast agreed to sell its stock to Jersey Standard for $761,000 with the understanding that Pacific Coast would produce, refine, and distribute oil for marketing and sale by Iowa Standard representatives. W.H. Tilford and H.M. Tilford, two brothers who were longtime employees of Standard Oil, assumed the leadership of Iowa Standard and Pacific Coast, respectively.

Drawing on Jersey Standard's strength, Pacific Coast immediately built the state's largest refinery at Point Richmond on San Francisco Bay and a set of pipelines to bring oil from its San Joaquin Valley wells to the refinery. Its crude production rose steeply over the next decade, yielding 2.6 million barrels a year by 1911, or 20 times the total for 1900. The bulk of Pacific Coast's holdings were in the Coalinga and Midway fields in the southern half of California, with wells rich enough to supply Iowa Standard with an increasing volume of crude but never enough to satisfy its many marketing outlets. Indeed, even in 1911 Pacific Coast was producing a mere 2.3 percent of the state's crude, forcing partner Iowa Standard to buy most of its crude from outside suppliers such as Union Oil and Puente Oil.

By that date, however, Pacific Coast and Iowa Standard were no longer operating as separate companies. In 1906 Jersey Standard had brought together its two West Coast subsidiaries into a single entity called Standard Oil Company (California), generally known thereafter as Socal. Jersey Standard recognized the future importance of the West and quickly increased the new company's capital from $1 million to $25 million. Socal added a second refinery at El Segundo, near Los Angeles, and vigorously pursued the growing markets for kerosene and gasoline in both the western United States and Asia. Able to realize considerable transportation savings by using West Coast oil for the Pacific markets of its parent company, Socal was soon selling as much as 80 percent of its kerosene overseas. Socal's head chemist, Eric A. Starke, was chiefly responsible for several breakthroughs in the refining of California's heavy crude into usable kerosene, and by 1911, Socal was the state leader in kerosene production.

The early strengths of Socal lay in refining and marketing. Its large, efficient refineries used approximately 20 percent of California's entire crude production, much more than Socal's own wells could supply. To keep the refineries and pipelines full, Socal bought crude from Union Oil and in return handled a portion of the marketing and sale of Union kerosene and naphtha. In the sale of kerosene and gasoline, Socal maintained a near-total control of the market in 1906, supplying 95 percent of the kerosene and 85 percent of the gasoline and naphtha purchased in its marketing area of California, Arizona, Nevada, Oregon, Washington, Hawaii, and Alaska, although its share dipped somewhat in the next five years. When necessary, Socal used its dominant position to inhibit competition by deep price cutting. By the time of the dissolution of the Standard Oil Trust in 1911, Socal, like many of the Standard subsidiaries, had become the overwhelming leader in the refining and marketing of oil in its region while lagging somewhat in the production of crude.

From 1911 to World War II: Growth As an Independent Company

In 11 short years the strength of Standard Oil and a vigorous Western economy combined to increase Socal's net book value from a few million dollars in 1900 to $39 million. It was in 1911, however, that Jersey Standard, the holding company for Socal and the entire Standard Oil family, was ordered dissolved by the U.S. Supreme Court in order to break its monopolistic hold on the oil industry. As one of 34 independent units carved out of the former parent company, Socal, sporting a new official name of Standard Oil (California), would have to do without Standard's financial backing, but the new competitor hardly faced the world unarmed. Socal kept its dominant marketing and refining position, its extensive network of critical pipelines, a modest but growing fleet of oil tankers, its many oil wells, and, most helpfully, some $14 million in retained earnings. The latter proved useful in Socal's subsequent rapid expansion, as did California's growing popularity among U.S. citizens looking for a fresh start in life. The state population shot up quickly, and most of the new residents found that they depended on the automobile—and, hence, on gasoline—to navigate the state's many highway miles.

The years leading up to World War I saw a marked increase in Socal's production of crude. From a base of about 3 percent of the state's production in the early part of the century, Socal rode a series of successful oil strikes to a remarkable 26 percent of nationwide crude production in 1919. The company expanded

Key Dates:

1879: Pacific Coast Oil Company is founded in California.

1900: Pacific Coast is purchased by the Standard Oil Trust.

1906: Pacific Coast is merged with Standard Oil of Iowa to form Standard Oil Company (California), known as Socal.

1911: The Standard Oil Trust is ordered dissolved by the U.S. Supreme Court, and Socal emerges as an independent firm officially called Standard Oil (California).

1926: Socal merges with Pacific Oil Company, a division of Southern Pacific Railroad Company; company name is changed to Standard Oil Company of California.

1930: Socal strikes oil in Bahrain, beginning the firm's involvement in the Middle East.

1933: Company gains drilling rights in Saudi Arabia.

1936: Socal sells 50 percent of its drilling rights in Saudi Arabia and Bahrain to the Texas Company (later Texaco Inc.), forming a joint venture called the California-Texas Oil Company (Caltex); the Saudi arm of the Caltex venture is later called Arabian American Oil Company (Aramco).

1948: 30 percent of Aramco is sold to Standard Oil Company (New Jersey) and 10 percent to Socony-Vacuum Oil Company.

1961: Socal purchases Standard Oil Company of Kentucky to market gasoline in the southeastern United States.

1970s: Company is rocked by the OPEC oil embargo and the nationalization of a number of Caltex holdings.

1980: The government of Saudi Arabia nationalizes Aramco.

1984: Socal changes its name to Chevron Corporation, Chevron having become the firm's main marketing brand; company purchases Gulf Corporation for $13.2 billion.

1993: Chevron forms joint venture with the Republic of Kazakhstan to develop the huge Tengiz oil field.

1996: Company sells its natural gas business to Natural Gas Clearinghouse, gaining a 27 percent stake in a firm later called Dynegy Inc.

2000: Chevron combines its worldwide chemical operations with those of Phillips Petroleum Company, forming a 50–50 joint venture called Chevron Phillips Chemical Company.

2001: Chevron acquires Texaco in a $45 billion deal, forming ChevronTexaco Corporation.

States about a possible shortage of domestic crude supplies. A number of the major oil companies began exploring more vigorously around the world. Socal took its part in these efforts but with a notable lack of success—37 straight dry holes in six different countries. More internationally oriented firms, such as Jersey Standard and Mobil, soon secured footholds in what was to become the future center of world oil production, the Middle East, whereas Socal, with many directors skeptical about overseas drilling, remained content with its California supplies and burgeoning retail business.

In the late 1920s Socal's posture changed. At that time Gulf Corporation was unable to interest its fellow partners in Iraq Petroleum Company in the oil rights to Bahrain, a small group of islands off the coast of Saudi Arabia. Iraq Petroleum was then the chief cartel of oil companies operating in the Middle East, and its members were restricted by the Red Line Agreement of 1928 from engaging in oil development independently of the entire group. Gulf was therefore unable to proceed with its Bahrain concession and sold its rights for $50,000 to Socal, which was prodded by Maurice Lombardi and William Berg, two members of its board of directors. This venture proved successful. In 1930 Socal geologists struck oil in Bahrain, and within a few years, the California company had joined the ranks of international marketers of oil.

Bahrain's real importance, however, lay in its proximity to the vast fields of neighboring Saudi Arabia. The richest of all oil reserves lay beneath an inhospitable desert and until the early 1930s was left alone by the oil prospectors. But at that time, encouraged by the initial successes at Bahrain, Saudi Arabia's King Ibn Saud hired a U.S. geologist to study his country's potential oil reserves. The geologist, Karl Twitchell, liked what he saw and tried on behalf of the king to sell the concession to a number of U.S. oil companies. None was interested except the now adventurous Socal, which in 1933 won a modest bidding war and obtained drilling rights for a £5,000 annual fee and a loan of £50,000. After initial exploration revealed the fantastic extent of Arabian oil, Socal executives realized that the company would need access to markets far larger than its own meager foreign holdings, and in 1936 Socal sold 50 percent of its drilling rights in Saudi Arabia and Bahrain to the Texas Company, later Texaco, the only other major oil company not bound by the Red Line Agreement. Thus was created the California-Texas Oil Company (Caltex). Once the oil started flowing in 1939, King Saud was so pleased with his partners and the profits they generated for his impoverished country that he increased the size of their concession to 440,000 square miles, an area the size of Texas, Louisiana, Oklahoma, and New Mexico combined.

Postwar Expansion

Socal and the Texas Company agreed to market their products under the brand name Caltex and developed excellent representation in both Europe and the Far East, especially in Japan. The new partners realized soon after the end of World War II, however, that the Saudi oil fields were too big even for the both of them, and in 1948, to raise further capital, they sold 40 percent of the recently formed Arabian American Oil Company (Aramco) for $450 million—30 percent going to Standard Oil Company (New Jersey), forerunner of Exxon Corporation,

further in 1926 with the acquisition of the Pacific Oil Company, a division of Southern Pacific Railroad Company, a merger that led to the adoption of the name Standard Oil Company of California. As the national production leader, Socal found itself in a predicament that would be repeated throughout its history—an excess of crude and a shortage of outlets for it. For most of the other leading international oil companies, the situation was reversed, crude generally being in short supply in a world increasingly dependent on oil. Particularly in the aftermath of World War I—of which the British diplomat George Curzon said ''the Allies floated to victory on a wave of oil''—there was much anxiety in the United and 10 percent to Socony-Vacuum Oil Company, forerunner of Mobil Corporation—leaving the two original partners with 30 percent each. With its crude supply secure for the foreseeable future, Socal was able to market oil around the world, as well as in North America's fastest-growing demographic region, California and the Pacific Coast. As later Chairman R. Gwin Follis put it, Saudi Arabia was a "jackpot beyond belief," supplying Caltex markets overseas with unlimited amounts of low-priced, high-grade oil. By the mid-1950s Socal was getting one-third of its crude production out of Aramco and, more significantly, calculated that Saudi Arabia accounted for two-thirds of its reserve supply. Other important fields had been discovered in Sumatra and Venezuela, but Socal was particularly dependent on its Aramco concession for crude.

On the domestic scene, Socal by 1949 had grown into one of the few American companies with $1 billion in assets. No longer the number one domestic crude producer, Socal was still among the leaders and had recently made plentiful strikes in Louisiana and Texas, as well as in its native California. In addition to its original refineries at Point Richmond and El Segundo, Socal had added new facilities in Bakersfield, California, and in Salt Lake City, Utah. Socal's marketing territory included at least some representation in 15 western states and a recent, limited foray into the northeastern United States, mainly as an outlet for some of its cheap Middle Eastern oil. The heart of Socal territory was still west of the Rocky Mountains, where the company continued to control about 28 percent of the retail market during the postwar years, a far cry from the 90 percent it owned at the turn of the century but still easily a dominant share in the nation's leading automotive region.

In the two decades following the war the U.S. economy became completely dependent upon oil. As both a cause and an effect of this trend, the world was awash in oil. The Middle East, Latin America, and Southeast Asia all contributed mightily to a prolonged glut, which steadily lowered the price of oil in real dollars. The enormous growth in world consumption assured Socal of a progressive rise in sales and a concomitant increase in profits at an annual rate of about 5.5 percent. By 1957, for example, Socal was selling $1.7 billion worth of oil products annually and ranked as the world's seventh largest oil concern. Its California base offered Socal a number of advantages in the prevailing buyer's market. By drawing upon its own local wells for the bulk of its U.S. sales, Socal was able to keep its transportation costs lower than most of its competitors, and California's zooming population and automobile-oriented economy afforded an ideal marketplace. As a result, Socal consistently had one of the best profit ratios among all oil companies during the 1950s and 1960s.

California crude production had begun to slow, however, and along with the rest of the world Socal grew ever more dependent on Middle Eastern oil for its overall health. The rich Bay Marchand strike off the Louisiana coast helped stem the tide temporarily. By 1961 Socal was drawing 27.9 million barrels per year from Marchand and had bought Standard Oil Company of Kentucky to market its gasoline in the southeastern United States. But the added domestic production only masked Socal's increasing reliance on Saudi Arabian oil, which by 1971 provided more than three-quarters of Socal's proven reserves. As long as the Middle Eastern countries remained cooperative,

such an imbalance was not of great concern, and by vigorously selling its cheap Middle Eastern oil in Europe and Asia, Socal was able to rack up a perfect record of profit increases every year in the 1960s. By 1970, 20 percent of Socal's $4 billion in sales was generated in the Far East, with Japan again providing the lion's share of that figure. The firm's European gas stations, owned jointly with Texaco until 1967, numbered 8,000.

Challenge of OPEC Beginning in the 1970s

The world oil picture had changed fundamentally by 1970, however. The 20-year oil surplus had given way in the face of rampant consumption to a general and increasing shortage, a shift soon taken advantage of by OPEC members. In 1973 and 1974 OPEC effectively took control of oil at its source and engineered a fourfold increase in the base price of oil. Socal was now able to rely on its Saudi partner for only a tiny price advantage over the general rate and it was no longer in legal control of sufficient crude to supply its worldwide or domestic demand. The sudden shift in oil politics revealed a number of Socal shortcomings. Though it had 17,000 gas stations in 39 U.S. states, Socal was not a skilled marketer either in the United States or in Europe, where its former partner, Texaco, had supplied local marketing savvy. In its home state of California, for example, Socal's market share was 16 percent and continuing to drop and Socal had missed out on both the North Sea and Alaskan oil discoveries of the late 1960s. Furthermore, the OPEC-spawned upheaval included the nationalization of a number of Caltex holdings in the Middle East, and in 1978 Caltex Oil Refining (India) Ltd. was nationalized by the government of India. A further blow to Socal's overseas operations came in 1980 when the government of Saudi Arabia nationalized Aramco.

Socal responded to these problems by merging all of its domestic marketing into a single unit, Chevron USA, and began cutting employment, at first gradually and later more deeply. Also, Socal stepped up its domestic exploration efforts while moving into alternative sources of energy, such as shale, coal, and uranium. In 1981 the company made a $4 billion bid for AMAX Inc., a leader in coal and metal mining but had to settle for a 20 percent stake. In 1984 Standard Oil Company of California changed its name to Chevron Corporation, tying the company more directly with its main marketing brand. Also in 1984, after a decade of sporadic attempts to lessen its dependence on the volatile Middle East, Chevron Corporation met its short-term oil needs in a more direct fashion: it bought Gulf Corporation.

The $13.2 billion purchase, at that time the largest in the history of U.S. business, more than doubled Chevron's proven reserves and created a new giant in the U.S. oil industry, with Chevron now the leading domestic retailer of gasoline and, briefly, the second largest oil company by assets. Certain factors made the move appear ill-timed, however. Oil prices had peaked around 1980 and begun a long slide that continued until the Gulf War of 1990, which meant that Chevron had saddled itself with a $12 billion debt at a time of shrinking sales. As a result, it was not easy for Chevron to sell off assets as quickly as desired, both to reduce debt and to eliminate the many areas of overlap created by the merger. Chevron eventually rid itself of Gulf's Canadian operations and all of Gulf's gas stations in the northeastern and southeastern United States, paring 16,000 jobs in the meantime, but oil analysts pointed to such key figures as profit per employee and return of capital as evidence of Chevron's continued poor performance.

Developments in the 1990s

In the early 1990s Chevron began publicizing its environmental programs, a response in part to public pressure on all oil companies for more responsible environmental policies. From 1989 to 1993 Chevron Shipping Company had the best overall safety record among major oil companies. In 1993, while transporting nearly 625 million barrels of crude oil, Chevron Shipping spilled an amount equaling less than four barrels. During this same period, Chevron utilities supervisor Pete Duda recognized an opportunity to convert an abandoned wastewater treatment pond into a 90-acre wetland. Fresh water and new vegetation were added to the site, and by 1994 the area was attracting a variety of birds and other wildlife, as well as the attention of the National Audubon Society, *National Geographic,* and the California Department of Fish and Game. The conversion saved Chevron millions, as conventional closure of the site would have cost about $20 million.

Financially the company began the 1990s with less than glowing returns. Chevron's 1989 results were poor, and in that year's annual report, Chairman Kenneth Derr announced a program to upgrade the company's efficiency and outlined as well a five-year goal: ''a return on stockholders' investment that exceeds the performance of our strongest competitors.'' The company also took important new initiatives. In 1993 Chevron entered into a partnership with the Republic of Kazakhstan to develop the Tengiz oil field, one of the largest ever discovered in the area.

In 1994, five years after Derr's announcement, Chevron had met its goal for stockholders, largely through restructuring and efforts to cut costs and improve efficiency. From 1989 to 1993 Chevron cut operating costs by more than $1 per barrel and the company's stock rose to an 18.9 percent return, compared with an average of 13.2 percent return for its competitors. The company celebrated this achievement by giving 42,000 of its employees a one-time bonus of 5 percent of their base pay.

After meeting its five-year goal, Chevron continued its cost-cutting and efficiency efforts. In December 1995 the company announced a restructuring of its U.S. gasoline marketing. It combined regional offices, consolidated support functions, and refocused the marketing unit toward service and sales growth. One example of the company's new efforts toward marketing was a joint initiative with McDonald's Corporation. In April 1997, as a response to ''one-stop shopping'' marketing trends, Chevron and McDonald's together opened a new gas station and food facility in Lakewood, California. The two companies shared the space, and customers could order food and pump gas at the same time. They could pay for the order with a Chevron card. More Chevron/McDonald's facilities were planned for California and elsewhere in the United States.

Chevron also cut its refining capacity, where margins were especially low in the early 1990s. Capacity dropped by 407,000 barrels a day from 1992 to 1995. The company helped reduce its refining capacity by selling its Port Arthur, Texas, refinery in February 1995 to Clark Refining & Marketing Inc. Chevron controlled 10.2 percent of U.S. refining capacity in 1992 but just 7.5 percent by 1995. These measures seemed to improve the company's fortunes, as its earnings jumped in 1996 to more than $2.6 billion, an all-time high. Stockholder return for the year was 28.5 percent. High gasoline prices also contributed to Chevron's huge profits. The company was able to take advantage of high crude prices by increasing production at its Kazakhstan and West African facilities. Also during 1996, Chevron sold its natural gas business to Houston-based NGC Corporation, gaining a 27 percent stake in the Houston-based energy marketer and trader, which changed its name to Dynegy Inc. in 1998. Late in 1997 Chevron sold the marketing side of Gulf Oil (Great Britain) Limited to a unit of Royal Dutch/Shell Group in a deal that included 450 service stations in the United Kingdom and three fuel terminals.

Cracks in the OPEC cartel and more efficient energy exploration technologies led to an oil glut and plunging oil prices in 1998 and 1999. With prices falling to as low as $10 per barrel, several major oil companies responded with a wave of megamergers that transformed the industry. Chevron, however, completed only two smaller acquisitions in 1999, picking up Rutherford-Moran Oil Corporation, a small U.S. independent with proven oil and gas reserves in the Gulf of Thailand, and Petrolera Argentina San Jorge S.A., the number three oil company in Argentina. The company made unsuccessful bids for both Atlantic Richfield Corporation and Amoco Corporation (both of which eventually were subsumed within BP p.l.c., the successor of British Petroleum Company PLC) and entered into advanced merger talks with Texaco in mid-1999. The latter discussions failed at least in part because the two sides could not agree on who should head up the combined firm. Meanwhile, Chevron exited from offshore California production in early 1999 when it sold its share of the Point Arguello project, located offshore near the city of Santa Barbara, and the rest of its California offshore properties to Venoco Inc. At the end of 1999 Derr retired from Chevron after 11 years as chairman and CEO, with Vice-Chairman Dave O'Reilly taking over those positions.

Formation of ChevronTexaco in the New Century

In addition to the spate of megamergers, the period around the end of the millennium was also noteworthy for the number of major joint ventures that were formed between various petroleum companies. For its part, Chevron combined its worldwide chemical operations with those of Phillips Petroleum Company, forming a 50–50 joint venture called Chevron Phillips Chemical Company LLC. Created in July 2000, the new venture began with about $6.1 billion in total assets and $5.7 billion in annual revenues. The two companies anticipated annual cost savings of about $150 million from the combination, partly from the elimination of about 600 positions, or 10 percent of the combined workforce.

A few months after the consummation of this merger, Chevron belatedly joined the megamerger bandwagon with the announcement of the merger of Chevron and Texaco, the longtime Caltex partners. The deal was struck despite the spike in oil prices, which had reached about $30 a barrel by the time of the merger announcement in October 2000, and the paramount rationale for the combination was the potential for substantial cost savings—initial estimates were for $1.2 billion in annual savings. Structured as a Chevron takeover of Texaco, the merger was completed on October 9, 2001, with Texaco shareholders receiving .77 shares of common stock in ChevronTexaco Corporation, the new name adopted by Chevron Corporation. The final value of the deal was $45 billion, including $38.3 billion in Texaco stock and $6.7 billion in Texaco debt. Texaco Inc. became a subsidiary of ChevronTexaco. Also becoming a wholly owned subsidiary of the newly enlarged firm was Caltex Corporation, which had moved its headquarters from Texas to Singapore in 1999 to be closer to its core markets. ChevronTexaco began with a market capitalization of $97 billion, enabling it to join the ranks of the so-called supermajor oil firms, which included Exxon Mobil Corporation, BP, and Royal Dutch/Shell. Headquarters for the company remained in San Francisco, but plans were soon made for a move to a nearby San Ramon business park during 2002. Heading up ChevronTexaco were O'Reilly as chairman and CEO along with two vice-chairmen, Richard Matzke, who had been Chevron vice-chairman, and Glenn Tilton, who had become chairman and CEO of Texaco in February 2001.

In approving the merger, the Federal Trade Commission ordered the divestment of stakes in two refining and marketing joint ventures inherited from Texaco: Equilon Enterprises LLC and Motiva Enterprises LLC. These interests were transferred to a trust prior to completion of the merger. Then in February 2002 Shell Oil Company and Saudi Refining, Inc. purchased the interests for $2.26 billion in cash and the assumption of $1.6 billion in debt. Meanwhile, in October 2001, the development of the Tengiz field in Kazakhstan received a boost when a new pipeline came online. Previously much of the crude oil from the field had been shipped by rail through Russia to the seaport of Ventspils, Latvia. The new 900-mile, $2.6 billion pipeline, built by the Caspian Pipeline Consortium, 15 percent owned by ChevronTexaco, ran from the Tengiz field westward through Russia to the Black Sea port of Novorossiysk. This represented a much less costly form of transportation for exporting the crude oil. Another development in late 2001 came through ChevronTexaco's equity stake in Dynegy. Energy trading giant Enron Corporation was on the verge of bankruptcy, with its stock price plunging, amid allegations of accounting and other improprieties. In November Dynegy announced an agreement to buy Enron for about $9 billion, and ChevronTexaco committed to inject an additional $2.5 billion into Dynegy in support of the merger. With the continuing collapse in Enron's stock price, however, Dynegy canceled the deal later in November. This led to Enron declaring bankruptcy and also suing Dynegy for withdrawing from the takeover, with a countersuit soon following.

The initial postmerger integration efforts led ChevronTexaco to suffer a net loss of $2.52 billion for the fourth quarter of 2001. This included $1.17 billion in charges related to the merger, including severance payments for some of the 4,500 employees who lost their jobs as a result of the merger, facility-closure costs, and other expenses. The company took an additional $1.85 billion in writedowns of energy, mineral, and chemical assets as it looked closely at the combined operations and pared back on investments. ChevronTexaco was now aiming to achieve annual cost savings of $1.8 billion by 2003. For

the year, the company reported net income of $3.29 billion on revenues of $104.41 billion. Looking to the future, analysts were expecting the company to pursue another significant acquisition in order to keep up with the other supermajors, each of which continued to grow aggressively. Possible acquisition candidates included Burlington Resources Inc., Conoco Inc., Marathon Oil Corporation, and Phillips Petroleum. Conoco and Phillips, however, soon announced their own merger, although ChevronTexaco was reportedly considering stepping in with an offer for one of the two firms, both of which were attractive as being among the last independent midsize energy concerns.

Principal Subsidiaries

Chevron U.S.A. Inc.; Chevron Capital Corporation; Chevron Pipe Line Company; The Pittsburgh & Midway Coal Mining Co.; Chevron Overseas Petroleum Inc.; Texaco Inc.; Chevron Canada Limited; Chevron International Limited (Liberia); Chevron Nigeria Limited; Caltex Corporation (Singapore); Chevron U.K. Limited.

Principal Competitors

Exxon Mobil Corporation; BP p.l.c.; Royal Dutch/Shell Group; TOTAL FINA ELF S.A.

Further Reading

Barrionuevo, Alexei, "Chevron and Phillips Petroleum to Form Venture with $5.7 Billion in Revenue," *Wall Street Journal*, February 8, 2000, p. A4.

Barrionuevo, Alexei, and Thaddeus Herrick, "Texaco to Sell Stakes in Two Joint Ventures," *Wall Street Journal*, October 10, 2001, p. A4.

Blackwood, Francy, "Chevron Environment Effort: Think Locally, Act Globally," *San Francisco Business Times*, November 4, 1994, p. 2A.

Brady, Rose, and Peter Galuszka, "The Scramble for Oil's Last Frontier," *Business Week*, January 11, 1993, pp. 42+.

Calvey, Mark, "Executive of the Year 2001: ChevronTexaco CEO David O'Reilly Runs Well-Oiled Machine," *San Francisco Business Times*, December 31, 2001.

"Chevron, Phillips to Form Giant Chemical JV," *Oil and Gas Journal*, February 14, 2000, pp. 24–25.

"Chevron Scaling Back Point Arguello amid Exit," *Oil and Gas Journal*, November 30, 1998, pp. 26–28.

"Chevron, Texaco Agree to Merge in All-Stock Deal," *Oil and Gas Journal*, October 23, 2000, pp. 28–30.

"Chevron, Which Met Its Five Year Goal of Achieving the Highest Total Return to Stockholders Among Its Competitors," *Oil and Gas Journal*, January 10, 1994, p. 4.

Cook, James, "Hungry Again," *Forbes*, March 7, 1988, pp. 68+.

Culbertson, Katherine, "Share of U.S. Refining Capacity Controlled by Top 4 Majors Dwindles, API Study Says," *Oil Daily*, July 31, 1996, p. 1.

Fan, Aliza, "Analysts Praise Chevron Restructuring As Bold Move to Boost Downstream," *Oil Daily*, December 19, 1995, p. 3.

Folmer, L.W., *Reaching for a Star: Experiences in the International Oil Business*, Austin, Tex.: L.W. Folmer, 1993, 243 p.

Herrick, Thaddeus, "ChevronTexaco Vows Not to Cut Output," *Wall Street Journal*, October 17, 2000, p. A3.

Hidy, Ralph W., and Muriel E. Hidy, *History of Standard Oil Company (New Jersey): Pioneering in Big Business, 1882–1911*, New York: Harper & Brothers, 1955.

Howe, Kenneth, "Chevron's Turn to Play?: Oil Giant Could Be Jumping on the Merger Bandwagon," *San Francisco Chronicle,* August 21, 1998, p. B1.

"Hunting the Big One," *Economist,* October 21, 2000, p. 71.

James, Marquis, *The Texaco Story: The First Fifty Years 1902–1952,* New York: The Texas Company, 1953, 118 p.

Klaw, Spencer, "Standard of California," *Fortune,* November 1958.

Kolbenschlag, Michael, "The Luxury of Time," *Forbes,* September 14, 1981, pp. 42 + .

Lazarus, David, "Vice Chairman Chosen to Lead Chevron," *San Francisco Chronicle,* September 30, 1999, p. B1.

Liesman, Steve, "Chevron and Texaco Argue That Size Isn't Everything: Companies Dissent, for Now, from Oil Industry's Megamerger Mindset," *Wall Street Journal,* December 30, 1998, p. B4.

Linsenmeyer, Adrienne, "Chevron's Oil Crisis," *Financial World,* October 30, 1990, pp. 26 + .

Louis, Arthur M., "Deal's Done on Chevron-Texaco Merger," *San Francisco Chronicle,* October 17, 2000, p. A1.

Mack, Toni, "Can Ken Derr Turn Chevron Around?," *Forbes,* November 27, 1989, pp. 49 + .

Mellow, Craig, "Big Oil's Pipe Dream," *Fortune,* March 2, 1998, pp. 158–60 + .

Miller, William H., "Chevron Bridges the Gulf," *Industry Week,* May 12, 1986, pp. 65 + .

Palmer, Jay, "Here Comes Chevron!: The Once-Lagging Oil Giant Steps Up the Pace," *Barron's,* May 6, 1991, pp. 16 + .

Petzinger, Thomas, *Oil and Honor: The Texaco-Pennzoil Wars,* New York: Putnam, 1987, 495 p.

Quirt, John, "Socal Is Looking Homeward," *Fortune,* March 10, 1980, p. 66.

Racanelli, Vito J., "Bigger Really Is Better: Benefits of Chevron's Acquisition of Texaco Seem Underappreciated," *Barron's,* May 28, 2001, pp. 19–20.

Sampson, Anthony, *The Seven Sisters: The Great Oil Companies and the World They Made,* New York: Viking Press, 1975, 334 p.

Shannon, James, *Texaco and the $10 Billion Jury,* Englewood Cliffs, N.J.: Prentice Hall, 1988, 545 p.

Shao, Maria, "Ken Derr's Got the Money—but What Will He Do With It?," *Business Week,* September 5, 1988, p. 27.

Texaco Today: The Spirit of the Star, 1902–1992, White Plains, N.Y.: Texaco Inc., 1992, 40 p.

Wilson, James W., et al., "The Chevron-Gulf Merger: Does It Still Make Sense?," *Business Week,* January 21, 1985, pp. 102 + .

—Jonathan Martin
—updates: Terry Bain, David E. Salamie

CNET Networks, Inc.

150 Chestnut Street
San Francisco, California 94111
U.S.A.
Telephone: (415) 364-8000
Fax: (415) 395-9207
Web site: http://www.cnet.com

Public Company
Incorporated: 1992 as CNET, Inc.
Employees: 1,900
Sales: $285.8 million (2001)
Stock Exchanges: NASDAQ
Ticker Symbol: CNET
NAIC: 514191 On-Line Information Services

Founded in 1992 as an online source of technology-related news and information, CNET Networks, Inc. has expanded through acquisitions and alliances, as well as internally, to become a multimedia technology and e-commerce information source. Technology-minded professionals and consumers alike can access CNET's informative content on the Internet, through broadcast and streaming media, and in print. CNET Networks owns two of the top Internet portals for technology news, information, and e-commerce services: CNET.com and ZDNet.com. It also owns TechRepublic, an online destination for IT professionals, and the online comparison-shopping site mySimon.com. Other online brands falling under the CNET Networks umbrella include Gamespot, an online source of computer games and gaming information; Download.com, a source for computer software; and News.com, an online source of technology news.

CNET's ventures in broadcast media include streaming and broadcast radio programming as well as streaming broadband interviews and video product reviews. CNET Radio, which was formed in January 2000 in partnership with radio station owner AMFM Inc., was the first all-tech radio format in the United States. The company exited long-form television production in September 2001 when it ceased production of its ''News.com'' television show, which was shown every week on CNBC since

1999. The company's video production unit, CNET Media Productions, planned to produce broadband product demonstrations and webcasts for business clients. The company also would continue producing streaming broadband interviews with technology executives for CNET Networks' News.com web site and video product reviews for CNET.com.

CNET acquired the print magazine, *Computer Shopper,* as part of its acquisition of Ziff Davis Media Inc. and ZDNet in 2000. With a circulation of more than 500,000, *Computer Shopper* contains about 75 product reviews in each monthly issue, along with feature articles on buying technology products.

CNET Networks also is active in technology e-commerce, creating marketplaces that bring together buyers and sellers of technology products and services. Its Swiss affiliate, CNET Data Services (CDS), licenses access to its multilingual product database of more than 600,000 items to online computer retailers, resellers, distributors, wholesalers, and other sales channels. CNET Networks also operates CNET ChannelOnline, an online marketplace that is marketed as a subscription-based application service provider (ASP) platform. It is powered by the company's CDS product catalog and provides access to detailed product descriptions and real-time pricing and availability from suppliers.

Developing Online Web Site and Cable TV Programs: 1992–95

CNET, Inc. was founded in 1992 in San Francisco by 27-year-old Halsey Minor, who was previously involved in investment banking and publishing. Minor obtained financial backing for the company from venture capital firm Tiger Management and its managing director, Shelby Bonnie. In 1993 Bonnie became CNET's chief financial officer and chief operating officer. Minor was the firm's chairman and CEO until March 2000, when Vice-Chairman Bonnie succeeded him as CEO, with Minor remaining as chairman. In 2001 Bonnie became CNET's chairman and CEO, and Minor became chairman emeritus.

By 1994 CNET was in the process of launching a new cable network, CET: The Computer Network. Its first production was a show called ''CET Central,'' which ran for several hours each weekend. The start-up cable network received a significant investment from Microsoft cofounder Paul Allen in 1994, and in 1995 USA Networks became a minority investor. USA Networks subsequently agreed to show CET programming on its USA and Sci-Fi cable channels.

Kevin Wendle, an original member of the Fox Broadcasting team and an Emmy Award-winning producer, was hired as president of CET Networks. In 1995 the network was developing two shows in addition to "CET Central." One was called "The Web" and focused on the Internet, and the other consisted of multimedia software and product reviews. CNET also launched a web site that was designed to be a leading source of information about computer technology and digital media. By mid-1995 CET Online had more than 43,000 registered users. Hewlett-Packard, IBM, and MCI were among the advertisers on CET Online, and the company had to create a separate department to support advertisers. After four months the number of CNET employees working on the web site grew from 6 to more than 85.

Creating More Online Resources: 1996–98

In 1996 CNET entered into a joint venture with E!Entertainment Television to create E!Online. At first E!Online was a web site that provided entertainment news. In 1997 E!Entertainment Television bought out CNET's 50 percent interest in E!Online for $10 million.

Meanwhile, traffic at CNET's web sites was increasing, due in part to the weekly airing of "CET Central" on the USA and Sci-Fi channels. CNET Online (www.cnet.com) was the company's flagship site and was receiving nine million hits a day in mid-1996. It offered technology news, game reviews, technical support, bulletin boards, and product reviews. It also delivered streaming audio reviews and offered an online look at CET Central's studio. Other web sites operated by CNET included Shareware.com, an archive with more than 170,000 free software titles, and Search.com, a portal that collected Internet search engine programs.

After CNET went public in 1996, the company decided to focus on the Internet as its principal media platform. It cut back on plans to operate a 24-hour cable TV channel, while developing three new cable TV programs. One was "TV.com," which featured presidential son Ron Reagan as a correspondent. Another was "The Web," in which young hosts discussed cool

web sites. The third was called "The New Edge" and examined how technology was affecting our daily lives.

Newly launched web sites in 1996 included News.com, a source of technology news; Download.com, a library of software demo titles; and BuyDirect.com, a site that let users register, purchase, and download software. In 1997 CNET launched Snap! Online, an Internet portal designed to compete with America Online, which then had 12 million subscribers. Targeting novice Internet users, Snap! Online included a free CD-ROM tutorial. It also organized Internet content into channels for news, sports, entertainment, and other topics. In 1998 Snap! obtained a $5.9 million investment from NBC, which also gained an option to acquire a 60 percent interest in the web portal for an additional $38 million. Snap! subsequently became a component of NBCi, the network's interactive business venture.

In mid-1998 CNET launched Shopper.com, a comparison-shopping site for computer and technology products. More than 60 participating computer retailers listed their products on Shopper.com. CNET then collected a fee from the retailers based on the "pay-per-click" advertising model. Shopper.com offered users a database of 100,000 products and one million prices.

CNET's revenue in 1998 was $56.4 million, an increase of 69 percent over 1997 revenue of $33.6 million. Net income for 1998 was $2.6 million (later reclassified to $3 million), compared with a net loss of $24.7 million in 1997. At the end of 1998 CNET's web sites were generating 8.2 million page views a day. The company's multiple revenue sources led analysts to predict that CNET would remain profitable for the next several years.

Developing Brand Identity and E-Commerce: 1999

Throughout 1999 CNET added e-commerce capabilities through acquisitions. Following the acquisition of NetVentures Inc. and its ShopBuilder (www.shopbuilder.com) online store creation system for $12 million, CNET launched a store-hosting service for small and mid-sized merchants at www.store.com. The service helped resellers of unbranded computer systems build their own online stores and benefit from CNET's marketing clout.

CNET also acquired KillerApp Corp. in March 1999 for $46 million. The company owned and operated KillerApp.com, an e-commerce web site that provided online comparison shopping services for computers and consumer electronics products.

Other acquisitions in 1999 included Sumo Inc., an Internet service directory that listed Internet service providers (ISPs) and web hosting services, for $29 million in stock, and Internet search firm SavvySearch Ltd. for $22 million. Both acquisitions improved CNET's search engine capabilities.

During 1999 CNET formed an alliance with America Online to provide it with online computer buying guides. As part of the alliance CNET paid $14.5 million for the exclusive right to provide co-branded computer buying guides on America Online and CompuServe for two and one-half years and to be the exclusive provider of free-to-download software on AOL.com. An agreement with RealNetworks resulted in Snap.com being used as a search tool to locate audio and video files by users of RealPlayer G2 and on all of RealNetworks' sites.

Key Dates:

1992: CNET, Inc. is founded by 27-year-old Halsey Minor as a source of technology information.
1994: The company's fledgling cable channel receives a significant investment from Microsoft cofounder Paul Allen.
1995: USA Networks becomes a minority investor in CNET and shows its program, "CET Central," on its USA and Sci-Fi cable channels.
1996: CNET becomes a public company.
1997: CNET introduces Snap! Online, an Internet portal and search service.
1999: CNET launches a $100 million national brand-building campaign.
2000: CNET debuts CNET Radio, acquires comparative shopper mySimon.com, and changes its name to CNET Networks, Inc.; CNET acquires Ziff Davis Media Inc. for $1.6 billion—the acquisition includes ZDNet, *Computer Shopper* magazine, the SmartPlanet online service, and part ownership of Red Herring Communications.
2001: CNET acquires TechRepublic Inc., an online destination for information technology (IT) professionals, from Gartner, Inc.

CNET also increased its advertising and branding efforts in 1999. After beginning the year with an advertising budget for a national branding campaign estimated at $45 million, the company announced that it would spend $100 million on advertising to build CNET's brand and make it synonymous with technology. Such a commitment meant that the company was putting growth before profits. The ensuing campaign featured the tagline: "CNET: The source for computers and technology."

More Acquisitions, Mergers, and Alliances: 2000–2001

In March 2000 CNET, Inc. changed its name to CNET Networks, Inc. The company continued to be active in broadcast media, launching the weekly television program "News.com" on CNBC in the fall of 1999 as well as the CNET Investor Channel. In January 2000 CNET formed an alliance with radio station owner AMFM Inc. to create CNET Radio, the first all-tech radio format in the United States.

CNET made its largest acquisition to date in January 2000 when it acquired comparison-shopping site mySimon.com for $736 million in stock. MySimon.com was founded in April 1998 by Michael Yang and Yeogirl Yun and launched later in the year as a comparison shopping engine. After attempting to license its virtual learning agent (VLA) technology to web portals, mySimon.com refocused in 1999 to become a shopping destination. In mid-1999 the company launched a multimillion-dollar advertising campaign that featured a humorous character named Simon and the tagline, "The future of shopping is here." Following the acquisition, mySimon.com added product reviews and recommendations as well as more product categories. In the fourth quarter of 2000 mySimon.com generated more than half of CNET Networks' total leads to merchants, with more than half of those leads representing nontechnology products.

CNET Networks made an even larger acquisition in the second half of 2000 when it acquired Ziff Davis Media Inc. in a transaction valued at approximately $1.6 billion. The acquisition featured the merger of two leading technology portals, CNET and ZDNet. Following the acquisition CNET Networks became the eighth largest Internet property with 16.6 million unduplicated users, according to Media Metrix. In addition to gaining the web portal ZDNet.com, CNET also got *Computer Shopper* magazine, the SmartPlanet online service, and part ownership of Red Herring Communications. Japanese computer giant Softbank Corp., which owned half of Ziff Davis, owned 17 percent of the new company.

With an international presence in 25 countries, CNET Networks ranked among the top five international networks in terms of global footprint. In the fourth quarter of 2000 the company acquired the remaining interest in its joint venture with AsiaContent.com for $6 million to gain full ownership of seven CNET web sites in Asia. The company also formed a European sales network to improve cross-border marketing opportunities in nine European countries.

CNET's acquisitions boosted its revenue in 2000 to $264 million, compared with $112.3 million for 1999. Acquisition costs and interest expense resulted in a net loss of $484 million for the year, compared with net income of $416.9 million in 1999.

Noting that an economic slowdown was affecting the technology market, CNET lowered its revenue forecast for 2001 as early as February and announced that it would lay off 190 employees, or about 10 percent of its workforce. In April the company announced that it would acquire TechRepublic, an online destination for IT professionals, from technology research firm Gartner, Inc. for $23 million. The acquisition of TechRepublic added 1.5 million registered IT professionals to CNET Networks' base of 3.4 million professionals, which represented 66 percent of the IT professional market, according to Nielsen/NetRatings.

Reaching a broader audience of technology minded consumers, CNET teamed with *Fortune* magazine to co-produce two special issues of the magazine in 2001. Dubbed the *Fortune/CNET Technology Review,* the June and November 2001 issues of *Fortune* and a related web site (www.fortune.cnet.com) provided a comprehensive technology resource that combined product reviews and information with articles about business trends and technology applications.

CNET altered its broadcast and broadband media strategy in the second half of 2001. The company ceased production of its weekly broadcast television show, "News.com," in September and announced that it would increase its emphasis on broadband and radio. CNET was a leading provider of broadband content on the Web, with some five million streams per month. The company broadcasted interviews with technology executives and opinion leaders on a daily basis at its CNET News.com site (www.news.com). It also posted video product reviews online at www.cnet.com. In addition, the company's corporate production unit, CNET Media Productions, produced broadband product demonstrations and webcasts for corporate clients. Although CNET exited long-form television programming and discontinued the ''News.com'' television program, it continued to provide technology coverage for CNBC's other business programs.

Meanwhile, 2001 was proving to be a difficult year financially. The company reported a pro forma loss of $218.1 million for the second quarter and announced that it would lay off an additional 285 employees, or about 15 percent of its staff. Losses in the third quarter were even greater, reaching $1.4 billion. In spite of the loss, company Chairman and CEO Shelby Bonnie appeared confident about the future, stating, ''Our business performed very well in a challenging business climate. We stabilized our revenues while significantly reducing our long-term cost structure, and we have more than sufficient financial resources to meet our capital needs for the foreseeable future.''

For all of 2001 CNET Networks reported net revenue of $285.8 million, down from 2000 pro forma net revenue of $427.7 million. The company's adjusted loss, excluding special and noncash items, was $77 million, compared with pro forma adjusted income of $22.4 million in 2000. In January 2002 the company predicted that its first quarter revenue would be 10 to 15 percent below that of the previous quarter, indicating that 2002 would be another difficult year for CNET Networks. The lowered revenue forecast was due in general to the economic slowdown and more specifically to a depressed market for technology advertising.

Principal Divisions

Media; International Media; Channel Services; mySimon.

Principal Competitors

International Data Group Inc. (IDG); INT Media Group, Inc.; United Business Media PLC (U.K.); Ziff Davis Media Inc.

Further Reading

Andrews, Whit, ''NBC Buys into CNET's Web Hub, Snap,'' *Internet World,* June 15, 1998, p. 1.

——, ''NBC Seals Net Deal,'' *Internet World,* May 17, 1999, p. 1.

——, ''Net Money: Reorganized CNET Makes Ambitious Bet on Snap Site,'' *Internet World,* May 11, 1998, p. 46.

Atwood, Brett, ''CNet Sets Sights on Cable-TV Market,'' *Billboard,* April 6, 1996, p. 87.

Bachman, Katy, ''CNET Joins with AMFM to Launch All-Tech Format,'' *Mediaweek,* January 10, 2000, p. 8.

Bemiker, Mark, ''CNET Plans More Cable Programming, Picks Up Online Users,'' *Broadcasting & Cable,* July 24, 1995, p. 35.

Bing, Michelle, ''CNET-Computer News You Can Use,'' *Online,* September-October 1998, p. 90.

Brown, Rich, ''USA Logs on to CNET: Cable Company Invests in Computer Channel,'' *Broadcasting & Cable,* March 27, 1995, p. 23.

Callahan, Sean, ''CNET Aims to Own @@Category,'' *Business Marketing,* August 1, 1999, p. 4.

——, ''CNET Buys Arch Rival ZDNet,'' *B to B,* July 31, 2000, p. 1.

Clark, Philip B., ''4: CNET.com,'' *B to B,* April 30, 2001, p. 21.

''CNET,'' *Brandweek,* October 4, 1999, p. 60.

''CNET Backs Ad Initiative with $100 Mil,'' *Adweek Western Advertising News,* July 5, 1999, p. 8.

''CNET: Can Tech Guru Handle Wine, Too?,'' *Business Week,* October 30, 2000, p. 116.

''CNET CEO Steps Down, Enters Incubator,'' *San Francisco Business Times,* March 17, 2000, p. 10.

''CNET Goes for Broke,'' *Business Week,* July 12, 1999, p. 36.

''CNET Offers E-Store Hosting,'' *Content Factory,* August 6, 1999.

''CNET: Revenge of the Preppies,'' *Fortune,* June 21, 1999, p. 112.

''CNET's Paper Chase,'' *Forbes,* June 3, 1996, p. 62.

''CNET Spins a Wider Web,'' *Business Week,* March 27, 2000, p. 48.

''CNET Targets Consumer Market with Launch of Snap! Online,'' *Electronic Advertising & Marketplace Report,* July 1, 1997, p. 3.

''CNET to Acquire Ziff-Davis, Inc. for Stock,'' *Business Publisher,* July 31, 2000, p. 1.

''CNET to Lay Off 190,'' *San Francisco Business Times,* February 9, 2001, p. 78.

Feuerstein, Adam, ''CNET Clicks on E-Commerce,'' *San Francisco Business Times,* March 5, 1999, p. 3.

Gardner, Elizabeth, ''CNET's Comparison Shopping Site Asks Stores for Clickthrough Fees,'' *Internet World,* October 26, 1998, p. 4.

''Gartner Group Sells TechRepublic After Less Than One Year,'' *Business Publisher,* April 16, 2001, p. 3.

Guglielmo, Connie, ''CNET: Minor's Major Move,'' *Inter@ctive Week,* March 13, 2000, p. 14.

''Halsey Minor's Major Plans,'' *Business Week,* July 26, 1999, p. EB39.

Higgins, John M., ''CNET Cuts Unusual Deal with USA Networks,'' *Multichannel News,* June 17, 1996, p. 63.

Kuchinskas, Susan, ''Changes.com: CNET Revamps Site and Channels,'' *Mediaweek,* March 1, 1999, p. 40.

Maddox, Kate, ''BtoB Q&A: CNET's Bonnie Still Bullish on Internet,'' *B to B,* June 11, 2001, p. 8.

''Minor Makes Major Changes,'' *Communications Today,* March 13, 2000.

Moran, Susan, ''Analysts See CNET Sustaining Profits Over the Long Term,'' *Internet World,* March 29, 1999, p. 42.

Negus, Beth, ''Wired and Inspired,'' *Direct,* October 1, 1996, p. 34.

Oberlag, Reginald, ''NBC Continues TV/Internet Convergence with Snap! Alliance,'' *Shoot,* August 14, 1998, p. 22.

Pack, Thomas, ''CNET Drops TV Show to Focus on Broadband,'' *EContent,* November 2001, p. 9.

''Quick Hits,'' *Business Marketing,* January 1, 2000, p. 8.

Rich, Laura, ''Snap! Goes CNET,'' *Adweek Eastern Edition,* June 23, 1997, p. 45.

Schrage, Michael, ''Halsey Minor,'' *Adweek Eastern Edition,* March 23, 1998, p. IQ22.

''Tech Sites Merge As Net Eats Computer Publishing,'' *Communications Today,* July 20, 2000.

Tedesco, Richard, ''NBC Snaps Up CNET's Snap!,'' *Broadcasting & Cable,* May 24, 1999, p. 66.

——, ''Snap Crackles, Pops with Higher Profile,'' *Broadcasting & Cable,* May 24, 1999, p. 72.

Virzi, Anna Maria, ''Separate Commerce Ventures for Globe.com, Cnet,'' *Internet World,* February 8, 1999, p. 8.

Wilmott, Don, ''A Front Door to the Web,'' *PC Magazine,* November 18, 1997, p. 66.

—David P. Bianco

COMMERZBANK

Commerzbank A.G.

Kaiserplatz
60261 Frankfurt am Main
Germany
Telephone: (49) 69-1362-0
Fax: (49) 69-2853-89
Web site: http://www.commerzbank.com

Public Company
Incorporated: 1958
Employees: 39,463
Total Assets: $432.81 billion (2000)
Stock Exchanges: Frankfurt Düsseldorf Hamburg Munich
    Berlin Stuttgart Bremen Hanover Antwerp Brussels
    Paris Tokyo Luxembourg Amsterdam Basel Bern
    Geneva Lausanne Zurich London Vienna
Ticker Symbol: CRZBY
NAIC: 522110 Commercial Banking; 522210 Credit Card
    Issuing (pt); 522120 Savings Institutions (pt); 522293
    International Trade Financing (pt); 522291 Consumer
    Lending; 523110 Investment Banking and Securities
    Dealing; 523120 Securities Brokerage; 523999
    Miscellaneous Financial Investment Activities (pt);
    522310 Mortgage and Nonmortgage Loan Brokers

Commerzbank A.G. has long been one of Germany's leading commercial banks, one of the small number of large and powerful institutions that has dominated Germany's highly stratified banking industry. Although its size and strength nearly led to its demise after World War II, those qualities also allowed Commerzbank to bounce back quickly and take part in West Germany's astounding economic recovery. Since German reunification and the emergence of the European Union, Commerzbank has struggled to maintain its independence in an era of consolidation in the European banking industry.

Banking in the Era of
German Unification: 1870–1914

Commerzbank began in 1870 in the port city of Hamburg under the name Commerz- und Discontobank. Founded by a group of bankers and Hanseatic merchants, its primary purpose was to finance foreign trade. The years 1870–72 were boom years for German banking; during this time many commercial banks were founded to take advantage of the business opportunities afforded by the recent unification of Germany and the prosperity that followed its victory in the Franco-Prussian War. Many of these banks were short-lived, springing into existence to profit from the speculative frenzy of the moment, but Commerzbank, along with Deutsche Bank and Dresdner Bank, survived to become one of the three largest banks in West Germany today.

During its early years, however, Commerzbank remained relatively small. Although it became a major shareholder in the London and Hanseatic Bank when that bank was founded in 1872, in order to obtain representation in the world's financial capital, Commerzbank did not participate much in the rapid expansion of German overseas banking during the 1880s and 1890s. Its larger Berlin-based rivals took the lead in German ventures into South American and foreign European markets. Despite its specialization in foreign trade, Commerzbank's name also is notably absent from the list of major participants in the Deutsche-Asiatische Bank, which was founded in Shanghai in 1889 and firmly established German financial presence in the Far East.

Commerzbank took a step up in 1892, when it opened a branch office in Berlin. Following the political centralization inherent in the establishment of the Second Reich, many German banks had gravitated to Berlin, making it the nation's financial capital. All of Germany's major banks were based there, and Commerzbank completed its bid to join their ranks in 1904 when it acquired Berliner Bank. Its Berlin operations quickly came to supercede those in Hamburg in importance. At that time, German banking was dominated by nine Berlin-based institutions that became known as the *Berliner Grossbanken*.

Bank Mergers Between the Wars: 1918–45

The influence of the *Grossbanken* grew substantially during World War I and again in the years immediately following the armistice, though for vastly different reasons. From 1914 to 1918, public borrowing to finance the war effort supplanted private-sector loans as the banks' main source of business, and the government naturally chose firms with large capitalization

Company Perspectives:

Commerzbank's six basic strategic goals: to consolidate the Bank's position as a European integrated financial institution; to achieve a stronger position in selected investment–banking products; to realize broader and more intensive cooperation with Generali; to become market leader in e-commerce banking; to develop the Bank's international business beyond Europe's borders; to allocate equity capital to reflect the growth potential of business areas.

to supply the sums of money that it required. This forced the banks to consolidate; large institutions absorbed smaller ones and smaller banks reached "community of interest" agreements with each other.

The inflation crises of the early 1920s, on the other hand, so threatened the German banking industry that the badly weakened banks were forced to merge with each other merely to survive. In 1920, Commerz- und Discontobank merged with Mittledeutsche Privatbank of Magdeburg, which was then one of Germany's most important regional banks and had long been active in building up a branch network. This new institution changed its name to Commerz- und Privatbank and, later that year, acquired Vereinsbank Wismar. In 1924, Commerzbank had 246 branch offices, compared with only eight in 1913, a staggering rate of growth that well outpaced the other *Grossbanken* during this time.

Commerzbank enjoyed a period of relative prosperity in the latter half of the decade, increasing its capital from 42 million Reichsmarks in 1924 to 60 million in 1928, and its reserves from 21 million Reichsmarks to 35.6 million. In 1929 it acquired another Berlin bank, Mittledeutsche Creditbank. It also helped facilitate American investment in Germany during this time. In 1927 it negotiated a loan of $20 million from Chase National Bank and re-lent the money to German firms. Such moves were regarded with some suspicion, as they blurred the traditional line between banks and investment companies. Commerzbank helped solve this public relations problem in 1928 by joining with Chase National to form General Mortgage and Credit Corporation for the sole purpose of increasing foreign investment in Germany.

Commerzbank changed its name to its current form, Commerzbank Aktiengesellschaft, in 1940. During the years of Nationalist Socialist rule, the *Grossbanken,* now numbering six, continued to dominate German banking. In 1944, their assets totaled more than 28 billion marks, more than all of Germany's other banks combined. Not only did they play a substantial role in financing the Nazi war effort, but thanks to Germany's universal banking system they were able to hold major interests in and place their executives on the boards of directors of the industrial concerns, like Krupp, Siemens, and IG Farben, that supplied hardware to the German military.

Reorganization and Global Expansion: 1945–80

After World War II ended in Europe in April 1945, Allied occupation authorities began investigating the German banking

industry as part of their effort to punish war criminals. They found that not only had the *Grossbanken* provided financial support to the ruling Nazis, but that they had helped plunder the assets of financial institutions in occupied countries and that companies under their control had employed slave labor. Although Commerzbank's sins were not the most grievous to be discovered, the occupation authorities decreed that all of the *Grossbanken* would be broken up into a total of 30 smaller institutions. The Allied authorities also hoped that decentralizing the German banking industry would limit its ability to finance future military buildups and that it would encourage U.S.-style competition. As a U.S. diplomat told the *Wall Street Journal* in 1955, "It wasn't merely vengeance we sought. We hoped that by modeling the German banking system after ours, where banks are usually confined to a single state, we'd be able to do a service to the competitive system."

The new West German government resisted this decree, but eventually gave in under severe political pressure. In 1952, the surviving *Grossbanken*—Commerzbank, Deutsche Bank, and Dresdner Bank—were each dissolved into three smaller banks. Commerzbank was broken up into Commerzbank Bankverein, Commerz- und Credit-Bank, and Commerz- und Disconto-Bank. In addition, Chancellor Konrad Adenauer promised that the banks would not be re-amalgamated for at least three years.

In 1955, Chancellor Adenauer's promise expired and plans were laid for the reconstitution of what would become known as West Germany's Big Three. On July 1, 1958, Commerzbank resumed business, now headquartered in Düsseldorf (during the 1970s, it would gradually shift its operations to Frankfurt). Thanks to the size and strength of its constituent banks, Commerzbank was quickly able to regain the position of eminence that it had held 15 years earlier. The survival of Germany's universal banking system also helped; as one German bank official told *Time* in 1962, an American equivalent of a Big Three bank would be like "a combination of Chase Manhattan, First Boston and Merrill Lynch."

In the late 1960s, Commerzbank joined the worldwide trend among financial institutions toward internationalizing its business. In 1967 it joined with Irving Trust Company, First National Bank of Chicago, Westminster Bank, and Hongkong & Shanghai Banking Corporation to form the International Commercial Bank in London. In 1970, it entered into a semi-merger with Credit Lyonnais, France's second largest bank, and Italy's Banco di Roma in order to both counter increased competition from large U.S. banks and meet the needs of European companies that had expanded their business overseas. The resulting institution had $18 billion in deposits and 3,000 branches, making it the largest banking organization in Europe and the fourth largest in the world. Differences in national banking laws and traditions prevented the three banks from effecting a full-fledged merger, but they did agree to coordinate management practices and integrate all competing operations outside their home countries. Commerzbank also formed an investment advising company in Tokyo in 1973 and the Financial Corporation of Indonesia in 1974.

At home, the Big Three continued to wield considerable influence in German business through shareholding and corporate directorships, just as they had before the end of World

<table>
<tr><td colspan="2">

Key Dates:
</td></tr>
<tr><td>1870:</td><td>Commerz- und Discontobank is founded in Hamburg.</td></tr>
<tr><td>1892:</td><td>Commerzbank opens a branch in Berlin.</td></tr>
<tr><td>1904:</td><td>Commerzbank acquires Berliner Bank.</td></tr>
<tr><td>1920:</td><td>Commerz- und Discontobank merges with Mittledeutsche Privatbank.</td></tr>
<tr><td>1928:</td><td>Commerzbank joins with Chase National Bank to form General Mortgage and Credit Corporation.</td></tr>
<tr><td>1967:</td><td>Commerzbank joins with Irving Trust Company, First National Bank of Chicago, Westminster Bank, and Hongkong & Shanghai Banking Corporation to form the International Commercial Bank in London.</td></tr>
<tr><td>1981:</td><td>Walter Seipp becomes chairman of Commerzbank.</td></tr>
<tr><td>1995:</td><td>Commerzbank acquires a 75 percent stake in Jupiter Tyndall.</td></tr>
</table>

War II. Commerzbank owned substantial interests in breweries, department store chains, and construction companies. In the 1970s, however, the Social Democratic Party's rise to power and widespread anxiety over the scope of the Big Three's influence convinced the banks to divest themselves of their holdings to prevent possible nationalization.

But the public and politicians did a quick about-face in the mid-1970s, when the oil boom generated fears that Middle Eastern interests would use their petro-dollars to muscle into strategic German industries. In January 1975, Commerzbank purchased a sizable stake in GHH, a machinery concern, to help ward off a possible Arab takeover, by acquiring a 25 percent interest in Regina Verwaltungsgesellschaft, a holding company owning 25 percent of GHH. The move also helped Commerzbank move into the insurance business through Regina's links with Allianz Insurance Gruppe. In addition, in December of that year, it joined Dresdner Bank, Bayerische Landesbank, and five other partners to buy a 25 percent stake in Daimler-Benz from Deutsche Bank, which had purchased the shares at the urging of Chancellor Helmut Schmidt to keep them out of the hands of an Iranian concern. Once the panic had passed, Commerzbank resumed its policy of selling off its business holdings. In 1980, it sold a 32 percent stake in Kaufhof, Germany's second largest retailer, to the Union Bank of Switzerland and Metro-Verwegensverwaltung, a German-owned Swiss supermarket concern.

Recovery and Prosperity: The 1980s

But the Kaufhof sale was also a way of raising cash at a time when Commerzbank was struggling badly. German banks in general fared poorly at the beginning of the new decade compared with their British, U.S., and Japanese counterparts, but Commerzbank suffered in particular from overexpansion in the late 1970s and heavy investments in fixed-interest securities, which turned sour when interest rates did not decline as predicted. The bank's profits shrank to virtually nothing, and in 1980 it failed to pay a dividend for the first time in its history. Chairman Robert Dohm resigned late that year after suffering a heart attack.

Paul Lichtenberg, Dohm's predecessor, became interim chairman and immediately began searching for a permanent replacement. He was able to woo Walter Seipp, vice-chairman of Westdeutsche Landesbank, who assumed the chairmanship in 1981. A lawyer by trade, Seipp had worked for Deutsche Bank from 1951 to 1974 before joining Westdeutsche Landesbank and had built a strong reputation for himself in both international and domestic banking circles. Under his direction, Commerzbank increased its loan loss provisions in 1982 when faced with the possible default of $250 million worth of loans to Poland. The bank did not pay out another dividend until 1983, but by 1984 it had returned to financial health.

From there, Commerzbank resumed its ambitious ways. In 1984, it continued to divest its nonbank holdings by selling its stake in the Kempinski luxury hotel group to Saudi Arabian interests. But it also joined Westdeutsche Landesbank, Bayerische Landesbank, and its Big Three rivals to form Deutsche Wagnisfinanzierung, a venture capital company. In 1986, responding to a new trend among West German companies toward raising money through the securities markets rather than by borrowing from banks, it raised $200 million in fresh capital through a floating-rate note issue. Commerzbank chose a propitious moment to float the new offering, doing so at a time when the market for floating-rate bonds denominated in European currencies was strong.

In 1988, Commerzbank sold its stake in Deutsche Wagnisfinanzierung to Deutsche Bank. That same year it also purchased a 40 percent stake in Leonberger Bausparkasse, West Germany's fourth largest savings and loan, from the Stuttgart insurer Allgemeine Rentenstalt Lebens- und Rentenversicherung. Commerzbank put the crowning touches on its international investment banking network by opening offices in Tokyo in 1987 and New York in 1988. By 1988, its commercial banking network had branches in Brussels, Antwerp, Paris, Madrid, Barcelona, London, Hong Kong, Tokyo, Osaka, New York, Chicago, Atlanta, and Los Angeles.

Commerzbank had always been the smallest of the Big Three banks, but the very fact that it was one of those select three counted for a great deal in the West German banking industry, where the drop from the first tier to the second was steep. Historically, Commerzbank was a latecomer, joining the major league of German banking long after its rivals had done so. When the European economy became fully integrated at the end of 1992, it presented West German financial institutions with a whole new set of challenges. Commerzbank had to be quick to adapt to change this time.

International Banking and the Reunified Germany: The 1990s

Commerzbank entered the 1990s intent on gaining ground on its two main rivals, Deutsche Bank and Dresdner Bank. The reunification of Germany in 1989, in reestablishing a single German currency and opening up a substantial unexploited market in the east, provided Commerzbank with the opportunity to expand its domestic banking network significantly. In October 1990 the bank earmarked DM 500 million for the creation of 120 new branches in the former East Germany over a three-year period, with the aim of seizing a share of the new market larger than that of its competitors. The bank had already welcomed a flood of new customers, and capital, since the implementation of the monetary union plan the previous July, enjoying an influx of more than DM 2 billion in new deposits from approximately 80,000 new clients. In addition, the bank was positioning itself to become a major partner with the up-and-coming businesses in the east, lending nearly DM 1 billion to East German companies in the first year of reunification.

A bigger challenge for the bank came in 1993, when the Single European Market officially went into effect. Arriving on the heels of a widespread recession, European unification brought the promise of new opportunities for sustained growth, through the opening of international borders and a general relaxation of government regulatory policies. To take advantage of this new economic environment, however, as well as to counter the threats that came with increased competition, Commerzbank needed to alter its business model. In the early 1990s, the bank's new strategy focused mainly on the strengthening of its international scope. To this end, in 1995 Commerzbank acquired a 75 percent stake in Jupiter Tyndall, a British fund management firm. The move was part of a larger trend toward diversification among the major German banking houses; both Dresdner Bank and Deutsche Bank had already made forays into the U.K. investment banking world, and Commerzbank was eager to follow suit. The Jupiter venture was immediately followed by a bid for leading English brokerage firm Smith New Court. Unfortunately, Commerzbank was ultimately edged out by a competing bid by U.S. securities giant Merrill Lynch, and its dreams of outpacing its rivals in England were thwarted.

Undeterred in the pursuit of its goal of establishing a global presence, Commerzbank turned its attention to acquisitions further afield, with a view to increasing its holdings in the United States and Asia. It was particularly interested in gaining a foothold in Japan, where it hoped to take advantage of the deregulation of the Japanese finance industry in the late 1990s. While Commerzbank was busy scanning the overseas landscape for new opportunities, however, it also faced a significant threat from home. By the end of the decade a group of prominent Commerzbank shareholders, led by Klaus Peter Schneidewind and Clemens Vedder and organized under a holding company called Cobra, had become dissatisfied with the course the bank was taking. In 2000 they began pushing for Commerzbank to enter into merger talks with another European Bank, preferably one outside of Germany. Commerzbank was not eager to become absorbed into a foreign banking house, and went so far as to discuss a merger with Dresdner Bank, in the face of Cobra's fierce opposition. Although the Dresdner deal eventually fell through, the pressure to find a powerful partner remained in-

tense. At the beginning of the new century, the bank found itself struggling to maintain its independence in the face of mounting pressures to consolidate, while searching for a means of achieving effective growth in the highly competitive banking environment of the European Union.

Principal Subsidiaries

ADIG Allgemeine Deutsche Investment-Gesellschaft mbH; ADIG-Investment Luxemburg S.A.; Banque Marocaine du Commerce Exterieur, S.A. (Morocco); BRE Bank SA (Poland); Caisse Centrale de Reescompte, S.A. (France); CBG Commerz Beteiligungsgesellschaft Holding mbH; CFM Commerz Finanz Management GmbH; comdirect bank AG; Commerz Asset Managers GmbH; Comerz Futures, LLC (U.S.A.); Commerz Grundbesitz-Investmentgesellschaft GmbH; Commerz International Capital Management GmbH; Commerz NetBusiness AG; Commerz Securities (Japan) Co. Ltd. (Hong Kong/Tokyo); Commerzbank Asset Management Italia S.p.A.; Commerzbank (Budapest) Rt. (Hungary); Commerzbank Capital Markets Corporation (U.S.A.); Commerzbank Capital Markets (Eastern Europe) a.s. (Czech Republic); Commerzbank (Eurasia) SAO (Russia); Commerzbank Europe (Ireland); Commerzbank International S.A. (Luxembourg); Commerzbank (Nederland) N.V. (The Netherlands); Commerzbank (South East Asia) Ltd. (Singapore); Commerzbank (Switzerland) Ltd.; Commerzbank Investment Management GmbH; CommerzLeasing und Immobilien AG; Deutsche Schiffsbank AG; Erste Europaische Pfandbrief- und Kommunalkreditbank AG (Luxembourg); Hypothekenbank in Essen AG; Jupiter International Group PLC (U.K.); Korea Exchange Bank (South Korea); Montgomery Asset Management, LLC (U.S.); P.T. Bank Finconesia (Indonesia); RHEINHYP Rheinische Hypothekenbank AG; Unibanco - Uniao de Bancos Brasileiros S.A.

Principal Competitors

Bayerische Hypo- und Vereinsbank Aktiengesellschaft (HVB Group); Deutsche Bank AG; Dresdner Bank AG.

Further Reading

Eisenhammer, John, ''Commerzbank Predicts Big Surge in Earnings for West German Industry,'' *Independent* (London), August 2, 1994.

Fisher, Andrew, and Norma Cohen, ''Commerzbank's Foreign Ambitions Gain Strength,'' *Financial Times* (London), July 14, 1995.

Lebert, Rolf, and Tony Major, ''Commerzbank 'Should Seek Global Partner,' '' *Financial Times* (London), May 18, 2000.

—update: Steve Meyer

Comstock Resources, Inc.

5300 Town and Country Boulevard, Suite 500
Frisco, Texas 75244
U.S.A.
Telephone: (972) 668-8800
Fax: (972) 668-8812
Web site: http://www.comstockresources.com

Public Company
Incorporated: 1919 as Comstock Tunnel and Drainage
    Company
Employees: 48
Sales: $169.4 million (2000)
Stock Exchanges: New York
Ticker Symbol: CRK
NAIC: 211111 Crude Petroleum and Natural Gas Extraction

Comstock Resources, Inc. is a small independent energy company located in Frisco, Texas, involved in the acquisition, exploration, and development of oil and gas deposits. Comstock owns interests in some 500 producing wells, concentrated in three geographical areas: Southeast Texas, East Texas/North Louisiana, and the Gulf of Mexico. Management has opted to locate its wells close to existing means of transportation in order to improve profitability. Moreover, by narrowing its operations to specific areas, the company has enhanced its engineering expertise, leading to greater success in its drilling program. Because of these and other conservative practices, Comstock is one of the most cost-effective producers of oil and gas in the industry.

Company Origins in the Comstock Lode Discovery: 19th Century

Comstock Resources was originally named the Comstock Tunnel and Drainage Company, a Virginia City, Nevada, business that resulted from the famous Comstock Lode. The area first drew attention in 1859 when gold was discovered, leading to boomtowns such as Virginia City and other long-since-forgotten mining communities. Prospectors Pat McLaughlin and Peter O'Reilly were the first to find gold in an area called Six-Mile Canyon, but they were persuaded by Henry Comstock

that they had been working part of his claim. This bold piece of deception ensured that Comstock's name would be forever linked to the history of the U.S. West. While working these original gold deposits, miners were hindered by a blue mud that caked to their picks and shovels. Once assayed, the mud turned out to be high quality silver ore. What became known as the Comstock Lode was so rich in gold and silver that President Lincoln made Nevada a state, despite the area's sparse population, in order to tap into the region's immense wealth to help finance the Civil War. It was also instrumental in the growth of San Francisco, as well as the career of Samuel Clemens, better known by his pen name of Mark Twain. Efforts to work the Comstock Lode peaked in the mid-1870s, after which production fell off significantly. Although mining operations of the Comstock Tunnel and Drainage Company date back to 1863, it was not until 1919 that the business was officially incorporated in Delaware. By the 1980s, the mining operation was reduced to inactive gold and silver claims and the company's other assets limited to some historic buildings, 25 income-producing office projects, and 1,800 acres of undeveloped real estate. Its stock was only sold on a regional exchange "by appointment only," priced below $1. For 1986, the company generated less than $400,000 in revenues while posting a loss of $167,000.

In 1987, the Comstock Tunnel and Drainage Company was purchased by a group of Texas investors with plans to use the corporation in oil and gas exploration and production. The group included Miles Jay Allison, Comstock Resources' current chairman, president, and chief executive officer. He became involved in oil and gas immediately upon the completion of his studies from Baylor University in 1981. In addition to an undergraduate degree in business administration, he earned a master's degree in economics and a law degree from the school. He then spent six years as an oil and gas attorney for the Midland, Texas, firm of Lynch, Chappell, Allday and Alsup. In 1983, he cofounded Midwood Petroleum and gained experience acquiring and developing oil and gas properties. Before quitting the law firm he also became part of an investment group that in 1987 purchased the rights to Ewing Oil. Although better known as a fictional company in the long-running "Dallas" television series, Ewing Oil was actually founded in the mid-1970s by Dallas oilman Bobby Ewing.

Because of a slump in the oil and gas industry, Allison and other investors sought help in developing a revised business plan, turning to the real estate banking group of New York investment firm Donaldson, Lufkin & Jenrette (DLJ), where they worked with a vice-president named Timothy Bell. Deciding to search for an existing public company that controlled some valuable assets, they eventually settled on Comstock Tunnel and Drainage. In February 1987, Ewing purchased its first stake in the company, spending $1.7 million to acquire 1.2 million shares. In April, Bell left DLJ to become Ewing's chief executive officer, with Allison serving as president, then in July the company increased its stake in Comstock by buying an additional 2.2 million shares with $2.7 million worth of oil and gas properties in west Texas and Oklahoma. The company was renamed Comstock Resources, its shares were listed on the NASDAQ, and its headquarters were moved to the Dallas area.

Along with three other Ewing nominations, Allison and Bell were named to Comstock's seven-member board of directors, with Bell taking on the additional responsibilities as the company's chief executive officer. Originally, the plan was for Comstock to more aggressively exploit the company's mining and real estate assets. Its real estate was appraised and mining interests subjected to engineering studies as well as historical analysis by the University of Nevada, which indicated that a considerable amount of residual gold and silver was present in the company's mining claims on the old Comstock Lode. Bell hoped to find buyers for some of the real estate as well as joint venture partners to develop other sites that Comstock owned. On the mining side, he expected to either lease claims to third parties or work the claims directly. To help fund its activities the company was able to arrange a $14 million loan with Union Bank, a branch of Bank of Toyko.

New Leadership: Miles Jay Allison, 1988

Bell and Comstock's board of directors soon disagreed on the company's direction, however, and by the end of the first full year of operation in 1988, Bell resigned as both an officer of the company and member of the board. Allison was named acting president and CEO, responsibilities that would become permanent. Under his leadership, Comstock changed its focus to the oil and gas industry with which he was more familiar. Gradually all of the Nevada assets were sold off, so that eventually all that remained of the company's heritage was an old safe originally used to store silver mined from the Comstock Lode, which was now put on display in Comstock's new corporate headquarters in Texas.

Comstock looked to buy oil and gas-producing properties with significant remaining potential at distressed prices (generally in the $10 million range) resulting from the severe slumps of the 1980s. Allison and his management team targeted private oil and gas companies which owned desirable properties that fell between the cracks, either too small to attract large companies or too large to attract the interest of small companies. Allison's acquisition team, which featured both seasoned oilmen and finance people, followed a general script. "What we've got is a good broker chain," Allison explained to the *Dallas Business Journal* in 1994. "Companies know that we're serious buyers of oil and gas properties. When we evaluate a property, we make the first pass to see if we want to get serious, and then boom, boom, boom: It goes through the chain." As a result of such fast action, Comstock was able to lock up sizable reserves before they hit the radar screens of larger competitors.

From 1988 to 1990, Comstock acquired a considerable number of undeveloped reserves, located primarily in the Texas panhandle field. Despite posting net profits of over $1 million on revenues of $7.4 million in 1989, the company lacked the capital to drill as aggressively as it would have preferred. As a result, a large portion of its properties were leased to third parties. To improve its financial position, Comstock staged a public offering of stock in 1990, netting $13.3 million. After paying off its bank debt, the company was still left with $3.5 million to make further acquisitions and launch a three-year program that called for the drilling of 400 wells. As these wells began producing, revenues were to be used in the drilling of new ones. Moreover, in 1990 Ewing Oil was liquidated and its shareholders received the privately held company's 25 percent stake in Comstock.

During the early 1990s, Comstock was especially aggressive in pursuing acquisitions. In 1991, it acquired Tidemark Exploration in a cash and stock deal, which included interests in 190 Oklahoma and Arkansas wells. Also during that year, Comstock paid nearly $17.5 million to the Goodrich Oil Co. for 66 producing wells located in Louisiana, Texas, Oklahoma, and Arkansas. In 1992, the company acquired 120 producing wells in Oklahoma and Arkansas from Liberty Life Insurance Company. (During the course of that year, its stock also moved from the NASDAQ to the New York Stock Exchange.) Comstock was extremely active in 1993, completing several deals. Early in the year, it purchased a number of smaller properties located in Nebraska, south Louisiana, and along the Texas Gulf Coast. A more significant transaction occurred late in 1993 when Comstock acquired Stanford Offshore Energy, Inc. in a $6.2 million stock deal. Stanford owned interests in oil and gas wells located in offshore Louisiana, Texas, Mississippi, Oklahoma, and Kansas. Allison indicated to the press that the addition of the Stanford properties would likely double Comstock's revenues the following year. Interests in some of Stanford's properties were also held by Tierra Mineral Development, L.C., which Comstock purchased in a subsequent cash and stock deal. Other interests in Stanford held by MG Trade Finance Corp. were purchased in 1994. In that same year, Comstock acquired five gas wells located near the Texas Gulf Coast as well as oil and gas properties in the El Campo field in Texas and a gas processing plant located in the Texas Gulf Coast area. In addition to some smaller purchases in 1995, Comstock acquired 319 wells located in East Texas and North Louisiana from Sonat Exploration Company at a cost of $49.1 million.

Acquisition of Black Stone Oil: 1996

Comstock's investment in oil and gas properties resulted in significant gains in annual revenues, which grew from $2.7 mil-

Key Dates:

1859: The Comstock Lode is discovered in Nevada.
1963: The operations of The Comstock Tunnel and Drainage Company commence.
1919: The company incorporates in Delaware.
1987: Ewing Oil buys the company, changes its name to Comstock Resources, and moves the company's headquarters to Texas.
1988: M. Jay Allison becomes chief executive officer.
1996: Black Stone Oil Co. is acquired.
1997: Key assets from Bois d'Arc Resources are acquired.
2001: DevX Energy Inc. is acquired.

lion in 1991 to more than $22 million in 1995. The cost of expansion, however, held back profits, and, more importantly, Comstock's drilling program was not as successful as management had hoped. The company was forced to take significant write-downs on reserves during the first half of the 1990s. Nevertheless, Allison and his team stayed the course and were able in early 1996 to complete one of the company's most important acquisitions, the $103 million purchase of privately owned Black Stone Oil Co. Again, they were able to quickly spot an attractive target, which in the case of Black Stone boasted a newly discovered gas field in the Houston area, and make a preemptive bid before much larger competitors were able to act. In addition to adding gas-bearing fields capable of producing 100 million cubic feet of natural gas per day, Comstock also gained Black Stone properties that could produce nearly 6,000 barrels of oil per day. The company now owned an asset and reserve base that put it on a par with mid-cap-size independents. Black Stone also marked a turning point in Comstock's strategy, the company electing now to focus on growth through exploration and drilling rather than acquisitions. Moreover, Comstock began to narrow its focus to three primary geographical areas of activity. In 1996, it sold off a number of non-strategic oil and gas properties for $9 million. For the year, Comstock posted significant gains over the previous year, due mainly to Black Stone. Revenues grew by more than 200 percent, totaling almost $70 million, and net income exceeded $24 million.

Despite its publicly stated shift in emphasis to exploration, by the end of 1997 Comstock again grew significantly through acquisitions. This time it paid Bois d'Arc Resources and its partners $205 million in cash for offshore oil and gas interests. In addition to gaining a stake in 37 wells and eight Gulf of Mexico production facilities, Comstock also acquired interests in six properties that had not yet been drilled but had already been explored using 3-D seismic technology. Altogether engineers estimated that the Bois d'Arc deal added 14.7 million barrels of oil and 30.4 billion cubic feet of natural gas to Comstock's reserves. In addition, the company entered into an exploration joint venture with the principals of Bois d'Arc that proved highly lucrative. Of the 39 wells drilled under this agreement in the next two years, 26 would prove successful.

Comstock posted more strong results in 1997, reporting $88.6 million in revenues and $21.7 million in net profits. Growth was now almost entirely the result of exploration efforts. Comstock's only significant acquisition in 1998 was the purchase of some working interests in offshore Louisiana oil and gas properties. Despite a drop in oil and gas prices in 1998, Comstock continued to show modest growth for the year, reporting revenues of $93 million and net earnings of $17.2 million. A decrease in oil and natural gas production in 1999, although offset somewhat by a rebound in oil prices, resulted in a loss of revenue. Total sales for the year fell to $90.1 million, and the company posted a $4.7 million net loss. The stage was set, however, for a significant increase in oil and gas prices in 2000 that would lead to a record year for Comstock. Revenues grew by 88 percent, totaling $169.4 million, and net earnings of $38.9 million more than made up for the previous year's shortfall.

Coming off a strong performance in 2000, Comstock was able to complete another major acquisition in 2001—the $93 million purchase of DevX Energy. The company picked up oil properties in East and South Texas, Kentucky, Oklahoma, and Kansas. More significantly, Comstock added to its natural gas reserves, which management believed was important because virtually every new power plant in the United States relied on natural gas to generate electricity. Although natural gas prices would weaken in 2001, prompting Comstock to cut back on its gas drilling program, the company was pleased with its long-term position and elected to simply wait for prices to improve. Price swings were a given in the industry, but Comstock had demonstrated an ability to operate in all conditions. Moreover, when rivals faltered, Comstock was ready and able to pick up additional properties at reasonable prices.

Principal Subsidiaries

Comstock Oil & Gas, Inc.; Comstock Offshore, LLC; DevXEnergy, Inc.

Principal Competitors

Apache Corporation; BP Amoco plc; Royal Dutch Petroleum Company.

Further Reading

Corwin, Jeff, "Jay Allison & Comstock Resources: Energy Drive," *Baylor Business Review,* Fall 1999, pp. 2–5.

Genusa, Angela, "Energy Company Sticks with Plan for Fast Growth," *Dallas Business Journal,* June 17, 1994, p. C16.

Kinder, Lesley, "Harvesting in the Shade of Giants," *Oil & Gas Investor,* March 1990, p. 54.

Lampman, Dean, "Ewing Oil Raises Stake in Nevada Mining Unit, Pursues Restructuring," *Dallas-Forth Worth Business Journal,* November 9, 1987, p. 1A.

Robertson, Jeffrey W., "Comstock Resources, Inc.," *Oil & Gas Investor,* June 1998, p. 72.

Steffy, Loren, "Comstock Raising $14 Million for 400-Well Drilling Project," *Dallas Business Journal,* April 16, 1990, p. 4.

Toal, Brian A., "Orphans of the Street," *Oil & Gas Investor,* September 1990, p. 50.

—Ed Dinger

Corporate Express, Inc.

One Environmental Way
Broomfield, Colorado 80021-3416
U.S.A.
Telephone: (303) 664-2000
Fax: (303) 664-3474
Web site: http://www.corporate-express.com

Wholly Owned Subsidiary of Buhrmann N.V.
Incorporated: 1986 as Business Express
Employees: 20,468
Sales: $6.72 billion (2001)
NAIC: 323116 Manifold Business Form Printing; 453210
   Office Supplies and Stationery Stores; 454110
   Electronic Shopping and Mail-Order Houses; 561110
   Office Administrative Services

Corporate Express, Inc., wholly owned by the Dutch firm Buhrmann N.V. since October 1999, is the world's largest supplier to businesses of office products, including office supplies, computer and imaging supplies, computer peripherals, and office furniture. Mainly serving large corporations, Corporate Express is the market leader in North America and Australia and holds the number two position in Europe. More than three-quarters of the firm's revenues are generated in North America, where the company's customers are served from 257 offices and through 42 distribution centers with more than six million square feet of space. In addition to its office products business, Corporate Express also operates several complementary manufacturing and services businesses: Corporate Express Document & Print Management, Inc., a manufacturer of forms; ASAP Software Express, Inc., which is a leading provider of services related to software licenses; and Corporate Express Promotional Marketing, Inc., a provider of customized corporate and brand products.

From Czechoslovakia, with Love

The company was founded in Boulder, Colorado, by Jirka Rysavy (pronounced YER-kah RIS-ah-vee). Born in Czecho-slovakia in 1954, the son of a civil engineer and an educational researcher, Rysavy became a hurdler for the Czech national team, competing in international track and field events. While attempting to reach the Olympics, Rysavy was forced out of competition because of injuries. In 1984, after earning a master's degree in engineering the previous year at the Technical University of Prague, he extended his travel visa and never returned to Czechoslovakia.

Barely speaking English, Rysavy spent a year in solitude in a remote part of Eastern Europe. After that, he traveled the world, sleeping on park benches and living on $3 a day, eventually finding himself in Boulder, Colorado, where he worked in a print shop for $3.35 an hour. After saving up $600, he started his own company, Transformational Economy, or Transecon, which sold recycled paper. Rysavy made $100,000 before taxes in his first year of business. Investing $30,000 of that money into a new venture following his strict vegetarian diet, Rysavy created Crystal Market, a natural foods retailer store, which made $2.5 million in sales in its first year. For a man with no business experience from a non-capitalist country, Rysavy was working wonders.

Planning to continue growing his foods business with additional health food markets, Rysavy got sidetracked when one of his neighbors in Boulder decided to sell an office supply store. Rysavy obtained the heavily indebted store in November 1986 for $100 and the assumption of $15,000 in overdue accounts payable. After renaming it Business Express and installing a computer system to track customers and sales, Rysavy realized that he would not be able to make the store successful by remaining a retail outlet. He noticed the successful accounts that a few local companies had with the store that bought supplies in large quantities. Moving quickly away from retail and towards corporate accounts, the company within a year had made $2 million with a pretax margin of 14 percent.

In the fall of 1987, after seeing the success of his corporate strategy, Rysavy hired a researcher to collect material on the office supply industry. By December, Rysavy had a pile of research materials and spent two weeks on the beach in Hawaii wading through all of it. He discovered huge problems in the industry as a whole: thousands of office supply companies were

Company Perspectives:

Whatever a business needs to get business done, Corporate Express supplies it. Through our office supplies, furniture, computer and imaging supplies, PC software, document and print management and promotional products, we prepare companies and organizations around the world for work every day.

At Corporate Express, we provide our customers with what they need, when and where they need it—and always with the best service that they can possibly imagine.

sharing a $100 billion market, split up among local markets and not selling enough volume to get deep discounts from manufacturers. Moreover, with the number of office products being produced growing at an enormous rate, most stores were overburdened with huge, slow-turning inventories.

Watching Staples and Office Depot begin to boom about the same time in the small business and home business retail market, Rysavy decided to try the same thing on a bigger scale by serving large corporations, companies with 100 or more employees, which accounted for $30 billion of the industry annually. In 1988, after selling his health food store to Mike Gilliland for $300,000 (Gilliland went on to make Wild Oats Markets, Inc. into a natural grocery store chain worth $200 million), Rysavy invested it all and managed to leverage the $12.8 million price tag on the office products division of NBI Inc., a Denver-based company with a loss of $1 million on sales of $20 million. Desiring to repeat with NBI the strategy that had worked for his small Boulder store, Rysavy needed to install a computer system to analyze NBI's market and customers. Boyhood friend and computer software developer Pavel Bouska came from Munich to Colorado to help in 1988.

Clearing the Hurdles: 1992–97

In 1992, with Bouska's computer system up and running, the newly named Corporate Express, Inc. (changed from Business Express in 1990) had attained 10 percent operating margins and would reach $65 million in sales by 1995. Striking out for the territories, Rysavy acquired his first companies outside of Colorado. The $31.6 million company acquired Trick & Murray, a $15 million office supply company, merging it with two other acquisitions in the Seattle area. In order to convince Trick & Murray to sell, Rysavy promised in three years to reach sales of $300 million. But at the end of 1992, the company posted revenues of $420 million. A year later, revenues rose to $520 million and the company continued its skyward climb. In 1994, after going public through an initial offering of nine million shares at $7 per share, the company completed six acquisitions in exchange for 1.7 million shares of stock swapped and revenues skyrocketed to $1.15 billion. Among these was the acquisition of New Jersey-based Hanson Office Products, which was purchased from the U.K. firm Hanson PLC.

In 1995, the company moved forcefully into the international market with several foreign acquisitions. With over 14,000 employees in over 500 locations, the company's revenues reached an unprecedented $1.89 billion. Analysts estimated the company would reach $3 billion in the year 2000. They were wrong.

With two acquisitions in 1996, the company became a major player in the distribution of desktop software to corporations, both domestically and internationally. In February, the company acquired Young, a distributor of computer and imaging supplies and accessories, in a 4.4 million share stock swap. In October, Corporate Express acquired France's leading supplier of computer software, the Paris-based company Nimsa, in a 1.1 million share stock swap and $2.3 million in cash. That month, the company also acquired a 51 percent interest in The Chisholm Group in the United Kingdom.

In order to deliver all of its product lines more efficiently, the company created its own delivery system. In March 1996 the company acquired U.S. Delivery Systems, Inc. (USDS), the largest local same-day delivery service in the United States, in a 23.4 million share stock swap. USDS was later renamed Corporate Express Delivery Systems, Inc. (CEDS); subsequently acquired delivery companies were merged into CEDS. Strengthening its domestic delivery infrastructure, the company acquired, in November, United TransNet, Inc. (UTI), the second largest same-day delivery service provider in the United States, in a 6.3 million share stock swap.

In 1996, the company acquired 104 firms, including 46 domestic office product distributors, 32 international office product distributors, and 11 delivery service companies for a total of $241.9 million in cash and approximately 3.6 million shares of stock swapped. Of the 32 international acquisitions, nine were in Canada, seven were in the United Kingdom, five were in Australia, and three were in New Zealand. With five acquisitions in Germany, two in Italy, and one (Nimsa) in France, Corporate Express entered the markets in those countries for the first time. In November, the company purchased the remaining 49 percent interest in The Chisholm Group in a stock swap and with options of up to $3.3 million, pushing the international operations of the company to account for approximately 18 percent of the company's total revenue. Another 1996 acquisition was Buffalo Grove, Illinois-based ASAP Software Express, Inc., a major distributor of software.

From the company's inception, it had been uniquely focused on the development and deployment of innovative technology. In its early years, Corporate Express introduced inventory management systems far more sophisticated than those of many large corporations, systems that could electronically track sales and inventory by item and accurately predict future sales and inventory requirements. The company's belief in the competitive power of technology caused it to routinely reinvest much of its profits into the development of these proprietary information management systems. In 1996, approximately 300 systems architects and engineers were on the payroll of Corporate Express, showing the strength of the company's commitment to ongoing systems development and implementation.

In September, the company unveiled and began to implement a major upgrade to its proprietary global electronic commerce system. The company released ISIS 3.0, a new generation of hardware, software, and networking capabilities. When

Key Dates:

1986: Jirka Rysavy acquires an office supply store in Boulder, Colorado, for $100; he renames it Business Express and reorients it toward corporate accounts.
1988: Rysavy acquires the office products division of Denver-based NBI Inc. for $12.8 million.
1990: Business Express is renamed Corporate Express, Inc.
1992: Revenues reach $420 million.
1994: Company goes public through an IPO, selling nine million shares at $7 per share; following the completion of six acquisitions, revenues skyrocket to $1.15 billion.
1996: Company enters the local same-day delivery service market with the purchase of U.S. Delivery Systems, Inc., which is later renamed Corporate Express Delivery Systems, Inc.; ASAP Software Express, Inc. is acquired.
1998: Overly rapid expansion leads to falling profits and a sagging stock price; company launches restructuring involving the closure of 100 offices and the elimination of 1,700 jobs.
1999: Corporate Express is acquired by Buhrmann N.V. for $2.3 billion and becomes a subsidiary of the Dutch firm.
2001: Corporate Express acquires the North American office products operations of U.S. Office Products Company.

completed, it would be a dynamic program integrating all facets of the company's processes, organizational structure, systems, and customer service. The three-tier client/server computer architecture was the backbone of the company's Corporate Supplier model, seamlessly integrating the customer's desktop with the company's distribution and service capabilities.

The back end of the system consisted of the actual Corporate Express company infrastructure, controlling product inventory, pricing, contracts, business practices, and delivery. Each customer account was customized by facility, price, supplier, and item. The centralized structure also allowed the consolidation of all customers' orders and invoicing, a capability especially valuable to corporations with multiple locations, as well as potentially providing a direct interface to their general ledger system. In addition, the back end system continually tracked and analyzed cost and demand patterns, allowing the company to forecast optimal reorder times and quantities, enabling the company to turn its inventory well in excess of the industry average and offering the customers a higher level of service.

At the front end, the customer's desktop, the system offered order entry featuring powerful search and display capabilities, rapid price lookup, customized order and payment approval, routing, and a secure connection for electronic commerce, allowing orders to be transmitted via a full range of traditional or electronic connections. The system was available to the customer without charge in a variety of formats, including a customized interface with customers' Intranet facilities. Certain key customers began testing an Internet version of the system in late 1996.

Within five years, the company's revenues had grown from $32 million to a staggering $3.2 billion, a 58 percent increase over 1995 revenues of $1.89 billion, blowing analysts' previous-year estimates away, and the company declared a 50 percent share dividend of its common stock, giving each shareholder an additional share of stock for every two shares held.

In 1997, the company continued its skyrocketing growth rate with more acquisitions. January saw the company acquiring Hermann Marketing, Inc. (HMI), the largest privately held supplier of promotional products to large corporations in the United States, Canada, the United Kingdom, and the Netherlands, in a 4.6 million share stock swap. HMI was soon renamed Corporate Express Promotional Marketing, Inc. Also in January, the company acquired Sofco-Mead, Inc. (SMI), one of the largest suppliers of janitorial and cleaning supplies in the United States, in a 2.6 million share stock swap. The company that same month moved into its new world headquarters in Broomfield, Colorado, which consisted of four interconnected octagons totaling 160,000 square feet of space; located at One Environmental Way, the building reflected Rysavy's commitment to the environment in that all materials for the building were chosen with the environment in mind.

By February, Corporate Express had acquired 15 additional companies, including St. Paul Book and Stationery, Inc. The St. Paul, Minnesota-based company was founded in 1851 and was one of the largest and oldest independent contract stationers in the United States. By June, the company had already acquired 13 additional companies for a total of $24.7 million. Two of the companies were contract stationers in Italy. Katro S.p.A. and Asite S.p.A. were purchased and consolidated into a new 120,000-square-foot distribution center located in Milan. Two other contract stationers were acquired in Cologne and Leipzig, Germany. The remaining nine acquisitions were in North America, including Everything for the Office, a $20 million-a-year contract stationer in Minneapolis, Minnesota.

September brought a definitive merger agreement with Data Documents Incorporated, a leading provider of forms management services and systems and custom business forms to large corporate customers, in a $195 million stock swap. The Omaha, Nebraska-based Data Documents added 85 new locations to the company and it would later be combined with several other acquired companies to form Corporate Express Document & Print Management, Inc.

By mid-1997, the company employed some 27,000 people and operated from approximately 700 locations throughout the world, including 80 distribution centers located in the United States, Canada, Australia, New Zealand, Germany, France, Italy, and the United Kingdom. Customers were able to select desired products and place orders by various means of electronic commerce, telephone, or fax, and receive next-business-day delivery via the company's fleet of over 10,000 delivery vehicles.

Consolidation Difficulties, Loss of Independence: 1998–99

Trouble consolidating the numerous acquisitions began in 1997 and accelerated in 1998, and Corporate Express's earnings started to fall below analysts expectations and its stock price started to sag. The most troubling areas were operations in the United Kingdom and Corporate Express Delivery Systems. The consolidation of the latter was particularly nettlesome as it proved extremely difficult to create a national delivery service from the combination of many small, regionally based firms. Revenues at the delivery unit grew to more than $700 million by 1998, but the operation was losing money. Corporate Express was further troubled by a high debt load that had been incurred as a result of the acquisitions spree.

Under increasing pressure from shareholders, Rysavy began relinquishing power at the company. Robert King, who had been hired as president and COO in 1993, took over the CEO position in September 1998, with Rysavy remaining chairman. Before joining Corporate Express, King had been chief executive of Dallas-based FoxMeyer Health Corporation, a distributor of pharmaceuticals and healthcare products. In December of that year the company launched a major worldwide restructuring involving the closure of 100 offices and the laying off of 1,700 employees, or 6 percent of the global workforce. The company also announced that it was seeking to reduce its ownership interest in the delivery unit or to sell it outright. The restructuring involved a charge of $55 million, and an additional $60 million loss was recorded from the operations of the delivery business, which had been declared a discontinued operation. As a result, Corporate Express reported a net loss for the fiscal year ending in January 1999 of $73.3 million. Revenues for the year totaled $3.75 billion.

By early 1999 the company's stock price had plunged to under $5.50, having traded for as high as $30 in June 1996. Takeover rumors had been swirling for months, and in January 1999 two investment management companies that together held 7.1 percent of Corporate Express's shares, Marlin Management LLC and Brahman Management LLC, urged that Rysavy be ousted from the company board and that a merger with another company be explored. In February Rysavy stepped aside as chairman of the firm but remained on the board as chairman emeritus. A new chairman was not named, but the company said that King would ''assume additional executive responsibilities.'' The company also reiterated its plans to sell the delivery unit and also said that it was seeking to sell its Sofco janitorial supplies subsidiary, which had annual sales of $160 million in fiscal 1998. In June 1999 Corporate Express sold Sofco to U.S. Foodservice for $56 million.

In July 1999 Corporate Express agreed to be bought by Buhrmann N.V., a Dutch firm that owned one of Corporate Express's main U.S. rivals, Chicago-based BT Office Products, and was also involved in paper merchanting and the distribution of graphic systems in Europe. Rysavy and one other director on the seven-person board voted against the merger. Shareholders also filed class-action lawsuits objecting to the deal, but these suits failed to derail the merger or to change the main terms of the transaction, which was completed in October. Buhrmann paid $9.70 in cash per Corporate Express share, or $1.1 billion, and also assumed $1.2 billion in Corporate Express debt. One month prior, Corporate Express sold Corporate Express Delivery Systems to United Shipping & Technology Inc. for about $60 million.

New Life As Subsidiary: Early 21st Century

With the merger, Rysavy's involvement in Corporate Express ended, although the founder managed to insist that the firm remain headquartered in Broomfield. Operating as a wholly owned subsidiary of Buhrmann, Corporate Express absorbed the operations of BT Office Products during 2000, further strengthening its position as the leading business-to-business supplier of office products in the United States. In addition to maintaining its number one position in the Australian market through its ownership of a 52 percent interest in Corporate Express Australia Ltd., Corporate Express, Inc. also bolstered its position in Europe through the amalgamation of Buhrmann office supplies operations there and became the number two player in that market. Already in 2000, under the stewardship of Buhrmann, Corporate Express began growing again through several smaller acquisitions in Europe and Australia, most notably the purchase of ANFA S.A., which marked the company's entrance into the French market. Revenues for 2000 surpassed the $6 billion mark, with $4.7 billion generated in North America and $1.33 billion in Europe and Australia.

Corporate Express continued its resurgent growth in 2001, completing two significant acquisitions. In May the firm purchased the North American office products operations of U.S. Office Products Company in a $172 million transaction. U.S. Office Products had filed for Chapter 11 bankruptcy protection, then began selling off its assets. Based in Washington, D.C., U.S. Office Products was the fifth largest supplier of office products to businesses, generating about $1 billion in sales from 16 distribution centers and more than 90 sales offices. Its focus on serving small and mid-size businesses made for a good fit with Corporate Express's concentration on larger companies. Also in May 2001, Buhrmann announced that it would cut between 1,000 and 1,200 jobs worldwide in response to weakening economic conditions that were resulting in softening sales of office products. In the other acquisition completed in 2001, Buhrmann purchased the office supplies operations of Netherlands-based Samas-Groep N.V. for EUR 321 million. This deal strengthened Corporate Express's position in the Benelux countries, Germany, the United Kingdom, and Ireland. In late 2001 Mark Hoffman was promoted from president to president and CEO of Corporate Express's North American operations following the departure of King, while Rudi de Becker, who had joined the company through the Samas-Groep acquisition, was selected to head up Corporate Express Europe. Revenues increased 11 percent in North America in 2001, reaching $5.22 billion, and in Europe sales increased 13 percent, to $1.5 billion.

Principal Subsidiaries

ASAP Software Express, Inc.; Corporate Express Document & Print Management, Inc.; Corporate Express Promotional Marketing, Inc.; Corporate Express Australia Ltd. (52%); Corporate Express Ges.m.b.H. (Austria); Corporate Express Belgium N.V.; Corporate Express Denmark; ASAP Software S.A.S. (France); Corporate Express France/ANFA S.A.; Corporate Express Deutschland GmbH (Germany); Corporate Express Hungary; Corporate Express Holding (Ireland) Limited; Corporate Express SpA (Italy); Corporate Express Luxembourg/Eugène Hoffmann Sarl; Corporate Express Europe B.V. (Netherlands); Buhrmann Office Products Nederland B.V. (Netherlands); Corporate Express Document Automatisering B.V. (Netherlands); DocVision B.V. (Netherlands); Corporate Express New Zealand Ltd. (52%); Corporate Express Polska Sp.z.o.o. (Poland); Corporate Express Svenska AB (Sweden); Corporate Express Ltd. (U.K.).

Principal Divisions

Corporate Express Imaging & Computer Graphic Supplies.

Principal Competitors

Office Depot, Inc.; Boise Office Solutions; OfficeMax, Inc.; Staples, Inc.; Moore Corporation Limited; Guilbert S.A.

Further Reading

Accola, John, "Corporate Express to Buy Rival for $250 Million," *Denver Rocky Mountain News,* March 6, 2001, p. 5B.

——, "Office Product Giant Merges: Corporate Express Set to Buy Omaha Company for Nearly $200 Million," *Denver Rocky Mountain News,* September 12, 1997, p. 1B.

Avery, Susan, "Can Consolidated Continue?," *Purchasing,* October 17, 1996, p. 93.

Edgerton, Jerry, "These Six Small Stocks Promise Big Gains," *Money,* Winter 1996, p. 66.

Everitt, Lisa Greim, "Investors Push for Ouster, Merger Critics Say Corporate Express Is Rudderless," *Denver Rocky Mountain News,* January 5, 1999, p. 1B.

"The Hottest Entrepreneurs in America," *Inc.,* December 1995, p. 35.

"Jirka Rysavy: Chairman and CEO, Corporate Express," *Chain Store Age Executive with Shopping Center Age,* December 1995, p. 54.

"Jirka Rysavy, Corporate Express," *PI,* September 1996.

Ketelsen, James, "Learning the Hard Way," *Forbes,* December 18, 1995, p. 130.

Laderman, Jeffrey M., "Don't Worry, Be Bullish," *Business Week,* August 4, 1997, pp. 28–29.

——, "Three IPOs That'll Let You in on the Ground Floor," *Business Week,* June 6, 1994, p. 108.

Leib, Jeffrey, "Fixing a Wounded Company: Growing Too Fast Led to Trouble for Corporate Express," *Denver Post,* March 7, 1999, p. J1.

——, "Office Suppliers Plan to Merge: Dutch to Take Over Corporate Express," *Denver Post,* July 14, 1999, p. C1.

——, "Supply Firm Maps Layoffs: Corporate Express Cutting 1,700 Jobs," *Denver Post,* December 10, 1998, p. C1.

Locke, Tom, "Corporate Express Inc. Executive Finds Meditation Key to Success," *Boulder (Colo.) Daily Camera,* March 18, 1997.

Martin, Katrina, "Corporate Express Makes Deal to Divest Delivery-Service Unit," *Denver Post,* September 10, 1999, p. C4.

Mullins, Robert, "Supply Firms Take New Owners, Battle with Chains," *Business Journal-Milwaukee,* April 15, 1995, p. 2A.

Raabe, Steve, "Company Founder Steps Aside: Corporate Express Seeks Investors, Tries to Refocus," *Denver Post,* February 9, 1999, p. C1.

——, "Corporate Express Buys 17 Companies," *Denver Post,* February 5, 1997, p. D1.

Richter, Konstantin, and Erik Siemers, "Buhrmann Is Buying Corporate Express in Agreement Valued at $1.1 Billion," *Wall Street Journal,* July 14, 1999, p. B8.

Rutledge, Tanya, "Office Products Giant to Build Mega-Project," *Houston Business Journal,* October 25, 1996, p. 1A.

Schine, Eric, "The Mountain Man of Office Gear," *Business Week,* May 5, 1997, pp. 114, 116–17.

Schonfeld, Erick, "Delivering Growth," *Fortune,* September 4, 1995, p. 137.

Svaldi, Aldo, "Corporate Express Shares Rebound from March Fall," *Denver Business Journal,* July 4, 1997, p. 4A.

Tejada, Carlos, "Corporate Express's Chairman Resigns," *Wall Street Journal,* February 8, 1999, p. B4.

——, "Corporate Express Urged to Replace Chairman Rysavy," *Wall Street Journal,* January 5, 1999, p. B8.

Vasquez, Beverly, "Corporate Express Turns 100: Dealmaking Flurry Makes Boulder Office Supplier Nation's Largest," *Denver Business Journal,* February 28, 1997, p. 6B.

—Daryl F. Mallett
—update: David E. Salamie

Direct
FOCUS Inc.

Direct Focus, Inc.

1400 NE 136th Avenue
Vancouver, Washington 98684
U.S.A.
Telephone: (360)694-7722
Fax: (360) 694-7755
Web site: http://www.directfocusinc.com

Public Company
Incorporated: 1986 as Bow Flex of America, Inc.
Employees: 398
Sales: $363.9 million (2001)
Stock Exchanges: NASDAQ
Ticker Symbol: DFXI
NAIC: 339999 All Other Miscellaneous Manufacturing

Direct Focus, Inc. is a Vancouver, Washington, direct marketing company originally dedicated to the manufacture and marketing of the Bowflex exercise machines. Since building up its sales operation, the company has expanded to market other products, developed either internally, such as a high-tech air mattress, or externally through acquisition, such as the fitness products gained through the purchase of Nautilus, StairMaster, and Schwinn fitness equipment. Direct Focus has achieved spectacular results, due in large part to its sophisticated direct marketing model. The company employs what it calls a "two-step" approach. Customer interest is generated through one-minute television commercials and infomercials, which generally appear on cable channels, as well as through print advertising. Once customers inquire about a product, Direct Focus follows up with response mailings and outbound telemarketing to convert interest into sales. The Internet has also become an important tool, generating an increasing level of sales while fitting in nicely with the company's overall marketing effort. Not only do product web sites generate interest and provide a depository of detailed information, they offer a chance to close a sale at any time of day. While Bowflex and the air mattresses are sold exclusively through the company's direct marketing operations, Nautilus, Schwinn, and StairMaster fitness products are sold to health clubs and sporting goods retailers. In addition, Direct Focus is testing the possibility of selling nutritional supplements and is active in searching for new products that it can sell through direct marketing.

Conception of Bowflex: 1979

The Bowflex exercise machine was invented by Tessema Dosho Shifferaw, who was born in Ethiopia, the son of a prominent army general. He was a teenager attending college in California when in September 1974 the Ethiopian government, headed by Emperor Haile Selassie, was toppled by a socialist revolution. Shifferaw's father, mother, and brother were jailed, and his father was ultimately executed. Shifferaw, who came from a rich and influential family and was well positioned for a political career, now found himself penniless in a foreign land. He moved to San Francisco and drove a cab to earn his way through San Francisco City College, where he studied industrial design. It was in 1979 that he first conceived of a new weight training machine that relied on a system of "power rods" and pulleys to provide increased resistance, as well as being easy to store.

Shifferaw spent several years refining the product, while lining up a group of investors, who incorporated Bow Flex of America, Inc. in California in 1986. They then hired Brian R. Cook, the current chairman and chief executive officer of Direct Focus, to form a company and develop the Bowflex technology commercially. Cook was a certified public accountant who earned a bachelor of arts degree in business administration from Western Washington University. He had worked as an accountant for Peat, Marwick, Mitchell & Co., then served as the chief financial officer for a manufacturer of industrial fasteners and held a number of financial and managerial positions at Sea Galley Stores, a restaurant chain. From 1986 to 1987, Bow Flex developed its first product and secured a patent on the power rod and pulley technology. Initially, Cook approached retailers about carrying the new machine but received a tepid response. He also made an early attempt to use direct marketing but in 1988 signed an exclusive distribution deal with Schwinn Cycling and Fitness, producing a new model called the Schwinn Bowflex.

The Schwinn arrangement lasted five years, during which Cook and his young company were able to mature and learn the fitness business. When Schwinn began to experience serious financial difficulties in the early 1990s, it appeared that the future for the Bowflex machine was dim. In order to induce Cook and another executive to stay on with the company, Shifferaw cut them in on a share of his royalties. When Schwinn went bankrupt in 1993, Cook was then able to terminate the exclusive distribution arrangement. In order to stand on its own, the company, which changed its name to Bow Flex, Inc., began to develop a direct marketing program to sell its new generation of the Bowflex system, the Power Pro line, funded by $2 million raised through a public offering on the Toronto Stock Exchange. From 1993 to 1995, Bow Flex refined its marketing approach and infrastructure. Although sales showed little improvement between 1994 and 1995, increasing from just $4.4 million to $4.8 million, the company turned a $510,000 loss in 1994 into a modest $15,000 net profit in 1995. More importantly, the company was now poised in 1996 to launch its first widespread direct marketing campaign, which helped to support the new Motivator line, an entry level Bowflex system. Revenues in 1996 almost doubled the results of the previous year, climbing to $8.5 million, while net income improved to $693,000.

Infomercials Launched in 1997

In 1997, Bow Flex introduced a "zero-down" financing program through a third party finance company, and it also tripled its advertising budget to about $9.5 million in order to launch its first infomercials, resulting in a sharp spike in sales. Revenues grew by 134 percent, to $19.9 million, and net income showed even more impressive improvement, topping $2.4 million. Clearly the company had developed a solid direct marketing operation and protected its Bowflex franchise by refusing to sell it through any other avenues. Corporate philosophy maintained that if customers knew that Bowflex was available at a store, they would be less likely to respond to the advertising call for immediate action. Nevertheless, the company had to face the reality that no matter how polished the sales operation, the life of a home fitness product rarely lasted for more than ten to 15 years. Constant improvements and the introduction of new models was part of the program as well, but Cook recognized the need for diversity. By now the company was in reality a direct marketing business that happened to sell a fitness product. There was no reason that the company's approach could not be applied to other products.

In late 1997 the company began to review possible new products to market. To reflect the changing nature of its business, in May 1998 Bow Flex changed its name to Direct Focus, Inc. In August of that year, it began to test market a second product, a high-end airbed mattress that permitted users to adjust the firmness on either side of the bed. Unlike most direct marketers, Direct Focus preferred higher cost, high quality products. The new airbed system, under the brand name "In-

stant Comfort," was a good fit within that approach. Moreover, the mattress market was large, representing over $7.5 billion in annual retail sales in the United States. Late in 1998, Direct Focus also diversified within the fitness sector when it acquired the Nautilus line of equipment from Delta Woodside Industries at a cost of $18.8 million, which included $16 million in cash and the assumption of $2.8 million in liabilities. Acquiring Nautilus, the best-known brand name in the fitness industry, was considered a coup for Direct Focus. A textile and fabric manufacturer, Delta Woodside had purchased Nautilus in 1993 with the intent of selling sportswear apparel under the Nautilus label, an idea that failed to pan out for the company, which then licensed the Nautilus name to other apparel companies. The business had been on the block for several months before Direct Focus stepped in and was able to pick up Nautilus at what was considered a highly reasonable price.

In 1998, Direct Focus posted results that were again a dramatic improvement over the previous year, with revenues totaling $63.1 million and net profits reaching nearly $12.5 million. The company encountered one problem in 1998 when it was sued by Soloflex, a prime competitor in the home fitness market. Soloflex alleged that Direct Focus copied its marketing strategies, stole marketing slogans, and made misleading, negative claims about the Soloflex system. Moreover, Soloflex named Randy Potter, Direct Focus's vice-president for marketing, as a defendant in the suit. Before joining Bow Flex of America in 1991, Potter had served as a Soloflex model. The matter would be settled a year later when Direct Focus agreed to pay $8 million.

It was an active year for Direct Focus in 1999. The company netted $15.1 million on a public offering of stock, which now began trading on the NASDAQ. It also took over Nautilus in the beginning of the year and initiated efforts to incorporate it into its business mix. It cut the workforce at the Nautilus plant in Virginia by 50 employees and introduced new products for sale under the Nautilus name: a weight bench and a strength station. Rather than direct marketing, Nautilus equipment, for both the home and clubs, were sold to specialty fitness and upper end sporting goods retailers. In addition, Direct Focus decided to apply the Nautilus name to its airbed mattresses, which now became known as the Nautilus Sleep System and was launched in December 1999. Like Bowflex it would be exclusively sold through the company's direct marketing operation, which began in 1999 to experience tangible benefits from its Internet site. Until late in the year the site was purely informational, lacking the ability to conduct sales transactions online, yet email leads from the site resulted in 10 percent of the company's overall sales. For the year, Direct Focus again posted impressive results: Revenues for 1999 more than doubled the previous year's total, exceeding $133 million, while net income climbed to $20.3 million. Investors, however, remained somewhat skeptical of the company, opting to wait to see how successful it would be in leveraging the Nautilus name. As a result, Direct Focus stock was considered undervalued by management, prompting the company to institute a buyback program in early 2000.

Direct Focus augmented its Internet business by introducing online credit in 2000. Direct Focus was hardly a dot-com business, but the Internet was such a natural fit with its direct marketing operation, and cost less per sale, that the company was fully committed to maximizing its e-commerce potential. Direct Focus introduced new products under the Nautilus label, including a number of multi-functional home-gym machines, but the major revenue producer for the company remained the direct sale of Bowflex. With the Internet now providing 25 percent of all direct sales, Direct Focus produced revenues of nearly $224 million and net income of $41.6 million in 2000. That kind of rapid growth was now hard to ignore, and *Business Week* ranked Direct Focus at the top of its list of "Hot Growth Companies" for 2000.

Schwinn Fitness Products Acquired in 2001

Direct Focus aggressively pursued external growth in 2001. It signed a deal with Champion Nutrition, a California manufacturer of nutritional supplements that gained prominence after signing an endorsement deal with baseball star Mark McGuire. Direct Focus agreed to loan $3 million to Champion and gained a 15-month option to purchase the company for $6 million. Champion planned to use the money, as well as names from the Bowflex customer database, to ramp up its marketing efforts. In effect, Direct Focus would have a chance to determine if the supplements business achieved synergy with its fitness products before having to decide if it wanted to buy Champion. Also in 2001, Direct Focus became reconnected to Schwinn. In June, a former Bow Flex executive who had gone to work for Schwinn, Kevin Lamar, returned to the company, taking over as president, an unoccupied slot in the organization. He had gone over to Schwinn in 1989 and was instrumental in building up a fitness equipment business.

The 106-year-old Schwinn was now once again in financial straits and Direct Focus offered $140 million for the company, although it was only interested in acquiring the fitness operation and had a partner, Huffy Corp., ready to purchase the cycling division for $68.3 million. Rather than accept the offer, however, Schwinn filed for Chapter 11 bankruptcy protection in July 2001 and other suitors for the cycling division weighed in. In September, Direct Focus completed a successful bid for the Schwinn fitness division, agreeing to pay $65 million in cash, a significant reduction on its pre-bankruptcy offer. As with the Nautilus acquisition, Direct Focus was able to acquire a solid brand at minimal cost, adding both the Schwinn and Trimline labels and a popular line of cardio-equipment, including treadmills, stationary bikes, and steppers. It was expected that Direct Focus would tab one or more of its new aerobic machines to join Bowflex and the Nautilus Sleep System as products sold exclusively through its successful direct marketing operation. In the meantime, another prominent exercise brand appeared on the company's radar screen, StairMaster Sports/Medical, Inc., which had also been forced into bankruptcy and was on the block. In court filings the only potential purchaser listed was Direct Focus, which stood to yet again pick up a major brand at distressed prices. In January 2002 the company successfully bid $25 million to acquire StairMaster and its line of stair-climbing machines, elliptical trainers, and treadmills.

Shortly after the StairMaster announcement, Direct Focus released its 2001 results, again showing massive gains over the previous year. Revenues for the year totaled almost $363.9 million and net income grew to $66.6 million. Following a year in which it made two significant acquisitions, Direct Focus still had no debt and nearly $52 million in cash at its disposal. It was now positioned as a leading manufacturer of fitness equipment with the ability to sell directly to customers as well as through retailers in both the home and club markets. Moreover, its direct sales operation was now finely tuned and the company actively looked for new product ideas to feed into the system. Not only was it generating ideas internally, the company's success resulted in a constant pitch of products from outside sources. Direct Focus remained thorough in its evaluation of new products, however, and it was likely that it would not stray far from its current product lines, nor would it act too hastily. It was unlikely that the company could continue to maintain its accelerated pace of mounting revenues and profits, but there was no reason to doubt its ability to continue a steady upward trend.

Principal Competitors

Sybex International; Icon Health & Fitness, Inc.; Select Comfort Corporation; Soloflex.

Further Reading

Binole, Gina, "When Buff Isn't Enough," *Business Journal-Portland,* April 20, 1998.

"Brian R. Cook, Direct Focus, Inc.," *Wall Street Transcript,* June 2001.

"Direct Focus Flexing Its Marketing Muscle," *Business Week,* May 29, 2000, p. 184.

Frost, Bob, "Innovations: The Good Earth," September 15, 1999, http://www.cafezine.com.

Goldfield, Robert, "Bowflex Bunch Braces for New Growth Spurt," *Business Journal Portland,* March 3, 2000, p. 1.

——, "Bowflex to Muscle Up with Nautilus," *Business Journal-Portland,* November 20, 1998, p 1.

——, "Nautilus Sales Bolster Growth of Direct Focus," *Business Journal-Portland,* May 14, 1999, p 5.

——, "When 'Salary + Bonus' Fails to Tell the Whole Story," *Business Journal-Portland,* August 17, 2001, p 1.

—Ed Dinger

Dorsey & Whitney LLP

50 South Sixth Street, Suite 1500
Minneapolis, Minnesota 55402-1498
U.S.A.
Telephone: (612) 340-2600
Fax: (612) 340-2868
Web site: http://www.dorseylaw.com

Partnership
Founded: 1912
Employees: 1,773
Gross Billings: $254 million (2000 est.)
NAIC: 541110 Offices of Lawyers

One of the world's major law firms, Dorsey & Whitney LLP has approximately 700 lawyers who practice from offices in Minneapolis (its headquarters), New York City, Denver, Vancouver, Seattle, Salt Lake City, Tokyo, Shanghai, Hong Kong, London, Brussels, Toronto, Washington, D.C., and elsewhere Its rapid growth in the 1990s added hundreds of lawyers. The partnership's best known lawyer is Walter Mondale, the head of its Asian practice who served as President Jimmy Carter's vice-president and, later as the U.S. ambassador to Japan from 1993 to 1996. Dorsey & Whitney's longest-running major client is the First Bank National Association, formerly called the First National Bank of Minneapolis. Other representative clients include Northwest Airlines, Mayo Clinic, and Aetna Life & Casualty.

Origins and Early Law Practice

The firm began as a two-man office in Minneapolis in 1912. In 1929 the firm then known as Junell, Dorsey, Oakley & Driscoll, headed by John Junell, James E. Dorsey, Robert S. Oakley, and Robert Driscoll, had 11 lawyers. Dorsey (1889–1959) had been admitted to the bar in 1914 after earning an A.B. in 1910 at the University of Minnesota and an LL.B. at Harvard in 1913. By 1936 the renamed firm of Junell, Driscoll, Fletcher, Dorsey & Baker had 20 lawyers. In 1940 the partnership was called Fletcher, Dorsey, Barker, Colman & Barber, but in the early 1940s it became Dorsey, Colman, Barker, Scott & Barber.

The firm's early practice seemed fairly typical, with its banking, insurance, and utility clients. In the 1920s it was counsel for the First National Bank of Minneapolis and was located in the First National-Soo Line Building. Several other large law firms in their early history were located in buildings owned by a major bank client. Clients in 1929 included the First Minneapolis Trust Company, Minneapolis Street Railway Company, Ocean Accident & Indemnity Company, and the W.B. Foshay Company.

In 1940 the firm's growing insurance practice included being special or local counsel to Equitable Life Assurance Society, New York Life Insurance Company, The Great-West Life Assurance Company, and four other insurance companies or departments. New clients added by 1945 included Piper, Jaffray & Hopwood; Pittsburgh Coal Company; the Minnesota Group Investment Bankers Association of America; and the Mayo Clinic in Rochester, Minnesota.

Post-World War II Developments

The firm grew slowly in the immediate postwar era, reaching a total of 24 lawyers in 1950 and 31 in 1955. It continued to serve long-term clients such as Cargill, Inc.; Donaldson Company, Inc.; and the Otter Tail Power Company. By 1965 it had almost doubled in size to have 59 lawyers under the name of Dorsey, Owen, Marquart, Windhorst & West.

The Dorsey firm continued its rapid growth, expanding from 77 lawyers in 1970 to 164 in 1980. During that time the firm opened new Minnesota offices in St. Paul, Rochester, Wayzata, and Chaska. The last two offices later were closed. By 1980 the firm was renamed Dorsey, Windhorst, Hannaford, Whitney & Halladay. In the early 1980s the firm began its expansion outside of Minnesota with new offices in Billings, Great Falls, New York, and Paris.

This rapid postwar growth not surprisingly was accompanied by specialization. As late as 1965 the firm described itself in the *Martindale-Hubbell Law Directory* as having a "General Practice." Just ten years later it had a "General Practice, including Patent, Trademark and Copyright Law. International Business and Taxation Law, State, Municipal and Public Authority Financing."

In 1984 name partner Arthur B. Whitney, Jr., retired after about 40 years at the firm. As head of the firm's public finance

---

Company Perspectives:

Because business doesn't stop at 5 p.m. in your time zone, you need a law firm that works 24 hours a day. A firm whose capabilities don't stop at domestic borders. A firm whose dedication to client service is a global priority.

Dorsey & Whitney LLP is that law firm.

Because we have locations worldwide we are able to offer you outstanding service wherever your business and legal needs take you.

---

department, Whitney had helped rewrite part of the Minnesota Constitution that granted the state government authority to issue general obligation bonds. One of Whitney's other contributions was assisting in drafting laws to form the St. Paul Port Authority.

In 1985 firm attorney Robert Helmick became the new volunteer president of the U.S. Olympic Committee (USOC), and four years later he received a permanent appointment as a member of the Executive Board of the International Olympic Committee (IOC). After allegations in *USA Today* that clients with Olympic ties had paid him at least $127,000 in legal fees, Helmick in 1991 resigned as USOC president due to an appearance of conflict of interest but remained on the IOC board.

One of Dorsey & Whitney's clients was the famous Mayo Clinic in Rochester, Minnesota. In 1986 the clinic's parent Mayo Foundation decided to partially pay bondholders who had invested $39 million in the Charter House, a retirement home occupied mostly by former patients at the clinic. The foundation made this decision to avoid public relations and legal problems that could have developed. Dorsey & Whitney also represented First Bank Minneapolis, which served Mayo and was trustee to the Charter House bondholders. In addition, there were allegations of conflict of interest since the law firm also served as bond counsel, but Dorsey & Whitney was replaced by Kirtland & Ellis when Charter House faced Chapter 11 bankruptcy proceedings.

Dorsey & Whitney in January 1988 merged with the 15-lawyer Washington, D.C. firm of Busby, Rehm and Leonard. With the U.S. economy rapidly growing in the 1980s, many law firms added to their ranks and opened new domestic and international offices. Thus it was not surprising that John B. Rehm said in the *Washington Post* on October 22, 1990, that his small firm "saw larger firms moving in and we couldn't offer the same services . . . We began to feel that the day of the boutique was ending. I hate to say it . . . but I'm afraid economic pressures are driving us to bigger and bigger firms."

By 1990 the firm also added new offices in Missoula and London. Its client list included Porsche Cars North America, Inc.; Super Valu Stores, Inc.; Ford Motor Company; and General Mills, Inc.

Developments in the 1990s and the New Millennium

In 1994 and 1995 Dorsey & Whitney helped Computer Network Technology (CNT) Corporation to finally start selling its products in South Korea. The law firm worked with federal officials, such as the U.S. ambassador to South Korea, to overcome South Korean requirements that had prevented CNT's expansion.

Dorsey & Whitney in 1995 opened an office in Hong Kong, in part because it was on neutral ground between rivals Taiwan and the People's Republic of China. Previously the firm had flown a lawyer from the United States to serve clients with Asian interests, but then decided it was better to have an actual office to work with clients such as Hormel, ADC Telecommunications, and Fourshift Corporation.

This was part of the firm's increasing international practice. By August 1996, 52 of the firm's 372 attorneys were practicing full-time in international law, up from 26 two years earlier. In addition to Hong Kong, the firm maintained foreign offices in Brussels and London. It helped United Health Care Corporation operate in South Africa.

In 1995 Dorsey & Whitney and public relations firm Mona Meyer McGrath & Gavin, a subsidiary of the United Kingdom's Shandwick International, formed a new Crisis Management Group to assist clients in preventing and dealing with emergencies. The two firms had worked together before. For example, both had served Northwest Airlines when it faced bankruptcy.

Meanwhile, the U.S. Supreme Court in 1997 made a landmark ruling that involved a Dorsey & Whitney attorney. In 1988 the firm had represented Grand Metropolitan when it made a bid to acquire Pillsbury. Although firm lawyer James O'Hagan was not involved in this transaction, he gained information about the pending deal to buy Pillsbury stock. Once the deal was announced, Pillsbury stock value shot up. O'Hagan then sold his stock for a nice $4.3 million profit.

O'Hagan was convicted of several counts of mail fraud and money laundering in violation of securities law and was sentenced to 41 months in prison. That was overturned in the Eighth Circuit Court of Appeals, but then the Supreme Court ruled that O'Hagan's conviction should stand. This case validated the misappropriation theory, which states corporate outsiders cannot use confidential information to make money in the stock market, and thus aided the Securities and Exchange Commission in its enforcement efforts.

Although Dorsey & Whitney represented organizations such as the Mayo Clinic, Fairview Hospitals, and United HealthCare, which favored less tobacco use, it also represented tobacco manufacturer Philip Morris in the late 1990s. Some argued that law firms representing both sides of a major controversy had a conflict of interest. A Mayo Clinic spokesperson admitted there were some concerns, but the clinic decided not to object, so long as the firm's lawyers working for the tobacco company did not have anything to do with the clinic. On the other hand, the University of Minnesota got rid of its Dorsey & Whitney attorney when the tobacco industry, also served by the firm, requested its medical records. In any case, several other large Minnesota law firms also represented both tobacco companies and healthcare organizations.

In 1998 Tom Moe retired after serving as Dorsey & Whitney's managing partner since 1989. Under his leadership the firm grew from 339 lawyers to 439 and increased its revenue from $84 million to $170 million in 1998, which made it the nation's 60th largest law firm in the *American Lawyer's* annual ranking.

With a strong American economy humming along, in 1998 Dorsey & Whitney discussed a merger with Seattle's Bogle &

Key Dates:

1912: The firm is founded in Minneapolis.
1983: The Billings office is opened.
1988: The firm gains a Washington, D.C. office through a merger.
1992: The Denver office is started.
1995: The firm's Hong Kong office is opened; the firm and Shandwick International cooperate to start the Crisis Management Group.
1999: New offices are opened in Vancouver, Anchorage, and Tokyo.
2001: The Billings office is closed; the Shanghai office is opened.
2002: The firm starts Dorsey Health Strategies as a healthcare consulting group.

Gates. When the talks collapsed, Dorsey initially hired 16 lawyers from Bogle & Gates. About a week later the 108-year-old Seattle firm decided to call it quits. By 1999 Dorsey had added from the closed firm a total of 50 lawyers to its Seattle office and also started a 12-person Anchorage office and a Vancouver office.

Meanwhile, Dorsey & Whitney in 1999 expanded its Denver operation by leasing offices in the Republic Plaza, which had the highest lease rate of any structure in the metro Denver area. By that time the Denver office had about 40 lawyers, up from 12 in just three years. Only the firm's offices in Minneapolis, New York, and Seattle were larger.

The firm's Asian practice expanded in the late 1990s under the leadership of Walter Mondale, former vice-president and ambassador to Japan. To complement its Hong Kong and Tokyo offices, in 2001 it opened a Shanghai office to serve the growing economy of the People's Republic of China. Its Asian clients included Toyota, Mitsubishi, and Nomura Securities.

According to Thomson Financial Securities Data, Dorsey & Whitney was the nation's top law firm from 1996 through 1999 for the number of domestic mergers and acquisitions. In 2000 its 244 deals earned the firm the number two ranking, but then in 2001 it returned to the number one spot with 287 completed deals. Dorsey & Whitney was one of the few big law firms that in 2001 increased its number of completed mergers and acquisitions. With the recession starting in March 2001, the total number of domestic deals declined from 11,000 worth $1.74 trillion in 2000 to only 7,500 deals worth $819 billion in 2001.

In the late 1990s and early 2000s, Dorsey & Whitney represented Great Plains Software when it was sold to Microsoft, the Florida Senate during the 2000 election controversy, and Nanopierce Technologies Inc. in a patent dispute.

Very rapid expansion caused the firm to move to new headquarters in Minneapolis. By 2002 the firm had left the Pillsbury Center where it had been since 1981 and moved to the newly built 27-story office building located along Nicollet Mall. Dorsey & Whitney, the anchor tenant of the new building, occupied seven floors and had the option to expand.

The firm's expansion also was seen in its national and international rankings. Based on its 1997 gross revenues of $148.5 million, it was ranked as number 58 in the United States. The *American Lawyer* ranked the firm number 56 for its 1999 gross revenues of $201.5 million. In 2000 Dorsey & Whitney increased to $254 million gross revenues, a healthy 26 percent increase from the year before, and rose to number 53. In 2000 its annual profits per partner increased 17.5 percent from 1999 to reach $370,000. Its 2000 rank based on its profits per partner was number 154.

In November 2001 the *American Lawyer,* in cooperation with London's *Legal Business,* published The Global 100 list of the world's largest law firms. Dorsey & Whitney was ranked as number 57 based on its 601 lawyers, number 64 for its gross revenue of $254 million, and number 99 for its average profits per equity partner of $370,000.

Principal Competitors

Davis Polk & Wardwell; Jones, Day, Reavis & Pogue; Skadden, Arps, Slate, Meagher & Flom.

Further Reading

Asher, Mark, and Christine Brennan, "Helmick Quits As President of USOC," *Washington Post,* September 19, 1991, p. B1.

Bailey, Jeff, and Richard Gibson, "Mayo Clinic to Bail Out Retirees' Home, Hoping to Avoid a Messy Legal Battle," *Wall Street Journal,* November 24, 1986, p. 1.

Biskupic, Joan, "High Court Agrees to Review Ruling in Insider Case," *Washington Post,* January 18, 1997, p. B1.

Coffman, Keith, "Tech Firm Lands Punch in Patent Feud Intellectual Property Rights at Root of Dispute Between Nanopierce, Inventor," *Denver Post,* December 14, 1998, p. E6.

"Dorsey & Whitney Adds 50 Lawyers to Seattle Office," *Seattle Post-Intelligencer,* March 3, 1999, p. E1.

Falstad, Jan, "Large Minneapolis Law Firm Closing Its Billings Office," *Billings Gazette,* November 15, 2001, p. 4C.

Freeborn, Dan, "Creighton Magid Melds Law, Public Relations," *Star Tribune* (Minneapolis), November 27, 1995, p. 8D.

Fryer, Alex, "Top Area Law Firm to Close—Bogle & Gates to End Practice on March 31," *Seattle Times,* February 4, 1998, p. A1.

Kerr, John, and Jennifer Dominitz, "US v O'Hagan: A Landmark Securities Law Decision," *International Financial Law Review,* October 1997, p. 67.

Klas, Mary Ellen, "Litigation Means Growing Taxpayers' Tab for Lawyers," *Palm Beach Post* (West Palm Beach, Fla.), December 1, 2000, p. 19A.

Levy, Melissa, "Dorsey & Whitney to Anchor New Tower on the Nicollet Mall" *Star Tribune* (Minneapolis), June 30, 1998, p. 1A.

Meyers, Mike, "International Law No Cinch; Dorsey & Whitney, Faegre & Benson Face Challenges in Crossing Globe," *Star Tribune* (Minneapolis), March 2, 1995, p. 1D.

——, "Mondale Provides Insights into Dealing with Japanese . . .," *Star Tribune* (Minneapolis), January 24, 1997, p. 1D.

Peterson, David, "Tobacco Trial Lands Law Firms in Odd Spot . . .," *Star Tribune* (Minneapolis), February 15, 1998, p. 1B.

Pheifer, Pat, "Arthur Whitney, 81; Was Senior Partner at Dorsey and Whitney," *Star Tribune* (Minneapolis), March 25, 1996, p. 4B.

Phelps, David, "Dorsey & Whitney Opening Office in Shanghai," *Star Tribune* (Minneapolis), February 23, 2001, p. 3D.

——, "Dorsey Forms Health-Oriented Unit," *Star Tribune* (Minneapolis), January 12, 2002, p. 2D.

——, "Law Firm and PR Agency Team Up to Create Crisis Management Group for Their Clients; Dorsey & Whitney Joins Mona Meyer in Unique Effort," *Star Tribune* (Minneapolis), September 14, 1995, p. 1D.

——, "Law Firms Are Following Their Clients into International Markets; Twin Cities-Area Firms Finding Opportunities Around the World," *Star Tribune* (Minneapolis), August 5, 1996, p. 1D.

Rebchook, John, "Law Firm Leases Republic Space Minneapolis-Based Dorsey & Whitney Takes Downtown Office," *Denver Rocky Mountain News,* May 25, 1999, p. 4B.

Savona, Dave, "Washington Opens the Korean Door," *International Business,* September 1995, p. 36.

Walsh, Sharon, "Prosperous Law Firms Are Bracing for Stormier Economic Conditions; Leaner Times Bring More Scrutiny to Hiring, Cuts in Spending," *Washington Post,* October 22, 1990, p. F1.

—David M. Walden

Dow Jones & Company, Inc.

World Financial Center
200 Liberty Street
New York, New York 10281
U.S.A.
Telephone: (212) 416-2000
Fax: (212) 416-4348
Web site: http://www.dowjones.com

Public Company
Incorporated: 1930
Employees: 8,100
Sales: $1.77 billion (2001)
Stock Exchanges: New York
Ticker Symbol: DJ
NAIC: 511110 Newspaper Publishers; 511120 Periodical
    Publishers (pt); 514191 On-Line Information Services;
    514110 News Syndicates

Dow Jones & Company, Inc. is best known for publishing the *Wall Street Journal* in its U.S., Asian, and European versions and for the worldwide stock market intelligence it provides. Like much of the business-journalism industry, Dow Jones has diversified from print to online newspapers and information retrieval. The company's three main product divisions are information services, business publications, and community newspapers. Although business information and journalism have been the core of Dow Jones in the past, electronic publishing that packages a range of financial information services and community newspaper segments are its future.

Company Origins

The popular reputation of Dow Jones & Company as one of the leading publishers of business news, information services, and community newspapers came nearly a generation after the founding fathers, Charles Henry Dow and Edward Jones, arrived in New York City from Rhode Island in 1879, with a liking for journalism and an ear for financial gossip. In their own day the two men were not especially well known outside trade circles. Dow had worked for a number of newspapers before moving to New York City, where he teamed up with Edward Jones and Charles Bergstresser to found Dow, Jones & Company in 1882. In 1885 Dow became a member of the New York Stock Exchange, where he formulated what would be called the Dow theory of stock market movements. He launched the *Wall Street Journal* in the summer of 1889 with Jones, a fellow journalist. Knowledge of the very earliest years of the company is sketchy.

Dow is said to have traded only infrequently on the exchange and to have taken his seat as a favor to a friend in immigration difficulties. Yet Dow's membership put him in a good position to observe the exchange and to overhear tips. Dow apparently wrote most of the copy for the early issues of the *Journal,* working only part-time at the newspaper, while Edward Jones edited the news-bulletin service and acted as managing editor. Reporters Thomas Woodlock and Charles M. Bergstresser covered Wall Street. Many of Dow's early articles were editorials, and information gleaned by Jones in the hotel bars formed the core of the news service.

Dow and Jones joined in a news-exchange agreement with Clarence Barron, the proprietor of the Boston News Bureau. Barron had begun to publish a financial newspaper in Boston two years before the *Wall Street Journal* was founded, and the two offices, the *Journal*'s in New York and *Barron's* in Boston, reinforced one another's coverage, with the aggressive Barron expanding into Philadelphia with his *Financial Journal* in 1896.

Edward Jones left the *Wall Street Journal* in January 1899. The family relationship between Dow and his cousin by marriage, Charles Bergstresser, who was also a partner in the firm, might have precipitated Jones's departure. Jones continued to live a good life on Wall Street, and his eulogy of Dow three years later was respectful and even loving, calling his former partner a "tower of strength" and one of "the most honest exponents" of financial journalism.

In 1900 the stockholders of Dow Jones, members of the Dow and Bergstresser families, and a few company employees received $7,500 each in addition to $1.20 a share in annual dividends. In March 1902 Clarence Barron purchased Dow,

Jones & Company—including the news agencies in Boston and New York and the *Wall Street Journal*—for $130,000. Dow and Bergstresser resigned their directorships. There was no public announcement, only the appearance of names for the first time on the *Journal*'s masthead. Although Barron had bought the company, he listed Dow, Bergstresser, Woodlock, and J.W. Barney, not himself. In December of the same year, Charles Dow died of a heart attack at age 51 in his Brooklyn home.

In 1905 Charles Otis was elected president, and F.A. Russell was named to the board of directors. Both Jessie Barron, Barron's wife, and Sereno Pratt were reelected directors of the company, and John Lane and Hugh Bancroft were added to the board.

Bancroft and the Barrons' daughter, Jane, married in 1907, and when Clarence Barron became ill, his son-in-law assumed increasing responsibilities in the New York offices. By 1911 the elder Barron's health had improved, but newspaper circulation, advertising, and profits were down, which precipitated a bitter quarrel between Barron and Charles Otis. Barron also fought with Bancroft and soon drove out President Otis and Director Sereno Pratt. On March 12, 1912, he reinstated himself in their places.

When Clarence Barron stormed into the editorial office of the *Journal* in March 1912 following his election to the presidency, the staff was terrified. Although lore has it that Barron harassed some employees into quitting, he is said never to have fired anyone. According to his contemporaries, Barron was a flamboyant and eccentric figure whose genius for journalism, along with his tough-mindedness, drove the ensuing prosperity of the publication.

The Great Depression and the Wartime Years

In 1921 Barron hired Kenneth Craven (Casey) Hogate, a second generation newspaperman. Later in 1921 Clarence Barron died, leaving an estate of $1.5 million to his daughter Jane Bancroft, who in 1918, at her mother's death, had inherited the majority shares. Hugh Bancroft was elected president and Casey Hogate, vice-president. Bancroft and Hogate managed a steadily prospering company until the stock market crash of 1929, when the paper began to sustain severe losses in circulation and advertising.

By 1932 the company had dropped the comma in its name. Despite the Great Depression, on June 27, 1932, Dow Jones & Company published an 80-page edition of the paper celebrating

its 50th anniversary and its new building on Broad Street. Although Hugh Bancroft's name continued to be listed as president, Casey Hogate was chiefly responsible for running the company in the Depression era, as Bancroft's health deteriorated.

In 1938 Richard Whitney—former president of the New York Stock Exchange, whose name was synonymous with the careless profiteering accused of causing the stock market crash—provided the *Journal* with a significant scoop when he telephoned the newsroom and confessed fraud before turning himself in to authorities. In the post-crash years, *Journal* editorials defended the financial community and free enterprise and supported the formation of the Securities and Exchange Commission (SEC) and regulatory legislation while condemning Whitney's behavior and Wall Street fraud. Hogate, meanwhile, struggled with a low in circulation in 1938 of 28,000.

About this time, with Barney Kilgore as president and William Kerby and Buren McCormack as directors in the company, Hogate took a risk with the *Journal* in order to revive the paper. He moved from strictly financial reports to include general news as well. Although Hogate fell into ill health, his formula worked, and his policy was carried out by the others. Kilgore, meantime, made the decision to produce the Monday morning paper on Sunday instead of Saturday so that the news would be fresh.

Throughout the war years the *Journal* became increasingly news oriented, as political and economic news became inextricably mixed with the fate of the markets. Although at the beginning the editorials were staunchly antiwar, even isolationist, the editorial policy became supportive in due course. After the armistice the trend toward news orientation, developed during the war years, remained with the paper.

Developments in the 1950s, 1960s, and 1970s

On December 21, 1949, Jane Bancroft, the last of the original Barron family, died in Boston. Throughout her life Jane Bancroft had been involved deeply in the growth of the paper, and her last acts had been to create an employee profit-sharing pension plan and to approve the postwar reorganization of Dow Jones.

Bancroft's daughter, Jane Cook, assumed her mother's place on the board, and before the end of 1949 Treasurer William Kerby drafted the new Dow Jones management chart, with Kilgore as president and chief executive officer. At this time the company portfolio included the Dow Jones News Service (in the United States and Canada); a commodity news service; the *Journal,* with editions in New York, Dallas, and San Francisco; and *Barron's,* a weekly periodical that continued to struggle with lagging circulation until 1955, when editor Robert Bleiberg turned the situation around. In the 1950s the *Journal*'s layout was modernized, using more two-column heads and readers' letters, cartoons, and drawings. In 1953 new equipment was used to set stock and bond quotations, which made it possible eventually to publish simultaneous editions of the newspaper, with identical news content and typographical quality, anywhere in the United States.

The *Journal*'s longstanding conservative editorial stance was disrupted when it supported the U.S. Supreme Court's decision in *Brown v. Board of Education of Topeka,* the historic civil rights case of 1954. Kilgore stayed at the helm of the

Key Dates:

1882: Charles Henry Dow, Edward Jones, and Charles Bergstresser found Dow, Jones & Company.

1885: Charles Henry Dow becomes a member of the New York Stock Exchange.

1889: Charles Henry Dow and Edward Jones begin publishing the *Wall Street Journal.*

1902: Clarence Barron purchases Dow, Jones & Company.

1949: Barney Kilgore becomes president and CEO of Dow Jones & Company.

1966: William Kerby succeeds Kilgore as president and CEO.

1978: Warren Phillips becomes chairman, president, and CEO of Dow Jones.

1987: Dow Jones launches *Professional Investor Report.*

1993: Asia Business News debuts.

1995: European Business News is started.

1996: *Wall Street Journal Interactive* goes online.

1997: Dow Jones enters into television agreement with CNBC.

Journal through John F. Kennedy's presidency, and the paper's editorial policies continued to take on issues of widespread social consequence. The *Journal* reporters, too, became increasingly well known to political leaders. Notoriety was good for business. In 1961 circulation came close to 800,000, with total advertising revenues of $47.7 million. The estimated value of Dow Jones stock was $235 million.

Technology moved the paper forward into the information services industry. By the 1960s facsimile pages of newspapers could be transmitted by coaxial cables and microwave transmitters. By the end of 1964 Dow Jones reported news-ticker clients in 676 U.S. cities and 48 of the 50 states. This business provided the company with the highest revenue after the *Journal.* With the advice of professional portfolio managers, the company began to move further into allied industries, venturing, for example, into textbooks with its purchase of Richard D. Irwin Inc. in 1975.

The change of leadership traditionally had been smooth at the company helm, and so it was when Kilgore handed over the reins to William Kerby in March 1966. Under the new management Vermont Royster directed editorial policy, and Executive Editor Warren Phillips headed news operations. Within two years the newspaper operation produced 94 percent of Dow Jones's profits, and it reached 1.5 million readers by 1978, when Warren Phillips became chairman, president, and chief executive officer. Dow Jones's operation of the *National Observer* never took off, and it ceased publication in 1977, when losses totaled $16.2 million after 15 years of existence. Its purchase of *Book Digest* magazine proved to be disappointing. In 1980 the company was reorganized along product lines into seven divisions under Phillips. While the main product lines had remained steady for nearly a century, revenue potential favored electronic publishing and information services, not the slow-growth textbook and community newspaper segments.

Transition to Electronic Publishing in the 1980s

After being the company's most lucrative business for a century, the *Journal* began to lose strength during the late 1980s, and electronic publishing became Dow Jones's primary growth sector. The *Journal*'s circulation fell from its 1983 high of 2.11 million to 1.95 million in 1989, a decrease of 7.5 percent. In March 1989 advertising revenues were down for the 19th straight month. For the first quarter of 1989, operating income of business publications fell 33 percent, and profits were down 13 percent in its community newspaper chain. The company had been through difficult times before, but the volatility of the world political and financial scene was changing the financial journalism business. The marketplace was placing increasing emphasis on user-friendly, computerized, fast news delivery. Phillips, observers said, needed to bring the *Journal* in line with the "real time" requirements of fast-breaking financial news.

The October 1987 stock market crash also had a negative impact on the *Journal*'s financial advertisement revenue. Phillips countered flat revenues by revamping the look of the *Journal,* expanding it from two to three sections. But all at Dow Jones was not bad. In 1989 *American Demographics,* owned by the company, reported a 10 percent growth in revenues and circulation. The European and Asian editions of the *Wall Street Journal* reported modest growth in circulation, *Barron's* reported steady circulation, and the *Far Eastern Economic Review* and *National Business Employment Weekly* were holding their own. Dow Jones also acquired Telerate, a real-time quote service, and sold its textbook division, Richard D. Irwin, for $135 million. The start-up of Telerate's foreign-exchange trading service accounted for some of Dow Jones's downturn in earnings in 1989 and 1990. In 1997 the company sold *American Demographics* and its associated publications to Cowles Media.

Dow Jones News/Retrieval, a market leader in online databases, was one of several businesses the company brought together to form the Information Group, which grew to 835 employees and $177 million in revenues by 1989. The Information Group had developed an innovative online searching system that made Dow Jones's electronic database more accessible than those of its closest competitors. The major problem with the electronic publishing business had been executives' reluctance to learn computer access codes in order to gain information. Dow Jones's system delivered the information to subscribers automatically. The Dow Jones system ranked and weighed articles by the number of times the user's access term occurred, delivering a text search with more specific targeting capability rather than a lengthy list of peripherally related articles.

Another information service owned by the company was the Dow Jones News Service, called the Broadtape, which supplied information to brokerages, banks, investment houses, and corporations. *Professional Investor Report* was started in 1987 as a companion product to the Broadtape, focusing on daily trading activity, and it became profitable in its second full year of operation, with a reported 29 percent growth in subscribers. The Dow Jones News Service changed its name to Dow Jones Newswires in 1996. Other company services included Dow-Vision, launched in 1990 as a customized newswire merging information from several databases; and DowPhone, a subscription-based telephone information service for investors, providing stock quotes, news reports, and investment analysis. JournalPhone was a 900-number (pay-per-call) installation derivative of DowPhone offering business and financial news updates. Dow Jones Voice Information Network was the satellite delivery system that provided customized news and information to about 75 voice-service providers.

Changes in the 1990s

During this transition to electronic publishing, Phillips retired from his company positions, first as chief executive officer in January 1991 and then as chairman the following July. Peter R. Kann—a 25-year veteran of the newspaper whom Phillips appointed publisher of the *Journal,* as well as president and chief operating officer of Dow Jones & Company—became the new chairman and chief executive officer.

By 1990, with a multiplicity of news-service products and its acquisition of Telerate, Dow Jones had positioned itself in the global financial market to expand into intercultural databases. Telerate's foreign exchange operation was the highest risk, most intensely competitive of such ventures. There were about a dozen other Telerate products, including SportsTicker, a sports news service. In 1994 Dow Jones sold an 80 percent share of its successful SportsTicker enterprise to the sports network ESPN. But Dow Jones & Company faced many other challenges during the early and mid-1990s, not the least of which was relatively stagnant growth in its *Wall Street Journal* subscriber base. New ventures, moreover, met with mixed success. In 1993 the company, in alliance with the Hearst group, launched the successful magazine *Smart Money*. In 1994 Dow Jones and American City Business Journals launched *BIZ,* a monthly magazine for small business. *BIZ* was discontinued in 1995.

Hoping to strengthen its television presence, Dow Jones launched Asia Business News (ABN) in November 1993 and European Business News (EBN) in February 1995. In partnership with ITT Corp., Dow Jones announced plans in 1996 to purchase the New York television station WNYC from New York City for $207 million. With the acquisition complete, the partnership launched a combination business and sports channel, named WBIS+, in January 1997. Later that year Dow Jones and ITT agreed to sell WBIS+ to Paxson Communications for $257.5 million.

In 1996, despite heavy criticism, Dow Jones promised to spend $650 million on its lagging Telerate service. Dow Jones's first major move to invigorate its market share was to rename the service Dow Jones Markets. Kenneth L. Burenga, company and *Wall Street Journal* president, was appointed chief executive officer of Dow Jones Markets.

The press, market analysts, and even investors were critical of such a large reinvestment in the information delivery service, which had been quickly losing market share to competitors. Although the policy of the Bancroft family had long been that of noninterference with Dow Jones operations, in part to protect the editorial integrity of its news publications, a few of the younger generation of Barron heirs, including the executive director, William Cox III, began to ask questions and make demands of their investments. Cox later resigned.

Despite rumors that Dow Jones could be subject to takeover, the vote-controlling segment of family ownership (the family owned 30 percent of total shares and 70 percent of vote-controlling shares) stood behind the management's $650 million decision. Although the company's earnings would slip because of the reinvestment, Dow Jones was committed to its online market, hoping that long-term earnings potential would outlive any short-term squabbles among investors. To shore up this potential, Dow Jones formed an alliance with Microsoft to upgrade the PC software for Dow Jones Markets.

Subscriber base for the *Wall Street Journal* had been stagnant throughout much of the 1990s, but ad lineage had increased overall. Still, high newsprint prices cut into profits for the paper until 1996, when advertising lineage increased 13.9 percent, circulation increased slightly, and newsprint prices leveled off. Perhaps more significant for Dow Jones was the early success of *Wall Street Journal Interactive,* the Internet edition of the venerable paper. The interactive edition was launched in April 1996, and with more than 70,000 subscribers by early 1997, it was the largest paid publication on the Internet (where consumers were accustomed to accessing information for free).

The *Wall Street Journal,* however, suffered a setback in 1997, when a federal jury in Houston found the paper guilty of libel and ordered them to pay $223 million in damages to MMAR Group Inc., a failed investment company. The suit was filed shortly after MMAR folded. MMAR claimed that the *Journal* had committed libel while describing MMAR's difficulties with a major client. But the *Journal* did not agree. "We were chronicling the difficulties of this company," said Managing Editor Paul Steiger. "We did not cause them."

In the late 1990s, despite criticism that it had stagnated somewhat and was no longer capable of making good, quick decisions in the modern marketplace, Dow Jones was a profitable company that had expanded impressively into electronic publishing. It remained, moreover, a respected source of business information and traditional journalism, areas that had established its core business identity from the days of Dow, Jones, and Bergstresser.

Adapting to the Information Age: Toward the 21st Century

By mid-1997 it was clear that Dow Jones Markets was never going to recover from its sluggish beginning. Even with the infusion of $650 million to revamp the struggling subsidiary, the service still lagged behind its major competitors, which were proving far more adept at adapting to rapidly evolving online technologies. Dow Jones's earnings for the first quarter of 1997 revealed a significant decline in the profitability of its financial information services; operating income for the division dropped to $7.5 million, compared with $46.1 million in the first quarter of 1996. By early 1998, Chairman Peter Kann conceded defeat, and Dow Jones Marketing was finally sold in 1998, at a write-off of $922 million.

As the decade neared an end, Kann came under increasing pressure to find new ways to offer Dow Jones shareholders a better return on their investment. In addition to the Dow Jones Marketing disaster, the company's television operations were floundering, with losses of $48 million in 1996 alone. To help shore up its flagging television business, the company entered into a partnership with NBC in December 1998. The move was designed to consolidate the two companies' television news services in Europe and Asia, with the aim of cutting operation and distribution costs and bolstering the global presence of each company. Under the terms of the agreement, CNBC earned the rights to broadcast Dow Jones features worldwide. In addition, Dow Jones gained a stronger foothold in the U.S. television market through the integration of its news stories into CNBC's national programming.

During this time the company also began divesting itself of some of its less vital business sectors. In December 1999 it sold Dow Jones Financial Publishing Corp. to Wicks Business Information, LLC, and in February 2002 it sold four of its Ottaway Newspaper interests to Community Newspaper Holdings for $182 million. The sale of these business units, however, did not signal a wholesale streamlining of the company's holdings. Peter Kann was still eager to carve out a niche for Dow Jones in the highly lucrative technology sector. In June 2000 the company entered into a joint venture with Excite@Home to create Work.com, a business network offering a range of news and services that catered to specific industries. Unfortunately, the new venture was hit hard by the decline in Internet advertising revenues, along with the general lack of funding, in the wake of the technology stock crash, and was forced to terminate operations in March 2001 (Excite eventually folded its own operations in February 2002). While overall the company saw decreased sales in 2000–2001, it remained profitable due in large part to the revenues earned by its most prominent holding, the *Wall Street Journal.* In the aftermath of some of its recent failures, Dow Jones could still take some comfort in the continued high performance of its core businesses.

Principal Subsidiaries

Dow Jones Newswires, Inc.; Wall Street Journal; Barron's; Ottaway Newspapers, Inc.

Principal Divisions

Information Services; Business Publications; Community Newspapers.

Principal Competitors

Bloomberg L.P.; Gannett Co., Inc.; Reuters Group PLC.

Further Reading

Bernicker, Mark, "ESPN Buys 80% of SportsTicker," *Broadcasting & Cable,* November 14, 1994, p. 47.

Brown, Rich, "Countdown to WBIS Debut; Just What the Focus of New Dow Jones ITT Station Will Be Remains Unclear," *Broadcasting & Cable,* August 5, 1996, p. 62.

Carvell, Tim, "Family Disunion at Dow Jones: The Owners Are Restless," *Fortune,* February 17, 1997, p. 25.

Chakravarty, Subatra N., "Fortune's Wheel," *Fortune,* February 10, 1997, p. 16.

Cohen, Jodi B., "Online Early and Still Going," *Editor & Publisher,* November 16, 1996, p. 26.

Dutt, Jill, "Dow Jones & Co. Earnings Plummet," *Washington Post,* April 10, 1997, p. C2.

Hackney, Holt, "Dow Jones: More Than the Journal," *Financial World,* July 4, 1995, p. 22.

King, Angela G., "Dow Jones Financial News Service Decision Draws Controversy," *Knight-Ridder/Tribune Business News,* February 26, 1997, p. 226B1059.

——, "Dow Jones to Pump $650 Million into Troubled Telerate Service," *Knight-Ridder/Tribune Business News,* January 21, 1997, p. 121B1060.

"More Bad News for Dow Jones," *Time,* March 31, 1997, p. 64.

Saloman, Jr., R.S., "The Outdated Dow Jones," *Forbes,* April 7, 1997, p. 132.

Spurgeon, Devon, "Dow Jones Teams Up with NBC; Companies Hope to Stem Losses Abroad with TV-Internet Partnership," *Washington Post,* December 10, 1997, p. C15.

—Claire Badaracco
—updates: Terry Bain, Steve Meyer

Edeka Zentrale A.G.

New York Ring 6
22297 Hamburg
Germany
Telephone: (49) 40-6377-0
Fax: (49) 40-6377-4575
Web site: http://www.edeka.de

Cooperative Company
Incorporated: 1908
Employees: 190,000
Sales: $29.4 billion (2000)
NAIC: 422490 Other Grocery and Related Products
Wholesalers; 445110 Supermarkets and Other Grocery
(Except Convenience) Stores; 452910 Warehouse
Clubs and Superstores

As a cooperative company, Edeka Zentrale A.G. is made up of a network of small retailers who purchase food and general goods as a group. Small shops that are part of the co-op can be found all across Germany, in rural as well as urban regions. Edeka, or EdK as it is also known, is the German acronym for "Central Purchasing Co-op of the Association of German Retail Co-ops."

The Rise of Food Co-ops in Germany: 1900–33

Edeka's direct predecessor was established in October 1907 with only 800 marks in capital, at a time when co-ops were a new idea. Fritz Borrmann and Karl Biller were its first managers. This company, the Association of German Retail Co-ops, was soon joined by other co-ops all over the country. At a meeting in May 1908, a statute was presented to 80 representatives of 23 organizations, and Edeka itself was formally born.

From its first year, Edeka was financially successful, and by 1910 it was able to establish an advertising division. EdK did not at first have its own brands, but in 1911 it purchased several famous brands. However, the young company soon felt the strength of its competitors, the industry's big retailers. The large retailers pressured suppliers not to sell Edeka goods at a discount, arguing that EdK was too small to receive the discounts big retailers were given. As a result, 44 supply companies boycotted EdK.

In its first years, EdK was very careful abut giving loans and credits to its members, making all money transfers in cash rather than using credit. But it was soon clear that the co-op needed a bank. After long and intense discussion, the Genossenschaftsbank Edeka (Edeka Co-op Bank) was founded to provide loans to Edeka's small retailers.

During the months before World War I, the German economy was in a state of chaos. The government partially restricted free trade, and city and county administrations were ordered to confiscate goods if necessary. People rushed into shops and bought as much food as they could. As a co-op, Edeka's local, decentralized structure meant that it handled the crisis in a steady and reliable fashion. For this, the organization earned a strong reputation among consumers, and within the next several years, many Edeka shops were founded. Local administrations sought Edeka's cooperation, and some city governments even tried—unsuccessfully—to unify all small retailers into a single co-op.

Finally, in 1918 EdK gained legal recognition as a co-op and as a trader that bought large quantities of goods and, therefore, was entitled to discounts. With this legal status, there was no question any more about its official place in the German economy.

After World War I, while free trade was still restricted, EdK's members increased from 194 in 1918 to 578 by 1923. As terrible inflation wrought economic havoc, Edeka had to come up with ways to lessen its impact. One way was to issue 20-mark "saving coupons," to strengthen the company's financial base. Edeka suggested that each co-op member purchase at least one coupon each week, and it promised to pay 6 percent interest. Edeka also made a call for solidarity in 1923, when it needed a new office and a warehouse and asked each retailer to contribute 20 marks. Edeka, like many other companies, also began to issue its own money in another effort to combat inflation. EdK retailers were obliged to accept EdK money, which they could use to buy supplies from the central organization. This measure helped insure that people would be able to shop at Edeka.

In 1924, EdK introduced several new policies for members. Each member store was required to use the name "Edeka" and to post an Edeka sign prominently. Shops also were required to sell Edeka brands. In its continuing effort to cope with inflation, in 1925 Edeka restricted its loans to not more than 5,000 Reichsmarks per shop, and limited the liability of each shop to 7,500 Reichsmarks. A year later, in 1926, new regulations required that all financial transactions be conducted in cash. This was an advantage for Edeka, since immediate payment, in cash, reduced its financial risk. By this time, EdK supplied a wide range of goods aside from food, like soap, floor wax, candles, and other products.

In a concerted effort to help small retailers, who often lacked experience as well as financial resources, EdK sent trained managers to member stores in trouble. During the Great Depression, customers trusted Edeka because of their experience during and after World War I, when Edeka's special role as a co-op ensured a stable and reliable market.

Government Regulation During the Nazi Years: 1933–45

After Adolf Hitler came to power in 1933, the whole economy was restructured and the government tried to organize institutions to regulate all sections of the economy. This effort was not entirely successful with EdK because of its decentralized organization.

After March 1934 it became illegal to import goods from foreign companies that were not part of a German company. To cope with this regulation, EdK was eventually forced to establish branches in Italy, Greece, and Turkey. Edeka also formed a subsidiary, Edeka Import and Export, a co-op with limited financial liability.

During the first years of Nazi rule, the large retailers once again tried to persuade the government to prevent Edeka from enjoying the discount and other advantages of bigger companies. Between 1936 and 1939 Edeka was confronted with intense regulations and controlled prices. At this time Edeka added cigarettes to its goods, which then included some 400 items. Despite huge losses, EdK proved to be a stable company, even when in 1943 its Berlin headquarters office was bombed and burned down. At a time when thousands of companies failed, Edeka was able to stay in business, and its food stamps remained valid until February 1945, when Germany's food industry collapsed.

Postwar Recovery: 1945–60

After the war, the partition of Germany cut off almost all communication between the eastern and western zones. The situation in Berlin was especially confusing, leading Edeka to establish a second headquarters in Hamburg.

A new generation of managers met in Bad Godesberg in 1945 to reestablish an active Edeka. Their first effort failed, but a second meeting in March 1946 in Goettingen made it clear that Edeka would continue to work. The company's first annual report, for 1945, was written by both headquarters, in Berlin and Hamburg.

Of the 524 co-ops that existed before World War II, 201 in West Germany and 125 in East Germany survived the war. In 1952, however, the East German state brought an end to all Edeka co-ops in East Germany when it forbade governmental companies to deliver to the private sector. But the situation in the West improved: in 1950 the central office counted 225 co-ops with a total turnover of DM 15 million. Each co-op encompassed an average of 124 small retailers.

The 1950s, the years of the economic miracle, were a time of tremendous growth for all sectors of the economy. During this time more than 20 percent of all small retailers were part of Edeka, and the co-op expanded vigorously, constructing warehouses in Braunschweig for tins and vegetables, in Cuxhaven for fish, and in Kempten for cheese.

Edeka also continued to introduce new ideas and systems to customers and small retailers: Edeka stores were among the first to introduce self-service, since new packing machines enabled EdK to sell packaged goods. By 1958, 7,000 of 40,500 stores offered self-service. Frozen food and fruits were introduced in 1955, and special diet and health foods were introduced in 1957.

Product Innovations, Corporate Restructuring: 1960s–80s

EdK did not stop its modernization. Shops continued to change to self-service. In 1962 delegations of the co-op traveled to the United States to compare the Edeka system to similar American companies. Meanwhile, Europe took its first steps toward the Common Market. Edeka joined the Union of Food Co-ops (UGAL) in Brussels. From the foundation of UGAL in 1963, EdK helped lobby for co-op interests in the European market.

In its ongoing effort to sell a greater variety of goods, EdK started to sell meat in 1963. The wider range of EdK's goods enabled the co-op to survive in smaller villages and towns, since it meant that neighborhoods could buy all of their necessary food, such as bakery products, fruits, frozen food, and dairy products, from an Edeka store. In 1968 Edeka for the first time began to sell general household goods such as can openers and pens.

But competition was fierce, especially in the early 1960s, and many smaller retailers failed. To survive, EdK had to improve its weak points. Restructuring the stocking system through the use of rolling shelf containers helped retailers stock a wider variety of goods in the same space, helping mitigate rising rents. By 1965 regional computer centers were established to simplify communication among small retailers and Edeka's head office. Another important initiative to compete with other companies was education. EdK established a training center and started an international educational program in cooperation with Swiss and Austrian retailers in 1965.

Two years later two new subsidiaries were founded to help with the real estate problems of small retailers, especially retailers located in downtown areas. All of these organizational and educational steps, however, could not prevent the failure of 2,500 small retailers between 1968 and 1970.

Edeka decided to tighten its organizational structure; five regional offices were created, in Hamburg, Cologne, Frankfurt, Stuttgart, and Munich. Since 1970 each regional office was financed equally by the Edeka bank and the co-ops. Despite this change, however, Edeka was heavily criticized by the department of monopolies, which saw the size of the organization as proof of its monopolistic hold on the retail industry. Edeka claimed that it simply represented small retailers and did not, as state officials assumed, dominate them.

In the economic turmoil that followed the oil shock in 1973, small retailers had a particularly hard time in Germany. Public opinion turned away from Edeka and from co-ops in general, which were seen as old-fashioned. Edeka began to concentrate more on public relations, and it recruited employees through workshops and cooperation with local schools. By 1975, 6,000 trainees worked in shops all over Germany. Three of every four EdK shops were remodeled between 1965 and 1975. In 1978, Edeka entered an agreement with the department store Horten in which Edeka rented space in 58 department stores and set up food shops. The agreement came at a time when almost no Edeka stores had survived in the rapidly changing downtown areas. The EdK-Horten arrangement helped many retailers to survive, as renting one section of a department store was much cheaper than the rent for a separate street-level shop.

At the beginning of the 1980s, EdK was the biggest independent group of small retailers in Europe, with 18,200 small retailers who owned 20,300 shops. By the end of 1988, Edeka had 11,000 members who operated a total of 13,150 stores and had total sales of more than DM 20 billion. Some of this drop can be accounted for by the trend toward fewer, larger stores in the retail industry.

By the end of the 1980s each member was part of a regional co-op; together, these regional co-ops ran 22 wholesale businesses for the individual stores, and each was a member of Edeka Zentrale, the holding company. The regional co-ops were also members of Edekabank, which handled both credit and insurance for Edeka members. In addition to supplying individual retailers and operating their own meat processing facilities, Edeka wholesale businesses supplied hotels and large restaurants. After surviving more than 80 years of tumultuous change, Edeka remained a powerful force in the German retail industry.

European Unification: The 1990s

The formation of the Single European Market in 1993 had an understandably profound effect on the German food industry. In addition to exposing retailers to increased competition from rivals in neighboring countries, the opening of national borders also forced companies to comply to a host of new laws, which were enforced by the newly centralized governing body of the European Union. Since the integrated economy required an enormous degree of standardization to be effective, such areas as procurement, distribution, and food quality became subject to increased regulation.

To prosper in this highly competitive climate, Edeka was compelled to undergo its own transformation during the 1990s. The company recognized three keys to maintaining its role as a leading food retailer in Germany. The first key to Edeka's future success lay in the implementation of new technologies into its retail business model. In 1997 the company introduced an electronic pricing information system in its Baden-Wurttemberg outlet; the success of the venture led the company to launch the system in five additional stores the following year. In anticipation of the arrival of a single European currency in 1999, the system was designed to scan prices in both Deutschmarks and Euros. The company also made its official entrance into the world of e-commerce in 2000, when it joined the WorldWide Retail Exchange, an extensive Internet resource geared toward establishing an online marketplace for distributors and retailers around the globe. As a way of providing new incentives to its customers, Edeka introduced a computerized card for its shoppers in 2001, allowing them to accumulate bonus points with their purchases.

The second key to Edeka's success involved expansion of its market reach. The company made a number of strategic acquisitions in the late 1990s, most notably in 1998, when its retail division enjoyed overall growth of 19.2 percent. In 1999 the company entered into merger talks with Tengelmann Warenhandelsgesellschaft OHG, the fifth largest food seller in Germany. Tengelmann, which owned a number of well-known grocery chains throughout Germany (including Tengelmann and Kaiser's), had not done well in the unified economy, suffering losses of more than DM 200 million in its retail operations. The two sides reached an agreement in late 1999, wherein the Tengelmann stores became absorbed into the Edeka retail network.

At the same time, Edeka focused on consolidating its holdings, in order to streamline operating costs and increase efficiency. To this end, the company undertook a major restructuring in the late 1990s. The plan called for the reduction of its regional wholesalers by half, from 12 to six, as well as the closure of more than 300 of its food stores nationwide. Overall, Edeka hoped to increase operating profits by up to DM 500 million annually. These changes aside, the company was still performing extremely well in comparison to its competitors. The combination of the restructuring plan, strategic expansion, and the introduction of a wider selection of products placed Edeka in a very good position to remain Germany's leading food retailer well into the 21st century.

Principal Competitors

METRO AG; REWE-Zentral AG; Tengelmann Warenhandelsgesellschaft OHG.

Further Reading

"Edeka Poised for Radical Restructuring," *Global News Wire* (abstracted from *Die Welt*), May 23, 2001, p. 14.
Edeka: 75 Jahre immer in Aktion, Hamburg: Edeka, 1982.
"Edeka Thinks Future Mergers Make Sense," *Global News Wire* (abstracted from *Frankfurter Allgemeine Zeitung*), May 18, 1999, p. 21.

—update: Steve Meyer

Electricidade de Portugal, S.A.

Avenida José Malhoa, Lote A/13
1070-157 Lisbon
Portugal
Telephone: 351-21-726-3013
Fax: 351-21-726-5029
Web site: http://www.edp.pt

Public Company
Founded: 1976
Employees: 14,867
Sales: $3.61 billion (2000)
Stock Exchanges: Lisbon New York
Ticker Symbol: EDP
NAIC: 513322 Cellular and Other Wireless
    Telecommunications; 221122 Electric Power
    Generation, Transmission and Distribution; 524210
    Insurance Agencies and Brokerages; 531210 Offices
    of Real Estate Agents and Brokers; 551112 Offices of
    Other Holding Companies

Electricidade de Portugal, S.A. (EDP) has emerged from its background as Portugal's state-controlled electricity monopoly to become a publicly traded holding company with international subsidiaries and ambitions to broaden its reach into other utility markets. The production and distribution of electricity still account for most of EDP's revenues. The company has a combined generating capacity of over 7,500 MW. Because Portugal has few fossil fuel energy resources, EDP relies heavily on hydroelectric power, supplemented by thermoelectric plants that burn imported natural gas, fuel oil, and coal to ensure a stable power supply during periods of low rain. The company has been active in the Brazilian power sector since 1996. EDP recently acquired a stake in a Spanish utility, and also has holdings in Guatemala, Morocco, Cape Verde, and Macau. Domestically, EDP's telecommunications unit, Onitelecom, is vying to become one of the main phone service providers in Portugal. In addition, the company's partnerships give it a role in various wastewater and gas projects, while it also capitalizes on its technical expertise to provide engineering and information technology (IT) services.

A State Electricity Monopoly: 1976–87

The first known use of electricity in Portugal occurred in 1878, when the royal family imported six voltaic arc lamps from Paris for a birthday celebration. In 1891 a company received a concession from the Lisbon Municipality to provide gas and electricity to the city, and small electrical installations followed in several buildings. The city of Braga was lit up by a northern electrical company in 1893, and through the early 1900s municipalities entered into concession contracts with local companies for electricity distribution, while the government licensed power plants. In the 1940s a set of nationwide electrification rules was adopted, making possible the formation of the Companhia Nacional de Electricidade to connect small generating systems across Portugal, followed by the construction of more large-scale plants after 1950. In 1960 the various companies that were supplying Portugal's primary electric network merged into the Companhia Portuguesa de Electricidade. After the Portuguese dictatorship was overthrown in the 1975 revolution, the Marxist government nationalized the country's power generation and transmission capabilities. The following year Electricidade de Portugal was formed with the goals of increasing the use of electricity in Portugal, improving the national grid, and establishing a single tariff.

In the 1980s the turbulence of economic and political change combined with a rapid rise in demand for electricity to create a decade of turmoil for EDP. Electricity investment more than tripled between 1976 and 1980 as the state utility tried to keep pace with demand. As one of the few Portuguese institutions with international credibility, EDP managed to secure loans from the World Bank and other sources, which it invested in improving its generating capacity. However, municipalities had stopped paying their power bills in the revolutionary climate, while at the same time the escudo was being steadily devalued by inflation. As a result, EDP's debt reached alarming levels.

One of the utility's more pressing problems was its reliance on imports for power generation. Although Portugal had 44 hydroelectric plants in 1981, their production had to be supplemented by a series of fuel oil power stations that had been constructed under the pre-1975 dictatorship. Most of the fuel for the thermonuclear plants had to be imported, with energy im-

Company Perspectives:

"The EDP Group ranks among Europe's major electricity operators, as well as being one of Portugal's largest business groups.

As a multidisciplinary organization whose activities extend to such diverse areas as telecommunications and the internet, it presents itself as a natural and competitive participant in other business segments, such as gas, water and the provision of services in the engineering and information systems' fields.

The EDP Group's mission today is no longer limited to the electricity sector: it is a leading protagonist in the Portuguese economy's internationalization drive. It is increasingly committed to markets with high growth potential, such as Latin America, Africa and Asia.

The EDP Group never ceases to grow. Always with three fundamental concerns: serving our customers better, defending the interests of our shareholders, meeting the aspirations of our workforce."

—Francisco de la Fuente Sánchez, chairman

ports accounting for about a quarter of total imports in the early 1980s. As the government invested in expansion of its hydroelectric capacity, it began searching for domestic fuel, and considered options such as coal-burning and nuclear power plants. Although the nuclear option was never pursued, EDP did have one small coal-burning plant at Tapada do Outeiro in the north and constructed a second coal plant at Sines in the south.

Restructuring and Liberalization: 1987–98

In 1987 a new government, led by the center-right Social Democrats, came to power and began loosening the state's control over economic activity. The Social Democrats passed laws allowing the private sector to generate electricity and talked of liberalizing, deregulating, and restructuring the energy sector. They appointed José Manuel Castro Rocha head of EDP with the hope that he would rescue the utility after a decade of neglect. When Rocha took over, EDP had an accumulated debt of Esc 1.05 trillion and an annual loss in 1987 of Esc 5.9 billion. The situation at the utility improved greatly during Rocha's five-year tenure. Energy imports, while still much higher than desirable, accounted for only 8 percent of Portugal's total imports in 1989. The following year EDP became a state-controlled public company and reported a net profit of Esc 10.3 billion. Debt was expected to fall below the Esc 1 trillion mark by the end of 1991.

At the same time, Portugal's newly liberalized, expanding economy was attracting foreign investment. International companies played a particularly prominent role in plans to bring natural gas to Portugal. In 1990 the country called for tenders to build an import terminal and pipeline for liquefied natural gas. The pipeline would supply a natural-gas fueled power plant at Tapada do Outeiro that was to be constructed by a consortium led by Germany's Siemens. A second gas-fired plant was to be built after a decade or so, which some of the bidding companies felt was an insufficient guarantee of demand for natural gas.

Gaz de France won the bidding process in mid-1991, but after nearly two years of negotiations over prices, risk-sharing, and construction of the second gas-fired plant, the deal fell through. Portugal remained without natural gas for the time being, and the future of the Tapada de Outeiro plant was in doubt.

Joaquim Silva Correia become EDP's new president in 1992. Under his direction the utility experienced a major restructuring, made significant progress in debt reduction, and increased its hydroelectric capacity. The turnaround in debt repayment came in December 1993, when EDP sold two coal-fired power units that were being constructed in Pego, a city north of Lisbon. The Tejo Energia consortium, led by the United Kingdom's National Power, acquired the units for Esc 170 billion. The deal cut EDP's debt service costs and allowed the company to focus investment on distribution rather than generation. EDP's financial situation continued to improve over the next four years, as interest rates fell and municipalities began paying their neglected power bills. By the end of 1995, the company's debt was down to Esc 678.7 billion.

Reorganization of the utility was officially completed in September 1994. The EDP Group became a holding company for 22 separate units, with the CPPE (Companhia Portuguesa de Producao de Energia) subsidiary in charge of production and the REN (Rede Electrica Nacional) subsidiary controlling transmission, distribution, and services. The restructuring gave the various components of the electricity sector more control over decision-making and daily operations, promoting better management. Profits in 1995, at Esc 66.3 billion, were more than double the previous year, an improvement attributed to greater operating efficiency. EDP was also working to improve its tariff structure. During the 1980s, industry had been charged particularly high rates in order to keep domestic rates artificially low. In a gradual effort to remedy the distorted structure, tariffs were reduced 30 percent for industry and 10 percent for domestic customers in the four years leading up to 1996. An independent regulator for the energy sector, known as ERSE, also began operation in late 1996 as part of continued efforts on the part of the government to make the electricity system more liberal and competitive. ERSE planned to push tariffs down even closer to the European Union average, improve the transparency of electricity distribution costs, and ensure that the distribution subsidiary REN bought power from producers on a lowest-price-first basis.

The next step in EDP's evolution was privatization. The Social Democrat government had been planning to privatize the regional units of the company, but after a Socialist government gained control at the end of 1995, they decided to sell a stake in the holding company itself. EDP president Silva Correia departed that fall, with the former banker and government official Antonio de Almeida taking his place. In June 1997 Almeida presided over Portugal's largest privatization yet: 30 percent of EDP was sold for Esc 368 billion. The offering met with enthusiastic public response, and was oversubscribed 37 times by retail investors. The Spanish utilities Endesa and Iberdrola had hoped to gain a share of their Portuguese neighbor, but the institutional share of the IPO went mainly to Portuguese investment institutions. EDP's share price rose 38 percent on the first day of trading on the Lisbon exchange, where it was the largest company. The company was also traded as U.S. depositary receipts on the New York Stock Exchange.

The offering was seen as a sign that Portugal had attained the status of a developed investment market.

After the privatization, Almeida announced that EDP would continue to improve efficiency, mainly by centralizing operations such as accounting and purchasing at the group level and further reducing its employees from 16,000 to 13,000. EDP had also recently carried out its first international foray. In November 1996 the company formed a consortium with Spain's Endesa and Chile's Enersis to buy 70.2 percent of the Rio de Janeiro electricity distributor CERJ. EDP would build on its Brazilian holdings over the next few years. Plans for natural gas also came to fruition during this period. With Gaz de France out of the picture, several large state-controlled Portuguese companies formed the Transgas consortium and finally brought gas to Portugal in 1997. A pipeline was constructed to import gas from Algeria to Tapada do Outeiro, where the long anticipated natural-gas fired power plant was still under construction. Projected to provide up to one fifth of Portugal's electricity, the Tapada plant was finished in the fall of 1998 by the Turbogas consortium, which included PowerGen of the United Kingdom and Siemens of Germany.

Branching Out Internationally: 1998–2002

In early 1998 a disagreement arose over EDP's search for a strategic partner. Company President Almeida preferred an alliance with the Spanish electricity company Endesa, but the Portuguese government, worried about the possible expansion of foreign influence, preferred a German power group. In the end, Almeida was replaced as chairman by Mario Cristina de Sousa, and a smaller Spanish utility, Iberdrola, was chosen for a partner. EDP and Iberdrola hoped to cooperate on expansion in Brazil and invest jointly in production on the Iberian peninsula, but the main fruit of their alliance was the August 1998 purchase of 80 percent of the Guatemalan electricity distributor EEGSA (Empresa Electrica de Guatemala).

A host of other acquisitions and alliances helped EDP expand its reach in the late 1990s. The company gained control of the São Paulo distributor Bandeirante in the fall of 1998,

acquired control of the Brazilian utilities Escelsa and Enersul by purchasing a 73 percent stake in the investment consortium Iven in August 1999, and also teamed up with Thames Water of the United Kingdom to develop water and wastewater projects in Portugal, Chile, and Brazil. These acquisitions came in spite of the fact that CERJ, EDP's original Brazilian investment, was performing poorly due to low tariffs and the devalued Brazilian real. Domestically, EDP also formed a new telecom unit, Oni, hoping to capitalize on the coming liberalization of Portugal's telecommunications market, and proceeded with construction of a second natural gas-fired plant in Carregado.

However, EDP was suffering under tariff pressure from ERSE. The independent EDP regulator cut tariffs 6.5 percent in 1998, bringing them close to the European Union average, and imposed another 6.4 percent cut in 1999. The cuts hurt EDP's performance on the Lisbon exchange and caused sharp falls in revenue in 1998 and 1999, with 1999 net income standing at EUR 520 million. Another financial blow came in November 1999 when the Portuguese conglomerate Sonae, one of EDP's largest customers, began buying its power from the Spanish utility Endesa.

Nevertheless, EDP moved ahead with growth and diversification. The Onitelecom unit became fully operational in 2000, as international and long-distance fixed-line services were liberalized that January. Although the unit lost money in its first two years of operation, it acquired 589,000 voice and 372,000 internet customers by the end of 2001. EDP also bought a 14 percent stake in the Portuguese oil and gas utility GALP early in 2000. The move gave EDP a chance to coordinate further gas-fired generation projects and was seen as a sign of the company's desire to offer multi-utility services. Outlining his vision for the company, EDP's new Chairman Francisco Sánchez was quoted in the *Financial Times* as saying, "The future of our business lies in satisfying the basic utility needs of a large base of customers. A big reduction in costs can be achieved by adapting the commercial network we already have to the integrated supply of power, gas and water." Net income in 2000 was EUR 520 million, a slight improvement over the previous year.

The government, which had held just over half of EDP since 1999, reduced its share further in October 2000 with the EUR 1.6 billion sale of an 18 percent stake. But the state was wary of relinquishing too much control over Portugal's electricity system; despite its minority holding, it retained a "golden share" that gave it veto power over major policy decisions. In addition, the state bought 70 percent of REN, the distribution subsidiary, in 2001 so that it could maintain control of the domestic grid.

In 2001 EDP ended its strategic alliance with Iberdrola in response to rumors that Iberdrola might merge with its larger competitor Endesa. EDP intended to independently seek electricity generation and distribution assets in Spain, and soon became involved in a drawn-out battle for control of a small Spanish utility, Hidroeléctrica del Cantábrico. The bidding war involved EDP and the German utilities RWE AG and Energie Baden-Württemberg AG (EnBW). In an initial agreement, EDP bought a 20 percent stake and EnBW received 60 percent, but EDP subsequently pursued an arrangement where it could play the dominant role in the management of its fellow utility on the Iberian peninsula. The companies reached an agreement in

December 2001 under which EDP had a controlling 40 percent and EnBW 35 percent of Hidrocantábrico, with two Spanish financial institutions holding the remaining shares. Results in 2001 showed a drop in net profit to EUR 451 million, due to losses in the telecom unit and a smaller contribution from REN. As EDP entered 2002, it faced the challenge of holding its market share in a sector that was growing ever more competitive. Although the company retained a monopoly on the domestic market, after January 2002 small and medium-sized companies were allowed to buy from other electricity suppliers. While actively pursuing acquisitions and opportunities for diversification, EDP also needed to concentrate on its core business of electricity generation. The company announced its intention to cut costs over the next four years as the Iberian electricity market became increasingly integrated.

Principal Subsidiaries

Companhia Portuguesa de Produçao de Electricidade, S.A.; EDP Energia (60%); EDP Distribuiçao; EDP Internacional; EDP Brasil, Bandeirante (Brazil; 96%); IVEN (Brazil; 73%); Companhia de Electricidade do Estado do Rio de Janeiro (CERJ; 19%); EEGSA (Guatemala; 17%); ONI Telecom Infocomuniçoes (67%); REDAL (Morrocco; 29%); CEM (Macau; 22%); ELECTRA (Cape Verde; 31%); REN (30%); Tejo Energia (10%); Turbogás (10%); GALP Energia (14%); EDP Aguas; Hidroeléctrica Del Cantábrico, S.A. (40%).

Principal Competitors

Endesa Group; Iberdrola; Portugal Telecom.

Further Reading

"Cerj Tops Auction Prices," *FT Energy Newsletters - Power in Latin America*, November 1, 1996, p. 1.

"EdP and Iberdrola to Inject New Energy into Strategic Alliance," *FT Energy Newsletters - European Energy Report*, August 13, 1999, p. 1.

"EdP Details Post-Sale Restructuring," *FT Energy Newsletters - Power in Europe*, April 11, 1997, p. 3.

"EDP Float Leaves Nothing for the Spanish," *FT Energy Newsletters - Power in Europe*, June 20, 1997.

"EdP Loses Its Head," *FT Energy Newsletters - Power in Europe*, July 26, 1996, p. 1.

"EdP Running Hard to Keep," *FT Energy Newsletters - Power in Europe*, February 3, 2000, p. 5.

Elkin, Michael, "EdP's Bid Gets Boost for Cantabrico," *Daily Deal*, March 6, 2001.

"Iberdrola-Teco-EdP Consortium Wins Guatemala Distributor," *Global Power Report*, August 7, 1998, p. 18.

McClosky, Gerard, "Energy Faces the Nuclear Plunge," *Financial Times (London)*, March 30, 1982, p. VI.

Mulligan, Mark, "European Venture Wins Chile Water Stake," *Financial Times (London)*, November 25, 1999, p. 34.

"Portugal Prepares for EdP Sell-off by Establishing First Watchdog," *FT Energy Newsletters - European Energy Report*, July 5, 1996, p. 1.

"Portugal Sells 18% of State Utility for $1.4 Bil," *Electric Utility Week*, October 30, 2000, p. 19.

"Regulator Bans Iberian Love Affair," *FT Energy Newsletters - Power in Europe*, June 5, 1998, pp. 3–4.

Valladares, Mayra Rodriguez, "EdP's International Ambitions," *Privatisation International*, December 1999, p. 23.

White, David, "The Infrastructure: Natural Gas; Link-up Will Cost More Than $2bn," *Financial Times (London)*, April 16, 1997, p. 8.

Wise, Peter, "Anxious to Gather an Electric Security Blanket: Portugal," *Financial Times (London)*, November 6, 1998, p. 4.

——, "EdP Branches Out in Bid to Sell All Things to All Men," *Financial Times (London)*, October 5, 2000, p. 34.

——, "EdP Reveals Cost-Cutting Plans," *Financial Times (London)*, March 20, 2002, p. 39.

——, "EdP Sees Sharp Fall in Revenue As Tariffs Are Cut," *Financial Times (London)*, December 8, 1998, p. 30.

——, "EdP Takes Lead in Hidrocantabrico Deal," *Financial Times (London)*, December 6, 2001, p. 20.

——, "EdP to Seek Acquisitions After Split from Iberdrola," *Financial Times (London)*, January 22, 2001, p. 27.

——, "Investors Flock to Portugal Power Sale," *Financial Times (London)*, June 17, 1997, p. 19.

——, "Lisbon Replaces Chairman of EdP," *Financial Times (London)*, March 11, 1998, p. 26.

——, "New President for EDP Before Offer Next April," *Financial Times (London)*, July 23, 1996, p. 26.

——, "Portugal: Oil-Import Cuts Are the Main Incentive," *Financial Times (London)*, November 4, 1991, p. VII.

Woodford, Julian, "Electricidad de Portugal," *Utility Europe*, March 1, 2000, p. 24.

—Sarah Ruth Lorenz

Eli Lilly and Company

Lilly Corporate Center
Indianapolis, Indiana 46285
U.S.A.
Telephone: (317) 276-2000
Fax: (317) 276-3492
Web site: http://www.lilly.com

Public Company
Incorporated: 1881
Employees: 41,000
Sales: $11.54 billion (2001)
Stock Exchanges: New York Boston Cincinnati NASDAQ
Philadelphia Basel Geneva Zurich Tokyo London
Ticker Symbol: LLY
NAIC: 325412 Pharmaceutical Preparation
Manufacturing; 339112 Surgical and Medical
Instrument Manufacturing; 422210 Drugs and
Druggists' Sundries Wholesalers

Eli Lilly and Company discovers, develops, manufactures, and markets ethical drugs (those requiring a doctor's prescription) for a wide variety of human ailments. It has research and production facilities in many nations, and its products are sold in 159 countries. It introduced the world's first commercial insulin in the 1920s, and in 2002 was the leading producer of products for those with diabetes. Its best-selling antidepressant, Prozac, continues to be a controversial drug, even though it lost its U.S. patent protection in 2001. Like many other large corporations, Lilly has numerous collaborations or joint ventures with other firms. As a major player in the pharmaceutical industry, Lilly has faced many controversies such as the high cost and advertising of prescription drugs. The company's subsidiary Elanco Animal Health sells animal health products in over 100 countries.

Lilly's Origins and Community Commitments: 1870s–1960s

Despite its huge domestic and international operations, Lilly continued to maintain a close allegiance to the U.S. Midwest and wielded significant influence in its native city. For instance, in 1971 *Forbes* magazine prepared a profile of the company, but because Lilly did not want the article published, an Indianapolis newspaper refused to sell *Forbes* photographs of the Lilly family.

Much of this community loyalty stemmed from Lilly's long history of paternalism and generosity. In 1876, Colonel Eli Lilly, a Civil War veteran, built a laboratory in Indianapolis and began to manufacture ethical drugs. The business established itself successfully with the innovation of high-quality gelatin-coated capsules, and it was not long before Colonel Lilly was able to serve Indianapolis in a variety of ways. He served as president of the Commercial Club to help in the development of the city and chaired a committee to help the indigent during the financial panic of 1893. He also donated his own personal funds to build a children's hospital in memory of his 13-year-old daughter who died of diphtheria.

This civic consciousness was inherited by the second and third generation of Lilly management. During the Depression, the Colonel's grandson, Eli Lilly, refused to lay off any employees. Instead, he had them help with general maintenance of the facility until they could return to their normal jobs.

The Lilly family in 1937 established the Lilly Endowment to provide financial support for educational, cultural, and religious institutions. The family donated $5 million worth of rare books to Indiana University, and later the Smithsonian Institution acquired a family coin collection worth $5.5 million. The endowment also funded new buildings, music schools, student centers, and laboratories in most colleges and universities in Indiana and in several other states.

Lilly also laid the foundations for its reputation for marketing ingenuity in those early years. After the 1906 San Francisco earthquake, the company sent as much of its stock as it could to the disaster area at the request of sales personnel and wholesalers. Since then the ready availability of Lilly's products was central to its marketing strategy. That and aggressive advertising campaigns, plus its large, eager sales force, have been the keys to its marketing success. Its sales marketing department was formally established around 1922.

Besides being a pioneer in pharmaceutical marketing, Lilly was known for its development of many important drugs. In the 1920s, Lilly began selling the world's first commercially available insulin that would benefit millions with diabetes. In the years ahead it would remain the leading manufacturer of insulin, commanding at least 75 percent of the U.S. market in the early 1990s.

In the 1920s, the company produced a liver extract for the treatment of pernicious anemia. In the 1930s, Lilly laboratories synthesized barbituric acids, essential to the production of drugs used in surgery and obstetrics. In 1955 Lilly manufactured 60 percent of the Salk polio vaccine. But the company's greatest contribution to human health was in production of penicillins and other antibiotics that revolutionized the treatment of disease.

Throughout this era of innovation and expansion and up until the late 1980s, Lilly's management remained a constant. Every president and almost every member of the board of directors was either a direct descendant of Colonel Lilly or a native of the Midwest, if not of Indiana. After the colonel's death in 1898, his son Josiah Lilly ran the company for the next 34 years. He was succeeded by son Eli and later by Josiah, Jr. During the 16-year presidency of Eli Lilly, sales rose from $13 million in 1932 to $117 million in 1948. After Eli relinquished his executive powers to his brother, he became the titular chairperson of the company. Upon his death at age 91, he had lived to see the company reach $1 billion in sales.

Business in the 1970s and 1980s

Josiah, Jr.'s presidency marked the last reign of a direct family descendant, followed by presidents Beesley, Beck, Wood, and Lake. Richard Wood, who advanced to the CEO position in 1973, was the third of seven company presidents to be an "outsider." He was, of course, born and raised in Indiana and was a longtime Lilly employee.

In 1971 members and descendants of the Lilly family owned $1 billion of the $4 billion in company stock, while the Lilly Endowment (controlled by the family) owned another $900 million. Furthermore, the endowment resisted making large disbursements, and it was not until the 1969 Tax Reform Act that the endowment was forced to loosen its 25 percent hold on stock. Still, in 1979 the endowment continued to hold 18.6 percent of company shares.

Lilly's conservative management paralleled the outspoken ideology of the Lilly Endowment, although the company and the endowment were separate and distinct organizations. During the 1960s, the Lilly Endowment professed a specific political mission. It supported anticommunism, free enterprise, and limited government. Despite what some have called an anachronistic approach to business, no one can dispute Lilly's financial success.

While the rest of the drug industry in the 1970s was depressed, Lilly doubled in size. When the pharmaceutical business was hit hard by competition from generic drugs that flooded the marketplace after the expiration of patents for drugs discovered in the 1950s and 1960s, Lilly diversified into agricultural chemicals, animal-health products, medical instruments, and beauty-care products.

Meanwhile, Lilly increased its expenditure on research and development of pharmaceuticals, spending $235 million in those areas in 1981 alone. The immediate result was three new drugs: Ceclor, an oral cephalosporin antibiotic; Dobutrex, a heart-failure treatment; and Mandol, an injectable cephalosporin effective against a broad spectrum of hospital-acquired infections. The release of the new cephalosporins represented a significant step for Lilly. The company had always been dominant in the antibiotic market, but competition from Merck, SmithKline, and foreign drug companies threatened Lilly's supremacy. With the new drugs, the company was able to recapture hegemony of the cephalosporin market; of the $3.27 billion in company sales in 1985, $1.05 billion was from the sale of antibiotics.

A similar success story resulted after the company bought Elizabeth Arden for $38 million in 1971. At first glance, the purchase of the beauty-care company seemed an unwise move. Elizabeth Arden had been a money loser and continued to lose money for five years after Lilly acquired it. Lilly management seemed to have no idea of the intense competition in the beauty industry. But, in an unusual move, Lilly hired outsiders to fill its subsidiary's top executive positions, and by 1982 Elizabeth Arden's sales were up 90 percent from 1978, with profits doubling to nearly $30 million.

The introduction of several new drugs in the late 1970s and early 1980s increased Lilly's sales and challenged the market boundaries of competing products. Lilly released Nalfon, an anti-inflammatory drug, to compete with Merck's top selling Indocin. In addition, the company introduced Cinobac, an antibacterial agent used to treat urinary-tract infections; Eldisine, a treatment for childhood leukemia; Moxam, a potent new antibiotic licensed from Shionogi, a Japanese drug company; and Benoxaprofen, an antiarthritic introduced in the United Kingdom. Moreover, the company in 1982 introduced Humulin, the first healthcare product made from recombinant DNA technology. This breakthrough promised to protect Lilly's majority share of the insulin market.

During this time, the initial flurry over the possible hazardous side effects of a popular analgesic called Darvon seemed to have subsided. Critics had charged that the drug introduced in 1957 was both ineffective and had the dangerous potential for abuse, but Lilly mounted an educational campaign on proper use of the drug and continued to hold 80 percent of the prescription analgesic market. Darvon generated annual sales of $100 million.

With a 19 percent increase in sales in 1978, a 24 percent return on equity, and impressive results from Wood's foreign-market campaign, Lilly's prospects seemed excellent. Then, however, company growth began to fall short of projected figures. In 1982, a miscalculation of inventory and expected sales caused Lilly to produce far more Treflan (a soybean

Key Dates:

1876: Colonel Eli Lilly starts making ethical drugs in Indianapolis.
1881: Company is incorporated.
1886: Lilly hired its first scientist, Ernest Eberhardt, to establish one of the first pharmaceutical research and development programs.
1923: Eli Lilly and Company begins selling Iletin, the first commercially available insulin.
1940s: Lilly becomes one of the first companies to begin mass producing penicillin.
1950s: Lilly introduces two important antibiotics: erythromycin and vancomycin.
1960s: Lilly introduces cephalosporin antibiotics and anticancer drugs vincristine and vinblastine.
1971: The company buys cosmetics manufacturer Elizabeth Arden.
1977: IVAC Corporation is acquired.
1978: Cardiac Pacemakers Inc. is acquired.
1980: Company acquires Physio-Control Corporation.
1982: Lilly introduces Humulin, the company's human insulin and the first human-healthcare item made by recombinant DNA technology (genetic engineering).
1987: Eli Lilly sells Elizabeth Arden cosmetics business to Fabergé for $657 million.
1987: FDA approves the use of Prozac for treating depression.
1996: Zyprexa is introduced as a new treatment for schizophrenia.
1998: Company dedicates its new laboratories for clinical research at Indiana University Medical Center in Indianapolis.
1999: Takeda Chemical Industries, Ltd. and Lilly launch Actos, an oral diabetes agent that acts as an insulin sensitizer.
2001: Patent protection for Prozac ends in the United States, opening competition from generic versions.
2002: Lilly becomes the fourth major drug company to offer big discounts for needy patients.

herbicide) than it could sell. With the patents expiring on Treflan and two animal products, and with the overproduction of Treflan, income from agricultural products suddenly did not look as promising as it once had. Furthermore, profits from Moxam had to be shared with Shionogi, the Japanese partner in the joint venture. In addition, the patent on Keflin, an injectable cephalosporin that had been generating $100 million in sales, expired in November 1982.

Lilly's diversification into medical instruments through the acquisition of IVAC Corporation, a manufacturer of systems that monitored vital signs and equipment for intravenous fluid infusion, and Cardiac Pacemaker, a manufacturer of heart pacemakers, cost Lilly $286 million in stock, a significant investment with an unknown potential for profits. Also, since the combined assets of its medical instrument subsidiaries and Elizabeth Arden represented only 20 percent of the entire company, their projected profits were not expected to have a substantial effect on company profits as a whole. Elizabeth Arden was, in fact, later sold to Fabergé, Inc. for $657 million in 1987.

Of more concern, however, was the re-emerging specter of Darvon's addictive qualities. Ralph Nader's consumer-advocacy group demanded a ban on Darvon because of its alleged associations with suicides, overdoses, and misuse by addicts. Joseph Califano, the U.S. Secretary of Health, Education, and Welfare, harshly criticized the sincerity of Lilly's educational campaign and went so far as to recommend that Darvon and other propoxyphene products not be prescribed unless there really was no alternative, and then only with care. The FDA charged that Lilly's educational campaign actually amounted to ingenious marketing in that Lilly sales representatives not only gave doctors educational material that emphasized the drug's positive attributes but also conveniently left samples. The result of this litigation was that Darvon was not removed from the market, and it was proven safe and effective when used as directed.

To the company's dismay, Darvon was not the only drug to cause a controversy. Oraflex, the U.S. version of Benoxaprofen, was withdrawn from the market in August 1982. Only one month after the FDA approved Oraflex, a British medical journal documented five cases of death due to jaundice in patients taking the drug. The FDA accused Lilly of suppressing unfavorable research findings. Initial warnings about the possibility of inconsequential side effects were later amended to include the threat of jaundice, but only after the company had already applied for FDA approval. Package inserts were amended to recommend a reduced dosage for elderly patients.

At a time when drug-regulation reform would have allowed companies to interpret the results of their own lab tests, the Oraflex controversy represented a major disaster. Furthermore, publicity for the drug, which was projected to be a $100 million seller (prescriptions for Oraflex increased by 194,000 in just one month), had been unwittingly distorted. Reports from outside the company had falsely claimed that the drug could cure arthritis.

On August 21, 1985, the Oraflex controversy culminated when the U.S. Justice Department filed criminal charges against Lilly and Dr. William Ian H. Shedden, the former vice-president and chief medical officer of Lilly Research Laboratories. The Justice Department accused the defendants of failing to inform the government about four deaths and six illnesses related to Oraflex. Lilly pleaded guilty to 25 criminal counts, which resulted in a $25,000 fine. Shedden pleaded no contest to 15 criminal counts and was fined $15,000. All 40 counts were misdemeanors; there was no charge against Lilly of intentional deception.

Lilly was cited as a defendant in a lawsuit filed against drug manufacturers and distributors of diethylstilbestrol (DES). The drug, which was prescribed to pregnant women during the 1940s and 1950s to prevent miscarriages, caused vaginal cancer and related problems in the children of the patients. Lilly was the first and largest manufacturer of DES, and it was estimated that 40 percent of the drug came from Lilly production facilities. In 1981, a court ordered the company to pay $500,000 in damages to one plaintiff, and in 1985 Lilly was ordered to pay $400,000 to the first male seeking damages in a DES-related case. Other claims asked for damages totaling in the billions of dollars.

In the early 1980s Lilly continued acquiring manufacturers of medical devices and diagnostic equipment. Lilly added both Physio-Control Corp. and Advanced Cardiovascular Systems Inc. through share exchanges in 1980 and 1984, respectively. Hybritech, a California diagnostic products company, was purchased for $350 million in 1986. Lilly added Devices for Vascular Intervention, Inc., and Pacific Biotech, Inc., in 1989 and 1990, respectively. These companies (along with Origin Medsystems, a 1992 acquisition) constituted Lilly's Medical Devices and Diagnostics Division, which contributed about 20 percent of the pharmaceutical corporation's annual revenues in the early 1990s. Heart Rhythm Technologies, Inc. was acquired in 1992. But even this new business interest had its problems, not the least of which was intense competition from Abbott Laboratories.

While Wood concentrated on these domestic acquisitions, Lilly's competitors had expanded internationally, where two-thirds of the world's pharmaceutical market awaited. Although Lilly's top two drugs, Ceclor (an antibiotic) and Prozac (an antidepressant introduced in 1987) were highly profitable, the company's $1 billion annual investment in research and development did not yield any new blockbuster breakthroughs.

The 1990s and the New Millennium

By the beginning of the decade, the company's star antidepressant Prozac had become a major medical, legal, and social controversy. Many reported relief from the sufferings of depression. About two million individuals worldwide had taken the drug by the summer of 1990. However, some said Prozac caused them to become suicidal. Lawsuits were filed and some politicians argued that their opponents were unstable because they took Prozac. Those who thought they were hurt by Prozac formed support groups in several states, while Lilly and the FDA continued to defend the drug's usefulness and safety. Eventually several books were written about the pros and cons of using drugs such as Prozac to treat depression and other mental illnesses.

In 1991, Wood abdicated Lilly's chief executive office and chose Vaughn D. Bryson, a longtime executive, as his successor. Lilly's employees reportedly appreciated Bryson's management style, which was much less formal than that of his predecessor. Unfortunately for Bryson, however, patent expirations, a dearth of new drugs, and general volatility in the pharmaceutical industry combined to thwart his stint at the top. The company lost over 30 percent of its market value during his 18-month tenure. Worse, the corporation recorded the first quarterly loss in its history in the fall of 1992. Wood, who had retained Lilly's chairmanship, orchestrated a boardroom revolt to oust his protégé in 1993.

In June of that year, Randall Tobias was selected CEO and chairperson. Unlike all his predecessors, Tobias was recruited from outside Lilly's employee roster. The former vice-chairman of American Telephone and Telegraph Co. had served on Lilly's board since 1986 and was by his own admission inexperienced in pharmaceuticals. Nonetheless, after just six months at Lilly's helm, Tobias announced a reorganization of the venerable drug company.

His plan included divestment of the profitable, but distractive, Medical Device and Diagnostics Division, through which he hoped to raise $550 million. A cost-reduction program included the elimination of 4,000 employees through early retirement. Tobias planned to use these savings to acquire the distributors needed in a pharmaceutical industry that was increasingly influenced by budget-conscious managed care organizations. In line with this focus, Lilly announced its plan to acquire PCS Health Systems Inc., America's largest pharmacy benefit manager, from McKesson Corp. for $4 billion in mid-1994. Tobias, who had orchestrated AT&T's overseas expansion, also worked to expand Lilly's international sales from their 1993 level of about 39 percent of total revenues.

Tobias's plan also focused Lilly's research and development on five broad disease categories: central nervous system diseases, endocrine diseases (including diabetes and osteoporosis), infectious diseases, cancer, and cardiovascular diseases. In line with these strategic imperatives, Lilly in 1995 released Lys-Pro, a new type of insulin for the treatment of diabetes, in 1995, and Zyprexa (olanzapine), indicated for schizophrenia, in 1996.

In 1996 the FDA approved Lilly's Gemzar as the nation's first drug to treat pancreatic cancer. Two years later the FDA approved using Gemzar for nonsmall-cell lung cancer. According to the company's web site, in 2002 over 85 countries had approved Gemzar and almost 80 percent of U.S. patients with pancreatic cancer used Gemzar.

In 1997 the FDA authorized using Evista to help prevent osteoporosis in postmenopausal women. Evista sales in 2000 of $552 million made it one of the company's major products. Other new products were Humalog, a human insulin analog, and ReoPro, a cardiovascular product discovered and developed by Centocor.

After the U.S. Food and Drug Administration in 1997 eased rules on mass media advertising for prescription drugs, Lilly and others in the pharmaceutical industry increased their spending on TV spots. Lilly spent $7 million in direct-to-consumer (DTC) promotionals in 1999. The following year $46.5 million was spent, mostly for Prozac as the end of its patent protection neared.

Although the evidence was not conclusive, television ads in particular were linked to increasing consumer sales, but perhaps with a hidden cost. "The issues raised by DTC advertising are serious," said health policy researcher Steven Findlay in *Marketing Health Services* in spring 2000. "They touch upon questions of public health, corporate responsibility, advertising ethics, and consumers' capacity to understand complex medical and pharmaceutical information."

In August 2001 Lilly lost U.S. patent protection for Prozac after a series of legal conflicts. At that point Barr Laboratories gained a six-month exclusive right to make a generic Prozac equivalent. Declining Prozac sales in the fourth quarter of 2001 led to a 14 percent reduction in company revenues. In January 2002 the U.S. Supreme Court rejected Lilly's final patent appeal without comment, which opened the door to several other companies making generic versions of the antidepressant drug. Thus ended a major chapter in Lilly's history.

The same month the federal government settled an investigation of Lilly violating its own privacy policies by releasing email addresses of over 600 Prozac patients. According to the *New York Times*, the "case is the first the Federal Trade Commission has pursued over suspected unintentional violation of a Web site's privacy policies."

Lilly reported $10.86 billion in net sales and $3.05 billion in net income in 2000, both figures up from $10.0 billion in net sales and $2.72 billion in net income the previous year. There was a significant change in the source of its income. In 1996 Prozac accounted for 34 percent of its net sales, but that declined to 24 percent in 2000. Meanwhile, its newer products (Zyprexa, Evista, Actos, Humalog, Gemzar, and ReoPro) increased to bring in 41 percent of all 2000 sales. Zyprexa, approved for schizophrenia and the acute manic phase of bipolar conditions, in the fourth quarter of 2000 surpassed Prozac as the company's number one selling product, with over $2 billion in 2000 sales. In 2000 the company listed 30 trademarked pharmaceuticals on its web site. A few of those were trademarked by other companies that Lilly worked with in joint operations.

In December 2001 Lilly had several new products that it planned to launch by 2004. They included Forteo to reverse osteoporosis, Cialis for male erectile dysfunction, Atomexetine to treat attention deficit disorder, Duloxetine for depression and urinary incontinence, an olanzipine and fluoxetine combination to fight depression, Alimta to treat a form of lung cancer called mesothelioma, and a PKC beta inhibitor to treat diabetic eye problems. Lilly expected that these and several other products in the pipeline would keep the company prosperous in the years to come.

Principal Subsidiaries

Eli Lilly International Corporation; Eli Lilly Interamrica, Inc.; Eli Lilly de Centro America, S.A. (Guatemala); Eli Lilly Compania de Mexico, S.A. de C.V.; Dista Mexicana, S.A. de C.V.; EPCO; Eli Lilly Industries, Inc.; Eli Lilly and Company (Taiwan), Inc.; CBI Uniforms, Inc. (50%); ELCO Management Corp.; Eli Lilly S.A. (Switzerland); Elanco Animal Health; Sphinx Pharmaceuticals Corporation; Control Diabetes SVC; Lilly ICOS LLC.

Principal Competitors

GlaxoSmithKline; Pfizer Inc.; Novo Nordisk.

Further Reading

Bian, Tonda R., *The Drug Lords: America's Pharmaceutical Cartel,* Kalamazoo, Mich.: No Barriers Publishing, 1997.

Bliss, Michael, *The Discovery of Insulin,* Chicago: University of Chicago Press, 1982.

Bottcher, Helmuth M., *Wonder Drugs, A History of Antibiotics,* London: Heinemann, 1963.

Breed, Allen G., "Women Form National Group to Support Prozac Users," *Provo Herald* (Provo, Utah), August 28, 1990, p. C5.

Clark, Roscoe Collins, *Threescore Years and Ten: A Narrative of the First Seventy Years of Eli Lilly & Company,* Chicago: R.R. Donnelley, 1946.

"Eli Lilly Puts Another Notch in Health Care's Belt," *Corporate Growth Report,* July 25, 1994, pp. 7363, 7374.

Findlay, Steven, "Do Ads Really Drive Pharmaceutical Sales?," *Marketing Health Services,* Spring 2000, pp. 20–25.

Greising, David, "Randall Tobias Takes a Pruning Hook to Lilly," *Business Week,* January 31, 1994, p. 32.

Hass, Nancy, "Serious Medicine," *Financial World,* November 9, 1993, pp. 32–34.

Kramer, Peter D., *Listening to Prozac,* New York: Viking Press, 1993.

Kronholm, William, "FDA Ends Barriers to Advertising Prescription Drugs," *Salt Lake Tribune,* September 16, 1985, p. D2.

"Lilly and Schering Offer Modest 4Q Results," *Chemical Market Reporter,* January 28, 2002, p. 2.

"Lilly Plans to Offer 8 New Drugs . . . ," *Los Angeles Times,* December 24, 2001, p. C6.

"Lilly Privacy Violation Charges Are Settled," *New York Times,* January 19, 2002, p. C3.

Madison, James H., *Eli Lilly: A Life, 1885–1977,* Indianapolis: Indiana Historical Society, 1989.

Moskowitz, Milton, et al., "Lilly," in *Everybody's Business: A Field Guide to the 400 Leading Companies in America,* New York: Doubleday Currency, 1990, pp. 176–77.

Petersen, Melody, "Lilly Joins 3 Other Giants on Discounts," *New York Times,* March 6, 2002, p. C12.

Scott, Carlee R., "Eli Lilly & Co. Agrees to Buy Hybritech Inc.," *Wall Street Journal,* September 19, 1985, p. 8.

"Supreme Court Rejects Lilly Appeal," *Chemical Market Reporter,* January 21, 2002, p. 4.

Swann, John P., *Academic Scientists and the Pharmaceutical Industry: Cooperative Research in Twentieth-Century America,* Baltimore: Johns Hopkins University Press, 1988.

Szegedy-Maszak, Marianne, "The Career of a Celebrity Pill," *U.S. News & World Report,* August 6, 2001, pp. 38–39.

Teitelman, Robert, "Wilting Lilly," *Financial World,* May 3, 1988, pp. 36–39.

Waldholz, Michael, and Gregory Stricharchuk, "Fight Between Generic and Major Drug Firms Heats Up As Stakes Rise," *Wall Street Journal,* October 4, 1989, pp.A1, A22.

"Watson to Sell a Generic Prozac," *Wall Street Journal,* January 30, 2002.

—updates: April Dougal Gasbarre, David M. Walden

communications

Emmis Communications Corporation

40 Monument Circle, Suite 700
Indianapolis, Indiana 46204
U.S.A.
Telephone: (317) 266-0100
Fax: (317) 631-3570
Web site: http://www.emmis.com

Public Company
Incorporated: 1980 as Emmis Broadcasting Corp.
Employees: 3,143
Sales: $470.62 million (2001)
Stock Exchanges: NASDAQ
Ticker Symbol: EMMS
NAIC: 513112 Radio Stations; 513120 Television
   Broadcasting; 513111 Radio Networks; 511120
   Periodical Publishers; 511130 Book Publishers

Emmis Communications Corporation is a diversified media company with interests in radio, television, and publishing. The Indiana-based firm operates about two dozen radio stations, including market leaders in New York and Los Angeles, 15 television stations that broadcast all of the major commercial networks, and niche-market magazines including *Texas Monthly, Duncan's American Radio,* and *Country Sampler.* Most Emmis properties are located in the United States, though the company also has interests abroad including two radio stations in Argentina. Publicly traded Emmis is run by its founder, Jeffrey Smulyan, who controls a majority of the firm's voting stock.

Beginnings

Emmis Communications got its start in 1979 when Jeffrey Smulyan and two partners purchased a radio station in Shelbyville, Indiana. After renaming it WENS-FM ("Lite Rock 9700") and moving it to Indianapolis, they put the station on the air in July 1981 after a number of regulatory hurdles had been cleared. Smulyan, who had a legal degree from the University of Southern California, had long been interested in radio, having operated a station in Indianapolis in the mid-1970s that his

father purchased for him. That station, WNTS-AM (News-Talk-Sports) was a small operation that was noteworthy for the presence of future TV talk show host David Letterman (who would later become a board member and 1 percent owner of Emmis). The entity formed to manage WENS was named Emmis Broadcasting, after an unpublished novel Smulyan had written called "The Emmis Region"—Emmis also being the Hebrew word for "truth."

Within six months of entering the market WENS was earning a respectable 7 share in the Arbitron ratings, and in 1983 the company purchased a second station, WLOL in Minneapolis, for $6 million. The next year KSHE in St. Louis and KMGG in Los Angeles were also bought for a combined total of $20 million. The company, which had taken in only $500,000 in revenues in 1982, reported $22.6 million in sales for the fiscal year ending in 1985.

That year found Smulyan in disagreement with partners Mickey Maurer and Bob Schloss over the expansion he was plotting for the company. An acrimonious split ensued, with Smulyan buying the pair out for a total of $21.3 million. The buyout was financed with a $61 million capitalization in which $11 million in private stock and $50 million in high-yield "junk" bonds were offered. Morgan Stanley and Cigna Insurance Co. invested a total of $8 million, with Smulyan holding on to 55 percent of the company. The cash that was left over was earmarked for expansion, and new stations were soon purchased in New York, Boston, San Francisco, Chicago, and Houston.

Smulyan's instincts for what worked in radio were strong, and he excelled at taking underperforming stations and rebuilding them until they generated a positive cash flow. A newly acquired station often underwent a format change which was promoted with cash give-away contests and advertising in a variety of media. Substantial research was done before a new acquisition was made which included taking listener surveys, examining the competition, and looking at the market's available advertising dollars and potential for growth.

One of Emmis's greatest successes took place in Los Angeles, where the company converted sleepy KMGG into KPWR ("Power 106"), which featured a then unusual mix of urban contemporary dance music that appealed to African American, Latino, and white teenagers. Within six months KPWR had moved from 24th to number one in the 80-station market, a stunning turnaround.

Getting a Toehold in New York: 1986

In 1986 Emmis became the largest privately held radio group when it purchased three stations from Doubleday Broadcasting for $53.6 million. They included WAPP-FM and WHN-AM in New York, and WAVA-FM in Washington, D.C. Smulyan had been looking to get into New York for some time, as it and Los Angeles comprised the top two markets in the United States. The company later changed the name of WAPP to WQHT, which began programming a similar mix of music to KPWR, and also repositioned country-formatted WHN as the nation's first all-sports station, WFAN. For Smulyan, a diehard sports fan, this was the realization of a longtime dream, and he began pumping money into the station to make it a hit, though its early results were not encouraging.

In 1988 Emmis acquired half ownership of Duncan's American Radio, Inc., publisher of American Radio, a leading broadcasting industry statistical publication. Other activities by this time included Emmis Research, a consulting firm that studied audiences and made recommendations to broadcasters, and *Indianapolis Monthly,* a 53,000 circulation magazine that focused on living in the city.

The year 1988 also saw Emmis make its largest acquisition to date when it bought five stations from the National Broadcasting Company (NBC), a move forced by federal ownership restrictions that became an issue when NBC was purchased by General Electric in 1986. Emmis obtained WJIB-FM in Boston, WKQX-FM in Chicago, KYUU-FM in San Francisco (later changed to KXXX), and WYNY-FM and WNBC-AM in New York. Emmis could only keep two of its four New York stations after the deal, and soon sold WYNY to Westwood One, Inc. for $39 million, moving WQHT-FM's signal to WYNY's more desirable 97.1 megahertz. WNBC-AM was shut down after 62 years in operation and its powerful 50,000 watt clear channel frequency assigned to Emmis's WFAN, at which time the old WFAN frequency was also sold. Having earlier racked up millions in losses, WFAN now clicked, due in part to the

addition of WNBC's New York Knicks and Rangers games as well as popular morning personality Don Imus. Emmis also bought adult-contemporary formatted KKHT-FM in Houston during 1988, which later became known as KNRJ.

The following summer Jeff Smulyan led a group that included Morgan Stanley & Co. and Emmis board member Michael Browning in purchasing the Seattle Mariners baseball team for an estimated $76 million and assumption of $12 million in debt. Afterwards Emmis sold KNRJ for $30 million and KXXX of San Francisco for $18.5 million to give Smulyan cash to finance the deal and to help lower Emmis's $220 million in debt. Emmis also secured a new credit line worth $185 million.

With interest payments eating up more and more of his company's revenues, in 1990 Smulyan decided to sell WLOL to Minnesota Public Radio for $12 million, and to take a $1 million pay cut. Despite such measures, when the company's year-end figures were tallied in early 1991 a record loss of $23 million was reported on revenues of $94.7 million. A few months later, in June, WAVA of Washington, D.C., was sold for $20 million.

Sale of WFAN: 1991

At the end of 1991, with both Emmis's and his own finances continuing to deteriorate, Smulyan put the money-losing Mariners on the block and sold WFAN to Infinity Broadcasting for $70 million, a record price for an AM station. The divestiture was a painful one, as WFAN was one of the most profitable broadcasting operations in the country. Soon afterwards, a deal was worked out to sell the Mariners for $120 million to a group of Seattle-area investors. At the end of 1992 Boston's WJIB was also sold.

In 1993 Smulyan arranged for issuance of $90 million in notes to help pay down the company's debt. That August Emmis made its first acquisition in several years when it bought Atlanta magazine from American Express Publishing Corp. The monthly magazine, founded in 1961, had 60,000 subscribers.

The company's finances were now on the mend, and at the end of the year an initial public offering of 3.4 million shares of common stock was readied. Some 540,000 of them were Smulyan's, who would retain control of two-thirds of the voting stock. The sale took place at the end of February 1994 and brought in $52.9 million, which was largely earmarked for debt reduction.

Emmis was now eager to get back into the acquisition game, as a recent FCC ruling that raised the number of radio stations a company could own gave it new opportunities for expansion. The first deal to be struck was for a pair of Indianapolis stations, news/talk WIBC-AM and oldies-formatted WKLR-FM, bought from Horizon Broadcasting Corp. for $26 million. Later in the year Emmis also bought a 24.5 percent stake in Talk Radio U.K., a joint venture of several media and investment companies that planned to start a new commercial station in Britain. In December Emmis bought another New York area station, WRKS-FM ("KISS-FM"), from Summit Communications for $68 million. The acquisition gave Emmis two of the top five stations in the market, and within a year WRKS and WQHT held positions one and two.

Key Dates:

1979: Jeffrey Smulyan and two partners buy a radio station near Indianapolis.

1981: WENS-FM begins broadcasting on July 4, soon earns a 7 market share.

1983: Company purchases WLOL of Minneapolis.

1985: Smulyan buys out partners for $21.3 million, issues $50 million in bonds.

1986: Three stations are acquired for $53.6 million from Doubleday Broadcasting.

1987: WFAN-AM, country's first all-sports station, is launched in New York City.

1988: Five station acquisition deal is completed with NBC; WFAN takes WNBC's frequency.

1991: Emmis's losses mount due to over-leveraging; WFAN is sold for $70 million.

1994: Back in financial health, Emmis goes public on the NASDAQ.

1998: Company buys six TV stations, changes name to Emmis Communications.

1998: New corporate headquarters opens in Indianapolis.

2000: Emmis purchases 15 television stations from Lee Enterprises for $562.3 million.

2001: Worsening economy forces layoffs and sales of two Denver radio stations.

In late 1995 Emmis sold its interest in Talk Radio U.K. for just under $3 million, due to a lack of control in the venture. The next year saw the company finalize plans to construct a new $15 million office and broadcast facility in downtown Indianapolis, aided by city funding of $9.5 million for infrastructure and a parking garage. Passage of the 1996 Telecommunications Act by the U.S. Congress, which further deregulated the industry, led to more acquisitions in the fall when Emmis reached a deal to buy three radio stations in St. Louis from Zimco, Inc. for $42.5 million. The company reported revenues of $103.3 million for the year ending in February, 1997, with earnings a healthy $15.4 million.

In May 1997 Emmis reached an unusual deal with Tribune Co. to swap that company's New York FM station, WQCD, for two television stations which Emmis purchased at Tribune's behest. The arrangement, which cost Emmis $140 million, allowed Tribune to avoid paying capital gains taxes. The acquisition of jazz-formatted WQCD made Emmis the third largest operator in the New York radio market. Also in the spring, Emmis bought two more Indianapolis stations, WTLC-FM and AM, from Panache Broadcasting of Philadelphia for $15 million.

In August the acquisitions continued with the purchase of Network Indiana and the AgriAmerica Network from Wabash Valley Broadcasting Corporation, both of which offered informational and talk programming within the state. Later in the year Emmis's publishing portfolio was expanded with the purchase of *Cincinnati Magazine* from CM Media. *Cincinnati* had circulation of 30,000.

The company re-entered the European market in November when it led a coalition of investors that purchased a seven-year license to run Hungaria Radio Rt. ("Slager Radio") of Hungary. The newly created national network would be managed by Emmis, which owned a 54 percent stake in the $20 million operation. In January 1998 Emmis spent $37 million to buy Mediatex Communications Corp., parent company of magazine publisher Texas Monthly, Inc., and two other subsidiaries. The 25-year-old *Texas Monthly* had 300,000 subscribers.

Moving into Television: 1998

In early 1998 Emmis Broadcasting reached an agreement to purchase six television stations and three radio stations from SF Broadcasting and Wabash Valley Broadcasting. The TV stations were in Fort Myers, Florida; Mobile, Alabama; Green Bay, Wisconsin; Terre Haute, Indiana; New Orleans; and Honolulu, Hawaii, while all three radio stations were located in Terre Haute. Five of the six television stations were Fox Network affiliates, with the Terre Haute one aligned with CBS. To finance the $397 million deal, and others that were expected to follow, Emmis issued five million shares of class A stock and arranged for $750 million in credit from a consortium of banks. The company's class B stock remained in the hands of Smulyan, who now had 66.4 percent voting control. At the same time the company changed its name to Emmis Communications Corporation, reflecting its diversification into print media.

In December Emmis opened its new seven-story corporate headquarters in downtown Indianapolis, which contained space for the company's local broadcasting and publishing operations. The building had 23 radio and television production studios, eight news rooms, three atriums, and an employee fitness center.

In January 1999 Emmis joined with 11 other broadcasters to invest $500,000 in USA Digital Radio, Inc. of Columbia, Maryland, which was developing technology to help radio stations broadcast "CD Quality" audio over the air. Several months later the company launched a quarterly offshoot of *Texas Monthly,* entitled *Texas Monthly Biz,* which used the subscriber list of recently purchased *Texas Business.* Another print media acquisition was closed in April when Emmis bought Sampler Publications, Inc., owner of several bimonthly craft and decorating magazines including *Country Sampler,* which had circulation of more than 500,000.

In June Emmis announced the acquisition of WKCF-TV of Orlando, Florida, a WB Network affiliate, for $191.5 million. A complicated deal to purchase six radio stations and a TV station in St. Louis from Sinclair Broadcast Group was also announced. The stations were acquired through former Sinclair head Barry Baker, who had retained options to buy them which he assigned to Emmis for "a nominal fee." The purchase price was to be determined by a committee of independent appraisers. In October Emmis sold 4.2 million shares of Class A common stock and 2.8 million shares of convertible preferred stock for $378 million. Liberty Media Group bought an additional 2.7 million shares for $150 million, which gave it 14 percent of the company. Controlling interest remained in Jeffrey Smulyan's hands.

In November Emmis invested $15 million to acquire 75 percent ownership of two top radio stations in Argentina, Radio 10 and FM News, and also donated its Terre Haute AM station WTHI to Word Power, Inc., a religious broadcasting concern.

Some $5 million more was spent to purchase 2 percent of BuyItNow.com, a web-based retailer.

In January 2000 Sinclair Broadcast Group filed a $40 million lawsuit against Emmis and Barry Baker over his assignment of stations to Emmis, which was soon met by a $300 million countersuit. Also in January, *Los Angeles* magazine was acquired from the Walt Disney Company. *Los Angeles,* with circulation of 183,000, was one of the six largest publications of its type in the country. Later in the year Emmis joined with Creative Street to introduce *Game Warden Wildlife Journal,* a new conservation-themed quarterly magazine based on a television program.

In May the company reached an agreement to buy 15 television stations from Lee Enterprises, Inc. for $562.5 million. The stations, which comprised eight network affiliates and seven satellite operations, were located in Oregon, New Mexico, West Virginia, Hawaii, Arizona, Nebraska, and Kansas. A short time later another swap deal was made in which Emmis received three radio stations in Phoenix from Hearst-Argyle in exchange for a television station to be purchased later. Next, Emmis scooped up two radio stations located in Phoenix and Denver from Clear Channel Communications and AM/FM, Inc. for $108 million.

The spring of 2000 saw Emmis resolve its legal dispute with Sinclair Broadcast Group. The settlement gave Emmis clearance to purchase the six St. Louis radio stations for $220 million, while forfeiting claims to the television station. The company subsequently traded four St. Louis stations to Bonneville International Corp. for country formatted KZLA-FM in Los Angeles. Emmis worked its magic there once again, reformatting KZLA to play modern country music, and it soon became the most listened to station of its type in the United States.

In September the company added another Denver station, adult contemporary KALC-FM, acquired from Salem Communications Corp. for $98.8 million. The same month an Emmis-led group launched Local Media Internet Venture, Inc. LMIV would offer links to 185 radio stations owned by the venture's five partners and offer streaming audio for online listening. Emmis was also a partner with 16 other television station owners in iBlast Networks, which was working on plans for offering streaming video content over the Internet.

In January 2001 Emmis sold WTLC-AM and the trademark, logo, and call letters of its Indianapolis-based WTLC-FM to Radio One, Inc., which would continue to operate the station at a different location on the dial. Emmis took in $8.5 million on the sale, afterwards using the 105.7 FM frequency for newly created WXYB, a "soft adult contemporary" station.

High Debt Causing Problems Again: Early 2000s

Although Emmis had taken a conservative tack during the unprecedented radio consolidation that followed passage of the Telecommunications Act of 1996 (largely because the memory of its earlier financial crisis was still fresh), the company was feeling more and more pressure from Wall Street to add to its holdings. Emmis had always sought underperforming, reasonably priced properties that it could develop into ratings leaders, but the company was now starting to pay some of the inflated

prices of the overheated market just to stay in the game. Consequently, its debt grew, eventually reaching more than $1 billion.

In early 2001 Emmis began to feel the effects of the dot.com bust, as advertising dollars from this important sector dried up. In March the company cut 120 jobs in its television station group, though this was attributed partly to the consolidation of operations at the stations acquired from Lee Enterprises.

With its stock taking a beating the company began making plans to spin off its TV group, but the move was put on hold after the terrorist attacks of September 11, 2001. The provision of advertising-free news coverage during the ensuing days, and the economic downturn that came soon after, put an even tighter crimp in the company's revenue stream. In December Emmis's majority-owned Hungarian radio venture lost its license to broadcast because the company had missed a loan payment. Emmis soon announced plans to institute a 10 percent pay cut for its entire workforce and to sell off non-strategic assets, though acquisition of a small book publisher, Guild Press of Indiana, was nonetheless completed during this period. Early in 2002 the company sold its two Denver, Colorado radio stations for a total of $135 million. Emmis continued to have trouble keeping within its loan covenants, however, and with outstanding debt of nearly $1.3 billion and reduced earnings it was once again in a precarious position. In April 2002, the company raised $120 million by selling four million new shares of stock.

While Emmis Communications was experiencing difficulties in the wake of a slowdown in the U.S. economy and the 9/11 terrorist attacks, the company had recovered from a similar situation in the early 1990s and had several options on the table. It also held a number of valuable assets, including leading radio stations in several major markets and a successful publishing division, and its founder and CEO Jeffrey Smulyan was a seasoned veteran of the radio business whose instincts had proven correct numerous times in the past.

Principal Subsidiaries

Emmis License Corporation; Emmis Television License Corporation; Emmis Radio License Corporation; Emmis License Corporation of New York; Emmis Radio License Corporation of New York; Emmis Radio Corporation; Emmis Meadowlands Corporation; Emmis Publishing Corporation; Emmis Escrow Corporation; Emmis Escrow Holding Corporation; SJL of Kansas Corp.; Emmis Television License Corporation of Wichita; Topeka Television Corporation; Emmis Television License Corporation of Topeka; Emmis International Broadcasting Corporation; Emmis Latin America Broadcasting Corporation; Emmis South America Broadcasting Corporation; Emmis Argentina Broadcasting, S.A.; Emmis Buenos Aires Broadcasting, S.A. (Argentina); Votionis, S.A. (Argentina; 75%); Slager Radio Rt. (Hungary; 59.5%); Emmis Hungarian Holding Co. (Hungary).

Principal Competitors

Clear Channel Communications, Inc.; Cumulus Media, Inc.; Infinity Broadcasting Corp.; Citadel Communications Corp.; Cox Enterprises, Inc.; Entercom Communications Corp.

Further Reading

Bachman, Katy, "Emmis Singing the Blues Over Sinclair," *Mediaweek,* January 24, 2000, p. 14.

Block, Valerie, "Emmis Finds Groove: Has Few Rivals in Black Radio Market," *Crain's New York Business,* November 16, 1998, p. 3.

Cobo, Lucia, and Geoff Fosie, "Emmis Broadcasting: The Perils of Smulyan," *Broadcasting and Cable,* February 18, 1991, p. 54.

Crawford, Amanda J., "Sinclair Selling Last 6 of Its Radio Stations," *Baltimore Sun,* June 23, 2000, p. 2C.

Dooms, Tracy M., "Smulyan Denies Reports That Morgan Stanley Will Take Control of Emmis," *Indianapolis Business Journal,* September 23, 1991, p. 4.

——, "WFAN Sale May Bring Emmis $70 Million," *Indianapolis Business Journal,* December 16, 1991, p. 3A.

Edelhart, Courtenay, "Indianapolis-Based Media Company Buys Stake in Internet Retailer," *Indianapolis Star and News,* November 17, 1999.

"Emmis Pursuing Rare Stock Move," *Indianapolis Business Journal,* June 19, 2000, p. 1.

"Emmis Writes New Chapter," *Indianapolis Business Journal,* July 17, 2000, p. 9.

Hebert, Emily, "Hungarian Radio License May Be Boon for Emmis," *Indianapolis Business Journal,* November 10, 1997, p. 13.

——, "Smulyan Shopping Overseas," *Indianapolis Business Journal,* September 29, 1997, p. 1A.

Higgins, Will, "Emmis Considers a Major Acquisition," *Indianapolis Business Journal,* June 15, 1987, p. 5A.

——, "1985 Enterprise Awards: Jeff Smulyan," *Indianapolis Business Journal,* January 6, 1986, p. 14.

——, "WENS' Jeff Smulyan & the $61 Million Deal," *Indianapolis Business Journal,* November 11, 1985, p. 1A.

Horgan, Sean, "Communications Company Opens World Headquarters in Indianapolis," *Indianapolis Star and News,* December 19, 1998.

Johnson, J. Douglas, "Mr. Radio Goes Major League," *Indiana Business,* October 1, 1989, p. 8.

Jones, Tim, "Small Indianapolis-Based Broadcast Company Survives in Sea of Big Fish," *Chicago Tribune,* February 6, 2000.

Kneale, Dennis, "NBC Agrees to Sell Emmis 5 Radio Stations," *Wall Street Journal,* February 22, 1988.

Knight, Dana, "Indianapolis-Based Emmis Communications Gives Stock in Return for Pay Cuts," *Indianapolis Star and News,* November 16, 2001.

——, "Indianapolis-Based Media Company Ponders TV Spinoff Proposal," *Indianapolis Star and News,* June 27, 2001.

Kukolla, Steve, "Emmis Completes Refinancing to Pay Down $90 Million of Debt," *Indianapolis Business Journal,* July 5, 1993, p. 4A.

——, "Healthy Emmis May Have Bigger Appetite for Growth," *Indianapolis Business Journal,* July 4, 1994, p. 5.

——, "WZPL Seen As Target for Emmis After Its Initial Public Offering," *Indianapolis Business Journal,* January 3, 1994, p. 3A.

Lauria, Peter, "Emmis Exits Denver with Rich Payday," *Daily Deal,* February 14, 2002.

"M's Owner's Mound of Debt Radio Company 'Can Survive,' Smulyan Says," *Seattle Post-Intelligencer,* February 20, 1991, p. B6.

Moss, Linda, "WFAN Scores with Sports After Losses," *Crain's New York Business,* April 17, 1989, p. 3.

Parets, Robyn Taylor, "Risk-Taking Broadcaster Hits Top of Charts," *Investor's Business Daily,* November 1, 1994, p. A6.

Peers, Martin, "Emmis Stops Watching Radio Deals from the Sidelines," *Wall Street Journal,* November 9, 1999, p. B4.

Pletz, John, "Emmis Scores Big with Television Play," *Indianapolis Business Journal,* April 6, 1998, p. 7.

Purdy, Janet, "Connecting with Listeners in Top Markets," *Investor's Business Daily,* January 23, 1996, p. A6.

Randall, Laura, "Emmis Stock Hammered on Plan to Buy Lee Stations," *Hollywood Reporter,* May 9, 2000, p. 6.

Rettig, Ellen, "Emmis Stock Wins Analysts' Acclaim," *Indianapolis Business Journal,* December 20, 1999, p. 1.

Rush, Jill, "Is Emmis Over-Leveraged? Smulyan, Others Say No; Cash Flow Strong Enough to Handle $194 Mil Long-Term Debt," *Indianapolis Business Journal,* March 6, 1989, p. 1A.

Sherwin, Bob, "Jeff Smulyan—Start with Confidence—The New Mariner Owner Is Off and Running, Looking for Ways to Make the Team a Winner," *Seattle Times,* March 25, 1990, p. 9.

Swiatek, Jeff, "Indianapolis-Based Radio Stays Tuned to Acquisitions," *Indianapolis Star and News,* December 22, 1999.

Wang, Karissa S., "TV's True Believer: Jeff Smulyan," *Electronic Media,* January 22, 2001, p. 40.

Weaver, Gregory, "Indianapolis-Based Radio, Television Company Warns of Drop in Revenue, Profits," *Indianapolis Star and News,* February 27, 2001.

—Frank Uhle

Energis plc

Carmelite
50 Victoria Embankment
London EC4Y 0DE
United Kingdom
Telephone: +44 20 7206 5555
Fax: +44 20 7206 5500
Web site: http://www.energis.co.uk

Public Company
Incorporated: 1993
Employees: 3,500
Sales: $1.18 billion (2001)
Stock Exchanges: London NASDAQ
Ticker Symbol: EGS.L (London); ENGSY (NASDAQ)
NAIC: 513310 Wired Telecommunications Carriers;
    513322 Cellular and Other Wireless Telecommunications; 514191 On-Line Information Services

Energis plc is a leading provider of telecommunications and e-commerce solutions to the business market in the United Kingdom. Since 1999, the company has embarked on an aggressive strategy to expand into Continental Europe, resulting in a significant presence in Germany, the Netherlands, Switzerland, Ireland, and Poland. In 2001, Energis launched the interactive portal BrightBlue, its first service aimed at consumers.

Rapid Expansion As a Telecommunications Service Provider: 1993–97

Energis plc was founded in March 1993 as a private company by National Grid Group, which was an electrical utility in the United Kingdom. At the time the company was conceived, it decided to focus on telecommunications, which represented a mature market for conventional voice services and a high growth market for enhanced voice and advanced data services. The company anticipated strong growth in corporate data networks, but it did not expect the spectacular growth that occurred during the rest of the decade in corporate internets and intranets, call centers, and the huge volume of data that companies would be transmitting to manage and run their businesses.

By mid-1994, most of Energis's national telecommunications network had been constructed. The company decided to build the most modern network possible and based its fiber-optic network architecture exclusively on the Synchronous Digital Hierarchy (SDH) standard. It also saved considerable time and expense by building its network primarily across the National Grid Group's electricity transmission infrastructure. Within 19 months of beginning construction of its network, Energis was able to bring its first services to market. Even before it completed its core network, Energis won its cornerstone contract with the BBC (British Broadcasting Company).

In December 1997, Energis became a public company, with shares trading on the London Stock Exchange and the NASDAQ. Net proceeds from the flotation were approximately £200 million. The company used the proceeds to reduce its debt to the National Grid; it also capitalized £190 million of inter-company loans from National Grid and issued £60 million worth of convertible preferred shares to the National Grid. By March 31, 1998, the end of Energis's first fiscal year, the convertible preferred shares owned by the National Grid were worth £1.6 billion if fully converted.

Energis reported turnover, or revenue, of £167.9 million for its first fiscal year as a public company ending March 31, 1998. That compared to revenue of £97.1 million for 1996–97, £42.8 million for 1995–96, and £4.6 million for 1994–95. In 1997–98, basic telephony contributed £99.9 million, a 67 percent increase over the previous year, while revenue from advanced services increased by 82.4 percent to £68 million. Growth of basic telephony revenue was attributed to an increase in Energis's customer base and connected customer sites as well as a focus on increasing sales through resellers and aggregators. Advanced services—a higher margin business than basic telephony—benefited from a deliberate sales and marketing focus and from working with existing customers to introduce value-added services such as Energis's Virtual Private Network service, CustomNet, and Frame Relay and ATM data services.

By the end of its first fiscal year as a public company, Energis's national network stretched over 5,000 kilometers. It was built primarily across the National Grid's electricity transmission infrastructure as well as along the main distribution lines

Company Perspectives:

Energis is a communications company with a passion, help-ing business customers achieve their goals. This has moved our focus towards providing a comprehensive range of in-ternet and advanced data services—supported by fast, reli-able, broadband national networks. We are rapidly develop-ing businesses in selected Continental European markets, building on our proven UK business model. Our aim is to be the leading e-business and advanced telecoms solutions provider in Europe.

of some regional electricity companies and through the London underground. Through a capacity sharing agreement with Scot-tish Telecom, Energis was able to serve customers in Scotland. The company secured an International Facilities license in De-cember 1996 and owned capacity in 11 submarine cables. Energis also established correspondent relationships with major overseas telecommunications operators to deliver traffic abroad and to carry their traffic back to the United Kingdom.

Added Capacity and Services in the United Kingdom: 1998–99

Network expansion plans for 1998–99 called for extending the basic network an additional 1,450 kilometers and connect-ing the national network to Britain's key metropolitan areas. That would enable Energis to connect directly with its cus-tomers' sites, thereby reducing interconnect payments and in-creasing the speed and depth of its services.

In April 1998, Energis formed a joint venture called MetroHoldings Ltd. with Deutsche Telekom and France Tele-com. MetroHoldings planned to invest £100 million over the next five years to expand its network across London and then into other metropolitan areas in the United Kingdom. In Sep-tember 1998, the MetroHoldings network went live in London with the completion of three fiber-optic rings. That same month, MetroHoldings finished the second phase of its metropolitan area network program by concluding construction of networks for businesses in Birmingham and Manchester.

In 1998–99, Energis began to benefit even more from explo-sive growth in Internet and data communications. For its fiscal year ending March 31, 1999, the company's revenue from ad-vanced services—including data communications and Internet services—nearly tripled to £77.4 million. Overall, Energis re-ported revenue of £285.5 million for fiscal 1998–99, a 70 percent increase over the previous year. Although the company had yet to turn a profit, it managed to reduce its loss before taxes by 50 percent to £31.1 million, and its EBITDA (earnings before inter-est, taxes, depreciation, and amortization) was a positive £49.7 million. During the fiscal year, Energis's national network added nearly 1,500 kilometers to reach more than 6,500 kilometers. With the National Grid reducing its holdings in Energis to 49 percent in terms of shares, the company was able to join the FTSE 100, Britain's national stock index, in March 1999.

As part of its strategy to grow its advanced services busi-ness, Energis acquired Planet Online Ltd. for £75 million in

August 1998. Established in Leeds in 1995, Planet Online was the largest independent Internet service provider (ISP) in the United Kingdom that was focused on the business market. Later in the year Energis and Planet Online supplied the network and connectivity for Freeserve, a free Internet service launched by Dixons Store Group, England's largest electrical retailer.

Rapid Expansion in Continental Europe: 1999–2000

Fiscal 1999–2000 was a good year for Energis. The com-pany reported a 73 percent increase in revenue to £494 million. EBITDA increased 86 percent to £92.3 million, and the firm's operating loss before taxes and interest (EBIT) was reduced to £7.1 million.

In May 1999, Energis and Viridian Group plc, the parent company of Northern Ireland Electricity, formed a joint venture called nevada tele.com to build a new telecommunications net-work in Northern Ireland. Like Energis's U.K. network, the Northern Ireland network was built with SDH broadband fiber-optic transmission technology. It was to be built over Northern Ireland Electricity's infrastructure. Service in Belfast began in February 2000, with the rest of the country to follow.

In other U.K. developments, MetroHoldings Ltd. completed nine more metropolitan area networks to serve business com-munities in Birmingham, Manchester, Leeds, Bristol, and other cities. In November 1999, Energis acquired the U.K. company Datarange Communications from SFA Inc. of Maryland for £15 million. Founded in 1987, Datarange offered a complete range of network integration services, including design, consultancy, implementation, and support, which Energis could now offer to its business customers.

During fiscal 1999–2000, Energis expanded the services of-fered by its Internet division, Planet Online. In June 1999, Planet Online also began offering application service provider (ASP) services, starting with Windows Office 2000 and Exchange 2000. In November 1999, Energis acquired streaming audio and video technology for Planet Online by investing £15 million in Geo Interactive Media of Israel. Half of the investment went toward a 5.6 percent interest in the company, while the other half gave Energis the exclusive four-year European rights to Geo's audio and video streaming technology. That enabled Planet Online to launch itself as a media Internet service provider in the United Kingdom and Europe. The technology also enhanced Planet Online's web hosting and related services. In November 1999, Planet Online launched a new e-commerce platform that offered customers a customizable electronic storefront, backed by a full range of services from payment to product delivery. As part of Energis's desire to move into the hosting of vertical and sector-specific applications through Planet Online, Energis invested £7.5 million in online brokerage firm Broker-to-Broker Networks Inc. in January 2000.

With its core U.K. business doing well, Energis expanded into the Continental European market with confidence. During fiscal 1999–2000, the company invested £449 million in Euro-pean-based acquisitions. Its first European acquisition came in August with the purchase of Netherlands-based, pan-European carrier Unisource Carrier Services for about £60 million. Unisource provided international wholesale voice services, managed bandwidth, and Internet transit services to alternative fixed line and wireless telecommunications operators in Europe as well as to Internet service providers (ISPs). The acquisition gave Energis a pan-European backbone network and points of presence in ten European countries and in the United States, as well as an existing customer base. Following the acquisition, Unisource was renamed Energis Carrier Services.

In November 1999, Energis acquired EnerTel for £352 million. Renamed Energis NV following the acquisition, EnerTel was the Netherlands largest fixed line network alternative to the country's national telecommunications operator KPN. Energis made a similar acquisition in Germany in March 2000 when it purchased carrier24 for about £20 million. Carrier24 was a start-up company formed in May 1999 as an alternative network. At the time it was acquired by Energis, carrier24 was Germany's third largest telecommunications network by reach and had licenses to operate in Austria, Luxembourg, and Switzerland. After obtaining a license to operate in Poland, Energis formed a consortium there with the National Grid and local Polish companies to provide long-distance telephone service.

Energis extended its Continental Europe strategy even further with the December 1999 acquisition of a controlling interest in German Internet service provider BusinessOnline. Established in 1994, BusinessOnline was headquartered in Berlin and had offices in four other German cities. It was a rapidly growing business with revenues of £1 million for the first ten months of 1999. The acquisition of BusinessOnline, together with services offered by Planet Online through Energis Carrier Services, gave Energis a stronger Internet and data services presence in Europe, while at the same time strengthening its direct sales channels and services across Europe. Energis also announced it was investing in the construction of six data centers in Europe, with data centers in Frankfurt and Amsterdam expected to be operational by the spring of 2000.

Improved Business Mix in 2000–01

During fiscal 2000–01, Energis improved its business mix in favor of higher margin advanced services, data communica-

tions, and IP-based products. For the year, sales of advanced, data, and Internet services increased 86 percent and accounted for 70 percent of the company's total revenue. Overall revenues increased 70 percent to £840.4 million, with advanced, data, and Internet services contributing £585.5 million. EBITDA rose 53 percent to £141.7 million, while the company's operating loss (EBIT) deepened to £38.2 million. Internationally, Continental European markets accounted for 19 percent of overall revenue, compared to 10 percent in the previous fiscal year.

In May 2000, Energis acquired a 45 percent interest in Eurocall Ltd. for £20.25 million. Founded in 1995, Eurocall was a leading independent switchless reseller based in Manchester, England. Its customer base of small and medium-sized business enterprises (SMEs) was located in northern and middle England. The acquisition gave Energis a foothold in the SME market and allowed the company to offer SMEs a more comprehensive portfolio of telecommunications services.

In mid-2000, Energis re-branded two of its key businesses, Planet Online and Datarange, to take advantage of the Energis brand. Planet Online was renamed Energis Squared and positioned as an e-business solutions provider that offers a complete portfolio of Internet services and connectivity to customers across Europe. Datarange, which specialized in network integration, was renamed Energis Integration Services. Around this time the company also launched Energis Mobile, which offered Energis-branded mobile phone services in association with Orange, the United Kingdom's fastest growing mobile phone operator.

Taking advantage of its position as the primary IP (Internet Protocol) supplier to the U.K. travel industry, Energis launched the Energis Travel Network in July 2000. The Energis Travel Network was an end-to-end IP solution for travel companies and tour operators. Energis estimated that by allowing tour operators to connect directly to the Energis Travel Network for a flat annual fee, it would save the U.K. travel industry more than £15 million annually.

Energis continued to develop its metropolitan area networks and its pan-European strategy in 2000–01. In November 2000, the company completed metropolitan fiber optic rings in Glasgow and Edinburgh, Scotland. In Germany, Energis formed Energis Deutschland to combine its acquisitions and Internet data center there, while in Poland NG Koleje Telekomunikacja (NGKT) was renamed Energis Polska. Energis Polska was in the process of building a broadband fiber optic network to connect the largest towns and cities in Poland as well as a new data center in Warsaw. In January 2001, Energis acquired a 75 percent interest in Ision Internet AG of Hamburg, Germany, for about $742 million (EUR 800 million) in cash and stock. Ision was a leading web hosting and ASP company with a customer base of more than 800 companies.

New initiatives for 2001 included the creation of Energis Interactive, a joint venture with software developer Graham Technology. Energis Interactive's principal project in 2001 was the launch of BrightBlue, a consumer portal for content providers. It was Energis's first entry into the consumer market. At the beginning of the year the company signed a carrier agreement with interactive digital satellite TV provider British Sky Broadcasting. The four million homes served by Sky would be able to access a broad range of services offered on BrightBlue through interactive TV, the Internet, and mobile phones. Among the services offered on BrightBlue when it launched in November 2001 were shopping, banking, travel, betting, and employment.

Meanwhile, Energis's CEO since 1996, Mike Grabiner, resigned suddenly in May 2001 and was succeeded by COO David Wickham. Around the same time Energis announced that its chairman, Gordon Owen, was also resigning.

In July 2001, Energis merged four of its U.K. companies—Energis, Energis Mobile, Energis Squared, and Energis Integrated Services—to form a single, unified organization. This restructuring enabled the company to provide an integrated approach to all of its customers' e-commerce, IT services, and telecommunications requirements.

For the six months ending September 30, 2001, Energis reported a 33 percent increase in revenue to £487.9 million. Higher margin advanced and Internet services accounted for 70 percent of revenues. While difficult market conditions slowed revenue growth, the company strengthened its financial position by reducing capital expenditures, realizing cost savings, and increasing its medium-term debt facility from £600 million to £850 million. However, market conditions continued to deteriorate for the rest of 2001, and in November the company announced it would cut 350 jobs in the United Kingdom, Germany, and the Netherlands, leaving it with a workforce of 3,500 employees. Further cost-cutting measures were announced in January 2002, when the company lowered its estimates for the fiscal year.

There was no doubt that Energis faced a challenging business environment in 2002. The company was confident its market position and financial condition would enable it to weather the downturn in the telecommunications market. It would have to wait for improved market conditions to see if revenue growth would return to previous levels.

Principal Subsidiaries

Energis Carrier Services (Switzerland); Energis Netherlands; Energis Deutschland (Germany); Energis Polska (Poland); Energis Interactive (50%); MetroHoldings Ltd. (50%); nevada tele.com (50%).

Principal Divisions

Energis Integration Services; Energis Mobile; Energis Squared.

Principal Competitors

British Telecommunications plc; Cable & Wireless plc; COLT Telecom Group plc; KPN Telecom Broadcast (Netherlands).

Further Reading

"British Telecoms Firm Energis Extends Debt Financing, Cuts 350 More Jobs," *Knight-Ridder/Tribune Business News*, November 13, 2001.

Brown, Malcolm, "The Power of Energis," *Management Today*, January 1994, p. 76.

"Concern for Energis As Executives Depart," *New Media Investor*, May 24, 2001, p. 4.

"Date Set for BrightBlue Launch," *Inside Digital TV*, August 10, 2001.

"Energis Acquires Ision," *ISP Business News*, January 1, 2001.

"Energis Cuts Deeper," *Computer Weekly*, November 15, 2001, p. 4.

"Energis Expands," *InformationWeek*, August 9, 1999, p. 97.

"Energis Explores Wireless Possibilities with Orange," *Telecoms Deal Report*, August 4, 2000.

"Energis Fights Back with EnerTel Purchase," *Telecoms Deal Report*, November 18, 1999.

"Energis Offers Mobile Service," *Communicate*, July 2000, p. 15.

"Energis Opens Travel Network," *New Media Age*, July 27, 2000, p. 14.

"Energis Pursues European Strategy with Acquisition," *Telecoms Deal Report*, March 16, 2000.

"Energis' Success Hinges on European Presence," *Broadband Networking News*, April 10, 2001.

"It's a BrightBlue T-Future," *New TV Strategies*, January 2001, p. 3.

"New Energis Network 'Will Save Millions,'" *Travel Trade Gazette UK & Ireland*, July 24, 2000, p. 2.

West, Janet Anne, "BrightBlue Adds New Hue to BSkyB," *Electronic Media*, February 26, 2001, p. 18.

—David P. Bianco

Everlast Worldwide Inc.

1350 Broadway, Suite 2300
New York, New York 10018
U.S.A.
Telephone: (212) 239-0990
Fax: (212) 239-4261
Web site: http://www.everlast.com

Public Company
Incorporated: 1992 as TI Sportswear, Inc.
Employees: 271
Sales: $36.9 million (2000)
Stock Exchanges: NASDAQ
Ticker Symbol: EVST
NAIC: 339920 Sporting and Athletic Goods Manufacturing

Everlast, a brand name all but synonymous with the sport of boxing, has been reborn after being acquired in the year 2000 by longtime licensee, Active Apparel Group, which subsequently changed its name to Everlast Worldwide Inc. In addition to its corporate headquarters in Manhattan, the company has manufacturing facilities in the Bronx and Moberly, Missouri, where it produces a wide range of boxing equipment: from trunks, robes, and gloves to protective mouthpieces and protective cups, as well as speed bags and heavy bags for training. Everlast also offers complete boxing rings. Although sales to the limited market of professional prizefighters have a minor impact on the balance sheet, a continued connection of the Everlast name with boxing is instrumental in maintaining worldwide recognition for the label. Brand awareness is key to the company's more lucrative activities: the production of sportswear products and the licensing of the Everlast name to an array of other items, from watches to fitness equipment. Active Apparel's founder, George Horowitz, owns close to 22 percent of the company and serves as chairman, president, and chief executive officer.

Establishment of Everlast: 1910

A 17-year son of a tailor, Jacob Golomb, and his wife Hannah founded Everlast in the Bronx in 1910 to manufacture swimsuits. The name of the company was derived from his guarantee that the outfits would last an entire summer. Within a few years he began to produce other sports equipment and opened a shop in the Bronx to sell his wares. An avid fight fan, Golomb also began to make boxing equipment, and within a few years his store became known as Boxing Headquarters. The connection of the Everlast name with champions began in 1916 when future heavyweight champion Jack Dempsey turned to Golomb for equipment. According to his biographers, Dempsey was unheralded when he arrived in New York in 1916, but apparently Golomb recognized the boxer's potential and granted him credit on training gear. Dempsey failed to launch his professional boxing career at this time, however, and returned to the West, where in reduced circumstances he picked fruit, dug ditches, and washed dishes. A new manager, Doc Kearns, provided Dempsey with a second chance, and it was late in 1917 that the boxer began to make a name for himself after a pair of noteworthy fights in San Francisco. He returned to the New York area in 1918, knocking out the number one contender in Harrison, New Jersey, which resulted in a title fight against Jess Willard on July 4, 1919. Dempsey, forever grateful to Golomb, was wearing Everlast boxing gloves on the day he became the heavyweight champion of the world. For years he freely endorsed Everlast products.

To replace the trunks secured by a leather belt that most boxers wore, Golomb introduced trunks with an elastic waistband in the mid-1920s. He continued to add to his line of boxing equipment, so that by the 1930s Everlast's ties to the sport were deeply ingrained. With all the great fighters wearing Everlast trunks and robes and fighting with Everlast gloves, the company gained the reputation as ''The Choice of Champions.'' To the general public, Everlast and its distinctive concave logo became virtually synonymous with boxing.

After Jacob Golomb died in the 1950s, the business was taken over by his son David. In 1958, David Golomb sold a half-interest to Ben Nadorf, but it remained very much a private business. Nadorf was instrumental in expanding Everlast and opening a second manufacturing operation in Moberly, Missouri, in 1966. It was in Moberly that Everlast produced complete boxing rings, including ropes, turnbuckles, corner stools, and 12-inch gongs to mark the rounds of a fight.

Long dominant in boxing, Everlast was not quick to adapt to the changing world of the 1960s and 1970s. The sport of boxing remained popular, but young boys no longer received a pair of boxing gloves in much the same way they would a baseball glove or a basketball. Moreover, the company faced increased pressure from foreign companies that now made copycat boxing equipment, which was carried by the modern sporting goods chains, as opposed to the smaller stores that Everlast traditionally preferred. Apparel companies, however, recognized that the Everlast label possessed international recognition, promoted by its recognizable logo, which was seen during countless fights on television: on the waistbands on trunks, the cuffs on gloves, and the stanchions supporting the ring turnbuckles. Everlast also received free play when it appeared in the advertising of other products. Despite the company's lack of interest in actively promoting itself, the Everlast label had achieved an incredible level of recognition. Virtually without trying, the company had created a brand with a penetration that others could only dream about. With its longtime connection to boxing, Everlast possessed an athletic and tough image, as well as associations to an edgy world. In others words, it had the making of becoming incredibly hip, a brand in a category all by itself with immense untapped value.

Beginning of Licensing: 1980s

It was in 1983 that the company first agreed to license the Everlast name. Apparel maker Gerson & Gerson licensed the label to market a line of novelty women's shorts and robes. To promote the items, Gerson employed models who shadowboxed in department stores wearing skimpy tank tops and shorts, a campaign that failed miserably. According to a 1990 *Forbes* article, "To many shoppers, the soft-porn approach seemed only slightly more upscale than mud-wrestling. . . . Everlast learned an important lesson: If you're selling macho by association, go light on the macho. Capitalize on the scrappy image without offending the target market with lurid images of boxing mayhem." Licensing became an increasingly more important source of income for Everlast as boxing equipment sales tapered off, although sales of sports equipment such as punching bags, wrestling mats, and pommel horses to schools and gyms remained steady. Relying primarily on an outside agent, Everlast by the end of the 1980s licensed its name to more than a dozen companies, its logo found on a wide range of sportswear as well as sports products such as equipment bags. Everlast merchandise was sold in such upscale department stores as Bloomingdale's, Macy's, and Nordstrom, and not found in mass merchandisers such as Kmart. In addition, during the 1980s Everlast sought to take advantage of a fitness boom and began manufacturing some new exercise items, including ankle and wrist weights for women, exercise wheels, and other home items.

Everlast became associated with its chairman and current chief executive, George Horowitz, in 1992 when the company asked him to launch a line of women's sportswear under the Everlast label. Born in Brooklyn Horowitz actually grew up far more interested in boxing than in women's apparel and essentially became involved in the garment industry by chance. His father introduced him to boxing, and, according to Horowitz, he developed a passion for the sport by the time he was five years old. He often attended fights with his father at Madison Square Garden, where he became familiar with the Everlast logo in the ring. Horowitz graduated from Long Island University during the height of the Vietnam War, and instead of going on to law school he elected to take a draft exemption by teaching social studies in the New York public school system as well as indulging his interest in sports by coaching basketball and track. When New York fell into a severe financial crisis in the mid-1970s, Horowitz, who lacked tenure, lost his job. To support himself and his pregnant wife, he sold insurance for a year, a job he was glad to leave when presented in 1976 with an opportunity to help start an apparel company called Golden Touch Imports with a family friend. It was only because of this unanticipated set of circumstances that Horowitz established a career in fashion.

Horowitz started out as the vice-president of operations at Golden Touch, which did about $1 million in business in its first year. Fifteen years later it was a $250 million international concern and Horowitz was part owner, although not the major partner. He struck out on his own in 1990, starting up his own company to produce no-name activewear and sportswear. In 1992, he formally incorporated the business as TI Sportswear, Inc. In that same year Everlast approached him about licensing the Everlast label for women's sportswear. Upon receiving the license he changed the name of his company to Active Apparel. In the early days, when the company was staffed by just three people, Horowitz hired Rita Cinque as a consultant. She soon disbanded her own three-year-old business to join the new firm and became instrumental in the quick rise of Active Apparel, which took full advantage of the Everlast license.

Everlast originally asked Horowitz if he was capable of doing half a million dollars in business under the Everlast label during the first year. When he was able to generate $6.7 million in sales for 1993 by focusing on the theme of women's empowerment, followed by $12 million in 1994, Horowitz solidified his relationship with Golomb and Nadorf. Proving to be a tireless promoter of the Everlast women's line, he crisscrossed the country and even became involved in women's boxing. To take advantage of Active Apparel's success in transforming a traditionally male-dominated brand into a lucrative women's line of clothing, he soon signed a licensing agreement with Converse. In 1995, he took Active Apparel public, offering initial shares at $6.25 and netting $4 million. He took the company in a different direction in 1996 when he obtained a license from MTV based on a popular dance show and launched The Grind Line collection. Everlast, however, remained the most lucrative part of Active Apparel's business, and Horowitz eagerly strengthened his ties to the boxing label. Late in 1997, Active Apparel began to sell a line of bathing suits under the Everlast Woman brand. To focus all the company's attention on Everlast, Horowitz soon jettisoned Converse and MTV. He subsequently landed the Everlast menswear license as well, leading to even more robust business for Active Apparel. Promotional efforts were stepped up, leading to "Everlast Week"

Key Dates:

1910: Jacob Golomb establishes Everlast as a swimsuit manufacturer.

1917: According to legend, contact with Jack Dempsey leads to Everlast's involvement in boxing.

1958: Ben Nadorf becomes co-owner with Golomb's son, David.

1966: Everlast opens manufacturing facility in Moberly, Missouri.

1983: Everlast begins licensing its name.

1993: George Horowitz and Active Apparel Group gain Everlast license for women's sportswear.

2000: Active Apparel acquires Everlast, forms Everlast Worldwide.

activities conducted at major retailers. The company also opened concept stores in Bloomingdale's.

Falling out of Favor in the 1990s

While the licensing business, spearheaded by Active Apparel, was doing well for Everlast in the 1990s, its traditional boxing equipment business was deteriorating rapidly. Its shoes were of poor quality, essentially generic products made in Pakistan with the Everlast logo stitched on. Furthermore, the company's robes and trunks had not kept current with changing styles and its gloves no longer appealed to professional fighters. They were not considered to be "punchers' gloves," nor were they durable, leading some to call them "Neverlast." Other companies took advantage of the decline in Everlast, including new glove manufacturers Grant and Reyes. Rather than answer the upstart competition by improving the quality of their boxing equipment, the company allegedly turned to unsavory means of maintaining its market dominance. In 1998, Grant's founder, Grant Elvis Philips, sued in federal court, accusing Everlast of conducting a smear campaign against him. He claimed that Everlast personnel spread a number of nasty rumors about his operation: that it illegally smuggled products into the country, lacked product-liability insurance, bribed fighters to wear Grant Gloves, and produced gloves that were so defective they could lead to injuries, even death. According to Grant, Everlast was also responsible for a whispering campaign that suggested he was the illegitimate son of a Nevada boxing promoter and that he was known to steal Everlast gloves out of dressing rooms so that boxers would have to fight wearing Grant gloves. Some months later the suit would be settled, with Everlast paying an unspecified amount of money.

Much of the reason that Everlast was out of step with the contemporary boxing scene was that its leadership was aging. After David Golomb died at the age of 74 in 1995, 80-year-old Nadorf bought the remaining half of the business. In the late 1990s, a number of large companies approached him about acquiring Everlast. Because he was concerned that the company might be broken up, and he wanted someone with a genuine passion for boxing and truly understood the Everlast brand, he turned to Horowitz, who was excited about the possibility of buying the company. In the fall of 2000, the two parties reached

an agreement on a $60 million cash and stock deal. Active Apparel changed its name to Everlast Worldwide, with Horowitz serving as chairman and chief executive and Nadorf holding the title of president of the Everlast Sporting goods division.

Horowitz was quick to initiate changes, foremost of which was to restore Everlast's reputation in the boxing world. He replaced 1950s-era sewing machines with new models and computerized the ordering and inventory systems. He also hired consultants to help redesign Everlast equipment. Well-known trainer Teddy Atlas served as the connection to the fighters, trying out new equipment and offering suggestions to the Everlast designers. Horowitz also hired a noted hand surgeon, Dr. Charles Melone, to help in the design of gloves, making sure they conformed to the hand and offered proper protection. Atlas, in turn, made sure the gloves felt right from the boxer's point of view. Horowitz became a frequent visitor to major fights, bringing along Everlast factory workers as well. Boxers were also invited to visit the Everlast offices and factories. Well-known boxers Sugar Ray Leonard and Shane Mosley were hired as spokesmen for Everlast. Moreover, the company became heavily involved in grass roots efforts and gave away boxing equipment around the world.

Horowitz brought licensing in-house, which prompted a lawsuit in December 2000 from the company's former agent, Joan Hanson & Co., alleging breach of contract. To run the licensing operation he hired Hal Worsham, who had considerable experience with Converse, where he headed international licensing. Worsham had also been involved in marketing at BF Goodrich Dunlop, Fisher-Price, and Hanna-Barbera. In order to support licensees and the introduction of new products, Horowitz stepped up the company's marketing efforts, from developing new packaging to engaging in advertising for the first time in many years. He forged sponsorship deals with major boxing broadcasters HBO and ESPN so that the Everlast logo would be prominently displayed on mat rings and corner posts. He was also keen to take advantage of product placement opportunities. The 2001 film *Ali*, which was based on the career of famed boxer Muhammad Ali, featured the Everlast logo throughout, and although the producers needed Everlast in order to maintain period accuracy and were prepared to pay for period Everlast equipment, Horowitz willingly donated the items. The result was in many ways a two-hour Everlast commercial and a rare case in which a movie's product placement was fully justified by the story.

Horowitz viewed the Everlast brand as a "sleeping giant," and there was no doubt that the label was nothing less than an American icon. Despite a lack of enthusiasm from Wall Street, which bid down the company's stock by a third over the course of the first 15 months, there was every reason to believe that with Horowitz's unbridled enthusiasm for Everlast, the label's high recognition factor, and untapped international licensing opportunities, the "Choice of Champions" was positioned to enjoy even greater success in the years to come.

Principal Subsidiaries

Active Apparel New Corp.; Everlast Sports Manufacturing Corp.; Everlast Fitness Manufacturing Corp.; American Fitness Products, Inc.

Principal Competitors

Bollinger; Grant; NIKE, Inc.; Reebok International Ltd.; Reyes Holdings, Inc.

Further Reading

Abend, Jules, "Active Apparel Acquires Everlast," *Bobbin,* October 2000, p. 6.

Cassidy, Hillary, "George W. Horowitz," *Sporting Goods Business,* October 11, 2000, pp. 34–37.

Gerbasa, Thomas, "Everlast: Comeback of The Year," *Maxboxing.com,* December 24, 2001.

Griffin, Cara, "Don't Call It a Comeback," *Sporting Goods Business,* January 2002, p. 14.

Hauser, Thomas, " 'Everlast': The Choice of Champions," *SecondsOut .com,* March 7, 2002.

Millman, J., "Swimsuits, Yes; Perfumes, No," *Forbes,* July 23, 1990, p. 81.

Strauss, Gary, "Boxing-Equipment Marketers Step in Ring, Grant Takes Legal Jab at Everlast," *USA Today,* September 21, 1998, p. 5B.

Zack, Ian, "Please Pass the Smelling Salts," *Forbes,* March 4, 2002, p. 92.

—Ed Dinger

Florida Gaming Corporation

3500 NW 37th Avenue
Miami, Florida 33142
U.S.A.
Telephone: (305) 633-6400
Fax: (305) 633-4386
Web site: http://www.fla-gaming.com

Public Company
Incorporated: 1976 as Lexicon Corp.
Employees: 373
Sales: 12.5 million (2000)
Stock Exchanges: OTC
Ticker Symbol: BETS
NAIC: 711219 Other Spectator Sports

Florida Gaming Corporation bills itself as the world's largest jai-alai operator in the world. At the company's Miami and Fort Pierce Jai-Alai facilities, called frontons, customers can wager on live matches as well as on televised horse races and greyhound races. Jai-Alai at Fort Pierce is offered on a seasonal basis, while Miami matches are presented year-round and transmitted by satellite to 62 parimutuel wagering locations in Florida, Connecticut, and Rhode Island, in addition to 25 locations in Mexico, Central America, and Austria. The Miami fronton also houses the Crystal Card Room, where small-stakes poker and dominoes are played.

Origins in 1976

The corporate lineage of Florida Gaming can be traced back to the Lexicon Corporation, which had no connection to jai-alai or gambling. It was cofounded in 1976 by Michael Levy, a Georgia Tech engineering graduate who in the early 1970s was involved in pioneering computer efforts. Working with Harris Corporation he designed a microcomputer-based utility-control system. He then went to work for Miami's Milgo Electronics, a data modem manufacturer, before striking out on his own with Lexicon, which was established to manufacture a handheld language translator that Levy helped to design and patent. The company went public and Levy, at the age of 32, became president and CEO. Lexicon

enjoyed some early success but efforts at developing other products failed to pay off. Among a number of attempts, it tried marketing a talking scale and became a defense contractor selling missile parts. In 1988, Levy created a subsidiary called Sports-Tech, which created a video-editing system for professional and college football coaches. The business secured enough early customers to warrant spinning off Sports-Tech in 1989 and taking it public. In the end, however, Lexicon failed to find a suitable business mix, never managed to top the $20 million mark in annual sales, and slowly faded. By 1993, the company was on its way to being delisted by the NASDAQ. Lexicon was sold to Freedom Financial Corp., and Levy resigned as both an officer and director of the company. Several months later he launched a new company, SportsLine USA, an early Internet business, which would later merge with CBS and become one of the most successful sports web sites.

Freedom Financial was almost exclusively owned by W. Bennett Collett, a businessman with a checkered background. He grew up in Kentucky during the Depression, his family forced to live off the dollar-per-day wages his mother earned as a domestic worker. During high school, Collett toiled in coal mines and saw mills before working his way through Ohio State, where he studied business and accounting. After a turn as an accountant, he struck out on his own, becoming primarily involved in insurance and banking. He served as principal shareholder and chief executive officer of 11 small banks across the country. According to the *Miami Herald,* "He was sued for fraud by the Securities and Exchange Commission in 1979. The SEC alleged Collett headed a group of investors who acquired companies and gutted them by causing them 'to transfer valuable assets for inadequate consideration.'" Although Collett settled the matter without admitting guilt, he signed an order of permanent injunction, pledging not to violate SEC anti-fraud regulations. At the same time, Collett, according to the *Herald,* was also coming under fire from the Indiana Department of Insurance, which "forced Collett's Pilgrim Life Insurance into liquidation. In 1981, the department sued Collett personally, claiming he had stripped Pilgrim of its liquid assets." He reportedly settled the suit for $175,000 two years later. According to the *Herald,* "Collett says he never paid to settle a suit in Indiana. He does acknowledge paying $75,000 to the estate of

Company Perspectives:

The Florida Gaming Corporation had its various companies produce one mission statement: to provide for over 75 years the very best the sport of jai-alai has to offer. We remain dedicated to this goal. While Florida Gaming offers other forms of wagering, such as poker and dominoes at Miami Jai-Alai, and simulcast betting on horse and dog racing at Ft. Pierce, there is one thing our patrons can count on: the opportunity to see jai-alai played at its highest level. We provide this top-notch sports entertainment for the public's enjoyment.

an insurance company in Maryland to settle charges against him there. In all, four of Collett's insurance companies ended up in liquidation.'' He established Freedom Financial Corporation in 1985 to serve as a bank holding company, but by 1988 sold off its banking subsidiaries. Collett attempted to take Freedom Financial public in 1990 with the intention of raising $10 million, but, according to the *Herald,* ''state regulators in New Jersey, Indiana, and Kentucky killed'' the offering because ''the prospectus issued to potential investors failed to disclose that Collett had been the subject of at least six prior legal actions.'' According to Indiana Securities Division Commissioner Mark Maddux, as quoted by *Business First-Louisville,* Collett ''had a history of bad relations with people who have invested in his entities. There's just been a long history of disgruntled investors in this person's companies.'' Despite being unable to take Freedom Financial public, Collett gained the benefits of a publicly traded, listed company when Freedom Financial acquired Lexicon, which by 1993 was nothing more than a shell corporation.

Introduction of Jai-Alai to United States

Collett used Lexicon to enter the jai-alai business, a choice that appeared curious at first glance, since the glory days of the sport were long past. Jai-Alai is derived from the ancient game of handball. The contemporary game traces its origins to the Basque provinces of Spain and France during the 15th century. The Basque version of handball, or ''pelota vasca,'' was played against a wall called a fronton, from which the name of a modern jai-alai facility is derived. The three-walled jai-alai court is known as the cancha. ''Jai-Alai'' itself means ''merry festival,'' alluding to the tradition of playing the games during religious and holiday festivals. As the game evolved, bare hands were protected by leather gloves, then replaced by wooden paddles and ultimately the cesta, a long, hooked woven basket made of birch strips used for catching and throwing, which was introduced in the mid-19th century. It was the cesta that allowed jai-alai players to hurl the ball (''pelota'') at speeds clocked as high as 175 miles per hour. The advent of the cesta completely changed the nature of the game. The ball was extremely hard, requiring granite walls, and the speed necessitated courts that were 172 feet long.

Jai-Alai was introduced in the United States at the St. Louis World's Fair in 1904, and Florida became the home of the nation's first Jai-Alai fronton in 1924. Ten years later, wagering

on the sport was legalized in the state. In the 1970s, the ''spectacular seven'' scoring system was introduced to shorten the length of games in order to increase the frequency of wagering. Essentially bettors bet on a player in a singles match, or two-man team in a doubles match, in a round-robin format that featured eight players or teams playing to seven points. As with horse racing, bettors could make win, place, and show wagers, as well as a variety of ''gimmick'' bets such as the quinella (picking two numbers to finish in the win and place positions), the exacta (picking two numbers to finish in the win and place positions in exact order), and the trifecta (picking three numbers to finish in the win, place, and show positions in exact order).

Although Connecticut and Rhode Island also became havens for jai-alai in the United States, the sport was generally associated with Florida. With little competition from other professional sports or gambling outlets, jai-alai flourished in the state, reaching a peak in popularity in the late 1970s and early 1980s. A number of factors would intervene, however, that severely hurt the business. Jai-Alai suffered a game-fixing scandal in the late 1970s, then in 1988 the players went on strike for two years. Although replacements were brought in, attendance suffered because fans had to cross picket lines to enter the frontons. In addition, major professional sports entered the territory. For a number of years the Miami Dolphins were the lone professional franchise, but they were soon followed by the Tampa Bay Buccaneers and Jacksonville Jaguars in football. The National Basketball League awarded franchises to Miami and Orlando, while Major League Baseball and the National Hockey League expanded to Miami and Tampa Bay. Moreover, jai-alai faced ever-widening competition for gambling dollars. No longer contending with just horse and dog tracks, the fronton also competed against casinos and bingo halls operated by Native American tribes and casino ships that offered gaming three miles offshore. Perhaps the biggest impact, however, was caused by the introduction of the state lottery, which siphoned off many of jai-alai's traditional blue-collar, two-dollar bettors.

The amount wagered at a gambling facility, termed the ''handle,'' was in steady decline at Fort Pierce Jai-Alai when Collett and Lexicon agreed to pay $3 million in February 1994 to acquire the inter-track wagering facility. Two months later Lexicon changed its name to Florida Gaming. Collett was not alone in developing a sudden interest in entering the jai-alai business, as within months jai-alai licenses increased dramatically in value. A referendum calling for the creation of 47 casinos, including the state's 30 parimutuel sites, was on the ballot in the November 1994 election. Twice before, in 1978 and 1986, Florida voters had rejected casino gambling, but in the past the parimutuel forces were left out of the equation and campaigned against the initiatives. Now jai-alai and racing interests were united in support of the referendum known as Proposition 8.

Collett told the press, ''I'd like to say we knew this casino referendum was a possibility then, but in truth, we had no clue,'' adding that the fronton had been purchased because he ''thought we could turn this into a very profitable business.'' According to SEC filings made by Florida Gaming, however, the company ''participated in a Florida lobbying group that collected signatures to place a referendum before the voters of Florida in November 1994 to amend the Florida Constitution to permit casino gaming.'' Clearly, Florida Gaming's interest in jai-alai was related to the possibility of opening a casino, and in October 1994 the company signed a joint venture agreement with Casino America, Inc., to build and operate a casino at the Fort Pierce fronton if the referendum passed. Casino America was one of the nation's largest operators of riverboat casinos. The forces supporting Proposition 8 launched an advertising campaign in the weeks before the election, but Florida voters again rejected casino gambling.

Florida Gaming did not give up on the possibility of becoming involved in the casino business, retaining hope that the idea would ultimately take hold in Florida while at the same time seeking an alternative entry. In June 1995, the company signed an agreement with Centrum X Corporation, gaining first refusal rights to develop and manage a casino on the Tonkawa Indian Reservation in Oklahoma. Two months later Florida Gaming agreed in principle to acquire EagleVisions Gaming Group of the Americas Inc., which was headed by the former chief of the Mystic Lake Casino Complex in Minnesota. Also in August 1995, Florida Gaming signed an agreement to run a casino for the Ponca Tribe in Douglas County, Nebraska. None of these efforts to become involved in Native American casinos panned out. In addition, the company attempted in 1997 to become involved in Las Vegas, agreeing to pay $14.5 million for the Bourbon Street Hotel and its shuttered casino, a small property located a block from the famed Las Vegas strip. Collett vowed to spend as much as $6.5 million to renovate Bourbon Street, but the deal was never finalized and the property was sold to another party in 1998.

Approval for Low-Stakes Poker Rooms: 1997

Although Florida voters rejected casino gambling, legislators decided in 1996 to allow parimutuels to open low-stakes poker rooms in their facilities, pending local approval, starting January 1, 1997. The tables only permitted $10 maximum pots, of which the state received 10 percent, yet parimutuels were hopeful that they could make a profit out of poker. On December 31, 1996, Florida Gaming acquired WJA Realty Limited Partnerships, which owned jai-alai facilities in Tampa, Miami, and Ocala. The deal made Florida Gaming the largest jai-alai operator in the world, as well as one of the largest poker room operators in Florida.

Although the company's handle increased dramatically, from $25 million in 1996 to over $125 million in 1997, Florida Gaming lost over $4 million for the year. Much of that shortfall was due to the cost of building card rooms, but other factors

were also involved. Poker played for a maximum $10 pot essentially eliminated raises and hardly generated the kind of enthusiasm necessary from bettors to make the business thrive. More importantly, the health of jai-alai was jeopardized because state taxes were based on the amount wagered rather than the amount of actual revenues. This formula may have worked at a time of much larger handles (which totaled $414 million statewide in 1986–87 and fell to $180 million in 1995–96), but now it was having a devastating effect on jai-alai operations, which might lose money and still have to pay taxes. Rates were lowered but the move still did not solve the problem.

Florida Gaming endured a difficult 1998. In February, the company agreed to sell the real estate of its Tampa Jai-Alai facility, which had been in business since 1953, for $8.3 million. Nevertheless, the company elected to retain the jai-alai license, which could still prove valuable in the event of casinos becoming legal in Florida. The price of Florida Gaming stock, which traded at a high of $17.25 in 1995, dropped below $1.35 in July 1998, shortly before the *Miami Herald* published a scathing recap of Collett's past business dealings. The article also questioned the relationship between Freedom Financial and Florida Gaming: ''In recent years, money and property has flowed between Florida Gaming and Freedom Financial. The largest deal was last fall, when Freedom sold a Georgia real estate development called Tara Club Estates to Florida Gaming for $6.4 million.'' In response, Collett denied any impropriety but promised to sever financial ties between the companies as soon as he was able to finalize the sale of the Tampa Jai-Alai property and pay off some debts. The *Miami Herald*, however, was not alone in its criticism of the relationship between Freedom Financial and Florida Gaming. The NASDAQ also made note of the situation when announcing that Florida Gaming would be delisted in August 1998.

Florida Gaming in the New Century

Florida changed the tax laws so that jai-alai profits were taxed rather than the handle, but the move came too late to save Tampa Jai-Alai. In fact, the entire jai-alai industry was on the verge of collapse. In 1987, there had been 12 frontons operating in Florida, but by July 1998 there were only five, and Florida Gaming began looking to sell its Ocala operation. It was not until August 2000 that the company was able to complete a sale of the fronton. In the meantime, Florida Gaming lost over $2 million in 1998 but rebounded in 1999, posting a profit of more than $1.5 million.

Florida Gaming streamlined its business in 2000, operating just two jai-alai frontons, one in Fort Pierce for a summer season and one in Miami that operated year-round. Coupled with further tax breaks from the state, the company, and the sport of jai-alai, appeared to be stabilizing. The halcyon days were definitely in the past but jai-alai remained enough of a draw to stay alive, at least in Miami with its heavy influx of tourists. In addition, technology allowed jai-alai matches to be simulcast for wagering in 62 parimutuel sites in Florida as well as locations in Connecticut, Rhode Island, Mexico, Central America, and Austria. In February 2002, Florida Gaming signed an agreement to broadcast its Miami Jai-Alai matches over the Internet, using streaming video. World Gaming Services would also offer viewers gaming options. In addition to jai-alai, Florida Gaming continued to draw income from its poker and domino tables, as well as inter-track wagering. The company also retained its Tampa Jai-Alai license. It was likely that Florida Gaming would only use the license in the event that the state finally approved casino gambling. Until that time the company would have to be content with the limited possibilities of the jai-alai business and its poker tables.

Principal Subsidiaries

Florida Gaming Centers, Inc.; Tara Club Estates, Inc.

Principal Competitors

Isle of Capri Casinos, Inc.; Ocala Breeders; Florida Lottery.

Further Reading

Cottrell, Bill, "Florida Tax Break Bill Aims at Reviving Jai Alai Industry," *Tallahassee Democrat,* April 24, 1998.

Faiola, Anthony, "After Going to the Dogs, Tracks Cash in on Casinos," *Times-Picayune,* October 23, 1994, p. A3.

Hershey, Steve, "Lottery, Casinos Take Jai Alai Out of the Game," *USA Today,* July 1, 1998, p. 11C.

Keefe, Robert, "Jai Alai Owners Plan to Merge," *St. Petersburg Times,* July 11, 1996, p. 1E.

Miller, Eric, "Sports Firm Dropped by Nasdaq Market, Sells Tampa, Fla., Jai-Alai Arena," *Tampa Tribune,* July 31, 1998.

Ostrowski, Jeff, "Jai Alai's Big Gamble," *South Florida Business Journal,* July 25, 1997, p. 1.

Poppe, David, "Florida Gaming Looks for New Deal to Avert Trouble," *Miami Herald,* July 27, 1998.

Sharp, Deborah, "Casino Backers Betting on Fla.," *USA Today,* October 26, 1994, p. 11A.

—Ed Dinger

FORTIS

Fortis, Inc.

P.O. Box 8837
Suite 1201, The Fortis Building
139 Water Street
St. John's, Newfoundland A1B 3T2
Canada
Telephone: (709) 737-2800
Fax: (709) 737-5307
Web site: http://www.fortisinc.com

Public Company
Incorporated: 1987
Employees: 2,500
Sales: C$394.9 million (2001)
Stock Exchanges: Toronto
Ticker Symbol: FTS
NAIC: 221111 Hydroelectric Power Generation (pt);
221121 Electric Bulk Power Transmission and
Control (pt); 221122 Electric Power Distribution (pt);
53121 Offices of Real Estate Agents and Brokers;
531312 Nonresidential Property Managers; 551112
Offices of Other Holding Companies

Fortis, Inc., through its subsidiaries, is the leading distributor of electricity in the Province of Newfoundland and the Province of Prince Edward Island, and the leading commercial distributor of electricity in the country of Belize. Fortis was created in 1987 as a holding company, with Newfoundland Light & Power Company, Limited as its chief subsidiary. Since then it has branched out into other power industry segments and diversified into the real estate and telecommunications industries. The company posted steady growth in the mid-1990s, as it expanded its power holdings into the United States and Central America.

Bringing Light to Canada in the Late 19th Century

Although Fortis is a relatively new company, its core subsidiary and predecessor, Newfoundland Light & Power Co., boasts a rich history dating back to the 1880s. By that time, Edison's breakthrough electric lamp had been introduced as had his design for an entire electrical supply system. Demand for Edison's sys-

tem was immediate and overwhelming. Not exempt from the clamor to develop an electric system were Edison's northern neighbors in Newfoundland (which did not actually join the Canadian confederation until 1949). In fact, it was on October 19, 1885, that residents of Newfoundland's port city of St. John's saw an electric light demonstrated for the first time. That event sparked a concerted drive to bring electricity to St. John's and throughout the rugged, sparsely populated Newfoundland region.

Among the first communities along the North American coast to develop an electric system was St. John's, a relatively wealthy town of about 31,000 people who were mostly of English or Irish descent. In May 1885, five men—Alexander McLellan Mackay, John Steer, Walter Baine Grieve, Edwin John Duder, and Moses Monroe—incorporated themselves as Newfoundland Electric Light Company Limited. Through that venture, the investors planned to develop "an electric light station or stations in St. John's and elsewhere in Newfoundland."

Spearheading the effort were Monroe and Mackay. Mackay served as the company's first president until 1892, at which time he was succeeded by Monroe. Mackay had moved to Newfoundland in 1857 to head the local division of the New York, London, and Newfoundland Telegraph Company. He became a Newfoundland citizen and achieved notable success as a politician there. Monroe was a successful businessman and was operating a successful wholesale venture at the time.

The fledgling electricity company, which became known as St. John's Electric Light Company, strung electric wires and converted an old warehouse into a power station. By October 1885 the company was already burning electric street and store lamps. Despite initial glitches—one telephone office employee was blown six feet away from the switchboard when electric lines came into contact with the phone lines—the company was an early success. Several companies signed up for electric lighting service and, significantly, St. John's Electric secured a lucrative street lighting contract with the city. By 1887 St. John's Electric was supplying electric lighting to about 50 companies and by 1888 was fueling about 25 street lamps that replaced antiquated gas lamps.

Once the company had proven the viability of electric lighting, growth was rapid. In 1889 the company installed a new plant near its first generation building to produce power for incandescent lamps. The advanced system consisted of two horizontal steam engines that drove a shaft connected to two dynamos. The contraption was capable of producing a total of about 330 amps at 125 volts (a very small amount of power by modern standards). Demand for electricity surged and within a few years generation capacity was again increased. In addition to lighting, St. John's Electric began producing power for other uses, including an electric street car in the early 1890s. The company also realized demand growth as a result of an unfortunate 1892 fire, which burned much of the city and severely damaged the competing gas company's infrastructure.

St. John's Electric and most of Newfoundland were rocked by financial turbulence during the mid-1890s. One result was that ownership and control of the electric company changed hands before the turn of the century. Simultaneously, other events were transpiring that would have an impact on the future of St. John's Electric Light Co. Among them was the creation of a street railway company by entrepreneur and statesman Sir Robert Gillespie Reid.

Reid had moved to Newfoundland in 1890, by which time the 48-year-old was already a multimillionaire. He took on the construction of a regional rail system as a new challenge beginning in 1890 and by the early 1890s had effectively built a rail network in and around St. John's. The importance of the development of St. John's Street Railway Company was that the venture entailed the development of a hydroelectric station and other infrastructures that were eventually integrated with the original operations of St. John's Electric Light Co.

Revamping the Power Infrastructure: 1900–50

Electric power was supplied to the St. John's region during the early 1900s primarily through a company named Reid Newfoundland, which was headed by the Reid family and had effectively absorbed St. John's Light Electric Light Co. As the number of applications for electricity increased, demand rose and Reid Newfoundland expanded capacity. Despite that growth, Reid Newfoundland enjoyed only spotty profitability from its electric power operations. In fact, the Reids tried to

jettison the division in the 1910s. By the 1920s, moreover, the electric infrastructure was becoming outdated and needed an overhaul. Reid Newfoundland incorporated a subsidiary named St. John's Light and Power Company that consisted of its electricity-related assets. It sold that company, by means of a relatively complex transaction, in 1924 to Montreal Engineering. The company was reincorporated as Newfoundland Light and Power Co.

New ownership of the power company was welcomed by many, because it was assumed that the new owners would inject the capital needed to update the aging system. Indeed, Montreal Engineering boasted wide experience in the North American light and power industry. Its expertise became evident at Newfoundland Light and Power as the company invested heavily and upgraded the system during the 1920s and 1930s. It boosted capacity, renovated the street car system, and launched a drive to increase consumption of electricity in St. John's and outlying areas. The company's main power generation station, for example, was upgraded during the mid-1920s to produce more than twice as much power as it had delivered prior to 1924. Customers were given incentives to use electricity, for example, to heat their homes, and electricity prices dropped as the aggregate volume of consumption rose.

Also boosting consumption for Newfoundland Light and Power was increased use of electricity by the company's major consumer outside of St. John's: the Bell Island iron works. Expansions at that facility during the late 1920s and 1930s, combined with other growth in the region, significantly boosted electricity output. Furthermore, during World War II electricity demand increased and the company expanded with additional hydro generation plants. After the war, the street car service was terminated to make way for the increasingly popular automobile. Despite that loss of power use, demand for Newfoundland Light and Power's electricity would rise as the postwar economy boomed; immediately following the war, though, consumption declined as use by local military installations diminished.

Just as important to the company as evolving power needs during the late 1940s and 1950s were striking political changes. In 1949, shortly after the tram service was stopped, Newfoundland became a Canadian province. For Newfoundland Light and Power and its 135-member workforce, that meant that the company was suddenly subject to regulatory control by the national government. Furthermore, it played a part in the formation of a labor union at the company, Local 1620 of the International Brotherhood of Electrical Workers (IBEW). It was with those changes that the company met the challenges of the 1950s and 1960s, most paramount of which were population growth and increased consumption of electricity per capita.

Postwar Expansion: The 1950s and 1960s

Indeed, the population of St. John's increased from about 50,000 in 1950 to 80,000 by the mid-1960s. Similarly, the company's power output grew more than threefold between 1947 and 1957. Power output during the late 1950s and 1960s, moreover, increased rapidly as Newfoundland Light and Power labored to extend its services outside of St. John's and throughout Newfoundland. The company constructed several new generation facilities and updated infrastructure throughout the period. New infrastructure included an innovative steam plant during the mid-1950s and replacement of incandescent street lights with high-efficiency mercury-vapor lamps during the early 1960s. Meanwhile, the company overcame memorable obstacles to progress, including a devastating sleet storm that wreaked havoc on the electricity delivery systems.

It was during the 1950s and 1960s, when Newfoundland Light and Power began reaching outside of its traditional boundaries near St. John's, that its potential service offerings began to overlap with those of other power companies. Since the early 1900s, in fact, several smaller electric companies had emerged in more rural areas of Newfoundland. United Towns Electric (UTE), for example, had supplied power to areas outside of St. John's since the early 1900s. UTE had grown in part by purchasing other rural power companies, such as the Conception Bay Electric Company (which it bought in 1914), the Wabana Light and Power Company (acquired in 1931), and Public Service Electric Company (1932). As UTE grew, so did another regional power provider named Union Electric Light and Power Company (UELP). UELP had started in 1916 and, like UTE, had merged with or purchased several other power suppliers to become a major rural power company. By the 1960s both UTE and UELP had become major Newfoundland power suppliers.

During the early 1960s, UTE, UELP, and Newfoundland Light and Power—the three established private utility companies in Newfoundland—became physically joined when they linked power lines in various projects. The linking of the three companies started the ball rolling toward the inevitable merger of a province-wide utility company. Other factors driving the union included pubic pressure for uniform electric rates, territorial disputes between the three companies, and the need for an integrated provincial power grid system. That merger finally occurred in 1966, when executives at the three companies, with permission from regulators, agreed to become a single entity called Newfoundland Light & Power Company, Limited. The Newfoundland Light and Power moniker carried over primarily because that predecessor company was far and away the largest energy producer, with about 95,000 kilowatts of capacity, compared with 25,000 and 4,662 for UTE and UELP, respectively. The newly amalgamated company enjoyed a customer base of more than 80,000.

Executives spent the next few years consolidating operations and streamlining the 77 different rate categories into just three. Management and administrative operations were combined and the systems were updated to create a uniform, province-wide company. Meanwhile, electricity consumption in the region soared, particularly during the 1970s when the company encouraged customers to heat their homes with electricity. In 1974 alone, Newfoundland's electricity use surged more than 20 percent. To keep up with increased demand Newfoundland Light & Power added capacity and updated infrastructure. During the early 1980s rampant growth was squelched by the energy crises that pushed up electricity prices. Still, Newfoundland Light managed to post 5 percent annual consumption gains throughout the period and into the mid-1980s.

Diversification in the 1980s and 1990s

By the mid-1980s Newfoundland Light was generating about C$200 million in annual sales and capturing roughly

C$16 million in net income. Its growth was predictably stable during most of the decade and into the 1990s because of its status as a government-regulated and protected utility. Revenues increased quickly to C$244 million in 1985 but then rose steadily to C$250 million in 1987 and then to about C$308 million in 1990, about C$24 million of which was netted as income. During the same period, the company's customer base increased from about 170,000 to 184,000, and then to 192,000. By 1990 the company was operating about 30 generating plants and serving roughly 85 percent of the province's electricity consumers. It purchased most of the electricity it sold from the Newfoundland and Labrador Hydro Electric Corporation. After years of operating purely as a government-regulated utility, however, Newfoundland Light & Power embarked on a new course in the late 1980s and early 1990s.

The change was partially the result of a new president. In 1985 Angus Bruneau was hired to run the company. Bruneau differed from his immediate predecessors in that his background was not in the utility or government sector. Among other initiatives, Bruneau created an advisory council designed to improve the company's customer relations. More important, it was under Bruneau's leadership that Newfoundland Light & Power began the transformation from a regulated public utility to a private-sector company engaged in nonregulated business. In 1987 the company created a holding company—Fortis, Inc.—to purchase the assets of Newfoundland Light & Power Co. The move was designed to allow the company, through Fortis, to participate in non-utility ventures.

Thus Newfoundland Light and Power Co. had suddenly become a subsidiary of a larger company named Fortis, Inc. The change was somewhat superficial, as existing management remained entrenched. It was important, though, because it allowed the company to diversify and invest its resources in potentially higher-profit businesses. To that end, in 1989 Fortis established Fortis Properties as a real estate arm. During the early 1990s that division began purchasing shopping malls, retail and office buildings, and other commercial properties. That effort was viewed as a way to benefit from depressed real estate prices caused by an ugly commercial real estate downturn. Between 1989 and 1994, Fortis Properties' assets increased from C$6 million to C$87 million.

Also in 1989, Fortis purchased Newfoundland Building Savings and Loan. It used that bargain buy to form the foundation for a new subsidiary called Fortis Trust. Fortis Trust, a mortgage company, started out with C$5 million in mortgage assets but grew to C$60 million within four years (it would eventually be sold, in 2001, to Scotia Bank). In 1990 Fortis bolstered its utility holdings when it acquired Maritime Electric, the power generation company that served approximately 90 percent of the population of nearby Prince Edward Island. During the early 1990s, Fortis used its expertise and deep pockets to whip the utility into shape. Rates were cut on the island by about 9 percent and customer service was improved. Maritime was unique in that it was a private company almost exempt from government regulation and, therefore, complemented Fortis's goal of private-sector diversification.

In 1991 Fortis made its foray into the telecommunications business when Fortis Properties joined in a partnership with Unitel Communications to provide wireless and other alternative telecommunications services to Newfoundland. Unitel quickly built a C$30 million system in Newfoundland, which became the most successful Unitel operation in Canada. Fortis also attempted a venture into the gas pipeline industry when it made a bid for a Saskatchewan gas pipeline company. The effort failed but signaled the company's intent to diversify broadly. ''I jokingly say that at Fortis we have two rules,'' said Stanley Marshall, vice-president of corporate affairs, in a *Trade and Commerce Magazine* special supplement in 1994, ''one, we invest in nothing that grows, i.e. cucumbers, fish, anything like that; and two, where government invests our taxes, no further investment by Fortis is warranted.''

The impact of Fortis's diversification on sales was negligible during the early 1990s, given the immense size of its core Newfoundland Light & Power Co. operations. Revenues rose to about C$380 million in 1994, about C$31.3 million of which was netted as income. Each of its new divisions was posting steady gains, however, and its core utility company continued to show profits. Net income at Fortis Trust, for example, grew from about C$50,000 to nearly C$500,000 between 1990 and 1994, while profits at Fortis Properties increased from almost nothing in 1991 to more than C$1.2 million. Its core utility operations, meanwhile, supplied power to more than a quarter of a million customers in 1994. The company's long-term goal was increased efficiency in its utility operations and ongoing diversification into growth industries.

Expanding Power Holdings in the 1990s

Although electric utilities in Canada suffered a period of stagnant growth and high interest rates during the early 1990s, Fortis held to its belief that its future prosperity depended on the further expansion of its core business. The key was to find ventures that offered stability and steady growth over the long term. A projected merger between Fortis and Newfoundland and Labrador Hydro in 1993 was particularly appealing to shareholders, since the latter already supplied Fortis subsidiary Newfoundland Light and Power with most of its electricity and would provide for greater efficiency and cost savings. The deal fell apart in the face of charges of political favoritism, however, and the company's stock subsequently declined.

Fortis rebounded nicely the following year, when it purchased the remaining 68 percent of Maritime Electric. It was a conservative move compared with the bid on Newfoundland and Labrador Hydro, and it made sound business sense: Maritime was a proven performer, and it dominated the electricity market on Prince Edward Island. The company further increased its market share of the Canadian power industry in 1998, with the purchase of 50 percent of the Canadian Niagara Power Company. The deal was significant in that it expanded the company's reach into Ontario, where Canadian Niagara already had a sizable customer base and a yearly power generation of 650,000 megawatt hours. Even more attractive to Fortis was Canadian Niagara's license to sell electricity in the United States; Fortis built on its U.S. holdings in 1999, when it purchased two hydroelectric stations in New York State. The company subsequently created the FortisUS Energy Corporation, in order both to manage the new generating facilities and to establish a strong

foothold in power markets south of the border. FortisUS became a subsidiary of Maritime Electric and controlled a total of four hydroelectric stations in New York by 2002.

These acquisitions also served as the impetus for expanding the company's holdings outside of North America. One area with huge potential was in the country of Belize. By 2000 Fortis owned a 67 percent share of Belize Electricity Limited, the only commercial power distributor in the country, with a customer base of more than 50,000. In January 2001 Fortis acquired a 95 percent stake in Belize Electric Company Limited (BECOL), which owned the Mollejon hydroelectric plant. The Mollejon facility had a generating capacity of 80 gigawatt hours a year and was the sole commercial electricity supplier for Belize Electricity Limited.

The company's business dealings in Belize were not greeted with universal enthusiasm, however. In late 2001 the company's proposed dam project in the Macal River Valley came under fire from environmentalists both at home and abroad. One notable opponent was Robert Kennedy, Jr., who led a campaign against the dam's construction, citing the potential devastation to the country's wilderness areas. The company asserted that the dam would cause negligible damage to the environment and that it would help ensure that power rates in Belize remained affordable. Furthermore, greater generating capacity would allow Belize to become less dependent on power from Mexico, which was a dominant electricity supplier to the country. Although the opposition stirred up a great deal of media attention, by 2002 the government of Belize remained committed to the project, and Fortis had every hope that the venture would eventually reap huge rewards.

Principal Subsidiaries

Newfoundland Light & Power Company, Limited; Maritime Electric; Fortis Properties Corporation; Belize Electric Company Limited (BECOL) (95%); Belize Electricity Limited (67%); Canadian Niagara Power Company (50%); Caribbean Utilities Company Limited (Cayman Islands; 20%).

Principal Competitors

Enbridge Inc.; Hydro One Inc.; TransAlta Corporation.

Further Reading

Baker, Melvin, with Robert D. Pitt and Janet Miller Pitt, *The Illustrated History of Newfoundland Light & Power,* St. John's, Newfoundland: Creative Publishers, 1990.

Hebbard, Gary J., ''Fortis Inc. Focused on Service,'' *Trade and Commerce Magazine,* special supplement, 1994.

McCarten, James, ''Kennedy Decries Fortis Inc.'s Belize Dam Project; Company Cries Foul,'' *Canadian Business and Current Affairs,* November 1, 2001.

Redmond, Michael, ''Fortis 'Not in a Hurry,' '' *Financial Post,* January 19, 1991, p. 23.

Urlocker, Michael, ''P.E.I. Takeover Straightens Fortis's Path,'' *Financial Post* (Toronto), July 7, 1994, p. 21.

—Dave Mote
—update: Steve Meyer

Fulbright & Jaworski L.L.P.

1301 McKinney Street, Suite 5100
Houston, Texas 77010
U.S.A.
Telephone: (713) 651-5151
Fax: (713) 651-5246
Web site: http://www.fulbright.com

Limited Liability Partnership
Founded: 1919 as Fulbright & Crooker
Employees: 1,800
Gross Billings: $343 million (2000 est.)
NAIC: 541110 Offices of Lawyers

With almost 800 lawyers, Fulbright & Jaworski L.L.P. is one of the world's largest law firms. It serves corporations, nonprofit groups, government entities, and individuals in many parts of the world by offering expertise in litigation, antitrust, securities, international arbitration, and most other practice areas. In addition to its main office in Houston, Fulbright & Jaworski has offices in Hong Kong, London, Minneapolis, Los Angeles, New York City, Dallas, San Antonio, Austin, and Washington, D.C. Name partner Leon Jaworski, who died in 1982, is the firm's best known lawyer due to his role as the Watergate special prosecutor who helped end the presidency of Richard Nixon in 1974.

Origins and Early Years

R. Clarence Fulbright was born in New Boston, Texas, in 1881, earned two degrees from Baylor University in Waco, Texas, and then earned his J.D. at the University of Chicago. Admitted to the Texas bar in 1909, Fulbright in 1919 joined with John Henry Crooker to start their partnership. Born in Mobile, Alabama, in 1884, Crooker had no formal law school training. Admitted to the Texas bar in 1911, he served as a district attorney from 1914 to 1918 before teaming up with Fulbright.

After graduating from Baylor Law School and earning a master's degree from George Washington University, Leon Jaworski practiced law a few years before joining the Fulbright firm in 1931 in the midst of the Great Depression. He soon tried many lawsuits, often in behalf of some of Houston's more prominent families and businesses. In 1935 the firm made him its youngest partner.

Probably the young firm's main client was Houston's State National Bank, its only client listed in the 1929 *Martindale-Hubbell Law Directory*. The firm, then known as Fulbright, Crooker & Freeman, also had an office in the Transportation Building in Washington, D.C., which for many years was its only branch office.

In 1932 the Fulbright firm was counsel to local clients such as the State National Bank of Houston, the Houston Compress Company, Houston Merchants Exchange, Houston Daily Press, and the Houston Chamber of Commerce. Its insurance practice represented Exporters Insurance Company of New York, Aetna Insurance Company based in Hartford, Connecticut, Fidelity American Insurance Company, and the Insurance Company of North America.

Beginning in 1936, one of Leon Jaworski's better known clients was Glenn McCarthy. In his book *Confession and Avoidance,* Jaworski described his colorful client, the model for the oilman Jett Rink in the novel and movie *Giant*. In 1949 McCarthy built Houston's luxurious Shamrock Hotel, and at his peak in the 1950s he owned a radio station, a chemical plant, a men's clothing store, and a 15,000-acre ranch. Serving such business leaders helped the Fulbright firm to grow and prosper.

Post-World War II Practice

In the late 1950s the growing firm then named Fulbright, Crooker, Freeman, Bates & Jaworski earned $1 million, its largest fee up to that point, for representing Mrs. Libbie Moody Thompson, wife of Congressman Clark Thompson, in an estate case. In 1960 Leon Jaworski began serving Lyndon Johnson, his longtime friend, in lawsuits that challenged Johnson's right to appear on the ballot as candidate for both vice-president of the United States and for reelection as U.S. senator from Texas. Johnson won those lawsuits or had them dismissed. Jaworski continued to represent Johnson until he died.

Company Perspectives:

Predominant over our size and geographical reach is our strong belief in the personal relationship between attorney and client. The basic principles upon which Fulbright & Jaworski was founded remain intact, and the firm's strong confidence in its attorneys is steadfast. Mutual respect and a common desire to excel on behalf of each of our clients are present in every aspect of the firm's practice.

During the 1960s, Leon Jaworski was involved in some of the nation's most heated controversies. He assisted the U.S. Justice Department in prosecuting Governor Ross Barnett of Mississippi for defying court demands that blacks be allowed to attend the University of Mississippi. In 1962 James Meredith, with the help of federal troops, finally became the first black to attend "Ole Miss."

Following the assassination of President John F. Kennedy, Leon Jaworski served as special counsel to the Texas attorney general in a court of inquiry to examine the murder. The court's report supported the Warren Commission's conclusions that a single gunman killed the president, and Jaworski in his 1979 book *Confession and Avoidance* rejected conspiracy theories that opposed the Warren Commission's findings.

Leon Jaworski's best known legal contribution was his work as the special prosecutor who in 1973 and 1974 investigated President Richard Nixon's role in the Watergate scandal. Jaworski convinced the U.S. Supreme Court to rule that Nixon must turn over tape recordings, a decision that hastened the end of the Nixon administration. Facing imminent impeachment by the U.S. House of Representatives, Nixon in 1974 became the first American president to resign.

Meanwhile, the firm expanded by opening several branch offices, including London in 1974, Austin in about 1979, San Antonio in 1981, and Dallas in 1982. In 1985 the firm leased more than 250,000 square feet in Three Houston Center to prepare for its move to its new offices in early 1986. This move consolidated the firm's 160,000-square-foot offices in the Bank of the Southwest building and its 50,000-square-foot facility in the Commerce Building. Fulbright & Jaworski opened a Zurich, Switzerland affiliated office in the late 1980s but closed it in the 1990s.

Fulbright & Jaworski in 1985 brought in $87 million in gross revenue. That resulted in the *American Lawyer* ranking the firm as the nation's 17th largest law firm. Its $225,000 revenue per lawyer placed it as number 36 in the United States. The *National Law Journal* in September 1988 listed Fulbright & Jaworski as the nation's 11th largest law firm, based on its 453 lawyers. In the booming economy of the 1980s, the firm moved from its Houston headquarters in the Bank of the Southwest Building to new offices at 1301 McKinney Street.

Fulbright & Jaworski represented Texaco in a much publicized legal battle with Pennzoil. Houston's Baker Botts represented Pennzoil. The dispute was finally settled in 1988 when Texaco agreed to pay Pennzoil $3 billion.

The firm took a major step on January 1, 1989, when its merger with New York City's Reavis & McGrath became effective after ten months of negotiations. With 476 lawyers from the Fulbright law firm and 105 from Reavis & McGrath, the merged law firm's 581 attorneys made it the seventh largest in the United States. Probably more important, it strengthened the firm's national practice by adding the New York and Los Angeles offices of Reavis & McGrath. Gibson Gayle, Jr., Fulbright's managing partner, admitted in a November 11, 1988 *Houston Chronicle* article, "We have suffered in recent years from the absence of offices in New York and Los Angeles because it limited our ability to serve existing clients."

Another advantage of the Reavis & McGrath merger was pointed out by Bradford Hildebrandt, Reavis's advisor, in the February 1989 *American Bar Association Journal.* "Reavis' major claim to fame is its securities corporate practice. On the other hand, Fulbright is a major litigation firm. That's the kind of thing you look for in a merger. They have practices that clearly complement each other."

The merged firm ended 1989 on a high financial note. Its gross revenue of $183.2 million made it the largest law firm in Texas, overtaking Houston's Vinson & Elkins, which had the highest gross revenue in the previous three years. According to a *Texas Lawyer* survey, Houston had ten and Dallas had 12 of the state's major law firms.

With the nation's economy booming in the late 1980s, law firms also grew rapidly. According to the *American Lawyer,* in 1987 20 American law firms brought in revenues of at least $100 million, up from just five firms two years earlier.

Practice in the 1990s and the New Millennium

As the decade began, Fulbright & Jaworski defended Phillips after the corporation's Pasadena chemical plant near Houston exploded in 1989, resulting in 23 dead, 314 injured, and more than $1 billion in damages. Anne Pearson in the *Houston Chronicle* called the explosion "the Houston area's most deadly industrial accident in more than 40 years." By 1990 at least 160 lawsuits had been filed against Phillips, and the U.S. Occupational Safety and Health Administration (OSHA) had fined Phillips $5.7 million.

Meanwhile, the nation's slowing economy led to many large law firms thinning their ranks. For example, in 1992 the *National Law Journal* reported that about half of the nation's 250 largest law firms had shrunk. Fulbright & Jaworski was part of this trend, cutting back to 659 lawyers from 689 the year before. In 1994 the firm decreased to just 609 lawyers, while it was the nation's 16th largest law firm based on its gross revenues of $227 million, the highest of any Texas law firm.

When the Houston Oilers were almost ready to leave Houston in 1996, the city government hired Fulbright & Jaworski to help it lobby on several sports franchise bills in Congress and seek new sports franchises. The following year, MCI Communications Corporation used Fulbright & Jaworski when it sponsored the MCI Center in Washington, D.C., the newly opened home arena of the professional basketball team Washington Wizards.

Key Dates:

1919: The firm is founded in Houston.
1920s: The partnership then known as Fulbright, Crooker & Freeman opens its Washington, D.C. office, its first outside of Houston.
1931: Leon Jaworski, the best known of the firm's lawyers, joins the law firm.
c.1946: The firm is renamed Fulbright, Crooker, Freeman, Bates & Jaworski.
1973: Leon Jaworski begins serving as special prosecutor in the Watergate scandal.
1974: The partnership opens its first European office in London. 1976: The law firm changes its name to Fulbright & Jaworski.
1989: The firm merges with New York's Reavis & McGrath, making it the nation's seventh largest law firm with additional branch offices in New York and Los Angeles.
1991: The firm starts its first Asian office in Hong Kong.
2001: The Minneapolis office is opened.

The law firm also aided small start-up technology companies as they ventured forth in what some called the 1990s "new economy." For example, it helped WANTads.com, Inc. develop new sources of capital for its online listing of classified ads that competed with traditional newspaper ads.

In the late 1990s Fulbright & Jaworski became a world leader in the growing practice of international arbitration. More companies, especially in the energy field, agreed to arbitration to avoid legal conflicts because of different nations' laws. "Ten years ago, Texaco, Amoco and others did about 70% of their oil and gas exploration and production domestically—now it's 70% outside the U.S.," said John Bowman of Fulbright & Jaworski in the *Wall Street Journal* of May 10, 2000. Although arbitration results were confidential, some of the law firm's clients in this field included the French company Total SA in a dispute over a natural gas field off the coast of Ecuador, Mexican company Television Azteca in a conflict with National Broadcasting Company, and Houston energy company Coastal Corporation. The *Houston Chronicle* on May 20, 2001, reported that international arbitration accounted for about 20 percent of Fulbright & Jaworski's litigation practice.

Another example of the firm's role in the globalized economy was its service to Russia's Agency for Reconstruction of Credit Organizations (ARCO). In 1999 the newly created ARCO hired the Houston law firm as it took over Rossiyskiy Kredit Bank (RKB) and gained a moratorium that prevented creditors from filing lawsuits and seeking claims from RKB in Russia. After some creditors sought relief in U.S. courts, the U.S. Bankruptcy Court in New York City on October 11, 2000, ordered a permanent injunction against such efforts. "The ruling in New York represents the first time a bankruptcy court in the United States has given its assistance to the reorganization of a Russian bank," said RKB Chairman Alexander Livshits in an October 30, 2000 press release.

With more mergers and strategic alliances of corporations based in different nations, law firms in the 1990s often opened more branch offices around the world. In the *Washington Post* on December 8, 1997, Joel Henning of consulting firm Hildebrandt Inc. referred to "the growing nationalization and ultimately globalization of the legal marketplace. There are very few local clients, so it stands to reason that there will be very few local firms."

Fulbright & Jaworski's gross revenue increased 7.7 percent from 1999 to reach $343 million in 2000. Many other firms reported much faster growth, however, so Fulbright & Jaworski slipped from number 23 in 1999 to number 32 in the *American Lawyer*'s annual ratings of the 100 largest American law firms. It was the third largest law firm in Texas, behind Akin, Gump, Strauss, Hauer & Feld and Houston's Vinson & Elkins.

The firm's 2000 revenue of $343 million ranked it number 39 in the November 2001 listing of the world's 100 largest law firms compiled by the *American Lawyer* and London's *Legal Business*. At the same time, Fulbright & Jaworski was ranked number 31 based on its total of 767 lawyers. Only 1 percent of its lawyers worked outside the United States, compared with 28 firms that had at least 10 percent of their lawyers practicing outside their home countries. Its average profits per equity partner of $455,000 earned the firm a number 85 listing, compared with the top 25 firms where the average was at least $1 million.

After the three California cities of Burbank, Glendale, and Pasadena lost millions of dollars selling power to the state's electricity grid, they hired Fulbright & Jaworski in 2001 to try to regain some of that money from bankrupt Pacific Gas & Electric (PG&E) and struggling Southern California Edison. This was part of California's severe energy crisis, when some argued that consumers had been illegally overcharged up to $9 billion.

In 2001 technical and trade schools in Texas hired Fulbright & Jaworski to lobby the state legislature for separate funding that could benefit as many as 15,000 students. Thus the firm continued to make major contributions in its home state while serving many national and international clients.

Principal Competitors

Baker Botts, L.L.P.; Jenkins & Gilchrist; Vinson & Elkins L.L.P.

Further Reading

Barnett, John, "Law Firms to Merge/Fulbright to Become 7th Largest in U.S.," *Houston Chronicle,* November 11, 1988, p. 1.
Berkowitz, Harry, "Texaco Dispute Keeps Lawyers' Pockets Filled," *Houston Chronicle,* April 19, 1987, p. 1.
Boisseau, Charles, "Major Houston Law Firms Among Those That Have Downsized," *Houston Chronicle,* September 22, 1992, p. 3.
"Chronicle 100 Leading Companies of Houston . . . ," *Houston Chronicle,* May 20, 2001, p. 32.
"City Hires Sports Lobby," *Houston Chronicle,* March 21, 1996, p. 34.
Flood, Mary, "Texas Lawyers Make a Splash Outside of U.S.," *Wall Street Journal* (Eastern edition), May 10, 2000, p. A1.
"Fulbright & Jaworski Announces Decision in Favor of Rossiyskiy Kredit: Russian Bank Receives Assistance from U.S. Bankruptcy Court," *Business Wire,* October 30, 2000.

"Fulbright & Jaworski Leases 250,000 Square Feet in Three Houston Center for Relocation," *Houston Chronicle,* February 24, 1985, p. 2.

Gao, Helen, "Payment Sought from Utilities: 3 Area Cities Hire Law Firm to Collect Millions," *Daily News* (Los Angeles), June 24, 2001, p. N3.

Jaworski, Leon, with Dick Schneider, *Crossroads,* Elgin, Ill.: David C. Cook Publishing Co., 1981.

Jaworski, Leon, with Mickey Herskowitz, *Confession and Avoidance: A Memoir,* Garden City, N.Y.: Anchor Press/Doubleday, 1979.

Kay, Michele, "Trade Schools Making Case for State Aid," *Austin American Statesman,* March 4, 2001, p. J1.

Levinson, Brian, "Texas Law Firms Catch the Merger Wave," *Houston Chronicle,* June 14, 1987, p. 1.

Moss, Debra Cassens, "The Urge to Merge," *American Bar Association Journal,* February 1989, p. 40.

Pearson, Anne, "Ranks of Lawyers Sort Phillips Suits," *Houston Chronicle,* October 21, 1990, p. 9.

Pope, Kyle, "Fulbright & Jaworski Top-Grossing Law Firm," *Houston Chronicle,* July 10, 1990, p. 1.

Segal, David, "Enough Talent to Fill the New MCI Center," *Washington Post,* December 8, 1997, p. F07.

Shook, Barbara, "Texaco Resumes Appeal of $11 Billion Damages," *Houston Chronicle,* May 14, 1987, p. 1.

Stewart, James B., "Who's in Command of Texaco's Team? Me! No, Me! No . . . Oil Giant Declining to Say Which of 4 Law Firms Controls Pennzoil Case," *Wall Street Journal* (Eastern edition), December 6, 1985, p. 1.

"3 Houston Law Firms Make Top-20," *Houston Chronicle,* July 8, 1986, p. 10.

"Top Texas Law Firms Post Big Revenue Rise/Total for 25 Leaders Jumps to $3.3 Billion," *Houston Chronicle,* June 26, 2001, p. 2.

"2 Houston Law Firms Among Revenue Leaders," *Houston Chronicle,* July 4, 1987, p. 1.

—David M. Walden

Galyan's Trading Company, Inc.

2437 East Main Street
Plainfield, Indiana 46168
U.S.A.
Telephone: (317) 532-0200
Fax: (317) 532-0250
Web site: http://www.galyans.com

Public Company
Incorporated: 1946
Employees: 4,500
Sales: $482.5 million (2002)
Stock Exchanges: NASDAQ
Ticker Symbol: GLYN
NAIC: 451110 Sporting Goods Stores

Galyan's Trading Company, Inc. is an expanding chain of innovative sporting goods stores specializing in huge, splashy retail spaces. Stores include such activity areas as putting greens and indoor climbing walls, making Galyan's a leader in so-called retail-tainment, where the shopping experience is made into something of an adventure. Galyan's operates several dozen stores in the Midwest, upstate New York, Georgia, Texas, and Utah, with plans for rapid rollout of more stores in urban markets across the country. The stores sell a variety of major brand-name clothing and sports gear, outdoor equipment, and athletic shoes, plus some of its own Galyan's branded goods. Retailing giant The Limited bought the company in 1995, then sold most of Galyan's to a private investment firm. Galyan's shares are now traded on the NASDAQ. The Limited retains more than 20 percent of the company, and an additional 30 percent is owned by Freeman Spogli & Co.

Expanding a Family Business in the 1980s and Early 1990s

Galyan's Trading Company began as a single store founded in Indianapolis in 1946 by Albert Galyan and his wife, Naomi. Galyan's was originally a grocery that also sold hunting and fishing supplies. Gradually it evolved into a small, successful sporting goods store. Albert Galyan died in 1975, and management of the business passed to his son Pat Galyan.

In 1978, Pat Galyan and his wife bought the store outright from Naomi Galyan. Pat Galyan managed the business for six years before deciding to expand. The second Galyan's store opened in the Indianapolis area in 1983. Over the next decade, the chain expanded to four stores in Indiana. These were about 37,000 square feet each and sold a full array of sporting goods. The chain dominated the central Indiana market. Sales for the company in the early 1990s were estimated at around $15 million.

In 1993 the company announced plans to build a fifth store, in Columbus, Ohio. But this one was to be quite different from its predecessors. The Columbus store was sited between two large-format regional retailers, Kohl's and Meijer's, and it was almost twice as big as the other Galyan's, at 75,000 square feet. The new store was built on two levels and offered a complete line of sporting goods, from skis to canoes, as well as athletic shoes and apparel. It featured a modern design, with a glass façade and an open atrium decorated with an enormous steel tree, and it offered its customers a chance to climb on its 42-foot indoor climbing wall. Outside, the store had another 40,000 square feet for a full-sized volleyball court, basketball court, golf practice area, batting cages, and a running track. An additional 8,000 square feet was set aside for boating equipment. The store was huge, and it employed 150 to 200 people. The Columbus store was a breakthrough in sporting goods retailing. No one had put together such a theatrical retail space in sporting goods before. The new store was more than a flagship. Pat Galyan announced that it was a prototype for the rest of the chain, which he planned to expand. In an interview with *Sporting Goods Business* (September 1995), Galyan explained that in wanting to grow his company, he was stuck competing with so-called "big box" stores such as Sports Authority. What he decided to do was "design the ultimate category killer killer." In other words, he outdid even the mega-stores by being not only large, but adding the sense of adventure and fun with the attractive architecture and onsite sports areas. Galyan's also claimed to be more than a sporting goods store. Pat Galyan called his retail outlets "sports stores" and claimed to have a broader understanding of the sporting lifestyle and sport fashions than other retailers. "It's not just jocks and socks and hunting and fishing," he said.

With The Limited in the 1990s

After the Columbus store made its mark, Galyan's also retrofitted some of its Indiana stores and built one more, bringing the chain to six by 1995. Galyan's called itself "The World's Coolest Sports Store" and showed an impressive retail flair. Pat Galyan seemed to have a wide view of the sports market as he made plans to keep the chain growing. He wanted to make sure his stores provided for women customers, something he thought few of his competitors emphasized enough. In both the store design and in its apparel offerings, Galyan's intended to stand out as a retailer that would cater to women in the sports market. Galyan also hoped to attract aging customers, particularly with the sale of exercise equipment. He believed that the aging baby boom generation would find itself with more time and money to spend on sports and exercise and would buy at-home fitness equipment. Although the chain was still small, it already was thinking of a national market.

By 1994, Galyan's sales had grown substantially, to $52 million, up from $15 million just a few years earlier. Even so, the company did not have the funds to expand nationally by itself. In 1995 The Limited Inc. bought Galyan's for $32 million. The Limited operated almost 5,000 stores and had sales in 1994 of more than $7 billion. It ran its namesake The Limited stores, a mall stalwart, as well as Abercrombie & Fitch, Express, the lingerie chain Victoria's Secret, and Bath & Body Works. The company had longstanding experience in developing retail niches, although sporting goods was a departure for it. The Limited's chairman, Leslie Wexner, was enthusiastic about Galyan's and saw the chain becoming a market leader soon. The Limited announced that it would build as many as 50 new stores by 2000, bringing sales up to possibly $500 million. Pat Galyan would stay on as CEO of the chain, which was to remain headquartered in Indiana. Galyan claimed to be ecstatic about the deal, which partnered his company with one of the most knowledgeable retailers in the country.

Over the next two years, Galyan's opened two stores in Minneapolis-St. Paul and another in Kansas City. The new stores were from 80,000 to 100,000 square feet and continued the Galyan's theme of hands-on displays and tryout areas and dynamic, theatrical design. By 1996, sales had already doubled from two years earlier, to $108 million. But in 1997 Pat Galyan abruptly left his post as CEO, claiming that he wished to retire at the age of 47 to spend more time with his family. The Limited

claimed that there were no financial problems at Galyan's, that in fact the stores pulled in $300 per square foot, and led the market for sporting goods in every market the stores entered. But clearly the expansion of the chain had not gone as quickly as had first been estimated.

The company's new CEO was Joel Silverman. Silverman had an extensive background in retailing, having worked at Federated Stores and then run three different divisions of The Limited. He had a longstanding interest in sporting goods and was extremely enthusiastic about Galyan's. He instituted changes to give Galyan's a better management infrastructure, making each store more consistent with its partners in the chain, overhauling the budget and merchandising planning processes, and in general setting up the chain to operate on a national scale even though it was still small.

Nevertheless, there were several barriers to the quick expansion that The Limited had first envisioned for Galyan's. One was that the stores were very large, and working out the real estate deals to build them was complicated and sometimes slow moving. Mall stores including Victoria's Secret were generally quicker and easier to open than something as architecturally unique as Galyan's. By 1998, the chain had moved to a couple malls, and the company did not rule out more mall expansion rather than stand-alone units. Silverman claimed in an interview with *Sporting Goods Business* (August 10, 1998) that he was willing to wait before entering a new market, in order to make sure the real estate the company bought was "A-plus. We don't settle for anything less than the best." Staffing new stores was also perhaps more of a problem at Galyan's than at other chains The Limited ran. Galyan's wanted employees who were knowledgeable sports enthusiasts. It needed some 200 people for each new store. Silverman acknowledged that it might be difficult to attract enough suitable personnel when the chain started opening more stores, more quickly. Galyan's also was moving slower than predicted in bringing out its own brand. By 1998, only about 6 percent of the business was in Galyan's private-label goods. Most of this was in casual apparel. The company hoped to introduce more private-label goods, but was waiting to see what niches its major brand vendors neglected, to see where the best opportunity might be. Thus the chain was nowhere near opening the 50 new stores it had planned. In 1998 Silverman revised the growth scenario to predict that Galyan's would have close to 20 stores by the end of the century. But Silverman also averred that the chain could grow to a $2 billion business, and within only 15 years. Galyan's ended 1998 with sales of $220 million.

Continued Growth and an Initial Public Offering

In mid-1999, Galyan's had expanded to 18 stores, and The Limited sold 60 percent of its interest in the chain to a private investment firm called Freeman Spogli & Co. The Limited made approximately $190 million on the sale. The growth of the chain continued. The company opened a 170,000-square-foot store in the Chicago area as well as its third store in the Atlanta area. New stores were also underway in Buffalo, Denver, Detroit, and Grand Rapids, Michigan. CEO Silverman claimed that Galyan's was doing better financially than most of its competitors, some of whom were seeing declining sales and closing underperforming units. Not only was Galyan's' revenue growing because of its new stores, but sales at stores open at least a

Key Dates:

1946: Albert and Naomi Galyan open their first store.
1975: Albert Galyan dies; son Pat begins to run the store.
1978: Pat Galyan buys the store from his mother.
1983: The chain begins to expand.
1994: A huge new Galyan's design premieres in Columbus, Ohio.
1995: The Limited buys the six-store chain.
1997: Pat Galyan retires.
1999: The Limited sells its stake in the chain to investment firm Freeman Spogli.
2001: The company begins selling its stock with its initial public offering on the NASDAQ.

year (a key measure of retail performance) also were growing at around 10 percent. In addition, Silverman announced that Galyan's would probably go public soon, when it had opened about 30 stores.

The company continued to do well, with another 10 percent gain in sales at stores open at least a year recorded for 2000. The company began selling its stock on the NASDAQ in 2001. The initial public offering raised about $115 million for the chain, which was to be used to pay down debt and to fund further expansion. The stock sale left The Limited with about 22 percent of Galyan's, and Freeman Spogli with another 30 percent. The chain opened more stores in urban markets across the country. It opened a store in Plano, Texas, in 2001, followed by others in Rochester, New York, and in Salt Lake City. By mid-2002, Galyan's had 26 stores in 16 states.

Principal Competitors

The Sports Authority, Inc.; Foot Locker, Inc.; Gart Sports Company; Recreational Equipment, Inc.

Further Reading

''Galyan's Secures Funding for Aggressive Expansion,'' *DSN Retailing Today,* July 9, 2001, p. 3.

Kaufmann, Martin, ''A Service Culture Permeates Galyan's,'' *Sporting Goods Business,* February 2002, p. 31.

''Limited Enters Sporting Goods Business in a Big Way,'' *Apparel Industry,* September 1995, p. 18.

McEvoy, Christopher, ''Joel Silverman,'' *Sporting Goods Business,* August 10, 1998, p. 34.

——, ''Pat Galyan Calls It Quits: Limited Still Bullish on Chain,'' *Sporting Goods Business,* July 21, 1997, p. 11.

Molinari, Elena, ''Galyan's Scores Modest Gain in Its Debut,'' *Wall Street Journal,* June 28, 2001, p. C19.

''Spinoff and Sale by the Limited,'' *New York Times,* May 4, 1999, p. C7.

Troy, Mike, ''Galyan's Debuts Atlanta Units, Plants Seeds for Greater Growth,'' *Discount Store News,* August 23, 1999, p. 6.

——, ''Public Offering in the Offing for Galyan's Trading Co.,'' *Discount Store News,* May 24, 1999, p. 6.

Wilson, Marianne, ''Bat, Putt, Dribble or Climb at Galyan's,'' *Chain Store Age,* December 1994, p. 92.

Wolf, Barnet D., ''Try-It-Buy-It Style Store Planned by Indiana Sporting Goods Chain,'' *Columbus Dispatch,* December 21, 1993, p. 1D.

—A. Woodward

Georgia-Pacific Corporation

133 Peachtree Street, Northeast
Atlanta, Georgia 30303-5605
U.S.A.
Telephone: (404) 652-4000
Fax: (404) 584-1470
Web site: http://www.gp.com

Public Company
Incorporated: 1927 as Georgia Hardwood Lumber
    Company
Employees: 75,000
Sales: $25.02 billion (2001)
Stock Exchanges: New York
Ticker Symbol: GP
NAIC: 321211 Hardwood Veneer and Plywood
    Manufacturing; 321212 Softwood Veneer and
    Plywood Manufacturing; 321213 Engineered Wood
    Member (Except Truss) Manufacturing; 321219
    Reconstituted Wood Product Manufacturing; 327420
    Gypsum Product Manufacturing; 322110 Pulp Mills;
    322121 Paper (Except Newsprint) Mills; 322130
    Paperboard Mills; 322210 Paperboard Container
    Manufacturing; 322232 Envelope Manufacturing;
    322233 Stationery, Tablet, and Related Product
    Manufacturing; 322291 Sanitary Paper Product
    Manufacturing; 326140 Polystyrene Foam Product
    Manufacturing; 326199 All Other Plastics Product
    Manufacturing; 421310 Lumber, Plywood, Millwork,
    and Wood Panel Wholesalers; 421330 Roofing,
    Siding, and Insulation Material Wholesalers; 422110
    Printing and Writing Paper Wholesalers; 422130
    Industrial and Personal Service Paper Wholesalers

Georgia-Pacific Corporation is a leading manufacturer and distributor of paper-based consumer products, pulp, office paper, packaging, and building products. Overall, it ranks as the world's second largest forest products company, trailing International Paper Company. The company holds the number one position worldwide in tissue products, producing paper towels, paper napkins, and bath and facial tissue under such brands as Quilted Northern, Angel Soft, Brawny, Sparkle, and Vanity Fair. Its Dixie business is the leading North American brand of disposable tableware, including plates, cups, and cutlery made of paper, plastic, and foam. Georgia-Pacific's bleached pulp and paper segment holds the number two position in North America in communications paper and the number three position in market pulp. The company's Unisource Worldwide, Inc. subsidiary is one of North America's largest distributors of printing and imaging paper, packaging systems, and related supplies. In packaging, Georgia-Pacific is a major North American producer of containerboard, corrugated containers, and other packaging products. The company's building products segments ranks first in North America in structural wood panels, second in gypsum wallboard, and third in lumber. Other building products made by Georgia-Pacific include siding, decorative panels, hardboard, particleboard, and fiberboard. In addition, the company runs a building products distribution business that is one of the largest suppliers of such products to lumber and building materials dealers and major do-it-yourself warehouse retailers. Unlike most other major forest products firms, Georgia-Pacific does not own any timberlands, having sold off its timber holdings in 2001.

Early Decades of Geographic and Operational Expansion

Although its operations in the 21st century range widely, the company's beginnings were in lumber distribution. Georgia Hardwood Lumber Company began operation in 1927 in Augusta, Georgia, as a hardwood lumber wholesaler with $12,000 in start-up funds provided by its founder, Owen R. Cheatham. During its first decade in business, the company began lumber manufacturing in addition to its wholesaling activities. Cheatham focused on expanding the company's milling capabilities in the southern United States (the company was operating five sawmills in the South by 1938), a strategy that allowed it to become the largest supplier of lumber to the U.S. Army during World War II. The company's purchase of a plywood mill in Bellingham, Washington, in 1947 coincided with plywood's growing popularity in the construction industry and gave the company a strong competitive advantage.

Company Perspectives:

Georgia-Pacific Mission: *Through excellence in all we do, the resourceful people of Georgia-Pacific grow our value and create wealth for our investors by providing value-added forest products that enable our customers and consumers to enhance where they live, work, and play.*

Georgia-Pacific Vision: *Georgia-Pacific will be a premier worldwide manufacturer and marketer of choice for value-added forest products. Employees will choose us because we reward excellence and we believe people make the difference. Customers and consumers will choose us because we provide superior products and services at competitive prices. Investors will choose us because we will consistently deliver returns in the top quartile of all major companies.*

Additional plywood mills in Washington and Oregon were purchased in 1948, as well as another plywood plant in 1949, to support this growing business area. The company changed its name in 1948 to Georgia-Pacific Plywood & Lumber Company to reflect more accurately its geographic and operational expansion. The following year the company went public with a listing on the New York Stock Exchange.

In 1951, the company changed its name again, to Georgia-Pacific Plywood Company. Cheatham gradually developed a reputation as an industry maverick. Over the next six years, he conducted a $160 million timberland-acquisition program in the western and southern United States. To finance this program, he borrowed heavily from banks and insurance companies expecting that the proceeds gained from the timber in the future would more than cover the required return on their investment. In order to be closer to these newly purchased resources, the company moved its headquarters from Georgia to Olympia, Washington, in 1953, and then again to Portland, Oregon, the following year.

Over the next decade, Cheatham used his financing model several times to acquire additional forest acreage and manufacturing facilities, including Coos Bay Lumber Company and Hammond Lumber Company in 1956. That same year the company's name was changed, for the third time since its founding, to Georgia-Pacific Corporation. Subsequent purchases of Booth-Kelly Lumber Company in 1959 and W.M. Ritter Lumber Company in 1960 took the company to the number three position in its industry.

The company's unorthodox approach to growth was evident in other areas as well. It opened a kraft pulp and linerboard mill in Toledo, Oregon, in 1957, and its first resin adhesive plant at Coos Bay, Oregon, in 1959. The latter manufacturing operation was intended at first to supply the resin required for the company's plywood-production business but gradually grew large enough to supply resin to other plywood manufacturers as well. Georgia-Pacific was also one of the first manufacturers to use wood byproducts rather than timber in pulp production. The company continued to pioneer in the development of plywood products, eventually shifting away from the traditional use of Douglas fir to a process using less-expensive southern pine.

This wood previously had been considered inappropriate for use in plywood because of its high resin content.

During the 1960s, Georgia-Pacific embarked upon another series of acquisitions by buying several lumber and paper companies across the country. These included Crossett Lumber Company (Crossett, Arkansas) in 1962; Puget Sound Pulp and Timber Company (Bellingham, Washington), Vanity Fair Paper Mills (Plattsburgh, New York), St. Croix Paper Company (Woodland, Maine), and Fordyce Lumber Company (Fordyce, Arkansas) in 1963; Bestwall Gypsum Company (Paoli, Pennsylvania) in 1965; and Kalamazoo Paper Company (Kalamazoo, Michigan) in 1967. With the purchases of Puget Sound Pulp and Timber and Vanity Fair Paper, Georgia-Pacific entered the tissue business. After building its first corrugated-container plant in Olympia in 1961, the company added a series of additional manufacturing facilities for lumber, paper, and chemical products over the course of the rest of the decade.

Struggles in the 1970s

Upon Cheatham's death in 1970, Robert B. Pamplin, who had worked with Cheatham since the company's inception, became chairman and chief executive officer. Although the company's building-products business benefited from the housing boom of the early 1970s, its paper and pulp interests struggled because of low prices and sluggish demand. To bolster its manufacturing operations, the firm expanded production of two new building materials, polyvinyl chloride (PVC) and particleboard, the former through a joint venture with Permaneer Corporation. Georgia-Pacific opened its own PVC manufacturing plant in 1975. When the cost of oil increased soon afterward, however, the company's prices for its PVC-molding products proved to be too high to compete effectively with wood moldings, resulting in significant losses.

It was also during this period that the firm was required by the Federal Trade Commission (FTC) to defend its acquisition of 16 small firms in the South that supplied the company with 673,000 acres of the southern pine used to make plywood. Charging that the acquisitions tended to create a monopoly, the FTC issued a consent order in 1972 that forced Georgia-Pacific to divest 20 percent of its assets. This step resulted in the formation of a spinoff company called Louisiana-Pacific Corporation. The order also prohibited the firm from acquiring any other softwood plywood companies and imposed restrictions on timberland purchases in the South for five years and on plywood mill acquisitions for ten years.

A slump in the housing industry in 1973 and 1974 depressed the company's lumber and plywood business. Georgia-Pacific continued to post record profits, however, largely because of the growth of its chemical, pulp, and paper operations. These areas experienced slowdowns as well by the middle of the decade. Nevertheless, the company moved forward in its long-range program to increase manufacturing capacity across the board. It expanded through vertical integration into the production of additional chemicals derived from wood wastes, such as chlorine, phenol, and methanol. The 1975 acquisition of Exchange Oil & Gas Corporation enabled the company to become more self-sufficient by developing its own reserves of important raw materials required for the operation of its chemical plants.

Key Dates:

1927: Owen R. Cheatham founds Georgia Hardwood Lumber Company in Augusta, Georgia, as a hardwood lumber wholesaler.

1938: After expanding into lumber manufacturing, the firm now operates five sawmills in the South.

1947: Expansion to the West Coast begins with the purchase of a plywood mill in Bellingham, Washington.

1948: The company's name is changed to Georgia-Pacific Plywood & Lumber Company to better reflect the geographic and operational expansion.

1949: Georgia-Pacific Plywood & Lumber Company goes public.

1951: The company is renamed Georgia-Pacific Plywood Company.

1956: The company's name is changed to Georgia-Pacific Corporation.

1957: Company expands into pulp and paper sector with the opening of a kraft pulp and linerboard mill in Toledo, Oregon.

1963: Georgia-Pacific expands into the tissue business with the acquisitions of Puget Sound Pulp and Timber Company and Vanity Fair Paper Mills.

1972: A Federal Trade Commission consent order forces the company to divest 20 percent of its assets, which are spun off as Louisiana-Pacific Corporation.

1982: Headquarters are relocated to Atlanta, Georgia.

1990: Great Northern Nekoosa Corporation is acquired.

1997: Timber operations are split off into a separate operating group, the Timber Company, with its own common stock.

1999: The company acquires Unisource Worldwide, Inc., a major distributor of printing and imaging paper and supplies.

2000: Fort James Corporation is acquired for $7.7 billion in stock and cash plus the assumption of $3.3 billion in debt.

2001: Georgia-Pacific sells four fine-paper mills to Domtar Inc. for $1.65 billion; Timber Company is merged into Plum Creek Timber Company, Inc., marking Georgia-Pacific's exit from the timber business.

In 1976 president Robert Flowerree succeeded Robert Pamplin as chairman and chief executive. A 25-year Georgia-Pacific veteran, Flowerree had been instrumental in taking the company into the chemical business. He was also considered to be more cautious than his predecessors. Under his leadership, the firm expanded its building products to include roofing materials, which it began to produce in a converted paper mill.

By 1978, the company was drawing three-quarters of its sales from the southern and eastern United States. This shift away from the West was instrumental in the decision to move the headquarters of the firm back to Georgia, specifically to Atlanta, 150 miles away from its original location. The relocation, completed in 1982, caused many employees to leave the company, and several senior executives chose to retire rather than make the move. This shift left the firm vulnerable at a critical time, particularly in the growing chemical area.

Turnaround in the 1980s

The dawning of the 1980s brought with it another housing slump, but Georgia-Pacific was able to use its chemical business to maintain overall growth. Its plywood products, however, were slowly losing competitive ground to new and cheaper materials, such as waferboard and oriented-strand board, which were being manufactured and sold aggressively by such firms as Louisiana-Pacific and Potlatch Corporation. Until then, Georgia-Pacific had not placed significant emphasis on these materials, with only one plant producing waferboard and another producing oriented-strand board. Most of its capital expenditure was directed instead toward upgrading existing facilities and buying timberlands.

In 1982, T. Marshall Hahn, Jr., who had succeeded Flowerree as president in 1976, became chief operating officer. When he became chairman and chief executive officer one year later, following Flowerree's early retirement, he faced several serious problems. Demand for paper was strong, but only in the area of higher-quality products, not in the basic linerboard and kraft paper sectors in which Georgia-Pacific concentrated. Although an upturn in the construction industry augured well for the company's building products business, the high interest rates on the debt the firm had used to fund expansion severely limited its freedom to take advantage of opportunities in that area. Furthermore, its chemical business, once the firm's star division, fell on hard times as sales dropped significantly. This business was sold to Georgia Gulf Corporation in 1984, followed by the sale of Exchange Oil & Gas in 1985. The company retained its specialty chemicals business, which continued to deliver good returns.

Hahn instituted a series of measures designed to get the company back on its feet. These included reviewing the health of its assets, improvement of cost controls and productivity, and continued investment in areas such as the pulp and paper business, which could insulate the company from future economic calamities and provide a hedge against cyclical upturns and downturns in the various industries in which the company operated. In 1984, Georgia-Pacific acquired a linerboard mill, several corrugated container plants, and over 300,000 acres of forest from St. Regis Corporation. It converted two paper plants to the production of higher-margin products, such as lightweight bleached board and white paper used by copiers and computer printers. It also successfully expanded a wood products mill in South Carolina and a plant in Florida to produce lattice and fencing materials, which were in heavy demand.

In 1986, the company entered the premium bathroom tissue market through the introduction of Angel Soft bath tissue. By the end of 1987, Georgia-Pacific's tissue and towel operation, combined with its production of linerboard, kraft, and fine papers, enabled the company to achieve higher profitability in paper products than in wood products for the first time in its history, despite tough competition from major consumer products companies such as the Procter & Gamble Company. Other elements of Hahn's turnaround strategy included further decentralization of the company's operations, which forced plant managers to compete with each other for capital funds, and the addition of several building materials distribution centers nationwide to capitalize on the growing trend toward remodeling and do-it-yourself projects.

During the last few years of the decade, the company made further acquisitions. These included U.S. Plywood Corporation and selected assets of the Erving Distributor Products Company in 1987 and Brunswick Pulp & Paper Company and American Forest Products Company in 1988. Its most controversial purchase, however, commenced in 1989 with an offer to buy Great Northern Nekoosa Corporation of Connecticut, a competing producer of pulp, paper, containerboard, lumber, and plywood.

Early to Mid-1990s: Acquisition of Great Northern Nekoosa and Cost-Cutting Initiatives

Originally incorporated in 1898 as the Northern Development Company but soon renamed Great Northern Paper Company, the predecessor to Great Northern Nekoosa had begun producing newsprint in 1900. By 1924, it was manufacturing corrugated paper and a decade later began a gradual transition from wrapping paper to business paper production. The company expanded its pulp and paper operations over the next 40 years. In 1970, the Great Northern Paper Company and the Nekoosa Edwards Paper Company merged to become Great Northern Nekoosa Corporation. Great Northern Nekoosa acquired several firms subsequently to enhance the company's manufacturing and distribution capabilities, including Heco Envelope Company in 1973; Pak-Well in 1975; Leaf River Forest Products in 1981; Barton, Duer & Koch, and Consolidated Marketing, Inc. in 1982; Triquet Paper Company in 1983; Chatfield Paper Company in 1984; J&J Corrugated Box Corporation and Carpenter Paper Company of Iowa in 1986; Owens-Illinois's forest products company in 1987; and Jim Walter Papers in 1988. By 1989, Great Northern Nekoosa was operating 55 paper mills and paperboard converting plants, 83 paper distribution centers, one plywood plant, and two sawmills.

Great Northern Nekoosa was a particularly attractive candidate for acquisition because of its depressed stock price. Georgia-Pacific saw the combination of the two companies as an opportunity to achieve economies of scale and other cost savings. In Hahn's opinion, the acquisition would enable Georgia-Pacific to add manufacturing capability at less expense than by building its own plants. On the other hand, Great Northern Nekoosa viewed Georgia-Pacific's $3.74 billion bid as a hostile takeover attempt. It attempted to halt the proposed buyout with a series of lawsuits and an extensive search for another buyer. All of these measures failed, however, and the purchase was completed in March 1990. Georgia-Pacific assumed a significant amount of debt as a result, but was able to eliminate part of the burden through the subsequent sale of several mills and some timberland to Tenneco, the John Hancock Mutual Life Insurance Company, and the Metropolitan Life Insurance Company.

With its hard-fought acquisition of Great Northern Nekoosa complete, Georgia-Pacific held market leadership positions in containerboard, packaging, pulp, and communication papers and was a major producer of related products, such as tissue, kraft paper, and bleached board. The most significant threat to the company's continued growth would be the economy's ef-

fects on its key business areas. Although the firm's diversification into paper and pulp manufacturing was intended to help it survive cyclical downturns in lumber and housing construction, its new business areas were also highly cyclical in nature, with peaks and valleys lagging only months behind those occurring in lumber and housing.

Paper prices fell soon after Georgia-Pacific closed the Great Northern Nekoosa deal, but true to plan, the declining paper market was offset by record profits in the company's building products division, which posted profits of $432 million in 1990 despite low levels in housing starts. Georgia-Pacific was also able to reduce a significant amount of the $8 billion debt it saddled through its Great Northern Nekoosa purchase, thanks to the company's healthy cash flow. Despite these favorable signs, net income fell to $365 million in 1990, down from $661 million in 1989.

Prices of Georgia-Pacific shares on the New York Stock Exchange fell almost 50 percent in 1990 in response to investors' fears that the company might be acquiring too much debt. To ease this concern, the company took out a two-page ad in national magazines to convey the message that the company had significant cash flow to pay down its debt and had laid the groundwork for a strong future.

Despite Georgia-Pacific's intentions, profits took a dive in 1991 when the bottom dropped out of both the building materials and pulp and paper markets. The company reported a net loss of $151 million, compared to profits of over $3 million the preceding year. Georgia-Pacific continued to rely on its substantial cash flow to pay shareholders and pay down its debt in 1991.

In 1991, the company also reorganized its building products division along product lines, as opposed to its previous method of management along geographical lines. It also completed the expansion of its Ashdown, Arkansas, paper mill with the addition of the world's largest and fastest paper machine. A.D. (Pete) Correll, who joined Georgia-Pacific's paper division in 1988 after being wooed from his position at the Mead Corporation, was elected president and chief operating officer.

Despite its continuously healthy cash flow and record-breaking profits in its building products division, the company posted losses again in 1992. In response to the recession, which continued to affect Georgia-Pacific's key businesses, management chose to focus on keeping costs down and reducing debt. Georgia-Pacific did this by paring down its "nonstrategic" assets, selling its Butler Paper distribution operations (acquired as part of its purchase of Great Northern Nekoosa) to Alco Standard Corporation in 1993 and its roofing manufacturing business to Atlas Roofing Corporation the following year. Also divested in 1994 was its envelope manufacturing business (another Great Northern inheritance), which was sold to Sterling Group Inc. (which would later emerge as Mail-Well, Inc.). Proceeds from these sales went to further reduce the company's debt.

By the time that Correll succeeded Hahn as Georgia-Pacific's chairman and CEO during 1993, the company's financial outlook began to look brighter. Housing starts were on the rise again, and lumber production remained far below demand. Lumber prices began rising to record highs in October 1993. Georgia-Pacific had grown to become the largest supplier of building lumber in the United States and was perfectly poised to benefit from improvements in the economy. The pulp and paper market, meanwhile, began a strong recovery in 1994, enabling the company to return to profitability after two years in the red. The improving conditions led the firm during 1994 to launch a two-year, $1.75 billion capital improvement program, focusing primarily on expanding its strongly performing engineered wood products operations. Surging pulp and paper prices enabled Georgia-Pacific to post record profits of $921 million on record revenues of $14.31 billion in 1995. The pulp and paper market began to enter another slump, however, late that year.

While the market was still surging, Correll launched a number of initiatives aimed at making Georgia-Pacific the most cost-efficient company in the industry. A major restructuring of the building products distribution operation, aiming at cutting costs and increasing sales, began in 1994. This led to the announcement in mid-1995 that 60 of Georgia-Pacific's 130 building products distribution centers would be closed by early 1997. Later in 1994 the company launched the Mill Improvement Program to cut costs and increase efficiency at the firm's 14 large pulp and paper mills. A little more than two years later, the mills had each identified cost savings of $20 million to $40 million per year. Finally, in mid-1995 the building products manufacturing operation launched Operation Complete, eventually identifying nearly $200 million in cost savings and productivity improvements at the 140 facilities of that company unit.

Georgia-Pacific used some of its profits from the heady results of 1995 to bolster its gypsum wallboard capacity. It paid about $350 million in early 1996 to acquire nine wallboard plants from Domtar Inc., based in Montreal, Canada. Moving quickly to counter the effects of the sliding paper prices, Correll, in May 1996, launched a three-year effort to reduce overhead costs by $400 million. The effort included a hiring freeze and an early retirement program for salaried employees. In late 1996, Georgia-Pacific announced that it would sell a number of operations based in Martell, California, including 127,000 acres of timberland, a sawmill, and a particleboard plant, to Sierra Pacific Holding Co. The $320 million deal closed in early 1997.

Late 1990s into Early 21st Century: Enter Fort James, Exit Timber

Seeking to increase its overall market value and to free its timber operations from the financial gyrations of its wildly cyclical pulp, paper, and building products businesses, Georgia-Pacific, in December 1997, split off its timber operations into a separate operating group with its own common stock. Georgia-Pacific Corporation essentially became a holding company for two operating groups, Georgia-Pacific Group (all operations other than the timber operations) and the Timber Company (the timber operations), with two classes of common stock for the two groups. The preexisting common stock was redesignated as the common stock of Georgia-Pacific Group, while company shareholders received shares of newly created Timber Company stock.

The late 1990s were also noteworthy for two significant acquisitions. In June 1998, Georgia-Pacific acquired Indianapolis-based CeCorr Inc. for about $190 million plus the assumption of $92 million in debt. CeCorr produced corrugated sheets at 11 sheet feeder plants, with the sheets sold to other firms for conver-

sion into corrugated containers. CeCorr was the leading independent maker of corrugated sheets in the United States with 1997 revenues of $282 million. In mid-1999, Georgia-Pacific acquired Unisource Worldwide, Inc. for about $850 million plus the assumption of $785 million in debt. This acquisition was secured through an unsolicited offer that bested a previously agreed upon bid by UGI Corporation. Based in Berwyn, Pennsylvania, Unisource was a leading North American distributor of printing and imaging paper and supplies, with revenues for the fiscal year ending in September 1998 of $7.42 billion. Georgia-Pacific thus returned in a major way to the paper distribution sector it had been involved in briefly—and more modestly—when it owned Butler Paper from 1990 to 1993.

Also in 1999, Georgia-Pacific combined its commercial-tissue business with Wisconsin Tissue, the commercial-tissue unit of Chesapeake Corporation. The resulting joint venture, Georgia-Pacific Tissue, LLC, was 95 percent owned by Georgia-Pacific and 5 percent by Chesapeake and was managed by Georgia-Pacific. As part of the deal, Chesapeake received $755 million in cash from Georgia-Pacific. The joint venture, kept separate from Georgia-Pacific's consumer-tissue operations, focused on selling paper towels and tissues to institutions. Meantime, the Timber Company during 1999 sold 194,000 acres of timberlands in northern California for about $397 million and 390,000 acres in Maine and 440,000 acres in New Brunswick, Canada, for about $92 million.

Seeking to gain a more significant presence in the consumer market as a hedge against the wild cycles of its core paper, pulp, packaging, and building products operations, Georgia-Pacific, in November 2000, acquired Fort James Corporation for about $7.7 billion in stock and cash plus the assumption of $3.3 billion in Fort James debt. Fort James's key products included Brawny paper towels, Quilted Northern bathroom tissue, Vanity Fair napkins, and Dixie plates, cups, and cutlery. Based in Deerfield, Illinois, the company had been formed in August 1997 through the merger of James River Corporation of Virginia and Fort Howard Corporation. Fort James had posted profits of $516.5 million in 1999 on revenues of $6.8 billion. The addition of Fort James made Georgia-Pacific the number one tissue maker in the world. To placate antitrust authorities and complete the transaction, however, the company had to agree to sell its commercial-tissue unit, Georgia-Pacific Tissue, LLC, because of the commercial-tissue operations it was gaining from Fort James, which included the Preference and Envision brands. In March 2001, the unit was sold to Svenska Cellulosa Aktiebolaget SCA for $852 million, with Georgia-Pacific paying Chesapeake $237 million to cover deferred capital gains and for its equity interest in the venture.

Continuing its drive to focus more on consumer products, Georgia-Pacific announced in March 2001 that it would close its pulp mill in Bellingham, Washington. Then, in August, the firm sold four fine-paper mills to Domtar Inc. for $1.65 billion in the largest divestiture in company history. This left Georgia-Pacific with four white paper mills and two pulp mills. The company was looking to unload the pulp mills as well as its specialty chemicals unit. In June, meanwhile, the firm announced it would close three gypsum plants and reduce its gypsum wallboard production by 45 percent in response to industry-wide overproduction that was driving prices down. A divestment even larger and more significant than the sale to Domtar came in October 2001 when Georgia-Pacific completed the merger of the Timber Company into Plum Creek Timber Company, Inc. in a transaction valued at about $4 billion. This marked the exit of Georgia-Pacific from the timber business.

Late in 2001, Georgia-Pacific entered into talks with Willamette Industries Inc. regarding a possible joint venture of the companies' building products businesses or the sale of Georgia-Pacific's building products operations to the other firm. Willamette was seeking a way to extricate itself from a hostile takeover bid from Weyerhaeuser Company, but early in 2002 Willamette backed away from a transaction with Georgia-Pacific and agreed to a merger with Weyerhaeuser. Part of Willamette's concern about a deal with Georgia-Pacific was the possibility of exposing itself to asbestos liabilities. In 1965, Georgia-Pacific had acquired Bestwall Gypsum, which made some gypsum products containing asbestos, which can cause lung disease and other diseases. Georgia-Pacific's use of asbestos was discontinued in 1977, and the firm had manufactured no products containing the substance since then. Lawsuits began to be filed against Georgia-Pacific in the mid-1980s, but it was not until late 2001, when large jury awards began making headlines and several major companies had been forced into bankruptcy because of their asbestos liabilities, that the issue began to seriously affect Georgia-Pacific. From early December 2001 to late January 2002, the company's stock lost more than one-third of its value as a result of investor concern about the firm's asbestos liability. Acting to halt the crisis, Correll announced that the firm would take a fourth quarter 2001 charge of $350 million for anticipated asbestos claims through 2011. The move was intended to quantify the company's asbestos risk and show that Georgia-Pacific was nowhere near the brink of bankruptcy. Correll emphasized that a third-party study had shown that the company's total liabilities through 2011 were expected to amount to less than $1 billion.

Whether these moves would be sufficient to lay to rest the asbestos concerns remained to be seen, but Georgia-Pacific was in any event continuing with its drive to transform itself into a consumer products concern. It appeared likely, but not certain, that the company would spin off of its building products operations, and there was also speculation about a divestment of the Unisource paper distribution subsidiary. Seeking further growth for its consumer products, Georgia-Pacific was pursuing endorsement deals with major names, such as stock-car racing legend Richard Petty, who was inked as a new Brawny spokesperson. One other challenge facing Georgia-Pacific in the early 21st century was servicing its high debt load, which stood at $12.2 billion in early 2002.

Principal Subsidiaries

Arbor Property and Casualty Limited (Bermuda); Arkansas Louisiana & Mississippi Railroad Company; Ashley, Drew & Northern Railway Company; Blue Rapids Railway Company; Brown Board Holding, Inc.; Brunswick Pulp & Paper Company; Brunswick Pulp Land Company, Inc.; CeCorr, Inc.; Color-Box, LLC (58%); Fordyce and Princeton R.R. Co.; Fort James Corporation; GNN Timber, Inc.; GPW Timber, Inc.; G-P Gypsum Corporation; G-P Maine, Inc.; G-P Receivables, Inc.; Georgia-Pacific Childcare Center, LLC; Georgia-Pacific Development Company;

Georgia-Pacific Foreign Holdings, Inc.; Georgia-Pacific Holdings, Inc.; Georgia-Pacific Investment Company; Georgia-Pacific Resins, Inc.; Georgia-Pacific Shared Services Corp.; Georgia-Pacific Tissue Real Estate Company, LLC; Georgia-Pacific West, Inc.; Georgia Temp. Inc.; Gloster Southern Railroad Company; Great Northern Nekoosa Corporation; NPC Timber, Inc.; NPI Timber, Inc.; North American Timber Corp.; Phoenix Athletic Club, Inc.; The Saint Croix Water Power Company (Canada); Southwest Millwork and Specialties, Inc.; The Sprague's Falls Manufacturing Company (Limited) (Canada); St. Croix Water Power Company; Tomahawk Land Company; Unisource Worldwide, Inc.; XRS, Inc.

Principal Competitors

International Paper Company; Weyerhaeuser Company; Stora Enso Oyj; Smurfit-Stone Container Corporation; MeadWestvaco Corporation; The Procter & Gamble Company; Boise Cascade Corporation; Kimberly-Clark Corporation; UPM-Kymmene Corporation; Jefferson Smurfit Corporation; USG Corporation.

Further Reading

Bell, John, "Georgia-Pacific's Paper Profits," *Journal of Business Strategy,* May/June 1997, pp. 36–40.

"The Best of Everything," *Forbes,* March 15, 1977.

Bond, Patti, "Georgia-Pacific Chief Slams Analysts," *Atlanta Journal/Constitution,* January 25, 2002, p. F1.

——, "Georgia-Pacific Puts Down New Roots," *Atlanta Journal/Constitution,* July 22, 2000, p. F1.

——, "Reinventing Georgia-Pacific Is Correll's Big Mission: Bold Move into Tissue, Paper Towels Wins Praise," *Atlanta Journal/Constitution,* November 4, 2001, p. E1.

Brooks, Rick, "Georgia-Pacific Is No Longer a Paper Tiger," *Wall Street Journal,* July 18, 2000, p. B8.

Calonius, Erik, "America's Toughest Papermaker," *Fortune,* February 26, 1990.

De Lisser, Eleena, "Georgia-Pacific Plans New Class of Stock Tied to Its Profitable Timber Business," *Wall Street Journal,* September 18, 1997, p. C27.

Deogun, Nikhil, and Dean Starkman, "Georgia-Pacific Nears Buying Fort James," *Wall Street Journal,* July 17, 2000, p. A3.

Ferguson, Kelly H., "Georgia-Pacific: Deals, Debt, and Redirection," *Pulp and Paper,* March 1994, pp. 34–35.

Foust, Dean, "Georgia-Pacific Turns Paper into Gold," *Business Week,* August 15, 1988, p. 71.

Gold, Jackey, "Culture Shock," *Financial World,* February 20, 1990.

Grimes, Ann, "Plum Creek Timber Agrees to Buy Georgia-Pacific Unit in Stock Deal," *Wall Street Journal,* July 19, 2000, p. A6.

Hagerty, James R., "No-Nonsense Paper Firm Bets on 'Calming Sandalwood': Georgia-Pacific, Tired of Commodity-Price Gyrations, Focuses on Branding," *Wall Street Journal,* December 14, 1999, p. B4.

Harte, Susan, "Accepting the Challenges with Confidence: Correll Faces Unprecedented Demands As He Takes the Reins at Georgia-Pacific," *Atlanta Constitution,* December 1, 1993, p. D1.

Henderson, Barry, "Critics' Choice: Georgia-Pacific Is Poised for a Rebound After Panned Purchase," *Barron's,* August 23, 1999, pp. 19–20.

"Is Georgia-Pacific Pruning at the Top?," *Business Week,* November 15, 1982, p. 38.

Kimelman, John, "Knock on (Composite) Wood: Georgia-Pacific Is Poised for a Sharp Cyclical Recovery," *Financial World,* July 19, 1994, pp. 36–37.

Mitchell, Cynthia, "Leading Georgia-Pacific Out of the Woods," *Atlanta Journal/Constitution,* July 20, 1997, p. D4.

Norvell, Scott, "Southern Comfort for a Timber Giant," *New York Times,* March 23, 1993, p. 6.

Pamplin, Robert B., *Heritage,* New York: Mastermedia, 1994, 520 p.

Reier, Sharon, "New Math vs. Old Culture," *Financial World,* March 22, 1988.

Roots, Atlanta, Ga.: Georgia-Pacific Corporation, 1988.

Ross, John R., *Maverick: The Story of Georgia-Pacific,* Portland, Ore.: Georgia-Pacific Corporation, 1978, 318 p.

Scredon, Scott, and Rebecca Aikman, "Georgia-Pacific Bets on Paper to Smooth Out Its Swings," *Business Week,* April 15, 1985, pp. 120+.

Terhune, Chad, "Georgia-Pacific Hopes Its Streak of Bad Luck Will End," *Wall Street Journal,* January 28, 2002, p. B3.

——, "Georgia-Pacific Says Asbestos Charge Will Result in Net Loss for Fourth Period," *Wall Street Journal,* January 25, 2002, p. A5.

Thomas, Emory, Jr., "Georgia-Pacific May Embark on a Spending Spree," *Wall Street Journal,* December 12, 1994, p. B4.

"Unrest at Georgia-Pacific," *Business Week,* November 24, 1980, p. 147.

Wiegner, Kathleen K., "A Tale of Two Companies," *Forbes,* March 6, 1978.

—Sandy Schusteff
—updates: Maura Troester, David E. Salamie

Gericom AG

Industriezeile 35
4021 Linz
Austria
Telephone: (+43) 732-7664-690
Fax: +43 732 7664 113
Web site: http://www.gericom.com

Public Company
Incorporated: 1990 as S plus S Marketing, Engineering
    and Computerproduction GesmbH
Employees: 296
Sales: EUR 539.88 million ($431.9 million) (2001)
Stock Exchanges: Frankfurt Neuer Markt
Ticker Symbol: GRO
NAIC: 334111 Electronic Computer Manufacturing;
    334119 Other Computer Peripheral Equipment
    Manufacturing

Fast-rising Gericom AG aims to become Europe's leading manufacturer and distributor of mobile computing and communications products. Based in Linz, Austria, Gericom has captured leading shares of notebook computer sales in much of the German-speaking market through its policy of selling competitively priced systems through the retail sales channel—including supermarketers Lidl, Metro, and others—as well as through its web-based channels. Gericom sells a wide variety of basic notebook computer configurations, which are then adaptable on a built-to-order basis. As with most of the company's competitors, Gericom does not manufacture its computers, but instead contracts with third-party manufacturers such as Compal, FCI, and others, which provide the core computer systems. Gericom then finishes the notebooks in its Linz facility, adding price-sensitive components and customizing the computers for individual national markets. Approximately 70 percent of Gericom's sales come from its Gericom-branded notebook computers. Gericom also designs and distributes portable digital assistance and so-called "pocket PCs," LCD screens, complete "no-name" computer systems (which are marketed under such third-party brand names as Network,

Highscreen, and other private-label brand names), mobile telephones, as well as major-name printers and accessories. Founded in 1990 by Chairman and CEO Hermann Oberlehner, Gericom went public in 2000 with a listing on the Frankfurt Stock Exchange's Neuer Markt. Oberlehner continues to hold nearly 70 percent of the company's stock, however. In 2001, Gericom generated nearly EUR 540 million; the company expects to double that figure by as early as 2003.

Big Fish in the Austrian Pond in the Early 1990s

Hermann Oberlehner had been working for Voest Alpine Stahl in the late 1980s, then worked briefly as CEO of a German computer manufacturer, when he became interested in founding his own company. Oberlehner's idea was to produce not only desktop computer systems, but also low-cost mobile computer systems, a market Oberlehner predicted was to grow strongly over the coming decade. Oberlehner started up his company in Linz, Austria, in 1990, giving it the name S plus S.

S plus S began producing its first computer systems in 1991, assembling its systems from components manufactured by third-party suppliers. The following year, however, the company hit on an essential part of the strategy that was to help it become one of Austria's leading computer makers before the middle of the decade. At the time computers remained expensive and had found little penetration into the home computer market. Most computer sales came through specialized computer resellers channels, which tended to feature prominent and international brand names, or through smaller integrators, which assembled individual systems based on third-party components. Instead, S plus S decided to pursue the consumer market, and in 1992, the company reached its first contracts to sell computer systems and equipment through the retail supermarket and appliance store circuit. Among the company's earliest customers were such retail chains as MediaMarket, Saturn, Lidl, and Metro.

If most of the company's products featured third-party and private-label brand names, a growing number of its products, and especially its mobile computers, began to feature a new brand name: Gericom, which stood for "Germany Industry

Company Perspectives:

The perspectives: We plan to exploit the whole European market for our products and to establish the Gericom trademark synonymously with mobile data processing and communications in Europe; we aim to increase our position at the cutting edge of the rapidly growing mobile computing and communications sector and reshape the future market decisively; extending our role now and in the future as one of the leading business enablers in the field of mobile computing and communications, we will target new groups and markets along with our sales partners.

Computer.'' The expansion into the consumer retail market enabled S plus S to extend its product line, so that by 1993 the company boasted a full range of products from the low-end components to high-end systems. The company also began designing its own components. In 1993, the company began producing computer monitors through a plant in China.

With its sales growing rapidly, S plus S was forced to move to new facilities in 1994. In that year, also, the company decided to phase out its production of its own-label desktop computer systems (the company continued to produce computer systems for third-party and private labels, however) and refocused the Gericom brand name as a notebook computing specialist. This move coincided with the rising strength of the mobile computer market in general, as a new generation of processors, including the first generation of Intel Pentium processors, coupled with larger, higher-quality active matrice LCD screens, larger hard drives, as well as the preparation of Windows 95, combined to enable the production of notebook computers that were able to rival their desktop counterparts in performance.

Before long, ''Gericom'' had become nearly synonymous with notebook computers in much of the German-speaking world. By then, S plus S operated subsidiaries in Germany and Switzerland. Yet the company had also successfully expanded into the Eastern European region, with offices in the Czech Republic, Slovakia, Poland, Croatia, and Romania. Back at home, S plus S was gaining quickly on notebook computer industry leaders such as Compaq, Toshiba, and IBM.

By 1995, S plus S had posted more than 1.2 billion Austrian shillings (approximately $62 million) in sales. The company's fast rise was aided in several key strategic elements. Countering the weight of its name-brand competitors—which typically commanded high prices for their systems—S plus S offered systems featuring competitive performance at far lower prices. S plus S also proved highly aggressive in being first to market with new components, especially new-generation processors. As a result, S plus S was able to boast of offering the fastest available notebook systems, often beating out its competitors by several months. If the traditional notebook-buying market, typically made up of corporate customers, remained brand sensitive, a growing new market of consumer purchases raced to S plus S's performance claims.

Yet S plus S also was working to match its quality levels to those of its competitors. In 1995, S plus S reached an agreement

with Kapok Computers, one of the largest manufacturers of notebook computers in Taiwan (and a supplier of basic systems to many of the brand-name systems as well). The cooperation agreement with Kapok now gave the Gericom brand not only a boost in quality, but in configuration flexibility as well.

European Notebook Leader for the 21st Century

The rising popularity of the Gericom brand name enabled S plus S to extend its own marketing channels. While the company continued to expand through the retail market, in 1996 it began targeting the small and mid-sized business markets as well. The company's growing importance in German-speaking Europe and in Eastern Europe was underlined when it won a cooperation agreement with Intel on the development of the market for that company's Pentium processors. The agreement enabled S plus S to become the first European notebook maker to feature the Pentium II processor in 1998. S plus S was also the first computer company to feature a notebook design with an integrated 15-inch LCD screen.

The Gericom range was expanded again when the company reached a manufacturing agreement with another major Taiwanese notebook computer maker, Compal. By then, a growing proportion of mobile computer product manufacturing had been turned over to a small circle of mostly Taiwanese manufacturers; most of S plus S's competitors had adopted a similar product development policy of personalizing and branding the basic notebook computers produced by Compal, Kopak, and others.

By 1997, S plus S had topped EUR 138 million (approximately $110 million) in sales. By the end of that year, the company also had risen to challenge global leader Compaq as the Austrian market's leading seller of PCs, with more than 60,000 desktop and notebook systems sold under the Gericom and third-party labels. The company also had begun to branch out from its computing specialty, adding a line of digital cameras, which, like its notebook computers, were targeted at the consumer retail market. By 1998, with sales rising to nearly EUR 230 million, Oberlehner, who continued to control more than 96 percent of the company's shares—with the remainder belonging to other company executives—began planning to take his company public.

Yet those plans were put on hold in 1999 after an earthquake in Taiwan destroyed much of the company's notebook computer supply. The aftershock devastated S plus S's plans for growth; in that year the company limped to just EUR 235 million in sales. Nonetheless, the year did not hold only bad news for S plus S. In that year, the Gericom brand took the lead as the largest independent maker of notebook computers for the European market. A significant factor in claiming that title continued to be the company's policy of being first to market with new components, including the Pentium III processor released in 1999.

S plus S opened a new distribution channel in 1999 with the development of its first e-commerce sites, targeted at both the consumer and small business markets. The company also had begun to seek to capitalize further on the strong Gericom brand name. In that year the company reached an agreement with Palmax to develop a Gericom-branded personal digital

Key Dates:

1990: Hermann Oberlehner founds S plus S Marketing, Engineering and Computerproduction GesmbH in Linz, Austria.

1991: Company begins production of the first desktop and notebook computer systems.

1992: Company begins to distribute its own brand and third-party and private-label branded systems through the consumer retail sector.

1993: S plus S expands its product line to include a full range of computer systems and components.

1994: S plus S decides to focus its Gericom brand production on notebook computer systems.

1995: Company reaches agreement on developing and manufacturing with Kapok Computer of Taiwan.

1997: The company enters a product development and manufacturing agreement with Compal, of Taiwan.

2000: Company changes its name to Gericom AG and goes public on the Frankfurt Stock Exchange's Neuer Markt.

2001: Gericom successfully enters the U.K. and French markets.

assistant. The company also began designing an LCD-based desktop computer. Meanwhile, after producing one of the first notebook computers with integrated DVD drive in 1998, the company claimed a new first, launching a notebook model with an integrated CD-R drive.

By the beginning of 2000, S plus S once again was forced to expand its production capacity, adding a new facility in Linz. Yet S plus S had already begun to eye further growth, targeting in particular the French and U.K. computer markets on its way toward its goal of becoming one of Europe's major notebook computer makers. In mid-year, the company put its plans for a public listing back on track, pledging to complete its initial public offering (IPO) by the end of the year. To prepare for this, S plus S converted to a limited liability company, then changed its name, to Gericom AG.

The collapse of the high-tech stock market in 2000 did not deter Gericom from making its IPO on the Frankfurt Stock Exchange's Neuer Markt in November 2000. Nonetheless, the company was forced to satisfy itself with an initial share price lower than that for which it had initially hoped. The company also reduced the level of its initial free-float, releasing just 25 percent to the public (an additional 5 percent was floated in 2001). Nonetheless, the company could expect strong growth in its share price, matching its own revenue growth, which topped EUR 331 million for the year.

With the capital raised from its IPO, Gericom went ahead with its entry into the United Kingdom and France, maintaining its target on the retail consumer market. The company also was boosted by the successful launch of its digital camera models— Gericom quickly captured a leading share of Austrian digital camera sales. Meanwhile, Gericom's notebook computer sales remained the company's driving force, and by early 2001, the company had nearly extended its leadership position to the German market, in which it tailed only Toshiba in numbers of notebooks sold. Helping to boost the company's sales was the launch of what the company claimed as the world's first one-gigahertz notebook computer.

Gericom continued seeking to expand its range of products, announcing its plans to release a new "pocket PC" handheld computer, as well as its development of a so-called "webpad" in conjunction with Abocom, expected to reach the market in late 2002. This latter device, which was expected to boast computerlike performance in a smaller, lighter format than traditional notebook computers, was seen as a particularly promising direction for the computer market in the coming years.

By the end of 2001, Gericom had made strong inroads into France and the United Kingdom, which together provided some 11 percent of the company's sales. Germany remained the company's strongest market, at more than 60 percent of sales, while Austria accounted for 20 percent of sales. Yet Gericom was already well on its way to becoming a "total European" brand.

By the end of 2001, Gericom seemed to have become a victim of its own success as a late-year surge in demand strained its production capacity. Yet the company was already taking steps to increase its capacity, investing as much as $60 million in a 40 percent stake of a new notebook manufacturing facility in China. By the end of the year the company had beat out its own sales forecasts, jumping to nearly EUR 540 million. With such strong growth, Gericom seemed likely to reach its revised target of doubling its sales by 2003.

Principal Competitors

Dell Corporation; International Business Machines Corporation; Toshiba Corporation; Compaq Computer Corporation; NEC Corporation; Fujitsu Limited; Acer Inc.; Medion AG.

Further Reading

"Gericom: Von der Linzer 'Quetsch'n' zur europaweit bekannten Marke," *Die Presse,* September 26, 2001.

"Gericom: Von Top bis Flop ist alles möglich," *Wirtschaftblatt,* October 18, 2000.

Kolar, Gabriele, "Gericom Plans Chinese Plant," *Reuters,* October 16, 2001.

Shannon, Victoria, "Gericom's Sales Surge," *International Herald Tribune,* June 19, 2001.

—M.L. Cohen

Glacier Water Services, Inc.

2651 La Mirada Drive, Suite 100
Vista, California 92083
U.S.A.
Telephone: (760) 560-1111
Fax: (760) 560-3333
Web site: http://www.glacierwater.com

Public Company
Incorporated: 1991
Employees: 276
Sales: $59.2 million (2000)
Stock Exchanges: American
Ticker Symbol: HOO
NAIC: 454210 Vending Machine Operators

Located in Vista, California, Glacier Water Services, Inc. is the largest operator of self-service water vending machines in the United States, with more than 15,000 units located in 35 states. Most of the company's business is tied to supermarkets, especially in Sunbelt states, where its vending machines are located outdoors, but the development of an indoor unit has allowed Glacier Water to make inroads in northern states. The coin-operated machines rely on a combination of techniques, including micron filtration, reverse osmosis, carbon absorption, and ultraviolet sterilization, in order to remove impurities and ''polish'' the taste of water drawn directly from local municipal sources. Once a week each unit is tested and serviced, but aside from this maintenance, the system is self-sufficient. Customers provide their own containers, although in many cases the retail outlets where the units are located also sell plastic jugs. The price per gallon ranges from 15 cents to 50 cents, depending on local competition, making the company's water an inexpensive alternative to bottled water sold in stores or delivered to homes.

Early History of
Water Vending Machines: 1900s–80s

The history of the vending water machine is tied to the Dixie Cup, invented by Lawrence Luellen in Boston in 1908. Luellen's original idea was to market a vending machine that could dis-

pense a clean cup of cold water for a penny. He developed the porcelain ''Luellen Cup & Water Vendor,'' which included a reservoir of water perched above an ice container along with a stack of nested paper cups. These one-piece pleated cups would become known as Dixie Cups. To exploit his device, Luellen recruited a number of investors and formed the American Water Supply Company of New England in April 1908. Because it cost too much to manufacture the machine, the directors of the new company elected instead to focus on marketing Luellen's paper cup, which could be sold next to a standard water fountain.

The first practical water vending machine was not developed until the mid-1970s and was intended to provide purified water in bulk rather than a cup of chilled, untreated water. Not only had water purification techniques been developed, but there was also a rising concern about the safety of drinking water that was pivotal to the creation of the water vending machine industry. Since the early 1960s, with the publication of Rachel Carson's seminal book *Silent Spring,* the public had become increasingly concerned about the level of contaminants found in the nation's water supply. A spate of environmental legislation resulted, including the Safe Drinking Water Act in 1974. Much of the early growth in water vending machines took place in California, which offered a favorable demographic. The state's large number of Latino and Asian immigrants came from countries where drinking water was unquestionably dangerous, and they were already in the habit of boiling water to remove impurities. Because water vending machines were both convenient and inexpensive, this lower-income immigrant population provided the bulk of customers in the formative years of the water vending machine industry. Middle- and upper-class consumers, for their part, were driving the quick rise in the bottled water market.

The founder of Glacier Water Services was Robert G. Miller, whose original business, Bottle Water Vending Inc., was established in 1983. It subsequently changed its name to GW Services, Inc. The company designed and built water vending machines, some of which it sold to others. It operated the remainder, placing the units outside supermarkets, which received a monthly share of revenues. While competitors developed units made out of steel, Miller opted for longer lasting fiberglass. GW Services soon began to expand beyond the

Company Perspectives:

Our mission is to be a great company by forming strategic partnerships with retailers to provide consumers with the highest quality, value-priced water dispensed from machines that are consistently clean, attractive, and reliable; ensuring that our employees are focused on service, quality, integrity, and safety; and producing profitable growth at a level that consistently enhances shareholder value.

California market, entering Arizona in 1984, then Nevada in 1986. By the following year, the company had nearly 900 units in operation, generating $5.6 million in revenues. In 1988, it moved into Texas and Florida, other Sunbelt states with a heavy Latin immigrant population.

Glacier Water Services: 1990s

In the spring of 1990, poor health forced Miller to relinquish day-to-day control of GW Services. In October 1991, he was replaced as chief executive officer by Jerry Welch, who had previously been the top executive at Stars to Go, a video rental business. A month later, on November 19, 1991, Glacier Water Services, Inc. was formed as a Delaware corporation to serve as a holding company for GW Services in preparation for making an initial public offering (IPO) of stock. The IPO was primarily arranged to allow Miller, whose health continued to deteriorate, to liquidate his 50 percent stake in the business and bring order to his estate. Two months before the IPO took place Miller resigned as chairman of the board, replaced by Welch in January 1992. On March 13, 1992 Glacier Water sold two million shares, netting $12 million and becoming the first publicly traded water vending machine company in the industry. By now the business was generating more than $23 million in annual revenues, with 3,300 units in operation. It was number one in the industry, its closest competitor, Aqua-Vend, boasting 2,900 vending machines.

In addition to allowing Miller to clean up his estate, the IPO helped to fund the expansion of Glacier Water, not only to northern states but also within existing territories. In August 1992, the company announced that it had signed a deal to place its machines in front of 250 Wal-Mart Stores in Glacier Water's five-state territory. It was the first time that a water vending machine company entered the mass merchant retail section. In support of its plan to expand into northern states, where year-round outdoor vending was not practical, the company also introduced its Model 1W, an indoor unit that could be mounted directly on a wall. Despite these promising developments, Welch suddenly announced his resignation, maintaining that the company did not need as many full-time executives as it currently had. Although he remained as a consultant and a board member, he was replaced as CEO by the company's president, Duke Bushong, and chairman by Peter T. Dixon, a senior executive vice-president of Loeb Partners Corp., one of the company's major investors. Several months later, in April 1993, however, Welch was again elected chairman of Glacier Water, and when Bushong resigned in September 1994 Welch also reassumed his role as chief executive officer.

No matter who was leading the company, the goal of Glacier Water was clear: solidifying its grip on the top position in the water vending machine industry. To support this end, management focused on bolstering four areas: operations, finance, marketing, and human resources. More marketing people were especially needed to expand into new territories, and additional staff would be needed to work in the field servicing the units. The customer base for vending machine water was also growing, as more middle-class consumers opted for the service rather than spend money on more expensive bottled water. Moreover, the market for purified water in general continued to grow at a significant pace, prompting the company to seek new geographical territories as well as to broaden the range of retail establishments where water vending machines could be placed. Supermarkets (in particular the Vons California chain, which accounted for as much as 13 percent of total revenues) would continue to provide the most suitable locations, but drugstores, convenience stores, and other establishments would also be targeted. The major source of customers, however, would remain in the company's home state of California: with just 12 percent of the country's population, California accounted for 30 percent of all purified water sales.

In 1993, Glacier Water paid $450,000 to acquire Vend Pure H2O Associates of Lubbock, Texas, adding 75 water vending machines. In general, however, the plan at this stage was to grow internally rather than pursue acquisitions or joint ventures. In 1993, Glacier Water entered the New Mexico market and that year deployed 1,114 new units systemwide. The company also initiated a pilot program in Taiwan, ultimately concluding, however, that it was not yet ready to commit to an international program. In 1994, Glacier Water added 1,945 machines and entered Louisiana and Mississippi. The following year Georgia was included and the total number of machines increased by 1,793. In 1996, Glacier Water grew beyond the Sunbelt, adding Illinois to its base of operations and overall increasing the number of vending machines systemwide by 646. At the end of 1996, the company also signed an important agreement with Ralph's Grocery Company, a major California supermarket chain, to place water vending machines at their locations. As of December 31, 1996, the company had a total 9,164 units deployed, placing it well ahead of its closest rival Aqua-Vend, which had only a third as many. Annual revenues grew from $30.6 million in 1993 to more than $46 million in 1996. Net income during this period grew from $2 million in 1993 to $3.3 million in 1996.

In March 1997, Glacier Water grew by external means, paying approximately $9 million to acquire its closest rival, Aqua-Vend, part of San Francisco-based McKesson Corporation's McKesson Water Products Company. For McKesson, selling Aqua-Vend provided funding that allowed it to expand upon direct delivery and grocery sales of its bottled water products. For its part, Glacier Water in a single stroke added 3,000 water vending machines located in California, Texas, Nevada, Florida, Louisiana, Alabama, and Mississippi. Approximately 600 of the units, however, would be removed as part of an integration plan that laid out balanced territories for the overall system. The increased number of vending machines added significantly to revenues of Glacier Water, exceeding $57 million for 1997. Although the company had many rivals in the water vending machine sector, some 40 small companies across the country, none boasted more than a 5 percent market share. Glacier Water now estimated that it accounted for three-quarters of all water sold through vending machines.

Entering the Mexican Market: 1998

In 1998, Glacier Water opted to enter the Mexico market, creating Glacier de Mexico. By the end of the year it had placed 144 vending machines in Mexico City (adding another 434 machines the following year). Prospects for the company appeared bright in 1998, a fact that was reflected by the price of its stock, which peaked at $32 per share in April 1998. A few months later, however, it would face the challenge of adverse publicity. In September 1998, a yearlong study on the quality of vending machine water (sold by Glacier Water and two dozen other companies) was released by the Environmental Toxicology Bureau of Los Angeles County. It found that 93 percent of all vending machines contained 163 times more bacteria than tap water, and that many units were poorly maintained. Some had dirty spigots or filters so old that they were incapable of removing contaminants. In defense of its operations, Glacier Water maintained that it inspected and maintained its units once a week. Management also pointed out that in order to lower bacterial levels, chlorine would have to be reintroduced to the water, while noting that a major reason consumers opted for its water was because of their dissatisfaction with the taste of chlorine. The fact that the report ''found no clear evidence of danger for consumers'' was overshadowed by the allusion to bacterial levels. Because consumer confidence in the product was paramount, Glacier Water was quick to call for a mandatory state inspection program, which it suggested could be funded by charging the owners $20 to $40 per machine. Although California had licensed and regulated water vending machines since 1989, it had relied on a self-inspection system that only required the reporting of results every six months. With the most machines deployed, Glacier Water had the most at stake if the industry lost credibility, but with the greater resources the company was also better able to afford the fee-based inspection program it promoted. In fact, it stood to benefit, since the expense added another barrier for companies attempting to rival its supremacy.

Glacier Water spent $125,000 in public relations fees combating the negative publicity that resulted from the county study. It faced other unforeseen charges as well in 1998, which was clearly a disappointing year for the company. It was accused of patent infringement and paid $675,000 in legal ex-

penses. It spent $800,000 in an unsuccessful test of the efficacy of media advertising, performed in San Diego and Phoenix during the summer months. Moreover, the company took a one-time charge of nearly $1 million related to the removal of 1,450 underperforming machines, to be relocated over the ensuing months. As a result of these difficulties, revenues fell slightly and the company posted a loss of $3.3 million.

Over the next two years, Glacier Water continued to struggle. In 1999, it reported more disappointing results. Although revenues showed a modest improvement, increasing to $56.7 million, the company net loss grew to $7.2 million. In September 1999, Welch resigned, replaced as CEO by Chief Operating Officer Jerry Gordon, who had started in the company as a salesman, and as chairman by Richard Kayne. Under their management in 2000, the company would have to make a tough decision on its Mexican operation, which was not performing up to expectations. In the first half of the year, it generated just $246,000 in revenues, resulting in a net loss of $558,000 for the period. By August, the decision was made to terminate the operation, take a $1.4 million restructuring charge, and return the vending machines to the United States for redeployment. Weeks before Glacier Water reported a loss of $6 million for fiscal 2000, Gordon resigned ''to pursue other opportunities for personal reasons,'' according to a statement released by Chairman Kayne.

In May 2001, Glacier Water hired a new chief executive, Brian McInerney, a former executive of Honeywell International. A month later the company had a new chairman when the board elected Charles A. Norris. He was familiar with the industry, having served as president of McKesson Water Products and overall having spent 20 years in the bottled water industry. He had also served as chairman and director of the International Bottled Water Association. The company's new management team elected to pay off long-term debt and concentrate on internal growth, adding machines to current territories. By early 2002, however, Glacier Water Services announced a major acquisition, picking up Pure Fill Corp. and its subsidiaries. Pure Fill had been in the water vending machine industry for more than 15 years and operated 1,625 units in 13 states. Because the Pure Fill assets complemented Glacier Water's other assets, McInerney expressed optimism that the acquisition would help to accelerate the company's return to profitability. In any case, Glacier Water was even more of a dominant player in the water vending machine industry, now boasting more than 15,000 units under its control. It was also clear that the demand for its product—inexpensive, clean drinking water—would only grow in the years to come.

Principal Subsidiaries

GW Services, Inc.; Glacier Water Trust I; GW Services International, Inc.

Principal Competitors

The Coca-Cola Company; Culligan Water Technologies, Inc.; Danone; Nestlé S.A.; Water Island.

Further Reading

''Glacier Water,'' *San Diego Daily Transcript,* January 11, 1993, p. 4.

"Glacier Water Services," *Wall Street Transcript,* October 11, 1993.

"Glacier Water Services," *Wall Street Transcript,* January 9, 1995.

Fine, Howard, "Embattled Water Vendors Defend Industry," *Los Angeles Business Journal,* September 14, 1998.

Hong, Peter Y., "State Inspection of Drinking Water Machines Sought," *Los Angeles Times,* October 1, 1998, p. 3.

Kraul, Chris, "Saturating the Market," *Los Angeles Times,* May 25, 1996, p. D3.

McSwane, David Z., William A. Oleckno, and Larry M. Eils, "Drinking Water Quality Concerns and Water Vending Machines," *Journal of Environmental Health,* June 1994, p. 7.

Sternman, Mike, "Treated-Water Vending Rides In-Store Wave," *Supermarket News,* July 12, 1993.

"Water Sales Make Splash at Retail," *Discount Store News,* September 21, 1992.

—Ed Dinger

Golden West Financial Corporation

1901 Harrison Street
Oakland, California 94612
U.S.A.
Telephone: (510) 446-3420
Fax: (510) 446-4256
Web site: http://www.worldsavings.com

Public Company
Incorporated: 1963
Employees: 6,103
Total Assets: $55.7 billion (2000)
Stock Exchanges: New York
Ticker Symbol: GDW
NAIC: 551111 Bank Holding Companies

Golden West Financial Corporation, the third largest savings and loan association, or thrift, in the United States, grew in stature due to the leadership of husband-and-wife team Marion and Herbert Sandler. Over a period of nearly four decades, the pair took a two-office operation with $38 million in assets to one with 450 locations and assets of $58 billion. One of the largest mortgage lenders in the country, Golden West focuses primarily on individual home buyers.

Striking Gold: 1960s–70s

Marion and Herbert Sandler formed a holding company, Golden West Financial Corporation, in 1963, to acquire Oakland, California-based Golden West Savings. The couple financed the $4 million deal primarily with bank loans; additional funds came from Marion's family money. The two-office operation had $38 million in assets at the time of the purchase. Golden West Savings had been in operation since 1929. In 1975, another California firm, World Savings, merged with Golden West Savings.

World Savings, established in Madera in 1912, had become a subsidiary of Trans-World Financial Corporation in 1959. Trans-World also acquired Guardian Savings and Loan of Colorado that year, renaming it World Savings of Colorado. The Sandlers combined the savings and loan subsidiaries of World

Savings and Golden West and began operating under the World Savings name. Comprised of 107 offices in California and Colorado, the new entity had assets of $1.8 billion.

Federal legislation changes in the 1980s expanded business opportunities available to savings and loans (S&Ls). The financial institutions were given the freedom to set their own interest rates, hitherto held under a ceiling by regulators. In addition, S&Ls were allowed to offer customers checking accounts and expand their loan activities, both consumer and commercial. The following year, in 1981, the right to originate adjustable rate mortgages (ARMs) was granted. World Savings established ARMs as its principal mortgage instrument. Regulation changes were not the only things afoot in the S&L industry as the new decade began.

By 1981, Marion and Herbert Sandler's S&L topped 130 branches with $5.2 billion in assets. The fifth largest publicly held S&L was notable for its strong performance record. Earnings per share had increased at a rate of 24 percent a year since 1966, according to a 1981 *Fortune* magazine article by A.F. Ehrbar.

The Sandlers, wrote Ehrbar, had historically avoided unnecessary risks. Marion, a former Wall Street S&L analyst, was company president and held the reins of the liability or deposit side of the business. Herbert, a real estate attorney, was chairman and oversaw the lending operations. The married couple shared the title CEO. In addition to their conservative business practices, Ehrbar attributed the company's stellar growth to the fact that the Sandlers were "uncommonly aggressive competitors."

Beginning late in the 1970s, however, some of that conservatism seemed to take a back seat to more speculative ventures. Adept at anticipating interest rate trends, Herbert Sandler had adjusted their business mix accordingly, making fewer mortgage loans when interest rates were low and more when they were on the rise.

Sandler also tried his hand at investment securities, putting borrowed money and cash into those instruments instead of writing mortgage loans. The balancing act helped Golden West extend an impressive string of year-to-year earnings growth even as, industrywide, S&Ls reported declining profits.

Company Perspectives:

Golden West Financial Corporation's vision is to create long-term value for customers, shareholders, employees, and neighbors by providing high quality consumer financial services through our World Savings and Atlas subsidiaries.

Volatile Decade for the Industry: 1980s

Golden West and its competitors' operating revenues were hit hard by high short-term interest rates in 1980. It was a dreadful year for many S&Ls: profits and stock values plummeted. Golden West managed to post slight quarterly increases, though some were as small as a penny a share. Consequently, its shares maintained or rose in value. According to Ehrbar, gains made in heavy trading of short- and intermediate-term securities, such as Treasury bills and notes, and mortgage-backed certificates, instruments similar in some ways to bonds, compensated for declines in operating results.

"In other words, the Sandlers may have created the illusion of rising profits by closing out hedge positions or selling securities on which they had capital gains, while hanging onto the ones in which they had capital losses," wrote Ehrbar. He noted that the move was legal and allowable under generally accepted accounting principles, but because S&Ls were able to keep details of such transactions private, shareholders and other interested parties were in danger of being left in the dark about the true status of a company's financial health. As the decade of the 1980s began, some S&Ls had begun to fall under the weight of failed trading ventures. The Sandlers could not totally sidestep the industry woes; during 1982, company stock traded as low as $3 per share.

World Savings grew through expansion in 1982, acquiring bank holding company First S&L Shares. The deal brought in 48 new branches and $1.3 billion in assets from Majestic Savings of Colorado and Commerce Savings of Kansas. In 1985, two additional offices and $272 million in deposits were added with the purchase of Texas-based Bell Savings Banc.

By 1987, the Sandlers had grown their business to 195 offices with assets of nearly $13 billion. The couple held about 8 percent of the stock, valued at around $75 million. The operation was one of the most profitable thrifts in the country. Earnings per share had grown an average of 30 percent a year since 1980. Stock was trading at around $30 per share. Golden West succeeded, according to a November 1987 *Forbes* article, because they had stuck to what they knew best and ran a highly efficient operation. While other thrifts had expanded into commercial, construction, real estate development, and consumer lending, Golden West held to residential mortgage loans, which made up 96 percent of its portfolio. Expenses were kept in check. The corporate offices made do without a receptionist, relying on visitors to announce themselves via a telephone. The total number of employees was lower than comparably sized thrifts. Managers knew that keeping at or below budget factored in significantly during bonus time.

Although the Sandlers kept a meticulously close watch on how employees and branch offices served their customers, they held back on offering new products and services others in the

industry were quick to promote. World Savings had no automated teller machines, for example. When compared with the competition in other ways, World Savings exceeded industry averages in return on equity and return on assets. Its ratio of nonperforming assets was 0.62% of total assets in 1987, or less than half the average rate for a healthy thrift operation. S&L giant H.F. Ahmanson's rate, for example, was 1.58%, according to *Forbes*.

Even though they were slow to follow some industry trends, the Sandlers kept abreast of one that was creating bigger and bigger competitors: consolidation. To keep up, they began opening small loan production offices in new territories, including New Jersey, Florida, and Virginia, and were on the lookout for opportunities to buy other financial companies.

The next year, 1988, proved to be bleak for S&Ls. By October, 103 thrifts had been closed or merged. The total number of S&Ls that failed during the 1980s would top 850. But Golden West continued to thrive and ended the decade with $19.5 billion in assets, savings offices in six states, and lending operations in 18 states. In addition, a second subsidiary, Atlas, was established in 1989 to provide investment products and services.

Golden West Continuing to Shine: 1990s–2000s

The 1990s started much as the 1980s ended: S&Ls were still hurting, particularly in five states. The California, Texas, Arizona, Kansas, New York, and New Jersey markets accounted for a lion's share of the total industry's losses early in the year. According to a 1990 *San Francisco Business Times* article, troubled real estate markets and investment debacles contributed to the problems. The Sandler operation, though, continued to stay the course, maintaining its traditional offering of savings deposit accounts and single family mortgages.

World Savings moved on its expansion plans in 1990. It gained $457 million in assets and six offices when it purchased New Jersey-based Community Federal Savings. World headed down the coast the next year, acquiring a failed Florida operation. Beach Federal held $1.5 billion in assets and 16 offices. Also in 1991, World entered Arizona, purchasing Security Federal Savings' three branches and $148 million in deposits. As 1992 began, Golden West Financial Corporation held assets of $25 billion. Return on equity over the past five years had averaged nearly 20 percent. The branches of World Savings and Loan numbered 230.

Although the 300 largest U.S. thrifts gained ground in 1994, the industry as a whole declined. According to a May 1995 *American Banker* article, some in the industry maintained that the S&Ls were being hurt by downward pressure on mortgage rates caused by the activity of huge secondary market players, Fannie Mae and Freddie Mac. The government-sponsored enterprises (GSEs) were intended to help make home mortgages affordable for low- to middle-income buyers.

Mid-sized thrifts were hurt the most by thin profit margins, making them targets for buyout by the larger players. The three largest thrifts—all California-based—increased their assets in 1994: top-ranked H.F Ahmanson & Co.'s Home Savings of America by 6 percent, to $53.4 billion; number two ranked Great Western Bank by nearly 11 percent, to $39.7 billion; and third-ranked Golden West Financial Corporation's World Savings by 10 percent, to $31 billion. Even the biggest players saw

---

Key Dates:

1912: World Savings is established in Madera, California.

1929: Golden West Savings is established in Oakland, California.

1959: World Savings of California becomes a subsidiary of Trans-World Financial Corporation.

1963: Golden West Financial Corporation is formed to acquire Golden West Savings.

1975: World Savings merges with Golden West; the combined businesses use the World Savings name.

1981: World Savings makes adjustable rate mortgages (ARMs) its major mortgage product.

1989: World Savings, surviving a rash of S&L failures, ends the decade with assets of nearly $20 billion.

1990–91: The company expands through acquisition of financial institutions in New Jersey, Florida, and Arizona.

2000: Savings branches are opened in eight states; lending offices are opened in 32 states.

---

their deposits drop, though, hurt by the trend toward investment products such as mutual funds.

By 1996, nearly 30 years since the company went public, Golden West Financial's assets had reached $35.8 billion, and the company operated in nearly half the states. Herbert and Marion Sandler, both in their mid-60s, were subjects of speculation: Would the golden couple retire? In a July 1996 *American Banker* article Barton Crockett asserted that some of the conjecture was driven by their involvement in outside interests, including international human rights causes. In addition, some competitors were wondering if the pair had lost their golden touch. Return on equity during 1994 and 1995 had been below its historic average in the mid-teens. The Sandlers held 18 percent of the company, valued at the time at around $566 million.

Buyout speculation was running rampant in California in 1997. The two largest thrifts were embroiled in a hostile takeover bid. Golden West, which had been generating growth internally, seemed to be outside the fray. The company's traditional mortgage market, efficient operation, and dearth of new technology made it a less attractive buyout target. Consolidation continued into 1998, and the purchase of Ahmanson by Seattle-based Washington Mutual Inc. made Golden West Financial the largest independent thrift in California.

Golden West had golden days on Wall Street in 2000. "There is a love affair going on with this stock," said Thomas Hain at Lehman Brothers, in a July 2000 *American Banker* article. "They are in a sweet spot right now in the mortgage business, and that is driving extraordinary earnings compared to other thrifts. They are the best ARM lender, and they have superior interest rate management."

But the love affair ended abruptly by year-end. Investors pulled back from ARM-dependent thrifts when signs of a new refinancing boom surfaced. ARMs' initial low interest rates and low down payments drew many first-time buyers, especially those without funds for other types of loans. But as interest rates for fixed loans improved, those buyers would switch over, diminishing thrifts' ARM portfolios.

The roller coaster ride continued for the thrifts in 2001, and ARM demand appeared questionable for the year to come. The company's mortgage lending unit produced $20.8 billion in loans in 2001, the vast majority from ARMs. But Golden West Financial Corporation, still led by Marion Sandler, as chairman and CEO, had a history of producing strong results even in difficult environments.

Principal Subsidiaries

Atlas Securities; World Savings and Loan.

Principal Competitors

Washington Mutual Inc.

Further Reading

Agah, M., "Golden West Financial," *RBC Capital Markets (US),* January 4, 2002.

Agosta, Veronica, "Thrifts' Decline Sparks Value Debate," *American Banker,* November 5, 2001, p. 23.

Bergquist, Erick, "Stiff-ARMed: Calif. Thrifts Take a Beating on the Street," *American Banker,* January 11, 2001, p. 11.

Boroughs, Don L., "Eating Humble Pie, Making Lots of Bread," *U.S. News & World Report,* April 6, 1992, pp. 50+.

Carlsen, Clifford, "World Savings Struts Its 1990 Assets, Earnings," *San Francisco Business Times,* April, 26, 1991, pp. 1+.

Cornwell, Ted, "Golden West: All-Time High in '01," *National Mortgage News,* February 4, 2002, p. 9.

Crockett, Barton, "Golden West's Golden Couple Retiring? No Way," *American Banker,* July 17, 1996, pp. 1+.

Ehrbar, A.F., "The Mysteriously Profitable S&L," *Fortune,* June 29, 1981, pp. 94–99.

Goodman, Jordan E., "Six Gems Amid the Rubble of Financial Services," *Money,* January 1991, pp. 55+.

Heins, John, "Boring Is Better," *Forbes,* November 16, 1987, pp. 167+.

Padgett, Tania, "Golden West, Rate Hopes Keep Thrift Stocks Rising," *American Banker,* July 26, 2000, p. 24.

Prakas, Snigdha, "ARMs Helped Top 300 U.S. Thrifts Build Assets As Industry Slipped," *American Banker,* May 17, 1995, p. 10.

——, "Golden West Plugs Along Profitably Amid Deal Mania," *American Banker,* April 22, 1998, p. 9.

——, "Will Great Western Bidding Put Golden West in Play?," *American Banker,* February 25, 1997, p. 13.

Schifrin, Matthew, "What's the Payback?," *Forbes,* January 6, 1992, p. 144.

Serwer, Andrew Evan, "Some Savings and Loans Are Doing Fine, Especially in California," *Fortune,* October 10, 1988, pp. 25+.

Shaw, Jan, "Sheshunoff Lauds World Savings," *San Francisco Business Times,* October 1, 1990, p. 14.

—Kathleen Peippo

Grupo Transportación Ferroviaria Mexicana, S.A. de C.V.

Avenida Periferico Sur 4829, Piso 4
Mexico City, D.F. 14112
Mexico
Telephone: (525) 447-5836
Toll Free: (800) 849-6145
Fax: (525) 447-5739
Web site: http://www.tfm.com.mx

Joint Venture of Transportación Maritima Mexicana, S.A.
de C.V., Kansas City Southern Industries Inc., and the
Mexican federal government
Incorporated: 1996
Employees: 4,500
Sales: $667.8 million (2000)
NAIC: 482111 Line-Haul Railroads

Grupo Transportación Ferroviaria Mexicana, S.A. de C.V. (TFM), which means ''Mexican Railway Transportation'' in English, is the principal Mexican railroad, hauling cargoes over a main-line network of 4,282 kilometers (2,661 miles). This line—almost all of it single-track—runs between Mexico City and Nuevo Laredo, from where it crosses the Rio Grande and connects to other rail lines in the United States and Canada. TFM handles 60 percent of all rail traffic crossing the U.S.-Mexican border and has access to nearly 70 percent of Mexico's population. Spurs or trackage rights link the main line to such important industrial cities as Guadalajara, Monterrey, Puebla, and Querétaro, and to Mexico's three main seaports: Lázaro Cárdenas, Tampico, and Veracruz. Grupo TFM is jointly owned by Transportación Maritima Mexicana (TMM), which translates as ''Mexican Maritime Transportation''; Kansas City Southern Industries Inc. (KCSI), a holding company that owns—wholly or partly—four U.S. railway lines; and the federal government of Mexico.

The Mexican Railway System: 1837–1996

In 1837, the Mexican government granted Francisco Arrillaga, a wealthy Spanish-born merchant, a concession to con-

struct the nation's first railroad, between Mexico City and Veracruz, its chief port. This project was never effected for a variety of reasons and ended with Arrillaga's death. In 1857, a grant to Antonio Escandon gave him the right to build a line through Mexico City from the Gulf of Mexico to the Pacific Ocean. Escandon had to sell his concession to the government of Emperor Maximilian, which then granted it to a British company that it subsidized and that completed a line between Mexico City and Veracruz in 1872.

In 1880, the Mexican Congress approved a 99-year concession to enterprises who would undertake to build three rail lines. The most important of the three was awarded to Ferrocarril Central Mexicano (Mexican Central Railroad), which was incorporated that year in Massachusetts. Mexico Central completed, in 1884, a line running from Mexico City to Nuevo Laredo, bordering Texas, as well as another one to Ciudad Júarez. Two years later, Mexico Central was connected to U.S. lines running as far north as Chicago. By 1890, there were several branch lines, including Monterrey-Matamoros and San Luis Potosí-Tampico. But in the early 1900s, the two largest U.S. concessionaires merged, creating alarm among nationalist Mexicans. Accordingly, in 1908 the federal government bought out the owners and became the main shareholder of the newly created Ferrocarriles Nacionales de México (FNM), with authority over 11,157 kilometers (6,933 miles) of line.

The Mexican revolution that began in 1910 disrupted the nation's railway system so severely that some lines did not function normally until 1920. There was no service at all in the north between 1914 and 1916. Some $400 million in debt, the FNM was restructured in 1926 as a private company, with the federal government holding 51 percent of the shares. With the private investors unwilling to continue bearing their share of the load, the FNM was nationalized in 1937. The federal government now assumed administration of the system for the first time. The northern line, which covered the most developed part of the country, was profitable, but other lines were not. The FNM suffered from debt, obsolete equipment, administrative inexperience, corruption, and sabotage.

To reduce political pressures that were incompatible with making the system profitable, the FNM became a formally independent public corporation at the end of 1940, but it was once again tied closely to the government in 1948. Deficits and labor trouble were chronic problems, with a major and bloody strike in the 1950s and a history of derailments due to poor maintenance. The FNM lacked enough capital to modernize its facilities and was unable to raise its low rates in the face of opposition by pressure groups. In 1987, the federal government decided not to pay out operating subsidies any longer, but it still had to carry the load for amortization of debt, interest, and financing capital expenses. By 1996, the FNM was hauling only 12 percent of all freight in its service area, compared to 20 percent a decade earlier (and 37 percent in the United States by U.S. railroads).

Privatization of the FNE: 1996–97

In spite of its problems, the FNM would have remained a politically sacrosanct government monopoly but for the economic crisis and ensuing peso devaluation of late 1994. The badly pressed federal government secured, in 1995, a constitutional amendment that permitted the privatization of the nation's railway system and made plans for the piecemeal auctions of three main lines and several short lines. Regarded as the "jewel in the crown" was Ferrocarril del Noreste, S.A. de C.V. (FNE, or Northeast Railway), which consisted of 19 percent of the nation's trackage but 38 percent of its traffic (of which 70 percent was international traffic). A joint venture of Union Pacific Corp. and Empresas ICA—Mexico's largest construction company—was expected to submit the winning bid, in December 1996, for this section of the system, but its $527 million offer was far short of an 11.07 billion peso bid (about $1.4 billion) by Grupo TFM, which had recently been established and was 51 percent owned by TMM and 49 percent owned by KCSI. (Jorge Serrano, chairman and chief executive of TMM, also held these posts for Grupo TFM.) For this sum the partners won 80 percent of the 50-year concession awarded to the operating company FNE—which was renamed TFM—plus an option to run the line for another 50 years. The federal government retained the other 20 percent but said it would sell this stake within two years.

TMM and KCSI shareholders and creditors immediately questioned how these companies could afford to make such a bid and still recoup their investment, and other observers questioned the Mexican government's own credibility. Accordingly, after TMM and KCSI made a down payment of $560 million at the end of January 1997, the government reduced its claim on the partners by contributing about $200 million of the rest for a total of 24.6 percent of the shares of Grupo TFM, with TMM retaining 38.5 percent and KCSI 36.9 percent. The government said it would remain a partner for up to seven years before liquidating its shares in a public stock offering or selling them back to Grupo TFM, whose officials had pledged to invest $200 million in 1997 to improve the line and an average of $125 million per year for the next five years. Morgan Stanley Co. extended a $150 million revolving credit line and a $325 million loan over 12 years and helped the partners raise another $400 million through the sale of notes and debentures. After paying out the remaining $860 million, Grupo TFM officially took control of the northeast line in June 1997.

TFM inherited lower labor costs, because the federal government had compelled the 8,700-member workforce of the line into retirement and then let the new owners rehire only those they considered necessary: about 4,500. These staffers received a wage increase averaging 25 percent. A Monterrey-based centralized sales force—something the FNM did not have in place—went to work signing up six classes of customers: automotive, agricultural, chemicals, industry (forest products and manufacturing), minerals, and intermodal. Security improved with the creation of a new police force that had the authority to arrest and prosecute thieves, vandals, trespassers, and stowaways attempting to cross into the United States. Most of the 371 locomotives were rebuilt and modernized by privatized locomotive shops. By late 2000, freight trains that four years earlier had averaged 60 hours for the 700-mile trek to Mexico City from the Texas border were making the trip in 34 to 41 hours. Average train speed had improved from 11.2 to 16.1 miles per hour.

An essential link to the United States was Texas Mexican Railway, also jointly owned by TMM and KCSI. This "Tex-Mex" line linked Nuevo Laredo to Laredo, Texas, and Matamoros to Brownsville and Corpus Christi, Texas. It then—by means of trackage rights—continued north as far as Beaumont, where it connected to the Kansas Southern Railway line. By late 1999, TFM was handling about 60 percent of all cross-border rail traffic between the United States and Mexico, most of it over the Laredo bridge. TFM operated the Mexican side of this single-track bridge. However, Union Pacific remained its chief customer at the Laredo gateway and was vocal in its complaints about congestion. A new Tex-Mex yard near the gateway, completed in 1999, increased the number of rail cars capable of crossing the bridge on a single day from 1,300 to 3,000.

Seeking Trucking Business: 1999–2001

TFM, KCSR, and Tex-Mex introduced at the International Intermodal Expo held in Atlanta in April 1999 a new intermodal service that they called the NAFTA Express. The new venture aimed to win truck-hauling business for cross-border traffic, particularly automotive parts into, and finished vehicles out of, Mexico. (Automobiles and auto parts were by far the biggest categories of such traffic.) "Mexico has always been looked upon by shippers and carriers as a black hole when it comes to moving equipment down there," a TFM executive told John Gallagher of *Traffic World*. "Most of the units going down had no tires by the time they came back up." He said that the former 31-day cycle for auto parts moving between Laredo and Mexico City had been cut to 12 days and that expenses on theft claims had been cut by nearly 80 percent. TFM was also said to be receiving the lion's share of exports of Corona beer being shipped to the eastern half of the United States.

Key Dates:

1884: The main line (Mexico City-Nuevo Laredo) of what would become Transportacion Ferroviaria Mexicana (TFM) is completed.
1908: This line and others are nationalized by the Mexican government.
1996: Transportación Maritima Mexicana, S.A. de C.V. (TMM) and Kansas City Southern Industries Inc. (KCSI) enter the winning bid for the Northeast railway line.
1997: Grupo TFM officially takes possession of the line.
1999: TFM introduces an intermodal service in order to win truck-hauling business.
2001: Two of five planned TFM intermodal service hubs are in operation.

A 2000 TFM plan called for five regional intermodal hubs: in Nuevo Laredo, Monterrey, Querétaro, San Luis Potosí, and Toluca. "Truck conversions are one of our biggest goals," a TFM marketing executive told Lawrence H. Kaufman of *Railway Age* in 2001. "We're still educating the U.S. shipper as to the actual availability of rail in Mexico and the service that TFM can provide" by means of the major corridors into Mexico from Chicago, Dallas, Houston, Los Angeles, and eastern gateways. TFM's service included pre-cleared trains that bypassed customs services at the border. The Toluca and San Luis Potosi terminals were in operation by late 2001.

By late 1999, TFM's five-year capital-investment plan totaled $731 million, with the annual sum expected to peak at $229.8 million in 2000. Long-term lease agreements for 4,720 freight cars brought the fleet to more than 11,000 cars by mid-2000, a 69 percent increase. A TFM yard with capacity to hold 950 cars had been completed at Nuevo Laredo, just south of the U.S. border. An alliance between KCSR and Canadian National Railway Co. allowed TFM to carry finished goods from Mexico all the way to Canada. The company had a goal of $1.5 billion in revenue by 2005, with 60 percent of the growth expected from cross-border traffic and the remainder from traffic within Mexico and growth through Mexican ports.

Grupo TFM was reportedly considering an initial public offering of shares on the New York Stock Exchange before the end of 2001, but these plans were shelved because of falling prices for existing stocks. By May 2001, the company had placed about $750 million worth of bonds on international markets.

TMM and KCSI announced in June 2001 that they would acquire the Mexican government's stake in Grupo TFM later in the year. Payment for the government's share of the company was estimated at about $249 million, less about $81 million representing the proceeds from the sale of a redundant 18-mile rail line to the government. The purchase was to be through a combination of cash and debt financing. In its annual filing with the Securities and Exchange Commission, however, KCSI reported that it and TMM actually held a call option to buy the Mexican government's share by July 31, 2002. The partners also, in March 2002, sold Grupo TFM the common stock of Mexrail, Inc. for $31.4 million. Mexrail owned the Texas Mexican Railway and the northern (U.S.) half of the Laredo international railway bridge.

Principal Competitors

Burlington Northern Santa Fe Corp.; Celadon Group; Grupo Ferroviario Mexicano, S.A. de C.V.; Union Pacific Corp.

Further Reading

Aguayo, Jose, "The Little Railroad That Hopes It Can," *Forbes,* April 21, 1997, pp. 58, 60.
"Consortium Says Mexican Rail Bid Is a Sound Investment," *Journal of Commerce,* December 10, 1996, pp. 1A, 3B.
Los ferrocarriles de Mexico 1837–1987, Mexico City: Ferrocarriles Nacionales de Mexico, 1987.
Gallagher, John, "KCS's NAFTA Express," *Traffic World,* April 26, 1999, pp. 35–36.
——, "New Sheriff at Tex Mex," *Traffic World,* November 8, 1999, pp. 35–36.
"Kansas City Southern Expands Its Holdings in a Mexican Railroad," *Wall Street Journal,* June 14, 2001, p. A10.
Kaufman, Lawrence H., "Mexico: Land of Opportunity," *Railway Age,* February 2001, pp. 40–1.
Sutter, Mary, "Mexico Rejuggles Rail Privatization to Keep It on Track," *Journal of Commerce,* February 10, 1997, pp. 1A, 2B.
——, "TFM Officially Takes Control of Mexico's 1st Privatized Rail," *Journal of Commerce,* June 23, 1997, p. 1A.
Vantuono, William C., "Cross-Border Bonanza," *Railway Age,* October 2000, pp. 31–6.
——, "In Mexico, A Railway Revolution," *Railway Age,* October 1997, pp. 35–8, 42–3, 45, 48, 50–2, 79.
——, "Mike Havarty, Railroader of the Year," *Railway Age,* January 2001, pp. 33, 36, 40, 43.
——, "A Railroad Renaissance South of the Border," *Railway Age,* October 1998, pp. 31–4, 36–7, 40–4, 46.

—Robert Halasz

GUS plc

Universal House
Devonshire Street
Manchester M60 1XA
United Kingdom
Telephone: (0161) 273-8282
Fax: (0161) 277-4056
Web site: http://www.gusplc.com

Public Company
Incorporated: 1917 as Universal Stores (Manchester)
Limited
Employees: 69,708
Sales: £6.04 billion ($8.56 billion) (2001)
Stock Exchanges: London
Ticker Symbol: GUS
NAIC: 442110 Furniture Stores; 443112 Radio,
Television, and Other Electronics Stores; 448140
Family Clothing Stores; 452990 All Other General
Merchandise Stores; 454110 Electronic Shopping and
Mail-Order Houses; 541512 Computer Systems
Design Services; 541860 Direct Mail Advertising;
561450 Credit Bureaus

GUS plc, formerly the Great Universal Stores plc, is one of the leading retailers in the United Kingdom and also is a supplier of business services. The company's largest division by revenues, generating about two-thirds of the total (and about 36 percent of overall profits), is Argos Retail Group, which includes catalog showrooms, mail-order catalogs, and e-commerce web sites. The group includes the leading U.K. catalog retailer, Argos, which has about 460 outlets located throughout the United Kingdom and the Republic of Ireland. Catalogs run by the group include the U.K.-based Argos Additions, Choice, Kays, and Great Universal, along with Wehkamp in The Netherlands and Halens in Sweden. Argos Retail Group also operates one of the top U.K. retail web sites, jungle.com, seller of electronic equipment and accessories. Outside of Argos Retail, GUS owns upscale retail clothing brands Burberry (known for its plaid fashions) and Scotch House and maintains a retailing operation in South Africa consisting primarily of about 430 Lewis furniture stores and more than two dozen Best Electric specialty electronics outlets. Responsible for about 16 percent of revenue but around 37 percent of profits is the Experian division. Operating in 50 countries, but most prominently in North America, Experian is best known for its credit reporting service, which maintains credit information on more than 200 million consumers and 14 million businesses in the United States. Other Experian services include direct marketing and the processing of consumer transactions. GUS's Reality division handles logistics, e-commerce, and customer services functions both for Argos Retail Group and for outside clients.

Early 20th-Century Origins

The company's history began in Manchester in 1900. Three brothers, George, Jack, and Abraham Rose, started a general dealing and merchanting business called the Universal Stores. By 1917, when Universal Stores (Manchester) Limited was registered as a limited, or incorporated, company, it supplied a wide range of consumer goods. Increased success accompanied a move into mail order in the 1920s. The Roses, who had previously relied on newspaper advertising of single items, began to draw up catalogs instead. Early versions were small in format but bulky, containing about 100 pages, with one product illustrated on each page. Agents were recruited to promote sales via the catalog and were allowed discounts on their own purchases. Customers paid by installment, usually over a period of up to 20 weeks. Sometimes the credit club method was employed, by which members paid a weekly sum and drew lots to determine the order in which they would receive their chosen goods. The catalog, the commissioned agent, and installment credit have remained the characteristic institutions of mail-order operations. Another form of direct selling by credit had been established earlier. This was the tallyman—or salesperson collector—system, which was later used by some GUS subsidiaries. The salesperson made regular home visits to collect installments and deliver goods.

Universal Stores grew rapidly toward the end of the 1920s. Profits averaged £244,000 over the three years from 1929 to 1931, reaching a peak of £411,000 in 1931. The company added

Company Perspectives:

GUS is focusing its skills and resources on the three areas of consumer understanding, choice and service in order to satisfy an even more discerning consumer.

Understanding: Through our information solutions business, Experian, we help companies understand the particular needs and circumstances of their customers in order to make better decisions at every point of contact.

Choice: Through our many retail brands, we enable customers to match the shopping experience to their own lifestyles and aspirations.

Service: Through our outsourcing business, Reality, we help companies manage every aspect of their relationship with customers in order to deliver on their brand promise.

the word "Great" to its title—and dropped "(Manchester)"—in 1930 and successfully went public in 1931. A combination of falling demand—induced by the Great Depression—and poor stock control reduced profits by half in 1932 and resulted in a small loss in 1933. The Roses, who had benefited considerably from the public issue, felt obliged to pay nearly £100,000 out of their own pockets to maintain the dividend at its previously anticipated level. Several members resigned from the board in late 1932, and three new directors, including Sir Philip Nash as chairman, were appointed to represent the interests of the U.K. securities firm Cazenove's clients. The most significant change precipitated by this crisis was the appointment of a new joint managing director, Isaac Wolfson, along with George Rose, who resigned two years later. Under Wolfson's leadership, GUS was to make the lengthy transition from the unpromising circumstances of 1932 to its current financial strength.

Wolfson's Career at GUS Beginning in the 1930s

Wolfson was born in Glasgow in the late 1890s, starting his career as a salesman for his father's modest furniture business. Moving to London in 1920, he traded on his own account, selling such items as clocks and mirrors and also building up an informal private banking practice. By 1932 Wolfson had become merchandise controller of GUS, having first met and impressed George Rose at a trade exhibition in Manchester. Wolfson specified that not all of his time would be devoted to his employer, and his remuneration consisted at least in part of an option to buy GUS shares from the Roses. When the share price fell heavily in 1932, the option was exercised with the assistance of both his father-in-law, Ralph Specterman, and of his stockbroker friend, Sir Archibald Mitchelson, who later succeeded Nash as chairman of the company. Although Wolfson would not advance to chairman until after World War II, he has been credited with transforming the company over the course of his half-century career. A 1994 profile of GUS in *Management Today* characterized Wolfson as "the secretive financial wizard who turned GUS from a small trading operation in Manchester into one of Europe's three largest mail order companies."

GUS soon recovered. Despite high unemployment, the majority of working-class consumers enjoyed rising real incomes, and the company had prospects of increased sales once the internal problems were under control. By 1934 the new 150-page catalog claimed to be the largest of any mail-order house in Europe. A few years later GUS took over the similar business of its Manchester neighbor Samuel Driver. Acquisitions, however, were not confined to mail order. A Wembley-based furniture concern, with large factory and warehouse capacity, had already been added to the company. Midland and Hackney, a recent amalgamation of two of the oldest established installment-purchase furniture businesses in the country, joined GUS in 1934. A feature of this firm that made it an attractive proposition was its substantial debts in installment purchases. Collection of outstanding debt and mortgaging of properties—wholly owned properties were mortgaged, then rented back—could unlock valuable cash resources. In 1938 Alexander Sloan of Glasgow, with 20 shops and a tallyman—an installment selling business—and two other similar Scottish concerns, were brought into the group. These 1930s acquisitions were on a cash basis and were financed by a combination of retained profit and debenture issues. Altogether, more than £2 million was raised in this way in 1936 and 1938. Expansion into the retail trade in the prewar years was not very successful in the short run, however. Profits fell in 1935, and thereafter grew more slowly than assets until after the outbreak of World War II.

Acquisitions Paced by Post-World War II Growth

GUS's profits were maintained during the war. By the late 1940s it had emerged as the owner of a large chain of furniture shops, while the mail-order base had been strengthened further by the purchase of Kays of Worcester in 1943. Jays and Campbells, with nearly 200 furniture outlets, was bought in 1943 for £1.2 million, after the previous owners had run into trouble with wartime price control legislation. In 1945 the British and Colonial Furniture Company sold a controlling interest to GUS for around £1 million. This included some 75 Cavendish and Woodhouse stores in the United Kingdom and a larger number in Canada. Another important furniture business, Smarts, was taken over in 1949, again for about £1 million. The purchase of Jackson's followed soon after. Also in 1949 the company expanded into South Africa with the purchase of Lewis Stores Group, a furniture retailer. By fiscal 1953–54 furniture sales, mainly by installment buying, accounted for about a third of the company's expanded profits of some £15 million.

The major acquisitions of the 1940s owed much to three major factors. One was that wartime trading restrictions, regulating allocation and use of raw materials, plus controls on capital and on profit margins in distribution, were a less severe constraint for GUS—which was accustomed to working on lower margins—than for retail concerns with weaker and more traditional management. Another was that Wolfson was sufficiently confident and farsighted to anticipate a postwar housing boom and a strong demand for furniture on credit. A final consideration was that after the war many retailers continued to hold properties at prewar valuations. Current values understated the potential for a buyer aware of the possibilities of property sales, or mortgage-and-leaseback deals with insurance companies. Property revaluation strengthened the balance sheet of the buyer and lifted the price of its shares.

In the postwar years GUS and Wolfson, who had become chairman in 1946 on the death of Mitchelson, quickly gained a

Key Dates:

1900: Three brothers launch a general dealing and merchanting business called the Universal Stores.

1917: The company is incorporated as Universal Stores (Manchester) Limited.

1930: The name of the firm is changed to The Great Universal Stores Limited.

1931: The company goes public.

1932: The involvement of the Wolfson family in the business begins with the appointment of Isaac Wolfson as a managing director.

1943: Kays of Worcester, a mail-order house, is acquired.

1946: Isaac Wolfson becomes company chairman.

1949: South African furniture retailer Lewis Stores Group is acquired.

1955: Upscale clothier Burberry's (later Burberry) is acquired.

1977: Revenues reach £1 billion and profits amount to £100 million for the first time.

1987: Isaac Wolfson retires and his son, Leonard, takes over as chairman.

1996: Leonard Wolfson retires and his cousin, David Wolfson, steps into the chairmanship; Experian is acquired for £1 billion.

1997: A real estate joint venture is formed with British Land Company.

1998: Two major acquisitions are completed: Metromail Corporation (for £560 million) and Argos (£1.9 billion).

2000: David Wolfson retires, ending an era of management by members of the Wolfson family; the company restructures into three core units: Argos Retail Group, Experian, and Reality.

2001: The company changes its name to GUS plc.

higher public profile. The new leader's growing reputation rested on the rapid growth of the firm and especially on his success as a practitioner of the takeover bid. Some of the techniques employed in the acquisitions of the 1950s were already familiar—notably the targeting of companies with undervalued properties and the sale, with or without leaseback, of selected properties. A major new element was the creation of new, mostly nonvoting, shares, of which GUS issued more than five million in a new "A" class via a stock split in 1952. Eventually the "A" shares vastly outnumbered the ordinary, allowing the Wolfson family to maintain control with a minority of the total stock. For the larger takeovers of the 1950s GUS offered a combination of cash and "A" shares. Bids on this basis were frequently acceptable and recipients, such as the directors of the women's clothing group Morrison's in 1957, announced their willingness to hold GUS "A" shares as a long-term investment. Similar offers succeeded in some cases where the bid was resisted or contested, as in 1954 with Jones and Higgins, the drapers and house furnishers. Probably the most publicized disputed takeover was for control of Hope Brothers in late 1957, for which Debenhams was also competing. As GUS grew and flourished, the "A" shares were a highly marketable security. As the *Economist* observed, on July 26, 1958,

their holders were generally "content with bigger dividends, scrip issues and high market values."

In 1955 the family created a trust, the Wolfson Foundation, to hold its shares. The entity grew to become one of the United Kingdom's largest philanthropies, with major beneficiaries including Oxford, Cambridge, and University College. The positive press arising from these donations was perceived as a foil to the veil of secrecy that surrounded GUS. For although the firm was more profitable and paid higher dividends than most of its peers, its stock price lagged behind many competitors' throughout the 1950s and 1960s. Analysts blamed the lower valuation on the Wolfsons' tight-fisted voting control and the dearth of public communication.

Acquisitions promoted the company's growth in the 1950s, and at times did so at a hectic pace. During fiscal 1953–54, 350 retail outlets were added to the existing 870. In the fiscal year 1957–58, the contribution of new subsidiaries exceeded the total increase in profits. Takeovers preserved the record of unbroken profit growth. Expansion of this kind resulted in diversification of trading interests. By the early 1960s the established base in mail order and furniture had been broadened not only by large investments in drapery and men's and women's clothing, but also by stakes in footwear, hotels, electrical goods, builder's merchants, food retailing, and a travel agency. Two of the less predictable of these purchases were perhaps most significant for the future of GUS. The arrival in the group of Burberry's in 1955 signaled a move into more specialized and upmarket areas of the clothing trade, and the absorption in 1957 of Whiteaway Laidlaw, an export drapery and finance company, pointed in some new directions. By the beginning of the 1960s the board had indicated its awareness of reduced opportunities for growth by takeover and of the need for expansion within the existing structure.

Pace of Geographic Expansion Quickening in the 1960s and 1970s

From the 1960s to the early 1980s the company experienced major acquisitions, more disposals, and increasing concentration on a reduced number of principal sectors. The high degree of diversification, however, was a factor in spreading risk and in enabling the group to avoid any setback to the growth of profits. The chairman complained in 1974 of 18 changes in hire-purchase—or installment buying—regulations over the previous 19 years. A further contribution toward smoothing the retail cycle came from GUS's own accounting practice, by which revenue from hire-purchase sales was not credited to profit until after the final installment was paid. Thus, when such sales were rising, debt provision rose faster than profit, but when they were falling, profits were boosted by sales made before the downturn. An additional factor in the stability of GUS's profit growth was the rising share from overseas, which reduced dependence on the performance of the U.K. economy. Until the early 1960s there were only modest earnings abroad, mainly from stores in the United Kingdom and the Commonwealth markets of Canada and South Africa. Then entry into both the United States and continental Europe helped to lift the overseas contribution of total profits to around 10 percent by the end of the 1960s and to 12.5 percent ten years later.

Much of GUS's postwar growth had been in the sector in which it achieved early market leadership—mail order. Even here, some expansion was bought by absorbing smaller competitors, although the last occasion—until the late 1990s—was the acquisition of John Myers in 1981. A proposed deal with Empire Stores was blocked on antimonopoly grounds in 1982. By then GUS held a position of strength in a market that had expanded since the war to a point where mail order represented perhaps 8 percent of nonfood retail sales in the late 1970s. Before the war, mail order had been popular mainly in northern England and Scotland, in rural areas, and among low-income groups. Starting in the early 1950s, it expanded both geographically and socially. The fastest phase of growth occurred in the late 1950s and 1960s before alternative sources of credit became more readily available in shops. The worst setback to the mail-order market was felt in the early 1980s, when recession and unemployment had a negative impact on installment buying. Some of GUS's techniques were unchanged—for example, the reliance on commissioned agents. The major catalogs were transformed into color-printed, 1,000-page, 26,000-item publications. Computerized stock control was introduced, along with automated storage buildings. The stock itself was to a large extent designed and manufactured to the company's own specifications. Deliveries were handled increasingly by GUS's own national distribution network, which included the White Arrow fleet.

Apart from its home-shopping division, GUS also was expanding vigorously in the 1970s and 1980s in property and finance and was disposing of its less successful retail interests. Two important milestones were passed in 1977, when turnover first reached £1 billion and profits £100 million. A new orientation toward property became apparent in the growing tendency to retain the owned property and longer leaseholds when a subsidiary was sold, as in the cases of the Paige clothing shops and Times Furnishing in 1986. By then, the company had long since discarded the image it had sported during earlier phases of growth. Its shares had once been regarded as volatile and speculative, and concern was sometimes expressed about the size of borrowings. By the early 1990s, criticism came from a different angle. The group made appearances on lists of British firms with "cash mountains." Some well-known GUS characteristics did not change at all—the relatively conservative accounting policies and the ungenerous rationing of public information about its activities. Shareholders had to wait a long time for full lists of subsidiaries and even longer for breakdowns of turnover or profit by sector.

Management Changes in the Late 1980s and Early 1990s

Sir Isaac Wolfson, made a baronet in 1962 for his charitable activities, stepped down as cochairman in 1986 in favor of his son Leonard, Lord Wolfson of Marylebone, who had become joint managing director in 1963 and later cochairman. In contrast with his acquiring father, Lord Wolfson was credited with a shrewd program of strategic divestment, shedding more than 2,000 shops via the sale of such chains as Waring & Gillow, the Houndsditch Warehouse, and Times Furnishing. The new leader kept the units' real properties, renting them back to their new owners in a move that essentially transferred these businesses into GUS's real estate management division.

Some industry analysts observed that competition within GUS's core mail-order business was heating up in the mid-1990s. The U.K. mail-order market's share of nonfood retail sales decreased from 6 percent in 1980 to little more than 3 percent in 1994, and challenges from French and German catalog powerhouses began to encroach on GUS's home turf. Nonetheless, the British firm maintained a 40 percent share of the nation's catalog sales and, more important, earned more than two-thirds of the industry's profits.

GUS surprised many observers in 1995 when it extended voting rights to all shareholders and appointed four nonexecutive directors. One of the new board members, Lord (David) Wolfson of Sunningdale, a cousin of Leonard's, had served the company as chairman of the Home Shopping Division from 1973 to 1978, but was believed to have had a disagreement with Leonard that precipitated his departure. David Wolfson went on to serve as chief of staff for Margaret Thatcher from 1979 to 1985 and returned to retailing in 1989 when he joined NEXT plc and subsequently helped turn that fashion chain's fortunes around. The "family reunion" at GUS sparked speculation with regard to the line of succession and, indeed, the 69-year-old Leonard relinquished the day-to-day responsibilities of the chairmanship to David in the summer of 1996. Leonard was given the title of honorary president.

Late 1990s and Beyond: Expanding Business Services, Acquiring Argos

With David Wolfson at the helm, GUS shook off its reputation as a "sleeping elephant," beginning an era of major acquisitions and significant changes in the mix of activities in which the firm was involved, including a rapid expansion in the area of business services. In December 1996 the company made its first major acquisition in more than three decades, the £1 billion ($1.7 billion) purchase of Experian Corp., one of the three major U.S. credit reporting groups. Experian was known for most of its history as TRW Information Systems and Services Inc. It had been a subsidiary of TRW Inc. until November 1996 when TRW spun the unit off, as Experian, to Thomas H. Lee Co. and Bain Capital Inc. for $1.01 billion. Just one month later, the two Boston investment firms turned around and sold Experian to GUS. Experian thus moved from one conglomerate in the United States to another in the United Kingdom with only a brief interregnum of independence, but the more consumer orientation of GUS appeared to be a better fit than that of industrially minded TRW. Experian was merged with GUS's existing CCN Group, which specialized in marketing databases, and its headquarters was moved to Nottingham. Though bold, the acquisition of Experian had a major drawback; the company announced in December 1996 that its nearly 50-year string of uninterrupted profit increases had come to an end.

GUS's commitment to expanding its financial and business services activities was soon evident as a series of acquisitions was completed in the late 1990s. To help fund the acquisitions drive, Wolfson tapped some of GUS's long dormant financial resources. In February 1997 GUS formed a joint venture, called BL Universal PLC, with the British Land Company PLC to manage the retail conglomerate's £900 million real estate portfolio. British Land paid GUS £230 million for its 50 percent stake in BL Universal, which began selling off some of the properties it owned, sending more cash GUS's way. In the first of the post-Experian acquisitions, GUS paid about £182 million in April 1997 for Direct Marketing Technology Inc., a Schaumburg, Illinois, provider of direct marketing services to the U.S. catalog industry. Then in early 1998 SG2, the largest check and debit card processor in France, was acquired from Société Générale for £70 million. Later that year GUS acquired Metromail Corporation for £560 million ($930 million). Based in Lombard, Illinois, Metromail had been spun off from printing firm R.R. Donnelley & Sons Company in 1996 and was a major U.S. database marketing firm. In addition to this vast expansion of its information and financial services activities, GUS also added onto its core cataloging operations with the purchase of Innovations, a catalog of gadgets, from Burton Group plc (later known as Arcadia Group plc) in November 1997 for £20 million. Then in early 1998 the company expanded its personal finance operations, which had consisted of offering home and auto insurance to customers of its catalog operations, by forming a joint venture between GUS Home Shopping and Capital Bank, a subsidiary of Bank of Scotland. Among the new financial services that were launched through this venture over the succeeding few years were personal loans and store and credit cards.

In February 1998, in the boldest move of the David Wolfson era, GUS launched the first hostile takeover in company history, a £1.68 billion cash bid for Argos. With Argos management fighting strenuously to maintain their firm's independence, GUS secured its prize in April by increasing its bid to £1.9 billion. GUS thus gained a major retailer in Argos, which operated more than 400 catalog showrooms throughout the United Kingdom and the Republic of Ireland at high-street (in-town) locations. Argos had been looking to expand into home shopping and delivery, and GUS would be able to take the retailer in that direction by leveraging its burgeoning direct marketing services operation and launching Argos direct-mail cataloging activities. This expansion into direct-mail cataloging also represented a needed deemphasizing of GUS's traditional—and declining-in-fortunes—agency catalogs (ones in which individual, commission-receiving agents sell products to consumers, mainly those who are unable to secure credit). The acquisition of Argos resulted in GUS going into debt for the first time in more than 40 years. Meanwhile, GUS sold off its Canadian furniture retailing chains in 1998.

In mid-2000 the long-running era of Wolfson family leadership at GUS came to an end with the retirement of David Wolfson, whose tenure, however brief, proved to be utterly transformative. He left behind a company the largest division of which in terms of profits was Experian and which was involved in multiple selling channels. Taking over as nonexecutive chairman was Victor Blank, who had been on the company board since 1993 and was a former chairman of Charterhouse plc. Running the firm on a day-to-day basis, however, would be John W. Peace, who had previously been in charge of Experian.

Also during 2000, GUS divided its operations into three main units: Argos Retail Group, which included Argos, the various cataloging operations, e-commerce activities, and related financial services (insurance, banking, loans, and credit cards); Experian, including the credit bureau, consumer transactions, and database marketing operations; and the newly formed Reality, which specialized in logistics, e-commerce, and cus-tomer services for both Argos Retail Group and third-party clients. Falling outside these three units were the retailing operations in South Africa and Burberry. GUS announced in late 2000 that it was planning to offer a partial IPO of Burberry stock by mid-2002—a possible prelude to a full divestment. Burberry had been revitalized and turned into a hot brand in the late 1990s under new managers, and the "'s" had been dropped from the name to make it snappier. Other developments in 2000 included a decision to gradually withdraw from vehicle financing and a somewhat belated drive into e-commerce. In regard to the latter, GUS had nine U.K. e-commerce web sites by mid-2000, including sites for Argos and Kay's, but its online revenues doubled overnight with the purchase of jungle.com in September of that year for a post-Internet bubble bargain price of £37 million. Claiming to be the second most recognized online retailer in the United Kingdom, after Amazon.com, jungle.com sold a wide range of electronic equipment and accessories, including computers, games, and music.

During 2001 GUS sold two noncore home shopping businesses in continental Europe: Universal Versand in Austria and Vedia in Switzerland. In July the company changed its name to GUS plc, officially adopting the name by which it was already best known. In the immediate wake of the events of September 11, 2001, a downturn in consumer spending in the United States hit Experian particularly hard. The company was buoyed, however, by strong results from Argos Direct, the catalog and e-commerce arm of Argos, and by strong Christmas 2001 results from Burberry. In March 2002 GUS announced that Experian had agreed to purchase ConsumerInfo.com from Homestore.com, Inc. for $130 million. ConsumerInfo.com was the leading U.S. supplier of online credit reports.

Principal Subsidiaries

Experian Limited; Argos Limited; Jungle Limited; GUS Home Shopping Limited; Kay & Co. Limited; Morses Limited; Family Hampers Limited; All Counties Insurance Company Limited; Whiteaway Laidlaw Bank Limited; Argos Card Services Limited; Reality Group Limited; Reality Solutions UK Limited; White Arrow Express Limited; Burberry Limited; The Scotch House Limited; Woodrow-Universal Limited; General Guarantee Finance Limited; Experian France S.A.; Experian Information Solutions Inc. (U.S.A.); Experian Services Corporation (U.S.A.); Experian Marketing Solutions Inc. (U.S.A.); Burberry USA; Wehkamp B.V. (Netherlands); GUS Ireland Limited; Lewis Stores (Pty) Limited (South Africa).

Principal Divisions

Experian; Argos Retail Group; Reality; Burberry; South African Retailing; gusco.com.

Principal Competitors

Littlewoods plc; Arcadia Group plc; NEXT plc; Otto Versand GmbH & Co.; N Brown Group plc; Marks & Spencer p.l.c.; House of Fraser PLC; Equifax Inc.; Trans Union LLC.

Further Reading

Aris, Stephen, *The Jews in Business,* London: Jonathan Cape, 1970.

Barker, Thorold, and Peggy Hollinger, ''GUS Ends Uncertainty with £37m Jungle Buy,'' *Financial Times,* September 2, 2000, p. 12.

Beck, Ernest, ''Burberry Parent Is Planning Partial IPO of Unit to Cash in on Brand's Identity,'' *Wall Street Journal,* December 4, 2000, p. B9C.

Berner, Robert, and Ernest Beck, ''Metromail's Data Are Spoils of Takeover War,'' *Wall Street Journal,* March 30, 1998, p. B1.

''Big British Retailer Seeks Stores Here to Sell British Goods,'' *Wall Street Journal,* January 8, 1949, p. 2.

Buckingham, Lisa, ''GUS Catalogues £1bn Deal,'' *Guardian,* November 15, 1996, p. 19.

Buckley, Neil, ''A Tempting Glimpse of Freedom at GUS,'' *Financial Times,* July 16, 1993, p. 17.

Bull, George, and Anthony Vice, *Bid for Power,* London: Elek Books, 1958.

Cowe, Roger, ''Agents Go the Way of Cold War Warriors,'' *Guardian,* December 6, 1996, p. 26.

——, ''Grandpa GUS Is Strong But Old-Fashioned,'' *Guardian,* July 21, 1989, p. 18.

Ellison, Sarah, ''Burberry Cuts Down on Plaid Patterns As It Helps Push Up Sales of Parent GUS,'' *Wall Street Journal,* June 6, 2001.

Fickenscher, Lisa, ''Experian and British Credit Firm Merged in Push for Global Scope,'' *American Banker,* November 15, 1996, pp. 1–2.

——, ''Experian, Not Just a Credit Bureau, Emerges As a Data Base Powerhouse,'' *American Banker,* April 6, 1999, p. 1.

——, ''Former TRW Unit Has New Name, New Life,'' *American Banker,* January 20, 1998, p. 14.

''GUS: The Olde Curiosity Shoppe,'' *Guardian,* July 19, 1991, p. 13.

Harris, Clay, and Peggy Hollinger, ''Pesky Tortoise Runs Hostile Hare All the Way to the Wire,'' *Financial Times,* April 25, 1998, p. 19.

Hollinger, Peggy, ''The GUS Supertanker Changes Course,'' *Financial Times,* February 4, 1998, p. 21.

——, ''An Open-Minded Risk-Taker at the Helm,'' *Financial Times,* November 15, 1996, p. 21.

——, ''An Outbreak of Symbiosis: Is GUS's £1.6bn Bid for Argos As Good As Some Say?,'' *Financial Times,* February 7, 1998, p. 5.

Kleinman, Mark, ''Can Argos Hold onto a Position of Strength,'' *Marketing,* September 27, 2001, p. 13.

Koshetz, Herbert, ''British Retail Giant Plans U.S. Branches,'' *New York Times,* December 9, 1964, pp. 71 + .

Laurance, Ben, ''GUS Shares Soar on Founder's Death,'' *Guardian,* June 22, 1991, p. 10.

Morais, Richard C., ''Street Cred,'' *Forbes,* December 15, 1997, pp. 100–02.

Nelson, Fraser, ''Thatcher Aide Turns Sleepy GUS into Tiger,'' *Times* (London), February 4, 1998, p. 27.

Newman, Aubrey, ''A Wealth of Generosity,'' *Guardian,* June 22, 1991, p. 21.

Patten, Sally, ''Peace Takes the Quiet Approach at GUS,'' *Times* (London), December 1, 2001, p. 51.

Pitcher, George, ''GUS Has Direct Marketing Clout That Argos' Dreams Are Made Of,'' *Marketing Week,* April 16, 1998, p. 21.

Springett, Pauline, ''GUS Frees £900m Asset,'' *Guardian,* February 17, 1997, p. 15.

Voyle, Susanna, ''Duddy Breaks Cover with Argos's Success,'' *Financial Times,* January 26, 2002, p. 16.

Woolcock, Keith, ''The Great Universal Mystery,'' *Management Today,* November 1994, pp. 48–52.

—Gerald W. Crompton
—updates: April D. Gasbarre, David E. Salamie

Harrods Holdings

87-135 Brompton Rd.
Knightsbridge
London SW1X 7XL
United Kingdom
Telephone: (+44) 20-7893-8524
Fax: (+44) 20-7225-6599
Web site: http://www.harrods.com

Private Company
Incorporated: 1889 as Harrod's Stores Limited
Employees: 4,000
Sales: £486 million ($770 million) (2001 est.)
NAIC: 452110 Department Stores

Harrods Holdings represents one of the most prestigious names in shopping history, operating the famed Harrods department store at Knightsbridge, London. The seven-story, 111,000-square-meter building, which includes more than 74,000 square meters of selling space, features 330 departments—Harrods has a long-established reputation for selling ''all things, for all people, everywhere.'' The company also operates a fleet of 47 delivery trucks. The Knightsbridge store remains one of London's biggest tourist attractions, receiving as many as 300,000 visitors per day. Beyond its flagship store, Harrods Holdings operates a number of in-store boutiques in other department stores, such as in the Takashimaya department store in Singapore. There are also Harrods shops in a number of airports, including in Heathrow Airport in London, the Hamburg and Frankfurt airports in Germany, and elsewhere. One of the latest additions to the company's retail chain is a shop opened on the *Queen Elizabeth II* cruise ship operated by Cunard Line. Harrods Holdings also includes the Harrods Casinos online gambling venture; property development arm Harrods Estates; and a helicopter service, Air Harrods, which operates from London's Stansted airport (the company was refused permission to add a heliport to its Knightsbridge store). Harrods Holdings is part of the financial empire owned by the controversial executive chairman Mohammed Al-Fayed, whose interests also include *Punch* magazine, the Fulham football (soccer) club, and the Ritz Hotel

in London. A private company, Harrods has long been rumored to be investigating a public offering—a move that appeared more likely in 2002 as Al-Fayed was reportedly facing financial difficulties. The company sales, already hard hit following the hoof-and-mouth epidemic of early 2001, plunged further with the sharp drop-off in tourism after the September 11 terrorist attacks in the United States; nonetheless, the company posted nearly £500 million for the year.

Founding a Retailing Classic in the 19th Century

In 1849, wholesale tea merchant Charles Henry Harrod decided to enter the retail arena, taking a lease on a small grocery store in the village of Knightsbridge, near London (the village was later swallowed up by its neighbor). The Great Exhibition of 1851 brought about dramatic changes in the area, and Harrod's business prospered. By 1853 he acquired the shop outright, giving it his own name, then began buying up a number of other shops in the neighborhood. Harrod also began expanding the range of goods offered at the store.

In the late 1850s, Harrod began to transition ownership of the store to his son, Charles Digby Harrod, selling it to him in installments. By 1861, the younger Harrod, then 20 years old, became the owner of the store. Charles Digby stepped up his father's expansion of the store's offerings, adding new ''departments'' selling furniture, perfume, china, and glassware. By 1867, Harrod had hired five employees to help sell the widening variety of goods featured at the store. By the beginning of the 1870s, the store's payroll had jumped to 16 employees.

Harrod continued building up its range of goods; in 1874, after buying up two adjacent buildings, the store moved to larger quarters. By the end of that decade, the store boasted more than 100 employees. After the store was destroyed by fire in 1883, Harrod rebuilt and reopened a new, five-story building that was to form the core of one of London's most popular landmarks. Two years later, the store's founder, Charles Henry Harrod, died.

Charles Digby Harrod sold the store to a limited liability company in 1889, which then floated the company as Harrod's Stores Limited. (Harrod died in 1905.) In 1891, the company took on a new managing director, Richard Burbidge, who became the driving force behind Harrod's transformation into not merely one of the world's largest department stores, but also a leading force in the U.K. retail industry.

Burbidge set out to expand the Knightsbridge store, purchasing the land surrounding the store to begin a dramatic expansion. At the turn of the century, Harrods—as it was now known—boasted 80 departments staffed by some 2,000 employees. Burbidge meanwhile transformed the nature of the goods sold at the store, moving to attract a more upscale trade. By the early years of the new century, Harrods was to become synonymous with the British upper class. Other additions during the decade included the construction of a ten-acre warehouse in 1894; the warehouse was later dressed up with a façade similar to the Knightsbridge store. That same year saw the first of what was later to become a U.K. Christmas tradition, the annual Harrods Winter Clearance sale. In 1898, Harrods installed the city's first escalator, complete with attendants waiting at the next floor with glasses of brandy for customers overcome by the experience.

Harrods continued to expand the range of goods and departments featured at its store. The company's motto became ''Omnia Omnibus Ubique'' (Everything for Everybody Everywhere). Among the most famous items sold by the store was an airplane, sold in 1917; the company also sold an alligator, as a gift to Noel Coward. The tradition of offering unusual items continued throughout the century: in the 1980s, the store sold a baby elephant as a gift for then U.S. President Ronald Reagan.

As the United Kingdom prepared for the outbreak of World War I, Harrods began to expand beyond its single store. In 1914, the company acquired retailer Dickins & Jones, on London's Regent Street, founded in 1790. That acquisition proved the first of several, including Rackmans, based in Birmingham, which had begun as a drapery shop in 1851 before expanding into a regionally based chain of department stores; and DH Evans, founded in 1879. Another expansion move came with the company's first attempt to export the Harrods name, when it set up a Harrods store in Buenos Aires, Argentina, in 1916. The two stores shared directors through World War II, but by the end of the war they had become separate companies, and by the 1960s, Harrods sold off the rest of its interest in the Argentinean store.

In the meantime, Harrods' position among the United Kingdom's upper crust was given an official seal when it received then-Queen Elizabeth's warrant as supplier of china, glass, and ''fancy'' goods to the royal household in 1938. The warrant was promptly incorporated into Harrod's trademark, as well as being posted outside its Knightsbridge store. In 1955 Harrods received another warrant from the new Queen as supplier of provisions and other household items; the following year, the Duke of Edinburgh gave the store the warrant as his outfitter.

Fighting over the Jewel in the Crown in the 20th Century

Having built up a retail network operating throughout the United Kingdom, Harrods itself was bought up by House of Fraser in 1959. That company had also been founded in 1849, by Hugh Fraser in Glasgow, Scotland. In the 1940s, the Fraser store, now led by another Hugh Fraser, began expanding, adding new stores. By the time Fraser went public in 1948, the company had built up a network of 15 House of Fraser stores. In 1953, House of Fraser made its first acquisition, of the Binns chain of retail stores.

The acquisition of Harrods by a Scottish company raised a considerable fuss in England; nonetheless, Harrods immediately became Fraser's ''jewel in the crown.'' House of Fraser continued to expand during the 1960s, acquiring other retail chains, such as the Army & Navy chain, the Dingles retail chain, and other department stores. The Fraser family had used its retail holdings as a springboard to amassing a variety of other financial holdings, which were later placed into a holding company, Scottish Universal Investments (SUITS). SUITS also held 30 percent of House of Fraser.

The Harrods story turned sordid in the 1970s as others began to covet Fraser's ''jewel.'' House of Fraser had entered a period of decline as shoppers began to avoid department stores in the 1970s. A new generation of Frasers had taken the helm since the mid-1960s—in the form of Sir Hugh Fraser, whose gambling debts had begun to eat away at his personal fortune. Fraser began selling off his shares in SUITS in order to pay off his debt; then sold off the rest of his stake to friend Roland ''Tiny'' Rowland, head of South African conglomerate Lonrho. Rowland had assured Fraser that his interest in SUITS was purely as an investment. Yet Rowland's true purpose—that of a takeover of Harrods through gaining control of House of Fraser—was quickly revealed. A bitter battle ensued to keep Harrods from Rowlands hands, who had built up a 30 percent stake in House of Fraser.

Rowland was finally thwarted in the early 1980s when the British mergers and monopolies commission barred him from acquiring House of Fraser. Instead, Rowland sold his 30 percent of the company to friends Mohammed and Ali Al Fayed in 1984. Rowland claimed to have merely ''parked'' his shares with the Al Fayeds. Yet in 1985, the Fayed brothers reached an agreement with House of Fraser to acquire the outstanding 65 percent of the company, in a deal worth some £615 million. With full control of the company, the Fayeds delisted House of Fraser from the London stock exchange.

Rowland counterattacked in a campaign to smear the Fayeds, and even managed to convince friends in the British government to launch an investigation into the Fayeds' finances. The report, completed in 1988, was left unpublished by the British government. The following year, however, Rowland managed to obtain a copy and promptly published it in one of his newspapers. Yet no criminal charges were ever brought against them, and the mere fact of battling Rowland won the Fayed brothers support among some members of the British government.

Investment in Harrods and other parts of the retail empire had fallen off under House of Fraser in the late 1970s and early 1980s. The Fayeds, however, turned that trend around; the

Key Dates:

1849: Charles Henry Harrod, a wholesale tea merchant, rents a small grocery store in Knightsbridge.

1853: Harrod buys his store, which now operates under his name, and begins to acquire neighboring shops.

1861: Harrod sells store to his son, Charles Digby Harrod, who begins expanding the range of merchandise.

1874: Harrod buys two adjacent buildings and expands store.

1883: Store burns down; Harrod rebuilds it as a far larger, five-story building.

1889: Harrod sells store to a limited liability company which takes the company public as Harrod's Stores Limited.

1891: Richard Burbidge is hired as managing director and begins transformation of Harrods into London landmark.

1914: Harrods acquires retailer Dickins & Jones.

1916: Harrods store opens in Buenos Aires but later becomes independent from main store.

1938: Harrods is awarded royal warrant from Queen Elizabeth.

1955: Duke of Edinburgh awards Harrods warrant as his outfitter.

1959: House of Fraser acquires Harrods.

1985: Fayed brothers acquire House of Fraser in a takeover battle with Roland "Tiny" Rowlands.

1988: House of Fraser begins to sell off a number of its department store assets.

1994: Fayed brothers spin off House of Fraser as a public company, keeping only Harrods.

1996: Harrods cancels plans for public listing.

2002: Harrods announces its interest in opening a Harrods store in Chicago as part of a new international expansion campaign.

Harrods "jewel" was given particular attention, as the company now spent nearly $400 million on renovations of the store, a program which included adding two additional floors of selling space and restoring the building's original Edwardian-period façade. Another change, meant to help the store reinforce its upscale image, was the institution of a customer dress code, banning ripped jeans and backpacks from the store. The result of these moves was a vast boost not only in sales, but also in the important sales-per-square-foot measure. By the mid-1990s, the Harrods Knightsbridge store had one of the highest sales per square foot in all of the United Kingdom.

Prestige Brand in the 21st Century

House of Fraser had begun a new attempt to export the Harrods' brand during the takeover battle at the beginning of the 1980s, opening an in-store boutique in Japan's Mitsukoshi department store in 1983. The Fayeds continued this move, leveraging the Harrods' name with the opening of a number of duty-free airport stores, beginning with Frankfurt airport in 1986. Other airport boutique locations included London's Heathrow airport, opened in 1990, and the airport at Hamburg,

opened in 1993. In that year, also, Harrods opened an in-store boutique at the Takashimaya department store in Singapore.

Harrods emerged as the Fayeds primary interest in the 1990s. During the late 1980s, Fayed-led House of Fraser had begun to sell off a number of the company's holdings, such as a group of ten department stores sold to Sellar Morris Properties in 1988 for £6.5 million, and another group of stores spun off a year later in a £6 million management buyout. Many of the company's properties were converted to other uses—one such was the transformation of the Barkers department store in Kensington into a far smaller store; the freed-space was then leased out to another company. By the early 1990s, House of Fraser had cut out nearly half of its former retail empire. The company's continued investment in its Harrods flagship began to drain on House of Fraser's accounts, even as the company, already suffering from an increasingly "dowdy" image, was hit by a recession at the beginning of the decade.

In 1994, the Fayeds placed their entire holding in House of Fraser—excluding the Harrods store and boutiques—on the London Stock Exchange. The Fayeds reformed the company under the Harrods Ltd. name. Two years later, Harrods began preparing its own public listing, proposing to list up to 20 percent of the company's shares, which would have valued the company at more than £2 billion. At the time, the company planned to invest the money raised in such an offering in stepping up the expansion of the Harrods name worldwide. The company also planned to convert Harrods' warehouse, located next to the store, into a five-star hotel. Yet the plan to go public was put on hold, in part because the company's financial advisors insisted that the controversial Fayed brothers would have to play a more distant role if they hoped for a successful public offering.

The suspension of the public offering also sidelined the company's international expansion plans. The following year, Mohammed Al Fayed faced personal tragedy when his son Dodi was killed in a car accident in Paris with Princess Diana. Al Fayed was later to gain renewed controversy when he began raising a question of a conspiracy surrounding the accident. Meanwhile, the company faced a setback in Argentina, when it attempted to retrieve the Harrods brand name from the by now reportedly dilapidated Buenos Aires store. The lawsuit was rejected; yet the company took steps to protect its brand name in other Latin American markets.

Harrods Holdings by then included Fayed's holdings of such properties as publishing group Liberty Media, which included *Punch* magazine, as well as Viva Radio, acquired in 1996; and the executive jet service Hunting Business Aviation, bought in 1995. In 1998, the Harrods name was placed on a new joint venture, Harrods Energy, with Thailand oil company PTT Exploration & Production.

The company returned to the retail front with plans to launch an online shopping service in 1999. The following year, Harrods teamed up with Gaming Internet to launch Harrods Casino, with plans to extend the Harrods name on the Internet to travel and auction web sites. In 2000, also, Harrods reached an agreement with BskyB to begin broadcasting an interactive shopping program hosted by Harrods.

Meanwhile, the company opened a new Harrods boutique on the *Queen Elizabeth II* cruise ship, operated by Cunard Line, in 2000. Yet the company was severing ties with the British royal family as its warrants came up for review. In 2000, the Duke of Edinburgh announced that he was not renewing his warrant for Harrods; by the end of that year, the company had announced that it would not pursue renewals of its other royal warrants, which were due for review in 2001. At the end of 2000, the company removed the warrants from its store façade and redesigned its logo and other materials to accord with its new royalty-free status.

By the beginning of 2002, Harrods once again seemed to be preparing for a public listing. In February of that year, the company announced its interest in returning to an international expansion of the Harrods name, starting with the city of Chicago, where the company was negotiating to build a store on that city's State Street. In April 2002, the possibility of listing appeared to take on force when journalists received a fax announcing Harrod's intention to go public. Yet that fax was quickly revealed as an April Fool's joke perpetrated by Mohammed Al Fayed himself.

Nonetheless, analysts had already begun to question the health of Fayed's finances. The Harrods flagship had seen declining sales and profits at the turn of the millennium, especially in the wake of the September 11, 2001 attacks that had brought the company's crucial tourist trade to a near standstill.

In order to finance its expansion, the company required fresh capital, if only to help the company pay off its mounting debt load. The question remained whether Al Fayed would be able to step back from a day-to-day operating role in order to ensure the success of an eventual public offering.

Principal Subsidiaries

Harrods Ltd; Harrods Casino; Harrods Estates; Air Harrods.

Principal Competitors

Arcadia Group Plc; Debenhams Plc; House of Fraser Plc; James Beattie Plc; Marks and Spencer Plc; N Brown Group Plc; New Look Plc; Next Plc; Otto Versand Gmbh & Co.; Selfridges Plc.

Further Reading

Aitken, Ian, "Harrods: Once the Preserve of the Toff, Fayed's Emporium Is Now a Mecca for Vulgarians," *New Statesman*, May 24, 1999.
"Chairman Mo's Red Ink," *Economist*, February 9, 2002, p. 29.
Dawley, Heidi, "Big Sale at Harrods?," *Business Week*, June 24, 1996.
Grant, Lorrie, "Chicago Officials Set Sights on Luring Harrods," *USA Today*, February 18, 2002, p. 4B.
"Harrods Troubles Fayed Empire," *The Age*, February 18, 2002.
Kay, William, "Harrods 'Float' Plan an April Fool Hoax," *Independent*, April 1, 2002, p. 13.

—M.L. Cohen

Hongkong Land Holdings Limited

8th Floor
One Exchange Square Central
Hong Kong
Telephone: (852) 2842 8428
Fax: (852) 2845 9226
Web site: http://www.hkland.com

Public Company
Incorporated: 1889 as The Hongkong Land Investment
and Agency Company Ltd.
Employees: 700
Sales: $213.00 million (2001)
Stock Exchanges: London Singapore
Ticker Symbol: HKLD
NAIC: 233110 Land Subdivision & Land Development;
531110 Lessors of Residential Buildings; 531120
Lessors of Nonresidential Buildings; 531311
Residential Property Managers; 531312 Nonresidential
Property Managers

Hongkong Land Holdings Limited is one of Hong Kong's foremost property investment, development, and management companies. Through its three operating companies, Hongkong Land owns and manages approximately five million square feet of office and retail space in Hong Kong's central business district, as well as three commercial developments in Singapore, two in Vietnam, and one in Thailand. The company also develops and manages residential properties, albeit on a smaller scale, in HongKong, The Philippines, and Mainland China. The company's primary shareholder is the Jardine Matheson Group, a British conglomerate.

Late 1800s: Hongkong Land's First Taipan

The company's origins date back to 1864 when Catchik Paul Chater, a native of Calcutta, arrived in Hong Kong to become a clerk with the Bank of Hindustan. After two years with the Indian bank, Chater formed his own brokerage firm with backing from the wealthy Sassoon family of Iraq, then active in Hong Kong for more than three generations. By 1870 Chater's early trading success put him on the road to becoming one of Hong Kong's great *taipans,* or illustrious merchants, who made their fortunes in trading opium and tea, or simply land.

In 1870 Chater bought and leased his first piece of property to the Victoria Club on Hong Kong Island. Over the next ten years, he developed a number of sites on the island's core central business district.

Today, the district's warren of skyscrapers, tightly packed from harbor front to the foot of the hill sloping down from Hong Kong Island's Peak district, is packed with shoppers and workers. This bustle owes much to Paul Chater's early efforts to develop the area to such an extent that he would later be described as "one of the most powerful and beneficent figures in the Empire."

During the 1870s Chater worked tirelessly to develop the Hong Kong harbor, providing new wharves for use by the colony's expanding trading and manufacturing businesses. He also did not neglect real estate opportunities in Kowloon, across the bay from Hong Kong Island. In 1884 Chater founded the Hong Kong and Kowloon Wharf and Godown Company to continue developing the Kowloon coastline. Two years later, in 1886, Chater arranged a merger of his new company with wharves held by Jardine Matheson, the British trading giant, in Kowloon.

Aside from aligning his own fortunes with those of a great trading company, Chater foresaw opportunities to develop commercial sites on Hong Kong Island itself, adjoining the harbor. Attempting this was difficult as Hong Kong Island had so little land at that time on which to build. To create space, Chater joined in various land reclamation projects, the results of which greatly changed Hong Kong's coastline. The cost of reclaiming land was high, but demand for space in Hong Kong was as acute in the 1880s as more than a century later.

Hong Kong property developers could foresee high land prices and handsome investment returns from land they reclaimed. Chater was not disappointed. In 1887, he began pursuing the 57-acre Praya Reclamation Project in the central district, on which stand many of Hong Kong Island's most prestigious buildings, including the Mandarin Oriental Hotel. To argue his case for reclamation, Chater bypassed the Hong

Company Perspectives:

The company's mission is to invest in, develop and manage property and infrastructure assets in Asia that build sustainable streams of value for our shareholders.

Kong governor, Sir William Des Voeux, and traveled personally to London to conclude negotiations with the Colonial Office. The Hongkong Land Investment and Agency Company was incorporated in March 1889 to facilitate the Praya project.

To maintain his ties with Jardine Matheson, Chater lured James Johnstone Keswick, an early *taipan* with the trading company, to Hongkong Land. Chater and J.J. Keswick became permanent joint managing directors of the new company. Hongkong Land's first issue of shares in 1889 yielded a mere HK$250,000 in working capital. The fact that the issue was almost solely taken up by European investors provoked anger among many Chinese investors, who promptly established a rival real estate company. Chater and Keswick responded to this challenge by making a further share issue of 25,000 HK$100 shares, doubling Hongkong Land's working capital and providing for a reserve fund of HK$1.25 million.

The company's funds were soon used up, however, in getting work underway at the Praya Reclamation Project. In 1890, land worth HK$800,000 was purchased and mortgage loans of HK$1.3 million were made. Shareholders received a 7 percent dividend at year-end. At the annual general meeting in Hong Kong's city hall, shareholders protested against the low return for an allegedly expensive share issue a year earlier. To quell the criticism, Keswick once again justified his nickname, "James the Bloody-Polite," calming nerves in the audience and urging the shareholders to sit tight for future rewards from their real estate investment.

True to Keswick's word, the returns for Hongkong Land shareholders grew over the next decade. The annual dividend stood at 8 percent for much of the 1890s, rising to 10 percent in 1898 and 12 percent in 1899. Notable among Hongkong Land's early developments was the New Oriental building, completed in 1898 on the recently reclaimed land stretching from Des Voeux Road to the fashionable Connaught Road.

1900–65: A Growing Portfolio

Soon skyscrapers were added by Hongkong Land to the reclaimed site, earning Chater a knighthood in 1905. Between June 1904 and December 1905, the company built five tall buildings, each either five or six stories in size, which dwarfed the other buildings in the colony. Bolstered by the success of the Praya Reclamation Project, Chater completed the adjoining Praya East Reclamation Project in 1921, in time to profit from the establishment of the giant Hongkong Electric on the site. Before his death in 1926, Chater was the guiding light for Hongkong Land.

In the years before World War II, the company built up a property portfolio in the colony worth HK$11.34 million in 1941 and comprising 13 key properties in the central business district. The Japanese occupation of Hong Kong suspended operations at the company, which reclaimed its properties in September 1945, finding most in remarkably good structural condition.

After the war Hongkong Land sold off much of its noncore central portfolio, including badly damaged properties in the Peak district. It then set its sights on key developments in the business district itself.

The company's first large development project was the adding of three stories to Marina House, first completed in 1935. Then, in 1950, Hongkong Land completed a HK$7 million redevelopment of 11 and 13 Queen's Road Central, turning the complex into the nine-story Edinburgh House. The building of Jardine House was completed in 1958, following renovations to the earlier Jardine Building, purchased in 1955. In the same period, the company erected the 13-story Alexandra House on a triangular site formed by Des Voeux Road, Chater Road, and Ice House Road.

During this period, Hongkong Land was involved in work to establish much of the colony's skyscraper waterfront known worldwide. Also in 1958, Hongkong Land demolished the King's and York buildings, first erected in 1905, to make way for Swire House. The Queen's Building, once the crown in the company's portfolio, was torn down and replaced by the giant Mandarin Oriental Hotel, opened in 1963. The completion of the Prince's Building in 1965 brought to nine the number of major office and commercial blocks that the company then owned on Hong Kong's prestigious waterfront and in the central district.

1965–80: Name Change, Diversification

In 1965, Hongkong Land began developing low-cost residential homes for sale, especially in the colony's Kwun Tong and Shaukiwan districts. The company later made investments in southeast Asia, purchasing properties in Australia, Hawaii, Indonesia, Thailand, Singapore, and Malaysia. Returning to core commercial property, Hongkong Land completed in 1972 and 1975, respectively, The Excelsior Hotel and World Trade Centre developments, on land first purchased by Jardine Matheson in 1841.

In 1970, however, Hongkong Land gained world attention by paying a record price of HK$258 million for reclaimed land on Connaught Road, along Hong Kong's waterfront. Company Chairman Henry Keswick, a descendant of J.J. Keswick, made the bid before announcing plans for a 50-story development on the site, the Connaught Centre. The building was completed in 1973 and was renamed Jardine House in January 1989.

The construction of the Connaught Centre prompted a change of name from Hongkong Land Investment and Agency Company to The Hongkong Land Company. This change coincided with expansion for the group through the purchase of Humphrey's Estate and Finance in 1971, and the Dairy Farm Ice and Cold Storage Company a year later. Before 1986, when Hongkong Land sold the company, Dairy Farm grew to become the colony's largest department store chain, and Australia's third largest.

In 1973, Hongkong Land bought a 49 percent stake in the Oriental Hotel in Bangkok. This diversification was made

Key Dates:

1866: Catchik Paul Chater, a bank clerk in Hong Kong, forms his own brokerage firm.

1870: Chater buys and leases his first piece of Hong Kong property.

1884: Chater founds the Hong Kong and Kowloon Wharf and Godown Company to develop the Kowloon coastline.

1886: Chater merges his company with wharves owned by British trading company Jardine Matheson.

1887: Chater pursues and wins a 57-acre reclamation project in the central district of Hong Kong.

1889: The Hongkong Land Investment and Agency Company Ltd. is formed and makes its first issue of shares; Chater and James Johnstone Keswick—head of Jardine Matheson—are joint directors.

1941: Hongkong Land holds 13 important properties in Hong Kong's central business district, worth a total of HK$11.34 million.

1965: Hongkong Land begins developing low-cost residential homes in Hong Kong.

1971: The Hongkong Land Investment and Agency Company is renamed ''The Hongkong Land Company.''

1982: In an effort to hedge against depressed property prices, Hongkong Land diversifies, buying stakes in Hong Kong Telephone and Hongkong Electric.

1984: Hongkong Land undergoes reorganization, selling its noncore holdings; the company changes its place of incorporation to Bermuda.

1986: The company's residential properties are sold off.

1987: Jardine Matheson establishes Jardine Strategic Holdings, which becomes Hongkong Land's primary shareholder.

1995: Hongkong Land completes its first development in Vietnam.

1996: The company starts its first two developments in The Philippines.

1997: The company starts its first development in Singapore.

2001: Hongkong Land starts development in Thailand.

against a backdrop of a slumping property market affected by a bearish Hong Kong stock market in 1973. A general tightening of credit in the economy as a whole, and controls imposed on commercial rents, encouraged Hongkong Land's strategy.

A year later, Mandarin International Hotels was established, to be followed by the building of the Manila Mandarin and the Jakarta Mandarin in the late 1970s. In 1987, Mandarin Oriental International Limited was demerged from Hongkong Land and given its own stock market listing on the Hong Kong stock exchange. With seven hotels in southeast Asia, and contracts to operate a number of Mandarin hotels in North America, the company remained a formidable force in the global hotel trade.

In 1976 Hongkong Land completed work on a 36-story development to join Alexandra House to Prince's Building, Swire House, the Mandarin Hotel, and the Connaught Centre, by a series of interlocking footbridges. This effort was soon supplanted by the Central Redevelopment, Hongkong Land's masterplan for redeveloping the colony's Core Central business district. This meant the demolition of five old buildings owned by the company—Gloucester Building, Windsor House, Lane Crawford House, and behind them Marina House and Edinburgh House—to make way for the Landmark. This giant complex entailed the building of two 47-story office blocks, Gloucester Tower and Edinburgh Tower, both to be surrounded by a five-story shopping development. Completed in two stages, in 1980 and 1983, the Landmark served as a focus for Hong Kong's business and shopping centers.

Late 20th Century: Recession, Heavy Debt, Reorganization

Despite the colony's property boom in 1980 and 1981, the effects of the world recession and high unemployment rates on domestic commerce and real estate prices depressed market conditions at the beginning of 1982. Property prices in Hong Kong plunged, and hesitation among investors, combined with generally weakened purchasing power, left the property market in a depressed state. Hongkong Land's reaction in 1982 was to diversify out of its traditional areas of property development and investment and to purchase large stakes in Hong Kong Telephone Company and Hongkong Electric Holdings.

It was the legacy of the early 1980s property boom, however, which led to the company's acquiring the last major site in Core Central, near the Connaught Centre, for HK$4.7 million in February 1982. Work began shortly after on Exchange Square, the colony's largest commercial development up to that time.

The heavy borrowing to finance the Exchange Square project helped lead Hongkong Land into financial difficulties when the colony's property market crashed in 1983. The slump in demand for large residential units and commercial office space produced a property recession in 1984. As a reaction, Hongkong Land underwent a major reorganization to reduce its substantial borrowing. In 1984 gearing—the amount of borrowing in relation to a company's equity or shareholder's funds—stood at an uncomfortably high 103 percent.

Hongkong Land sold most of its overseas properties and noncore investments, including its stakes in Hong Kong Telephone and Hongkong Electric. By the end of 1986, the company had brought gearing down to a manageable 31 percent without greatly reducing its presence in Core Central, the heart of its property portfolio.

Ambitious restructuring continued with the demerger of Dairy Farm in 1986 and Mandarin Oriental in 1987 from the company's core holdings. At the same time, Jardine Matheson set up Jardine Strategic Holdings, a public company, which became Hongkong Land's principal shareholder.

Hongkong Land's residential portfolio was sold off in 1986, as were Harcourt House and Windsor House a year later. As a result, company gearing fell to a mere 6 percent of shareholders' funds in 1987.

Tower Three of Hongkong Land's ambitious Exchange Square project was opened in 1988, following the earlier opening of Towers One and Two in 1985. This brought office rentals in the complex up to three times their 1985 level.

In 1989, Hongkong Land acquired Fu House, which stood between two other Hongkong Land buildings, the Bank of Canton Building and No. 9 Ice House Street. The three buildings were demolished to make way for the company's newest development of 500,000 square feet. Also in 1989, Hongkong Land Holdings Limited was incorporated in Bermuda, with The Hongkong Land Company becoming a wholly owned subsidiary.

Hongkong Land headed into the last decade of the century in financially sound condition, despite a persistent draining off of Hong Kong's personnel and resources due to fears of what might happen when ownership of the colony reverted back to China in 1997. Some analysts speculated that the company itself was prepared to sell its way out of Hong Kong. HongKong Land had already taken precautionary measures in view of the coming Chinese reclamation, moving its corporate home to Bermuda. In 1991, it looked to build an asset base outside Hong Kong, acquiring 25 percent of Trafalgar House PLC, a large British construction company. But real rumors about the company's exodus started in 1992, when HongKong Land sold one of its office towers in the colony's central business district. The sale of the tower—Nine Queen's Road—led many to speculate that it was only the beginning of a gradual sell-off.

The rumors proved untrue, however. HongKong Land remained firmly rooted in Hong Kong, despite tense relations between its largest shareholder, Jardine Matheson Group, and the Chinese government. It also, however, began making investments in other Asian countries. In 1995, the company finished its first development in Vietnam, a commercial building in Hanoi. In 1996, the company initiated two residential projects in the Philippines, a high-rise condo project in Manila and a joint venture formed to develop middle-income housing.

Further non-Hong Kong investments followed. In 1997, HongKong Land began construction of a commercial complex in Singapore, a seven-story office building with an adjoining mall. Then in 1998, HongKong Land completed its second Vietnamese development, also in Hanoi. In 2001, HongKong Land entered Thailand, partnering with a Thai property developer to refurbish and manage a retail center in Bangkok. That same year, the company partnered with two other development companies to build a second commercial development in Singapore.

Not all of HongKong Land's investments were successful. Its investment in Trafalgar House, particularly, proved to be a costly mistake. The company sustained loss after loss, and by the time HongKong Land sold its majority stake in 1996, it had lost more than $3 million.

In late 2000, HongKong Land offered to buy back up to 260 million of its shareholder-owned shares, a number that represented approximately 10 percent of the company's issued shares. Although the official reason given for the buyback program was a desire to increase the company's gearing and create a better

capital structure, many industry watchers suggested that the real reason was to strengthen Jardine Matheson's control of the company. Maintaining control was of extreme importance to the group's controlling family, the Keswicks—descendants of J.J. Keswick, who had merged Jardine Matheson with Chater's fledgling company back in the late 1800s. The Keswicks had maintained rigid control of Jardine and its holdings—including Hong-Kong Land—for more than a century through a complex and unusual cross-shareholding agreement, which also made the company virtually immune to takeover attempts.

Looking Ahead

As of early 2002, HongKong Land had a residential property development underway in Hong Kong, due for completion in 2004. The company also was developing a residential property in Beijing, as part of a joint venture with the Vantone Group, a mainland China investment company. As the new century unfolded, it appeared that HongKong Land had no surprises in store for industry watchers or investors. According to a June 13, 2001 *South China Post* interview with the executive director, Ian Hawksworth, the company planned to continue focusing on Hong Kong and Singapore as bases for commercial development. The company also was looking at Shanghai as a potential development target, according to the article.

Principal Subsidiaries

Hongkong Land China Holdings Limited; Hongkong Land Limited; HongKong Land International Holdings Limited; HongKong Land Infrastructure Holdings Limited; The Hongkong Land Company Ltd.; The Hongkong Land Property Company Ltd.; HKL (11 Chater Road) Limited; HKL (Esplanade) Pte Limited (Singapore); HKL (Prince's Building) Limited; Foundasia (HK) Limited; Mulberry Land Company Limited; Asia Container Terminals Limited (28.5%); Bonus Plus Company Limited (50%); King Kok Investment Limited (40%); Normelle Estates Ltd. (50%); Grosvenor Land Property Fund Limited (50%).

Principal Competitors

Hutchison Whampoa Ltd.; Kerry Properties Limited; New World Development Company Limited.

Further Reading

Clifford, Mark, "The Taipan's Last Chance," *Business Week* (International Edition), April 26, 1999, http://www.businessweek.com/1999/99_17/b3626011.htm?scriptFramed.

Criswell, Colin, *The Taipans of Hong Kong,* Oxford: Oxford University Press, 1981.

Hongkong Land 1889–1989, Hong Kong: Hongkong Land, 1989.

Irvine, Steven, "An Obsession with Control," *FinanceAsia,* July/August 2000, p. 21.

—Etan Vlessing
—update: Shawna Brynildssen

Husky Energy Inc.

707 8th Ave. SW, Box 6525, Station D
Calgary, Alberta T2P 3G7
Canada
Telephone: (403) 298-6111
Fax: (403) 298-7464
Web site: http://www.huskyenergy.ca

Public Company
Incorporated: 1938 as Husky Refining Co.
Employees: 2,500
Sales: C$6.63 billion (2001)
Stock Exchanges: Toronto
Ticker Symbol: HSE
NAIC: 211111 Crude Petroleum and Natural Gas
    Extraction; 213112 Support Activities for Oil and Gas
    Operations; 324110 Petroleum Refineries

Husky Energy Inc. is one of the top integrated oil and natural gas concerns in Canada, carrying out extraction, transport, storage, upgrading, marketing, and retail operations. Most of the company's production activity occurs in western Canada, where Husky's holdings include natural gas reserves in British Columbia, oil and gas fields in the southern regions of Alberta and Saskatchewan, and oil sands deposits in northeast Alberta. In addition, Husky has a long history of working with heavy oil, extracting and refining it into asphalt to be marketed for road construction projects across North America. Alternatively, the heavy crude is sent to the company's Lloydminster Upgrader on the Alberta-Saskatchewan border to be converted into light synthetic crude appropriate for transportation fuel. Other mid- and upstream activities at Husky include the Hussar gas storage facility in Alberta and a network of 580 gas stations operating under the Husky and Mohawk brand names. With an eye toward long-term growth, Husky has begun exploration and development projects off the east coast of Canada, and holds interests in the Terra Nova and White Rose projects. Husky also has exploration and production joint ventures in China. Although headquartered in Calgary, Alberta, the company has been majority owned by a Hong Kong businessman, Li Ka-Shing, and his family since 1986. Li's associate John C.S. Lau, president and CEO of Husky, was instrumental in bringing financial stability to Husky after he joined the company in 1992. Li's son Victor is co-chairman of the board.

The Nielson Era: 1938–78

Husky Energy's roots are in Wyoming. It was there that Glenn Nielson, a rancher from Cardston, Alberta, convinced a farm supply cooperative and a Montana contractor to join him in purchasing two heavy oil refiners. The facilities were organized into the Husky Refining Co. on January 1, 1938, with headquarters in the small town of Cody. The company expanded slowly in the prewar years, with annual revenues in the hundreds of thousands of dollars. Husky Refining gradually acquired tracts of oil-rich land, waiting to develop them until it had enough revenue to proceed without debt. By 1940 the company's assets also included a small chain of gas stations and a trucking line.

The demand for heavy oil skyrocketed during World War II, allowing the young company to attain financial stability for the first time. When the war had run its course, Nielson's Canadian background reasserted itself, and in 1946 he moved one of his refineries to Alberta. Husky Oil and Refining Ltd. was incorporated in Canada the following year as a wholly owned subsidiary of the U.S. company. With headquarters in Calgary, the Canadian company processed heavy oil, producing bunker fuel for railroads and asphalt for highways. In 1953 the Canadian branch separated from its U.S. parent and was renamed Husky Oil Ltd. Both companies went public independently. Operations in Canada gradually outpaced activities south of the border until, in 1960, the Canadian company bought all shares of the U.S. unit.

During the 1960s Husky Oil Ltd. grew into a true integrated company, with producing, refining, and marketing divisions. About C$35 million was invested in the development of heavy oil operations and reserves in the Lloydminster area, and Husky also began exploring for conventional oil. By the end of the decade the company was a major regional presence, with annual revenues in 1970 of about C$175 million. A few years later the OPEC oil embargo pushed oil prices higher and made further expansion possible. Husky bought the marketing and refining assets of Union Oil Company in 1976, an acquisition that included a retail network in western Canada and a refinery in Prince George, British Colombia. Profits that year reached C$30 million on revenues of C$522 million. In the late 1970s Husky began considering a major new undertaking: the construction of an expensive upgrader that could convert heavy oil into synthetic light oil. The company began looking for partners who, like Husky, desired a new outlet for their heavy oil production.

As the company entered 1978, the Nielson family expected to lead Husky comfortably into its fifth decade. But by the end of the year, an outside entrepreneur would have seized control after a month of whirlwind takeover bids. At the beginning of June 1978, Glenn Nielson was chairman of Husky, while his son Jim acted as CEO. The two owned only about 20 percent of the company, but ran it like a private family firm. Then, on June 9, they got a message that Wilbert Hopper, president of the state oil and gas company Petro-Canada, wished to meet with them. He offered to buy out the Nielsons at a C$9 premium over the last recorded trading price. The Nielsons refused; besides the huge tax liability that would face them after such a deal, they did not want the independent Husky absorbed by a concocted state conglomerate. So, acting quickly, they turned to Dr. Armand Hammer, chairman of the Los Angeles-based multinational Occidental Petroleum Corp. Occidental arranged a higher counterbid and also structured the deal to reduce tax consequences for the Nielsons. Both Occidental and Petro-Canada made formal offers and waited for shareholders to accept.

But in the end, control of Husky went to an outsider: Bob Blair, CEO of Alberta Gas Trunk Line Co. Ltd., a company dealing in natural gas pipelines and petrochemicals. Blair had a reputation as a nationalist, progressive oilman with ties to the Liberal Party. He had been buying shares in Husky since early in 1978, and managed to acquire a controlling 37 percent stake by the end of June. The two major contenders were forced to abandon their bidding war. Under Blair's ownership, the Nielsons stayed on as consultants, but soon, dissatisfied with their reduced role at Husky, sold out their share and moved back to Wyoming to concentrate on other enterprises.

Turbulent Expansion: 1979–91

By May 1979, Alberta Gas Trunk Line held 68 percent of Husky. Blair renamed AGTL "Nova Corp." in 1980. That year Marathon Oil Co. made an offer for Husky, but the transaction was abandoned at the request of U.S. Steel, which was engaged in a friendly takeover of Marathon. So Nova began pouring money into Husky, which in 1982 ranked 13th in Canadian oil

production. Husky acquired a small producing company, Candel Oil Ltd., built a new refinery at Lloydminster, and moved into an elegant new office complex in downtown Calgary. Exploration began in North Africa, Indonesia, Australia and offshore Newfoundland. Bigger was better throughout the 1980s. Husky did, however, get rid of its Denver-based U.S. subsidiary in 1984. The unit's oil and gas production operations were sold to Marathon Oil Co. and the downstream operations, to a group of investors that included three former Husky executives. The transaction helped reduce Husky's growing debt.

Husky's expansion policy began to appear ill-advised in the second half of the decade, when Arab nations flooded the world market with cheap oil. Husky recorded its first year-end loss in 1986, and share price plummeted. Soon Husky was looking for a private partner to prop up the company's finances. The company found a willing investor in Li Ka-shing, a Hong Kong billionaire with holdings in Canada and a friendly business relationship with Blair. In a deal worth about C$855 million, Li bought a 43 percent stake in Husky Oil through his Hutchison Whampoa trading company. Li's family acquired another 9 percent, and 5 percent was purchased by the Canadian Imperial Bank of Commerce. Nova was left with a 43 percent stake. Husky was delisted from the stock market, but Blair continued to run the company. With restored optimism, Husky looked for good returns in the coming decade.

Continued expansion and low oil prices, however, prevented Husky from attaining financial prosperity. In particular, the Lloydminster Bi-Provincial Upgrader project, initiated in 1988, was a financial black hole for many years. In theory, the upgrader was to make a profit on the differential between the prices of heavy and light oil. If the differential was wide enough and the upgrading process fairly efficient, Husky could make money converting heavy oil into light. But both the high cost of the project and the uncertainty of oil prices discouraged potential industry partners from joining Husky on the project. Consequently, Husky President Art Price turned to the government. Early in 1984 he succeeded in convincing the Liberal-controlled federal government to provide financing, but the deal fell through when the Progressive Conservatives gained control in the fall elections.

After negotiating for several more years and trimming the price of construction, Husky finally won a deal. In 1988 the provincial governments of Alberta and Saskatchewan, together with the federal government, agreed to fund 75 percent of the estimated C$1.2 billion cost of constructing an upgrader. Even though Husky only provided one quarter of the equity for the deal, it was to receive half of the profits. Blair insisted that the jobs and tax revenue generated by the upgrader would make the deal worthwhile for all parties. The upgrader would process 46,000 barrels per day of heavy crude, a welcome development in a market that was oversupplied with heavy oil. Husky commenced construction of the upgrader, persevering over the next few years despite about C$300 million in cost overruns.

Expansion continued into the 1990s amid poor performance. In 1988, Husky carried out a takeover of Canterra Energy Ltd., a large Calgary-based conventional oil company, in a deal that made Husky one of the ten largest oil and gas producers in Canada. The company also built a gas-processing plant north of

Key Dates:

1938: Glenn Nielson founds Husky Refining Co. in Cody, Wyoming.
1946: Nielson moves some Husky operations to Alberta, Canada.
1953: The U.S. and Canadian companies separate and go public.
1960: Canadian Husky Oil Ltd. acquires all shares of the U.S. unit.
1978: Entrepreneur Bob Blair acquires a controlling share in Husky Oil.
1987: Burdened with the debt of expansion, Blair sells a majority stake in Husky to Hong Kong investor Li Ka-Shing.
1991: Li acquires all but 5 percent of Husky and installs new management.
1998: Husky invests heavily in acquisition and development of properties offshore Newfoundland.
2000: Husky merges with Renaissance Energy and goes public.

Calgary, but lost out on a potentially lucrative supplier for the plant. In 1990 Shell Canada Ltd. and Husky were battling over who would develop a major gas discovery near the town of Caroline, a village 100 miles northwest of Calgary. Once partners, the two companies now had competing proposals for development. The town of Caroline favored Shell's proposal, which would build a new gas plant nearby. Husky, on the other hand, wanted to transport the gas 35 miles by pipeline to its Ram River gas plant. Shell's plan won approval that fall from the Alberta Resources Conservation Board.

Hong Kong Taking Charge: 1992

By 1992, it was clear that Blair's aggressive expansion had only pulled Husky further into debt. The company lost C$315 billion in 1991. Once again, Li stepped in with an offer from his Hutchison Whampoa holding company. He negotiated a deal late in 1991 to buy Nova's remaining 43 percent stake in Husky for approximately C$325 million. Li then took a stronger hand in management of the company. He sent John Chin-Sung Lau to Husky in 1992 as vice-president. Although Lau had no experience in the oil industry, he had successfully turned around some of Li's other businesses with a strict focus on efficiency and profits.

Lau's first years at Husky were rocky, and employees felt that Lau and President Art Price were competing for their loyalty. Price eventually resigned in mid-1993, and Lau became CEO. Now the undisputed leader, he set about ridding the company of useless undeveloped properties, laid off hundreds of employees, and scrapped the company's ''quality work environment'' initiative. *Canadian Business* wrote that Husky was gaining a reputation as a bad place to work, marred by reports of sexual harassment and disrespect toward female employees. A former employee was quoted as saying, ''Lau was very hard-nosed, all teeth and claws. He was very abrasive.'' Nevertheless, by 1996 Husky was performing better and Lau was de-

claring himself willing to give employees more access to management. The company made a C$35 million profit in 1996 on revenues of C$2.11 billion.

The Lloydminster upgrader was also emerging from years of dismal performance. The upgrader began operation in 1992 and lost C$140 million in the first three years of operation, due to the fact that the cost of upgrading was higher than the heavy oil-light oil price differential. The federal and provincial Alberta governments sold their stakes in the project in 1994, but Husky and the Saskatchewan government held on to 50 percent stakes in the hopes that the facility would eventually turn a profit. Eventually the upgrader reorganized to operate more efficiently, the price differential improved, and the upgrader made a combined C$26 million in 1996 and 1997. Saskatchewan managed to recover all the money it had put into the project and sold its interest to Husky for C$310 million in 1998.

Looking Eastward: Late 1990s

With a financial situation that looked fairly secure in the short term, Husky began to focus more attention on projects that held promise for long-term profits. The Canadian oil industry began extensively developing properties off the east coast of Canada by the late 1990s. Husky had a minority interest in the second project in the area, Terra Nova, and was the operator and majority holder for a third project, White Rose. Both properties were located in the Jeanne d'Arc Basin just offshore of Newfoundland. Husky had been exploring in the east coast area since 1982 and then invested heavily there in 1998 and 1999. Extensive work at Terra Nova began in mid-1998, when a floating production and storage system was constructed. Production commenced there in January 2002 after delays. The White Rose project was in an earlier stage of development. Husky, working with partner Petro-Canada, struck oil on the site in 1999, but subsequent drilling in 2000 was less promising. After carefully reconsidering the prospects at White Rose, Husky announced in March 2002 that it would move ahead with development.

The company was also looking even farther east, working on projects in China. In April 1998 Husky began testing production from wells in the Pucheng oil field in Henan province, in a joint venture with China National Petroleum Corp. In late 2000 the company also signed an agreement to develop two fields in the South China Sea with the China National Offshore Oil Corporation. Other expansion included the purchase of Mohawk Canada Limited for C$102 million in July 1998. The acquisition added about 300 gas stations and an ethanol plant to Husky's assets. Profits were rising steadily after 1998, with net earnings in 1999 reaching C$43 million on revenues of C$2.79 billion.

In the summer of 2000 Husky took a step that catapulted it into the leading ranks of Canada's oil and gas producers. The company merged with a smaller public oil concern, Renaissance Energy Ltd., for approximately C$3.02 billion. The combined company, renamed Husky Energy Inc., took over Renaissance Energy's listing on the Toronto Stock Exchange. When the deal was announced, there was some negative reaction to the idea of a large private company swallowing a small public company, and Husky tried to build trust by releasing an unprecedented amount of information about its finances and operations. When the deal went through, Li and his family controlled about 70 percent of the new public company. Husky's leadership said that Renaissance, which worked primarily with small low-risk oil pools in Western Canada, would provide steady income to finance capital development at the offshore Newfoundland fields, expand retail stations in Canada, and work with oil sands in Alberta.

Results for 2000—earnings of C$464 million on revenue of C$5.09 billion—reached record levels, and were followed in 2001 with earnings of C$201 million on revenues of C$6.63 billion. Now that Husky was an attractive investment, Li was interested in selling. There was speculation in the fall of 2001 that France's TotalFinaElf was a potential buyer, but talks were postponed. In the early months of 2002 Husky confirmed that it was in talks with PetroChina, a massive company that could easily raise the funds to buy Husky. The company's future ownership was up in the air, as Li showed himself open to selling the firm he had helped guide to prosperity.

Principal Subsidiaries

579518 Alberta Ltd.; 147212 Canada Ltd.; Pounder Emulsions' Operations Ltd.; Husky BPU Operations Ltd.; Husky Oil Limited; Husky (U.S.A.) Inc.; HOI Resources Co.; Longridge Resources Inc.; Avid Oil & Gas Ltd. (38%); Carnduff Gas Limited (94%); Husky Energy International Sulphur Corporation; Husky Oil China Ltd.; Husky Oil (Madura) Ltd (Alberta); Husky Oil Overseas Ltd. (Cayman Islands).

Principal Competitors

Imperial Oil Ltd.; Shell Canada Ltd.; Petro-Canada.

Further Reading

Bayless, Alan, "Husky Plans to Buy Polysar's Canterra for $329.2 Million," *Wall Street Journal*, June 17, 1988, p. 1.
——, "Nova, an Alberta Corp., Plans to Sell Husky Oil Control to Hong Kong Group," *Wall Street Journal*, December 4, 1986. p. 1.
Burton, Brian, "Making the Grade: Husky Oil Steps Boldly Where the Multinationals Wouldn't Go," *Oilweek*, November 16, 1992, p. 20.
Carey, Susan, "Marathon Oil to Buy Husky's U.S. Subsidiary," *Wall Street Journal*, March 30, 1983, p. 1.
Carlisle, Tamsin, "Husky Oil Agrees to $2.06 Billion Plan to Purchase Renaissance Energy Ltd.," *Wall Street Journal*, June 20, 2000, p. C21.
Ferry, Jon, "Canadian Oil Giants Square Off over Gas Discovery," *Oil Daily*, February 6, 1990, p. 1.
"Heavy Oil Suffers in Downturn," *Petroleum Economist*, April 1998, p. 56.
Hutchinson, Brian, "Energy Roughneck," *Canadian Business*, August 1996, pp. 20–23.
"A Joint Venture of Canada's Husky Oil and China National Petroleum Corp.," *Oil and Gas Journal*, April 6, 1998, p. 3.
Ludwick, Laurie, "Husky Upbeat on Upgrader's Future," *Financial Post*, August 6, 1994, p. 4.
McMurdy, Deirdre, "A Billionaire's Bargain," *MacLean's*, November 4, 1991, p. 48.
Morton, Peter, "Shell Bests Husky in Bid to Develop Big Gas Field," *Oil Daily*, September 7, 1990.
Pike, David, "Canada's Husky Oil Comes in from the Cold in Bid to Charm Shareholders," *Oil Daily*, June 22, 2000.
Reid, Wes, "Husky's Offshore Leverage Boosted with Renaissance," *Oilweek*, September 4, 2000, p. 1.
Sharpe, Sydney, "Scratching at the Door," *Financial Post*, March 29, 1997, p. 12.
"Takeover Dogfight," *Canadian Business*, September 1988, p. 158.
Warn, Ken, "Husky in Talks with Chinese Oil Group," *Financial Times*, February 20, 2002, p. 33.
Watson, Laurie, "Operation Upgrade," *Saskatchewan Business*, May-June 1995, p. 17.

—Sarah Ruth Lorenz

Information Holdings Inc.

2777 Summer Street, Suite 209
Stamford, Connecticut 06905
U.S.A.
Telephone: (203) 961-9106
Fax: (203) 961-1431
Web site: http://www.informationholdings.com

Public Company
Incorporated: 1996 as Information Ventures L.L.C.
Employees: 468
Sales: $105.3 million (2001)
Stock Exchanges: New York
Ticker Symbol: IHI
NAIC: 511120 Periodical Publishers; 511130 Book
    Publishers; 511140 Database and Directory
    Publishers; 511210 Software Publishers

Information Holdings Inc. (IHI) provides a wide range of information products and services, including reference works, journals and other subscription services, and electronic databases on CD-ROM and over the Internet. Its principal fields of activity include intellectual property management, especially patent and trademark information, and scientific, technical, and medical (STM) and professional publishing. Since beginning operations in 1997, the company has grown through acquisitions as well as internally. Its strategy for growth has been to acquire businesses in niche markets, increase revenue and profits organically through new product development, improve operating efficiencies, and attract and retain superior management.

Began Operations in 1997

Information Ventures L.L.C., the predecessor to Information Holdings Inc. (IHI), was formed in December 1996 as a limited liability corporation by Mason P. Slaine, a publishing entrepreneur and former president of Thomson Financial Services, and venture capital firm Warburg, Pincus Ventures, L.P. Slaine had been involved in several successful publishing ventures, starting in 1982 when he and other partners acquired Dealers'

Digest, Inc., a financial publishing company, for $800,000. Four years later they sold it for $40 million. Slaine's second venture, Rand Data Services, Inc., was a financial information company that he founded in 1987 with an equity investment of $1.5 million. In 1988, it was merged into The Thomson Corporation's Securities Data Company, Inc., for which Slaine and his associates received $25 million over the next several years. Slaine followed that up with a successful turnaround at *Chemical Week* magazine, which he and a partner acquired for $9.5 million in 1988 and sold in three stages between 1991 and 1996 for $23 million. From 1994 to 1996, Slaine served as president of Thomson Financial Services, where he oversaw numerous acquisitions and increased the company's revenue from $407 million to $790 million.

It was undoubtedly Slaine's ability to create value in acquired publishing properties that enabled him to attract the financial backing of Warburg, Pincus for Information Ventures. With Slaine as its president and chief executive officer (CEO), the company acquired CRC Press from The Times Mirror Co. in January 1997 and began operations. CRC Press was a mid-sized scientific, technical, and medical (STM) and professional publisher. From its beginnings in Cleveland, Ohio, at the start of the 20th century as the Chemical Rubber Company, CRC Press became highly regarded in the STM field with the publication of such titles as *The Handbook of Chemistry and Physics*, published annually since 1913. At the time it was acquired by Information Ventures, CRC Press was headquartered in Boca Raton, Florida.

Information Ventures completed two related acquisitions at the same time it acquired CRC Press. One was St. Lucie Press, a professional publisher, and Auerbach, a provider of technology-oriented print and electronic subscription-based products, which was acquired from The Thomson Corporation.

In July 1997, the company acquired MicroPatent, one of the largest commercial providers of patent information in the world and a leading source of intellectual property information products and services. MicroPatent was established in 1989 as a joint venture between British CD-ROM publisher Chadwyck-Healey Ltd. and microfilm patent publisher OPUS Publications Inc. of New Haven, Connecticut. Also located in New Haven, MicroPatent introduced its first CD-ROM with patent information at the end of 1989. For as little as $60, libraries could purchase data for 150,000 patents on one disc. In 1992, the company began creating Patent Technology Centers, the first of which opened in February 1992 at the U.S. Patent and Trademark Depository Library in Science Park, New Haven. The MicroPatent Patent Technology Center was a computerized, CD-ROM-based system for researching information on U.S., European, and Patent Cooperation Treaty (PCT) patents. Companies could use the Patent Technology Center as a research tool to track competitive developments in their industry. MicroPatent hoped to provide such tools to all 73 U.S. Patent and Trademark Depository Libraries.

Other CD-ROM products developed by MicroPatent included *Who Invented What,* which was launched in 1993 and contained full-text abstracts of every patent issued in the United States during the previous year. The company also issued subject-oriented CD-ROMs, including Chemical PatentImages and BioTech PatentImages, both of which were offered as current subscriptions with monthly or biweekly updates and optional-purchase backfiles.

In 1994, MicroPatent offered Patent BBS, a free online service that provided information on new patents worldwide. It was the company's first online service offering. In 1995, the company introduced World Patent Alert, a series of 32 electronic newsletters that tracked emerging technology developments around the world and offered fully searchable information on U.S., European, and world patents up to one month before other online services. The 32 separate electronic newsletters were available monthly on diskette or over the Internet.

Before the end of 1995, MicroPatent's Patent Server was up and running on the Internet. It contained more than 1.5 million patent documents in image form and allowed users to do full-text searches of every patent issued in the United States during the previous two weeks. Users could also view, purchase, and receive copies of any patent issued since 1975. MicroPatent offered a range of additional services through Patent Server.

The company also introduced MarkSearch in 1995. It was a new research tool for U.S. trademarks and consisted of a six CD-ROM set available for $1,950 per year. It contained fully searchable text and images of every live trademark registered by the U.S. Patent and Trademark Office since 1884—more than 1.5 million trademarks in all. In 1996, MicroPatent published the Trademark Checker, a low-cost ($199) CD-ROM that contained the complete U.S. database of federal trademarks dating back to 1884. For an additional $699, customers could subscribe to monthly updates to Trademark Checker. By the end of 1996, MicroPatent made Trademark Checker available to subscribers over the Internet.

In 1997, MicroPatent began offering commercial patent information for free over the Internet at its patent web site, PatentWeb. The company provided free access to its Online Gazette, formerly priced at $600 per year, which contained summary information on each of the approximately 2,500 U.S. patents issued each week. MicroPatent anticipated that free access to its Online Gazette would increase demand for its PatentImages downloading business.

Company Reorganization and IPO: 1998

In 1998, Information Ventures reorganized from a limited liability corporation to a Delaware corporation for the purpose of going public. The new corporation, Information Holdings Inc. (IHI), assumed control of all of the assets of Information Ventures when it went public on August 7, 1998. The company's stock was traded on the New York Stock Exchange and offered at an initial price of $12 per share. Net proceeds of approximately $51 million were set aside for general corporate purposes, including acquisitions.

During 1998, IHI strengthened its position in the STM and professional markets by acquiring a line of engineering titles from Krause Communications, the McGee line of business titles, and a line of advanced mathematics titles from Addison Wesley Longman. IHI also replaced the senior management of CRC Press and implemented plans to increase CRC's frontlist of new titles and editions from 280 titles in 1998 to between 350 and 400 in 1999. Some of that increase was due to the acquisition of mathematics, statistics, and chemical titles of Chapman & Hall from Wolters Kluwer N.V. in August 1998. CRC also had a backlist of some 4,000 titles. By revising its operating procedures, CRC was able to reduce direct costs and improve overall gross margins from 65 percent in 1997 to 74 percent in 1998. For all of 1998, CRC contributed 83 percent of IHI's revenue, while MicroPatent contributed 17 percent.

For 1998, IHI reported revenue of $46.7 million, up from $34.9 million in 1997. Net income in 1998 was $4.8 million, compared to a net loss of $4.9 million in 1997. The improvement in net income was attributed primarily to increased gross profits of $11.6 million and increased interest income.

Strengthening the Intellectual Property Business: 1999

IHI's intellectual property business initially consisted of MicroPatent and its Internet- and CD-ROM-based patent information products. During 1999, MicroPatent released PatSearch

FullText, an Internet-based resource that included full-text patent documentation for U.S., European, and world patents of the current year. MicroPatent also made its Special Collection of more than 25 million patent copies from more than 45 patent authorities worldwide available commercially.

In 1999, IHI made several acquisitions that strengthened its position in the intellectual property field. Optipat, Inc. and Faxpat, Inc., two companies that provided print and Internet-delivered patent information to the legal and corporate markets, were acquired in January and June, respectively. Master Data Center, Inc. was acquired in August. Founded in 1971, Master Data Center specialized in patent and trademark management, including portfolio management software and payment services. The next month IHI acquired the Corporate Intelligence business of Innovator Corp. and formed CorporateIntelligence.com, an Internet-focused business unit.

By the end of 1999, IHI's intellectual property business included patent information services offered through MicroPatent, Optipat, and Faxpat, and patent annuity services offered through Master Data Center. In addition, IHI was developing Trademark.com, which would enable full trademark searches to be performed over the Internet. The company was also developing an Internet-based patent licensing service that would provide a marketplace for patent holders and qualified buyers.

IHI's other principal business was scientific and technology information, consisting of CRC Press. CRC published two major groups of products, reference books and subscription services. In 1999, CRC published 404 new titles, compared to 282 in 1998, mainly in the areas of life sciences, hard sciences, environmental sciences, and information technology and business. CRC's subscription services included newsletters published by its Food Chemical News division, 17 journals in selected scientific areas, Auerbach products published for the information technology market, and electronic databases available through site licenses or on CD-ROM. CRC's electronic databases were focused on chemistry, food chemistry, information technology, and engineering and included chemical dictionaries as well as electronic versions of its major print products.

For all of 1999, IHI's intellectual property businesses contributed 30 percent of revenue, while its scientific and technology information businesses provided 70 percent of revenue. IHI reported revenue of $58.8 million for 1999, an increase of 26 percent. Net income was $6 million.

Introducing New Intellectual Property Services and Entering the IT Learning Market: 2000

New developments in IHI's intellectual property businesses in 2000 were primarily Internet-based initiatives. The company launched CI.com (CorporateIntelligence.com) to provide access to existing Internet services. In June, CI.com launched Trademark.com, a web-based database of trademark information. On Trademark.com users could search a comprehensive set of U.S. federal, state, and common law databases over the Internet. This marked the first time that information on more than 800,000 common law trademarks was available on the Web.

In the area of patent technology licensing services, IHI launched PATEX.com, an Internet exchange for licensing patents and technology that was operated jointly with BTG International Inc., a commercial technology provider. PATEX.com included both the Internet licensing of patent rights and a service that facilitated more complex licensing transactions. During 2000, PATEX.com was offered as a free service with more than 15,000 patents and technologies available for licensing. In 2001, PATEX.com began generating revenue through listing fees and transaction fees for licensing transactions that were completed through the service.

In November 2000, IHI entered the information technology (IT) learning market with the acquisition of Transcender Corporation for $60 million. The company was a leading provider of online IT certification products, including exam simulations for certifications from major hardware manufacturers and software publishers. Transcender's customer base consisted primarily of IT professionals seeking certification in various product areas and programming languages.

For 2000, IHI reported revenue of $73.3 million, an increase of 24.7 percent over 1999. IHI's intellectual property businesses accounted for 41 percent of revenue, while CRC Press contributed 53 percent. Transcender provided the remaining 6 percent of IHI's revenue in 2000. For the year net income rose to $7.1 million.

Numerous Acquisitions in 2001

IHI grew internally as well as through acquisitions in 2001. In February, it launched a full-service licensing and consulting division, LPS Group (Licensing Products and Services), as part of its intellectual property group. LPS offered a wide range of online and offline services, including portfolio mining, portfolio mapping, contingency patent licensing, and general IP consulting. It also included the PATEX.com licensing exchange and a new exchange, Patent Triage, for patents that were ready to be abandoned.

In March 2001, IHI announced two European-based acquisitions. One was GSI Office Management GMBH, a German-based provider of intellectual property management software, in which IHI took a 49 percent interest with an option to acquire the remaining 51 percent in three years. The other European-based acquisition involved the IDRAC business of IMS Health. Based in France, IDRAC was a leading provider of regulatory and intellectual property information to pharmaceutical companies worldwide. Founded in 1993, IDRAC developed and maintained an international regulatory affairs database for the pharmaceutical industry.

In May 2001, IHI announced it had added the U.K.-based publisher Parthenon Publishing Group Ltd. to its scientific and technical information group. Parthenon was acquired for $8 million and became part of CRC Press. Its publishing program was focused on medical and environmental reference works and included books, journals, and electronic products.

IHI's final acquisition in 2001, was Liquent Inc., a provider of electronic regulatory publishing solutions to the life sciences industries. Its flagship software product was CoreDossier. Liquent's software and services were used by 33 of the world's top 50 biopharmaceutical companies to assemble and publish regulatory reports and dossiers. IHI completed its tender offer for Liquent in December 2001, and in February 2002 Liquent and IDRAC combined their operations. The new organization was known as Liquent/IDRAC in Europe and as Liquent in the United States and elsewhere.

For 2001, IHI reported revenue of $105.3 million, an increase of 43.7 percent over 2000. Net income increased to $7.8 million. The company generated strong growth in 2001 and projected earnings in 2002 would double. It also enjoyed a strong financial position with more than $50 million in cash and investments and no debt. The company planned to grow internally as well as through further acquisitions.

Principal Subsidiaries

CorporateIntelligence.com; CRC Press LLC; GSI Office Management GMBH (Germany; 49%); IDRAC (France); Liquent, Inc.; Master Data Center Inc.; MicroPatent LLC; Parthenon Press (U.K.); Transcender LLC.

Principal Divisions

Intellectual Property Group; IT Learning; LPS Group; Scientific and Technical Information; Trademark.com.

Principal Competitors

Academic Press; Chemical Abstract Service (American Chemical Society); CCH Corsearch (unit of Wolters Kluwer, Netherlands); Computer Packages, Inc.; Derwent Information; European Patent Office; John Wiley & Sons, Inc.; McGraw-Hill Companies, Inc.; Thomson & Thomson.

Further Reading

"Complete U.S. Patent Library Now Available on the Internet," *Information Today,* October 1995, p. 53.

"Database Race to the Web," *Information Today,* September 1996, p. 22.

"Electronic Newsletters Track Emerging Technologies," *Online,* March-April 1995, p. 9.

"Free Online Service from MicroPatent Offers Instant Access to Emerging Technologies," *Information Today,* July-August 1994, p. 3.

"Free Patent Searching Offered by MicroPatent," *Link-Up,* September-October 1994, p. 19.

Hurst, Jill Ann, "The New Kid on the Trademark Block," *EContent,* October 2000, p. 51.

"IBM, MicroPatent Add to Free Patent Information Offerings," *Information Today,* February 1997, p. 1.

"International Cooperation Yields Unified Format for Patents," *Information Today,* November 1991, p. 24.

"MarkSearch Trademark Research System from MicroPatent," *Information Today,* October 1995, p. 31.

"MicroPatent," *Online,* May 1999, p. 14.

"MicroPatent Abstracts Disc Covers 10 Technology Areas," *Link-Up,* March-April 1993, p. 13.

"MicroPatent Donates Patent Technology Centers," *Information Today,* April 1992, p. 30.

"MicroPatent Intros Complete Chemical Patent Collection on CD-ROM," *Information Today,* May 1992, p. 30.

"MicroPatent Loads Biotechnology Patents," *Link-Up,* November-December 1992, p. 23.

"MicroPatent Makes Available Collections of Patent Documents," *Information Today,* March 1999, p. 32.

"MicroPatent Presents Automated Patent Searching on CD-ROM," *Information Today,* December 1989, p. 23.

"PATEX," *EContent,* August 2000, p. 10.

"PatSearch FullText Now Available on the Web," *Information Today,* January 1999, p. 21.

Quint, Barbara, "Trademark.com: A New Alternative for Trademark Searchers," *Information Today,* June 2000, p. 30.

"U.S. Trademark Library Now on CD-ROM," *Information Today,* February 1996, p. 28.

—David P. Bianco

International Paper Company

400 Atlantic Street
Stamford, Connecticut 06921
U.S.A.
Telephone: (203) 541-8000
Fax: (203) 358-6444
Web site: http://www.internationalpaper.com

Public Company
Incorporated: 1898
Employees: 113,000
Sales: $26.36 billion (2001)
Stock Exchanges: New York Montreal Swiss Amsterdam
Ticker Symbol: IP
NAIC: 113110 Timber Tract Operations; 113210 Forest Nurseries and Gathering of Forest Products; 321113 Sawmills; 321210 Veneer, Plywood, and Engineered Wood Product Manufacturing; 322110 Pulp Mills; 322121 Paper (Except Newsprint) Mills; 322130 Paperboard Mills; 322212 Folding Paperboard Box Manufacturing; 322215 Nonfolding Sanitary Food Container Manufacturing; 322233 Stationery, Tablet, and Related Product Manufacturing; 422110 Printing and Writing Paper Wholesalers; 422130 Industrial and Personal Service Paper Wholesalers

International Paper Company (IP) is the world's largest producer of paper, packaging, and forest products. Within specific industry segments, the firm is the world's leading producer of printing and writing papers and of bleached packaging board, as well as the second largest maker of containerboard in the United States. IP owns or manages about 12 million acres of forestlands in the United States, primarily in the South, and owns, manages, or has an interest in nearly 11 million acres in other countries. The company holds majority ownership of Auckland, New Zealand-based Carter Holt Harvey, one of the largest forest-products companies in the Southern Hemisphere. IP also operates a distribution business—operating in North America as xpedx and in Europe as Paperteries de France, Scaldia (Neth-

erlands), and Impap (Poland)—which distributes printing paper, packaging, and graphic arts products to industrial wholesalers and end users. Nearly 80 percent of the products distributed are made by other companies. International Paper began as a major player in its core industry and expanded through mergers, acquisitions, and product development. By the early 21st century, IP had operations in nearly 50 countries and was exporting its products to more than 130 nations.

Early History

Established on January 31, 1898, the firm resulted from a merger of 17 pulp and paper mills located throughout five northeastern states. The new company had one million acres of timberlands, with the properties ranging as far north as Canada, and streams running through the properties were used to run the mills with hydroelectric power. By 1900, the mills provided 60 percent of U.S. newsprint. In 1903, in order to enhance its research and development efforts, the company opened the Central Test Bureau in Glens Falls, New York.

The company's power interests played a dominant role in its early years. As household electricity demand grew in the 1920s, the firm established large hydroelectric plants and power companies. At one time, it produced enough electricity to light all of New England and most of Quebec and Ontario. In 1928 International Paper & Power Company was organized in Massachusetts to acquire International Paper. IP continued to operate as a subsidiary of International Paper & Power. In 1935 the United States passed the Public Utility Holdings Act, making it illegal for an organization to run both an industrial firm and a power company. The law signified the end of International Paper's involvement in the energy and power business. Instead, the company began to focus on key areas such as paper and packaging.

The company expanded into the southern United States in the 1920s and 1930s, primarily because trees could be grown more quickly and in greater volume than they could in the North. It also maximized its use of the trees through the kraft process, which involved use of a very strong pulp to manufacture packaging materials.

In June 1941 a new company was incorporated to acquire the assets of International Paper & Power Company. The new parent company was named International Paper Company to reflect the change from a paper and power company to a manufacturer devoted solely to paper. During World War II, International Paper did what it could to support the war effort. Its contributions included the development of nitrate pulp for use in explosives and the development of a waterproof board called V-board—victory board—which was used to make boxes to send food and other supplies to the troops. The new technology, along with the wartime inventions of other manufacturers, led to increased competition after the war. As a result, IP began to invest more capital in research and development. Shortly after the war, it established the Erling Riis Research Laboratory in Mobile, Alabama.

An emphasis on packaging products also characterized the firm's progress in the 1940s. In December 1940 it acquired the Agor Manufacturing Company, which included three subsidiaries and four container plants in Illinois, Kansas, Massachusetts, and New Jersey. In June 1941 IP merged the Southern Kraft Corporation with its main business. Previously a subsidiary, Southern Kraft owned eight kraft board and paper mills in the southern United States. IP also bought the assets of a shipping-container maker, the Scharff-Koken Manufacturing Company.

In 1947 IP merged with Single Service Containers Inc., a manufacturer of milk containers, and in 1952 it founded the International Paper Company Foundation, a nonprofit organization developed to support charitable, educational, and scientific efforts. IP acquired the capital stock of a specialty coated paper manufacturer, A.M. Collins Manufacturing Company, of Philadelphia, in 1955. In 1957 the latter merged with IP. In 1958 IP bought Lord Baltimore Press, Inc., a Maryland manufacturer of cartons and labels.

IP's Canadian subsidiary, Canadian International Paper Company, also made its share of acquisitions in the 1950s. These included Brown Corporation in 1954; Hygrade Containers Ltd. in 1955; and Anglo American Paper Company, Mid-West Paper Ltd., Vancouver Pacific Paper Company, and Victoria Paper Company in 1959.

1960s and 1970s: Diversifying Beyond the Core, with Mixed Results

During the following decade, new technology improved both product design and manufacturing processes. In 1962, for example, IP began using computers to control paper machines at its mill in Georgetown, South Carolina. A year later, it introduced polyethylene-coated milk cartons. In addition to new products, the 1960s presented IP with challenges, including development of new production and management techniques. Since 1943 IP had been headed by the Hinman family; John Hinman was chief executive from 1943 to 1962, and his son, Edward B. Hinman, held the post from 1966 to 1969. Various associates appointed by the elder Hinman ran the company from 1962 to 1966.

During the 1960s IP continued to grow internally and took giant leaps toward diversification—many of them in haste—and learned that bigger is not always better. IP had emphasized production efficiency as a means of increasing output for most of the century. IP's production muscle came at the expense of marketing expertise, which lagged. The production emphasis led to overexpansion of paper plants, which in turn resulted in low profit margins. To increase profitability, IP diversified, with little success, into areas as far ranging as residential construction, prefabricated housing, nonwoven fabrics, consumer facial tissue, and disposable diapers. It also moved into lumber and plywood but found equally little success in those areas. White paper, paperboard, and pulp still accounted for more than half of the company's sales during the early 1970s; converted paper products comprised one-third; lumber, plywood, and other building products totaled 9 percent; and the remaining sales came from real estate, packaging systems, and nonwoven fabrics.

By 1971 IP's long-term debt, which had been almost nonexistent in 1965, reached $564 million. When Edward Hinman took over in 1966, the company's greatest asset was its large share of real estate, including eight million acres that it owned and 15.5 million that it leased. In 1968 Hinman sought the help of Frederick Kappel, formerly chairman of AT&T. The two ran the company together, but after earnings declined by 30 percent in 1970, Kappel and a team of outside directors replaced Hinman the following year with Paul A. Gorman, another AT&T executive. Gorman faced the challenge of returning the company to profitability.

Gorman started the long-term task by setting up a $78 million reserve to cover write-offs of inefficient facilities; closing a specialty mill in York Haven, Pennsylvania; and closing various plants in Ecuador, Italy, Puerto Rico, and West Germany. In 1972 he also sold most of Donald L. Bren Co., a southern California house builder acquired in 1970, and Spacemakers Inc., a prefabricated-housing subsidiary. The company also sold its interest in C.R. Bard, Inc., a medical equipment manufacturer.

From 1966 to 1972, IP had spent $1 billion to increase its paper-making and -converting capacity by 25 percent. During the early 1970s the paper industry headed toward cyclical recession.

IP laid off 7 percent of its employees. Gorman felt that the firm needed more financial control and saw to it that decisions made by the company's manufacturing groups were reviewed from a financial, marketing, and manufacturing perspective. In addition, all projects had to show a minimum after-tax profit of 10 percent. Ailing plants were improved, sold, or shut down. Gorman also reorganized international operations on a product line basis. His efforts were successful. Earnings of $69 million in 1971 were the lowest in ten years, despite record earnings just two years earlier, but they jumped 30 percent the first six months of 1972.

In 1973 J. Stanford Smith joined IP as vice-chairman. Previously a senior vice-president with General Electric, Smith eventually would replace Gorman as chairman. Smith felt that one way to increase profitability was to develop natural resources on the company's land. He devised a plan to purchase General Crude Oil Company, which IP did in 1974 for $489 million. The business was unsuccessful, however, in locating major oil or gas deposits on IP's land. Five years later, in order to raise capital for acquisitions and internal growth, the company sold General Crude Oil's oil and natural gas operations to Gulf Oil Corporation for $650 million. In addition, IP sold a Panama

City, Florida, pulp and linerboard mill to Southwest Forest Industries for $220 million.

Early 1980s: Major Plant Modernization Program

Between 1975 and 1980, IP's operating profits were mediocre. Again it turned to new management for help, and in 1979 Edwin Gee stepped in as chairman. A chemical engineer, Gee recognized that many of the company's 16 pulp and paper mills—all built in the 1920s and 1930s—were wasting labor and energy. Immediately, he instituted a $6 billion program to modernize the plants. Gee's goal was to turn the world's largest paper company into one of the lowest-cost producers of white paper and packaging materials, thus making it one of the most profitable papermakers as well.

To raise money for Gee's plan IP sold its remaining interest in General Crude Oil Company for $763 million and used the profits to buy Bodcaw Company of Dallas in 1979. Bodcaw added a highly efficient linerboard mill in Pineville, Louisiana, and 420,000 acres of prime timberland. In 1981 IP sold Canadian International Paper for US$900 million. In addition, Gee increased the research-and-development budget and reduced IP's labor force by 20 percent. By 1982 he had raised US$2 billion, aided by sales of land, timber, and other subsidiaries.

After determining that only two of the six major packaging mills were operating efficiently, Gee sold one mill, shut down three others, and invested $600 million in the Mansfield, Louisiana, mill. In April 1981 IP unveiled a new southern pine plywood and lumber manufacturing plant in Springhill, Louisiana. The $60 million facility, the brainchild of Gee, featured the latest computerized process controls and supplied the containerboard mill in Mansfield plus paper and pulp mills at Camden, Arkansas, and in Bastrop, Louisiana.

In the same year, John Georges became chief operating officer. His solution to IP's production problems was not to build new plants but to remodel existing facilities. The company also spent $500 million on remodeling a Georgetown, South Carolina, mill, changing its product focus in the process. Instead of brown linerboard, a cyclical product, part of the plant was set up to make white papers. The white paper business was to offer a faster-growing and more stable market.

In addition, Georges began a $350 million project to convert another mill in Mobile, Alabama. The 60-year-old facility, which housed the company's last remaining newsprint machine, was also remodeled to produce white papers in 1985, thus marking the end of the company's longstanding newsprint business. In 1987, newsprint prices began a steady decline.

A recession in the early 1980s meant further delays but the investments began to bear fruit in the mid-1980s. As a result of new automation, IP's production costs decreased 11 percent between 1981 and 1987 and its mills were able to use 25 percent less energy. Georges was named chairman in 1985, succeeding Gee.

Late 1980s to Mid-1990s: Diversifying Geographically and in Product Mix

The appointment had been preceded in 1984 by a decline in linerboard and pulp prices and a 14-year low in earnings. The white-paper market seemed to be one of the few that was profitable, so Georges hired a team of scientists and technicians to promote business in that area. Their work led to a major acquisition in 1986: Hammermill Paper Company. The $1.1 billion purchase increased IP's white-paper capacity by 750,000 tons and provided the technology to produce premium paper lines. Georges also reduced the number of salaried employees from 12,000 in 1981 to 9,200 in 1988, and streamlined management. Under his leadership, the firm also acquired Anitec Image Technology Corporation, maker of photographic film, papers, and darkroom chemicals; Avery Corporation, a Chicago-based envelope manufacturer; and Kendall Company's nonwoven fabrics division. IP also purchased Masonite Corporation, maker of composite wood products, in 1988. As a result, profits improved in 1988 and set a record in 1989.

In addition to the company's recovery, however, it also weathered several crises. These included a 1984 fire that destroyed its Nacogdoches, Texas, plywood-manufacturing plant, causing $32.5 million in damages. The facility reopened in 1986 after being equipped to produce oriented-strand board. In 1987, to protest inadequate wages and benefits, 2,200 workers went on strike at paper mills in Alabama, Maine, Mississippi, and Wisconsin.

Under Georges's leadership, the watchword at IP in the late 1980s and early 1990s was diversity, both in geography and product mix. His aim was to lessen the firm's vulnerability to the cyclical nature of its core paper, packaging, and forestry operations. Many of the international acquisitions that Georges pursued were aimed at expanding IP further into the area of specialty products, which generally produce higher margins. These products included photographic paper and films, specialty industrial papers, molded-wood products, laminated products, and nonwoven fabrics such as disposable diapers. Although similar in some ways to the firm's diversification of the 1960s, this round of expansion proved more successful.

Heading into its overseas spending spree, International Paper already owned box-manufacturing facilities in Italy, the Netherlands, Spain, Sweden, and the United Kingdom. In 1989 it acquired three major European manufacturers: Aussedat-Rey, the second largest paper company in France; the Ilford photographic-products division of Ciba-Geigy; and Germany's Zanders Feinpapiere AG, a high-quality coated-paper company. In 1990 IP bought the French operations of Georgia-Pacific Corporation.

The following year, in addition to bolstering its domestic base with the purchase of two U.S. paper companies—Dillon Paper and Leslie Paper—and its European holdings with the acquisition of Scaldia Paper BV of the Netherlands and the packaging equipment business of Dominion Industries Ltd., IP gained a presence in the Pacific Rim through a $258 million purchase of a 16 percent interest in the leading New Zealand forest products company, Carter Holt Harvey Ltd. (CHH). IP increased its stake in CHH in 1992 to 24 percent by investing an additional $298 million. Not only dominant in its home market, CHH was a major exporter of forest products to Australia and Asia. Also in 1992, IP paid $209 million for an 11 percent stake in Israel's Scitex Corporation Ltd., a world leader in color electronic-imaging equipment. The stake was increased to 12 percent the following year. The company also purchased

Kwidzyn from the government of Poland for $150 million and the promise to invest $75 million more in the firm, the country's largest white-paper manufacturer and operator of one of the most modern paper mills in Eastern Europe.

IP's diversification program appeared to pay off in the early 1990s when the paper industry encountered one of its worst cyclical downturns in 50 years. While competitors Boise Cascade Corp. and Champion International Corp. posted huge losses, IP continued to report profits, albeit smaller than those of 1988–90. Sales in 1992 hit a record $13.6 billion, although earnings were reduced substantially by a $263 million restructuring charge for the closure and consolidation of 20 underperforming mills and sales offices worldwide. In 1993 IP folded its North American distribution business into ResourceNet International, with more than 250 locations.

IP continued to expand aggressively in the mid-1990s. In 1994 ResourceNet International picked up two paper-distributing companies in Mexico, while in the area of liquid packaging, a new plant was built in Brazil and a joint venture was formed in China to build and operate a plant near Shanghai. IP made its biggest purchases yet in 1995, however. The firm spent $1.15 billion to attain majority control of Carter Holt Harvey and $64 million to acquire DSM, a producer of ink and adhesive resin based in the Netherlands. IP attempted to acquire Holvis AG, a Swiss fiber and paper company, for $422 million but was rebuffed by the Holvis board. Late in 1995 IP announced a $3.5 billion purchase of Federal Paper Board Company, based in Montvale, New Jersey, and the 15th largest paper company in the United States. Federal Paper specialized in bleached paperboard used for cigarette cartons, laundry detergent, and other consumer products, and, added to IP's packaging operations, gave IP about one-third of the bleached board market. Through the transaction, IP gained mills in Augusta, Georgia; Riegelwood, North Carolina; and Versailles, Connecticut.

Fittingly, the Federal Paper acquisition was consummated nearly simultaneously with the announcement of Georges's retirement as chairman and CEO, both of which occurred in early 1996. Georges's diversification program had increased non-U.S. sales to 30 percent of total revenues by 1994. While IP's core paper, pulp, and paperboard businesses accounted for 78 percent of sales in 1988, they accounted for only 52 percent of sales by 1994. During the same period, IP's specialty products' share of sales increased from just 3.7 percent to 17.3 percent. Overall, during Georges's leadership tenure, annual revenues at the company quadrupled to nearly $20 billion.

Late 1990s into 21st Century: Restructurings and Major Acquisitions

John T. Dillon, previously president and COO, succeeded Georges as chairman and CEO of International Paper. In addition to working to consolidate the Federal Paper acquisition, Dillon's initial months of leadership focused on divesting some operations, in part to offset the approximately $800 million in long-term debt incurred with the purchase of Federal Paper. In the most significant divestment of 1996, International Paper sold off about 300,000 acres of timberlands in Oregon and Washington, booking a $592 million pretax gain in the process. Also in 1996, IP took a $515 million restructuring and asset impairment charge as part of an ongoing cost-cutting program. A large proportion of the charge went toward the writing off of assets in the company's struggling imaging products business, maker of printing plates, films, chemicals, and paper for the photography and commercial printing market. With market conditions suddenly deteriorating after a record-setting year for the paper industry in 1995, IP saw its net earnings drop to $303 million in 1996 from the $1.15 billion of the previous year.

Conditions failed to improve in 1997, and Dillon responded mid-year with a major restructuring plan that aimed to divest more than $1 billion in underperforming assets or businesses. By mid-1998 IP had sold its imaging products business; Veratec, its nonwovens business; two of its four box plants in California; and small paper mills in France and Colombia. The company's workforce was reduced by about 10 percent. Restructuring and other charges led to a net loss of $151 million for 1997. Among the other charges that year was $150 million set aside as a legal reserve as part of the settlement of a class-action lawsuit brought against Masonite Corporation. The suit alleged that pressed-wood exterior siding made by Masonite was failing prematurely, allowing moisture to be retained and causing damage to the underlying structure. In September 1996 a jury found that the siding was defective, leading to the settlement in January 1998. Two other similar suits—one also involving siding, the other a roofing material—against Masonite were settled in similar fashion in January 1999.

Concurrent with the restructuring efforts were targeted acquisitions. IP's North American distribution business, which changed its name from ResourceNet International to xpedx in January 1998, expanded in July of that year with the purchase of the Mead Corporation's Zellerbach distribution unit for about $261 million in cash. This acquisition increased xpedx's 1998 revenues to $5.2 billion, a 22 percent increase over the previous year. The combination was expected to result in annual savings of $100 million in operating costs, and IP shut down 25 facilities and eliminated about 1,000 jobs following the deal's closure. Also added in 1998 was Weston Paper and Manufacturing Company, acquired through a stock deal valued at $232 million. Based in Terre Haute, Indiana, Weston operated 11 corrugated-container plants in the South and Midwest. In December 1998 International Paper expanded in eastern Europe with the purchase of Svetogorsk AO, a Russia-based pulp and paper firm.

Dillon moved beyond these smaller deals in April 1999 with a blockbuster stock-swap acquisition of Union Camp Corporation for about $7.9 billion, including the assumption of about $1.6 billion in Union Camp debt. Although much larger than the previous several acquisitions, this deal was also targeted in the sense that Union Camp's operations meshed so well with those of International Paper. Two of Union Camp's strengths—uncoated paper and containerboard—were strengths of IP as well. Union Camp's Alling and Cory distribution business was merged into xpedx. The merger also added 1.6 million acres of timberlands to IP's holdings, with most of the new lands adjacent to the previously held ones. Union Camp also held a 68 percent stake in Bush Boake Allen, Inc., a leading producer of flavors and fragrances, and this concern was seen as complementary to IP's Arizona Chemical unit, a product of an early diversification effort dating back to the early 1930s. In the wake of the Union Camp acquisition, IP eliminated more than 3,600 jobs from its workforce and closed a number of unprofitable plants in an effort to eliminate excess capacity.

IP's acquisition spree continued in 2000, with the company picking up Shorewood Packaging Corporation in March for about $640 million in cash plus assumed debt of $280 million and Champion International Corporation in June for about $5 billion in cash and $2.4 billion in IP stock and the assumption of $2.8 billion in debt. Both acquisitions involved third parties. In the case of Shorewood, that company had been fending off a hostile takeover by Chesapeake Corporation before agreeing to be acquired by IP. The addition of Shorewood greatly expanded IP's position in the high end of the consumer packaging sector, making it a leading provider of high-quality printing and paperboard packaging for home entertainment, cosmetics, health and beauty, pharmaceutical, sporting goods, tobacco, and other consumer products. Champion had agreed to be acquired by UPM-Kymmene Corporation of Finland in February 2000 in a stock-swap deal originally valued at $6.6 billion. UPM's stock had fallen significantly in price, reducing the value of the deal, by April 2000, which is when IP stepped in with its first offer, a combined cash and stock transaction valued at $6.2 billion. UPM responded with an all-cash offer of $70 per share, or $6.8 billion. But in May International Paper emerged the winner of a tense takeover battle with a revised offer of $75 in cash and stock, or $7.4 billion.

Champion was a company with 1999 revenues of $5.27 billion and papermaking capacity of 4.79 million tons a year. It ranked as the second largest producer of magazine paper and the sixth largest maker of office paper in North America. Champion (and Shorewood) had distribution operations that were absorbed by xpedx postmerger. The five million acres of U.S. timberlands controlled by Champion greatly increased IP's land holdings. Champion also had key assets outside the United States. Its Weldwood of Canada Limited subsidiary was a manufacturer of pulp, lumber, plywood, and engineered wood products with operations centered in British Columbia and Alberta. Brazil-based Champion Papel e Celulose Ltda. was one of South America's leading makers of office paper and a major producer of magazine paper with a total of 600,000 tons of annual capacity. IP also gained the significant timber holdings in Canada and Brazil controlled by these two companies, and even more importantly it now had a major presence on three continents: North America, Europe, and South America. International Paper also gained a new headquarters through the Champion deal as the company moved its head offices to the former headquarters of Champion in Stamford, Connecticut, later in 2000.

During 2000 IP also launched a major divestiture program. It was originally aimed at eliminating $3 billion in assets but this figure was increased to $5 billion following the acquisition of Champion. The divestitures were slated to be completed by the end of 2001. The program had a number of goals: cutting down the debt incurred from the string of acquisitions; paring the company's operations to three core areas: paper, packaging, and forest products; and reducing capacity in an attempt to break free of the ups and downs of the paper industry cycle. In November 2000 IP sold its interest in Bush Boake Allen for $640 million. During 2001, IP completed a series of divestitures, selling its petroleum and minerals business, 265,000 acres of forest lands in Washington and 800,000 acres in east Texas,

Masonite Corporation, Zanders Feinpapiere, a hydroelectric facility in the state of New York, a water company in Texas, and its flexible packaging business. The company also closed down a number of mills and announced plans to lay off about 3,000 workers in the United States, or about 10 percent of the workforce there. By early 2002 International Paper was still attempting to sell a number of businesses, including Arizona Chemical, its industrial packaging business, its chemical cellulose unit, its decorative products unit, and its oriented strand board facilities.

For 2001 IP reported revenues of $26.36 billion, a decline from the previous year's total of $28.18 billion. Thanks to restructuring and other charges of $1.12 billion and losses on the sales of businesses totaling $629 million, the company posted a net loss of $1.27 billion for the year. Despite this volley of red ink, under the continued leadership of Dillon, International Paper had made great strides in its ambitious restructuring program, and it remained the world's largest forest products company while appearing to have transformed itself into a much nimbler, more competitive, and potentially more profitable giant.

Principal Subsidiaries

Sustainable Forests, LLC; Carter Holt Harvey (New Zealand; 50.4%); International Paper S.A. (France; 99.92%); Weldwood of Canada Limited.

Principal Operating Units

Coated and Supercalendered Papers; Consumer Packaging; Distribution (xpedx); European Papers; Forest Products; Forest Resources; Industrial Papers; Industrial Packaging; Lumber Products; Panels & Engineered Wood Products; Printing & Communications Papers.

Principal Competitors

Georgia-Pacific Corporation; Weyerhaeuser Company; Stora Enso Oyj; MeadWestvaco Corporation; Boise Cascade Corporation; Smurfit-Stone Container Corporation; UPM-Kymmene Corporation; Jefferson Smurfit Corporation; Svenska Cellulosa Aktiebolaget SCA.

Further Reading

Byrnes, Nanette, and Michael Arndt, "John Dillon's High-Risk Paper Chase," *Business Week,* January 22, 2001, pp. 58, 60.

Deutsch, Claudia H., "International Paper Offers $6.2 Billion for Champion," *New York Times,* April 26, 2000, p. C2.

Heinrich, Thomas, "Product Diversification in the U.S. Pulp and Paper Industry: The Case of International Paper, 1898–1941," *Business History Review,* Autumn 2001, pp. 467-505.

"IP Buys Zellerbach Merchant from Mead," *Pulp and Paper,* August 1998, pp. 15, 17.

"IP Planning to Take a $500-Million Charge," *Pulp and Paper,* April 1996, p. 23.

Killian, Linda, "A Walk in the Woods," *Forbes,* September 30, 1991, pp. 78–79.

Kimelman, John, "Slash and Build: While Restructuring at Home, International Paper Is Investing Overseas," *Financial World,* April 13, 1993, p. 28.

Loeffelholz, Suzanne, "Putting It on Paper," *Financial World,* July 25, 1989, p. 26.

Osborne, Richard, "An Unpretentious Giant: John Georges Has Quietly Built International Paper into a Diversified $15 Billion Corporation," *Industry Week,* June 19, 1995, pp. 73–76.

Palmer, Jay, "No Lumbering Giant: International Paper Races to New Peaks in Earnings," *Barron's,* January 2, 1989, p. 13.

"Pulp Friction," *Economist,* November 11, 1995, p. 66.

Starkman, Dean, "International Paper Has Its Work Cut Out for It," *Wall Street Journal,* May 15, 2000, p. A4.

——, "Shorewood Agrees to International Paper Acquisition," *Wall Street Journal,* February 17, 2000, p. C15.

Sullivan, Allanna, "International Paper Shutting Plants to Cut Supply," *Wall Street Journal,* October 19, 2000, p. A4.

Welsh, Jonathan, "International Paper Settles Suit on Masonite Siding," *Wall Street Journal,* July 15, 1997, p. B3.

——, "International Paper Unveils Revamping and Posts Better-than-Expected Results," *Wall Street Journal,* July 9, 1997, p. A4.

——, "IP Agrees to Acquire Union Camp Corp.," *Wall Street Journal,* November 25, 1998, p. A3.

Willoughby, Jack, "Paper Tiger: A Dow Dowager No More, International Paper Works Itself into Fighting Trim," *Barron's,* July 9, 2001, pp. 21–22.

Young, Jim, "International Paper Co.: Worldwide Expansions Gear for Economic Recovery," *Pulp and Paper,* May 1994, pp. 32, 35.

—Kim M. Magon
—update: David E. Salamie

Invacare Corporation

One Invacare Way
Elyria, Ohio 44035-4196
U.S.A.
Telephone: (440) 329-6000
Toll Free: (800) 333-6900
Fax: (440) 366-9008
Web site: http://www.invacare.com

Public Company
Incorporated: 1971
Employees: 5,400
Sales: $1.05 billion (2001)
Stock Exchanges: New York
Ticker Symbol: IVC
NAIC: 339111 Laboratory Apparatus and Furniture
    Manufacturing; 339113 Surgical Appliance and
    Supplies Manufacturing

Invacare Corporation is a world leading maker and distributor of non-acute healthcare products for people requiring home healthcare, for those needing rehabilitative care, and for persons with temporary or permanent disabilities. Among the company's products are power wheelchairs, manual wheelchairs, motorized scooters, seating and positioning products, crutches, canes, walkers, manual and electric home care beds, respiratory products for the home, and safety equipment, such as shower chairs and grab bars. Acquisitions and innovative products have fueled Invacare's success. It was the first firm to produce a motorized wheelchair with computerized controls.

1885 to the 1970s: From Fay Manufacturing Company to Invacare Corporation

The roots of Invacare can be traced back to 1885, when Fay Manufacturing Company was founded in the Cleveland suburb of Elyria by Winslow Lamartine Fay and began making tricycles. Competition from the newly introduced two-wheeled ''safety'' bicycle reduced demand for tricycles, leading Fay to transform his tricycle design into a line of mobility devices for persons with disabilities. The new products featured hand levers and treadles for steering and pedaling. The products proved successful, in part because they filled an existing need—the Civil War had left thousands of veterans with amputated limbs who needed help getting around. Following on this success, Fay developed specialized carts that were precursors to the modern wheelchair.

Looking to pursue other business opportunities, Fay sold his company to Arthur L. Garford in 1891. Soon after, Garford hired George Cushing Worthington to manage the firm's plant operations. Worthington became a key employee at the company, designing a line of bicycle-wheeled rolling chairs. His influence was great enough that when Garford elected to rename the company in 1899, he chose the moniker the Worthington Manufacturing Company. Worthington was named president in 1902, and five years later the firm was renamed the Worthington Company.

In 1917, Fred W. Colson, a Worthington vice-president, engineered the merger of Worthington with the Machine Parts Company to form the Colson Company, majority owned by Colson, who also served as company president. The Colson Company continued to make wheelchairs and tricycles—as well as the automotive parts that had been made by Machine Parts Company—but it soon expanded its product line to include stretchers, service carts, and bicycles and scooters for children.

During the Great Depression of the 1930s, Colson fell upon hard times. The firm went into receivership in 1933 and was reorganized as the Colson Corporation, with new management and with Neely Powers serving as president. The company once again specialized in tricycles, wheelchairs, and automotive parts until World War II, when Colson produced ''Mighty Mouse'' rockets for the U.S. Navy.

In the postwar era, the firm struggled shifting back to civilian production, and in 1953 a weakened Colson was purchased by the Pritzker family of Chicago. The manufacture of bicycles and tricycles was halted and the company was moved out of Elyria. The wheelchair division of Colson, however, was purchased in 1957 by three veteran employees: W.C. ''Court'' Shea, Charles ''Chuck'' Hazelton, and W.J. Pivacek. The three men renamed the division Mobilaid Inc. and concentrated primarily on the manufacture of wheelchairs. Much smaller than

---

Company Perspectives:

Invacare Corporation's mission is to provide, worldwide, the highest value in mobility products and home medical equipment for people with disabilities and those requiring home health care. To accomplish this, the company focuses on two basic fundamentals—innovation and distribution. The company's name, in fact, stems from the slogan ''Innovation In Healthcare.'' The company is managed on a decentralized basis by an operating committee. Invacare continuously strives to achieve excellence through improved products, processes and service. The breadth and depth of the company's distribution system, together with the continuous search for new channels and expansion opportunities has allowed Invacare to literally explode new products into the marketplace. Internally, Invacare employs its technological and personnel resources to their maximum potential. Externally, the company seeks to add value through acquisitions and partnerships with companies that provide synergistic relationships.

Colson, Mobilaid had annual revenues of about $150,000 in the late 1950s. A key development in this period was the procurement of a large government contract to supply wheelchairs to the Veterans Administration.

In 1967, Mobilaid formed a subsidiary called the Rolls Equipment Company, which was charged with selling the company's products under the Rolls brand directly to hospitals and surgical equipment companies. By 1970, Mobilaid had grown substantially and was producing nearly 40,000 wheelchairs per year. The following year, Boston Capital Corporation (BCC) purchased both Mobilaid and Invalex Company, a maker of walkers, safety side rails, and other home healthcare products that had operations in Long Beach, California, and Lodi, Ohio. BCC merged these companies later in 1971 to form Invacare Corporation.

Transitioning from investment firm to healthcare company, BCC changed its name first to BCC Industries Inc. and then to Technicare Corporation; it also moved its headquarters to Cleveland. In addition to Invacare, Technicare also owned Ohio-Nuclear Inc., which achieved tremendous success with a new line of CT scanners in the mid-1970s. By 1977, Ohio-Nuclear accounted for $125 million of Technicare's overall sales of $164.4 million, while Invacare contributed only $17 million. With Invacare's slow sales, muddled management, and lack of new product development becoming a financial drain, Technicare decided to sell the company. But in 1978, Johnson & Johnson purchased Technicare for $87 million in stock. The following year, Johnson & Johnson, which had purchased Technicare mainly to gain the CT scanner business of Ohio-Nuclear, announced that it intended to sell Invacare. Two groups of investors stepped forward with offers to buy Invacare but both deals fell through. Then A. Malachi Mixon appeared on the scene.

1980s: A Company Turnaround Under Mixon's Leadership

Mixon, a 39-year-old head of marketing at Ohio-Nuclear's CT scanner division, former Marine Corps artillery officer who served in Vietnam, and Harvard Business School graduate, immediately decided to buy Invacare when he heard it was for sale. But with only $10,000 of his own money to invest, financing the acquisition of a company that cost $7.8 million seemed almost impossible. Undeterred, Mixon arranged for two real estate brokers to purchase Invacare's facility on Taylor Street, and then lease it back to the company. Then, Mixon arranged for a $4.3 million loan from First Chicago Bank. The remainder of the needed money came from his own resources, loans from friends, and issuing shares of stock to various local investors. While structuring the financing of Invacare, Mixon included a 15 percent interest in the company for himself.

When Mixon and his group officially assumed control of Invacare on December 28, 1979, the company had a low standing within the healthcare products industry. Sales were stagnant at approximately $20 million, far lower than the $124 million sales figure of its chief competitor, Everest & Jennings. Furthermore, Mixon's leveraged buyout resulted in a $6.5 million debt, and the high interest rate of nearly 25 percent was devouring Invacare's modest $1.2 million in profits.

During the first year as chief executive officer at Invacare, Mixon devoted a significant amount of time to studying the company's product line. After eliminating the manufacture of those items that were either obsolete or unprofitable, he pushed Invacare's engineering department to develop highly innovative products. Mixon believed that Everest & Jennings, which had over an 80 percent share of the world's wheelchair market, not only was growing complacent with its position within the industry but also was losing touch with its customers.

In 1982, Mixon's emphasis on new product development paid off when Invacare was the first in the industry to introduce a motorized wheelchair with computerized controls. Invacare's computer controls could be easily adapted to suit the individual needs and requirements of the severely disabled. The wheelchair quickly became an industry standard, and Invacare suddenly found itself in an intense competition with Everest & Jennings for the larger share of the wheelchair market.

Everest & Jennings responded to Invacare by reducing its prices, but cost-effective production methods enabled Invacare to match its competitor's prices. At the same time, Mixon had worked hard to improve Invacare's distribution network: inexpensive financing, volume discounts, 48-hour delivery, funds for cooperative advertising, and prepaid freight convinced more than 6,000 home healthcare dealers in the United States that Invacare was the better of the two companies. In a short time, Invacare had equaled and then surpassed Everest & Jennings' share of the wheelchair market. Invacare's ever expanding product line, which now included items such as cardiovascular exercise equipment and oxygen concentrators, and its policy of stocking parts for the products of its competitors, soon placed the company in a league of its own.

In the beginning of 1984, it appeared that Invacare's rapid growth and enviable financial success would continue unabated. During that year, Mixon decided to enter the European market for home healthcare products, and acquired a British firm that manufactured wheelchair and patient aids and a West German producer of wheelchairs. Mixon also determined that it was an

Key Dates:

1885: Fay Manufacturing Company is founded in Elyria, Ohio, by Winslow Lamartine Fay and begins making tricycles; the company soon finds success through a line of mobility devices for persons with disabilities.

1891: Fay sells his company to Arthur L. Garford, who soon hires George Cushing Worthington to manage the firm's plant operations.

1899: The firm is renamed the Worthington Manufacturing Company.

1907: The company's name is changed to Worthington Company.

1917: Worthington merges with the Machine Parts Company to form the Colson Company.

1933: During the Great Depression, the firm goes into receivership and is reorganized as the Colson Corporation.

1953: Colson is purchased by the Pritzker family of Chicago and moved from Elyria.

1957: Colson's wheelchair division in Elyria is purchased by three veteran employees and renamed Mobilaid Inc.

1971: Boston Capital Corporation (later known as Technicare Corporation) purchases Mobilaid and Invalex Company, a maker of home healthcare products, and merges the two firms to create Invacare Corporation.

1978: Johnson & Johnson acquires Technicare and its Invacare subsidiary.

1979: An investment group led by A. Malachi Mixon purchases Invacare for $7.8 million.

1982: Company becomes the first to introduce a motorized wheelchair with computerized controls.

1984: Company goes public and enters the European market for home healthcare products.

1992: Poirier S.A., the leading wheelchair maker in France, is acquired.

1997: Invacare is rebuffed in hostile bid for Healthdyne Technologies Inc.

1998: Suburban Ostomy Supply Company, Inc. is acquired for $132 million.

1999: Denmark-based Scandinavian Mobility International A/S is acquired for $142 million.

appropriate time to take the company public in order to underwrite the expenditures for Invacare's quick growth, offer employee stock options that would attract highly qualified managers, and provide Invacare's original group of investors with some liquidity for their initial stake in the company.

Later in 1984, however, Invacare was hurt by a series of unexpected events. When the company discovered it had less inventory than was reported in its books, it was forced to take a charge against earnings that resulted in a financial loss for fiscal 1984. In addition, because of manufacturing defects in the company's oxygen concentrator, Invacare was forced to recall the product and suffered a loss of approximately $1.5 million in sales. To compound company problems, in 1985 the U.S. government changed its formulas for Medicare reimbursement. The

new requirement led wheelchair dealers to sell more chairs than they leased, which resulted in a disincentive for dealers to purchase better built, but more expensive, reusable wheelchairs. Invacare's sales dropped precipitously, and its profitability was threatened. Not surprisingly, the company's initial stock, offered at $11 per share just one year earlier, plummeted to less than $4 by mid-1985.

Mixon was convinced that a significant part of Invacare's problems could be attributed to a lack of manufacturing efficiency and quality control problems. He was determined never to allow another Invacare product to suffer the embarrassment of a recall by the federal government. Mixon called on Joseph B. Richey to rectify the manufacturing problems at Invacare. Richey was a former associate of Mixon's at Ohio-Nuclear and was head of that company's research and development department and was also one of the initial investors in the 1979 buyout of Invacare and a member of the Invacare board since 1980. He joined Invacare in an executive capacity in 1994 as senior vice-president of product development. Richey first concentrated on finding Invacare's quality control problems. The company's sales force was required to submit monthly reports detailing customer complaints about its products. With these reports, Richey then began to correct the problems that occurred during production.

Simultaneously, Richey implemented a program in statistical process control methods for company employees. Another quality control measure involved sending Invacare's own certified representatives to check the plants of its suppliers; this policy led to a reduction in the number of suppliers but a higher and more consistent quality of product parts. Richey's strategy paid off handsomely as Invacare reduced the rejection rate of its supplier's parts to less than 2 percent. But Richey had said numerous times that Invacare's goal should be to measure rejection rates as Japanese companies do—in parts per million. One of the most important aspects of Invacare's determination to improve the quality control of its products involved a switch from purchasing to manufacturing the electronic control systems on its motorized wheelchairs. Richey went directly to the National Aeronautic and Space Administration's (NASA) Lewis Space Center and purchased much of the equipment NASA used to test its controls on the space shuttles. The result of employing such sophisticated quality control equipment led to the perception that Invacare's power wheelchairs were the most reliable in the industry.

With all its improvements in quality control, Invacare was well-prepared to meet an unexpected challenge in 1986. Wheelchair manufacturers in Taiwan started to sell their products in the United States that year at nearly 20 percent below the normal price structure. Invacare's response was to construct a new manufacturing plant in Reynosa, Mexico, in addition to its facilities in Elyria, Ohio. Although Mixon denied that there was a plan to shut down the Elyria plant or relocate jobs to Mexico, the consequence was that Elyria employees became more productive and efficient in light of the prospect of losing their jobs. Invacare's new plant in Mexico produced wheelchairs at a much lower cost and almost eliminated the Taiwanese manufacturers from the U.S. domestic market. With its quality control problems solved and no other company to challenge its dominance of the wheelchair market, Invacare grew quickly. In 1986 the company reported profits of $3.4 million on revenues of $111 million.

By 1989, Invacare's revenues jumped to over $186 million. An important aspect of its success was the decentralized management structure emphasized by Mixon. Each of the key officers in the company was given complete authority to make the changes necessary for the respective divisions they supervised to meet their sales goals. This organizational setup encouraged a fast-paced, high-pressure work environment, but management was given full authority to meet the dual responsibilities of efficiency and productivity. In addition, Invacare not only hired disabled people to help design and test its products, but the company also provided a stock sharing plan for its employees that helped create a sense of ownership, empowerment, and accountability.

1990s: Growing Toward $1 Billion in Sales Through Acquisitions

The next two years, 1990 and 1991, were watershed years for Invacare. In 1990, the company introduced a total of 53 new products, including significant innovations in wheelchair design with the introduction of microprocessors for power wheelchairs and the first wheelchair designed for use on airliners. Invacare also created its Action Technology division in which highly flexible wheelchairs made of light composite materials were designed for active users. By 1991, Invacare stock had climbed to $25 per share. That year, the company launched an advertising campaign to sell its products directly to consumers. Although still relying heavily on dealers to market its products, Mixon successfully anticipated that a large segment of the disabled population was looking for products allowing them to lead a more active life. Invacare reported revenues of more than $263 million for fiscal 1991. Invacare's successes made it one of the top 50 firms to invest in during the decade of the 1990s, according to *U.S. News and World Report.*

In 1992, Invacare was known by industry analysts as the leader in manufacturing wheelchairs and home care medical equipment. The company was manufacturing a comprehensive line of wheelchairs, including pediatric and sports models, quad canes, scooters, and walkers in the most up-to-date ultralight materials. With its oxygen concentrators, medical beds, nebulizers, cushions, and positioning systems, Invacare produced the broadest line of items in the home healthcare industry. The company had expanded to include 19 manufacturing facilities in the United States and over 10,000 dealers distributing its products throughout the world, including Mexico, Canada, New Zealand, and Europe. In 1992 international sales accounted for approximately 23 percent of Invacare's total revenues.

Invacare experienced another banner year in 1993. Sales increased to $365 million while earnings were reported at over $22 million. From 1979 through 1993, the company had achieved an annual growth rate of over 23 percent and was listed in *Forbes* as one of the 200 best small companies in America and in *Business Week*'s ''250 Companies on the Move.'' From October 1991 to the end of 1993, Invacare made seven major acquisitions, including Canadian Posture and Seating Centre, Inc. (Kitchener, Ontario); Hovis Medical Limited (Mississauga, Ontario); Perry Oxygen Systems, Inc. (Port St. Lucie, Florida); Poirier S.A. (Tours, France); Top End (Pinellas Park, Florida); Dynamics Controls Ltd. (Christchurch, New Zealand); and Geomarine Systems, Inc. (Carmel, New York). Although Dynamic Controls, a

manufacturer of power controls for wheelchairs, and Geomarine Systems, a manufacturer of low air loss therapy mattress replacement systems, were important in expanding the company's product line and increasing the cost effectiveness of its manufacturing operations, it was the purchases of Top End Wheelchair Sports and Poirier that were most significant.

Top End products included road racing and tennis wheelchairs, and a water ski for disabled people. Top End Action wheelchairs were used in over 200 sports events during 1993, including the National Veterans Wheelchair Games, NBA-sponsored wheelchair basketball games, Easter Seals wheelchair tennis camps, and numerous other competitive and recreational sports events. The acquisition of Top End gave Invacare valuable exposure to the growing active user wheelchair market.

Purchased for $57.3 million in October 1992, Poirier was the leading maker of wheelchairs in France and the leading maker of lightweight wheelchairs in Europe. The addition of Poirier doubled Invacare's European sales, and the company's headquarters were made the new base for Invacare's European operations. These acquisitions helped increase sales to $411.1 million by 1994, a year in which Gerald B. Blouch was named chief operating officer, with Mixon remaining chairman, president, and CEO.

Throughout the 1990s, the company pursued acquisitions that tended to: grow market share in or extend existing product lines (called tactical); expand the firm into new, complementary product segments (strategic); and/or open up new foreign markets for selling the company's products (geographic). During 1995 and 1996 Invacare completed more than a dozen acquisitions. One area of expansion was specialty seating systems and cushions, and the 1995 acquisitions of PinDot Products, Inc. (Northbrook, Illinois), Bencraft Limited (Birmingham, England), and Special Health Systems (Ontario, Canada) all contributed to that expansion. In early 1996, Invacare acquired Frohock-Stewart, Inc. (Northboro, Massachusetts), a manufacturer of Aurora brand bath safety products that were sold to mass retail outlets, such as Home Depot and Eagle Hardware. This marked Invacare's entry into the retail market, although home medical equipment dealers remained the core market. The Aurora line of products was soon expanded to include such Invacare mainstays as canes, walkers, and wheelchairs, while the retail channels broadened to include Wal-Mart, Sears, and other major retailers. Also purchased in 1996 was Healthtech Products, Inc. (St. Louis), a maker of beds and patient room furniture for nursing homes and other institutions.

A number of acquisitions outside North America extended Invacare's geographic presence during this period. European purchases included Beram AB (Gothenburg, Sweden), a distributor of wheelchairs and other rehabilitative products, and Paratec AG (Basel, Switzerland), maker of the Kuschall brand of active wheelchairs, both bought in 1995; and Fabriorto, Lda. (Oporto, Portugal), a producer of wheelchairs, beds, and walking aids purchased in early 1996. Invacare's presence in the Australasian region was significantly bolstered as well, in a follow-up to the purchase of Dynamic Controls in 1993. Invacare bought Thompson Rehab (Auckland, New Zealand) in July 1995, gaining a manufacturer and distributor of power and manual wheelchairs. The following month the company acquired another Auckland firm, Group Pharmaceutical Limited, which distributed Invacare products in New Zealand. In July 1996, Invacare purchased the leading maker of power wheelchairs in Australia, Roller Chair Pty. Ltd. (Adelaide). The person responsible for integrating all of these foreign acquisitions was Blouch, who was placed in charge of international operations in December 1993 and was promoted from COO to president in November 1996.

In January 1997, Invacare made an offer to acquire Healthdyne Technologies Inc., a maker of products for adult sleep disorders and sleep apnea monitors for infants, for $12.50 a share, or $163 million, in what would have been the company's largest acquisition to date. Healthdyne's board rejected the offer as too low, turning the bid into a hostile one. Invacare subsequently raised its bid three times, eventually offering $15 a share, or $190 million, in June. Two months later, after this final offer was rejected, Invacare called off its takeover attempt. (Healthdyne was later purchased by Respironics Inc. for about $370 million.)

In addition to this disappointment, 1997 was also noteworthy for the difficult environment in which Invacare had to operate, resulting in below average sales growth for the company of about 5.5 percent. Increasing competition, a strong dollar that dampened sales in Europe, and uncertainty created by a Medicare budget debate combined to wreak havoc. Invacare responded with a major restructuring involving plant closures, the elimination of unprofitable product lines, asset writedowns, and increased bad debt reserves. In connection with the restructuring, the firm took a pretax charge of $61 million, resulting in net income of just $1.6 million for the year, compared to $38.9 million for 1996. In September 1997, Invacare moved into a new $5 million headquarters building in Elyria.

As healthier growth returned in the last two years of the 1990s, Invacare rounded out its acquisitive decade with its two biggest deals ever. In January 1998, the company acquired Suburban Ostomy Supply Company, Inc. (Holliston, Massachusetts) for about $132 million in cash. Suburban Ostomy was a leading wholesaler of disposable medical products for the home healthcare market, primarily in the areas of ostomy, incontinence, and diabetes and wound care. This move into ''soft goods'' was part of the company's effort to provide its customers with one-stop shopping for home healthcare products. During 2000, Suburban was renamed Invacare Supply Group. In July 1999, Invacare spent approximately $142 million in cash to buy Scandinavian Mobility International A/S (SMI), which was based in Copenhagen, Denmark. SMI was one of the largest European makers of bed systems and mobility aids for the home care and institutional markets. Also during 1999, Invacare began retooling its product line toward the eventual goal of selling all products under the Invacare name. The aim was to make the Invacare name synonymous with home healthcare products. In conjunction with this effort, the company logo was redesigned and the tag line ''Yes, you can'' was adopted to emphasize the firm's ''can-do'' spirit.

New Goal and New Spokesperson for the New Millennium

By 2000, Invacare was the clear leader of the home healthcare product market. Under the continued leadership of Mixon,

Invacare had acquired 35 companies since the Mixon-led group bought the company in 1979. These acquisitions, along with innovative new product development, helped the company surpass the $1 billion revenue mark for the first time in 2000, a remarkable achievement for a company that had had revenue of only $19 million two decades earlier. Earnings for 2000 were a record $59.9 million. In June 2000, Invacare moved its stock listing from the NASDAQ to the prestigious New York Stock Exchange. Mixon, meantime, set a goal of achieving $2 billion in sales by 2005.

A key to reaching this target would be to achieve success in the effort to make Invacare a household name. Toward that end, in late 2001 the company signed up legendary golfer Arnold Palmer to be the company spokesperson in a $5 million marketing campaign. Although 72-year-old Palmer did not need to use the company's products, he was chosen for his image as an older American maintaining an active lifestyle. Sales for 2001, however, were discouraging, increasing by only 4 percent as the weakening economic climate, particularly after the events of September 11, led customers to cut back on purchases. Despite this setback, the longer term forecast for Invacare remained bright. Demographic trends were in the company's favor, in terms of the continuing aging of the U.S. and European populations, as were the increasing efforts to have the elderly live at home rather than in nursing homes.

Principal Subsidiaries

Invacare Ltd. (U.K.); Invacare Canada Inc.; Invacare Deutschland GmbH (Germany); Invacare International Corporation; Invacare Trading Company, Inc. (U.S. Virgin Islands); Invamex, S.A. de R.L.C.V. (Mexico); Invacare Credit Corporation; Invatection Insurance company; Lam Craft Industries; Invacare Poirier S.A. (France); Dynamic Controls Ltd. (New Zealand); Quantrix Consultants Ltd. (New Zealand); Dynamic Europe Ltd. (U.K.); Sci Des Hautes Roches (France); Sci Des Roches (France); Mobilite Building Corporation; Genus Medical Products USA, Inc.; Invacare Florida; Infusion Systems, Inc.; Invacare New Zealand Ltd.; Invacare AG (Switzerland); Healthtech, Inc.; Invacare Portugal Lda. (Portugal); Production Research Corporation; Suburban Ostomy Supply Company, Inc.; Roller Chair Pty. Ltd. (Australia); Silcraft Corporation; Invacare Supply Group; The Aftermarket Group, Inc.; Invacare Holdings Denmark ApS; Scandinavian Mobility International ApS (Denmark); Invacare EC-Hong A/S (Denmark); Invacare A/S (Denmark); Invacare AB (Sweden); Invacare NV (Belgium); Scandinavian Mobility Niltek A/S (Denmark); Scandinavian Mobility Radius A/S (Denmark); EC-Invest A/S (Denmark); Invacare Holdings AS (Norway); Groas A/S (Norway); Invacare Rea AB (Sweden); France Reval SA; Matia SA (France); R2P S.a.r.L. (France); Scandinavian Mobility GmbH (Germany); France Reval GmbH (Germany); Invacare B.V. (Netherlands); Samarite B.V. (Netherlands); Revato B.V. (Netherlands); Scandinavian Mobility Medical Services B.V. (Netherlands); Invacare Australia Pty, Ltd.; Adaptive Switch Laboratories, Inc.; Adaptive Research Laboratories, Inc.; Garden City Medical; Hatfield Mobility Limited (New Zealand); Pro Med Equipment Pty, Ltd. (Australia); Pro Med Australia Pty, Ltd.; Invacare, S.A. (Spain); Invacare Holdings Two AB (Sweden); Invacare Holdings AB (Sweden); Invacare Holdings

CV (Netherlands); Invacare Holdings BV (Netherlands); Invacare Verwaltungs GmbH (Germany); Invacare GmbH and Co. KG (Germany); Invacare Holdings Two BV (Netherlands); Invacare Holdings (New Zealand).

Principal Competitors

Sunrise Medical Inc.; Hillenbrand Industries, Inc.; Kinetic Concepts, Inc.; Graham-Field Health Products, Inc.

Further Reading

Bendix, Jeffrey, "Invacare Rolls to Number One," *Cleveland Enterprise,* Spring 1991.

Butler, Charles, "Mal Bonding," *Sales and Marketing Management,* July 1995, pp. 66–72.

Byrne, Harlan S., "The Right Rx," *Barron's,* July 18, 1994, p. 19.

Freeman, Anne M., "The Energizer," *Medical Industry Executive,* February/March 1992, pp. 28–31.

Gleisser, Marcus, "Invacare Corp. Purchase of Medical Supplier Feeds 22.1 Percent Increase in Sales," *Cleveland Plain Dealer,* June 22, 1999, p. 30S.

——, "Invacare Seeking to Buy Danish Wheelchair Maker," *Cleveland Plain Dealer,* July 2, 1999, p. 1C.

Johnson, Terrence L., "Invacare Corp. Broadens Its Base," *Cleveland Plain Dealer,* April 21, 1996, p. 3J.

Kissling, Catherine L., "Invacare Pushing to Reduce Costs, Get Edge on Rivals," *Crain's Cleveland Business,* May 19, 1986, p. 3.

Krouse, Peter, "Invacare Hits $1 Billion Annual Sales," *Cleveland Plain Dealer,* January 23, 2001, p. 1C.

Lipin, Steven, and Matt Murray, "Invacare Makes a $163 Million Offer to Acquire Healthdyne Technologies," *Wall Street Journal,* January 13, 1997, p. B6.

Love, Steve, "Invacare Signs Up Palmer as 'Lifestyle' Spokesman," *Cleveland Plain Dealer,* October 23, 2001, p. C1.

Morrow, David J., "Vehicles for Market Share: Wheelchair Makers Are Trying to Expand Their Turf," *New York Times,* January 21, 1998, p. D1.

Murray, Matt, "Invacare Expects Showdown with Healthdyne over Bid," *Wall Street Journal,* July 30, 1997, p. B4.

Palmeri, Christopher, "Wheel-to-Wheel Combat," *Forbes,* February 15, 1993, pp. 62–64.

Peric, T.S., "Mixonian Alchemy," *Cleveland Magazine,* 1993 reprint.

Pfaff, Kimberley, "Health for the Masses: Medical-Goods Company Courts an Emerging Market," *HFN—The Weekly Newspaper for the Home Furnishing Network,* January 29, 1996.

Phillips, Stephen, "Acquisition Gives Invacare Access to Retail Market," *Cleveland Plain Dealer,* January 16, 1996, p. 1C.

Prinzinsky, David, "Invacare Wheels into Lead with Healthcare Products," *Crain's Cleveland Business,* October 15, 1990.

Rodengen, Jeffrey L., and Anthony L. Wall, *The Yes, You Can of Invacare Corporation,* Fort Lauderdale, Fla.: Write Stuff Enterprises, 2001, 192 p.

Santiago, Raquel, "Invacare Introducing New Brand Plan: Marketing Strategy to Bring Products Under One Name," *Crain's Cleveland Business,* July 19, 1999, p. 2.

——, "Invacare Sees Growth Avenue in Retail Sales," *Crain's Cleveland Business,* March 3, 1997, p. 3.

Scott, Jennifer A., "Money Games: To Invacare Corp.'s Mal Mixon and His Close Circle of Friends, Venture Capitalism Is a Hobby That More Than Pays for Itself," *Small Business News-Cleveland,* June 1, 1995, p. 12.

Shingler, Dan, "Invacare Pursuing Growth with Gusto," *Crain's Cleveland Business,* January 1, 1996, p. 1.

——, "It's the Midas Touch," *Crain's Cleveland Business,* October 21, 1991.

Vickers, Jim, "Master Innovator: A. Malachi Mixon III, Balancing Innovation and Growth," *Small Business News-Akron,* September 1, 2000, p. S6.

Yerak, Becky, "Going to the People: Invacare Is Pushing into Retailing to Sell Its Home Health Products," *Cleveland Plain Dealer,* June 1, 1997, p. 1H.

——, "Invacare CEO Reflects on Bid: Elyria Firm Still Plans to Enter New Field Without Healthdyne," *Cleveland Plain Dealer,* August 10, 1997, p. 1H.

——, "Invacare to Increase Cost-Cutting," *Cleveland Plain Dealer,* September 10, 1997, p. 1C.

——, "Serial Entrepreneur: From a $10,000 Investment, Invacare CEO Mal Mixon Has Built a Powerhouse in Medical Equipment. Now, Even As He Drives His Company Toward the $1 Billion Mark, He Works to Help Other Ventures Get off the Ground," *Cleveland Plain Dealer,* September 14, 1997, p. 1H.

—Thomas Derdak
—update: David E. Salamie

Jamba Juice Company

17100 17th Street
San Francisco, California 94103
U.S.A.
Telephone: (415) 865-1200
Toll Free: (800) 545-9972
Fax: (415) 865-1294
Web site: http://www.jambajuice.com

Private Company
Incorporated: 1990
Employees: 210
Sales: $97.2 million (2000)
NAIC: 722211 Limited-Service Restaurants

Based in San Francisco, Jamba Juice Company has more than 350 company and licensed stores spread across 23 states and the District of Columbia that serve some 20 varieties of smoothies, 24 to 32 ounce drinks that the company positions as healthy meal replacements. Most of the blenderized concoctions rely on frozen or fresh fruit, supplemented with such optional ''boosters'' as bee pollen, ginseng, brewer's yeast, and wheat grass. In addition, Jamba sells vegetable soups, breads, and gourmet soft pretzels. The bulk of the chain's outlets are located in California, where juice bars have long been a staple. In order to expand rapidly across the United States, Jamba has taken on regional franchise partners, although the company has been reluctant to initiate overseas franchising.

Pursuit of a Dream: 1989

The individual behind the founding of Jamba Juice was Kirk Perron, who at an early age harbored a desire to start his own business. ''I was inspired because my parents never owned their own home,'' he told *QSF Magazine* in a 1999 profile. ''My parents both worked at blue collar jobs and I knew that wasn't the way to get ahead. So, I started developing ideas about retail business—the wheels started turning pretty early on.'' Rather than engaging in high school sports, he began investing in real estate, accumulating a $12,000 down payment by turning to the adults he knew from school, including his bus driver, a librar-

ian, and a guidance counselor. At the age of 16, he also began working at supermarkets—bagging groceries at Vons and ultimately becoming an assistant store manager at Safeway—and in the process he gained ten years of valuable retail experience. Perron was 25 in 1989 when he quit his management position at Safeway, electing to spend his days working out and bicycling, supported by his real estate ventures and a late-night job stocking grocery shelves. Often after exercising, he bought a smoothie at his health club, a drink he found far more nutritious and satisfying than a frozen drink he might buy at a convenience store after one of his long bicycle rides. Still looking to realize his childhood dream of running his own business, Perron soon decided to open a store to sell smoothies.

With a determination bordering on evangelical zeal, Perron recruited people to help him launch the business that would one day become Jamba Juice. He met his future director of research and development, Joe Vergara, at a Safeway store. Vergara was already involved in the juice bar business, managing a handful of stores in San Luis Obispo, California. He often went shopping for good deals on overripe bananas and was buying a dozen cases at a Safeway when Perron struck up a conversation that ultimately led to Vergara's involvement in the new venture. Another person impressed by Perron's passion was Kevin Peters, who helped him scout for the location of his first store and would become director of partnership development. A fourth person who would be credited with cofounding Jamba was Linda Ozawa Olds, the later head of marketing.

Although his colleagues believed in his vision of a healthful fast-food restaurant that relied on the sale of smoothies, Perron was less successful with the bankers, who quickly dismissed such a concept. To fund the business, Perron had to sell a small apartment building and borrow money from his mother and her boyfriend, in all scraping together $115,000. He then secured a 700-square-foot location in San Luis Obispo and in April 1990 launched his smoothie business, originally called Juice Club. During the first weekend the store was extremely busy, serving some 1,600 customers, but Juice Club was far from an overnight success. During the first year, daily sales hovered around the $500 level, and it was not certain that Juice Club would succeed, although some people already began to inquire about obtaining a franchise. Gradually, the store built up a loyal base of customers, many of whom visited several times a week to buy the store's unique menu of smoothies, which were given such exotic names as Pacific Passion, Boysenberry Bliss, and Protein Berry Pizazz.

By the end of the second year, Juice Club was turning a profit and Perron was ready to expand. After failing to secure a Small Business Administration loan, he decided to grow through franchising. The second Juice Club opened in Irvine, California, and by the autumn of 1994 there were 16 franchises. Already, however, Perron recognized that franchising was not the best way to grow the Juice Club concept. Not only did he risk losing quality control—and it was the quality of the product that created customer loyalty—he lacked the necessary funding to make a franchise chain profitable. The franchisees had to foot the entire bill for land and facilities, resulting in a franchise fee too modest to allow the parent company to provide the necessary management training or monitor the quality of the product. For Perron, choosing profit over quality was simply not an option. Clearly what Juice Club needed was sufficient capital to own and operate all of its outlets—to bankroll its own destiny. Rather than seek out investors, however, investors sought out Perron. In September 1994, he received a telephone call from venture capitalist Bob Kagle, a general partner in Technology Venture Investors (TVI) and Benchmark Capital. By chance, Kagle had come upon the recently opened Juice Club in Palo Alto while on his way to lunch, attracted by the long line that stretched outside the store. He was struck by the zeal of the customers, later telling the *Los Angeles Times,* "It seemed like everyone had a tremendous sense of affirmation about buying this smoothie." He canceled his appointments in order to conduct some impromptu research, asking questions and taking notes, and ultimately concluding that there was a growing market for healthy drinks like the smoothie and that Juice Club had a chance to define the category in a way similar to what Starbucks had done with coffee. In fact, Kagle enlisted Starbucks' chairman and CEO, Howard Schultz, to participate in an initial $3 million round of funding for Juice Club. After meeting with Perron and finding that they shared similar values, Schultz subsequently agreed to join the board. Perron also turned to Starbucks' real estate brokers to co-locate some outlets with Starbucks, since the two franchises were not in direct competition. With Schultz's blessing, Juice Club was able to raise a further $19 million from seven venture groups, one of which was Microsoft cofounder Paul Allen's Global Retail Partners. A wider group of investors would ultimately invest an additional $44 million in the business.

From Juice Club to Jamba Juice: 1995

Perron was now well positioned to take his business to a new level. He moved his corporate headquarters to San Francisco, increased the staff from 17 to 40, and changed the name of Juice Club to Jamba Juice Company. With a lot of imitators entering the business, all of whose names began with the word "juice," Perron wanted to distinguish the company from the pack. Moreover, Jamba Juice became a store concept that offered a hipper, festive, more Starbuck-like quality, a decided move away from a bland health store look. The word "jamba" means "to celebrate" in Swahili, and in turn Jamba Juice celebrated a healthy lifestyle. The brightly colored decor of the new stores and the smoothie names contributed to the effort to brand the Jamba Juice sensibility. Perron was also quick to recognize infringements and displayed a willingness to go to court to prevent rivals from copying Jamba's store layout, packaging, or drink names.

While Juice Clubs gradually made the transition to the Jamba Juice concept over the next two years, Perron initiated a site acquisition and development plan to roll out new Jamba Juice outlets at an accelerated pace, with a goal of reaching the 1,000 mark in a few years. He believed it was important to stake a claim in the fast-growing juice segment of the restaurant industry. By mid-1996, the chain had 30 stores, all located in California, 18 of which were company owned. A year later that number would virtually double, and California would top the 300 mark in total juice bars, with any number of competitors cropping up. In August 1997, Jamba took an initial step in expanding outside the state when it signed a licensing deal with Whole Foods Market of Austin, Texas, a major natural and organic foods grocery chain. Whole Foods' staff, trained by Jamba personnel, were to operate juice stands under the Jamba name and logo. The agreement allowed for Jamba outlets in four supermarkets, two of which would be established in California. Whole Foods supermarkets in Boulder, Colorado, and Tempe, Arizona, were chosen as the first non-California Jamba Juice locations, with the ultimate goal of placing juice bars in all of the Whole Foods 75 supermarkets spread across 17 states and the District of Columbia. In addition to tapping into the organic and natural food store sector, Jamba targeted two other locales that management believed were fertile territories for its concept: universities and airports.

Jamba's infrastructure evolved along with its menu. In order to retain them for an extended period, store managers were treated as quasi-owners. Not only did the company pay managers a percentage of a store's profits as an incentive, Jamba developed a retention plan, which it labeled "J.U.I.C.E." In essence, a percentage of a store's cash flow was placed in a retention bonus account, which would be awarded after three years. Should managers agree to another three-year term, they would be granted a three-week paid sabbatical. Moreover, employees in managerial positions received stock options. Jamba workers also received considerable training before being allowed to work alone, and were encouraged to make decisions in order to address customer problems without the need to seek managerial approval. It was Jamba's focus on the needs of its customers that led to changes on the menu. While they waited for their smoothies to be prepared, many customers were known to visit neighboring shops to buy a bagel. The drinks may have been adequate meal replacements from a nutritional point of view, but they lacked what was called the "chew factor." Jamba turned to the research and development firm of Mattson & Co., which produced a number of new food options. After much fine tuning, the chain introduced the results of that effort in 1998: the Jambola, a four-ounce, high-nutrient bread that was

Key Dates:

1990: Juice Club opens in San Luis Obispo.
1995: The store changes its name to Jamba Juice.
1996: Thirty stores, both franchised and company owned, are in operation throughout California.
1997: A licensing agreement is signed with Whole Foods Market to open Jamba Juice bars in Whole Foods supermarkets in both California and other states.
1998: Jambola bread is introduced.
1999: Jamba Juice acquires its main competitor, Zuka Juice; Souprimos soup line is introduced.
2000: Paul Clayton is named CEO.

toasted and, accompanied by a smoothie, created a "Power Meal." Rather than deal with the difficulties of a fresh-baked product, Jamba chose to have the Jambolas produced by a third party and delivered frozen to stores, where they would be prepared in a conveyor toaster oven.

Over the next two years, Jamba added to its food offerings, all the while introducing new smoothie concoctions. In 1999, a line of vegetable soups, Souprimos, was launched. Because customer feedback indicated that the product fell short on taste, Jamba decided to improve flavor and consistency by including some fat to the recipes. In early 2000, the chain added gourmet soft pretzels to its menu. In addition to the traditional salted pretzel, Jamba offered two exotic flavors, Apple Cinnamon and Sourdough Parmesan. Smoothies and soups were then combined with either the breads or pretzels to produce what the chain now called Jamba Meals.

Acquisition of Zuka Juice: 1999

The Jamba chain boasted some 125 outlets in early 1999 when Perron negotiated a merger with one of Jamba's main competitors, Zuka Juice, which totaled nearly 100 stores, 25 of which were company owned. Zuka had been launched in Provo, Utah, in 1995 by Dave Duffin, who now elected to join forces with Perron rather than battle over the same territory and see the smoothie business degenerate into something like the 1990s bagel wars, which resulted in overexpansion and the bankruptcy of several aspiring chains. The addition of Zuka gave Jamba a presence in the Northwest as well as in Texas and Nevada. Only in Utah, where the brand was well entrenched, would the Zuka name be retained. To further accelerate growth, Jamba also began opening stores with major franchising partners. Jamba Hawaii Partners looked to open outlets in Hawaii, while a joint venture called Heartland Juice Company was created to bring Jamba Juice to Illinois, Minnesota, and Wisconsin. Although there would be some concern about the success of smoothies in cold climes, doubts would be eased considerably when the first store that opened in Chicago quickly developed into one of the most profitable units of the entire chain. Although there was already some interest at this time in franchising Jamba Juice overseas, the focus remained on the domestic market.

Perron was eager to take Jamba public, a move that would allow his equity partners a chance to realize a return on their sizeable investments in the company. In preparation for such a move, in January 2000 he brought in a seasoned fast-food executive, Paul Clayton, to take over as the chief executive officer. Clayton had 16 years of experience at Burger King as well as some time with McDonald's in Germany. Thoughts of an initial public offering (IPO), however, would have to be postponed due to the poor results of most restaurant stocks in 1999. Under Clayton, Jamba continued to focus on internal growth while it waited for market conditions to improve. It introduced a catering service, which it called Jamba Go Go, and became involved in delivery by teaming up with Waiter.com, an Internet ordering and delivery service (with a minimum order of $60). To build on Jamba's strong West Coast presence, Clayton continued to look for suitable development partners in order to enter new markets. The Jamba concept was also undergoing constant tweaking, with decor changes and an ongoing search for foods to complement smoothies in order to appeal to consumers who were less likely to view a smoothie as a desirable meal replacement.

By the summer of 2001, the Jamba chain had grown to some 330 units, far short of the 1,000 that Perron had envisioned yet still a significant increase over the 75 units the chain numbered just three years earlier. Sales were growing significantly, and there appeared to be a significant upside to the number of outlets the company could expect to open in the coming years. Whole Foods Markets was enjoying success with its 25 Jamba Juice stands and expected to expand the concept to its other 50 stores. In addition, Jamba began testing similar outlets inside California health clubs, which if successful offered great future growth potential. A major reason behind the success of the Chicago store, in fact, was its proximity to a large health club. Clearly, Jamba needed to be located close to its core customers, primarily college campuses, health food stores, and health clubs, as well as airports where travelers were receptive to the idea of a smoothie as a quick nutritious meal replacement. Clayton hoped to add 60 to 70 new stores each year for the next several years. This plan was given a significant boost in early 2002 when Jamba signed a licensing agreement with Sodexho, a major foods and facilities management company. Sodexho already ran Jamba outlets at Loyola Marymount University and the University of Nevada, but in addition to opening Jamba Juice stores at additional colleges it was considering the possibility of transferring the idea to its healthcare and corporate services divisions.

Prospects appeared bright for Jamba. There remained ample room for growth, both in the United States and overseas. Moreover, the category was not yet dominated by any major players and the Jamba concept was attractive enough to provide a competitive edge. What remained uncertain was investor response to Jamba's seemingly inevitable IPO. Would they view Jamba and its smoothies as the next Starbucks? Or would they simply dismiss smoothies as a fad?

Principal Subsidiaries

Zuka Juice.

Principal Competitors

Planet Smoothie Franchises, LLC; Smoothie King Franchises, Inc.

Further Reading

Adams, Michael, "Kirk Perron: Jamba Juice," *Restaurant Business,* March 15, 1999, p. 38.

——, "Smoothie Operator," *Restaurant Business,* October 10, 1996, p. 80.

Carlsen, Clifford, "Juice Club Given Fresh Cash, Will Pour into New Markets," *San Francisco Business Times,* June 17, 1996.

——, "Juicy Growth Deals Have Jamba Ready to Peel Out," *San Francisco Business Times,* May 3, 1999.

Cavanaugh, Connie Brewer, "Paul Clayton: Ex-KB Prexy Becomes a Smoothie Operator As Jamba Juice's Chief Exec," *Nation's Restaurant News,* January 2000, pp. 56–57.

Hanushevsky, Andy, "Kirk Perron Freshly Squeezed," *QSF Magazine,* January 1999.

Plotkin, Hal, "Seeking Quality, Juicer Squeezes Out Franchises," *Inc.,* July 1997, p. 25.

"Retail Entrepreneurs of the Year: Kirk Perron," *Chain Store Age,* December 2001, p. 66.

Ruggless, Ron, "Jamba Juice: Smoothies Sail Full Steam Ahead," *Nation's Restaurant News,* May 11, 1998, pp. 96–100.

Seo, Diana, "Getting All Juiced Up," *Los Angeles Times,* May 17, 1997, p. D1.

—Ed Dinger

Kikkoman Corporation

250 Noda
Noda, Chiba 278-8601
Japan
Telephone: 81-471-23-5111
Fax: 81-471-23-5200
Web site: http://www.kikkoman.co.jp

Kikkoman International, Inc.
50 California Street
Suite 3600
San Francisco, California 94111
U.S.A.
Telephone: (415) 956-7750
Fax: (415) 956-7760

Public Company
Incorporated: 1917
Employees: 2,640
Sales: $2.8 billion (2000)
Stock Exchanges: Tokyo
NAIC: 311941 Mayonaisse, Dressing, and Other Prepared
Sauce Manufacturing; 312130 Wineries; 311999 All
Other Miscellaneous Food Manufacturing; 325412
Pharmaceutical Preparation Manufacturing; 325998
All Other Miscellaneous Chemical Product and
Preparation Manufacturing

Kikkoman Corporation is the world's largest and most famous producer of soy sauce. It is the best-selling soy sauce brand in Japan, and virtually the only soy sauce with an international presence. Some 20 percent of its revenue derives from overseas sales, and about half of its profits come from its U.S. market. The company makes a variety of other products besides soy sauce, including Mann's Wine, one of the most popular labels in Japan, health foods such as vegetable juices and brown rice under the Del Monte brand label, and a slew of biotechnology products such as the enzyme luciferase, which is used in food production facilities to test for microorganisms. In addition, Kikkoman owns and operates the Colza restaurant chains along with the Nakanakaya chain of pubs, and also runs a wine garden in the heart of downtown Tokyo. The company's five main divisons are soy sauce, products related to soy sauce, wine and liquor, Del Monte (Kikkoman acquired that company's Far Eastern division in 1990), and biotechnology. Kikkoman maintains production facilities in Japan, Singapore, Taiwan, and the Netherlands, and two factories in the United States, one in Walworth, Wisconsin, and another in Folsom, California. U.S. marketing and sales are overseen by Kikkoman International, Inc., in San Francisco.

Ancient Roots

Kikkoman Corporation was founded in 1917 in Noda, Japan, but the company's roots go back to the 17th century. Around 1650, a number of families began to produce food seasonings from the plants and crops of their small, intensely cultivated growing fields. One of these products was soy sauce, a concoction primarily made from soybeans that was used to enhance the flavor of countless dishes, from soup to skewers of chicken. Many of these family-operated businesses located their operation next to the Edo River, so that freshly made soy sauce could be delivered as quickly as possible to customers in the capital of Edo, present-day Tokyo. During the time that Japan was open to outside trade, Dutch ships from half a world away bought soy sauce in the city of Nagasaki. These Dutch traders shipped the soy sauce back to The Netherlands, where the new taste became the overnight sensation for the upper classes.

Over the years, some of the families who produced soy sauce grew in wealth, prominence, and influence and contributed many astute business leaders that helped develop Japan's economy into one of the strongest in the Orient. However, by the end of the 19th and beginning of the 20th centuries, there were over 1,000 soy sauce companies competing for a rather limited Japanese market. In order to ensure the survival of their businesses, eight families producing soy sauce and other food seasonings in Noda banded together and formed Kikkoman Corporation in 1917.

From the very beginning, the production of high-quality soy sauce was the cornerstone of Kikkoman's success. The ingredients of soy sauce and the method of its production have been the same for nearly 400 years. Soy sauce is made from three simple ingredients—soybeans, wheat, and salt. The soybeans, rich and full of protein, are first steamed and then mixed with wheat, previously crushed and roasted. This mixture of soybeans and wheat is then combined with something similar but not identical to yeast, which serves as a catalyst for the culturing process. The result is a dry mash, known as *koji.* According to the traditional brewing procedure, brine is next added to the *koji* in order to make *moromi.* Moromi is a strong, even potent concoction, which remains in fermentation casks or tanks. During fermentation, the *koji* acts as an enzyme and changes the protein of a soybean into an amino acid while also transforming the starch of the wheat into sugar. After a short time, the *moromi* turns a startling reddish brown, and lactic acid cocci and yeast activate all the combined factors that make and distinguish the flavor, color, and aroma of soy sauce.

Kikkoman Corporation not only maintained the traditional manner of making soy sauce but also continued the historical method of careful atmospheric and temperature control that enables the brewing processes to take place. In the old days, master brewers took extensive precautions in brewing the soy sauce and spent long hours monitoring its progress. Buckets known as *kakioke* and paddles called *kaibo* provided these brewing experts with all they needed to control the entire process. After four centuries, the quality-control process was refined through the development and cultivation of microorganisms that made production much more efficient.

Kikkoman in the Early 20th Century

After its founding in 1917, Kikkoman Corporation became known as the biggest soy sauce producer in Japan. The company sold exclusively to consumers in Japan and, since virtually every person used some form of soy sauce during a meal, revenues grew rapidly during the 1920s. Kikkoman began to expand its product line at this time and produced such variations as soy sauces for meat, noodles, fish, and chicken. By the end of the 1930s the company had grown so large that a brand-new plant, named Goyogura, was constructed in Noda; it was specifically developed and designed to preserve the traditional manner and techniques of brewing soy sauce. The Goyogura plant was designated to produce soy sauce for the emperor of Japan and the entire imperial retinue.

During the early part of World War II, the company's Japanese market remained high, but as the war progressed there was less and less food to eat, and consequently the demand for soy sauce decreased. By the end of the war, the company's production facilities in Noda had almost come to a complete halt. The postwar years were harsh ones for the entire Japanese population. Food shortages, lack of fuel, and a ruined economy contributed to years of privation. However, with the help of the United States and other countries, Japan slowly rebuilt its country and economy.

Postwar Expansion

Kikkoman revived its fortunes along with the rest of Japanese business in the late 1940s. By the early 1950s the company was selling large amounts of soy sauce and other seasonings both to the domestic market in Japan and to the new burgeoning markets around the Pacific Rim. In the Asia-Pacific region, countries including Australia, New Zealand, Malaysia, Taiwan, and Korea began to open their doors to such Japanese companies as Kikkoman. Within a very short time, Kikkoman's soy sauce was used on many different kinds of food, including fried noodles, fried rice, barbecued beef, roasted lamb, fish, fowl, and the entire range of vegetables. Chefs in those countries began to notice how soy sauce awakened the flavor of food, and soon the popularity of the product had spread across the Pacific Ocean to the United States.

In 1957, the company took a big step in its international development by establishing Kikkoman International, Inc., in San Francisco, California. The company's first subsidiary outside of mainland Japan, Kikkoman International was a marketing operation that helped popularize soy sauce in the United States. Although interest started slowly, soy sauce soon found its way into the recipes of chefs at glamorous restaurants as well as into common lunchtime meals. Soy sauce began to be used on distinctly American cuisine such as hamburgers, Caesar salads, and barbecued baby pork ribs. As its presence in the United States grew, and its share of the food seasonings market increased, Kikkoman began to introduce other items such as teriyaki sauce and tofu in order to stir Americans' imaginations. By the end of the 1950s, the company was firmly established on the West Coast of the United States, and sales of its products were increasing rapidly.

By the 1960s, Kikkoman Corporation was ready to initiate a major expansion program in both the domestic and international markets. In 1962, the company created Tone Coca-Cola Bottling Company, Ltd., a soft drink bottling company located near Tokyo. This venture signaled the company's entry into a market not directly related to soy sauce and food seasonings. In one of its most important decisions, Kikkoman arranged to produce and market a number of Del Monte products for the Japanese market. The first of these items included a variety of Del Monte juices and tomato products. Kikkoman's advertising campaign for Del Monte products caused the brand to become a household name throughout the Japanese islands. In 1964, Kikkoman formed Mann's Wine Company, Ltd., for the purpose of producing and distributing its own wine labels in Japan. To complement the formation of this company, management at Kikkoman also created a laboratory in order to develop sophisticated technology that would allow the use of domestically grown grapes to produce distinctive and unique Japanese wines. In addition, Mann's Wine Company began to import various brandy and champagne labels to market for domestic consumption. The decade ended on a high note when Kikkoman invested in the Japan Food Corporation, a large trading firm that provided greater access to overseas markets.

The 1970s witnessed a continuation of the policies set by the company during the 1960s. The ever-increasing demand for its products led Kikkoman to design and construct its own U.S.-based manufacturing facility. Located in Walworth, Wisconsin, in the heart of the Upper Midwest, the plant began making soy sauce and other food products in 1972. During the same year, Kikkoman initiated its operation of a chain of restaurants located in major cities across West Germany. Named Kikkoman Daitokai (Europe) GmbH, the venture garnered immediate popularity. Kikkoman Daitokai was the company's entry into the restaurant business, and, since revenues were increasing rapidly, management decided to open a chain of similarly styled restaurants in Japan. The Colza restaurant chain began operating in 1974 in Tokyo, specializing in *teppanyaki*—prepared grilled foods—and the Kushi Colza restaurant chain opened during the same year, specializing in vegetables and various meats heated on skewers of bamboo. This style of food, called *kushiyaki,* is one of the most popular in Japan. Since the restaurant chain within Germany had performed so well from its opening in 1974 through 1979, the company established Kikkoman Trading Europe GmbH in Dusseldorf to take advantage of the growing demand for Japanese products such as soy sauce.

Kikkoman's markets in the Asia-Pacific region grew in importance during the 1980s. The use of so many different kinds of food seasonings in countries such as Korea, China, Malaysia, and Australia led the company to establish a production facility in Singapore, called Kikkoman (S) Pte. Ltd., in 1983. As consumer demand continued to grow, the company added a fully automated plant located in Chitose, Japan. Both the facility in Singapore and the one in Chitose made products for the Asia-Pacific region. The European arm of Kikkoman's operations also expanded during the 1980s. The company grew its restaurant business by creating Kikkoman Restaurants S.A., a subsidiary based in Switzerland.

Perhaps the most important development during the 1980s was the company's commitment to laboratory research and development. Kikkoman established a state-of-the-art research facility that would remain on the cutting edge of technological sophistication in the food industry. Kikkoman's laboratory focused on applying biotechnology and enzymology to create new seasonings and foods. One of its most significant achievements included the improvement of a proprietary microorganism employed in the production of soy sauce. Other accomplishments were just as impressive. Scientists were able to create an enzyme that produced gallic acid, normally used within the semiconductor and pharmaceutical industries. Initially created for industrial

production, this enzyme developed into one of the company's most lucrative commercial products. Company researchers were also the first to isolate luciferase and produce it for industrial use. Luciferase is an enzyme that enables fireflies to glow, and scientists at Kikkoman's laboratory used it to detect various microorganisms in water and food. Luciferase also found commercial applications in hospitals and in the semiconductor industry. Another research success involved the development of the *Oretachi* orange, a fruit that is resistant to cold temperatures. Based on cell-fusion techniques, this knowledge was exported by Kikkoman to help orange growers around the world.

International Growth in the 1990s and After

In the 1990s, Kikkoman continued to expand its international operations. The company purchased the perpetual marketing rights for the Del Monte brand label covering the entire Asia-Pacific region, except for the Philippines. After this agreement was reached in 1990, the company made a concerted effort to increase sales throughout the region. During the same year, Kikkoman entered into a joint venture and established President Kikkoman, Inc., a soy sauce production facility based in Taiwan. The company also formed Kikkoman Trading (S) Pte. Ltd., a subsidiary that marketed products made in both Japan and Singapore, in addition to the whole line of Del Monte products, to the countries around the Pacific Rim. In 1992, Kikkoman Australia Pty. Limited was formed to take advantage of the market demand in Australia and New Zealand. This Australian subsidiary was able to help make Kikkoman's soy sauce the highest selling oriental food seasoning ingredient in the country.

International growth was particularly important to Kikkoman as its domestic market stagnated. The bubble that had sustained the Japanese economy through the 1980s had burst, and the country was plagued by a long recession throughout the 1990s. Domestic consumption of soy sauce was not burgeoning, and Kikkoman needed to find new products and new markets. In 1995, the company gained a new president and CEO, Yuzaburo Mogi. Mogi was an outspoken businessman who was also vice-chairman of Japan's Association of Corporate Executives (*Keizai Doyukai*) and chairman of the Committee on Infrastructure for New Industries. He spoke in front of the World Economic Forum in Davos, Switzerland, in 1997 about topics thought unusual in a Japanese corporate leader: taking risks, innovating broadly, deregulating the Japanese economy. Mogi railed against the sometimes stultifying management style of Japanese companies, and he converted Kikkoman's top executives to an incentive-based pay system in 1996. Mogi struggled to bring more products to market, and to do it faster. The company investigated ways to invigorate Japan's soy sauce market by developing brand extensions such as a deluxe soy sauce and a new sauce for beef, which was growing in popularity. But markets outside of Japan seemed to be the company's best bet.

Kikkoman enjoyed a strong presence in the United States, where its only significant competitor was La Choy, a chemically processed soy sauce. In the mid-1990s, Kikkoman changed its U.S. advertising agency. Eventually the San Francisco agency Foote, Cone & Belding put out a series of animated television advertisements which aimed to reach a mainstream audience. The thrust of the messages was how easy it was to cook with

Kikkoman sauces, and the animated spokesperson was notable for not appearing to be Japanese. Kikkoman also upped its production capability in the United States, breaking ground for a new plant in Folsom, California, in 1997. The Folsom plant was designed to serve the Western United States and the Canadian market. That same year, Kikkoman began building a soy sauce plant in the Netherlands to serve its European market.

The company also continued its biotechnology research. After Kikkoman purchased Del Monte's Asian business in 1990, the company began research into new tomato varieties. Kikkoman researchers evolved a new method of inoculating tomato plants against a common virus, and developed hardier and juicier tomatoes. Kikkoman also continued to develop and market enzymes for industrial use. By 1997, the company had a stable of 12 enzymes it sold to other food manufacturers, laboratories, and cosmetic manufacturers. Kikkoman also developed soy-based pharmaceuticals, such as the estrogen product Isoflavon.

By 1999, the company was enjoying strong growth in its U.S. market. Approximately 50 percent of its operating profits for the first half of 1999 came from the United States. But other Japanese companies were attracted to the hot American market as well. The Yamasa Corp. and the San-J Corp. both began producing soy sauce in the U.S. in the 1990s. Kikkoman, which had about 50 percent of the U.S. soy sauce market, faced losing market share to these companies. Kikkoman also competed with U.S. firms such as Nabisco and Lawry's over condiments and marinades. In 2000, Kikkoman launched a new, $7 million advertising campaign in the United States, again demonstrating how easy it was to cook with Kikkoman products. The company also began cross-promoting its sauces with Reynolds brand aluminum foil and with Hefty brand food storage bags. Sales for 2000 were over $2.8 million, a surge of more than 30 percent over 1999. Net income rose only slightly.

Principal Subsidiaries

Kikkoman Ajinomingei Co., Ltd.; Kikkoman Business Development Inc.; Kikkoman Restaurant, Inc.; Mann's Wine Co., Ltd.; Manns Wine Pub Co., Ltd.; Nippon Del Monte Corporation; Pacific Trading Co., Ltd.; Seishin Corporation; Sobu Butsuryu Co., Ltd.; Sobu Service Center Inc.; Tone Coca-Cola Bottling Co., Ltd.; Japan Food Corp. (Aust) Pty. Limited; Japan Food Canada Inc.; Japan Food (Hawaii), Inc.; JFC Hong Kong Limited; JFC International Inc.; Kikkoman Australia Pty. Limited; Kikkoman Daitokai (Europe) GmbH; Kikkoman Foods, Inc.; Kikkoman International Inc. (USA); Kikkoman Restaurants S.A.; Kikkoman (S) Pte. Ltd.; Kikkoman Trading Europe GmbH; Kikkoman Trading (S) Pte. Ltd.; President Kikkoman Inc.

Principal Competitors

Yamasa Corp.; San-J Corp.

Further Reading

"Company Profile," Forbes, January 7, 1991, pp. 267–68.
"Company Profile," Forbes, January 3, 1994, pp. S21–S22.
Conan, Kerri, "Soy Sauce," Restaurant Business, October 10, 1993, p. 97.
Kelly, Jane Irene, "A Real Character," Adweek, May 31, 1999, p. 4.
"Kikkoman Set to Break Ground on New US Production Facility," Nation's Restaurant News, January 20, 1997, p. 52.
"More Than Oriental," Prepared Foods, October 1992, p. 64.
Reyes, Sonia, "Kikko-man Returns for Condiment Aisle Spin," Brandweek, April 3, 2000, p. 8.
Ryan, Nancy Ross, "All About Soy Sauce," Restaurants & Institutions, November 15, 1994, p. 83.
Takagawa, Michael K., "Kikkoman Adds Takagawa to Team," Nation's Restaurant News, August 3, 1992, p. 136.
Tanikawa, Miki, and Robert McNatt, "A Saucy Little Condiment Hits It Big," Business Week, September 20, 1999, p. 6.
Voight, Joan, "Battle for Sauce Is Brewing," Adweek, March 11, 1996, p. 2.
Yates, Ronald E., The Kikkoman Chronicles, New York: McGraw-Hill, 1998.

—Thomas Derdak
—update: A. Woodward

Kmart Corporation

3100 West Big Beaver Road
Troy, Michigan 48084-3163
U.S.A.
Telephone: (248) 463-1000
Toll Free: (800) 63-KMART; (800) 635-6278
Fax: (248) 463-5636
Web site: http://www.kmartcorp.com

Public Company
Incorporated: 1912 as S.S. Kresge Company
Employees: 252,000
Sales: $37.03 billion (2001)
Stock Exchanges: New York Pacific Chicago
Ticker Symbol: KM
NAIC: 452910 Warehouse Clubs and Superstores;
  452990 All Other General Merchandise Stores;
  454110 Electronic Shopping and Mail-Order Houses

Kmart Corporation, which entered 2002 as the second largest U.S. discount retailer (behind Wal-Mart Stores, Inc.) with over 2,100 outlets in 50 states, Guam, Puerto Rico, and the Virgin Islands, once so dominated the discount store marketplace that few believed any competitor could shake its mighty grip. Yet too much diversification, too little attention to its core business, and brutal competition—particularly from the mighty Wal-Mart—led to a prolonged state of decline and ultimately to a filing for Chapter 11 bankruptcy protection in January 2002. The company soon announced a host of changes in upper management, the planned closure of hundreds of stores, and various efforts at improving operations in a massive turnaround effort that was far from guaranteed of success.

Kresge Red Fronts and Green Fronts: 1899 to 1929

The giant Kmart Corporation grew from a Detroit five-and-dime store opened in 1899. Its proprietor was Sebastian Spering Kresge, a former Pennsylvania tinware salesman, who along with a partner, John McCrory, adopted the chain-store idea first used by Frank W. Woolworth. When Kresge and McCrory dissolved the partnership they had formed in 1897, McCrory took over the stores in Memphis, and Kresge maintained those in Detroit, forming S.S. Kresge Company. Kresge's eponymous outlet sold costume jewelry, housewares, and personal grooming aids. Its success encouraged him to open a second store in Port Huron, Michigan, the same year; others followed in rapid succession. By 1912, when Kresge incorporated his company in Delaware with a capitalization of $7 million, there were 85 stores producing annual sales of $10.3 million. Four years later he reincorporated in Michigan, this time with a $12 million capitalization. In 1918 the firm went public with a listing on the New York Stock Exchange.

Always in high-traffic, convenient locations, Kresge Red Front stores featured open displays of merchandise with items systematically associated. Following their founder's abhorrence of credit, they kept their prices to thrifty nickel and dime limits, until inflation after World War I made the cost of many items too high. Undaunted, Kresge opened a chain of Green Front units in 1920, all selling merchandise at prices ranging between 25 cents and $1. He also acquired Mount Clemens Pottery, to supply the stores with ever popular inexpensive dinnerware.

In 1924 the company's 257 stores generated annual sales of $90 million. Convinced this success should go hand in hand with corporate responsibility toward the less fortunate, the company founder established the Kresge Foundation, making an initial contribution of $1.3 million plus securities worth $65 million.

The following year Kresge resigned the presidency he had held since 1907 to concentrate on long-range goal-setting as company chairman. His planning bore fruit in January 1929, when a Kresge store opened in the United States' first suburban shopping center, Country Club Plaza, in Kansas City, Missouri, thereby anticipating a shift in shopping patterns by some 15 years.

Another long-range goal crystallized in September 1928, with the formation of a Canadian subsidiary that opened the country's first Kresge store the following May. Based in Kitchener, Ontario, the initial venture was so successful that the company's $5 million investment financed another 18 stores in locations from Winnipeg to Montreal by the end of 1929. These brought the total number of Kresge stores to 597, together yielding sales of $156.3 million.

Weathering the Great Depression: 1930–40

The company's orderly expansion changed after 1929, when the Depression-era stock market plunged the price of Kresge stock from $57.50 per share to an eventual low of $5.50. This was a severe blow to company management, which had pledged its support by taking turns to buy the deflated stock, gambling on its bottoming out at $26. Kresge found himself at a loss, having promised to buy 100,000 shares he could no longer afford, and the company took them off his hands. By 1936, however, the chairman had bought back at cost his own shares plus the 251,306 others owned by the management.

The Depression also brought falling sales as well as inventory losses through the failure of suppliers' businesses. Competition also increased; the scramble for the retail dollar fueled rivalry from Sears, Roebuck and prompted other chains to open department store "bargain basements." Forced to broaden its inventory to meet this threat, Kresge had to raise its prices, so that Green Front stores had many items selling for up to $3 despite their former $1 ceiling.

With the Depression over by 1940, there were 682 stores in 27 U.S. states, plus 61 in Canada. Together, the stores produced 1940 sales of $158.7 million. As the decade advanced, many homeowners moved out to the suburbs from inner-city locations; the retailers followed. Kresge management cautiously opened one suburban shopping center store in 1947, adding to the first one that had opened in 1929. Three more followed in 1948. By 1953 there were about 40 suburban stores in the United States, plus one in Canada.

Massive Expansion: 1950s

By the mid-1950s Chairman Sebastian Kresge was long retired from active company management. An operating committee of 16 executives appointed by the board of directors steered the corporate strategy. Although the committee frequently combined smaller stores in high-volume areas to provide better selection and more efficient service, there were 616 U.S. stores by 1954, plus 74 in Canada. Many of the units featured modern conveniences such as air conditioning, self-service displays, and shopping baskets. All these operations combined to reach sales figures totaling $337.9 million in 1954—up from $223.2 million in 1945.

Although the variety store image still guided company activities during the 1950s, pricing limits were fading away, with the concept of discount retailing coming to the fore in its stead. Kresge offered economical private-label products ranging from clothing to house paint. The variety of brand-name offerings

also broadened to include electric appliances, radios, and lawn-mowers.

In the late 1950s food grew into the largest single department, warranting training in food management for all store managers. Many stores had delicatessens, and Kresge in-store luncheonettes provided shoppers with a large assortment of snacks, lunches, and dinners devised by the test kitchen at the company's Detroit headquarters. By 1958 these mini-restaurants were so popular that at least one new or remodeled facility opened alongside a delicatessen counter in some Kresge store each week.

A wider variety of merchandise plus higher pricing brought a need for a layaway plan allowing customers to save for expensive items. It was, however, still against company policy to offer credit, although competitors were luring customers in this way.

In 1959, coinciding with the opening of the first Kresge store in Puerto Rico, Harry Blair Cunningham succeeded to the presidency of S.S. Kresge Company. Cunningham, aged 58, had been with Kresge since 1928. A former newspaper reporter, he had worked his way up from trainee status through the store manager ranks, eventually becoming general vice-president. Twin assignments went with this position: one was to tour all of Kresge's U.S. stores, assessing the future position of the company and its competitors in the variety store industry; the other was to prepare himself for the company presidency, when Franklin Williams would retire in two years' time.

Cunningham's travels convinced him that Kresge's competitors were not other variety chains, but the new discounters aiming for fast inventory turnover, which they could achieve by lower markups on a large assortment of small items. Discounting, in fact, was a return to Sebastian Kresge's basic merchandising philosophy, which would be a bulwark against competition in the future, just as it had been in the past. Cunningham, after a period of testing, concluded that higher sales volume, rather than higher markups, would boost the company's profits, which had dropped during the 1950s.

The Birth of Kmart: 1960s

In 1962 the company opened its first discount store in the Detroit suburb of Garden City, calling it Kmart. Within a year, there were 17 others. Unlike Kresge stores, Kmarts were not placed in shopping centers but were built in plazas by themselves, to avoid internal competition and also to provide ample parking. To ensure a 25 percent annual pretax return on investment, each store featured decor that was pleasant, though not extravagant, and each aimed for eight inventory turnovers per year. The Kmart stores were an instant success; by 1963, there were 63 facilities, 51 of which provided repair and maintenance service for automobiles. Three years later, the number of Kmarts had swelled to 122.

The Kmart introduction still left the company with a number of older Kresge stores, still on long leases, which were too small to display Kmart's expanded merchandise lines. Numerous Kresge stores, mostly in deteriorating business areas, were re-named Jupiter Discount Stores and converted to facilities offering a limited variety of low markup, fast-moving merchandise

Key Dates:

1897: Sebastian Spering Kresge and John McCrory form partnership to open five-and-dime stores in Detroit and Memphis.

1899: Partnership is dissolved, and Kresge takes over the Detroit stores, forming S.S. Kresge Company.

1912: S.S. Kresge Company, with 85 stores and $10.3 million in sales, is incorporated.

1918: Company goes public with a listing on the New York Stock Exchange.

1929: First store in Canada opens; a Kresge store is opened in the first suburban shopping center in United States; store total reaches 597 and sales hit $156.3 million.

1962: First discount store, called Kmart, opens in the Detroit suburb of Garden City.

1977: With Kmarts accounting for almost 95 percent of sales, the company changes its name to Kmart Corporation.

1984: Diversification into specialty retailing begins with purchase of Home Centers of America (renamed Builders Square) and Walden Book Company.

1985: First celebrity product line is introduced—the Jaclyn Smith line of clothes.

1987: Martha Stewart's association with Kmart begins; most U.S. Kresge and Jupiter stores are sold to McCrory Corporation.

1989: PACE Membership Warehouse Inc. is acquired.

1990: Wal-Mart surpasses Kmart in sales.

1991: First Super Kmart opens in Medina, Ohio, featuring a full-service grocery store and general merchandise; 90 percent stake in OfficeMax is acquired.

1992: Borders book superstore chain is acquired.

1994–95: Numerous noncore assets are shed, including PACE, OfficeMax, Sports Authority, Borders Group, and 860 auto service centers.

1995: More than 200 U.S. stores are closed.

1997: The Big Kmart format debuts; the Martha Stewart Everyday line of bed and bath products is launched.

1998: Kmart sells its stores in Canada to Hudson's Bay Company.

2001: Declining sales amid intense competition leads to liquidity crisis and halts in shipments from major vendors.

2002: Kmart files for Chapter 11 bankruptcy protection, becoming the largest retailer ever to do so; company announces that it will close 284 stores.

such as clothes, drugstore items, and housewares. By 1966 there were almost 100 Jupiter stores in operation.

In 1965 the company underwent several changes. One involved the sale of longtime subsidiary Mount Clemens Pottery. Another was the acquisition of Holly Stores, a retailer of women's and children's clothing that had been a Kmart licensee since 1962, and was operating clothing departments in 124 Kmarts, Kresges, and Jupiters at the time of the acquisition. The same year, the company acquired Dunhams Stores Corporation, a sporting goods supplier already operating under license in 42 Kmarts. Dunhams then became Kmart Sporting Goods, Inc.

S.S. Kresge Company's sales for 1965 reached a record $851 million, representing a 23.6 percent gain from 1964. There were 895 stores, of which 108 were in Canada. Although discount retailing had gained momentum somewhat later in Canada than in the United States, the Canadian subsidiary had opened its first Kmart in London, Ontario, in 1963. At the same time, while inner-city deterioration in Canada had not reached the same level as in U.S. cities, the company turned some of its smaller, older Canadian stores into Jupiters.

The successful Canadian operations made a large contribution to the total sales figures for 1966, which topped $1 billion for the first time, reflecting a 28 percent rise over 1965. Company founder Sebastian Kresge did not live to see this triumph. He died in September 1966 at the age of 99, having retired from the company chairmanship only three months earlier. Also in 1966, the famous "Blue Light Special" was invented by a Kmart manager in Fort Wayne, Indiana, who was seeking a way to make it easier for his customers to find the Christmas wrapping paper that he was clearing; the Blue Light Special went on to be adopted chainwide and become an American icon. Meantime, spurred by its Canadian success, the company found another international opportunity in Australia, via a joint venture: Kmart (Australia) Limited, with retailer G.J. Coles & Coy, Limited. The 1968 undertaking, in which Kmart held 51 percent of the shares, produced five Australian Kmarts by 1970.

By 1969 S.S. Kresge Company had decided against purchasing the licensee of its automotive departments, instead opening another subsidiary called Kmart Enterprises, Inc., to operate the departments, now so popular that 56 had opened in that year alone. That year the number of company stores stood at 1,022, sales at $4.6 billion, and average profit per store at $42,358.

Further Diversification: 1970s

As the 1960s ended, an economic slowdown posed challenges for S.S. Kresge. The company resorted to heavier-than-usual promotional markdowns in December 1969 and January 1970 that shaved profit margins. Other problems included the difficulty of keeping to a 25 percent annual rate of sales gain for an ever expanding number of stores; the fact that the rate of sales growth in a store slowed as the store aged; and the increase in inventory that came from formerly licensed in-store departments. All these factors led to an earnings slowdown in 1970's first quarter, bringing company stock down 11.5 points in one day. Still, sales for 1970 reached almost $2.2 billion.

In 1972 Cunningham was succeeded as chief executive by Robert E. Dewar, a former company lawyer and president since 1970. The presidency was filled by Ervin Wardlow, whose forte was merchandising.

The three upper managers hurdled these challenges with strategies forged under Cunningham's tenure, such as the centralized buying for both Kresge and Kmart stores that reduced possible in-house conflict between variety store and discount divisions. The company also expanded its management training program, so variety store managers could switch to discount facilities with ease. Meticulous crafting of the training program guaranteed each store manager could make decisions about products, promotions, pricing, and locations to ensure the store's competitiveness. Other policies included limiting each store to one entrance and exit, thus reducing staff needs and escalating sales per employee, and designing smaller stores of 65,000 to 70,000 square feet, adequate for smaller, more affluent shopping communities. All of these changes gave the company a chance to upgrade merchandise while phasing out leased departments on all items except shoes.

The course charted for the 1970s brought Kresge an annual sales growth of 22 percent from 1972 to 1976, with 1976 sales totaling $8.4 billion. The company, however, was not without its failures. A fast-food drive-in chain called Kmart Chef, set up in 1967, closed in 1974 after having peaked at just 11 units. The costly credit card operation, used by only 9 percent of Kmart's customers, was withdrawn the same year, while a $65 million purchase of Planned Marketing Associates, an insurance company renamed Kmart Insurance Services Inc., brought a loss of $8 million in 1975, although a modest profit of $344,000 was recorded for 1976. By this time the company's 1,206 Kmarts were accounting for almost 95 percent of sales. For this reason, shareholders changed the company name to Kmart Corporation in 1977.

Bolstering a Faded Image: 1978–89

The late 1970s saw changes in Kmart's seemingly impregnable position. New competitors with more inviting stores made company facilities seem shoddy, and specialty stores began to stock Kmart staples such as sports equipment, drugs, and personal grooming aids. Changes in public taste showed up in lagging profits, which sank 27 percent in 1980 on record sales reaching $14.2 billion. Other warning signals showed in plunging inventory turnover, which dropped from the 8 times annually level of the 1960s to 3.8 times by 1979. Utility bills, wages, and other overhead costs soared because of inflation, but fierce competition prevented the company from raising its discount prices.

Kmart responded by cutting the number of scheduled new stores in favor of remodeling existing units and restocking them with more fashionable merchandise. It also installed a computer system to handle inventories, orders, shipments, and other procedures that could speed up delivery times to each store. Other changes included the 1978 sale of the company's 51 percent interest in Kmart (Australia) Limited to G.J. Coles & Coy for a 20 percent stake in G.J. Coles & Coy (known as Coles Myer Ltd. following a 1985 merger), thus closing out Kmart's ownership of the Australian Kmart stores.

Bernard M. Fauber succeeded Dewar as chairman and chief executive in 1980. Fauber steered the company through an economic slowdown and into diversification that year, with purchase of a 44 percent interest in a Mexican discount chain, as well as a joint venture into Japanese mass-merchandising with Japan's biggest retailer, The Daiei, Inc. Kmart also bought Texas-based Furr's Cafeterias Inc., a 76-unit chain that was a natural outgrowth of the cafeterias in Kmart stores.

In 1984 Kmart expanded its acquisition program and diversified into specialty markets. Because Kmart had already been experimenting with its home improvement departments, a logical move was the $88.2 million purchase of a nine-unit Texas chain called Home Centers of America, Inc. Kmart made Home Centers' operations into warehouse-type stores, changing the name to Builders Square. Next came the Walden Book Company (Waldenbooks), costing $300 million for 845 stores that had produced sales of $417 million in 1983. An Oregon-based chain of 164 drugstores called PayLess joined the growing lineup in 1985.

There was another change in 1985—this one in Kmart strategy when apparel division president Joseph Antonini launched a new line of clothes named for and designed by actress Jaclyn Smith that helped turn apparel into the company's fastest-growing business. By the time he succeeded to the company chairmanship in 1987, Antonini's strategy had added racing driver Mario Andretti to the list for automotive accessories promotions, Fuzzy Zoeller for golf products, and domestic doyenne Martha Stewart for kitchen and housewares support. The celebrities helped the bottom line—profits for 1987 rose 19 percent, to reach $692 million on total sales of $25.6 billion. Other factors in year-end figures were the sale of all U.S. Kresge and Jupiter stores to McCrory Corporation (the business founded by Sebastian Kresge's original partner); the $238 million sale of Furr's Cafeterias and another cafeteria chain called Bishop Buffets, Inc., to Cavalcade Foods, Inc.; and the disposal of Mexican interests.

New ventures in 1988 included a partnership with Bruno's Inc., a food retailer, which generated the American Fare hypermarket near Atlanta in 1989; purchase of a 51 percent ownership interest in Makro Inc., which operated membership warehouses; and launch of Office Square, a discount office supply chain. In 1989 Kmart acquired PACE Membership Warehouse Inc. and the remaining 49 percent of Makro, converting Makro stores to PACE formats. It also opened Sports Giant, a group of sporting goods stores, and finished the year with sales of $27.7 billion and income of $800 million.

Beleaguered but Not Beaten: Early 1990s

The company changed its logo from red and turquoise to red and white, with "mart" written within the larger "K" in 1990. Next came the acquisition of The Sports Authority into which it rolled the Sports Giant stores. Kmart also began a long overdue six-year overhaul of its stores (including openings, closings, enlargements, and refurbishings) to help shore up its image. By this time, Wal-Mart had emerged as a credible threat and overtook Kmart in sales and market share in 1990. The following year, Kmart opened the first Super Kmart Center in Medina, Ohio, combining a full-service grocery store with the Kmart general merchandise selection and opening 24 hours a day, seven days a week. Still believing diversification was a good investment, the company purchased a 21.6 percent interest in OfficeMax, an office supply chain, in 1990 then increased the stake to 90 percent in 1991. By 1992 Kmart was still in an acquisition mode, buying 13 stores in the Czech Republic and Slovakia's Maj department store chain; Borders book superstores as a complement to Waldenbooks; and Intelligent Electronic's Bizmart chain. Sales for 1992 hit $34.6 million, a healthy notch above 1991's $32.5 billion, and Kmart's workforce reached an all-time high of 373,000.

Realizing that Kmart's future lay in its core retail business, the company began shedding noncore assets and sprucing up its stores. In 1993 Kmart sold 91 of its 113 PACE membership Warehouses to Wal-Mart. In 1994 came the spinoff of Office-Max and the Sports Authority (keeping a quarter interest in the former and 30 percent of the latter); the sale of PayLess Drug Stores (retaining 46 percent interest) and its 22 percent interest in Coles Myer Ltd.; an alliance to open stores in Mexico and Singapore; and the launch of Kathy Ireland's apparel line. Sales for 1993 had hit a high of $37.7 billion with income of $941 million; sales for 1994 fell to $34.6 billion but the big news was a staggering loss of $940 million.

More serious than ever in its reorganization, Kmart's newest journey began with the appointment of Floyd Hall, former chairman of Target stores, as president, CEO, and chairman of the board in June 1995. Next came the spinoff of the Borders Group (Borders and Waldenbooks' combined corporate name), the sale of its remaining interest in OfficeMax and the Sports Authority, and the divestment of 860 auto service centers to the Penske Corp. With widespread rumors of bankruptcy, the downgrading of its rating, and analysts predicting Kmart's demise, many wondered if the nearly 100-year-old retailer could survive increased competition from both Wal-Mart's and Target's newer, snazzier stores. Hall set out to prove Kmart not only was not going under—but had just begun to fight.

Short-Lived Comeback: Late 1990s

After closing 214 stores, disposing of its Czech, Slovak, and Singapore properties, and pledging to reduce expenses by $600–$800 million, Kmart was ready to prove its retail mettle. Its new merchandising credo centered around four simple words: brands, consumables, convenience, and culture. To help achieve its goals came a new advertising campaign featuring comedian Rosie O'Donnell and director Penny Marshall, a massive shakeup in upper management, and the launch of a multiyear $750 million remodeling program. The latter involved the introduction of the Big Kmart format, which was cleaner and brighter and featured wider aisles for easier shopping. Other key changes were the addition of a section of consumable goods conveniently located near the front of the stores and an increased emphasis on the children's and home furnishings departments. By the end of 1998, 1,245 of the company's stores (or 62 percent of the total) had been converted to the Big Kmart format.

Another important initiative was an expansion of popular brand-name and private-label lines, particularly the 1997 launch of the Martha Stewart Everyday line of bed and bath products through a strategic alliance between Kmart and Martha Stewart Living Omnimedia L.L.C., which Stewart had formed earlier that year to oversee her growing empire. The Martha Stewart line was expanded to include garden and patio products as well as baby products in 1999, and that year the line generated more than $1 billion in sales. Proving successful as well was the launch of a line of Sesame Street children's apparel and juvenile products.

Also in 1997, Kmart announced the sale of its remaining interest in Thrifty PayLess to Rite Aid, refinanced its debt load, started leasing out hundreds of its largest parking lots, and built a hip new three-story Kmart in Manhattan near Greenwich

Village. The firm also sold its interest in its Mexican joint venture and sold Builders Square to Leonard Green & Partners for a mere $10 million. Further retrenchment came in February 1998 when Kmart sold its 112 stores in Canada to Hudson's Bay Company for US$167.7 million (the stores were either closed or converted to other formats, mainly Zellers).

Through these and other moves, Hall succeeded in saving Kmart from oblivion, and the firm returned to profitability in the fiscal year ending in January 1998, posting net income of $249 million on sales of $32.18 billion, and stayed in the black for the following two years. By 1999 Hall was confident enough of the company's future to announce plans to open 400 stores over the next five years, with half of the units to be Super Kmart Centers. About 100 new stores were opened in 1999, the same year that Kmart ventured into e-commerce with the formation of BlueLight.com, a joint venture formed by Kmart, Softbank Corp., Yahoo! Inc., and Martha Stewart Living Omnimedia. Kmart also signed agreements in 1999 with Fleming Companies, Inc. and SuperValu Inc. to distribute grocery items to its stores. Despite this string of positive developments, underlying and significant problems remained, and Hall's expansion program quickly proved to be premature.

Falling into Bankruptcy, Early 21st Century

Hall retired as chairman, president, and CEO in early 2000. Hired as the new chairman and CEO was 39-year-old Charles C. "Chuck" Conaway, who had been president and COO of CVS Corporation, the giant drugstore chain. Conaway moved quickly to implement major changes as Kmart's financial performance began to once again head south. He shook up senior management, announced that 72 underperforming stores would be closed, and launched a $1.7 billion program to improve the supply chain and attempt to resolve the chain's chronic problem of keeping items in stock. The new initiatives continued in 2001. The company inked a deal with Fleming, making that firm the exclusive supplier of food and consumables for Kmarts and Super Kmarts. The Martha Stewart Everyday line was expanded even further, and an agreement was reached to develop a new and exclusive line of Disney children's clothing. On the marketing side, Conaway brought back the Blue Light Special—which had been shelved in 1991—in an attempt to instill some excitement into the stores, and prices were permanently trimmed on 38,000 everyday items in a new "Blue Light Always" pricing strategy.

This last maneuver, an ill-advised attempt at beating Wal-Mart at its own game that was launched in August 2001, proved to be a critical mistake. Not only did Wal-Mart move quickly and ruthlessly to match or undercut the prices, but Kmart also compounded its mistake by simultaneously and drastically cutting back its distribution of expensive advertising circulars. Customers used to the circulars simply stopped shopping at Kmart, and same-store sales fell throughout the final months of 2001, including during the crucial holiday selling season. The declining sales resulted in a liquidity crisis and halts in shipments from major vendors, leading the company to file for Chapter 11 bankruptcy protection on January 22, 2002, becoming the largest retailer ever to do so.

Just prior to the filing, James B. Adamson was named Kmart chairman, with Conaway remaining CEO. Adamson had been a

Kmart director since 1996 and had previously served as chairman and CEO of Advantica Restaurant Group, Inc., owner and operator of mid-priced restaurant chains, such as Denny's. In March 2002 Conaway resigned and Adamson took on the position of CEO as well. That month, Kmart announced that it would close 284 underperforming stores, resulting in the elimination of 22,000 jobs and a charge of more than $1 billion. As the company attempted to emerge from bankruptcy by mid-2003, its biggest challenge was to find a niche to occupy. Many observers were doubtful that a major discount chain could find such a niche given the strengths of the two main rivals: Wal-Mart with its rock-bottom prices and extensive grocery aisles and Target with its discount prices for slightly upscale products. In February 2002 Kmart launched a new advertising campaign featuring television commercials directed by Spike Lee and sporting a ''family values'' theme and the tagline ''Kmart. The Stuff of Life.'' In a company press release, Steven Feuling, a senior marketing vice-president, said that ''Kmart's goal with this campaign is to build an emotional bond with the consumer by re-establishing the role Kmart plays in its shoppers' lives.'' Whether this campaign and the company's other initiatives would be enough to save Kmart remained to be seen.

Principal Competitors

Wal-Mart Stores, Inc.; Target Corporation.

Further Reading

Brauer, Molly, ''Kmart Posts Profit, Denies Buyout Rumor,'' *Knight-Ridder/Tribune Business News,* November 21, 1996.

Byrne, Harlan S., ''New Look at Kmart: The Retailer Goes Upscale and Its Earnings Follow Suit,'' *Barron's,* May 11, 1987, pp. 8+.

Coleman, Calmetta Y., ''Grand Designs: Ask Ms. Stewart's Advice for How to Improve Kmart,'' *Wall Street Journal,* May 1, 2000, pp. A1+.

Fauber, Bernard M., ''Kmart's New Directions,'' *Discount Merchandiser,* November 1983, pp. 34+.

Gallanis, Peter J., ''Next Chapter in Kmart's Book Reads Refinement, Expansion,'' *Discount Store News,* March 6, 2000, pp. 51+.

Halverson, Richard, ''Leaner, Meaner, Cleaner: Nearly $1 Billion in Cost Cutting Has Goosed Earnings and Improved Efficiencies,'' *Discount Store News,* December 9, 1996, p. 27.

Hays, Constance L., ''Kmart to Close 284 Stores; 22,000 Jobs Will Be Cut,'' *New York Times,* March 9, 2002.

Hazel, Debra, ''Kmart: Is the Rebound Real?,'' *Chain Store Age,* May 1997, pp. 45–48.

Johnson, Jay L., ''Kmart's Solution,'' *Discount Merchandiser,* November 1999, pp. 27+.

''Kmart: It All Begins and Ends in the Store,'' *Discount Merchandiser,* August 1986, pp. 106+.

''Kmart Rises from Would-Be Fall, but Others Not So Lucky,'' *Discount Store News,* July 1, 1996, p. 59.

Koudsi, Suzanne, ''Attention Kmart Bashers: The Folks at BlueLight Are Turning the Troubled Retailer into an Online Force. And Wal-Mart Is Watching,'' *Fortune,* November 13, 2000, pp. 213+.

Kresge, Stanley Sebastian, *S.S. Kresge Company and Its Builder, Sebastian Spering Kresge,* New York: Newcomen Society in North America, 1957, 32 p.

——, *The S.S. Kresge Story,* Racine, Wis.: Western Publishing, 1979, 373 p.

''Kresge's,'' *Fortune,* June 1, 1940.

''Kresge's Triple-Threat Retailing,'' *Business Week,* January 29, 1966.

Kruger, Renée, ''Big Plans at Kmart,'' *Discount Merchandiser,* June 1997, pp. 20+.

Lieback, Laura, ''Kmart's To-Do List: Succession, Status, Stability,'' *Discount Store News,* March 9, 1998, pp. 22+.

——, ''A New Day Dawns for Kmart,'' *Discount Store News,* March 22, 1999, pp. 23+.

Main, Jeremy, ''Kmart's Plan to Be Born Again, Again,'' *Fortune,* September 21, 1981, pp. 74+.

Mammarella, James, ''The Martha-ization of Kmart's Home,'' *Discount Store News,* December 9, 1996, p. H3.

Mayer, Caroline E., ''Budget Retailer Kmart Tries to Dress Up Its Bargain-Basement Image,'' *Washington Post,* October 4, 1987, p. H1.

Merrick, Amy, ''Expensive Ad Circulars Help Precipitate Kmart President's Departure,'' *Wall Street Journal,* January 18, 2002, pp. B1, B6.

——, ''Kmart Lays Out Plans to Trim Its Size, Increase Efficiency in Bankruptcy Filing,'' *Wall Street Journal,* January 23, 2002, pp. A3, A6.

——, ''Kmart Says CEO Conaway Resigned, Adds Post to Cart of Chairman Adamson,'' *Wall Street Journal,* March 12, 2002, pp. A3, A10.

——, ''Kmart Store Closures Will Include Many of Its New Ones,'' *Wall Street Journal,* April 5, 2002, p. B4.

Mitchell, Russell, and Amy Dunkin, ''How They're Knocking the Rust Off Two Old Chains: As Other Old-Line Mass Merchandisers Struggle, Woolworth and Kmart Soar,'' *Business Week,* September 8, 1986, pp. 44+.

Muller, Joann, ''Kmart's Last Chance,'' *Business Week,* March 11, 2002, pp. 68–69.

——, ''Kmart: The Flood Waters Are Rising,'' *Business Week,* January 28, 2002, p. 106.

Muller, Joann, and Ann Therese Palmer, ''Kmart's Bright Idea,'' *Business Week,* April 9, 2001, pp. 50+.

Muller, Joann, and Diane Brady, ''A Kmart Special: Better Service,'' *Business Week,* September 4, 2000, pp. 80, 82.

Naughton, Keith, ''Bright Lights, Big City Won't Cut It for Kmart,'' *Business Week,* May 26, 1997, p. 57.

Perman, Stacy, ''Attention KMartha Shoppers,'' *Time,* October 6, 1997, pp. 55–58, 60.

Sanger, Elizabeth, ''Value at a Discount: Kmart Can Still Deliver the Goods,'' *Barron's,* February 28, 1983, pp. 24+.

Schlesinger, Jacob M., ''Kmart's New Look Seems to Be Taking Hold,'' *Wall Street Journal,* September 2, 1986.

Schwadel, Francine, ''Kmart Is Trying to Put Style on the Aisle—Will Upscale Image Confuse Core Customers?,'' *Wall Street Journal,* August 9, 1988.

Sellers, Patricia, ''Attention, Kmart Shoppers,'' *Fortune,* January 2, 1989.

''S.S. Kresge Expansion Is Costly,'' *Barron's,* September 7, 1936.

Taub, Stephen, ''Can Kmart Come Back Again?,'' *Financial World,* March 31, 1983, pp. 50+.

Wellman, M.G., ''Kmart's Repositioning for Growth,'' *Discount Merchandiser,* April 1988, pp. 40+.

''When 2 Cents = $380 Million,'' *Forbes,* April 1, 1970.

—Gillian Wolf
—updates: Taryn Benbow-Pfalzgraf, David E. Salamie

La Poste

4 Quai du Point du Jour
92777 Boulogne-Billancourt Cedex
France
Telephone: (+33) 1-41-41-66-66
Fax: (+33) 1-41-41-78-57
Web site: http://www.laposte.fr

Government-Owned Company
Incorporated: 1990
Employees: 320,000
Sales: EUR 17.03 billion ($13.6 billion) (2001)
NAIC: 491110 Postal Service; 541614 Process, Physical
   Distribution, and Logistics Consulting Services;
   522120 Savings Institutions

France's La Poste has expanded beyond its position as that country's postal service to become one of the top three logistics, corporate services, and financial providers in Europe, behind Germany's Deutsche Post and ahead of the United Kingdom's Concordia. The government-owned, yet independently operated company holds the number three position for electronic mail services in Europe, the number three spot in the European parcels and logistics sector, and one of the top positions in the French financial services market. These activities combined to produce more than EUR 17 billion in 2001. Among the company's assets is its network of more than 17,000 post offices, which provide mail services, financial services, and Internet access and e-mail services throughout France. The company's Geopost subsidiary, formed in 2000 and located in the United Kingdom, handles the company's parcels and logistics wing, while express mail services are provided through Chronopost International and Tat Express. Since 2001, La Poste has gained controlled of Deutsche Paket Dienst, giving it entry into Germany, as well as adding to its operations in France and England; the DPD acquisition gave La Poste the number two spot in Europe's business-to-business parcel delivery market. Other subsidiaries and participations include Brokers Worldwide, which offers collection, preparation, and other services to U.S.-based international mail dispatchers; Dynapost, which is the French market leader in corporate mail processing; Europe Airpost, formerly the Aéropostale partnership with Air France; INSA, which specializes in print distribution; and Mediapost, the leading French direct mail advertising service.

Roman-Era Postal Roots

The history of the postal service in France goes back to the time of Julius Caesar, who mentions in his *De Bello Gallico* a mail service running along the Rhone valley in Gaul. The province then benefited from Emperor Augustus's creation of the *cursus publicus,* which was at first restricted to carrying administrative mail. Private messages were carried by *tabellarii,* personal slaves or freedmen in the service of patrician families. During the Middle Ages, the state postal service disappeared, giving way to various private mail services. Messages were carried between abbeys by monks; the messengers of the University of Paris carried letters between the University's numerous foreign students and their families in Europe, and aristocrats and rich merchants such as Jacques Coeur employed messengers for their private correspondence. Messengers were appointed by municipalities, initially restricted to carrying mail between municipal officials, but by the 14th and 15th centuries they were also entrusted with private letters. The royal postal service remained one of many postal services for a long time. King Louis XI, who reigned from 1461 to 1483, reintroduced the Roman post house system, a relay system whereby horses could be changed along the route. King Louis XII, who reigned from 1498 to 1515, established such relays every seven leagues along royal roads. In 1533 permanent postal routes were created between France, England, and Switzerland.

On May 8, 1597, a royal edict created *relais de louage,* a stagecoach service intended for private use. This system was merged with the *poste aux cheveux* in 1602. The controleur général of the posts, Guillaume Fouquet de la Varane, appointed in 1595, played a major part in establishing a royal monopoly on the collection, carriage, and delivery of mail, with varying rates according to weight and destination. However, Louis XIII, who reigned from 1610 to 1643, gradually contracted the service to individuals in an attempt to raise funds for the royal treasury. During the reign of Louis XVI—from 1643 to 1715—various post-related positions were sold as special offices. Later, however, under the influence of minister Jean-Baptiste Colbert, the superintendent of the posts, Jérome de Nouveau, sought to abolish postmasters' offices. This took place in 1662. In 1668 the secrétaire de la guerre (minister of war), François-Michel Letellier, Marquis of Louvois, took the role of superintendent of the posts, left vacant after the death of de Nouveau in 1665.

Louvois entirely reorganized the postal service, placing it under two authorities. The superintendent, a government minister, was to set postage rates, while the fermier général was contracted by the royal treasury to administer the postal service. The first contract for the latter function was drawn up between the state and the Pajot and Rouillé families, who occupied this position for more than 50 years. The fermier générale included more than 800 post offices in France as well as offices in Rome, Genoa, Turin, and Geneva. There were six postal routes, covering the six major French highways, along which mail was carried by postcoaches. In 1738 the Grimod and Thiroux families took on the role of fermier général, which they retained until the 1789 revolution. During this period post was delivered between towns but not within them. The poste aux chevaux (horse post) was operated by postmasters who ran posthouses—these were often inns—and were responsible for carrying mail, while there were around 1,000 post offices in France, headed by salaried directors, which were responsible for collecting and dispatching correspondence. In 1759 C.H. Piarron de Chamousset obtained from the king the right to undertake local postal delivery in Paris. The service proved so profitable that the crown soon decided to recover the rights and to extend local delivery throughout France. The so-called Petite Poste (intra-town post) was extended by royal decree in 1786 throughout France, eventually covering all French municipalities. The 1789 revolution did not affect the mail service until 1793, when it became a state-owned agency. Financial difficulties prompted the government to revert to the contract system several years later. State control of the posts was established definitively in 1804 with the creation of a directorate general under the Ministry of Finance. Antoine-Marie Chamans, Count of La Valette, remained in charge of the posts from this date until the fall of the First Empire in 1815, when he gained a place in history by escaping from prison, disguised in his wife's clothes, the day before he was due to be executed.

Forming the Modern Postal Service in the 19th Century

The Restoration period brought several major changes in the postal service. A royal decree of February 24, 1817, made possible the introduction of the money order, which allowed funds to be delivered at one post office upon receipt of an order transmitted from another. From April 1, 1830, postal collections and deliveries were made every second day from and to homes in every municipality in France. This was the first appearance in France of the modern postman, and brought the end of rural isolation. During the reign of Louis-Philippe, mail transport was accelerated by the introduction of the railway. In 1842 mail was carried on the Strasbourg-Basel line. In 1845 mail began to be sorted in designated wagons during the train journey from city to city. Soon this method of transport replaced the horse post, which officially ended in 1873. A major improvement was due to Etienne Arago, a famous scientist and director of the posts under the Second Republic, who was responsible for the introduction of the fixed postage rate and the postage stamp, based on the English innovation of the penny post. On August 24, 1848, the National Assembly decreed that a single postage rate should be charged regardless of distance, though varying with the weight of the letter. In December 1848 another decree marked the introduction of the first three French postage stamps. In the first year after the reform, postal traffic jumped from 122 million to 158 million letters per year. During the Second Empire, rapid improvements were made in postal services abroad, especially by boat, when regular postal links were established with Indochina in 1861; the United States, Mexico, and the West Indies in 1864; and South America and West Africa in 1866.

After a short period during the siege of Paris by the German army in 1870 when a pigeon post operated, the postal service extended its role during the Third Republic. The postal service, controlled by the Ministry of Finance, and the telegraph service, controlled by the Ministry of the Interior, were combined under a single administration, the Ministry of Posts and Telegraph, headed by Adolphe Cochery. Later, however, the postal and telegraph services were attached to several other ministries until 1906, when an undersecretariat of posts and telegraph services (P&T) was reestablished as a single ministry within the government. On April 9, 1881, a new state institution was created, the Caisse Nationale d'Epargne (National Savings and Loans), with a separate budget, which was supervised by the posts and telegraphs undersecretariat. Savers could use any post office in the country as a savings bank. At the same time, this gave the state vast sums of money to finance large social and housing programs. In 1900 deposit accounts at the Caisse Nationale d'Epargne totaled FFr 3.5 billion. Following the example of Austria (1883), Switzerland (1906), Germany (1909), and Belgium (1913), under the law of January 7, 1918, the French posts and telegraphs undersecretariat was allowed to operate a current account service. In the face of violent opposition from the French banks, the undersecretariat was not allowed to offer interest-bearing accounts. The funds accumulated by postal current accounts were placed in the custody of the Public Treasury.

Developing in the 20th Century

In the 20th century, an airmail service was introduced. The first attempt to transport mail by air took place in July 1912, near Nancy in Lorraine. The airplane, carrying 40 kilograms of mail, flew for 17 minutes. On October 15, 1913, the same pilot, Lieutenant Ronin, flew from Paris to Bordeaux carrying an urgent letter to the steamship Peru, bound for the West Indies. During World War I the development of airmail services was suspended. In 1918 the Paris-Le Mans-St. Nazaire route began to be exploited for the use of the U.S. Army. Several state-subsidized private firms carrying airmail, such as the Compagnie Aéropostale and the Compagnie Farman, appeared in 1919. At the end of the year, the pilot and airplane-builder Pierre Latécoère made the first international airmail delivery, to Barcelona, Spain. The service was soon extended to Rabat, Morocco, by way of Alicante and Malaga. In 1922 the pilot Maurice Nogues established the first commercial Paris-Bucharest-Constantinople-Ankara airlink, and in February 1930 the first postal airlink between France and Indochina. Jean Mermoz made the first direct mail-carrying flight between France and South America on May 12, 1930. On September 2, 1930, Dieudonné Costes and Maurice Bellonte flew from New York to Paris without stopping. In 1939 the airmail service consisted of four routes covering 11 French municipalities with daily flights.

The French P&T was affected severely by World War II: by the end of the war, 25 percent of post offices, 50 percent of mailwagons, and 75 percent of Paris's post vans had been lost, destroyed, or stolen. Old German warplanes were used to start up airmail services again. During the 1950s and 1960s the P&T concentrated on improving existing services, introducing motorized postal delivery and mechanical sorting. Postal codes, included in addresses to facilitate sorting, were introduced in 1964. In 1973 the first automatic sorting center opened in Orléans. In 1961 a helicopter service was introduced to deliver mail to the islands off Brittany. At the same time, postal services began to be rationalized; first Sunday and then Saturday afternoon deliveries were withdrawn.

It was only since the 1970s that national P&Ts began to experience competition from new communication techniques. Between 1976 and 1985, international mail traffic decreased by 10 percent because of growing recourse to telecommunications. Meanwhile, European Economic Community (EEC) regulations were introduced to control competition between data and written material transmission services. This led to the French government's decision to separate telecommunication and postal services. The reform law of 1971 separated the Direction Générale des Télécommunications (DGT) from the Direction Générale de la Poste (DGP). In 1990 the two entities adopted new names—La Poste and France Télécom, respectively—in recognition of their new legal status.

At that time, La Poste and France Télécom became *exploitants autonomes de droit public*, state-owned and largely autonomous. The powers of the ministry in charge of these were clearly defined: general regulation of the sector, planning contracts between La Poste and the state, and protection of employees' status as civil servants. Postal and telephone rates were no longer set by the ministries of finance and posts and telecommunications. The financial status of La Poste was markedly different from that of the DGP. In 1923 a law had been passed that separated the budget of the postal services from that of the state. This, however, allowed the state to levy large sums of money from the mail service's profits in order to subsidize government electronic and space programs. The 1990 reform law granted La Poste a totally independent budget. The question of reduced postal rates for the press, which represented half the public subsidies given in total to that sector, was also solved by the reform, which obliged the state to contribute to press rates subsidies.

Other subsidies needed to be found to finance loss-making post offices in rural areas; in 1990 there were 17,000 post offices, 12,000 of which were based in areas with fewer than 10,000 inhabitants. The 1990 reform aimed to support the structurally loss-making postal services by developing La Poste's expertise in financial services. La Poste's share of current account funds had been diminishing steadily for 40 years; it fell from 30 percent of total current account funds in 1950 to 12 percent in 1988. Traditional savings products were also facing serious competition from new stock-exchange-oriented savings products. The 1990 reform authorized La Poste to act as an insurance company in offering all types of personal insurance. A major difference remained between La Poste and the French banks, however; the first was barred from making real estate loans unless the borrower had previous savings, as well as from making consumer loans, the two types of loans for which there was growing demand.

Diversified Services Provider for the New Century

Meanwhile, the P&T began to develop a marketing policy, since it was allowed to establish individualized contracts for mail services with major private clients, generally corporate. The 1980s were characterized by the development of new services: telecopy (facsimile, or fax) services were launched in 1981. Chronopost, a rapid delivery service of correspondence and goods with guaranteed time limits, began in 1986. The P&T started to explore services such as gift or advertisement delivery or company mail, whereby special prices could be negotiated for large mailings. In 1990 computerized scanners were installed for post-code sorting.

La Poste became an independent, public sector company in 1991. The group began to step up its financial services offerings, to the extent that by the middle of the decade financial services represented nearly one-fourth of its revenues. Yet, in 1997, La Poste was forced to detach its financial services products from its mail services in a move designed to reduce its competitive advantage. This policy placed La Poste in line with most of its European counterparts. Meanwhile, La Poste was facing increasing competition in its mail and parcel delivery services as more and more of the segment was opened to competition.

As a response, La Poste began diversifying its operations in the late 1990s. Logistics and corporate mail services, not only in France, but across Europe, became a core company direction; in 2000, La Poste created a new subsidiary, GeoPost, based in the United Kingdom, to oversee its growing logistics holdings. In that year, also, La Poste acquired full control of its Aéropostale air freight partnership with Air France, which was renamed Airpost and then focused on providing postal traffic services. La Poste also took steps to gain a major share in the Internet communication and e-commerce delivery markets; in 2000 La Poste rolled out a free e-mail and Internet access service located in its network of offices. Meanwhile, La Poste had been building up its position in the European parcel deliveries market. After buying up Denkhaus, with operations in Germany and the Benelux countries, in 1998, La Poste began acquiring a stake in Deutsche Paket Dienst (DPD), a major rival to Deutsche Post in Germany, which also held leading positions in the United Kingdom and France. By 2001, La Poste had gained full control of DPD, giving it one of the leading positions in the European market.

That acquisition, however, was not without its glitches—by the end of the year, it had become apparent that La Poste had overpaid some EUR 100 million for DPD. The resulting write-off—combined with preparations for the passage to the Euro-dollar in 2002 and disruptions resulting from the September 11th attacks in New York City and Washington, D.C.—forced La Poste to report its first annual loss since 1996, of EUR 95 million.

A parliamentary report released at the end of 2001 recommended that La Poste spin off its financial services wing into a separate subsidiary, in order to ensure its survival against the new banking services giant created with the merger of Caisse des Depots et Consignations and Caisse d'Epargne. The spinoff would allow La Poste to offer a complete range of financial services, including providing home and other loans, and would enable many of the group's loss-making rural offices to become profitable. In the meantime, La Poste began lobbying for the right to shut down a large proportion of those offices—many of which served towns with populations of fewer than 2,000, in favor of reorienting the network toward more densely populated towns of more than 10,000.

Principal Subsidiaries

Brokers Worldwide; Dynapost; Europe Airport; Geopost; INSA; Media Post; SF2 (50.1%); Sofipost Holding Company; Sopassure (50.01%); STP.

Principal Competitors

Deutsche Post World Net (DPAG); Consignia plc; TPG NV (TP); Die Schweizerische Post; Canada Post Corp.; Australian Postal Corp.; Post Office Ltd.; La Poste (Belgium); Maroc Telecom; Communications Authority of Thailand; Entreprise des Postes et Telecommunications Luxembourg; Magyar Posta Rt; Hellenic Post-ELTA SA; Malawi Posts and Telecommunications Corp.

Further Reading

Barberi, Jean-Luc, "Un 'mammouth' en panne," *Expansion*, December 4, 1997, p. 76.

Chauvigny, *Les Grands Moments de La Poste,* Paris: France-Empire, 1988.

Dupuy, Héléna, "La Poste veut sa place dans le trio de tête européen," *La Tribune*, April 4, 2002.

Fabre, Thierry, "La Poste mene sa guerre d'independance," *Expansion*, October 10, 1994, p. 82.

Fourre, Jean-Pierre, *Rapport à l'Assemblée Nationale Relatif à L'Organization du Service Public des Postes et des Telecommunications,* Paris: Imprimerie Nationale, 1990.

Histoire d'une Réforme, Paris: Ministry of Posts, Telecommunications and Space, 1990.

Rolland, *Chronologie de l'Histoire des Postes,* Paris: SNSL, 1975.

Vaille, *Histoire Générale de la Poste de Louis XI à 1789,* 5 volumes, Paris: Presses Universitaires de France, 1950.

Vingt Siècles d'Histoire de la Poste, Paris: Ministère des PTT, 1954.

—William Baranès
—update: M.L. Cohen

AIR LIQUIDE ™

L'Air Liquide SA

75, quai d'Orsay
75321 Paris Cedex 07
France
Telephone: (+33) 1 40 62 55 55
Fax: (+33) 1 40 62 54 65
Web site: http://www.airliquide.com

Public Company
Incorporated: 1902
Employees: 30,800
Sales: EUR 8.3 billion ($6.64 billion) (2001)
Stock Exchanges: Euronext Paris; OTC
Ticker Symbol: AI; AIQUY
NAIC: 325120 Industrial Gas Manufacturing

L'Air Liquide SA (Air Liquide) is the world's leading producer of industrial gases, with operations in 60 countries that together produced more than EUR 8.3 billion in sales in 2001. Industrial and medical gases and accompanying services represent more than 80 percent of Air Liquide's sales. The company's home base, France, accounts for 23 percent of its sales. The Americas produce 33 percent of sales, while the rest of Europe adds 27 percent. The Asia/Pacific region, where the company is also present through subsidiary Société d'Oxygène et d'Acetylène d'Extrême-Orient, represented 15 percent of the company's sales. The company's products find multiple applications in a diversity of products. The areas of chemistry, industry, agriculture, pharmacy, electricity, biology, papermaking, glassmaking, and medicine all use industrial gases. Since the late 1990s, Air Liquide has also stepped up its activities in "wet" chemicals products, such as hydrogen peroxide, ammonium hydroxide, and acids used in semiconductor production and in other industries. Founded in 1902, Air Liquide attempted to seal its world leadership with the acquisition of Britain's British Oxygen Corporation; the deal fell through in 2000, however, after failing to win FTC approval. Shortly after, Air Liquide fought off an attempted takeover by Suez Lyonnaise des Eaux in 2001. Instead, Air Liquide had continued growth through smaller-scale acquisitions and internal growth initiatives, such as the opening of small site production facilities designed to provide products for specific customers.

Chemicals Industry Pioneer at the Turn of the 20th Century

Georges Claude received his diploma in chemistry from the School of Physics and Chemistry in 1889. From 1896 to 1902 he worked as a chemist at Compagnie Française Houston-Thompson. While employed there he attempted to develop a process for handling acetylene. The chemical, discovered only a few years earlier, posed several difficulties for industrial use; in particular the expense of production and storage made it economically unfeasible for wide-scale use. At the age of 26, Claude solved these problems and discovered a method for liquefying acetylene. Professor Land, a German chemist, had succeeded earlier in separating oxygen and nitrogen. However, the gases converted by Land's "counter-current procedure" contained 40 percent impurities. The triumph of Claude's process, acclaimed by the Academy of Science and Chemistry, returned gases with less than 1 percent impurities.

Claude's research led him to believe that air gases, produced and stored economically, could serve as viable and inexpensive sources of energy. He envisioned oxygen and nitrogen as sources of power for combustion engines. Claude's process for separating air gases resulted in the emission of large quantities of heat. However, many of his early experiments failed. They were expensive to undertake and the young chemist had no financial resources of his own to rely upon. Good ideas, Claude realized, needed financing if they were to become anything more than ideas.

Paul Delorme, a former schoolmate and coworker at Houston-Thompson, encouraged his friend Frédéric Gallier to match his own financial contribution to Claude's research. In November 1902 Delorme and Gallier each contributed FFr 50,000 to the fledgling enterprise; the company was formally constituted, and Paul Delorme was named president, a position which he held until 1945. The bulk of the company's original 26 shares were entrusted to Claude.

During the early years the company suffered from financial hardships, but the business skills of Paul Delorme carried L'Air Liquide through these difficult times. In 1903 Delorme issued 725 new shares and offered 100 of these shares for sale. By the third quarter of 1906, L'Air Liquide had overcome its financial problems, and during that year the company earned its first dividends. Since that time L'Air Liquide continued to prosper.

International Growth Before World War II

Under the direction of Delorme, L'Air Liquide established plants in Belgium and Brazil in 1906, and continued to expand into overseas markets; plants were set up in Spain (1910), Japan (1911), and Canada and Sweden (1913). One of the earlier inventions of Claude, neon lighting, appeared on the streets of Paris in 1910. (He had applied for the first patent on neon tubes in 1907.) In 1908 L'Air Liquide began producing oxygen and later became one of the largest producers in Europe. Immediately prior to and during World War I, Claude designed machinery to improve the production of ammonia. His work with liquid oxygen at this time led to technological innovations in explosives.

The interwar years were ones of continued overseas expansion for L'Air Liquide. Plants were established in Greece, Singapore, Hong Kong, Malaysia, Portugal, and Senegal. In this period Claude concentrated his efforts on the separation and utilization of rare atmospheric gases. His engineering skills overcame the practical difficulties and Claude was able to improve on his process for separating hydrogen. Through several stages of cooling, using liquid carbon monoxide as the coolant, hydrogen was compressed. His success with hydrogen produced a lubricant which could be used for driving motors. Employing nitrogen, the gas was injected into the motor and provided an efficient lubricant down to -211 degrees Fahrenheit. No other lubricant product had proved to be so efficient at this temperature.

Claude regarded the oceans as the most abundant yet untapped source of energy on the globe, and during the 1930s he began experimenting with thermodynamic principles to take advantage of this energy source. His efforts in this area did not have any immediate practical results, but following World War II the Academy of Sciences used his principles of thermodynamics and started to build a thermodynamic plant off the coast of Cuba. An accident caused the project to be cancelled, but L'Air Liquide continued to develop oceanic products, including the manufacturing of special equipment for deep-sea diving.

Following World War II the French High Court accused Claude of collaborating with the Nazis. Unconfirmed charges claimed that the development of the "flying bomb" resulted from Claude's work. In his defense, Claude stated that he believed in German victory under the auspices of Pétain in Vichy France. The Court, however, sentenced him to life imprisonment and stripped him of all honors. He was released from prison in 1950.

During the 1960s gas sales declined, and most of the major industrial gases manufacturers began to diversify their compa-

nies. But Jean Delorme, Paul Delorme's son, believed the potential market for gases remained strong, and under his leadership L'Air Liquide did not follow the movement to diversification. This decision improved the company's leading position in the industrial gases market. At the same time, L'Air Liquide pursued a policy of expansion through cautious acquisition, Delorme seeking to acquire only companies with an established customer base.

Unlike most industries, gases producers usually performed well during a recession; the real cost of gases actually declined during the 1970s. With other fuel costs rising, the incentive to use combustion engines, which require oxygen, increased. Improved technologies resulted in the intensified use of more efficient combustion engines. Recession, though, adversely affected the customer base that consumed industrial gases. Heavy industry, like steel manufacturing, was adversely affected by the recession of the 1970s, resulting in the reduction of demand for L'Air Liquide products. This trend continued into the 1980s as European and U.S. steelmakers reduced their capacities. In order to compensate for its losses, L'Air Liquide sold its unprofitable sectors.

Technological innovations posed another major threat to L'Air Liquide's markets. For example, new technologies allowed steel manufacturers to do away with blast furnaces and the oxygen used to power them. However, L'Air Liquide recognized that these innovations resulted in more efficient blast furnaces which, in turn, have maintained a demand for oxygen.

Welding accounted for as much as 11 percent of L'Air Liquide's sales by the end of the 1980s. This sector traditionally used oxy-acetylene in all its welding equipment. Oxy-acetylene, the hottest and most concentrated fuel gas, provided light before the invention of the electric light bulb. Yet the welding market for L'Air Liquide began to decline as laser technology provided cleaner, safer machinery, replacing the traditional gas-fueled torch.

Restructuring for the Next 100 Years

The smallest customers of industrial gases producers tended to be hospitals which purchased gases in cylinders. U.S. industrial gases manufacturers largely left this market to the smaller producers. In Europe the larger manufacturers tended to sell cylinder gases, and then lease the cylinder. To some degree this practice insulated them against cyclical changes in the marketplace. However, the demand for cylinder gases, mainly oxygen and acetylene, was usually met by local producers since these gases could not be liquefied and were dangerous to transport. Reductions in social security drug reimbursements and lower healthcare expenditures led some gases manufacturers in Europe to believe that the market could decline in this sector. These governmental policies, along with exchange rate fluctuations, contributed to declining profits and sales for L'Air Liquide in the late 1980s.

As early as 1916 L'Air Liquide entered into a joint venture with Rockefeller and Hollingsworth to form L'Air Reduction Company in the United States. After World War II, however, the French government forced L'Air Liquide to sell its U.S. holdings in order to assist France in diminishing its war debts.

Key Dates:

1902: L'Air Liquide is founded for the production of liquid acetylene based on a process developed by Georges Claude.

1906: Air Liquide opens plants in Brazil and Belgium.

1908: Company begins production of oxygen.

1969: Air Liquide opens U.S. subsidiary.

1986: Company acquires Big Three Industries, based in Texas, and becomes second largest industrial gas producer in the United States.

1990: Company begins five-year restructuring program to reduce costs and adopt a decentralized organization.

1994: Air Liquide begins power cogeneration activities, including acquisition of power generation company Bayou Cogen and construction of new plants in Italy, the Netherlands, and France.

1999: Air Liquide and Air Products and Chemicals agree to joint acquisition of British Oxygen Corporation; the acquisition is rejected in 2000 by the FTC, however.

2001: Air Liquide rejects takeover offer by Suez Lyonnaise des Eaux, acquires full control of Hede Nielsen A/S in Denmark.

Not until 1969 did L'Air Liquide return to the United States. The highly international character of L'Air Liquide made the company susceptible to parity changes between the French franc and the U.S. dollar. Efforts to increase L'Air Liquide's share of the U.S. market contributed to this volatility in the late 1980s. As L'Air Liquide's presence in the U.S. market grew, this vulnerability increased in importance. The limiting effects of the European Monetary System made this a lesser concern in the European markets; these markets accounted for 53 percent of the net sales of L'Air Liquide and were to remain the company's largest market into the new century.

L'Air Liquide, however, acquired Big Three Industries of Texas in 1986 for $1.6 billion. This acquisition made L'Air Liquide the second largest industrial gases manufacturer in the United States. The deal, financed by cash and U.S. borrowing, increased the company's U.S. market from approximately 14 to 20 percent. However, the Federal Trade Commission (FTC) required L'Air Liquide to divest part of its holdings by selling certain sections of the company to ensure free competition and guard against monopolization of the industry within the United States by L'Air Liquide.

Air Products and Chemicals, Inc., a leading U.S. competitor hoping to acquire a portion of L'Air Liquide's customer base, had begun building small plants, approximately one-eighth the size of the larger L'Air Liquide sites. Air Products believed that the structure of the larger firm slowed down its ability to respond quickly to changing market conditions. Air Products hoped this would give it a competitive edge against L'Air Liquide.

Nevertheless, L'Air Liquide expected to maintain a substantial share of its customer base in the United States. First, the size of the company allowed for large expenditures on research and development. Second, the nature of the industrial gases market enticed companies to build plants next to established customers. Traditionally, the customer and the supplier entered into long-term contracts for 15 to 25 years. The supplier installed pipelines to the customer site and pumped the gases directly to the plant, alleviating expensive shipping costs.

AGA of Sweden and L'Air Liquide dissolved a 15-year cooperative agreement in the mid-1980s. The decision not to renew the agreement resulted in the increased presence of L'Air Liquide in Belgium and Luxembourg, while AGA increased its holdings in Germany, Holland, and The Netherlands. The termination of the agreement also reduced a number of constraints that Air Liquide faced when pursuing market opportunities throughout Europe, though the monopoly of the British market by BOC continued to make the United Kingdom virtually inaccessible. Nevertheless, Air Liquide boasted an impressive record during the decade, more than doubling its markets. During this time sales in the United States, Canada, Australia, Asia, and Africa increased from 20 to 36 percent, while the gas sector alone accounted for approximately 66 percent of net sales.

Although technological innovations potentially threatened the continued use of gases, L'Air Liquide exhibited its capability to adapt to changing market conditions. In 1985 the company entered into a joint venture with Whemo Denko of Japan to supply NASDA, the Japanese Space Agency, with liquid hydrogen. In addition, the rapidly growing electronics industry in Japan required vector gases, nitrogen and hydrogen. The purification techniques developed by L'Air Liquide provided quality products for this market, with less than one part per billion of impurities. L'Air Liquide quickly took second place to Nippon Sanso in this Japanese market.

Declining sales, as a result of the recession of the early 1990s, encouraged Air Liquide to adopt a vast reorganization and cost-cutting plan, including shedding some 10 percent of its international workforce. In 1993, the company reorganized its operations into a decentralized, regionally focused structure in an effort to bring the company closer to its customers. The ultimate goal of the company's new strategy was to step up its level of services, with the expectation that customers would be willing to pay more for the added value.

In the mid-1990s, Air Liquide value-added strategy expanded to include cogeneration activities, including the acquisition of power generation company Bayou Cogen in 1994. The company built a new power generation plant in Texas, while acquiring generation capacity in Milan, Italy. By 1995, Air Liquide was capable of producing more than 500 megawatts. In that year, the company commissioned two new plants, in Rotterdam, the Netherlands, and in Fos-sur-Mer in France. By then, the company had increased its operations in the Far East as well, when it acquired full control of Société d'Oxygène et d'Acetylène d'Extrême-Orient. The following year, Air Liquide stepped up its activities in Eastern Europe, moving into Poland.

Air Liquide began stepping up its activities within the semiconductor industry by entering the "wet" chemicals sector, manufacturing products such as hydrogen peroxide, ammonium hydroxide, and acids used as cleaning agents during the semiconductor manufacturing process. By then, the company had found another lucrative market for its gas products as the automobile industry began adding airbags as standard features in their new automobiles.

By the late 1990s, Air Liquide had established itself as the world-leading producer of industrial gases. In 1999, the company made an attempt to gain a still greater share of the market when it purchased the Dutch, Belgian, and German operations of the United Kingdom's British Oxygen Corporation (BOC). Later that year, Air Liquide moved to acquire BOC outright, in a purchase offer made in cooperation with the United States' Air Products and Chemicals. Despite BOC's agreement to be acquired, the deal, worth $11.4 billion, was rejected by the FTC in the United States; in 2000, BOC, Air Liquide, and Air Products called off the proposed acquisition.

The following year, Air Liquide found itself the object of a takeover approach, when Suez Lyonnaise des Eaux offered to buy up Air Liquide for EUR 53 billion. The offer was quickly declined by Air Liquide, which preferred to remain independent and dedicated to its core product, rather than become part of a diversified group.

As it prepared to celebrate its 100th anniversary in 2002, Air Liquide continued to build up its global position through smaller-scale acquisitions. In September 2001, the company reached an agreement to acquire full control of Hede Nielsen A/S, based in Denmark (Air Liquide had acquired a 43 percent stake, as well as operational control of Hede Nielsen in 1992). Then, in October 2001, the company purchased six subsidiaries from debt-laden Messer Griesheim, of Germany, in a deal worth EUR 185 million. That acquisition expanded Air Liquide's operations in South Africa, South Korea, Brazil, and Argentina, while enabling it to establish new operations in Egypt and Trinidad & Tobago. Despite the difficult economic climate at the turn of the century, Air Liquide showed every sign of continuing to lead its market in the years to come.

Principal Subsidiaries

L'Air Liquide SA; Air Liquide International; Société Chimique de la Grande Paroisse (64.79%); Compagnie Française de Produits Oxygenes (99.85%); Société d'Oxygène et d'Acetylène d'Extrême-Orient; Société Anonyme de Fabrication de Genilis (99.99%); Société Industrielle des Gaz de l'Air (99.96%); SOGIF (98.84%); Compagnie Industrielle Commerciale et Financiere des Gaz; CRYOLOR (79.99%); ALM (60%); SEPAL (50.95%). The company also has subsidiaries in the following countries: Argentina, Australia, Austria, Belgium, Cameroon, Canada, Denmark, Gabon, Ghana, Greece, Italy, Luxembourg, The Netherlands, Nigeria, Paraguay, Portugal, Senegal, Sweden, Tunisia, the United Kingdom, the United States, and Germany.

Principal Competitors

Air Products and Chemicals, Inc.; Airgas, Inc.; BOC Group; Linde AG; Mitsui Chemicals, Inc.; Nippon Sanso Corporation; Praxair, Inc.; Valley National Gases Incorporated; S.A. White Martins.

Further Reading

Hunter, David, "For Air Liquide, Growth Through Decentralization," *Chemical Week*, June 7, 1995, p. 44.

Jemain, Alain, *Les Conquerants de l'Invisible*, Editions Fayard, Paris: 2002

Minder, Raphael, "Air Liquide Abandons Earnings Guidance," *Financial Times*, February 26, 2002.

100 Years of Inspiration—The Air Liquide Adventure, Paris: L'Air Liquide, 2002.

—update: M.L. Cohen

Ligand Pharmaceuticals Incorporated

10275 Science Center Drive
San Diego, California 92121-1117
U.S.A.
Telephone: (858) 550-7500
Fax: (858) 550-7506
Web site: http://www.ligand.com

Public Company
Incorporated: 1987 as Progenx Inc.
Employees: 356
Sales: $48.1 million (2000)
Stock Exchanges: NASDAQ
Ticker Symbol: LGND
NAIC: 325412 Pharmaceutical Preparation Manufacturing

Operating out of San Diego, California, Ligand Pharmaceuticals Incorporated discovers, develops, and markets new drugs, concentrating on cancer, skin diseases, hormone-related diseases, osteoporosis, metabolic disorders, cardiovascular diseases, and inflammatory diseases. Ligand's drug development program relies on the company's expertise on the way hormones work, in particular intracellular receptor (IR) technology. Receptors in the human body permit cells to respond to hormones or other chemical messengers. Similar to IR technology is STAT technology, which Ligand uses to target a receptor located on the surface of a cell rather than the interior. In essence, Ligand develops drugs that attach to a receptor in order to affect the body in a manner similar to the way a hormone naturally acts. In recognition of the company's expertise in this field, a number of larger and more established global pharmaceutical companies have forged collaborative relationships, including Pfizer, Glaxo Wellcome, American Home Products, SmithKline Beecham, Eli Lilly, Abbott Laboratories, Warner-Lambert, and Elan Corporation.

Formation of Ligand: 1987

Ligand was originally called Progenx, Inc., formed in September 1987 by Brook Byers, partner in the San Francisco venture capital firm of Kleiner Perkins Caufield & Byers. The new company licensed monoclonal antibody technology in order to develop cancer detection and therapy products. While raising $1.6 million in seed money, Byers recruited a chief executive to run the business, settling on Howard Birndorf, a man well seasoned in launching biotechnology start-ups, many of which Byers had previously funded. Although earning a graduate degree in biochemistry, Birndorf also displayed an entrepreneurial spirit, having once helped a friend to establish a chain of shoe stores. He launched his first biotechnology company, Hybritech, in 1978, teaming with medical doctor Ivor Royston. The two men drew up a business plan based on a model they found in a "how-to" book, then convinced Byers's firm to commit to $300,000 in funding. After taking Hybritech public in 1984, Birndorf departed, and two years later Eli Lilly & Co. purchased the company in a $485 million deal. Although Royston remained dedicated to research, Birndorf found that he loved nurturing start-ups, then turning over management to others to take to the next stage. Forsaking a scientific role, he was involved in the creation of Gen-Probe, Gensa, and Idec, becoming recognized as an expert in start-ups and often hired to speak to groups of entrepreneurs. Byers told the *Los Angeles Times,* "I really like doing start-ups with Howard because he can get more done in the first year than some people can get done in the first two years. And, in the competitive world of biotech, lead time is all-important."

In January 1988, Birndorf joined Progenx, which was housed in a far-from-luxurious office located at the La Jolla headquarters of General Atomic. A year later the company shifted its emphasis to IR work, licensing technology from the Salk Institute. In December 1989, it also changed its name to Ligand, an allusion to the scientific term for the chemical complex that forms around a central atom or molecule. As expected, Birndorf's stay at Ligand was short term. In 1991, he left to take on yet another start-up challenge, Neurocrine Biosciences, and was replaced by David Robinson, an executive with 20 years of experience at major pharmaceuticals.

Like Birndorf, Robinson also took an unusual path to becoming a chief executive. Born in Indianapolis, he suffered hardships during his childhood, moving to St. Louis after his father died. His mother struggled to support the family of seven from the wages she earned as a government clerk, forcing Robinson to go to work at the age of 12. Through high school and three years of college, he worked as a janitor at a YMCA, then drove a factory forklift. He got married in 1970 and dropped out of school to travel the world with his wife, eventually landing in Sydney, Australia. There, Robinson completed his undergraduate education, studying political science and history, and became involved in the pharmaceutical industry when he took a job as a sales representative for Schering AG. To further his career he decided to earn an M.B.A. at the University of South Wales, but after he became a rep for Abbott Laboratories, influenced by his brother who already worked for the company, Robinson found himself transferred to Chicago in the middle of his M.B.A. program. Six months later, however, he was returned to Australia and was able to complete his M.B.A. before embarking on a number of stops for Abbott. He worked in Chicago a second time, then moved to Puerto Rico to become commercial director, followed by a promotion to the general manager level in Montevideo, Uruguay, where he stayed from 1980 to 1982. Next he became regional director of Abbott Europe and moved to Paris. After two years, he left Abbott and returned to the United States to assume the presidency of Adria Laboratories, located in Connecticut, a position he held for three years before becoming chief operating officer of Adria's corporate parent, Erbamont N.V. The position required a heavy travel schedule, as Robinson commuted from his home in Connecticut to offices in Columbus, Ohio, and Milan, Italy. In the meantime, he and his wife had a second child, and after two years as COO he elected to step down in favor of replacing Birndorf at Ligand.

Ligand in 1991, with no sales and only 71 employees, was still very much a small company, especially compared to Erbamont and its $1 billion in annual revenues and 9,000 employees. When Robinson became chief executive he expected to make a success of the business within five years, then turn over the reins to another executive. Success, however, would not come quickly and Robinson remained with Ligand well after his five-year limit.

First Collaborative Agreement: 1991

In 1991, Ligand signed its first research and collaboration agreement with a major pharmaceutical partner when it teamed with Pfizer Inc. to develop osteoprosis therapies. In June 1992, Ligand and Allergan Inc. agreed to work together on skin disorders, in particular Kaposi's sarcoma, caused by AIDS. Under terms of the deal, Allergan paid $20 million to gain a stake in Ligand. In the spring of 1992, Robinson was also preparing to make an initial public offering (IPO) of Ligand's stock, but when biotech stocks fell off, the IPO had to be

postponed. By the end of the year, underwriters for the offering found a novel way to attract investors. *Barron's* described the concept in a 1994 article: "The crux of the revised deal was the creation of two classes of stock—A and B shares—with similar voting rights. The venture capitalists and insiders who owned stock prior to the IPO could convert 25% of their holdings to A shares, but the remainder would be of the B class. The IPO, in turn, would be only of A shares, and that class alone would trade over the counter. The kicker: If, at the end of two years, Ligand's stock, initially offered at $11, was below $15.875, the company would issue additional shares to each Class A holder to make up the difference in total value.... The revised offering succeeded: Ligand sold 3.75 million Class A shares, netting more than $38 million."

Essentially, Robinson had two years to build value in Ligand in order to meet the target stock price. In September 1992, he negotiated another collaboration, this time with the English pharmaceutical Glaxo Wellcome, to develop drugs for the treatment of atherosclerosis. Glaxo agreed to also invest $10 million in Ligand, gaining a 6 percent stake in the company. Because of these deals with established drug companies, Ligand was able to book revenues despite not yet having any products to sell. The company's balance sheet boasted $5.5 million in revenues for 1992, and a $14 million net loss, and $16.1 million in revenues in 1993, with losses growing to $19.5 million. As Ligand approached the two-year mark after the IPO, when its stock needed to average $15.875 over a 60-day period, the company failed to excite investors and the price lingered under $12, despite its best efforts. In the days leading up to the test period, Ligand agreed to work with Abbott Laboratories to work on treatments for inflammatory diseases, and the pharmaceutical division of American Home Products, Wyeth-Ayerst, to research the use of sex steroids in such areas as hormone replacement, anti-cancer therapy, and gynecological diseases. Moreover, Ligand secured the Canadian rights to market the kidney cancer drug Proleukin from Chiron Corp. Proleukin also provided a way for Ligand to build a sales force, albeit a three-man-operation at first, in preparation for the time when the company's own products were ready to market. In November 1994, Ligand converted Class A shares into Class B Shares and issued additional shares to Class A holders to fulfill its IPO promise. The net effect was that insiders lost value, as the ownership of non-insiders grew from 25 percent to 30 percent.

Acquisition of Glycomed: 1995

Early in 1995, Ligand used some of its stock to acquire Glycomed Inc., a struggling California biotech, in a deal valued at $57 million. The company also entered into another research and development collaboration, this time with SmithKline Beecham to work on blood disorders. Ligand gave its new sales force more business in 1995 by acquiring the Canadian rights to sell Photofrin, a bladder cancer drug. In June 1995, Ligand and Allergan made an initial public offering of their cancer research joint venture, Ligand and Allergan Ligan Retinoid Therapeutics Inc. (ALTR), offering $32.5 million in stock. The deal allowed Ligand to buy back the company in five years, but just two years later Allergan elected to pull out of the venture and the two parties divided up the compounds developed by ALTR in order to pursue them separately. Ligand exercised an option to buy all

Key Dates:

1987: Progenx Inc. is formed.
1989: The company's name is changed to Ligand Pharmaceuticals.
1991: David Robinson becomes chief executive.
1992: The company goes public.
1995: Glycomed Incorporated is acquired.
1998: Seragen Inc. is acquired.
1999: Ligand has two drugs approved by the FDA in the same week.

the shares of ALTR, while Allergan paid $8.9 million to gain a one-half interest in ALTR's assets and technologies. Ligand continued to engage in research with Allergan on Kaposi's sarcoma, as well as treatments that could prevent blindness.

Ligand landed yet another major drug development deal in October 1997, when Eli Lilly & Co. agreed to pay approximately $200 million over eight years to use IR technology in such areas as diabetes, obesity, and cardiovascular diseases. Supported by so many corporate sponsors, Ligand was well positioned to stay afloat while it waited for its first drug candidates to proceed through clinical trials in order to obtain approval from the Federal Drug Administration. In the spring of 1998, the company's Panretin capsules, used to fight Kaposi's sarcoma, produced excellent results in Phase II of the process. Prospects for Ligand's future appeared quite bright. Early in May 1998, SmithKline Beecham agreed to a collaboration deal to develop oral drugs to prevent obesity. A few days later Ligand acquired Seragen Inc., a Boston biotech, in a $35 million cash and stock transaction. Not only did Ligand pick up Seragen's manufacturing operation, it acquired the rights to Ontak, a drug awaiting Food and Drug Administration (FDA) approval for use in treating cutaneous T-cell lymphoma (CTCL). Ontak was a good fit for Ligand because of the CTCL drugs it already had in clinical trials, Targetin gel and Targetin capsules. Although the market for CTCL drugs was limited, Ligand was now well positioned to take advantage of the niche. Robinson was so pleased with the Seragen acquisition that he predicted that Ligand would become a profitable business by the end of 1999. He improved his chances to meet that goal when in October 1998 he forged an alliance with Elan Corporation, an Ireland-based pharmaceutical. In order to acquire an 8 percent stake in Ligand, Elan agreed to purchase $20 million in common stock as well as to buy as much as $110 million in the company's zero coupon convertible notes. In addition, Elan granted Ligand the exclusive rights to market its drug Morphelan in the United States and Canada. Morphelan, a solid

once-a-day morphine drug for use by HIV and cancer patients, was in Phase III clinical trials.

To prepare for the next stage in Ligand's growth, the company began an effort in late 1998 to beef up its sales capabilities in the United States, establishing a 20-person sales force. That number would be doubled in 1999 when in the space of a single week Ligand received FDA approval on two drugs, Panretin gel and Ontak. Although neither held out the prospect of gaining blockbuster status, obtaining approval for two drugs in one week was a notable achievement. By the end of 1999, Ligand also received FDA approval for Targretin, a drug to treat patients with a rare form of lymphoma. It held much greater potential than Ligand's other products, estimated to generate as much as $100 million per year. Should clinical trials show that Targretin was effective against breast cancer, however, that number would likely grow to $300 million in annual sales.

Despite these positive developments, Ligand did not turn profitable in 1999, nor would it in the foreseeable future. Robinson, who had only planned on running Ligand for five years, was still at the helm after ten. Nevertheless, the company was inching its way towards profitability. Sales from its products were steadily improving, while other drugs made their way through the clinical trial process. Moreover, Ligand was still able to attract major pharmaceuticals to enter into collaborative research agreements. Organa and Bristol-Myers Squibb both signed pacts in 2000. Exactly when Robinson would finally be able to step away from what he considered a successful company, however, remained uncertain.

Principal Subsidiaries

Glycomed Incorporated; Allergan Ligand Retinoid Therapeutics, Inc.; Seragen Incorporated.

Principal Competitors

Arena Pharmaceuticals; AstraZeneca; Gilead Sciences; IDEC Pharmaceuticals Corporation; Vertex Pharmaceuticals.

Further Reading

Gupta, Udayan, "Small Pond, Big Paychecks," *Wall Street Journal,* April 13, 1994, p. R7.
Johnson, Greg, "Expert on Biotechnology Start-Ups Prefers the Cutting Edge," *Los Angeles Times,* April 19, 1988, p. 8.
Webb, Marion, "Ligand Expects to Leap into the Black," *San Diego Business Journal,* May 18, 1998, p. 1.
——, "Success Is His Paradigm for Life," *San Diego Business Journal,* May 18, 1998, p. 8.
Wyatt, Edward A., "As Easy As A and B," *Barron's,* October 3, 1994, p. 20.

—Ed Dinger

Lloyds TSB Group

Lloyds TSB Group plc

71 Lombard Street
London, EC3P 3BS
United Kingdom
Telephone: (44) 20-7626-1500
Fax: (44) 20-7356-1731
Web site: http://www.lloydstsbgroup.co.uk

Public Company
Incorporated: 1865 as Lloyds Banking Company Limited
Employees: 77,540
Total Assets: £236.5 billion (2001)
Stock Exchanges: London New York
Ticker Symbol: LLOY (London); LYG (New York)
NAIC: 522110 Commercial Banking (pt); 522210 Credit
   Card Issuing (pt); 522120 Savings Institutions (pt);
   523991 Trust, Fiduciary, and Custody Activities (pt);
   522320 Financial Transactions Processing, Reserve,
   and Clearinghouse Activities (pt); 522390 Other
   Activities Related to Credit Intermediation (pt);
   522220 Sales Financing (pt); 522291 Consumer
   Lending; 522292 Real Estate Credit (pt); 522310
   Mortgage and Nonmortgage Loan Brokers; 524113
   Direct Life Insurance Carriers; 525110 Pension Funds

Lloyds TSB Group plc is one of the Big Four British clearing banks in the United Kingdom. Through the bank and its subsidiary and associated companies, Lloyds offers a wide variety of international banking and financial services. It has almost 3,000 branches throughout the United Kingdom, and its international business is conducted through approximately 500 offices in 47 countries, including the United States, Canada, Japan, Australia, Brazil, and Egypt. Long considered a conservative banking house, Lloyds has grown increasingly innovative since the early 1970s, often taking the lead among the Big Four clearing banks in offering new financial services and products and in developing an international presence. The present company arose from a merger of Lloyds and the TSB Group, a deal that catapulted the company into its present position as the second largest bank in Britain.

The Birth of a Banking Giant

Sampson Lloyd II worked for 40 years in the family iron trade in Birmingham before founding Taylors and Lloyds in partnership with John Taylor in 1765. Taylor was a wealthy Unitarian who was a maker of buttons and snuff boxes; Lloyd was a prominent Quaker whose father had settled in Birmingham in 1698. Each man's eldest son was also a partner in the bank, and two of Lloyd's other sons eventually joined it as well.

Taylors and Lloyds opened its accounts in June 1765. Just five years later, the bank's two junior partners set up their own banking house in London with two other businessmen, forming Hanbury, Taylor, Lloyd and Bowman. This bank then served as the Birmingham house's agent. In 1775 the Birmingham bank had 277 customers.

Sampson Lloyd II had apprenticed to a Quaker businessman in Bristol before joining his father's iron firm. He was married twice and had six children. Little is known of his son and partner Sampson III, who was the last Lloyd to be a partner in both the Birmingham and London houses. Sampson III and his wife had 16 children and were known to have entertained James Boswell and Dr. Samuel Johnson. Sampson's half-brother Charles was the more important of the two, best known for his intellect and remarkable memory. In the final years of the 18th century and the early years of the 19th, Charles was the principal figure in the Birmingham bank. Charles tried mightily to mold his eldest son, Charles II, into a banker, but his efforts failed. His second son, James, became a partner in the Birmingham bank in 1802 and was followed in the mid-19th century by his own three sons.

Strategic Partnerships in the 19th Century

The Bank of England had a monopoly on joint-stock banking until 1826, when Lord Liverpool, the prime minister, sponsored a new law allowing joint-stock banking, except within a 65-mile radius of London. Seven years later, joint-stock banks were allowed within the 65-mile circle, but in 1844 a stricter law virtually stopped further joint-stock banks from being founded. During those brief lenient years, 120 "joint-stocks" were founded in England and Wales and of these, 20 eventually became part of the Lloyds group. By the time they amal-

Company Perspectives:

We aim to set an example in the conduct of our business. We demand honesty and integrity in everything we do, and will not do business if our standards are endangered. We greatly value our good reputation.

gamated with Lloyds, these 20 banks had a total of approximately 350 offices.

John Taylor died just ten years after founding Taylors and Lloyds. His son John, Jr., was 27 at the time of the bank's founding and remained a partner in both the Birmingham and London banks until he died in 1814. His oldest son, John, never entered banking and his two other sons, James and William, were the last Taylors involved with the firm. When James died in 1852, his son was offered partnerships in the Birmingham and London houses but turned both down. Thus the Taylor family's connection to the bank ceased. The Birmingham bank became Lloyds and Company, and the London house became Hanburys and Lloyds. The latter merged with Barnetts, Hoares and Company in 1864 to form Barnetts, Hoares, Hanbury and Lloyds. This transaction brought Barnetts, Hoares' sign, a black horse, to Lloyds, where it continues to be the bank's symbol.

In 1865 Lloyds and Company, joined by Moilliet and Sons, was incorporated as Lloyds Banking Company Limited. With the Birmingham bank's change to joint-stock ownership, there came an infusion of new blood into the company. The first chairman of Lloyds Banking Company, Timothy Kenrick, was a Unitarian businessman and a director of the Midland Railway Company. Although he had married into a banking family, he had no banking experience, but was widely respected in Birmingham for both his business acumen and philanthropic activities. During Kenrick's term as chairman, the bank absorbed four other banks.

Sampson Samuel Lloyd, a great-great-grandson of Sampson Lloyd III, became chairman in 1869. He oversaw Lloyds' mergers with seven banks, including its two London agents, Bosanquet, Salt and Company and Barnetts, Hoares, Hanbury and Lloyd, both in 1884. After these amalgamations, which gave Lloyds a foothold in London and entrance to the clearing-house system of clearing checks and settling balances, the bank was known as Lloyds, Barnetts and Bosanquets Bank Limited. Although the bank's branches were all within a 50-mile radius of Birmingham and the head office remained in that city, its center of activity was rapidly shifting to London. Beginning in 1899, Lloyds' board would meet alternately in London and Birmingham, but by 1910, the board met only in London and all head office business also was transferred there.

Two years after the two important London mergers, Sampson Lloyd handed over the chairmanship to Thomas Salt, whose family had been in banking for generations. Salt had been a director of the bank since 1866, when the bank at which he was a junior partner, Stafford Old Bank, was sold to Lloyds. Early in Salt's term, the bank took the title of Lloyds Bank Limited. In Salt's 12 years as chairman, the bank absorbed 15 banks and grew from 61 offices in 1886 to 257 in 1898.

Also deserving of credit for this growth was Howard Lloyd, who served as general manager from 1871 to 1902. A direct descendant of Sampson Lloyd II, Howard Lloyd held many jobs in the bank, gradually working his way up to secretary and, finally, to general manager. Lloyd successfully oversaw the melding of Lloyds' two London agents into the Lloyds framework, calling those two amalgamations ''the most important forward step of the bank's history.'' At the end of his tenure in 1902, the bank had 267 offices. Lloyd was fond of saying that Lloyds Bank was to be not necessarily the biggest bank, but the best bank. He stands out in the history of Lloyds as a tireless administrator who handled an impressive variety of functions.

Modernization: 1900–45

John Spencer Phillips became chairman in 1898. The eldest son of a rector, Phillips had been a partner in the Shrewsbury and Welshpool Old Bank, which was acquired by Lloyds in 1880. He became a member of Lloyds' board and served as deputy chairman for eight years before assuming the chairmanship. Nine years before becoming chairman, Phillips had been instrumental in negotiating the amalgamation of the Birmingham Joint Stock Bank, which had long been considered Lloyds' chief competitor in that city. The last chairman to act also as chief executive, Phillips oversaw 15 amalgamations. An excellent public speaker, he was the first to offer commentary on national economic affairs at the annual meeting.

In June 1903, Lloyds opened secret merger negotiations with the Manchester and Liverpool District Bank, but public sentiment against the merger was so strong that the idea was dropped. Manchester citizens were particularly outspoken, objecting to their city's losing its separate identity.

After Phillips died in office in 1909, he was succeeded by Richard Vassar-Smith. His 13 years were a period when, for some time, Lloyds was the biggest bank in England. A director of the Worcester City and County Bank, Vassar-Smith was selected to become a director of Lloyds Bank when the smaller bank was absorbed by Lloyds in 1889. Vassar-Smith was heavily involved in governmental discussions about wartime preparations, and he served as chairman of the 1917 Treasury Committee on Financial Facilities. In recognition of his contributions to the war effort, he was made a baronet in 1917.

World War I saw the formation of the Big Five, a group of large clearing banks that included Lloyds. Although the banks still called themselves the London clearing banks, they were in fact national banks.

Several key acquisitions and amalgamations marked Vassar-Smith's years as chairman. In 1914 Lloyds absorbed the Wilts and Dorset Banking Company, which had 200 offices, many in areas where Lloyds already had a branch. In 1918 came the merger of two huge banking concerns: Lloyds with its 888 offices merged with the Capital and Counties Bank, which had 473 offices. Although there was substantial overlap of office locations, each did have offices in areas in which the other had little or no representation. Capital and Counties also had attractive foreign connections. It participated in a bank in France as well as in agencies for banks in Canada, Mauritius, and Brazil. The amalgamated bank, whose title remained Lloyds Bank

Limited, had a board of directors consisting of the 19 members of Lloyds and seven from the Capital and Counties board. In 1918 Lloyds had just more than 13 percent of all bank deposits in Britain.

Poet T.S. Eliot joined Lloyds' colonial and foreign department at the head office in 1917, where he worked as a bank clerk. When Eliot's health deteriorated in the fall of 1921, the bank gave him a three-month leave, during which he finished *The Waste Land.* He left Lloyds for a better-paying job at another bank in 1925.

In the year and a half after the end of World War I in November 1918, there was a sharp upturn in economic activity, but it was succeeded by a lengthy recession. The bank's business mirrored these broad swings in the economy. With the end of the war, official restrictions on branch openings were lifted and, in 1919, Lloyds opened or reopened 203 offices. The bank also acquired the 34 offices of the West Yorkshire Bank that year.

With the 1921 acquisition of Fox, Fowler & Company, the last country bank to issue its own note, Lloyds added 55 additional branches and agencies in Somerset, Devon, and Cornwall. By 1923, Lloyds had become a banking giant, with 1,626 offices throughout England.

Nationwide, public concern was mounting over the large number of bank amalgamations, which came to a quick halt after the Treasury Committee on Bank Amalgamations issued its report in 1918. The committee's recommendations for minimizing future amalgamations, although never formally made law, became the country's unwritten law. Henceforth, every amalgamation would require treasury approval. The treasury usually permitted the acquisition of small banks by large concerns, but it was clear that the amalgamation of any two of the Big Five would not be permitted.

Lloyds averted a serious banking crisis with its 1923 takeover of Cox & Company, West End army bankers with branches in India, Burma, and Egypt. Lloyds also took over

Henry S. King & Company, which Cox had recently acquired. These amalgamations were made by order of the Bank of England to avoid an expected run on Cox & Company.

After Vassar-Smith's death in 1922, J.W. Beaumont Pease, who had served as deputy chairman throughout Vassar-Smith's tenure, succeeded him. Another direct descendant of Sampson Lloyd II, Pease had been a partner in the established and prosperous private bank of Hodgkin, Barnett, Pease, Spence & Company of Newcastle upon Tyne. When that bank amalgamated with Lloyds in 1903, Pease was elected to Lloyds' board.

During Pease's lengthy term, Lloyds gained a reputation for its conservatism. When Pease retired in 1945, Lloyds had 60 more branches than when he took office. Although the bank had expanded during the 1920s to nearly 1,950 branches in 1931, many had to be closed during the Depression and World War II.

The Depression made its most serious dent in Lloyds' lending business, with a two-fifths loss of income in this area. Total earnings reflected this loss, with a two-fifths reduction in the overall figure. In 1933, gross profits fell to their lowest level since the turn of the century. Economizing measures were instituted, including a renewed dedication to mechanization and the development of a standard formula for determining which branches were to be closed. In the mid-1930s, approximately 20 branches a year were mechanized, using machines that would post entries on an account and strike a balance.

In the late 1930s, elaborate plans were drawn up to keep the bank functioning in case of war. The clearing banks issued a war preparation report stipulating that in case of war, all ordinary competition between banks would cease entirely. Throughout the war, 641 Lloyds offices were damaged and 32 destroyed. Of the latter, the vaults were destroyed in only two. Between 1940 and 1945, 214 offices were closed and seven opened (a number of those closed were reopened after the war). In addition, three Lloyds branches were overrun by enemy troops during the war: in Jersey and Guernsey in the Channel Islands and in Rangoon, Burma.

Throughout World War II, deposits and the total number of accounts increased each year. Deposits doubled between 1939 and 1945, but with prices rising steadily, real growth was considerably less. Lending activity fell, but this was offset by an increase in investments, especially treasury deposit receipts. For the period 1939–45, gross profits tripled. Lloyds had inherited the army's business from Cox & Company; at one point during the war, the influx of newly commissioned officers forced the army pay department to work seven days a week.

Postwar Boom: The 1940s and 1950s

Lord Balfour of Burleigh succeeded Pease as chairman in 1946. A member of an old Scottish family, he had been named chairman of the National Bank of New Zealand in 1938 and also served as a director of other banks and organizations. Lord Balfour, or ''B of B'' as he was called, started the practice of having regular dinners at which the chairman, a few directors, and small groups of managers could freely exchange ideas.

The immediate postwar years brought an upturn in the economy. Between 1945 and 1951, total loans almost tripled. Deposits, however, increased by only about a third, a considerably slower rate of growth than during the war, and virtually no real growth at all due to inflation.

Sir Oliver Franks, who had served as Britain's ambassador to the United States from 1948 to 1952, succeeded Lord Balfour as chairman in 1954. The former head of an Oxford college, Franks was one of the finest intellects ever to serve the bank as chairman. Due to the essentially conservative nature of the bank and continued governments controls, however, Franks was not able to make as many changes as he would have liked.

In 1958 the government abolished restrictions on bank lending and the clearing banks did away with their self-imposed limits on competition among themselves. Lloyds continued to expand. Its total number of branches in 1959 was 1,851, compared to 1,711 in 1951, and its employees had increased from 17,690 in 1951 to 20,160 in 1959.

After Oliver Franks's retirement in 1962, Harald Peake, a director since 1941 and a vice-chairman since 1947, was elected chairman. Peake had a varied background in business, having served as chairman of a steel company and director of many other companies. He was a key player in negotiating the purchase of property from the Commercial Union Assurance Company, which allowed for expansion of the head office.

International Expansion in the 1960s and 1970s

During the 1960s Lloyds developed rapidly. In 1963 it set up Lloyds Bank Property Company to conduct property development schemes that would incorporate branch premises, and in 1967 Lloyds acquired Lewis's Bank from Martins Bank. Lewis's had branches in ten Liverpool department stores. Altogether the bank opened 456 new branches, bringing the total at decade's end to 2,307.

Peake is best remembered for a failed attempt at merging Lloyds with Barclays and Martins Bank, a move the monopolies commission deemed would be against the public interest. Barclays finally acquired Martins, making Lloyds the smallest of the Big Four London clearing banks rather than the third largest among the Big Five.

Eric O. Faulkner, who had spent 32 years in banking at Glyn, Mills and Company and was considered something of a radical, was elected chairman of Lloyds in 1969. He provided a new perspective on how the bank should continue to grow.

One of Faulkner's priorities was the development of an international banking group. He created Lloyds Bank International by merging Lloyds Bank Europe with the Bank of London and South America to form the Lloyds and Bolsa International Bank in 1971, in which Lloyds held a 51 percent interest. Two years later, it became a wholly owned subsidiary, marked by a name change to Lloyds Bank International. Lloyds expanded its geographic base considerably during the next several years to include West Germany, Switzerland, the Middle East, Australia, Canada, and the United States in its international network. Early in 1986 Lloyds Bank International was merged with the clearing bank to better meet the demands of a worldwide financial market.

To handle its growing volume of transactions, Lloyds became the first British bank to transfer all of its branches to a common computer accounting system in October 1970. This helped immensely as the bank adjusted to the government's introduction of decimal currency in February 1971.

Competition among banks intensified after the Bank of England radically changed its control of the banks in 1971, when it introduced a new policy that included removal of a maximum ceiling on bank lending. In this newly competitive environment, Faulkner oversaw many new business ventures. An insurance department was established in 1972, and a year later Lloyds Leasing was started.

By 1978 Lloyds Bank International had offices and subsidiaries in 43 countries. By the end of that year, a little more than half of Lloyds Bank Group's consolidated balance was attributable to the bank's many subsidiaries. In a 1971 interview with *The Banker,* Faulkner echoed Harold Lloyd's words of nearly a century ago when he said, "All these objectives for our domestic business amount simply to being not the largest but the best of the clearing banks."

Sir Jeremy Morse succeeded Faulkner as chairman in 1977. At 47, he was one of the youngest chairmen of a clearing bank in recent history. Morse had served as chairman of the deputies of the International Monetary Fund's Committee of Twenty, where he was involved in efforts to reform the world's monetary system. He had served as Lloyds' deputy chairman for 16 months before assuming the chairmanship.

Diversification in the 1980s

In 1979 Lloyds became the first clearing bank to move into the home loan market. Seeking to fill a gap in the home-loan services offered by the British building societies, Lloyds announced that it would consider loans greater than £25,000 and up to £150,000. The building societies' maximum home loans were £25,000.

Two years later Lloyds Bank and American Express announced plans to issue a joint sterling traveler's check from their offices and branches around the world. Lloyds Bank further diversified in 1982 with the creation of Blackhorse Agencies, a real estate agency business that had as its nucleus a Norfolk-based practice acquired by Lloyds. By 1989, Blackhorse had 563 offices. Competition between the big London banks intensified in the mid-1980s when Lloyds and other clearing banks announced that they would begin offering free banking for clients whose current accounts remained in the black.

In 1986 Lloyds Bank PLC offered £1.27 billion in a hostile takeover bid for Standard Chartered PLC, Britain's fifth largest bank, but was rebuffed after East Asian and Australian investors made last-minute purchases of Standard Chartered shares. Although Standard Chartered's profits had lagged behind other large British banks for some time, Lloyds was sorry to lose the chance to acquire Standard Chartered's many interests in the Far East, especially in Hong Kong.

Just three months after its unsuccessful bid for Standard Chartered, Lloyds announced that it would start its own brokerage firm rather than acquire a brokerage firm, as the other Big

Four clearing banks had done. That same year, Lloyds formed a new subsidiary, Lloyds Merchant Bank, to handle its capital market and merchant banking operations.

In 1987 Lloyds announced that it would move 1,400 head office staff from London to Bristol, where it would build a two-phase office development in a park-like setting. Due to the impact of Third World loan losses, Lloyds Bank incurred a pretax loss in 1987 of some £248 million, compared to profits of £700 million the year before. Lloyds Chairman Jeremy Morse told the *Wall Street Journal* in early 1988 that Lloyds was "refocusing" its international business on more profitable services such as foreign exchange, trade finance, investment management, and private banking and that it was moving away from wholesale lending to countries and large corporate borrowers.

In 1988 Lloyds' profit figures were handsomely turned around, with both pre- and post-tax profits at record levels. The biggest Third World debtor, Brazil, resumed interest payments in 1988 and several other countries began programs to reduce their debts.

That year Lloyds became the second British bank to offer a debit card, a card that linked directly to a user's bank account, allowing transactions to be debited just as if a check had been written. Also in 1988, Lloyds made a bold competitive move when it began offering interest on basic checking accounts. Although the idea was common in the United States, British banks had competed mainly by cutting fees and adding new services. Analysts saw the move as a predictable response to the building societies' chipping away at the bank's dominance in checking accounts. At year's end, Lloyds acquired a controlling interest in Abbey Life Group PLC, a British life insurer, by merging five of its businesses with Abbey Life to create Lloyds Abbey Life. This bold move into a new market was a part of Lloyds' strategy to attract new business and raise earnings by offering customers a wider range of services.

The Merger with TSB Group in 1995

The British banking industry was hit hard by a recession in the early 1990s. Many businesses throughout England were caught off-guard, and the resulting high numbers of loan defaults and bankruptcies, along with a significant decline in demand for business and mortgage loans, put an enormous amount of pressure on Lloyds. Although Lloyds was still able to enjoy tremendous profit margins—the bank's net earnings exceeded £1 billion in 1993—its market share value began to slip by 1994, as more investors turned away from retail banking in favor of the more robust securities trading sector. The bank was faced with a difficult decision: It could either turn its profits over into high dividends for its shareholders, or it could try to jumpstart its sagging business through strategic acquisitions.

To the surprise of nobody, Lloyds chose the latter course. Still smarting from its failed bid to take over Midland Bank in 1992, Lloyds set its sights on a much larger prize: the TSB Group. In many respects, the union represented a perfect fit. One key advantage of the merger was geography; whereas Lloyd's 1,800 branches helped give the bank a dominant position in southern England, TSB was a major presence in the north, with 1,100 branches in northern England and Scotland.

The two banks also catered to two distinct segments of the banking industry, with Lloyd's serving a predominantly wealthy client base, while TSB focused exclusively on the middle-class market.

Most important, the deal created a much larger banking entity, one that could remain competitive in the emerging global economy. The market capitalization of the joint enterprise was nearly £15 billion, and the scope of its combined operations made it the second largest bank in England. At the same time, the restructuring allowed the new company to streamline much of its operational costs, making room for a projected savings of £350 million per year by the end of the decade. The decision to close 150 bank branches in September 1996 did create a great deal of concern among labor groups, who feared that the bank might eventually close up to 1,000 branches and terminate more than 10,000 positions. The lack of overlap between the Lloyds and TSB networks, however, along with the group's continued commitment to its core retail banking business, proved these worries to be unfounded.

The genius behind the merger was Sir Brian Pitman, former Lloyds CEO and new chairman of Lloyds TSB. As CEO of Lloyds Bank, Pitman presided over a remarkable period of growth, wherein the bank's overall market capitalization increased from £1 billion in 1983 to more than £20 billion in 1996. Pitman's emphasis on shareholder value as the bank's primary objective, and his strict focus on the retail banking sector, were considered instrumental to this success.

Pitman's philosophy quickly paid off for Lloyds TSB, and by mid-1997 the group was poised for another merger, with a surplus of more than £1 billion to spend. The banking climate was beginning to change in England, however. Regulators, already wary of a lack of competition in the British banking industry, were resistant to further domestic mergers among the nation's top banks. Although the prospect of an international merger was appealing to shareholders, the relative inexperience of Lloyds TSB, and British banks in general, in foreign financial service markets made it difficult to find a suitable overseas partner.

At the same time, it was becoming clear that overseas expansion was unavoidable in the early years of the new millennium. Fiscal 2002 witnessed a steep decline in Britain's high-end financial service market, as a number of customers, many of them young professionals, began moving their accounts abroad. Lloyds TSB was hit particularly hard by this trend, and its market share dropped from 17 percent in 2001 to 12 percent in 2002. The challenge for Lloyds TSB clearly lay in adapting its services to cater to a new generation of wealthy clientele and in finding a way to gain a foothold in the international banking market. Heading into the new century, a significant overseas merger seemed especially critical.

Principal Subsidiaries

Lloyds TSB Bank plc; Cheltenham & Gloucester plc; Lloyds Bank (BLSA) Limited; Lloyds TSB Commercial Finance Limited; Lloyds TSB Leasing Limited; Lloyds TSB Private Banking Limited; The Agricultural Mortgage Corporation PLC; The National Bank of New Zealand Limited; Lloyds TSB Bank (Jersey) Limited; Lloyds TSB Scotland plc; Lloyds TSB General Insurance Limited; Scottish Widows Investment Partnership Group Limited; Abbey Life Assurance Company Limited; Lloyds TSB Insurance Services Limited; Lloyds TSB Life Assurance Company Limited; Lloyds TSB Asset Finance Division Limited; Black Horse Limited; Scottish Widows plc; Scottish Widows Annuities Limited.

Principal Competitors

Barclays PLC; HSBC Holdings plc; Prudential plc.

Further Reading

Gapper, John, "Uncertainty Reigns in Absence of a Transaction—The Greatest Concern Over Lloyds Bank: What Will It Do with Its Money," *Financial Times* (London), February 11, 1994, p. 23.

Mackintosh, James, "High Street Banks Lose Share of Richer Clientele; Financial Services Lloyds TSB Worst Hit by Drift Towards Online Services and Offshore Investment," *Financial Times* (London), February 4, 2002, p. 3.

Rodgers, Peter, "The Bank That Wants to Be Just Like Coca-Cola; Lloyds-TSB's New Chairman Is Inspired by a Soft Drink Company," *Independent* (London), September 21, 1996, p. 20.

Sayers, R.S., *Lloyds Bank in the History of English Banking,* Oxford: Clarendon Press, 1957.

Smith, Alison, and Patrick Harveson, "The Bank That's About to Say Yes: The Likely Shape of a Merged Lloyds-TSB Group Is Already Becoming Clear," *Financial Times* (London), October 10, 1995, p. 19.

Winton, J.R., *Lloyds Bank: 1918–1969,* Oxford: Oxford University Press, 1982.

—update: Steve Meyer

Mayer, Brown, Rowe & Maw

190 South LaSalle Street
Chicago, Illinois 60603
U.S.A.
Telephone: (312) 782-0600
Fax: (312) 701-7711
Web site: http://www.mayerbrown.com

Partnership
Founded: 1881
Employees: 1,500
Gross Billings: $590 million (2001 est.)
NAIC: 541110 Offices of Lawyers

Mayer, Brown, Rowe & Maw is one of the world's largest law firms, based on both its revenue and number of lawyers. Chambers & Partners in 2001 rated the law firm, at that pre-merger time known as Mayer, Brown & Platt, as one of the top ten in North America. The Chicago-based firm also has offices in Houston, New York City, Los Angeles, Charlotte, Palo Alto, London, Frankfurt, Cologne, Paris, and Washington, D.C, and affiliated offices in Beijing and Shanghai. Its lawyers specialize in most areas of domestic and international law but are particularly well known for their corporate, banking, securities, tax, real estate, litigation, appellate, and information technology practices. One of the firm's oldest historic clients is Continental Illinois Bank, and at the turn of the millennium it represented 25 of the world's largest banks. Other clients include nonprofit organizations, multinational corporations such as Dow Chemical, AOL Time Warner, BMW, and Oracle, and national, state, and municipal governments. On February 1, 2002, Mayer, Brown & Platt merged with Rowe & Maw, a London-based firm with offices in Manchester and Brussels, to form the new partnership of Mayer, Brown, Rowe & Maw. The merged firm, with more than 1,300 lawyers worldwide, is just one example of the consolidation of the legal profession. As their corporate clients merged, so did some of the law firms. Such huge professional firms play a key role in the world's economic and political developments such as globalization, privatization of former state-owned enterprises, and the technological changes in the Information Age.

Origins and Early History

Levy Mayer (1858–1922), the lead name partner of Mayer, Brown, Rowe & Maw, was born in Richmond, Virginia, and attended public schools in Chicago. Following his graduation from Yale Law School in 1876, Mayer worked as an assistant librarian at the Chicago Law Institute.

In 1881 Levy Mayer joined the Illinois Bar and began practicing law with Adolf Kraus and William S. Brackett. The firm was renamed Kraus & Mayer and then Kraus, Mayer & Stein after Brackett retired. In 1893 the partnership became known as Moran, Kraus, Mayer & Stein. When Stein became a judge and Kraus retired, the firm became Moran, Mayer & Meyer. Carl Meyer, a graduate of Yale University, had studied law under Levy Mayer before joining the bar in 1890. After Judge Moran died and Alfred S. Austrian and Henry Russell Platt joined the firm, it was known as Mayer, Meyer, Austrian & Platt.

In 1913, just before the onset of World War I, *Hubbell's Legal Directory* listed Mayer, Meyer, Austrian & Platt with 11 lawyers with their offices in Chicago's American Trust Building. Partners included Isaac H. Mayer, who had joined the bar in 1886 and became a specialist in trademarks and unfair competition.

Levy Mayer helped form several companies, including Sears Roebuck & Company in Chicago, Hart Schaffner & Marx, the Great Lakes Transit Corporation, the Chicago Packing & Provision Company, Ltd., The Chicago & Northwest Granaries Company Ltd., and the Pan American Commission Corporation.

By 1910 Levy Mayer had assisted six Chicago banks when they merged into what became known as Continental Illinois Bank & Trust Company. For several decades the Chicago law firm provided most of the bank's legal advice, with Carl Meyer serving as its (and the Federal Reserve Bank of Chicago's) general counsel. Similar close relationships existed between New York City banks and law firms. For example, Chase Manhattan Bank and its predecessors used Milbank Tweed and Citibank relied on Shearman & Sterling.

Levy Mayer also assisted in merging sugar companies, chewing gum businesses, and distilling firms. He also success-

Key Dates:

1881: Levy Mayer starts his law practice in Chicago.
1970: The firm's Washington, D.C. office is started.
1974: Mayer, Brown & Platt opens a new branch office in New York City.
1982: The Houston office is opened.
1985: The firm opens its Los Angeles office.
2001: The firm merges with the Paris law firm of Lambert & Lee and the Frankfurt office of Gaedertz.
2002: Mayer, Brown & Platt on February 1 merges with London's Rowe & Maw to form Mayer, Brown, Rowe & Maw.

fully represented business interests that were sued, such as large meat packing companies in the 1912 Packers' Trial and the owners of the Iroquois Theatre after a major fire.

Post-World War II Developments

In 1950 the law firm headed by senior partners Isaac H. Mayer and Carl Meyer had 22 partners, up slightly from its 17 partners in 1940. By 1960 the firm, renamed Mayer, Friedlich, Spiess, Tierney, Brown & Platt, included 28 partners and 27 associates but still had no branch offices. New name partner H. Templeton Brown had graduated from Harvard Law School and had been admitted to the bar in 1926.

The firm rapidly grew in the 1960s, reaching 55 partners and 36 associates in 1970. In the 1970 *Martindale-Hubbell Law Directory* the firm also listed a European Office in Paris that later was closed. In addition, in 1970 the firm opened its Washington, D.C. office. This was part of a general trend for outside firms to start offices in the nation's capital to help their corporate clients deal with the growing number of federal laws and agencies, such as the 1964 Civil Rights Act and the U.S. Office of Economic Opportunity.

Following the Nixon administration's beginning of diplomatic ties with the People's Republic of China, the law firm's Everett L. Hollis in 1972 was one of the first outsiders to explain the workings of capitalism to the communist nation. Hollis, with a few other Americans, met in Peking (now Beijing) in an informal seminar to clarify the way Wall Street really worked. Such contacts paved the way for future economic ties between the two nations.

In 1974 the firm opened its New York City office, mainly to work with its longtime client Continental Bank. In 1975, however, the bank hired its first inside general counsel, a major step in decreasing the bank's historic dependence on the Chicago law firm. "Largely gone are the relationships that spawned some of the country's most prosperous firms," wrote James B. Stewart in 1984 in the *Wall Street Journal*. When Continental Bank faced possible bankruptcy in 1984, the law firm could have closed or expanded its New York practice. It decided to remain and eventually built a major branch office there.

The law firm in the post-World War II era played a significant leadership role in the bar. For example, partner Justin

Armstrong Stanley served as president of both the Chicago Bar Association in 1967 and the American Bar Association in 1976. See Terence C. Halliday's book *Beyond Monopoly* for a sociological study of the Chicago Bar Association.

Like many large law firms, the renamed Mayer, Brown & Platt saw tremendous growth in the 1980s as the economy boomed and numerous mergers and acquisitions occurred. In 1982 it added a new office in Houston, in part to deal with oil, natural gas, and other energy issues. In 1985 its Los Angeles office opened its doors, and by 1990 other branches had been founded in London and Tokyo. This first Asian branch later was closed.

Law Practice in the 1990s and Beyond

In 1991 Mayer, Brown & Platt chose a woman as its managing partner, one of the first large law firms to do so. In 1997 Mayer, Brown & Platt's Mickey Kantor, the former secretary of the U.S. Department of Commerce, began serving David and Simon Reuben and their company Trans World. The Reuben brothers had built Trans World in Russia into the world's third largest aluminum producer, with additional investments in steel, coal, chrome, and other raw materials. The Russian government investigated Trans World for alleged money laundering, organized crime connections, and other misdeeds. By 2000 the Reubens had sold most of their business.

Fortune on June 12, 2000, said the Trans World story, "filled with bribes, shell companies, profiteers, and more than a few corpses," was a "vivid illustration of how Russia's criminal class has dismantled the promise of the post-Soviet era." It also was an example of the role of large American law firms in the transition to capitalism after the Soviet Union disintegrated in 1991.

In the 1990s Mayer, Brown & Platt increased the capacity of its New York City office. By 1999 the New York office had 165 lawyers who served mostly financial institutions such as Morgan Stanley Dean Witter, Lehman Brothers, the Bank of Nova Scotia, and CIBC Oppenheimer. After three partners and ten associates of Gordon Altman Butowsky Weitzen Shalov & Wein left to join Mayer, Brown & Platt in 1999, the Chicago-based firm increased its ability to counsel mutual fund managers. Writer Matthew Goldstein concluded that by 1999 the firm's Manhattan office had "become one of the biggest success stories among out-of-town firms."

The firm in 1998 acquired the seven-lawyer Charlotte, North Carolina firm of Blanchfield Cordle & Moore, which specialized in tax and litigation matters. By March 2000 this branch office had grown to 30 lawyers.

Mayer, Brown & Platt also expanded overseas. On April 1, 2001, it merged with the Frankfurt, Germany office of Gaedertz, a well known corporate law firm. The two firms shared some mutual clients such as ITW and Credit Suisse First Boston before the merger. This new German office pushed the firm's total number of lawyers past 1,000, which included more than 75 lawyers in Europe. The firm represented the following clients as part of its German practice: Daimler-Benz in U.S. product liability litigation, NBC Europe in German cable matters, and Enron in German and European Union energy issues, as well as Deutsche Bank, Deutsche Telekom, Lufthansa, Bosch, and Monsanto.

While growing internationally, Mayer, Brown & Platt continued to play a major role in its home city of Chicago. According to a *Chicago Sun-Times* story that used records using a Freedom of Information Act request, Chicago paid the firm $3.8 million in fees from 1997 through 1999. Although the city had its own staff of 280 lawyers, it increasingly relied on outside help, spending $42.3 million on outside counsel from 1993 to late 1999. Mayer, Brown & Platt received more than any other law firm in what the newspaper called "the gravy train of pinstripe patronage." Chicago's top lawyer justified using more outside counsel because of increased litigation and conflicts of interests.

Also close to home, the law firm twice represented the Illinois state government when it opposed efforts by Native American tribes trying to gain land. Based on the Treaty of Prairie du Chien of 1829, Oklahoma's Ottawa Tribe in 1998 was trying to get the state government to turn over 1,280 acres near Chicago's western suburbs and threatened a lawsuit as a last resort. In 2000 the Miami Tribe filed a lawsuit trying to get land it said was theirs under the 1805 Treaty of Grouseland. The 2,250-member tribe estimated that the land located in 15 counties was worth about $30 billion in 2000. In both these cases some speculated that the tribes wanted the land for casino sites.

The law firm also continued its leadership in the mergers and acquisitions field. For example, in 1999 it advised Burlington Northern Santa Fe Corporation in its merger with Canadian National Railway Company. In 2001 it represented iPCS Inc. when it was acquired by AirGate PCS Inc. for $802.8 million, George Weston in its $1.765 billion acquisition of Bestfoods Baking Company, and Devon Energy Corporation in its $3.1 billion acquisition of Mitchell Energy.

In its first Global 100 listing, the *American Lawyer* in its November 2001 issue ranked Mayer, Brown & Platt as the world's 21st largest law firm based on its number of lawyers (884) and 11th based on gross revenue of $533.5 million. With 324 equity partners, the firm also was ranked 49th for most profits per partner ($725,000).

Mayer, Brown & Platt on February 1, 2002, merged with London's Rowe & Maw to create the new firm of Mayer, Brown, Rowe & Maw. The two firms had earlier shared several important clients, such as the Bank of America, Aon, Ernst & Young, and GE Power Systems. Founded in 1895, Rowe & Maw was well known for its corporate, construction, pension, insurance, property, and employment practices. Chambers & Partners nominated Rowe & Maw as the "UK Law Firm of the Year in 2000." It reported revenues of $80 million for its fiscal year that ended April 2001. The merged firm's London office, with more than 300 lawyers and 600 staff, served clients such as

Cable & Wireless Communications, EMI, ICI, Reuters, Unilever, and AstraZeneca.

The merged law firm of Mayer, Brown, Rowe & Maw in 2002 faced plenty of competition, including two large international law firms that each had about 3,000 lawyers (Clifford Chance and Baker & McKenzie). Eleven other firms had between about 1,000 and 2,000 lawyers, according to the Global 100 list of November 2001.

Principal Operating Units

Finance; Construction and Engineering; Employment; Corporate; Intellectual Property and Information Technology; Pensions and Financial Services; Real Estate; Litigation; Dispute Resolution.

Principal Competitors

Sidley Austin Brown & Wood; Baker & McKenzie; McDermott, Will.

Further Reading

Bakke, Dave, "Unsettled Property/Oklahoma Tribe Eyes Casino in DeKalb County," *State Journal Register* (Springfield, Ill.), November 1, 1998, p. 1.

Behar, Richard, "Capitalism in a Cold Climate," *Fortune*, June 12, 2000, pp. 194–216.

"Carl Meyer, Attorney for 64 Years, Dies," *Chicago Tribune*, May 29, 1954.

Dettro, Chris, "Tribe, Illinoisans at Battle Over Land; State Plans to Assist Landowners in Lawsuit Filed by Miami Indians," *State Journal Register* (Springfield, Ill.), July 24, 2000, p. 9.

Goldstein, Matthew, "Chicago Law Firm Finds That NYC Is Its Kind of Town," *Crain's New York Business*, August 30, 1999.

Goldstein, Tom, "New Head of A.B.A. Justin Armstrong Stanley," *New York Times*, August 12, 1976, p. 18.

Halliday, Terence C., *Beyond Monopoly: Lawyers, State Crises, and Professional Empowerment*, Chicago: University of Chicago Press, 1987.

"I.H. Mayer, 103, Dies; Oldest Yale Graduate," *Chicago Tribune*, September 25, 1967.

Machalaba, Daniel, and Steven Lipin, "Burlington Northern Agrees to Merger—Canadian National Rail Deal for $6 Billion Will Form Leader in North America," *Wall Street Journal*, December 20, 1999, p. A3.

Salisbury, Harrison E., "Peking Takes Stock of Wall Street Ways," *New York Times*, June 10, 1972, p. 37.

Spielman, Fran, "Clout-Heavy Law Firms Cash in City Fees in 6 Yrs. Top $42 Million," *Chicago Sun-Times*, December 5, 1999, p. 9.

Stewart, James B., "Legal Landmark: Major Banks Loosen Links to Law Firms, Use In-House Counsel—Ties of Continental Illinois to Mayer, Brown & Platt Erode Since Penn Square—A Way to Cut Costs in Half," *Wall Street Journal*, April 26, 1984, p. 1.

—David M. Walden

McKesson Corporation

One Post Street
San Francisco, California 94104
U.S.A.
Telephone: (415) 983-8300
Fax: (415) 983-7160
Web site: http://www.mckesson.com

Public Company
Incorporated: 1928 as McKesson & Robbins
Employees: 23,000
Sales: $42.01 billion (2001)
Stock Exchanges: New York
Ticker Symbol: MCK
NAIC: 422210 Drugs and Druggists' Sundries
    Wholesalers; 422990 Other Miscellaneous Nondurable
    Goods Wholesalers

McKesson Corporation on its web site describes itself as "the world's largest supply management and healthcare information technology company." With industry-leading operations in the United States, Canada, and Mexico, the company is North America's largest pharmaceutical wholesaler. It specializes in distributing drugs and other healthcare products to hospitals, pharmacies, and retail stores including Wal-Mart and ShopKo. Its robotic and Internet-based technologies have led to a 99.9 percent customer order accuracy. As part of the growing healthcare industry, McKesson ranks as number 35 in the 2001 *Fortune* 500 list.

Origins and Changes in the 1800s and Early 1900s

In 1833 John McKesson and partner Charles Olcott founded Olcott & McKesson, a wholesale and import drug company in Manhattan that provided herbal products. Twenty years later with the addition of Daniel Robbins and the death of Olcott, the firm changed its name to McKesson & Robbins. Yet this was just the beginning of the changes experienced by McKesson. When John McKesson died in 1893, the McKesson heirs left the company in order to form the New York Quinine and Chemical Works. By 1900 McKesson & Robbins had partially consolidated its industry by convincing several large wholesale drug distributors to become McKesson subsidiaries.

In 1926, McKesson & Robbins was sold to Frank D. Coster. The ownership transition plunged McKesson & Robbins into 13 years of disrepute attributed directly to its new owner and his crime-prone family. Coster, whose real name was Philip Musica, was the son of a New York importer of Italian foods. The Musica family had prospered in the import trade primarily by bribing dock customs officials to falsify shipment weights. When the Musica team was arrested in 1909, Philip paid a $5,000 fine and served five months in prison for the crime.

The prison experience did not reform the criminal family, however, and they were again arrested in 1913 on similar charges. This time, a hair importing business started after Philip Musica left prison had racked up $500,000 in bank debt based on virtually nonexistent security. A bank investigation revealed that the supposedly valuable hair pieces being used for collateral were in fact only worthless ends and short pieces of hair. The Musica family was caught trying to escape on a departing New Orleans ship. Once again, Philip was the scapegoat for the family escapades; he served three years in prison. When he was released in 1916 he worked for the District Attorney's office as an undercover agent named William Johnson.

During World War I, Musica began a poultry business, but his entanglement with the law was not over. After evading conviction for a 1920 murder, he changed his business interests from poultry to pharmaceuticals, posing as president of Adelphi Pharmaceutical Manufacturing Company in Brooklyn. In spite of many "second chances," Musica appeared unable to avoid a life of crime; his new venture, a partnership with Joseph Brandino, was actually a front for a bootlegging concern.

When Adelphi failed, Musica changed his name to Frank D. Coster. Hoping to put his criminal past behind him, Coster managed to establish himself as a respectable businessman by starting a hair tonic company that had a supposedly large customer list. With this apparently firm collateral, Coster seemed a viable acquirer when he offered to purchase McKesson & Robbins in 1926. In fact, for 13 years thereafter, Coster

233

was able to keep his identity a secret; he was even listed in *Who's Who in America,* where he was described as a businessman as well as a "practicing physician" from 1912 to 1914.

Coster went on an acquisition spree when the Great Depression weakened many competitors. In 1928 and 1929 alone, he added wholesale drug companies in 42 cities to McKesson & Robbins's American and Canadian operations. Five more firms were acquired from 1930 to 1937. Meanwhile, 1929 sales had reached $140 million, and the company earned $4.1 million in profits.

Coster's true identity was revealed in 1938 when a treasurer at McKesson & Robbins became concerned over the way the profits were being handled. That curiosity soon led to an investigation that revealed a $3 million embezzlement scheme perpetrated by Coster. Some of the money was used to pay blackmail fees to his former partner, Brandino, who had discovered Coster's true identity and threatened to expose him. In 1939 Coster shot himself and Brandino was convicted of blackmail.

Post-World War II History

The company reorganized in the early 1940s and returned to private ownership. Its operations were presumably closely held during this period. The company's calm and relatively quiet existence was intruded upon in 1967, however, when Foremost Dairies of California implemented a hostile takeover. Acrimony over the conduct of the buyout fostered an unhappy relationship between the managers of the new "partners" for several years after the merger. In fact, it was three years before McKesson offices were even moved to San Francisco, the headquarters of Foremost.

The new company formed by this merger, Foremost-McKesson, Inc., had no corporate strategy and appeared to be moving in several different directions at the same time. Rudolph Drews, head of the unified firm, was described by *Forbes* magazine as the "freewheeling" president who had acquired several diverse companies from "sporting goods to candy" after the merger with McKesson and who was better at making acquisitions than managing them. In 1974 Drews was forced from the corporation after a daylong board meeting; his management style was considered the cause for a "flattening" of earnings.

Drews's response, "I'll be back," after he was fired from Foremost-McKesson was no idle threat. Drews established his own corporate merger consulting business and found an opportunity in 1976 to orchestrate a takeover bid of his former company. Drews's middleman for the corporate raid was Victor Posner, a Miami multimillionaire who saw his own opportunity to buy out Foremost-McKesson. William Morison, who had succeeded Drews as president of Foremost-McKesson, worked hard to prevent Sharon Steel, Posner's Pennsylvania firm, from acquiring his company's stock. Although Posner was able to

obtain 10 percent of Foremost-McKesson's equity, he soon found that the price of the stock could be measured in more than dollars and cents.

Morison's defense strategy focused on a negative public relations campaign that targeted Posner and Sharon Steel. Careful, well-publicized research revealed that Sharon Steel Corporation had overstated its earnings for 1975 by 45 percent in order to support its takeover offer. According to *Forbes,* Posner was "scourged coast to coast" for his tactics as a "corporate marauder." Having repulsed Posner and Drews's takeover attempt, Foremost-McKesson stockholders approved a charter change that prohibited any "unsuitable" party from acquiring more than 10 percent of the company's common stock. An unsuitable party was defined as any business that might jeopardize Foremost's liquor or drug licenses.

Although the takeover crisis only lasted a few months, Foremost-McKesson suffered long-term consequences. The company had lost valuable time in executing the turnaround plans devised by the new president, William Morison. Morison was determined to make the company a more dynamic, streamlined operation. Up to this point, Foremost-McKesson had been viewed as two companies wedded together with no real direction or focus. Morison complained that "people on the East Coast think of us as McKesson the drug company, and people on the West Coast think of us as Foremost the dairy company, and we don't think either one really fits anymore." Morison hoped not only to turn Foremost-McKesson around operationally, but also to create a new corporate image. In 1977, Executive Vice-President Thomas E. Drohan compared the company to an elephant that, under the new direction of Morison, was now "off its knees and ambling noisily."

Morison had, in fact, worked to implement a reorganization in the midst of the 1976 battle to maintain autonomy. That year, Foremost-McKesson made two major acquisitions and sold or combined 11 of its less vital operations. Morison wanted to move the company away from its role of middleman as a wholesale distributor of pharmaceutical products, beverages, and liquor, and emphasize production of proprietary products. His objective was to streamline the company by selling its low-profit operations and investing $200 million into new businesses by 1990. Although the battle with Posner sidelined many of these goals, Foremost's acquisitions of C.F. Mueller Company, the country's largest pasta marker, and Gentry International, a processor of onion and garlic, were two significant acquisitions made in 1976 that met the objectives set by Morison.

Over the course of the two years before Morison's retirement, he reorganized the company into four major operating groups: drugs and healthcare, wine and spirits, foods, and chemicals, as well as a small home-building division. This new strategic plan was the first of its kind for Foremost-McKesson, and it was one factor that placed the company in a more comfortable position for the future.

Thomas P. Drohan, who was elected president upon Morison's 1978 retirement, continued his predecessor's strategy. Drohan's defense against corporate raids was to maintain a prohibitively high stock price. His management style focused on productivity and efficiency. Specifically, he automated in-

Key Dates:

1833: The partnership of Olcott & McKesson is founded.
1853: The business is renamed McKesson & Robbins.
1893: Founder John McKesson dies and his heirs leave the company.
1926: Frank D. Coster, a criminal whose real name was Philip Musica, buys the company.
1928: McKesson & Robbins is incorporated.
c.1940: The company becomes privately owned after Coster kills himself in 1939.
1967: Foremost Dairies takes over the company, which becomes Foremost-McKesson, Inc.
1970: The company moves its headquarters to San Francisco.
1976: The company avoids a hostile takeover, is reorganized, and acquires C.F. Mueller Company and Gentry International.
1979: Armor All Products is acquired as McKesson enters the car protection products industry.
1983: The company acquires Zee Medical, Inc. and sells C.F. Mueller and Foremost Dairies.
1984: The company is renamed McKesson Corporation.
1986: McKesson Chemical Division is sold to Univar Corporation.
1989: McKesson gains Wal-Mart Stores as a major customer.
1990: The company gains control of Medis Health and Pharmaceutical, Canada's major drug wholesaler.
1994: McKesson acquires Integrated Medical Systems Inc. and decides to sell PCS Health Systems to Eli Lilly & Company.
1998: The company acquires Red Line HealthCare Corporation.
1999: A January merger with HBO & Company creates McKesson HBOC Inc.; Kelly/Waldron & Company and Kelly Waldron/Technologies Solutions are acquired.
2000: McKesson acquires Prospective Health, Inc. and sells its Water Products business; the company renews its contract with ShopKo Stores for five years.
2001: The firm introduces Supply Management Online to increase its Internet capabilities.

ventory and stock procedures, allowing Foremost to reduce personnel costs by a third.

Drohan also redefined the company's "middleman" role in the distribution chain by establishing data processing procedures that would be valuable to both suppliers and customers, placing Foremost-McKesson in the position of acting as part of the marketing teams. This business strategy has been characterized by one *Harvard Business Review* analyst as a "value-adding partnership." Over the course of the 1980s, independent druggists were faced with competition from powerful mass and discount drug chains. Foremost-McKesson's value-adding partnership offered these small business owners—many of whom could not afford the computerized inventory controls that were a key to the national chains' success—the benefits of automated

systems without the expense. These practices catapulted the company to the vanguard of wholesale practices and contributed to average annual profit increases of 20 percent, ten times the rate recorded before 1976.

Neil Harlan succeeded to the chairmanship of Foremost-McKesson in 1979. A former army captain, Harvard business professor, and McKinsey & Company director, Harlan soon initiated a second restructuring, selling the pieces of the company that did not fit its distribution image. In 1983 alone, Harlan divested more than one-third of the conglomerate's holdings to focus on healthcare and retail products. Divisions sold included C.F. Mueller as well as Foremost Dairies and its food processing and residential construction subsidiaries.

In 1983 McKesson acquired Zee Medical, Inc. Formed in 1959, Zee Medical provided occupational safety and first-aid products. This McKesson subsidiary had grown rapidly after the federal government in 1971 increased workplace safety demands through OSHA. By around 2000 Zee Medical was a $100 million business that served more than 300,000 manufacturing plants, hotels, and other facilities.

Acquisitions made in the early part of the decade strengthened Foremost-McKesson's role as a major distributor of healthcare products. In 1982 the drug distribution business contributed $2.1 billion to the company's $4 billion in sales. Fueled by $90 million in acquisitions of distribution and distribution-related businesses, revenues increased steadily in the early 1980s. Harlan's aggressive consolidation helped make McKesson one of the leaders in wholesale distribution. His strategy was twofold; he believed that "any company that doesn't stick to what it does best is inviting trouble" and that "anybody who doesn't prepare [for a raider] is living in a dreamworld." A 1984 name change, to McKesson Corporation, reflected the declining influence of food operations.

Harlan, a popular leader, retired in 1986 and was succeeded by Thomas W. Field, Jr., formerly of American Stores Co., a national grocery chain. That same year, McKesson sold its poorly performing chemical distribution division, McKesson Chemical, to Univar Corp. for $76 million. Proceeds of the sale funded acquisitions of additional drug and healthcare product distributors, software firms, and medical equipment distributors. The company also raised funds for capital investments through the public offering of shares amounting to about 15 percent of subsidiary Armor All Products Corp. and a similar stake in prescription reimbursement division PCS Health Systems Inc. in 1986. Part of the proceeds went toward a $115 million expenditure on increased automation and efficient new distribution hubs.

McKesson had acquired Armor All, the company that launched the automotive protective market, in 1979. After suffering five years of limited profits, Armor All took off in the late 1980s. Within four years of entering the Japanese market in 1984, the product had captured one-fourth of the market. By the late 1980s, Armor All had achieved $126 million in annual sales and held 90 percent of the U.S. auto protectant market. Hoping to parlay its complete dominance of this category into continuously increasing sales, McKesson expanded Armor All's product line to include car waxes, detergents, and spray cleaners. By

1993, the products were offered in more than 50 countries. McKesson's bottled water subsidiary also paid off during this period: from 1980 to 1990, the American market for bottled water grew by 250 percent, and McKesson's Sparklett's brand enjoyed a number two ranking in that industry.

Although profits rose 33 percent and sales increased 46 percent over the course of CEO Field's term in office, he abruptly resigned in September 1989 amid difficulties related to McKesson's prescription reimbursement division, PCS Health Systems Inc. PCS managed pharmaceutical costs for the sponsors of corporate, government, and insurance healthcare plans by performing cost-benefit analyses of drugs and recommending the top candidates to its customers. Under pressure from insurance companies to cut costs, PCS had tried to reduce reimbursements to pharmacists and drugstore chains. When major customers—including Rite Aid Corp. and Wal-Mart Stores—balked at the cuts, McKesson scrambled to keep both its constituencies satisfied. Neil Harlan came out of retirement to serve as McKesson's interim CEO. Harlan was able to rejoin the ranks of the retired by the end of the year, when Alan Seelenfreund, a 14-year veteran of McKesson, advanced to chairman and CEO.

By 1990 McKesson was the industry leader in the drug wholesaling business. Its 27 percent market share was twice the percentage of its main competitor, Bergen Brunswig. McKesson in 1990 sold about 120,000 different products ranging from over-the-counter medicines to prescription drugs. Its customers included 2,500 hospitals, 14,000 independent drugstores, and 3,000 chain stores. Its annual sales of $7.6 billion and profits of $106 million came from the hard work of 15,800 employees.

Expansion and Changes in the 1990s and the New Millennium

Ironically, after causing such an uproar in the late 1980s, PCS evolved into a vital segment of McKesson's business in the early 1990s. During that time, PCS recorded sales and earnings increases of 50 percent annually, and although the company only contributed 2 percent of McKesson's annual sales, it brought in 20 percent of its profits. The parent company moved to transform PCS into what *Business Week* called "a full-fledged medical-services-management company" through the early 1994 acquisition of Integrated Medical Systems Inc., an electronic network designed to connect doctors, hospitals, medical laboratories, and pharmacies. Although these two acquisitions improved McKesson's operations, they also attracted the attention of an increasingly acquisitive pharmaceutical industry. In 1993, Merck & Co., then the world's largest ethical drug company, or producer of doctor-prescribed drugs, bought Medco Containment, a rival drug distributor, for $6.6 billion.

Merck's move prompted speculation that PCS and parent McKesson were the next logical takeover targets. McKesson's stock increased by more than 40 percent from July 1993 (when the Medco deal was announced) to February 1994. To a limited extent, that speculation became reality later that year, when McKesson agreed to sell PCS to Eli Lilly & Co. for $4 billion in cash.

McKesson used the sale as an opportunity to restructure its finances: The company gave shareholders $76 plus a new share

in McKesson in exchange for each old McKesson share they held. The remaining $600 million in proceeds from the sale were reinvested in the company.

CEO Seelenfreund looked to McKesson's future in the company's annual report for 1993. He noted, "In the competitive environment created by efforts to bring rising healthcare costs under control, the winners will be those organizations that have both the financial strength and the technological skills needed to improve the quality of care while cutting their own costs and those of their customers. McKesson is one of the few companies that possess both these strengths."

McKesson's expansion in the 1990s was fueled by several acquisitions. On November 17, 1998, it announced the acquisition of Red Line HealthCare Corporation, a Novartis subsidiary whose headquarters remained in Golden Valley, Minnesota. A distributor of medical services and supplies for extended care facilities, Red Line (www.redline.com) reported sales of about $375 million for the fiscal year that ended on August 31, 1998.

In January 1999 McKesson through a subsidiary completed its merger with HBO & Company (NASDAQ: HBOC) to form McKesson HBOC, Inc. The merged business that began operations on January 13, 1999 was "the world's largest healthcare services company," according to a press release.

In 1999 McKesson HBOC acquired two other companies. First it acquired Kelly/Waldron & Company and Kelly Waldron/Technologies Solutions, which provided market research, database services, and automated systems to help strengthen the corporation's sales and marketing efforts. The two acquired businesses had revenue of about $25 million in 1998. Later in 1999 McKesson acquired the Minneapolis company of Abaton.com, Inc., a private firm that offered Internet-based prescribing, laboratory requests and results, and related services to doctors' offices.

Prospective Health, Inc. (PHI)'s acquisition by McKesson HBOC was announced in a press release dated January 31, 2000. Headquartered in Palos Heights, Illinois, PHI and its 50 employees developed software for the healthcare industry.

About a month later, on February 29, 2000, McKesson announced the sale of subsidiary McKesson Water Products Company to Groupe Danone for $1.1 billion in cash. That was the final step that began in the 1980s to end the company's diverse operations. "This sale completes the company's transition to a focused healthcare company, with market-leading positions in healthcare information technology and supply management," said John H. Hammergren and David L. Mahoney, company co-CEOs and co-residents, in a February 29, 2000 announcement.

At the end of fiscal 2000, which ended March 31, 2000, McKesson HBOC reported total revenues of $36.7 billion, a 22.3 percent increase over its $30.0 billion in total revenues for fiscal 1999. The corporation's fiscal year 2000 total revenues came from four sources: 1) pharmaceutical distribution and services, $24.1 billion, 2) medical-surgical distribution, $2.7 billion, 3) $8.7 billion in sales to customers' warehouses, and 4) information technology, $1.2 billion. Including special items, the company in fiscal 2000 earned a net income of $723.7 million, up from $84.9 million the year before.

The company on July 24, 2000 announced it had signed a three-year contract with Wal-Mart Stores to continue providing pharmaceuticals for the chain of 1,773 Wal-Mart stores, 780 Supercenters, 466 SAM'S Clubs, and five Wal-Mart warehouses. A Wal-Mart executive praised McKesson for its innovative service and technological prowess that led to the renewal of a business relationship that began in 1989.

In September 2000 McKesson HBOC Information Technology Business signed an agreement to acquire the MED-Solution system of Montgomery, Alabama's Health Care Systems, Inc. This was part of the company's efforts to improve the reliability and safety of drug dispensing in hospitals and other institutions. Through its automated systems, the company planned to ensure that the right patients received the right medications at the right times. Adverse drug events that led to deaths and suffering were a major problem according to the Institute of Medicine's 1999 study called *To Err Is Human: Building a Safer Health System.*

In early December 2000 McKesson HBOC's Clinical and Biological Services announced a strategic alliance with DHP Ltd., an Abergavenny, United Kingdom clinical trial supplies company (www.dhpclin.com). This agreement resulted from increased globalization of the pharmaceutical and biotechnology industries that both companies served.

McKesson in late 2001 announced another expansion of its U.K. operations. In 1990 its Information Solutions business had started in the United Kingdom, but in 2001 it signed a $480 million ten-year contract to provide automated human resources and payroll systems to the government's National Health Service Information Authority. Such agreements helped McKesson look forward to a prosperous future, both in its home country and overseas.

Principal Subsidiaries

Millbrook Distribution Services Co.; Armor All Products Corp.; McKesson Service Merchandising Co.; Medis Health & Pharmaceutical Services Inc. (Canada); Zee Medical, Inc.; McKesson HBOC Pharmaceutical; McKesson HBOC Automated HLTCR; McKesson HBOC Medical Group; McKesson Healthcare Del Sys; McKesson Drug Co.; McKesson HBOC Health Systems; McKesson HBOC Corporate SLTNS; McKesson Aps; McKesson Bioservices; McKesson Pharmacy Systems; McKesson HBOC Extended Care; Med Management.

Principal Competitors

Cardinal Health, Inc.; AmerisourceBergen Corporation.

Further Reading

Byrne, Harlan S., "McKesson Corp.: Big Drug Distributor Bounces Back from a Bummer Year," *Barrons,* June 25, 1990, pp. 51–52.

Hof, Robert, "McKesson Dumps Another Asset: The Boss," *Business Week,* September 25, 1989, p. 47.

Johnston, Russell, "Beyond Vertical Integration: The Rise of the Value-Adding Partnership," *Harvard Business Review,* July/August 1988, pp. 94–101.

Mitchell, Russell, and Joseph Weber, "And the Next Juicy Plum May Be McKesson?," *Business Week,* February 28, 1994, p. 36.

Moskowitz, Milton, Robert Levering, and Michael Katz, editors, "McKesson," in *Everybody's Business: A Field Guide to the 400 Leading Companies in America,* New York: Doubleday/Currency, 1990, pp. 228–30.

Schlax, Julie, "Strategies: A Good Reason to Mess with Success," *Forbes,* September 19, 1988, pp. 95–96.

—updates: April Dougal Gasbarre, David M. Walden

Meridian Gold, Incorporated

9670 Gateway Drive, Suite 200
Reno, Nevada 89511-8997
U.S.A.
Telephone: (775) 850-3777
Toll Free: (800) 572-4519
Fax: (775) 850-3733
Web site: http://www.meridiangold.com

Public Company
Incorporated: 1996
Employees: 250
Sales: $115.4 million (2001)
Stock Exchanges: New York Toronto
Ticker Symbol: MDG (New York); MNG (Toronto)
NAIC: 212221 Gold Ore Mining; 212222 Silver Ore Mining

Meridian Gold, Incorporated mines for gold and silver. Based in Nevada, the company has gone as far as Chile and Kyrgyzstan in search of its fortune. It runs Chile's most productive gold mine, El Peñón. Another record find, at the Beartrack property in Idaho, wound up commercial production in 2001. Formerly the gold production unit of FMC Corp., Meridian was reincorporated in Canada in 1996.

Origins

One of Meridian Gold, Incorporated's precursors was FMC Gold Co., a subsidiary of FMC Corp., the Chicago-based industrial conglomerate. Based at first in Chicago and then in Reno, FMC Gold was active in Nevada; in 1972 the company discovered gold in Jerritt Canyon, near Gabbs in the west central part of the state. Ten years later, FMC discovered gold at nearby Paradise Peak. This mine was owned 30 percent by FMC and 70 percent by the Freeport McMoran Gold Co.

FMC's interests produced 223,500 ounces of gold in 1986. The volcanic rock in the area proved so difficult and expensive to drill, that the company tested hundreds of bits from 12 different manufacturers. The Paradise Peak Mine, on the other hand, was one of the world's lowest-cost producers of gold and silver, noted the *Engineering and Mining Journal*. Both of these mines were undergoing major expansion programs, and in 1989 they produced 332,000 ounces of gold for FMC.

Spun Off in 1987

In June 1987, FMC floated its gold mining unit as FMC Gold. The parent company was refinancing $1.2 billion in long-term debt at the time. The partial spinoff raised $95 million for FMC Corp., which retained 89 percent of the subsidiary's equity. FMC Gold's sales were $153.3 million that year.

In 1988, FMC added 15 new properties to its 20 already under investigation, including some along Nevada's Carlin Gold Belt. Exploration costs exceeded $13 million for the year. FMC Gold showed a profit of $61.2 million in 1988, up 22 percent.

Another of Meridian Gold Inc.'s predecessors was also having a good year. In November 1988, Meridian Gold Co., then a unit of Burlington Resources Inc., announced the discovery of two million ounces of gold at its Beartrack Joint Venture in Lemhi County, Idaho—the state's largest gold find to date. Colorado-based Canyon Resources Corp. was Meridian's partner in the venture. FMC Gold acquired Meridian Gold from Burlington Resources in a stock trade in May 1990.

FMC's costs per ounce nearly doubled at Paradise Peak in the spring of 1991, while production at Jerritt Canyon rose 24 percent. The company's Royal Mountain King mine in California was producing a modest amount of gold but losing money at it.

In November 1991, Larry D. Brady replaced Robert N. Burt as FMC Gold CEO when Burt was picked to be the CEO of FMC Corp., which then owned 79 percent of FMC Gold Co. Brady also became Burt's second-in-command at FMC Corp. For 1991, FMC Gold posted earnings of $7 million on sales of $139.4 million. More efficient production techniques and other cost-cutting measures helped the company's earnings in 1992.

In the five years since its 1987 spinoff, FMC Gold had suffered from lower gold prices ($340 an ounce; $100 an ounce lower than 1987) as its mines grew emptier. Its attempts to find

Company Perspectives:

Meridian has established itself as a different kind of gold company. We produce gold and silver ounces to accomplish our objective, but we focus on the quality of these ounces as measured by the profitability per ounce not the quantity of ounces produced. Historically, many gold companies were fixated on just the reverse. We have believed from the beginning that the best way to thrive in this business was to find gold deposits that were capable of making money.

Key Dates:

1981: FMC Gold begins operations.
1982: Gold is discovered at Paradise Peak.
1987: Twenty percent of FMC gold is floated on the stock market.
1988: Meridian Gold makes Idaho's largest gold find to date at Beartrack.
1990: FMC acquires Meridian.
1996: FMC Gold is reincorporated in Canada as Meridian Gold Inc.
1998: Gold is discovered at El Peñón, Chile.
2000: El Peñón operation is inaugurated.
2001: Commercial mining winds down at Beartrack.

new sources had proven fruitless, even after drilling hundreds of holes in the ground in Nevada, California, Montana, and New Mexico. The company was waiting for gold prices to recover before developing its Beartrack mine near Salmon, Idaho. Fortunately, the company did have $154 million in cash reserves to fund development and exploration. The dry spell prompted FMC to expand its search to Chile, Mexico, and Russia.

FMC Gold announced it was forming a $20 million joint venture in July 1995 with Kyrgyzstan's largest gold company, Kyrgyz Altyn, to expand an existing mine. FMC's Beartrack mine in Idaho went onstream around the same time and was expected to yield 90,000 ounces of gold a year through 2005.

FMC Gold's annual sales were $57.4 million in 1995; net income rose from $151,000 the year before to $2.3 million. The company was producing 200,000 ounces of gold a year at a cash cost of $200 an ounce. Thirty percent owned Jerritt Canyon, which produced three-sevenths of FMC's total output, had a much higher operating cost than Beartrack: $260 to $285 an ounce. Paradise Peak closed in 1994.

In September 1995, parent company FMC Corp. began looking for a buyer for its 80 percent stake in FMC Gold, in order to focus on its core business. When gold prices rose in early 1996, it began evaluating other options, such as selling just part of the company.

Going North in 1996

FMC Corp. ultimately decided on a unique course of action: relaunching FMC Gold Co. as a Canadian company. FMC Corp. offered 90 percent of its stake in FMC Gold, which was renamed Meridian Gold Inc. at this time. Conditions were somewhat less auspicious than at FMC Gold's 1987 flotation, as gold prices had fallen yet again (trading between $380 and $400 an ounce). The reincorporated company would continue to trade on the New York Stock Exchange while beginning a new listing on the Toronto Stock Exchange, which was considered the financial center of the mining world.

Because of market conditions, FMC Corp. reduced the minimum offering price 30 percent, from $284.6 million (C$370 million) to $201.9 million. The company raised C$267 million from the sale. The underwriters exercised an option to buy FMC Corp.'s remaining 10 percent interest in Meridian, bringing the final proceeds to C$295 million.

Meridian's leader was Brian Kennedy, a former military aviator. A longtime FMC Gold veteran, he aimed to double its

production after its reincorporation by seeking out new deposits on its own rather than buying from others. Due in part to exploration costs, which were accounted for as expenses, Meridian posted a $15.9 million loss in 1996 on sales of $76.2 million. The company had two major exploration projects underway, one named Rossi in the Carlin Gold Belt near Jerritt Canyon, and the other, El Peñón, in northern Chile. Barrick Gold Corporation later agreed to invest up to $15 million in Meridian's new Rossi property in Nevada in exchange for a 60 percent interest.

In July 1998, Meridian announced it had struck gold at El Peñón in a big way, finding very high grade deposits. The price of gold had soon fallen to $300 an ounce, but the quality of the find at El Peñón suggested Meridian could mine it for as little as $180 an ounce. The news made Meridian stand out among gold stocks, which were otherwise faring poorly, even though the company had begun to post losses.

El Peñón Opens 2000

El Peñón, located in Chile's Atacama desert, was officially inaugurated on January 21, 2000. It would be the country's most productive mine. In March, Meridian pulled out of the Venturina property in Chihuahua State, Mexico, a joint venture it had developed with International Northair Mines Ltd.

Meridian posted a net income of $40.6 million on sales of $128.3 million in 2000 after losing a combined $53 million in the previous two years. Sales of $128.3 million were greatly increased over 1999's $71.2 million. After hitting a 20-year low two years earlier, gold prices were climbing beyond $300 an ounce at the end of 2001, meaning more good news for Meridian.

Principal Subsidiaries

Compañia Minera Meridian (Chile); Jerritt Canyon Joint Venture (30%); Minera Meridian Peru S.A.C.; Rossi Joint Venture (40%).

Principal Operating Units

Beartrack Mine; El Peñón; Jerritt Canyon; Rossi.

Principal Competitors

Agnico Eagle Mines Ltd.; Barrick Gold Corporation; Kinross Gold Corp.; Newmont Mining Corp.; Placer Dome Inc.; Rio Tinto plc.

Further Reading

Bagnell, Paul, "Meridian Sees Golden Opportunity in Dry Spell," *Financial Post,* Sec. 2, July 31, 1998, p. 17.

Burns, Greg, "Writing FMC's Rule Book on Damage Control," *Business Week,* Special Report, October 31, 1994, p. 90.

Chow, Jason, "Gold Set to Hit US$300 an Ounce: BMO's Geoff Stanley: But Stocks in Sector May Not Keep Pace with Bullion Rise," *National Post,* September 25, 2001, p. C1.

Church, Foster, "Whistleblower: Corps Employee Claims He Was Silenced," *Portland Oregonian,* May 2, 1996.

"Costs Hit FMC Gold," *Mining Journal,* July 19, 1991, p. 57.

Critchley, Barry, "Miners See the Beauty in the TSE," *Financial Post* (Toronto), Sec. 3, February 15, 1997, p. 51.

Damsell, Keith, "Mine's Prospects Put Sparkle in Meridian," *National Post,* March 16, 1999, p. D3.

Fedeli, Patricia C., "Innovation Leads to Assets at the Paradise Peak Mine," *Engineering and Mining Journal,* January 1989, p. N25.

"FMC Gold Disposal?" *Mining Journal,* August 25, 1995, p. 142.

"FMC's Kyrgyzstan Involvement," *Mining Magazine,* July 1995, p. 50.

"FMC Starts Heap Leach at Paradise Peak," *Engineering and Mining Journal,* August 1988, p. 15.

"Gold Producing Industry Feels Mounting Pressure to Explore Consolidation," *National Post,* August 2, 1999, p. C3.

Gooding, Kenneth, "FMC Forced to Cut Meridian Gold Sale Price to $201M," *Financial Times* (London), Cos. & Finance: The Americas/Asia-Pacific, July 31, 1996, p. 26.

Hirschmann, Thomas, "Meridian Regains Altitude on Back of Chilean Find," *Financial Post,* Sec. 2, July 7, 1998, p. 22.

Kennedy, Peter, "FMC Gold to Be Relaunched in Canada in $370M Deal," *Financial Post* (Toronto), Sec. 1, News, July 6, 1996, p. 5.

——, "FMC Raises $267M As Venture Goes Canadian," *Financial Post* (Toronto), Sec. 1., July 25, 1996, p. 9.

Lashinsky, Adam, "All That's Gold Is Not Glittering; There's Little to Treasure Yet in FMC Spinoff," *Crain's Chicago Business,* November 2, 1992, p. 1.

——, "Splitsville? These Firms Fit the Bill; Like AT&T, They May Be Worth More in Pieces," *Crain's Chicago Business,* Finance Sec., October 2, 1995, p. 1.

"Meridian Pulls Out of Venturina," *Mining Journal,* March 31, 2000, p. 249.

"New Look to FMC Gold," *Mining Journal,* July 12, 1996, p. 34.

"North Americans Boost Gold Output," *Mining Journal,* March 3, 1989, p. 178.

"Record Idaho Gold Deposit Reported at Beartrack," *Engineering and Mining Journal,* January 1989, p. 7.

Schreiner, John, "Meridian Gets Aggressive," *Financial Post* (Toronto), March 21, 1997, Sec. 2, p. 24.

Thomas, David, "International Miners Home in on Canada," *Financial Post* (Toronto), Sec. 1, March 11, 1997, p. 1.

Wagstyl, Stephan, "Market Value Near $1 Billion Likely for FMC Gold Unit," *Financial Times* (London), Intl. Capital Markets & Cos., June 8, 1987, p. 30.

—Frederick C. Ingram

Merrill Corporation

1 Merrill Circle
St. Paul, Minnesota 55108
U.S.A.
Telephone: (651) 646-4501
Toll Free: (800) 688-4400
Fax: (651) 646-5332
Web site: http://www.merrillcorp.com

Private Company
Incorporated: 1968 as K.F. Merrill Corporation
Employees: 4,100
Sales: $649.5 million (2001)
NAIC: 323110 Commercial Lithographic Printing;
    323122 Prepress Services; 561410 Document
    Preparation Services

Merrill Corporation delivers diverse document management and communications services to the worldwide financial, legal, and corporate communities. Based in St. Paul, Minnesota, Merrill is the third largest financial printer in the world, behind industry mainstay Bowne & Co. and printing powerhouse R.R. Donnelley & Sons. While financial printing remains a core market and top revenue producer for the company, Merrill has steadily reduced its reliance on that volatile market. In 1996, financial printing provided slightly more than 36 percent of the company's revenues, corporate printing nearly 30 percent, commercial clients 21 percent, and document management services nearly 13 percent.

Merrill's services include typesetting, printing, reproduction, electronic filing, custom communications design, and publishing. The company prints prospectuses and other timely, transaction-based, and compliance documents for the worldwide financial community. Mutual funds and other investment vehicles are another important source of company revenue. The company's Merrill/May subsidiary is a leading provider of customized marketing, corporate identity, and franchise products. Document management services include document reproduction, litigation support, imaging, scanning, storage and retrieval, electronic SEC filing, and other document reproduction

services. Merrill has been at the technological forefront of the printing industry, using high-speed telephone-based data transmission to serve its clients through an innovative "hub and spoke" system, with typesetting and other services centralized at its St. Paul headquarters and sales and service centers operating in 42 offices in 31 cities in the United States. The company also operates five regional printing facilities, which handle approximately half of the company's printing needs. The remainder is contracted out to a network of printer "partners." Most of Merrill's revenues are domestic. However, the company has achieved a significant international presence through joint ventures in Canada, Europe, Asia, and South America. John W. Castro, principal architect of Merrill's growth, continues to lead the company as president and CEO.

Getting Started: 1968

Merrill and his wife, Lorraine, started their typesetting business in their home in St. Paul in 1968. Called K.F. Merrill, the company soon began serving the financial printing needs of the Twin Cities market. For most of the next decade, Merrill acted as the company's sole salesman, while also assisting in all phases of the business, from proofreading to delivering the final product. By the end of the 1970s, the company had grown to regional status and dominance of the St. Paul-Minneapolis market—without owning a single printing press. Toward the end of the decade, the company had about $1 million in sales and some 30 employees. Yet years of working 18-hour days had begun to take its toll on Merrill, by then in his 60s. After three heart attacks, he began looking for someone to take over the day-to-day operations of the company.

Merrill chose Chicago native John W. Castro, who joined the company in 1978 as production manager. Castro, only 29 years old at the time, already had printing experience stretching back to the mid-1960s. After graduating from high school, Castro had taken a construction job in order to earn money for college. Laid off from that job after six months, Castro took a friend's advice and applied for a pressman's job in a local manufacturer's print shop. There he developed a keen interest in graphic arts and printing, and particularly the newly developing application of electronics technology to the still traditional

---

printing industry. While working full time at the print shop, Castro managed to complete three years of college at Chicago's DePaul University. An offer of a job with a Chicago printing company, however, convinced Castro to leave college without a degree. The printing company placed Castro at the forefront of the still nascent computerized typesetting applications. As Castro's expertise grew, he began consulting for other printing companies looking to use the new technology, and in this role he met Kenneth Merrill.

Merrill offered Castro the job as Merrill's production manager. However, as Castro told *Minnesota Ventures,* Merrill "was really looking for a partner. And the thing I always thank him for is that he gave me a lot of immediate authority in the business, from day one." With Merrill's encouragement, Castro worked to transform the company, which was struggling to break even in spite of sales of more than $1 million.

Although dominant in its market, the company was faced with a new challenge. By the late 1970s, the financial printing industry's larger firms were beginning to expand nationally. Competitors such as industry leader Bowne & Co. were establishing printing operations in the Twin Cities area, responding to a similar expansion by their mainstay law firm and underwriter clients. Merrill, which relied on a single client for some 30 percent of its sales, soon faced a choice: to expand the company nationally or sell it to a competitor.

Named president of the company in 1981, Castro and a team of top executives weighed their options. They decided to build Merrill into a national printing operation, with an eye toward breaking into the New York market, the heart of the financial printing business. "[We] started to figure out where to grow this business," Castro told *Minnesota Ventures.* "We didn't have cash so we had to figure out a way to grow it that was different and less expensive than our competitors did it." What Castro came up with was a "hub-and-spoke" system based on that being deployed by the airline industry. Rather than imitate its competitors, which typically moved into a new market by establishing complete printing operations, Castro turned to his background in computerized typesetting and the developing technology in telephone data transmission.

Castro's approach would tackle two significant problems. Establishing printing operations in other regions required a great deal of capital. Printing, however, tended to be a volatile business, with demand for services following a peak and valley activity cycle. Building its own printing facilities would require Merrill not only to raise more cash than it had, but also to be able to absorb the costs of operating during low demand periods, while being able to supply clients during times of high demand. Castro determined that the company would avoid own-

ing its own printing presses, a policy the company followed through much of the 1980s. Instead, Merrill's typesetting and related operations were centralized at its St. Paul headquarters.

Expansion was driven by setting up far less capital-intensive sales and service centers in target markets. Customer orders were taken by a sales office, beginning in Chicago, and the project would be sent to the St. Paul headquarters using a dedicated analog phone line capable of transmissions of about 48 characters per minute. The finished product would be transmitted back to Chicago, where it was brought to a printer "partner," one of several local printing firms contracted to complete Merrill's orders. Successful expansion of the company, however, depended on overcoming still another obstacle. The financial printing industry remained somewhat of an "old boys club," with relationships between printers and clients stretching back decades or more. Bowne & Co., for example, had been in operation since 1775. Castro overcame this obstacle by aggressively recruiting the top salespeople in each market, paying top salaries, and relying on their ties with clients to bring Merrill business. In this way, Merrill essentially bought into the "buddy" system of the financial printing market.

Rising to the Top in the 1980s

Castro established Merrill as a lean, price-competitive organization, plowing earnings into enhancing its technology—particularly its data transmission capacity—instead of building printing presses. In contrast, its competitors were saddled with heavily unionized, capital intensive printing operations. Yet, as Castro pointed out to *Inc.* magazine, "The term 'financial printing' is kind of a misnomer. Three-quarters of the work performed is typesetting, not printing. How can others possibly keep up with us?" Printing often represented the largest cost associated with an initial public offering or merger agreement. Unburdened by the need for large cash outlays, Merrill was able to provide its services at lower cost. The company quickly moved to enter the crucial New York market, which accounted for nearly 40 percent of the industry's $630 million in yearly sales. "They used to laugh at us," Castro, who was named CEO in 1984, told *Minneapolis-St. Paul CityBusiness.* "Here's a company in Minnesota trying to compete with Wall Street and the deal doers."

Merrill caught the wave of the bull market of the 1980s, capturing clients among that period's flood of mergers, acquisitions, hostile takeovers, and initial public offerings. Sales grew quickly, reaching $8.3 million in 1983, and climbing to $25 million by 1985, as the company established sales offices in seven major markets. Much of its success lay in its use of technology, while its competitors struggled to convert their typesetting operations, hampered by union contracts requiring retraining of their employees. Merrill's employee base, which grew to 400 by the mid-1980s, remained non-union, while the company's employee-friendly policies kept them loyal to Merrill. By 1986, Merrill was printing a new prospectus—its own, as it went public, offering 1.7 million shares. The company was also moving to hedge its operations against a downturn in the financial market, expanding its commercial printing operations. Early in 1987, the company added advertising typography capacity to its Chicago office and acquired Financial Publishers, a company that produced newsletters for banks. Sales continued

Key Dates:

1968: K.F. Merrill Company is founded in St. Paul.
1982: Branch offices are opened in Denver and Chicago.
1983: A Los Angeles office is opened.
1984: John Castro becomes president and CEO; company name is changed to Merrill Corporation.
1985: Company acquires Adwest Corporation and opens offices in New York and Washington, D.C.
1986: Merrill acquires Appellate Printing, and completes its IPO.
1992: Company merges with Burrups Ltd. of London.
1996: Paul Miller replaces Kenneth F. Merrill as board chairman.
1997: Company acquires Superstar Computing and Total Management Document Service Center Business and has a two-for-one stock split.
1999: Merrill recapitalizes with DLJ, becomes a private company, reorganizes into five business sectors.
2000: Firm expands internationally with offices in London, Paris, and Frankfurt.
2001: Company forms Merrill/CPY as a strategic alliance with Chas. P. Young Company and begins a marketing and development agreement with TRION Technologies.

to rise, to $38.5 million and net income of $1.6 million in 1986, and to just under $50 million, with earnings of nearly $3 million, the following year. In less than a decade, Merrill had become the industry's sixth largest financial printer.

1987: Profiting from "Black Monday"

The so-called "Black Monday" stock market crash of October 1987 claimed the financial printing industry as one of its victims. Almost overnight, financial printing sales, which had grown to an estimated $800 million per year, shriveled to around $600 million. Merrill's stock slid from $14 to $4.25 per share, prompting the company to buy back a large chunk of its shares the following year. But Merrill, which still had about $9 million in cash from its IPO, was in better shape than its industry rivals. Within three years, three of its chief competitors—Sorg, Charles P. Young, and Pandick, Inc. (ranked fifth, fourth, and second, respectively)—would declare bankruptcy and go out of business entirely.

Merrill, too, was hit hard by the collapse of the financial printing market. But it had successfully expanded its corporate printing services, including products such as 10-Ks, 10-Qs, and annual reports, to account for about 60 percent of revenues by the end of the decade. The company's revenues grew, to $55 million in 1988 and to $63 million in 1989, returning profits of $4.5 million and $3.8 million, respectively. Then Merrill was forced to take a temporary earnings hit after writing off stock it had purchased in rival Sorg when that company declared bankruptcy. Nonetheless, the company continued to expand, opening new sales offices, including one in Atlanta, and purchasing for around $3 million the Chicago, Los Angeles, and San Francisco offices of then struggling Charles P. Young. That purchase also

included printing presses in Chicago and Los Angeles, marking Merrill's first company-owned presses. The cost of the acquisition, coupled with the writeoff of the Sorg stock, however, produced the company's first loss in ten years, of nearly $1.25 million on revenues of $69 million.

Growth During the Early 1990s

In the aftermath of the stock market crash, the printing industry quickly began to consolidate. When Pandick declared bankruptcy in 1990, Merrill negotiated an agreement to take over Pandick's Dallas printing facilities, allowing Merrill to expand its capacity at virtually no cost. The collapse of its competitors, as Castro told *Corporate Report Minnesota*, was "the easiest way to go from No. 6 in the market to No. 3." By then, however, Castro had skillfully led the company into diversifying its services, expanding its commercial printing capacity while adding new services such as reproduction and custom design. In this way, Merrill was well positioned for the next blow to the barely recovering financial printing industry. The recession of 1990 and the outbreak of the Gulf War combined to put a near halt to the transactions upon which financial printers depended.

Merrill acquired two small printing companies, Southeastern Financial Printing Corp. of Atlanta and Group Web, Inc., of St. Paul, in February 1990. The Group Web acquisition also included printing and binding equipment. By then, Merrill was handling approximately 25 percent of its own printing needs. Merrill was also moving into a new direction, legal publishing, through its Merrill/Magnus Publishing Corp. subsidiary, hoping to build on its knowledge of the legal community. Meanwhile, the company continued to expand its business by making acquisitions. In July 1990, Merrill acquired Sorg's former Illinois operation, S Printing Co., adding still more printing equipment to the company's in-house capacity. In that same month, the company also purchased Group Printing California, based in Los Angeles. These acquisitions, and Merrill's expanding share of the financial and corporate printing markets, which was reaching 14 percent, helped propel the company's sales past the $100 million mark for its 1991 fiscal year.

Another factor in Merrill's favor was the printing industry's practice of awarding contracts on a bid basis, generally from among three competing bids. With three of its principal competitors out of business, Merrill found itself receiving a greater number of invitations to bid on contracts. Moreover, the end of the recession meant also that there were many more contracts on which to bid. Financial printing once again began to supply a primary source of Merrill's revenues, soon accounting for more than a third of annual sales, up from a low of 21 percent of revenues at the beginning of the decade.

The company steadily gained ground in the first half of the 1990s. Its growth was further aided by a joint venture agreement made in 1992 with London-based Burrups Ltd., the leading European financial printer. Another acquisition, of May Printing Company for $25 million in 1993, also boosted revenues and strengthened the company's commercial printing business, by then the fastest-growing segment of company sales. Merrill's sales neared $150 million in 1993, bringing a net profit of nearly $9 million; by 1994, sales rose to $182 million, for a net income of over $13 million. The following year, with sales growing to $237 million, Merrill was again preparing new acquisitions, and in 1996 the company paid $33 million for the purchase of assets of Corporate Printing Co. of New York, and an additional $7.4 million in cash and notes for FMC Resource Management Corp., based in Seattle. These purchases helped raise Merrill's revenues to nearly $250 million for its 1996 fiscal year.

Continued Expansion in the Late 1990s and Beyond

Merrill in 1999 accepted a merger offer of over $500 million from Viking Merger Sub, Inc., an affiliate of DLJ Merchant Banking Partners II, a subsidiary of Donaldson, Lufkin, & Jenrette Inc. Merrill's shareholders approved this transaction in November, which left Merrill Corporation as the surviving entity. It also resulted in Merrill becoming a private company.

In 2000, Merrill launched www.merrilldirect.com as a business-to-business web site designed to allow companies and law firms to prepare financial documents online. In a press release, Merrill President and CEO John Castro said, "We are proud to be the first in the financial printing industry to become a complete online management resource for financial documents required by publicly traded companies."

Meanwhile, Merrill was expanding its document management services (DMS), designed mainly for law firms. In late January 2000, it announced an alliance with INTEGREX, an Owens Corning subsidiary with expertise in technology-based litigation support services. The next month, Merrill announced the start of its web-based UR-Law system that used Oracle technology to provide speedy access to text, video, audio, and emails stored online.

Such technological innovation helped Merrill gain new DMS clients. In January 2001, it announced a five-year contract with the law firm of Akin, Gump, Strauss, Hauer & Feld. That contract brought the number of Merrill's new DMS client sites for the year up to 23. In June 2001, the law firm of Morrison & Foerster LLP signed a similar five-year contract. The law firm's 11 offices in the United States soon gained the new Merrill technology and Merrill employees to run the systems. A Morrison & Foerster office administrator in Los Angeles praised Merrill for its "understanding of the culture of law firms" and its flexibility to meet the needs of its clients.

In an April 12, 2001 press release, Merrill Corporation announced that its Financial Document Services business had become the "first major filing agent to convert its EDGAR filings to the new Securities and Exchange Commission (SEC) web-based filing system which used the Extensible Forms Description Language (XFDL) format. The month before, when many public companies filed their annual SEC reports, Merrill submitted almost one-fourth of all HTML documents submitted to the SEC, far more than any of its competitors. Again the company reaped the rewards of its technology investments.

In early January 2002, Merrill Corporation announced a strategic alliance with CCBN, a Boston-based provider of Internet services to support communications between about 3,000 public companies and the investment community. As part of this arrangement, CCBN acquired some of Merrill's Investor Relations Edge product line.

For the fiscal year ending January 31, 2000, Merrill Corporation reported revenue of $587.7 million, up 15.3 percent over fiscal 1999. The company's revenue came from five sources: Financial Document Services ($259.2 million), Investment Company Services ($137.9 million), Managed Communications Programs ($98.2 million), Document Management Services ($77.3 million), and Merrill Print Group ($15.1 million). Merrill also reported a net loss of $17.6 million in fiscal 2000, compared to a net income of $26.5 million in fiscal 1999.

Merrill's 2001 sales were $649.5 million, a 10.5 percent increase over the previous year. It also reported a net income of $17.9 million. The company was ranked as number 473 in the 2001 *Forbes* Private 500.

Principal Subsidiaries

Merrill/May; Merrill Burrups Worldwide (50%); Quebecor Merrill Canada Inc. (49%).

Principal Competitors

Automatic Data Processing, Inc.; Bowne & Company, Inc.; R.R. Donnelley & Sons Company; Workflow Management.

Further Reading

Berry, Kathleen M., "Merrill Grows Fast As a Survivor Among Wall St. Printers," *Investor's Business Daily,* July 22, 1993, p. 36.

Biemesderfer, S.C., "Merrill Gets Streetwise," *Corporate Report Minnesota,* January 1992, p. 59.

Burcam, Jill P., "Merrill's Growth Business: Corporate Identity Management," *Corporate Report Minnesota,* July 1995, p. 19.

Cross, Lisa, "Balancing Business & Technology," *Graphic Arts Monthly,* July 2000, pp. 49–52.

Kurschner, Dale, "Merrill Corp: Technology Keeps It Alive," *Minneapolis-St. Paul CityBusiness,* November 4, 1991, p. 17.

——, "Merrill Weathers Storm in Financial Printing," *Minneapolis-St. Paul CityBusiness,* March 19, 1990, p. 13.

Marmor, Laurie, "Merrill Gains by Acquisitions Amid Industry Consolidation," *Investor's Daily,* August 10, 1990, p. 32.

O'Hara, Kelly, "John Castro, Interview," *Minnesota Ventures,* October 1992, p. 21.

Persinos, John F., "Pressing Business," *Inc.,* January 1985, p. 44.

Shipman, Catherine, "Local Printer Cuts Corners in Wake of Market Crash," *Minneapolis-St. Paul CityBusiness,* December 2, 1987, p. 9.

Youngblood, Dick, "Printing Firm Prospers, Thanks to Wise Use of Technology," *Star Tribune,* November 16, 1992, p. 2D.

—M.L. Cohen
—update: David M. Walden

Metatec International, Inc.

7001 Metatec Blvd.
Dublin, Ohio 43017
U.S.A.
Telephone: (614) 761-2000
Fax: (614) 761-4258
Web site: http://www.metatec.com

Public Company
Incorporated: 1985 as Discovery Systems, Inc.
Employees: 500
Sales: $77.28 million (2001)
Stock Exchanges: OTC
Ticker Symbol: META
NAIC: 334612 Prerecorded Compact Disc (Except Software), Tape, and Record Reproducing; 334611 Software Reproducing

Metatec International, Inc. creates, manufactures, and distributes CD-ROMs and DVD-ROMs. The company offers its customers a complete line of services that range from disc mastering and graphic design through replicating, packaging, and distribution. Metatec's clients, which number in the thousands, include such major names as CompuServe, General Motors, and Harcourt Brace. The publicly held company has factories at its headquarters in Dublin, Ohio, and in Breda, Netherlands.

Beginnings

Metatec traces its roots to 1985 when Jeffrey M. Wilkins founded Discovery Systems, Inc. to offer laserdisc-based video programs for employee training in the banking, fast food, and healthcare industries. Wilkins had earlier cofounded CompuServe, Inc. with his father-in-law, building it from a small data-processing concern into a leading information services and videotext company. After selling it to H&R Block in 1980 for $22.4 million, Wilkins stayed on as CEO until he was dismissed in 1985. Following an unsuccessful attempt to buy back the company, Wilkins assembled more than $10 million in venture capital and set out on a new tack. He formed Discovery Systems

in a suburb of Columbus, Ohio, where a new plant was built to produce laser discs. Unlike other companies in the nascent optical disc business, Discovery planned to develop content in addition to manufacturing the discs. To this end, the company soon bought Columbus-based Morning Star Video Productions.

During Discovery's first year Wilkins decided to begin manufacturing compact discs for outside clients, as the new CD format was starting to take off and there were still relatively few replication plants in the United States. The technology was similar to that of laser discs, and Wilkins quickly moved to license a CD manufacturing system developed by U.S. Philips Corp. and DiscoVision Associates.

Soon after entering the field, however, Discovery found its CD output abilities dwarfed by many newly arrived competitors. By 1988 wholesale prices for the discs had dropped by more than half, and the company, which had also branched out into recording and releasing albums by the likes of Cincinnati, Ohio's Pure Prairie League, found itself under siege from investors and creditors who sought millions of dollars in payments. The U.S. Bankruptcy Court in Columbus was petitioned to dissolve Discovery, but instead the judge approved a reorganization plan that included an infusion of new capital from Larry and Robert Liebert, Wilkins, and Silco Corp. of Lakeland, Florida, a publicly traded real estate firm. The Lieberts and Silco each controlled 48 percent of the company, with Wilkins owning the remainder.

The resuscitated company was renamed Discsystems and its focus was changed to the manufacturing of CD-ROM discs, which were compact disc lookalikes that could store large quantities of data (such as the contents of an entire encyclopedia), as well as sound and images, for use on a computer. CD-ROMs at this time were in wide use at institutions such as libraries, but were only just beginning to gain acceptance as a consumer format. The reorganized company found the CD-ROM business to be a steadier and more profitable one than manufacturing audio CDs, though the company continued to make some of the latter, primarily for syndicated radio programs.

Some months later Silco Corp. purchased the Lieberts' and Wilkins' shares of Discsystems, and the merged company's name was changed to Metatec. Wilkins, who was serving as president and CEO, later bought up shares of the firm, gaining control of more than 10 percent over the next few years.

Introduction of Nautilus in 1990

In 1990 Metatec introduced a "CD-ROM Magazine" called Nautilus. The multimedia disc, which included games, photos, sound files, and software demonstrations, was initially sold by subscription, but also reached some users when it was bundled with new computers. Several Nautilus spinoff discs were produced by Metatec during the early 1990s, including "Best of Sound Bytes Vol. 1" and "Best of Photography Vol. 1," priced at $49.95. A World Almanac and Book of Facts CD-ROM, based on the Pharos print version, was priced at $79.95.

In 1992 Metatec sold the remaining Silco real estate investments and eliminated its restricted Class B stock. The company had by this time developed relationships with several hundred clients, putting, for example, General Motors' parts catalog on CD-ROM for use by its dealers. Metatec's distinction in the CD-ROM market was its ability to put the data together for a customer, format it, and manufacture the discs, permitting one-stop shopping for clients. The company had also become the leading manufacturer and distributor of compact discs for the radio syndication market. Metatec was still losing money at this time, however, reporting a loss of $370,000 for fiscal 1992 on revenues of $17.1 million.

In the fall of 1993 the company announced a strategic alliance with CompuServe to produce CD-ROMs for the latter's online service. The discs contained multimedia programs that could be linked to information from the Web. The slow speeds of home Internet connections limited the amount and quality of audio and video that could be obtained online, but the higher capacity, faster CD-ROM could provide such features with ease.

By 1994 Metatec was beginning to see the need for increased manufacturing capacity, and it began construction of a 65,000-square-foot addition to its existing 55,000-square-foot facility in Dublin, Ohio. The new space would give the company the ability to manufacture 12 million discs per year, up from five million. A contract was also signed with Colorado-based Optimus Corp. to produce and distribute several CD-ROM titles including Fed Log, a federal parts and logistics information disc that sold an estimated one million units per year. Metatec's Nautilus was now reaching 12,000 subscribers who paid $11 a month.

In October 1994 Metatec bought Compact Disc Services, Inc. of Saratoga, California. CDSI offered CD-ROM publishing services to customers on the West Coast. For fiscal 1994 the rapidly growing company reported revenues of $28.9 million and net earnings of $1.69 million.

Deals with Harcourt Brace and IDG: 1995

In 1995 Metatec signed an agreement with Harcourt Interactive, a division of Harcourt Brace College Publishers, to help develop multimedia CD-ROM products that would complement various Harcourt Brace textbooks. The company also announced plans to work with International Data Group of Boston to create a CD-ROM magazine called Multimedia WorldLIVE!, based on IDG's publication *Multimedia World.* The first issue was released in July. In the fall Metatec folded the Windows-based version of its money-losing Nautilus into Multimedia WorldLIVE!, while continuing to publish a separate Macintosh version for a time. Multimedia WorldLIVE! was bundled with *Multimedia World* print copies, 100,000 of which were sold through subscriptions and on newsstands.

In the spring of 1996 Metatec announced another expansion of its Dublin plant, adding 80,000 square feet to the existing 120,000. The new space would be used to produce a data-storage version of the latest evolution of the optical disc, the DVD-ROM, which was expected to take off in the near future. Some $5 million was earmarked for the expansion and for purchasing new equipment. The company had also created a new division, the New Media group, which focused on applications that combined CD-ROMs and the Internet, an area which CEO Wilkins felt was the way of the future. One of the division's first ventures was called Metatec Access, which offered customers a complete package of design, programming, and manufacturing services for Internet-linked CD-ROMs. The initial response to these initiatives was not overwhelming, however, and late in the year the New Media division was shut down and its operations renamed Metatec Access Services. At the same time the company was experiencing a reduction in orders for CD-ROM supplements to magazines. Seeking new ways to capture business, Metatec began to increase the company's capabilities for packaging and distributing discs.

In late 1997 Metatec reached an agreement to provide financing to Optical Disc Corporation of California, a CD-ROM and DVD mastering system maker that had been supplying Metatec with equipment for ten years. Metatec was now making 40 million CD-ROMs per year for thousands of different customers. The company's forte was its quick turnaround time, with many discs mastered, pressed, and shipped within three days. Major clients of the firm included Hewlett-Packard, Sun, Microsoft, and Bell & Howell. Wall Street was not showing much interest in Metatec, however, and during 1997 the company bought back 1.1 million shares of its stock, seeking to shore up the sagging price.

Purchase of Imation CD-ROM Business: 1998

In the late summer of 1998 the company spent $39.8 million to acquire the CD-ROM Services business of Imation Corporation, which included replicating plants in Menomonie, Wisconsin, Fremont, California, and Breda, the Netherlands. Imation retained ownership of the Menomonie site and Metatec later transferred its equipment and employees to other facilities. The acquisition doubled Metatec's manufacturing capacity, and the firm, which now had ten sales offices in the United States and one in Europe, changed its name to Metatec International.

Key Dates:
1985: Jeffrey Wilkins founds Discovery Systems, Inc.
1988: Near bankruptcy, Wilkins gets help from new investors.
1989: Company becomes Metatec, Inc.
1990: Nautilus ''multimedia magazine'' is launched on CD-ROM.
1991: Stock moves to the NASDAQ exchange.
1993: Strategic alliance with CompuServe, Inc. is announced.
1998: Company purchases Imation's CD-ROM manufacturing business.
1998: Corporate name is changed to Metatec International.
2001: With losses mounting, Metatec lays off more than 40 percent of its workforce.
2002: California manufacturing plant is sold; stock moves to the OTC market.

Following the Imation purchase Metatec began to expand in Europe, first by doubling the capacity of the Breda plant and later by adding a sales office in Germany. In July 1999, the company bought the technology products and services business of SilverSpan from its bankrupt parent MegaSoft, renaming it Metatec Internet Products Group. The $314,000 acquisition gave Metatec the ability to distribute software and other information products over the Internet. SilverSpan's customers included Merrill Lynch, Motorola, and Dow Jones. During 1999 Metatec began yet another expansion in Dublin, devoting $7 million to a 155,000-square-foot fulfillment and distribution center next door to its existing facility.

Integration of the Imation businesses was proving problematic and costly, and Metatec reported a loss of $2.8 million for 1999 on earnings of $120 million. In early 2000 the company announced a reduction of 12 percent of its workforce, mainly at its Dublin headquarters. Wilkins stated that Metatec would not make any acquisitions in the near future and would concentrate on developing its core business of CD-ROM manufacturing. The DVD-ROM category was still not taking off, with only a small percentage of the company's revenues coming from it.

The year 2000 saw Metatec develop a new service for its customers, in which they could create online catalogs of their CD-ROMs with the company's software, and then use Metatec's fulfillment services for packaging and delivery of the orders. A seamless link would be made from their own web sites to a Metatec-hosted catalog page. The service was not intended for major e-commerce companies, but rather for ones which had little infrastructure in place to handle sales over the Web. Metatec hired Columbus-based Ultryx to help in the development of the new service.

In September 2000 Metatec introduced a new mini-CD-ROM called the Metatec DataCard. The disc's surface could be printed with business card information and cut into a variety of shapes, and it could be played in a computer's disc drive to display information or links to the Web. The new cards were popular, but

did not put a significant dent in the company's losses, which hit $18.4 million for the year, a figure which was largely attributed to a $16.1 million writedown of goodwill and assets.

The first half of 2001 saw Metatec let another 20 percent of its workforce go while streamlining manufacturing and reducing office space in continued efforts to stem the flow of red ink. The company also renegotiated hundreds of customer contracts and eliminated a number of other ''low margin'' ones. The tough situation only got worse after the terrorist attacks on the United States in September, and plans were soon announced to shut down the firm's California CD-ROM manufacturing facility, which was later sold to Medius Corp.

Metatec defaulted on a $20.2 million loan in October, and negotiations were held throughout the fall with its lenders to develop a new payment plan. In December an additional 20 percent reduction in the workforce was announced as the company continued to struggle. That month company founder Jeffrey Wilkins stepped down from the roles of CEO and president, and his place was taken by Christopher Munro, who had joined the company a year earlier as chief operating officer. Final figures for 2001 saw a further shrinkage of earnings, to $77.3 million, with losses hitting $29.9 million, two-thirds of which was due to restructuring and asset writedown costs. The company's battered stock was subsequently scheduled to move from the NASDAQ to the OTC market.

Reeling from the U.S. economic slowdown and the costly integration of Imation's CD-ROM operations, Metatec International struggled to pare its business down to the essentials and get back on track. With a drastically reduced workforce and its manufacturing recently consolidated, the company was looking to fresh leadership to bring it back to financial health.

Principal Subsidiaries

META Holdings, LLC; META Management, LLC; Metatec Worldwide, Inc.; Metatec International B.V. (The Netherlands).

Principal Competitors

Zomax, Inc. Cinram International, Inc.; DOCdata, N.V.; Technicolor Inc.

Further Reading

Block, Debbie Galante, ''Recently ISO Certified, Metatec Grabs Market Share of Quick Turn ROM Market,'' *Tape-Disc Business,* February 1, 1996, p. 36.

''Discovery Emerges from Chapter 11 with Infusion of Capital,'' *MacWeek,* May 23, 1989, p. 95.

Hall, Matthew, ''In on the Ground Floor . . . Again,'' *Ohio Business,* October 1, 1986, p. 26.

Hutheesing, Nikhil, ''When in Doubt, Diversify (CD-ROM Publisher Metatec Corp.),'' *Forbes,* February 28, 1994, p. 104.

McKenzie, Gia, ''Chris Munro, Metatec's New President and CEO: Champion of Supply Chain Management and 'Co-opertition,' '' *Tape-Disc Business,* January 1, 2002, p. 49.

Melvin, Chuck, ''CD-ROM Maker Seizes Spotlight,'' *Plain Dealer Cleveland Ohio,* January 11, 1998, p. 2H.

''Metatec Announces New Long-Term Financing Agreement,'' *Dow Jones News Service,* February 8, 2002.

"Metatec Reports Restructuring Strategy," *DVD News,* January 3, 2002.

Newpoff, Laura, "Inefficiency After Imation Deal Behind Metatec Cutback," *Business First of Columbus,* February 18, 2000, p. 9.

——, "Metatec Plots Plan to Reverse Fortunes," *Business First of Columbus,* November 26, 1999, p. 1.

——, "Metatec Readies New Service to Stem Losses, Expand Reach," *Business First of Columbus,* May 12, 2000, p. 6.

——, "Wilkins, Metatec on European Adventure," *Business First of Columbus,* July 2, 1999, p. 1.

"Ohio's Own," *Ohio Business,* December 1, 1985, p. 15.

O'Reilly, Tom, " 'Beyond Technology' (Metatec Corp.)," *Tape-Disc Business,* September 1, 1999, p. 20.

Pramik, Mike, "Founder Steps Back As Metatec's Financial Problems Mount," *Columbus Dispatch,* December 14, 2001, p. 1F.

——, "Metatec to Reduce Payroll by 80 Jobs," *Columbus Dispatch,* December 29, 2001, p. 1C.

Scott, Jennifer, "Costly Investments Seen Bearing Fruit," *Columbus Dispatch,* April 25, 1998, p. 1J.

——, "Metatec's Revenues May Double with Acquisition from Imation," *Columbus Dispatch,* June 16, 1998, p. 2C.

Turnbull, Lornet, "Metatec Will Trim 7 Percent of Local Staff," *Columbus Dispatch,* February 16, 2000, p. 1G.

Wolf, Barnet D., "Metatec Meets Technology: After a Long Struggle, Metatec's Vision for CD-ROMs Becomes a Commercial Success," *Columbus Dispatch,* July 26, 1993, p. 1.

—Frank Uhle

Millennium Pharmaceuticals, Inc.

75 Sidney Street
Cambridge, Massachusetts 02139
U.S.A.
Telephone: (617) 679-7000
Fax: (617) 374-7788
Web site: http://www.mlnm.com

Public Company
Incorporated: 1993
Employees: 1,330
Sales: $196.3 million (2000)
Stock Exchanges: NASDAQ
Ticker Symbol: MLNM
NAIC: 325412 Pharmaceutical Preparation Manufacturing

Millennium Pharmaceuticals, Inc. is a Cambridge, Massachusetts biotech company dedicated to the discovery and development of new drugs through the application of genomics, but what sets it apart from similar companies is its business model. Since its foundation in 1993, Millennium has been highly successful in landing lucrative research and development contracts with major pharmaceutical firms. Rather than signing blanket agreements, however, the company forms alliances that target specific diseases. This strategy allows it to forge lucrative relationships with a number of partners. Essentially Millennium leverages its advanced drug discovery technology platform to enable researchers to quickly identify genes that may be associated with a particular disease. Rather than being content to just collect royalties from pharmaceuticals, Millennium has designs on becoming a drug maker itself, although its few products are the result of acquisitions rather than internal development. Nevertheless, Millennium has built an organization that is now capable of discovering a new drug, taking it through clinical trials, and marketing it. The company concentrates on three fields: oncology, inflammation, and metabolic disease.

Business Background of Millennium's Founder: 1970s–80s

The driving force behind the creation of Millennium was its chairman and chief executive officer, Mark J. Levin. He grew up in St. Louis, the son of a businessman who owned several small shoe stores. Levin was forced to take on a great deal of responsibility early in life, following the death of his mother from cancer when he was 16. While maintaining his studies he cared for his three younger sisters and sold shoes for his father, ultimately earning a master's degree in chemical and biomedical engineering from an area school, Washington University. For a brief spell he stayed in St. Louis selling shoes, then in 1976 accepted an engineering position in Indianapolis with Eli Lilly. He next took a job in North Carolina, where his wife attended college, overseeing the setup of a new brewery for Miller Brewing Company, which provided him with exposure to a large production facility. A brief, unsuccessful stint owning a doughnut shop taught him the pitfalls of running a business. Levin and his wife moved to Massachusetts, where he took a job with the Foxboro Co. selling computers to biotech companies. He called on his former boss at Lilly, William Young, who now worked at Genentech, one of the pioneering biotechs, but instead of selling a process control system he found himself being offered a job.

In 1981 Levin relocated with his wife to San Francisco, where he gained experience managing a number of complex drug projects with Genentech. He then took a position in 1987 with the Mayfield Fund, a San Francisco venture capital firm, where he served as the co-director of its Life Science Group. His job was to identify new scientific ideas, then help form companies to exploit them. Rather than wait for someone to approach him with an idea, Levin kept up on research journals and made contacts with scientists. In this way he was instrumental in the creation of Cell Genesys, Inc. in 1987, Cyto Therapeutics, Inc. in 1988, Tularik, Inc. in 1990, and Focal, Inc. in 1991. While starting these companies and spending time with scientists, Levin became aware of research on the human genome. He visited the major genome centers in both the United States and Europe, meeting many of the prominent people in the field. It became clear to him that they believed all human diseases had some connection to genetics and that within the next decade the human genome would be sequenced. Levin recognized that genomics offered a way to produce a myriad of new drugs to cure specific diseases, as well as a business opportunity with significant potential. He was not alone in this belief, with differing business models developing to exploit genomics. Levin described the situation in a 2001 *Technology*

Company Perspectives:

We believe that by understanding how specific changes in genes relate to disease, we can deliver precisely the right medicine to precisely the right patient at precisely the right time. The catalyst for this vision is genomics; the force behind it, a unique blend of science and business innovation; the promise, breakthrough therapeutic and predictive medicines that can transform healthcare.

Review interview: "Some formed diagnostic companies by identifying mistakes or [diversity] in genes. Some built companies by compiling genomic information and selling the databases that arose from the information. Others realized that there were going to be important technologies to develop and you could sell these tools and form alliances around them. Millennium was focused from day one on building the biopharmaceutical company for the future by developing personalized therapeutic products."

Founding of Millennium: 1993

From 1991 to 1992 Levin laid the groundwork for Millennium, recruiting a team of top scientific advisers with commercial appeal who would found the company in 1993: Eric Lander, with the Massachusetts Institute of Technology; Jeffrey Friedman, of Rockefeller University; Raju Kucherlapati, of the Albert Einstein College of Medicine; and Daniel Cohen, chief scientist at Genset, a French biotech. From the outset the advisers knew that in the beginning they would have to team up with a large pharmaceutical to provide major funding and to develop drugs out of Millennium's research, then take them through trials and bring them to market. The founders also recognized that they would produce a great deal of intellectual property. David Stipp in a *Fortune* profile of the company outlined the potential of Millennium's genomic research: "Not only would it reveal thousands of disease-related genes in humans and germs, but also every single one might become a little patent factory. For starters, a gene and the specific protein it helps produce might be patented, providing molecular targets for developing traditional drugs. A separate patent might be awarded for a bioengineered drug generated by splicing the gene into a microbe. Another patent might cover novel medicines that directly affect the gene to ameliorate the disease it's involved with. Yet another might cover the gene's use in new diagnostics for spotting individual patient's predisposition to disease." As a result of this thinking, Millennium was determined to form partnerships that were narrowly defined, retaining as many rights as possible to the intellectual property the company produced, as well as earning royalties on any drugs that made it to market. Teaming with a number of companies targeting different diseases also served to spread the risk. In addition, Millennium chose to portray itself as a technology company involved in drug research, rather than an aspiring drug company, a label that was likely to drive away many investors.

At first, Levin turned to Mayfield for $8.5 million in seed money, then raised additional money from other venture capital funds. His wife, who was an executive search professional, spent months looking for a suitable chief executive for the company before concluding that her husband was the only candidate with enough vision to run the business. Although Levin intended to head Millennium on a temporary basis, as he had with earlier start-ups funded by Mayfield, he ultimately decided to stay on as the permanent CEO. In December 1993 Millennium Pharmaceuticals was incorporated. Levin leased space close to MIT and within six months the company recruited a team of 30 scientists. It also began to establish its technology platform, in many ways a testament to Levin's engineering background. A number of technologies, including robotics and computers, were combined with microbiology to create a complex, but efficient, production process. According to Stipp, Millennium began to "refine its platform. From major medical centers it obtained access to tissue samples from sick people—researchers extract DNA from such samples and scan it for genetic patterns correlated with diseases." It was this platform that Millennium offered to potential partners.

By March 1994 the first cash-rich pharmaceutical signed on with Millennium. Hoffmann-La Roche agreed to pay $70 million over a five-year term to develop drugs to treat type II diabetes and obesity, two target areas with the potential to generate large revenues. In July, Levin named Steven H. Holtzman as chief business officer for the company. Holtzman would be instrumental in the structuring of future agreements with pharmaceuticals, reserving as many rights as possible. Millennium's next major alliance, and Holtzman's first deal, came in October 1995, a $50 million joint venture with Eli Lilly & Co. focusing on atherosclerosis, the blocking of arteries by fatty deposits. Two months later Millennium signed a five-year, $60 million collaboration with Swedish pharmaceutical Astra AB, targeting inflammatory diseases such as asthma, hay fever, and bronchitis.

Public Offering in 1996

Millennium went public in 1996, netting $58 million. During the year the company's research efforts produced the first tangible results. A gene-based assay was produced for Roche to screen for obesity drug candidates. Millennium also identified a gene involved in the development of type II diabetes, triggering a milestone payment from Hoffman-LaRoche. Furthermore, a gene-based test developed for Eli Lilly and Company was used to identify atherosclerosis drug candidates.

Millennium was active on a number of fronts in 1997. In an $89 million stock transaction, it acquired Chemgenics Pharmaceuticals, which allowed Millennium to broaden its research into antibacterial drugs. The company also forged a new important alliance: a $218 million, five-year deal with Monsanto Inc. involving research into bioengineered crops. Unlike previous partnerships, the agreement with Monsanto was not as narrowly defined. Because it wanted to maintain its focus on drugs, Millennium essentially agreed to a technology transfer to a new Monsanto unit, Cereon Genomics, which was set up next door. Under this arrangement Millennium received a hefty payment from Monsanto yet was not saddled with the costs of adding personnel and equipment. Also in 1997 Millennium formed a pair of subsidiaries to enhance the value of the corporation. Millennium BioTherapeutics was established to develop therapeutic proteins, gene therapy, and antisense products. Lilly immediately signed a $70 million, five-year deal to develop medicines from proteins, in the process gaining an 18 percent stake in the subsidiary. Millennium next formed Millennium Predictive Medicine to produce diagnostic tests using bioinformatics and proteomics.

After gaining valuable experience in genomics, Millennium researchers developed a way to narrow down the number of target genes. Rather than conduct lengthy validation studies on each new gene, they concentrated on genes that reacted to known medicines. These so-called ''druggable'' genes were then studied, saving a considerable amount of time and effort. Needing a partner to put this new technique into use, Millennium turned to Bayer AG, which because it was late to embrace biotechnology was willing to assume some risk in order to catch up with its rivals. Bayer had been looking to team with a genomics company since late 1997 and by September 1998 agreed to a $465 million, five-year deal with Millennium. Under the terms of the agreement, Millennium was to deliver 225 genomics-based proteins targeting cardiovascular diseases, cancer, osteoporosis, pain, liver fibrosis, hematology, and viral infections. In addition, Bayer gained a 14 percent stake in Millennium. It would be allowed to cherry-pick the target proteins, but the rights of 90 percent of the proteins would revert to Millennium. Although it still had no products on the market, Millennium was able to post a $10.3 million profit for the year because of its pharmaceutical agreements.

More research deals would follow in 1999. Bristol-Myers Squibb agreed to a $32 million, five-year alliance with Millennium Predictive Medicine to develop diagnostic tests in oncology. The subsidiary also signed Becton Dickison to a $70 million, five-year strategic alliance. The parent company, meanwhile, moved closer to its goal of becoming a drug company capable of selling its own proprietary products when it agreed to a $750 million stock acquisition of LeukoSite Inc., providing latter-stage drug development capabilities as well as several possible drugs in clinical and late-stage preclinical development.

In June 2000 Millennium landed another major deal with a pharmaceutical company, which in the process forwarded its long-term aspirations. France's Aventis SA, Europe's fourth largest pharmaceutical, agreed to pay $450 million in a complex five-year deal that called for the two parties to create, develop, and market a new line of anti-inflammatory drugs to treat such diseases as rheumatoid arthritis, asthma, and certain allergies. The two companies would share profits equally in any drugs sold in the United States and Canada, and Millennium was to receive a royalty in all other markets. It was a highly advantageous deal for Millennium, but it was also of strategic importance to Aventis, which had been formed in a $25 million merger in 1999. A new management team conducted a thorough review of its operations to identify shortcomings. Establishing a relationship with Millennium was a quick and economical way for Aventis to fill its needs. Millennium then bolstered its ability to fulfill the Aventis agreement by paying $53 million to acquire Cambridge Discovery Chemistry, a British subsidiary with a large number of scientists experienced in pharmaceutical chemistry. Moreover, the addition of Cambridge Discovery extended Millennium's presence overseas.

Millennium had its first drug on the market in 2001, Campath, used to treat chronic lymphocytic leukemia, which it picked up in the LeukoSite acquisition. Although Campath was only expected to reach revenues of no more than $150 million a year, and Millennium had to share profits with two other companies involved in its development, it was still a major step for the company. As other products made their way through clinical trials, Millennium continued to forge partnerships with pharmaceuticals that might one day become rivals. Hoffmann-LaRoche reached a three-year agreement to develop diagnostic products for rheumatoid arthritis. Because of the expiration of an earlier deal with Hoffmann-LaRoche, Millennium was able to strike a new partnership to develop drugs and diagnostic tests for diabetes and obesity, this time with Abbott Laboratories for $250 million over five years. By the end of 2001 Millennium also completed the largest acquisition in its brief history, a stock swap valued at $2 billion for San Francisco-based Cor Therapeutics. The transaction was a clear statement that Millennium intended to one day become a major player in the pharmaceutical business. The Cor purchase brought with it a cardiovascular drug expected to generate $225 million for the year, a sales and marketing staff was experienced in launching a new product, as well as researchers working in heart disease, the most lucrative therapeutic area. Although some observers were critical of the Cor acquisition, others thought that Millennium had put itself in a solid position to realize future growth. It had ten drugs in human clinical testing and several others on the verge of entering that stage, a large well trained staff, $400 million in estimated annual revenues, and $2 billion in cash to cover losses incurred from an annual commitment of $500 million for research and development. In a December 2001 interview with *Technology Review,* Levin was candid about his lofty plans for Millennium: ''Over the next five to 10 years, our goal is to become a company that's leading the world in personalized medicines, a company that is leading the world in productivity, a company with a value of over $100 billion, a company that has five to 10 products on the market that are making a big difference in people's lives, a company with the strongest pipeline in the entire industry.''

Principal Subsidiaries

Millennium BioTherapeutics, Inc.; Millennium Predictive, Inc.; Cambridge Discovery Chemistry, Inc.

Principal Competitors

Amgen, Inc.; Genentech Inc.; Genzyme Corporation.

Further Reading

Aoki, Naomi, "Changing the Odds," *Boston Globe,* June 17, 2001, p. D1.

Blanton, Kimberly, "Biotech's Pied Piper," *Boston Globe,* June 13, 1999, p. F1.

"Custom-Made Medications," *Technology Review,* December 2001, p. 82.

Fisher, Lawrence M., "The Race to Cash in on the Genetic Code," *New York Times,* August 29, 1999, p. 1.

Moukheiber, Zina, "Biotools," *Forbes,* May 4, 1998, p. 170.

"A Pharma Star Is Born?" *Business Week,* September 25, 2000, p. 100.

Rosenberg, Ronald, and Alex Pham, "Biotech Thrives on the Hot Idea," *Boston Globe,* April 10, 1994, p. 77.

Stipp, David, "Hatching a DNA Giant," *Fortune,* May 24, 1999, p. 178.

Thiel, Karl A., "The Millennium Minuet," *Forbes,* May 31, 1999, pp. 80–81.

—Ed Dinger

Motorcar Parts & Accessories, Inc.

2929 California Street
Torrance, California 90503
U.S.A.
Telephone: (310) 212-7920
Fax: (310) 212-7581

Public Company
Incorporated: 1968
Employees: 834
Sales: $160.7 million (2001)
Stock Exchanges: Over the Counter
Ticker Symbol: MPAA
NAIC: 335911 Storage Battery Manufacturing

Motorcar Parts & Accessories, Inc. (MPA), based in Torrance, California, is a remanufacturer of replacement alternators, starters, and spark plug wire sets for vehicles imported from England, Germany, Italy, Japan, Korea, and Sweden. To a lesser extent the company is involved in remanufacturing parts for domestic cars and lights trucks. With alternators and starters accounting for approximately 98 percent of annual sales, MPA is a leading remanufacturer of starters and alternators in both the United States and Canada. Geared toward the do-it-yourself market, almost all of the company's products are sold under private labels, with only 1 percent marketed under the MPA trademark. Customers selling MPA parts under their private labels include such major retailers as AutoZone, CSK Automotive, The Pep Boys, O'Reilly Automotive, and Canadian Tire. In addition, General Motors sells MPA remanufactured products under its AC Delco label. By far, Autozone is MPA's largest customer, accounting for about half of all annual sales, followed by CSK Automotive in the 10 percent range. The company offers an extensive line of its primary products, more than 1,100 types of alternators and nearly 750 different starters. In addition to its California facility, MPA remanufactures auto parts in two company-owned plants located in Singapore and Malaysia.

Formative Years: 1940s–80s

MPA's founder, Mel Marks, became involved in the auto parts industry just after serving in the navy during World War II. Nineteen years old and looking for work, he answered an ad in the newspapers and was hired on as a shipping clerk with Beck/Arnley-Worldparts, a division of Echlin, Inc. The owner of the business took Marks under his wing and sent him to school to learn auto mechanics and gain a deeper understanding of the auto parts business, in particular parts for imports. Marks stayed with the company for 21 years, ultimately became a vice-president, traveled extensively to Europe, and established a number of contacts that would prove crucial when he decided to strike out on his own in order to take advantage of the increasing number of foreign cars in the United States. Britain pioneered the trend by shipping MG's and Austins into the U.S. market, followed by a brief influx of French and a far more sizeable invasion of Volkswagens from Germany. In the late 1960s, Marks started his import parts business, originally called Motorcar Parts and Associates, out of his home in Jerrico, New York. Without partners or financial backing, he relied heavily on his relationship with his U.S. and European contacts in order to function as an import car parts broker. Although he could have made a comfortable living as a broker, Marks was intent on building a company. In 1968, he incorporated Motorcar Parts & Accessories, Inc. in the state of New York and initially started doing business in Plainview, New York. His timing proved to be prescient, as the import trend only heightened in the 1970s when the Japanese began to sell large quantities of Toyotas, Nissans, and Hondas in the United States. In 1979, Marks was joined by his son, Richard Marks, who gained experience in the business by owning and operating his own import automotive parts store.

For almost 20 years, MPA acted as a distributor of imported auto parts. It was not until 1986 that the company became involved in remanufacturing starters and alternators for foreign cars, aimed at the do-it-yourself customer. A spike in foreign auto sales during the 1980s made such a move an attractive idea. As those vehicles began to age they would need replacement alternators and starters, anywhere from four to eight years after purchase. Moreover, the sale of imports continued to pick up in pace. In 1985, according to the research firm R.L. Polk & Co., there were 14.5 million import car registrations in the United States, but by 1992 that number grew to more than 22.3 million, meaning that MPA could look forward to an increasing need for replacement parts as these vehicles entered their so-called "prime repair age." Americans were also holding onto their cars longer, a fact that also boded well for MPA's entry into the remanufactured replacement parts business.

Domestic Remanufacturing Beginning in 1987

Initially the company conducted its remanufacturing efforts overseas at two plants run by foreign affiliates located in Singapore and Malaysia, but only separated by an hour's drive. Both businesses, MVR Products Pte Limited and Unijoh Sdn, Bhd, were 70 percent-owned by Mel and Richard Marks and 30 percent-owned by Vincent Quek, a Singapore resident. MPA provided the raw materials to the affiliates which remanufactured parts on an independent contract basis. Although the company's Asian affiliates enjoyed much lower labor costs, MPA also began remanufacturing in the United States in 1987, establishing a plant in Torrance, California.

The remanufacturing process involved a number of steps, starting with the procurement of used alternators and starters, known in the business as "cores." Most of the cores were obtained as trade-ins from direct customers in exchange for a credit against future purchases. General consumers were in turn encouraged by credits to trade in their used starters and alternators when they purchased new or remanufactured parts. As a supplemental source, MPA also purchased cores from brokers who specialized in the buying and selling of cores in the open market. Once received, the cores were assessed and stored, sorted by make and model for inventory purposes. Only when they were needed for the remanufacturing process would the cores be completely disassembled into component parts. Parts that could not be reused, either because they were damaged or were simply subjected to too much wear, were discarded and replaced with new components. Discarded parts were subsequently sold off as scrap. Reusable components were cleaned by specialized equipment and materials, in keeping with the specifications of that particular unit. This step was followed by thorough inspection and testing through MPA's quality control program, which was QS 9000 approved (the internationally recognized automotive quality system certification designation). Component parts that make the grade were then ready to be placed on an automatic conveyor for use in the assembly of a final starter or alternator. Further quality control testing was conducted throughout the assembly process by separate quality control personnel. Finished products were also subjected to testing to make sure they performed up to expectations. Using an electroplating process, MPA applied a chrome-style finish to each item to present a like-new appearance. MPA's re-

manufactured products were then either warehoused or packaged for delivery. The complete process, from receipt of the core to final assembly and testing, lasted about four days. The company's spark plug wire set business, launched in 1992, was a much less intricate process, involving components manufactured to MPA specifications by third parties. In short, terminals were attached to wire cut to required lengths. After testing, the final product was packaged under customers' private labels.

With the advent of CAD/CAM technology, MPA was able to move beyond the simple remanufacturing of starters and alternators. Company personnel now sought to re-engineer the items. Original equipment products were thoroughly analyzed and MPA isolated ways to improve performance. Computer-aided design technology was then used to design better component parts. Moreover, MAP sought to better serve its customers through its private label programs by tailoring products to specific geographical conditions or other special needs. The company also published a comprehensive catalog of import and world car starters and alternators that featured a product identification system to allow counter personnel to quickly locate part numbers. The catalog also provided a glossary of technical terms and an explanation guide to clarify instructions and note additional parts that might be required for the installation process. Helpful photographs to assist the novice were included as well.

As the flood of foreign vehicles that Americans purchased in the 1980s began to enter prime repair age in the 1990s, MPA saw its revenues and profits steadily climb. For fiscal 1992, the company generated $13.7 million in sales and $500,000 in earnings. There was clearly considerable room for growth, since the foreign vehicle aftermarket for alternators alone was $231 million in 1992 and was expected to increase to more than $325 million within four years. Even during periods of weak economic conditions, such as the early 1990s, MPA was well suited for growth, with consumers opting to keep their vehicles longer and save money by purchasing remanufactured parts. As a result, the company also chose to concentrate on recruiting retail automotive chains as customers, believing that these chains represented the fastest growing segment of the automotive aftermarket industry. In anticipation of increased business, MPA moved much of its New York operations to California, where manufacturing and warehouse space were consolidated in a new 125,000-square-foot facility. Administration and sales continued to operate in offices located in Woodbury, New York.

Going Public: 1994

In fiscal 1993, MPA reported $17.5 million in sales, a significant improvement over the previous year, as well as a $600,000 profit. To fuel the company's continued growth, Marks took MPA public in 1994, netting nearly $5.7 million in an initial offering of stock. He also secured a $5 million credit line from Wells Fargo bank. For fiscal 1994, MPA saw its sales improve to $20.6 million and net earnings top $1 million for the first time. Prospects appeared even brighter in fiscal 1995: MPA's plan to concentrate its sales efforts on major autopart retailers paid off when the AutoZone and Pep Boys chains signed on. To better serve its East Coast and southern markets, in May 1995 the company also established a 31,000-square-foot warehouse and distribution facility in Nashville, Tennessee. MPA then added the Canadian Tire chain as a customer in fiscal

1996, as well as Delphi, which chose MPA to supply remanufactured alternators and starters for imported vehicles under General Motors' AC Delco private label. Sales to these new customers helped to continue MPA's upward trend in sales and profits, resulting in revenues of $28.3 million in fiscal 1995 and $44.9 million in fiscal 1996. Net earnings grew to $1.6 million in fiscal 1995 and $3.6 million in fiscal 1996. The company's success in appealing to major retailers was reflected in the fact that more than 70 percent of MPA sales in fiscal 1996 were to the automotive chains, with the rest mostly attributed to the large warehouse distributors such as Parts, Inc. and Hahn Automotive.

Although remanufactured alternators and starters for imported cars was now an $800 million-a-year business, the domestic segment totaled $2.4 billion and offered MPA attractive growth possibilities. Leveraging its reputation as a market leader for imports, the company successfully launched a domestic program for remanufactured alternators and starters in fiscal 1997. To fund necessary factory upgrades, MPA made a secondary offering of stock in 1997. It also brought the Asian affiliates into the fold in a stock-for-stock merger that made MVR and Unijoh wholly owned subsidiaries. In 1998, the company opened a second Torrance manufacturing plant, as well as signed a lease on a larger facility in Nashville, which not only provided distribution and warehousing functions but also the manufacture of spark plug wire sets.

MPA continued to post impressive sales and earnings. In fiscal 1997, the company generated revenues of $86.9 million and a reported net profit of $5.5 million, followed by revenues of $113 million in 1998 and a net profit of $6.6 million. That trend would continue through much of fiscal 1999, but by the time the company prepared to report year-end results, questions by senior management and the board were raised about accounting procedures. The audit committee initiated an investigation, bringing in outside auditors, and by early August the company announced that because it discovered ''certain accounting irregularities'' it would have to restate its financial results for fiscal 1997, fiscal 1998, and the first three quarters of fiscal 1999. Net income was overstated by $2.68 million in fiscal 1997, nearly $600,000 in fiscal 1998, and $2.35 million for the first nine months of 1998. In the same company press release, it was also announced that Mel Marks would step down as MPA's chief executive officer, although he would remain as chairman. Investor reaction to this news was swift. Because MPA was unable to file an annual 10K financial report, the NASDAQ halted trading of the company's stock. Moreover, MPA was now in violation of debt covenants in its revolving credit facility, requiring it to enter into some negotiations with the lender.

Soon MPA also faced a class-action lawsuit, which alleged that for ''11 quarters in a row the company inflated its earnings by eliminating from its publicly issued financial statements the expenses for the used parts that were received during each quarter.'' Seeking to recover damages, the suit contended that the company took advantage of its rising stock price to make a secondary offering of stock in 1997, with Mel Marks and Richard Marks selling 100,000 and 150,000 shares, respectively, at a price of $16.63 per share. Following the announcement of a restatement of earnings and subsequent delisting by the NASDAQ, MPA shares were traded on the pink sheets at $1.50 per share.

In addition, MPA became the subject of an SEC investigation in early 2000. While that lingered, the class-action suit was settled in September 2001, with the plaintiffs receiving $7.5 million. Of that amount, $6 million was to be paid by the company's directors and officers and its insurance carrier. The balance would be raised by the company by selling 1.5 million shares of common stock to Mel Marks at $1 per share. Also in 2001, the founder of the company relinquished his position as chairman, although he stayed on as a director. He was replaced by Selwyn Joffe, who had been a director of the company since 1994 and had considerable executive experience at Wolfgang Puck Food Company as well as NetLock Technologies and Palace Entertainment. He and CEO Anthony Souza took over a company that suffered losses in both 2000 and 2001, yet MPA remained a company involved in a viable niche of the automotive aftermarket parts industry and continued to hold promise for a return to future profitability and growth.

Principal Subsidiaries

MVR Products Pte Limited; Unijoh Sdn, Bhd.

Principal Competitors

Champion Parts; Dana Corporation; Denso; Genuine Parts Company; Robert Bosch Gmbh; Universal Manufacturing.

Further Reading

Binkley, Christina, ''Motorcar Parts to Lower Its Earnings Since 1997 As Its Chief Executive Quits,'' *Wall Street Journal,* August 3, 1999, p. B10.

Maio, Patrick J, ''Filling Need For Import-Car Replacement Parts,'' *Investor's Business Daily,* July 1, 1994, p. A4.

''Motorcar Parts & Accessories, Inc.,'' *Wall Street Transcript,* October 3, 1994.

''MPA Features Used-Friendly Catalog Spark Plug Wire Sets at AAIW,'' *Aftermarket Business,* December 1, 1992, p. 32

—Ed Dinger

National Educationl Music Company

National Educational Music Co. Ltd.

1181 Route 22
Mountainside, New Jersey 07092-22807
U.S.A.
Telephone: (908) 232-6700
Toll Free: (800) 526-4593
Web site: http://www.nemc.com

Private Company
Incorporated: 1957 as New Jersey Educational Music
    Company
Employees: 75
Sales: $20 million (2001 est.)
NAIC: 532299 All Other Consumer Goods Rental

Located in Mountainside, New Jersey, National Educational Music Co. Ltd. (NEMC) is dedicated to providing musical instruments to schoolchildren. NEMC operates the only national franchised licensed band and orchestra instrument rental program in the United States, enabling local music stores to offer a high-quality rental program without the heavy burden of capital investment. NEMC affiliates, located in 46 states, pay a one-time lifetime franchise fee (or in some cases no fee at all), and in return receive an inventory of brand name instruments, which are either new or in ''like-new'' condition. To maintain a like-new level of quality, all returned instruments are completely refurbished and cleaned in a proprietary process by a staff of 45 repairmen. Should a franchised dealer already own an inventory of rental instruments, NEMC buys the stock at 100 cents on the dollar. NEMC also customizes rental documents for affiliates according to state regulations. Affiliates promote the rental program in their territory, aided by NEMC printed materials, and obtain the customer's initial payment. At that point, NEMC takes over the monthly billing, accounting, sales tax remittance, and collection on delinquent accounts.

Because NEMC's rental program is a true franchise operation, it complies with FTC regulations, which ensure that a dealer's territory is protected. Depending on rental volume, affiliates earn a commission that ranges from 19.5 percent to as high as 40 percent. Not only are parents assured that their children are receiving the highest quality of rental instruments from NEMC, they have the ability to cancel their contract at any time without further obligation, and if they reach the end of the rental agreement will own the instrument outright. NEMC also sells all band and orchestra instruments, including high-ticket items such as tubas and cellos, to organizations and individuals through a catalog, using its size to obtain the maximum discount from manufacturers and passing on some of the savings to its customers. NEMC also takes advantage of manufacturers' discounts when bidding on school instrument contracts. Aimed at schools and other organizations strapped by tight budgets, NEMC offers its Multi-Brand Lease Program, which allows the groups to fill all their musical needs on a lease-to-own basis. In addition, NEMC is involved in a limited amount of export sales.

Instrument Rental During the 1950s

NEMC's founder and president, Raymond Benedetto, grew up in New Jersey in the 1930s, playing the trumpet and idolizing the great trumpet players of the era's most popular big bands. As a high school student he began playing trumpet in 15-piece bands that played in local clubs. He continued to play professionally while studying music at Montclair State University. After earning a teaching degree in 1952, he went to work at a New Jersey public school, where for the next two years he served as a music director. His musical career was limited mostly to weekends and summers. He played in a swing band as well as house show bands that accompanied well-known singers who appeared in clubs in New Jersey, New York City, and the popular upstate New York resorts of the Catskills. During the Mambo craze, Benedetto took up the flute as a second instrument and joined a band playing Latin music that had an extended stay at a major New York City nightclub, the Queens Boulevard. Because the inflexibility of a school schedule prevented him from traveling to out-of-town engagements, he quit his teaching job. Although he played at the Queens Boulevard six nights a week, Benedetto felt restless during the days and decided to take a job at a large music store, Dorn and Kirschner, located in Newark, New Jersey, close to where he was living at the time. Taking advantage of his experience in the New Jersey public school system, he became the store's educational director, a position that put him in charge of renting musical instruments. The instrument rental business developed during the 1920s and 1930s and revolved around a rent-to-own concept akin to the installment plan made popular by the automobile industry and subsequently applied to furniture, home appliances, and other consumer goods. Dorn and Kirschner boasted one of the area's largest instrument rental programs, serving a sizeable section of central and northern New Jersey.

At first Benedetto took advantage of the flexibility that Dorn and Kirschner allowed in his schedule to play occasional out-of-town engagements, but as he became more fully committed to his position at the store he gradually cut back on his performing career. He soon began to entertain ideas of expanding the store's rental business, which evolved into a dream of one day creating a national instrument rental program. He approached the owners of the store with some of his thoughts but received a cool reception. The owners were second generation and quite content to continue doing business in the same way as their parents had. Feeling that he had reached a dead-end at Dorn and Kirschner, Benedetto decided to quit and strike out on his own.

Incorporation of New Jersey Educational Music Company: 1957

In 1957, Benedetto incorporated New Jersey Educational Music Company. Other than a name for his new instrument rental business, however, he had little else. He approached a distributor of musical instruments named Chris Kratt, with whom he had become slightly acquainted during his time at Dorn and Kirschner, and asked for credit in order to obtain an inventory of instruments. Much to Benedetto's surprise, and relief, Kratt extended $50,000 in credit, asking only for his signature. A loyal relationship between the two men ensued, lasting until Kratt retired years later. As Benedetto expanded his lines of instruments beyond what Kratt had to offer, he always made a point of first approaching the distributor who had been so crucial to the establishment of his business.

Working out of Summit, New Jersey, Benedetto forged his own rental program, starting out with several Dorn and Kirschner customers who wanted to stay on with him. He drummed up additional business by visiting schools and establishing relationships with band directors and music directors, who along with school administrators had the authority to decide on an instrument rental program. Benedetto then worked with his customers to demonstrate the instruments, either at school assemblies or individual music classes. The focus was on the most popular and most commonly rented school instruments: the trumpet, trombone, flute, clarinet, alto sax, and snare drum kit. The school itself would then serve as the contact to the parents and children. In the beginning, Benedetto worked out of the trunk of his car and garage. Each weekday, until mid-afternoon, he made his rounds to the schools, either seeking new business,

conducting demonstrations, or picking up and delivering instruments. He then returned home to do his own billing and to repair instruments. During that first winter working in his unheated garage, Benedetto cut the fingers out of a pair of gloves in order to type.

Benedetto's business was successful enough that he was soon able to afford a small storefront location in Summit. Roughly 15 feet by 30 feet in size, the space was just large enough to accommodate a desk and house his instruments. Benedetto continued to play the trumpet professionally, but because he usually worked until 11 p.m. he had to give up regular weeknight engagements and limit his playing to just the weekends. Dedication to the new business, however, paid off, as the reach of New Jersey Educational Music Company extended well beyond Summit. He was even approached by some music teachers in Long Island who were dissatisfied with their local instrument rental program and drove all the way to Summit to visit with him and ultimately become customers. Benedetto hired a part-time secretary in the late 1950s as well as a service repairman to come in a couple days each week. In 1963, because of increased business, he hired a full-time accountant to handle billing and other bookkeeping chores.

By 1965, Benedetto had outgrown his space and took a lease on a three-story building in Summit. At the outset, he only used the first floor and basement but eventually took over the other two floors. He created a full-fledged service department and hired three sales reps. Although Benedetto still went out on the road on occasion, he mostly confined his work to the office. The reach of his rental program now extended some 100 miles into such areas as Westchester and Connecticut, and he also began to think again about his dream of creating a national instrument rental program. In 1968, he took an initial step by changing the name of the company, which he felt sounded too regional, to National Educational Music Company. He then spent the next two years developing a franchised affiliate program that was unprecedented in the music industry. The concept was straightforward enough: franchisees, relieved of the burden of capital investment, simply sought out business on a commission basis. What Benedetto believed was the key element in his plan, however, was the quality of the instruments NEMC would provide. No longer would children be renting instruments priced by how beat up they were. His customers were to receive either brand new instruments or refurbished, like-new instruments, which to most people were indistinguishable from new. Affiliates were required to ship rental-returned instruments to the New Jersey facilities to ensure that refurbishing was done properly and in accordance with NEMC's high standards. What was more time consuming in the development of the affiliate plan, however, was the legal vetting that was required. Because Benedetto pursued a franchise approach he had to comply with FTC and state regulations and prepare a detailed Uniform Franchise Offering Circular.

Some two years after the company had proclaimed itself to be a national operation, at least in name, Benedetto's franchising plan was completed. The only question was whether or not to implement it. Both his accountant and lawyer advised against the idea, maintaining that Benedetto risked too much. Should his concept fail, he likely faced financial ruin. Nevertheless, Benedetto decided to take the chance, calling in his sales reps one day to inform them that starting with the next school year NEMC was making the switch to a license program. They were given the opportunity to become licensees and, although somewhat skeptical, all but one signed on.

Signing Affiliates, Expanding the Business: 1970s–90s

Rather than recruit franchisees by personal contact, Benedetto relied on advertising in trade publications of the music industry. His first marketing effort was a full-page ad in *Music Trades* featuring an unauthorized use of the Superman character. In reality the ad's photograph was of a local friend dressed up as the comic book hero. The essential pitch was that by signing on with NEMC a local music store owner would become a Superman of instrument rental sales. To create this ad, as well as brochures to mail to prospective affiliates, Benedetto turned to a local advertising agency, Falcone and Associates. From the outset, Benedetto could tell that his gamble to convert to an affiliate program was going to pay off. A Binghampton, New York, music store became the first NEMC franchise in 1970. Benedetto gradually added franchisees and by 1983 boasted affiliates in more than a dozen states. He outgrew the three-story building in Summit and moved to nearby Mountainside where a 3.5 acre site would accommodate his warehouse needs, as well as a service center and general offices.

In the late 1970s, Benedetto also expanded beyond his basic rental program. NEMC created the first mail-order catalog of band and orchestra instruments, copies of which were sent to band directors with the expectation that they would filter down to children looking to buy replacement instruments. It was during this time that NEMC also became involved in the school bid process and proved to be very successful in winning school contracts for the high-priced instruments that schools generally bought in order to fill out their bands and orchestras. Ultimately

NEMC began to use its maximum manufacturers discount to sell instruments to dealers as well.

The NEMC affiliate program grew at a comfortable and steady pace, with new franchises outnumbering the ones that dropped out due to normal attrition. To expand any faster would have required a much larger infrastructure and outlay of cash than Benedetto was interested in making. Nevertheless, by the early 1990s NEMC had affiliates in 46 states. The only states not represented were Hawaii, Wyoming, North Dakota, and Rhode Island. The success of NEMC was not lost on others involved in the musical instrument rental business. In the mid-1990s, a number of large dealers began satellite programs with smaller stores, essentially copying the NEMC approach on a limited scale, at most on a one- or two-state basis. None of this new breed of competition, however, attempted to launch an affiliate program comparable to NEMC.

Looking to the Future

NEMC faced a number of challenges at the turn of a new century. Because the company again outgrew its facilities, in 1998, it had to acquire some 10,000 square feet of warehouse space offsite. By 2002, Benedetto and a management team that grew up with the company had to decide whether to move again or build on to the current site. Although nearing retirement and taking steps towards a succession of power, Benedetto was still eager to fend off mounting competition and maintain a dominant position in a business that he pioneered. For a number of years he had been asked when he was going to take NEMC public. Such a move was a clear possibility for the future should the company's plans require a significant increase in capital. What was certain was that Benedetto was determined to remain a step ahead of the competition, which looked to copy his approach and emulate the success of NEMC.

Principal Divisions

Sales; Rental; Licensed Affiliate Program.

Further Reading

Calhoun, Firth, and Caroline Baer, "Musical Instruments; Noteworthy Savings," *Money,* April 1984, p. 34.
"NEMC Affiliate Commission Top $20 Million," *Music Trades,* February 1, 2001.
"NEMC Expands Repair Facility," *Music Trades,* April 1, 1994.

—Ed Dinger

National Public Radio, Inc.

635 Massachusetts Avenue NW
Washington, D.C. 20001-3753
U.S.A.
Telephone: (202) 513-2000
Fax: (202) 513-3329
Web site: http://www.npr.org

Private Nonprofit Corporation
Incorporated: 1970
Employees: 700
Operating Revenues: $143.8 million (2000)
NAIC: 513112 Radio Stations

National Public Radio, Inc. (NPR) is the world's first non-commercial, satellite-delivered radio system. As an organization consisting of member radio stations, NPR serves over 17 million Americans each week through some 555 public radio stations in the United States and Guam by distributing cultural and news programming, providing training and promotional services, and representing public radio interests before the Federal Communications Commission (FCC) and Congress.

Emergence of Public Broadcasting: 1940s–60s

Public broadcasting got its first boost with the FCC's decision in the 1940s to reserve a segment of the FM radio spectrum for educational stations. While various noncommercial educational stations had already developed throughout the country in the 1920s, many at America's universities, their financial well-being and integrity was threatened first by the Great Depression and later by commercial pressures. The first nonprofit community group to establish a public FM radio station was the Pacifica Foundation, which established a public station in Berkeley, California, in 1949.

Prompted largely by severe criticism of the quality of television programming, President Lyndon B. Johnson and Congress passed the Public Broadcasting Act in 1967, which sought to provide the nation with noncommercial radio programming of an educational nature. Soon thereafter, the Corporation for

Public Broadcasting (CPB) was formed as a government-sponsored corporation that derived its funding through the U.S. Department of Housing, Education, and Welfare.

Formation of NPR: 1970

In helping the many small educational radio and TV stations develop professional standards, CPB promptly formed two organizations: The Public Broadcasting Service (PBS) produced and distributed television programming, while National Public Radio (NPR) did the same for radio. The funds derived from Congress were allocated by CPB to PBS, NPR, and creative outsiders who helped introduce and implement new programs. NPR's original mission was to serve as a leader in national news gathering and production as well as to provide a national inter-connection between local noncommercial radio stations. Incorporated on February 26, 1970, NPR soon boasted over 90 charter member stations.

NPR's first programming foray consisted of live coverage of the Senate Vietnam hearings, which first aired in April 1971. This was quickly followed by the debut of a daily news program called *All Things Considered,* which would steadily grow in listenership and eventually enjoy tremendous success in providing listeners with weekday drive-time news and information. In fact, in 1973, *All Things Considered* garnered its first Peabody Award for NPR, which then built on the success of this program by extending it to weekends with *Weekend All Things Considered* in 1974, mornings with *Morning Edition* in 1979, and *Weekend Edition* and *Weekend Edition Sunday* in 1985 and 1987, respectively. Thus, an NPR news presence seven days a week was ensured. Over the years, NPR news programs provided member stations with live coverage of the Watergate hearings in 1973, as well as extensive reporting on presidential and Congressional elections and Supreme Court nominating procedures, including the Senate hearings on Judge Clarence Thomas in the early 1990s.

During its first five years in existence, NPR focused on production and distribution for its member stations. Public radio further benefited when, following NPR's merger with the Association of Public Radio Stations in 1977, NPR began providing member stations with training programs, management, and lobbying activities in Washington, D.C. NPR developed the first nationwide, satellite-delivered radio distribution network in 1979. This enabled smaller stations in rural areas to receive programming as easily as their city counterparts. It also provided NPR with a larger audience.

Funding: A Perennial Issue

From their inception, NPR and public broadcasting in general were plagued by internal and external funding pressures. In the early 1970s, President Richard Nixon, Vice-President Spiro Agnew, and their administration expressed disapproval of programming they regarded as politically controversial and biased. In 1973, Nixon vetoed a planned endowment to the CPB and encouraged member stations to become more autonomous, believing that local stations would naturally shift to more conservative programming.

While CPB struggled with budget cuts and bureaucracy, eased somewhat during the Carter administration but reinstated during the Reagan presidency, NPR faced severe financial problems, ending 1983 somewhere between $7 million and $9 million in debt. Moreover, NPR's CEO resigned during this time under allegations of mismanaging funds, and Congress began pressuring NPR to stabilize its financial situation. In addition to staff layoffs and cutbacks on programming, NPR sought a loan from CPB in order to retire its debt and restructure its financial backing.

By July 1983, the situation was indeed bleak; NPR was advanced $500,000 by CPB so that the former could meet its payroll. Further loans followed, with the proviso that ownership of NPR's equipment be shifted to a group of independent trustees to prevent seizure of the equipment by creditors. NPR also agreed to cut costs, raise the fees it charged member stations, and work to increase its contributions from listeners. The restructuring also involved a change in operating arrangements with NPR's member stations. Specifically, NPR sought money from the public and private sectors, while its member stations received CPB funds directly.

The 1990s and Beyond

In 1995, a member radio station receiving all of NPR's programming paid 10.2 percent of its revenues to NPR, according to Marc Gunther of the *New York Times*. This meant that when key stations had unsuccessful fundraising drives, or when Congress voted to cut the annual budget for public broadcasting, NPR also suffered.

Such a scenario came to pass in 1995 when, in its zeal to reduce the federal budget deficit, Congress agreed to reduce public broadcasting dollars from $285 million to $275 million in 1996 and to $260 million in 1997. As a result, NPR's new CEO Delano Lewis was forced to eliminate 20 positions and drop several programs, including a minority-oriented news program entitled *Horizons* and other cultural programs.

Delano Lewis was hired as NPR's president and CEO in 1994. As the former head of Chesapeake & Potomac Telephone with 20 years experience in that industry, Lewis had no previous background in broadcasting. His business acumen, however, was viewed as crucial to NPR's success in a competitive broadcast environment. In addition, Lewis had also served as a lawyer under Robert Kennedy's Justice Department, which led to positions with the Equal Employment Opportunity Commission, the Peace Corps, former Senator Edward Brooke, and Congressman Walter Fauntroy. Such Capitol Hill contacts could only help an organization which depended on Congressional goodwill. Finally, Lewis was the first African-American executive at NPR and was expected to lead the organization in more cultural programming and broaden its appeal to a wider range of listeners. As of the late 1990s, however, Lewis's primary achievement was to keep NPR solvent. He helped do this by expanding NPR's reach into different markets and by pursuing corporate and foundation support to bolster dwindling public dollars.

Some forays into new markets had already been initiated, since, in October 1993, NPR began broadcasting for six hours each day in Europe via satellite. Later that year, NPR partnered with CPB and Public Radio International in a venture known as "America One," which extended NPR's broadcasts in Europe to 24 hours a day via direct-to-home satellite.

In addition to expanding its markets, NPR under Lewis pursued corporate and foundation dollars with increased vigor. This took several forms, including "enhanced underwriting." In the early years of public broadcasting, public broadcasters were forbidden by law from accepting commercials; as commercial pressures mounted, the FCC relaxed rules regarding what public stations could broadcast. Kathy Scott, an NPR spokesperson, told David Barboza in the *New York Times* in 1995 that the organization's goal was to become more self-sufficient and that its new guidelines were changed "with an eye toward not passing up opportunities." While NPR did not interrupt programming, permit "calls to action" or comparative or qualitative language, it relaxed its policies regarding the inclusion of phone numbers in underwriter acknowledgments and broadcasting slogans. It also accepted grants earmarked for coverage of particular issues. For example, in 1994, the General Motors automaking subsidiary Saturn began sponsorship of *Car Talk,* an NPR call-in program on cars and car repair. In the late 1990s, concepts such as "brand leveraging" were also being reviewed along with revenue generation in the form of a record label called "NPR Classics," a music-ordering service, and individual station fundraising initiatives.

Keeping abreast of technology, the NPR web site was established in 1994 and, beginning in 1995, pioneered the use of technology known as audio streaming or RealAudio to allow users to hear prerecorded audio files of NPR programs. In 1996,

NPR began 24-hour service for the Armed Forces Radio and Television Service offering programs to military radio stations abroad. At that time, NPR broadcasted in over 140 countries around the world.

Lewis also worked to rid NPR of some negative publicity surrounding several discrimination lawsuits, hearkening back to the mid-1970s, when CPB was criticized for not hiring enough minorities to meet the requirements of civil rights legislation. A number of these lawsuits, alleging sexual discrimination against women, were settled out of court. In 1997, an African-American Muslim reporter based in Cairo filed a lawsuit alleging race and religious discrimination. After an April 1997 article summarizing the charges in *Time,* CEO Delano Lewis responded with a letter, quoting staff percentages of 29.2 percent minorities and 48 percent women and noting both minority and female representation in senior management positions. Said Lewis, ''the advancement of minorities and women is an ongoing commitment, and our record compares favorably with that of other broadcasters. I have made it my objective to ensure that our employees are treated with dignity and respect.''

From its inception, NPR has become famous for the high sound quality of its programs and its engaging radio personalities. Professionals such as *Morning Edition*'s host Bob Edwards, interviewer Terry Gross of the program *Fresh Air,* former *All Things Considered* host Susan Stamberg, reporter Nina Totenberg, and many others have received several awards for their work with NPR. NPR is also known for its ''quirky'' features such as Stamberg's perennial Thanksgiving presentation of her mother-in-law's cranberry relish recipe and David Sedaris's retelling of his stint as a Christmas elf at Macy's. Moreover, NPR has cultivated the distinctive sound of its broadcasts in such features as *Radio Expeditions,* which takes listeners on ''audio journeys'' to remote areas and includes wildlife recordings.

By the late 1990s, about 60 percent of NPR's operating income was derived from member stations' dues and fees, 2 to 3 percent from CPB and other governmental sources, with the remaining funding coming from corporate and foundation contributions. Funding concerns continued to vex NPR and public broadcasting in general. Ironically, contrary to its original purpose of serving as an outlet for alternative programming that could not survive commercially, NPR has needed to become more commercial in order to continue to provide that programming. Liberty Media, a subsidiary of Tele-Communications Inc.

(TCI), which already had a two-thirds interest in public television's Macneil/Lehrer Productions in 1996, expressed serious interest in similar funding of public radio programming in exchange for ''content.'' Such offers led to questions regarding the amount of control corporate sponsors would have on editorial and news coverage, as well as concerns over a possible backlash from listeners in the form of reduced donations.

In the convergence of electronic media (cable, computer, radio, television), public radio has also been looked to as a possible starting point for the National Information Infrastructure (NII), due to its existing network, listener base (according to Mitch Ratcliffe in *Digital Media,* 85 percent of U.S. homes can receive public radio), and proven abilities in community building. While the NII could certainly prove to be a boost for NPR, many industry observers regarded this as an unlikely scenario, due to the probable involvement of media conglomerates with more dollars and power than public radio. Given the competitive media climate of the late 1990s, however, it was certain that NPR would need to continue to search for options in its never-ending battle for funding.

The Changing Face of Public Radio: NPR in the Year 2000

In the late 1990s NPR undertook a series of unique business ventures aimed at capitalizing on the company's reputation for quality programming. In September 1997 NPR reached an agreement with Borders Books and Music to promote books and compact discs that had been featured on NPR. The plan called for the installation of specially designed Town Square kiosks in Borders retail outlets. The kiosks, which resembled radio towers, bore the NPR logo and included listening stations. In July 1999 NPR reached an agreement with America Online to allow its news stories to be carried on AOL's News Channel, a popular online news source. The integrated programming featured audio highlights from NPR broadcasts, and allowed listeners to submit their own commentary.

Meanwhile, the growing presence of corporate sponsorship in connection with NPR programming raised a number of questions about the path the company was taking. On the one hand, the Congressional budget cuts from the mid-1990s had inspired a movement away from federal funding altogether, something CEO Delano Lewis, with his business background, was supposed to spearhead. The challenge lay in striking a balance between NPR's tradition of unbiased reporting and the political agendas of its corporate backers. While NPR asserted that it maintained complete autonomy over the manner in which its stories were covered, certain grants, such as the Lila A. Wallace Fund's sponsorship of news coverage of campaign finance reform, clearly had an influence on the content of NPR's programming.

In April 1998 Delano Lewis suddenly announced his intention to retire. While he cited personal reasons for his decision, many in the industry speculated that the difficulty of establishing workable financial partnerships with major corporations ultimately proved frustrating to Lewis. Lewis's successor, Kevin Klose, took over in November 1998. From the start, Klose worked to improve relations with members of Congress, in an effort to reestablish the federal government's support for public broadcasting. Klose also devoted attention to expanding NPR's audience among younger listeners, and led a campaign to commit more money to creating web sites for affiliate stations, which would both help broaden exposure for popular programming and enable them to explore the retail possibilities of e-commerce. However, many local stations were wary of such a move, believing that Internet access to national programming would siphon listeners away from regional offerings.

The relationship between NPR and its affiliates became further strained in October 1999, when the company began charging the stations based on audience-base, rather than operating expenses. The increase in fees injected some much needed capital into the company's sagging budget, but it also weakened the financial stability of many of the smaller stations. However, supporters of the new system felt that increased accountability would inevitably result in stronger programming and greater choice, improving the company's product without undermining its commitment to unbiased reporting.

In the midst of these shifts in business strategy, NPR celebrated some significant milestones. The year 1999 marked the 20th anniversary of *Morning Edition* with Bob Edwards, and *All Things Considered* turned 30 in April 2001. The durability of these popular programs was crucial to maintaining NPR's reputation as a reliable source of intelligent radio broadcasting. At the same time, the company continued to seek out new opportunities to broaden its reach, particularly through the Internet, and in February 2000 NPR launched *All Songs Considered*, its first program created exclusively for web broadcasts. Heading into the heart of the technological era, NPR was clearly committed to exploring the possibilities of new media, but without sacrificing the integrity of its programming.

Principal Competitors

Infinity Broadcasting Corporation; Jones Media Networks, Ltd.; Westwood One, Inc.

Further Reading

Adelson, Andrea, "The Business of Public Radio," *New York Times*, April 5, 1999, p. C9.

Auderheide, Pat, "Will Public Broadcasting Survive?," *Progressive*, March 20, 1995, pp. 19–21.

Barboza, David, "The 'Enhanced Underwriting' of Public Broadcasting Is Taking a More Commercial Flair," *New York Times*, December 27, 1995, p. D2.

De Witt, Karen, "New Chief Wants to Widen NPR's Financial Base," *New York Times*, March 28, 1994, p. D6.

Duhart, Bill, "First Black Director Increases NPR Base," *Philadelphia Tribune*, April 19, 1994.

Gleick, Elizabeth, "Static on Public Radio: Seven Discrimination Cases in Two Years Have Taken Their Toll on NPR's Warm-and-Fuzzy Image," *Time*, April 7, 1997, p. 55.

Gunther, Marc, "At NPR, All Things Reconsidered," *New York Times*, August 13, 1995, p. H1.

Husseini, Sam, "The Broken Promise of Public Radio," *Humanist*, September/October, 1994, pp. 26–29.

Kaplan, Peter, "National Public Radio's New CEO Hopes to Win Friends on Capitol Hill," *Washington Times*, December 28, 1998.

Lewis, Delano, "Letters: NPR's Record on Employment," *Time*, April 28, 1997, p. 8.

Peterson, Iver, "Does National Public Radio Feel Pressure When Foundation Donors Specify Topics?," *New York Times*, February 3, 1997, p. D7.

Pressler, Margaret Webb, "NPR Chief Announces Resignation; Delano Lewis Cites Personal Reasons," *Washington Post*, April 4, 1998, p. E1.

Ratcliffe, Mitch, "Public Radio on the Digital Edge," *Digital Edge*, May 16, 1994, p. 3.

Speer, Tibbett L., "Public Radio: Marketing Without Commercials," *American Demographics*, September 1, 1996, p. 62.

Tedeschi, Bob, "PBS and NPR Find Unexpected Success Selling on the Web," *New York Times*, October 23, 2000, p. C12.

Tolan, Sandy, "Must NPR Sell Itself," *New York Times*, July 16, 1996, p. A17.

—Karen Troshynski-Thomas
—update: Steve Meyer

Navigant International

Defining Travel Management

Navigant International, Inc.

84 Inverness Circle East
Englewood, Colorado 80112-5314
U.S.A.
Telephone: (303) 706-0800
Fax: (303) 706-0505
Web site: http://www.navigant.com

Public Company
Incorporated: 1983 as Professional Travel Corporation
Employees: 5,000
Sales: $350.33 million (2001)
Stock Exchanges: NASDAQ
Ticker Symbol: FLYR
NAIC: 561510 Travel Agencies

Navigant International, Inc. is the number two travel management firm in the United States. The company offers complete planning, ticketing, accounting, tracking and reporting services for business travelers, and also books leisure travel through its NavigantVacations.com web site. Navigant has approximately 900 offices in the United States, Canada, the United Kingdom, and a dozen other countries that serve more than 13,000 clients in the corporate, government, and military sectors.

Beginnings

Navigant's roots go back to 1979, when Ed Adams borrowed $10,000 from his parents to buy a small travel agency in Denver, Colorado, called Travel Bazaar. A University of Colorado graduate, Adams was a newcomer to the field and soon decided to focus on providing travel arrangements for business flyers, seeing opportunity in the recent deregulation of the airline industry that had created a number of new carriers and lower fares. The strategy was a success, and in 1981 Adams acquired a second Denver agency, Metro Travel, and retained the new company's name for his business.

In 1983, Metro Travel joined with three other Colorado travel agencies, Bomarc, Ports Unlimited, and Tourizons, to form a company called Professional Travel Corporation (PTC).

The new firm, which was headed by Adams, was set up to focus exclusively on corporate work. Several years later, PTC also bought another small agency in the Denver area.

In 1989, the company won the regional travel account of Denver-based communications and financial services company U S West, Inc., worth upwards of $10 million in air ticket bookings. Because U S West had mandated that the work go to minority or women-owned firms if possible, PTC developed a loose network of such agencies to act as subcontractors for the job. The deal was worked out by three female vice-presidents at the company. PTC offered women significant opportunities for advancement, with females constituting half of the firm's employees and the majority of its executive committee.

The year 1990 saw PTC hire an outside firm to develop a new public relations strategy. In addition to targeting regional publications with press releases, the company offered the expertise of its executives to journalists who were writing on the travel industry. The concept worked well and brought PTC greater name recognition as well as plaudits within the industry. Over the next several years, the company also developed a weekly travel column for the *Rocky Mountain News* and a short TV and radio broadcast, dubbed "Tuesday Travel Tip," for Denver's KCNC-TV and KOA radio that featured CEO Ed Adams. PTC was now the largest agency in Colorado and the 25th largest in the United States, with over $100 million in air ticket billings. The company had 160 employees.

The 1990s: Developing New Technology

In addition to performing its main job of travel management, PTC also operated the Travel Related Electronic Capabilities Division, which offered such software products as Travel Commander (later known as AQUA) that monitored changes in airfare prices and scanned seat maps for preferred seating assignments. The division performed research on travel habits for use by both agents and clients.

In 1991, PTC began to offer online travel information through an electronic bulletin board called TrecNet. Company clients could also use it to transmit reservation requests and other messages directly to PTC. In October, the firm joined with six other large regional agencies to form SuperRegionals, an association that would establish standards for the industry, share information about management and accounting techniques, and lobby for common goals.

In February 1992, PTC bought United Security Travel Services of Washington, D.C., from USLICO, an insurance firm. United Security's business was 90 percent corporate, and the company had annual sales of $13 million. The move added four East Coast offices to the ten already established by PTC in Colorado. A new division, InterRes, was also formed during the year as a first step toward offering international travel services.

In 1993, PTC again worked with a group of minority- and women-owned agencies to win the $40 million national travel account of U S West, an expansion of the regional contract granted several years earlier. The company also teamed up with Foley's department stores to offer Foley's VacationPlus, which would consist of travel offices in nine Foley's locations in Colorado and New Mexico. In 1994, PTC won the $1 million account of the Defense General Supply Center of Richmond, Virginia, and also bought six Airline Ticket Express kiosks, which were located in Colorado King stores. The one-person offices, which accounted for $3.5 million in ticket sales, were updated after the acquisition.

In 1995, PTC won an exclusive ten-year contract to run an onsite travel agency at the new Denver International Airport. The office, open from 5:30 a.m. to 9:30 p.m., offered the company's customers the convenience of last-minute ticket pickup and easy itinerary changes. PTC also won a major contract with the U.S. Treasury Department during the year, taking a $6.5 million account away from industry leader American Express.

The year 1995 saw the airline industry move to reduce the commissions travel agents received for ticket sales, which had heretofore been 10 percent of their face value. The amount was reduced to a maximum of $50 for domestic flights, and the rate was later decreased to 8 percent. These changes had a major effect on travel agencies, and during the latter half of the 1990s a number of firms went out of business or were consolidated. PTC, which typically charged a flat fee for its services and gave clients back some of the commission money, was better positioned than many for survival. The company also had an advantage in that it offered broader services to its clients than just ticket booking, including handling accounting and managing other details specific to business travel. The company's focus was on "middle-market" clients who spent between $500,000

and $20 million per year on travel and who were concerned about getting the most for their money.

In January 1997, the company bought World Travel & Incentives (WTI) of Minneapolis, which had 110 employees and $50 million in sales. In addition to making travel arrangements, WTI ran travel incentive programs which companies used to help motivate employees to meet sales goals. After the merger, PTC began to offer the incentive programs to its own clients. At about the same time, the company was closing its VacationPlus offices in Foley department stores and moving their employees back to PTC's headquarters.

Sale to U.S. Office Products: 1997

Shortly after the WTI acquisition, Ed Adams sealed a deal to sell Professional Travel to U.S. Office Products (USOP) of Washington, D.C., in a stock swap. The publicly traded, two-year-old USOP had no other travel interests and was primarily engaged in acquiring office supply firms. USOP planned to offer PTC's services to its 250,000 corporate accounts. At the time of the deal PTC was writing $220 million in airline tickets per year and had 400 employees.

USOP made Ed Adams head of its Corporate Travel Services division, and he began formulating plans for rapid expansion, targeting "profitable regional agencies with strong management." Adams also wanted to change the firm's ratio of 80 percent business travel and 20 percent leisure, group, meeting, or incentive travel to a 70/30 or 60/40 split.

The first acquisitions were made in the spring, when Mutual Travel of Seattle, Super Travel of Houston, and Cal Simmons Travel of Washington, D.C., were purchased. The three had combined airline billings of $385 million, putting USOP's total for this industry yardstick at more than $650 million annually. The companies each retained their original names and identities after the purchase, though all were overseen by Adams. The goal of USOP was to ultimately reduce overhead by combining "backroom" operations among the agencies and by negotiating better deals with suppliers. During the remainder of the year, other acquisitions were made, including McGregor Travel of Stamford, Connecticut; Travel Consultants of Grand Rapids, Michigan; Omni Travel Services of Cambridge, Massachusetts; Evans Travel Group, Inc. of New Orleans; Travel Guide of Baltimore; Associated Travel Services, Inc. of Santa Ana, California; and Atlas Travel Services, Inc. of Vancouver, British Columbia. The total air ticket billings of the division, which had become the fifth largest travel group in the country, swelled to $1.4 billion.

While the division was growing, USOP's stock price was traversing a downward curve. At the beginning of 1998, in order to boost shareholder value, the decision was made to focus on operations rather than acquisitions. The company subsequently decided to spin off four of its divisions, Corporate Travel Services, Education, Print Management, and Technology Solutions. The travel spinoff was effected in June when one share of the unit, which had been renamed Navigant International, Inc., was distributed for every ten shares of USOP. Navigant, which would continue to be run by Ed Adams, also sold two million shares of stock on the NASDAQ exchange. At the end of its first

Key Dates:

1979: Ed Adams buys Travel Bazaar of Denver, Colorado.

1981: Adams purchases Metro Travel, which becomes the company's new name.

1983: Metro Travel and three other agencies merge to form Professional Travel Corporation (PTC).

1990: The firm develops its first major public relations campaign.

1992: PTC expands to the East Coast with the purchase of United Security Travel.

1995: PTC wins an exclusive ten-year contract for an office at the new Denver airport.

1997: Adams sells PTC to U.S. Office Products and begins a campaign of expansion.

1998: U.S. Office spins off its travel division, which becomes Navigant International.

1999: Web sites Navigant.com and NavigantVacations.com are launched.

2001: The acquisition of SatoTravel makes Navigant the second largest firm of its type.

2001: In the aftermath of the September 11 terrorist attacks, the company cuts its workforce by 20 percent.

fiscal year, the company reported revenues of $120.4 million and an increase in ticket bookings to $1.8 billion.

Within a month of becoming a stand-alone company, Navigant bought three more travel firms, Minneapolis-based TravelCorp, Inc.; Arrington Travel Center, Inc. of Chicago; and Atlas Travel Services, Ltd. of Houston. By year's end World Express Traveler, Inc. of Anchorage, Alaska; Jarvis Travel, Ltd. of Calgary, Canada; Bowers Worldwide Travel Service, Inc. of Phoenix; Chartrek International, Inc. of Norwalk, Connecticut; and Akra Travel, Inc. of Jacksonville, Florida, had been added as well.

1999: Taking to the Web

In April 1999, the company announced the formation of NavigantVacations.com, Inc., which would offer leisure travel packages and airline tickets over the Internet, focusing on sales to Navigant's existing customer base. The company's own web site, navigant.com, had been launched earlier in the year. Another site, cruisecenter.com, was added a few months later.

In May, the company appointed Thomas Nulty, head of Navigant subsidiary Associated Travel, to the position of president, with Ed Adams continuing to serve as CEO and chairman. Nulty had overseen the tenfold growth of Associated during the 13 years before it joined Navigant.

In the summer, the company announced plans to rebrand all of its subsidiary companies with the Navigant name. The company also joined Woodside Travel Trust, the largest international corporate travel management purchasing alliance. More acquisitions were taking place as well, with Navigant buying Forbes Travel and Couch-Mollica of Pittsburgh and Moran Travel of Boston.

In August 1999, the company raised its credit facility to $125 million from $60 million, giving it further funding for expansion. In the fall, Navigant sold 22.5 percent of NavigantVacations.com to Och-Ziff Capital Management Group for $15 million, using the money to help develop the web site. Acquisitions during the latter half of the year included First Travelcorp of Raleigh, North Carolina; Cornerstone of Marlboro, Massachusetts; Lovejoy-Tiffany of Ann Arbor, Michigan; Dollinger Travel of Rochester, New York; Travel Resources of Toronto; and Oaks Travel of Houston. The company's goal at the time of its spinoff had been to boost its penetration in the top 25 markets, and the firm had gone from having offices in fewer than ten cities to operating offices in 21 cities in only a year and a half. Analysts praised Navigant's purchases, noting that the acquisitions were uniformly well-managed and profitable.

In 2000, Navigant initiated a lawsuit against Navigant Consulting of Chicago over the use of its name. The Illinois firm, which had adopted the name second and was also involved in a shareholder lawsuit, was sometimes confused with Navigant International. During the winter, the company acquired two British agencies, M.D. Travel Management Ltd. and MSW Group. M.D. Travel was one of the United Kingdom's top ten travel management firms. Navigant had begun consolidating its operations, and by spring had closed a number of redundant facilities and eliminated 130 positions from its workforce of 3,500. The company was now organized into eight geographic regions, with the Denver headquarters providing the backbone of accounting, purchasing, data storage, and administrative support services.

In August 2000, Navigant made its first acquisition in South America, buying K.R. International of Brazil, the fifth largest agency in Rio de Janeiro. The firm specialized in managing travel for the oil industry. An additional Canadian firm, GTS Global Travel Solutions, was purchased in October. GTS was one of Canada's largest corporate travel companies. In October, Navigant also completed the sale of $80 million in senior secured notes.

The following summer, the company spent $45 million to buy SatoTravel, the seventh largest travel management firm in the United States. Arlington, Virginia-based Sato specialized in working with government agencies and large corporations and had a half-dozen call centers around the United States and offices in 13 countries. Unlike previous acquisitions, Sato kept its name after the merger. The purchase made Navigant the second largest firm of its type in the United States, behind only American Express. After the deal, Navigant would have more than 6,000 employees and write $4.2 billion in airline ticket bookings. Later in the summer another agency, Meritek Travel of St. Louis, was also acquired.

The terrorist attacks on the United States in September 2001 had an immediate effect on Navigant, as business travel fell off dramatically in the weeks afterward. By the end of the month, the firm announced a 20 percent reduction in its workforce and a trimming of salaries to executives of 12 percent and to associates of 5 percent. A freeze in capital expenditures was also implemented. The cuts were considered temporary measures until the company's business returned to normal. The attacks had come as business for the year was already declining and airlines were again reducing their ticket commissions. One bright spot for the company was the renewal of a five-year Sato contract with the U.S. Navy worth $400 million in annual air billings.

Navigant International had grown into the second largest travel management firm in the United States over a short period of time. While it continued to consolidate operations and deal with the aftereffects of the September 11 terrorist attacks and the slumping economy, the company possessed many strengths, including a carefully chosen group of agencies, a strong technological base, and a seasoned leadership team.

Principal Subsidiaries

AQUA Software Products, Inc.; Associated Travel Services of Texas, Inc.; Associated Travel Services of Texas, Ltd.; Atlas Travel GP, Inc.; Atlas Travel Services Corp.; Cornerstone Enterprises, Inc.; Envision Vacations, Inc.; FireVine, LLC; International Travel Resources, Inc.; K.R. Agencia de Viagens Ltda. (Brazil); Navigant Cruise Center, Inc.; Navigant International Canada Inc.; Navigant International/North Central, Inc.; Navigant International/Southwest, LLC; Navigant International/ South Central, L.P.; Navigant International/Southeast, Inc.; Navigant International/Northeast, Inc.; Navigant International/ Northwest, Inc.; Navigant International/Rocky Mountain, Inc.; Navigant International UK Holdings, Inc.; Navigant International/United Kingdom Limited; Navigant UK Limited; NavigantVacations.com Holdings, Inc.; Scheduled Airlines Traffic Offices, Inc.; Sato Travel srl (Italy); Sato Seyahat ve Turizm Ltd. Sti. (Turkey).

Principal Competitors

American Express Company; Carlson Wagonlit Travel; WorldTravel BTI; Rosenbluth International Inc.

Further Reading

Brisson, Mary, "Professional Travel," *Business Travel News*, November 9, 1992, p. 33.

Bunn, Dina, "Professional Travel Cuts Parental Ties," *Rocky Mountain News*, January 15, 1998, p. 6B.

Draper, Heather, "Navigant to Buy SatoTravel," *Rocky Mountain News*, June 8, 2001, p. 1B.

——, "Traveling in the Fast Lane—Navigant Challenges Industry, Focusing on Corporate Services," *Rocky Mountain News*, February 21, 2001, p. 6B.

Gonzalez, Erika, "Traveling Man: Ed Adams Looks Ahead, Hitches Agency to Office Products Firm," *Rocky Mountain News*, February 9, 1997, p. 5F.

Lassiter, Eric, "USWest Taps Professional Travel, Subcontractors," *Travel Weekly*, March 1, 1993, p. 35.

Mahoney, Michelle, "Women Put Travel Firm Sky-High," *Denver Post*, October 16, 1990, p. 1C.

"Navigant and Nulty Are Flying High," *Denver Business Journal*, July 28, 2000, p. 3A.

"Navigant Plans Layoffs, Pay Cuts in Light of Sharp Reduction in Travel Demand," *Dow Jones Online News*, September 21, 2001.

Ng, Melissa, "Dawn of a New Mega? USOP Adds 3 Agencies," *Travel Agent*, May 12, 1997, p. 8.

"Professional Travel Corp.: Best Public Relations Campaign, Over $5 Million in Sales," *Travel Weekly*, July 29, 1991, p. 37.

"Professional Travel's DIA Location Is 'Great Marketing Piece,'" *Travel Weekly*, April 24, 1995, p. 68.

Rundles, Jeff, "Hospitality Tourism: Professional Travel Corp.," *Colorado Business*, August 1, 1991, p. 55.

Schwab, Robert, "CEO Who Sold His Business Happy Now As an Employee," *Denver Post*, May 22, 1997, p. C1.

Wada, Isae, "U.S. Office Products on Buying Spree," *Travel Weekly*, May 19, 1997, p. 47.

——, "USOP Intends to Assemble $3B Network," *Travel Weekly*, March 27, 1997, p. 4.

Whitney, Daisy, "Englewood, Colo.-Based Firm Offers Comprehensive Travel Services," *Denver Post*, December 5, 1998.

Williamson, Richard, "Bricks and Sticks Travel Services Provider Navigant Enjoys Unique Niche in Online, Offline Worlds," *Rocky Mountain News*, January 24, 2000, p. 1B.

Zeiger, Dinah, "Leading the Flock: A Short History of Navigant," *Colorado Business*, May 1, 2001, p. 24.

—Frank Uhle

Neptune Orient Lines Limited

456 Alexandra Rd.
NOL Bldg. #06-00
119962 Singapore
Telephone: (+65) 278-9000
Fax: (+65) 278-4900
Web site: http://www.nol.com.sg

Public Company
Incorporated: 1968
Employees: 8, 734
Sales: S$8.51 billion (US$4.74 billion) (2001)
Stock Exchanges: Singapore New York Frankfurt
Ticker Symbol: NEPS
NAIC: 488510 Freight Transportation Arrangement;
483111 Deep Sea Freight Transportation; 541614
Process, Physical Distribution, and Logistics
Consulting Services

Neptune Orient Lines Limited (NOL, or NOL Group) ranks among the world's top five shipping companies and is the largest shipping company in its Singapore home market. NOL is a worldwide provider of container shipping and logistics services, and operates one of the industry's largest fleet of tankers for petroleum and other liquid and dry bulk transport; the company also operates a charter vessel service. Shipping, both containers and tankers, represents by far the largest share of the company's revenues, accounting for 72 percent of the company's sales of nearly US$4.75 billion in 2001. Logistics, including the company's supply-chain management and overland container rail transportation services in the United States, added 15 percent to the company's sales. Charter services provide another 9 percent to the company sales. In addition to APL, the company's chief subsidiaries include American Eagle Tankers, the company's crude oil transport division, with a fleet of 25 Aframax tankers; and Neptune Associated Shipping (NAS), formed in March 2002, which consolidates the company's fleet of 22 clean petroleum product tankers. NOL is a public company listed on the Singapore stock exchange, with additional over-the-counter trading conducted through the New York and Frankfurt exchanges. The Singapore government, long NOL's controlling force, maintains a 33 percent share of the company. The company has been led since 1999 by Flemming Jacobs, formerly of rival Maersk.

19th-Century Shipping Power

While Neptune Orient Lines was incorporated only in 1968, its largest component, APL, carried its history back to the mid-19th century. In the year 1848, William Henry Aspinwall—who was later to become one of the founders of the Society for the Prevention of Cruelty to Animals—won a ten-year mail delivery contract between Panama and Oregon. Aspinwall set up the Pacific Mail Steamship Company that year; the following year, the company got an added boost when, with overland routes blocked by heavy snow, the 49ers rushing to the California Gold Rush were forced to take passage on Pacific Mail ships. In 1850, Pacific Mail sealed its monopoly of the Panama-Oregon route when it acquired two steamships from rival Empire City Line.

Aspinwall's other interests included part ownership of the Panama Railroad Company, which enjoyed exclusive railroad rights across the Panama Isthmus. By 1855, the Panama Railroad had begun operations linking the Atlantic and Pacific oceans. A journey that had previously taken four days to accomplish was now possible in just four hours, cutting the total transport time between San Francisco and New York to as little as three weeks. In 1865, Pacific Mail extended its own operations to cover that entire route when it acquired eastern counterpart Atlantic Mail Steamship Company.

Pacific Mail opened a sea route to the Far East in 1867, using a specially prepared vessel to begin regular service from San Francisco to Hong Kong and Yokohama, while adding feeder lines to other destinations in Japan and China. Government subsidies enabled Pacific Mail to increase the frequency of its service and to add newer and more modern ships, including an order of 11 new ships delivered in 1873. The cost of the company's fleet expansion, coupled with the onset of an economic depression, enabled financier Jay Gould to take a controlling interest in Pacific Mail, which was then acquired by

Gould's Union Pacific Railroad in 1885. The following decade, Pacific Mail was taken over again, now by Southern Pacific Railroad. That company extended Pacific Mail's service to include direct routes to Honolulu, Kobe, Nagasaki, and Shanghai.

The opening of the Panama Canal in 1912 presented opportunity for U.S. shipping companies; yet because railroad operators were prohibited from providing shipping through the canal—to discourage the formation of a monopoly—Pacific Mail was locked out of use of the canal. Unable to compete in the newly possible east-west shipping route, Southern Pacific decided to sell off Pacific Mail's fleet. Most of the company's ships were acquired by Grace Line, owned by W.R. Grace, which then acquired the company outright in 1916. That company invested heavily in Pacific Mail and by 1920 the company boasted a fleet of 46 steamers.

Presidents' Line in the 1920s

By then, Pacific Mail was facing competition from another rising steamship company, Dollar, owned by Captain Robert Dollar. Launched in 1900, Dollar had become a leading shipper across the Pacific. In the 1920s, the Dollar family began shares in its competitors, and by 1924 had acquired Pacific Mail from Grace Line. By then, the Dollar company had begun its practice of naming its vessels after American presidents—in 1925, its President Harrison became the first to begin operating a route around the world. Dollar continued making acquisitions, and succeeded in gaining nearly full control of the Pacific shipping routes by the end of the decade.

The effects of the Depression, coupled with losses from the wreck of one of its vessels in 1937, brought the Dollar company to bankruptcy in 1938. The company was then taken over by the U.S. government, which, during the 1940s added more than 30 new ships to its fleet. The government owners maintained the tradition of naming its vessels after presidents, underscored by the renaming of the company as American President Lines (APL). During the war, APL's fleet was converted to supporting the war effort; returned to civilian duty following the war, the company once again became a leader in the passenger trade.

In the mid-1950s APL was held by the Natomas Company, owned by Texas oilman Ralph Davis. Under Natomas, APL began converting its operations to container shipping. Just being introduced in the late 1950s, container shipping promised to revolutionize international shipping, offering faster roll-on roll-out times, with small crews, and safer passage for the goods being transported. It also promised some salvation for shipping companies staring down a new threat—the inauguration of the first passenger jet service by Pan American Airlines in 1958. By the middle of the next decade, passenger traffic rates among shipping lines had been cut in half, and were to continue to dwindle as the passenger jet industry took off.

APL's conversion to container shipping took place over the course of a decade—by the beginning of the 1970s, container shipping accounted for nearly 60 percent of the company's operations. During the decade that followed, APL prepared to embrace another revolution in the shipping industry, which was then beginning a transition to becoming part of a larger logistics industry. By the end of the 1970s, APL had developed an ''intermodal'' operation capable of linking truck, rail, and sea shipments. This shift led the company to abandon its around-the-world cargo service and instead to concentrate on its Pacific sea service.

In 1979, the company became the first U.S. firm to provide rail links between its port operations and cities in the interior of the country. The company was behind the growth of containers themselves, which reached 45 feet in length at the beginning of the 1980s, and later extended to 53 feet. In 1984, APL added a new concept, that of the ''stacktrain,'' which enabled containers to be stacked two-deep on special-purpose railcars. By then, parent Natomas had been acquired by Diamond Shamrock, which then spun off APL as a public company in 1983.

Container-based shipping had by then become the dominant mode of shipping goods. In the late 1980s, APL and other companies began seeking to extend the size of their container ships in order to maximize their profit potential. Yet ships faced a logistical barrier to growth—passage through the Panama Canal was restricted to ships of less than 33 meters in width, a size that had become an industry standard, even for ships that were never to use the canal. In 1988, however, APL began operating the new C10 class of containership, which, at 39 meters, was too wide to pass through the Panama Canal. Other carriers were to adopt the C10 design—a trend that was to force the Panamanian government to begin preparations to enlarge the canal at the turn of the millennium.

After opening offices in Shanghai, Tianjin, and Dalian in China in 1993, APL continued to expand its Far Eastern operations, opening a route to Ho Chi Minh City in Vietnam, as well as an office there. The company also entered the Global Alliance agreement with other carriers, which enabled it to begin offering services to Europe and South and Central America. By the mid-1990s, APL had grown to become the second largest container shipper in the United States, with a rail-based logistics network that stretched across the entire country. Yet APL's margins were equally stretched, as the shipping industry went through a wave of consolidations, new vessels began to appear, capable of carrying as many as 6,000 containers and more, resulting in overcapacity and intense pricing pressures. After changing its name in 1996 to APL Ltd.; the company was acquired by Neptune Orient Lines in a deal worth more than US$825 million.

Singapore-Based Shipping Giant in the 21st Century

Neptune Orient Lines (NOL) was a far smaller and much younger regional shipper controlled by the Singapore government. Set up in 1968, NOL bought its first ship, the Neptune

Key Dates:

1848: William Henry Aspinwall helps found Pacific Mail Steamship Company to service mail delivery contract between Panama and Oregon.

1865: Pacific Mail acquires Atlantic Mail Steamship Company, giving the company a route stretching from New York to San Francisco; company begins freighter service across the Pacific.

1893: South Pacific Railroad acquires Pacific Mail.

1916: Grace Line acquires most of Pacific Mail's fleet, then begins expansion of company.

1924: Pacific Mail is sold to Dollar Line, which launches around-the-world service the following year.

1938: Dollar Line goes bankrupt and Pacific Mail is taken over by U.S. government, which renames company American President Lines (APL).

1952: Ralph Davies leads an investment group to acquire APL for US$18 million.

1959: APL begins transforming its fleet to containerships.

1968: Singapore-based Neptune Orient Lines (NOL) is founded; buys its first ship the following year.

1971: Neptune begins first charter service route and also begins providing clean petroleum product tanker shipping.

1981: NOL goes public on the Singapore stock exchange.

1994: NOL creates American Eagle Tankers to operate its crude oil tanker business.

1997: NOL acquires APL in the largest acquisition ever made by a Singapore company.

2001: NOL acquires GATX Logistics, which is integrated into its growing APL Logistics subsidiary.

Topaz, the following year. In 1971, NOL began operating a charter route, and soon after began building a fleet of clean petroleum product tankers. By 1974, NOL had begun to spread out beyond its home region, moving across the Pacific to open an office in the United States. Nonetheless, the bulk of NOL's operations were in the intra-Asian market, with a strong component operating within the Asian-European trade market.

NOL went public in 1981 on the Singapore stock exchange; the company's stock was later to be sold as over-the-counter shares on the New York and Frankfurt exchanges as well. The Singapore government remained a major shareholder, and by the end of the century still held about one-third of NOL's stock through its investment company Temasek Holdings. The stake enabled the Singapore government to maintain control of the growing shipping firm.

NOL began expanding in the 1990s, moving into crude oil transport. In 1994, the company regrouped its crude oil operations under a new subsidiary, American Eagle Tankers, which began offering both lightering (barged-based goods transportation) and voyage chartering services. American Eagle started out with just three ships and by the end of the decade had grown to a fleet of 25 ships. The subsidiary quickly extended its range, becoming particularly active in the U.S. Gulf and the Caribbean, as well as on transatlantic and North Sea and Mediterranean routes.

The worldwide shipping industry entered a period of consolidation in the mid-1990s. Part of the motivation behind the series of mergers, such as that between P&O of the United Kingdom and Nedlloyd, of the Netherlands, was the heavy investment that companies were facing as they began replacing aging fleets with the larger, newer generation of vessels. In order to fund such large-scale investments, the companies themselves began seeking a larger scale.

NOL's acquisition of APL in 1997 placed it among the top five in its industry worldwide. While some analysts criticized the company for paying too much in the deal, worth US$825 million, others praised the company for taking the opportunity for gaining scale far faster than would have been possible through organic growth. NOL not only more than doubled in size, it also expanded its operations worldwide—with APL's prized cross-U.S. railway-based logistics link helping the company complete an around-the-world service operation.

The APL acquisition had been the largest ever made by a Singapore company. It also led the company to posting the largest-ever losses in that country's history, as NOL, hard hit by the Asian economic crisis, saw its losses mount to more than US$250 million in 1998. Between 1997 and 1998 the company's total losses topped US$460 million, while the company's debt swelled past US$4 billion.

In 1999, NOL went in search of a new CEO, bringing in Flemming Jacobs, who had formerly worked for rival Maersk. Jacobs immediately set to work rescuing the sinking company, shedding a number of noncore operations acquired with the APL purchase, raising US$500 million in equity funding, and paying down more than half of the company's debt by 2000. Among the assets sold was Stacktrain, bought by Pacer International for US$315 million. The company also began trimming its workforce, which had grown to more than 10,000 employees after the acquisition, cutting out more than 1,000 jobs.

By 2000, NOL was once again posting profits. At that time, NOL began preparing to boost its logistics component, which it viewed as its major growth area. As Jacobs stated in a company press release, "This is the third of the three steps we identified to take the company into the future. The first two steps—strengthening the financial base of the company and strengthening the organization of the liner business and how we serve our customers—are now well established. Concurrently, we have prepared ourselves for the third step—focusing on our Logistics business."

For this, the company hired outside consultants to assist its APL Logistics subsidiary in planning its expansion. Then, in 2001, APL Logistics made its first major acquisition, that of GATX Logistics, one of the largest logistics providers in the U.S. market. The US$210 million acquisition gave NOL some 21 million square feet of warehouse space in a network operating across North and South America, while boosting APL Logistics revenues by more than 70 percent. The GATX acquisition also brought the company an online logistics subsidiary, Direct Logistics. That same year, the company added German freight forwarding and distribution operator Mare Logistik & Spedition GmbH.

APL remained NOL's single largest operation, and that division continued to grow. After joining Mitsui OSK Lines and Hyundai Merchant Marine Co. to form the New World Alliance, APL also inaugurated additional container shipments between Europe and North America, as well as new container services to Latin America. The company also began serving ports on the Red Sea directly from Asian ports. Supporting this growth was the expansion of the company's container stock, which topped 450,000 containers in service.

The softening of the world economy at the turn of the century, and particularly since the destruction of the World Trade Center in September 2001, hit the company hard, and by the end of 2001 the company posted a loss of US$57 million, while its revenues barely advanced to US$4.74 billion for the year. As a result, the company disposed of its Direct Logistics operations, which had suffered from the collapse of much of the Internet market.

Although NOL remained pessimistic about its prospects in 2002, it continued to make moves to streamline its operations and enhance its profitability. Among these was the creation, in March 2002, of a new subsidiary named Neptune Associated Shipping (NAS) which grouped all of the company's petroleum product tanker operations, previously operated through various subsidiaries. By then, NOL's operations stretched to more than 100 countries, served by one of the world's largest fleets of containerships and Aframax tankers. Neptune Orient Lines was ready to sail into the new century.

Principal Subsidiaries

American Eagle Tankers Inc. Limited; APL Limited; Neptune Associated Shipping (NAS); APL Logistics Singapore Pte Ltd; Centenary Shipping (Pte) Ltd (60%); Globe King Company Limited (Hong Kong); Golden Sol Investment Pte Ltd; Intidaya Properindo 90 90 53 53 (Indonesia); Milky Way Shipping Inc (Panama); Neptank Pte Ltd; Neptune Iota Lines Ltd; Neptune Realty Management Pte Ltd; Neptune Shipmanagement Services (Pte) Ltd; NOL (Australia) Pty Ltd; NOL (China) Co Ltd; NOL (Germany) GmbH; NOL Infotech (Australia) Pty Ltd; NOL (Hong Kong) Co Ltd; NOL (Japan) Ltd; NOL Management Services (Hong Kong); NOL (Netherlands) Rederij B.V.; NOL Singapore Agency (Pte) Ltd; NOL (United Kingdom) Ltd; OCWS Logistics Pte Ltd; Specargo Forwarding (S) Pte Ltd; Trident Travels Ltd; Trident Towers Realty Pte Ltd; Trilith Shipping Pte Ltd; Trilithon Shipping Pte Ltd; Trident Districentre Pte Ltd (75%); Titan Company Pte Ltd (Cayman Islands); Tsui Ching Ltd (Hong Kong).

Principal Competitors

A.P. Moller; B + H Ocean Carriers Ltd.; Bolloré SA; Evergreen Marine Corporation (Taiwan) Ltd.; Frontline Ltd.; Golar LNG Ltd; Hanjin Shipping Co., Ltd.; Mitsui O.S.K. Lines, Ltd.; Nippon Yusen KK; OMI Corporation; P&O Nedlloyd Plc; Stena Line; Stolt-Nielsen SA.

Further Reading

Batchelor, Charles, "Choppy Waters Ahead," *Financial Times*, April 24, 1997.

Dolven, Ben, "High Seas, High Stakes," *Far Eastern Economic Review*, May 11, 2000.

Shamen, Assif, "One Foot out of the Water," *Asiaweek*, May 12, 2000.

Tan, Angela, "NOL Chief Aims to Beat the Odds," *Reuters*, June 8, 1999.

Tet-sieu, Choong, "Neptune Orient Line's American Adventure," *Asiaweek*, May 23, 1997.

—M.L. Cohen

NEW LINE CINEMA
New Line Cinema, Inc.

888 7th Avenue
New York, New York 10106
U.S.A.
Telephone: (212) 649-4900
Fax: (212) 649-4966
Web site: http://www.newline.com

Wholly Owned Subsidiary of AOL Time Warner Inc.
Incorporated: 1967
NAIC: 512110 Motion Picture and Video Production;
   512120 Motion Picture and Video Distribution;
   512220 Integrated Record Production/Distribution

New Line Cinema, Inc. is a leading producer and distributor of films. The company made its reputation producing horror films and other low-budget niche movies. Its early hits were the *Nightmare on Elm Street* movies of the 1980s. Later, as a subsidiary of Turner Broadcasting and then as a subsidiary of entertainment conglomerate AOL Time Warner, the company has produced films that rival major studio releases for production and advertising budgets. New Line operates a subsidiary company, Fine Line Features, which produces films for an art house audience. The company has a television arm, New Line Television, and a music division, New Line Music. New Line International Releasing coordinates publicity and marketing for New Line films overseas, where the company does substantial business.

Exploiting a College Niche: 1960s–70s

New Line Cinema began as a distribution company that showed films on college campuses. The company was founded by Robert Shaye in 1967. Shaye was born in 1940, the son of a wholesale grocer. Shaye first got behind a movie camera when he was 15, producing a training film for his father's grocery. He attended the University of Michigan, where he earned a bachelor's degree in business. He eventually earned a law degree from Columbia University in New York, and then traveled to Sweden on a Fulbright scholarship to study copyright law. But he remained interested in film, and made an award-winning

movie before he was 25. Living in lower Manhattan in the mid-1960s, Shaye found a way to combine his interest in movies with his legal training. He was invited to a viewing of a film called *Reefer Madness,* a quasi-documentary film made in the 1930s dramatizing the evils of marijuana. The film, made as a serious anti-drug vehicle, came off as howlingly funny to the drug-tolerant youth of the 1960s. Shaye had a hunch *Reefer Madness* would be a hit at college campuses across the country. In addition, he knew that the film's copyright protection had expired, meaning that he could legally show it for his own profit. Shaye founded New Line Cinema with an initial investment of only $1,000. Its corporate address was Shaye's Manhattan apartment, a scruffy fifth-floor walkup. The gamble paid off. *Reefer Madness* was a hit, and Shaye's company eventually made $2 million off distributing the film.

New Line Cinema continued distributing films to campuses through the 1970s. Shaye picked films that appealed to a college audience and were somewhat outside the mainstream of popular culture. New Line brought John Waters's bombastic creation *Pink Flamingos* to campus audiences, along with the horror film *Night of the Living Dead.* New Line also distributed foreign films that had a limited mainstream audience, such as the 1977 French film *Madame Rosa,* and the 1978 French-Belgian *Get Out Your Handkerchiefs.* Both these films won Academy Awards for Best Foreign Film. Yet the film distribution business was up and down for New Line, with Shaye constantly casting about for the next hit. In the early 1980s, Shaye decided to produce films as well as distribute.

Rising to a New Level with Freddy: 1980s

New Line had distributed George Romero's *Night of the Living Dead,* a low-budget 1968 film that became a classic in the horror genre. Thus the company had an understanding of horror's appeal to its core youth audience, as well as an idea of what could be done with just a couple million dollars for production. Robert Shaye was on the lookout for a film his company could produce, wanting more control over his product than he had just by distributing. In 1982 he got hold of the script to *Nightmare on Elm Street,* written by Wes Craven. Craven had previously directed two horror films known for their goriness,

---

Company Perspectives:

New Line Cinema is one of the largest independent produ-
cers, acquirers, and distributors of theatrical motion pic-
tures in the world. Founded in 1967, today the studio has a
domestic marketing and distribution organization; a home
video division; a television production and distribution or-
ganization; an international division; and merchandising,
music and new media subsidiaries that fully exploit New
Line's film properties and franchises. New Line's program-
ming refreshes AOL Time Warner's libraries and provides
valuable programming for its cable networks, in particular
TNT, TBS and HBO.

Last House on the Left, and *The Hills Have Eyes,* as well as
other low-budget movies for big screen and for television.
Shaye liked the script, and paid $14,000 for it. New Line
produced the movie, spending less than $2 million to make it.
Nightmare on Elm Street came out in 1984, and was an instant
hit. The film brought in more than $26 million. New Line
quickly followed up with an Elm Street sequel in 1985. This one
too was made on a limited budget, $2.5 million. It went over
even better than the original, and grossed $30 million.

New Line's success in the 1980s was closely tied to the
popularity of the *Nightmare on Elm Street* movies, of which
there were six. The company promoted the films with personal
appearances by actor Robert Englund, who played the burned
and disfigured killer Freddy Krueger. Each succeeding film
drew a large audience. The fourth in the series, the 1989 *Dream
Master* grossed around $50 million in its first six months. By
1991, the combined Elm Street films had brought in some $500
million in worldwide sales. Even though New Line seemed to
have an unstoppable product in the Elm Street series, the company did not deviate from its early financial strictness. The
movies were all made for under $6 million. New Line timed the
release of its films carefully, so that they did not compete with
the major studios' big releases. Though a new Elm Street film in
the late 1980s was bound to have a big opening because of its
loyal following, New Line typically debuted during a dull time,
such as at the end of summer, when no blockbusters were
around to distract from it.

New Line Cinema went public in 1986, made newly visible by
the first two Elm Street movies. Its revenues were $26.5 million
that year. The company also branched into television. It produced
Freddy's Nightmares with Lorimar Telepictures. The show was
hosted by actor Englund, though New Line was careful to monitor how much the Freddy character appeared on the show, so as
not to dilute his popularity. The arrangement with Lorimar meant
that company took the financial risk, and New Line and Lorimar
split the profits from syndication of the series.

New Line had more than Freddy Krueger in its arsenal. The
company bought the rights to the 1974 horror film *The Texas
Chainsaw Massacre* for $75,000 and in 1986 put out a sequel,
The Texas Chainsaw Massacre 2. This was followed by the
1990 film *Leatherface: Texas Chainsaw Massacre III.* These
were, like the Elm Street films, produced on a relatively low

budget and geared towards a youthful audience. The company
also produced other movies similar to what it distributed in the
1970s to college campuses. New Line produced *Torch Song
Trilogy* in 1988. This was a movie by Harvey Fierstein, based
on his Broadway play about a drag queen. New Line managed
to keep production costs for this film down to only about $5
million. Other films the company produced were equally low-
budget, and an eclectic mix. New Line produced children's
films, such as *Babar: The Movie* and *Suburban Commandos,*
assorted horror films, and softer movies such as *Torch Song
Trilogy* that looked for an art house audience.

Transformation in the Early 1990s

The company had a huge mass-market hit in 1990 with its
release of *Teenage Mutant Ninja Turtles.* The movie, based on a
comic and television show about four pizza-loving warrior
turtles, was a must-see for children worldwide, and it became
the highest grossing film ever for an independent studio. New
Line's revenue rocketed up to approximately $150 million, and
the company began investing in other entertainment ventures. In
1991, New Line bought a 20 percent share in RHI Entertainment Inc., a company that made television miniseries and made-
for-TV movies. RHI brought with it a library of films that could
be syndicated. New Line wanted a bigger toehold in the fast-
growing television movie market, and was also looking to
syndicate shows in Europe. Also in 1991, New Line acquired a
company called Nelson Entertainment Group. The deal gave
New Line home video and foreign rights to a substantial collection of films, some 600 in all. As part of the arrangement, New
Line also became a backer of filmmaker Rob Reiner. The
company signed on to back Reiner's next 11 films, for 17.5
percent of the profits.

New Line had become a more powerful company in the
early 1990s. It had a worldwide distribution arm, a television
and home video business, and its own singular brand of new
movies. In 1993 the company caught the eye of media mogul
Ted Turner. Turner owned a string of leading cable television
companies, including CNN, TNT, and the Cartoon Network.
His Turner Broadcasting System (TBS) announced in August
1993 that it was buying New Line for over $500 million. The
acquisition also brought TBS another film production company,
Castle Rock Entertainment.

A Bigger Player in the Late 1990s and After

New Line became a unit of Turner Broadcasting in 1994.
The company began working on a slightly bigger scale, spending more to develop and promote its films. But it was still a
small studio compared to such established Hollywood giants as
Warner Brothers. The company had revenues of $400 million in
1994. It stayed with films for a youthful audience, such as its
1994 *The Mask,* taken from a comic book and starring Jim
Carrey. This film had conventional marketing, including tie-ins
with McDonald's, and merchandising deals with a toy maker
and a video game producer. New Line also made less splashy
films in the mid-1990s, and tried promoting them in unusual
ways. For its 1995 *My Family,* a film about a Mexican American family, New Line advertised on Latino television stations
and displayed posters in Mexican groceries. For another 1995
release, *Friday,* the film's musical stars attended street fairs in

several cities. New Line's budgets for its films were still relatively low, yet it did splurge on occasion. In 1995 the company's development arm paid $4 million for the script for *The Long Kiss Good Night*, nearly setting a record.

In 1996, New Line's parent company, Turner Broadcasting, was acquired by the media conglomerate Time Warner Inc. for over $7 billion. Time Warner quickly dissolved Turner's film unit, Turner Pictures, into its Warner Brothers studio. Next it announced that it was considering selling New Line Cinema. Though a host of investors were named as interested, the sale did not go through. New Line continued to put out its signature mix of films, with some successes and some flops. It did well with the critically acclaimed *Boogie Nights* in 1997, a movie about the rise and fall of a male porn star. A mass-market hit was the 1997 *Austin Powers, International Man of Mystery*. This spy spoof quickly earned over $55 million, and New Line licensed a slew of tie-in merchandise to capitalize on its popularity. This was followed by a sequel in 1999, which made over $200 million in the domestic market. Other mid-1990s films did not fare so well for New Line. It had a string of flops, including *The Long Kiss Good Night*, which the studio had paid so dearly for. In addition, New Line began spending significantly more to make movies. Though it had built its reputation for films made for under $10 million, by the mid-1990s, it was spending closer to $50 million for some films, close to what larger studios lavished on their product. This meant that even films which did well at the box office did not recoup as much. New Line spent $45 million to make *The Cell* in 1999, and it grossed around $60 million. Financially, this movie was only a modest success. Then in 2000, New Line spent $80 million for a film starring actor Adam Sandler, *Little Nicky*. The company spent another $35 million on marketing, and the poorly received movie grossed only around $45 million.

In 2000, New Line's parent, Time Warner, merged with America Online, forming the new mega-media company AOL Time Warner. Under terms of the new deal, New Line's top brass no longer reported to Ted Turner, as they had ever since he bought the company in 1994. They became responsible instead to the president of Time Warner, Richard Parsons. Time Warner had earlier wanted to jettison New Line, and now its finances seemed to come under increasing suspicion. In an article in the *Los Angeles Times* (December 1, 2000), New Line President Michael Lynne admitted that "as a general rule, New Line has had its

greatest success with pictures in the $30-million to $40-million range that have made a lot of money." He declared the company's focus would remain on genre films made for under $15 million, as well as mainstream films in the $25 million to $50 million range. New Line protected itself from significant loss by pre-selling foreign rights to its movies. Nevertheless, it was clear that New Line had deviated from this general rule several times recently. Not only had *Little Nicky* cost $80 million, but a mainstream comedy, *Town & Country*, originally budgeted for $55 million, ended up costing closer to $90 million.

In January 2001, New Line lost 100 employees as part of a trim dictated by new parent AOL Time Warner. Several months later the company underwent a management restructuring. Michael Lynne became co-chairman and co-CEO along with founder Robert Shaye, the production manager was replaced, and the company's divisions streamlined. As 2001 drew to a close, AOL Time Warner's top management made several announcements in the press concerning their excitement about Warner Brother's upcoming release of *Harry Potter and the Sorcerer's Stone*. This was almost guaranteed to be a whopping success, since it was based on the new titan of children's literature, J.K. Rowling's book of the same name. At the same time, New Line was preparing to release its most expensive and undoubtedly riskiest film yet, the first of three movies based on J.R.R. Tolkien's *Lord of the Rings*. The studio, which had prided itself on its low budget successes, had gambled $270 million to make the three films back-to-back. The danger of course was that if the first film flopped, the second two were bound to be duds. New Line had committed to the films in 1998, before the AOL Time Warner merger, and it had been Robert Shaye's suggestion to the director that they make all three. It seemed rather ominous that AOL Time Warner's chief operating officer had not thought to tout the films, favoring *Harry Potter* in his press interviews. But New Line had worked assiduously to offset its financial risk. It had gotten major distributors to pay up some $160 million in advance for *Lord of the Rings*, and it worked with a worldwide marketing and distribution network to coordinate the release country by country. The movie spawned over 40 licensed products, and New Line entered joint marketing deals with major corporations such as Barnes & Noble, Burger King, and General Mills. New Line had a lot riding on the success of *Lord of the Rings*. Fortunately the film opened to a wave of critical and public acclaim in December 2001. The next two films in the trilogy were due to be released in December 2002 and December 2003, respectively. The company seemed to have at least these two hits lined up, and so for the short term had proven its worth to its new parent.

Principal Subsidiaries

New Line Music; Fine Line Features.

Principal Divisions

New Line Home Video; New Line Television; New Line Theatrical Distribution; New Line International Releasing.

Principal Competitors

Sony Pictures Entertainment; Universal Studios; Fox Filmed Entertainment.

Further Reading

Andersen, Kurt, "Ted Goes to Hollywood II," *Time*, August 30, 1993, p. 65.

Angwin, Julia, and Martin Peers, "AOL Time Warner Narrows Loss, Meets Targets," *Wall Street Journal*, April 19, 2001, p. A3.

Coleman, L., "Picking Your Targets," *Forbes*, January 21, 1991, p. 72.

Eller, Claudia, "Latest Flop Caps a Painful Year at New Line Cinema," *Los Angeles Times*, December 1, 2000, p. C1.

Goldsmith, Jill, and Charles Lyons, "New Line Realigns," *Daily Variety*, March 29, 2001, p. 1.

Grover, Ronald, "Nightmares, Turtles—And Profits," *Business Week*, September 30, 1991, pp. 52–56.

Gubernick, Lisa, "It's Great for a Date," *Forbes*, February 6, 1989, pp. 110–14.

Harris, Dana, et al., "Can B.O. Postman 'Ring' Twice?" *Variety*, November 26, 2001, p. 1.

Heuton, Cheryl, "New Line's New Dream Is Television," *Channels*, July 16, 1990, p. 8.

Horn, John, "Crossed Swords, Cold Cash," *Newsweek*, December 10, 2001, p. 78.

"Interactive Multideals," *Economist*, August 21, 1993, p. 50.

Jensen, Jeff, "Licensing Assault Readied for Cult Hit 'Austin Powers'," *Advertising Age*, June 8, 1998, p. 8.

——, "New Line's 'Boogie Nights' Challenges Movie Marketer," *Advertising Age*, November 10, 1997, p. 8.

Rotenier, Nancy, "Cool Guy," *Forbes*, June 5, 1995, p. 168.

Stanley, T.L., "New Line Hits Street for Niche Pics," *Brandweek*, April 17, 1995, p. 14.

Tyrer, Kathy, "From Zero to Hero," *Adweek*, March 21, 1994, p. 6.

—A.Woodward

Norm Thompson Outfitters, Inc.

3188 Northwest Aloclek Drive
Hillsboro, Oregon 97124
U.S.A.
Telephone: (503) 614-4600
Toll Free: (800) 547-1160
Fax: (503) 614-4601
Web site: http://www.normthompson.com

Private Company
Incorporated: 1949
Employees: 608
Sales: $200.0 million (2001 est.)
NAIC: 454110 Electronic Shopping and Mail-Order
  Houses; 452990 All Other General Merchandise
  Stores

Norm Thompson Outfitters, Inc. is a specialty retailer of casual and outdoor clothing, unique gifts, and gourmet foods, which are sold primarily through mail-order catalogs. Norm Thompson also sells its merchandise on its web site and at a handful of retail and outlet locations in Oregon. The company publishes four catalogs under the titles Norm Thompson, Early Winters, Solutions, and Waterfront Living. Together, the catalogs offer approximately 2,600 items. Aside from its operations in Oregon, Norm Thompson also operates a distribution center in West Virginia.

Origins

In its original guise, Norm Thompson reflected the interests of its founder and namesake, Norm Thompson. An avid sportsman, Thompson retired shortly after the end of World War II and devoted his newly found free time to his greatest passion, fly-fishing. He started his company in 1949 more as a hobby than a business; an enterprise whose scope and aims were modest. Thompson ran two-inch advertisements in outdoor magazines, hawking his hand-tied fly-fishing ties. After a year, Thompson ended his involvement with the homespun enterprise and passed control of the company to his son-in-law, Peter Alport.

When Alport inherited control of the company in 1950, he made his living running an advertising agency in Portland, Oregon. Like his father-in-law, Alport treated the company primarily as a hobby. He operated the company alongside his advertising agency, dividing his attention between the two concerns. Although Norm Thompson's initial development may have suffered because of a lack of focused attention, meaningful strides were achieved during Alport's first years in control.

Debut of First Catalogue: 1951

In 1951, Alport produced the first Norm Thompson catalogue, introducing what would become the company's signature trait. The first catalogue showcased the company's narrow line of fly-fishing gear, but in later years the catalogues expanded, as Norm Thompson began to reflect the interests and personality of Alport. Alport and his friends immersed themselves in the lifestyle of 1950s adventurers, a lifestyle based on the African safari hunting trips made famous by Ernest Hemingway and Charles Ritz. By the late 1950s, Norm Thompson's product line had expanded beyond fly-fishing gear to include high-end outdoor gear and apparel.

The first major turning point in Norm Thompson's development occurred in 1965, when John Emrick joined the company. Emrick's first discovery was a discouraging one. For 16 years, the company had been treated as a sidelight venture, as a hobby rather than a business. Although unique, the company's high-end merchandise could never attract more than a small, albeit devoted, following. Largely because of its small target audience and its casual management, Norm Thompson was financially destitute when Emrick joined the firm, its prospects bleak unless sweeping change was implemented.

Emrick emerged as the company's savior shortly after his arrival. He convinced Alport to redefine and to broaden the company's focus, arguing that Norm Thompson was best suited as an outfitter of outdoor apparel, gear, and accessories. Emrick also persuaded Alport to lend his full attention to the company. In 1966, Alport dissolved his advertising accounts and began focusing exclusively on the management of Norm Thompson.

Company Perspectives:

Norm Thompson is committed to having a positive impact on the environment. Our goal is to prove that sustainability is the right thing to do for the planet—and for commerce. We will, therefore, ensure that the choices we make in our day-to-day business take into account the environment around us, as well as our stakeholders and profitability. Specifically, we will strive to follow principles of sustainability to: Meet the needs of the present without compromising the ability of future generations to meet their needs; Secure a high quality of life within those means; Meet the criteria of The Natural Step.

With the implementation of the new strategy proposed by Emrick, Norm Thompson began to take on the trappings of a genuine corporate concern. Alport's frequent trips to Europe and elsewhere gave the company access to goods rarely seen by U.S. consumers. Alport imported tweeds and natural fibers from England, which defined Norm Thompson's image as a "country gentleman" look. By the mid-1970s, Alport's constant purchasing trips abroad had helped the company to realize Emrick's vision. Norm Thompson had become an outfitter carrying a diverse collection of apparel, gear, and accessories targeted toward a much larger target audience.

Emrick's positive influence over the fortunes of Norm Thompson was rewarded in his selection as the company's president in 1971. His control over the company was strengthened four years later, when Alport, after a 25-year association with the company, passed away. Following Alport's death, Emrick continued operating the company under new ownership, first by a company called Parker Penn and later by a group of investors that included Emrick himself. During the period punctuated by Emrick's rise to the presidency, Alport's death, and the switches in ownership, Norm Thompson experienced significant change. It was during the 1970s when the company emerged as an innovator, a role that would describe it into the 21st century.

From its start, Norm Thompson catered to an exclusively male audience. As the company entered the mid-1970s, however, its catalogues began to carry gift and apparel items geared for female customers. Research, conducted under the increasingly influential Emrick, revealed that women were browsing through the company's catalogues and placing order calls to Norm Thompson operators. The company reacted to this discovery because of the emphasis Emrick placed on the needs and desires of Norm Thompson's customers, a perspective that represented a fundamental change in the corporate philosophy espoused by Alport. Alport focused on merchandise, believing that unique items would attract customers. Emrick, in contrast, focused on customer service, believing that listening to what the customer wanted should dictate the type of merchandise that appeared in company catalogues.

The adoption of Emrick's customer-oriented philosophy led to pioneering changes in the way Norm Thompson operated. In 1975, Emrick solicited the help of outside vendors to create a computer system that could facilitate the company's newly adopted customer-oriented approach. During the ensuing three years, the company developed its own software that was operated and maintained without outside assistance. Also in 1975, the company established online communications with customers, which allowed company operators to inform customers about product availability while the customers were on the telephone line. The utilization of computer systems to bridge the gap separating a catalogue company and its customers was novel at the time. Most direct response companies of Norm Thompson's ilk viewed computer systems as accounting or order-taking aids, but Emrick used the technology to create a marketing tool that enhanced the interactive relationship between company and customer. Said Emrick, in an April 1996 interview with *Direct Marketing,* "If you focus on great service and great products and stay connected to what's happening with technology, you will succeed in this business."

Against the backdrop of strategic change and growth, Norm Thompson began to flower into a robust enterprise. The policy of responding to the demands of customers expanded product lines and, by necessity, expanded the company's catalogue offerings. In 1965, the company mailed its first fall season catalogue. In 1967, a spring catalogue was added. By 1973, the company was producing four catalogues: spring, fall, winter, and Christmas.

Norm Thompson's innovative customer-service system was in place before the end of the 1970s. By blending its own sophisticated direct response system along with other developments of the era, such as credit cards and toll free telephone numbers, the company entered the 1980s as a vibrant mail-order firm, its customers and product selection growing steadily. Emrick, who would later couple his customer-service zeal with a passion for environmental concerns, had fashioned Norm Thompson into the type of company that later would be hailed by industry observers. As the company entered the 1980s, however, its diminutive stature and private-ownership status kept it from public awareness. Soon Norm Thompson's anonymity would be shed, and Emrick's achievements revealed, but before public scrutiny cast its eye toward the small company based in Hillsboro, Emrick was already making plans to pass control of the company to someone else.

According to *Oregon Business,* Emrick began making plans for a year's sabbatical as early as 1982. Emrick, according to reports, wanted to turn his company over to another individual by the time he reached 50 years old. Aside from a desire for more free time, Emrick believed that Norm Thompson's growth during the latter half of the 1970s and the early 1980s demanded a more professional managerial structure. In 1988, he met the individual he believed could spearhead the necessary transformation of the business.

Ron Decker joined Norm Thompson in 1989, as the mail-order retailer neared the $50 million-in-sales mark. The process of transferring power from Emrick to Decker took a surprisingly long time, as both executives moved methodically through the first change in Norm Thompson's leadership in a quarter century. By mid-1992, Emrick was ready to take his sabbatical, his only contact with the company reduced to one monthly telephone call with Decker and attendance at an occasional board meeting.

Key Dates:

1949: Norm Thompson begins selling his hand-tied fly-fishing ties.
1950: Peter Alport, Norm Thompson's son-in-law, takes control of the company.
1951: The first Norm Thompson catalogue is introduced.
1965: John Emrick joins the company.
1975: Peter Alport dies, passing stewardship to Emrick.
1996: Norm Thompson's new, ''green'' headquarters opens.
1999: The company's new web site debuts.

Growth in the 1990s

Decker's influence over Norm Thompson did not last long. Emrick returned to guide the company through much of the 1990s. During the latter half of the decade, Norm Thompson, long the innovator in terms of customer service, added a new dimension to its corporate personality, becoming a leader in progressive environmental practices. In 1996, the company unveiled its new, ''green'' headquarters near Portland, Oregon. The site, design, and materials were selected because of their minimal environmental impact, resulting in a state-of-the art facility that served as a model for other environmentally minded companies to follow. The building's heating, ventilation, and air-conditioning system realized roughly 40 percent reductions in energy use by using the heat produced by the facility's occupants and equipment. Ceiling tiles were made from recycled telephone books and newspapers. Flooring in the lobby consisted of wood salvaged from railroad boxcars.

Under Emrick's direction, Norm Thompson pursued other progressive objectives that were hailed by the environmental movement. The company partnered with the Alliance for Environmental Innovation to study the feasibility of using recycled paper in its catalogs. Norm Thompson began using 10 percent recycled-content paper, which represented a pioneering move in an industry saddled with a woeful record of excessive paper consumption. Norm Thompson also pledged to offer only plastic products free of polyvinyl chloride (PVC) and 100 percent organic cotton in its products.

As the company neared its 50th anniversary, there was one area where the otherwise progressive and innovative Norm Thompson fell short of expectations. In 1998, sales surged past the $150 million mark, but the company had yet to establish a presence on the Internet commensurate with its stature. As other catalog companies threw themselves headlong into electronic commerce, Norm Thompson conspicuously refrained from establishing anything more than a token presence on the Internet. At the company's flagship store in Portland, customers could choose from roughly 1,300 different products. Through the company's catalogs, customers could select from 2,600 different products. On the Internet, however, Norm Thompson customers were limited to 75 items. Competitors such as L.L. Bean and J. Crew had long since established substantial web sites befitting the scope of their catalog offerings. In the business press, critics wondered why Norm Thompson had not yet followed suit.

In 1998, Emrick and his other top executives finally decided that the Internet represented a legitimate and vital method of shopping. Their decision led to the October 1999 debut of a web site that gave Norm Thompson customers full access to the company's myriad gifts, apparel items, and specialty foods. ''I wish we'd started a year earlier than we did,'' Emrick confided to *Business Journal—Portland* in an October 8, 1999 interview. Emrick was confident, however, that his company had not fallen behind its competitors because of its belated foray into electronic commerce. The company, he argued, had spent the time valuably, revamping its image and its merchandise selection so that it remained attuned to the needs and desires of its customers in the 21st century.

Principal Competitors

Lands' End, Inc.; L.L. Bean, Inc.; Spiegel, Inc.

Further Reading

Back, Brian J., ''Norm Thompson's Love of Community,'' *Business Journal—Portland,* October 13, 2000, p. 18.
Eisler, Gary, ''The Mail Order Tax War,'' *Oregon Business,* October 1990, p. 109.
Fundak, Lydia, ''Norm Thompson: Looking Beyond the Bottom Line,'' *Direct Marketing,* April 1996, p. 14.
Goldfield, Robert, ''E-Commerce Convert,'' *Business Journal—Portland,* October 8, 1999, p. 21.
Harding, Elizabeth U., ''Hello? Your Order Has Arrived,'' *Software Magazine,* February 2001, p. 6.
Hill, Robert L., ''Letting Go of the Reins,'' *Oregon Business,* May 1992, p. 44.
Hogue, Kendra, ''Norm Thompson Adjusting to Postal Rate Hike, Cuts Staff,'' *Business Journal—Portland,* March 4, 1991, p. 1.

—Jeffrey L. Covell

NTN Corporation

3-17, 1-chome
Kyomachi-bori
Nishi-ku
Osaka 550-0003
Japan
Telephone: (81) 6-6449-3612
Fax: (81) 6-6443-6966
Web site: http://www.ntn.co.jp

Public Company
Incorporated: 1927 as NTN Manufacturing Company, Ltd.
Employees: 12,619
Sales: $2.7 billion (2001)
Stock Exchanges: Tokyo
NAIC: 332999 All Other Miscellaneous Fabricated Metal Product Manufacturing (pt); 336399 All Other Motor Vehicle Parts Manufacturing (pt)

NTN Corporation is one of Japan's largest manufacturers of bearings, second in domestic market share only to longtime rival Nippon Seiko, and one of the largest exporters of friction-reducing products in the world. As a natural extension of its bearing business, it is also Japan's principal manufacturer of constant-velocity joints, which are used in automobile transmissions, railway cars, construction machinery, and steel manufacturing equipment.

Origins and Growth: 1920s–30s

NTN traces its lineage back to Nishizono Ironworks, a factory located in the city of Uchibori in Mie Prefecture, which began developing and manufacturing ball bearings in 1918. The Japanese bearings industry was then in its infancy; Nippon Seiko had become the nation's first producer of ball bearings no more than several years earlier. In 1923 Nishizono Ironworks merged with Osaka-based Tomoe Trading Company to manufacture and sell bearings under the brand name NTN. Four years later, however, the partnership broke up and the Nishizono side

of the operation, retaining the NTN name, set up a privately owned company called NTN Manufacturing Company, with an initial capitalization of ¥50,000. It reorganized as a joint-stock company in 1934, and three years later it changed its name to Toyo Bearing Manufacturing and offered shares to the public for the first time.

Also in 1937 Japan invaded Manchuria, beginning eight years of war in the Far East. What little export trade Japanese bearing makers had conducted to this point ended by 1941; but as war increased the demand for bearings and companies made rapid advances in manufacturing techniques, production increased 22-fold between 1937 and 1944, and producers prospered. In 1938 Toyo Bearing established a domestic subsidiary, Showa Bearing Manufacturing Company, in Mukogun, Hyogo Prefecture. The next year Toyo Bearing absorbed Showa Bearing, which became its Mukogawa plant, and merged its operations with those of its newly constructed plant at nearby Kuwana.

Postwar Revival and Diversification: 1950s–70s

By the end of World War II, however, U.S. bombing raids and shortages of steel and other raw materials had brought Japanese bearing makers to a near standstill. The industry began to revive in the late 1940s, as the shattered nation rebuilt, and domestic demand for its products, as well as demand from other Asian nations, increased. In 1950 Toyo established a separate marketing arm, NTN Sales. The company emerged from these years as one of Japan's five largest bearing makers, along with Nippon Seiko, Koyo Seiko, Fujikoshi Kozai, and Asahi Seiko. Together, these firms accounted for 80 percent of the nation's bearing output in 1951. In 1954 NTN was awarded the first Deming Prize, for statistical quality control.

Toyo began to diversify its product lines during the 1950s and continued to do so into the next decade, although all of its products related to its mainstay, bearings. In 1956 it began manufacturing expansion compensating bearings. In 1961 it entered into a licensing agreement with the West German bearing company INA Wälzlager Schaeffler, under which Toyo produced needle bearings using Wälzlager Schaeffler's technology. The two set up a joint venture, NTN Wälzlager Europa, to market the needle bearings in Europe. In 1963 Toyo secured a similar licensing pact with the British firm Hardy Spicer to produce Birfield-type constant-velocity universal joints. The next year it obtained a license from another British company, GKN Transmission, to manufacture its constant-velocity joints in Japan and formed NTN Bearing-GKN to do so; in 1965 it began producing pipe fittings and oil-impregnated sintered bearings.

Such growth and diversification as Toyo underwent in the 1960s might be expected to create unwieldy corporate management, but the company avoided this problem by creating subsidiaries to handle new products, thus distributing the decision-making load through a decentralized command structure. In 1961 Toyo created Kongo Bearing Company to handle the production of pillow blocks. The next year, it founded Senyo Kosakuki Kenkyujo, which made ball bearing equipment. This trend continued into the 1970s; in 1971 it created Toyo Bearing Okayama Company to manufacture roller bearings and automotive tapered bearings, and the next year it founded Shohin Kaihatsu Kenkyusho to manufacture other automotive equipment. The company also changed its name to NTN Toyo Bearing Company in 1972.

International Expansion in the 1970s and 1980s

After riding out the effects of sluggish demand at home, especially in automotive industry, Toyo began pursuing the export market in earnest in the 1960s. In 1963 it established its first sales subsidiary outside Japan—NTN Bearing Corporation of America, followed in 1964 by NTN France. In 1968 it established a sales subsidiary in Canada, NTN Bearing Corporation of Canada. A manufacturing subsidiary, NTN Manufacturing Canada, followed in 1973. In 1971 it founded American NTN Bearing Manufacturing Corporation and opened a plant in Schiller Park, Illinois, its first manufacturing operation in North America. It also established a sales subsidiary in Hong Kong, NTN Trading—Hong Kong, and a West German manufacturing subsidiary, NTN Kugellagerfabrik.

Like its compatriots, NTN made its mark in the high-volume sector of the European and U.S. markets, exporting ball and roller bearings used in automobile parts and electrical equipment. The Japanese bearing exporters became successful enough and their products pervasive enough to produce resentment among their competitors, especially in Great Britain. In 1972 the British government, acting on complaints from its own bearing industry that the Japanese had captured almost one-fifth of the domestic market for standard ball bearings and over two-thirds of the market for bearings for small electric motors, pressed Japanese companies to restrict their exports for two years; but European bearing makers could not avoid the fact that these bearings were of superior quality—a far cry from the 1950s, when Japanese bearing companies were plagued by a scarcity of high-grade steel. In fact, many European companies were buying Japanese bearings, including those made by NTN Kugellagerfabrik, for their own use. NTN Toyo's overseas expansion continued unabated in the mid-1970s. In 1975 it established two sales subsidiaries in Latin America, NTN de Mexico and Panama-based NTN Suramericana. It also opened another factory in Illinois, this time in Elgin.

In fiscal 1977, however, NTN Toyo posted an operating loss of nearly ¥1 billion, as a strong yen made exports prohibitively expensive. Most of its bearings sold in foreign countries were still made in Japan, not by overseas subsidiaries, making them vulnerable to exchange rate fluctuations. In addition, NTN Toyo and other Japanese bearing makers were fined by the European Economic Community for dumping, the practice of gaining an unfair advantage by selling one's products at less than fair value. In 1978 the company was forced to suspend dividend payments for the first time in 12 years.

The strong yen soon weakened, and NTN Toyo's exports surged once again. Strong domestic demand from automobile manufacturers, themselves experiencing an export boom because of the weak yen, also served to boost sales. In fiscal 1979 the company posted a profit of ¥3.4 billion with strong increases in sales and all of its overseas plants reported to be running at full capacity.

With its financial health restored, NTN Toyo targeted its constant-velocity-joint business and its operations in the United States for expansion in the 1980s. In 1982 it added a facility for producing the automotive joints to its Okayama plant. It also entered into a joint venture with the Korean automaker Hyundai Motors, under which Hyundai would manufacture the joints on a license from NTN Toyo. In 1983 NTN Toyo licensed its constant-velocity-joint technology to two more foreign companies, Lepco Company of Australia and Taiway of Taiwan.

The company focused on producing tapered roller bearings in the United States over the next two years. It expanded its Elgin plant in 1984 to increase its capacity to produce the tapered bearings. The next year, it entered into a joint venture with Detroit-based Federal-Mogul Corporation—one of NTN's many U.S. distributors—to manufacture tapered bearings and cylindrical roller bearings. The new company was called NTN-Bower Corporation, with the second name coming from a division of Federal-Mogul, and was given two Federal-Mogul plants and a related research facility. NTN Toyo controlled 60 percent of the joint venture. In 1987 NTN Toyo exercised its option to buy the remaining 40 percent of NTN-Bower and became sole owner.

In 1985 NTN opened its Nagano works, specializing in precision miniature bearings. The following year, the company built its Kuwana plant, Japan's first plant dedicated to bearings for use in aerospace products.

By increasing its manufacturing capacity in the United States, NTN Toyo reduced its reliance on bearings exported from Japan for its presence in the U.S. market. It could not cut that reliance entirely, and its bearing exports caused some friction. In 1987 the U.S. bearing manufacturer Timken brought a suit before the U.S. Department of Commerce charging that NTN Toyo, Koyo Seiko, and other Japanese bearing makers were dumping their goods. The Commerce Department found

Key Dates:

1923: Nishizono Ironworks merges with Tomoe Trading Company to form NTN.
1927: Nishizono splits with Tomoe to form NTN Manufacturing Company.
1937: NTN reorganizes as Toyo Bearing Manufacturing.
1938: Showa Bearing Manufacturing Company is formed.
1950: NTN Sales is formed.
1961: Toyo joins with INA Wälzlager Schaeffler to form NTN Wälzlager Europa.
1963: NTN Bearing Corporation of America is formed.
1972: Toyo Bearing Manufacturing becomes NTN Toyo Bearing Company.
1989: NTN Toyo is renamed NTN Corporation.
1990: NTN forms NTN USA Corp.
2001: NTN launches Management System Transformation Project.

the Japanese companies guilty and ordered NTN Toyo to pay a fine of 47 percent of the price of the products it had exported to the United States.

In 1988 the company established a technical center in Ann Arbor, Michigan, and once again expanded its U.S. manufacturing operations, adding a bearing-hub production facility to its Elgin plant. It also entered into a joint venture to manufacture constant-velocity joints in Australia with Borg-Warner Australia and GKN Transmission. The new company was called Unidrive and was 50 percent owned by Borg-Warner Australia, with 30 percent going to GKN and 20 percent to NTN Toyo.

In 1989 NTN Toyo shortened its name to NTN Corporation. The company also established NTN Driveshaft in Columbus, Indiana, to manufacture constant-velocity joints and opened a new research and development center.

By the late 1980s, NTN was still able to achieve substantial success by doing one thing very well and sticking to it. While other large corporations viewed far-flung diversification as the key to success, NTN continued to make nothing but bearings and bearing-related products. Since becoming a major exporter in the late 1960s, its presence in foreign markets caused occasional controversy, which was not unexpected. What counted was that NTN had found its bearings and was sticking to them.

International Competition in the 1990s

The emergence of the global economy in the 1990s presented a number of unique challenges to NTN. On the one hand, the dissolution of traditional economic boundaries exposed the company to increased competition from foreign companies, especially in regions where NTN had always held a formidable market share. At the same time, the proliferation of multinational manufacturing operations in the United States, Europe, and Asia, particularly in the automobile and computer industries, made it clear that a strong international presence would be more critical than ever to the company's long-term success. Since globalization was having a major impact on the ball bearing industry, with bearing specifications being determined

more and more by international standards, it became imperative for the company not only to consolidate its existing overseas operations, but also to strive for the further expansion of its businesses into emerging markets.

One region where the company aimed to centralize its operations was in the United States. In 1990, to facilitate the expansion of its manufacturing and sales capabilities in North America, the company invested $50 million to form NTN USA Corp., with the aim of creating a holding firm for its existing U.S. subsidiaries. The new company, headquartered in Delaware, assumed complete control over the stock of the existing businesses. At the same time, NTN established an office to oversee the manufacturing operations of the existing plants. One of the company's primary goals was to commence production of constant-velocity joints in North America. The company took further steps to enhance its U.S. presence by acquiring the ball bearings division of Federal-Mogul, a Michigan-based machine tool manufacturer, in 1996.

NTN's expansion during this period was not limited to North America. In February 2001 the company entered into a partnership with FAG Kugelfischer Georg Schafer AG, a German manufacturer, to market ball and roller bearings in both North America and Europe. The agreement outlined a number of joint research and development projects, in addition to establishing a system by which the two companies could pool their procurement and sales resources. Furthermore, the deal laid the groundwork for the creation of manufacturing operations in Hungary and Portugal. Closer to home, NTN was busy firming up its presence in Southeast Asia with the formation of NTN Manufacturing Company Limited, a bearing and CV joint manufacturing facility based in Thailand, in February 2000.

In order to manage its international expansion, which was dubbed the "Four Base Production and Sales System," NTN was compelled to undergo a restructuring at the beginning of the new century. NTN implemented the first major change in May 2000, when it absorbed the NTN Sales Corporation into the parent company. A far more radical step came in April 2001, when NTN launched its Management System Transformation Project, with the aim of streamlining its operations both in Japan and abroad. The plan called for the creation of a Program Office responsible for the management of numerous subprojects, each of which was designed to increase efficiency and improve customer service. With these changes already in place by the beginning of the new century, NTN was poised to meet the challenges involved with remaining an industry leader in the highly competitive international marketplace.

Principal Subsidiaries

Higashinihon NTN Service Corp.; Kyoei NTN Corp.; NTN Kongo Corp.; NTN Engineering Plastics Corp.; NTN Powder Metal Corp.; NTN Mikumo Company Ltd.; NTN Precision Forging Co., Ltd.; NTN Casting Corp.; NTN Kishiwada Corp.; NTN Hirano Corp.; NTN Kinan Corp.; NTN USA Corp. (U.S.A.); NTN Bearing Corp. of America (U.S.A.); NTN Driveshaft, Inc. (U.S.A.); American NTN Bearing Mfg. Corp. (U.S.A.); NTN-Bower Corp. (U.S.A.); NTN-BCA Corp. (U.S.A.); NTN Bearing Corp. of Canada Ltd.; NTN Sudamericana, S.A. (Panama); NTN Walzlager (Europa) G.m.b.H. (Germany); NTN Kugellagerfabrik (Deutschland) G.m.b.H. (Germany); NTN Bearing (U.K.) Ltd.; NTN France S.A.; NTN Transmissions Europe (80%); NTN Bearing-Singapore (PTE) Ltd.; NTN China Ltd. (Hong Kong); NTN Bearing-Thailand Co., Ltd. (49%); NTN Manufacturing (Thailand) Co., Ltd.; NTN Bearing-Malaysia Snd. Bhd. (70%); NTN Korea Co., Ltd.

Principal Competitors

Koyo Seiko Co., Ltd.; MINEBEA Co., Ltd.; NSK Ltd.

Further Reading

"Bearing Maker NTN Teams Up with Germany's FAG," *Japan Economic Newswire,* February 27, 2001.

NTN Company Profile, Osaka, Japan: NTN Corporation, 1990.

"NTN Sets Up Holding Company in U.S.," *Japan Economic Newswire,* August 30, 1990.

—Douglas Sun
—update: Steve Meyer

OAO NK YUKOS

26 Ulansky Pereulok
103045 Moscow
Russia
Telephone: (+7) 095 232 3168
Fax: (+7) 095 755 5393
Web site: http://www.yukos.com

Public Company
Incorporated: 1993
Employees: 85,000
Sales: $8.5 billion (2000)
Stock Exchanges: MICEX RTS MSE OTC Bulletin
    Board
Ticker Symbol: YUKO; YUKOY (OTC)
NAIC: 211111 Crude Petroleum and Natural Gas
    Extraction; 213112 Support Activities for Oil and Gas
    Operations; 324110 Petroleum Refineries

OAO NK YUKOS is the second largest of Russia's integrated oil companies, with an estimated 11.8 billion barrels of oil reserves in its western Siberian fields and an average production of one million barrels a day. With holdings in numerous sectors of the oil industry, the company accounts for 15 percent of oil produced and 15 percent of oil refined in Russia, and also operates a domestic retail network of approximately 1,200 gas stations. Oil extraction at YUKOS is carried out by three main production units. Yuganskneftegas, in western Siberia, accounts for 62 percent of total production. Remaining production is shared between the Tomskneft association in Central Siberia and the Samaraneftegas association in European Russia. Refining occurs at five separate facilities. The Novokuybyshevsky, Kuybyshevsky, and Syzransky refineries are located in the Central Volga region, while two more refineries are located east of the Ural Mountains in the cities of Achinsk and Strezhevoi.

YUKOS is a company with international reach. It exports 45 percent of its crude oil to Asia and Europe. In addition, foreign companies are partners in several development, production, and field services enterprises. The company's shares are traded as level one American Depository Receipts (ADRs) in London, Frankfurt, Munich, Berlin, and in the United States on the OTC Bulletin Board. Domestically, YUKOS is listed on the three major Russian exchanges: the Russian Trading System, the Moscow Interbank Currency Exchange, and the Moscow Stock Exchange. The company is headed by Mikhail Khodorkovsky, who, after going through a period of rocky relations with investors, is gradually regaining credibility with efforts to improve corporate governance and transparency. Khodorkovsky and his affiliates hold about 69 percent of the company.

A State-Held Company in the Early 1990s

YUKOS was formed in the early 1990s as part of the post-communism process of transforming state concerns into joint stock companies. When the USSR fell apart at the end of 1991, dozens of individual local oil concerns existed. The entire oil sector was in need of restructuring, as production had fallen since the mid-1980s due to poor maintenance and technical problems. It was decided to assemble a limited number of large integrated companies from the various pieces of the oil industry. Following a presidential decree on privatization in April 1993, NK (Neftyanaya Kompaniya, or "oil company") YUKOS was formed as a joint stock company uniting the Yuganskneftegas production concern, three refineries in the Central Volga region, and several smaller operations relating to the sale of refined products. YUKOS's major competitors, created under the same decree, were LUKOIL and Surgutneftegas.

While YUKOS's daughter companies went through the process of privatization, the parent company remained state-owned. The government chose Sergei Muravlenko, former head of Yuganskneftegas, to lead the company. In its first year of operation, YUKOS developed a joint venture with Shell and the Canadian company Fracmaster. The first joint venture in the Russian oil industry, the "Yuganskfracmaster" partnership worked on well stimulation in the western Siberian fields. A second joint venture, "Yusat," focused on refining. In an agreement with Eser Foreign Trade of Istanbul, the Yusat venture allowed Siberian crude to be processed at Turkish refineries. The retail end of business was also developed early on. In 1993 YUKOS began building service stations in the Moscow area.

Company Perspectives:

Yukos' mission is to become one of the locomotives of the Russian economy and to assist the country in emerging from economic crisis. "Leadership. Progress. Responsibility." These are the components of our company's success.

Yukos' activity is directed toward the generation of profit in conjunction with ceaseless development and the consideration of the interests of society and the government. Yukos relies on the professionalism of its employees, innovation, initiative and the creative efforts of a whole collective.

Production levels at YUKOS declined substantially in 1994 and 1995 due to the destabilizing effect of sweeping structural changes in the Russian economy. Nevertheless, exports increased gradually, making use of an already existing link to the Druzhba pipeline into Western Europe. With a total 1994 production of 198 million barrels, YUKOS accounted for 11 percent of Russia's oil output that year.

As the economy began to stabilize near the end of 1995, YUKOS directed the proceeds from exports toward the rehabilitation of idle wells and the production of new anti-corrosive pipelines. That fall the company grew substantially when the production concern OAO Samaraneftegas, along with several affiliated research, development, and marketing organizations, became part of YUKOS. With the acquisition, YUKOS moved past Surgutneftegas to become the second largest company in terms of oil reserves. But growth only exacerbated management problems at YUKOS. Each daughter company had its own management philosophy, often based on Soviet traditions such as meeting quota and dealing in barter rather than profitability. As a result, the company fell behind on payment of salaries and amassed a $3.5 billion debt to the Russian treasury.

New Ownership, Active Leadership: 1995–98

Financial difficulties led to the privatization of YUKOS in a series of auctions. In early 1995, the cash-strapped Russian government had offered shares in state-held assets as collateral for loans from a select group of private banks. When the government defaulted on its loans, state companies fell into private hands. A controversial auction in December 1995 resulted in the sale of a controlling stake in YUKOS to Menatep Bank for $350 million. The modest price for such considerable assets was alleged to be a result of close connections between the government and the head of Menatep, Mikhail Khodorkovsky. Khodorkovsky was a former Communist Youth League leader who became a prominent player in the post-1991 privatization process. It was expected that he would now redirect his attention from Menatep to YUKOS, as he announced plans to clean up the company's finances, court foreign loans, increase export revenues, and solve the problem of back taxes.

Khodorkovsky replaced Muravlenko as CEO in May 1996 and was elected to the board of directors. In December 1996 another "open auction" allowed Menatep to increase its holdings in YUKOS to an estimated 85 percent. With foreign investors and other competitors excluded from participation in the auction, a previously unknown company with, as the *Wall Street Journal* reported, obvious connections to Menatep paid $160 million for a substantial stake in YUKOS.

In 1997 YUKOS managed to restructure its tax debt in negotiations with federal and regional governments. Khodorkovsky pushed for the adoption of accounting and management methods that matched Western standards and produced a plan to address environmental problems by replacing more pipeline. He also traveled abroad that spring in an effort to lure foreign financial support, and eventually won an $800 million loan from an international syndicate. The loan, secured by oil exports and pledges of YUKOS stock, was used to acquire a controlling stake in the state-owned Eastern Oil Company. Eastern Oil, the 12th largest producer in Russia, operated several concerns in central Siberia, including the Tomskneft production entity and the Achinsk refinery.

Khodorkovsky's success in finding foreign support led to a conflict with Amoco Corporation. Back in 1993, Amoco had won a tender to develop the massive Priobskoye field in western Siberia, with an estimated four billion barrels in reserves. After four years of talks and more than $100 million already invested in the project, Amoco had not yet established a concrete joint venture. Now that YUKOS had found financial support elsewhere, the Russian company asserted its right to develop the field independently. Negotiations with Amoco neared a breakdown point. After a brief revival of talks, Amoco officially renounced its plans for Priobskoye in August 1998.

Retrenching During Crisis and Conflict: 1998–2000

In early 1998 YUKOS announced plans to merge with AO Sibneft, the seventh largest oil company in Russia. Industry observers marveled at the potential size of the new holding company, to be called AO Yuksi—its reserves would be greater than those of Royal Dutch/Shell. However, the merger was doomed by economic problems on the horizon. With oil prices falling, YUKOS defaulted on a $500 million loan after failing to meet its export targets. The merger was called off amid concerns over the financial status of both companies.

In August 1998 an economic crisis leveled the Russian economy. The country had been dependent on oil exports for producing foreign currency and tax revenues. Squeezed by low oil prices, the whole economy collapsed as the ruble plummeted in value and the government defaulted on its debts. Khodorkovsky emerged from the crisis with significantly weakened control over YUKOS. Menatep Bank had collapsed and defaulted on loans, which meant that shares pledged as collateral ended up in the hands of Western banks. Germany's West Merchant Bank, Daiwas of Japan, and the Standard Bank of South Africa together gained control of 32 percent of YUKOS.

In the midst of this bleak situation, YUKOS saw a need for fundamental change. In late 1998 the company initiated a major reorganization of its operations to match a Western model. Western consulting firms were brought in and advised a switch from geographic management to management based on the separation of upstream, downstream, and corporate business activities. Two management companies were created: YUKOS EP (Exploration and Production) and YUKOS RM (Refining

<table>
<tr><td colspan="2">Key Dates:</td></tr>
<tr><td>1993:</td><td>A presidential decree creates YUKOS from several separate oil entities.</td></tr>
<tr><td>1995:</td><td>The production concern OAO Samaraneftegas becomes part of YUKOS.</td></tr>
<tr><td>1996:</td><td>Mikhail Khodorkovsky acquires YUKOS and becomes CEO.</td></tr>
<tr><td>1997:</td><td>YUKOS acquires Eastern Oil Company.</td></tr>
<tr><td>1998:</td><td>YUKOS begins a major reorganization after the Russian economic crisis.</td></tr>
<tr><td>1999:</td><td>Conflict with investors tarnishes YUKOS's reputation.</td></tr>
<tr><td>2001:</td><td>YUKOS regains investor confidence with a new focus on public relations and open communication.</td></tr>
</table>

and Marketing). The central *apparat,* or organization, under the name YUKOS Moscow, worked on forming a broader development strategy. The day-to-day management of production concerns was handed over to individual facilities, and noncore activities were spun off into limited partnerships. Many employees were transferred to these partnerships, lowering payroll costs for YUKOS.

The reorganization was successful in that it lowered the cost of production by almost half. Daughter companies, which had been set up to be self-sufficient, now benefited from the efficiency of centralized repair and construction activities. In a later stage of the reorganization, YUKOS began working with the oil field services firm Schlumberger Ltd. A continuing partnership with Schlumberger helped maintain efficient practices in the Priobskoye oil field and in the area of information technology services. While these changes would improve YUKOS's bottom line in the future, year-end results for 1998 were poor. The company reported a net loss of $680 million.

The following year brought an attempt by Khodorkovsky to make up for the shares that had been lost to foreign banks, a move that sparked allegations of wrongdoing from investors. Specifically, he decided in April 1999 to issue 77 million new shares in YUKOS's three production subsidiaries, more than doubling the number of shares in the companies. The new shares were sold to little-known offshore companies that were suspected, according to the *Washington Post,* of having ties to YUKOS. Investors had long had poor relations with Khodorkovsky, alleging that he stripped profits from subsidiaries by buying their oil at rock-bottom prices and then exporting the same at open-market prices; now the conflict erupted into the open. Billionaire investor Kenneth Dart was the most prominent voice of investor discontent. He owned a 10 percent stake in the production subsidiaries, and accused Khodorkovsky of attempting to dilute his holdings. Khodorkovsky in turn excluded Dart's representatives from shareholder meetings. The chairman of the Russian Securities Commission launched an investigation into the affair and eventually resigned in protest against the conduct of YUKOS. The conflict was not settled until December 1999, when Dart sold his shares and YUKOS managed, in negotiations with shareholders, to regain control over 90 percent of its subsidiary stock.

Emphasizing Transparency in the New Millennium

With YUKOS firmly under the control of its management and the economic crisis receding into the past, 2000 promised to be relatively calm as well as profitable. Net income in 1999 had reached $1.3 billion, which exceeded competitor LUKOIL's earnings despite YUKOS's lower production level. Strong oil prices made even better results likely for 2000, and prompted YUKOS to move ahead on several fronts. The company continued developing the Priobskoye oil field, planning to invest $1.6 billion over the next five years to tap the massive field's reserves. In June YUKOS announced plans to build a pipeline from Angarsk, Siberia, to Beijing, in an agreement with the oil pipeline monopoly Transneft and China National United Oil Corp. The project, expected to begin in 2005, would cost about $1.7 billion.

Some analysts questioned whether YUKOS had the assets to support its investments. The conflict with Kenneth Dart was still fresh in investors' minds and had the potential to complicate attempts to find international financing. Consequently, YUKOS took steps to demonstrate the sincerity of its new investor-friendly image. In June the board of directors approved a corporate governance charter that provided for quarterly U.S. GAAP financial reporting, a transparent management structure and "arm's-length" transactions with all parties. The board also authorized payment of the company's first dividend. YUKOS's actions paid off in August, when the company won a $50 million syndicated loan from Western banks. Khodorkovsky summarized YUKOS' new approach in a meeting with reporters early in 2001. According to the *New York Times,* he sat at company headquarters under a sign reading, "Honesty, Openness, Responsibility," and told reporters, "There has been a change in mentality. People now understand that transparency, good relations with investors and honest behavior in the market in the short term is to your advantage."

Results for 2000 seemed to corroborate Khodorkovsky's new strategy. Net income was $3.3 billion on net revenues of $8.5 billion. Average daily production had increased by 10,000 barrels per day over the previous year, and now stood at 991,000 barrels per day. High oil prices and increased exports were major drivers behind the year's financial success. In 2001, YUKOS continued to capitalize on its strong standing with more acquisitions. In June the company bought a 27 percent stake in the Lithuanian Mazheikiu Nafta refinery, with the understanding that YUKOS would supply crude there and upgrade the Lithuanian facilities. Another acquisition followed in October, when YUKOS paid $30 million for 22 percent of the Anglo-Norwegian engineering group Kvaerner ASA. Kvaerner was expected to help develop the Priobskoye field. The deal, which rescued Kvaerner from financial difficulties, marked a turnaround from the days when Russian companies were courting Western investors.

December brought a mild check on YUKOS's aggressive expansion. In a compromise with the Russian government, the six major oil producers agreed to cut their oil exports by 150,000 barrels per day. The decision was made in a concession to the OPEC countries, who were trying to maintain world oil prices at a high level. YUKOS had opposed the cut, preferring to expand exports as much as possible. Under the deal, companies remained free to export larger volumes of refined oil. YUKOS had shown an ability to adapt in the first decade of its existence, and would likely be able to adjust its mix of production, refining, and retail activities to market conditions.

Principal Subsidiaries

OAO Yuganskneftegas (91.7%); OAO Tomskneft VNK (75%); OAO Samaraneftegas (94.8%); OAO Novokuybyshevsky NPZ (91.4%); OAO Kuybyshevsky NPZ (95.2%); OAO Syzransky NPZ (94%); OAO Achinsky NPZ (42.3%); East Siberian Oil and Gas Company (68%).

Principal Competitors

OAO Gazprom; OAO LUKOIL; OAO Surgutneftegaz; OAO Sibneft; OAO Tatneft.

Further Reading

Bahree, Bhushan, and Jeanne Whalen, "Russia's Yukos Starts to Win Over Its Doubters," *Wall Street Journal*, May 4, 2001, p. A13.

"The Bear Is on a Buying Spree," *Business Week*, November 12, 2001, p. 56.

Brzezinski, Matthew, "Oil Firms in Russia Delay Union," *Wall Street Journal*, May 14, 1998, p. A14.

——, "Oil Giants in Russia Will Merge," *Wall Street Journal*, January 20, 1998, p. A12.

Brzezinski, Matthew, and Gregory White, "Amoco Could End Up Out in the Cold After Its Siberian Partner Is Snapped Up," *Wall Street Journal*, December 9, 1997, p. A19.

Crow, Patrick, "Outlook for Yukos," *Oil & Gas Journal*, May 12, 1997, p. 36.

Cullison, Alan, "Russian Oil Firm Gets Syndicated Loan," *Wall Street Journal*, August 15, 2000, p. A23.

——, "Russian Watchdog Sues Oil Giant, Seeks Probe of Share Shufflings," *Wall Street Journal*, July 22, 1999, p. A22.

"Dart Sells Out of Yukos," *Oil Daily*, December 21, 1999.

Dracheva, Marina, and Michael Ritchie, "Teaming of Russian Giants in Caspian Prompted by Politics, Not Oil," *Oil Daily*, August 2, 2000.

Gaddy, Dean E., "Fresh Opportunities Arise in Russia As Country's Oil Majors Respond to Lessons Learned from the 1990s," *Oil and Gas Journal*, February 25, 2000, pp. 23–26.

——, "Russian Oil Major Yukos Implements Western-Style Reorganization," *Oil and Gas Journal*, June 14, 1999, p. 21.

Galuszka, Peter, "This Oil Giant Is Refining Its Act," *Business Week*, May 13, 1996, p. 116F.

Gill, Patrick, "YUKOS Buys Nafta Stake, Posts Results," *Russia Journal*, June 22, 2001, p. 12.

Gorst, Isabel, "Yukos Forges Partnerships in Its Russian Base and Abroad," *Petroleum Economist*, April 1994, p. 1.

Helmer, John, "Government, Producers Reach Oil Export Compromise," *Russia Journal*, December 7, 2001, p. 2.

Hoffman, David, "Out of Step with Russia?," *Washington Post*, April 18, 1999, p. H01.

Liesman, Steve, "Russian Crisis Yields Foreigners Big Oil Stake," *Wall Street Journal*, September 16, 1998, p. A17.

——, "Russia Sells Oil Interest to Bank Menatep," *Wall Street Journal*, December 24, 1996, p. A6.

Liesman, Steve, and Allanna Sullivan, "Amoco's Russia Oil Venture Stumbles," *Wall Street Journal*, September 11, 1997, p. A2.

Obut, Tina, Avik Sarkar, and Sankar Sunder, "Comparing Russian, Western Major Oil Firms Underscores Problems Unique to Russian Oil," *Oil and Gas Journal*, February 1, 1999, p. 20.

"Pipeline Will Move Siberian Crude Oil to China," *Oil and Gas Journal*, June 12, 2000, p. 75.

Rohlfs, Doug, "Yukos Courts Chevron to Help Develop Big Siberian Field," *Oil Daily*, February 7, 2000.

"Russia to See Its First Merger of Oil Majors," *Oil and Gas Journal*, January 26, 1998, p. 42.

Tavernise, Sabrina, "Fortune in Hand, Russian Tries to Polish Image," *New York Times*, August 18, 2001, p. C3.

Whalen, Jeanne, "Russian Oil Firm's Shares Double Since Profit News," *Wall Street Journal*, August 8, 2000, p. A19.

——, "Russia's Yukos Posts a Strong '99 Profit," *Wall Street Journal*, July 17, 2000, p. A30.

Young, David, "An Arranged Marriage," *Oil and Gas Journal*, December 10, 2001, p. 36.

—Sarah Ruth Lorenz

Panalpina World Transport (Holding) Ltd.

Viaduktstrasse 42
CH-4002 Basel
Switzerland
Telephone: +41-61 226 11 11
Fax: +41-61 226 11 01
Web site: http://www.panalpina.com

Private Company
Incorporated: 1918
Employees: 11,586
Sales: SFr 6.88 billion ($4.27 billion) (2001)
NAIC: 488510 Freight Transportation Arrangement;
   481112 Scheduled Freight Air Transportation; 483111
   Deep Sea Freight Transportation

Private, Switzerland-based Panalpina World Transport (Holding) Ltd. is one of the world's leading integrated freight forwarding and logistics companies, with operations spanning nearly 400 offices in 65 countries. The company's primary activities involve air and sea freight forwarding and shipping services, and Panalpina has built up an impressive fleet to support its operations. Intercontinental air freight accounts for some half of the company's activities, conducted in large part through subsidiary ASB Air, rebranded in 2001 after the company took full control of its SwissGlobalCargo partnership with struggling Swissair. The company's sea freight, which included a fleet of more than 500,000 containers, operates under the ASB Sea brand. Once Europe's leading freight forwarder and logistics concern, Panalpina has slipped in the ranks because of the ongoing consolidation of the industry. The company has fought back, extending its services reach into its competitors' core parcel delivery sector. Panalpina also has targeted the North American and inter-Asian market for its future growth and has set up a partnership with U.S. freight forwarder AIT Worldwide. Supporting these efforts, in 2001, the company restructured its operations into a regional structure comprising Europe, North and South America, Asia, and Africa/Middle East/Commonwealth of Independent States (CIS; former Soviet states).

Panalpina is owned by the Ernst Göhner Foundation and is led by CEO Bruno Sidler and Chairman Gerhard Fischer.

Late 19th-Century Rhine River Transporter

The earliest component of the later Panalpina World Transport was founded as Hans im Obersteg & Co. AG, in 1895, as a freight forwarder operating out of Switzerland. That company, which formed the basis of the later Panalpina Switzerland subsidiary, focused on the Rhine river market. In 1918, a holding company that later coined the Panalpina name was established to cover the Rhine shipping route. That company bought Hans im Obersteg in the 1930s, at which time it took its first steps into maritime shipping.

The future Panalpina continued to extend its operations into the maritime shipping market in the years prior to World War II, and it also began international forwarding activities at this time. After the war, the company found its services in strong demand as the international transport market grew strongly. During the 1950s, the company, which had been operating under a number of brand names, regrouped its subsidiaries under a single holding company, changing its name to Panalpina World Transport, emphasizing its commitment to markets beyond its home base in Swtizerland. Indeed, that country was to represent an increasingly smaller segment of the company's revenues, to the extent that, by the beginning of the next century, Switzerland represented no more than 2 percent of Panalpina's sales.

Panalpina grew strongly throughout the boom economic years of the 1950s and 1960s, establishing itself as one of the European continent's leading freight forwarders. Panalpina also was expanding steadily beyond Europe, forming the basis of a worldwide network that was to include nearly 400 offices in 65 countries before the end of the century. During this time Panalpina made its first moves into the North American market.

The rise of the airline industry, particularly with the success of the Boeing 747 airplane and the popularization of air travel, opened a new opportunity for growth for the company. In 1973, Panalpina launched a new subsidiary, Air Sea Broker, which brought the company into the growing air freight field. That company focused on air charter brokering, with a chief target being the growing oil industry in West Africa; Air Sea Broker also acted as a ship's agency coordinator. By the end of the decade, the company had grown into a leading coordinator in the intercontinental shipping market.

In the early 1980s Panalpina continued to expand its international operations, including strengthening its position in North America. The company gained a larger share of that market in 1984 when it acquired Rohner, Gehring & Co. That company was then merged with Panalpina's other U.S. holdings, forming a new subsidiary, Panalpina Inc.

European Leader in the 1990s

The 1980s saw Panalpina grow into a worldwide force in freight forwarding, particularly in the air freight segment. Air Sea Broker had begun a shift away from the traditional freight forwarder's role of booking space on other carriers' flights to taking control of its own network of charter flights. Working with Cargolux, Panalpina took out long-term contracts on several of that company's chartered freighters. Over the course of the decade the company built up a worldwide network of cargo flights flying under the Air Sea Broker name. By the end of the 1980s, the company was carrying as much tonnage as many of the world's airlines. The company now began to refer to itself as an "integrated forwarder."

As Panalpina grew during the decade, it was able to use its buying power to persuade operators such as Cargolux to set up new routes to serve a wider range of Panalpina's expanding operations. As one industry consultant told *Air Cargo World:* "Panalpina was prepared to do something no other forwarder would do, which is assume some of the prospective capacity risk. That created a whole new channel for just-in-time business." Through the late 1980s, Cargolux had stepped up its development in such markets as South America, Southeast Asia, Australia, and West Africa.

Panalpina's position as an integrated forwarder took a big step ahead when the company launched its very own 747 route between Luxembourg and Huntsville, Alabama. The route, which grew to seven flights per week, was operated using an airplane owned by Atlas Air and operated by Cargolux crew personnel, but was dedicated to Panalpina coordinated freight shipments. Inaugurated in 1990, this route marked the first of a number of similar Panalpina-controlled freighters that enabled the company to set up a worldwide heavyweight air freight network. That same year the company extended its reach into Africa with the acquisition of Interfreight, a business that had generated a strong cross-continental network.

Through the mid-1990s Panalpina continued to grow organically, building up its market position to that of Europe's freight forwarding leader. Yet the beginning of a consolidation drive toward the end of the decade was soon to push the

company out of the number one spot. Meanwhile, Panalpina was facing increasing competition as express and parcel delivery operators such as Federal Express and UPS began to add freight operations.

Full-Service Integrated Forwarder in the 21st Century

Panalpina was forced to fight back. As CEO Sidler told *Air Cargo World:* "I don't think we can become another FedEx or UPS. But I am convinced we can carve out a sizeable chunk of business. We are now reversing the tables. These boys went for our piece of the market, and we are not just standing there like a rabbit in front of a snake. We are doing something, we are fighting back." In 1999, Panalpina announced that it was forming a joint partnership with SAirLogistics, the cargo division of SAirGroup, parent company of Swissair.

The new company, called SwissGlobalCargo, took over all of Air Sea Broker's air activities, as well as the Austrian, Italian, and Swiss operations of SAirLogistic's Jacky Maeder Group cargo subsidiary. Significantly, the joint venture also gave Panalpina its own air charter for the first time. Panalpina held a 55 percent stake in the partnership, while SAirGroup acquired a 10 percent stake in Panalpina—a move that prompted speculation on a possible future public offering of Panalpina. The launch of SwissGlobalCargo created the industry's first fully integrated air freight services group. In addition to offering door-to-door services, SwissGlobalCargo was able to promise guaranteed delivery times and "integrated hardfreight," freight contracts with no weight limits. Said CEO Sidler of the joint venture: "For a long time we have differentiated ourselves from other forwarders with Air Sea Broker, but it has been very hard to make the breakthrough to being seen as an integrated forwarder. The perception among our customers was that we were not bad, but that we could not really offer true door-to-door service. But now people will look at us differently. Using Swissair, we can fine-tune the network so we can offer true door-to-door services."

Panalpina soon found itself in full control of SwissGlobalCargo as Swissair floundered at the turn of the millennium. In May 2001, Panalpina bought out its partner in SwissGlobalCargo, and subsequently announced its intention to change its subsidiary's name to ASB Air. At the same time, Swissair sold back its 10 percent stake in Panalpina to parent Ernst Göhner Foundation.

Panalpina continued to eye its global expansion, targeting specifically the U.S. and inter-Asian market. The company expected much of its near-term growth to come through organic expansion, including the setting up of a partnership agreement with U.S.-based freight forwarder AIT Worldwide in 2001. The company hoped to establish similar partnerships elsewhere, without ruling out making acquisitions to boost its presence in the Asian market.

In order to bring its operations closer to its local markets, Panalpina underwent a reorganization at the beginning of 2002 that turned over much of its decision-making to four regional divisions: Europe, North and South America, Asia, and Africa/Middle East/CIS. Although the company's headquarters in

Key Dates:

1895: Hans im Obersteg & Co. AG, a forwarding company based in Switzerland, is established.

1918: Panalpina's predecessor company is founded.

1930s: Panalpina acquires Hans im Obersteg and expands into maritime shipping and international forwarding.

1954: The company reorganizes under a single name, Panalpina World Transport.

1973: Panalpina launches the Air Sea Broker subsidiary, which grows to become a leading air-based freight forwarder.

1984: Company acquires Rohner, Gehrig & Co. of the United States, then regroups all of its U.S. operations under a single Panalpina Inc. subsidiary.

1990: Company inaugurates Air Sea 747 chartered freight flights between Luxembourg and Huntsville, Alabama.

1999: The creation of SwissGlobalCargo joint venture with SAirLogistics enables Panalpina to become an integrated logistics company.

2001: Panalpina takes full control of SwissGlobalCargo, renaming the subsidiary ASB Air.

2002: Panalpina reorganizes and adopts a regional operational structure.

Basel continued to guide overall development of the group, as well as coordination with the Air Sea companies, each regional division was given its own chief executive officer in order to respond to the specific demands of its market.

Principal Subsidiaries

Europe: Panalpina Management AG; Panalpina Finance Limited Jersey; Panalpina AG; Air Sea Broker AG; Pantainer AG; Panalpina Insurance Broker AG; Hausmann Transport AG; SGC SwissGlobalCargo AG; Jacky Maeder AG; Avalog AG; Panalpina Welttransport GmbH (Germany); Air Sea Broker (ASB Deutschland) GmbH (Germany); SGC SwissGlobalCargo (Deutschland) GmbH (Germany); Panalpina Aktiengesellschaft (Austria); Panalpina Welttransport GmbH (Austria); Jacky Maeder Luftfracht GmbH (Austria); Panalpina World Transport N.V. (Belgium); Air Sea Broker Belgium N.V.; Panalpina World Transport B.V. (Netherlands); Panalpina Luxembourg S.A.; Panalpina France Transports Internationaux S.A.; Panalpina World Transport Limited (U.K.); SGC SwissGlobalCargo U.K. Ltd.; Panalpina World Transport (Ireland) Ltd.; Panalpina World Transport ZAO (Russia); Panalpina World Transport Ltd. (Russia); Panalpina Trasporti Mondiali S.P.A. (Italy); Panalpina Transportes Mundiales S.A. (Spain); Panalpina Transportes Mundiais Lda. (Portugal); Pantrans Transitarios S.A. (Portugal); Panalpina AB (Sweden); Panalpina Logistics AB (Sweden); Panalpina World Transport Nakliyat Ltd. Srk. (Turkey). North, Central and South America:

Tramo Holding Inc. (Canada); Panalpina World Transport (Eastern) Ltd. (Canada); Panalpina Inc. (Canada); Panalpina Inc. (U.S.A.); Management Logistics Services, Inc. (U.S.A.); Hensel, Bruckmann & Lorbacher, Inc. (U.S.A.); SGC Swiss-GlobalCargo, Inc. (U.S.A.); World Freight Corporation (U.S.A.); Panalpina Transportes Mundiales S.A. (Argentina); Panalpina Ltda. (Brazil); Management Logistics Services Comercial Ltda. (Brazil); Panalpina Chile Transportes Mundiales Ltda.; Panalpina Servicios Aduanales (Chile); Panalpina Transportes Mundiales S.A. (Chile); Panalquito, Panalpina Transportes; Mundiales Ecuador S.A.; DAPSA Depositos Aduaneros Santa Fé Panalpina S.A. de Bogotá (Colombia); Invertrans S.A. Santa Fé de Bogotá (Colombia); Panalpina S.A. Santa Fé de Bogotá (Colombia); Panalpina Transportes Mundiales, S.A. de C.V. (Mexico); Panalpina S.A. (Panama); Panalpina Transportes Mundiales S.A.(Peru); Patrasa S.A., Agencia de Aduana (Peru); Panalpina Transportes Mundiales C.A. (Venezuela); Panalpina C.A. (Venezuela); Inversiones Ortrac C.A. (Venezuela); Panalpina Uruguay Transportes Mundiales S.A.; Asia and Australia: Panalpina China Limited (Hong Kong); Panalpina World Transport (India) Pvt. Ltd.; PT Panalpina Nusajaya Transport (Indonesia); Panalpina World Transport (Japan) Ltd.; Panalpina Korea Ltd.; Panalpina Transport (Malaysia) Sdn. Bhd.; Panalpina World Transport (Singapore) Pte. Ltd.; Panalpina World Transport Ltd. (Taiwan); Panalpina Taiwan Ltd.; Panalpina World Transport (Thailand) Limited; Panalpina World Transport (Pty) Limited (Australia). Africa, Near and Middle East: Panalpina Transportes Mundiais-Navegaçao e Transitos, S.A.R.L. Luanda; Panalpina Transports Mondiaux Congo SARL; Panalpina Transports Mondiaux Gabon S.A.; Panalpina (Ghana) Limited Accra; Panalpina World Transport (Nigeria) Limited; Panalpina Gulf LLC (Dubai); (Panalpina Qatar) WLL; Panalpina (Bahrain) WLL.

Principal Competitors

APL Limited; BAX Global Inc; CNF Inc.; Deutsche Post AG; EGL, Inc.; Exel plc; Expeditors International of Washington, Inc.; FedEx Corporation; Fritz Companies, Inc.; GeoLogistics Corporation; Kuehne & Nagel International AG; Deutsche Lufthansa AG; Nippon Express Co., Ltd.; Preussag AG; Stinnes AG; TNT Post Group N.V.; United Parcel Service, Inc.; UTi Worldwide Inc.

Further Reading

Conway, Peter, "Chartering New Courses," *Air Cargo World,* July 1999.

Hailey, Roger, "Panalpina in Regional Split," *Lloyd's List,* October 1, 2001.

"Panalpina Concentrates on Rapid Growth Curve," *Neue Zurcher Zeitung,* May 5, 2001.

"Restless Panalpina Looks to Organic Growth or Shopping Spree," *Lloyd's List,* May 14, 2001.

"SwissGlobalCargo: Panalpina, SAirGroup in Partnership," *Shippers Today,* July 1999.

—M.L. Cohen

Panamerican Beverages, Inc.

Torre Dresdner Bank
Piso No. 7, Calle 50
Panama City
Panama
Telephone: (507) 223-8723

Panamco LLC
701 Waterford Way, Suite 800
Miami, Florida 33126
U.S.A.
Telephone: (305) 929-0800
Web site: http://www.panamco.com

Public Company
Incorporated: 1945
Employees: 28,500
Sales: $2.65 billion (2001)
Stock Exchanges: New York
Ticker Symbol: PB
NAIC: 312111 Soft Drink Manufacturing

Panamerican Beverages, Inc., also known as Panamco LLC, is the world's second largest bottler of Coca-Cola soft drink products and the leading beverage bottler in Latin America. Based in Panama City and in Miami, Florida, Panamco boasts a relationship with The Coca-Cola Company stretching back more than 60 years. Entering the 21st century, the two companies are more closely linked than ever: Panamco is one of an elite group of "anchor" bottlers for the soft drink giant, and Coca-Cola owns nearly 25 percent of Panamco, with two seats on Panamco's board of directors. Panamco's operations stretch across a major portion of Latin America, holding exclusive Coca-Cola bottling licenses in most of Mexico (excluding Mexico City), the states of Sao Paulo and Mato Grosso do Sul in Brazil, most of Colombia, half of Guatemala, and all of Venezuela, Costa Rica, and Nicaragua. Apart from the Coca-Cola line, Panamco also produces, markets, and distributes other Coca-Cola brands, including Beat, Delaware Punch, Frescolita, Hit, Sprite, Fanta, Kuat, Quatro, Lift, and Canada Dry. Altogether, Coca-Cola products account for 90 percent of Panamco's revenues, which topped $2.65 billion in

2001. The rest of its sales come from sales of beer, including the Heineken and Kaiser labels in Brazil, and Regional in Venezuela; bottled water, including the Risco, Premio, Agua de Lourdes, Crystal, Manantial, and Top labels; and other soft drinks, including regional specialties such as Keloco (Mexico), Club K (Colombia), and Powerade (Costa Rica). Panamco has long succeeded in navigating the often turbulent waters of its Latin American markets, in part by maintaining a decentralized structure of more or less autonomous, country specific subsidiaries. The company has been listed on the New York Stock Exchange since 1993, and reports its earnings in U.S. dollars. In 2000, Panamco moved its main headquarters from its longtime home in Panama City to new offices in Miami, Florida. With little room for additional geographic expansion—the company already had captured nearly 25 percent of the continent's total soft drink market—Panamco was targeting initiatives to encourage an increase in soft drink consumption. Most of Latin America's markets have per capita consumption rates of less than half of their neighbor to the north. Yet with a far larger proportion of the population under the age of 30, the Latin American beverage market remains an area with strong potential for future growth.

Family-Owned Bottler in the 1940s

In 1941, the American Albert H. Staton led a group of investors in acquiring a number of Coca-Cola bottling franchises in Mexico. That group migrated to Panama during the years of World War II and, in 1945, the company incorporated as Panamerican Beverages. By then the company, which became a family-run concern, began expanding into other Latin American markets in order to shield itself from the risks of operating with a single market in the often turbulent Latin American region. The company acquired its first Coca-Cola bottling franchise in Brazil in 1944. A year later, Panamco moved into Colombia as well.

In 1950, Panamco gained the franchise for the state of Sao Paulo, one of the most important markets in Brazil. This franchise provided the launch pad for the company's expansion into other parts of Brazil. Over the next several decades, Panamco succeeded in establishing itself as a major Coca-Cola bottler in its three core markets of Mexico, Brazil, and Colombia. For

Key Dates:

1941: Albert H. Staton leads a group of investors in acquiring a small Coca-Cola bottling operation in Mexico.

1944: Panamco acquires a Coca-Cola bottling franchise in Brazil.

1945: Panamco incorporates in Panama and acquires a bottling franchise in Colombia.

1950: The company acquires the Coca-Cola bottling and distribution franchise for Sao Paulo, Brazil.

1993: The company is listed on the New York Stock Exchange.

1994: The acquisition of Refrigerantes de Santos gives Panamco production and distribution rights to Coca-Cola and distribution rights to Kaiser and Heineken beer in the coastal region of Sao Paulo.

1995: Panamco is named one of Coca-Cola's anchor bottlers; it acquires Embotelladora Tica and 85 percent of the Costa Rican soft drink market.

1996: The company acquires Embotelladora del Valle S.A. and Industrias del Atlantico SA and gains 100 percent control of the Costa Rican Coca-Cola market.

1997: The company enters Venezuela with the $1.1 billion purchase of Coca-Cola y Hit de Venezuela, the country's leading bottler; it enters Nicaragua through the acquisition of Embotelladora Milca, that country's only Coca-Cola bottler.

1998: The company buys the leading Coca-Cola bottler in Guatemala, Embotelladora Central SA, for $39 million.

1999: Panamco suffers its first ever net loss, which reaches $59 million for the year.

2002: The company announces that it has returned to profitability, posting $118 million in net profit on $2.65 billion in revenues for the 2001 year.

much of this period, Panamco operated in its markets through three primary subsidiaries, Azteca in Mexico, Indega in Colombia, and Spal in Brazil. Over time, the company opened up the capital of these subsidiaries to local minority shareholders. This policy helped the company continue to build its position, despite the recurring waves of political and economic turmoil that affected these markets in the last decades of the 20th century.

Indeed, Panamco's close ties to the Latin American community helped it to survive where many other companies failed. As Chairman and CEO Francisco Sanchez-Loaeza told *Industry Week:* "Many American and European companies come to Latin America to do business, but the vast majority of them are not successful. The problem is they do not understand the complexities of the Latin American business environment. Companies that have been here a while and understand the culture, they survive."

Panamco did more than just survive. By the early 1990s, the company had grown to become the world's largest Coca-Cola bottler outside of the United States, and the largest bottler in Latin America. Part of Panamco's success was due to Coca-Cola's vast marketing campaign, with an advertising budget among the largest in the world, which helped impose the brand as one of the few truly global brands and make it one of the world's top beverages. Panamco also had capitalized on the strength of Coca-Cola's expanded portfolio, which included such brand names as Sprite, Fanta, and Hit, as well as a number of brands and flavors specific to the Latin American market (Colombian consumers, for example, prefer apple-flavored soft drinks). The company also added sales of bottled mineral water.

By 1993, Panamco had topped $1 billion in revenues for the first time. The company now prepared to move to a new level of operations. For this, the company abandoned its family-owned status and opened its capital to outside investors. In 1993, the company went public on the New York Stock Exchange, where it sold more than 15 million shares. The company also adopted U.S.-based GAAP accounting principles and began reporting its financial statements in U.S. dollars.

In 1994, the Mexican economy entered a crisis when the peso was sharply devalued. Yet Panamco maintained its course, and even stepped up its investments in that country, modernizing production facilities and rolling out new packaging, such as disposable plastic bottles. As Sanchez-Loaeza told *Industry Week:* "We didn't panic and that helped us. We operated much the same as if nothing were wrong. During the devaluation we didn't reduce investments, especially in assets that could generate volumes. We suffered less than our competitors because we invested in new markets. We spread the risk, and it minimized damage from the crisis. It's a long-term business we're in and we always see it that way."

Similar economic difficulties faced the company in Brazil, where inflation had hit double-digit rates. Yet there too Panamco maintained its investment program, including the acquisition of Refrigerantes de Santos, giving it production and distribution rights to Coca-Cola and distribution rights to Kaiser and Heineken beer in the coastal region of Sao Paulo. Meanwhile, the company made a new public offering of more than six million shares, raising funding to pursue the buyout of its major subsidiaries, increasing its stake in Azteca to 74 percent and its position in its Colombian holding companies to 88 percent. Panamco now prepared itself for a still more dramatic expansion program.

Bottling Champion in the New Century

A major step in Panamco's growth came in 1995 when The Coca-Cola Company named its largest Latin American bottler as one of its exclusive class of "anchor bottlers." In this way, the Atlanta-based soft drink maker took a direct interest in Panamco's growth—building its participation in the company to include a 16 percent voting share—while pledging to contribute financial and marketing muscle to Panamco's expansion plans in the region.

The anchor bottler designation was followed by an important acquisition for Panamco. At the end of 1995, the company acquired Embotelladora Tica, based in Costa Rica, marking the company's first expansion beyond its longtime core markets of Mexico, Colombia, and Brazil. Meanwhile, in its primary base Panamco continued to go from strength to strength, building its market share in Mexico to 69 percent, in Colombia to 51 percent, and in Brazil to 54 percent. The Tica acquisition, meantime, gave Panamco an 85 percent share of the Costa Rican soft drink market.

At the same time, Panamco continued its policy of buying out minority partners in its local subsidiaries. By 1995, the company had achieved 85 percent and 97 percent of its Brazilian and Colombian subsidiaries, respectively. The company was also busy on its product development, introducing Fresca and Risco purified bottled water in Mexico; Cherry Coke and another Coca-Cola brand, Guarana Tai, in Brazil; and the apple-flavored Lift drink in Colombia. The company also continued implementing a strategic marketing and distribution plan, placing 57,000 coolers—for a total of 132,000 company-owned coolers—in its Latin American markets.

Panamco began preparing for the consolidation of the Latin American bottling market, where the Coca-Cola franchise branch counted more than 100 bottling companies. Panamco expected to become a motor behind the creation of a smaller number of far larger and more profitable bottling companies. In 1996, the company increased its coverage of the Costa Rican market, paying $14 million to acquire Embotelladora del Valle S.A. and Industrias del Atlantico SA.

Panamco's position as one of only eight Coca-Cola anchor bottlers worldwide also placed it in primary position to acquire new franchises in its operating territory. Such was the case in 1996 when the company took over two franchises in Colombia that had been held previously by competing bottlers. By the end of that year, Panamco's revenues had doubled in the short period since its public offering, topping $2 billion for the first time.

In 1997, Panamco entered a new market, Venezuela, when it paid $1.1 billion for Coca-Cola y Hit de Venezuela, that country's largest soft drink bottler. Soon after, Panamco entered another Latin American market, buying up Embotelladora Milca in Nicaragua. That $42 million purchase gave Panamco 100 percent control of the Nicaraguan Coca-Cola products market as well—and a 78 percent share of the country's overall soft drinks market. Meanwhile, Panamco continued building up its shares in its regional subsidiaries, boosting its ownership of its Mexican subsidiary to 95 percent. The company also more than doubled its placement of coolers and vending machines, topping 320,000 company-owned units. In addition, Panamco launched its new "100 meters rule," establishing a company goal of offering its soft drinks within 100 meters of every consumer. Rolled out at first in Mexico, the "100 meters rule" was quickly extended to all of the company's operating areas.

Panamco turned to Guatemala in 1998, buying up that market's leading Coca-Cola bottler, Embotelladora Central, S.A., for $39 million. That purchase gave the company a 40 percent share of the Guatemalan soft drink market and helped cement the company's implantation in Central America. The company then joined its Guatemalan, Costa Rican, and Nicaraguan operations under an integrated management structure in order to achieve greater regional synergy. Another strategic acquisition came in September 1998, when Panamco paid $48 million for Refrigerantes do Oeste, SA, based in the state of Mato Grosso do Sul, where it held a market share of more than 49 percent.

Panamco's rise was cut short in 1999, however, when it reported its first ever net loss, reaching $60 million for the year. The company responded by an extensive cost-cutting exercise, which included the elimination of nearly 3,500 jobs. Despite its difficulties, Panamco maintained its longstanding commitment to investment. As part of its "100 meter rule," the company continued its aggressive placement of coolers, adding more than 75,000 new coolers and vending machines that year, bringing the company's total number of such outlets to more than 666,000. Panamco also began exploring nontraditional distribution routes, such as street corner and even traffic light sales.

Soft drink consumption in Latin America, where much of the economy was hard hit by a lingering recession and a series of natural disasters, continued to shrink at the turn of the millennium. Nonetheless, Mexico proved to be the company's bright spot, posting increases of some 20 percent in revenues. This helped the company reduce its losses somewhat, to just $14 million for the year. By 2001, Panamco appeared to have completed its turnaround, posting a net income of $188 million. Part of the company's success came through strong increases in sales of bottled water, one of its fastest-growing product lines. Yet Coca-Cola remained the true motor for Panamco's growth as it eyed further expansion throughout Latin America in the coming years.

Principal Subsidiaries

Panamco Mexico, S.A. de C.V.; Refrescos do Brasil S.A. (Brazil; 90%); Panamco Colombia, S.A. (97%); Embotelladora Coca-Cola y Hit de Venezuela S.A.; Embotelladora Panamco Costa Rica, S.A.; Embotelladora Milca, S.A. (Nicaragua); Embotelladora Central, S.A. (Panamco Guatemala).

Principal Competitors

Bavaria S.A.; Companhia de Bebidas das Américas; Coca-Cola FEMSA, S.A. de C.V.; Cervecería Nacional, S.A.; Embotelladora Andina S.A.; Grupo Continental, S.A.; Pepsi-Gemex, S.A. de C.V.

Further Reading

Michaels, Anthony J., "Coke's Monster Bottler Has Latin Fizz," *Fortune,* December 11, 1995, p. 204.

"New Coke Bottler Hopes to Boost Profits in Venezuela," *Panorama,* July 1, 1997.

"No Fizz to Panamerican Beverages Results," *South Florida Business Journal,* November 2, 2000.

Van Yoder, Steven, "Thirst for Success," *Industry Week,* May 15, 2000.

—M.L. Cohen

Paul, Weiss, Rifkind, Wharton & Garrison

1285 Avenue of the Americas
New York, New York 10019-6064
U.S.A.
Telephone: (212) 373-3000
Fax: (212) 757-3990
Web site: http://www.paulweiss.com

Private Partnership
Founded: 1923
Employees: 1,052
Gross Billings: $185 million (2000 est.)
NAIC: 541110 Offices of Lawyers

Paul, Weiss, Rifkind, Wharton & Garrison is a globally oriented, full-service law firm with headquarters in New York City and other offices in Beijing, Hong Kong, London, Paris, Tokyo, and Washington, D.C. The firm's core practice is concentrated in the areas of litigation and corporate law, including mergers and acquisitions and public and private financing. It is also prominent in such fields as antitrust, communications, corporate reorganization, employee benefits and executive compensation, entertainment, environmental regulation, intellectual property, new media and the Internet, personal representation, real estate, and tax and bankruptcy.

Progressive Politics: 1923–50

Jewish lawyers who entered practice in New York City a century ago found it difficult to join non-Jewish law firms and impossible to become partners; instead they formed their own all-Jewish ones. The firm that eventually became Paul, Weiss, Rifkind, Wharton & Garrison was founded before World War I as a general commercial practice for a small group of wealthy Jewish entrepreneurs of German origin, such as the Straus family, who owned Macy's department store, and the Cullman family of tobacco merchants later associated with Philip Morris Companies. One of these lawyers was Samuel William Weiss. In 1923, his son Louis started his own firm with a Columbia University Law School classmate, John F. Wharton, a Protestant. They intended their firm, Weiss & Wharton, to be one in which Jews and Gentiles could work together as partners, em-

ployees, and clients. They merged with the earlier firm a few years later, and it now became Cohen, Cole, Weiss & Wharton. Wharton was a specialist in theatrical law who became the sole trustee of the trusts that controlled the rights to Cole Porter's songs after the composer's death.

With the coming of the Roosevelt Administration's New Deal, Cohen, Cole, Weiss & Wharton emerged as a firm stocked with partners identified with liberal politics and the fortunes of the Democratic party. One of its lawyers, Walter Pollak, represented the "Scottsboro Boys"—four young Alabama black men convicted of raping a white woman and sentenced to death in a cause celebre of the 1930s. Lloyd K. Garrison, great-grandson of the abolitionist William Lloyd Garrison and former dean of the University of Wisconsin Law School, joined the firm in 1945 and represented such clients as poet Langston Hughes, playwright Arthur Miller, and physicist J. Robert Oppenheimer in cases involving their left-of-center political views. Another acquisition was Randolph Paul, a tax lawyer who left the U.S. Department of the Treasury in 1944 and, along with Garrison, added his name to the firm. This brought the firm's roster of lawyers to 13.

Paul, Weiss became the first major New York law firm to take a woman partner, Carolyn Agger—albeit in the firm's Washington office, established in 1946, rather than in New York. In 1949, it hired William I. Coleman, Jr., a black graduate—first in his class—of Harvard University Law School who had served as law clerk to Supreme Court Justice Felix Frankfurter. A Philadelphia native, Coleman came to New York because, he said, no firm in Philadelphia would hire him, and went to work at Paul, Weiss mainly because no other New York firm offered him a job. Also in 1949, Paul, Weiss became the first major Wall Street firm to move its headquarters to midtown Manhattan.

A Galaxy of Stars: 1950–80

A major impetus to the firm's growth and prosperity was the entry of Simon Rifkind in 1950. Rifkind drafted New Deal legislation in the 1930s and served as a federal judge in the 1940s before leaving the bench to buttress his family's finances. When he joined Paul, Weiss, the firm had a dozen partners but only one engaged in trial work. Rifkind extended the firm's presence in

Company Perspectives:

Our objectives are, by pooling our energies, talents and resources, to achieve the highest order of excellence in the practice of the art, the science and the profession of the law; through such practice to earn a living and to derive the stimulation and pleasure of worthwhile adventure; and in all things to govern ourselves as members of a free democratic society with responsibilities both to our profession and our country.

litigation and was invaluable as a "rainmaker" bringing in new business for the firm. He never retired and died in 1995 at the age of 94. It was at Rifkind's urging that Adlai Stevenson, after the second of his two unsuccessful bids for the U.S. presidency, combined his small Chicago law firm with Paul, Weiss in 1957. This alliance dissolved after John F. Kennedy was elected president in 1960, because Stevenson and his three Chicago partners all joined the new administration. About this time the Washington office, directed by Agger, merged with the law firm of her husband, Abe Fortas, who later became a Supreme Court justice. (By 1970 Paul, Weiss had recreated the Washington office, which was mainly devoted to tax practice.)

In his posthumously published autobiography, Arthur Liman, who rejoined Paul, Weiss in 1963, after a brief stint in the Manhattan district attorney's office, recalled that at the time the firm had some 20 partners and about 50 lawyers working out of a single building on Madison Avenue. "The lion's share of the practice was generated by Rifkind himself, and a lot of it consisted of litigation," he wrote. "We had only a few corporate clients, but the younger partners, spurred by Rifkind, wanted to build the firm not just in tax, litigation, and entertainment law, where we already shone, but in the corporate field as well." Rifkind recruited Morris Abram, who had helped argue the cases in which the Supreme Court voided racially discriminatory voting districts and established the one-person, one-vote principle. He also brought in Theodore Sorenson, one of President Kennedy's closest aides. The succeeding Johnson Administration also provided talent in the form of former Supreme Court justice and ambassador to the United Nations Arthur J. Goldberg and Attorney General Ramsey Clark, a Texan whom Rifkind hoped would attract oil companies to the firm.

Paul, Weiss's new stars found it difficult to adjust to the more mundane, although more lucrative, environment of private law practice. Abram resigned to become president of Brandeis University but returned after a brief, tempestuous tenure on campus. Clark's politics had turned far to the left, and he departed from Paul, Weiss after only three years, later telling Benjamin Weiser of the *Washington Post,* "I found the commercial law practice unpleasant, the role that money played in it unpleasant, and the issues that were chosen by the clients—it wasn't how I wanted to spend my time." Sorenson unsuccessfully sought the Democratic party nomination for the Senate before finding fulfillment as the firm's first international lawyer; in 1993 he drafted a constitution for Tajikistan, one of the new nations emerging from the former Soviet Union. Goldberg—the prize catch who briefly took third place on the firm's name, after "Paul, Weiss"—never really adjusted to private practice.

Described in Paul Hoffman's book *Lions in the Street* as having "an ego as big as the Bronx," he ran unsuccessfully for governor, then left to establish his own Washington practice.

The star system antagonized many of the hard-working associates at Paul, Weiss, who comprised two-thirds of its 110 lawyers in 1970. Plush new quarters on Park Avenue could not obscure the firm's reputation as a "sweatshop" where the associates labored ten or more hours a day in hopes of one day becoming a partner. Still, the firm's prestige remained high among idealistic law students, since it was willing to hire young lawyers despite knowing that they might remain only a short time before going into teaching or government service. Liman wrote that Paul, Weiss remained intensely concerned with political issues as well as making money, representing both "libeled, rich clients who could comfortably afford our services and poor ones who couldn't afford to pay anything. . . . We have also taken on pro bono appeals in capital punishment cases. We brought the first environmental cases—opposing a proposed nuclear plant on the Hudson River. We have handled First Amendment and voters' rights cases. Every economical and social upheaval in the country has found its way into our office—the quiz show scandals, the salad oil fraud that nearly toppled American Express, the civil rights movement, the criminal case against Spiro Agnew, the asbestos cases, the back-office crisis on Wall Street in the 1960s, the takeover mania of the 1980s." Even Goldberg shook up the status quo by representing Curt Flood in a lawsuit that eventually established free agency for major league baseball players.

Liman credited Rifkind for a collegial atmosphere at Paul, Weiss, which had no managing partner to run the firm either alone or at the head of a small executive committee. "In his view," Liman wrote, "every associate who came to work at Paul, Weiss should have the same opportunity to become a partner and to build a practice, and each partner, even the newest, should be free to choose and develop his or her own clients, subject only to the rules of conflict of interest. This open-door policy has clearly been one of the reasons Paul, Weiss has consistently been able to attract top law school graduates, and why, conversely, we have never lost a partner to another firm."

The Liman Years and After: 1980–2000

By the 1980s, Liman himself was becoming as legendary a lawyer as Rifkind as well as his successor in rainmaking. In the words of another attorney, Liman was the glue binding Paul, Weiss together. By the time he appeared on the national stage in 1987 as special counsel to the Senate select committee that investigated the Iran-Contra scandal, Liman had acquired a reputation as perhaps the most outstanding white-collar defense attorney of his generation. (He later recruited a committee member, Senator Warren Rudman of New Hampshire, for the firm.) Among Liman's clients were mutual-fund embezzler Robert Vesco; John Zaccaro, the husband of vice-presidential candidate Geraldine Ferraro, who was accused of misusing funds from court-entrusted estates; magnates such as Steve Ross of Warner Communications Inc. (and subsequently Time Warner Inc.) and Herbert Siegel of Chris-Craft Industries, Inc.; and such especially rough diamonds as corporate raiders Carl Icahn and Ronald Perelman.

Key Dates:

1923: Louis Weiss and John F. Wharton open a law firm that soon merges with an older one.
1950: Simon Rifkind joins the firm and quickly establishes his leadership.
1957: Adlai Stevenson is the first of several prominent Democrats to join the firm.
1989: Arthur Liman, now the firm's leading partner, represents junk-bond king Michael Milken.
1994: Jeh Johnson becomes Paul, Weiss, Rifkind, Wharton & Garrison's first black partner.

Writing for *Institutional Investor* in 1989, Frederic Dannen declared that Liman had "the ineffable aura of a star for the simple reason that he rarely loses a case." At the head of a ten-lawyer team, Liman defended wealthy junk bond consultant Michael Milken against insider-trading charges. This case contributed to record profits for Paul, Weiss, but did not enhance his reputation. His client eventually pleaded guilty to five of the 98 felony charges on Liman's assurance that the two-year sentences would run concurrently. Instead, Milken was sentenced to serve time consecutively, although in the end he only spent 22 months in custody.

Paul, Weiss suffered a more severe blow to its reputation in 1993, when federal regulators investigating the extensive savings and loan failures that marked the end of the 1980s accused the firm of fraud and misappropriation of funds in connection with the demise of Miami-based CenTrust Savings Bank, whose collapse cost taxpayers more than $1.7 billion. Beginning in 1983, more than 55 Paul, Weiss lawyers represented CenTrust at a cost of $12 million and, according to the government, became involved in the shady investments and financial dealings of the bank's chairman (who later went to prison) at the expense of depositors. Paul, Weiss denied any wrongdoing and settled the case at a cost of $45 million. Most or all of that sum was covered by an insurance pool formed in 1971 by 21 New York law firms.

Paul, Weiss had 333 lawyers in 1988, of which 82 were partners. The firm grossed about $161.5 million that year and netted $65 million, according to the magazine the *American Lawyer*. The ensuing recession ended the Wall Street hyperactivity that had brought so much business to the firm in the 1980s, and about 40 associates were let go. Even so, Paul, Weiss remained among the nation's 15 most profitable big law firms in the mid-1990s, according to the *American Lawyer*. Among its major clients were such powerhouses as Continental Grain, Goldman, Sachs & Co., Time Warner, Viacom, and Sumitomo Corp.

Liman died of cancer at the age of 64 in 1997 but left behind such well-regarded protegees as Mark Belnick, Martin Flumenbaum, and Robert Schumer. Management of the firm remained decentralized. Instead of appointing a managing partner, it continued to be headed by a managing committee, elected each year, which in turn appointed the other committees that together ran the firm. A small committee of influential partners—also elected annually—determined each partner's share of the profits.

In his autobiography, Liman wrote that when he entered the firm in 1957, his "class" consisted of five associates, four of whom eventually became partners, but that by the late 1990s, out of an incoming group of between 30 and 40 associates, only five would make it to partner. In 1957, there was only one woman associate in New York, and she was also the firm's only African American lawyer. By 1997, he declared, "Paul, Weiss now has nine female partners and more than 75 female associates—not a perfect ratio, but better than where we were." But a national survey that year asking 1,255 female lawyers at 77 large firms to assess working conditions for women ranked Paul, Weiss dead last. Its response was to hire a management consultant in order to try to improve its image. The firm did not have a black partner until 1994, when Jeh Johnson—a protegé of Liman and Abram—was promoted. Another African American lawyer, Ted Wells, was named partner and co-chairman of the firm's 150-lawyer litigation department in 2000. Described as one of the nation's premier trial lawyers, he was the first partner in 30 years to be brought in to Paul, Weiss from another firm.

Paul, Weiss had about 500 lawyers in 2001. In 1999, it signed a ten-year lease renewal for 391,975 square feet of space at 1285 Avenue of the Americas, an office building between West 51st and 52nd streets in midtown Manhattan.

Principal Competitors

Cravath Swane & Moore; Davis Polk & Wardwell; Proskauer Rose LLP; Shearman & Sterling; Simpson Thacher and Bartlett; Skadden Arps Slate Meagher & Flom; Sullivan & Cromwell; Weil Gotschal & Manges.

Further Reading

Barrett, Paul M., and Dean Starkman, "Legal Beat: Paul Weiss Faces Future After a Star Partner's Death," *Wall Street Journal,* July 29, 1997, pp. B1, B6.

Dannen, Frederic, "Arthur Liman for the Defense," *Institutional Investor,* December 1989, pp. 116+.

Dorsen, David, "Paul, Weiss, Goldberg—What Kind of Ticket Is That?" *New York,* April 13, 1970, pp. 44–6.

Galen, Michele, "Got Big Deals, Big Problems, Big Bucks? Get Arthur Liman," *Business Week,* May 15, 1989, pp. 112, 114.

Goldstein, Matthew, "Better Representation for Women?" *Crain's New York Business,* June 15, 1998, p. 16.

Himelstein, Linda, and Gail DeGeorge, "The Mud on a Fancy Law Firm," *Business Week,* August 16, 1993, pp. 91–2.

Hoffman, Jan, "Outsider? Insider? A Lawyer Wins As Both," *New York Times,* January 12, 2000, p. B2.

Hoffman, Paul, *Lions in the Street.* New York: Saturday Review/Dutton, 1973.

Jensen, Ruth Henley, "Paul Weiss Pact Remains Puzzling," *National Law Journal,* October 11, 1993, p. 9.

Kaufman, Jonathan, "As Blacks Rise High in the Executive Suite, CEO's Often Are Jewish," *Wall Street Journal,* April 22, 1998, pp. A1, A12.

Liman, Arthur L., *Lawyer: A Life of Counsel and Controversy,* New York: Public Affairs, 1998.

Weiser, Benjamin, "Putting Power into Practice," *Washington Post,* March 27, 1994, pp. H1, H6.

Wetzler, Cynthia Magriel, "Theodore Sorenson Maintains Optimism," *New York Times,* April 23, 1995, Sec. 13 (Westchester), p. 21.

—Robert Halasz

⊞ Pitney Bowes

Pitney Bowes Inc.

One Elmcroft Road
Stamford, Connecticut 06926-0700
U.S.A.
Telephone: (203) 356-5000
Fax: (203) 351-6059
Web site: http://www.pitneybowes.com

Public Company
Incorporated: 1920 as Pitney-Bowes Postage Meter
   Company
Employees: 29,000
Sales: $4.12 billion (2001)
Stock Exchanges: New York
Ticker Symbol: PBI
NAIC: 333313 Office Machinery Manufacturing; 334290
   Other Communications Equipment Manufacturing;
   514199 All Other Information Services; 522298 All
   Other Nondepository Credit Intermediation; 561110
   Office Administrative Services

Pitney Bowes Inc. (PB) is the world's largest manufacturer and supplier of postage meters and mailing equipment. The company originally built its reputation on its postage meter invention and other paper-mail processing products, but has been expanding its scope to keep up with the electronic information age. With respect to product development, PB's main areas of focus now lies in traditional paper mailing systems, electronic billing and mailing systems, and computer software solutions. The company also provides business support services and financial services to customers worldwide. PB remains the world's leader in the production and leasing of postal meters, which are used by postal services in countries around the world. PB controls about 85 percent of the U.S. postage meter market, and about 60 percent of the entire world market. More than a quarter of the firm's revenue derives from its non-mail-related businesses.

The Early Years

Pitney Bowes' beginnings can be traced to the year 1902, when Arthur Pitney patented his newly created postage-stamp-ing machine. He then spent the next 12 years fine-tuning it and attempting to gain acceptance and financial backing for the product from the postal service. Pitney's machine offered a solution for the U.S. Post Office, which was confronted with the impracticality of the adhesive postage stamp in the face of the increasing volume of mail. The postage-stamping machine would stamp the mail at its source, while also keeping track of the amount of postage used. This method helped save labor and also decreased costs for both the postal service and the businesses using the machine. Although the machine achieved impressive results when tested by the post office in Pitney's hometown of Chicago in 1914, ultimate approval did not come until after World War I.

Meanwhile, in New York, Walter Bowes's Universal Stamping Machine Company was doing brisk business with the U.S. Postal Service, providing stamp-canceling machines on a rental basis. Bowes also had some international success, selling his machines in Germany, England, and Canada. In 1917 Bowes moved his operations to Stamford, Connecticut, a location which evolved into the company headquarters for years to come. Although Bowes's machine was profitable, he worried that Pitney's similar invention would render it obsolete. Thus, in April 1920, the two men decided to pool their resources.

The merger of Pitney's American Postage Meter Company and Bowes's Universal Stamping Machine Company created the Pitney-Bowes Postage Meter Company. The day after the merger officially took effect, Pitney and Bowes succeeded in pushing legislation through Congress to allow all classes of mail to be posted by meters instead of stamps, and the Pitney-Bowes postage meter was licensed for use throughout the postal system.

By 1922, PB had branch offices in 12 cities and 404 postage meters in operation. In the same year, Bowes's previous international experience paid off and PB's postage meter was approved for use in England and Canada. PB experienced early growing pains, however. As the meter gained exposure in the early 1920s, demand for the machines began to outpace the company's ability to manufacture, distribute, and service them. Also, it was thought in many quarters that PB enjoyed a government-created monopoly. Thus, in its first decade of existence, PB's scope of operations was limited by government regula-

---

Company Perspectives:

Pitney Bowes' products, solutions and people power our customers' businesses, everyday. Our brand is known as the leader in mail and document management solutions. Our mission statement drives everything we do to power business: Pitney Bowes will deliver shareholder and customer value by providing leading-edge global, integrated mail and document management solutions for organizations of all sizes.

---

tion—lobbied for by PB's competition—restricting PB from reaping the advantages of its technologically superior product.

Expansion Efforts in the Early and Mid-1900s

In 1924, Arthur Pitney retired from the company after a dispute with Bowes and started a company of his own, manufacturing postage-permit machines to compete with PB's meters. Even without Pitney, the company name remained Pitney-Bowes, due to the recognition factor the name had earned throughout those first four years. After the cofounder's departure, however, uncertainty reigned at PB, and Walter Wheeler II, Bowes's stepson, was promoted from New York branch manager to general manager in Stamford in an attempt to utilize new leadership and find new direction.

PB's share of the market was still uncertain because of the postal service's equivocation on postal regulations. Permit mail required counting to assess fees, while metered mail did not; but the postal service, wary of establishing a monopoly for PB, required all mail to be counted. Although PB's future hung by a thread during the early and mid-1920s, by 1927 the company had 2,849 meters in operation and branches in 20 cities. Finally, after a Congressional hearing at which Arthur Pitney testified by letter against preferential treatment for the system he invented, a bill to impose uniform regulations on permit and metered mail was killed in the Senate. The postal service was free to exercise its preference for the more efficient, reliable, and safe postage meter. From that point on, first-class mail was posted only by meter or adhesive stamp.

Pitney-Bowes began to grow and diversify, producing machines for stamping, counting, canceling, and metering mail. PB's 1929 profit of $300,000 represented a 100 percent increase over that of the previous year. The company expanded abroad as well, establishing cross-licensing and patent-sharing agreements with similar firms in Great Britain and Germany. Throughout the 1930s, government restrictions on the metered-mail business eroded, and Pitney-Bowes's field of operations grew wider. By the end of 1933 there were 9,620 PB postage meters in service.

The Great Depression meant retrenchment at Pitney-Bowes, as it did in most sectors of the economy. PB was fortunate to be in a growth industry and did not face critical financial difficulties, but its profits shrunk considerably during these years. The company was forced to cut wages by 10 percent and also suspended stockholder dividends. The union movement received a boost during the Depression, but found little support at PB, which had provided benefits to its employees for years. PB

emerged from the Depression earlier and healthier than most firms, partly due to the nature of its product, and partly due to the leadership of Walter Wheeler. He became the company president in 1938.

Pitney-Bowes's success in the industry and the further relaxation of postal service restrictions on metered mail stimulated competition in the production of postage meters. Many small firms sought a share of the market, as did some heavy hitters, including IBM and NCR. Nonetheless, PB consistently kept ahead of its competition. Its development of the omni-denomination meter in 1940 was a breakthrough in the industry. Not only was PB prospering, with over 27,000 meters in service in 1939, but the U.S. Postal Service had a $2 million budget surplus in fiscal 1939, largely due to the efficiency of the metered-mail system.

Like most other large manufacturers, PB converted its plant to defense production during World War II. PB's wartime priorities, as established by Walter Wheeler, were maximum production of war goods, maintenance of meters in operation to handle American mail, and planning for postwar manufacture of new products. The production of postage meters was completely halted during the war. Instead, PB manufactured replacement parts for guns, aircraft, and radios, and was a four-time recipient of the Army-Navy "E" Award, given for excellence in wartime production.

Post-World War II Diversification

In 1945, anticipating the broadening of its product base, Pitney-Bowes Postage Meter Company shortened its name to Pitney-Bowes Inc. By the end of 1947, the number of PB postage meters in service had more than doubled to over 60,000 in less than ten years. PB expanded and modernized its plant and office space in Stamford to accommodate projected growth. Two years later, PB introduced a desktop postage meter, which brought small business customers within its reach. Further diversification continued with the acquisition of the Tickometer Company, whose namesake product counted paper items such as labels and tickets. PB simplified the Tickometer machine's design and promoted its use for many new purposes. For the most part, though, PB limited its diversification to fields related to those functions performed in mail rooms.

Throughout the 1940s and 1950s, Wheeler worked hard to maintain good labor-management relations and progressive incentive, benefit, and profit-sharing plans. This was reflected in a high rate of productivity at PB, and in the decision of the majority of workers not to seek union representation. The wisdom of this strategy was demonstrated by PB's continual out-performance of its competition during those years.

By 1957, however, due to the virtual disappearance of domestic competition, PB was faced with government antitrust action. The company cooperated fully with investigators. Wheeler even went so far as to prepare a 12-volume history of Pitney-Bowes and submit it to the Department of Justice. Wheeler maintained, as he always had, that it was PB's productivity, efficiency, and personnel relations that made it difficult for other companies to compete, not anti-competitive practices. PB eventually agreed to sign a consent decree that required the

Key Dates:

1902: Arthur Pitney patents his postage-stamping machine.
1920: Pitney's American Postage Meter Co. and Walter Bowes's Universal Stamping Machine Co. merge to form Pitney-Bowes (PB).
1940: Company develops omni-denomination meter.
1957: Company faces government antitrust suit.
1979: PB acquires Dictaphone Corp.
1982: PB enters fax machine market.
1995: Company sells Dictaphone and Monarch subsidiaries.
2001: PB spins off fax and copier division as Imagistics International.

company to license its patents to any manufacturer who wished to compete, at no charge.

In 1960, when Walter H. Wheeler retired as president and chief operating officer, PB had 281,100 postage meters in service and metered mail accounted for 43 percent of U.S. postage. PB's gross income was over $57 million. Furthermore, products other than postage meters accounted for 20 percent of the company's gross income, a result of PB's increasing diversification measures.

Entering the 1960s, diversification became an even more important facet of PB's strategy. Because PB no longer had a monopoly in the postage-meter market, diversification into new product areas was necessary for company growth. In 1967, the company established a copier-product division whose first product was a tabletop office copier. Although PB was a latecomer to a market already dominated by Xerox, its copiers had two advantages: they were reasonably priced, and included excellent service packages. Service had long been a hallmark of PB's operations because the U.S. Post Office never allowed PB to sell its meters, only lease them. PB was responsible for the day-to-day operations of every meter it leased, so a large service fleet was already in place. This service team made expansion into other markets much more manageable.

The following year, PB acquired Monarch Marking Systems, which soon grew into the largest U.S. supplier of price marking, merchandise identification, and inventory control equipment and supplies. By the end of the decade, PB's sales of postage meters, while still growing, accounted for only just over 50 percent of its total sales. Pitney Bowes dropped the hyphen from its name in 1970.

The 1970s and 1980s

In the early 1970s, PB began to experience financial losses that stemmed from a joint venture with Alpex Computer Corporation to manufacture point-of-sale terminal systems. PB was forced to write off its 64 percent investment in the venture, at a loss of $42 million. More modest losses from this venture continued to mount for several years, due to disputes with the Internal Revenue Service over allowable write-offs and an $11 million lawsuit filed by Alpex.

By the late 1970s, however, PB was back on track. The company established leasing companies in the United States and in the United Kingdom in 1977 to support marketing efforts for its business products. This was a record year for the company, with both postage meters and price-marking systems posting record sales. In 1979 PB made a major acquisition, adding the Dictaphone Corporation and its subsidiaries Data Documents and Grayarc to the company, for a $124 million price tag. The purchase made PB the worldwide leader in sales of voice-processing and dictation equipment, while still enjoying a 90 percent controlling share of the postage-meter market.

In the early 1980s, PB made moves to solidify its standing as the country's leader in the mail-room and office equipment market. It first filled a gap in its copier line in 1981 by arranging a marketing agreement with the Ricoh Company of Japan to make its tabletop model available in the United States. This increased the number of copier models marketed by PB to eight. PB also received a $111 million contract from the post office to help further automate the handling of mail by developing computers to "read" envelopes and parcels. PB then entered the facsimile machine market in 1982, and soon became the leader in new placements of facsimile equipment. The company became one of the top suppliers of fax machines to large and medium-sized businesses in the United States, and began seeking new international markets by the late 1980s.

Keeping in line with company policy to compete mainly in markets in which it was guaranteed a prominent share, in 1987 about 80 percent of the company's sales were in industry segments that PB led. The Data Documents subsidiary, however, deviated from this standard, and was sold in 1988. The company also laid off 1,500 workers, underwent a costly retooling in 1989, and began to push more sophisticated mailing systems, like its Star system, which picked the most efficient carrier method for each package. In addition, PB got a boost from the U.S. Post Office, which began pushing big mailers to use barcode envelopes.

The 1990s and Beyond

Entering the final decade of the century, PB saw its sales surpass the $3 billion mark for the first time in company history, topping off at $3.2 billion in fiscal 1990. Furthermore, the company's extensive sales force had earned PB a 45 percent share of the market for fax machines in corporate America. Following the course charted by that success, the company continued to penetrate the domestic market for business machines with the introduction of another line of copiers in 1991. This line of machines, the 9000 series, was targeted mainly at large businesses. The year 1991 also saw the introduction of computerized software programs focusing on automated freight management, address and mail list management, and medical records transcription.

The 1990s ushered in the "information age," which included an increase in communications by electronic means, in the form of both facsimile and electronic mail. PB attempted to keep pace with the world's new communication needs, shifting its operations from a mechanical base to that of computerization and software solutions. In order to ease the transition, the company instituted a program of self-directed work teams on both the production floor and in the management ranks. PB also trained its management and sales teams to become proficient in the use of computers. The changes helped to integrate the ideas and actions of everyone in the company, while also technologically enabling PB to more easily expand its scope in line with technological advances.

Meanwhile, PB worked to maintain its standing as the country's leading producer of mail-room equipment. In fact, its work in that area was honored in 1993, when the company was featured in the National Postal Museum in Washington, D.C., a recognition of numerous PB innovations throughout history. The company also continued to expand worldwide, nailing down deals with three other countries in 1994. PB introduced its popular Paragon mailing system in Germany, while it also began to aid China and Mexico in the modernization and automation of their postal systems.

The following year, PB sold its Dictaphone subsidiary to an affiliate of Stonington Partners, a New York investment group, for $450 million. The company also divested its Monarch Marking Systems subsidiary, selling it for $127 million. More sales and service offices were opened in Europe, and product development efforts utilizing new technology continued. An important introduction in late 1995 was a computerized mail tracking and accounting system called PostPerfect.

PB promoted a new chief executive in May 1996, Michael Critelli. The change in leadership came after a slump in the company's stock price, and a siphoning off of its customers to competitors. PB lost approximately 2 percent of its customers over the first nine months of 1996, and it was becoming increasingly apparent that the company would have to move fast to prevent further slides as electronic mail became more widely used. PB's customers were primarily large businesses. These big companies generated over 40 percent of all U.S. mail, and serving them had long made PB one of the most profitable business supply companies. But it was more difficult for PB to reach smaller businesses, and this is where new competitors began to see opportunity. By 1996 PB was making a concerted effort in this area, marketing smaller postage meters and cutting-edge electronic mail technology. By 1997 PB had developed software that converted mailing lists into addressed envelopes with postage printed on a personal computer. Other companies too, such as the California-based E-Stamp Corp., also developed such a system. Postal Service regulation made the implementation of PC-based metering slow, and technical problems abounded. Hand-addressed mail or mail bound outside the United States could not be simply metered using the software, and even the size and design of the metered mark (called the "indicium") was contentious. Yet the PC-generated indicium was capable of encoding far more information than a typical bar code, which could allow an individual letter to be tracked easily. PB, E-Stamp, and its European competitor Neopost Inc. vied in the late 1990s to come up with easy-to-use and efficient PC-based meters that could be utilized by any business large enough to have a computer. PB's outlook changed, then, from a near-monopoly company with little to worry about to a much more entrepreneurial enterprise trying to break a new market with new products.

Pitney Bowes also divested some businesses and acquired others. In 1997 the company sold part of its leasing portfolio to

GATX Corp. for $460 million. Because PB had always leased its office equipment, it had gradually built up a business leasing other equipment for its customers, including large items such as airplanes, railcars, and barges. It sold off this portion of its business to GATX, a Chicago-based company that specialized in leasing transport, mostly because it did not fit with the company's core business model. In 1998 PB sold its subsidiary, Colonial Pacific Leasing Corp., to Capital Services, a division of General Electric. Colonial Pacific specialized in leasing equipment to small and mid-sized companies. Though the unit was profitable, PB preferred at this point to rid itself of businesses that were not closely related to mail and messaging. It also sold off a mortgage servicing company it owned, Atlantic Mortgage & Investment Corp., for roughly $490 million. PB had a record year in 1999, with revenue growing 8 percent, to $4.4 billion. The company's profits also grew sharply, topping $1 billion for the first time. The company bought two smaller firms in 2001, paying $24 million for Alysis Technologies Inc. in March, then buying a unit of Danka Business Systems for $290 million the next month. Alysis, based in California, made software for billing over the Internet. PB acquired the international business of Danka, which provided document management services. It made other international acquisitions too, buying the French mailing company Secap and some overseas business units of Bell & Howell's International Mail and Messaging Technologies. At the end of 2001, PB spun off its fax and copier division, forming a new publicly traded company called Imagistics International Inc.

By the end of 2001, PB seemed to have come through all the changes of the 1990s well, and was poised for more growth in the decades to come. Though the volume of regular mail had dropped due to the increase in faxes and electronic mail, PB had shown itself able to adapt its business. It had promising new markets in administering mail services for clients and in developing more and varied electronic mailing and bill-paying products. While about three-quarters of PB's revenue came from its traditional postage meter business by 2001, its non-mail business was growing quickly. The company expected to find more ways to serve its key markets even as technology altered the terrain.

Principal Subsidiaries

Adrema Leasing Corporation; Adrema Maschinen und Auto-Leasing GmbH (Germany); Adrema Mobilien Leasing GmbH (Germany); Andeen Enterprises, Inc. (Panama); Artec International Corporation; B. Williams Holding Corp.; Cascade Microfilm Systems, Inc.; Chas. P. Young Health Fitness & Management, Inc.; Datarite Systems Ltd. (U.K.); Dodwell Pitney Bowes K.K. (Japan); ECL Finance Company, N.V. (Netherlands); Elmcroft Road Realty Corporation; Financial Structures Limited (Bermuda); FSL Valuation Services, Inc.; Harlow Aircraft Inc.; Imagistics International Inc.; Informatech; La Agricultora Ecuatoriana S.A. (Ecuador); Norlin Australia Investment Pty. Ltd.; Norlin Industries Limited (Canada); Norlin Music (U.K.) Ltd. (England); PB Forms, Inc.; PB Funding Corporation; PB Global Holdings, Inc.; PB Leasing Corporation; PB Leasing International Corporation; PB CFSC I, Inc. (Virgin Islands); PBL Holdings, Inc.; PB Nikko FSC Ltd. (Bermuda); PB Nihon FSC Ltd. (Bermuda); Pitney Bowes AG (Switzerland); Pitney Bowes Australia Pty. Limited; Pitney

Bowes Austria Ges.m.b.H. (Austria); Pitney Bowes of Canada Ltd.; Pitney Bowes Management Services Canada Inc.; Pitney Bowes Credit Australia Limited; Pitney Bowes Credit Corporation; Pitney Bowes Data Systems, Ltd. (U.K.); Pitney Bowes de Mexico, S.A. de C.V.; Pitney Bowes Deutschland GmbH (Germany); Pitney Bowes Espana, S.A. (Spain); Pitney Bowes Finance, S.A. (France); Pitney Bowes Finans Norway AS (Norway); Pitney Bowes Finance plc (U.K.); Pitney Bowes Finance Ireland Limited; Pitney Bowes France S.A.; Pitney Bowes Holdings Ltd. (U.K.); Pitney Bowes Holding SNC (France); Pitney Bowes Insurance Agency, Inc.; Pitney Bowes International Holdings, Inc.; Pitney Bowes Italia S.r.l. (Italy); Pitney Bowes (Ireland) Limited; Pitney Bowes Leasing Ltd. (Canada); Pitney Bowes Macau Limited; Pitney Bowes Management Services, Inc.; Pitney Bowes Management Services Canada, Inc.; Pitney Bowes Management Services Limited (U.K.) Pitney Bowes Oy (Finland); Pitney Bowes Limited (U.K.); Pitney Bowes Properties, Inc.; Pitney Bowes Real Estate Financing Corporation; Pitney Bowes Servicios, S.A. de C.V. (Mexico); Pitney Bowes Shelton Realty, Inc.; Pitney Bowes Svenska Aktiebolag (Sweden); Pitney Bowes World Trade Corporation (FSC) (Virgin Islands); RE Properties Management Corporation; Remington Customer Finance Pty. Limited (Australia); Remington (PNG) Pty. Limited (Papau New Guinea); Remington Pty. (Australia); ROM Holdings Pty. Limited (Australia); ROM Securities Pty. Limited (Australia); Sales and Service Training Center, Inc. TECO/Pitney Bowes Co., Ltd. (Taiwan; 50%); Time-Sensitive Delivery Guide, Inc.; Towers FSC, Ltd. (Bermuda); Universal Postal Frankers Ltd. (U.K.); Walnut Street Corp.; 1136 Corporation; 75 V Corp.

Principal Divisions

Mailing and Integrated Logistics; Office Solutions; Capital Services.

Principal Competitors

E-Stamp Corp.; Neopost Inc.; Francotyp-Postalia.

Further Reading

Anders, George, "It's Digital, It's Encrypted—It's Postage," *Wall Street Journal*, September 21, 1998, pp. B1, B6.

Babyak, Richard J., "Low-Cost, High-Tech," *Appliance Manufacturer,* March 1994, p. 36.

Cahn, William, *The Pitney-Bowes Story,* New York: Harper and Brothers, 1961.

Darlin, Damon, "Innovate or Die," *Forbes*, February 24, 1997, p. 108.

Day, Charles R., Jr., "Faceless But Fantastic," *Industry Week*, November 15, 1993, p. 7.

Deutsch, Claudia H., "Despite Mail Tumult, Pitney Bowes's Long-Term Outlook Is Strong," *New York Times*, November 10, 2001, pp. C1, C2.

——, "Not Your Father's Postage Meter," *New York Times*, August 18, 1998, pp. D1, D4.

Dugan, I. Jeanne, " 'Small Business Is Big Business'," *Business Week*, September 30, 1996, p. 117.

Hitchcock, Nancy A., "Can Self-Managed Teams Boost Your Bottom Line?: How Pitney Bowes Establishes Self-Directed Work Teams," *Modern Materials Handling,* February 1993, p. 58.

Marcial, Gene G., "Stamp of Approval?" *Business Week*, April 24, 1995, p. 75.

Murray, Matt, "GE Capital Services Agrees to Acquire Pitney Bowes Operation for $800 Million," *Wall Street Journal*, October 13, 1998, p. B8.

Paley, Norton, "Fancy Footwork," *Sales & Marketing Management,* July 1994, p. 41.

Taylor, Thayer C., "Does This Compute?" *Sales & Marketing Management,* September 1994, p. 115.

Welsh, Jonathan, "Pitney Bowes Plans Sale, Move of Leases in Pact with GATX Totaling $1 Billion," *Wall Street Journal*, August 22, 1997, p. A4.

Zuckerman, Laurence E., "It's a New Brand of E-Mail," *New York Times*, April 28, 1997, p. D5.

—Robin Carre
—updates: Laura E. Whiteley, A. Woodward

PORTAL™

Portal Software, Inc.

102000 S. De Anza Boulevard
Cupertino, California 95014
U.S.A.
Telephone: (408) 572-2000
Fax: (408) 572-2001
Web site: http://www.portal.com

Public Company
Incorporated: 1985 as Portal Communications Co.
Employees: 1,486
Sales: $154.8 million (2002)
Stock Exchanges: NASDAQ
Ticker Symbol: PRSF
NAIC: 511210 Software Publishers

Since it was first established in 1985 as an Internet service provider, Portal Software, Inc. was guided by the vision that the Internet would fundamentally change the way business was done. The company's founder, John E. Little, was interested in providing companies with a flexible software platform that would handle customer management and billing. With the introduction of Infranet, the software solution that formed the basis of Portal's product line, in 1996, Portal began to focus exclusively on software. Infranet attracted the attention of telecommunications carriers and other companies that wanted to provide a wider range of Internet-based services. Portal expanded its customer base through partnerships with more than 140 companies, including leading technology innovators and system integrators. As of 2002, Portal had more than 420 customers for its customer management and billing software solutions, more than all of its competitors combined.

Internet Connections and Infrastructure Software: 1985–96

Portal Software, Inc. was founded in 1985 as Portal Communications Co. It was one of the first companies to offer public Internet connections. The company was started in a house in Cupertino, California, by John E. Little, a Princeton graduate in electrical engineering and computer science. After working as a

consultant for a few years on the East Coast, he relocated to Silicon Valley from New Jersey. Little wanted to sell infrastructure software that would handle routine transactions for Internet businesses. At the time, there was little demand for such services, so Portal offered public Internet connections.

Over the next several years, Portal began getting more requests for its software. Companies seeking venture capital financing were often referred by the venture capital firms to Portal for basic business functions such as customer management and billing. The company also picked up clients when Little spoke at industry conferences.

In late 1993, Portal began focusing more intently on developing and marketing real-time customer management and billing (CM&B) software. In 1994, the company changed its name to Portal Information Network. By the beginning of 1996, software accounted for about half of its business, and Internet service, the other half.

Software Solutions Replacing Internet Service: 1996–99

In May 1996, Portal shipped its first off-the-shelf version of Infranet, its CM&B software package. One of the first customers to choose Infranet was telecommunications provider Sprint Corp. Portal's Infranet System, as it was called, would allow Sprint customers, including ISPs and carriers, to deliver commercial services over the Internet quickly. Infranet included five core applications that authorized credit card purchases, created databases to track customer statistics, monitored consumer use of the system, collected and processed payments, and managed the system. Businesses using Infranet to manage their customer transactions had the ability to modify their customer interfaces and business processes, implement a set of standard business objects, and connect to various external systems. Analysts noted that gaining Sprint as a customer was a major coup for Portal. They also noted that Infranet's use of object technology allowed it to be easily adapted to other computer systems and represented an advance over one-off and proprietary solutions.

When Portal shut down its ISP service in October 1996, it had been seeking a buyer for its customer base for about a year.

That was when the decision to focus on software solutions for ISPs was made. With Portal selling Infranet to larger ISPs, the company did not want to be competing with them. Sprint took over Portal's ISP customers, which numbered about 5,000. At the time Portal had about 50 employees.

In the first four months of 1997, Portal received orders for Infranet from four major international ISPs: CompuServe and Citizens Telecom in the United States, Australia's OzEmail, and France's Grolier Club-Internet. They selected Infranet to provide customer management and delivery capabilities. Portal also signed CAP Gemini Group, Europe's largest systems integrator, as a distribution and support channel partner. In addition, Microsoft and Portal formed an alliance to run the Infranet platform on the Microsoft Commercial Internet System. Later in the year, the iPass Alliance, the largest Internet access network in the world with more than 100 ISPs, agreed to work with Portal to provide its members with Infranet software to help improve their billing systems.

In October 1997, Portal changed its name to Portal Software, Inc. Starting with fiscal 1997 ending January 31, virtually all of Portal's revenue came from the licensing of Infranet and related services. For fiscal 1997 Portal reported revenue of $5 million, with $3.9 million from license fees and $1.1 million from services. Services revenue was derived from systems integration and other consulting activities, maintenance agreements, and training of customers and partners. Portal reported a net loss of $2.3 million in fiscal 1997 and had not shown a quarterly or annual profit since 1994, when it began focusing on software. For fiscal 1998, Portal's revenue nearly doubled to $9.4 million while its net loss increased to $7.6 million. License fees contributed $6.9 million in revenue and services contributed $2.5 million. During fiscal 1998, Portal gained U S West Inc. and Cincinnati Bell Information Systems as customers for Infranet.

In 1998–99, Portal gained more customers, including Juno Online Services, which had more than five million free e-mail accounts. Juno planned to use Infranet to manage tracking, order taking, and customer tracking. Portal also signed a worldwide distribution agreement with American Management Systems Inc., which was a major integrator for telecommunications companies and large corporations. Infranet was recognized for its real-time, flexible billing solutions that allowed online service providers to track use and adjust their pricing.

During the year, Portal formed several alliances with other manufacturers, a strategy for growth that the company would pursue over the next several years. Through an alliance with original equipment manufacturer (OEM) SkyWave Inc., Portal was able to make a version of Infranet available to providers of Internet telephony services. Another alliance with Verifone Inc., a subsidiary of Hewlett-Packard Co., resulted in the integration of Verifone's vPOS payment software into the Infranet system. The result was that Portal customers could have direct connections to financial institutions for online payment processing.

For fiscal 1999, Portal reported revenue of $26.7 million, a 283 percent increase over 1998. Revenue was evenly split between license fees ($13.5 million) and services ($13.1 million). Costs and expenses also increased, with research and development spending doubling to $11.3 million in 1999 from $5.6 million in 1998. Sales and marketing expenses also increased substantially, from $5.4 million in 1998 to $14.1 million in fiscal 1999. As a result, the company's net loss grew to $17.1 million.

Going Public: 1999–2001

By February 1999, when Portal filed its initial registration statement with the Securities and Exchange Commission (SEC) for its initial public offering (IPO), there were approximately 80 companies using Infranet. They included ISPs, such as Concentric Network Corp. and UUNet Technologies; online enterprises, including Juno Online Services and Palm.net; and online divisions of telecommunications carriers, such as BellSouth Corp. and U S West Inc. These customers represented Portal's target market of providers of advanced communications services worldwide. Portal also had established a series of partnerships with systems integrators, such as Andersen Consulting LLP, Cap Gemini Group, NTT Software Corp., and PricewaterhouseCoopers LLP, and with hardware and software manufacturers, including Cisco Systems, Compaq Computer, Hewlett-Packard, Microsoft, Oracle, and Sun Microsystems.

When Portal went public in May 1999, Cisco Systems bought three million shares of Portal for $39 million, which represented 4 percent of the company's shares. In April, the company opened a new European headquarters in Slough, United Kingdom. Later in the year, Portal moved its U.S. headquarters into a new four-story building on De Anza Boulevard in Cupertino that it purchased from Symantec Corporation. Toward the end of 1999, Portal opened a wholly owned subsidiary in Tokyo, Japan. Partners in the subsidiary included three distributors: Bussan Systems Integrations Co. Ltd., Itochu Techno-Science Corp., and NTT Software Corp.

Portal's customer base for Infranet grew to more than 200 companies by the end of fiscal 2000. The company's target market had grown to include not only the online service divisions of traditional telecommunications providers and online and Internet service providers, but also wireless service divisions, application service providers (ASPs), and companies that used the Internet to provide entirely new types of communications services. Portal's Infranet technology gave these customers scalability and reliability, enterprise integration and interoperability, comprehensive functionality and ease of use, and flexibility and improved time to market. Infranet allowed customers to manage the customer life cycle, including account creation and service provisioning, authentication and authorization, activity tracking, rating and pricing, billing and accounts

---

Key Dates:

1985: Portal Communications Co. is established as an on-line service and one of the first Internet service providers (ISPs).
1994: The company changes its name to Portal Information Network.
1996: Portal ships its first version of Infranet software and shuts down its Internet service.
1997: The company changes its name to Portal Software, Inc.
1999: Portal becomes a public company.
2000: Portal introduces a version of its customer management and billing software for cable TV companies.

---

receivable, customer management, and reporting. Business benefits to the customer included increased revenue, reduced costs, and improved customer service.

Portal offered customers several capabilities and features as optional additions to the basic Infranet solution. These included Infranet IPT, introduced in September 1998, for providers of Internet telephony services. Infranet DNA, introduced in fiscal 2000, was an option for customers requiring high availability and fault tolerance; it used remote, limited scope satellite installations of Infranet to handle user authentication, service authorization, and event queuing. During normal operation, the satellite installations of Infranet were updated in real time from the customer's main database. If the main database went offline, the satellite installation provided continuous operation of the customer's service and avoided denial of access. Infranet MultiDB was another option introduced in fiscal 2000. It was aimed at customers with very high subscriber counts and enabled the distribution of accounts across multiple databases in a single Infranet installation.

For fiscal 2000, Portal reported revenue of $103 million, nearly four times the previous year's revenue. Portal's dramatic growth in revenue reflected the changing nature of Internet service providers and the introduction of new Internet-based services that required flexible CM&B software that could scale from hundreds to millions of users and that was adaptable to a wide range of services. Portal continued to spend a sizeable portion of its revenue on research and development, while managing to reduce its net loss from $17.4 million in 1999 to $7.6 million in 2000.

After one year as a public company, Portal had grown to more than 750 employees. Approximately one-third of its workforce was in sales and marketing, and nearly one-third was in engineering. Portal maintained a direct sales force in 13 states and internationally in Australia, Canada, China, France, Germany, Hong Kong, Japan, Malaysia, Singapore, Spain, and the United Kingdom. Portal also pursued its sales efforts through its strategic partners.

During fiscal 2001, Portal's customer base more than doubled to some 420 companies. The company gained several large international customers, including iAdvantage, which owned and operated five Internet service centers in Hong Kong, China,

and Singapore. Japan's NTTPC Communications, a subsidiary of Japan's largest telecommunications group NTT, selected Infranet to support several new business initiatives. Telekom Malaysia, the country's leading telecommunications carrier, deployed Infranet to support the further expansion of its ISP, TMnet. Other new business in Asia came from Shanghai Telecom and China's Liaoning Telecom. Israel's national telecommunications provider, Bezeq, chose Infranet to provide customer management and billing for its high-speed DSL service.

Portal reported record revenue of $268.3 million for fiscal 2001. The company also reduced its net loss to $2.3 million, even as spending on research and development more than doubled to $57.7 million and sales and marketing expenses more than doubled to $128.7 million. During fiscal 2001, Portal made one of its few acquisitions, purchasing Solutions42, a developer of third generation (3G) technology, for about $200 million.

Declining Revenues: 2001–2002

Portal began fiscal 2002 by announcing a new multi-year contract with America Online, under which America Online licensed Infranet to support a wide range of services. Later in the year, Time Warner Cable licensed Infranet to allow its subscribers to independently select services from various ISPs. Cidera, a provider of broadband content via satellite, chose Infranet to offer its customers real-time, activity-based billing in an open, scalable environment.

Internationally, several wireless providers joined Portal's customer base, including Vodafone UK and Australia's Telstra OnAir. Finland's Nokia Networks announced it would build Portal's Infranet software into its mobile networks and also resell the software to its infrastructure customers. Taiwan's eASPNet, a consortium formed by leading Taiwanese and Asian companies, selected Infranet to support the rapid rollout of new services, include Internet data centers and ASPs.

During the year, Portal formed a global strategic alliance with IBM. The focus of the alliance was to provide wireless service providers with a comprehensive 3G-ready infrastructure platform by integrating IBM's WebSphere Everyplace Suite with Portal's Infranet. Another alliance formed in 2001 involved Reliacast Inc., a developer of audience management software and the intelligent delivery of content. Reliacast planned to integrate its audience management solution with Portal's Infranet to create a comprehensive audience management and billing solution for the delivery of live and cached web-based events.

In mid-2001, Canadian wireless operator TELUS Mobility implemented Infranet to manage real-time revenue sharing with its more than 80 content providers. Later in the year TELUS used Infranet to offer its customers pay-per-use billing and extended its contract with Portal. TELUS became the first announced customer for Portal's Infranet Content Connector, a new billing interface that linked communications providers, content providers, and value-added service providers.

For fiscal 2002, Portal reported a 42 percent decline in revenue to $154.8 million. On a pro forma basis, the company's net loss was $85.9 million. Pro forma results excluded a restructuring charge of $71 million, the write-off of purchased technology and goodwill of $199.2 million, the amortization of acquisition-related costs of $35.4 million, and another $4 million write-off for impairment of equity investments. Taking those charges into account, Portal had a net loss of $395.5 million for fiscal 2002.

Looking ahead to 2002–03, Portal expected its business to be affected by the slowdown in capital expenditures by telecommunications companies and content providers. In February 2002, the company strengthened its management team by hiring Glenn R. Wienkoop as president and chief operating officer. Wienkoop had more than 20 years of experience in the technology industry, having served in executive positions with Measurex Corp., SDRC (Structural Dynamics Research Corp.), and Cognex Corp.

Principal Competitors

Alopa Networks, Inc.; Amdocs Ltd.; Ceon Corp.; Convergys Corp.; Connext Inc.; Kenan Systems Corp.; Sigma Data Systems, Inc.; Telcordia Technologies, Inc.

Further Reading

"AMS in Distribution Deal with Portal Software," *American Banker,* April 28, 1998, p. 13.
Andrews, Whit, "Buying & Selling," *Internet World,* April 13, 1998, p. 20.
"At the High End of the B2B Market, Portal Software, Inc. Has Shown That It Intends to Be a Major Player in Japan," *Japan-U.S. Business Report,* December 1999, p. 30.
Bucholtz, Chris, "Built-in Billing," *Telephony,* August 25, 1997, p. 25.
——, "E-Entrepreneurs Make Their Mark," *Telephony,* October 6, 1997, p. S24.
——, "Elevating the Platform," *Telephony,* April 7, 1997, p. 32.
——, "Real Time Inches Toward Big Time," *Telephony,* January 5, 1998, p. 8.
——, "Sprint Selects Off-the-Shelf Fast Infranet Solution," *Telephony,* May 20, 1996, p. 16.
"China's Liaoning Telecom Selects Portal Software to Support the Largest Provincial Public Communications Network," *China Telecom,* February 2001, p. 15.
"Cidera Enhances Range of Global Satellite-Based Services with Portal Software," *Wireless Satellite and Broadcasting Newsletter,* March 2001, p. 2.
"Cisco Systems Inc.," *Internet World,* May 17, 1999, p. 4.
"Entrepreneur of the Year," *San Francisco Business Times,* June 30, 2000, p. 4.
Graebner, Lynn, "Portal Software to Expand into New Space in Cupertino," *Business Journal,* July 30, 1999, p. 12.
"iAdvantage Chooses Portal Software to Support Asia Business Expansion," *China Telecom,* September 2000, p. 17.
"IBM and Portal Software Form Global Strategic Alliance," *EDP Weekly's IT Monitor,* March 5, 2001, p. 8.
"Infranet Adds ICP for Circuit-Switched Billing," *Computer Telephony,* October 2000, p. 28.
"Israel's National Telco Implements Portal Software for New High-Speed DSL Services," *ISP Business,* November 2000, p. 9.
"Japan's NTTPC Chooses Portal Software to Support Rollout of New ISP Services," *Japan Telecom,* October 2000, p. 15.
"Juno Takes on Customer Mgm't," *InternetWeek,* August 31, 1998, p. 18.
"Leading Canadian Wireless Operator TELUS Mobility Signs Multi-Million Dollar Contract with Portal Software," *Canadian Corporate News,* December 18, 2001.
Maclachlan, Malcolm, "Portal Breaks Net Connection, Leaves Customers Wondering," *Business Journal,* October 21, 1996, p. 7.
Matsumoto, Craig, "Portal Offers Passageway to Doing Business on Line," *Business Journal,* January 8, 1996, p. 20.
McElligott, Tim, "Download: NightFire, Portal Go the ASP Way," *Telephony,* April 24, 2000.
——, "Download: Portal Stirs the Pot," *Telephony,* August 21, 2000.
McKenna, Ted, "Telus Mobility Switches off the Meter, Gives Web Customers Pay-Per-Use Billing," *Telecommunications,* January 2002, p. 34.
Neil, Stephanie, "Powering up Customer Relationships," *PC Week,* May 11, 1998, p. 69.
"The OSS Challenge," *CED,* November 2001, p. SS1.
"Portal Extends Services to Cable," *Business Journal,* March 3, 2000, p. 28.
"Portal Software Unveils Infranet Cable & Satellite," *Wireless Satellite and Broadcasting Newsletter,* August 2001, p. 16.
"Portal, Verifone Linking Payments Products," *American Banker,* November 12, 1998.
"Reliacast Teams with Portal Software to Offer First Comprehensive Solution for Advanced Web-Based Content Delivery," *Information Superhighway Newsletter,* April 2001, p. 3.
Rendleman, John, "IP Telephony Vendors to Strengthen Offerings," *PC Week,* April 13, 1998, p. 102.
"Shanghai Telecom Chooses Portal Software to Support Further Expansion," *China Telecom,* January 2001, p. 6.
Smetannikov, Max. "Billing Systems Become Strategic," *Inter@ctive Week,* December 13, 1999, p. 52.
"Taiwan's eASPNet Chooses Portal Software to Support Fast Roll-Out of ASP and Internet Data Centers," *Information Superhighway Newsletter,* June 2001, p. 1.
"Telekom Malaysia Chooses Portal Software's Infranet," *Asia Pacific Telecom,* October 2000, p. 14.
"Telus Debuts Pay to Play," *Wireless Week,* July 23, 2001, p. 22.
"Time Warner Cable Licenses Portal Platform," *High-Speed Internet Access User,* March 2001, p. 13.
Vizard, Michael, "Portal Software CEO John Little Extols the Virtues of Managing Web Customers," *InfoWorld,* December 14, 1998, p. 49.
Walker, Meg, "Nokia Wraps Billing Software into Networks," *TechWeb,* March 7, 2001.
Wilson, Carol, "Duo Teams to Package Broadband Services," *Inter@ctive Week,* June 12, 2000, p. 16.

—David P. Bianco

Prairie Farms Dairy, Inc.

1100 N. Broadway Street
Carlinville, Illinois 62626
U.S.A.
Telephone: (217) 854-2547
Fax: (217) 854-6426
Web site: http://www.prairiefarms.com

Private Company
Incorporated: 1962
Employees: 3,000
Sales: $1.1 billion (2001 est.)
NAIC: 311511 Fluid Milk Manufacturing; 311512
Creamery Butter Manufacturing; 311520 Ice Cream
Manufacturing

Prairie Farms Dairy, Inc. is one of the largest bottlers of fluid milk in the United States and one of the largest dairy cooperatives in the Midwest, with nearly 800 members. In addition to fluid milk products, Prairie Farms produces cottage cheese, butter, yogurt, dips, sherbet, and ice cream, including the North Star brand of novelty ice cream products. The company also processes and distributes orange juice. Prairie Farms operates in 13 states, including the operations of its five joint ventures. A subsidiary, PFD Supply, distributes over 2,400 food and paper products to fast-food restaurants, including McDonald's and Burger King.

Pooling Resources to Form a Dairy Cooperative: 1930s–40s

Prairie Farms Dairy originated in 1932 as one of 12 dairy cooperatives formed under the umbrella of the Illinois Producers Creameries through the encouragement of the Illinois Agricultural Association. At that time small farmers each owned a few cows, using the milk for personal use and selling the excess sour cream butterfat to independent creamers. The cooperatives allowed individual farmers to pool their farm-separated cream and negotiate a better market price through the influence of a group. The cooperative organized three collecting stations, in Carlinville, Palmyra, and Piasa, where farmers took their cream for delivery to a butter-churning plant in Bloomington.

In 1937 the Producers Creamery of Carlinville formed and organized to open a butter-churning plant in Carlinville. The board of directors found a site for the plant and raised capital by selling Class A preferred stock to local farmers for $25 per share. To manage the cooperative the board hired Fletcher A. Gourley, a man whose commitment to the cooperative's farmers and employees created an atmosphere of family loyalty.

Gourley's first responsibilities involved obtaining a $3,000 loan from the Carlinville National Bank and purchasing the building and equipment. In 1938 the Carlinville plant began production. The company traveled to farms to purchase cream, though the collecting stations at Palmyra and Piasa continued to operate. In 1939, its first full year in operation, the Creamery collected seven million pounds of farm-separated cream for processing into butter. Butter was sold under the Prairie Farms name (as it did at all of the cooperatives) for ten cents a pound. That year the cooperative recorded revenues of $84,000 and net income of $3,400. While other cooperatives struggled, Gourley's calm, thoughtful management style helped to guide the Carlinville cooperative along a profitable path. The company recorded steady growth of revenues and earnings, allotting 20 percent to 50 percent of earnings to member patronage.

The advent of World War II changed the public's dairy needs. The Illinois Producers Creameries chose the Carlinville creamery for installation of one of four roller dryers to produce powdered milk. In 1943 the Producers Creamery of Carlinville began to collect whole milk for this purpose and to sell cream and a minor quantity of bulk milk as well. That year sales more than doubled to $537,000. In 1945, the company installed a condenser to make sweetened condensed milk for ice cream manufacturers. To reflect its more diversified product line, the company took the name Prairie Farms Creamery of Carlinville. Prairie Farms processed 24 million pounds of whole milk and nine million pounds of cream in 1945; sales exceeded $1 million.

Prairie Farms continued to diversify its product line in the postwar era. The company reported its first significant sales of bulk milk in 1946 and began to sell packaged milk in 1949.

Construction was completed on a new plant in May 1947 when Prairie Farms purchased a bottling machine for packaging milk in paper cartons. Before production started in June 1949, the company contracted with Dressel-Young Dairy in Granite City to package milk.

These were difficult years and Prairie Farms reported the only loss of its history in 1947, at $10,574 on $1.85 million in sales. By 1950 company operations solidified with continued sales of butter, cream, bulk milk, condensed milk, milk powder, and the first significant sales in packaged milk, cottage cheese, ice cream, and ice cream mix. New operations required the company to expand its facility with a cooler and ice cream hardening room in 1949 and a general storage room in 1951. Sales fluctuated, but in 1952 Prairie Farms commenced a steady pace of increasing revenues, rooted in mergers, acquisitions, and consolidations, as well as internal growth.

1954 to 1977: Mergers and Acquisitions Supporting Steady Growth

Between 1954 and 1962, Prairie Farms expanded through five mergers and five acquisitions, involving dairies in middle and southern Illinois and one in Lafayette, Indiana. In addition to expanding Prairie Farms market area, mergers and acquisitions facilitated the shift from production of non-grade milk toward Grade A milk, a process which began in 1948.

Changes in the dairy industry prompted consolidation as well. New technology for homogenization, sanitation, and other functions required small dairies to consolidate in order to compete. Also, home milk delivery faded in favor of supermarket-based sales, changing the dynamic of competition. Acquisition gave the small dairies a market for valuable assets that might have little worth otherwise. Gourley's method of acquisition involved letting a seller approach him and convince him of the merits of a partnership. He assisted sellers in improving the operations at their dairies. This stance earned Gourley a reputation as a fair negotiator.

One of the most significant transactions concerned a 1957 merger with Prairie Farms Dairy of Carbondale, an operation with $3.3 million in annual sales. The merger created a new entity, Prairie Farms of Southern Illinois. Prairie Farms then merged with Prairie Farms of Olney; that dairy reported $2.5 million in sales the previous year. In 1962 Prairie Farms of Southern Illinois merged with Prairie Farms of Western Illinois and Danville Producers Creamery and incorporated as Prairie Farms Dairy, Inc. In 1963 Prairie Farms recorded revenues of approximately $16 million.

During the 1960s Prairie Farms discontinued certain operations, eventually becoming a processing-only cooperative. In 1963 the company halted the purchase of farm-separated cream and discontinued production of condensed milk and milk powder. The company began to purchase milk by the tank-load from cooperatives in Wisconsin and Minnesota. As the company raised its standards of quality, Prairie Farms halted the purchase of non-grade milk by 1970.

With the acquisition of Aro-Dressel Foods in 1967 Prairie Farms made a noteworthy entrance into the St. Louis market as 60 percent of that company's bottled milk sales were based in St. Louis. The acquisition involved a significant ice cream mix operation and a fast-food supply operation in Granite City, Illinois. Prairie Farms formed a new subsidiary in 1969, PFD Supply, to separate the fast-food supply business from other operations at Granite City. PFD customers included McDonald's, Burger King, Wendy's, Ponderosa, and Bonanza restaurants.

From 1964 to 1977 Prairie Farms completed 33 acquisitions and three mergers. While most of the dairies were located in Illinois, Prairie Farms purchased two dairies each in Iowa, Indiana, and Nebraska, and three in St. Louis. Many of the acquisitions were attractive for their customer accounts. Acquisitions included a distribution company, a Dairy Queen ice cream mix operation, and five ice cream companies. Prairie Farms formed its Ice Cream Specialties subsidiary with the acquisition of three ice cream companies in St. Louis and Lafayette, Indiana, with aggregate sales of $5 million and covering markets in 13 states. A key merger involved the Peoria Producers Dairy in 1972, adding $4 million in sales. That year sales reached $78.2 million. By 1978 Prairie Farms reported sales of $206 million, after processing 913.5 million pounds of milk into dairy products.

Joint Ventures, Major Strategy for Growth During the 1980s

Between 1978 and 1989 Prairie Farms slowed its acquisition pace and changed to a strategy of growth through joint ventures. In October 1978 Dairymen and Prairie Farms each paid half of the acquisition costs for Ideal Dairy and American Dairy in Evansville, Indiana, and combined the two companies under the name Ideal American. Prairie Farms transferred a recent acquisition, Owensboro Ice Cream & Milk in Owensboro, Kentucky, to the joint venture for its distribution capabilities. Dairymen supplied milk to the operation and Prairie Farms provided management.

In the Hiland Dairy joint venture with Mid-America, formed in October 1979, Mid-America supplied milk and other ingredients and Prairie Farms supplied management to handle operations. The venture combined Mid-America's milk processing expertise and Prairie Farms' bottling expertise. Hiland operated dairy processing facilities in Oklahoma, Missouri, Kansas, and Arkansas. In 1985 Mid-America Dairymen and Prairie Farms purchased two Arkansas dairies, College Club Dairy in Fayetteville and ACEE Dairy in Fort Smith for the Hiland venture.

Prairie Farms formed two joint ventures in 1981. Muller-Pinehurst, formed with Midwest Dairymen, served dairies in Illinois. Roberts Dairy, formed with Mid-America, served markets in Iowa, Nebraska, Kansas, and Missouri. Prairie Farms transferred its holdings in Iowa and Nebraska to Roberts Dairy.

Key Dates:

1932: Local farmers form cooperative to negotiate price received for cream.

1938: Producers Creamery of Carlinville opens butter manufacturing plant.

1943: The company begins to produce powdered milk for wartime uses.

1945: Cooperative is renamed Prairie Farms Creamery; sales exceed $1 million.

1949: Prairie Farms opens its first milk bottling plant.

1962: Growth through mergers and acquisitions leads to incorporation as Prairie Farms Dairy.

1970: Transfer to Grade A milk processing concludes as company halts purchase of non-grade milk.

1978: Prairie Farms forms the first of several joint ventures.

1989: The company acquires Pevely Dairy, the largest and oldest independent dairy in St. Louis.

1999: Prairie Farms reports $1.1 billion in revenues and net income of $50.2 million.

2001: Cooperative members receive total patronage of $28.5 million.

In both ventures Prairie Farms provided management while the partner supplied milk.

Prairie Farms purchased only six dairies between 1981 and 1989. Notable among them was the Pevely Dairy Company, the oldest and largest independent dairy in the St. Louis area, purchased in June 1989. Pevely processed and distributed milk, ice cream, cottage cheese, and yogurt to markets in southeastern Missouri, southern Illinois, and areas of Kentucky and Tennessee. The acquisition included five milk-processing plants. Family owned and operated since the company's founding in 1887, Pevely continued to be led by members of the Kerckhoff family, who decided to sell the company to remain competitive. The Pevely acquisition added approximately $60 million in annual sales to revenues at Prairie Farms.

PDF Supply grew as an important source of revenues, serving independent restaurants as well as fast-food chains. By 1989 PFD Supply recorded $218 million in sales delivering over 1,200 items, including fresh and frozen meat, dairy products, frozen fish and seafood, produce, carbonated beverages, cleaning supplies, plastic cutlery, and paper products. Two warehouses, one in Granite City, Illinois, and a new warehouse in Lebanon, Indiana, served over 800 chain restaurant locations, with deliveries being made within a 400-mile radius of each warehouse. The Lebanon warehouse supplied only McDonald's restaurants, however. PFD Supply's customers were located in Illinois, Missouri, Indiana, Kentucky, Tennessee, and parts of Mississippi, Arkansas, and Kansas. The subsidiary made deliveries of at least 100 cases to each location three times per week, with larger and more frequent deliveries being made to McDonald's locations.

New leadership took the helm at Prairie Farms in 1988 when Gourley stepped down as CEO and general manager after 50 years at the helm. During that time Gourley oversaw the growth of Prairie Farms from a small cooperative to a large, multi-state operation with $165 million in assets and over $500 million in annual revenues. He wrote the *Prairie Farm News* (originally *Co-op Producer*), the cooperative's newsletter, since its inception in 1943. Gourley took the positions of senior vice-president and COO until his death in 1991. Leonard J. Southwell replaced Gourley as CEO. Southwell joined Prairie Farms in 1964 through the acquisition of Equity Union Creamery, where he served as general manager.

1990s: Prairie Farms Among Top Fluid Milk Bottlers

Prairie Farms expanded through merger, acquisition, and joint venture during the 1990s, though many of the acquisitions were transacted for joint ventures. The Steffens Dairy in Wichita, the Gold Spot Dairy in Enid, Oklahoma, and the Gilt Edge Dairy in Norman, Oklahoma, became part of Hiland Dairy, while Fairmont-Zarda in Kansas City, Missouri, became part of Roberts Dairy. Madison Dairy Butter, a joint venture formed in July 1993, operated a butter plant in St. Louis. Prairie Farms purchased Food Service Systems to expand operations at the PFD Supply subsidiary. The company acquired three distribution centers in 1994 to support general operations in Illinois and Kentucky. In addition to expanding the company's reach to Galesburg, Michigan, and Lima, Ohio, Prairie Farms strengthened its presence in Indiana through four acquisitions and a merger with Allen Dairy Products.

One of the attractions of a merger or acquisition involved the availability of capital to upgrade equipment and make processing plants more efficient. This was the case for Allen Dairy Products, a cooperative of 95 milk producers in northeast Indiana and northwest Ohio. After acquisition by Prairie Farms in January 1994, Prairie Farms added new equipment and began expansion of the Fort Wayne facility. The facility was expanded by 12,000 square feet to double the size of the storage cooler where the installation of conveyer belts improved order fulfillment functions. The cooler packed 110,000 gallons of milk daily for distribution.

Prairie Farms' investment in facilities and infrastructure increased considerably during the late 1990s. In 1997 the company invested $11.6 million on plant equipment, including silos, blow molding, case packer and stacker equipment, and plastic milk bottle filling lines for 8-ounce, 12-ounce, and half-gallon containers. Capital investment of $17 million in 1998 included $8 million for an ultrahigh temperature processing plant in Granite City. The plant processed soft-serve ice cream mix, half-pints of milk for vending machines, half-and-half cream, and five-gallon bags of milk. Prairie Farms spent $14 million on similar projects in 1999.

In the late 1990s Prairie Farms became one of the top five fluid milk bottlers in the country. In 1994 Prairie Farms recorded $800 million in revenues, but surpassed the $1 billion mark when revenues from joint ventures were counted. Prairie Farms' operations alone passed the $1 billion mark in 1999, with $1.05 billion in revenues; joint ventures added $685 million in revenues.

In the fall of 2000 Southwell retired as CEO, being replaced by Roger Capps, a 23-year veteran of Prairie Farms. Capps inherited leadership of a cooperative in a strong financial position, carrying small amounts of long-term debt. Prairie Farms placed 15th among the 150 largest privately held companies in the St. Louis area, based on its fiscal 2000 revenues. Operating income of $52.1 million yielded net income of $43.1 million. Net income from joint ventures reached $25.9 million. Prairie Farms paid $28.5 million in patronage to cooperative members, the equivalent of $1.93 per hundredweight of milk.

While Prairie Farms did not omit the possibility of future growth through mergers or acquisitions, the company engaged in only one transaction at this time. The Prairie Farms joint venture Hiland Dairy purchased Farm Fresh Dairy Division of Farm Fresh, Inc. in April 2001. The acquisition included a state-of-the-art plant in Chandler, Oklahoma, one of the newest dairy processing facilities in the country. The facility handled the processing of milk, cottage cheese, yogurts, and manufactured ice cream and frozen desserts in bulk or in packages. The facility also bottled fruit juices and spring water.

Principal Subsidiaries

PFD Supply, Inc.; Ice Cream Specialties, Inc.; Pevely Dairy Company; Hiland Dairy Foods (50%); Roberts Dairy (50%); Muller Pinehurst (50%); Ideal American (50%).

Principal Competitors

Associated Milk Producers, Inc.; Dairy Farmers of America; Land O'Lakes, Inc.

Further Reading

"Combined Case Packer/Stacker Saves Space," *Dairy Foods,* September 1997, p. 12.

Dobson, W.D., "Competitive Strategies of US Fluid Milk Processors: A Case Study," *Agribusiness*, September 1992, p. 425.

Fusaro, Dave, "Only Semi-Retired at 76," *Dairy Foods,* December 2000, p. 13.

"Hiland and Roberts Form New Company," *Ice Cream Reporter*, March 20, 1997, p. 1.

"Hiland Dairy Acquiring Farm Fresh," *Ice Cream Reporter*, April 20, 2001, p. 2.

"LeDuc, Doug, "Dairy Aims to Increase Sales with Expansion," *Knight Ridder/Tribune Business News*, September 28, 1998.

——, "Prairie Farms Dairy Merges with Allen Dairy Products Cooperative," *Knight Ridder/Tribune Business News*, January 4, 1994.

Mans, Jack, "Capital Commitments: 1997's Gonna Be a Good Year," *Dairy Foods*, June 1997, p. 76.

Norris, Melinda, "Roberts, Hiland Dairies Team Up on Ice Cream," *Omaha World-Herald Company*, January 25, 1997, p. 38.

"150 Largest Privately Held Companies," *St. Louis Business Journal*, March 23, 2001, p. 34.

"P.F.D. Supply," *Institutional Distribution*, February 1990, p. 96.

Powell, Jeff, "Powell Takes Roberts Diary into 21st Century," *Dairy Foods,* December 2000, p. 16.

Prairie Farms Dairy, Inc. Economic Impact of a Dairy Cooperative, Research Report Number 12, second printing, U.S. Department of Agriculture: Washington, D.C., 1982.

"Steffen Dairy Foods Gets Third Owner in Six Years," *Wichita Business Journal*, October 18, 1991, p. 3.

Steyer, Robert, "Dairy Co-ops Drop Ban on Farmers' Use of BST," *St. Louis Dispatch*, May 5, 1994, p. 1C.

Stroud, Jerri, "Big Hike in Cost of Milk," *St. Louis Dispatch*, October 8, 1989, p. 1A.

——, "Milk Merger Pevely Agrees to Buyout by Prairie Farms; Terms Undisclosed," *St. Louis Dispatch*, June 14, 1989, p. 1E.

—Mary Tradii

Proskauer Rose LLP

1585 Broadway
New York, New York 10036
U.S.A.
Telephone: (212) 969-3000
Fax: (212) 969-2900
Web site: http://www.proskauer.com

Private Partnership
Founded: 1878 as Rose & Putzel
Employees: 1,100
Gross Billings: $250 million (2000 est.)
NAIC: 541110 Offices of Lawyers

Proskauer Rose LLP is among the largest American law firms and one of the top ten based in New York City, offering a wide variety of legal services to major clients throughout the United States and the world. Unlike some of New York's elite firms, it cannot rely on traditional ties to old money or the big investment banks that are a source of fat fees. Instead, Proskauer Rose has grown and profited by serving corporations in such down-to-earth areas as labor and employment law. It also is one of the few major firms with a healthcare practice and is active in sports management, representing the interests of owners of professional sports franchises. The firm also has wide experience in such areas as corporate finance, mergers and acquisitions, real estate transactions, bankruptcy and reorganizations, taxation, litigation and dispute resolution, and intellectual property.

A Century of Law Practice: 1878–1978

William R. Rose, founder of the firm that became Proskauer Rose, was born in New York City in 1854 and was admitted to the bar in 1875. In 1878, he and his friend Gideon Putzel founded the firm of Rose & Putzel. Until 1908, the partners were largely engaged in a personal, family, and real estate practice catering to Jewish families. Clients included businessmen engaged in such fields as textiles, breweries and distilleries, and cigars and cigarettes. Probably the most important early client was Henry Siegel, who established the large Siegel-Cooper department store at 620 Sixth Avenue in Manhattan.

Putzel died in 1907 and was succeeded as partner by Benjamin Paskusz, who had joined the firm in 1898. After he dropped the "z" from his name, the firm became Rose & Paskus. Rose's son Alfred L. Rose joined the firm in 1911, when it had four other lawyers besides the partners. Rose & Paskus was general counsel to Gimbel Brothers, proprietors of the Herald Square alternative to Macy's department store, and to members of the Gimbel family. It also represented such noted theatrical producers of the era as Abraham Erlanger and Charles Frohman. The adoption of the federal income tax in 1913 gave Rose & Paskus a new line of business in which Paskus excelled. By 1915, the firm had clients in all major U.S. cities and also in a number of European cities. May Department Stores Co. became a regular client in 1920.

By 1923, both partners of Rose & Paskus were deteriorating in health. Rose's son, who became a partner in 1919, helped pick up the slack and recruited a close friend, Norman Goetz, who joined the firm as a partner in 1925. In-house lawyers Lawrence Coit, Sylvan Gotschal, and Walter Mendelsohn were also made partners in 1926. The younger Rose became a specialist in real estate, corporate, and probate law. Mendelsohn, who died in 1995 at the age of 98, was cited in his *New York Times* obituary as "a driving force in virtually every facet of the firm's growth. A trust, estates and corporations specialist, he was credited with everything from creating the firm's structure of departments in the 1920s to establishing branch offices in the 1970s."

In 1930, a much more public figure, Joseph M. Proskauer, joined the firm, which now became Proskauer, Rose & Paskus. A Democratic party stalwart and friend of former governor Al Smith, Proskauer was a state appeals-court judge before retiring from the bench to resume the practice of law. Active in civic and charitable organizations (and later in raising funds for the new state of Israel), Proskauer presumably recruited clients from his large roster of acquaintances. An experienced trial lawyer, he represented in court such large firms as Bethlehem Steel Co., Cities Services Co., National City Bank, Loew's Inc., Radio Corporation of America, Union Carbide & Carbon Co., and Universal Pictures. He defended banks and stockbrokers in several cases involving their liabilities and Warner Brothers Pictures Corp. and other companies against shareholder suits.

He also served as counsel to public utilities that were opposing government actions deemed to unfavorably affect their interests. In addition, Proskauer successfully represented, on appeal, the aunt of Gloria Vanderbilt, who won custody of her niece from the girl's mother in a celebrity case of the 1930s.

The firm was renamed Proskauer, Rose, Goetz & Mendelsohn in 1942. Proskauer died in 1971, Goetz in 1972, and Rose in 1981. Proskauer, Rose, Goetz & Mendelsohn gained a new partner in 1954, when George M. Shapiro, counsel to Governor Thomas E. Dewey, left government service. Shapiro had played an important role in drafting such significant legislation as the establishment of the state's university system, the New York City Transit Authority, and the Waterfront Commission. Charles D. Breitel was Shapiro's original boss in Albany. After serving as Dewey's counsel, he became chief judge of New York and, in 1978, facing mandatory retirement at the age of 70, also joined Proskauer, Rose, Goetz & Mendelsohn. In the same year a federal judge, Marvin E. Franklen, rejoined the firm as a managing partner.

Expansion in the 1980s

Proskauer, Rose, Goetz & Mendelsohn opened a Los Angeles office in 1979, and by 1988 this office was staffed with 30 lawyers. By 1989, there was also a San Francisco office. In 1988, the firm recruited Arnold Burns, second-in-command at the U.S. Department of Justice, to head its Washington office. This office doubled in size within a year. In New York, Proskauser Rose Goetz & Mendelsohn (the commas appear to have been dropped by then) hired 15 lawyers in 1987 from Schwartz Klink & Schreiber, a firm which was dissolved. Nine of these lawyers were in litigation; the others were in corporate, securities, tax, and real estate law. At least seven Botein Hays & Sklar lawyers joined the firm when their own firm closed its doors at the end of 1989 because of a loss of business during the recession. In 1990, Proskauer Rose Goetz & Mendelsohn affiliated itself with a Paris-based firm, Dubarry, Gaston-Dreyfus, Leveque, Le Douarin, Servan-Schreiber, so that each could represent the other's foreign clients in court. Proskauer Rose had now grown to about 400 lawyers, compared to about 250 in 1987.

One of the clients of Proskauer Rose Goetz & Mendelsohn was the National Basketball Association. David J. Stern, a rising star in the firm who in 1974—at the age of 32—became its youngest partner ever, helped arrange the 1976 merger with the American Basketball Association that put an end to the rivalry between the established professional league and its feisty, but undercapitalized, rival. Stern left the firm to join the NBA in 1978 and became its commissioner in 1984. Gary Bettman, also a Proskauer Rose Goetz & Mendelsohn lawyer, joined the NBA as Stern's assistant in 1981 and became the first commissioner of the National Hockey League in 1993. Randy Levine, another of the firm's lawyers, was major league baseball's chief negotiator for the five-year agreement with the players' union signed in 1996. Another Proskauer Rose client was Madison Square Garden, the venue for many New York sporting events. Proskauer Rose was credited by some observers with saving the 1998–99 NBA season in hard bargaining with the players. In 2000, the firm scored another success when its client Robert Wood Johnson IV made a successful bid to purchase the New York Jets of the National Football League.

Proskauer Rose Goetz & Mendelsohn's presence in sports management was only one facet of its prominence in labor and employment practice, "an area of law," according to Matthew Goldstein of *Crain's New York Business,* "that many of Manhattan's largest firms have historically considered too grubby." Its clients in this field were solidly in management's corner. "We are on the opposite side of almost everything," a founding partner of a pro-union law firm active in labor and employment practice told Goldstein. In 1991, Proskauer Rose, Goetz & Mendelsohn entered another "grubby" field when it brought in Ronald Storette and Lowell Gettman to head a new practice in immigration and naturalization law.

Proskauer Rose in the 1990s

Proskauer Rose Goetz & Mendelsohn moved from its Park Avenue headquarters in 1990 to a new 43-story office building at 1585 Broadway, between West 47th and 48th streets. This made the firm a pioneer in the still raunchy Times Square area, but its options were limited because it wanted a lot of space with the ability to accommodate state-of-the-art wiring and computer fixtures. Taking a 20-year lease, the firm occupied 11 stories and 365,000 square feet of the building but found itself the sole tenant as recession put a crimp on business activity in the city and drove the building's developer into bankruptcy. Citing such conditions as an incomplete facade, unfinished paving, unreliable elevators, and unwashed windows, the firm began withholding rent in the fall of 1991. For a time it took over the building maintenance, but it was able to yield that role after Morgan Stanley Group, Inc. bought the building. Morgan Stanley made the building its worldwide headquarters in 1995 but remained its only other tenant, although by 2000 the Times Square area had attracted many other legal, financial, and information services firms. Proskauer Rose Goetz & Mendelsohn opened branch offices in Paris and Boca Raton, Florida, during the mid-1990s. However, it closed its 16-lawyer San Francisco office in 1995.

When another of the city's leading law firms, Shea & Gould, broke up in early 1994, Proskauer, Rose, Goetz & Mendelsohn added 20 of the firm's lawyers. Five of them joined as partners: Shea & Gould corporate department head Arnold S. Jacobs, former litigation head Leon Gold, real estate specialist Law-rence J. Lipson, corporate lawyer Allen R. Williams, and litiga-tor Richard M. Goldstein. They and the other 15 were said to have brought substantial business with them. Lipson, who be-came co-chair of the firm's real estate practice, reportedly brought in $6 million worth of fees in 1997 alone. In 1995, John Gross, formerly head of insurance litigation practice for Ander-son Kill & Olick, joined the firm to assume its practice in that field. He brought four associates with him.

The firm, which became simply Proskauer Rose in 1997, had close ties to New York City Mayor Rudolph Giuliani in the 1990s. Gross and Burns were friends of Giuliani dating back from his tenure as a federal prosecutor in the 1980s. Gross was treasurer of the mayor's campaign committee in 1989, 1993, and 1997. Levine became a deputy mayor in his administration, and Proskauer Rose partner Saul Cohen was one of his leading fundraisers and became president of the Rudolph Giuliani Cen-ter for Urban Affairs when he left office at the end of 2001. The firm was outside counsel to the city's office of labor relations, a position that dated back to the administration of Mayor Edward Koch (1977–89).

Proskauer Rose established a new-media practice, called iPractice, and in 1999 decided to cut its normal $450-an-hour fee for new-media and Internet policy. It expressed a willing-ness to take stock in a company instead of fees, an unprece-dented action for the firm. "We have targeted this particular industry because of the potential it has for our corporation practice," Alan Jaffe, Proskauer Rose's chairman, told Gold-stein, "and because we feel it is an industry that is indigenous to New York City." Proskauer Rose's clients in this field included two local Internet companies, 24/7 Media Inc. and iTurf Inc. "I know some of our clients we are doing work for are not going to make it," Arnold Levine, the chairman of iPractice, told Gold-stein. "But we're hoping that there will be clients whose success more than outweighs those that don't make it."

Proskauer Rose also was expanding in neighboring New Jersey. In 1998, the firm had only three lawyers working in the state, housed in a small office in Clifton since 1989. By late 1999, there were 15 lawyers doing business from a brand new office building in downtown Newark. Earlier in the year, Proskauer Rose had added a group of eight labor lawyers from a New Jersey firm, including one who brought with him Pruden-tial Insurance Co. of America, a major new client for the firm.

Proskauer Rose was ranked eighth among New York-area law firms in 2001, according to *Crain's New York Business*, with 457 lawyers, of whom 116 were partners. Unlike most of these firms, it had no banking and commerce practice, but also unlike most of them, it had a healthcare practice, with 17 attorneys. The firm had only nine female and minority partners in 1997, ranking 55th

among 77 national firms in a survey on working conditions for women. The firm was employing, in early 2002, 550 lawyers in Boca Raton, Los Angeles, Newark, Paris, and Washington. Its clients included companies in many industries, including chemi-cals, entertainment, financial services, healthcare, hospitality, information technology, insurance, internet, manufacturing, me-dia and communications, pharmaceuticals, real estate investment, sports, and transportation.

Principal Competitors

Cravath, Swane & Moore; Davis Polk & Wardwell; Paul, Weiss, Rifkind,Wharton & Garrison; Shearman & Sterling; Simpson, Thacher and Bartlett; Skadden Arps, Slate, Meagher & Flom; Sullivan & Cromwell; Weil Gotschal and Manges.

Further Reading

Abramson, Jill, "As a Former Deputy Attorney General Joins Private Firm, Ethics Issue Surfaces," *Wall Street Journal,* June 29, 1988, p. 52.

Breznick, Alan, "New Law Causing Migration," *Crain's New York Business,* September 30, 1991, pp. 1, 38.

"David J. Stern," in *1991 Current Biography Yearbook,* New York: H.W. Wilson, 1991.

"Dewey's Counsel to Practice Here," *New York Times,* December 9, 1954, p. 30.

Felsenthal, Edward, "Life After Shea & Gould," *Wall Street Journal,* February 28, 1994, p. B3.

Gabriel, Frederick, "Carrying Ball for Proskauer," *Crain's New York Business,* December 16, 1996, p. 19.

"Gary Bettman," in *1999 Current Biography Yearbook,* New York: H.W. Wilson, 1999.

Goldstein, Matthew, "New York Law Firms Go Poaching to Build Up Their Jersey Offices," *Crain's New York Business,* September 13, 1999, p. 21.

——, "Not Quite Alley Cats," *Crain's New York Business,* September 6, 1999, p. 3.

——, "Power Lineup Gets Law Firm Off Bench," *Crain's New York Business,* July 27, 1998, p. 4.

Goldstein, Tom, "Park Avenue Judges," *New York Times,* December 8, 1978, p. D4.

Klein, Chris, "It's a Neon Sunrise," *National Law Journal,* July 21, 1997, pp. A1, A9.

McDowell, Edwin, "Law Firm Is No Longer Lonely in Refurbished Tower on Times Square," *New York Times,* August 23, 2000, p. B8.

Proskauer, Joseph Meyer, *A Segment of My Times,* New York: Farrar, Straus, 1950.

Rose, Alfred L., *Proskauer Rose Goetz & Mendelsohn: The Early Years, 1875–1930,* New York: Proskauer, Rose, Goetz & Men-delsohn, 1982 (microfiche).

Rosenberg, Geanne, "A Touchdown for Proskauer," *National Law Journal,* January 31, 2000, pp. B1, B3.

"Walter Mendelsohn," *New York Times,* October 16, 1995, p. 37.

—Robert Halasz

Pueblo Xtra International, Inc.

1300 NW 22nd Street
Pompano Beach, Florida 33069
U.S.A.
Telephone: (954) 977-2500
Fax: (954)979-5770
Web site: http://www.puebloxtra.com

Wholly Owned Subsidiary of Cisneros Group
Incorporated: 1955 as Pueblo International
Employees: 4,800
Sales: $622 million (2001 est.)
NAIC: 445110 Supermarkets and Other Grocery (Except Convenience) Stores

Based in Pompano Beach, Florida, Pueblo Xtra International, Inc. is a holding company for subsidiaries involved in supermarkets and video rental stores in Puerto Rico and the U.S. Virgin Islands. The company operates 42 supermarkets in Puerto Rico and six in the Virgin Islands. Through its franchise rights with Blockbuster, Inc., Pueblo Xtra operates 24 video rental stores in Puerto Rico and two in the Virgin Islands, most of which are located near its supermarkets. In addition, 15 of its Puerto Rican supermarkets feature in-store video rental outlets. Pueblo Xtra is a subsidiary of the Cisneros Group, a privately held Venezuelan conglomerate, better known for its extensive Latin American media holdings.

Origins of Pueblo Xtra

The history of Pueblo Xtra is very much the story of Harold Toppel, the son of Russian immigrant parents. He was born and raised in the back of the family's small grocery store in Franklin, New Jersey. The store was a major part of his everyday life in the 1930s and early 1940s. He worked there while growing up, to the point that by the time he was an adult he "detested the grocery business." After graduating from high school in 1941, he worked in a number of factories before leaving for the University of Delaware to study mechanical engineering, a field which he soon discovered was not as exciting as he had imagined.

After the United States entered World War II, Toppel was drafted into the military and served with General George Patton's 4th Armored Division of the Third Army in Europe. When he resumed his education at the University of Illinois following the war it was as a business major, studying marketing and business administration. There he also gained some experience working in the cigarette and candy vending machine business, and considered devoting himself to that line of work before ultimately concluding that he lacked the necessary political, and possibly underworld, connections. Instead he went to work for Lever Bros. selling soap at $65 a week, a job which introduced him to a small Rahway, New Jersey, supermarket operator, who offered him a job. Overcoming his childhood antipathy for the grocery business, he accepted the position and quickly discovered that the job actually suited him.

In 1950, Toppel and three partners pooled their resources to create the National Grocery Company. They opened their first supermarket in Metuchen, New Jersey, with Toppel serving as manager. By 1953, the company opened three more stores and two of the partners were bought off for $300,000. The following year, Toppel sold his interest for $50,000 in cash and $25,000 in deferred payments. He took a trip to San Juan, Puerto Rico, in late 1954, and rather than getting his mind off of business he soon recognized that the island was untapped territory for supermarkets. The only competition were larger stores that concentrated on canned goods. Toppel decided to invest his $50,000 in opening the first complete supermarket on the island, and in order to conduct his business he incorporated Pueblo International in Delaware in 1955. At the behest of his mother, he also allowed his older brother George, who ran a New Jersey haberdashery store, to gain an equity position for $20,000. The first unit of what became the Pueblo Supermarkets chain was located in the Puerto Nuevo section of San Juan and opened on April 25, 1955. With 5,000 square feet of retail space, it grossed $30,000 in the first week, an amount that would double within a year. In 1957, a third Toppel brother joined the business and a second supermarket was opened.

By 1960, the Pueblo chain grew to six stores and Toppel decided to take the company public at $12.50 per share. After initially selling over the counter, it soon gained a listing on the

---

Company Perspectives:

Pueblo is the foremost supermarket chain in Puerto Rico and the U.S. Virgin Islands, known for its variety, quality and freshness in all its products.

New York Stock Exchange. With Pueblo Supermarkets now well established, Toppel began to accumulate other properties, starting in 1963 when he acquired the largest commercial bakery in the Caribbean, Wholesome Bakeries of Puerto Rico. In that same year, Pueblo Supermarkets spread to the Virgin Islands, when it opened its first outlet in Charlotte Amalie, St. Thomas. In 1965, Toppel attempted to transfer his success in the Caribbean to the mainland, acquiring a 90 percent stake in the pioneering grocery chain H.C. Bohack Co. He returned to the United States to serve as Bohack's chairman, but after several months he knew that the chain was not the vehicle for expansion he had hoped for. Moreover, he came to the realization that Puerto Rico was now his home.

Doing Business in New York City in the Late 1960s

Toppel unloaded the Bohack business and looked elsewhere for a better entry into the American market, in particular New York City. In early 1967, he acquired a 50 percent stake in the ten-store Great Eastern Food Markets grocery chain. Several months later he purchased Hills-Korvette, adding its 57 supermarkets to the 20 Pueblo Supermarkets now operated in Puerto Rico and the Virgin Islands. Toppel's hope was to use his acquired supermarkets to tap into the estimated one million Puerto Ricans that lived in New York City, with the intention of becoming the nation's largest importer of Puerto Rican food products. That dream, however, was not realized. By the early 1980s, the company began to shed its New York operation in order to focus its mainland activities on southern Florida with its large Latin population.

In 1983, Pueblo introduced its Xtra warehouse-style supermarkets, opening a 70,000-square-foot unit in Hato Tejas; it was by far the largest supermarket in Puerto Rico. Xtra was also introduced in the southern Florida market where its sheer size, especially its extensive produce section, sparked a revolution in area merchandising. By now Toppel had relinquished day-to-day control of the business, although he continued to serve as chairman of the board and retained a large stake in the operation. At the end of 1984, Pueblo consisted of 44 supermarkets located in Puerto Rico, the Virgin Islands, and Florida, generating more than $475 million in annual revenues. Although the Xtra stores promised to provide economies of scale, resulting in lower prices to lure more customers, the cost of opening the large stores was so high that it took several years before they became profitable.

Late in 1987 a management group that included Toppel announced its intention to take Pueblo private through a leveraged buyout funded by investment bankers. The purpose of the move was to shelter the company from shareholder pressure for a period of time in order to improve the underlying cost structure. Afterwards, according to Toppel's plan, the company would again go public, allowing certain investors to cash out at

a more lucrative price. The first step of this plan was accomplished by June 1988 when shareholders approved a $125.5 million buyout offer from First Boston Corp. and the Metropolitan Life Insurance Company. Now, as a private concern, Pueblo expanded into the video business even as management pared down operational costs. In 1990, the company won an exclusive franchise to Puerto Rico and the Virgin Islands from Blockbuster Entertainment, opening its first video store that year in Carolina, Puerto Rico. In addition to stand-alone stores, Pueblo offered in-house video stores in many of its supermarkets. In Florida, however, the company's supermarket video rentals, which began in the late 1980s, faced stiff competition and by mid-1992 were discontinued. Moreover, the Florida Xtra stores struggled in a tight market, made even more competitive by warehouse clubs that added produce to their grocery offerings.

By 1993, Pueblo's major investors were eager to realize a profit and settled on a number of options. They decided that the first choice was to sell the business and, if that proved unsuccessful, to make a public issuance of stock or to borrow money in order to pay down debt so that the company was in a position to issue dividends to shareholders. Management produced a written offering that was shared with 60 prospective buyers, resulting in several serious candidates who then studied the company's books and visited its operations. In May 1993, private auction bids were submitted, and the eventual successful bidder was the Venezuelan Cisneros Group. Its $426.5 million offer, backed by Chase Manhattan and Morgan Stanley, was the largest transaction in the history of Puerto Rico. As a result, Pueblo International became a subsidiary of Pueblo Xtra International, Inc., which in turn became a subsidiary of the Cisneros Group. Although he would remain as chairman emeritus, Toppel relinquished control of the business he founded some 40 years earlier. He remained involved in his family's investment firm as well as philanthropic endeavors.

Cisneros Brothers' 1960s Rise to Power

The Cisneros Group was a privately held conglomerate controlled by brothers Ricardo and Gustavo Cisneros. Like Toppel, theirs was a second generation immigrant success story, with the exception that their parents were immigrants to Venezuela, rather than the United States. Their father, Diego Cisneros, left Cuba for Venezuela decades before Castro's revolution of the late 1950s. Starting out as a truck driver, Diego Cisneros obtained a Pepsi bottling concession in 1940 that made him a wealthy man and led to the formation of the Cisneros Group in 1953. The entry into television came in 1961 with the launching of Venevision. Diego's sons, educated in the United States, began to chart their own course to wealth and political power in the 1960s, a time when Venezuela began to enjoy the benefits of large oil deposits. Gustavo became chairman and CEO of the Cisneros Group in 1968 and along with his brother, who became chief operating officer in 1970, built the conglomerate into a vast enterprise, owning supermarket and department store chains, a beer company, African mining interests, numerous Burger King and Pizza Hut franchises, and media interests that included part ownership of Univision, the country's largest Spanish-language television network. The Cisneros empire also included American companies Evenflo, makers of baby products, and Spalding, the 100-year-old sporting goods manufacturer.

Key Dates:

1955: Pueblo International is formed and opens its first supermarket in Puerto Rico.
1960: The company goes public.
1963: First Pueblo supermarket opens in the U.S. Virgin Islands.
1983: Pueblo Xtra warehouse stores are introduced.
1988: The company is taken private.
1993: Cisneros Group acquires the company.
1996: Pueblo supermarkets are closed in Florida.
1998: Hurricane Georges causes major damage to the company's operations.

Being owned by the Cisneros Group offered great promise for Pueblo Xtra. Management planned to improve its buying power as well as expand its Xtra warehouse supermarkets in south Florida. Moreover, the company hoped to take advantage of the Univision connection to obtain a discount, allowing Pueblo Xtra to advertise on television for the first time. These ambitious ideas, however, were shelved in the wake of a financial catastrophe in Venezuela, triggered by the failure of the country's second largest bank, Banco Latino, that led to a run on a number of other institutions. Ricardo Cisneros, who a year earlier had become Banco Latino's chairman, fled the country for Miami after arrest warrants were issued for him and 82 others, who faced charges of fraud, misappropriation, and publishing false bank balances. In addition to bad publicity that was fueled by a rival media group, the Cisneros Group suffered major losses in Venezuela, which forced it to sell off businesses in order to concentrate on its core media and entertainment interests.

Pueblo Xtra was one of the Cisneros businesses that appeared destined for the block. In August 1995, the parent company announced its intention to auction off Pueblo Xtra, but by January 1996 it changed course, opting instead to retain the business but focus on the Puerto Rican and Virgin Island operations. The eight Florida Xtra stores were put up for sale. Unable to find suitable buyers, Cisneros simply closed down the operations later in the year, thus severing Pueblo Xtra's ties to the mainland, although the company continued to maintain its corporate headquarters in Pompano Beach, Florida.

With the loss of the Florida stores, Pueblo Xtra's annual revenues dipped below $1 billion. Management concentrated on growing sales at its remaining stores, which, unlike the early days when Harold Toppel opened the first supermarket on Puerto Rico, now faced stiff competition from rival chains. To improve profitability, in 1997 the company launched its own Pueblo brand of products, which would grow to more than 300 items, ranging from canned goods to bread. Management's efforts were severely set back in September 1998 when Hurricane Georges devastated the region, causing extensive damage to most of the chain's stores. The company initiated a rebuilding program that would last well past 2000. Not only did sales suffer because so many of the supermarkets were not fully operational, but the Hurricane had an adverse effect on the economy of Puerto Rico, which further weakened revenues. Because Pueblo Xtra's stores were more extensively damaged than those of its competitors, the company also faced the prospect of winning back customers that had developed a loyalty to other supermarkets. Moreover, regional competition in groceries was growing even stiffer, with the addition of warehouse clubs, megastores, and discount stores. Although the prospects for Pueblo Xtra were far from dire, its future was certainly cloudy. Industry rumors suggested a sale of the chain to Wal-Mart, denied by all parties, was in the works. The Cisneros Group, after emerging from a rough patch in the mid-1990s, was even more of a major media player with its new ties to satellite television provider DirecTV. It was more in the news for its battles with Rupert Murdoch over the Latin American market than for its interests in the grocery business. Whether Pueblo Xtra would remain worth keeping to the Cisneros Group was undoubtedly an open question.

Principal Subsidiaries

Pueblo International, LLC; Pueblo Entertainment, Inc.; Xtra Super Food Center, Inc.

Principal Competitors

Kmart Corporation; Walgreen Co.; Wal-Mart Stores, Inc.

Further Reading

De Cordoba, Jose, "Troubled Empire: A Conglomerate Reels from Bank's Failure and Caracas Politics," *Wall Street Journal*, November 16, 1994, p. A1.

Gigante, Lucienne, "Reinventing Pueblo Supermarkets," *Caribbean Business*, March 1, 2001, p. 18.

Goodman, Cindy Krischer, "Xtra CEO Gets Boost with Acquisitions by Cisneros," *Miami Daily Business Review*, August 6, 1993, p. 6.

Jaffe, Thomas, "Viva el Pueblo," *Forbes*, June 4, 1984, p. 42.

Nemy, Enid, "Grocer Boy Finds Island Treasure," *New York Times*, May 18, 1969, p. 18.

Vogel, Thomas T., Jr., "Latin Clan Scours for Media Deal," *Wall Street Journal*, September 18, 1996, p. A14.

Zwiebach, Elliot, "Pueblo Is Considering IPO, Sale," *Supermarket News*, January 25, 1993, p. 1.

—Ed Dinger

Puerto Rico Electric Power Authority

Avenue Ponce De Leon 17½
Puerto Rico
Telephone: (787) 289-3434
Fax: (787) 289-4665
Web site: http://www.prepa.com

Government-Owned Company
Incorporated: 1941 as Puerto Rico Water Resources
    Authority
Employees: 10,200
Sales: $1.99 billion (2000)
NAIC: 221121 Electric Bulk Power Transmission and
    Control

Puerto Rico Electric Power Authority (Prepa) is a government-owned utility responsible for the distribution of electricity to 1.3 million residential and business customers of Puerto Rico. Although it generates most of its own power, Prepa has in recent years turned to independent power producers to provide additional sources of electricity in order to keep pace with the island's increasing demand. Prepa is directed by a nine-member government board, seven of which are appointed by the Governor of Puerto Rico, subject to Senate approval. The remaining two board members represent the clients and are chosen through an election supervised by the Consumer Affairs Department. The government board is responsible for appointing an executive director to oversee the operations of the utility, which for administrative purposes divides Puerto Rico into seven regions, serviced by more than 10,000 employees.

Private Companies Supplying Electricity in Early 20th-Century Puerto Rico

Electricity was initially generated in Puerto Rico for private lighting systems, the first of which was installed as early as 1893. Over the next two decades other private companies cropped up in the island's larger urban areas. The first public power plant, a hydroelectric facility, was established in 1915, the same year that the Electric Light Anonymous Society established Puerto Rico's first public street lighting system, located in the capital city of San Juan. To prepare for visiting royalty, eight lamp posts with some 600 incandescent lamps were installed. Other small street lighting systems soon followed. It was not until 1908 that the government of Puerto Rico became involved in the production of power through a small agency, the South Coast Irrigation Service, which required electricity for a regional irrigation system. The agency built a hydroelectric plant, making use of the waters in the Carite Lake that also flowed into the system's irrigation channels. A second Carite hydroelectric plant was opened in 1922.

As Puerto Rico created other artificial lakes and generating plants, a new government agency under the auspices of the Department of the Interior was created in 1926 to manage the emerging electric power system: Water Resources Use. Three years later the agency placed into service its first hydroelectric plant, followed in 1937 by a second facility. It was also in 1937 that the government purchased the privately owned Ponce Electric Company, setting the stage for the acquisition of all of the island's private power companies, which were incorporated into the public system. A network of power lines began to crisscross Puerto Rico as a distribution system evolved. Taking advantage of funding made available from the Puerto Rico Reconstruction Administration, part of the United States' New Deal legislation of 1935 to reduce unemployment and stimulate economic growth, Water Resources opened two new hydroelectric plants in 1941. The agency was superceded in May 1941 by the creation of Puerto Rico's first public corporation and Prepa's original incarnation, The Puerto Rico Water Resources Authority (PRWRA). The Authority was incorporated in order to gain the ability to float bonds and raise the financing necessary to meet the island's rising need for power and an expanded distribution infrastructure. The concept of an "Authority" had been made popular in recent years with the rise of The Port Authority of New York, which had been able to successfully fund the building of the George Washington Bridge and other major projects. PRWRA's reliance on hydroelectric power plants accounted for the "Water Resources" in its name.

PRWRA continued the process of consolidating power plants, in 1945 purchasing the island's two main electric systems, Puerto Rico Railway Light and Power Company and the

Company Perspectives:

Our Mission: To provide electric energy services to clients in the most efficient, cost-effective and reliable manner, without affecting the environment.

Mayagüez Light Power and Ice Company. To this point in the history of Puerto Rico, electricity was essentially confined to urban areas, with just 12 percent of the rural population having access. PRWRA began a major push to rectify this situation in 1946, financed by its own means as well as government money. Further funding would come from the Rural Electrification Administration of the United States starting in 1952.

In the second half of the century, hydroelectricity was replaced by petroleum burning turbines in Puerto Rico. PRWRA experimented briefly with nuclear power in the early 1960s but settled on oil. A new oil-burning power plant in the early 1970s would be the last of any kind to be built on the island for a generation. As a result, PRWRA found itself highly dependent on petroleum and its derivatives, which generated 98 percent of all electricity on the island. Because just 2 percent of the utility's power was produced by water, the government in 1979 changed the name of PRWRA to the Puerto Rico Electric Power Authority. Two years later, Prepa acquired the electric system owned by the municipality of Cayey, an act which finally consolidated all of the island's electric system under the control of a single utility.

Prepa's position as a monopoly was strengthened by the 1978 passage of the federal Power Utilities Regulatory Act that only permitted independent energy producers to sell to an area's monopoly utility. Over the next dozen years, Prepa did not increase its production capacity, despite a mounting demand for power on the island, and by the 1990s had a poor reputation. Not only did its customers have to pay high rates, they had to endure frequent blackouts, which lasted on average nearly ten hours. Customers on the mainland, by contrast, experienced about four hours of outages in an entire year. Prepa customers were further frustrated when they attempted to telephone the utility, usually forced to wait 90 minutes before talking to a representative. Much of Prepa's problems could be attributed to geography. Operating on an island, unlike the mainland, it was unable to tap into a neighboring supply of energy during an emergency. It desperately needed a reserve capacity, but because Prepa had not built a new power plant in 20 years it was not able to keep up with the current need for electricity, let alone provide a buffer for peak periods of usage or to account for plants going offline due to maintenance or breakdowns. Furthermore, the system was aging and much of its transmission lines were above ground and exposed. It was also evident that Prepa would be simply unable to meet the island's energy needs by the end of the century. It considered investing in a battery energy storage system to provide reserve power, but there was little doubt that what was needed was new power plants. Because a new facility required several years lead time before it could be operational, Prepa had to take immediate steps in order to avert an eventual shortfall. If businesses could not count on a consistent supply of electricity, they would not choose to conduct business in Puerto Rico, which would have a devastating effect on the island's economy. Moreover, Prepa desperately needed to upgrade its oil-burning power plants and find cleaner fuels. The Environmental Protection Agency (EPA) levied a heavy fine against the utility in 1993. As late as 2001, Prepa plants occupied the top four spots on EPA's list of polluters, based on the release of toxic chemicals into the local environment.

Prepa's Government Board was well aware that changes needed to be made at Prepa, but an additional incentive was provided by the passage of the Energy Policy Act in 1992, which permitted independent companies to build power plants and sell energy directly to residential and business customers. The best way to fend off potential competition was to improve Prepa, and the first priority was to find newer and cleaner sources of energy. Because Prepa needed at least 1,000 additional megawatts by the year 2000, and it could only supply 40 percent of that total by upgrading facilities and building new plants, the utility had to find private suppliers. A cogeneration committee was formed with representation from eight government agencies to help Prepa select among a number of proposals. The concept of cogeneration called for excess heat resulting from the production of electricity to be used to produce steam, which could also be distributed and sold. In the end, two private power producers were selected: EcoElectrica, a natural gas fired system, and Applied Energy Systems (AES), a coal-power plant.

Shortly after the passage of the Energy Policy Act, Prepa named a new executive director, Miguel A. Cordero, who was well familiar with the utility's operations. In the early 1970s, he started out with Prepa as a line supervisor, overseeing maintenance crews. In his new capacity, Cordero was quick to fast-track plans for building new plants, as well as introduced new computer technology to help existing plants become more fuel efficient. The maintenance program was also improved, with more regular checkups also improving efficiency. Moreover, Cordero cut staff while increasing productivity and took efforts to enhance customer relations as well as environmental compliance.

Hurricane Georges and Its Aftermath: 1998

Until new sources of electricity came online, however, Cordero could not address the primary need of Prepa. The devastation wrought by Hurricane Georges in 1998 revealed other shortcomings that required attention. With winds that reached 130 miles per hour, the hurricane was the worst to strike Puerto Rico in 70 years. Because so much of Prepa's transmission lines were above ground, most of the island was plunged into darkness. Five days after the winds subsided, less than a third of Prepa's system was operational, and it was estimated that 85 percent of the population was without power. Even two weeks after Georges struck, almost a third of the electric system remained out of commission. It was not until 73 days had passed that Prepa finally returned to fully operational status. Making the best of a catastrophe, Cordero used the opportunity to upgrade more than 10,000 downed poles and several telecommunications towers, ensuring that in the future they would be able to withstand 120 mile-per-hour winds. The utility also developed an improved, detailed emergency plan for restoring power to the island in future disasters.

As Prepa waited for its private energy providers to come online, it looked to take advantage of its system in order to

Key Dates:

1893: Puerto Rico's first electric lighting system begins operation.
1908: The island's first government-funded power plant is built.
1941: Puerto Rico Water Resources Authority (PRWRA) is established.
1979: PRWRA changes name to Puerto Rico Electric Power Authority.
1992: Energy Policy Act permits private companies to sell electricity.
2000: EcoElectrica natural gas burning plant comes on-line.

generate other revenue streams. A natural gas pipeline built by Prepa for the EcoElectrica project, connecting the new gas-fired power plant to a major new storage facility, had the potential of being extended to other parts of the island. The pipeline could also be rented to private industry or even sold. Moreover, it could be used to convert older oil-burning power plants to natural gas. Another attempt at diversification was the purchase of the Commonwealth Oil Refining Corp. (Corco) in Guayanilla and the Union Carbide refinery in Peneulas. Should there be a spike in oil prices, Prepa would now be able to turn to crude stored at Corco until prices returned to more reasonable levels. Prepa also took steps to become involved in the communications business by constructing a fiber optic system using its distribution system as the basic infrastructure. Prepa would then act as a wholesaler, renting unused capacity to commercial interests. The utility even planned to make its fleet of helicopters available for rental. The thrust of all these initiatives was to lower Prepa's expenses in order to reduce Puerto Rico's high energy costs.

The EcoElectrica natural gas-burning plant started operations in the summer of 2000, providing more than 500 megawatts of power, or 17 percent of Puerto Rico's demand. The AES coal-powered plant was delayed in becoming operational, its opening pushed back to the summer of 2002. Once online it was expected to contribute 15 percent of Prepa's capacity. As a result of these private suppliers, the system would go from being 98 percent dependent on crude oil to just 67 percent, a significant step towards fuel diversification as well as creating a much cleaner system. Prepa's plans were hindered, however, by problems with the utility's $200 million natural gas plant initiative, the Repowering San Juan Project, which was supposed to take advantage of the EcoElectrica natural gas storage facility and provide an additional 320 megawatts of power. After construction began, the developer abandoned the project, which led to litigation, and work came to a halt.

In 2001, Prepa, under the leadership of a new executive director, Hector Rosario, appeared well situated to meet the island's energy demands until 2007. Looking beyond that date, as well as continuing the effort to lower Prepa's reliance on oil and improve system efficiency, Rosario prepared to ask for bids on a third cogeneration plant to be built in the western part of Puerto Rico, which was not yet served by a local power plant. Escalating oil and natural gas prices, however, forced him to postpone the completion of an expansion plan that called for $34 million for the upgrading of Prepa headquarters, the remodeling of other buildings, and the construction of a plaza. With Prepa barely staying ahead of Puerto Rico's energy demands and still too dependent on the price swings of crude oil, Rosario was committed to first devoting the utility's money to improving its transmission and distribution system. A reliable and ample supply of electricity was not only important for Prepa's financial well-being, the future economy of Puerto Rico also depended upon it.

Further Reading

Alfaro, Aura N., "A Mightier Prepa," *Caribbean Business,* May 6, 1999, p. 18.
Diaz, Alexander F., "Turning It On," *Caribbean Business,* January 11, 1996, p. 12.
Gigante, Lucienne, "Leading the Way," *Caribbean Business,* May 17, 2001, p. 22.
——, "Prepa Looking to Make Money," *Caribbean Business,* July 27, 2000, p. 4.
Schell, Mari Carmen, "It's Time to Energize Puerto Rico," *Caribbean Business,* September 2, 1993, p. 1.
Tangeman, Michael, "Power Island," *Latin Finance,* September 1998, pp. 67–8.

—Ed Dinger

QUALCOMM Incorporated

5775 Morehouse Drive
San Diego, California 92121-1714
U.S.A.
Telephone: (858) 587-1121
Fax: (858) 658-2100
Web site: http://www.qualcomm.com

Public Company
Incorporated: 1985
Employees: 6,500
Sales: $2.7 billion (2001)
Stock Exchanges: NASDAQ
Ticker Symbol: QCOM
NAIC: 334220 Radio and Television Broadcasting and
    Wireless Communications Equipment Manufacturing
    (pt)

QUALCOMM Incorporated (Qualcomm) is a wireless communications company dedicated to the creation of innovative mobile phone systems. Its patented code division multiple access (CDMA) technology is used by telecommunications companies across the globe and has played an integral role in the development of a single international standard for wireless communications. Qualcomm's Third Generation technologies have combined mobile communications with Internet and email access, providing cell phone users with a range of data transfer capabilities. This integration of wireless and information technologies remains the company's primary goal heading into the 21st century.

The Birth of Mobile Communications in the 1960s

In 1959, two former engineering classmates at the Massachusetts Institute of Technology, Irwin Jacobs and Andrew Viterbi, reunited at an academic conference and resowed the seeds of a friendship that during the 1960s evolved into a consulting business and then, in 1968, into Linkabit, a San Diego-based manufacturer of digital communications equipment. After graduating from MIT in 1959, Jacobs had become a

professor of electrical engineering and in 1965 authored *Principles of Communication Engineering,* later described as "the first comprehensive textbook on digital communications." Viterbi had gone into research, helping to design the telemetry equipment of the first successful U.S. satellite, Explorer I, and playing a pioneering role in developing the potential of digital transmission technology for the telecommunications systems of space and satellite equipment.

At Linkabit, Jacobs and Viterbi applied their considerable talents to developing satellite communications applications for the television industry and by 1980 had transformed tiny Linkabit into a thriving communications enterprise with more than 1,000 employees and more than $100 million in sales. In August 1980, Linkabit merged with M/A-COM, forming M/A-COM Linkabit, a developer of cable television, data transmission, and other electronics technologies. Although Jacobs had risen to M/A-COM's executive vice-presidency by 1983, mobile satellite communications technology had developed to the point where both he and Viterbi saw a golden opportunity to create a new business with the potential to dominate its industry. If they could work out the as-yet-unsolved technical obstacles, Jacobs and Viterbi reasoned that the wireless mobile communications (WMC) market was so young—and so complex—that they could grab an insurmountable three- to five-year headstart over any future competition.

Revolutionizing the Trucking Industry: 1985–88

In 1985 they left M/A-COM (which was later sold and broken up) to form Qualcomm Inc., a provider of contract research and development services and which *Business Week* later described as a "tiny military house." Their real goal, however, was a full-fledged integrated research-to-manufacturing business, and they began to cast about for an application of digital satellite communications with commercial potential. Military uses were considered first but Jacobs soon decided that the transportation industry offered the best opportunity for building a WMC-based company.

If there was any segment of the U.S. transportation industry that needed the help of wireless, long-distance communications it was the trucking industry. Valuable shipping time was routinely lost as truckers pulled off the road to call into their dispatchers with updates on their location and expected arrival, and dispatchers' inability to precisely monitor and coordinate their fleets' schedules meant many "deadhead" miles as truckers wasted return trips with empty trucks that could have been used to haul more freight. Moreover, shippers themselves often had to act as ersatz dispatchers, continually checking in with trucking companies to see if their shipments would arrive on time. To solve these problems, between 1985 and 1988 Jacobs and Viterbi began developing a wireless, two-way messaging and positioning system that would enable trucking firms to closely track their drivers' progress while enabling drivers and dispatchers to send messages to each other.

Christened OmniTRACS, the system would lease the capability of existing communications satellites to create continent-wide coverage. Qualcomm's proprietary signal processing technology meant that OmniTRACS could operate without interfering with other satellite transmissions, and the position-reporting component would use either the federal government's Global Positioning System (GPS) satellites or a signal generated on a leased satellite using Qualcomm's own automatic satellite position-reporting system. Down on earth, a keyboard-and-terminal hardware and software package would be located next to the driver in the cab and a huge integrated network management facility in San Diego would route messages between truckers and dispatchers.

By 1988 Qualcomm was ready to unveil OmniTRACS to the public. Jacobs invited 300 trucking industry leaders to San Diego for a demonstration of the 30-pound device. It worked, and within months Qualcomm had signed up its first customer—Schneider National Inc. of Wisconsin, one of the largest long-haul truckers in the country. The Schneider contract alone was worth $20 million and involved 5,000 trucks, and by the end of 1989 Qualcomm's revenues had soared to $32 million. Qualcomm established OmniTRACS systems for Canada and Europe, and in August 1991 OmniTRACS enjoyed its first profitable month. On the eve of Qualcomm's initial public stock offering as a public corporation in the fall of 1991, it

landed a deal to launch OmniTRACS for Brazil's and Japan's trucking industries, and by early 1992 more than 23,000 Omni-TRACS terminals had been installed worldwide by some 150 transportation companies and 50,000 trucks and their dispatchers were generating 400,000 messages and position reports each day. By 1993 Jacobs was being anointed by *Fleet Owner* magazine as "The Man Who Changed Trucking."

Revolutionizing the Cell Phone Industry: 1989–91

In the late 1940s, AT&T's Bell Laboratories conducted the first test to determine the commercial feasibility of cellular communications technology. In 1970 the Federal Communications Commission (FCC) set aside radio frequencies for land mobile communications and by 1977 had announced the construction of two cellular development systems in Baltimore/Washington and Chicago. A U.S. cellular phone industry began to emerge in the 1980s, and by 1985 some 300,000 Americans were making cell phone calls from their car phones. It was clear to Jacobs and Viterbi that the analog transmission technology with which the cellular industry had started would eventually be replaced by digital signals (which transformed the electrical signals of the traditional phone into the zeros and ones of computer technology), and they began to develop a new standard that they hoped would become the sole medium by which all cell phone calls would eventually be made. In 1989, however, the Cellular Telecommunications Industries Association adopted a cell phone standard developed by Sweden's Ericsson called time division multiple access (TDMA), which divided phone conversations into blocks of digital data that were streamed one after the other over specific radio frequencies, allowing cell phone channels to carry three to six times as many callers as traditional analog systems.

Jacobs and Viterbi's own standard, called code division multiple access (CDMA), took a different approach. Instead of assigning an entire frequency channel to each cell phone call, CDMA tagged each conversation with a code that could be identified and retrieved only by the phone of the intended recipient. Once coded, the call was divided into ten different digital pieces that were then transmitted across all available cell phone channels. By thus using the cellular frequencies more efficiently, voice quality could be sustained over greater distances, reducing the number of antennas needed to cover a given territory and cramming twice as many conversations onto the airwaves as TDMA phones—and ten times as many as analog phones.

The catch was twofold: The cell phone industry had already adopted TDMA, and Qualcomm's CDMA was untested and, as far as the industry was concerned, thus only a theory. In 1989 Jacobs nevertheless pitched CDMA's advantages before the Cellular Telecommunications Industries Association. He was given a cool reception but resolved to rally the financial support of key industry firms to conduct a series of tests that would conclusively establish the superiority of CDMA over TDMA. The wireless division of Pacific Telesis agreed to commit $2 million toward a CDMA trial, and throughout 1989 Qualcomm lined up some $30 million to construct limited CDMA test networks in San Diego and New York City. While Qualcomm closed licensing or development agreements with such companies as Nokia, Motorola, Northern Telecom, and Sony; estab-

Key Dates:

1965: Irwin Jacobs publishes *Principles of Communication Engineering*.
1968: Irwin Jacobs and Andrew Viterbi found Linkabit.
1980: Linkabit merges with M/A-COM to form M/A-COM Linkabit.
1985: Qualcomm Inc. is formed.
1988: Qualcomm launches the OmniTRACS messaging system.
1993: U.S. Telecommunications Industry Association adopts Qualcomm's CDMA technology as a cellular standard.
1999: Qualcomm reaches settlement in a patent-infringement suit with L.M. Ericsson.
2002: China Unicom agrees to implement Qualcomm's CDMA technology.

lished international CDMA partnerships in Europe, Japan, and Canada; and convinced AT&T and Nynex to adopt the CDMA standard for their cellular service, it continued to test CDMA's call quality, coverage area, and call capacity.

In November 1991, 14 international and domestic cellular carriers and manufacturers conducted a large-scale field validation test of Qualcomm's CDMA technology. The tests were conclusive enough to convince the Cellular Telecommunications Industries Association to reopen the cellular standard debate. Buoyed by the news that its technology might indeed become the new cellular standard, Qualcomm nevertheless faced a daunting challenge. A national CDMA infrastructure simply did not exist, and to make CDMA cell phones a commercial reality a huge base station and network system had to be created—at Qualcomm's expense. To help raise the funds, Qualcomm went public in December 1991, generating $53 million.

While Jacobs and Viterbi were recasting Qualcomm into a cellular industry giant, they also were pursuing other cutting-edge technologies. In 1991, Qualcomm continued research on high-definition television (HDTV) signal processing components, data link systems, specialized modems, and custom VLSI (very large scale integrated) circuits, as well as a number of classified communications-related research projects for the U.S. government. It also formed a joint venture with satellite-maker Loral Corporation to develop a network of low earth orbit satellites called Globalstar that would use CDMA technology to provide—beginning in 1998—mobile communications service to regions of the world that could not be economically served by ground-based cellular systems. It also unveiled Eudora, a cross-platform email software program originally licensed from the University of Illinois that by 1997 claimed some 18 million Internet users.

CDMA Approaching Critical Mass: 1992–94

Although 1992 represented the third straight year in which Qualcomm suffered a net loss, its sales continued to climb and its future continued to brighten. In 1992 it prepared for the rollout of CDMA in 1993 by signing a technology agreement with Nokia and a licensing agreement with Northern Telecom; by promoting CDMA in Korea, Australia, Switzerland, and Germany; and by opening regional offices in Pittsburgh, Dallas, Atlanta, Salt Lake City, and Washington, D.C. It secured a license from the FCC to tailor CDMA technology for the new personal communications service (PCS) niche of the cellular industry and created a PCS corporate group to create applications for this market. By bundling traditional cellular phone service with paging, messaging, fax, and email service all from a single all-purpose "pocket communicator," PCS appeared to have become the future of CDMA and of the cell phone industry as a whole.

Sales of OmniTRACS meanwhile leaped 68 percent over 1991 to 36,000 installed units and 200 trucking customers in North America. In 1992, OmniTRACS' first and largest customer, Schneider National Inc., renewed its OmniTRACS contract; Qualcomm added Werner Enterprises, one of the five largest truckload carriers in the United States, to its stable; and Mexico, Japan, and Brazil committed to adopting the Omni-TRACS system in 1993.

The tidal shift toward the CDMA cellular standard began to snowball in 1993: The U.S. Telecommunications Industry Association adopted CDMA as a cellular standard; three Bell regional operating companies and Alltel Mobile Communications placed orders with Qualcomm and its partners for CDMA handsets and infrastructure equipment; and major telecommunications firms conducted tests of CDMA service. Internationally, companies in Korea and the Philippines placed orders with Qualcomm for CDMA systems, and Chile, China, India, Malaysia, Pakistan, and Russia signed memoranda edging them closer to the adoption of Qualcomm's CDMA technology for the wireless local loops (WLL) that would take the place of traditional copper wire for connecting telephone switching centers to homes in the developing world. OmniTRACS, however, remained—for the time being—Qualcomm's money machine, and the company sold 62 percent more units in 1993 than it had the year before. Moreover, 50 new trucking firms adopted the system—including J.B. Hunt, the largest truckload carrier in the United States.

In 1994 the CDMA rollout anticipated for 1993 was delayed until 1995 while the FCC began auctioning off PCS licenses to potential service providers and Qualcomm battled off patent suits brought by competitors who claimed it had lifted its CDMA technology from their own research. A growing number of U.S. cellular carriers—now including AirTouch, GTE, Sprint, and Ameritech—prepared to deploy or test CDMA-based PCS service in major American markets, and the International Telecommunications Union adopted CDMA as one of four global wireless communications standards. Moreover, China and Argentina began testing CDMA cellular systems, and Qualcomm opened offices in Beijing, New Delhi, and Buenos Aires. With more and more companies signing onto the CDMA/PSC standard, Qualcomm moved to fill the void of manufacturers offering CDMA/PCS equipment by partnering with Sony Electronics to create Qualcomm Personal Electronics, a joint venture to manufacture and market up to a million PCS cell phones a year.

OmniTRACS, meanwhile, had increased its customer base to 425 and by the end of 1994 was processing 2.5 million trucking messages and position reports every day on 13,000 OmniTRACS units in 25 countries. Qualcomm augmented its OmniTRACS software offerings by acquiring Integrated Transportation Software Inc. in 1994 and continued to integrate the 10,000 customers of Motorola's CoveragePLUS ground-based radio operation that it had acquired in late 1993 into its OmniTRACS network. Qualcomm's long-planned Globalstar satellite communications system also got a welcome boost when Qualcomm signed the largest development contract in its history—valued at $266 million—to develop Globalstar's ground communications equipment and telephones.

Qualcomm's "Arrival": 1995–97

For all the billions spent on development, testing, equipment, and marketing, by mid-1995 CDMA still remained, in large part, an unknown quantity. In a feature article on Qualcomm's battle to establish CDMA as the cellular standard, Britain's *Economist* magazine described CDMA as a "clever—but fiendishly complicated and unproven—technology" that was still "a good year away from the market" and one that might never be made to work as well as the thoroughly operational TDMA standard. Moreover, despite 1995 earnings estimated at only about $30 million, Wall Street investors had driven Qualcomm's stock valuation to an atmospheric $2.4 billion. What is more, Qualcomm was entering a telephone equipment market in which it was dwarfed by such giants as AT&T, NEC, and Motorola.

Nevertheless, by July 1995 Qualcomm could claim that 11 of the 14 largest telephone carriers in the United States had committed to CDMA. In addition, 12 cell phone suppliers, including Motorola, NEC, Mitsubishi, Matsushita, and Sony, had each paid Qualcomm $1 million for its CDMA technology, and six manufacturers—including AT&T, Northern Telecom, and Motorola—had each surrendered $5 million for the right to make CDMA network equipment. From its CDMA royalty fees and microchip sales alone Qualcomm stood to profit handsomely in the years to come. In August 1995, it raised $500 million in a public stock offering to fund its transformation from a cellular standard licenser to a cellular phone maker.

By partnering with virtually every major telecommunications carrier and manufacturer in as many markets as it could, Qualcomm sought to translate the CDMA PCS market from an idea into a foregone conclusion almost overnight. In late 1995 the first telephone calls on a commercially installed system using CDMA were made by Primeco customers, and AirTouch announced plans to launch the first commercial CDMA system in Los Angeles.

Qualcomm's equipment joint venture with Sony received an $850 million order for handheld phones in 1996, and by mid-year a Qualcomm/Sony truck departed from San Diego for the East Coast with thousands of PCS phones ready for delivery to Primeco customers. When it was discovered that a software bug rendered the phones' menu screens inoperable, however, a Qualcomm team was dispatched to the Primeco warehouse with the software fix. Four days later, the 40,000 handsets had been reprogrammed and overnighted to Primeco's anxious retail outlets. With a potentially damaging PR gaffe evaded, in March 1997 Qualcomm introduced its newest PCS handset, the Q phone. Motorola sued Qualcomm for stealing the Q phone design from Motorola's own StarTAC phone, but a San Diego court ruled in Qualcomm's favor a month later.

By mid-1997, 57 percent of all digital wireless systems under construction used Qualcomm's CDMA standard, which now boasted some four million users, and Primeco and Sprint had agreed to spend $850 million over the next two years to buy Qualcomm/Sony handsets. Handsets and equipment orders from China, Korea, Russia, and Chile were expected to add another $500 million to Qualcomm's coffers, and Qualcomm made plans for new equipment factories in Asia and Latin America. In June 1997, it opened a Moscow sales office and could claim that it had licensed CDMA to more than 45 leading telecommunications manufacturers worldwide.

Because it was wedded to the CDMA standard, however, Qualcomm's fortunes as a cellular phone maker were threatened by its larger phone-making rivals, who had long offered handsets for every cellular standard. Nevertheless, by the end of its 1997 first quarter, Qualcomm's sales were a full 165 percent greater than a year earlier and, with the penetration of the U.S. wireless communications market expected to increase from 16 percent to 48 percent by 2006, Qualcomm appeared to have plenty of room to grow. Its one-time cash cow, OmniTRACS, had in the meantime grown to encompass 200,000 terminals at 800 transportation companies in 32 countries worldwide. When Qualcomm announced in May 1997 that San Diego's Jack Murphy sports facility had been officially renamed Qualcomm Stadium, Jacobs and Viterbi's dream of building a communications business that could dominate its industry appeared to have been fulfilled beyond anyone's rosiest expectations.

Cellular Technology in the 21st Century

As the millennium approached, Qualcomm continued to work tirelessly to establish CDMA as the global standard for cellular communications. As the sole producer of CDMA, however, the company encountered a great deal of opposition from the nation's phone industry, which was wary of relying on a single supplier for its cellular technology. Qualcomm responded to this resistance by loosening its licensing restrictions, making CDMA technology available to a range of manufacturers, many of them in Asia. The reasoning was simple: By broadening the production capacity for CDMA, Qualcomm hoped to make prices more competitive, thereby providing the major telecommunications corporations with a wider range of choices. At the same time, Qualcomm saw this strategy as a means of establishing a more powerful presence for CDMA technology in the global marketplace.

In the late 1990s the company undertook a series of initiatives designed to expand its reach into emerging cell phone markets in Asia. The biggest prize was China, where the number of cell phone users was projected to exceed 70 million by the year 2000. Despite a number of promising tests of CDMA technology in the Chinese marketplace, however, China continued to favor GSM, which was still the industry standard in Europe. After failing in its initial bid to forge a strategic alliance with China Unicom, one of the country's largest cell phone companies, Qualcomm signed research-and-development deals with seven Chinese cell phone manufacturers in June 2000, in the hope that the increased presence of CDMA on the production level might stir up greater interest among the larger Chinese telecom companies.

The competitive advantage held by GSM technology in the late 1990s, however, still posed a serious threat to the future of CDMA. Companies like Ericsson, reluctant to give Qualcomm the opportunity to promote CDMA as an alternative to GSM in Europe, successfully lobbied regulators to maintain a single European standard, effectively closing the door on foreign competition. The conflict came to a head in 1998, when Ericsson introduced a new technology that was based on CDMA, but not compatible with it. A patent infringement lawsuit ensued, with the two companies reaching a settlement in March 1999. The agreement created a new standard in Europe, one that would allow for compatibility among the various competing technologies.

The agreement with Ericsson turned out to be a watershed moment for Qualcomm. No longer distracted by concerns of being shut out of international cell phone markets, the company was able to devote more attention to the development of its Third Generation, or 3G, wireless technologies. The company had already set the stage for the creation of its 3G products in November 1998, when it joined with Microsoft to create Wireless Knowledge, a joint venture dedicated to the integration of data transfer capability with mobile communications. The new technology, known as High Data Rate, or HDR, would allow subscribers to access the Internet and email accounts from their cell phones. In April 2000 Qualcomm purchased a 10 percent share of Net Zero, with the intention of making the Internet provider the first to utilize HDR in the United States.

The company achieved another breakthrough in January 2002, when Verizon Wireless launched the nation's first 3G mobile phone service, called Express Network, using Qualcom's patented CDMA2000 technology. That same month Qualcomm finally reached an agreement with China Unicom to implement CDMA as the Chinese telecom's standard. Having established a foothold in China, Qualcomm then turned its attention to other emerging markets. It invested $200 million in the Indian company Reliance Communications Ltd., with the aim of laying the foundation for the introduction of CDMA to the subcontinent. The long-awaited acceptance of CDMA on the international stage, combined with the meteoric development of 3G technology in the United States, put Qualcomm on firm ground heading into the new century.

Principal Subsidiaries

SnapTrack, Inc.; Wireless Knowledge, Inc. (50%).

Principal Divisions

QUALCOMM CDMA Technologies; QUALCOMM Technology Licensing; QUALCOMM Internet Services; QUALCOMM Wireless Business Solutions; QUALCOMM Digital Media; QUALCOMM Ventures.

Principal Competitors

Motorola, Inc.; Nokia Corporation; Texas Instruments Incorporated.

Further Reading

Aguilera, Mario, "CDMA Gets the Press While OmniTRACS Pulls the Qualcomm Wagon," *San Diego Transcript,* January 6, 1995.
Armstrong, Larry, "Qualcomm: Unproven, But Dazzling," *Business Week,* September 4, 1995.
Bauder, Don, "Analysts See Growth in Asian Markets As Key for Qualcomm," *San Diego Union-Tribune,* January 20, 2002.
Crawley, James, "Telecom Valley," *San Diego Union-Tribune,* March 1, 1994.
Davies, Jennifer, "Chinese Tap CDMA Technology; Network Launch Aids Qualcomm," *Los Angeles Times,* January 9, 2002.
——, "Verizon, Qualcomm Team Up for a First," *San Diego Union-Tribune,* January 29, 2002.
Douglass, Elizabeth, "Tracking Trucks Is Big Business for Qualcomm," *San Diego Union-Tribune,* April 14, 1989.
Flanigan, James, "Torpedo That Hit Qualcomm Carried a Message," *Los Angeles Times,* July 12, 1998.
Krause, Reinhardt, "Qualcomm vs. Ericsson Reaches a Critical Stage," *Investor's Business Daily,* February 18, 1999.
Maggs, John, "Telecom Firm's Recipe for Success: Add Competition; Qualcomm Advances Its Technology by Sharing," *Journal of Commerce,* November 7, 1997.
Mele, Jim, "The Man Who Changed Trucking," *Fleet Owner,* October 1993.
"Qualcomm Spars with Motorola," *Business Week,* April 21, 1997.
"Satellite System Helps Trucks Stay in Touch," *New York Times,* June 5, 1991.
Schine, Eric, "Qualcomm: Not Exactly an Overnight Success," *Business Week,* June 2, 1997.
"Shorts Circuited," *Economist,* July 29, 1995, p. 45.
Therrien, Lois, "Cellular Phones: The Static Is Getting Louder," *Business Week,* January 28, 1991.
"Trucking Looks to the Sky for Its Future," *Industry Week,* April 3, 1989.

—Paul S. Bodine
—update: Steve Meyer

Quanta Computer Inc.

No. 188, Wen Hwa 2nd Road
Kuei Shan Hsiang
Tao Yuan Shien
Taiwan
Telephone: 886-2-03-327-2345
Fax: 886-2-03-327-1511
Web site: http://www.quantatw.com

Public Company
Incorporated: 1988
Employees: 1,200
Sales: NT$131.09 billion (2001)
Stock Exchanges: Taiwan
Ticker Symbol: QCI
NAIC: 334110 Computer and Peripheral Equipment
Manufacturing

Quanta Computer Inc. operates principally as a manufacturer and designer of notebook personal computers, ranking as the largest producer of notebooks in the world. Quanta also makes LCD desktop personal computers, computer components, Internet appliance devices, servers, and cellular phones. The company's notebooks are produced and designed for major computer manufacturers such as Dell, Compaq, Gateway, Apple, IBM, Sony, Hewlett-Packard, Sharp, Siemens, and Fujitsu. Dell ranks as the company's most important customer, accounting for approximately half of annual sales.

Origins

Hailed as the "Laptop King," Barry Lam built a business empire and a fortune that befitted his epithet. He was born in Shanghai, raised in Hong Kong, and received his education in Taiwan, where he earned a degree in engineering. In his early career, Lam worked as a pocket-calculator salesman and as an engineer for several computer makers based in Taiwan, before striking out on his own as an entrepreneur. Although he deserved much of the credit for the success of his entrepreneurial creation, Lam was also indebted to circumstance, to the time

and the place of Quanta's corporate birth. The rise of his company was part of a general trend unique to Taiwan, representing a case study of success in the evolution of the country's electronics industry.

For years, Taiwanese electronics firms produced equipment under contract for other manufacturers, generally U.S. companies. Their existence as such provided a means for survival, but the profits were meager. Contract manufacturing represented the bottom of the profit scale, well below the margins recorded by engineering-driven firms who designed electronics goods. Taiwan's importance to the global electronics industry, and its own wealth as a manufacturer within the vast marketplace, increased exponentially after the country's manufacturers began to assist in the creation process. This evolutionary leap, which was largely a Taiwanese phenomenon, occurred during the 1990s, when Taiwan, long the home of "ghost," or contract manufacturers, assumed its more pivotal role as the base for designer-manufacturers. The Taiwan government aided in the development of its high-technology industry, providing tax and venture capital incentives, which helped speed the country's technological maturation. Barry Lam's Quanta helped lead the way toward the more lucrative end of the business. By the beginning of the 21st century, Taiwan accounted for 25 percent of the desktop computer production in the world and 55 percent of the notebook computer production in the world. Lam's Quanta, on its own, accounted for one-seventh of global notebook computer production, making its mark not only as the leading manufacturer but also as a capable engineering and design firm.

Lam's rise toward dominance began modestly. With the help of a colleague, C.C. Leung, Lam founded Quanta in May 1988, using less than $900,000 in capital to start the company. The lack of resources relegated Lam's initial operations to a small space located in Shin-Lin, an old industrial district in Taipei. In a building, on the sixth floor, Quanta began its existence, endeavoring to become one of the first companies of its type on the small, island nation.

At the time of Quanta's formation, few firms in Taiwan were involved in the production or design of what would become known as notebook computers. Lam, however, threw himself into the task of developing a portable personal computer (PC), laboring in the cramped, "office-factory" in Taipei. In November 1988, six months after starting Quanta, Lam completed work on his first version of a portable personal computer, a notebook prototype remembered as a bulky, briefcase-sized machine. He took his creation to trade shows, hoping to spark interest.

Although the reaction to Lam's awkward prototype was not immediate, orders for the Quanta machine gradually arrived. In August 1989, the company opened its first genuine production facility, a building located in Linkou, a suburb of Taipei. The following year, Quanta began production of its first commercial notebook PC, a machine that featured an Intel 386 processor.

Early 1990s Growth

Quanta's success became measured by the stature and number of its customers and by what services the company performed for them. The design work completed by the company's engineers increased, as major U.S.-based customers agreed to let Lam's Quanta construct, and in some cases, help design their notebook computers. During the first half of the 1990s, Quanta secured contracts with important customers such as Apple Computer and Gateway, Inc. To better serve these customers, Lam established a network of offices to serve his clients. In 1991, an after-sales office was established in Fremont, California. In 1994, an office was established in Augsburg, Germany. A turning point in the company's history occurred in 1996, when Quanta reached an agreement with Dell Computer Corporation. For years, Dell ranked as the company's largest customer, accounting for a significant portion of annual revenue and profit totals.

Lam prided himself on presiding over a design firm, as opposed to a pure contract manufacturing operation. Quanta's engineers, whose ranks swelled as the company blossomed into global force, increasingly lent their talents in the design of notebook computers sold under the brand names of U.S. and other foreign manufacturers. Although the major, well-known computer companies were reticent about disclosing the contributions of ghost designer-manufacturers, Quanta, in many instances, was the company behind the prolific growth of portable PCs during the latter half of the 1990s.

In 1995, Quanta reached an agreement with Apple Computer that called for Lam's engineers to exhibit their talents on the design side of notebook production. Apple Computer, wishing to reduce costs and development time on its new Epic line of PowerBook notebooks, turned to Quanta to co-develop the product. Based on the success of this agreement, a lasting partnership was formed that saw Quanta engineers assume much of the responsibility for the design of later generations of Apple Computer's notebooks. For the company's G4 notebook, released at the start of the 21st century, Quanta's 500 engineers in Taiwan accounted for half of the design work that went into the highly popular model.

Quanta also was credited for salvaging the fortunes of California-based Hewlett-Packard Company. In 1999, the U.S. industry giant was close to shuttering its notebook division when company executives decided to hire Quanta in a last ditch effort to keep the Hewlett-Packard name in the notebook computer market. Quanta applied its production and engineering talents to the Hewlett-Packard cause, taking over nearly all the responsibilities previously assumed by the Palo Alto company. Quanta assembled the hardware, installed the software, tested the final product, and even began shipping the Hewlett-Packard notebook computers to customers. Hewlett-Packard's success in the notebook computer market quickly improved, impressing the company's director for notebook operations. Turning to Quanta, according to the Hewlett-Packard director in a November 5, 2001 interview with *Business Week*, "saved our business." He noted that the intervention of Quanta represented "the biggest turnaround in Hewlett-Packard's history."

Lam, who took Quanta public in 1998, registered much of his success because of the company's nimble and sophisticated manufacturing operations. Quanta's competitors based in the United States typically engaged in a number of manufacturing activities, whereas Lam specialized exclusively on designing and manufacturing notebook computers. In this specific area, Quanta excelled, its notebook assembly factory in Linkou representing a paradigm of efficiency, adaptability, and profitability in the computer industry. Lam's assembly lines mass-produced notebook computers 24 hours a day, able to accommodate different product specifications and configurations for the company's various customers. Dell, which accounted for half of the company's annual sales, had its own secured floor at Quanta's Linkou facility, where Quanta engineers performed between 60 and 70 percent of the design work on Dell's Latitude models.

Emergence of a 21st-Century Giant

By 2000, little more than a decade after Lam had set out in his cramped office in Taipei, Quanta was exuding considerable strength. The company's roster of customers was impressive, comprising essentially all the major notebook manufacturers in the world. Among Quanta's customers were Dell, Compaq, Apple, Hewlett-Packard, IBM, Sony, Sharp, Fujitsu, and Siemens. The company had also begun to vertically integrate and diversify its operations, seeking to add alternative revenue streams to its mainstay business. In February 1999, the company formed Quanta Storage Inc., a subsidiary that manufactured data storage devices such as CD-ROM drives and DVD drives. In July 1999, Quanta Display Inc., a producer of liquid crystal display (LCD) panels, was formed. In March 2000, the

Key Dates:

1988: Lam starts Quanta with $900,000 in capital.
1989: The company's first production facility is opened.
1996: Dell Computer becomes a Quanta customer.
1998: Quanta converts to public ownership.
2001: Quanta becomes the largest manufacturer of notebook computers in the world.

company created Quanta Network System Inc., a manufacturer of web pads with wireless data transfer capability, personal digital assistants (PDAs), and cellular phones.

In 2001, Quanta stood apart from the rest of the computer industry, the same year the company achieved global dominance. The year marked the most debilitative market crash in the history of the high-technology industry, yet Quanta displayed energetic growth, recording double-digit increases in sales as other computer makers endured crippling declines in business. During the year, Lam anticipated shipping four million notebook units, a 50 percent increase from the total recorded in 2000. Quanta vaulted past Toshiba to become the world's largest producer of notebook computers, its factories accounting for one-seventh of all notebooks sold worldwide. Although the company's forays into cellular phones and Internet devices had yet to generate any appreciable profits, Quanta represented a glowing success story at a time many computer makers chose to forget.

As Quanta embarked on its future in the 21st century, the company continued to garner praise for its high level of efficiency in an increasingly competitive market. In 2002, production was being shifted to China, where Quanta hoped to realize a 10 percent reduction in costs. Plans called for an $18 million investment in plant improvements in China, part of the company's goal to reach $10 billion in sales from operations in China and Taiwan by 2004. In the years ahead, analysts maintained, Quanta's biggest challenge consisted of keeping its lead as growth in the notebook market declined, reaching the same

saturation point experienced by makers of desktop personal computers. Prices of notebooks were expected to fall, and consequently, profit margins were expected to shrink, giving Lam a considerable obstacle to surmount if he hoped to retain his title as the Laptop King.

Principal Subsidiaries

Quanta International Ltd. (British West Indies); LINKO Computer GmbH (Germany); Access International Co.; Quanta Storage Inc.; Quanta Display Inc.; Quanta Investor Inc.; Advanced International Investor Inc.; Quanta Network Systems Inc.; QCE Computer B.V. (Netherlands); Quanta Manufacturing Inc.; Quanta Service Inc.; Quanta Computer USA, Inc.; Q-Lily Computer Inc.; QCH Inc.

Principal Competitors

Solectron Corp.; Celestica Inc.

Further Reading

"Barry Lam," *Business Week,* January 14, 2002, p. 61.

Gore, Andrew, "Apple to Polish PowerBooks; New Line to Be Developed by Taiwan PC Manufacturer," *PC Week,* October 16, 1995, p. 39.

"Hitching a Ride on the Wireless Web," *Business Week,* August 7, 2000, p. 58J.

Hung, Faith, "Compaq Signs Major Laptop Deal with Taiwan's Quanta," *Electronic Buyers' News,* July 10, 2000, p. 4.

——, "Quanta Holds Course in Turbulent Times—EMS Provider to Make Headway Where Others Have Foundered," *EBN,* December 17, 2001, p. 48.

"Laptop King," *Business Week,* November 5, 2001, p. 48.

"Quanta Computer Obtains iMac PC Orders from Apple," *Taiwan Economic News,* December 7, 2001, p. 46.

"Quanta's Quantum Leap," *Business Week,* November 5, 2001, p. 79.

"Quanta to Serve As Sole OEM Supplier of Notebook PCs for Gateway," *Taiwan Economic News,* December 19, 2001, p. 13.

Tanzer, Andrew, "Made in Taiwan," *Forbes,* April 2, 2001, p. 64.

—Jeffrey L. Covell

QUEBECOR INC.

Quebecor Inc.

612 Rue St. Jacques
Montréal, Quebec H3C 4M8
Canada
Telephone: (514) 877-9777
Fax: (514) 877-9757
Web site: http://www.quebecor.com

Public Company
Incorporated: 1965
Employees: 58,000
Sales: US$7.31 billion (2001)
Stock Exchanges: Toronto
Ticker Symbol: QBR.A
NAIC: 511110 Newspaper Publishing; 511120 Periodical
Publishers; 511130 Book Publishers; 513210 Cable
Networks; 513120 Television Broadcasting; 323110
Commercial Lithographic Printing; 323113
Commercial Screen Printing; 322122 Newsprint Mills

Quebecor Inc. is a vertically integrated company with two main related businesses: commercial printing, and media. Quebecor World, its printing division, is the world's largest commercial printer, with over 150 printing plants on five continents. The company's media arm oversees Sun Media, one of the largest newspaper publishers in Canada; runs Vidéotron, Quebec's largest cable television service; operates a commercial television network in Quebec, TVA; and owns dozens of Canadian book publishers, several internet companies, and a chain of music stores and video rental clubs.

Getting a Start in the 1950s with Papers and Presses

Pierre Péladeau, Quebecor's founder, president, and chief executive officer, bought his first newspaper in 1950 when he was 25 years old. His father had been successful in business, but lost his fortune by the time of his death when his son was only ten. His mother managed to send Péladeau to an exclusive school and he continued his education at elite universities. At an early age, Péladeau decided he would control his own financial destiny. "I always created my own jobs," Péladeau told *Forbes.* A graduate of McGill University with a degree in law and of the University of Montreal with a master's degree in philosophy, Péladeau borrowed C$1,500 from his mother to buy the ailing weekly *Le Journal de Rosemont,* and worked hard to make the paper a success. In 1953 Péladeau bought his first printing press. More dailies and printing presses followed, until Péladeau had built the beginnings of his empire.

A 1964 strike at Quebec's leading French language daily, *La Presse,* gave Péladeau a big opportunity. In *La Presse*'s absence, Péladeau launched his own daily, *Le Journal de Montréal.* The tabloid, which featured graphic pictures of crime scenes, heavy sports coverage, pin-up girl photos, and no editorials, met with immediate success. *La Presse*'s return to the stands seven months later slowed but did not halt that success. In fact, circulation rose during the following years until *Le Journal* became Quebec and North America's leading French language daily in the late 1970s, a status it maintained into the 1990s.

After an entrepreneurial beginning and incorporation in 1965, Quebecor Inc. pursued a decade long course of acquisition and expansion that aimed to consolidate the company's leading position in the fields of publishing and printing in Canada and the United States. In the ten years after 1965, over 100 subsidiaries were added to the Quebecor empire. The location and business activity of Quebecor's subsidiary purchases indicated the success of the company's stated strategic objective: "[To] Broaden its reach across North America and overseas; to acquire additional product market share and diversity; to target and acquire underperforming assets that are geographically well situated and improve their performance; and to achieve a size that maximizes the benefits of economies of scale."

In 1967, Péladeau founded *Le Journal de Quebec,* and later added an entertainment magazine and the *Winnipeg Sun* to his newspaper holdings. Labor lawyer Brian Mulroney, eventually to become Canada's prime minister, worked out *Le Journal*'s first labor agreement. Péladeau's generous dealings with labor cemented his positive reputation with the public. In 1972, Péladeau offered shares in Quebecor on the Toronto Stock Exchange.

International Reach in the 1970s and 1980s

In 1977, Péladeau gambled in the U.S. newspaper market by launching the *Philadelphia Journal*. But this venture turned out to be one of Péladeau's few misjudgments of the market and the competition. He thought the extensive sports coverage and tabloid format used in *Le Journal* would be a big hit in Philadelphia. Yet the paper's competition simply increased its sports coverage and cut advertising rates to squeeze Péladeau out of the market. Five years later, at a loss of US$14 million, the paper closed its doors.

In the next several years, Péladeau undertook a more aggressive campaign to establish a presence in the U.S. market and to take the number one position in Canada. He saw that technology and economies of scale were becoming increasingly important to success in the printing and publishing industries due to changes in technology and a more competitive world economy. His strong customer orientation and grasp of client needs, both in business-to-business and consumer markets, were great assets in the strategic expansion of Quebecor. Quebecor invested in emerging technologies, allowing retailers and advertisers to regionalize product offerings and prices. Bar code technology allowed the creation of large databases from which computers could determine demographic buying patterns, making it possible to tailor publications to specific regions, neighborhoods, or even individuals. These technologies required specialized capabilities, including binding techniques that allowed customized compilation of pages destined for different markets.

Péladeau and British publishing magnate Robert Maxwell teamed up in 1987 to form Mircor Inc., a joint subsidiary created to purchase—for C$320 million—a 54 percent stake in Donohue Inc., a leading forest products company in Quebec. Quebecor took a 51 percent share of the newly formed Mircor. The Donohue acquisition gave Quebecor its status as one of the most vertically integrated communications companies in the world, for it allowed the company to do everything from cutting the tree to distributing the printed product. Donohue supplied paper for Quebecor's journals and magazines and for direct mail advertising for its retail clients.

In 1988, Quebecor bought almost all of the printing assets of BCE Inc., the owner of Bell Canada, for C$161 million and a 21 percent share of Quebecor capital stock. The acquisition expanded Quebecor's printing capabilities and brought in lucrative contracts for printing telephone directories, currency, and passports. This acquisition made Quebecor first in printing in Canada and gave the company significant economies of scale, positioning it well for success in the increasingly competitive and technology driven industry.

More Acquisitions in the Early 1990s

In 1990, Quebecor bought Maxwell Communication Corporation's 14 U.S. printing operations, forming the basis of Quebecor Printing. The US$510 million deal included a non-competition agreement and the purchase by Maxwell of a 25.8 percent interest in Quebecor Printing for US$100 million. According to Michael Crawford in *Canadian Business,* the purchase gave Quebecor access to a C$744 million customer list and rotogravure presses tailored to U.S. advertisers and catalogue companies. Only a year later, Robert Maxwell's death revealed his holdings to be in a financial mess. Quebecor bought back its shares from Maxwell for US$94.8 million, US$5.2 million less than Maxwell had paid for it, giving Quebecor 100 percent ownership of Quebecor Printing.

Quebecor was not immune from the recession in the early 1990s. Plummeting newsprint prices in 1991 created heavy losses at Donohue, substantially eating into Quebecor's revenues. Advertising was down as well, putting pressure on the publishing and printing segments. In anticipation of the North American Free Trade Agreement (NAFTA), Quebecor established a foothold in Mexico by buying Mexican printer Graficas Monte Alban S.A. The move was another step forward in Quebecor's determination to become a truly North American company and gave Quebecor a presence in all three North American countries. Graficas printed books for Mexican and South American publishers. With about 200 employees and annual sales of US$4.5 million, Graficas was not a large acquisition. Nevertheless, it provided a starting point from which to learn the Mexican market and expand holdings in the fast growing nation of 80 million people.

Quebecor expanded further in 1992 as it made large investments in its printing facilities and took Quebecor Printing Inc. public with an initial public offering that left the parent company with a 67.57 percent share of its printing subsidiary. Proceeds from the offering were used to reduce bank debt. In the same year, Quebecor won two lucrative five-year contracts to print and bind Canadian telephone directories. The value of the contracts over five years was estimated at a combined total of C$505 million.

In 1992 and 1993, Quebecor Printing acquired Arcata Graphics, San Jose, and three major Arcata Corporation printing plants, bringing in clients such as *Reader's Digest, Parade,* and *TV Guide.* The acquisition of these plants substantially expanded Quebecor's market share and capacity in producing catalogues, magazines, and books. Advanced web offset publication, special binding, ink jet printing, and shorter run production capabilities were some of the technologies enhanced by the purchase. In 1994, Quebecor completed its buyout of Arcata when it exercised its option to buy the company's outstanding shares. The final acquisition added five book manufacturing

Key Dates:

1950: Pierre Péladeau buys his first newspaper, *Le Journal de Rosemont.*
1964: Péladeau launches *Le Journal de Montréal.*
1965: Company incorporates as Quebecor Inc.
1972: Quebecor goes public.
1987: Company takes stake in paper firm Donohue.
1990: Printing business is launched with acquisition of Maxwell Communication Corp.'s U.S. printing operations.
1997: Pierre Péladeau dies.
1999: Quebecor acquires Sun Media; printing division merges with World Color Press.

plants and a distribution facility to Quebecor, making the company the second largest book fabricator in the United States.

The strategic importance of Quebecor's expansion of its printing operations and move into the U.S. market was apparent from financial figures. By the end of 1993, U.S. sales represented more than 73 percent of Quebecor Printing's revenues and 64 percent of Quebecor Inc.'s revenues.

Quebecor's launch of *Le Magazine Provigo* with Provigo supermarkets in early 1993 was another example of Quebecor management's insight into consumer trends and changing markets. Four years before the magazine was introduced, Quebecor had approached the supermarket chain with the idea of differentiating itself from competitors by producing a monthly magazine on nutrition and health, with bits about local sports and entertainment celebrities. Quebecor hoped the magazine would join its information and distribution networks with Provigo's large target market to produce an effective advertising vehicle. Though Provigo was not ready to make the investment at the time, increased competition and narrowing profit margins in the retail grocery business eventually compelled Provigo to embrace the more upscale image offered by the magazine.

Quebecor Printing continued its international expansion with purchases and contracts in France, India, and Lebanon. Quebecor chose France because it was strategically situated to serve the European market, the world's second largest market for printed products after the United States. In 1993, Quebecor acquired 70 percent of the shares of commercial printer Groupe Fécomme for about US$12 million. The concern was renamed Imprimeries Fécomme-Quebecor S.A. The operation included three printing plants that made magazine covers, advertising inserts and circulars, and direct mail. Quebecor signed a letter of intent a few months after the Fécomme purchase to buy 49 percent of the shares of Groupe Jean Didier, the largest printer in France, for US$27.6 million. The deal was completed in early 1995. The company produced magazines, catalogues, and inserts. With the two acquisitions, Quebecor established a significant foothold in Europe.

A partnership was formed in 1993 with Tej Bandhu Group in India to construct a printing plant, called Tej Quebecor Printing Ltd., for printing the majority of telephone directories in India. With a population of 850 million, the establishment of a subsid-

iary in India provided great potential for future expansion. In 1994, Quebecor was awarded a contract to produce bank notes for the central bank of Lebanon. The job specified at least 29 million large denomination pound notes. The new issue represented the first time Lebanon had printed its currency outside of England since its independence in 1943.

On the domestic front, 1994 saw the loss of one of Quebecor's major contracts, the printing of the U.S. edition of *Reader's Digest,* the largest paid monthly circulation magazine in the United States. Quebecor lost the US$20 million-a-year, ten-year contract to its major U.S.-based competitor, R.R. Donnelley & Sons Co. Donnelley was the largest commercial printer in North America and the world, with three times the revenues of Quebecor Printing. The contract was apparently awarded to Donnelley because of the company's technological capabilities in targeting advertising to specific subscriber groups. Another factor in the loss of the contract may have been the refusal of some unionized workers at Quebecor Printing of Buffalo Inc., where the magazine was printed, to accept a ten-year no-strike/no-lockout amendment to the contract. Quebecor planned to make up the lost volume with growth in book printing.

Continued Growth After Founder's Death: Late 1990s

Pierre Péladeau was 71 in 1996, and beginning to talk about leaving his company to his sons. Though Péladeau himself was evidently not in the best of health, Quebecor was still active, making acquisitions and entering new markets. Quebecor Printing's revenue was over $3 billion by the mid-1990s. Quebecor's pulp and paper subsidiary, Donohue, made a $1.1 billion acquisition in 1995, and was on the lookout for another major opportunity. Péladeau's second son, Pierre-Karl, left Quebecor's communications division in 1995 to head Quebecor Printing Europe. Within a few years, this subsidiary had made enough acquisitions to rank it as one of the largest printing companies in Europe. In late 1996, Quebecor made a bid for the Toronto Sun Publishing Company, which sold Sun papers in Toronto, Edmonton, Calgary, and Ottawa. Toronto Sun had a slim profit margin, and Péladeau was sure his company's management could convert the newspaper chain into much more of a money-maker. However, Péladeau himself was a controversial figure, and several of the newspaper's columnists voiced outrage at the prospect of his owning the company. Péladeau had made an anti-Semitic comment in a magazine profile in the early 1990s which he had not retracted; he was viewed as favoring Quebec separatism; and he made no bones of his past as an alcoholic and as a manic-depressive. Eventually the Toronto Sun was sold to its own management team, and took the name Sun Media.

Pierre Péladeau died of a stroke in December 1997. He was succeeded by Pierre-Karl Péladeau. Within a year, Quebecor renewed its offer for Sun Media, which this time was accepted promptly. Quebecor paid C$983 million (US$680 million) for Sun and the combined media company became the second largest newspaper group in Canada. Quebecor filled the late 1990s with other significant acquisitions as well. The company moved into book publishing beginning in 1997, and within a few years Quebecor had bought up five major Quebec publishers. The company also moved into television, buying the French-language network TQS. In 1999 the company launched a New Media division, capitalizing on the boom in Internet communications. Quebecor invested in various fledgling electronic commerce projects, and created a new company, Nurun, which was the largest so-called Web integrator in Canada, and a leader in the European market as well.

The largest acquisition of all was Quebecor's deal in 1999 to merge with its rival commercial printer World Color Press. World Color was quite similar in its operations to Quebecor Printing, producing magazines, catalogs, books, direct mail circulars, and other printed goods at plants principally in the United States. The new combined company had roughly 175 printing facilities on five continents, and vaulted to the number one spot in the worldwide commercial printing industry. Quebecor's printing division changed its name to Quebecor World after the merger.

Quebecor's partially owned paper subsidiary, Donohue, also made a major acquisition, buying Texas-based newsprint and specialty paper maker Champion International in 1998. Then in early 2000, Quebecor announced it was selling its stake in Donohue to a third company, Abitibi-Consolidated. Quebecor then took an 11 percent share in Abitibi. Quebecor's management became embattled with Abitibi over the next year, when it insisted that Abitibi's CEO step down. Quebecor eventually dropped its demand, and then sold off its stake in the company. The move allowed Quebecor to pay off debt it took on when making another major purchase, the Quebec cable television station Groupe Vidéotron. Quebecor began the new millennium seemingly having accomplished the goals it set out decades ago. It was a truly global company, a powerhouse in media of all sorts, with paper and printing facilities around the world.

Principal Subsidiaries

Quebecor World Inc.; Quebecor Media Inc.; Sun Media; Groupe Vidéotron Itée; Nurun Inc.; TVA Group Inc.

Principal Competitors

Southam Inc.; R.R. Donnelley & Sons Co.; Dai Nippon Printing Co., Ltd.

Further Reading

"Abitibi's Big Holder Is Seeking Backing to Oust the CEO," *Wall Street Journal*, November 3, 2000, p. B8.

Bomberger, Paul, "Donnelley Planning Big Expansion Here," *Intelligencer Journal*, September 15, 1994, p. A1.

"Business," *Time Canada*, September 27, 1999, p. 68.

"Business Brief—Quebecor Inc.: Mexican Printer Is Acquired by a Unit of the Company," *Wall Street Journal*, January 7, 1992, p. 2.

Coles, Alex, "Quebecor Inc.—Sanford Evans Communications Ltd. Restructures Its Direct List Brokerage Services," *Business Wire*, February 22, 1993.

Crawford, Michael, "Prey for the Paper Tiger," *Canadian Business*, November 1993, p. 22.

De Santis, Solange, "Quebecor Appears to Win Battle to Buy Sun Media As Torstar Won't Top Offer," *Wall Street Journal*, December 22, 1998, p. B2.

Dougherty, Kevin, "The Powerful World of the Péladeaus," *Financial Post*, March 21, 1992, p. 2S16.

Dunn, Brian, "Provigo and Quebecor Launch Magazine for Grocery Shoppers," *Montreal Gazette*, March 1, 1993, p. C15.

Gray, Alan, "Quebecor Makes Paper, Prints on It and Distributes the Published Product," *Montreal Gazette*, March 22, 1993, p. F8.

Jenkison, Michael, "Their Day in the Sun," *Alberta Report/Newsmagazine*, August 19, 1996, p. 19.

McIntosh, Andrew, "Pierre Péladeau to Quit Quebecor—Next Year," *Montreal Gazette*, April 29, 1994, p. 1.

Palmeri, Christopher, "Nietzsche's Out God's In," *Forbes*, December 10, 1990, pp. 40–41.

"A Peace Pact at Abitibi," *Maclean's*, December 25, 2000, p. 143.

"The Péladeau Ship Sails On," *Maclean's*, January 12, 1998, p. 34.

"Quebecor Earnings Fell 89 Percent in Quarter, Revenue Declined 9 Percent," *Wall Street Journal*, February 13, 1992.

"Quebecor Finalizes Arcata Deal," *Graphic Arts Monthly*, August 1994, p. 21.

"Quebecor Inc. Sells Its 11% Abitibi Stake for $393.4 Million," *Wall Street Journal*, June 8, 2001, p. A6.

"Quebecor Printing Gets Contract," *Wall Street Journal*, September 29, 1992, p. B8.

"Quebecor Printing Gets 5-Year Contract to Print Directories," *Wall Street Journal*, July 6, 1992, p. 27.

"Quebecor Scraps Demands for Management Shake-Up," *Wall Street Journal*, December 15, 2000, p. A4.

"Quebecor Unit Acquires Plant," *Wall Street Journal*, January 23, 1992, p. 4.

"Quebecor Unit Sets Initial Public Offering of 14 Million Shares," *Wall Street Journal*, April 13, 1992, p. C11.

"The Rationale Behind the Big Acquisition," *Graphic Arts Monthly*, August 1999, p. 12.

"Reader's Digest Selects Donnelley As Printer for Its U.S. Edition," *Wall Street Journal*, September 14, 1994, p. A4.

Rojo, Oscar, "Canadian High-Tech Firms Heading Overseas," *Toronto Star*, April 4, 1994, p. F3.

"Separatism, No: Quebecor to Acquire Sun Media," *Editor & Publisher*, December 12, 1998, p. 19.

Wells, Jennifer, "Péladeau's Power Play," *Maclean's*, August 5, 1996, p. 38.

—Katherine Smethurst
—update: A. Woodward

Reckson Associates Realty Corp.

225 Broadhollow Road
Melville, New York 11747
U.S.A.
Telephone: (631) 694-6900
Toll Free: (888) RECKSON; (888) 732-5766
Fax: (631) 622-6790
Web site: http://www.reckson.com

Public Company
Incorporated: 1994
Employees: 311
Sales: $540.47 million (2001)
Stock Exchanges: New York
Ticker Symbol: RA
NAIC: 233110 Land Subdivision and Land Development;
531312 Nonresidential Property Managers

Reckson Associates Realty Corp. is the largest commercial landlord on Long Island and owns, develops, acquires, constructs, manages, and leases office and industrial properties throughout the tri-state metropolitan area of New York City. A real estate investment trust (REIT), it owns a number of suburban office parks, but its holdings also include a few Manhattan office buildings and a large selection of industrial properties.

The Private Company: 1968–95

William Rechler, his brother Morton, and their brother-in-law Jack Wexler established an aluminum furniture business in 1946 and developed the collapsible aluminum beach chair. In 1956 they sold the business and bought 32 acres of property, including docks, along Newtown Creek, a four-mile-long tidal inlet of the East River that separates western Brooklyn from western Queens. The location was not only on the water but was close to the Williamsburg Bridge, linking Brooklyn to Manhattan; to a tunnel connecting Queens with midtown Manhattan; and to the still-uncompleted Long Island Expressway. By the end of 1958 they had established a $12 million industrial park with at least nine tenants engaged in manufacturing or distribution and warehousing. Morton Rechler and Wexler subse-

quently started their own development business, while William Rechler, in partnership with Walter Gross, bought 400 acres of property in Hauppauge, Long Island. By 1964 their Vanderbilt Industrial Park in Hauppauge was the second largest in the United States.

In 1968 William Rechler and his sons Donald and Roger founded Reckson Associates. This company completed the Airport International Plaza, an industrial park in Bohemia, Long Island, in 1971. When Metropolitan Life Insurance Co. leased a site for office space, Reckson Associates began to enter this field. It purchased and retrofitted a 100,000-square-foot manufacturing site in Syosset, Long Island, formerly occupied by Grumman Corp., converting it into the 200,000-square-foot North Shore Atrium, a remodeled split-level office complex, in 1978, and enabling the company to charge tenants about five times per square foot what it cost them to buy. "It was unheard of at the time," Donald Rechler later told Alan J. Wax of *Newsday.* "It was the first recycling of an old industrial building . . . That was where we learned high-yield value creation." Thereafter Reckson focused its acquisition strategy on finding industrial space that when converted—generally to office buildings—could be leased at much higher rents.

The following year the company purchased land for the construction of the million-square-foot Huntington Melville Corporate Center. In 1981 they purchased the land for the million-square-foot Nassau West Corporate Center at Mitchel Field. This project was completed in 1985. The Omni, a 575,000-square-foot luxury office building in this center, was completed in 1990. These developments were further examples of the company's modus operandi—recycling poorly performing properties into profitable office sites.

The enterprise, officially the Reckson Group, went public in 1995 as Reckson Associates Realty Corp. a real estate investment trust (REIT). Falling property values during the recessionary early 1990s had raised Reckson Group's debt level to 80 percent of its market capitalization. "When values shrank, we couldn't grow anymore," Donald Rechler, the chief executive officer, explained to Glenn Jochum of *LI Business News.* "In order to go public, we took a 20 to 25% discount on our real estate. We took less money than it was worth to get it into the public arena, because of the advantage it gave us to be on the

Company Perspectives:

We are in the business of improving the quality of life in the workplace through innovation, design excellence and providing premier service.

NY Stock Exchange. . . . The day we went public we had a $150-M [credit] line at our disposal with no strings attached. . . . Our options were to cut back and be landlords or make the move and grow the company.''

Reckson Associates netted $162 million in its initial offering of stock, and its debt level of $122.9 million immediately fell to 26 percent of market capitalization. Following this conversion, Reckson Associates Realty Corp. became the sole general partner of Reckson Operating Partnership L.P., contributing substantially all of the net proceeds of the stock offering in exchange for about 73 percent of the operating partnership. All properties acquired by the company were held by or through the operating partnership. Reckson's portfolio at this time consisted of 72 properties—all on Long Island—containing 4.5 million square feet of space, 92 percent leased, with a yield of more than 8 percent a year.

Headlong Suburban Expansion: 1996–98

Within six months Reckson Associates had used the infusion of funds to acquire two million square feet of office and industrial space. This included its entry into Westchester County, New York, by means of its $83 million purchase of the 935,000-square-foot portfolio of Halpern Enterprises, including six of the seven office buildings in the Tarrytown Office Center. Reckson then signed on Halpern's executives in order to gain in-house expertise in local management, leasing, and construction. Jon Halpern was put in charge of the new Westchester division. Later in 1996, the company entered Connecticut by acquiring Landmark Square, a six-building office complex in Stamford, Connecticut, for about $77 million from the F.D. Rich organization. It then hired F.D. Rich III as managing director of its new southern Connecticut division. Reckson Associates ended the year with 110 properties encompassing about 8.8 million square feet of space. During the year the company raised $146 million from two additional stock offerings. (The company raised another $811 million from the public sale of stock between 1997 and 1999.) Its revenues rose from $61.27 million in 1995 to $96.14 million in 1996 and its net income from $3.45 million to $17.53 million.

Reckson Associates reached across to the other end of Fairfield County, Connecticut, in 1997, when it purchased a 452,000-square-foot office and warehouse complex in Shelton from the F.D. Rich organization for $26.95 million. Then it entered New Jersey with the purchase of five office buildings from Sy Heller for $56 million. By May 1997 it held 138 properties with a total of 12.3 million square feet of office and industrial space and also owned or controlled 170 acres within the tri-state New York City metropolitan area. It also acquired ten buildings in Vanderbilt Industrial Park and purchased the Melville building that became its headquarters. In *Fortune*, a mutual fund manager described Reckson to David Whitford as,

in his estimation, ''the best run REIT in the country. . . . They buy an empty building or a dirty building, fix it up, and then get an increase in revenue because of the improvements.'' Despite its free spending, the company was maintaining one of the lowest debt-to-market-capitalization ratios in the industry (11 percent, according to a company executive). By the end of the year Reckson had purchased, for $80 million, Royal Executive Park, a six-building complex in Rye Brook, New York, near the Connecticut border and at the other end of Westchester County from Tarrytown.

During 1997 Reckson Associates also formed a joint venture with Morris Cos. to develop big-box industrial space: buildings of at least 150,000 square feet with ceiling heights of 30 feet or more. The company invested more than $200 million in this operation before selling its share of the partnership in 1999 for $300 million in cash, stock, and assumed debt to American Real Estate Investment Corp. The sale included 28 industrial buildings with some 6.1 million square feet of space, 111 acres of land, and options for an additional 259 acres. Also in 1997, the company spun off Reckson Service Industries, Inc., which became FrontLine Capital Group and Reckson Strategic Venture Partners, LLC (RSVP). Its equity held indirectly by FrontLine, RSVP was a real estate venture-capital fund investing primarily in real estate and real estate operating companies outside Reckson's core office and industrial focus. FrontLine developed a portfolio of Internet-based business services for small and medium-sized companies.

Into Manhattan: 1999–2001

Reckson Associates ended 1997 with 155 properties encompassing 13.6 million square feet of space and net income of $34.64 million on revenues of $153.4 million. Its portfolio grew to 189 properties with 21.4 million square feet of space in 1998, when it earned $37.9 million in net income on revenues of $266.37 million. During the year the company, through its newly formed Metropolitan Partners, LLC, moved to enter Manhattan for the first time with a bid of $734 million for Tower Realty Trust Inc., a rival REIT. The deal took six months to finalize and did not close until 1999, when Reckson paid for Tower with a combination of stock, cash, and the assumption of debt for 4.6 million square feet of property. The newer office buildings included 100 Wall Street, 810 Seventh Avenue, and 120 West 45th Street. The older buildings at 90 Broad Street and 286, 290, and 292 Madison Avenue were sold to S.L. Green Realty Corp., a Manhattan-based REIT specializing in such properties. Additional Tower office developments in Arizona and the Orlando, Florida, area were also sold, for about $231 million. The architect of the deal, Scott Rechler—Roger's son—now became co-chief executive officer of the company at the age of only 31. He shared the title with his uncle Donald, who remained chairman of the firm, while Scott remained president, the position he had assumed in 1997. Five other Rechlers were also working for the company.

Later in the year the company agreed to purchase 919 Third Avenue and reached an agreement to acquire another Manhattan office building, 1350 Avenue of the Americas, for $126.5 million. Both deals were laborious. Negotiations for the latter building included some 50 members of the Minskoff family. Purchase of the 1.4-million-square-foot Third Avenue building

Key Dates:

1968: William Rechler and his sons establish Reckson Associates to deal in Long Island real estate.
1978: Reckson begins converting industrial buildings into office complexes.
1995: Reckson becomes a publicly traded real estate investment trust (REIT).
1996: The company enters the Westchester County and Connecticut markets.
1997: Reckson Associates enters the New Jersey real estate market.
1999: The company becomes a Manhattan landlord by purchasing Tower Realty Trust Inc.
2001: The collapse of a spun-off subsidiary, FrontLine Capital Group, leads to a net loss of $57 million for Reckson.

required the assumption, in 2000, of a mortgage for about $278 million that was in default from a group of Japanese investors. In 2001 the company sold a 49 percent interest in this property to the New York State Teachers' Retirement System for $220.5 million, of which $122.1 million consisted of its share of secured mortgage debt, with the remaining $98.4 million distributed to the company for a gain of $18.9 million.

Reckson Associates reached maximum size of 189 properties and 21.4 million square feet in 1999, when its revenues rose to $403.15 million and its net income to $60.27 million. Its portfolio size remained almost unchanged in 2000, when it earned $86.03 million on revenues of $509.94 million. Heavy borrowing for acquisitions brought the company's interest expenses to a record $96.3 million in 2000. During the year the company formed a joint venture with Teachers Insurance and Annuity Association, contributing eight suburban office properties for a 51 percent majority-ownership interest. Its partner contributed about $136 million for its interest. As a result, Reckson realized a gain of about $15.2 million.

Clouding Reckson Associates' fortunes in 2001–02 was the collapse of FrontLine Capital Group, to which Reckson had earmarked $163 million in loans. Once a high flier on the NASDAQ stock exchange, FrontLine foundered when the technology boom ended in 2000. HQ Global Workplaces, Inc., a majority-owned subsidiary that FrontLine turned to as its fallback when the Internet boom faded, became the world's largest office-suites rental business but plunged into the red when the U.S. economy fell into recession. Because of FrontLine's problems, Reckson lost $166.1 million in valuation reserves during 2001 and as a result sustained a net loss of $57.87 million despite record revenues of $540.47 million. Its market capitalization reached a new high of $3.3 billion, but its indebtedness came to about $1.3 billion (including long-term debt of $884 million) for a debt-to-market capitalization ratio of 41 percent. During the year the company sold five office properties for $82.1 million and its interest in a property trust for $35.7 million, with much of the net proceeds used to repay loans. While Scott Rechler struggled to restructure FrontLine, Re-

ckson's own stock price was suffering because investors disapproved of the amount of time he was spending to attend to FrontLine's problems.

As of the end of 2001, Reckson Associates owned 182 properties (including 11 joint-venture properties) encompassing about 20.6 million square feet of rentable space, all of which was being managed by the company. These holdings included 42 top-grade suburban office properties located within the company's ten office parks. Another 17 office properties were in New York City (five), Stamford, Connecticut (eight), and White Plains, New York (four). In addition, the company held 103 industrial properties, of which 72 were within its three industrial parks, and an office building in Orlando, Florida, plus a partnership in the Omni. Reckson also owned about 254 acres of land in 12 separate parcels earmarked for future development and was under contract to purchase, in 2002, parcels in Valhalla and Rye Brook, New York. Since its initial public offering of stock, the company had developed or redeveloped 14 properties encompassing about 2.1 million square feet of office and industrial space.

Principal Subsidiaries

Metropolitan Partners, LLC; Omni Partners, L.P.; RANY Management Group, Inc.; Reckson Construction Group, Inc.; Reckson FS Limited Partnership; Reckson Management Group, Inc.; Reckson Operating Partnership, L.P.

Principal Competitors

Equity Office Property Trust; Mack-Cali Realty Corp.

Further Reading

Anastasi, Nick, "Reckson Tops on Island," *LI Business News*, May 5, 1997, pp. 1+.
Croghan, Lore, "After Fast-Track Success, FrontLine Hits End of Line," *Crain's New York Business*, February 4, 2002, pp. 25, 29.
Feldman, Amy, "Developers Are Bearing Express to the Suburbs," *Crain's New York Business*, August 19, 1996, p. 20.
Hegarty, Liam, "Reckson Acquires Shelton Property in $26.9 Million Deal," *Fairfield County Business Journal*, April 28, 1997, pp. 1+.
Holusha, John, "Reckson Invests Heavily in Its Manhattan Portfolio," *New York Times*, October 31, 1999, Sec. 8, p. 11.
Jochum, Glenn, "REITs: The Second Generation," *LI Business News*, December 25, 1995, pp. 1+.
Krisher, Bernard, "Industrial Park, Dream of 3 Men, Lures Top Firms," *New York World-Telegram and The Sun*, December 2, 1958, Brooklyn section, pp. 1–2.
Martinez, Barbara, "He'll Take Manhattan—If He Can," *New York Times*, May 26, 1999, p. B14.
"Reckson Sells a Stake in New York Building for About $221 Million," *Wall Street Journal*, December 24, 2001, p. B3.
Wax, Alan J., "Aggressive Reckson Associates Amasses Billion-Dollar Portfolio, Becomes LI's Biggest Property Company," *Newsday*, February 10, 1997, pp. C8–C9, C12.
——, "He'll Take Manhattan," *Newsday*, March 15, 1999, pp. C8–C9.
——, "Quotes: Reckson Associates Realty Corp. Has Reached," *Newsday*, August 10, 1999, p. A43.
Whitford, David, "Picking His Way to the Top," *Fortune*, March 31, 1997, p. 172.

—Robert Halasz

Rentokil Initial Plc

Elcourt, East Grinstead
West Sussex RH19 2JY
United Kingdom
Telephone: (+44) 1342 833022
Fax: (+44) 1342 833029
Web site: http://www.rentokil-initial.com

Public Company
Incorporated: 1925 as Rentokil Limited
Employees: 96,000
Sales: £2.24 billion ($3.58 billion) (2001)
Stock Exchanges: London OTC
Ticker Symbol: RTO
NAIC: 561210 Facilities Support Services; 561621
Security Systems Services (Except Locksmiths);
561710 Exterminating and Pest Control Services;
812331 Linen Supply Services; 561499 All Other
Business Support Services

Rentokil Initial Plc is one of the world's leading services companies operating in seven primary areas: Hygiene, including linen supply services, the company's largest division, providing 31 percent of sales; Security, the second largest segment, with 23 percent of sales; Facilities Management; Pest Control, the company's historical base of operations; Tropical Plants rental and maintenance; and Conferencing. Together these activities generated nearly £2.24 billion in sales in 2001. The United Kingdom remains the company's headquarters and single largest market, at 51 percent of sales. The rest of Europe adds 29 percent of the company's sales, while Rentokil Initial's North American activities generate about 13 percent of sales. The company is also active in the Asia/Pacific region, where the company hopes to focus its future growth. Rentokil Initial's growth has long been led by CEO Clive Thompson—known as "Mr. 20 Percent" for his longtime insistence that Rentokil grow at least 20 percent per year. Since the late 1990s, however, the company has abandoned that target, settling for growth rates of just 15 percent and lower. In order to counter its slumping margins, the company, which claimed to have made more than 300 acquisitions since the early 1980s, began shedding a number of its noncore operations, including its plant hire, temporary staffing, and distribution operations. The sell-off, which slashed some 30 percent of the company's turnover, generated more than £620 million and has provided the company with a strong war chest to pursue growth in its chosen markets. Among its acquisitions at the turn of the century was the purchase of Ratin A/S, which held 32 percent of Rentokil Initial's stock. Much of its acquisition interest has gone toward bolt-on purchases, including 12 businesses in 2000. Rentokil Initial is traded on the London Stock Exchange and on the U.S. OTC market.

Exterminating Origins: Early 20th Century

Rentokil Initial was the result of the hostile takeover by Rentokil Plc of far larger BET, and its Initial brand name, in 1996. Both companies traced their roots back to the turn of the 20th century and had established themselves as leaders in their respective markets. The merged company, renamed Rentokil Initial, combined Rentokil's expertise in pest control services and its 1990s foray into security services with BET's broader base of business services, including linen rentals, cleaning, and catering.

Rentokil's origins lay in pest control. In 1902, Georg Neumann, a pharmacist working in Aalborg, Denmark, developed a type of bacteria that proved to be deadly for rats and mice. Neumann dubbed his poison Ratin and set up his own company, Bakteriologisk Laboratorium Ratin, in 1902. Neumann's discovery soon caught the attention of the Sophus Berendsen company, which decided to introduce the poison to the British market as well as the other Scandinavian countries. The first U.K. sales office for Ratin opened in 1906 and proved a popular product, for which Sophus Berendsen retained the exclusive U.K. license. In the 1920s, the British arm took on greater importance and began moving toward providing pest control services, rather than simply selling the Ratin poison system. In 1927, the sales office incorporated as the British Ratin Company, led by Karl Gustav Anker-Petersen. In 1928, Petersen abandoned sales of Ratin and converted the company fully to pest control services, beginning the company's expansion throughout the United Kingdom.

Company Perspectives:

Our aim is to substantially outperform the support services sector as measured by shareholder return over a five-year period. We target to achieve this through a continual drive to improve the quality of our service delivery and technical leadership, the quality of our culture and management and the quality of our earnings. Our strategy is to continue developing our business services in the major developed economies of the world, with a range of high growth and quality driven services, which generate cash and are in less cyclical markets, using the strength of the Rentokil and Initial brands.

World War II and the scarcity of food stocks brought a new urgency to the pest control industry, and particularly the extermination of insects. As growing numbers of its customers began requesting insect control services in addition to the company's rodent control services, British Ratin branched out, acquiring Chelsea Insecticides Ltd. to inaugurate its new division. This move brought British Ratin in competition with another company, Rentokil Ltd.

Rentokil had been founded in 1925 by Harold Maxwell Lefroy. As a professor of entomology at the Imperial College in London, Lefroy had been asked to find a way to eliminate a death watch beetle infestation at Westminster Hall. Lefroy, assisted by Elizabeth Eades, came up with a formula in 1924, dubbed "Ento-Kill." Since a similar name had already been registered as a trade name, Lefroy instead named his insecticide Rentokil. The following year, Lefroy started up a business, Rentokil Ltd., to sell his preparation. Lefroy, however, was killed in a laboratory accident the following year, and the company's operations were taken over by Eades.

Rentokil began offering its own extermination services during World War II, focusing on woodworm and dry rot control. That segment was incorporated as a separate subsidiary, the unglamorously named Woodworm and Dry Rot Control Ltd., established in 1952. By then, British Ratin had begun expanding its insecticides division, establishing a dedicated subsidiary, Disinfestation Ltd. At the beginning of the 1950s, that company began preparing a move into the market for control of woodworms, launching its first treatment products in 1952.

British Ratin, which still counted Sophus Berendsen as its major shareholder, acquired Rentokil Ltd. in 1957. Yet it was the Rentokil name that was to carry on the company's banner. In 1960, the company reorganized, adopted the new name of Rentokil Group Ltd. By 1962, all of the company's U.K. operations had been rebranded under the single Rentokil Ltd. name.

Going Public, Moving Beyond Pest Control: 1969

Rentokil went public in 1969. The public offering enabled the company, which until then had specialized in pest control, to branch out into other services. Soon after its stock market listing, Rentokil acquired Rashbrooke Chemical Co., forming the basis of Rentokil's Hygiene division. The following year, the company paid £1 million to acquire another hygiene ser-

vices business, Thames Services. Meanwhile, Rentokil continued to invest in its pest control systems and during the 1970s succeeded in establishing itself as the U.K. leader in the sector. By then, too, Rentokil had succeeded in extending its reach beyond the United Kingdom, beginning with Australia in 1965, and built up an especially strong position in the European market. Pest control and hygiene services were to remain the core of the company's offerings until the mid-1990s; however, during the 1980s, the company began to branch out into a variety of diversified services offerings.

The company had rested on its laurels somewhat during the 1970s, which led to the ouster of its senior management at the beginning of the 1980s. Placed in charge of the company was Clive Thompson, then 40 years old, who started with the company as a director before being named chief executive officer in 1983. Thompson took Rentokil on an acquisition spree, pledging to achieve a per-year growth rate of 20 percent or more—the pledge was to earn him the moniker of "Mr. 20 Percent" for years to come. Over the next decade and a half, Rentokil made some 300 acquisitions, taking the company into a variety of new areas, such as tropical plant rental and maintenance; office machinery and equipment maintenance; office cleaning services; healthcare, including washroom services; and distribution.

In 1991, the company moved into textile and industrial laundry services by acquiring that division from Electrolux, of Sweden. Two years later, Rentokil moved into the security services sector with its £76 million acquisition of Securigard, which also marked the company's entry into the parcels delivery sector with subsidiary A to Z Parcels. The Rentokil name now represented a wide variety of business services—yet the name's connotations tended to form a handicap for entry into a number of business sectors.

Rentokil solved that problem in 1996 when it launched a hostile takeover of BET, a business services company three times its size. As Rentokil had diversified into new business areas, BET had become an increasingly tough competitor. Formerly known as British Electric Traction Company, founded in the 19th century, when it had been one of the United Kingdom's foremost transportation services providers, BET had transformed itself into a diversified business services provider. In the 1930s, BET had started up a laundry services wing, called Advance Services; the company also acquired a shareholding in a small towel services company, Initial Towel Supply.

New Initials for the 21st Century

Initial had been started by A.P. Bigelow, an American living in England, in 1903. Bigelow not only rented towels, a novelty at the time in London, he also adopted a policy of personalizing towels—so that each towel belonged only to a single customer. Bigelow began placing customers initials on the company's towels, and soon adopted the name Initial Towel Supply Company. Initial went public in 1928, and Bigelow returned to the United States.

Following World War II, Initial achieved strong growth, and succeeded in establishing itself as the United Kingdom's leading linens rental company. Initial also branched out internationally, spreading throughout Europe and into the United States as

Key Dates:

1902: Georg Neumann discovers bacteria-based rat and mice poison, called Ratin, then sets up company, Bakteriologisk Laboratorium Ratin.

1903: Initial Towel Supply is founded by A.P. Bigelow.

1906: Sophus Berendsen opens sales office for Ratin in the United Kingdom, which becomes the British Ratin Company in 1927.

1924: Harold Maxwell Lefroy develops insecticide, originally named Ento-Kill.

1925: Lefroy incorporates business as Rentokil; BET (British Electric Traction Company) sets up Advance laundry services subsidiary.

1928: British Ratin switches focus from sales of poison to offering pest control services; Initial goes public on London Stock Exchange.

1940s: Both British Ratin and Rentokil begin offering insect control services.

1952: Rentokil spins off insect control services into new subsidiary, Woodworm and Dry Rot Control Ltd.

1957: British Rain acquires Rentokil, then takes on new name, Rentokil Group Ltd., in 1962.

1969: Rentokil goes public, then acquires Rashbrooke Chemical Co., which forms the basis of a new Hygiene division.

1982: Sir Clive Thompson takes over leadership of Rentokil, leads company on acquisition trail of more than 300 companies in less than 20 years.

1985: BET takes over Initial Towel Supply, merging it with its own Advance linen services subsidiary; new subsidiary retains Initial name.

1991: Rentokil enters textile and industrial laundry services by acquiring that division from Electrolux.

1992: Rentokil moves into security services sector with its £76 million acquisition of Securigard, which also marks the company's entry into the parcels delivery sector with subsidiary A to Z Parcels.

1996: Rentokil launches hostile takeover of BET, and changes name to Rentokil Initial.

2001: Restructuring of company shaves 30 percent of sales while providing Rentokil with £1.5 billion for future acquisitions.

The controversial BET takeover—a number of analysts questioned the possible synergies of the merger—tripled Rentokil in size and gave it operations in a number of new areas. It also gave the company the strong Initial brand name, which Rentokil promptly added to its own, renaming the company Rentokil Initial Plc that year. CEO Thompson had more than made good on his promise to achieve at least 20 percent growth that year. Nor was Rentokil's quest for growth undiminished: by 1997, the company was back on the acquisition trail, adding the textile services divisions of France's Generale des Eaux, itself in the process of transforming into Vivendi Universal. The company continued its acquisition drive through 1998, adding ten more companies to its various services divisions.

Yet the BET addition saddled Rentokil Initial with a number of BET's underperforming, low-margin businesses, which in turn dragged down Rentokil Initial's overall picture—by 1999 Thompson was forced to face public humiliation as he revealed that Rentokil was unable to meet its 20 percent growth target that year. Thompson now faced public derision as "Mr. Substantially Outperform," as Rentokil Initial formally dropped its longtime 20 percent per annum growth targets.

Rentokil Initial took the axe to itself at the end of the century, redefining its core business areas and shaving off a number of its newly noncore activities. By the end of 2001, the company had succeeding in raising more than £620 million in a series of selloffs that had trimmed nearly 30 percent of the company's annual revenues as well. Boasting a war chest in excess of £1.5 billion, Rentokil Initial nonetheless showed no signs of slowing down in its acquisitions. Throughout 2001, the company added a series of some 18 bolt-on acquisitions, including a number of companies in the Asian market countries, where Rentokil Initial hoped to see strong future growth. The company also moved to make its stock more liquid: after longtime shareholder Sophus Berendsen, which itself had grown into a leading Scandinavian textile services company, spun off its 32 percent of Rentokil Initial into a dedicated holding company, Ratin A/S, Rentokil Initial moved to acquire that company, ending the two companies' long relationship.

Thompson announced his intention to step down as chief executive at the end of 2002, taking on the position of non-executive chairman instead. By then, too, Rentokil Initial expected to have completed its restructuring around a new, more limited core of business services.

Principal Subsidiaries

United Kingdom: Dudley Industries Ltd; Initial A to Z Couriers Ltd; Initial Aviation Security Ltd; Initial Catering Services Ltd (75%); Initial City Link Ltd; Initial Contract Services Ltd; Initial Electronic Security Systems Ltd; Initial Hospital Services Ltd; Initial Security Ltd; Initial Style Conferences Ltd; Rentokil Ailsa Environmental Ltd; Rentokil Facilities Maintenance Ltd; Rentokil Initial Management Services Ltd; Rentokil Initial Services Ltd; Rentokil Initial UK Ltd; Rentokil Insurance Ltd; Rentokil IT Hygiene Ltd; Rentokil Office Machine Maintenance Ltd; Retail Cleaning Services Ltd (51%); Rentokil Initial Pty Ltd (Australia); Rentokil Initial GmbH Austria; Rentokil Initial (Bahamas) Ltd; Rentokil Initial (Barbados) Ltd; Initial Cleaning NV (Belgium); Initial Euroblan NV (Belgium); Initial

well as Australia. BET, meanwhile, continued to develop its own linen services wing, along with a growing variety of business services. That company also steadily increased its shareholding in Initial, building up a 40 percent stake by the mid-1980s. In 1985, BET launched a full-fledged takeover of Initial, then merged its Advance Services subsidiary under the Initial brand name.

BET ran into trouble by the end of the 1980s, however, as its debt blossomed to more than £600 million. By the time the recession of the early 1990s was underway, BET was floundering, sinking into losses by the beginning of the decade. In 1991, BET brought in a new CEO, John Clarke, who struggled to restore the company's health. Yet its stock price remained low, leaving it open to Rentokil's hostile takeover in 1996.

Friswit NV (Belgium); Initial GMIC Security NV (Belgium); Rentokil Initial NV (Belgium); Rentokil Tropical Plants NV (Belgium); Rentokil Initial Canada Ltd; Ecotex sro (Czech Republic); Rentokil Initial A/S (Denmark); Rentokil Initial Ltd (Ireland); Rentokil Initial Ltd (Fiji); Oy Rentokil Initial AB (Finland); Initial BTB SA (France; 97%); Initial Rouch Intermodal SA (France); Rentokil Initial Delta Protection SA (France); Rentokil Initial SA (France); Rentokil Initial Martinique SARL; Bilger-Schwenk AG (Germany); Initial Adrett GmbH (Germany); Rentokil Initial GmbH (Germany); Rentokil Initial Hellas EPE (Greece); Rentokil Initial Guyana Ltd; Rentokil Initial Hong Kong Ltd; PT Calmic Indonesia; PT Rentokil Indonesia; Rentokil Initial Italia SpA; Rentokil Jamaica Ltd; Rentokil Initial Kenya Ltd; Celcure (M) Sdn Bhd (Malaysia); Rentokil Initial (M) Sdn Bhd (Malaysia); Initial Dienstverlening Nederland BV (Netherlands); Initial Varel Security BV (Netherlands); Rentokil Hokatex BV (Netherlands); Rentokil Initial BV (Netherlands); Rentokil Initial Ltd (New Zealand); Rentokil Initial Norge AS (Norway); Rentokil Initial (Philippines) Inc; Rentokil Initial Portugal-Servicos de Proteccao Ambiental Lda.

Principal Competitors

ARAMARK Corporation; The Davis Service Group Plc; Ecolab Inc.; ISS-International Service System A/S; Mitie Group PLC; Penauille Poly Services SA; Protection One, Inc.; Rollins, Inc.; SC Johnson Commercial Markets, Inc.; Securicor plc; Securitas AB; Serco Group plc; The ServiceMaster Company; Sodexho, Inc.; Steiner Corporation; Swisher International, Inc.

Further Reading

Cope, Nigel, "Sir Clive Thompson—Rentokil's Chief Longs," *Independent*, September 3, 2001, p. 13.

Croft, Jane, "Rentokil Declares £1.5 Bn War Chest," *Financial Times*, August 30, 2000.

Felsted, Andrea, "Rentokil Damps Bid Speculation over Securicor," *Financial Times*, December 5, 2001.

——, "Rentokil Hunts for New Chief Executive," *Financial Times*, March 1, 2002.

Maunsell, Nevill Boyd, "How Houdini Sir Clive Thompson Escaped the CBI Curse," *Birmingham Post*, August 31, 2001, p. 19.

"Rentokil Initial: Missed the 20%," *Economist*, August 7, 1999.

"Sir Clive Rats on Mr. Twenty Per Cent," *Independent*, August 19, 1999, p. 17.

Urquhart, Lisa, "Sir Clive Thomson: Mr. Rentokil Takes a Dive," *Financial Times*, June 26, 2000.

—M.L. Cohen

Rodale, Inc.

33 East Minor Street
Emmaus, Pennsylvania 18098-0099
U.S.A.
Telephone: (610) 967-5171
Fax: (610) 967-8963
Web site: http://www.rodale.com

Private Company
Incorporated: 1930
Employees: 1,300
Sales: $500 million (2001 est.)
NAIC: 511120 Periodical Publishers; 511130 Book
   Publishers

Rodale, Inc. is a leading U.S. publisher of health- and sports-related magazines and books. Known for the monthly publications *Men's Health* and *Prevention,* the family-owned operation also publishes the popular magazines *Runner's World, Bicycling,* and *Backpacker.* The company branched out into new markets in 2001 with *Organic Style* and *MH-18.* Rodale Books provides a significant portion of the company's revenues, with approximately 100 new titles a year and a backlist of more than 500 titles, including the best-selling *Dr. Shapiro's Picture Perfect Weight Loss* and *The Wrinkle Cure. The Doctor's Book of Home Remedies,* one of its most popular titles, was a brisk seller around the world.

Out of the Depression

J.I. Rodale began his professional life not on a farm, but in a New York City accounting practice. He and his brother Joe formed Rodale Manufacturing in 1923. The company produced commercial and residential electrical connectors but it would provide the means to launch Rodale's more earthy enterprises. Emmaus, Pennsylvania, a borough near Allentown, eventually lured Rodale Manufacturing to relocate through offers of lower costs and free factory space.

J.I. Rodale soon began publishing a humorous reader from a corner of the factory floor. However, it proved too humorous to last a second issue. Nevertheless, other magazines with such lively titles as *The Clown* (later *The American Humorist*), *You Can't Eat That* (later *Health Guide*), *Everybody's Digest,* and *True Health Facts* appeared before 1940. *Fact Digest* was the most successful of the lot, selling 100,000 copies at one point.

During the Great Depression, most families had dirt yards and education was as scarce as good jobs. Most people were more concerned about merely eating than eating right. But J.I. Rodale felt that something was fundamentally lacking with the ways Americans looked after their farms and themselves. He was inspired to buy a 60-acre farm after Sir Albert Howard, considered the founder of the modern organic farming movement, published his findings in 1940. Following 40 years of research in India, Howard believed that the living organisms that made soil useful needed to be nourished with compost, the way the natives Howard observed returned all animal and vegetable matter to the earth. He also felt this made for more healthful produce. Howard also strongly opposed artificial fertilizers and pesticides.

Rodale began publishing *Organic Farming and Gardening* in 1942, while developing techniques on his farm near Emmaus. The magazine was born into controversy; however, it remained an enduring success, counting a million readers more than 50 years after its debut. An interest in nutrition and other areas of personal health led to the launch of *Prevention* in 1950; it eventually garnered an audience of more than 3.5 million to become the country's leading health magazine. *Prevention* was originally printed on uncoated paper with few graphics and carried mostly mail-order advertising.

J.I. Rodale attained some celebrity, and died while appearing as a guest on the *Dick Cavett Show* in 1971. His son Robert, who was born in 1930, would lead the company for the next 20 years.

Building Upon Success in the 1970s

Robert Rodale was an editor at Rodale before becoming its leader in 1971. He was also skilled with a shotgun and landed a trip to Mexico City with the 1968 U.S. skeet shooting team. He became known for the sensational growth the company experienced under his leadership.

Rodale continued the research efforts initiated by his father at the Rodale Research Center (originally the Soil and Health Society, founded in 1947), which operated a 333-acre farm in Maxatawny, Pennsylvania. Regenerative agricultural techniques were the focus of this center, which, in cooperation with the USDA, USAID, and other institutions, examined a variety of environmental and economic issues. Rodale also founded the Rodale Institute, a nonprofit organization that sought to make science "not just *for* the people, but *by* the people as well."

Inspired by the cycling at the 1968 Olympics, Rodale bought *Bicycling* magazine in 1977 and turned it into the hottest thing on wire wheels. Another editorial innovation was *The Prevention Index,* an annual survey of American health trends used by media, government agencies, and corporations.

As health foods and nutritional supplements became more available in specialty stores and supermarkets, *Prevention* had to formulate a new strategy for the 1980s to accommodate dwindling mail-order advertising. However, its efforts to interest media buyers for national accounts seemed doomed by the magazine's earlier criticisms of processed food. The magazine also began occupying checkout counters, spurring previously nonexistent single copy sales. In the early 1990s, Rodale would focus more on retail sales to counter increasing postal rates.

Competition drove Rodale out of two categories in 1987. It sold *Practical Homeowner* magazine as its interest area became too crowded, and also sold *Children,* which struggled amid a field of parenting copycats. However, the company was fertile with new ideas. Rodale tested what would become one of the fastest-growing magazines in print, *Men's Health,* in 1988. Its circulation would quadruple in the early 1990s, reaching one million in 1994.

Going Global in the 1990s

Eventually, the company was able to export viable versions of its domestically successful magazines in Europe, Asia, and South Africa. Robert Rodale's international expansion plans brought him to the Soviet Union to work on a publishing joint venture with state publishing agency Vneshtorgizdat and a state farm. The pioneering collaboration eventually produced *The New Farmer* (*Novii Fermer*) with a circulation of 50,000 in spite of huge obstacles. For example, the magazine was printed in Finland due to a lack of quality presses in the U.S.S.R. Tragically, Robert Rodale was killed in a Moscow car accident in September 1990.

Ardath Harter Rodale succeeded her husband Robert as chairman and CEO of Rodale Press after his death. Ardath Rodale immediately formed an advisory board including her children, several executives, and Robert J. Teufel, a longtime employee and trusted advisor, who served as chief operating officer and president.

For the previous 30 years, Ardath Rodale had designed office space for the company. (True to the company's origins, existing vacant buildings were often renovated and reused.) AIDS awareness projects had become the focus of her extensive community service after her son, David, died from the disease in 1985. Ardath Rodale wrote the "Reflections" column for *Prevention* and the syndicated "Awakenings" column for the *Chicago Tribune* and published the inspirational text *Climbing Toward the Light* in 1989. Her thoughts on spirituality in modern life were featured in *Embracing Our Essence: Spiritual Conversations with Prominent Women.* She also lectured on health, the environment, and relationships. "Our mission is to show people how they can use the power of their bodies and minds to make their lives better," said Ardath Rodale. " 'You can do it,' we say on every page of our magazines and books."

Revenues were about $250 million when Ardath Rodale assumed the company's leadership. The company continued to launch many new magazine and book titles. Rodale developed *Straight Talk,* a magazine for teens, with the National Education Association, and marketed it to schools in 1991. The company tested *Young Executive,* designed to help men attain corporate distinction, in 1992. *Rodale's Scuba Diving* fared better. The company even presented a cable television show based on its *Bicycling* magazine.

While the depressed economy of the early 1990s was not kind to Rodale's startups, the company fared fairly well otherwise, except perhaps for *Prevention* magazine, which saw ad revenues dip. The venerable *Runner's World,* launched in the mid-1960s, experienced a huge increase in advertising, however. Rather than discounting rates, the company focused on innovative promotional tie-ins to keep sponsors enthusiastic. In addition, magazines that led their categories weathered depressions best, and Rodale had unloaded underperforming titles in competitive fields. The company credited consumer loyalty to its high standards.

Although group publisher George Hirsch had two years earlier predicted to the contrary in the *Wall Street Journal,* in 1993, Rodale entered the lucrative and competitive women's service market with its own *Healthy Woman.* However, this venture failed within a few months. Rodale launched *Heart and Soul,* aimed at black women, with Reginald D. Ware, a black entrepreneur who had spent years developing the concept. *Heart and Soul* attracted advertisers, but four years after its debut had yet to become profitable.

Rodale pursued cautious growth by acquisition in the mid-1990s. In the spring of 1995, Rodale Press bought a share in Abenaki Publishers with plans to introduce new fly fishing magazines. Rodale spent $15.8 million to buy *New Woman* from K-III Communications Corp. in August 1997.

Sales increased considerably—more than 50 percent—under Ardath Rodale's tenure. By 1996, Rodale Books had sold 20 million copies, reaching one-fifth of all American homes and providing half of Rodale's income. *Green Pharmacy, Low-Fat Living,* and *New Choices in Natural Healing* were among the most popular offerings of its 500 titles in print.

A British version of *Men's Health* was immediately successful. However, other international ventures frustrated Rodale, prompting them to hire the consulting firm Braxton Associates. They found that Rodale's traditional, decentralized working methods, while fostering creativity, made communications even more complicated overseas. In 1997, Rodale began distributing a Spanish-language version of *Men's Health* in cooperation with Editorial Televisa, based in Mexico City.

In late 1996, AT&T canceled its web venture with Rodale called the HealthSite after only a few weeks. Rodale Press created a new marketing division in 1997 and applied a new, decentralized approach to its online operations. Its web site for *Men's Health* featured an online form for ordering back issues and article reprints.

Setbacks in the Late 1990s

Although sales had risen considerably in the 1990s, several of Rodale's publications were dragging down profits in the late 1990s. In response, the company sold off underperforming magazines and reorganized some divisions, in addition to changing its name to simply Rodale, Inc. In 1998 Rodale sold its American Woodworking Group, which included the magazine *American Woodworker,* to Reader's Digest Association for $20 million. The same year Primedia purchased the company's *Quiltmaker* and "Quilter's Newsletter," and Clotilde bought the company's *Quilts and Other Comforts* catalog. *Heart & Soul,* Rodale's health and beauty magazine for African American women, was sold to BET. In 1999, a downturn in what had

been the booming bicycling market led Rodale to combine its sales and marketing forces for *Bicycling* and *Mountain Bike,* resulting in the layoff of 20 people, the first ever for the almost 70-year-old company.

Organic Gardening, Rodale's flagship publication, was also experiencing difficulties. Readership and advertising had been falling since 1997, and Maria Rodale, Ardath's daughter, was brought in to revive the title. She was put in charge of the new Organic Living division, which ran *Organic Gardening* and the company's gardening book titles. In addition, she began developing a new entry into the women's glossies: *Organic Style.*

The company's purchase of *New Woman* was also proving a disappointment. After two years of investment in the magazine's editorial, marketing, and circulation departments, Rodale closed the 30-year-old title in January 2000. Rodale ended 1999 with a disappointing 46.6 percent drop in sales, to $267 million.

New Life in the New Millennium

Rodale continued to revamp its product line, its organization, and its image in the early 2000s. Most importantly, Steven Murphy took over as president for retiring Bob Teufel in April 2000. Soon thereafter, the former Disney Publishing executive restructured the company, abandoning the format divisions for ones organized by content: Men's Health, Women's Health, Sports and Fitness, Organic Living, and Books. His intent, he said, was to transform Rodale into a multimedia company.

Support for this new focus came from Maria Rodale, seen as the heir-apparent to CEO Ardath Rodale. "Maria wants a much harder-edged company," *Folio* quoted one Rodale employee as saying. "She wanted to bring in what she calls 'New York cool.'" Maria encouraged that new image with her magazine *Organic Style,* which launched in August 2001. The health and lifestyle magazine for women went head-to-head with Time Inc.'s *Real Simple* and Hearst's *O.*

Revenues were still on the rise in 2001 for the company's top seller, *Men's Health.* Hoping to expand on that magazine's 33-country success story, Rodale launched *MH-18,* a version of *Men's Health* for teenage boys.

By 2001, Murphy's changes seemed to be bearing fruit. Streamlining operations had cut the company's workforce from 1,300 to 800 and saved an estimated $40 million. Despite the soured economy, company sales had reached approximately $500 million in 2001, and the privately owned company had reportedly returned to profitability. Early in 2002, Murphy was promoted to chief executive officer, although Ardath Rodale remained as chairman.

Principal Divisions

Men's Health; Women's Health; Sports and Fitness; Organic Living; Books.

Principal Competitors

The Hearst Corporation; Meredith Corporation; Reader's Digest.

Further Reading

Bamford, Janet, and Jennifer Pendleton, "The Top Fifty Women-Owned Businesses," *Working Woman,* October 1997.

Calvacca, Lorraine, "Fits and Stops for Rodale Start-Ups," *Folio,* October 1, 1996, p. 20.

Carey, Robert, "Exercising Your Options," *Incentive,* June 1995, pp. 30–34.

Donaton, Scott, "Boys Will Be Boys But, Says *Men's Health,* It's No Fad," *Advertising Age,* March 7, 1994, p. S3.

——, "Rodale Press Nurtures Growth with Spinoffs," *Advertising Age,* September 14, 1992.

D'Orio, Wayne, "Rodale's New Challenges," *Folio,* October 1999, p. 43.

Foege, Alec, "Emmaus on the Hudson," *Mediaweek,* July 16, 2001, p. 20.

Freeman, Laurie, "Trash to Treasure," *Advertising Age,* June 24, 1991, p. 36.

"Getting Better: Rodale Press," *Chief Executive,* December 1995, pp. 12–13.

Hochwald, Lambreth, "Database Partnerships," *Folio,* August 1, 1994, pp. 52–53.

——, "Sub Promotion Still Hard to Read," *Folio,* March 15, 1994.

Hodges, Jane, "After Suffering Setbacks, Rodale Tries Decentralizing," *Advertising Age,* February 17, 1997, p. 22.

"How Rodale Takes Care of Its Health," *Business Week,* July 23, 2001, p. 79.

Jaben, Jan, "Publishers Beware," *Business Marketing,* December 1991, pp. 29–30.

Kavanagh, Mick, "Men Slip Between the Covers," *Marketing,* April 13, 1995, pp. 27–29.

Kaplan, Michael, "Rodale's New Attitude," *Folio,* November 2000, p. 57.

Lucas, Allison, "Exercising Your Options," *Sales and Marketing Management,* December 1995, p. 14.

Manly, Lorne, "Fly Fishing Lures Rodale," *Folio,* June 1, 1995, p. 36.

Masterton, John, "*Prevention* Passes Physical," *Folio,* February 1991, pp. 55–56.

McCullagh, James C., "Publishing Opportunities in Russia," *Folio,* June 1, 1996, pp. 77–87.

McGrath, Mike, ed., *The Best of Organic Gardening,* Emmaus, Pa.: Rodale Press, 1996.

Milliot, Jim, "Rodale Promotes Murphy," *Publishers Weekly,* January 21, 2002, p. 14.

Mummert, Hallie, "Naturally Successful," *Target Marketing,* March 1994, pp. 10–16.

Peterson, Lisa C., "Dressed for Health and Success," *Food Management,* June 1996, pp. 52–58.

Popper, Margaret, "Take It to the Tube," *Folio,* January 1, 1993, pp. 58–62.

Reilly, Patrick M., "Magazine Launching Moves Timidly," *Wall Street Journal,* p. B1.

——, "Rodale Finds Clean Living Gives a Healthy Tone to Ad Levels," *Wall Street Journal,* p. B1.

Rodale Press, Inc., "Who We Are," Emmaus, Pa.: Rodale Press, n.d.

"Rodale Sues Poll Firm, Baxter International Over Health Survey," *Wall Street Journal,* April 22, 1993.

Rosch, Leah, "Heart and Soul Shows Healthy Symptoms," *Folio,* November 1, 1994, p. 30.

Rosenfield, James R., "In the Mail," *Direct Marketing,* December 1992, pp. 19–20.

——, "Pets, Pests, and Paranoia: Direct Marketing in All Its Glory," *Direct Marketing,* September 1996, pp. 50–55.

Simon, Virginia, "The Arithmetic of Going Green," *Target Marketing,* January 1993, p. 29.

Teufel, Robert J., "The Rodalization Process," *Journal of Direct Marketing,* Spring 1996, pp. 2–3.

Wynter, Leon S., "Business and Race," *Wall Street Journal,* June 14, 1993, p. B1.

Yorgey, Lisa A., "American Direct Mail Overseas," *Target Marketing,* September 1997.

—Frederick C. Ingram
—update: Susan Windisch Brown

Sasol Limited

1 Sturdee Avenue
Rosebank
Johannesburg 2196
Republic of South Africa
Telephone: (27) 11-441-3111
Fax: (27) 11-788-5092
Web site: http://www.sasol.com

Public Company
Incorporated: 1979
Employees: 30,800
Sales: $5.4 billion (2001)
Stock Exchanges: NASDAQ Johannesburg
Ticker Symbol: SASOY (NASDAQ)
NAIC: 325110 Petrochemical Manufacturing (pt); 212112
Bituminous Coal Underground Mining; 324119 All
Other Petroleum and Coal Products Manufacturing
(pt); 213113 Support Activities for Coal Mining;
211111 Crude Petroleum and Natural Gas Extraction;
325920 Explosives Manufacturing

Sasol Limited was formed in 1979 to hold the assets of the South African Coal, Oil and Gas Corporation (Sasol) and its subsidiaries. For years its principal product was synthetic fuel, a business that enjoyed significant government protection in South Africa during the apartheid years. The transition to democracy in the 1990s has forced the company to search for products that could prove more competitive in the global marketplace, and as of the new millennium Sasol is focusing primarily on its petrochemical business, as well as on efforts to convert natural gas into crude oil.

Origins and Growth: 1950–80

The South African Coal, Oil and Gas Corporation (Sasol) was established in 1950 as part of the process of industrialization that the South African government considered essential for its economic development and autonomy. The fact that South Africa had no domestic oil reserves made the country extremely vulnerable to disruption of supplies coming from outside, albeit for different reasons at different times. Although it was generally much more expensive to produce oil from coal than from natural petroleum, the political as well as economic importance of achieving as much independence as possible in this sphere was sufficient to overcome any objections. Early attempts to attract private capital, foreign or domestic, were unsuccessful, and it was only with state support that the project could start.

The first Sasol installation opened in 1955, but had to overcome initial technical problems that delayed successful operation for more than a year. Financial success was possible only because a system of tariff protection and subsidy operated. This was in addition to profits from the sale of byproducts of the process as feedstock for the production of other chemicals and, from 1966, Sasol's involvement in National Petroleum Refiners of South Africa (Natref), which refined imported petroleum. With the industry functioning, private finance became available, and Sasol was successfully privatized in 1979.

As international oil sanctions threatened South Africa's oil supplies and African nationalists targeted Sasol installations, the company remained in the domestic political foreground. Political considerations also became international. Opposition to the continued involvement of U.S. finance and technology in the undertaking, for example, led in 1986 to the withdrawal of the American multinational Fluor from its South African subsidiary, which had provided initial construction and engineering support for Sasol installations. This had no practical effect in South Africa, as Fluor's place was taken by a European consortium. Already a major industrial enterprise when it went into the private sector, Sasol continued to grow, maintaining and expanding its role not only as the supplier of an increasing proportion of South Africa's fuel requirements, but also as a major producer of explosives, polymers, fertilizers, and other chemicals, and as a provider of technical services at home and abroad.

Industrialization in South Africa After World War I

It was only after World War I revealed just how vulnerable to external events the South African economy was because of its reliance on imports, that substantial efforts were made to promote domestic industrial development. Earlier moves in that direction had been strongly opposed by the mining industry on the grounds that domestically produced goods would be more expensive than imports. There were some small-scale producers of consumer goods such as shoes and textiles but no attempts had been made to move beyond gold and coal mining to make use of some of the country's other varied and abundant mineral resources to establish an industrial economy. Between 1911 and 1916, some iron works using electric furnaces and scrap metal from the mines and railways operated, but were of no real significance.

In 1922 a blast furnace was built in Newcastle, Natal, and a steelworks at Vereeniging, Transvaal, but it was with the formation of the Iron and Steel Corporation (Iscor) in 1929 that the foundations of an industrial economy were firmly laid. It rapidly became clear that development would be hampered by the fact that there were no known petroleum reserves in the country. In addition to the fact that Afrikaners—people of Dutch origin— were moving increasingly into the world of finance previously dominated by Britons, more immediate political considerations also came to the fore.

South Africa in the 1920s and 1930s experienced serious political, economic, and social problems as more and more poor white Afrikaners, unable to secure even a minimal living in the agricultural sector, sought work in towns—work that was in conspicuously short supply. In 1925 the Pact Government—a coalition of the South African Labour Party representing skilled, primarily British workers, and the National Party representing strongly anti-British Afrikaner nationalists—moved away from the policy of laissez-faire, making it possible to impose protective tariffs on imports. By protecting and promoting domestic industries, the move was expected to create more jobs. Other policies were put in place to ensure that as many new jobs as possible would go to white rather than black workers.

Although there was considerable debate about direct government involvement in manufacturing, government finance of essential infrastructure had never been seriously questioned. The railway network had been built and continued to be run as a nationalized enterprise, and in 1922 the Electricity Supply Commission (ESCOM) had been set up to provide electricity for the entire country. By the time Iscor was formed, although some mining financiers were beginning to show some interest in investing in industrial development, domestic risk capital was not easily available, and there was a growing aversion to allowing foreign capital to increase its hold on the economy. Many Afrikaner nationalists, including members of the government, did not feel that they could trust British or other foreign capitalists to be sufficiently loyal to South Africa to operate such a fundamentally important industry in the true interests of

the country. The growing number of Afrikaner financiers wanted a share in the profits of industrialization, but, having to build on a predominantly agricultural capital base, did not have the large amounts of finance needed. State-provided capital was considered preferable, all the more with regard to the conversion of coal to oil, as private sector efforts to raise the necessary initial funds came to naught.

Deriving Oil from Coal: The Late 19th and Early 20th Centuries

Research into the possibility of converting coal into oil had been going on in Europe for many years. Some of the scientific basis for the process was discovered at least as early as 1875, with further major progress reported in 1890. There was particular interest in the development of a commercially viable process in Germany where, in 1913, Friedrich Bergius (who would share in the 1931 Nobel chemistry prize for his work in this field) first patented an effective means of producing a substance similar to oil by liquefying coal and increasing its hydrogen content under pressure—hydrogenation.

Continued German interest in the search for an economical means of producing oil from coal led, in 1923, to the discovery of an alternative process based on gasifying rather than liquefying coal. Franz Fischer and Hans Tropsch at the Kaiser Wilhelm Institute for Coal Research at Mulheim developed a process in which synthesis gas—sometimes referred to as water gas—produced from coal was combined with hydrogen in the presence of a catalytic agent under controlled temperature and pressure conditions.

In a free market climate, the comparatively high cost of synthetic fuels made them totally uneconomical. World War II had reinforced concern about South Africa's economic vulnerability. The government was now much more interested in the establishment of a coal-to-oil capability than it had been when the idea was first mooted in the 1920s.

Initially there was greater interest and hope in the development of the production of oil from shale deposits than from coal. With the help of German experts, the possibility of exploiting the torbanite deposits at Ermelo was extensively explored. The South African Torbanite Mining and Refining Company (Satmar) was formed in 1932 "to refine and market indigenous petrol obtained by blending petrol from oil shale, alcohol from maize and molasses, and benzol from Iscor." These shales were capable of producing 20–100 gallons of oil per ton, but the company could only operate profitably by refining imported crude oil to supplement the shale operations.

In collaboration with Anglo-Transvaal Consolidated (Anglo-Vaal), Satmar acquired the South African rights to the Fischer-Tropsch process. Tenders were invited for the construction of the necessary plant, but capital was not forthcoming. As late as 1938 the South African government continued to hope that the possibilities of deeper drilling might yet lead to the discovery of oil or that Ermelo's torbanite could be made to produce oil economically. Coal-to-oil schemes were still considered uneconomical, but the government did agree that it made sense to test South African coal in both the Bergius hydrogenation and the Fischer-Tropsch gasification processes.

Government Economic Initiatives in the 1940s and 1950s

After World War II, shales still produced only small quantities of oil, natural petroleum still could not be found, and coal-to-oil conversion looked increasingly attractive. In 1947 a regulatory licensing framework was established for anyone interested in moving in that direction. The only applicant was Anglo-Vaal, which acquired a license in 1949 and elaborated a scheme, initially estimated to cost £13 million, for the opening-up of a new coal mine to ensure a steady supply for a Fischer-Tropsch plant with an annual output capacity of 260,000 tons, including 76 million gallons of motor fuel.

By early 1950, having spent some £400,000 in preliminary work, Anglo-Vaal sought government support in the form of a guarantee of £16 million debentures to be issued by the Industrial Development Corporation (IDC), which had been set up by the government in 1942 to help finance industry. After considerable debate, the IDC was allowed to provide the necessary funds or guarantees, with additional support from American banks. By 1955, the fully mechanized Sigma colliery was ready to supply 7,600 tons of coal daily, 3,200 tons of which were to be gasified in Lurgi generators to produce some three million cubic meters of gas for the Fischer-Tropsch plant, which was expected to produce 55 million gallons of motor fuel and 16 million gallons of other products annually. Some of these products—ammonia, tar, phenols, and creosote—were byproducts of gasification, while others—alcohols, acetone, and paraffin waxes—were produced in the Fischer-Tropsch units. Over the years, that process proved extremely versatile. By varying temperature, pressure, and the catalytic agents used, a wide range of organic compounds could be synthesized, making it important for the chemical industry throughout the world. Byproducts were also important for the South African undertaking, but it was only in that country that the process had been used extensively to produce fuel.

In what was to become known as Sasol I at Coalbrook—subsequently Sasolburg—two Fischer-Tropsch units operated. One used a fixed bed catalyst of the kind the Germans had employed during the war and was provided by the German firm Argbeit-Gemeinschaft Lurgi und Ruhrchemie (Arge). This process, based on a well tried and tested technique, operated without difficulty. The second unit, a fluid bed system, had been developed and installed by the American firm of M.W. Kellogg. This had never before operated on an industrial scale, and created technical difficulties which were not resolved until 1957. The original estimated cost of £13 million had risen to £18 million by the time IDC support was sought, and actual costs by the time the

system was functioning were significantly more than £40 million. The integration of the fixed and fluid bed systems was expected to produce considerable economic and technical advantages. The difficulties experienced in bringing the fluid bed unit onstream meant that any such benefits were slower to materialize than anticipated. Over the years, however, research and development led to the emergence of a unique production technique, ultimately to be known as the Sasol-Synthol process.

With underlying government support in the form of a tariff on imported petroleum and a sliding price scale for Sasol's own produce geared to world petroleum prices, Sasol was able eventually to show profits. At the time of its formation, hope that it could be profitable in its own right, without artificial protection, was not without justification. In addition to the greater efficiency expected from and finally achieved by process integration, the five units installed by Arge had the same capacity as 75 of the smaller units used in wartime Germany. Considerable immediate savings were made in the amount of equipment and instrumentation required. Less tangible, but nonetheless important, was the widespread belief that American oil reserves were nearing depletion. Supplies from the Middle East were thought to be at risk because of the fear of Soviet influence.

Toward a Post-Apartheid Economy: 1964–94

South Africa did not experience any difficulty in importing the crude oil it needed, although the means by which this was done, and the prices paid, were at times shrouded in secrecy. Strong international pressure to restrict supplies began to have an impact in 1964, when Kuwait banned all petroleum exports to South Africa. OPEC followed suit in 1973. Iran was South Africa's major supplier until the revolution of 1979 and the National Iranian Oil Company (NIOC) had a 17.5 percent share in Natref when it was formed. The French firm Elf Aquitaine (later to become Total Fina Elf S.A.) was also a major shareholder, but Sasol was in control with 52.5 percent. After the revolution, NIOC tried unsuccessfully to sell its shares, which were in effect absorbed in South Africa, Sasol's Natref holding rising to 63.63 percent.

The oil crises of 1974 and 1978 provided a substantial boost for Sasol, higher world prices not only enabling it to increase prices, but also making the cost of production closer to, or even lower than the world oil price. At the end of 1979, for example, Sasol's production cost was estimated to be about $30 per barrel at a time when world spot prices were about $10 per barrel higher. Although such differentials were not sustained, prospects in the 1970s were sufficiently good to lead Sasol to embark on the construction of a second installation, Sasol 2, at Secunda in 1976. By the time this installation came onstream in 1980, work had already begun on Sasol 3, also at Secunda. This third unit came onstream in 1982. Still based on the Fischer-Tropsch process, the new plants, like Sasol 1, were capable of producing a range of chemicals as well as synthetic fuel.

In 1979 it was decided to take Sasol public, with 70 percent of its shares being placed on the market. Initially, some R 490 million were raised by private placement of shares, with another 17.5 million shares made available to the public. South African institutional investors, pension funds, and large companies took the lead. Small investors were attracted by promises of preferential allocation treatment, and foreign investors were particularly interested because they were allowed to make their purchases using the financial rand, while dividends would be paid at the ordinary commercial exchange rate. At the time, the financial rand was at a discount in excess of 30 percent as against a more normal rate of about 12 percent. The public issue was more than 30 times oversubscribed. Foreign investors did not do as well as they hoped out of the allocation.

In 1983, on the basis of the expanded capacity provided by Sasol 2 and 3, Sasol Limited was able to begin moving beyond the provision of feedstock for the country's chemical industry into the production of fertilizers and various specialty chemicals. Existing producers did not welcome this competition.

Still a relative newcomer to the industry, Sasol was nonetheless part of the general effort to increase South African specialty chemical output. In addition to saving substantial amounts of foreign exchange by reducing reliance on imports, Sasol also planned to produce for export. In 1990, major investment plans were approved for the company to expand production of a range of products that would contribute to this end.

In relations with its workers, Sasol was facing, like most other South African enterprises, increasing pressure from African trade unions for improvements in pay, working conditions, and housing. A nine-day strike in 1989, for example, was resolved by the payment of a food allowance for African workers not living in hostel accommodation. More serious industrial action in 1987 resulted in Sasol's being criticized by the Industrial Court for using "rough and ugly tactics" in dealing with a strike by members of the Chemical Workers' Industrial Union. The company was, the court held, more interested in forcing capitulation than in negotiating a financial settlement. A subsequent appeal, however, found the company's actions justified.

Apart from specific trade union issues, Sasol was also a major target for political activists seeking to put pressure on the South African government to bring the apartheid system to an end. In June 1980, for example, there was a well-coordinated attack on Sasolburg, showing evidence of detailed knowledge of the plant and its weak security points. Bombs placed in the offices at Fluor, then constructing Sasol 2 and 3, were defused only a short time before they were set to explode.

During this period Sasol placed considerable emphasis on research and development, which had been the platform for considerable technological advance. On this basis it not only built up its manufacturing base within South Africa, but also provided technical services abroad. Most notable was technical support for some U.S. gas companies and general consultancy for a gasification plant in North Dakota, successfully commissioned in 1984.

By the beginning of the 1990s the company was calling for the expansion of synthetic fuel production in South Africa. It turned to government and other industries to provide the large amount of capital required, but it was not forthcoming.

After Apartheid: 1994–2001

As the apartheid system was being dismantled in the early 1990s, Sasol was searching for ways to remain competitive in the emerging free market economy. Deregulation and the end of government protection made it clear that the company would no longer be able to survive on the profits from its synthetic fuel business. In 1993 synthetic fuel still accounted for 41 percent of the company's profits, much of which were in the form of government subsidies. The government's plan to gradually phase out these subsidies—which amounted to R 1.1 billion annually—by 1997 left the company little choice but to focus more intently on products that could be competitive in the global economy.

The most obvious solution involved the expansion of the company's petrochemical business. In many respects, chemicals made far more business sense: International demand was far higher, and specialized chemicals could sell for nearly $1,000 a ton in the free market, compared to $200 per ton of synthetic fuel. With significantly lower operating costs, Sasol had a distinct edge over its European competitors. The key, however, was gaining a foothold in previously unexplored global markets. To this end, the company entered into a number of strategic partnerships with overseas corporations in the mid-1990s. These agreements included deals with Merichem for the production of phenolics and with DHB for the manufacturing of explosives. In 1995 Sasol joined forces with the German chemicals firm Schumann, giving the joint company control over one-fifth of the international wax market, and its 1998 acquisition of AECI made it the third largest producer of explosives in the world.

By 1995, chemical production accounted for 31 percent of the company's operating profits, with income from chemical exports reaching nearly $400 million, more than double the figure for the previous year. In spite of this shift toward petrochemicals, however, Sasol remained committed to developing an economically viable synthetic fuel throughout the 1990s. Much of the company's efforts remained focused on the possibilities of coal. By 1995 Sasol had succeeded in lowering the operating costs of its synthetic fuel reactors significantly, and it became conceivable that its product might become competitive with standard crude oil. At the same time, Sasol began exploring the possibilities of alternative forms of fuel conversion, most notably natural gas. In 1999 the company entered into a $1 billion agreement with Chevron to construct a natural gas processing plant in Nigeria, with the eventual goal of producing synthetic crude oil at the rate of 30,000 barrels a day. By 2000 the joint venture emerged into a new company, Sasol Chevron Holdings, dedicated to establishing similar natural gas-to-oil refineries around the world.

Clearly, Sasol was finding its way quite well as it took its first steps into the global economy. Investors were not blind to the company's potential; Sasol's stock price rose 50 percent between 2000 and 2001, prompting the Dow Jones World Sustainability Index to name it the second best performer of the year. While Sasol was still feeling its way in the post-apartheid economy at the beginning of the new millennium, it had every reason to feel confident that its past success in South Africa was going to translate into future success worldwide.

Principal Subsidiaries

Sasol Oil (Pty) Ltd.; Sasol Technology (Pty) Ltd.; Sasol Chemical Industries Ltd.-Operations Division; Sasol Mining (Pty)

Ltd.; Sasol Synthetic Fuels (Pty) Ltd.; Sasol Petroleum International (Pty) Ltd.

Principal Divisions

Sasol Alpha Olefins; Sasol Fertilizers; Sasol Fibres; Sasol Fuel Oil; Sasol Solvents; Sasol Carbo-Tar; Sasol Ammonia; Sasol Akrylo; Sasol Minchem; Sasol Mining Explosives (SMX); Sasol Gas; Sasol Engineering Division; Sasol Amsul; Sasol Synfuels International (Pty) Limited.

Principal Competitors

ChevronTexaco Corporation; Galp Energia, S.G.P.S., S.A.; Royal Dutch/Shell Group.

Further Reading

Ashurst, Mark, "Sasol Rides Out Upheaval in South Africa," *Financial Post* (Toronto), May 7, 1996.

Mallet, Victor, "Chevron, Sasol Join for Gas-to-Liquid Fuel Project," *Financial Times* (London), June 10, 1999.

Rich, Motoka, "New Role for Sanctions-Beaters Sasol: South Africa's Oil-from-Coal Concern Leads Way in Chemicals Industry Revamp," *Financial Times* (London), December 13, 1996.

Rutherford, Stuart, "Glug! Glug! Down It Goes," *Financial Mail* (South Africa), September 25, 1998.

—Simon Katzenellenbogen
—update: Steve Meyer

Idee che creano valore

Seat Pagine Gialle S.p.A.

via Saffi 18
10138 Turin
Italy
Telephone: (+39) 011-4351
Fax: (+39) 011-435-2722
Web site: http://www.seat.it

Public Company
Incorporated: 1925
Employees: 2,452
Sales: EUR 1.96 billion ($1.57 billion) (2001)
Stock Exchanges: Milan
Ticker Symbol: SPG
NAIC: 514191 On-Line Information Services; 511140 Database and Directory Publishers; 323119 Other Commercial Printing

Seat Pagine Gialle S.p.A. bills itself as Italy's leading "new economy" company—Seat controls Tin.it, the country's leading Internet Service Provider, as well as Virgilio, the leading Internet portal in Italy. Seat also provides business-to-business (B2B) Internet services through subsidiaries including Mondus, Gialle Viaggi, and Gialle Lavoro. Yet Seat also calls itself a "multi-platform media company" embracing such interests as publishing Yellow Pages, White Pages, and other directories (its historic core), which are available in print and online editions; retail office supplies through its Buffetti stores; call centers and directory assistance, which includes its German subsidiary, telegate, one of Europe's leading directory assistance companies; direct marketing, through its Gialle Dat@ subsidiary; information marketing and related business services, through NetCreations, an email marketer based in the United States and acquired in 2001; and television broadcasting, through its ownership of La 7, Italy's third largest and only independent broadcaster, which operates the La 7 and MTV Italy channels. Faced with losses at the beginning of 2002, Seat announced a strategic restructuring of its operations, with plans to shed its Business Information division, including France-based subsidiary Consodata; its B2B Internet branch; and other

holdings. The company also expected to reduce its number of subsidiaries—from more than 200 to just 75, including a reduction in the number of its Internet companies from 32 to just five remaining subsidiaries. These cuts also would include the trimming of its workforce, including a 50 percent reduction of its Internet-based staff. The company expects these and additional cost-cutting moves to produce overall profits by as early as 2003. Seat Pagine Gialle trades on the Italian stock exchange and is led by CEO Paolo Dal Pino. In 2001 the company posted sales of EUR 1.6 billion ($1.57 billion).

Telephone Directory Publisher in the 1920s

As Italy's telephone system developed through the early years of the 20th century, the various telephone companies operating at the time began implementing new services for their customers. The growth in numbers in people possessing telephone services led to the need for directory services to maintain lists of their names, addresses, and telephone numbers. One of the first to offer this service was SIP, the telephone operator serving Turin, which, together with printer Gianni & Cie, began publishing a list of the company's local subscribers in 1925. That operation later evolved into the Seat Pagine Gialle group.

The company grew quickly over the following decade, gaining the licenses to print telephone directories from four of the five telephone operators of the period. Then, in 1936, the company's printing operations were taken over by STET (for Societa Finanziaria Telefonica). The bombing of Turin during World War II caused heavy damage to the company, which was forced into bankruptcy. Following the war, however, Seat quickly rebuilt and by the end of the 1940s had begun acquiring directory publishing operations throughout Italy.

Seat came to control more and more of the market, and by 1954, the company became the only directory publisher to offer nationwide directory coverage. Soon after, in 1957, the country's telephone system was reorganized, with the remaining five regional operators bundled into a single government owned and operated entity, STET. STET became the holding company for Italy's various telecommunications interests, including Telecom Italia, the fixed line operator, and Seat, the directory publishing arm.

345

Seat had concentrated on publishing ''white pages'' of subscriber lists. In 1966, the company added a new service that had caught on elsewhere in the world, those of ''yellow pages.'' Featuring listings of businesses, the yellow pages, known as ''Pagine Gialle'' in Italy, became an important generator of advertising revenue for the Italian government—and the single largest generators of advertising revenue in all of Italy. In the late 1970s, Seat Pagine Gialle, as it became known, began diversifying beyond telephone directories. The company at first concentrated on print media, such as the ''Annuario'' (Yearbook) first published in 1977, then later added third-party ad-based media publishing in the 1980s, and electronic media, such as CD-ROMs and online databases, in the 1990s. During this time, STET's monopoly on the Italian telecommunications market helped it become one of the country's largest companies; by the 1990s, STET's market capitalization was estimated to be worth up to $20 billion.

Privatized Multi-Platform Media Company in the New Century

Yet by then, too, the Italian government was under pressure to privatize many of its holdings, including STET, in order to bring the country in line with its European Community partners. At the same time, EC rules also forced the government to attack the mountain of debt piled on top of its IRI holding company, which acted as the immediate parent of STET. The approach of the single currency market at the end of the 1990s placed an additional urgency on the reduction of this debt load, which reached levels of more than $12 billion in the mid-1990s.

Political battles, and particularly resistance from the government's Communist Party members, dragged out the privatization process. But by 1996, the government had at last agreed in principle to the privatization of its ''jewel in the crown,'' STET. A key part of the privatization included the spinoff of a number of STET's noncore assets, including the Sirti engineering division, the Italtel manufacturing joint venture with Germany's Siemens, and Seat, the directory publishing division, into separate, government-controlled companies. These companies were then expected to be privatized in their turn.

Seat was spun off at the end of 1996 and began preparing for its transition into the private sector. This, too, became a source of political tension. In 1995, the Italian government had set up a new newspaper advertising subsidiary under Seat, called MMP. That company, however, was an immediate money-loser, with losses ranging from L 25 billion (worth approximately $15 million) in 1995 to more than L 180 billion in 1996. At the same time, a number of the company's advertising contracts had led some observers to criticize MMP as a funding source for newspapers controlled by the country's various political newspapers.

In order to proceed with the Seat privatization, the Italian government agreed to shut down MMP and absorb its losses. The government moved to dismantle other roadblocks, including an agreement by Telecom Italia—slated to be merged into STET, which was then to adopt the Telecom Italia name for its overall operations—to acquire at least a 20 percent stake in Seat. By April 1997, the Italian government had narrowed down the bidding pool to three consortiums: one led by the United States' ITT; a second led by the United States' GTE; and a third, led by Banco Commerciale Italiana (which later changed its name to IntesaBei) and including publishing company De Agostini and investment group Investimenti Associati. At the same time, Telecom Italia pledged to acquire as much as a 20 percent share of Seat, a condition viewed as a prerequisite for successfully launching Seat as a publicly listed company.

The Banco Commerciale Italiana group won its bid for Seat. By August 1997, the last hurdle in Seat's privatization was cleared when the acquiring consortium and Telecom Italia reached a two-part agreement. The first part of the agreement gave Seat a ten-year extension on its directory publishing contract with Telecom Italia, maintaining that link between the two companies until at least 2007. The second part included Telecom Italia's agreement to acquire 20 percent of Seat from the consortium, a move that also gave Telecom Italia two seats on Seat's board of directors. At that time, Seat was listed on the Italian stock exchange, with a market value of more than L 3.2 trillion. Seat's primary shareholders now included the Banco Commerciale consortium (which placed its shares under a holding company, Ottobi), Telecom Italia, and the Italian government. The privatization of Telecom Italia followed in October that same year, giving that company a market value of L 24 trillion.

Seat had not been idle while it waited for its ownership structure to be sorted out. The company had been quick to recognize the growing importance of the Internet and other alternative delivery vehicles, such as CD-ROMs, in the mid-1990s. The company placed its Pagine Gialle online in 1996. That service enabled the company to broaden into the portal market, with the acquisition of web-services group Matrix and the launch of Virgilio. That site quickly became the Italian market's largest Internet portal and helped Seat gain a more than 70 percent share of all of the country's Internet advertising spending.

Seat reported its first full year of revenues in 1998, topping L 1.7 trillion and producing profits of L 155 billion. By then, Seat had begun to prepare for further growth. In 1999, the company absorbed its holding company, renaming itself Seat Pagine Gialle S.p.a. Seat then began to expand its operations. In that year it acquired a stake in the Buffetti office supply retail chain, in part to expand the company's electronic commerce offerings.

After acquiring Buffetti, Seat turned to the Internet provider market, buying up a controlling stake in McLink. At the beginning of 2000, the company added Kompass Italia, part of Kompass International, in keeping with its strategy to boost B2B operations. The company also raised its stake in Buffetti to more than 92 percent in a friendly takeover. By the end of 2000, however, Seat had transformed itself into one of Italy's most powerful multi-platform media players.

Key Dates:

1925: Turin telephone operator SIP and printer Gianni & Cie publish the first telephone directory.

1936: STET, or Societa Finanziaria Telefonica, takes over the telephone directory publishing business.

1954: Directory publishing company, later known as Seat, now covers all of Italy.

1957: Government-controlled STET takes monopoly of Italian telephone market.

1996: Italian government announces its intention to spin off Seat as part of the privatization of STET; Pagine Gialle is placed online.

1997: Seat is spun off as a publicly listed company.

1998: Seat reports first-year profits of L 155 billion on sales of more than L 1.7 trillion.

1999: Seat acquires Buffetti office supplies company and McLink, an Internet service provider.

2000: Seat merges with Tin.it, as Telecom Italia acquires a 61 percent controlling share; the company acquires TDL Infomedia (U.K.), Consodata (France), telegate AG (Germany), and television broadcaster TeleMonteCarlo.

2001: Seat acquires NetCreations in the United States; the company restructures its operations.

2002: Seat announces a new strategy, including disposal of parts of its business information and business-to-business services operations.

That transformation took place with the merger of Seat with Telecom Italia's Internet service provider Tin.it, the largest ISP in Italy. The deal, valued at more than $50 billion, gave Telecom Italia control of 61 percent of Seat and created one of Europe's largest Internet-oriented companies in what many saw as a shrewd marriage of content and access, much in the vein of the larger AOL-Time Warner merger of that same year.

The deeper pockets of the newly enlarged Seat enabled it to go on a shopping spree, as the company sought to boost a number of existing operations and expand into new territory. One of these new areas was the television broadcasting market, which the company entered with the purchase of TeleMonteCarlo 1 & 2. Following the purchase—which was at first blocked by the Italian government—Seat relaunched its television subsidiary as La 7 and its two stations as news-oriented La 7 and MTV Italia. Other important acquisitions that year included the Thomson Directory publisher TDL Infomedia of the United Kingdom and Germany's telegate, one of Europe's leading directory assistance companies, based in Germany.

Seat attempted to acquire its Swedish telephone directory counterpart Eniro in 2001, but the offer of some EUR 3 billion was rejected by Eniro's parent Telia. Instead, Seat went shopping in the United States, coming up with NetCreations, an email marketing company. The company also took a controlling share of French marketer Consodata.

Seat, however, had started losing money—nearly EUR 1 million on sales of EUR 1.92 billion in 2000. The company's losses continued through 2001, forcing the company to restructure its operations and adopt a number of new strategic objectives. Among these was a streamlining of its core operations, with planned sales of parts of its Business Information and B2B Internet divisions, its holding in Italian satellite television provider Viasat, and various other Internet-related interests. At the same time, the company announced a series of cost-cutting initiatives, such as the creation of a centralized purchasing system and the reduction of its subsidiaries from 215 to just 75, including a reduction of its Internet-related businesses from 32 to just five. Seat also moved to reduce staff, cutting out half of its Internet-related payroll.

These moves, to be carried out during 2002, were expected to return the company to profitability by 2003. Seat also began a revamp of its television broadcasting unit, including the launch of more competitive programming, to bring that subsidiary into profitability by 2004. Seat Pagine Gialle had nonetheless successfully transformed itself from a publisher of television directories into a multi-platform and Internet-ready media company for the 21st century.

Principal Subsidiaries

Euredit S.A. (France); Gialle Voice S.p.A; telegate AG (Germany); TDL Infomedia Ltd. (U.K.); Thomson Directories Ltd. (U.K.); Gruppo Buffetti S.p.A. (96%); Gialle Lavoro S.p.A.; Gialle Viaggi.it S.p.A.; Italbiz.com Inc. (U.S.A.; 72%); Matrix S.p.A. (67%); Tin Web S.r.l.; Consodata S.A. (France; 91%); Databank S.p.A. (93%); Kompass Italia S.p.A.; Gialle Professional Publishing S.p.A.; Editoriale Quasar S.r.l. (51%); Gruppo Editoriale Faenza Editrice S.p.A. (60%); Gruppo Editoriale JCE S.p.A. (65%).

Principal Competitors

Deutsche Telekom AG; DoubleClick Inc.; Infostrada S.p.A.; Mediaset SpA; Omnicom Group Inc.; PubliGroupe Ltd; Tiscali S.p.A.; yesmail.com, inc.

Further Reading

Levene, Abigail, "T. Italia Internet Plan Stokes Italy E-Fever," *Reuters,* February 11, 2000.

Prentice, Heather, "Seat PG to Cut Internet Jobs, Units, Sees Growth," *Reuters,* February 14, 2002.

"Seat Pagine Gialle Reports Loss, TeleMonteCarlo Battle Heats Up," *Yellow Pages & Directory Report,* March 28, 2001.

Sullivan, Ruth, "Italy's Telecom Giant to Be Split and Sold," *European,* August 8, 1996, p. 18.

"T. Italia Gets the Ball Rolling on Seat Deal," *Reuters,* April 7, 2000.

—M.L. Cohen

Seitel, Inc.

50 Briar Hollow Lane, 7th Floor West
Houston, Texas
U.S.A.
Telephone: (713) 881-8900
Fax: (713) 881-8901
Web site: http://www.seitel-inc.com

Public Company
Incorporated: 1982 as Seismic Enterprises Inc.
Employees: 128
Sales: $163.81 million (2000)
Stock Exchanges: New York Toronto
Ticker Symbol: SEI
NAIC: 213112 Support Activities for Oil and Gas
Operations

Seitel, Inc. develops and markets seismic data to the petroleum industry. Seitel owns the largest publicly available library of seismic data in North America, a database that contains one petabyte (one quadrillion bytes) of seismic information. The company captures, or "shoots," measurements of sonic reverberations off underground rock formations, which scientists use to ascertain the likely existence of oil or gas. Seitel is paid to shoot these seismic surveys, then stores the information in its library, later licensing the maps to other oil and gas exploration companies. Through its wholly owned subsidiary DDD Energy, Inc., Seitel also is engaged in the exploration and production of oil and gas wells. In exchange for cash and seismic information, DDD Energy secures an ownership stake in exploration and production activities. Seitel operates primarily in California, Texas, Louisiana, and the Gulf Coast.

Origins

Seitel's robust growth during the 1990s was attributable to the influence of the company's motivational leader, Paul A. Frame. A native of Crown Point, Indiana, Frame, above everything else, prided himself as a salesman without rival. His family owned a shoe store in Crown Point, giving Frame the opportunity to hone his skills in sales. While in high school, Frame sold shoes at his family's store and enjoyed success, but the family business, he soon realized, could never support his lofty ambitions for the future. In an interview with *Success* magazine in May 1995, Frame reflected on the reasoning that forced him to leave Crown Point and the family shoe store: "Based on my ability—and I was as good a shoe salesman as there is—I could only make so much money. I needed to find a product with a higher unit price to make my time more valuable."

After leaving Crown Point, Frame shifted his focus from shoes to commodities of a much higher value: diamonds and gold. He attended Indiana University, earning a degree in economics in 1969, and began a career as a jewelry broker. His stints in the diamond and gold industries lasted for roughly a decade after he left Indiana University, ending abruptly after Frame endured a near-death experience. In 1979, just before Christmas, Frame was working as a wholesale diamond salesman, visiting a client in Stockton, California. Frame concluded his meeting, returned to his car, and was ambushed. Hidden behind his car were three assailants, waiting for Frame to return so they could steal his collection of diamonds. Frame was clubbed in the head three times. His sports coat was used to bind his arms and he was thrown into the car, a .45 caliber pistol cocked and pointed at his head. The thieves, with Frame in the car, drove off. They stole the diamonds and locked Frame in the trunk of the abandoned car. Eventually, Frame popped the trunk open and escaped, vowing never to sell diamonds again.

Acquiring Its Future Leader in 1984

As the 1980s began, Frame started a new chapter in his sales career. From shoes in the 1960s to jewels in the 1970s, Frame devoted the 1980s to marketing seismic maps and selling data used by oil and gas explorers to improve their odds of discovering viable wells. The progression was incongruous, but for someone ingrained with the concept that selling was selling, no matter the commodity being sold, Frame hardly blinked as he threw himself into the business of selling scientific data.

Frame's introduction into the realm of geophysics occurred after he arrived in Houston, Texas, in 1984, with several pieces of furniture and $10,000 in a bank account. He soon met an entrepreneur named Herman Pearlman. Pearlman invited Frame on a three-day yachting trip. Frame accepted the invitation, and by the time the offshore trip was over, Pearlman had secured the employment of the most important executive in his company's existence.

In 1982, two years before meeting Frame, Pearlman had helped start a company called Seismic Enterprises Inc., a seismic information company. Pearlman, who had earlier founded a television production company called Telepictures Inc. (later acquired by Time Warner Inc.), applied the strategic underpinnings of television syndication to the operation of a seismic data concern. Similar to the library of television shows controlled by a syndication company, a seismic information company controlled content that could produce a recurring revenue stream. The financial success of a company such as Pearlman's Seismic Enterprises hinged on selling data to oil and gas companies. The crucial component of success was marketing. By the end of his trip with the then 37-year-old former metals broker, Pearlman had found the salesman to make his fledgling company a genuine financial success.

In 1984, Pearlman hired Frame as Seismic Enterprises' vice-president of marketing. Frame's initial task was to build and market the company's database of information. Six months later, Pearlman converted the company to public ownership, using the proceeds raised from the initial public offering to fuel the young company's rise from obscurity toward national recognition. Although every other seismic information company pursued this same goal, Pearlman and Frame decided to take a different route. Unlike its competitors, Seismic Enterprises did not use its meager supply of capital to purchase seismic equipment. Nor did the company rely on capturing—"shooting"—surveys exclusively for one customer. Instead, Frame searched for small groups of energy exploration firms who wanted to survey a particular area. Once a collection of clients had been signed, Seismic Enterprises hired a contractor to execute the geophysical shoot.

The atypical approach adopted by Pearlman and Frame enabled their small company to survive in an industry occupied by firms exponentially larger than their Houston-based concern. According to the terms of the deals brokered by Frame, Seismic Enterprises' initial customers paid for roughly 70 percent of the cost to obtain the data. For their investment, the oil and gas companies who ordered the seismic survey paid for the first look at the data captured, securing rights that generally ranged between 60 and 90 days. From the start, however, Seismic Enterprises retained the ownership rights to the surveys, which served as the source of the company's profit stream. After the initial 60-

to 90-day period passed, the company resold the data to other interested oil and gas exploration firms, enabling Frame to recoup the company's initial 30 percent investment. Once the company's capital outlay was recouped, it began to make money.

In 1987, the same year Frame was named president, Seismic Enterprises was renamed Seitel, Inc. At the time, the company was generating less than $7 million in revenue. Its stock was trading at $1 per share. In the coming years, Seitel's financial stature swelled exponentially, as Frame, newly appointed to the more powerful position of company president, began to exert his influence on Seitel's salespeople. An avid listener of motivational tapes, Frame expected everyone beneath him in the company's hierarchy to share in his passion for sales. He demanded much and, more often than not, his sermons paid dividends. Every morning at seven o'clock, Frame presided over a strategy meeting that included all of the salespeople within the organization and the company's geophysicists. The hour-and-a-half meetings became known as "shark tanks" throughout the industry. Specific goals were set, and if they were not met, the guilty party had little chance of surviving the wrath of Frame. "A marketing intelligence network, that's what I brought to this company," Frame remarked in a December 16, 1994 interview with the *Houston Business Journal,* referring to the spirit of success he instilled in Seitel's sales force. It was a marriage of marketing and geophysics, with Frame presiding as the preacher of successful salesmanship.

By the end of the 1980s, shortly after Pearlman appointed Frame president, Seitel was starting to show signs of the robust growth that would define the company in the following decade. In 1989, Seitel supplied data to 91 oil companies. The company derived half of its revenues from supplying seismic maps under initial contracts, typically contracting with groups of four or five firms. The other half of revenues came from the licensing of the same data to the other companies at a later period, once the original rights had expired. Frame built a library of data that was licensed much like syndicated television programs.

By the beginning of the 1990s, few observers could ignore the meaningful strides achieved by the Frame-led Seitel. By 1991, the company's success in selling its proprietary data to energy concerns in its operating territory of Texas, Louisiana, and the Gulf Coast belied recessive economic conditions. Seitel's market share in the area had risen from 1 percent in 1985 to 10 percent by 1991. During the same period, the market for seismic information in Seitel's service territory had plummeted from more than $600 million a year to less than $350 million a year. Seitel was bucking a formidable trend. All the accolades were accorded to Frame and his conviction that skillful marketing would fuel the company's success, whether the company sold shoes, diamonds, or seismic data.

Frame's resounding success earned him promotion in 1992, when he was named Seitel's chief executive officer. By the following year, a telling measurement of his successful presidency could be taken. Between 1987—the year Frame was named president—and 1993, Seitel's revenues septupled and its stock price increased 32-fold. In 1993, the amount the company posted in profits nearly equaled the $7 million recorded in revenues in 1987. The gains were impressive, enabling the company to carve a position for itself in the $3 billion-a-year

Key Dates:

1982: Seismic Enterprises, the predecessor to Seitel, is founded.
1984: Paul Frame is hired as vice-president of marketing.
1987: Frame is named president.
1992: Frame is appointed chief executive officer.
1993: Seitel forms DDD Energy, using the subsidiary to enter the exploration and production business.
2002: Frame is named chairman.

seismic data production and sales industry. In 1987, Frame had set a goal of reaching $30 million in sales in five years. With that objective surpassed, he declared a new goal for the company in 1993, one that would spark concern among his growing list of customers.

Diversification in 1993

Frame, whose aggressive sales approach had become known throughout the industry, became an iconoclast of sorts when he made a controversial decision in 1993. He formed DDD Energy, Inc., a Seitel subsidiary, to serve as the company's exploration and production unit. Frame intended to invest in the oil and gas wells his customers dug, a proposal that alarmed some of Seitel's customers, who began to perceive Seitel as a competitor. Traditionally, oil and gas service companies did not own interests in wells, and neither did they participate in drilling and exploration. Frame was breaking barriers, but he steadfastly maintained that Seitel's customers should not feel threatened by his bold diversification. In a typical deal brokered by DDD Energy, the company contributed cash, information from its database (by then the second largest publicly available library in the country), and new surveys. In return, Seitel, through DDD Energy, generally gained a 20 percent stake in the well.

By the fall of 1994, nearly 50 oil and gas exploration companies had signed agreements with Seitel. Of the first 25 wells drilled under investment partnerships with Seitel, oil or gas was struck an impressive 22 times, far exceeding industry averages. Encouraged by his initial success, Frame declared that by 1997 Seitel's oil and gas earnings would eclipse the profits derived from selling seismic data. As he guided the company into the mid-1990s, Frame set a new financial goal. He promised to build Seitel into a $1 billion-in-sales company.

Although it took several years, concerns about Seitel's equity interests in exploration and production properties dissipated. DDD Energy, like Seitel's seismic mapping activities,

grew during the latter half of the 1990s, becoming a meaningful contributor to revenues and earnings. Late in the decade, Frame decided to spin off DDD Energy through an initial public offering. At the time he filed with the Securities and Exchange Commission in November 1999, Seitel had invested roughly $150 million through DDD Energy. Frame filed for the spinoff to enable Seitel to focus exclusively on its core business of marketing seismic data, but unfavorable stock market conditions prompted Frame to withdraw from the scheduled IPO.

By 2000, Seitel's revenue volume reached $163.8 million, having increased from $106 million in 1996. The company entered the 21st century with what was believed to be the largest nonproprietary seismic data library in North America. In September 2000, Seitel announced plans to make its data available to its customers via the Internet. Although the goal of reaching $1 billion in sales remained a distant dream, Frame's unflagging zeal for sales promised to deliver continued growth to the company. In February 2002, Seitel's 20th anniversary, Frame was named chairman of the company.

Principal Subsidiaries

Seitel Delaware, Inc.; Seitel Data Corp.; DDD Energy, Inc.; Matrix Geophysical, Inc.; SEIC, Inc.; Seitel Canada Holdings, Inc.; Seitel Solutions, Inc.; Solutions, LLC; Seitel Management, Inc.

Principal Competitors

Petroleum Geo-Services ASA; Schlumberger Limited; Baker Hughes Incorporated.

Further Reading

Fletcher, Sam, ''Seitel to Spin Off 90% of DDD in IPO,'' *Oil Daily,* November 5, 1999, p. 32.

Greer, Jim, ''Seitel Reveals IPO Vision for DDD Subsidiary,'' *Houston Business Journal,* November 19, 1999, p. 6.

——, ''Seitel Shows Seismic Success, Insiders Sell Shares of Stock,'' *Houston Business Journal,* November 25, 1991, p. 9.

MacDonald, Elizabeth, ''Wildcat,'' *Forbes,* March 18, 2002, p. 32.

Palmeri, Christopher, ''Shark Tank: Paul Frame Built Seitel, Inc.'s Sales to $50 Million in Practically No Time,'' *Forbes,* October 10, 1994, p. 108.

Rouffignac, Ann, ''Seitel Chief Creates Glitz, Glamour, and Controversy,'' *Houston Business Journal,* December 16, 1994, p. 8.

''Rumbles for Seitel,'' *Business Week,* August 14, 2000, p. 141.

''Seitel Plans Eagle IPO,'' *Oil Daily,* June 4, 1997, p. 7.

Warshaw, Michael, ''Shark Tank Selling,'' *Success,* May 1995, p. 52.

—Jeffrey L. Covell

serco

Serco Group plc

Dolphin House, Windmill Road
Sunbury-on-Thames, Middlesex TW18 7HT
United Kingdom
Telephone: +44 (0) 1932 755900
Fax: +44(0)1932 755 854
Web site: http://www.serco.com

Public Company
Incorporated: 1929 as RCA Ltd.
Employees: 32,500
Sales: $1.15 billion (2000)
Stock Exchanges: London
Ticker Symbol: SRP
NAIC: 488111 Air Traffic Control; 488119 Other Airport
    Operations; 488190 Other Support Activities for Air
    Transportation; 488210 Support Activities for Rail
    Transportation; 488310 Port and Harbor Operations;
    488330 Navigational Services to Shipping; 488390
    Other Support Activities for Water Transportation;
    488490 Other Support Activities for Road Transporta-
    tion; 488991 Packing and Crating; 525910 Open-End
    Investment Funds; 541330 Engineering Services;
    541611 Administrative Management and General
    Management Consulting; 541614 Process, Physical
    Distribution, and Logistics Consulting Services;
    561110 Office Administrative Services; 561210 Facili-
    ties Support Services; 561320 Temporary Help Ser-
    vices; 561330 Employee Leasing Services

Serco Group plc provides facilities management and other engineering services for a variety of governmental and industrial clients in Great Britain and 34 other countries around the world. Unlike traditional support services companies, which typically limit themselves to areas such as catering or cleaning, Serco undertakes the management of complex tasks. Its interests range from testing nuclear weapons to managing parking meters to operating tourist attractions. About 60 percent of turnover comes from within the United Kingdom. Serco has grown as government agencies have privatized more and more services. Despite numerous diversified acquisitions since the 1990s, facilities management accounts for nearly 90 percent of business.

Origins

Serco's history begins in 1929, when the Radio Corporation of America (RCA) established a U.K. subsidiary, RCA Ltd., to service the growing film industry in Britain. In the late 1950s, RCA supplied radomes (a dome structure for protecting radar antennas) for the Ballistic Missile Early Warning System (BMEWS) at RAF Flyingdale in Yorkshire. RCA Ltd. supplied most of the workers needed during its construction and won a contract to maintain the facility. The company would maintain this relationship into the new millennium.

In the 1980s, the U.K. Ministry of Defence used this program as a model for its privatization of operation and mainte-nance functions at defense facilities. The cost-cutting of Prime Minister Margaret Thatcher's administration in the 1980s pro-vided many other opportunities for RCA Ltd. By the early 1980s, the company also was managing traffic light systems. The European Space Agency (ESA), formed in 1975, provided another area of expansion. RCA Ltd. contracted to maintain ESA's computer networks and satellites.

1987 Management Buyout

General Electric (GE) acquired RCA in 1986. RCA Ltd.'s managers bought their unit from GE for $24 million in 1987. The newly independent company was named Serco Limited. Serco, led by Chairman George Gray, who had been with the company since 1964, listed on the London Stock Exchange as Serco Group plc in 1988.

Revenues during Serco's first full year as a public company were about £47 million, producing profits of £3.6 million. Al-though Serco provided support services to private sector clients such as British Aerospace and Marks and Spencer, the U.K. Ministry of Defence accounted for nearly half of the group's turnover.

In 1989, Serco began branching out to Asia and the Pacific Rim and launched an expansion into civil government and commercial markets. Several small acquisitions, together worth £1.4 million, in 1990 brought Serco into the management of

351

Company Perspectives:

Culture and Values: While our products and processes make us stand out from our competitors, what makes us really different is our culture. What we believe is central to how we view the business and, consequently, how we run the company. At the heart of our culture is the belief that success is an outcome, not a goal. Success comes from focusing on customers, staff and investors and treating them all fairly. Serco is what it is because of what we believe in and how we apply those beliefs.

---

central government facilities in Australia and New Zealand and bolstered the company's business with local governments inside the United Kingdom.

The *Times* observed that Serco was unique in not limiting itself to one or two discrete areas of support, such as catering or cleaning. The company began running hospitals for Britain's National Health Service (NHS). Total revenues approached $200 million by 1991. In May of that year, Serco entered a new market by acquiring Community Leisure Management. A couple of months later, the company and European Handling Management formed the Serair joint venture to provide an array of support services for airlines.

Serco entered the air traffic control business by acquiring most of International Aeradio Limited (IAL) (apart from loss-making health operations) from British Telecommunications for £12.25 million ($18 million) in April 1992. IAL, which provided management services for airports, including air traffic control, had 900 employees in Germany, Sweden, Russia, and the Middle East. The buy brought Serco into the civil airport services market.

Mid-1990s Expansion

Serco continued to acquire companies, enter new markets, and form new structures in the mid-1990s. In 1993, the same year it entered the North American market, Serco bought Building Management Scotland; it soon obtained contracts to operate parts of the United Kingdom's traffic signal system. The Serco Institute was created in 1994. The launch of Serco Investments followed the next year.

Pretax profits grew 21 percent in 1995 to £15.2 million as turnover rose 24 percent to £323.3 million. During the year, Serco announced new contracts worth £600 million, including a £180 million deal to manage ship movements and provide specialist support at three Ministry of Defence ports. Similar profit and turnover increases were reported in 1996, spurred by increased outsourcing demand in Australia.

In the mid-1990s, Serco bid on several projects, particularly defense-related ones, as part of various consortiums. In October 1996, a group including Serco, Cobham plc, and Bristow Helicopter won a £400 million, 15-year contract to establish and operate a training school for the British military's helicopter pilots. It was the largest contract the Ministry of Defence had yet awarded under the government's private finance initiative (PFI).

In the spring of 1997, a joint venture with Docklands Light Railway took over the operation and maintenance of the ten-year-old automated railway. Serco also had, as did British Telecommunications, a contract to handle railway telephone inquiries.

Serco moved into the U.S. state and local public services market via the acquisition of JL Associates in 1998. In Europe, it bought out the remaining shares of Serco Newsec AB, a Swedish joint venture. It also acquired Tecnodata, a technical services company active in continental Europe, in a deal worth up to £9.3 million.

The company expected the Asian financial crisis to result in increased demand for outsourced services, particularly in Japan, which was seen as ripe for economic reform. The domestic support services industry had grown considerably in the 1990s, reported Britain's *Financial Times,* and expanded its range of offerings. Some estimates valued the U.K. market at £10 billion a year.

New Capital in 1999

As Serco's chief executive, Richard White, searched for new business, he pointed out to skeptical potential clients that the company's first job had been to provide the country with a four-minute warning in case of nuclear attack. Because of its strong reputation, Serco could choose the most lucrative opportunities, which were usually the most complex as well. White replaced Serco Chairman George Gray upon his retirement in 1999, and was himself succeeded by former CFO Kevin Beeston.

In early 1999, Nomura International, the European division of a Japanese investment bank, established a £1 billion ($1.7 billion) fund along with Serco for the purpose of bidding on and financing large public infrastructure projects. Two major projects coming up for bidding were those for Britain's National Air Traffic Control System and portions of the London Underground.

Serco bought the support services subsidiary of DASA, DaimlerChrysler's aerospace division, in August 1999. It paid DM 53 million (£18 million) for Elekluft, which specialized in military and aerospace customers. Its origins were similar to Serco's—it was formed in 1961 to install and support German air defense radar systems. Elekluft billed about DM 150 million a year and had added payroll, technical documentation, and other services to its repertoire.

After earnings and turnover growth slipped slightly in 1998, Serco was again approaching its by then customary 20 percent returns in 1999. Expansion was coming in the United Kingdom and Australia. "It is a far bigger market than we can possibly address," said CEO Kevin Beeston. The company continued to renew 90 percent of its contracts. According to one analyst quoted by the *Financial Times,* Serco's main constraint was finding enough qualified managers. In December 1999, a consortium of Serco, BNFL, and Lockheed Martin won a ten-year £2.2 billion contract to manage two of Britain's Atomic Weapons Establishment facilities.

Serco continued to acquire companies. It bought the consulting firm Quality Assurance Associates in 2000 and the technical consulting division of AEA Technology in 2001. The latter

Key Dates:

1929: RCA Ltd. is formed to service the British movie industry.
1958: Ballistic Missile Early Warning System (BMEWS) work begins.
1987: RCA Ltd. is bought out by managers after GE acquires its parent company.
1988: Renamed Serco, the company lists on the London Stock Exchange.
1997: Serco joint venture begins running Docklands Light Railway.
1999: Nomura International and Serco set up a £1 billion infrastructure fund.

deal, worth £76.8 million, was Serco's largest yet. AEA Technology focused on science and safety-based services.

Serco aimed to expand its business in the United States. The company already had air traffic control contracts with the Federal Aviation Administration. In 2001 it teamed with Lockheed Martin in bidding to build an astro-biology lab for NASA in California. Serco failed to win a 46 percent share of Britain's National Air Traffic Services (NATS), though it remained busy with contract renewals and new business such as its first ever contract to operate an immigration detention center.

Principal Subsidiaries

Aeradio Technical Services WLL (Bahrain; 49%); Baker Serco Wright Patterson (U.S.A.; 49%); Defence Management (Holdings) Limited (50%); Serco Docklands Limited; Great Southern Railways Pty Limited (Australia); International Aeradio (Emirates) LLC (United Arab Emirates; 49%); JBS Singapore Pte Limited (20%); Premier Prison Services Limited (50%); Serco Australia Pty Limited; Serco Belgium S.A.; Serco Facilities Management BV (Netherlands); Serco Facilities Management, Inc. (Canada); Serco France Sarl; Serco Gardner Merchant NZ (New Zealand; 50%); Serco Guardian (FM) Limited (Hong Kong; 50%); Serco-IAL Limited; Serco Management Services, Inc. (U.S.A.); Serco Research & Development Limited; Serco Systems Limited.

Principal Competitors

Capita Group plc; ISS A/S; Rentokil Initial plc; WS Atkins plc; Hunting plc.

Further Reading

Ahmed, Pervaiz K., Glenn Hardaker, and Martin Carpenter, "Integrated Flexibility—Key to Competition in a Turbulent Environment," *Long Range Planning* (London), August 1996, pp. 562+.

Barker, Thorold, "Serco Feels the Benefits from Complex Tasks; Support Services Group Highlights Accelerating Growth in UK Outsourcing Market," *Financial Times* (London), Companies & Finance, March 3, 2000, p. 28.

Batchelor, Charles, "Keeping Driverless Trains in Line: Operator Faces Stiff Penalties If Docklands Railway Fails to Provide Service," *Financial Times* (London), News UK Sec., March 27, 1997, p. 10.

——, "Penalties May Total Millions for Rail Operators," *Financial Times* (London), Back Page—First Sec., July 10, 1997, p. 30.

——, "Regulator Warns Rail Operators to Upgrade Systems," *Financial Times* (London), News UK Sec., June 19, 1997, p. 8.

Carruthers, Quentin, "Deals Lie Behind the Frontline," *Financial Times* (London), Survey—Private Finance Initiative, October 18, 1996, p. 7.

Crooks, Ed, and Juliette Jowit, "Engineering Groups May Bid to Run Railway," *Financial Times* (London), National News, November 1, 2001, p. 3.

Donaldson, Liza, "Interim Management: Troubleshooters for Hire in a Buyer's Market," *Industrial Relations Review and Report* (London), May 1993.

Dyer, Geoff, "Serco Lands £180 Million MoD Service Contract," *Financial Times* (London), UK Co. News, March 1, 1996, p. 20.

Felsted, Andrea, "Serco Hopes That the World Will Prove to Be an Outsourcer's Oyster," *Financial Times* (London), Companies & Finance UK, January 16, 2001, p. 30.

——, "Serco Soars Despite Air Traffic Loss," *Financial Times* (London), Companies & Finance UK, September 5, 2001, p. 21.

Foster, Angus, "Serco Pays £12 Million on Move into Civil Aviation Services," *Financial Times* (London), UK Co. News, April 11, 1992, p. 18.

Fuller, Jane, "Public Sector Work Aids Serco's 23 Percent Gain," *Financial Times* (London), UK Co. News, August 30, 1991, p. 17.

"Independent Hospitals Mean Welcome Tonic for Serco's Prospects," *Times,* Bus. Sec., December 17, 1990.

Martinson, Jane, "Australian Demand Helps Serco to £18 Million," *Financial Times* (London), Companies & Finance, March 5, 1997, p. 31.

Nicoll, Alexander, "MoD May Close Nuclear Warheads Assembly Plant; Defence BNFL Consortium Wins £2 Billion Contract to Manage Facilities," *Financial Times* (London), National News, December 2, 1999, p. 2.

Ostrovsky, Arkady, "Nomura Sets Up £1 Billion Infrastructure Fund; Investment Venture with Serco to Bid for Services Such As London Underground and Air Traffic Control," *Financial Times* (London), Companies & Finance, February 1, 1999, p. 20.

Pike, Alan, "A Stronger Emphasis Now on Partnership: Companies Are Depending More Than Ever on Managed Service Suppliers," *Financial Times* (London), Survey—Business Britain: Managed Services and Outsourcing, November 18, 1999, p. 1.

"Serco/Nomura," *Financial Times* (London), Lex Column, February 2, 1999, p. 24.

Tieman, Ross, "Consortium in 15-Year Deal to Train Forces' Helicopter Pilots," *Financial Times* (London), Back Page—First Sec., October 2, 1996, p. 18.

——, "More MoD Projects May Be Awarded to Private Sector," *Financial Times* (London), Front Page—First Sec., October 14, 1996, p. 22.

Voyle, Susanna, "Board Shuffle at Serco," *Financial Times* (London), People Sec., March 4, 1999, p. 12.

——, "Corporate Odd-Job Men Get Some Big Ideas of Their Own: Outsourcing Started with Cleaning and Catering But the Fashion Has Spread to White Collar Sectors," *Financial Times* (London), National News, September 18, 1998, p. 11.

——, "Outsourcing Expansion Buoys Serco," *Financial Times* (London), Companies & Finance, March 4, 1999, p. 30.

——, "Serco Hails Growth in Main Markets," *Financial Times* (London), Companies & Finance, September 3, 1998, p. 28.

——, "Serco Makes German Support Services Purchase," *Financial Times* (London), Companies & Finance, August 11, 1999, p. 21.

——, "Serco Sees Opportunity in Asia," *Financial Times* (London), Companies & Finance, March 5, 1998, p. 32.

——, "TBI Acquires Leading Airports Operator," *Financial Times* (London), Companies & Finance, May 21, 1999, p. 24.

—Frederick C. Ingram

Serono S.A.

Chemin des Mines 15bis
P.O. Box 54
1211 Geneva 20
Switzerland
Telephone: +41 22 739 3000
Fax: +41 22 731 2179
Web site: http://www.serono.com

Public Company
Incorporated: 1906 as Istituto Farmalogico Serono S.p.A.
Employees: 4,300
Sales: $1.24 billion (2001)
Stock Exchanges: Swiss New York
Ticker Symbol: SEO; SRA (New York)
NAIC: 325412 Pharmaceutical Preparation Manufacturing

Over nearly a century of activity, Serono S.A. has grown from a small pharmaceutical to the third largest biotechnology company in the world. The company first gained prominence as a producer of infertility treatments, and the fertility enhancer Gonal-F still accounts for nearly a third of the company's sales revenue. Serono's other major products target multiple sclerosis and growth and metabolism disorders. In the age of genetic engineering, Serono is positioning itself as a leader in the production of recombinant treatments, which are produced through DNA-splicing. Besides Gonal-F, the company has five other recombinant products on the market, including the multiple sclerosis treatment Rebif, the growth hormone Saizen, the AIDS wasting therapy Serostim, and the recently introduced infertility treatments Ovidrel and Luveris. In addition, Serono invests over 20 percent of its sales revenue in research and development in an effort to secure a healthy pipeline of new products. The company conducts research in the areas of breast and prostate cancer, gastrological and bowel disease, Hepatitis C, and rheumatoid arthritis.

Serono has headquarters in Geneva, a major operating center in Boston, and important manufacturing sites in Italy. Other production sites are located in Mexico, Puerto Rico, Israel, Switzerland, Spain, France, and Argentina. The company's major research and development laboratories are located in Geneva, Boston, and Israel. In addition, Serono's marketing subsidiaries are scattered across North and South America, Southeast Asia, and Europe. In all, Serono conducts operations in 45 countries and sells its products in 100. The company is led by Ernesto Bertarelli, who represents the third generation of his family to hold a head position at the company. The Bertarelli family holds just over half of Serono's stock and controls about 60 percent of the voting rights in the company.

Developing Infertility Treatments in Italy: 1906–77

In 1906 the Italian scientist Cesare Serono founded the Istituto Farmalogico Serono S.p.A. in Rome. In its early years, the company extracted proteins from chicken eggs to produce a product with a variety of medicinal applications. The chicken-egg extract remained the company's major product until 1949, when the breakthrough came that was to make Serono the world leader in the treatment of infertility. That year the chemist Piero Donini succeeded in extracting and purifying the first gonadotropin, a hormone that promotes egg and sperm production. The fertility enhancer Pergonal was developed on the basis of Donini's research. Production of the drug was a daunting operation. Thousands of liters of urine were collected annually from post-menopausal women to provide the raw material for extraction of the fertility-enhancing hormone.

The Vatican obtained control of the Istituto Farmalogico after Cesare Serono's death. Day-to-day management was in the hands of a man named Bertarelli who had worked his way up from financial comptroller to general manager. When Bertarelli died in 1965, the company's managers began turning to his son Fabio for advice. Three years later the board of directors invited the younger Bertarelli to take over the official management position.

Fabio Bertarelli had distanced himself from Serono as a young man. He fought in World War II with the Italian marines and was imprisoned by both the Germans and the Russians before escaping. After the war, he tried to work with his father at the institute but left shortly because of too much father-son conflict. He then gained some business experience selling glass and animal feed in Brazil, but by the early 1950s was back in

Italy racing sailboats and only occasionally working at Serono. Once he was in charge of the company, however, his entrepreneurial flair blossomed. Bertarelli's flexible, responsive management transformed the small Istituto Farmalogico Serono into an internationally known company with a commanding presence in the infertility treatment niche. The company's first foreign subsidiary, Serono Laboratories Inc., was established in Boston in 1971 to market Pergonal. Doctors at the Boston laboratory researched and endorsed the fertility treatment, broadening its use in the United States. Infertile couples were willing to spend large amounts of money to improve their chances of having a child, and sales both in the United States and Europe grew at a moderate pace through the 1970s.

Bertarelli's next success was to secure ownership of Serono. The notorious Italian investor Michele Sindona had gained control of the company in the late 1960s as the Vatican's shares somehow ended up with firms he owned. In the early 1970s, Bertarelli organized a syndicate of small investors to challenge Sindona's ownership. Sindona fled Italy in 1974 with warrants out for his arrest. His shares were dumped on the market and Bertarelli managed to gain control of about three quarters of Serono at a low price.

Bertarelli then shepherded Serono through a relocation to Switzerland. A diagnostics division under the name Hypolab SA had been established in Switzerland in 1973, where it produced and distributed diagnostic products and test kits. In 1977, after gaining control of Serono, Bertarelli moved the company's headquarters to Geneva, Switzerland, leaving behind the instability and melodrama of the Italian business climate. At that time the company's name was changed from Istituto Farmalogico Serono to Ares-Serono. A year after the move, the world's first test tube baby, Louise Brown, was conceived with the help of Pergonal. Sales of the infertility treatment soared. In order to keep a strong hold on the U.S. market, Serono designated the Boston complex its ''operational center'' in 1983.

Developing Biotechnology Capabilities in the 1980s and 1990s

Although Serono was prospering with infertility treatments, Bertarelli recognized that the firm would be left behind if it failed to keep pace with scientific advances. Traditional biological extraction processes were beginning to be replaced by recombinant manufacturing techniques based on genetic engineering. In 1984 a new production facility for Serono's pharmaceutical branch was inaugurated in Aubonne, Switzerland. Three years later the center began to work on the manufacture of recombinant drugs. The U.S. biotechnology firm Genentech was already challenging Serono with its success in that area of recombinant technology, and Serono's new genetic engineering facility would have to work hard to keep pace. The company turned to outside investors for support in 1987 when it went public on the Swiss Exchange. That year Serono posted record sales of $327.7 million, a 44 percent increase over 1986. By now the company had diversified beyond the infertility niche. Serono had a substantial portion of the European and U.S. market for growth hormones and was also active in the area of immunology. Sales of diagnostic products were up 30 percent in 1987. The diagnostics division was expanded considerably the following year with the acquisition of Baker Instruments, a U.S. diagnostics group. Serono invested heavily in this division over the next few years. Two fertility centers in the United Kingdom were also acquired in 1988, the Bourn Hall clinic and the Hallam Medical Center. Serono planned to use the facilities to learn more about the needs of doctors treating infertility.

Internal growth nevertheless had precedence over acquisitions. Serono's sales grew more than tenfold in the 1980s. Europe was still the company's most important market, accounting for 70 percent of sales in 1989. Italy alone provided more than half of Serono's revenues, with Spain in second place in Europe. Only one-fifth of the company's sales were made in the United States, a market that Serono hoped to concentrate more on in the coming decade. Technological improvement also remained a central concern. In the first half of 1989, Serono bought the method for producing human fertility hormones through genetic engineering from Integrated Genetics, started a genetic engineering plant near Madrid, and doubled its research and development capacity in Italy with a new building near Rome. Later that year, Serono launched its first recombinant product, Saizen, a treatment used for growth hormone deficiency in children. Saizen captured one fifth of the European market after four years, but was shut out of the U.S. market under the Orphan Drug Act—a rule that gives a competing firm a seven-year monopoly for drugs that combat obscure disorders.

Pergonal remained Serono's flagship product even as the company made efforts to diversify. The drug was being produced on a large scale through a system that relied on 110,000 volunteer urine donors in Italy, Spain, Brazil, and Argentina. However, a new genetically engineered gonadotropin known as Gonal-F had the potential to eclipse Pergonal. The first births attributed to Gonal-F occurred in 1992, but the hormone still faced several years of clinical trials. Meanwhile, reorganization efforts allowed the company to function more effectively. A new regional management structure was set up in 1991, with separate divisions for Europe, North America, Latin America, Japan, and the rest of the world. In the spring of 1992 Serono sold its nonprescription drugs unit to an Italian branch of American Home Products. Results for 1992 painted a positive picture. Net profit was $107 million on sales of $855 million. Sales had risen an average of 22 percent over the past decade.

The fast-paced growth came to a stop in 1993, when some of Serono's products were removed from government reimbursement lists in Europe. A change in Italy's health plan alone wiped out $250 million in annual sales. As a result, annual sales fell 12 percent in 1993 to $755.3 million. Serono cut its dividend in response and hurt many international investors. The

---

Key Dates:

1906: Cesare Serono founds the Istituto Farmalogico Serono in Rome.

1949: A Serono scientist isolates a fertility-enhancing hormone, the basis for Pergonal.

1965: Fabio Bertarelli begins to take control after the death of his father.

1971: Serono founds its first international subsidiary in Boston.

1977: Serono relocates to Switzerland.

1978: The birth of the world's first test-tube baby drives up sales of Pergonal.

1989: Serono's first recombinant drug, the growth hormone Saizen, hits the market.

1996: Ernesto Bertarelli becomes CEO; recombinant infertility treatment Gonal-F is launched.

2002: The recombinant multiple sclerosis treatment Rebif is approved for sale in the United States.

---

situation made it clear that heavy reliance on the European market would hurt Serono's bottom line.

The company started to get back on track in 1994 with a clearer focus on its priorities. Serono sold its diagnostics division to BioChem Pharma of Montreal. The division had recently returned to profitability after struggling for several years, but it was out of line with Serono's need to focus on biotechnology. In efforts to improve its biotech capabilities, Serono was investing the money it saved with lower dividends in research and development projects. One promising product was Rebif, a recombinant beta interferon with potential for the treatment of multiple sclerosis. Serono also bought the French biotechnology firm Sorebio in 1994 and, despite the resistance of minority shareholders, increased its stake in Israel's InterPharm Laboratories Ltd. from 76 percent to 100 percent. At the end of the year, sales were down 5 percent from 1993 as the reimbursement reductions in Italy and Spain continued to exact a toll on revenues. Net income fell 61 percent to $28.2 million. However, there was reason to believe that better times lay ahead for Serono, since sales outside of Spain and Italy were up 22.3 percent.

But before reaching secure profitability, Serono had to weather a period of transition from traditional to recombinant drugs. The difficulties of changing to a new production method contributed to a shortage of Pergonal in 1995. The recombinant Gonal-F was not yet on the market at the time, and Metrodin, an alternative infertility treatment introduced in 1993, was taking resources away from Pergonal production. The easier-to-inject Metrodin sold well but used up more urine during production than Pergonal. Because Serono anticipated an imminent transition to Gonal-F, the company was reluctant to expand its urine collection centers. As a result, fertility centers were unable to obtain adequate supplies of Pergonal and expressed dissatisfaction with what they saw as an attempt on Serono's part to profit from Metrodin's higher cost. Together with the drug reimbursement changes in Europe, the shortage held back Serono's earnings, although sales in 1995 grew slightly to $682.3 million from $636.8 million in 1994.

Secure in the Era of Genetic Engineering: 1996–2002

In 1996 new product launches and a change in company leadership were clear indicators of a new era at Serono. The infertility treatment Gonal-F was finally ready for the market, and an AIDS wasting therapy known as Serostim was also introduced that year. The product launches boosted Serono's sagging profits and represented a payback from years of heavy investment in research and development. CEO Fabio Bertarelli, however, was ill with cancer and would have to entrust Serono to the next generation. His son Ernesto Bertarelli took control in 1996 at the age of 31. Ernesto was a graduate of Harvard Business School with a passion for yacht racing and experience as a salesman, project manager, and financial analyst at Serono. Unlike his father, he had been involved in Serono since his early childhood, presenting awards to employees at age five and sitting with his father at budget meetings. Yet when Ernesto was indicated as his father's successor in 1993, some longtime Serono employees expressed concern about his lack of managerial experience. He had to prove that he could contribute more than glamour.

Ernesto Bertarelli began by instituting a more rigid management structure than was seen under his flexible, entrepreneurial father. His goal was to create a well-run company with a reputation for growth. He also planned to continue the trends toward product diversification and a growing reliance on genetically engineered products. Serono's strategy seemed to be working, as sales in 1996 reached $805 million. In 1997 sales of Gonal-F alone were $116 million, contributing to a net income that, at $87.8 million, was 64 percent higher than the previous year. In the next two years several acquisitions supported Serono's increased production of recombinant drugs. A laboratory in Geneva, together with the scientists employed there, was purchased from Glaxo-Wellcome in 1998 and renamed the Serono Pharmaceutical Research Institute. In 1999 a new facility, combining advanced production capabilities and research capabilities under one roof, opened in Corsier-sur-Vevey, Switzerland.

By the end of the 1990s momentum had shifted conclusively toward the new production techniques: In 1998 biotechnology products accounted for half of sales, while in 1999 that figure grew to 70 percent. However, Serono's new recombinant multiple sclerosis treatment, Rebif, could not be sold in the lucrative U.S. market. The drug was first launched in Italy, Argentina, and Brazil in 1997 and was allowed into the European Union in mid-1998. But it was shut out of the United States under the Orphan Drug Act, legislation meant to encourage biotechnology firms to develop treatments that had limited sales potential. Serono's U.S. competitor Biogen had orphan drug status for its rival treatment Avonex until 2003. Although the two treatments were based on similar beta-interferon technology, Serono believed it could challenge Biogen's monopoly by proving that Rebif was a more effective product. To that end, the company pitted Rebif against Avonex in a costly head-to-head trial beginning in 2000.

Meanwhile, Serono became less closely held on July 27, 2000, with a listing on the New York Stock Exchange. The listing raised about $1 billion for the company, while the Bertarelli family sold another $1 billion worth of its own shares.

The sale reduced the Bertarelli stake from 70 to just over 50 percent. The firm's name was also changed to Serono S.A. early in 2000. Sales that year continued their upward trend, reaching $1.14 billion. Rebif brought in $254 million in sales in Europe alone, where it accounted for over half of all new prescriptions. The results of the head-to-head trial with Avonex were announced in May 2001. The study overwhelmingly supported Rebif, showing that patients on Rebif had a 90 percent greater chance of avoiding a relapse than those treated with Avonex. On the basis of the study, Serono pushed to have Avonex's orphan status rescinded, finally winning approval from the U.S. Food and Drug Administration in March 2002. Two new recombinant treatments for infertility also came out in May 2001 under the brand names Ovidrel and Luveris. The products gave Serono a full line of recombinant treatments for every stage of the reproductive cycle. The following month Serono won the attention of the scientific community with a breakthrough in detecting mass-producing prions, the abnormal proteins that contribute to mad cow disease in cattle and Creutzfeldt-Jakob disease in humans. The detection process, reported in the journal Nature, could be used to develop more sensitive diagnostic tests in the early stages of the diseases.

The year 2001 was successful in the financial realm as well as the scientific. Sales reached $1.24 billion, with sales of the growth hormone Saizen up nearly 20 percent, Gonal-F up 15 percent, and Rebif sales up almost 50 percent. The only weak performer was the AIDS wasting therapy Serostim, which lost 8.6 percent in sales. Results for 2002 promised to be even better now that Rebif could be sold in the United States. With a diverse line of products and strong science to back them up, Serono had a reputation as a dynamic leader in the biotechnology industry. Bertarelli announced that Serono would maintain its leading position through research alliances with outside firms as well as internal development.

Principal Subsidiaries

Serono International S.A.; Serono Pharma Schweiz Zweigniedrlassung von Serono International S.A.; Laboratoires Serono S.A.; Laboratoires Serono S.A., succursale de Corseir-sur-Vevy; Ares Trading S.A.; Serono Argentina S.A.; Laboratorios Filaxis S.A. (Argentina); Serono Australia Pty Ltd; Serono Austria GmbH; Serono Benelux BV, Belgian Branch; Serono Produtos Farmaceuticos (Brazil); Serono Canada, Inc.; Serono de Colombia S.A.; Serono Pharma Services, s.r.o. (Czech Republic); Laboratoires Serono France S.A.; Sorebio S.à.r.l. (France); Simed S.A.; Serono Pharma GmbH (Germany); Serono Hellas A.E. (Greece); Serono Hong Kong Ltd; ASI Pharma Ltd; InterPharm Laboratories Ltd (Israel); InterLab Ltd. (Israel); Istituto Farmacologico Serono S.p.A. (Italy; 96.7%); Industria Farmaceutica Serono S.p.A. (Italy; 96.7%); Istituto di Recerca Cesare Serono S.p.A. (Italy; 96.7%); Istituto di Recerche Biomediche 'Antoine Marxer' RBM S.p.A. (Italy; 96.7%); Serono Pharm S.p.A. (Italy); Serono Japan Co. Ltd; Serono Korea Co. Ltd; Serono de Mexico S.A. de C.V.; Serono Produtos Farmaceuticos Lda (Portugal); Serono Singapore Pte Ltd; Serono South Africa (Pty) Ltd; Laboratorios Serono S.A. (Spain); Serono Nordic AB (Sweden); Serono (Thailand) Co., Ltd; Serono Benelux B.V. (The Netherlands); Serono Ilaç Pazarlama ve Ticaret A.S. (Turkey); Serono Pharmaceuticals Ltd (U.K.); Bourn Hall Clinic (U.K.); Filaxis International S.A. (Uruguay); Serono Inc. (U.S.A.); Serono Reproductive Biology Institute Inc. (U.S.A.); Serono de Venezuela S.A.

Principal Competitors

Genentech Inc.; Amgen, Inc.; Biogen Inc.; Schering AG; Akzo Nobel N.V.; Roche Group.

Further Reading

Adelson, Andrea, "A Fertility Drug Grows Scarce," New York Times, February 26, 1995, pp. 3–26.

"Ares Serono Proceeds with InterPharm Buyout," Israel Business Today, June 3, 1994, p. 1.

"Biotech Babies: Ares-Serono," Economist (US), March 13, 1993, p. 78.

Dullforce, William, "Ares Increases Net Earnings to Dollars 63.6m," Financial Times (London), March 5, 1991, p. 27.

——, "Swiss Drug Group Jumps 34 Percent to $15.1M Net," Financial Times (London), August 8, 1989, p. 25.

Goldman, Lea, "The Billionaire and the Orphan Drug," Forbes,, October 2, 2000, p. 168.

Hall, William, "Ares-Serono Boosts Net Income by 62%," Financial Times (London), March 2, 2000, p. 30.

——, "Ares-Serono Expects Boost from MS Drug," Financial Times (London), February 25, 1998, p. 24.

——, "Biotech Chief Profits from a Following Wind," Financial Times (London), August 20, 2001.

——, "Swiss Infertility Specialist Lifts Profits by 70%," Financial Times (London), August 19, 1996, p. 19.

Marsh, Peter, "Serono High on Drug of Success," Financial Times (London), October 17, 1989, p. 39.

Meyer, Thierry, "Laboratory Success the Key to Curing Ares-Serono's Financial Ills," Financial Times (London), March 26, 1996, p. 29.

Moore, Stephen D., "Drug Makers Battle Over MS Treatment," Wall Street Journal, November 9, 1998, p. B13.

Munk, Nina, "The Child Is Father of the Man," Forbes, August 16, 1993, p. 88.

Olson, Elizabeth, "Biogen Fights Rival Over Drug Claim," New York Times, July 12, 2001, p. W1.

——, "New Drug for Multiple Sclerosis Gains Approval from F.D.A.," New York Times, March 9, 2002, p. C2.

——, "Swiss Drug Maker Moves to the Brink of a Product Leap," New York Times, June 14, 2001.

Pilling, David, "Serono to Double External Research Spending," Financial Times (London), March 9, 2001, p. 30.

Rodger, Ian, "Ares-Serono Optimistic on Outlook for Year," Financial Times (London), June 28, 1994, p. 28.

——, "Ares-Serono Sells Its Diagnostic Division," Financial Times (London), May 6, 1994, p. 27.

——, "Ares-Serono Tumbles 61%, Halves Payout," Financial Times (London), March 22, 1995, p. 28.

——, "Price Cuts Take Toll on Swiss Drugs Group," Financial Times (London), March 22, 1994, p. 29.

"Serono Raises US Profile with Popular $1.8 bn NYSE Listing," Euroweek, July 28, 2000, p. 13.

"Smooth Sailing, So Far," Economist (US), June 10, 2000.

Studer, Margaret, "Ares-Serono Ripe for Takeover but Coy," Wall Street Journal, July 24, 1992.

—Sarah Ruth Lorenz

Silverstein Properties, Inc.

<table>
<tr><td>

521 Fifth Avenue
New York, New York 10017
U.S.A.
Telephone: (212) 490-0666
Fax: (212) 764-3265

Private Company
Founded: 1957
Employees: 100
NAIC: 233110 Land Subdivision & Land Development;
531110 Lessors of Residential Buildings &
Dwellings; 531120 Lessors of Nonresidential
Buildings; 531311 Residential Property Managers;
531312 Nonresidential Property Managers

</td></tr>
</table>

Silverstein Properties, Inc. is a family-owned corporation controlled by Manhattan real estate developer Larry A. Silverstein. Its portfolio in 2000 included 8.4 million square feet of space in New York City. A dynamic entrepreneur who has been described as an unquenchable optimist, Silverstein was only temporarily stunned by the September 2001 destruction of the twin towers of the World Trade Center, which he had leased just weeks before. The disaster claimed the lives of four members of his staff. A 47-story office building adjacent to the trade-center complex and owned by Silverstein Properties also collapsed as a result of the conflagration. The 70-year-old Silverstein quickly vowed to rebuild his destroyed building and submitted a plan for constructing four 50-story office buildings in place of the two 110-story towers.

Buying Manhattan Buildings: 1957–80

Larry Silverstein's father Harry was a real estate broker who made a precarious living by leasing loft space in lower Manhattan to rag-and-remnant traders in the garment business. This area, just south of Greenwich Village, would eventually become trendy SoHo after artists moved into the lofts, but at this time—the early 1950s—the pickings were slim. Larry Silverstein joined the business after earning a law degree but was able to survive only

because of his wife's salary as a teacher. "I suggested to my father that the guys making all the money were the owners, not the brokers," he later told Robin Finn of the *New York Times.* "And he said, 'But we have nothing.' I told him about syndicators like Lawrence Wein and Harry Helmsley. I said, 'Dad, if they can buy the Empire State Building like that, why can't we?' " In 1957 Silverstein convinced his father to buy an East 23rd loft building for which he had been acting as broker. They lacked the necessary capital, but, after many failed attempts, managed to secure a $15,000 loan for a down payment from one bank and a first mortgage of $350,000 from another. By this time the firm was Harry G. Silverstein & Sons, the other "son" being Bernard Mendik, who had married Harry's daughter Annette. They raised the other $250,000 by persuading 22 tenants to invest $10,000 apiece. After this undertaking proved successful the firm bought another East Side loft building, raising more money from banks and syndicate partners.

Harry Silverstein died in 1966. Larry Silverstein and Mendik continued acquiring properties as syndicators until economic conditions worsened in 1972. Five years later, the partnership was dissolved. Silverstein later blamed the break-up on the divorce of Mendik and his sister. Mendik said that one reason for the split was that Silverstein was interested in development, which he opposed as a too risky and protracted way of making money. The two established separate partnerships for the syndicated properties, but each continued to hold interests in the properties that the other administered as managing partner. Mendik remained a power in New York real estate until he sold his holdings to Vornado Realty Trust in 1997.

Silverstein's portfolio in 1978 contained about four million square feet of floor space and included 521, 529, 530, 689, and 711 Fifth Avenue, 44 Wall Street, and a shopping center in Stamford, Connecticut. In 1980 Silverstein Properties completed a $25 million renovation of the 33-story office building at 11 West 42nd Street, in collaboration with Tishman Speyer Properties. Also that year, Silverstein made two major acquisitions in the financial district of lower Manhattan. He purchased 120 Wall Street, remodeling it extensively, and acquired the leasehold to 120 Broadway for a reported $60 million.

Big-Time Developer: 1980–2000

The aforementioned were all existing buildings, but in 1980 Silverstein Properties also won the right to build a two-million-square-foot building on the last vacant lot of the World Trade Center complex in lower Manhattan. Although connected to the Trade Center plaza by an elevated walkway, it was not part of the original six-building complex. The entrepreneur who one developer later described to Lore Coughlan of *Crain's New York Business* as "the most optimistic man I've ever met. . . . [with] a riverboat gambler's instinct," started construction of the building—7 World Trade Center—in 1984 on speculation, having failed to sign on a major tenant. It was completed in 1986. The brokerage firm Drexel Burnham Lambert Inc. agreed to lease the entire 47-story building in 1985 but soon became snarled in an insider-trading scandal and eventually went out of business. In early 1988 the structure was still 87 percent vacant, but before the year was out Silverstein leased half the space to Salomon Brothers Inc. It was 80 percent leased by mid-1990.

In 1989 Silverstein Properties and General Electric Pension Trust agreed to construct and jointly own a 43-story Embassy Suites hotel. Located just north of Duffy Square, at the northern end of Times Square area, the building was erected in front of and above the venerable Palace Theater and included huge neon signs on part of the facade. During this period Silverstein also created, with two other developers, A & S Plaza, a million-square-foot shopping mall at Herald Square on the site of the former flagship Gimbel's department store. They also collaborated to put up the Park Avenue Court residential condominium on East 86th Street, over another former Gimbel's. By this time Silverstein controlled more than ten million square feet in 13 buildings.

The recession that gripped New York toward the end of the 1980s put a stop to further construction. Some of New York's biggest developers went bankrupt, and Silverstein's personal fortune—estimated at $375 million in 1988—began to erode. His company lost two Miami office buildings and its shares of the Embassy Suites and A&S Plaza properties to lenders. Another lender purchased the 120 Broadway office building to settle Silverstein's debt. In 1991 Silverstein Properties set aside 20 stories of the 34-floor office building at 120 Wall Street as tax-free headquarters for nonprofit groups that might otherwise leave the city. This program was only moderately successful until 1996, when nonprofits raised their participation in the building from 49,595 to 171,827 square feet. Even the loss of some Silverstein properties had its compensations, according to Croghan, who wrote, "Mr. Silverstein could have fought the lenders' moves to reclaim their buildings. But he did not. As a result, these lenders were willing to keep working with him. For instance, one of the lenders bought the outstanding loan on his building at 530 Fifth Ave., acting as his partner. Another let him continue to manage 120 Broadway, and in 1999 sold the building back to him."

By 1998 Silverstein and his backers were feeling sufficiently confident in downtown Manhattan's business climate to purchase the 52-story office building at 140 Broadway from Leona Helmsley for $191 million. The building, which dated from 1967, was 59 percent occupied at this time and needed some $60 million worth of renovation. Financing was provided by Silverstein's partner in the project, Morgan Stanley Dean Witter & Co.

During the 1980s Silverstein Properties acquired a major amount of space in a neglected area of midtown, occupied by warehouses and parking lots, west of the developed part of West 42nd Street and north of the new Javits Convention Center on West 34th Street. The slump in business activity, a necessary rezoning, and a subsequent lawsuit prevented Silverstein from developing this tract until 1999, when the company began construction of a $400 million, 1,700-unit rental residential project encompassing the entire block bounded by West 41st and 42nd streets and 11th and 12th avenues, just east of the West Side Highway and the Hudson River. Silverstein moved ahead on this project in the face of opposition by both the city and state, which for a time denied him tax-exempt financing because they wanted the site for an expansion of the convention center.

The first of the two brick-and-glass 40-story towers, 1 River Place, was completed in 2000. Designed with multiple angles and ribbon windows, it offered units with unusual layouts and unobstructed city and river views. Amenities were to include a fitness center with a gymnasium, Olympic-size swimming pool, two outdoor tennis courts, and three sun decks. By April 2001, 600 of the 921 units were rented. Silverstein smoothed his relations with the state in 2000 by agreeing to sell it most of the block between West 39th and 40th streets and 11th and 12th avenues.

The World Trade Center Disaster and Its Aftermath: 2001–02

By this time Silverstein had his eye on the millions of square feet of office and retail space in the World Trade Center complex, which its owner—the Port Authority of New York and New Jersey—was ready to lease for 99 years. Silverstein had wanted the twin towers for his own as far back as 1987, after finishing his 47-story building across the street. "I remember looking up at the towers one day," he told Croghan, "and thinking, 'That makes my building look like a peanut.'" To Finn he said, "Here I was with this beautiful . . . building, but when I walked outside I realized it was totally eclipsed by the towers and thought, 'Wouldn't it be wonderful to own that, too?' It was a compulsion with me.'' Early in 2001, Silverstein and his partner, Los Angeles-based real estate investment trust Westfield America, made a $3.22 billion bid for the lease. They met the deadline although Silverstein was in a hospital, his pelvis broken by a drunk driver only five days earlier. Soon he learned that the bid had fallen just short of the one made by Steven Roth of Vornado Realty Trust, the biggest owner of commercial real estate in Manhattan. In May, however, the Port Authority—exasperated by Roth's notoriously hard-line negotiating tactics—awarded the lease to Silverstein.

In retrospect, the auto collision that put Silverstein into the hospital should have served as an omen. Two months after the agreement was enacted, two hijacked airplanes plowed into the twin towers—1 and 2 World Trade Center, taking several thousand lives, including four employees of a recently established Silverstein Properties management office on the 88th floor of 1 World Trade Center. (Silverstein had an appointment at his dermatologist's office; his son had just arrived downtown when the first plane struck.) Hours later, Silverstein's evacuated 7 World Trade Center building also collapsed. Mayor Rudolph Giuliani had established a $13 million emergency command center in this building, and the installation included a giant, above-ground diesel-oil tank meant to fuel generators that would supply electricity to the 23rd-floor center in case of a power failure. When the fuel was set ablaze by debris from the twin towers the fire apparently irreversibly weakened the supports that held the building together.

Nine days after the disaster, Silverstein proposed building four 50-story office buildings in place of the twin towers and said he expected to rebuild 7 World Trade Center, too. In a telephone interview reported by Alan J. Wax of *Newsday,* he said, "It's more economically feasible to do 50-story buildings. . . . The New York City skyline would never be what it was when these towers soared to 110 stories. He said a memorial at the site "is necessary and totally appropriate," but added that not rebuilding the complex would "give a victory to these terrorists who are out to destroy our way of life."

Before long, however, Silverstein was embroiled in controversies with the insurers and with the Lower Manhattan Development Corporation, which was created to coordinate the redevelopment effort. He claimed to have a legal right to rebuild 7 World Trade Center, using the proceeds of an $861 million insurance policy and said he intended to build at about the same bulk and dimensions as the original edifice. The land beneath the building belonged to the Port Authority, however, and the insurer refused to say whether it would make the payment or take the case to court, citing the placement of the fuel tank in the building. One member of the development corporation indicated that this body preferred that Silverstein coordinate his

effort with an overall plan for the area rather than break ground on the first anniversary of the terrorist attack, as he hoped to do.

Concerning the main complex, Silverstein proposed building a memorial on six acres and constructing the four office towers plus a mall, museum, and performing arts center on the other ten acres. Silverstein carried a $3.55 billion insurance policy on the twin towers but claimed to be owed twice that sum because the terrorist assault, he argued, consisted of two events rather than one. Rebuilding, he told Finn, is "a no-brainer. The World Trade Center was responsible for $47 billion in gross wages in 2000, and unless we get it back, it's going to decimate the region financially."

Principal Competitors

Boston Properties, Inc.; Brookfield Properties Corp.; Tishman Speyer Properties, L.P.; Trump Organization.

Further Reading

Bagli, Charles V., "Developer's Pace at 7 World Trade Center Upsets Some," *New York Times,* January 31, 2002, pp. B1, B3.

Croghan, Lore, "After Five Decades, Larry Silverstein Grabs Real Estate's Golden Crown," *Crain's New York Business,* May 14, 2001, pp. 1+.

Dunlap, David W., "Wall Street Tower As a Site for a Service Association," *New York Times,* October 27, 1991, Sec. 10, p. 11.

Finn, Robin, "Undaunted and Planning the Next Great Skyline," *New York Times,* February 15, 2002, p. B2.

Fredrickson, Tom, "Silverstein Names Builder for Second 7 WTC," *Crain's New York Business,* January 14, 2002, pp. 3, 55.

Gabriel, Frederick, "Wall Street's New Tenants Aren't Interested in Profit," *Crain's New York Business,* December 23, 1996, pp. 13, 16.

Garbarine, Rachelle, "Rental Tower Seeks to Ride Times Square Wave," *New York Times,* May 12, 2000, p. B14.

Glanz, James, and Eric Lipton, "Burning Diesel Is Cited in Fall of 3rd Tower," *New York Times,* March 2, 2002, pp. A1, A8.

Horsley, Carter B., "A Steady Force In the Market," *New York Times,* July 26, 1978, p. D16.

Kennedy, Shawn G., "Theater-Hotel Partnership in Times Square," *New York Times,* March 1, 1989, p. D22.

Lueck, Thomas J., "New York Developers Feel a Chill," *New York Times,* September 19, 1990, p. D1.

Oser, Alen S., "Silverstein Properties: A Key Buyer of City Office Space," *New York Times,* May 13, 1981, p. A31.

——, "Sounding the Alarm on Mortgage Loans," *New York Times,* January 26, 1992, Sec. 10, p. 5.

Rice, Andrew, "Silverstein Plan Ready for Site; Payment on Hold," *New York Observer,* March 25, 2002, pp. 1, 10.

Rudnitsky, Howard, "The 2001 Deals of the Year: The World Trade Center Sale," *Institutional Investor,* January 2002, p. 82.

Wax, Alan J., "Developer Proposes 4 Buildings at WTC," *Newsday,* September 21, 2001, p. A72.

—Robert Halasz

Simmons Company

One Concourse Parkway, Suite 800
Atlanta, Georgia 30328-6188
U.S.A.
Telephone: (770) 512-7700
Fax: (770) 392-2560
Web site: http://www.simmonsco.com

Private Company
Incorporated: 1915 as Simmons Co.
Employees: 2,800
Sales: $727 million (2000 est.)
NAIC: 337910 Mattress Manufacturing

Simmons Company is one of the leading U.S. mattress manufacturers, selling one of the best-known brands of bedding, Beautyrest. The company operates 18 manufacturing facilities in the United States, licenses its name to foreign makers, and sells its products in over 100 countries across the globe. Simmons makes mattresses, box springs, bedding frames, and other sleep accessories. The company was responsible for popularizing several major innovations in bedding, including the innerspring mattress and the queen and king size mattress. A family business until the late 1970s, the company is now majority owned by a New York-based investment firm, Fenway Partners. A remaining percentage of the company is owned by Investcorp, a Bahrain-based investment firm which once owned 85 percent of the company, and by Simmons employees.

From Cheeseboxes to Mattresses

Simmons Company began as one of many projects of Wisconsin businessman Zalmon Simmons. Simmons was president of the Rock Island Railroad and of the Northwest Telegraph Company, and at one point was the mayor of Kenosha, Wisconsin. He entered the bedding industry circuitously in 1870, after purchasing a cheesebox factory that year. This became the Simmons Manufacturing Company. Zalmon Simmons was not interested in cheeseboxes; rather, he hoped to use the factory's equipment to manufacture a wooden telegraph insulator he had designed himself. In the meantime, he also owned a Kenosha

general store, and he took an unusual item in payment one day from a customer without cash money. This gentleman sold Simmons a patent for a woven wire bedspring. This unknown inventor was not the first person to patent a bedspring. At least one earlier patent was held by a New York inventor. But the technology was expensive, and mattresses in the 1870s were by and large stuffed with horsehair or cotton. Simmons went to work on the bedspring idea, and managed to bring down the cost of manufacturing each spring to around 80 cents. Nevertheless, the idea seemed before its time. The Simmons Company's most successful product was instead a fine brass bed. The company continued to make beds and ship them all around the world throughout the tenure of Zalmon Simmons.

Simmons's son, Zalmon Simmons, Jr., took over the company in 1911. The company incorporated as Simmons Co. in 1915. The younger Simmons became known as "The Chief" throughout his company. He was a legendary gambler, said to have bet an automobile a hole during a game of golf. He also seemed to have a flair for showmanship and advertising, and he brought his company to national prominence within a few short years. He did this by making the innerspring mattress something middle-class consumers could afford. Though Simmons Co. had held a mattress spring patent since the 1870s, it had turned to bed frames and let the idea languish. In 1900 a Canadian inventor patented a mattress with springs held within individual cloth pockets. His "Marshall ventilated mattress" was made by hand, and sold to luxury hotels. The unlucky Titanic was fitted with Marshall ventilated mattresses, as were other famous liners including the Lusitania and the Mauritania. It was Zalmon Simmons, Jr., who made the innerspring mattress a widely available item.

Simmons moved its company headquarters to New York in 1919, ready to make itself a national name. The company acquired a string of mattress makers at this time. It bought a firm in Atlanta, another in San Francisco, one in Montreal, and the Newark Spring Mattress Company in Newark, New Jersey. Despite the geographic spread of Simmons's new mattress firms, none of these made a mattress that Zalmon Simmons considered worthy of being promoted as a nationwide brand. The mattresses were still made by hand, often stuffed with the cuttings left over from tailor's shops and other cheap material.

Company Perspectives:

Simmons is the world's number one name in bedding—with $1 billion in worldwide sales. And the number one market share in accounts where we do business. Our history is one of innovation. Today more than ever, Simmons is dedicated to producing distinctive, consumer-benefit-driven products such as Simmons, Beautyrest, Simmons BackCare, Olympic Queen and various adjustable sleep products.

Simmons drafted one of the machinists from his original Kenosha factory to study the feasibility of making a spring mattress cheaply by machine. The machinist worked for three years, and finally revealed something similar to the Marshall ventilated mattress, with springs held inside individual cloth pockets. The equipment to make it was called the Beautyrest Pocket Machine, and the resulting mattress was the Beautyrest.

Simmons Co. listed its stock on the New York Stock Exchange in 1924. Two years later, the Beautyrest mattress debuted in a national advertising campaign. Simmons set a standard retail price for its new product, $39.50. This was nearly twice what consumers were used to paying for a mattress, but Simmons gambled that the public would soon find the Beautyrest worth it. Simmons recruited a host of luminaries to declare the value of a good night's sleep. Henry Ford, George Bernard Shaw, Thomas Edison, and many others, appeared in full-page Beautyrest ads. In its first year, the Beautyrest mattress brought in $3 million. By 1929, the company had sales of $9 million. The company was soaring, and made acquisitions in the furniture and textile industries that year.

Weathering the Depression

Zalmon Simmons, Jr., gave way the presidency of the company to his son, Grant Simmons, Sr., in 1929. Simmons's stock had been flying high, at close to $200 at the height of 1929. By 1932, it was almost worthless, at less than three cents a share. Grant Simmons, Sr., nursed the company through the bad years by borrowing money and by selling off the furniture companies his father had recently acquired. Simmons Co. became profitable again by 1935, and then entered a period of steadily growing sales. Simmons made great use of advertisement, often featuring a beautiful model or Hollywood star resting on a Beautyrest. The company funded sleep research in the 1930s, which tracked for the first time how the body actually moved in sleep. These studies continued after World War II at the Simmons-supported Sleep Research Center. Simmons also resorted to stunts to show how well-made its mattresses were. It devised a machine to hammer its products, and compared these to its competitors. The company took the Beautyrest to the circus and photographed an elephant standing on it. Even the elephant's bulk could not break the Beautyrest spring. The company continued to recruit famous people to speak on its behalf. Eleanor Roosevelt furnished her bedrooms with Beautyrest mattresses, and Simmons featured her in a full-page ad declaiming her satisfaction.

Simmons also came out with new products in the postwar era. It debuted the Hide-A-Bed sofa in 1940, the famous sofa with a mattress tucked inside. Grant Simmons, Sr., retired in 1957, and his son Grant Simmons, Jr., took over the company. In 1958 Simmons brought out another landmark in mattress history, the Beautyrest Supersize. The Supersize was the first queen- or king-size mattress widely distributed in the United States. By this time, the company was a national leader in bedding products, well-known and profitable. Company documents show the proverbial arrow on the sales chart climbing up and up from 1930 to 1970. Simmons had a profit of over $8 million in 1968, and very little debt.

The company diversified during this time period, too, particularly in the 1960s. By the late 1960s, Simmons had subsidiaries in a variety of businesses. A company that it bought in 1962, Thonet Industries, specialized in making wood furniture for public use. Simmons also ran a division that specialized in hospital furniture, and another that made patient handling equipment. Simmons's Juvenile Products Division made children's wooden furniture, including cribs. Simmons Co. also owned two high-fashion furniture importers and distributors. In the textile industry, Simmons owned Katzenbach and Warren, a high-end wallpaper and fabric wall covering manufacturer, and Greeff Fabrics, a manufacturer of fashionable upholstery and drapery fabrics. By 1970, Simmons had also diversified into the casket industry, owning one casket manufacturer and one manufacturer of metal casket linings. By 1970 Simmons had also diversified abroad, running foreign subsidiaries to make bedding in Canada, Mexico, Venezuela, Argentina, England, France, and elsewhere.

Tough Times and New Ownership in the 1970s and 1980s

The company had grown rapidly in the 1960s, and by 1970 it had become a multinational conglomerate in the mid-ranks of the *Fortune* 500. Much of the firm's diversification had been orchestrated by Grant Simmons, Jr., great-grandson of founder Zalmon. Chairman Simmons became unhappy with the decentralization of the company, which now had dozens of manufacturing plants all across North America. He implemented a management restructuring, which coincided with moving the company headquarters out of New York to Atlanta, Georgia. Some managers were let go or retired early, and the company got a new president, Robert Tyler. The move and management change took three years to complete, but by late 1975, Simmons had relocated to its new wooded headquarters. Grant Simmons explained to *Fortune* magazine (May 1976) how the move had energized the company and made executives more productive. Yet a look at the balance sheet showed something different. Earnings began falling in 1973, falling off 50 percent between that year and 1977. Sales for 1977 were just over $468 million, showing almost no increase over 1973. Perhaps most ominous, the company lost market share. It had been the number one bedding maker in 1974, with a market share of 21 percent. Its next nearest competitor, Sealy, had only an 11 percent share. But by 1978, Sealy had pulled ahead. Simmons's bedding operations began losing money in 1976, and its only profitable units were its international divisions and non-bedding subsidiaries.

Chairman Simmons responded to the company's evident stagnation by cutting the workforce, closing several plants, and reducing production capacity. Simmons also cut back the number

Key Dates:

1870: Zalmon Simmons operates Simmons Manufacturing, making various products.
1915: Company incorporates as Simmons Co.
1919: Headquarters are moved to New York City.
1926: Company debuts Beautyrest mattress.
1940: Hide-A-Bed sofa is introduced.
1958: Simmons begins selling queen and king-sized mattresses.
1975: Company relocates to Atlanta.
1979: Simmons is sold to Gulf & Western.
1985: Gulf & Western sells company to Wickes Co.
1986: Wesray Capital engineers first leveraged buyout of Simmons.
1989: Wesray group sells firm back to its employees.
1991: Merrill Lynch Capital Partners acquires most of company for $32 million.
1993: New chairman and chief executive is named; market share begins to rise.
2000: Charles Eitel becomes chairman and CEO.

of styles of mattresses the company manufactured, and endeavored to correct problems with quality control and inventory flow. Though Grant Simmons had promised that things would get better over 1978, the company continued its poor performance. In June 1978, the company's board asked Simmons to resign. The company was then headed by Theodore Greeff, who ran Simmons's Greeff Fabrics subsidiary. In 1979 the company was acquired by Gulf & Western, a large conglomerate which had been buying up Simmons stock since 1976. Simmons became a wholly owned subsidiary of that company.

Gulf & Western was a sprawling conglomerate that later metamorphosed into the movie company Paramount Communications. In 1985 Gulf & Western sold Simmons Co. to Wickes, another conglomerate with lumber and furniture holdings. Wickes, too, was on the verge of a major reorganization. Wickes held onto Simmons for only one year. In 1986, a management group and the investment firm Wesray Capital raised $120 million for a leveraged buyout of Simmons. Wesray was headed by William E. Simon, who was a former secretary of the U.S. Treasury, and his partner Ray Chambers, and was one of the major buyout firms of the 1980s. Seventeen Wesray partners, plus 18 Simmons executives, borrowed almost the entire purchase price to secure the company. Over the next two years, the new management sold off pieces of Simmons, until almost all the debt was repaid.

In 1989, the management group decided to try something Wesray had done successfully before with other companies it had taken over. This was to sell Simmons to its employees through an employee stock ownership plan, or ESOP. This was a seriously flawed deal that soon saw Simmons at the brink of bankruptcy and all the involved parties battling it out in court. Wesray engineered the sale to the ESOP, helping the employee entity borrow the purchase price, $241 million, just over twice the amount Wesray and partners had paid for the company in 1986.

Again the company was loaded with debt. But this time, its most valuable assets had already been sold off. Within four months, Simmons found itself with a $19 million shortfall, and it had to call an emergency meeting with Chemical Bank, the main underwriter of the deal. The bank and Wesray squabbled over who was responsible for the problems. Simmons's employees, the nominal owners of the company, were slow to understand the complexity of the buyout, which left their retirement accounts pegged to the now almost worthless Simmons stock. Unable to meet its debt payments, Simmons looked like it would go bankrupt. Then in March 1991 Merrill Lynch Capital Partners offered to buy 60 percent of the company for the astonishingly low price of $32 million. Employees were left with an approximately 30 percent share in the company. Simmons employees filed a class-action suit against Wesray and Simmons managers, which eventually settled out of court with a payment of about $15 million to the ESOP.

Recovery in the 1990s and Beyond

By the mid-1990s the company began to focus again on advertising and marketing. Simmons got a new chairman in 1993, Zenon Nie, and in 1994 the company switched to a new advertising agency. In 1996 Simmons came out with an evocative television ad, which showed a bowling ball dropped on a Beautyrest mattress and not knocking down ten bowling pins standing on it. Beautyrest sales increased by over 50 percent within a month of the ad's debut. The company also brought out a new mattress in 1996, its BackCare brand, which was also promoted with television advertising. The company's profits grew through the mid-1990s, and its overall sales growth was about double the mattress industry average. In March 1996, Merrill Lynch sold its stake in Simmons to a Bahrain-based investment group, Investcorp. The ESOP also sold part of its stake in the company, leaving it with 15 percent, and Investcorp with 85 percent. The investment group paid $250 million for its share of Simmons, and assumed some of the company's debt. By 1997, Simmons had sales of over $550 million, with a profit of about $50 million.

The company changed hands again in 1998 when a private investment firm, Fenway Partners, bought out most of Investcorp's share. The New York-based Fenway paid about $500 million for roughly 75 percent of the company. Simmons continued to boost its advertising spending and to recover market share. By 1998 Simmons reported it held over a 15 percent share of the bedding industry, putting it in the number two spot behind Sealy. The company continued to innovate in the late 1990s and into the new century. It hired a new advertising agency in 1999, and vowed to bring out a new campaign that would top even its successful bowling ball spots. Simmons came up with a new brand for the millennium, the Beautyrest 2000 NoFlip mattress. Zenon Nie resigned as chairman and chief executive in 2000, and he was replaced by Charles R. Eitel, formerly president of a fabric and flooring company. Simmons began licensing its name to a textile manufacturer in 2001 to make sheets, comforters, accessories, and window treatments under the Beautyrest, BackCare, and other Simmons brand names. Sales for 2000 were reported at over $727 million, and the company was vying for the lead in the bedding market that it had helped to revolutionize.

Principal Competitors

Sealy Corp.; Serta, Inc.; Spring Air Co.

Further Reading

"Haywin, Simmons Ink Licensing Deal," *Home Textiles Today,* May 21, 2001, p. 2.

Higgins, Kevin T., "Sleeping Beauty," *Marketing Management,* Summer 1998, p. 6.

Konrad, Walecia, "Nobody Is Resting Easy at Simmons," *Business Week,* December 9, 1991, p. 35.

Maher, Philip, "The Price of Peace After an LBO That Went Sour," *Mergers and Acquisitions,* November/December 1993, p. 33.

Siebert, T.W., "BBDO Follows the Bouncing Ball," *Adweek,* November 1, 1999, p. 5.

——, "Simmons Tests BBDO, Martin," *Adweek,* October 25, 1999, p. 5.

"Simmons: A Turnaround Proves Hard to Bring Off," *Business Week,* June 5, 1978, pp. 146–50.

Simmons Co., *Simmons Second Century,* New York: Simmons Co., 1970.

"Simmons Co. Likes It Down South," *Fortune,* May 1976, pp. 255–66.

"Simmons Co. Pushes a Simmons Out," *Business Week,* July 17, 1978, pp. 32+.

Stevens, Shannon, "Five-Zone Offense Set for Simmons Mattress," *Brandweek,* January 19, 1998, p. 3.

—A. Woodward

SOMERFIELD

Somerfield plc

Somerfield House
Whitchurch Lane
Bristol BS14 0TJ
United Kingdom
Telephone: (0117) 935-9359
Fax: (0117) 935-6566
Web site: http://www.somerfield.co.uk

Public Company
Incorporated: 1974 as Linfood Holdings Ltd.
Employees: 59,000
Sales: £4.61 billion ($6.64 billion) (2001)
Stock Exchanges: London
Ticker Symbol: SOF
NAIC: 445110 Supermarkets and Other Grocery (Except Convenience) Stores

Somerfield plc is a major grocery retailer in the United Kingdom, holding about a 7 percent share of the U.K. market. Unlike its major competitors who focus their energies on superstores located in edge-of-town sites, Somerfield concentrates on smaller "neighborhood" supermarkets—averaging less than 9,000 square feet per unit—located in-town ("high street" in British parlance). The firm's stores operate under two names: Somerfield, an upmarket modern grocery format where the emphasis is on fresh foods, and Kwik Save, one of the largest discount supermarket chains in the United Kingdom. In 2001 there were approximately 585 Somerfield units and 725 Kwik Save units. Among the Somerfield outlets were about 20 that were gasoline minimarkets operated in partnership with Total Fina Elf S.A.

1875–1970s: Sleepy Roots

Somerfield traces its roots back to a single small grocery store opened in Bristol, England, in 1875 by J.H. Mills. By 1900, with 12 J H Mills stores in the fold, J H Mills Ltd. was formed. Fifty years later, Tyndall, a finance house based in Bristol, gained majority control of the company and changed its name and the name of the supermarkets to Gateway. The name

was selected because Bristol was considered the "gateway" to England's West Country. At the same time, the stores were converted into self-service supermarkets.

Meantime, in 1964, Frank Dee purchased the wholesaler that had been part of J H Mills. He then developed the Frank Dee supermarket chain in northern England, which soon had 70 units. Associated Food Holdings Ltd. purchased the Frank Dee chain in 1970 and then four years later merged with Thomas Linnell & Company Ltd. to form Linfood Holdings Limited. In 1977 Linfood acquired Gateway, and the number of Gateway stores located throughout the country soon increased to 100.

Early 1980s: Rapid Growth Under Monk

By the early 1980s Linfood was doing about £1 billion a year in sales. It was at this point that the company began a short-lived period of rapid expansion. At the zenith of this era in the mid-1980s, the firm was England's third largest retailer of groceries and employed some 85,000 people. Leading the firm to this position was Alec Monk, who served as managing director from 1981 to 1989.

Monk was born in Wales in 1942, the son of a baker. After earning a degree at Oxford, he worked for Esso and then spent a number of years at Rio Tinto-Zinc (RTZ), a mining company, where he became a member of the board of directors at age 31. Apparently frustrated at RTZ, in 1977 Monk moved to New York and took a position with AEA Investors, a prestigious investment firm. After four years with AEA as a specialist in the buying and selling of midsized corporations, Monk was offered the post of managing director at Linfood Holdings. Monk admitted that before the offer he had never heard of Linfood, but he took the job and immediately began to shake things up.

When Monk arrived in 1981, he decisively reoriented corporate growth in the direction of retailing, eventually restricting wholesale activity to the cash-and-carry supply of independent grocers and caterers. Linfood had acquired a number of Carrefour retail superstores in 1978, and with these as a base Monk began to build his grocery empire. From the start, his reign was marked by continual corporate skirmishing, as Linfood bought one rival chain after another or was itself the object of takeover

---

Company Perspectives:

The Somerfield Group incorporates the Somerfield and Kwik Save supermarket business units which together operate over 1,330 stores nationwide.

Somerfield's focus is on its key strength as the U.K.'s biggest neighborhood supermarket offering easy to shop convenience in its smaller high street stores with a focus on its fresh food offer, modern ready meals and a quality range of wines.

Kwik Save operates as a distinct value brand building on its heritage as the nation's number one discount supermarket offering the biggest brands at lowest prices.

---

attempts. Just weeks after Monk had joined his new company, Linfood escaped the clutches of the aggressive James Gulliver when Gulliver's £87 million hostile bid failed to gain approval from the Monopolies and Mergers Commission.

Having survived this early battle, Monk began his own campaign of acquisitions. In 1983 Monk converted the Frank Dee supermarkets into Gateway outlets, and he also changed Linfood's name to Dee Corporation. In June 1983 Dee snapped up the 98 Keymarkets, topping Safeway's bid with a £45 million offer, and in 1984 followed up with the purchase of 41 Lennons stores for £25 million. At the end of that year, Monk and Dee made a quantum leap with the acquisition, for £80 million, of BAT's 380 International Stores. For the financial period ending in April 1985, Dee had amassed sales of £2.43 billion and profits of £64 million, making Monk one of the London financial world's most celebrated stars.

The Dee collection of stores included many small, older markets located primarily on the "high street"—that is, near the center of urban concentrations—as well as a growing number of supermarkets and a sprinkling of superstores (stores larger than 25,000 square feet and including nonfood items). By unifying many regional corporations into one organization, Monk was able to eliminate management positions, benefit from economies of scale in advertising and food distribution, and cut better deals with his wholesale suppliers. With each new acquisition, Dee gained not only additional clout in the marketplace but also the particular expertise of each chain, as one group might have specialized in fresh produce, while another had made a name for its meat departments.

Mid-1980s: The Herman's and Fine Fare Acquisitions

As Dee grew in size, its profits grew proportionately, and it appeared to those in the investment business that Monk might expand his retailing success indefinitely. When, in 1985, no further targets were available in the British food retailing sector, Monk decided to establish a U.S. base with the purchase of Herman's, the largest retailer of sporting goods in the United States, for $414 million. With 130 stores and a reputation for skilled management, Herman's seemed a good bet; but in retrospect the acquisition proved to be the beginning of the end for Monk and the Dee Corporation.

Like other tacticians before him, Monk had spread his forces too thin, and he compounded the error a few months later when he bought a very large and complex chain of 419 Fine Fare supermarkets. At the time—early 1986—both moves were generally praised, but a series of apparently unimportant events soon combined to thwart Monk's plans. First of all, both the Herman's deal and the £686 million Fine Fare purchase were financed by means of "vendor placings," in which new shares in a company are sold without first being offered to existing shareholders on a pro-rated basis. This technique, common in the United States, was new to Britain, and it inevitably angered the institutional investors who held large blocks of Dee stock. Their displeasure became an important, although subtle, drag on the price of Dee shares at a time when Monk was most in need of investor faith in his ambitious plans. The institutional managers felt abused by Monk, and their resentment seemed to color their assessment of his company's prospects.

Those prospects, however, no longer looked quite as outstanding from any angle. Monk's efforts to make Herman's into a nationwide sporting goods chain were a disaster from the beginning. As the chain expanded into new parts of the country it could not keep its shelves stocked efficiently and, when it did have merchandise, it was often poorly suited to varying local tastes. While sales went up, profits did not, and Monk soon found that he had transformed a well-run regional chain into a national mess.

Much more significant were the problems at Fine Fare, the chain that had boosted Dee into third place among British food retailers by sales (and largest in terms of square footage), but that proved to be much more difficult to integrate and streamline than Monk's earlier purchases. As it turned out, Fine Fare's stores were not in the excellent condition Monk had expected them to be, but suffered from deteriorated physical settings and widespread pilferage. In addition, Fine Fare's wide range of store formats, from vast suburban "hypermarkets" to hole-in-the-wall city locations, only added to Dee's already complex distribution and administrative problems. Converting all of these stores to Gateway's logo, accounting system, and corporate standards proved to be more difficult than Monk had envisioned, or at least more costly than investors were willing to pay for.

Late 1980s: Declining Fortunes and the Isosceles Takeover

For the year ending in April 1987, Dee's first after the big mergers, the company was expected to earn around £230 million on sales of £4.8 billion; when the figure came in at £192 million many already disenchanted analysts said that Monk had gone too far too fast. As a result, Dee's stock price faltered, drifting sideways while the market as a whole was booming along at a 45 percent faster clip. For the year and a half following the Herman's purchase, Dee's stock was dead last on the *Financial Times'* list of the 100 leading companies in Great Britain. Monk defended the prudence of his moves, noting that he had predicted all along that it would take three years for Dee to assimilate its new acquisitions fully, which by 1987 also included the country's fourth largest drug chain, Medicare, and two more American sporting goods outfits. He asked for patience and a little faith, two commodities always hard to buy on the world's stock exchanges. Monk might have come through the crisis if Dee's first half result for 1987–88 had been outstanding. However, the £64 million total announced in the fall of 1987 was 18 percent below the previous year's midterm figure, and rumors of a takeover immediately began to circulate through the city. When the October 19, 1987, crash ruined the Christmas selling season for Herman's, it was only an appropriate conclusion to Dee's dismal year.

Even the stock crash could not prevent the beginning of a prolonged and bitter bidding war for what was now characterized as an overly diversified, poorly managed conglomerate. In December 1987, a British confectionery company called Barker & Dobson (B&D) offered Dee shareholders the equivalent of about £2 billion for their stock, charging Monk with incompetence and promising to sell off unprofitable parts of the Dee network. Monk fought back vigorously, however, spending millions of pounds sterling in defense of his company and its future prospects. Second-half profits for the fiscal year ending April 1988 were substantially better, cutting the total annual decline to only 3 percent, and the chairman could point to the company's remarkable growth and the profits to be realized when all of its stores had organized themselves under the Gateway banner. When the votes were counted in the spring of 1988, Monk had won the battle easily and Dee appeared safe for the time being.

The grace period was short. Although Monk took steps to correct some of the problems Barker & Dobson had harped on, selling, for example, Dee's Spanish distributing business and the original Linfood wholesaling subsidiary, it was only a year later that the second wave of predators made its attack. Dee had changed its name in the summer of 1988 to Gateway Corporation, emphasizing its commitment to the retailing end of its business, but to David Smith it was still the same bloated, underpriced temptation. Smith had been a financial advisor to B&D during its unsuccessful bid, and, backed by a variety of large investors, including the British investment bank S.G. Warburg, he launched his own strike, under the name Isosceles PLC, in April 1989. After intense competition from a number of other bidders, including a company called Newgateway PLC, put together by the Great Atlantic & Pacific Tea Company and dealmaker Wasserstein Perella & Company, two U.S. companies—Isosceles emerged the winner in July of that year, buying up a bare majority of the stock to force out Monk and his board of directors.

Smith wasted no time implementing the policy B&D had urged two years before, selling off 61 of Gateway's largest superstores to the ASDA Group plc for £705 million and repositioning the company as an operator of mostly midsized, high-street retail outlets. Gateway would no longer try to compete with the big out-of-town and edge-of-town grocers, but would fill the somewhat smaller niche left in-town by the emergence of the suburban superstore.

The Gateway takeover, however, got off to a rocky start. In December 1989 Isosceles launched an offering to help unload some of its $2.1 billion in debt, but was unable to find buyers, and its 16 underwriters were left holding $848 million more in paper than they had expected. Further asset sales had been expected, including the divestments of Herman's, a group of 110 stores in Scotland and the north of England, and the F.A. Wellworth & Co. supermarket chain in Northern Ireland. But the only other immediate sale was that of the Medicare drugstore chain, which was sold for only £5 million in November 1989.

Early and Mid-1990s: The Troubled Isosceles Era

In 1990 the first Somerfield store was opened, with the new format positioned upmarket from Gateway and designed to compete more directly with the stores of rivals J Sainsbury plc, Tesco PLC, and Safeway plc. The more modern Somerfield stores were bright and placed a heavy emphasis on fresh foods. At the same time, the Somerfield line of private-label products was launched. The company launched Food Giant, a downmarket, discount chain, in 1991.

Although the launch of the Somerfield chain would prove to be a key development in the company's history, the early 1990s were most notable for the financial struggles of Isosceles stemming from the huge debt burden incurred in the 1989 takeover, from a deep and long-lasting recession, and from price wars in the grocery sector. Sales and profits fell, and the company was saved from bankruptcy only through the three separate restructurings of its debt that occurred by early 1994 as well as the laying off of 2,000 workers in 1992. There were also a number of management changes, with Smith departing in September 1991 and being replaced by Bob Willett, and Willett stepping aside a year later. David Simons, who had been finance director of the Storehouse apparel chain, began a longer-lasting stint as chief executive in January 1993.

Around this same time, Isosceles was finally able to unload some of its noncore holdings. In late 1992 the Wellworth chain was sold to Fitzwilton PLC for £122 million. In March 1993 Isosceles sold Herman's to a U.S. investor group led by Taggart/Fasola Group for an undisclosed sum. Simons also moved to center the company around the Somerfield format. In May 1994 the Gateway name began to disappear; a two-year, £200 million refurbishment program was launched to convert the remaining Gateway Foodmarkets into Somerfield Stores, and the Gateway Group, still owned by Isosceles, was renamed Somerfield Holdings. Next, Somerfield gained its independence from Isosceles through a flotation of Somerfield plc on the London Stock Exchange in August 1996. At the time the company was operating about 600 supermarkets. Through a complex series of financial maneuvers, Somerfield emerged as an independent, public company with only about £130 million in debt. Also in 1996 Somerfield began opening gasoline station minimarkets in partnership with Elf Aquitaine SA (later known as Total Fina Elf S.A.).

Late 1990s and Beyond: The Kwik Save Merger and Its Difficult Aftermath

In March 1998 Somerfield merged with Kwik Save Group plc, operator of nearly 900 discount grocery stores located throughout the United Kingdom. Founded in 1959 by Albert Gubay, a Welsh entrepreneur, Kwik Save had opened its first discount supermarket in Colwyn Bay, Wales, in 1965. The company grew over the decades both organically and through acquisitions, maintaining its position as the largest grocery discounter in the United Kingdom. Like Somerfield, Kwik Save concentrated on in-town locations, making for a good fit between the two chains. As Simons envisioned the merger, the combination would yield annual savings of £50 million through the closure of Kwik Save's head office, the pooling of back-office operations, and the increased clout the company would have with its suppliers. He also foresaw further savings from the conversion of at least some of the Kwik Save outlets to the Somerfield banner. Later in 1998 Somerfield entered discussions with struggling food wholesaler Booker plc regarding a possible takeover, but the talks ended without an agreement. In early 1999 Somerfield entered the home shopping market and began experimenting with a home delivery service.

Integrating the Kwik Save and Somerfield chains proved more difficult than anticipated, and Simons embarked on a major overhaul late in 1999. The company announced that it would sell about 500 stores, including as many as 140 of the larger Somerfield stores and about 350 underperforming Kwik Save outlets, in order to refocus the firm on smaller ''neighborhood'' stores. Simons also planned to eventually convert the remaining Kwik Save stores to the Somerfield banner. Unfortunately, finding buyers for the stores proved extremely difficult—although 46 larger Somerfield stores were sold in early 2000—and after seeking to take the company private with the backing of private equity firms, Simons was forced out. Alan Smith took over as chief executive in April 2000, having previously served as chief executive of Punch Taverns. Soon after, John von Spreckelsen was named executive chairman. Von Spreckelsen was a turnaround specialist who had most recently helped reverse the fortunes of Budgens plc, operator of convenience stores, as that firm's chief executive. The new leadership team retained Simons's emphasis on ''neighborhood'' stores but halted plans to sell any more stores and to eliminate the Kwik Save chain. Needing to concentrate on reviving sales and profits at its core operations, Somerfield also announced in June 2000 that it would halt further development of its home shopping unit.

Von Spreckelsen and Smith emphasized that the situation they had inherited at Somerfield had been so dire that a full recovery could not be expected until 2005. The executives felt that by the end of the fiscal year ending in April 2001 the company had at least been stabilized and was no longer in a death spiral. The operating loss for that year was £6.3 million, compared to £79.5 million for the previous year. For the first six months of the 2001/2002 fiscal year Somerfield was back in the black, posting an operating profit of £5.6 million. The company was beginning to see dividends from its commitment to an expensive multiyear program of store renovation in which a certain number of Somerfield and Kwik Save outlets were upgraded each year. Same-store sales growth appeared to have returned to both chains by the Christmas selling season of 2001. Other important initiatives in the attempted restructuring included the opening of a new flagship store in Kingswood (a suburb of Bristol) featuring high-quality fresh foods and ready-to-eat meals, the launch of a new high-end private label line called So Good, and the introduction of the company's first loyalty card, the Saver Card. Somerfield's recovery was by no means a certainty given the highly competitive and volatile nature of the food retailing market, but the company appeared to have a solid strategy for surviving and thriving.

Principal Subsidiaries

Somerfield Stores Limited; Somerfield Property Company Limited; Kwik Save Stores Limited; Colemans Limited; KS Insurance Limited.

Principal Competitors

Tesco PLC; J Sainsbury plc; ASDA Group Limited; Safeway plc; John Lewis Partnership plc; Wm Morrison Supermarkets PLC; Marks & Spencer p.l.c.

Further Reading

Batchelor, Charles, "Dee Buys International Stores Chain for £180m," *Financial Times,* November 23, 1984, p. 10.

——, "Dee Makes Agreed £23m Bid for Lennons," *Financial Times,* September 11, 1984, p. 27.

Bose, Mihir, "Knight Errantry and the Round Table," *Director,* February 1990, pp. 32–34, 37–38.

Churchill, David, "Climbing Up the League Table," *Financial Times,* November 23, 1984, p. 30.

——, "Dee to Acquire U.S. Sports Chain," *Financial Times,* March 21, 1986, p. 1.

——, "U.K. Food Group in £232.5m Bid for Booker McConnell," *Financial Times,* May 31, 1984, p. 1.

"Fishing on the Dee," *Economist,* December 26, 1997, p. 76.

"Group Launches Bid to Acquire Gateway Corp.," *Wall Street Journal,* April 19, 1989.

Hall, Trish, and Paul Hemp, "Grace Will Sell Herman's Stake for $227 Million: Dee Corp. of Britain Agrees to Pay $35.25 a Share for Sporting Goods Line," *Wall Street Journal,* March 21, 1986.

Hoggan, Karen, "Against the Tide," *Marketing,* October 27, 1988, pp. 36+.

Hollinger, Peggy, "Somerfield and Kwik Save Hope That Size Will Matter," *Financial Times,* February 17, 1998, p. 23.

——, "Somerfield Chief Hard at Work on Strengthening His Reputation," *Financial Times,* September 8, 1999, p. 22.

Johnson, Mike, "Gateway Lowers Sights," *Marketing,* February 13, 1992, p. 2.

Kay, William, "Leverage, Old Chap?: LBO Crunch Spreads Across the Atlantic," *Barron's,* October 29, 1990, pp. 18–19, 47.

Lublin, Joann S., "Gateway Gets a $3.03 Billion Buy-Out Offer," *Wall Street Journal,* June 20, 1989.

Mason, Tania, "Can Somerfield Build a Strong Brand Identity?," *Marketing,* February 21, 2002, p. 15.

Melcher, Richard A., and Leah Nathans Spiro, "An LBO That Went Over Like a Soggy Teabag: Can Wasserstein Salvage Its Stake in Britain's Isosceles Supermarkets?," *Business Week,* June 29, 1992, p. 54.

Nelson, Fraser, "Somerfield's Black Knight May Be Facing Checkmate," *Times* (London), November 12, 1999, p. 37.

——, "What Simons Says Goes As Somerfield Consumes Kwik Save," *Times* (London), February 20, 1998, p. 31.

Nicoll, Alexander, "Unravelling the Booker Saga," *Financial Times,* January 22, 1985, p. 20.

O'Keeffe, R. Kevin, "Why a U.K. Food Retailer Shifted Its Sights in the U.S.," *Mergers and Acquisitions,* July/August 1987, pp. 71+.

Price, Christopher, "Food for Thought at Somerfield," *Financial Times,* January 25, 1997, p. 5.

Simpson, Michele, "Somerfield's Gateway to Opportunity," *Marketing Week,* September 22, 1995, p. 25.

Sparks, Leigh, *Strategy in Retailing: The Development of Kwik Save Group P.L.C.,* Stirling, Scotland: University of Stirling, Institute for Retail Studies, 1988.

Tait, Nikki, "Barker & Dobson Bid for Dee Fails," *Financial Times,* February 20, 1988, p. 22.

——, "If You Don't Succeed, Hone Your Method: The Bid for Gateway," *Financial Times,* April 20, 1989, p. 33.

——, "Isosceles Wins £2 Billion Battle for Control of Gateway," *Financial Times,* July 14, 1989, p. 1.

Tait, Nikki, and Maggie Urry, "Can Isosceles Square the Vicious Circle of Debt?," *Financial Times,* October 4, 1990, p. 27.

Thornhill, John, "A Badly Timed Deal in an Evolving Marketplace: A Look at the Problems Facing Isosceles As It Plans a Reflotation of the Gateway Chain," *Financial Times,* May 28, 1992, p. 26.

Timewell, Stephen, "Isosceles: Anatomy of a Failure," *Banker,* March 1993, p. 52.

Urry, Maggie, "High Noon on the High Streets," *Financial Times,* December 18, 1987, p. 14.

——, "Why Gateway Believes It Is Leading a Retail Revolution," *Financial Times,* November 3, 1988, p. 27.

Warner, Liz, "Dee's Defence," *Marketing,* October 15, 1987, p. 27.

—update: David E. Salamie

Southwest Water Company

Southwest Water Company

225 North Barranca Avenue, Suite 200
West Covina, California
U.S.A.
Telephone: (626) 915-1551
Toll Free: (800) 301-3801
Fax: (626) 915-1558
Web site: http://www.southwestwater.com

Public Company
Incorporated: 1954 as Suburban Water Systems
Employees: 643
Sales: $104.74 million (2000)
Stock Exchanges: NASDAQ
Ticker Symbol: SWWC
NAIC: 221310 Water Supply and Irrigation Systems;
    551112 Offices of Other Holding Companies

Southwest Water Company owns and operates water and wastewater treatment systems, manages and operates water and wastewater treatment systems under contract, and provides utility submetering services. The company's regulated public utilities are operated through southern California-based Suburban Water Systems, New Mexico Utilities, Inc., and two utilities in Texas, Windermere Utility Company and Hornsby Bend Utility Company. Southwest Water's contract operations are conducted through ECO Resources, Inc., which operates in California, New Mexico, Texas, and Mississippi. The company's submetering activities are operated through Master Tek International, Inc., which serves customers in 30 states, coast to coast. Southwest Water serves more than one million customers, predominantly in California and Texas.

Origins

Southwest Water's corporate lineage stretches throughout much of the 20th century. The company's earliest predecessor began supplying water to customers in the Los Angeles area as early as 1907. A more direct route to Southwest Water's past began on December 10, 1954, when Suburban Water Systems—an integral component of the company's corporate structure in the 21st century—was incorporated.

From its birth as a regulated water utility, Suburban Water Systems benefited from the strident growth and development surrounding it. Operating in a regulated industry, Suburban Water Systems was dependent almost entirely on population growth within its service area for its own financial success. Rate increases only provided modest growth, whereas the establishment of new communities, the expansion of existing neighborhoods, and new industrial and commercial development could provide a substantial surge in the company's bottom line. Such was the case for Suburban Water Systems between the mid-1950s and the late 1960s. The Los Angeles area became the greater Los Angeles area, as the suburban sprawl that would later describe the region began to take shape. Officials at Suburban Water Systems witnessed their service area transform from agricultural use to residential, business, and industrial use, a conversion that added meaningfully to the company's stature.

The more than decade-long growth period experienced by Suburban Water Systems tapered off by the late 1960s. Population expansion within the company's service area slowed considerably, reaching its saturation point. Modest growth of the pace typical of a regulated water utility in a mature market set in, prompting company management to pursue opportunities elsewhere. Suburban Water Systems officials moved quickly, completing an acquisition just as business in the Los Angeles area began to lose its robust vigor. In 1969, Suburban Water Systems purchased New Mexico Utilities, Inc., a small water utility serving 800 customers. In 1975, the name of the combined businesses was changed to Southwest Water Company, with Suburban Water Systems and New Mexico Utilities, Inc. operating as its two subsidiaries.

In the decade after the name Southwest Water was adopted, growth was recorded at a measured pace, presided over by a leader whose contributions to Southwest Water's financial health were substantial. Anton C. Garnier, who would serve as Southwest Water's president, chief executive officer, and chairman as the company entered the 21st century, spent his entire

370

career at Southwest Water. Raised on a 1,000-acre farm established by his family in the late 19th century, Garnier attended Orange Coast College and San Diego State University. He served a two-year stint in the U.S. Army as a sergeant before joining Suburban Water Systems in 1968, the year before the company acquired New Mexico Utilities, Inc. Early in his career at the company, Garnier earned a Grade V water certificate, the highest level of certification awarded in California. Under Garnier's leadership, Southwest Water kept pace with changes in the water industry, and made the most adventurous leap in its history. During the mid-1980s, when the company operated as one of 18 investor-owned water companies, Garnier led Southwest Water into its first non-regulated business area.

Diversification in 1985

Southwest Water's regulated utility operations provided financial stability, but little opportunity for sizable growth. In New Mexico, the company was achieving gains in growth through the extension of water services and sewage collection services into new residential subdivisions and new commercial property. In southern California, the years of rampant growth had gone, as Suburban Water Systems' service area reached maturity in terms of population. By no means had the company's regulated utility operations lost their worth; rather, the water systems, particularly the assets operated by Suburban Water Systems, had become established and reliable profit generators—properties Garnier had no desire to disassociate Southwest Water from. Instead, Garnier wanted to complement the company's stable money earners with new growth opportunities.

In 1985, Southwest Water entered the contract water and wastewater management services industry by purchasing ECO Resources, Inc. Established in 1972 and incorporated two years later, ECO Resources operated and managed water and wastewater systems near Houston, Texas, that were owned by other entities, generating its revenues from contracts with the systems' owners. The acquisition opened a path toward new growth, both geographically and financially, positioning Southwest Water in an emerging industry that called upon the company's expertise. In 1986, Southwest Water collected $27.9 million in revenue, the bulk of which—$23.3 million—was derived from the company's utility subsidiaries, Suburban Water Systems and New Mexico Utilities, Inc. For the same year, the company's fledgling contract operations, conducted by ECO Resources, accounted for the remaining $4.6 million. A little more than a decade later, contract operations would constitute over half of Southwest Water's entire business, proving to be a source of substantial growth.

By the beginning of the 1990s, Southwest Water's regulated operations supplied water to more than 500,000 customers. As the mainstay of the company's business, the regulated operations, located in southern California's San Gabriel Valley and in New Mexico, served as a steady source of revenues and respectable profit margins. By this point, however, the emphasis was on building the company's contract operations by forging business relationships with cities, municipal utility districts, and private companies. Garnier's progress in this segment of the company's business enabled Southwest Water to reach a financial milestone in 1994, when the company celebrated its 40th anniversary by eclipsing the $50 million-in-sales mark, recording $50.9 million in sales and posting $1 million in net income.

Growth in the Late 1990s

During the latter half of the 1990s, Southwest Water enjoyed the best years in its history. The company's revenue volume nearly doubled during the five-year period, while its profits quadrupled. The growth was attributable to expansion within both segments of the company's business, as substantial gains were made in both regulated and non-regulated sectors. By the end of the decade, the company was ready to enter a new line of business, encouraged by the overwhelming success recorded during the late 1990s.

In the company's regulated utility operations, growth was achieved from modest increases in Suburban Water Systems' existing markets and through the acquisition of water and wastewater systems. In 1996, for example, the company purchased 49 percent of Windermere Utility Company, located near Austin, Texas. Sales efforts, aimed at securing new contracts and renewing existing contracts, provided substantial growth as well. From its base in the Houston area, ECO Resources was expanding its presence in Texas and broadening its geographic scope by securing contracts with utility districts and private companies in California, New Mexico, and Mississippi. One notable contact, obtained in 1995, forged a lasting relationship with the El Paso County Water Authority (EPCWA), a municipal utility district for whom ECO Resources operated water and wastewater systems.

By 1998, Southwest Water supplied water and wastewater services to nearly 750,000 people. The majority of the company's customers resided in California and Texas, where Southwest Water served 300,000 people in each state. Mississippi, with 110,000 customers, and New Mexico, home to 20,000 Southwest Water customers, represented the balance of the company's customer base. Combined, the company's territories of service produced record-high financial totals in 1998, with $72.1 million in revenues and $3.34 million in net income. During the year, the company increased its anticipated future revenues from contractual commitments to $70 million, the

Key Dates:

1954: Suburban Water Systems is incorporated.
1969: Suburban Water Systems acquires New Mexico Utilities, Inc.
1975: Suburban Water Systems changes its name to Southwest Water Company.
1985: ECO Resources, Inc. is acquired, providing entry into contract operations.
1996: A 49 percent stake in Windermere Utility Company is acquired.
2000: Master Tek International, Inc. is purchased, adding utility submetering to the company's business activities.

result of netting more than 20 new and renewed contracts for water and wastewater services. Southwest Water suffered its losses during the year, such as the decision by the City of Rio Rancho, located in New Mexico, not to renew the company's contract. The loss of Rio Rancho represented $4.5 million in business, but the successes outweighed the failures in 1998.

In 1998, Southwest Water secured more than a dozen new contracts, helping to compensate for unusually wet weather in California. The global weather phenomenon of El Niño was the cause for more than twice the normal seasonal rainfall during the first six months of 1998, leading to a decline in water sales of more than $2 million, but Garnier's decision to enter the contract business in 1985 compensated for the loss. The new contractual relationships Southwest Water secured in 1998 included a five-year, $1.6 million contract with the City of Dos Palos, California, to provide water treatment and distribution, meter reading, and wastewater treatment and collection services for the community's 8,000 residents. A similar arrangement was brokered for a Brazonia County municipal utility district in suburban Houston, giving the company a three-year, $900,000 contract.

In 1999, another year hailed as the best in the company's history, Southwest Water outstripped the accomplishments of the previous year. During the year, the company secured 20 new contracts and renewed contracts with 22 existing clients. A drier 1999 in California also produced gains in the company's regulated operations, leading to a 12 percent increase in water sales. In New Mexico, more good news was to be found, as residential and commercial development expanded the company's utility customer base by 16 percent. Early in the year, Southwest Water signed a five-year, $2.3 million contract with Discovery Bay, a community service district located east of Oakland, California, that added 8,000 new customers. The company also added 22,000 new customers in northwest Mississippi by signing a five-year, $4.1 million contract with the City of Olive Branch. Perhaps the most significant of the company's renewed contracts was a 20-year renewal with EPCWA, a $20 million agreement that included the financing, construction, and operation of a $6.7 million reverse osmosis water treatment facility.

Southwest Water's contract operations expanded by 16 percent in 1999, accounting for 53 percent of the company's total

revenues. Regulated utility business, which constituted the company's entire business before 1985, accounted for 45 percent of Southwest Water's revenue volume. Garnier would soon add another dimension to Southwest Water's operations, as the company prepared to enter the 21st century enjoying the most successful years in its history. New contracts continued to arrive in 2000, beginning with an agreement with Lamont, California, that was expected to generate $3.2 million in revenue during the ensuing five years. The addition of the contract in Lamont combined with the contracts signed in 1999 gave the company more than 60,000 new customers. On the regulated utility side of Southwest Water's business, the company's customer count increased as well in February 2000, when the City of West Covina's water distribution system was acquired, increasing the company's customer base in California by 11 percent.

Garnier steered Southwest Water in a new direction in 2000, engineering the company's first foray into a non-governmental market. In April 2000, Southwest Water purchased Master Tek International, Inc., a leading company in the submetering industry. Master Tek's customers were property owners of multi-family housing units for whom Master Tek provided utility metering, billing, and collection services, enabling property owners to bill individual utility usage. The company served customers in 30 states, greatly broadening Southwest Water's geographic scope, and generated approximately $6 million in annual revenues.

Southwest Water's record-setting year also included substantial gains in the company's regulated utility operations. In October 2000, the company acquired an additional 31 percent stake in Windermere Utility Company, bolstering the 49 percent interest the company acquired in 1996. Also in October, the company purchased 100 percent of Hornsby Bend Utility Company, a water utility situated adjacent to Windermere Utility. Collectively, the two companies were referred to as the "Texas Utilities." By the end of the year, thanks largely to the two acquisitions, Southwest Water recorded a 15 percent increase in its regulated utility customer base. The company's contract operations recorded a 29 percent increase in revenues, as compared to the total recorded in 1999.

Strengthened considerably by the achievements during 2000, Southwest Water posted an impressive 30 percent increase in its overall revenue. For the year, the company generated $104.7 million in sales and $5.3 million in net income. With more than one million customers residing in 30 states, the company represented a rising force in the water and wastewater services industry, its decision to diversify, while maintaining the financial stability engendered by regulated operations, holding it in good stead for its second half-century of business.

Principal Subsidiaries

ECO Resources, Inc.; Master Tek International, Inc.; Suburban Water Systems; New Mexico Utilities, Inc.; Hornsby Bend Utility Company; Windermere Utility Company (80%).

Principal Competitors

California Water Service Group; Lower Colorado River Authority; Western Water Company.

Further Reading

Bekey, Michelle, "Southwest Water Taps New Markets," *California Business,* July 1985, p. 37.

Burkhardt, Daniel A., "Water Is a Treasure," *Public Utilities Fortnightly,* November 15, 1991, p. 26.

Byrne, Harlan S., "Southwest Water Co.: Its Profits Flow from Its Nonregulated Businesses," *Barron's,* April 16, 1990, p. 41.

"Southwest Water Acquires Two Utilities in Austin Area," *Austin Business Journal,* October 6, 2000, p. 52.

—Jeffrey L. Covell

SPX Corporation

SPX Corporation

2300 One Wachovia Center
301 South College Street
Charlotte, North Carolina 28202-6039
U.S.A.
Telephone: (704) 347-6800
Fax: (704) 347-6900
Web site: http://www.spx.com

Public Company
Incorporated: 1911 as The Piston Ring Company
Employees: 14,000
Sales: $4.11 billion (2001)
Stock Exchanges: New York Pacific
Ticker Symbol: SPW
NAIC: 321918 Other Millwork (Including Flooring);
332212 Hand and Edge Tool Manufacturing; 332311
Prefabricated Metal Building and Component Manufac-
turing; 332313 Plate Work Manufacturing; 332912 Fluid
Power Valve and Hose Fitting Manufacturing; 333294
Food Product Machinery Manufacturing; 333319 Other
Commercial and Service Industry Machinery Manufac-
turing; 333412 Industrial and Commercial Fan and
Blower Manufacturing; 333415 Air-Conditioning and
Warm Air Heating Equipment and Commercial and In-
dustrial Refrigeration Equipment Manufacturing; 333511
Industrial Mold Manufacturing; 333991 Power-Driven
Handtool Manufacturing; 333994 Industrial Process Fur-
nace and Oven Manufacturing; 333995 Fluid Power Cyl-
inder and Actuator Manufacturing; 333996 Fluid Power
Pump and Motor Manufacturing; 334210 Telephone Apparatus Manufacturing; 334220 Radio and Television
Broadcasting and Wireless Communications Equipment
Manufacturing; 334290 Other Communications Equipment Manufacturing; 334519 Other Measuring and Controlling Device Manufacturing; 335312 Motor and Generator Manufacturing; 336399 All Other Motor Vehicle
Parts Manufacturing; 336413 Other Aircraft Parts and
Auxiliary Equipment Manufacturing; 541330 Engineering Services

With beginnings as an auto parts manufacturer, SPX Corporation has evolved over its 90-plus-year history into a wide-ranging
maker of various industrial products and a provider of related
services. The company's subsidiaries and units are divided into
four segments: technical products and services, industrial products and services, service solutions, and vehicle components. The
technical products and services segments includes networking
and switching products for storage, data, and telecommunications
networks; fire detection and building life-safety systems; television and radio transmission systems; and automated fare collection systems. The industrial products and services segments includes power transformers, industrial valves, industrial fluid
mixers and agitators, laboratory and industrial ovens and freezers,
hydraulic pumps, material handling systems, and electric motors
for industrial chemical companies, pulp and paper makers, laboratories, and utilities. The service solutions segment includes
diagnostic systems and service equipment, specialty service
tools, and technical and training information, primarily for North
American and European motor vehicle manufacturers. The vehicle components segment is a supplier of aluminum and magne-
sium die-castings, forgings, automatic transmission and small
engine filters, and transmission kits to automotive original equipment manufacturers. SPX has operations in 19 countries, with 14
percent of revenues coming from outside the United States.

Piston Ring Beginnings

SPX's foundations were laid on December 20, 1911, when
two friends, Charles E. Johnson and Paul R. Beardsley, each
deposited $1,000 in the National Lumberman's Bank of Muske-
gon, Michigan. The money was to serve as the initial working
capital of their new single product firm, The Piston Ring Company. Johnson, a mechanic, and Beardsley, a salesman, foresaw
the need for automotive parts for the burgeoning automotive
industry in Michigan. The two partners personally delivered the
first piston rings manufactured in their rented 30-by-60-foot
factory to the firm's first customer, Continental Motors Corporation. In its first years, the aptly named Piston Ring Company
devoted itself entirely to the production of piston rings for
leading engine builders. The advent of World War I brought a
huge increase in the demand for engine parts for the war effort,
and The Piston Ring Company responded by undertaking a
major plant expansion.

Company Perspectives:

We are a global multi-industry company that is focused on profitably growing our businesses that have scale and growth potential, enabling us to continue to grow sales, earnings and cash flow. Our strategy is to create market advantages through product and technology leadership, by expanding our service offerings to full customer solutions and by building critical mass through strategic acquisitions.

In the years between the two world wars, The Piston Ring Company began a series of acquisitions and expansions, a pattern of growth for the company for the next 60 years. In 1923 they bought the No-Leak-O Piston Ring Company, which allowed the firm to further increase its production of the crucial engine component. By 1925, they were able to begin exporting their product and to enter the increasingly lucrative replacement parts market. The acquisition in 1931 of the Accuralite Company, a maker of pistons and cylinder sleeves, would mark a crucial step for the growing firm. This diversification of their product line would become a fundamental component of the company's strategy in later years. In order to reflect this new diversity, the company also changed its name from the simple "The Piston Ring Company" to the more evocative "Sealed Power Corporation."

The post-World War II years were a period of major expansion for Sealed Power. In 1946 the company opened its first plant outside Muskegon with the construction of a piston ring machining facility at St. John's, Michigan, closer to the huge Detroit automakers than were its primary customers. Two years later the company built a cylinder sleeve machining facility in Rochester, Indiana, and in 1957 it added a Replacement Distribution Center in LaGrange, Indiana. This distribution center, which serviced 33 smaller distribution outlets in key cities throughout the United States and Canada, was indicative of the growing role of replacement parts marketing in the company's business strategy. By 1959, replacement parts accounted for about 50 percent of Sealed Power sales and served as an important hedge against the highly cyclical original equipment market. The automotive aftermarket is not only relatively free from the sharp ups and downs of the original parts industry but actually tends to increase during downturns in the original automotive market. When people are not in a position to buy new cars they have their old ones repaired instead.

Sealed Power's relatively rapid expansion in the 1950s led to the company's first public offering of common stock in 1955. The company also increased exports, distributing their original and replacement parts in 78 countries by the end of the decade. Even more significantly for their global presence, by the dawn of the 1960s Sealed Power had opened plants in Stratford, Canada, and in Mexico City. This expansion in both production and market diversity was accompanied by a major product breakthrough in 1956 when Sealed Power introduced the first stainless steel piston ring. The ring quickly achieved 100 percent original and replacement market acceptance, according to company sources.

Steady Growth in the 1960s and 1970s

At the beginning of the 1960s, in spite of product diversification over the previous 50 years, the sale of piston rings for both the original and replacement markets still accounted for over 65 percent of Sealed Power's sales. These sales made up about one-quarter of the total U.S. market for piston rings and made Sealed Power the second largest manufacturer of piston rings in the country. Cylinder sleeves and pistons made up the bulk of the company's remaining sales, although by this time it was also producing a variety of small engine parts, such as valves and tappets. By the end of the decade, Sealed Power, determined to decrease its reliance on a single product, implemented a planned program of product diversification. In 1968 the company acquired another cylinder sleeve plant in Mexico as well as the Consolidated Die Cast Corporation (later renamed Contech), a Michigan firm that produced precision die castings. During the next six years it acquired a manufacturer of valve tappets (later renamed the Hy-Lift Division), a manufacturer of transmission fluid filters (later renamed the Filtran Division), and a manufacturer of small alloyed castings. It had also opened a sealing ring plant in Franklin, Kentucky, a tappet facility in Zeeland, Michigan, and a new piston ring plant in Liege, Belgium, to serve the European market.

Sales rose steadily during the 1960s and 1970s as Sealed Power expanded. From annual sales of $25 million in 1960, the company's sales had grown to over $200 million by 1977. Although sales grew, earnings remained heavily dependent on fluctuations in the auto industry. In 1974, for instance, a year in which American car and truck production plummeted, earnings fell to $1.46 per share from the previous year's $2.19. Diversification had meant that piston rings made up a smaller percentage of sales than it had in the early 1960s; nonetheless, Sealed Power's original engine parts group, which now included sealing rings, valve tappets, and transmission filters in addition to the company's longstanding engine products, still accounted for 42 percent of sales in 1975. With over three-quarters of these sales coming directly from the auto industry, Sealed Power's fortunes were inextricably tied to that of the major American automakers. In a 1980 press release, company President Edward I. Schalon stated that "as a supplier of engine parts to the motor vehicle industry we are adversely affected by the proliferation of cars and trucks imported into the United States. This situation is compounded by the growing number of vehicles which bear domestic nameplates, but are powered by engines manufactured overseas."

Continuing Acquisitions and Diversification in the 1980s

Diversification continued to dominate Sealed Power's long-term business strategy in the 1980s. In early 1982, the company acquired Kent-Moore Corporation in a cash and stock transaction valued at $70 million. Kent-Moore, headquartered in Warren, Michigan, was a major manufacturer of specialized service tools, equipment, and diagnostic instrumentation for the transportation industry. An important step in Sealed Power's campaign to diversify its product line, the acquisition of Kent-Moore provided a new direction for Sealed Power's relationship with the auto industry. Although Kent-Moore dealt directly with the same automakers that Sealed Power had supplied since its beginnings in

Key Dates:

1911: The Piston Ring Company is founded in Muskegon, Michigan, to manufacture piston rings for automakers.

1931: Acquisition of Accuralite Company, maker of pistons and cylinder sleeves, marks first diversification of product line; company changes its name to Sealed Power Corporation.

1955: Company goes public.

1982: Kent-Moore Corporation is acquired.

1988: Company changes its name to SPX Corporation.

1989: Major restructuring is launched involving the sale of a majority stake in all of SPX's original equipment operations.

1993: Automotive replacement parts division is sold to Federal-Mogul; SPX regains full control of its original equipment operations.

1997: The Sealed Power Division, the company's founding business, is sold to Dana Corporation.

1998: General Signal Corporation, maker of products for the process control, electrical control, and industrial technology industries, is acquired for $2.3 billion.

2001: United Dominion Industries Limited, a diversified manufacturer of engineered products, is acquired for about $1.9 billion.

2002: Company headquarters are moved to Charlotte, North Carolina.

1911, the specialty tools that it produced relied on the introduction of new automotive models rather than on the volume of production. Each new car model required a set of specialized tools with which dealers could service the vehicles, and the Kent-Moore division worked directly with manufacturers before new vehicles were introduced. Kent-Moore also had significant overseas operations, including a partnership in Japan, that allowed Sealed Power to expand its foreign presence. In 1982, the first year of the acquisition, Kent-Moore contributed some $86 million to Sealed Power's $366 million sales total.

Sales continued to grow during the 1980s, topping $400 million in 1983 and placing Sealed Power on the *Fortune* 500. Earnings, however, continued to fluctuate. In 1983 and 1984, when domestic automobile production soared, Sealed Power's earnings rose an impressive 27 percent and 17 percent only to fall back again in 1985 and 1986 when both the original equipment and replacement markets flattened out. By 1985, as it became clear that the American auto industry would be unstable for at least the immediate future, stock analysts began to stress the advantages of the aftermarket. "At this point in the automobile cycle," a parts industry analyst for Merrill Lynch was quoted as saying in a 1985 *New York Times* article, "we believe that the aftermarket is more attractive than the original equipment segment." After the Kent-Moore purchase the proportion of sales contributed by each of Sealed Power's product groups began to shift. In 1982, the year of the Kent-Moore acquisition, aftermarket sales made up 39 percent of total sales, original equipment contributed 35 percent, and specialty service tools took over 22 percent of total revenues.

In 1985, Sealed Power further expanded its specialty tool product segment through the acquisition of the Owatonna Tool Company and its subsidiaries, later the Power Team and Truth divisions of SPX. Owatonna, a producer of specialty tools and electronic repair equipment, allowed Sealed Power to expand its market in this area. Power Team and Truth further diversified Sealed Power's product line with the addition of high-pressure hydraulic pumps and other equipment for industrial applications as well as window and door hardware for the home construction industry. Also acquired in 1985 was the V.L. Churchill Group of Daventry, England, a major supplier of specialty tools and service products in Europe, further expanding Sealed Power's overseas presence. In order to respond to the growing threat of Japanese automobile imports, Sealed Power also set up a joint agreement with the Riken Corp., Japan's largest manufacturer of piston rings, to allow Sealed Power to distribute Riken's engine parts for repair and maintenance of Japanese cars in the United States. Sealed Power continued its program of diversification and expansion through acquisitions into the late 1980s. In addition to a number of smaller businesses, the company purchased the piston ring operations of TRW in 1987, resulting in a reorganization and consolidation of Sealed Power's piston manufacturing plants and the laying off of some 400 employees.

The late 1980s were a critical period for Sealed Power. By 1988 Sealed Power's products ranged from piston rings to door hardware and were sold to a wide range of markets. Original equipment motor parts sales had fallen to only 28 percent of total company revenues, whereas replacement parts constituted 36 percent of sales, service products and specialty service remained steady at 22 percent of corporate volume, and window and door hardware now assumed 14 percent of total sales. In recognition of the changing nature of the company, the decision was reached to change the company name from the Sealed Power Corporation to the SPX Corporation. Robert D. Tuttle, then company chairman and CEO, stated in a press release that the name change was necessary because the Sealed Power name did not reflect the scope of the company's diversity in products and markets nor the range and depth of its vision of the company's future.

Acquisitions had greatly increased SPX's total sales, which rose from $250 million in 1980 to $632 million in 1989. Net income, however, failed to rise as consistently and the still considerable original equipment segment continued to be tied to the fluctuations in the automobile industry. The acquisition in 1988 of Bear Automotive Service Equipment Company increased SPX's presence in the specialty service equipment field. In 1989 the company reached a major crossroads—diversification had transformed it from an engine parts maker with some other interests, to a replacement parts and specialty service tool manufacturer that also made piston rings.

A rumor was reported in early 1989 that corporate raider Arthur Goldberg was making a move toward SPX and had actually purchased a 4 percent stake in the company. Whether or not these rumors were heeded by SPX management, they clearly thought that strong action was needed to maintain shareholder confidence in the now diffuse company. That action came in April 1989 when it was announced that the company would undergo a major restructuring. The key component of this restructuring would be the sale of a majority stake in all of SPX's original equipment operations.

A new partnership, to be called Sealed Power Technologies Limited Partnership, would be formed from four Sealed Power divisions specializing in original equipment manufacture. The partnership would be controlled by a joint agreement between Sealed Power, who would retain a 49 percent stake in the companies, and Goldman, Sachs & Co., a New York securities firm who would assume control of 49 percent of the partnership. The remaining 2 percent stake would be owned by company management. This partnership would operate independently of SPX's other operations and would leave SPX free to concentrate more heavily on its replacement and specialty service tools segments. In addition, SPX would establish an employee stock ownership plan, in an apparently defensive move, to make unfriendly takeovers more difficult. "The restructuring will allow SPX to concentrate fully on a market segment that has higher margins and is more resistant to recessions than the original equipment business," CEO Robert Tuttle was quoted as saying in an article in the *Grand Rapids Business Journal.*

Struggles in the Early 1990s

The resistance to recession that SPX believed it would gain from concentrating its resources on the automobile aftermarket and construction industries failed to materialize. Instead, 1990 proved a very poor year for all sectors of SPX, with the exception of such environmentally driven products as refrigerant recycling equipment from the Robinair division. Net income dropped from $23.6 million in 1989 to only $17.7 million in 1990 (not including income or losses from Sealed Power Technologies), mostly because of weak demand in the automotive replacement business and a major downturn in the housing industry. If 1990 was disappointing for the reorganized SPX, 1991 was disastrous. For the first time in over 50 years SPX recorded a net loss, totaling $19.4 million. Sales were down in all sectors, but continued losses in the Bear Automotive Service Equipment division were particularly worrisome.

Faced with increasing pressure to restabilize the company, Dale A. Johnson, SPX CEO since 1989, essentially reversed the restructuring that had taken place in the late 1980s. The first step in the repositioning of the company was the sale of the automotive replacement parts division to Federal-Mogul in September 1993. Then, in late 1993, the company decided to repurchase the outstanding 49 percent stake in the Sealed Power Technologies Partnership. With the reacquisition of the four divisions that had made up the partnership, in addition to the sale of SPX's door and window hardware division, SPX was firmly back into the original automotive equipment market. The restructuring itself, however, had demanded a substantial outlay, and SPX faced another substantial loss by the end of 1993. Johnson, commenting on the $40.6 million loss in a press release, maintained that "operating performance for 1993 was sharply impacted by steps taken to complete the strategy for transforming the company into a global market leader in specialty service tools and original equipment components for the motor vehicle industry."

As the new SPX emerged in 1994, its operations were tightly focused in two distinct arenas. Specialty Service Tools made up 54 percent of sales and were produced and distributed by the Automotive Diagnostics (created by the merging of Bear Automotive with the newly acquired Allen Testproducts), Dealer Equipment and Services, Kent-Moore, OTC, Power Team, and Robinair divisions of SPX. The Original Equipment Components Group, formed by the Acutex, Contech, Hy-Lift, and Sealed Power divisions, contributed 46 percent of revenues. A substantial recovery in the motor vehicle industry occurred in 1994, making SPX's re-entry into the original equipment market seem well timed. Sales surged past the $1 billion mark for the first time, registering at $1.09 billion, although net income was a fairly paltry $14.1 million.

Late 1990s and Beyond: Rapid Transformation into a Diversified Industrial Manufacturer

Midway through 1995, with the company again struggling to make a profit and in fact on its way to a net loss for the year of $5.3 million—and with the company stock price on the decline—Johnson was forced to resign from his position as chairman and CEO. Charles E. Johnson II, grandson of the company cofounder, was named interim leader (Dale A. Johnson was not related to the founding Johnson family). In December 1995 John B. Blystone was named SPX's new chairman, president, and CEO. Blystone was a longtime executive with General Electric Company with nearly 20 years of experience managing various businesses, most recently Nuovo Pignone SpA, a $2 billion conglomerate based in Florence, Italy.

Blystone had experience turning companies around, and he moved quickly to change SPX's fortunes. The company began to divest unprofitable or noncore operations and strengthen and grow the remaining core units. Among the first divestments, in a clear signal of a new era, was the company's Sealed Power Division, its founding business, which was sold to Dana Corporation in early 1997 for $223 million. Other early moves in the Blystone era were the consolidation of divisions to save costs and the elimination of 1,100 jobs by mid-1997. SPX posted a net loss of $62.3 million in 1996, but this resulted largely from the recording of unusual expenses, including a $67.8 million write-off of goodwill and $20 million in restructuring charges. The improved financial condition of the firm was evident from the operating profit of $24.6 million reported in 1996, a substantial gain over the $7.7 million figure of the preceding year.

Acquisitions, fueled by the firm's rich stock price, began to be sought to bolster the core units. During 1997 SPX acquired A.R. Brasch Marketing, producer of automotive owner's manuals and technical service and training materials, a company that fit perfectly alongside the specialty service equipment operations. In early 1998 SPX made a surprising $3 billion hostile takeover bid for Echlin Inc., a much larger auto parts supplier. SPX withdrew its bid after Dana Corporation stepped in with a richer offer. Undismayed, SPX succeeded later in 1998 with a $2.3 billion stock-and-cash takeover of General Signal Corporation, a firm with 1997 revenues of $1.95 billion, more than double the revenues of the acquirer. The acquisition, completed in October 1998, enabled SPX to substantially diversify its product portfolio beyond the automotive industry. Based in Stamford, Connecticut, General Signal was a leading maker of products for the process control, electrical control, and industrial technology industries, such as ultra-low-temperature laboratory freezers and industry valves and radio-frequency transmission equipment. Late in 1998 SPX announced a restructuring program. As part of its integration of General

Signal, SPX closed 18 manufacturing, sales, and administrative facilities and eliminated about 1,200 jobs. Substantial special charges related to the restructuring led to a net loss for the year of $41.7 million, but the company's revenues nearly doubled to $1.83 billion. Only about 14 percent of the sales were generated by the firm's founding sector, automotive parts.

SPX continued to restructure, divest selected units, and complete acquisitions in 1999. Four more facilities were closed during the year, leading to the cut of more than 600 additional jobs and a special charge of $38.4 million. Divestments included Best Power, a maker of uninterruptible power supplies that had been acquired in 1995, which was sold to London-based Invensys plc for $240 million; and the Acutex division, which produced solenoid valves and transmission products and was sold to Hilite Industries, Inc. for $27 million. In September 1999 SPX paid $86 million in cash to Rockwell International Corporation for North American Transformer, Inc., manufacturer of large power transformers. Revenues surged to $2.71 billion in 1999, while net income was a strong $101.5 million.

The story was similar in 2000 although there were no major divestitures and the company's acquisitiveness increased. Restructuring efforts led to the closure of ten manufacturing plants and sales offices, job cuts of more than 700, and $90.9 million in special charges. SPX spent about $225 million during 2000 to complete 21 acquisitions, most of which were small, strategic purchases. The largest of the bunch included Copes-Vulcan, a maker of control valves and turbine bypass systems purchased for $35 million; Pittsburgh-based Computerm Corporation, a producer of channel extension products, bought for $30 million; Fairfax, Virginia-based Varcom Corporation, a specialist in network management hardware, software, and services, acquired for $25 million; and Fenner Fluid Power, a division of Fenner plc of Yorkshire, England, specializing in medium-pressure hydraulic power system components, which was bought for $64 million. Also during 2000 SPX completed an initial public offering of 10.5 percent of class B stock in Inrange Technologies Corporation, a subsidiary specializing in the design, manufacture, marketing, and service of networking and switching products for storage, data, and telecommunications networks; it was actually Inrange that made two of the key 2000 acquisitions: Computerm and Varcom. SPX retained 100 percent of the class A stock and the remaining 89.5 percent of the class B, giving it voting power of about 98 percent. Proceeds of $128.2 million were raised through the offering. Revenues actually declined slightly for the year, to $2.68 billion—with the company feeling the impact of the midyear decline in the global economy—but net income increased 86.7 percent, totaling $189.5 million, although this figure was inflated by a $98 million gain on the issuance of Inrange stock.

In May 2001 SPX completed the acquisition of United Dominion Industries Limited in an all-stock transaction valued at about $1.9 billion, including the assumption of $876 million in debt. Based in Charlotte, North Carolina, United Dominion was a diversified manufacturer of flow technology, engineered machinery, test instruments, and other products. The firm had annual sales of about $2.4 billion. This acquisition marked a significant and further diversification of the SPX product mix. In April 2001 SPX announced that it planned to purchase VSI Holdings Inc., a Bloomfield Hills, Michigan-based provider of

integrated marketing services mainly to the automotive industry, for $197 million. SPX soon pulled out of the deal, however, leading VSI to file a class-action lawsuit on its own behalf and on behalf of the company's shareholders alleging breach of contract and requesting that the court require SPX to complete the acquisition. By early 2002 a court date for the trial had been scheduled for February 2003. Meanwhile, as the integration of United Dominion got underway, SPX announced in August 2001 that it would cut 2,000 jobs and close 49 manufacturing, sales, and administrative facilities by the end of 2002. That same month, the company announced that it would relocate its company headquarters from Muskegon to Charlotte, North Carolina. In a press release, Blystone explained the reasoning: "In choosing Charlotte, we considered total corporate costs, labor pool, access to metropolitan airports that offer better domestic and international flights, affordable housing, employment opportunities for dual income families and overall quality of life." The move was completed in early 2002.

The acquisition of United Dominion helped send SPX revenues soaring to $4.11 billion for 2001. Operating income of $420.3 million was a healthy increase over the $276.1 million figure of 2000 despite the special charges of $87.9 million taken during 2001, while net income for 2001 was $173 million. Through a continuous focus on cost-containment, efficiency, and the retention and acquisition of only those businesses with the highest value, Blystone had managed to maintain solid levels of profitability for SPX through the more uncertain economic times of the early 21st century. Since taking over leadership of the company in late 1995, Blystone had engineered both a remarkable financial turnaround and a major transformation in the mix of SPX operations, and had also laid the foundation for a bright future.

Principal Subsidiaries

A.R. Brasch Marketing Inc.; Aurora/Hydromatic Pumps Inc.; Edwards Systems Technology Inc.; Engineering Analysis Associates, Inc.; Fairbanks Morse Pump Corporation; Filtran Aftermarket Products; Fluid Technologies, Inc.; GCA International Corporation; General Farebox Service of Atlanta, Inc.; General Signal Corporation; Inrange Technologies Corporation; Kayex China Holdings, Inc.; Kodiak Partners Corp.; Kodiak Partners II Corp.; LDN, Ltd.; MF Development Corporation; Metal Forge Company, Inc.; New Signal, Inc.; The Potomac Group & Associates, Inc.; Revco Technologies, Inc.; SPX Minnesota Properties, Inc.; SPX Risk Management Co.; Toledo Trans-Kit, Inc.; United Dominion Industries Limited; Waukesha Electric Systems, Inc.; Data Switch Gmbh Elektronische Systeme Gmbh (Germany); Data Switch (UK) Limited; GCA Limited (U.K.); DeZurik International, Limited (U.K.); G.C. Evans (Holdings) Limited (U.K.); Hangzhou Kayex Zheda Electromechanical Co., Ltd (China); High Ridge Ireland Ltd.; IBS Filtran GmbH (Germany); JATEK, Limited (Japan) KK; Jurubatech (Brazil); Kent-Moore do Brasil Industria Commerce, Ltda. (Brazil); Leeds & Northrup Limited (U.K.); Lightnin Mixers Limited (U.K.); Lowener GmbH (Germany); Shenyang Stock Electric Power Equipment Company Limited (China); SPX Australia Pty., Ltd.; SPX Canada, Inc.; SPX (Europe) A.G. (Switzerland); SPX Europe GmbH (Germany); SPX France, S.A.; SPX Iberica, S.A. (Spain); SPX International, Ltd. (Barbados); SPX de Mexico S.A. de C.V.; SPX

Netherlands, B.V.; SPX (Shanghai) Trading Co. Ltd. (China); SPX Singapore PTE LTD; SPX U.K. Ltd.; Stock Japan Ltd.; Tau-Tron (UK) Limited; Tecnotest Srl (Italy); Telenex Europe Limited (U.K.); Valley Forge Technical Information Services GmbH (Germany); Ziton Limited (U.K.).

Principal Competitors

Robert Bosch Corporation; Dana Corporation; United Technologies Corporation; ABB Ltd.

Further Reading

Alexander, Dave, "Firm's Poor Showing Forces SPX Head to Quit," *Grand Rapids Press,* June 29, 1995, p. B7.

——, "Muskegon's Largest Corporation Leaving for Charlotte, N.C.," *Grand Rapids Press,* September 1, 2001, p. D3.

Blake, Laura, "SPX Sees Profit with Acquisition," *Grand Rapids Business Journal,* July 5, 1993, p. B7.

——, "Technology Keys SPX into Future," *Grand Rapids Business Journal,* December 12, 1994.

Burton, Jonathan, "The House That John Built," *Chief Executive,* May 1997, p. 24.

"Car Parts: A Replacement Bias," *New York Times,* April 15, 1985.

Deogun, Nikhil, "SPX to Buy United Dominion for $954 Million in Stock Deal," *Wall Street Journal,* March 12, 2001, p. A6.

Dorfman, Dan, "Money Follows Goldberg's Moves," *USA Today,* March 3, 1989, p. 4B.

"Greater Efficiency, New Items Spark Advance in Earnings of Sealed Power," *Barron's,* November 6, 1961, p. 21.

Lipin, Steven, "SPX Is Buying General Signal for $2 Billion," *Wall Street Journal,* July 20, 1998, p. A3.

Maher, Tani, "SPX Cannot Unseal Its Past," *Financial World,* September 6, 1988, p. 16.

Novoselick, Paul, "SPX Wins, Despite Losing Bid for Takeover," *Grand Rapids Press,* May 18, 1998, p. B4.

Sabo, Mary Ann, "SPX Looks for Come-from-Behind Win over Losses," *Grand Rapids Press,* April 24, 1997, p. A15.

"Sealed Power Corp. Extends Solid Earnings, Recovery of Final Half of Last Year," *Barron's,* March 16, 1959, p. 28.

"Sealed Power, Engine Parts Maker Revved Up for Record Earnings," *Barron's,* May 10, 1976, pp. 32, 34.

Sendler, Emily R., "SPX Agrees to Acquire General Signal in $2 Billion Deal for Stock and Cash," *Wall Street Journal,* July 21, 1998, p. A4.

——, "SPX Plans to Trim Sites, Jobs in Restructuring," *Wall Street Journal,* December 29, 1998, p. A4.

"SPX Corp. Selects Veteran of GE, Other Companies As Its New Leader," *Grand Rapids Press,* December 1, 1995, p. A17.

"SPX to Consolidate Bear, Allen Divisions," *Tire Business,* July 12, 1993, p. 5.

Turner, Mike, "The New Look of Muskegon's SPX," *Grand Rapids Business Journal,* April 17, 1989, p. B1.

Wieland, Barbara, "SPX Chief: 'The Rules Have Changed,' " *Grand Rapids Press,* November 14, 2000, p. A22.

—Hilary Gopnik
—update: David E. Salamie

Stillwater Mining Company

536 East Pike Avenue
P.O. Box 1330
Columbus, Montana 59019
U.S.A.
Telephone: (406) 322-8700
Fax: (406) 322-9985
Web site: http://www.stillwatermining.com

Public Company
Incorporated: 1992 as Stillwater Mining Co. Ltd.
Employees: 700
Sales: $277.38 million (2001)
Stock Exchanges: New York
Ticker Symbol: SWC
NAIC: 212299 All Other Metal Ore Mining

Stillwater Mining Company operates the world's only viable platinum and palladium mines outside Russia and South Africa. *Mining Magazine* describes SMC as the highest grade, lowest cost producer of platinum group metals (PGMs) in the world. PGMs include platinum, palladium, and rhodium, and are used in jewelry, dental alloys, electronic equipment, and their largest use—catalytic converters for controlling auto emissions.

Origins

The Stillwater Complex, located near the town of Nye in the Beartooth Mountains of southern Montana, has been mined for various minerals by various companies since the late 1800s. Prospectors first searched the area for gold in 1883 but nickel and copper were the first to be extracted. Chromite was first mined there in 1905; Anaconda Copper developed its Mouat chromite mine in World War II, and also mined for the strategically important mineral during the Korean War.

In 1967, Manville Products, a unit of Manville Corporation, a Denver-based provider of building products, began intensive exploration of the site and located deposits of platinum group metals (PGMs). In the next 20 years, Manville and its partners would spend $40 million exploring and developing the com-

plex. Johns Manville Corporation geologists discovered a 28-by-4-mile strip of viable PGM deposits in the early 1970s and named it the J-M Reef after their employer.

Chevron USA Inc. joined the Stillwater Mining Co. Ltd. (SMC) joint venture in 1979. Its Chevron Resources Co. unit would be the operator of the mine. Anaconda Minerals Co., a unit of Atlantic Richfield Co., joined in 1983. By 1984, the partners had agreed to spend another $45 million to open a mine on property still owned by Anaconda.

The tale was complicated by the bankruptcy of Manville Products and the decision of Atlantic Richfield Co., parent of Anaconda, to abandon metals mining altogether. Toronto-based LAC Minerals Ltd. bought Anaconda's one-third share and acquired a 5 percent net profit interest for $15 million in the autumn of 1985.

Located near Nye, Montana, Stillwater was launched as the only platinum and palladium mine in the United States. In fact, it was the only one in the world outside South Africa and the Soviet Union. As *Business Week* noted, the timing seemed perfect. Platinum and palladium were in very high demand. Western countries consumed six million ounces of the two metals every year, which were used in products as varied as jewelry, dental alloys, computer chips, and automotive catalytic converters. They were also used as a catalyst in petroleum refining and in manufacturing organic chemicals.

Prices began a steep rise in June 1985 on news of racial unrest in South Africa. Platinum was selling for about $360 an ounce in January 1986. One Manville executive quoted by *Business Week* speculated the price could hit $600 an ounce by 2000. Catalytic converters, required on new U.S. automobiles since 1975, also began to be mandated in West Germany and Australia in the late 1980s.

Opening of Stillwater Mine: 1986

Mining began in late 1986, and the mine was officially dedicated on August 14, 1987. Stillwater had 210 employees by the end of the year. Some of these came from neighboring states, whose mines were closing due to low silver prices.

Company Perspectives:

Not only are we a tremendous contributor to clean air throughout the world, but we have been good citizens during 14 years of operation in Montana. We have taken very good care of the environment where we operate. We have an impeccable record, with no environmental citations during this time. We have accomplished this because we believe preserving the quality of life in Montana is an inherent part of our responsibility to the communities in which we live and work.

Key Dates:

1967: Denver-based Manville Corp. begins looking for platinum in Montana's Beartooth Mountains.
1979: Chevron joins Manville in Stillwater Mining (SMC) joint venture.
1983: Anaconda Minerals joins SMC.
1985: LAC Minerals buys Anaconda's share.
1985: Platinum mining begins at Stillwater.
1994: SMC launches IPO on NASDAQ.
1995: Manville sells its remaining interest in SMC.
1998: Unprecedented "Good Neighbor Agreement" signed.
2001: SMC migrates from the American to the New York Stock Exchange.

Stillwater was expected to become fully operational in 1992 and produce 150,000 ounces of palladium and 50,000 ounces of platinum a year, together worth $30 million in 1986 prices. The Stillwater Mine was not the world's largest, but the PGM deposits found there were relatively accessible. There was a high ratio of palladium to platinum. Stillwater was only geared to produce 1 percent of the Western world's platinum supply, but accounted for more than 3 percent of the palladium market.

Stillwater had higher labor costs per miner than its counterparts in Russia and South Africa. Other costs included civic contributions to fund infrastructure and schools in local communities and the cost of environmental compliance in an area that was considered a pristine wilderness. SMC filed a $1.2 million reclamation bond with the state, later increased to $4.2 million; the mine was projected to be in operation for 20 to 30 years. SMC produced 6.3 tons (203,000 ounces) of platinum and palladium in 1989, 3.4 ounces of palladium for every one ounce of platinum. SMC had about 450 employees, three of them based at its Denver headquarters.

A number of important changes had occurred by this time. A new $6.8 million smelter was under construction 40 miles away in Columbus, Montana. Manville Corp. had become half owner in Stillwater, and the company was considering selling its interest in the mine.

Public in 1994

In September 1994, Manville Corporation had funded the placement of Chevron's 50 percent stake in SMC with private investors after Chevron decided to exit the mining business. Stillwater Mining Co. Ltd. then made an initial public offering on the NASDAQ exchange in December 1994. SMC aimed to take proceeds from the IPO to incorporate radical changes in mining methods and double production by mid-1997. The smelter product was then being sent to Metallurgie Hoboken Overpelt for removal of copper and nickel. The IPO raised about $54 million and reduced Manville's holding in SMC to 31 percent.

A new management team was installed as SMC underwent a restructuring. The investors were rewarded handsomely and quickly as platinum and palladium prices rose. SMC, which had by then spent $100 million to develop the mine, had not turned a profit since 1990 and lost $5.63 million on revenues of $53.8 million in 1993. In 1994, though, the company posted net income of $2 million on sales of $58.6 million. The share price, initially $13, doubled in eight months.

Manville Mining Co. sold its interest in SMC in August 1995, making SMC an independent company. Johns Manville Corporation still held a 5 percent royalty in the mine, which it sold to the Franco-Nevada Mining Corporation for $36 million in March 1998.

Platinum prices reached $400 an ounce in 1997. The palladium market was also tightening. The mine produced 271,000 ounces of palladium and 84,000 ounces of platinum in 1997, from 520,000 tons of ore. SWC moved its stock listing to the AMEX exchange during the year.

William E. Nettles was brought in to help turn the company around and appointed chairman and CEO in August 1997. The company's hedging policy (agreeing to sell future production at fixed prices) had prevented it from capitalizing on the upturn in PGM prices. After the changeover in management, the company made it a policy to hedge no more than 50 percent of production for no more than two years ahead, a strategy designed to placate investors seeking to take advantage of the "upside" of higher prices. Only 15 percent of the company's metals production would be sold forward in 2000.

By 1998, SWC was developing its East Boulder platinum mine in Montana's Absaroka Mountains. This was expected to cost $270 million. Two other expansion projects were in the works: expanding the Stillwater mine at a cost of $75 million and expanding the smelter and base metals refinery in Columbus, Montana. SMC lowered its palladium and platinum production costs to a record $147 per ounce in the second quarter of 1998, while producing a record 120,000 ounces. A fall in the price of gold made PGM mining that much more attractive to investors.

"Good Neighbor" in 1998

SMC and local citizens groups signed an unprecedented contract in August 1998. The "Good Neighbor Agreement" set out environmental and community protections beyond those required by law and aimed to head off the years of legislative and legal wrangling commonly associated with the impact of mining on communities.

Frank McAllister, formerly chairman and CEO of copper producer ASARCO Incorporated, took those roles at SMC in

February 2001 upon the retirement of William Nettles. Driven by demand from automakers, the price of palladium had reached $1,100 an ounce. Platinum had peaked at $625 an ounce the previous December. However, prices fell sharply during the year. In November, palladium was only selling for $320 an ounce. New sources of PGMs were being developed in Canada, the United States, and Zimbabwe.

As a result of the plunge in PGM prices, SMC scaled back plans for its East Boulder underground mine, halving its planned ore production rate to 900 tons a day. The company also terminated 500 contract employees and 30 of its own employees at the East Boulder mine. Rumors of a takeover (perhaps by other mining companies, including Lonmin plc or Impala Platinum Holdings Ltd.) abounded throughout 2000 and 2001.

SMC posted net income of $65.8 million on revenue of $277.4 million in 2001, both figures up from the previous year. The company produced a record 504,000 ounces of palladium and platinum. SMC had left the American Stock Exchange to trade on the New York Stock Exchange in June 2001 and had relocated its headquarters from Denver to Columbus, Montana.

Principal Operating Units

East Boulder Mine; Stillwater Mine.

Principal Competitors

Impala Platinum Holdings Ltd.; Lonmin plc; JSC MMC "Norilsk Nickel"; Northam Platinum Ltd.

Further Reading

Accola, John, "Sinking Money into Mine Pays Off; Early Investors See Shares' Value Double As Stillwater Digs Up Platinum, Palladium," *Denver Rocky Mountain News,* Bus. Sec., August 6, 1995.

Atchison, Sandra D., "Platinum: The Birth of an American Industry; The World's Only Mine Outside South Africa and the Soviet Union Is Opening in Montana," *Business Week,* January 27, 1986, pp. 64, 69.

Carey, David, "Stillwater Investor Lines Up Forces," *Daily Deal,* M&A Sec., November 2, 2001.

Carlyle, W. Matthew, and B. Curtis Eaves, "Underground Planning at Stillwater Mining Company," *Interfaces,* July/August 2001, pp. 50–60.

Chadwick, John, "Stillwater Doubling Output," *Mining Magazine,* November 1999, p. 290.

——, "Stillwater Expands," *Mining Magazine,* January 1996, p. 10.

Cothran, Tom, "In Big Sky Country," *Occupational Health & Safety,* October 1999, pp. 98–102.

Dayton, Stanley, "SMC Profiles the PGM Potential of Stillwater," *Engineering and Mining Journal,* July 1984, p. 9.

"Developments at Stillwater Pt/Pd Mine, Montana," *Mining Magazine,* June 1990, p. 400.

Draper, Heather, "McAllister Heads Up Stillwater As Mining Firm Is Poised to Soar," *Rocky Mountain News* (Denver), February 14, 2001, p. 2B.

Dyas, Keith, and Jerry Marcus, "Stillwater; Plans to Triple PGM Production by 2003," *Engineering & Mining Journal,* December 1998, pp. 20+.

Gallagher, Susan, "Western Mines Face a Host of Legislative, Economic Challenges," Associated Press, April 20, 1993.

Gooding, Kenneth, "Radical Changes for Stillwater—The Platinum Group Could Double Production," *Financial Times* (London), Intl. Co. News, December 5, 1994, p. 19.

Guerriere, Alison M., "Stillwater's Union Stirred Up As Cuts, Questions Proliferate," *American Metal Market,* December 13, 2001, pp. 1+.

Kennedy, Alan, "Stillwater Platinum-Palladium Mine," *Mining Magazine,* November 1987, p. 418.

Kramer, Becky, "Montana Mining Company Seeks Skilled Workers in Idaho," *Spokesman-Review,* June 29, 2001.

Lucchetti, Aaron, "Stillwater Mining's Hedging Policy for Metals Has Hurt Stock and Perhaps Profit This Year," *Wall Street Journal,* November 10, 1997, p. C2.

Marcial, Gene, "Stillwater Mining: Digging Its Way into a Buyout?" *Business Week Online,* Inside Wall Street Online, October 17, 2000.

"Marketing Stillwater PGMs," *Engineering and Mining Journal,* December 1998, p. 24.

McGuane, Thomas, "Extracting the Soul of a Western Town," *New York Times,* August 1, 1998, p. A13.

"Mining Platinum in Montana," *New York Times,* August 13, 1998, p. A22.

"Montana," *Engineering and Mining Journal,* October 1998, p. 38.

O'Connor, Gillian, "Glittering Prizes Made of Platinum: Gold Is Losing Its Lustre As Mining Groups Find Better Margins and Profits Elsewhere," *Financial Times* (London), Commodities & Agriculture, June 10, 1999, p. 42.

"A Promising Accord in Montana," *New York Times,* May 17, 2000, p. A22.

Schaffler, Rhonda, and Michael Holland, "Gold Producer Stillwater Mining Transfers to NYSE, Leaves AMEX," *Market Call,* CNNfn, June 26, 2001.

"Smoking the 'Peace Pipe' in Montana," *Engineering & Mining Journal,* August 2000, pp. 15+.

"Stillwater Float," *Mining Journal,* December 9, 1994, p. 417.

"Stillwater Gets an Early Start on Palladium-Platinum Mining," *Engineering and Mining Journal,* May 1987, p. 15.

"Stillwater: Getting to Grips with Its Potential," *Mining Journal,* November 10, 1995, p. 346.

"Stillwater PGM Output Rising, Expansion Lagging," *Metals Week,* Precious Metals Sec., December 20, 1999, p. 2.

"Stillwater Scales Back," *Mining Journal,* November 16, 2001, p. 375.

"Stillwater to Accelerate Expansion," *Mining Journal,* October 9, 1998, p. 272.

"Stillwater's Mine Runs Deep," *Business Week,* June 12, 1995, p. 82.

"Stillwater's PGM Expansion," *Mining Journal,* May 22, 1998, p. 393.

"Stillwater's President Leaves; Board Member to Be in Charge," *American Metal Market,* December 19, 2001, p. 4.

Todd, Joan C., "Stillwater Cleared to Develop Mine-Mill Complex," *Engineering and Mining Journal,* February 1986, p. 17.

——, "Stillwater Developers to Begin Construction of Mine Support Works," *Engineering and Mining Journal,* October 1986, p. 22.

Wheeler, Dennis, "Palladium: Metal of the Year," *On Wall Street,* January 1, 1998.

——, "Russia Crumbles; Platinum Soars," *On Wall Street,* April 1, 1997.

White, Lane, "Planning and Hard Work Drive Stillwater Mining's Growth," *Engineering & Mining Journal,* June 2001.

——, "Stillwater Adds a New Source to World Platinum Supplies," *Engineering and Mining Journal,* October 1987, p. 38.

Williamson, Richard, "Shining Future; Precious Metals Platinum and Palladium See Increasing Demand by Industry," *Denver Rocky Mountain News,* August 2, 1998, p. 2G.

Wroughton, Lesley, "Price Brightens Platinum Outlook," *Toronto Star,* Bus. Sec., May 15, 2001.

—Frederick C. Ingram

Taiwan Semiconductor Manufacturing Company Ltd.

121 Park Avenue III
Science-Based Industrial Park
Hsinchu 300
Taiwan
Telephone: +886-3-578-0221
Fax: +886-3-578-1546
Web site: http://www.tsmc.com.tw

Public Company
Incorporated: 1987
Employees: 14,500
Sales: $3.69 billion (2001)
Stock Exchanges: Taiwan New York
Ticker Symbol: TSM
NAIC: 334413 Semiconductor and Related Device
   Manufacturing

When Taiwan Semiconductor Manufacturing Company Ltd. (TSMC) was founded in 1987, it was a novel concept to have a dedicated foundry that produced microchips for other semiconductor companies. At the time, chips typically were produced in-house by giant integrated device manufacturers (IMDs) such as Intel Corp. and NEC Corp. When those companies had excess production capacity, they produced chips for other semiconductor design houses. With the advent of dedicated semiconductor foundries to supply design houses, TSMC and other foundries have paved the way for the development of fabless semiconductor companies that are strong on design but cannot afford the investment required for fabrication facilities.

Transforming Taiwan's
Semiconductor Industry: 1987–92

Taiwan Semiconductor Manufacturing Company Ltd. (TSMC) was formed in 1987 as a joint venture between the Taiwan government, which wanted to promote the development of the island's semiconductor industry, and Philips Electronics NV of The Netherlands. The company was set up by Morris Chang, who had been invited by the Taiwan government in 1985 to come to the island and help grow its semiconductor industry. Chang was born in China and educated at the Massachusetts Institute of Technology (MIT) and Stanford, where he earned a doctorate in electrical engineering. He was the president of General Instrument Corp. when he left to go to Taiwan.

When TSMC was founded in 1987, it was a major catalyst in transforming Taiwan's semiconductor industry. It provided state-of-the-art manufacturing processes that complemented Taiwan's strength in chip design. Between 1987 and 1992 TSMC gradually added to its foundry capacity by vertically integrating into related disciplines, including wafer sort testing in 1988, mask-making in 1990, and design services utilizing technology licensed from VLSI Technology in 1991. It also improved its process technology. After starting as a six-inch, 2-micron wafer-processing fabrication facility, or fab, it broke the 1-micron barrier in 1991.

TSMC originally was intended to service Taiwan's design houses, which were noted for their chip designs but did not want to get involved in manufacturing processes. TSMC, however, soon became an internationally oriented, profit-driven organization that supported the development of fabless semiconductor companies, that is, that did not own their own manufacturing facilities. Fabless semiconductor companies were strong on design, but they could not afford the large investment required to build their own fabrication facilities.

By 1992 TSMC was rated as the world's top silicon foundry, producing chips for other companies. TSMC employed 250 process engineers and was on the cutting edge of process technology. TSMC accounted for 80 percent of Taiwan's production of SRAM and also produced a variety of other semiconductor chips, including DRAM and EPROM. Revenue for 1992 was around $245 million.

Building New Facilities to
Expand Capacity: 1994–96

By 1994 demand for chips was exploding with new applications in multimedia and portable computing. At the beginning of the year TSMC announced plans to build a new eight-inch wafer fabrication facility, or fab, that would double the company's output to more than $1 billion worth of product a year. The new plant was the company's third fabrication facility and cost about $800 million to build. At the time TSMC was running several different processes for both logic and memory chips, and the company was running out of capacity.

In September 1994 TSMC went public on the Taiwan Stock Exchange. Before the end of the year TSMC announced an agreement with Advanced Micro Devices Inc. (AMD) to pro-vide foundry services for AMD's AM486 processors. For 1994 TSMC reported sales of $744 million and net income of $325 million. A 60 percent increase of worldwide semiconductor sales between 1992 and 1994 resulted in a global shortage of wafer fabrication capacity. About 60 percent of TSMC's sales were to fabless semiconductor companies, with the remaining 40 percent going to companies short of manufacturing capacity. TSMC's gross margin of 49 percent was the highest in the semiconductor industry.

In March 1995 TSMC announced that it would build another eight-inch wafer fab at a cost of $1.2 billion. The new plant, TSMC's fourth fab, was designed to operate at 0.4-micron initially and later at 0.25-micron, which was about one genera-tion ahead of the eight-inch 0.5- to 0.35-micron plants proposed by other Taiwan semiconductor manufacturers. Construction on the new eight-inch fab began in November 1995. Some of the funding for the plant came from deposits that customers made to ensure long-term fab capacity, an option that TSMC began offering to customers in mid-1995.

Between 1993 and 1995 TSMC nearly doubled its capacity to produce six-inch (150mm) wafers, from 665,000 wafers in 1993 to 1.2 million in 1995. Its six-inch fabs, including Fab 1, Fab 2A, and Fab 2B, were running at full capacity, producing 100,000 wafers per month. Fab 3, which produced eight-inch wafers, was expected to ramp to full capacity of 22,000 wafers per month in 1997 and 35,000 per month in 1998. Fab 4 was expected to come online in 1997 and ramp to full capacity of 25,000 eight-inch wafers per month in 1998. The construction of Fab 5 in Hsinchu was announced before the end of 1995.

In November 1995 TSMC and Altera Corp. announced a joint venture to build a wafer fabrication plant in the United States. After considering sites in Oregon and British Columbia, TSMC selected Camas, Washington, for the $1.2 billion plant. The plant would have the capacity of producing 30,000 eight-inch wafers per month, starting with line geometries of 0.35-micron and then migrating to 0.25-micron. By mid-1996 TSMC had signed on two more joint venture partners for the plant, to be called WaferTech; they were Analog Devices and Integrated Silicon Solutions Inc. (ISSI). Altera's $140 million investment gave it 18 percent ownership of WaferTech. Analog Devices

also owned 18 percent, ISSI owned 4 percent, private investors owned 3 percent, and TSMC owned 57 percent.

At the end of April 1996 TSMC became the first Taiwanese company to be listed on the New York Stock Exchange when it raised more than $500 million through the sale of 305 million ADR (American depository receipt) shares. At the time Philips Electronics owned about 35 percent of TSMC. For 1996 TSMC reported sales of $1.45 billion and net income of $718.5 million.

Facing Challenges in 1997

TSMC began 1997 anticipating a sales decline and a 50 percent drop in profits. The company announced it would cut prices due to excess capacity and fierce competition. United Microelectronics Corp. (UMC) of Taiwan recently had replaced longtime competitor Chartered Semiconductor Manufacturing Pte. Ltd. of Singapore as TSMC's primary rival by forming three independent foundry ventures in the past 18 months with several North American design houses. UMC also was aggres-sively cutting its prices. In March 1997 Donald Brooks, who had been TSMC's president since 1991, resigned and was replaced by TSMC Chairman Morris Chang. Brooks subse-quently joined TSMC rival United Microelectronics as presi-dent of its new International Operation unit, based in Sunny-vale, California.

Around this time TSMC announced an ambitious, ten-year expansion program that called for an investment of $14.5 billion in the construction of six eight-inch and 12-inch (300mm) fabrication facilities as well as other facilities. The company also announced a long-term commitment with the local Tainan government to establish a new Science-Based Industrial Park in Tainan in the southern portion of Taiwan. TSMC planned to construct Fab 6 there at a cost of $1.4 billion, starting in mid-1997. As the company had announced before, it had run out of space to expand at Hsinchu.

By mid-1997 TSMC was fully booked for the remainder of the year. It was experiencing strong demand from customers in the PC, consumer electronics, and communication IC (inte-grated circuit) sectors. It also was ramping up production for Japan's Fujitsu Ltd. as part of a deal signed in 1996.

In spite of the downturn in semiconductor demand in 1996, TSMC continued to be generous with its employees. Employees who worked for TSMC in 1996 received an employee-dividend distribution worth more than $100,000 per employee. TSMC transferred some 100 million shares of stock to the more than 4,000 employees who worked for the company in 1996. At the time TSMC stock was trading between $5 and $6 a share. For 1997 TSMC reported revenue of $1.37 billion as it continued to be the leader in the semiconductor foundry industry.

Semiconductor Sales Down in 1998

Although the forecast for 1998 called for sluggish growth in the global semiconductor industry, TSMC was fully booked for the first quarter and announced that it would increase its eight-inch wafer production by 40 percent to 1.67 million units for the year. The company planned to ramp up production at two eight-inch fabs and begin construction on several more plants, includ-

Key Dates:

Key Dates:

1987: Taiwan Semiconductor Manufacturing Company Ltd. (TSMC) is formed as a joint venture between the Taiwan government and Philips Electronics NV.
1994: TSMC becomes a public company.
1996: TSMC and joint venture partners begin construction of a wafer fabrication plant in Camas, Washington, called WaferTech.
1999: TSMC acquires a 33 percent interest in Acer Semiconductor Manufacturing, Inc.
2000: TSMC completes acquisition of Acer, acquires Worldwide Semiconductor Manufacturing Co. for $550 million, and takes control of WaferTech.

ing two at Taiwan's new scientific industrial park at Tainan. WaferTech was scheduled to begin production mid-year.

In the first quarter of 1998 TSMC entered into a licensing agreement with intellectual property (IP) vendor Artisan Components of San Jose, California. Under the agreement, TSMC would license Artisan's intellectual property and offer it directly to its foundry customers exclusively. The IP that Artisan would create for TSMC included memories, standard cells, and I/O (input/output) for its 0.25-micron process technology. The arrangements reflected the value of having foundry-ready IP available to customers to put into their own designs. TSMC began making Artisan's IP library available to its foundry customers in the second half of the year.

By mid-1998 the semiconductor manufacturing industry was experiencing considerable weakness, with an erosion in both prices and demand. TSMC was operating at 80 percent capacity after starting the year at full capacity. As a result, the company announced that it would cut its capital spending budget for 1998 from $1.3 billion to $920 million and projected that it would spend $800–$900 million in 1999. The company named a new president, F.C. Tseng, and announced plans to offer a copper-metallization process and move to 0.18-micron process technology in 1999. According to *Electronic Engineering Times,* TSMC was pushing its process technology at a rate that appeared to match its larger rivals, including Intel Corp., IBM, and NEC Corp.

Following its successful strategy of building for the future, TSMC entered into an agreement with Philips Electronics and EDB Investment of Singapore to build a $1.2 billion, joint venture fabrication facility in Singapore's Pasir Ris Wafer Fab Park in 1999.

The company realigned its international management team in October 1998. Ron Norris, president of TSMC's U.S. subsidiary based in San Jose, was promoted to senior vice-president of worldwide sales and marketing and relocated to the company's headquarters in Taiwan. Magnus Ryde, formerly vice-president of worldwide field operations at semiconductor manufacturing equipment maker KLA-Tencor Corp., was named the new president of TSMC-USA.

For 1998 TSMC's revenue reached $1.56 billion, a 14.6 percent increase over 1997. Profits declined, however, from $559.5 million in 1997 to $477.9 million in 1998.

Continuing to Seek Additional Capacity in 1999

TSMC's capital spending plans went through several revisions in 1999. Although sales declined in the second half of 1998, the company expected that results for 1999 would improve. With strong demand for its 0.25-micron wafers, TSMC's first quarter was significantly better than the first quarter of 1998. In February the company announced an agreement with Motorola, which was in the process of outsourcing up to 35 percent of its semiconductor production. Under the agreement TSMC would use Motorola's 0.25-micron and 0.35-micron CMOS logic processes, which typically were used for making microcontrollers, while Motorola would gain access to TSMC's technology at similar micron levels.

With TSMC making progress on 0.18-micron process technology, the company raised its capital spending budget for 1999 to $1.26 billion. The increase was intended to support the ramp-up of 0.18-micron capacity in Taiwan and later in the year at WaferTech. The company also was moving forward with copper-interconnect technology and planned to begin volume production in 2000. With orders for semiconductor capital equipment accelerating, the semiconductor foundry industry was again pursuing additional capacity. TSMC and its affiliate Vanguard International Semiconductor Corp. formed a $2 billion joint venture to build Taiwan's first 300mm-wafer fab. Construction began in 2000, with volume production slated for 2002.

In June TSMC invested $170 million in Acer Semiconductor Manufacturing Inc. (ASMI), about 30 percent of the company's shares. ASMI, a subsidiary of Taiwan computer company Acer Inc., manufactured chips in its foundry for IBM Microelectronics and Fujitsu Ltd. As part of its investment in ASMI, TSMC would provide its full support to transform ASMI into a dedicated foundry. TSMC also would manage the newly formed corporation, renamed TSMC-Acer Semiconductor Corp., with TSMC President F.C. Tseng as TSMC-Acer's chairman.

TSMC's sales and income in the second quarter of 1999 were the best it ever had, and sales in July 1999 were more than double those of July 1998. While the company was considering building a fabrication facility in Europe, it was concentrating its capacity-building efforts on its joint venture fab with Philips in Singapore and converting Acer into a dedicated foundry.

In September 1999 Taiwan suffered an earthquake that was the largest in the island's history. Following the quake TSMC issued status reports to its customers and formed a special task force to keep its customers informed of the status of their orders. The company also donated $7 million to relief efforts. Power on the island was fully restored within a week and almost all of the island's fabs were fully operational. After the recovery TSMC was functioning at 90 percent capacity.

As 1999 drew to a close, TSMC was experiencing wafer demand about 80 percent higher than in 1998. For 2000 the company predicted greater demand than supply and would be hard pressed to maintain its goal to have 10 percent more capacity than demand. With TSMC experiencing strong demand throughout 1999, the company reported sales of $2.35 billion and net income of $792 million. The firm's profit margin was about 33 percent.

Acquisitions Boosting Capacity in 2000

Just before the end of 1999 TSMC broke ground on the construction of its first 300mm-wafer processing plant, called Fab 12, in Taiwan. Fab 12 was scheduled to begin production in 2002. The company was planning to invest $2 billion in Fab 12, which would serve both as a fabrication base and a leading-edge research and development center.

In January 2000 TSMC completed its acquisition of TSMC-Acer, paying about $90 million for the remaining 70 percent interest in the company. The purchase gave TSMC access to more than 40,000 wafers per month of production. In the same month TSMC acquired Worldwide Semiconductor Manufacturing Co. (WSMC) for $550 million in stock. Established in 1996, WSMC was Taiwan's third largest foundry. It operated one eight-inch fab using 0.25-micron and 0.18-micron process technologies and had a second eight-inch wafer fab that would begin production in March 2000. TSMC estimated that the acquisition of TSMC-Acer and WSMC would result in an increase in production from 2.8 million eight-inch wafers to 3.4 million in 2000.

Through alliances with more than 40 library, semiconductor intellectual property, and design service companies, TSMC was able to offer a wide array of services directly to system-on-a-chip (SOC) designers. The company created a common Design-Service-Alliance umbrella to offer original equipment manufacturers (OEMs) and integrated device manufacturers (IDMs) end-to-end solutions at a lower cost than could be achieved by internal design teams or other partners. At the time IDMs accounted for 27 percent of TSMC's revenue, and OEMs accounted for just 3 percent.

At the end of March 2000 TSMC formally opened its Fab 6 in Tainan's Science-Based Industrial Park. It was the first of six fabs TSMC planned to build there and was part of a $4.4 billion capacity expansion program that would help double TSMC's sales in 2000. Fab 6 was TSMC's last eight-inch wafer facility; subsequent fabs would use 12-inch wafers.

In the second half of 2000 TSMC entered into a licensing agreement with National Semiconductor Corp. of Santa Clara, California. The deal marked the first time that a pure-play foundry licensed its process technology to a major integrated device manufacturer (IDM). Under the licensing agreement National would implement TSMC's technology at its South Portland, Maine fabrication plant only.

TSMC also completed its mergers with TSMC-Acer Semiconductor Manufacturing Co. and Worldwide Semiconductor Manufacturing Co., giving it a workforce of more than 13,000 employees. Once the company realized its customers required substantially increased capacity, TSMC moved quickly to support that demand. After reporting record sales of $2.1 billion for the first half of 2000, TSMC announced that its foundry capacity was fully booked through the end of 2001. For the year 2000 TSMC reported revenue of $5.3 billion, up 131 percent over 1999 sales, and profits of $1.9 billion.

Before the end of 2000 TSMC's joint venture fab in Singapore with Philips Electronics began producing its first silicon. The two companies also strengthened their alliance, with Philips acquiring $420 million worth of TSMC's preferred stock. In addition, the two companies renewed their cross-licensing agreements. In November TSMC announced that it would take full control of WaferTech in Camas, Washington, by buying out its joint venture partners there at a cost not to exceed $500 million. TSMC also continued to improve its process technology, developing a 0.13-micron test chip before the end of the year and becoming the first silicon foundry to begin shipping 300mm wafers. The 300mm wafers were produced at Fab 6 in Tainan, Taiwan.

Surplus of Global Capacity: 2001

During the first quarter of 2001 TSMC reduced its capital spending budget a couple of times, finally setting it at $2.1 billion for the year. Principal rival United Microelectronics Corp. also cut its capital expenditures for 2001 to $1.5 billion, down from $2.8 billion in 2000. TSMC cited lower demand for processed wafers in lowering its budget. During the first quarter TSMC was running at 70 percent of capacity, and in April the company announced that it would cut its production output to 50 percent of capacity. By mid-year both TSMC and UMC were running at about 45 percent of capacity, and TSMC announced that it would delay construction of two 300mm fabs that it had planned to build in 2001.

While production was down, TSMC continued with its efforts to improve its process technology. It appointed its first chief technology officer, Dr. Chenming Hu, a well-known scientist in the field of semiconductors. In August the first 300mm wafers for customers were produced at TSMC's Fab 12. The company also made some executive management changes, promoting Dr. F.C. Tseng to deputy chief executive officer and naming Dr. Rick Tsai as president and chief operating officer. Dr. Morris Chang remained the company's chairman and CEO.

The outlook for semiconductor demand began to improve in the fourth quarter of 2001, and TSMC announced plans to spend $20.2 billion to build six silicon wafer plants in Taiwan. With sales up in the fourth quarter, the company was running at nearly 50 percent of capacity, compared with 41 percent during the third quarter. For the year 2001 TSMC had sales of $3.6 billion, a decline of 24 percent over 2000, and profits of $378 million. For 2002 TSMC expected the momentum to continue, with utilization rates for the first quarter around 60 percent.

Principal Subsidiaries

TSMC North America; System on Silicon Manufacturing Co. Pte. Ltd. (Singapore; 50%); Vanguard International Semiconductor Corp. (Taiwan; 25%).

Principal Competitors

Advanced Semiconductor Manufacturing Corp.; Chartered Semiconductor Manufacturing Pte. Ltd.; Intel Corp.; NEC Corp.; Newport Wafer Fabrication Ltd.; Tower Semiconductor Ltd.; United Microelectronics Corp.

Further Reading

Arensman, Russ, and Brent Hannon, "Fortunate Fabs," *Electronic Business,* November 1999, p. 84.

Ascierto, Jerry, "TSMC to Buy 30% of Acer Fab," *Electronic News (1991),* June 14, 1999, p. 22.

"Betting Big on Chips," *Business Week,* April 30, 2001, p. 54.

Carroll, Mark, "Armed with 0.18-Micron Processes, TSMC and UMC Vow to Pick Up Pace in 2000," *Electronic Engineering Times,* December 6, 1999, p. 30.

——, "Brooks Assesses Taiwan at Close of TSMC Stint," *Electronic Engineering Times,* April 28, 1997, p. 30.

——, "Seeks to Complete Turnaround to Pure-Play Foundry—TSMC Buys Out Acer IC Fab," *Electronic Engineering Times,* January 10, 2000, p. 37.

——, "TSMC Buys WSMC, Pushing Foundry Consolidation," *Electronic Engineering Times,* January 10, 2000, p. 4.

Carroll, Mark, and Peter Clarke, "TSMC Boosts Capital Spending, Considers Euro Fab," *Electronic Engineering Times,* August 16, 1999, p. 33.

Carroll, Mark, et al., "United Microelectronics, TSMC and Chartered Try to Catch Process-Technology Leaders," *Electronic Engineering Times,* March 22, 1999, p. 14.

Chappell, Jeff, "TSMC Forming Alliances," *Electronic News (1991),* March 27, 2000, p. 30.

Chen, Sandy, "Acer Gives Control of Foundry to Rival TSMC," *Electronic Buyers' News,* July 19, 1999, p. 10.

——, "Morris Chang: Writing New Chapters in Industry, and in Transformation of Taiwan," *Electronic Buyers' News,* December 21, 1998, p. 46.

——, "TSMC Gets New President," *Electronic Buyers' News,* May 18, 1998, p. 6.

Clendenin, Mike, "After Big Sales Drops, TSMC's Up, UMC Off," *Electronic Engineering Times,* January 14, 2002, p. 4.

Cohen, Sarah, "Washington Fab Venture Lures 2 More," *Electronic News (1991),* July 1, 1996, p. 6.

Dorsch, Jeff, "Chip Recovery: It's for Real," *Electronic News (1991),* May 24, 1999, p. 1.

"Fast Chips, Faster Cleanup," *Business Week,* October 11, 1999, p. 129.

"First Taiwanese Company," *Television Digest,* April 29, 1996, p. 21.

"Foundry Formula Keeps the Profits Rolling on In," *Electronics Weekly,* January 19, 1994, p. 12.

Hachman, Mark, and Mark LaPedus, "Chip Suppliers Pressure Foundries to Expand," *Electronic Buyers' News,* October 25, 1999, p. 1.

Hardie, Christine, "Altera Deepens Ties with TSMC," *Electronic News (1991),* November 27, 1995, p. 4.

——, "Taiwan Semi Chooses Camas for U.S. Fab with $1.2B Tag," *Electronic News (1991),* March 18, 1996, p. 1.

——, "TSMC Eyes $14B Expansion," *Electronic News (1991),* April 14, 1997, p. 1.

Huang, Charlene, "TSMC Expedites Second 8-inch Wafer Fab," *Electronics,* March 13, 1995, p. 7.

Hung, Faith, "TSMC Becomes First Foundry to Process 300-mm Wafers," *Electronic Buyers' News,* November 20, 2000, p. 10.

——, "TSMC to Gain Full Control of WaferTech," *Electronic Buyers' News,* November 13, 2000, p. 14.

——, "TSMC to Sell $420M in Shares to Philips," *Electronic Buyers' News,* September 11, 2000, p. 10.

Lammers, David, "Fab 6 Puts TSMC in Running As Biggest Producer," *Electronic Engineering Times,* April 3, 2000, p. 18.

——, "Steps Up Capital Expenditures to Support Fabs in Taiwan, Washington State," *Electronic Engineering Times,* May 17, 1999, p. 4.

LaPedus, Mark, and Mark Hachman, "Taiwan Foundries Adopt New Look," *Electronic Buyers' News,* December 14, 1998, p. 1.

LaPedus, Mark, and Sandy Chen, "The Wafer Chase," *Electronic Buyers' News,* December 7, 1998, p. 48.

McLeod, Jonah, "U.S., Asian Chip Firms Solve Each Other's Problems," *Industry Week,* June 19, 1995, p. 65.

Morrison, Gale, "National Licensing TSMC Processes," *Electronic News (1991),* July 3, 2000, p. 10.

Murphy, Tom, "TSMC Starts 12-inch Fab Construction," *Electronic News (1991),* December 20, 1999, p. 1.

Ojo, Bolaji, "TSMC Seeks to Double Revenue in Europe," *Electronic Buyers' News,* August 2, 1999, p. 18.

"Profits Soar, But Not TSMC Stock," *Electronic Engineering Times,* August 7, 2000, p. 22.

Ristelhueber, Robert, "TSMC Using 0.18-Micron Process," *Electronic News (1991),* May 17, 1999, p. 4.

Robertson, Jack, and Robin Lamb, "Fabs Fall Victim to Capex Cuts As Demand Wanes," *EBN,* June 4, 2001, p. 3.

Siekman, Philip, "Taiwan Goes After the World's Chip Business," *Fortune,* May 14, 2001.

Souza, Crista, "TSMC Providing Single End-to-End Design Solution," *Electronic Buyers' News,* March 27, 2000, p. 48.

Tanzer, Andrew, "Silicon In, Cash Out," *Forbes,* March 13, 1995, p. 54.

Wade, Will, "TSMC Delivers First 300-mm ICs As Overcapacity Fears Grow," *Electronic Engineering Times,* December 22, 2000, p. 41.

—David P. Bianco

Takashimaya Company, Limited

1-5 Namba, 5-chome
Chuo-ku
Osaka 542-8510
Japan
Telephone: (6) 6631-1101
Fax: (6) 6631-9850
Web site: http://www.takashimaya.co.jp

Public Company
Incorporated: 1920 as Takashimaya Gofuku Store Co.,
  Ltd.
Employees: 10,070
Sales: ¥1.16 trillion ($9.94 billion) (2001)
Stock Exchanges: Tokyo Osaka
NAIC: 452110 Department Stores; 454110 Mail-Order
  Houses

Takashimaya Company, Limited is the oldest and one of the largest department store retailers in Japan. The company operates in three main segments: Department Store Business Operations, Affiliated Business Operations (which includes the Contract & Design, Corporate Customer Sales, and Direct Marketing divisions), and Group Affiliates' Operations (which encompasses the activities of the company's more than 85 domestic and overseas affiliates). Takashimaya's affiliates are involved in real estate, construction, wholesaling, and restaurant management.

1800s: Early Growth, International Trade

Takashimaya began in 1831. Like a number of Japan's leading department store retailers, the company originated as a small, specialty retailer of kimono, with the founder, Shinshichi Iida, opening the first store in Kyoto at the age of 27. The store had a sales space of only 3.6 square meters and specialized in Japanese formal wear—*gofuku*—supplying both kimono and related accessories. At the time, Japan was in the final 30 years of the feudal Edo period, and its economy was weak and in some confusion. In order to build a successful business, Iida laid

down four principles, which Takashimaya's management maintains to this day: high-quality goods, fair prices, honesty in sales, and care and courtesy to all customers.

In 1855 the store was expanded to include more cotton goods and a wider range of formal wear accessories. At this time the company employed 21 people. Japan was finally opened to Western influence in 1867 with the restoration of the Meiji Emperor, and Takashimaya began to stock a wider range of goods, including many household products. In 1876 links were formed with U.S. businesses that had come to Japan with the opening of the feudal society, and the company began to import goods from abroad, even targeting the small but growing foreign community in Kyoto. Toward the end of the 1880s Takashimaya moved to expand its overseas trading. Dealing chiefly in fabrics, the company began to export to Europe, with considerable success. Around the turn of the century Takashimaya took part in various European expositions, displaying fine silks and dyed fabrics, and won prizes for its displays in London, Barcelona, and Paris. In 1899 a sales office was established in Lyons, and a direct export business was founded. An office was opened in London in 1903.

The second Takashimaya store opened in eastern Kyoto in 1893, and a further store was opened in Osaka in 1898. The company established a small office in Tokyo in 1890, which became a full store in 1897. With the opening of an export office in Yokohama in 1900, Takashimaya's business extended into the two major commercial areas of Japan, the Kansai area around Kyoto and Osaka, and the Kanto area centered in Tokyo.

Early 1900s: Evolution of a Department Store

By the turn of the century Takashimaya employed more than 500 people. Traditional stores like Takashimaya began to expand their businesses as a precursor to becoming general merchandise department stores. Takashimaya, however, maintained a strong emphasis on its original fabrics and clothing business, and the company became famous for the quality of its dyeing and weaving. By importing European expertise in weaving and design, Takashimaya introduced new designs and its own clothing brands, while at the same time keeping full control of costs

Company Perspectives:

Over the years, the company has consistently adhered to a corporate philosophy of putting people first. In line with this philosophy, the company has made diligent efforts to offer consumers the means for a high-quality lifestyle through its products and services, as well as to respect its employees and practice corporate openness.

and the final retail price. To display these new designs, in 1909 Takashimaya opened an art exhibition area within its stores. This later became common practice among Japanese department stores, with many, including some Takashimaya outlets, maintaining permanent art exhibition areas.

In 1909 Takashimaya became an unlimited partnership and at the same time began to operate its stores as departmentalized general merchandise stores. The company expanded and modernized all of its outlets to keep pace with other new department stores. The number and range of goods sold was greatly expanded, and by the end of World War I, Takashimaya had six major stores and nine nonretail offices in Japan and overseas. In 1916 the new Tokyo store was opened and Takashimaya introduced a full home-shopping service to its wealthier customers. These customers were given their own accounts and were visited regularly by Takashimaya salespeople. The main items sold in this way were kimono, interior decorations, and furniture. Customers could order by mail, a telephone order service was established, and along with the other major department stores, Takashimaya provided a home-sales service to customers living in the northern and southern regions of Japan. Salespeople would visit wealthy customers living hundreds of miles away from the stores, thus providing a national sales coverage for the Takashimaya stores. Takashimaya Iida Limited was established in 1916 as a separate company, operating as an independent overseas trading arm for the Takashimaya group.

Takashimaya became a private stock company following the end of World War I, with the company taking the name Takashimaya Gofuku Store Co. Ltd. By this time the number of employees had reached 891, and Takashimaya stores had become full department stores. The small restaurant businesses that had operated in the stores since 1912 were formally incorporated and expanded, establishing an independent restaurant business in 1922 based in the newly opened Osaka Takashimaya Store. Immediately after World War I, all stores were equipped with elevators and escalators for the first time. Many of these new facilities were leased from major insurance firms, increasing the level of outside capital involved in the business.

Expanding the Customer Base, Battling Competition: 1920s–30s

In the Great Kanto Earthquake of 1923, Takashimaya's store in Tokyo was destroyed by fire, and a similar fate befell most other major department stores in the city. Out of the ashes, new department stores were built, which were larger and carried a far wider range of merchandise, making department stores available to a wider clientele and not only the most wealthy. Department stores became the general retail stores of Japan. Takashimaya's image was one of privilege, and to introduce its stores to a wider clientele, in 1926 the company began 10 Sen Kinitsu Markets, translated as "Everything for 10 sen," *sen* being a unit of a yen. The markets were opened in existing Takashimaya stores and were highly successful, selling simple household goods.

Takashimaya also expanded its nonstore retailing business, sending salespeople to a greater number of customers and increasing the availability of goods by mail order. Department stores also began to provide free home delivery services and bus services to transport customers to and from major rail stations. As the leading retailers in Japan at the time, department stores engaged in fierce competition as each one fought to establish a strong niche in the market. This competition was heightened by the entrance into the department store business of such major railroad companies as Tokyu and Hankyu, which opened "terminal department stores" at rail terminals. The advantages of these sites were clear and Takashimaya followed suit, opening a terminal store in Osaka in 1930. In the same year, Takashimaya changed its legal name to Takashimaya Co., Limited, dropping Gofuku Store, which indicated its roots in garment retailing. Takashimaya appointed its first outside director and became a public limited company in 1933, at the height of competition between Japanese department stores. This fierce competition affected many small retailers, not only in the major urban areas but also throughout the regions in which stores sent their traveling salespeople to people's homes. Takashimaya maintained an advantage through its upmarket image and through the development of a new cheap retailing business. The 10 Sen Kinitsu Markets within existing Takashimaya stores proved so successful as a low-price retail strategy that the company began a chain of stores selling low-priced household goods in 1931. Within a year, some 51 new outlets were opened.

Eventually public groups began to see the competition between department stores and their rapid expansion as being detrimental to Japanese retailing overall. In 1932 the Japan Department Store Association—founded in 1924—called for self-restraint in new store openings and the restriction of home visit sales, especially in the provinces. Even so, small retailers continued to complain, and in 1937 the Department Store Law, the original forerunner of the modern Large Store Law (1974) was promulgated to restrict the operations of large stores. As the law was aimed at department stores, the only large-scale retailers in existence at the time, Takashimaya made its new chain of low-price stores into a separate company, calling it Marutaka Kinitsu Store Ltd., and the new company continued to expand the chain store under the name Kinitsu. To get around restrictions on home selling, Takashimaya moved to expand its mail-order business, producing catalogs and advertising widely in national newspapers.

World War II and the Postwar Period: Destruction and Rebuilding

The Department Store Law effectively stopped the expansion of the department store chains, but capital became increasingly scarce as Japan reached the height of its military power during the late 1930s. From 1939 restrictions were placed on the supply of consumer goods, and a black market soon arose. Throughout this period, Takashimaya, along with some other

Key Dates:

1831: Shinshichi Iida establishes the Takashimaya clothing store in Kyoto.

1876: Takashimaya begins to import goods from abroad.

1893: The second Takashimaya store opens in eastern Kyoto.

1898: A Takashimaya store opens in Osaka.

1899: Takashimaya forms a direct export business.

1909: Takashimaya first opens an art exhibition area in its stores; the company becomes an unlimited partnership; the company begins to operate its stores as departmentalized general merchandise stores.

1916: A Takashimaya opens in Tokyo; Takashimaya Iida Limited is established to serve as an independent overseas trading arm for the group.

1922: Takashimaya establishes an independent restaurant business to handle the small eateries in its stores.

1930: Takashimaya changes its corporate name to Takashimaya Company, Limited.

1931: The company starts a chain of stores designed to sell low-priced household goods.

1933: Takashimaya becomes a public limited company.

1937: The Department Store Law is established in Japan, to restrict the operations of large stores.

1945: World War II ends; Takashimaya is left with only 21 of its original stores—only three of which are department stores.

1953: Takashimaya reintroduces mail-order service.

1956: Takashimaya joins the Intercontinental Group of Department Stores as Japan's representative.

1958: The company opens a shop in New York, becoming the first Japanese department store to do so after the war.

1959: Takashimaya Shoji Limited is established to manufacture brand-name products.

1990: Takashimaya forms High Retail System Co., Ltd. to open upscale convenience stores in urban areas; Japan's economy suffers a major downturn.

1993: Takashimaya opens a flagship U.S. store in New York.

1995: The company implements the first of three medium-term restructuring plans.

department stores, maintained a policy of setting fair prices, establishing an image of trustworthiness that still exists today. Takashimaya continued to expand its Kinitsu chain of stores and operated 106 outlets covering 39,000 square meters of sales space and employing more than 2,000 people by 1941. The ravages of war took their toll, however, and Takashimaya had lost all but 21 stores by the time the war ended in 1945. Of these, three were department stores and 18 were Kinitsu stores.

Takashimaya's outlets in both Osaka and Tokyo were badly damaged in air raids in March 1945, although enough remained for the company to continue trading. These stores were rebuilt and refurbished between 1945 and 1948, and small offices were opened in various parts of Japan including Shikoku, Hiroshima, Kyushu, and Hokkaido. In 1948 the Allied occupation authori-

ties abolished the original Department Store Law and department stores were finally free to consider opening new stores.

Takashimaya, however, chose to expand and improve its existing main stores in Osaka, Kyoto, and Tokyo, and even closed smaller stores in Kyoto and Wakayama in the early 1950s. In 1956 the Department Store Law was reintroduced by the new Japanese government. The 1956 law restricted the opening of new retail businesses larger than 1,500 square meters, regulated opening hours, and laid down minimum numbers of closing days. The expansion of all department stores was held back by this law, but by careful acquisition of sites and long-term negotiations with local retailers, Takashimaya opened three major new stores up to 1965, including Yokohama Takashimaya, which was established in 1959 at the west exit of Yokohama Station. The company already owned the site, and the new store was established as a separate company from Takashimaya. Further stores were opened in Sakai and Yonago, with the latter store also operating as a separate company.

1950s–90s: International Expansion and Diversification

During the 1950s and 1960s, Takashimaya began to expand its range of businesses. In 1956 Takashimaya became the Japanese member of the Intercontinental Group of Department Stores, an international body covering stores throughout the world. In the same year, this new contact enabled Takashimaya to become the first Japanese department store to hold an international fair for imported goods, the theme on this occasion being Italian. The company later exhibited the famous collection of anthropological photographs, "The Family of Man," in all of its stores, followed by other world famous art collections. In 1958 Takashimaya opened a store on New York's Fifth Avenue, the first of a number of overseas boutiques and restaurants, which later included stores in New York, Paris, Milan, and London.

Takashimaya Shoji Limited was established in 1959 to manufacture a range of exclusive brand-name products. Between 1960 and 1989, 34 of these brands were introduced, including formal wear, food products, cut diamond jewelry, and tableware, designed to be sold at the high-price, high-quality end of the retail market. Other subsidiaries were opened during the 1960s including real estate—Koei Real Estate Ltd.—and a housing and shopping development company, Toshin Kaihatsu Ltd. The latter company was responsible for the development of the Tamagawa Shopping Centre, which opened to the southwest of Tokyo in 1969. This was Japan's first major suburban shopping center development and had a Takashimaya Department Store at its center, with some 48,800 square meters of sales floor space, accounting for a little more than 50 percent of the total shopping center.

In 1971, Takashimaya formed the Hi-Land Group, a buying and development organization that allowed its members to source and buy products collectively and provided professional consultancy and advice, physical distribution facilities, and some financial support. All Takashimaya stores became members, and the group subsequently expanded to include many independent regional department stores. By 1990, the group included 40 member stores from all over Japan.

Takashimaya was the only company to successfully span the two major markets of Kanto and Kansai, although in each case the company often found its retail sales falling below that of the local stores, Daimaru in Osaka and Kyoto and Mitsukoshi in Tokyo. At the beginning of the 1990s, Seibu dominated the Tokyo department store market, but was competing at a slightly different level because of its shorter, less prestigious history.

Takashimaya maintained a significant advantage in its diversification strategies. In addition to operating a number of overseas boutiques and restaurants, it had introduced many overseas brands into the Japanese market. In 1959, the company acquired a license to manufacture and sell Pierre Cardin goods and in 1990 maintained exclusive licenses to manufacture 15 overseas brands, including Fauchon and Emanuel Ungaro. The store was also the exclusive importer of 12 major brands, including James Martin whiskey and Rosenthal tableware.

In 1990, Takashimaya's second main activity was nonstore retailing. The company first began mail-order retailing as long ago as 1899 and, following a curtailment of business during World War II, reintroduced a mail-order service in 1953 from the company's main Osaka store. In the 1980s Takashimaya began to expand its catalog sales, introducing a cable television shopping service and a number of multimedia catalogs, including videotapes and floppy disks. As a result, Takashimaya became the 14th largest nonstore retailer in Japan—this category included direct mail-order or catalog sales as well as home sales—and was far ahead of any other retailers also competing in the market. Takashimaya had the third largest mail-order business in Japan and in 1990 produced 1.45 million catalogs of various kinds, achieving sales of more than ¥65 billion.

Less widely known was Takashimaya's involvement in the interior design business. Based on the company's original fabrics business, Takashimaya had offered high-quality interior design services since 1878 and especially since the early 1970s had been involved in the design of numerous hotels and office and state buildings throughout the world.

For a period at the end of the 1970s and beginning of the 1980s Takashimaya's business benefited from a scandal at the Mitsukoshi Department Store, the company's leading rival in Tokyo, involving the selling of fake antiques and a rumored affair between the chairman and a younger woman. The scandal served to emphasize Takashimaya's reputation for trustworthiness and honesty, and Takashimaya briefly overtook Mitsukoshi as the most popular store at which to buy the obligatory, biannual gifts that are so important in Japanese society. For many consumers this was the first time they had considered using a store other than Mitsukoshi for such socially important purchases. Mitsukoshi later recovered its position as Tokyo's most prestigious store, but Takashimaya maintained a more modern image after the incident.

In 1990 Takashimaya formed High Retail System Co., Ltd. to open upscale convenience stores in major urban areas. Using a telephone-ordering system, customers were able to phone their shopping lists to the local store and receive delivery a few minutes later. The stores were geared to serve office areas and include various services such as color copying, in addition to offering basic convenience foods, drinks, and packaged meals.

Gifts also could be ordered by catalog from the main department store's full range.

End of the Century: Difficult Times

By the end of the 1980s, Japan's economy was a problem waiting to happen. Low interest rates, a seemingly endless stream of investment capital, and rampant speculation had combined to grossly overinflate real estate and stock values. At the beginning of the 1990s, the bubble burst. Interest rates rose, causing the flow of money to dry up and causing property and stock values to collapse. The resulting dramatic slowdown in consumer spending inflicted heavy damage on Takashimaya and its competitors alike. Net profit for the company plummeted, falling 74 percent in fiscal 1992, and another 78 percent in 1993.

Despite its ongoing financial woes, in 1993 Takashimaya opened a new store on New York's Fifth Avenue, replacing a small gift shop it had previously operated. With its prestigious location and its 20,500 square feet of space housing luxury clothing, home fashions, and a fine art gallery, the new store was Takashimaya's flagship store for the United States. One of the company's goals for the new store was to better establish its own lines of fashions and furnishings.

In 1995, as Japan's recession dragged on, Takashimaya established a three-year plan for restructuring its business and lowering operating costs. One of the first steps taken under the new plan was the merging of six group companies that managed department stores into one single entity, thereby eliminating redundancies and reducing expenses. The company also set new, lower limits for various budgetary items, such as advertising and distribution. At the same time, it implemented various measures designed to increase sales, such as extending its stores' operating hours, augmenting sales floor space, and expanding its product selection.

By the end of fiscal 1996, Takashimaya was beginning to see results from its efforts. Net sales for that year rose by 26 percent—but more significantly, net income rose by 208 percent from the previous fiscal year. Net income grew again in 1997, albeit at a more conservative rate. But in 1998, with Japan still plagued by an uncertain economic future, personal spending hit a new low, and the already challenging retail environment grew even tougher. Takashimaya's net profits decreased by 18 percent, and the company implemented its second short-term plan for restructuring. This second plan, like the first, involved cost-trimming measures and operational reforms. It also called for a renewed focus on the customer and a new, "socially open" corporate culture.

One of the first cost-cutting measures undertaken involved a partnership with Japan's second largest department store operator, Mitsukoshi Ltd. In March 2000, the two companies joined together to integrate many of their operations, including distribution, purchasing, and information systems. Takashimaya expected the partnership to result in cost savings of several billion yen. By early 2001, Japanese department store superpowers Daimaru and Matsuzakaya also had joined the distribution network.

In 2001, when Takashimaya's second three-year restructuring plan ended, Japan's economy was still weak, unemployment still high, and consumer confidence still low. Faced with these significant obstacles as it looked to bolster its shaky profitability, the company evolved a third plan. One of the plan's major components involved strengthening its department store business by concentrating its investments on the five large stores in Tokyo, Yokohama, Shinjuku, Osaka, and Kyoto. The plan also called for increasing the percentage of Takashimaya private-brand goods offered in the product mix, continuing to overhaul the company's divisional structure, reducing interest-bearing debt, and further trimming employment and related operating expenses.

Looking Ahead

The year 2001 was yet another difficult one for Takashimaya and its fellow Japanese retailers; according to Japan's Ministry of Economy, Trade and Industry, retail sales declined throughout the last four quarters of 2001, with an especially sharp drop of 4.5 percent in December. As 2001 gave way to 2002, there appeared to be no immediate relief in sight. Economists claimed that with the economy still weak and corporate earnings still on the decline, the pressure on retailers was likely to continue.

Takashimaya had so far remained profitable—something not all of its competitors had managed to do. How well it would continue to hold up under the ongoing economic slump, however, remained to be seen.

Principal Subsidiaries

A.T.A. Co., Ltd.; Century & Co., Ltd.; Fashion Plaza 21 Co., Ltd.; Georg Jensen Japan, Ltd.; Golden Spa New Otani Co.; Gourmail Co., Ltd.; Hotel Seagull Takashimaya Co., Ltd.; Kanto Telephone Communication Center, Inc.; Koei Real Estate Co., Ltd.; Nippon Craft Co., Ltd.; R.T. Corporation; Rosier Co., Ltd.; Shin-Nankai Store Co., Ltd.; Takashimaya Building Maintenance Co., Ltd.; Takashimaya Credit Co., Ltd.; Takashimaya Kosakusho Co., Ltd.; Takashimaya Logistics Service Co., Ltd.; Takashimaya Nippatsu Kogyo Co., Ltd.; Takashimaya Store Co., Ltd.; Takashimaya Sun Roser Co., Ltd.; Takashi-maya Tomonokai Co., Ltd.; Takashimaya Trading Co., Ltd.; Takashimaya Urban Freight Co., Ltd.; TAPP Co., Ltd.; Toshin Development Co., Ltd.; Yutaka Construction & Engineering Co., Ltd.; Takashimaya (California), Inc. (U.S.A.); Takashimaya Enterprises, Inc.; Takashimaya Fifth Avenue Corporation (U.S.A.); Takashimaya New York, Inc. (U.S.A.); Rodeo Drive Properties, Inc. (U.S.A.); S.A. Leroy (France); Takashimaya (France) S.A.; Takashimaya (Italia) S.P.A. (Italy); Takashimaya International Finance B.V. (The Netherlands); Kakashimaya Hong Kong Enterprises Limited; Ngee Ann Development Private Ltd. (Singapore); Takashimaya Advertising & Promotion PTE, Ltd. (Singapore); Takashimaya (Singapore) Ltd.; Toshin Development International (1995) PTE, Ltd. (Singapore); Dayeh Takashimaya Department Store, Inc. (China); Taipei Takashimaya International Co., Ltd. (China); P.T. Nowl Knitting Indonesia; P.T. Trisenta Interior Manufacturing (Indonesia); Takashimaya (Thailand) Co., Ltd.; Takashimaya Retailing Australia PTY, Ltd.; Takashimaya Australia PTY, Ltd.

Principal Competitors

The Daimaru, Inc.; Istean Co., Ltd.; The Seibu Department Stores, Ltd.

Further Reading

Nikkei Ryutsu Shinbun, *Kourigyo: Seme no Jidai,* Tokyo: Nihon Keizai Shinbun, 1989.
Nishiyama, Nobuo, "Takashimaya Foshon: Sekai no Tokusen Gurume wo Uru Butikku," in *Sutoa Aidentiti Senryaku* (Buren, ed.), Tokyo: Seibundo Shinkosha, 1987.
Okada, Yasushi, *Hyakkaten Gyokai,* Tokyo: Kyoikusha, 1988.
Takaoka, Sueaki, and Shuzo Koyama, *Gendai no Hyakkaten,* Tokyo: Nihon Keizai Shinbunsha, 1970.

—Roy Larke and Kota Nagashima
—update: Shawna Brynildssen

TALISMAN
ENERGY

Talisman Energy Inc.

Suite 3400
855 3rd Street S.W.
Calgary, Alberta T2P 5C5
Canada
Telephone: (403) 237-1234
Fax: (403) 237-1902
Web site: http://www.talisman-energy.com

Public Company
Incorporated: 1925 as Supertest Petroleum Corporation
Employees: 1,263
Sales: C$3.99 billion ($2.66 billion) (2000)
Stock Exchanges: Toronto New York
Ticker Symbol: TLM
NAIC: 211111 Crude Petroleum and Natural Gas
  Extraction

Talisman Energy Inc. is Canada's largest independent oil and gas exploration and production company. Proven reserves stood at 1.2 billion barrels of oil equivalent at the end of 2000. Talisman's main areas of operation are Canada, the British North Sea, Indonesia, Malaysia, and Sudan, with additional operations in Algeria, Colombia, Trinidad, and the United States. The company's involvement in the Sudan has been controversial because of the political situation in that war-torn African nation. Talisman emerged in 1992 after its former parent, British Petroleum Company plc, sold its 57 percent interest in the Canadian concern, which had been known as BP Canada. Since becoming independent, Talisman Energy has grown rapidly through a series of acquisitions under the leadership of James W. Buckee.

Early History of Supertest Petroleum and BP Canada

Talisman's roots can be found in the Supertest Petroleum Corporation, established on December 17, 1925, with the opening of a corner gas station in London, Ontario. The company immediately began building a network of gas stations, and in 1926 it bought the gas and oil interests of Ensign Oil Company,

based in Montreal. Growth for Supertest was slow during the economic depression of the 1930s, when unemployment and persistent economic downturns affected the ability of Canadians to buy and drive cars.

The rival British Petroleum Company plc (BP) made its first large foray into the Canadian market in 1953. BP, headquartered in London, England, had its earliest roots in the Middle East, where extensive gas and oil interests were found and exploited, in Iran and Saudi Arabia in particular. As early as 1926, the company considered expanding outside of the Middle East. Specifically, Arnold Wilson, who succeeded F.G. Watson as managing director of D'Arcy Exploration Company, a division of BP, told company directors that disappointment with drilling in Asia and Africa led him to consider drilling opportunities in Canada or South America. As it happened, BP did much to explore new opportunities before it entered the Canadian market in a substantial way. Between 1927 and 1930, company geologists showed considerable interests in possible fields in British Columbia, New Brunswick, and Alberta. The geologists, however, could not agree on whether potential gas and oil reserves in the Canadian hinterland warranted further investment toward drilling.

In 1953, BP bought a minority stake in Triad Oil Company, a small exploration company based in Calgary with large exploration holdings in western Canada. Four years later, BP entered the Quebec market. By 1960, when the company's first refinery opened for business in Montreal, BP had over 800 service stations in the French-speaking province. Now operating as rivals, both companies expanded during the 1950s and 1960s. Earlier, in 1959, Supertest merged into its own operations those of Reliance Petroleum Ltd., also based in Calgary. In 1964, BP bought the eastern Canadian interests of Cities Service, comprising 750 retail gas stations and a refinery at Oakville, Ontario. This acquisition brought to just under 1,800 the number of retail gas stations that BP had in Ontario and Quebec and added to its sales and service teams for home heating and the agricultural, commercial, marine, and aviation industries.

In 1969, BP's holding company in Canada was renamed BP Canada, and the principal marketing company was renamed BP Oil Ltd. Put another way, BP's Canadian operations now had two arms, an upstream arm (oil and gas exploration and production) and a downstream arm (refining and marketing). A year later, all BP's marketing and refining interests in western Canada were put under the corporate umbrella of BP Oil and Gas Ltd., including the interests of the former Triad Oil Company.

1971: Merger of BP Canada and Supertest

The discovery in August 1969 of giant oil reserves at Prudhoe Bay, Alaska, convinced BP headquarters in London that it had a significant future in northern Canada. In August 1971, BP Canadian Holdings Ltd., then BP Canadian Ltd., and a division of BP in Britain offered to buy a controlling interest in Supertest. The British parent exchanged for shares all of its petroleum marketing, refining, and exploration interests in Canada. These entailed all the outstanding stock of BP Oil Ltd.—an associate company mainly engaged in marketing and refining in eastern Canada—and a 65.9 percent interest in BP Oil and Gas Ltd. The BP offer was accepted by Corlon Investments Ltd., which then held an 83.7 percent stake in Supertest. It sold its entire stake for $10 a share. By November of that year, BP had bought 97.8 percent of Supertest, having paid $16.50 per share for that holding.

Immediately upon buying Supertest, the new company, BP Canada Ltd., set about securing new oil and gas acreage holdings in the Arctic Islands region of Canada. The idea was to explore for possible oil and gas reserves in the regions adjoining the 1969 Alaskan oil and gas discoveries. Once located, substantial oil and gas reserves would be extracted from the earth via drilling rigs and then refined downstream before being sold to consumers through a network of gas stations. Other oil companies tended to be specific about identifying and taking aim at specific oil targets. BP Canada, on the other hand, had a "shotgun," as opposed to a "rifle," approach. It explored in many places in search of leads and eventual discoveries.

Total acreage in 1970 for BP Canada amounted to 26.7 million gross acres, up from 19.3 million gross acres held a year earlier. Of particular interest was a 1.2 million acre tract of property purchased for exploration on Vanier, Emerak, and Prince Patrick Islands where actual drilling was to commence in 1971. BP Canada's net production of crude oil and natural gas in 1970 amounted to 18,582 barrels daily, up 17 percent on production a year earlier. Sales of natural gas had jumped 24 percent to an average of 62.4 million cubic feet per day, compared with production in 1969. In 1971, the company drilled its first Arctic well on Vanier Island, and labeled it "BP et al Panarctic Hotspur J-20." It then added two more, one on Prince

Patrick Island ("BP et al Panarctic Satellite F-68") and the other on Graham Island ("BP et al Graham C-52"). BP Canada also purchased considerable acreage holdings in northern Alberta and British Columbia for possible exploration and drilling in those regions.

A year later, the former offices of Supertest Investments and Petroleum in Calgary had been closed as management of the new company was moved to the Montreal-based headquarters of BP Oil and Gas Ltd. Production for the company jumped substantially in 1972. Sales of petroleum products averaged 94,400 barrels daily, whereas production of crude oil and natural gas was posted at an average 22,132 barrels daily. To accommodate this increased production, the company announced plans in 1972 to add a further 40,000 barrels per day of refining capacity at its Trafalgar Refinery facility in Oakville, Ontario. Products produced there would be marketed under the BP and Supertest brand names.

In April 1972, just months after the Supertest merger, company President Derek Mitchell, who had initially come to the position in 1966, outlined his business strategy to shareholders in the company's 1971 annual report: "Your company is now firmly established as a major marketer and refiner of petroleum products in Ontario and Quebec, is well placed as a producer of oil and gas in Western Canada, and has an important stake in the exploration activity rapidly gaining momentum in Canada's frontier areas." BP Canada was establishing upstream exploration and production facilities in western Canada to serve key downstream markets in Ontario and Quebec, where oil and gas products could be sold directly to consumers.

Surviving the Oil Shocks of the 1970s

By late 1972, the company was beginning to feel the effects of higher world prices for a barrel of oil caused by the efforts of the Organization of Petroleum Exporting Countries (OPEC) cartel. Essentially, a higher price paid for imported crude oil forced BP Canada to pay more for the energy reserves it required to replace petroleum products sold earlier downstream in the marketplace.

This trend worried Mitchell, who said in March 1973 in the company's 1972 annual report: "The comparative stability of the 1960s is giving way to a decade likely to be characterized by rising prices for petroleum and growing government interest in the industry's affairs, both at the political and at the technical levels." Mitchell's words were to prove prophetic. Throughout 1973, OPEC instigated production cutbacks and embargoes among its customers, which played havoc with the global oil industry. The price of oil on the global market went up, and the world supply seemed to be shrinking.

Turmoil and confusion gripped the oil industry. Responding, BP Canada began moving crude oil from western Canada to Montreal through the St. Lawrence Seaway, and later through the Panama Canal during the winter freeze-up. A thorn in the company's side was the growing involvement in the domestic oil industry by the Canadian government in Ottawa. Specifically, the government was calling on the industry to hold down anticipated price rises for Canadian oil products, which would grow costlier as they were affected by the rising world oil prices

Key Dates:

1925: Supertest Petroleum Corporation is founded with the opening of a gas station in London, Ontario.

1953: British Petroleum Company (BP) enters the Canadian market through the purchase of a minority stake in Calgary-based Triad Oil Company.

1969: BP's Canadian holding company is renamed BP Canada.

1971: BP acquires 97.8 percent of Supertest, which it renames BP Canada Ltd. and merges with its other Canadian interests.

1992: BP sells off its 57 percent stake in BP Canada to the public; BP Canada is renamed Talisman Energy Inc.

1993: James W. Buckee takes over the helm as president and CEO; Encor Inc. is acquired.

1994: Bow Valley Energy Inc. is acquired for C$1.82 billion, giving Talisman properties in the British North Sea and in Indonesia.

1996: Company completes three deals that substantially increase its North Sea production.

1997: Hostile bid for Wascana Energy Inc. is scuttled by a higher offer from Canadian Occidental Petroleum Ltd.; Talisman acquires Pembina Resources Limited from Loram Corporation for C$605 million.

1998: Company acquires Arakis Energy Corporation and its 25 percent stake in a major oil production project in Sudan for C$277.5 million.

1999: Rigel Energy Corporation is acquired for C$1.12 billion.

2001: Talisman acquires Petromet Resources Limited for C$823 million and Lundin Oil AB for C$504.8 million; the company announces major oil discoveries in Trinidad.

charged by OPEC member countries. Such restraint was meant to allow the government to develop a Canadian pricing policy to cushion the impact on consumers from rising world oil prices and provide an incentive for the domestic oil industry to develop new energy sources.

As a measure of the growing spread between domestic and world oil prices, a barrel of Canadian crude oil rose by 85 cents to around $4.50 in Toronto in the 12 months leading up to January 1, 1974. During that same period, the cost of imported crude oil rose by some $8 to over $11 a barrel in Montreal. BP Canada was making increased profits from selling petroleum products to consumers at higher prices, but it had to restore energy reserves it had sold off by buying imported crude oil at around twice the December 1973 level. According to the company, it was under-recovering its cost of crude oil by some $300,000 a day in the second half of 1973.

BP Canada might have been trading in crisis-ridden conditions in 1974, but it still managed to see profits rise 82 percent to $39.5 million that year. Even so, the company still found grounds to complain in its 1975 annual report about growing royalties and income taxes owed to Canada's provincial and federal governments. What is more, by the end of 1974, world oil prices had risen to five times the mid-1973 level. The unprecedented price hikes had led to increased production, and ultimately a glut in the world oil market. The net result: lower margins for BP Canada products in an ever more competitive market.

In 1975, the company began exploring for oil off Newfoundland, on Canada's easternmost seaboard. Also that year, the expansion of the Trafalgar Refinery was completed, but only after delays and cost overruns. A year later, BP Canada bought the remaining 65 percent stake in British Columbia Oil Sands Ltd. to take full control of the company. Paying $20 per share in the transaction, the company gained ownership of oil and gas acreage in the Yoyo, Kotcho, Cabin, and Louise gas fields of northeastern British Columbia. Cost-cutting measures that year included reducing the number of retail outlets selling BP petroleum brand products in Ontario and Quebec from just over 3,000 to around 1,800. The company also introduced BP no-lead gasoline at its remaining retail outlets.

Early in 1977, BP Canada signed an agreement with the Alberta Oil Sands Technology and Research Authority that would see the government body contribute half the $18 million cost of testing a sequential steam heating system to extract heavy crude oil (thick sludge used as highway asphalt) in the Wolf Lake area of Alberta. These tarlike deposits are filled with impurities but can be upgraded to light, valuable crude oil; the process is worthwhile if there is a $3 to $5 spread between the light and heavy crude oil variants. At the time, the price of oil on the world market was rising too quickly, compared with the price for domestically produced oil, to fully justify the development of heavy oil upgraders. The Wolf Lake project was noteworthy for its incentives to develop new sources of oil and gas in Canada. Companies such as BP Canada often had to extract heavier crude oil reserves at greater than average expense and longer than usual lead times before it could deliver a refined product to consumer markets in a light crude form.

BP Canada in the 1970s continued its thrust into the rugged terrain of the Monkman area in northeastern British Columbia. It now held interests from 25 to 64 percent in 204,000 acres and 100 percent of 94,000 acres in the region, which was thought to hold vast natural gas reserves. The British Columbia Petroleum Corporation announced plans to build a pipeline and plant facilities to bring the Monkman area natural gas to market in 1980.

In 1978, BP Canada saw its profits rise over the $40 million mark for the first time. This record, however, was reached at a time when the industry as a whole was experiencing a market glut because of excess refining capacity and reduced consumer demand for petroleum products due to the unexpected success of conservation measures. The Iranian revolution in 1979 caused yet another jump in the price of oil on the world market. BP Canada saw its offshore supply drop substantially because of embargoes. To replace the shortfall, the company arranged to send Canadian crude oil from western Canada to northern-tier U.S. refiners, who in turn would divert their imported oil to the Montreal refinery.

At this time, BP Canada also faced a glut in the natural gas market, then a key earner for the company. Production in 1979 was 109.5 million cubic feet per day, down from 122.7 million cubic feet per day a year earlier. Purchasers had essentially been unable to take all the gas they had contracted to buy. Sales of natural gas continued slowly in 1980, but the company did manage to post profits of $63.1 million for fiscal 1979, up 93 percent from the year before. A jump like that had company Chairman and CEO Mitchell defending the company's performance, given its persistent calls for less government control over the oil industry. Suspicions abounded in the 1970s that the oil industry as a whole was manipulating the OPEC crisis for its own profitable ends.

Developments in the 1980s

Speaking to shareholders, Mitchell repeated his company's call for regulatory restraint in the company's 1980 annual report: "There is no doubt that given appropriate policies—higher crude oil prices, a fair and stable tax and royalty system which will allow adequate netbacks to the industry, a commitment to allow companies to reap the fruits of their endeavors, and the encouragement of fuels substitution and energy conservation—Canada can again become self-sufficient in oil." If Mitchell sought government restraint, he ended up with greater intervention still. The Conservative government, entering the 1980 federal election, had proposed an 18-cents-a-gallon gasoline tax, to subsidize more expensive oil imports. That proposed excise tax in part led to the Conservative government's downfall at the polls. The incoming Liberal government introduced the National Energy Program in October 1980. It painted foreign oil companies as profit-hungry conglomerates and gave support to Canadian-owned companies such as Petro-Canada.

Company Chairman Mitchell complained in March 1981 in the company's 1980 annual report: "The government is now hell-bent on putting on a circus for the benefit of the media and the public. . . . The principal purpose will, doubtless, be to try to justify by propaganda and by 'trial' in the media the federal government's already well-demonstrated xenophobic prejudices against one of Canada's vital and most successful industries."

Although the Liberal government became a foul word in the BP Canada boardroom, the company's fortunes did not suffer. For the first time in 1980, gas from the Sukunka-Bullmoose area of northeastern British Columbia reached the market after many years of exploration. It was also announced that year that BP Canada's headquarters would move from Montreal to Toronto. The relocation served two purposes: it would remove the company from the separatist tensions then developing in Quebec and would place the headquarters in Ontario, where 70 percent of the company's assets were.

Profits for 1980 were posted at $104.3 million, a 56 percent advancement over the previous year. The rate of return on investment was 17.3 percent, a company record. Despite the government's aim to restrain foreign oil companies in Canada and support the domestic sector, the multinationals were doing better than ever.

Company Chairman Mitchell died suddenly on October 29, 1981, and was replaced by R. Hanbidge as president and CEO. A year later, BP Canada shelved plans to proceed with developing the Sukunka coal mine in northeastern British Columbia. Low coal prices on the world market accounted for the strategic

move. The company in 1984 completed work on its Wolf Lake project, which came onstream five months ahead of schedule and with a price tag of $110 million. Full production of 1,100 cubic meters of fuel per day was achieved in September 1985, and expanded production at Wolf Lake was forecast at 5,600 cubic meters per day by the end of the decade.

The falling price of oil on the world market hit BP Canada's earnings in 1985. Cash flow fell by 17 percent, and net profits fell by 55 percent to $20 million, compared with results for the year earlier. Continuing success at energy conservation during the 1980s also cut into production at BP Canada. In 1985, sales of light and medium oil were down by 10 percent on sales a year earlier, and 15 percent of production was lost during the first quarter of 1987. Also that year, production at the Wolf Lake project stood at 1,140 cubic meters per day, not far above production figures when the project came onstream in 1984.

For these reasons, the company attempted to curb its operating costs to maintain profitability. M.A. Kirkby, president of BP Canada, told shareholders in the 1987 annual report: "While we cannot control the worldwide prices of oil, gas and metals, we are constantly working to reduce our costs and to improve our netbacks within the market." Cost-cutting measures helped boost BP Canada's net profits to $44.6 million in 1987, an all-time high. But the very next year, net profits were down to $10.3 million. The main reason: world oil prices fell by 27 percent in 1988.

In 1989 David Claydon replaced Kirkby as president of BP Canada. That year, he ordered environmental audits of all BP Canadian operations in response to growing concerns about possible environmental damage from oil exploration and refining. The company also announced plans to boost its natural gas exploration and reserves, recognizing that natural gas was a clean-burning fuel considered more environmentally sound by consumers than oil or coal.

Early 1990s: From BP Canada to Talisman Energy

In 1991, mounting debt and losses prompted a management shuffle and a worldwide review of operations by the head office of British Petroleum in London. By mid-1992, BP announced it would sell off its 57 percent stake in BP Canada through a secondary offering of shares. The *Financial Times of Canada* reported that Canadian employees responded with a burst of applause on hearing the news. To sell its stake in a highly profitable company with prospects that greatly encouraged Canadian and American investors, BP in London clearly had priorities elsewhere.

Upon being sold in June 1992, Talisman's share price stood at C$13.00. At the end of July 1993, the share price had climbed to C$26.50. The company now had Jim Buckee at its helm as president and CEO. The British-born businessman, Oxford-educated and with a Ph.D. in astrophysics, transformed Talisman in the 1990s into a smaller company focused on oil and gas exploration and production. For example, the company sold its Wolf Lake oil sands assets to Amoco Canada Petroleum Company in April 1992. Talisman then bought Encor Inc. the following year, gaining a company that held the oil and gas assets that once belonged to TransCanada PipeLines Ltd. The purchase price comprised C$239 million worth of treasury shares.

No longer subservient to a British multinational parent, Talisman was now free to seek international operations. The company had already gained Encor's foreign activities in Algeria and Indonesia, but Buckee was seeking more substantial overseas holdings to balance Talisman's domestic operations. Bow Valley Energy Inc. was quickly identified as a prime target, and with a willing seller in the form of 53 percent owner British Gas PLC, a deal was soon struck. Talisman completed its acquisition of Bow Valley in August 1994, through a C$1.82 billion transaction consisting of C$627 million in cash, C$899 million in stock, and C$297 million in assumed debt. The purchase made Talisman the third largest gas producer in Canada but more importantly gave the company substantial properties in the British North Sea and in Indonesia, some of which were already in production and some of which were still at the prospecting stage. To reduce debt in the wake of the deal, Talisman sold off some assets, including a group of oil and gas fields in southwestern Saskatchewan inherited from Bow Valley.

During 1996, Talisman substantially increased its North Sea holdings through three transactions. In January, Goal Petroleum plc was acquired for C$275 million. The deal doubled Talisman's oil production from the North Sea to nearly 39,000 barrels of crude oil per day, nearly equal to its production in western Canada. Later in the year, Talisman purchased a 52 percent stake in the North Sea's Ross field, which was expected to come onstream in the late 1990s with 20,000 barrels per day for Talisman. In the third deal, the company paid British Petroleum more than C$100 million for controlling stakes in three North Sea fields, adding another 16,000 barrels a day to Talisman's production.

Late 1990s and Beyond: Controversy over Involvement in Sudan

Continuing its aggressive approach to expansion in 1997, a year in which the company gained a listing on the New York Stock Exchange, Talisman made a hostile C$1.56 billion bid for Wascana Energy Inc. The deal would have doubled Talisman's oil and gas properties in western Canada, but Canadian Occidental Petroleum Ltd. stepped in as a white knight with an offer that topped Talisman's, scuttling the bid. Talisman succeeded, however, with a C$605 million purchase of Pembina Resources Limited from Loram Corporation. Completed in October 1997, the transaction included Pembina's oil and natural gas operations in western Canada and Ontario with daily production of 10,000 barrels of oil and gas liquids and 92 million cubic feet of natural gas.

One year later, Talisman acquired Calgary-based Arakis Energy Corporation for C$277.5 million in stock. Already operating in such politically risky areas as Indonesia and Algeria, Talisman now gained Arakis's 25 percent stake in a major crude oil production and pipeline project in Sudan. Arakis had been attempting to develop the project since the 1990s but had been unable to raise the funds necessary to move the project forward because of the turbulent situation in Sudan, which was in the 42nd year of a civil war pitting the Islamic government of the north against mainly Christian and animist groups in the south. In late 1996, Arakis had brought partners into the project—China National Petroleum Corporation, which took a 40 percent stake; Malaysia's Petronas Carigali Overseas Sdn.

Bhd. (30 percent); and Sudapet Ltd., owned by the Sudanese government (5 percent). Ominously for Talisman, just three days after the company announced that it would purchase Arakis, the U.S. government launched cruise missiles at a purported nerve gas factory in the Sudanese capital of Khartoum. Talisman shares soon plunged by nearly a third before recovering, and the deal was completed. In managing the crisis brought on by the missile strike, Buckee emphasized the long-range potential of the project and that the revenues from the oil fields could help to alleviate some of the strife plaguing Sudan.

Talisman completed a noncontroversial acquisition in September 1999, purchasing Calgary-based Rigel Energy Corporation for C$1.12 billion—C$735.8 million in stock, C$57 million in cash, and C$329.4 million in assumed debt. This deal significantly increased Talisman's natural gas production in western Canada and its oil production in the North Sea. It also helped to catapult the company into the top spot among Canadian oil and gas production companies in 2000.

The purchase of Rigel received little notice compared to the reams of negative publicity that Talisman was receiving over its Sudanese operations—publicity that increased in intensity in 1999 when oil began flowing through the completed pipeline and the government of Sudan began receiving hundreds of millions of dollars in oil revenues. Talisman was accused of helping to fund the government in its war against the rebels in the south, a government that was widely accused of committing human rights violations against its own citizens. Among the allegations, the government was accused of condoning slavery and forcing villagers to relocate to make way for the oil project. Human rights and religious groups called for the U.S. and Canadian governments to place sanctions on Talisman and put pressure on investment firms to withdraw their investments in Talisman. The U.S. government imposed sanctions on Talisman in February 2000—banning the refinement of Sudanese oil in the United States—but the Canadian government elected not to impose sanctions, despite a scathing report by a government-appointed special investigator, John Harker. In his report, Harker wrote that "Sudan is a place of extraordinary suffering and continuing human rights violations, and the oil operations in which a Canadian company is involved add more suffering." Talisman continued to maintain that its involvement in Sudan would lead to improvements in the human rights situation and help bring peace, and it also signed the International Code of Ethics for Canadian Business and in early 2001 released its first corporate social responsibility report on its Sudanese operations.

By the end of 2000, Talisman Energy's annual revenues were approaching C$4 billion, and its proven oil and gas reserves had reached 1.2 billion barrels of oil equivalent, up from 485 million barrels in 1995. In May 2001, Talisman acquired Calgary-based Petromet Resources Limited for C$765.9 million in cash and the assumption of C$57 million in debt in a deal that further expanded the company's natural gas operations in Canada. Then in August of that same year, Lundin Oil AB was acquired for C$434.6 million in cash and $70.2 million in assumed debt. Based in Sweden, Lundin had oil and gas interests in the North Sea, Malaysia, Vietnam, and Papua New Guinea that were conveyed to Talisman. Crucially, Lundin's operations in Sudan, Russia, and Libya were divested prior to the completion of the purchase.

Pressure on Talisman to exit from Sudan increased following the events of September 11, 2001, particularly because the Sudanese government was accused of harboring and aiding the Al Qaeda terrorist network. The U.S. Congress began serious consideration of a bill that would strip Talisman of its New York Stock Exchange listing, a potentially devastating blow to the company. Then in November 2001 human rights activists in New York filed a class-action lawsuit against Talisman on behalf of southern Sudanese alleging that the company was complicit in human rights abuses in Sudan. Around this same time, Talisman announced that it had made major oil discoveries in Trinidad that could be as large or larger than its Sudanese operations. The Trinidad discovery, combined with the international operations newly acquired via the Lundin purchase, provided the potential pretext for the company's exit from Sudan. It appeared likely that Talisman could divest itself of its Sudanese operations without suffering a drastic reduction in oil output or revenues. It was unclear, however, whether the company would take advantage of this opportunity to rid itself of its Sudanese albatross.

Principal Subsidiaries

Talisman Energy (U.K.) Limited; Talisman North Sea Limited (U.K.); Talisman (Greater Nile) B.V. (Netherlands); Talisman (Corridor) Ltd. (Barbados).

Principal Competitors

Imperial Oil Limited; Canadian Natural Resources Limited; BP Canada Energy Company; PanCanadian Energy Corporation; Alberta Energy Company Ltd.; Nexen Inc.; Husky Energy Inc.; Petro-Canada; Conoco Inc.; Shell Canada Limited; Suncor Energy Inc.

Further Reading

Bott, Robert, "Fuelled for Takeoff: Jim Buckee's Talisman Energy Leads the Way As One of the Most Dynamic Oil and Gas Players in a Reborn Calgary Oil Patch," *Globe and Mail,* Report on Business Magazine, November 25, 1994, p. 50.

"BP Canada Cut Loose As British Parent Sells Stake," *Globe and Mail,* May 13, 1992.

"BP Plans Further Cutbacks," *Globe and Mail,* May 6, 1992.

Carlisle, Tamsin, "Talisman Agrees to Buy Rigel Energy in $563.2 Million Cash-and-Stock Deal," *Wall Street Journal,* August 24, 1999, p. B9.

——, "Talisman, Chasing Prized Natural Gas, to Buy Petromet in $469.7 Million Deal," *Wall Street Journal,* April 11, 2001, p. C14.

——, "Talisman Makes Purchase Offer for Bow Valley," *Wall Street Journal,* May 18, 1994, p. A3.

——, "Talisman Plans Unsolicited Bid for Wascana," *Wall Street Journal,* February 14, 1997, p. B23.

Chase, Steven, "Talisman Bids for Arakis Energy," *Globe and Mail,* August 18, 1998, p. B1.

——, "Talisman Cools on Quitting Sudan," *Globe and Mail,* May 3, 2000, p. B4.

——, "Talisman Stares Down Sudan Strike," *Globe and Mail,* October 9, 1998, p. B25.

——, "Talisman to Acquire Smaller Peer Rigel," *Globe and Mail,* August 24, 1999, p. B1.

Chase, Steven, and Jeff Sallot, "Heat Grows on Talisman over Sudan," *Globe and Mail,* May 4, 2000, p. A1.

Drohan, Madelaine, "Into Africa: Talisman Energy Wants Shareholders to Believe That Its Investment in Sudan Is Secure," *Globe and Mail,* Report on Business Magazine, September 24, 1999, p. 82.

——, "Sudan Play Bad Timing for Talisman," *Globe and Mail,* October 27, 1999, p. B2.

Fitz-James, Michael, "Talisman Turns the Tables: Responding to Social Protest Doesn't Necessarily Mean Backing Down," *Corporate Legal Times,* October 2001.

"Free of Stodgy Parents and Gushing Profits," *Financial Times of Canada,* July 31, 1993.

"Fueling a Fire," *Economist,* September 2, 2000, pp. 62–63.

Ingram, Mathew, "Talisman Deep in Sudan Quagmire," *Globe and Mail,* November 1, 1999, p. B2.

——, "Talisman Pumps Itself Up," *Globe and Mail,* October 14, 1996, p. B2.

Jang, Brent, "Talisman Bets on North Sea: Calgary Company Pays Over $100-Million for Controlling Stakes in Three Offshore Oil Fields," *Globe and Mail,* August 21, 1996, p. B1.

——, "Talisman Finds Huge Gas Pool in Alberta," *Globe and Mail,* August 15, 1997, p. B1.

——, "Talisman Looks Around for Bargains: Acquisitions Could Top $1-Billion," *Globe and Mail,* January 30, 1997, p. B1.

——, "Talisman to Buy Goal, Double Oil Output," *Globe and Mail,* December 16, 1995, p. B3.

Leitch, Carolyn, "Talisman Kills Wascana Bid," *Globe and Mail,* April 10, 1997, p. B1.

Lem, Gail, "Talisman Makes Bid for Encor," *Globe and Mail,* March 11, 1993, p. B9.

Motherwell, Cathryn, "Talisman Bids $1.8-Billion for Bow Valley," *Globe and Mail,* May 18, 1994, p. B1.

Nguyen, Lily, "Suit Filed in U.S. Against Talisman: Sudan Class Action Disappoints Firm," *Globe and Mail,* November 9, 2001, p. B3.

——, "Talisman Heralds "Major" Oil Discovery off Trinidad Coast," *Globe and Mail,* December 5, 2001, p. B1.

——, "Talisman Oil Find Could Add Major Area of Operation," *Globe and Mail,* November 7, 2001, p. B7.

Nikiforuk, Andrew, "Company Loves Misery," *Canadian Business,* March 20, 2000, p. 16.

——, "Oil Patch Pariah," *Canadian Business,* December 10, 1999, pp. 69–70, 72.

Pitts, Gordon, "NGOs to Confront Talisman CEO," *Globe and Mail,* October 16, 2001, p. B8.

"Religious Groups Challenge Oil Giant," *Christian Century,* April 19–26, 2000, p. 450.

Simon, Bernard, "Oil Company Defends Role in Sudan," *New York Times,* October 17, 2001, p. W1.

"Talisman Grapples with Negative Publicity over Its Oil Project in War-Torn Sudan," *Oil and Gas Journal,* January 17, 2000.

"Talisman in a Flurry of Changes," *Globe and Mail,* April 14, 1993.

Wallace, Bruce, "A Sliding Moral Scale," *Maclean's,* February 28, 2000, p. 25.

Willis, Andrew, "Streetwise Talisman Lost a Fair Fight," *Globe and Mail,* April 11, 1997, p. B11.

—Etan Vlessing
—update: David E. Salamie

TCF Financial Corporation

200 Lake Street East
Wayzata, Minnesota 55391-1693
U.S.A.
Telephone: (952) 745-2760
Fax: (952) 745-2775
Web site: http://www.tcfexpress.com

Public Company
Founded: 1923 as Twin City Building and Loan
   Association
Employees: 7,500
Total Assets: $11.35 billion (2001)
Stock Exchanges: New York
Ticker Symbol: TCB
NAIC: 522110 Commercial Banking; 551111 Offices of
   Bank Holding Companies; 522291 Consumer
   Lending; 522210 Credit Card Issuing

TCF Financial Corporation, a financial holding company that compares itself to large successful retailers instead of other banks, operates the fourth largest supermarket branch system in the United States. The company markets itself aggressively to middle- and lower-income customers with products such as Totally Free Checking accounts. The Minnesota-based company has banking offices in Minnesota, Illinois, Wisconsin, Indiana, Michigan, and Colorado and provides leasing and equipment finance, mortgage banking, discount brokerage, and investments and insurance sales through various affiliates.

Early Leadership: 1920s–60s

Twin City Building and Loan Association opened its doors on April 2, 1923, in downtown Minneapolis. "The firm was organized by a life insurance man who thought the savings business would feed his life business," Leonard Inskip reported in the *Minneapolis Tribune* in 1960. Back in the 1920s, real estate investors were also setting up savings and loans (S&Ls) as affiliated business ventures to drive up profits.

The operation, though, was not a sure bet. Public skepticism borne of the failure of other S&Ls initially made the hunt for investors a challenge. The membership fee was $2 per share, and investors in the savings and loan association would receive dividends at a rate of 7 percent.

But, persistence paid. By April of the next year, a second office had opened across the Mississippi River in neighboring St. Paul, Minnesota, and held nearly $50,000 in resources. During its second year of operation the Twin City Building and Loan Association grew nearly fivefold. The rapid growth prompted a move to larger facilities in both cities.

The economic hardships of the early 1930s cut into the association's earnings. In turn, interest rates were pared down, falling to a low of 2.5 percent. The mid-1930s introduction of a government insurance program for S&Ls proved to be a catalyst for growth in the industry and the Minnesota operation.

Twin City Building and Loan, upon receiving a federal charter in 1936, changed its name to Twin City Federal Savings and Loan Association. Its resources were $3.5 million at that time but grew to $10 million over the next three years.

Calendar years 1941 and 1942 proved to be stellar ones. Member accounts increased by over $7 million—a growth rate near if not at the top of the industry for the time period. By 1943, the operation's 20th year of business, the association was the seventh largest savings and loan in the nation, holding over $20 million in resources. During its first two decades, Twin City Federal disbursed to its members approximately $2.9 million in dividends while also financing 14,126 homes.

Roy W. Larsen, who had been on board from day one, led the company as president though its growth spurt. Assets doubled every few years: $50 million in 1946; $100 million in 1951; $200 million in 1955. Another man on hand in 1923, company Vice-President and Secretary Burch N. Bell, still served alongside Larsen as the 1960s approached.

In the fall of 1959, Twin City Federal had surpassed in terms of total size its biggest competitor in the Minneapolis/St. Paul

Company Perspectives:

TCF became a public company in 1986 and since that time we have had a simple and consistent philosophy of banking. Our strong conviction that our customers come first is the driving force that has made TCF one of the best performing banks in the country. We listen to our customers and we have provided the products and services they want. The results speak for themselves; over this time we have recorded some of the highest performance ratios among the top 50 banks in the country and posted record operating earnings for the last 11 years.

savings market. With year-end assets of $357 million, the S&L was also closing in on some of St. Paul's largest banks.

Twin City Federal's rapid rate of growth had been propelled by a number of factors. S&Ls could offer larger interest rates on savings accounts than banks, which were capped by law at a rate of 3 percent. Plus, Twin City Federal had been spending some $700,000 annually on self-promotion. Moreover, the post-World War II housing boom helped the S&L grow: most of its funds were dedicated to long-term mortgages. Finally, there was Larsen's leadership and drive to beat out competitors. ''Business is a game, and I have a competitive urge,'' he told Inskip. ''If I didn't like to win I would have quit years ago.'' He continued to man the helm even as others his age retired.

In 1960 Twin City Federal had about 26 percent of total assets held by the state's savings institutions. The bulk of the S&L's assets came from its savings account volume, primarily in the Twin Cities of Minneapolis and St. Paul. But about 20 to 25 percent came from customers outside the Twin Cities; from folks seeking more interest for their deposits than what local banks offered. ''It's not just that we pay a higher rate for money than the country people,'' Larsen said in the *Minneapolis Tribune.* ''A lot of people just don't want the rest of the people in their home town knowing how much money they've got salted away.'' Originating from rural northwestern Minnesota himself, Larsen led the urban operation for over four decades. Two other company veterans followed in the wake of his tenure. Under those early leaders, the company grew to $1 billion in assets, a milestone reached in 1972.

Storm on the Horizon: 1970s–80s

The new leadership of the 1970s inherited an operation which was at the top of the local thrift market ''thanks largely to an aggressive, personality-driven marketing strategy,'' wrote John R. Engen for *Corporate Report Minnesota.* A popular local radio host, an outspoken Twin's baseball manager, a gregarious Viking's football player, and droll comedian Jack Benny all promoted Twin City Federal. ''That and a strong branch network, sports team sponsorships, a few catchy jingles ('Tuck-abuckadayaway'), and the omnipresent premium giveaways add up to TCF's oldtime formula for success,'' observed Engen.

S&Ls had historically been tied to the strength of the economy and the home building industry: approximately 40 percent of all home loans were made by S&Ls at the beginning of the 1960s.

But by the late 1970s, many of the nation's thrifts, including Twin City Federal, were chasing commercial real estate ventures and other activities promising higher return on investment.

Skyrocketing inflation and interest rates eroded the value of traditional fixed-rate mortgage portfolios, according to Engen. Thrifts posted losses in the early 1980s. Margins shrunk, as interest paid out on savings accounts rose, but interest coming in on loans remained the same. Moreover, federal legislation had changed the lending and investment landscape, leaving S&Ls looking for new ways to drive up profits.

But by the mid-1980s, the cyclical nature of interest rates was the least of the S&L industry's problems: it was about to sink in a sea of red ink created from risky ventures and questionable business practices. The federal agencies regulating the S&Ls would be overwhelmed by the sheer number of thrifts that were insolvent or teetering on the brink.

The weight of ventures such as condominium conversions on the Upper East Side of Manhattan and interest rate swap contracts was about to kill off Twin City Federal. William Cooper, named CEO in the spring of 1985, was charged with keeping the operation alive.

Coming from a working class background, Cooper served as a Detroit police officer while studying to become an accountant during the mid-1960s. A CPA job with Touche Ross would lead him to Michigan National Bank, where he was mentored in retail banking by the company vice-chairman. He held executive positions with Huntington Bancshares in Ohio and American Savings & Loan Association in Miami before arriving in Minnesota.

Cooper returned Twin City Federal to the basics, cutting expenses and revamping the culture. He stripped the corporate headquarters of its luxuries, including expansive executive suites fragrant with orchids tended by flower ladies. Thirty-five upper level officers would retire or be fired during Cooper's first three years in command. Branch managers found their incomes tied tightly to performance.

Seeking capital, Twin City Federal went public in 1986, under the name TCF Banking and Savings, F.A. (TCF Bank). Meanwhile, Cooper continued to clean house. He shut down the company's New York real estate subsidiary, incurring a loss of more than $200 million; a $40 million race track construction loan was sold off; and a billion in interest rate contracts—used by his predecessor to lock in high rates—were canceled to the tune of $70 million.

While tearing down on one end of the spectrum, TCF built on the other. Totally Free Checking was introduced in 1986 to court low- and middle-income customers. Thrift patrons paid for their checks but incurred no other service fees on the noninterest- bearing accounts. Cooper believed that this strategy would drive up net interest margins. He intended to draw in a large number of small deposits, on which TCF paid little or no interest, and use that cheap source of money for higher-yielding consumer loans. By 1988 TCF's consumer loan portfolio—including home equity, credit card, and direct auto and recreational loans—had climbed to $1 billion from about $200 million in 1986.

Key Dates:

1923: Twin City Building and Loan Association is founded in Minneapolis, Minnesota.
1936: The business is granted a federal charter and changes its name to Twin City Federal Savings and Loan Association.
1943: Twin City Federal ranks as the seventh largest S&L in the nation, with $20 million in assets
1972: Twin City Federal reaches $1 billion in assets.
1986: Company goes public under name TCF Banking and Savings, F.A.
1987: TCF Financial Corporation is formed as a holding company.
1988: TCF opens first supermarket branch location.
1989: TCF switches to a federal savings bank and begins trading on the NYSE.
1997: Company converts to a national bank charter.
1999: TCF opens its one-millionth retail checking account.

Cooper also began an expansion drive. During 1987, TCF acquired approximately $300 million of insured deposits from an S&L in Illinois. The holding company TCF Financial Corporation was also formed. The next year, TCF entered the supermarket sector, opening a branch in an Eagan, Minnesota, Cub Foods store. At decade end, TCF converted to a federal savings bank, operating under the name TCF Bank Savings fsb, and company stock began trading on the New York Stock Exchange.

Despite Cooper's moves, TCF's future was still in the balance in 1990. The firm remained in the red, and federal regulators watched it closely. During a period of three years, from 1989 to 1991, the government seized 633 thrifts, and the industry faced ever tighter controls. "In those dark times TCF's management bought heavily into the stock while the board, under Cooper's direction, turned to stock-driven incentives as a bigger part of the pay formula," wrote Engen.

TCF, unlike so many others, survived. Entering the last quarter of 1991, TCF had reduced its nonperforming assets to $87.3 million, down from $156 million at the end of 1986. The company's commercial real estate portfolio was split about evenly between multifamily loans, such as for apartment buildings, and higher risk loans for retail development and office space. A record $1 billion in new mortgages was generated by TCF Mortgage Corporation, TCF Bank's mortgage lending subsidiary.

Warp Speed: Mid- to Late 1990s

By 1993, TCF had boosted its share of Minnesota's consumer banking market to 18 percent, up from 8 percent in 1986, according to a May 1993 *American Banker* article by Brian Hellauer. Its figures surpassed larger commercial banks Norwest Corp. and First Bank Systems Inc.

In addition to growing market share by aggressively selling its banking services, TCF was beefing up profits with technology. According to Hellauer, a lean data processing operation allowed the company to continue to service mortgages while other operations farmed the work out to third parties. Furthermore, TCF's widespread automatic teller machine (ATM) network generated income with each transaction.

"We charge for just about everything, and we charge for things other people don't charge for," Cooper told Hellauer. "We're very aggressive pricers, but we give people a lot of service—longer hours, a broader base of products, more access to ATMs."

Through the mid-1990s, TCF relied heavily on acquisitions to build business in Illinois, Wisconsin, and Michigan. In 1993, TCF acquired $960 million-in-assets Republic Capital Group, Inc. of Milwaukee, Wisconsin. The company also spent about $14.5 million to buy $220 million of deposits and 15 branches of the failed thrift First Federal Savings and Loan Association of Pontiac, Michigan. TCF added 39 offices in Michigan when it acquired a struggling $2.4 billion Great Lakes Bancorp in 1995.

By 1996 TCF was clearly on solid ground, ranked among the best-performing thrifts in the nation, according to *Corporate Report Minnesota*. It was the 14th largest savings bank in the United States, holding just over $7 billion in assets. But in 1997, Cooper led TCF's conversion from a thrift to a bank.

Also in 1997, TCF entered the leasing business through the acquisition of Winthrop Resources Corporation. The operation leased computers and other equipment to businesses nationwide. Additionally, banking operations were expanded to Colorado.

TCF directed a lot of attention to the Chicago area in 1997 and 1998, first purchasing the Bank of Chicago and then acquiring 76 bank branches in Jewel-Osco stores from BankAmerica Corp. The supermarket branches had failed to turn a profit under Bank of America: its upscale product was not in line with the profile of the typical Jewel customer. TCF turned the branches around by marketing products such as Totally Free Checking to modest-means customers.

"A small number times a large number equals a large number," Cooper told *Crain's Chicago Business* in 2000, citing the same strategy that had worked so well in the Twin Cities market. In terms of total number of branches in Chicago, TCF ranked second only to Bank One Corp.

Mixed Results: 1999–2002

From 1990 to 1998 TCF's stock rose spectacularly, exceeding the pace of even strong industry performers. But as its earnings growth slowed in 1998, the stock nosedived. A February 1999 *American Banker* article reported profits were hurt by a $10 million price tag to open 105 supermarket branches; mortgage prepayments; and the discontinuation of its indirect automobile lending operation.

"Cooper's investor-relations problems coincided with voter dissatisfaction with his politics," wrote John Engen in a June 2001 *American Business* article. In 1990, Cooper served as finance chairman for a Republican gubernatorial candidate. Arne Carlson's unexpected victory in strongly democratic Minnesota gave Cooper a solid foothold in the party, and in 1997, as party chairman, he helped bring in record contributions. But, another unexpected victory took the shine off Cooper's political star. Ex-professional wrestler Jesse Ventura defeated both the Democratic and Republican candidates for governor in 1998. Cooper was not shy about exchanging barbs with the colorful new governor. Engen wrote, "Mr. Cooper displayed a bumper sticker that said, 'Your governor is smarter than my governor.'" In 1999, Cooper stepped down as party chairman, but he remained politically active, serving as finance chair.

Meanwhile, TCF opened its one-millionth retail checking account. In other business sectors, TCF both expanded and contracted in 1999. Leasing operations grew with the establishment of TCF Leasing, Inc. But, the company sold off substantially all of its remaining automobile loan portfolio. Additionally, TCF sold its title insurance and appraisal operations and formed a strategic alliance with the buyer.

In 2000, TCF surpassed $1 billion in supermarket branch deposits. The Minnesota-based bank was the fourth largest operator of supermarket bank branches in the country with over 200.

TCF also ranked as the 16th largest issuer of Visa debit cards in the United States with 1.1 million cards in circulation—TCF had introduced the card that worked like a check to its Minnesota customers back in 1996. During 2000, TCF's debit card transactions produced $28.7 million in revenue, an increase of 47 percent over 1999.

TCF continued to apply technology as a means to draw customers: phone cards were introduced as part of a customer loyalty program and an Internet banking site was launched in 2000. As committed as ever to the concept of convenience, in 2001 TCF expanded Sunday hours to some of its traditional banking locations, a practice already in place in its supermarket sites. Its investment business was also expanded in 2001 with the introduction of a discount brokerage service. TCF had begun offering annuities in the 1980s and mutual funds in the 1990s.

TCF initiated some business activity outside its markets of Colorado, Illinois, Indiana, Michigan, Minnesota, and Wisconsin in the new millennium. Its venture capital unit planted seed money in new banks: the company's first two investments were made in Florida. TCF intended to invest between 5 and 25 percent of needed start-up capital. In addition to Florida, TCF was looking toward the Southwest for start-up bank locations, particularly in areas in which there had been a recent merger or buyout of a community bank, according to a February 2002 *American Banker* article.

Principal Subsidiaries

TCF Mortgage Corporation; Winthrop Resources Corporation; TCF Leasing, Inc.

Principal Competitors

Associated Bank-Corp.; U.S. Bancorp; Wells Fargo & Company.

Further Reading

Arndorfer, James B., Julie Johnsson, "Grocery Outlets a Real Jewel for TCF," *Crain's Chicago Business,* September 4, 2000, p. 1.

Chase, Brett, "High-Performing TCF Defies Banking Wisdom," *American Banker,* July 12, 1996, p. 4.

——, "TCF Bids for Respect with Conversion to Bank Charter," April 7, 1997, p. 6.

——, "TCF's Check Mastermind to Retire on New Year's Day," *American Banker,* October 6, 1997, p. 8.

——, "TCF Isn't Ready to Check Out of Supermarket Strategy," *American Banker,* February 25, 1999, p. 5.

Conroy, Bill, "Minnesota's S&Ls: Asset or Liability?" *Minneapolis-St. Paul CityBusiness,* October 21, 1991, pp. 1+.

Engen, John R., "CEO Cooper—Wrestled Ventura, Sluggish Earnings—Won't Budge," *American Banker,* June 15, 2001, p. 1.

——, "A Master of Marketing—Supermarketing, That Is," *American Banker,* April 4, 1994, pp. 6+.

——, "Pin Money," *Corporate Report Minnesota,* October 1996, pp. 46+.

Hellauer, Bill, "TCF Financial Finds Fees, Profits Catering to Mass Market," *American Banker,* May 10, 1993, pp. 1A+.

Inskip, Leonard, "Twin City Builds Pennies into 373 Million Dollars," *Minneapolis Tribune,* April, 24, 1960, pp. 9, 11.

Jackson, Ben, "Start-Up Investor TCF Says Control Is Not Its Goal," *American Banker,* February 4, 2002, p. 5.

——, "TCF Financial Introduces Sunday Hours," *American Banker,* October 26, 2001, p. 1.

Kimelman, John, "Thrifts Slow to Abandon Traditional Ways," *American Banker,* November 1, 1999, p. 25.

Leuty, Ron, "TCF Fills Its Shopping Bag with Old BofA Branches," *San Francisco Business Times,* September 15, 2000, p. 15.

Rieker, Matthias, "TCF Financial of Minnesota Wins Praise from Merrill," *American Banker,* May 10, 2001, p. 20.

Schafer, Lee, "Alive and Well Among the Living Dead," *Corporate Report Minnesota,* December 1988, pp. 51–54.

Schwab, Paul, "TCF Launches Discount Brokerage," *Business Journal—Milwaukee,* June 29, 2001, p. 9.

Silvestri, Scott, "TCF Plans to Stock Up on Store Branches," *American Banker,* September 12, 2000, p. 1.

Twenty Million in Twenty Years, Minneapolis: Jones Press and Twin City Federal Saving and Loan Association, 1943.

—Kathleen Peippo

Tishman Speyer Properties, L.P.

520 Madison Avenue
New York, New York 10022
U.S.A.
Telephone: (212) 715-0300
Fax: (212) 319-1745
Web site: http://www.tishmanspeyer.com

Private Partnership
Founded: 1978
Employees: 300
Sales: $205 million (1998 est.)
NAIC: 233110 Land Subdivision & Land Development;
531110 Lessors of Residential Buildings; 531120
Lessors of Nonresidential Buildings; 5313110
Residential Property Managers; 531312 Nonresidential
Property Managers

Tishman Speyer Properties, L.P. (TSP) is a large real estate developer—possibly the largest in the world—with headquarters in New York City and offices in several other U.S. cities and in European and South American countries. With a piece of both Rockefeller Center and the Chrysler Building, TSP has become Manhattan's most high-profile commercial landlord, thereby making its chief executive officer, Jerry Speyer—somewhat against his will—a celebrity developer. In addition to establishing office buildings in major urban locations, this private partnership creates mixed-use, retail, residential, and entertainment centers. It also provides planning services for large-scale developments and manages the conversion of under-utilized tracts of land into such developments.

Tishman Predecessors: 1898–1976

Julius Tishman was an immigrant peddler who began building small tenements in downtown Manhattan in 1898. In 1910 he built a nine-story luxury apartment building on the Upper West Side despite warnings that no well-to-do New Yorker would live north of 86th Street. The project was successful, and he made a small fortune erecting more apartment buildings in

this neighborhood during the next ten years. In 1923, he decided to put up an office building across from Penn Station, even though this area around West 34th Street and Seventh Avenue was mainly occupied by garment factories. Again, he was successful, and he followed by putting up more office buildings. Tishman Realty & Development Co. Inc. was established as a publicly traded firm in 1928, with Julius's son David as president. Shortly after, the Great Depression put an end to the firm's construction activities.

Tishman Realty & Development did not significantly renew its growth until after World War II, when it once again began constructing office buildings in New York City, including Manhattan's first fully air-conditioned office building and first metal-clad office building, under the direction of Norman Tishman, another of Julius Tishman's five sons. In 1950 the company began putting up office and apartment buildings on Wilshire Boulevard in Los Angeles, and within a few years it was the largest landlord in southern California. By 1958 the firm was operating 31 large office or apartment buildings and three shopping centers in five cities, with others under construction in Buffalo and Cleveland. In 1959 the company also began leasing office and factory equipment and aircraft. The following year it began constructing buildings for other developers as well as doing so for its own account, and a few years later it added a research subsidiary to help manufacturers apply new products and techniques.

Tishman Realty & Development moved into Chicago in 1962 to build the Gateway Center and soon had become the city's second largest office landlord. It divested itself of the last of its residential properties in 1967. By this time the company was under the direction of David's son Robert. After serving as the general contractor for the 100-story John Hancock Building in Chicago and for Renaissance Center in Detroit, the company won the contract to build the World Trade Center in New York.

The recession that began in 1970 hurt all developers, but Tishman Realty & Construction was especially hard hit because of the 44-story office building at 1166 Avenue of the Americas in midtown Manhattan that it completed in 1974. Two years later, with the building still vacant, Tishman defaulted on its construction loan from Citibank. This structure was said to have cost the company some $70 million to $80 million in cumulative losses—more money than had ever been lost before on a single building. Its management decided in 1976 to liquidate the company and use its assets for a cash distribution to the shareholders—of whom the largest group by far consisted of members of the Tishman family. Seventeen properties were purchased by the Equitable Life Assurance Society of the United States for $107.5 million. The remaining ones were sold for $78.5 million to Lazard Realty Inc., an arm of the investment house of Lazard Freres & Co. acting on behalf of a group of investors.

Making Its Mark: 1978–95

The nine Tishmans in executive positions had no intention of putting themselves out of work, however. Tishman Realty & Construction continued as a general-contracting subsidiary of Rockefeller Center Corp. under John L. Tishman until 1980, when 16 of the senior executive officers of the subsidiary bought it back. The former company's management and leasing operations became Tishman Management and Leasing Corp., with Alan V. Tishman in charge. The finance and development arm became Tishman Speyer Properties, with Robert V. Tishman—who had been president of the old company prior to liquidation—as chairman and Jerry Speyer, his son-in-law, as president and chief executive officer. All three successor companies took up quarters in the Tishman Building, the aluminum-clad high-rise at 666 Fifth Avenue that had served as the old company's flagship. Tishman Speyer started business with assets of $17 million from the dissolution of the old firm, a staff of 13, and two properties worth $65 million.

Tishman Speyer's first job, under contract to Lazard Realty as part of the sale, was to direct the land assemblage and construction of 520 Madison Avenue, a 38-floor slant-faced office tower clad in rose-colored granite. TSP took an equity interest in the property and moved its headquarters there after completion in 1981. The fledgling company also acquired and renovated five or six buildings at relatively low cost, tapping funds from the Lazard Realty-organized investment group. By 1981 Tishman Speyer had built enough equity from its projects to buy out this group. It then turned to Lester and Henry Crown of Chicago—the largest shareholders of General Dynamics Corp.—to fund joint ventures, forming both a development and

an acquisition partnership with the family, and also took on Equitable as a limited partner. By the spring of 1983 Tishman Speyer had developed 12 projects in New York, Chicago, Atlanta, Houston, and Stamford, Connecticut, worth $1.2 billion. TSP's net equity in these projects was believed to exceed $100 million.

In 1983 Tishman Speyer completed $300 million more in construction to put it among the top ten commercial developers in the United States. The firm developed five major projects in Chicago, including a $200 million tower for NBC, and completed a 28-story building at One Brickell Square in Miami, overlooking Biscayne Bay. The Crown brothers' connections enabled TSP to secure Chicago's Continental Illinois National Bank & Trust Co. as the anchor tenant for 520 Madison Avenue in Manhattan, which was named the Continental Illinois Center. In 1984 Tishman Speyer formed a syndication company that would allow individual investors not as well-heeled as Equitable or the Crown brothers, but capable of putting up at least $500,000, to participate in the ownership of existing properties through private limited partnerships.

Tishman Speyer was also sharing the wealth from about $550 million worth of real estate with some of its own employees. Managing partners Tishman and Speyer took 60 percent of the income and tax benefits, while three general partners and a dozen limited partners shared in the remainder, an arrangement that could double or triple their basic pay. In order to quench competition within the firm, this partnership interest applied to all of TSP's projects and not only to the ones in which a given staffer was engaged. The actual construction was in the hands of hired outside managers supervised by TSP. A company executive told Ronald Derven of *National Real Estate Investor* in 1988, "The people on our staff come from either a design or construction background. We look over the shoulders of our contractors—second-guessing them if you will—to anticipate problems before they become insurmountable."

Tishman Speyer had, in the mid-1980s, the daring to undertake Manhattan projects outside the usual locations, completing the Saatchi Building at 375 Hudson Street, north of the financial district, in 1985, and turning the ruins of the old Siegel-Cooper department store, at 620 Sixth Avenue in the Flatiron district, into a retail complex. In 1986 the firm completed a 54-story tower for Equitable on Seventh Avenue—the first major office building on this avenue and a trendsetter as developers began moving farther west in midtown. But sensing that the market for new buildings would not last, Tishman Speyer began withdrawing from further construction. "We put 7 million square feet of development on the shelf between 1985 and 1987," Speyer later told Peter Hellman for *New York*. "The market was *too* hot," he explained. "It was worrisome." Instead, TSP began acquiring existing buildings, including ones in Los Angeles, Miami, and San Francisco.

By the fall of 1987 Tishman Speyer's portfolio had grown to 25 properties, with 18 million square feet of space owned or managed by the firm and a cumulative market value of $4.2 billion. Only 30 percent of this portfolio was now in New York, because the managing partners considered building in Manhattan increasingly difficult and costly. TSP projects underway at this time included three in Florida, two in Chicago, one in

Durham, North Carolina, and a joint venture with Shearson Lehman Brothers Holdings Inc. to develop, finance, and market a $150 million office and apartment complex in Beijing for foreign executives and diplomats in China. This project collapsed in 1989, after Chinese security forces crushed a protest in Tiananmen Square.

By this time Tishman Speyer had begun work on its first foreign project, as developer of the MesseTurm, a 62-floor pyramid-crowned office tower in Frankfurt, Germany. It was completed in 1990 as the tallest building in continental Europe. The firm followed this up with some of the largest development projects in Berlin, capital of the reunified German republic. In 1996 TSP completed Friedrichstadt Passagen, a $500 million property with one million square feet of office, retail, and residential space fronting the city's historic Friedrichstrasse.

One Manhattan deal that proved attractive to Tishman Speyer was the purchase of 1301 Avenue of the Americas—the headquarters of J.C. Penney Co.—for $353 million in 1988. This 46-story, 1.8-million-square-foot tower was acquired in a joint venture with Trammell Crow Co. Once Penney moved to Plano, Texas, the prematurely aged 26-year-old building was vacant. The partners resurfaced the building's faded external panels and filled in the sunken entrance plaza, installing a Jim Dine sculpture. By late 1990, in spite of a recession, it was 80 percent rented by prestige tenants and had been renamed the Credit Lyonnais Building.

Spanning the World: 1995–2000

Tishman Speyer essentially marked time in the early 1990s as the U.S. economy slowly recovered from recession. One of its few losers was 1515 Broadway, a 54-story midtown Manhattan office tower purchased in 1985 in partnership with Equitable and other investors. This venture resulted in bankruptcy and an end to TSP's relationship with Equitable. By 1995, however, the firm was ready to raise its profile again in its own backyard, by paying $306 million, in partnership with Goldman, Sachs & Co. and David Rockefeller (who also brought in Europe's super-rich Gianni Agnelli and Stavros Niarchos), to purchase Rockefeller Center from Mitsubishi Estate Co., Ltd. and rescue it from imminent bankruptcy. Although the high-profile 12-building center included six million square feet of commercial and retail space, it was $900 million in debt, and Mitsubishi had incurred $2 billion in losses. Ninety percent of the space was leased, but at relatively low rates, while operating costs were high. Tishman Speyer wound up with only a 5 percent stake in the complex but, as manager, brought in blue-chip tenants such as Christie's International plc and Cablevision Systems Corp. as well as fashionable retailers Banana Republic, J. Crew, Kenneth Cole, and Sephora. The center turned profitable in 1998 and earned $45.3 million in 1999.

Another Manhattan classic dropped into the Tishman Speyer portfolio in 1997, when a TSP investment fund established in partnership with Travelers Group Inc. and Shearson Lehman Brothers purchased the mortgage of the Chrysler Building and adjoining 666 Third Avenue for $220 million. Speyer acknowledged that the 77-story Art Deco landmark was in need of renovation and said the firm anticipated spending about $100 million to replace elevators and the heating and air-conditioning systems. By 2000 the venerable tower was packed with tenants paying as much as $100 a square foot. The following year TSP and Travelers sold a 75 percent stake in the Chrysler Building to TMW, a German investment group, for a reported $300 million. TSP continued to manage and lease the building. Also in 1997, TSP and Travelers Group formed a joint venture for ten office buildings previously held by Travelers, including 125 High Street in Boston, a recently built 1.5-million-square-foot complex that included twin towers with an atrium between them, three restored 19th-century buildings, and a city fire station. The other properties consisted of buildings in Florida, California, and the Midwest, as well as one other building in Boston.

Tishman Speyer was also active in Europe and South America. In addition to the previously completed German projects, the firm was, in 1998, developing a three-million-square-foot Berlin mixed-use complex, including a new train station, and, with Sony Corp., a two-million-square-foot complex near Potsdamer Platz with retail, entertainment, and office space, including Sony's new European headquarters. TSP also was developing an office building in Krakow, Poland, and had developed properties in France and Great Britain. The firm had joined with Brazil's largest construction company to erect the nation's tallest building, a 36-story office tower in Sao Paulo. This was followed in 2001 with the announcement that the partners would join with Deutsche Bank to put up a four-tower office complex in the city. TSP had nine overseas offices in 2001.

Tishman Speyer took a trip down memory lane in 2000 when it purchased—in collaboration with a group that included the Crown family and TMW—the former Tishman Building at 666 Fifth Avenue. Also in 2000, Tishman Speyer completed 101 West End Avenue, a 35-story, twin-tower residential rental complex between West 64th and 65th streets in Manhattan.

Tishman Speyer was also active in California. In San Francisco, the firm purchased the Chevron Corp. buildings at 555 and 575 Market Street in 1998 for about $190 million after selling 525 Market Street the previous year. When Chevron moved out of the city and new-media businesses started to fail, however, the buildings began to empty. Construction of two office towers in Mountain View and Santa Clara was scheduled to begin in 2000. In southern California, Tishman Speyer purchased Santa Monica's MGM Plaza in 2000 for $353 million, with funding from partners who included Travelers. This six-building office complex covered a whole city block.

Tishman Speyer had, in 2001, offices in nine U.S. cities and in Berlin, Buenos Aires, Frankfurt, Krakow, London, Madrid, Paris, Sao Paulo, and Warsaw. Since its formation the firm had developed or acquired a portfolio of more than 48 million square feet of constructed area, valued at over $10 billion. According to Jerry Speyer in a *New York Times Magazine* entitled ''The Anti-Trump,'' TSP achieved an average annual rate of return of 47.5 percent between 1993 and 1998.

Principal Subsidiaries

Tishman Speyer Properties Inc.; Tishman-Speyer Realty.

Principal Competitors

Boston Properties, Inc.; Brookfield Properties Corp.; Equity Office Properties Trust.; Silverstein Properties, Inc.; Vornado Realty Trust.

Further Reading

Bagli, Charles V., "German Group Buys Stake in Skyscraper," *New York Times,* March 5, 2001, p. B1.

Blair, William G., "Tishman Company Back on Its Own Once More," *New York Times,* February 10, 1980, Sec. 8, pp. 1, 4.

Croghan, Lore, "Jerry Speyer Scores Two NY Landmarks," *Crain's New York Business,* May 15, 2000, p. 88.

——, "New Chrysler Bldg. Partner Helps Speyer Keep His Spire," *Crain's New York Business,* March 5, 2001, p. 4.

Derven, Ronald, "Tishman Speyer Celebrates 10 Years of Success," *National Real Estate Investor,* February 1988, pp. 96–98.

Ginsberg, Steve, " 'Anti-Trump' Plays a New Hand," *San Francisco Business Times,* August 11, 2000, p. 1.

Goldberger, Paul, "Equitable's New Tower: A Curious Ambivalence," *New York Times,* February 20, 1986, pp. B1, B5.

Greenberg, Jonathan, "This Just Might Amount to Something," *Forbes,* May 23, 1983, pp. 158, 163.

Hellman, Peter, "The Invisible Magnate," *New York,* October 16, 1995, pp. 35–39.

Horsley, Carter B., "New Office Tower to Rise at 520 Madison," *New York Times,* October 21, 1979, Sec. 8, p. 4.

Kindleberger, Richard, "Office Buildings Purchase May Lead to Resale," *Boston Globe,* February 15, 1997, p. F1.

Pacelle, Mitchell, "Chrysler Building Gets a New Owner As Tishman Speyer Wins Bidding War," *Wall Street Journal,* November 25, 1997, p. A6.

Scardino, Albert, "Tishman's Global Strategy," *New York Times,* October 10, 1987, pp. 43, 45.

Slatin, Peter, "Will Rock Drag Down New Owners?" *Crain's New York Business,* November 13, 1995, pp. 1, 31.

Thompson, Russell, and Matthew Williams, "How One U.S. Developer Has Found Happiness Overseas," *Barron's,* July 6, 1998, pp. 36–37.

"Tishman Matches Sales with Rental Income," *Business Week,* March 19, 1960, pp. 128–30, 132, 134, 137.

"Tishman Speyer: A Whole New Kind of Real Estate Empire," *Business Week,* August 12, 1984, pp. 104–05.

Traub, James, "The Anti-Trump," *New York Times Magazine,* December 20, 1998, pp. 62–68.

—Robert Halasz

Tokyu Corporation

5-6, Nanpeidai-cho
Shibuya-ku, Tokyo 150-8511
Japan
Telephone: (03) 3477-69603
Fax: (03) 5459-7061
Web site: http://www.tokyu.co.jp

Public Company
Incorporated: 1922 as Tokyo Kyuko Electric Railway
Company Ltd.
Employees: 4,445
Sales: ¥1,012.89 billion (US $8.10 billion) (2001)
Stock Exchanges: Tokyo
NAIC: 481111 Scheduled Passenger Air Transportation;
482111 Line-Haul Railroads; 485210 Interurban and
Rural Bus Transportation; 485999 All Other Transit
and Ground Passenger Transportation; 233320
Commercial and Institutional Building Construction

Tokyu Corporation operates railways, freight companies, bus companies, and a domestic airline in Japan. It is also involved in construction and real estate development, focusing on geographic areas that are served by its rail lines, and hotel ownership and other travel and leisure services. The company is the nucleus of the Tokyu Group, a group of more than 500 companies. Tokyu is one of Japan's relatively new conglomerates, unlike the long-established, finance-oriented groups such as Mitsubishi and Mitsui.

Early 1900s: Roots in Transportation

The story of Tokyu began in the rural town of Aoki in Nagano Prefecture in western Japan, where founder Keita Kobayashi was born in 1883. After completing primary school in his native village he attended high school in the nearby city of Matsumoto, where he spent a year before moving to Tokyo to attend what is now the law department of Tokyo University, the country's most prestigious university. He graduated in 1907 at the age of 24. While at the university Keita Kobayashi made the

acquaintance of a politician, Takaaki Katoh, who would later become prime minister of Japan. Katoh was an inspiration to the young Kobayashi and provided him with a prestigious position upon graduation with the civil service in the Agricultural Ministry. The following year Kobayashi took the name of his wife's family, Gotoh, which means "raider" in Japanese. The pun has been used by countless journalists alluding to Keita Gotoh's style of doing business.

By 1921 Gotoh was employed by the Ministry of Transport. He was involved in supervising Japan's national railway system, and was given a post as director of the newly privatized and ailing Musashi Railway. At the time Musashi Railway was a so-called paper company because it did not actually own or operate any trains, but possessed real estate and planning permission to do so. Gotoh not only turned the company around but in 1922 also bought a controlling interest in it for ¥50,000. This was to be the first of the many corporate buyouts that characterized Keita Gotoh's rise. In the same year, he founded Tokyo Kyuko Electric Railway Company Ltd., which absorbed Musashi Railway.

The following year Eichi Shibusawa, a leading Japanese industrialist and founder of Denenchofu Corporation, one of Japan's first electric railway companies, was looking for help in building and developing the railway arm of his company, Mekata Railway. He approached Ichizo Kobayashi, founder of Hankyu Corporation, who promptly recommended Gotoh. Gotoh not only accepted the offer, but following the Great Kanto Earthquake of 1923 he took control of its railway interests.

1920s–30s: Growth and Acquisition

The next five years saw ambitious construction projects realized, including a 13.2-kilometer line through the southwest section of Tokyo. The late 1920s and the 1930s in Japan were a time of rapid industrialization, and Gotoh realized that the key to a modern and industrialized Japan was an efficient infrastructure. In densely populated Tokyo and in Kawasaki and Yokohama, rail transport was becoming increasingly important. Gotoh's aggressive expansion policy continued as the Tokyu Corporation—as it was then named, "Tokyu" being an abbreviation of "*Tokyo Kyuko,*" or "*Tokyo Express*"—came to include the Ikejoh and Tamagawa lines and Tokyo Underground line. Gotoh became a pioneering force behind the most efficient underground railway system in the world by building, in 1937, an underground link from Shibuya to Shinbashi, both districts of Tokyo. Other acquisitions made around this time were Enoshima Electric Railways and Shizuoka Electric Railways companies, both outside Tokyo; Sotetsu Transport Company; and Kanto United Cars, a railway car manufacturer. In the decade before the end of World War II, Gotoh continued his policy of buying weak companies and turning them around. He also began exploiting the extensive lands his company owned around its railway lines. One of the first areas to be developed—which became one of Tokyo's most exclusive residential areas—was Denenchofu. During its first two decades, leading up to World War II, Tokyu was not only providing the crucial transport links to this area but also developing and constructing real estate.

About this time, another railway and real estate group was flourishing in Tokyo, the Seibu Group. The two companies became bitter rivals.

World War II: Starting Over

The years 1935 to 1945 were prosperous years. The Japanese war machine was in full gear and provided the various group companies with contracts in such areas as cargo, construction, and the manufacture of railway cars for the Japanese army. The saturation bombing of Tokyo during 1944 and 1945, however, proved disastrous for the company, severely disrupting the railway lines. The U.S. occupation proved equally disastrous. Like the other huge industrial and financial combines, or *zaibatsu,* Tokyu was dismantled under the Economic Decentralization Law imposed by General Douglas MacArthur. Rail and bus transportation networks were broken up and transferred to other companies. With its operations reduced, Tokyu Corporation attempted a new beginning as did the remnants of other Japanese companies. Although much of the infrastructure had been damaged or destroyed, Gotoh used this as an opportunity to modernize the company's enterprises and make inroads into new businesses to meet the various needs of consumers. Gotoh made the remaining businesses into subsidiaries, thus encouraging them to develop and prosper independently. In 1949, in order to raise capital for continued expansion, Gotoh floated Tokyu on the Tokyo stock exchange.

1950s–70s: New Markets

In the early 1950s Gotoh's son Noboru, born in 1920, began to rise through the ranks within the company. As his father was still the largest single shareholder in Tokyu, it was natural that Noboru Gotoh should succeed him at the helm of the company. Indeed, it was the young and dynamic Noboru who was en-

couraging his father to lead Tokyu into new markets. In 1934 Tokyu opened its first department store with the innovative idea of locating it in one of its Tokyo railway stations. In 1948 the Tokyu Department Store Company was formed to expand the chain nationwide and eventually overseas. Tokyu Tourist Corporation was established in 1956 to provide travel services both in Japan and overseas, and in 1960 Tokyu added the hotel business to its activities. Noboru Gotoh became president of Tokyu in 1958 at the age of 38. Keita Gotoh died in 1962, leaving his son clearly in charge of the group. Although Noboru was a less aggressive businessman than his father, he was perhaps more of a visionary and made ambitious plans for Tokyu both in Japan and overseas. He even healed the rift between Tokyu and Seibu by attending the opening of a new Seibu department store.

In 1953 Tokyu began the development of the real estate it owned around its Denentoshi line in Tokyo. The project spanned three decades and involved the development of a relatively sparsely populated suburb called Tama Denentoshi. As Tokyo grew as a center of business and government, and as residential real estate in centrally located areas became more expensive, the new development provided thousands of Japanese with the opportunity to own decent homes within commuting distance of their workplaces. Tokyu would later apply this domestically acquired experience on overseas projects in Seattle, Washington, and in Perth, Australia.

In 1961 Tokyu, under the leadership of Noboru Gotoh, branched out into two new areas of business: air travel, through the formation of Toa Domestic Airlines, later Japan Air System; and information services, through the formation of Tokyu Agency, which became one of the largest advertising agencies in Japan and, later, overseas. Tokyu also began manufacturing automobile parts in 1964 with the formation of Shiroki Corporation.

While the company branched out into these new areas, Tokyu's mainstay remained its railways, and although the latter did not experience growth as rapid as for some of the newer businesses, it provided steady growth along with a financially stable backbone for the group. In 1961 Tokyu established Izukyu Corporation, a railway line carrying tourists to the national park of Fuji-Hakone-Izu. In 1966 the opening of a new Tokyu railway in the Tama Denentoshi area brought the number of Tokyu lines in the Tokyo area to seven, totaling more than 100 kilometers. The Ueda Kotsu Company, operating a line in Nagano Prefecture, completed Tokyu's national railway network.

In the 1970s Noboru Gotoh led Tokyu into the car rental business through Nippon Rent a Car Tokyu and also dramatically expanded Tokyu's hotel network by forming two companies: Tokyu Hotel Chain, which operated luxury hotels such as the Tokyu Capitol Hotel in the heart of Tokyo, and Tokyu Inn Chain, which was set up in 1958 to cater to the economizing business traveler. In 1972 with the opening of the Hawaiian Regent Hotel in Honolulu, Tokyu Hotels International was established. By the mid-1970s Tokyu was once again a huge conglomerate and like many large companies used its financial clout for charitable as well as investment purposes. Tokyu Foundation for Better Environment was established in 1974 and, as its name suggested, was concerned with environmental issues, one of the first such organizations in Japan. This, along

Key Dates:

1921: Keita Gotoh becomes director of the Musashi Railway.

1922: Gotoh buys a controlling interest in the Musashi Railway; founds Tokyo Kyuko Electric Railway Company Ltd., which absorbs Musashi.

1923: Gotoh takes control of Mekata Railway.

1937: Gotoh's company, by then named Tokyu Corporation, builds an underground link from the Shibuya district to the Shinbashi district in Tokyo.

1945–47: Tokyu's operations are reduced by the Economic Decentralization Law during the U.S. occupation.

1948: The Tokyu Department Store Company is formed.

1949: Gotoh lists Tokyu on the Tokyo stock exchange.

1953: Tokyu begins developing the Tama Denentoshi area in Tokyo.

1958: Keita Gotoh's son, Noboru Gotoh, becomes president of Tokyu.

1960: Tokyu enters the hotel business.

1961: Tokyu forms Toa Domestic Airlines and Tokyu Agency, an advertising agency.

1980: Tokyu begins a period of aggressive overseas expansion.

1987: Tokyu Cable Television is formed.

1989: Noboru Gotoh dies; Jiro Yokota is Tokyu's president.

1995: Shinobu Shimizu becomes Tokyu Corporation's president.

2000: The Tokyu Group announces a major restructuring, to be led and overseen by Tokyu Corporation.

2001: Tokyu partners with Lend Lease Corp. of Australia to form a real estate investment firm.

with the Tokyu Foundation for Inbound Students, provided scholarships for postgraduate and research students. The Gotoh Museum contains a fine Japanese and Chinese art collection, including the original manuscript of what is recognized as the world's first novel, *The Tale of Genji*.

1980s: International Expansion

The 1980s were years of accelerated overseas expansion for the Tokyu Corporation. In 1980 Tokyu established Tokyu Zurich AG and in 1982 launched a large-scale residential development project in Jakarta, Indonesia. In 1983 Tokyu opened the Mauna Lani Bay Hotel and in the following year the Palau Pacific Resort, both in Hawaii. Tokyu was one of the leading developers in Hawaii. Early in 1986 Tokyu completed construction of a prestigious hotel/office complex in Vancouver. Again, Tokyu was one of the pioneer Japanese developers in a city that was to become one of the world's most lucrative real estate investment areas. In 1987 Tokyu branched out into television broadcasting with the formation of Tokyu Cable Television. As his father had done before him, Noboru Gotoh relied on the infrastructure base of Tokyu's railway lines to move into a new area of business. Cables were laid initially to span the Tama Denentoshi region, covering 600,000 households. A broadcasting center and studios were constructed in Tama Denentoshi, and to launch their activities a two-way Tokyu Cable Computer was developed. The system, which linked the center's host computer to each subscriber's home terminal, was designed to provide subscribers with diversified two-way information services.

Tokyu's railway and bus transportation business remained the nucleus of the group. In 1987 Japan National Railways (JNR), carrying 86 percent of Japan's passenger traffic, was privatized and split up into regional companies that were organized to be more cost-effective and profit-oriented. This in the late 1980s meant increased competition for Tokyu and the other private railway companies such as Seibu and Hankyu, and heralded a turbulent time both financially and politically for the usually steady Japanese railway industry. Tokyu, therefore, set about increasing its competitiveness through better service. This meant alleviation of overcrowding, greater passenger comfort, and greater speed and frequency of service. An example of investment toward these ends by Tokyu was the construction of triple tracks and station improvement along the heavily used Toyoko line between Tokyo and Yokohama.

By the mid-1980s Noboru Gotoh was approaching retirement. Like his father before him, his eldest son was rapidly rising within the Tokyu organization. Konsuke Gotoh was born in 1949, and by 1987 was a senior manager in Tokyu Construction. In an interview with the *Yomiuri Newspaper* shortly before his death in 1989, Noboru Gotoh stated that Tokyu was no longer a Gotoh family concern and that although he would give his son Konsuke the chance to take over the reins, he would like to see his son work his way up competitively. Although Noboru Gotoh became president at age 38, the Tokyu Corporation had grown and diversified tremendously since then. Its president was Jiro Yokota, but Konsuke Gotoh was fairly powerful within the organization.

1990s Through the Early New Century: Restructuring

In 1995, Jiro Yokota, plagued by health problems, stepped down from his post as president of Tokyu Corporation. He was succeeded by Shinobu Shimizu, who had previously been a senior managing director of the company.

The late 1990s saw major difficulties for the Tokyu Group, which by that time consisted of some 500 companies. With the financial crisis of 1998 and its far-reaching ramifications, the performance of many of the group's companies suffered. This decline, especially among the group's publicly traded companies, caused Tokyu's investment rating to be downgraded.

By 2000, feeling compelled to make major changes, the Tokyu Group announced the launch of a three-year restructuring. The process through which the group was to reorganize differed substantially from the way decisions had been made in the past—and placed Tokyu Corporation in a pivotal role. Previously, strategy decisions for the group had been made by an organization consisting of group companies' presidents. Under the 2000 plan, however, Tokyu Corporation, as the principal shareholder in the group's operations, was appointed to lead the entire restructuring. In the Tokyu Group's 2000 annual report, Shinobu Shimizu explained Tokyu Corporation's new responsibility: ''Regarding Tokyu Corporation's role, Tokyu will be positioned as, in effect, a holding company with a strategic decision-making function.''

As part of the restructuring, Tokyu identified two core businesses: the urban development business, which focused on growth in areas served by Tokyu's railway, and the group of Tokyu-branded businesses, which included the hotel, real estate, tourism, and airline businesses. The group began reshuffling its assets; one of the first major changes implemented was making the Tokyu Hotel Chain a wholly owned subsidiary of Tokyu Corporation. The group also began a thorough review of its underperforming and/or noncore companies, looking for those that should be consolidated and those that should simply be sold off.

Meanwhile, as part of the effort to develop areas served by its railway, Tokyu joined with Sony Corporation to develop a broadband network. The partnership, formed in 2000, gave Sony a 10 percent stake in Tokyu's cable television unit. The companies planned to use Tokyu's existing cable infrastructure, which had been put in place in the 1980s, as the basis for the new broadband system.

In mid-2001, Shimizu vacated the position of Tokyu Corporation president, assuming instead the position of chairman. The presidency was filled by Kiyofumi Kamijo.

Another significant development of 2001 was the formation of a joint venture with Lend Lease Corp. Ltd., the largest real estate company in Australia. Together, Tokyu and Lend Lease planned to establish an asset management firm specializing in Japanese real estate investments. The partners' initial investment vehicle was to be a Japanese real estate investment trust (J-REIT), which would consist mostly of Tokyu properties. The J-REIT, which was expected to be launched in 2002, was to be valued between $2 billion and $4 billion and listed on the Tokyo exchange.

Principal Subsidiaries

Tokyu Car Corporation; Izukyu Corporation; Japan Air System Co., Ltd.; Taiyo Aviation Co., Ltd.; Ueda Kotsu Corporation; Gumma Bus Corporation; Nippon Kotsu Co., Ltd.; Tokyu Land Corporation; Tokyu Construction Co., Ltd.; Tokyu U.S.A. Inc.; Tokyu Land Development (Hawaii), Inc.; Tokyu Department Store Co., Ltd.; Tokyu Store Chain Co., Ltd.; Tokyu Agency, Inc.; Tokyu Agency International, Inc.; Tokyu Trading Corporation; Tokyu Air Cargo Co. Ltd.; Tokyu Freight Service Co., Ltd.; Tokyu Hotel Chain Co., Ltd.; Tokyu Inn Chain; Tokyu Hotels International Co., Ltd.; Nippon Rent a Car Tokyu Co., Ltd.; Tokyu Cable Television Co., Ltd.; Tokyu Bunkamura, Inc.

Principal Operating Units

Transportation; Real Estate; Retail; Leisure and Services; Construction.

Principal Competitors

East Japan Railway Company; Keihin Electric Express Railway Co., Ltd.; Nippon Telegraph and Telephone Corporation.

Further Reading

''Tokyu Group Reform Efforts Hinge on Strength of Affiliates,'' *Nikkei Weekly,* August 6, 2001.
Tsushi, Kazunari, *Tokyu and Noburu Gotoh,* Tokyo: Pal Publishing, 1984.

—Dylan Tanner
—update: Shawna Brynildssen

NV Umicore SA

Broekstraat 31
Rue du Marais
B-1000 Brussels
Belgium
Telephone: (+32) 2-227-71-11
Fax: (+32) 2-227-79-00
Web site: http://www.umicore.com

Public Company
Incorporated: 1906 as Union Minière du Haut Katanga
Employees: 8,987
Sales: EUR 3.5 billion ($2.8 billion) (2001)
Stock Exchanges: Euronext Brussels
Ticker Symbol: UNIM
NAIC: 212231 Lead Ore and Zinc Ore Mining; 212234 Copper Ore and Nickel Ore Mining; 212222 Silver Ore Mining; 212291 Uranium-Radium-Vanadium Ore Mining; 331492 Secondary Smelting, Refining, and Alloying of Nonferrous Metal (Except Copper and Aluminum); 331419 Primary Smelting and Refining of Nonferrous Metal (Except Copper and Aluminum); 331411 Primary Smelting and Refining of Copper; 331423 Secondary Smelting, Refining, and Alloying of Copper

NV Umicore SA—known as Union Minière until late 2001—is one of the world's leading producers of zinc, precious metals, copper, and advanced materials. While its copper, zinc, and precious metals production units continue to represent the bulk of its revenues, the company has targeted Advanced Materials for growth, with a goal of doubling that division's revenues in 2002. Advanced Materials includes such metals and materials as germanium, selenium, and tellurium, used in applications such as semiconductors, electronics, optics, and other high-technology sectors. Part of the company's advanced materials production comes from a strong recycling division, which also recovers gold, platinum, and other precious metals. Umicore hopes that its name change will help the company shake its notoriety as Belgium's main mining operation in Africa—a market the company exited in the late 1960s. Umicore is listed on the Euronext Brussels stock exchange. Sales in 2001 topped EUR 3.5 billion ($2.8 billion).

Early 20th-Century Mining Giant

The Haut Katanga region of what later became known as the Belgian Congo (and subsequently Zaire, before being renamed Congo in the late 1990s) had long been recognized as a prime source of copper, zinc, and a variety of other metals and materials. In the later years of the 19th century, the Belgian government, propelled by King Leopold II, began laying the groundwork for the exploitation of the region's vast mineral deposits. Preliminary surveying was completed by 1901, and mining operations were begun a year later.

In 1906, Belgium's mining interests in the region were formalized with the creation of the Union Minière du Haut Katanga (UMHK), which was granted the right to exploit all of the region's copper deposits in an area that reached more than 20,000 square kilometers and included some of the world's richest copper deposits. UMHK also received permission to exploit the region's variety of minerals, which included silver, zinc, cobalt, cadmium, radium, uranium, germanium, and other precious minerals. Supporting its mining operations was the right to build dams and develop its own hydro-electric power systems. The company, backed by Société Generale, was placed under the leadership of Jean Jadot, who had helped build the railroad linking Peking (later Beijing) and Hankow (later Wuhan) in China, and Robert Williams, who had been one of the pioneering prospectors in the Katanga region. UMHK's position in the region was solidified when Belgium formally took control of what then became known as Belgian Congo.

UMHK originally mined and smelted copper ore in Katanga, shipping the smelted ores to Belgium to be refined. By the end of the decade, the company constructed refining facilities in Belgian Congo, and by 1911 began casting copper at Elisabethville, later renamed Lumbumbashi.

World War I and the German occupation of Belgium for the duration forced UMHK to move its headquarters to London.

From there, the company contributed to the British and American war efforts, providing vital metals and minerals. By the end of the war, UMHK had shipped more than 85,000 tons of copper to the United States and England and other Allied countries.

Following the war, UMHK began branching out from copper production, adding tin production in 1918, gold and silver refining in 1921, radium in 1922, and then beginning cobalt smelting operations in 1924. During the Depression years, the company's core copper market collapsed. In response, UMHK added another important unit, that of zinc production, which began operations in 1937.

Cut off from its headquarters after the German invasion of Belgium during World War II, UMHK began shipping directly to the Allied countries, supplying more than 800,000 tons of copper throughout the duration of the war. UMHK began providing another important mineral, uranium, in 1942, production of which continued until the end of the 1950s.

UMHK's shipments to the Allies had enabled Belgium to emerge from the war more or less debt-free. The company remained one of the most important industrial concerns in Congo, yet by the end of the 1950s the company's days had become numbered in that country. This was particularly so after Congo won its independence in 1960. The chaos and violence that followed independence, temporarily abated by the arrival of U.N. peacekeeping forces, came to a head with the rise to power of Joseph Mobutu in 1965.

After ruthlessly consolidating his grip on the newly renamed Zaire, Mobutu moved to take control of the country's foreign-run industries. In 1966, UMHK was forced to move its headquarters to Kinshasha (formerly Leopoldville). By the beginning of 1968, however, the entirety of UMHK's mining and smelting operations in Zaire had been nationalized. The company then found itself without any business.

New Mining Concern for the 21st Century

During the 1970s, Union Minière (which dropped the Haut Katanga from its name) operated as a subsidiary of Belgian conglomerate Société Générale, grouping its nonferrous metals, mining, and smelting interests. In the late 1980s, however, Union Minière began to reassert itself as a full-fledged opera-

tion. In 1989, the company announced its intention to merge with three other Belgian companies, Metallurgie Hoboken-Overpelt, a producer of copper, lead, cobalt, germanium, and other precious and special metals; zinc producer Vieille Montagne; and Mechim, an engineering firm.

The newly enlarged company, which began operations under the Acec-Union Minière name, represented more than 200 years of Belgian metals and minerals production. The Vieille Montagne site had been producing zinc since before the French Revolution. The Hoboken-Overpelt company had been formed through the mergers of two companies, both of which had been active in metals and minerals production since the late 19th century.

The enlarged company restructured at the beginning of the 1990s, flattening out its management and organizational structure as it absorbed the different entities involved in the merger. By 1992, the company simplified its name, to Union Minière.

Yet Union Minière ran into difficulties in the early 1990s as the worldwide economic slump cut deeply into the company's profits. By 1995, the company was forced to undergo a drastic streamlining of its operations. Over the next four years Union Minière was to shed nearly a dozen of its business units in an effort to restore its profits.

Union Minière nonetheless remained committed to its position as a multi-metals producer, covering more than 20 metals categories, including its industry-leading positions in silver and platinum refining (number two in Europe), manufacturing of palladium and rhodium (Europe's largest), and positions as number two in the world's zinc refining market and number two in European zinc production. The company was also stepping up its involvement in specialty metals and the recycling of precious metals—primarily from used electronics parts. The company's multiple areas of activity left it somewhat on the sidelines during the consolidation spree of the late 1990s that saw mergers among many of its rivals.

Suez's takeover of Société Générale in 1998 temporarily gave Union Minière a new parent company. Yet Suez quickly made it clear that it intended to sell off its more than 25 percent holding in the Belgian metals giant. By the end of December 2000, Suez had exited Union Minière's shareholding, leaving the company as an independent, publicly listed company with no single major shareholder.

As it entered the new century, Union Minière had been making strides in transforming itself into a "modern" metals producer, placing growing emphasis on precious metals reclamation through recycling, while also stepping up its involvement in the specialty metals spheres, such as the production of cobalt and germanium alloys. An example of this came with the 1999 launch of a lithium cobalt oxide plant in South Korea. In 2000, the company attempted to step up its advanced minerals operations with the takeover of U.S.-based Laser Power, a fiber optics company; that takeover attempt failed, however.

Despite its new focus on advanced minerals and specialty metals, the company remained equally committed to its long-standing leadership positions in such base metals production as copper rods and zinc. These divisions continued to account for a

Key Dates:

1906: Belgium government sets up the Union Minière du Haut Katanga (UMHK) to exploit mineral deposits in the soon-to-become Belgian Congo.

1911: UMHK begins casting copper, becoming a primary source of copper for Allied forces during World War I.

1918: UMHK branches out into tin production.

1921: UMHK begins gold and silver refining.

1922: UMHK adds production of radium.

1924: UMHK begins cobalt smelting operation.

1937: After the copper market collapses during the Depression, UMHK adds zinc mining and production.

1942: UMHK begins production of uranium.

1968: UMHK's Congo operations are nationalized by the Zaire government under the Mobutu dictatorship.

1970: UMHK becomes a subsidiary of Belgian conglomerate Société Génerale, which groups all of its smelting and mining interests under reformed Union Minière.

1989: Union Minière is now known as Acec-Union Minière after merging with three other Belgian companies.

1992: Company changes its name back to Union Minière.

1995: Union Minière undergoes far-reaching restructuring, selling off 12 divisions.

1998: Suez acquires Société Générale and announces its intention to spin off its holding in Union Minière.

2000: Union Minière becomes an independent, publicly listed company.

2001: The company changes its name to Umicore in order to break its link to former colonial mining activity and to emphasize its new focus as a modern specialty metals producer.

major share of the company's revenues, despite persistent profit pressures. As CEO Thomas Leysen told *American Metal Market:* "We're not totally against smelting and refining commodities. We just think that by doing that alone, for us it would be very difficult to achieve consistent above-average returns. I think the other parts of the business will tend to grow more rapidly. We can say that in relative terms this will gradually— but only very gradually—continue to shift the balance."

Nonetheless, in September 2001, Union Minière made a symbolic move to shed its longstanding image as a traditional metals producer by adopting a new name, Umicore. The name change also was meant to help the company divorce itself from

Union Minière's controversial role in the development—some called it exploitation—of Belgian Congo.

With its new name, Umicore expected to continue its transformation in the early years of the new century. Among the company's plans was the doubling of its Advanced Materials division in 2002. The company was inaugurating a new germanium tetracholoride production plant in North Carolina, completed at the end of 2001. Another addition to its Advanced Materials division came in December 2001 when Umicore acquired Hall Chemical Company, based in the southeastern United States. That company, which produced specialty chemicals by converting nickel, cobalt, and manganese, was renamed Umicore Specialty Chemicals-Arab.

At the beginning of 2002, continued pressure on copper prices and oversupply of zinc once again called into question Umicore's long-term presence in these two sectors. Urging continued consolidation of these markets, Leysen stated to *Reuters* that Umicore intended "to be a catalyst rather than a bystander in this process." At the same time, however, Leysen suggested that Umicore had not yet determined if it intended to be a buyer or a seller in any future consolidation move.

Principal Competitors

Anglo American plc; ASARCO, Inc; Asturiana de Zinc, S.A.; BHP Billiton Limited; De Beers Consolidated Mines Limited; Falconbridge Limited; Impala Platinum Holdings Limited; Inco Limited; Johnson Matthey Public Limited Company; Metaleurop SA; Grupo México S.A. de C.V.; Mitsubishi Materials Corporation; Mitsui Mining & Smelting Co., Ltd.; Noranda Inc.; Norddeutsche Affinerie AG; Outokumpu Oyj; Phelps Dodge Corporation; Rio Tinto Limited; Sumitomo Metal Mining Co., Ltd.; Teck Cominco Limited; Toho Zinc Co., Ltd.

Further Reading

Crols, Bart, "Union Miniere in Acquisition Talks," *Reuters,* May 16, 2001.

Michiels, Karel, "De historische fouten van Umicore," *De Standaard,* September 19, 2001.

Nguyen, Katie, "Umicore Sees Lower 2001 EPS, No Upturn Until 2003," *Reuters,* November 12, 2001.

Reynolds, Vicki, "Union Miniere Strategy Working Well," *American Metals Market,* January 17, 2001.

"Umicore Eyes Copper Sector Consolidation," *Reuters,* February 15, 2002.

Warden, Edward, "Umicore Won't Abandon Base Metals," *American Metals Market,* September 13, 2001.

—M.L. Cohen

United Pan-Europe Communications NV

Boeing Avenue 53
1119 PE Schiphol-Rijk
PO Box 74763
1070 BT Amsterdam
The Netherlands
Telephone: (+31) 20-778-9447
Fax: (+31) 20-778-8419
Web site: http://www.upccorp.com

Public Company
Incorporated: 1995 as United and Philips
    Communications
Employees: 11,385
Sales: EUR 1.01 billion ($942.6 million) (2000)
Stock Exchanges: Euronext Amsterdam NASDAQ
Ticker Symbol: UPC; UPCOY
NAIC: 513210 Cable Networks; 514191 On-Line
    Information Services

Not content with becoming one of Europe's largest cable television companies, with more than seven million subscribers, United Pan-Europe Communications NV (UPC) intends to become a "triple play" provider of broadband Internet and telephony services. The Amsterdam-based company has constructed a largely cable-based network spanning 17 countries in Europe as well as Israel. In total the company's cable network has a potential reach of 14 million households. UPC's many subsidiaries and diversified activities are structured into three primary divisions: UPC Media, which also includes its chello broadband Internet access subsidiary; UPC Distribution, which provides content production and distribution to the company's cable network; and Priority Telecom, the company's telephony services group, which provides fixed and wireless telephone access to the residential and consumer markets. Much of UPC's "Triple Play" strategy is based around its set-top television devices; the company's plans hit a snag, however, when the "da Vinci" set-top box being developed in conjunction with Microsoft (which also holds an 8 percent share in the company) was delayed. After an extraordinarily fast growth sprint in the late 1990s—the company made more than 16 acquisitions in just five years—UPC's high debt-load of more than EUR 8 billion, coupled with the collapse of the high technology stock market, left the company gasping for breath. From a high of EUR 80, the company's stock tumbled, reaching a low of just 25 Euro cents and threatening the company's continued listing on the Euronext Amsterdam exchange. CEO Mark Schneider, who is also the son of Gene Schneider, the U.S. cable television pioneer, resigned in April 2001; by the end of that year, much of UPC had come under the control of Liberty Media and its chief, John Malone, after that company gained control of UPC's parent, UnitedGlobalCom. UPC has since been led by John Riordan, who previously served as the company's president. In March 2002, UPC averted complete collapse by starting negotiations with its chief debtors for a debt-for-equity swap.

Old World Cable Television Pioneer in the 1980s

Gene Schneider had already brought cable television to the western United States when he began amassing cable television interests in Europe in the 1980s. Beginning in 1952, Schneider expanded throughout much of the American West, acquiring cable television franchises and existing companies, as well as merging with others, such as LVO Corporation in the late 1960s, until Schneider's empire had grown to become the eighth largest cable television operator in the United States. The company, now called United Cable Television Corporation, had also built up a small portfolio of international holdings, including cable television operators in Sweden, Norway, and Israel.

In 1989, Schneider merged his company into United Artists Communications, which was then a subsidiary of Tele-Communications Inc. (TCI), then led by John Malone. The new company was renamed United Artists Entertainment Company, with Schneider acting as chairman of the board until UAE's merger into TCI in 1991. As part of the initial 1969 agreement, TCI, which was focusing on building its North American operations, agreed Schneider and other executives of United Cable could keep the company's international cable television holdings. These were then placed into a new company, United International Holdings (UIH), later to be known as UnitedGlobalCom. UIH also contained a number of Blockbuster Video rental store franchises; these, however, were sold in the early 1990s.

414

Cable television remained a minor segment in the European television market in the late 1980s, although a few countries, such as the Netherlands, had already switched over nearly all of their television broadcasting to cable-based systems (in some parts of that country, cable-based television reached nearly 100 percent of the market). A number of the continent's largest markets remained largely undeveloped; such was the case in France and Germany. Nonetheless, the potential of cable television—and the potential broadening of cable-based services, such as Interactive Television and a nascent interest in consumer-oriented online networks, represented by America Online, CompuServe, and Prodigy—became clear by the middle of the 1990s.

UIH continued to build up its European holdings, buying minority interests in cable television franchises in Hungary, Ireland, Spain, and Malta, as well as controlling shares of cable television franchises in the Czech Republic and Portugal. In the mid-1990s, Schneider returned to the formula that had succeeded in building his former United Cable Television Corporation. In 1995, UIH reached an agreement with Philips Electronics to combine the two companies' cable television interests into a new company, UPC—which at that time stood for United and Philips Communications.

Under the terms of the merger, Philips added its three cable television holdings, Austrian Cable TV systems; Citécable, based in France and extended into Germany, Spain, and Portugal; and the Netherlands' KTE, the country's largest cable operator. For its part, UIH, in addition to its cable television holdings, added $75 million in cash, gave $50 million of its own stock to Philips; and placed a $133.6 million convertible note to make up the difference in value between the Philips and UIH holdings. The deal, formalized in July 1995, gave Philips and UIH each 50 percent of UPC.

Much of UPC's initial holdings were no more than minority interests in the companies involved. UPC worked quickly to correct this situation, beginning a buying spree that was to span five years and bring more than 15 cable television systems under the company's control. By the end of July 1995, the less than one-month-old UPC had launched its first acquisition, acquiring 50 percent of Dutch cable television operator A2000, which had recently acquired the cable television franchise for Amsterdam and a number of outlying towns from Philips.

In September 1995, UPC boosted its share in KTE to more than 96 percent. UPC's acquisition trail continued into 1996, taking the company to Norway, where the company boosted its 8 percent share of Norkabel to 100 percent. In Hungary, UPC boosted its participation in that country's Kabelkom to 50 percent, while in Sweden it acquired a 25 percent share—later sold—in a cable operator there. Meanwhile, UPC was also reshuffling its holdings, moving to sell off its Citécable franchises beginning in 1996.

Rising Convergence Star in the Late 1990s

Gene Schneider turned over the leadership of UPC to his son, Mark Schneider, that same year. The younger Schneider sought to go his father one better. Recognizing the potential of building a cable network to offer a full palette of integrated and interactive services, Schneider embraced the convergence fever then catching on across the telecommunications industry. The company began investing in replacing its existing cable networks with new fiber optics-based, broadband-ready systems.

In the meantime, Schneider stepped up the company's expansion. In January 1997, UPC bought 70 percent of Janco, which operated the cable television system in Oslo. UPC then merged Janco with Norkabel to create Janco Multicom; UPC's share of the new company stood at 87.3 percent (increased to 100 percent in 1998). By then, UPC had already built up Europe's largest network of cable television subscribers. At the end of 1997, the company, together with parent UIH, moved to take full control of UPC, buying out Philip's 50 percent share. UPC was now renamed United Pan-Europe Communications.

The new name revealed the breadth and depth of UPC's growing ambitions. As Internet use at last began to take off across western and central Europe, new technologies were promising high-speed data transmission. The number of so-called broadband applications appeared unlimited and companies raced to position themselves in what many anticipated would soon be a booming market. UPC now announced its intention to pursue a "Triple Play" strategy, with the goal of offering its customers services ranging from television programming to broadband Internet access to telecommunications services. As part of its strategy, UPC also began building up its own production division, including a planned EUR 30 million studio based in Amsterdam and capable of providing programming in 22 languages.

At the beginning of 1998, UPC acquired Combivision, which controlled the cable television franchise adjacent to the company's KTE subsidiary near Amsterdam. These companies were then merged, forming CNBH. UPC followed a similar pattern in Hungary, where it acquired the remaining 50 percent of Kabelkom from Time Warner Entertainment, then merged that company with Hungarian rival Kabeltel, to form Telekabel Hungary. UPC's share of the new company topped 79.25 percent.

The company's mergers and acquisitions drive continued through 1998. In August of that year, the company agreed to form UTH, combining all of its Netherlands-based broadband cable systems with the broadband and telecommunications holdings of newly formed energy company NUON. UPC acquired full control of UTH at the beginning of 1999. By then, UPC increased its shareholdings in Israel and Malta, then briefly gained a position in the Irish cable television market. At the end of 1998, UPC had added to its Hungarian interests, buying Monor Communications Group from UIH, gaining its telephone network in Hungary's Monor region and 75 percent of Tara Television. Parent company UIH also sold UPC its interest in Spain's IPS, a provider of programming to the Spanish and Portuguese markets.

Schneider had developed the basis of a new set-top system, dubbed "da Vinci," which would be capable of providing the triple-play convergence of entertainment, communications, and television that UPC sought. Da Vinci seemed to be coming closer to reality when Microsoft, eager to join in on what was by then widely considered the future of not only the Internet but also of television, acquired 6 percent of UPC and agreed to develop the set-top box.

Boom to Near Bust: Early 2000s

The time was ripe for UPC to spread its wings. In February 1999, Schneider took the company public with listings on the Amsterdam and NASDAQ stock exchanges, with an IPO price of EUR 29 per share. UIH retained 62 percent of UPC; Microsoft stepped up its holding to 8 percent.

Following the IPO, UPC began to put its Triple Play strategy into place. In March 1999 the company launched the "chello" broadband internet service in the Netherlands, Norway, France, Belgium, and Austria, before rolling it out to the rest of its European network. The company also prepared to launch chello as a separately listed public company. At the same time, UPC boosted its cable network, acquiring 100 percent of Time Warner Cable France, which had operations in Paris, Lyon, and Limoges.

After the introduction of its broadband Internet service, UPC put the next piece of its triple play strategy into effect, launching Priority Telecom, offering telephony services to the Netherlands market based on its UTH subsidiary's backbone. Meanwhile, the company's cable business continued to grow with the purchase of a cable television provider in Bratislava, from Siemens, for $41 million. The company also entered Poland in 1999, buying that country's @Entertainment, a provider of cable, direct-television, and programming, including ownership of local sports channel Wizja. In France, UPC expanded its network with the acquisition of Videopole and Réseaux Cables de France, giving it the fourth

and fifth largest cable television companies in that country. Throughout 1999, UPC added a number of other acquisitions to its belt, including Stjärn TV in Sweden and 13.3 percent of SBS Broadcasting, as part of a partnership agreement to develop joint-programming initiatives.

Paying for this activity was a EUR 1.5 billion bond offering, the largest ever in Europe; a secondary offering of 13.5 million shares, at EUR 59.75 per share; and a private debt offering of $1 billion in senior discount notes. At the same time, UPC teamed up with Microsoft and Liberty Media to form a joint-venture content and distribution partnership for the European market.

UPC appeared unstoppable as it rounded into the new century. At the end of 1999, the company announced its 50,000th chello subscriber (or, in UPC parlance, "revenue generating unit," as each customer represented the potential for multiple revenue streams depending on the number of UPC services to which they subscribed). In January 2000, the company's Priority Wireless division launched a broadband fixed wireless access network in Norway, marketing telephony and Internet services under the Priority and chello brand names. The company then increased its position in the Netherlands, buying K&T Group for $1.15 billion, and Telecal, a cable television provider, for $77 million.

After increasing its position in SBS Broadcasting, UPC made an offer for a full takeover of that company in March 2000 (abandoned soon after, however). That partnership meanwhile was preparing to launch a new series of themed television channels. At the same time the company completed the acquisition of Intercom France, and ElTele Ostfold and Vestfold in Norway. Meanwhile, UPC appeared to be finally making headway in its effort to break into the all-important German cable market, which had been dominated by Deutsche Telekom, when it announced its acquisition of EWT/TSS. The company also made its entry into the United Kingdom, with the acquisition of 25 percent of Telewest. UPC had, in addition, boosted its telecom branch, announcing its acquisition of global network services provider Cignal Global, based in the United States. The company also announced a plan to merge chello with fast-rising Excite@Home in order to create internationally operating broadband access and content provider "Excite chello."

UPC appeared to be riding high at the turn of the century. Yet by the beginning of 2001, the company was beginning to unravel. Saddled by a debt load topping EUR 8 billion, the company's shares were hammered by the collapse of the technology sector in general and an economic slowdown that appeared to be heading towards a new recession. Meanwhile, the company's da Vinci set-top had been delayed by Microsoft's inability to complete a product that worked—UPC was forced to abandon that system temporarily in favor of a different system. Yet set-top services had failed to excite the subscriber base—the company signed just 50,000 customers among a pool of more than seven million.

UPC had added problems at its fast-growing chello broadband Internet service, where Internet access speeds were increasingly becoming bogged down by an oversaturated network (that problem was shortly to be solved by the introduction of the DOCSIS protocol). But chello's dream of going public was forced on hold as the stock market continued to reject technology stocks. The company did go through with a public offering of 16 percent of Priority Telecom in order to comply with requirements involved with its Cignal Global purchase.

UPC restructured its operations at the beginning of 2001, combining its transactional television and broadband Internet operations into a single division, UPC Media, alongside its UPC Distribution and Priority Telecom divisions. The company began to show signs of rising sales by the end of the first quarter of that year; but it was too little too late for Mark Schneider. With the company announcing net losses of more than EUR 750 million, Schneider resigned from his CEO position.

UPC's fortunes continued to slip through the year. By the end of 2001, UPC's share price had dropped to just 25 Euro cents. The company was forced to abandon its plan to merge with Excite when that company's stock too had lost its value. By the end of 2001, UPC had gained a new majority shareholder, as John Malone-led Liberty Media once again bought out a Gene Schneider company. Taking control of UIH—and a major share in UPC as well—Liberty Media was building on its newfound interest in the European broadcasting and communications market. With John Riordan, a former associate of Malone, placed in the CEO spot at UPC, the two companies' relationship was certain to strengthen as the future unfolded. In the meantime, UPC, which faced financial ruin at the beginning of 2002, managed to stave off collapse as it entered negotiations with its major creditors to convert its massive debt—its legacy from its explosive growth in the 1990s—into restructured equity.

Principal Subsidiaries

@Entertainment, Inc. (Poland); @Entertainment Programming, Inc. (U.S.A.); A2000; BESY Praha s.r.o. (Czech Republic); chello broadband Australia Pty Ltd; chello broadband Chile Ltda; chello broadband do brasil Ltda; chello broadband GmbH (Austria); chello broadband S.A./N.V. (Belgium); chello broadband SRL (Argentina); chello broadband USA Inc.; Cignal Global Communications; Cignal Global Communications (Bermuda) Ltd.; Cignal Global Communications Australia Pty Limited; Cignal Global Communications Austria GmbH; Cignal Global Communications Belgium S.A.; Cignal Global Communications Canada Holding, Inc.; Cignal Global Communications Canada U.L.C.; Cignal Global Communications Carrier Services, Inc. (U.S.A.); Cignal Global Communications, Inc. (U.S.A.); Cignal Local Communications, Inc. (U.S.A.); Czech Link s.r.o. (Czech Republic); DattelKabel (Czech Republic);

Dattelkabel a.s. (Czech Republic); ElTele stfold/Vestfold (Norway); Eneco K&T Group; Gelrevision; INNET, spol. s.r.o. (Czech Republic); Intercomm Holding (France); Kabel Haarlem B.V.; Kabel Net Brno A.S. (Czech Republic); Kabel Plus A.S. (Czech and Slovak Republics; 95%); Kabel Plus Tel a.s. (Czech Republic); Melita Cable P.L.C. (Malta; 50%); Poland Communications, Inc.; PrimaCom AG (Germany; 25%); Priority Telecom (84%); Sat Net spol. s.r.o. (Czech Republic); SBS (13%); StjarnTVnatet AB (Sweden); Tebecai; Telekabel Graz Gesellschaft mbH (Austria); Telekabel Klagenfurt Gesellschaft mbH (Austria); Telekabel Wien Gesellschaft mbH (Austria); Telekabel-Fernsehnetz Region Baden Betriebsgesellschaft mbH (Austria); Telekabel-Fernsehnetz Wiener Neustadt/Neunkirchen Betriebsgesellschaft mbH (Austria); Tevel Israel International Communications Ltd. (47%,); UCI Enterprises, Inc. (U.S.A.); United International Investments GP (U.S.A.); UPC Belgium S.A.; UPC Ceska republika a.s. (Czech Republic); UPC Germany; EWT/TSS Group (Germany); UPC Magyarovszag Kft (Hungary); UPC Romania, Inc. (U.S.A.); UPC Sport s.r.o. (Czech Republic); UTH; Videopole (France).

Principal Divisions

UPC Media; UPC Distribution; Priority Telecom.

Principal Competitors

British Sky Broadcasting Group plc; Deutsche Telekom GmbH; Digitale Telekabel AG; France Telecom SA; Globo Cabo S.A.; Inmarsat Ventures plc; Matav-Cable Systems Media Ltd.; New Skies Satellites N.V.; PrimaCom AG; Telewest Communications plc; Yes Television plc.

Further Reading

Baker, Stephen, "Mark Schneider, United Pan-Europe Communications," *Business Week*, February 7, 2000.
——, "A 'Triple Play' for Control of Europe's Net," *Business Week*, December 13, 1999, p. 64.
Bickerton, Ian, "UPC Begins Critical Talks to Avoid Collapse," *Financial Times*, February 3, 2002.
——, "UPC's Rapid Rise and Fall," *Financial Times*, December 12, 2001.
Blau, John, "The Son Also Rises," *tele.com*, February 21, 2000.
Borowski, Christopher, "UPC out of Index and Near All-Time Lows," *Reuters*, February 14, 2002.

—M.L. Cohen

USA Interactive, Inc.

152 West 57th Street
New York, New York 10019
U.S.A.
Telephone: (212) 314-7300
Fax: (212) 314-7309
Web site: http://www.usanetworks.com

Public Company
Incorporated: 1982 as Home Shopping Club
Employees: 20,780
Sales: $5.28 billion (2001)
Stock Exchanges: New York
Ticker Symbol: USAI
NAIC: 512110 Motion Picture and Video Production;
     513210 Cable Networks; 514191 On-Line Information
     Services

The history of USA Interactive, Inc., formerly USA Networks, Inc., involves some of the media's biggest names, including Barry Diller, John Malone, Lowell Paxson, Edgar Bronfman, Jr., and Jean-Marie Messier. Its properties have ranged from cable TV networks to movie studios to electronic commerce companies. USA Networks, Inc. was formed in 1998 when Barry Diller acquired the cable networks USA Network, Sci-Fi Channel, and other assets from Edgar Bronfman's Seagram Co. and combined them with the Home Shopping Network and other assets. Ever the dealmaker, Diller entered into an agreement at the end of 2001 with Jean-Marie Messier of French media giant Vivendi S.A. to sell off USA's cable networks and movie studios and transform what remained of USA Networks, Inc. into an electronic commerce company called USA Interactive, Inc.

Diller Building His Media Empire: 1995–98

Media mogul Barry Diller became the chairman and CEO of the newly formed USA Networks, Inc. in 1998. Prior to that Diller's distinguished career included serving as chairman of the board of Paramount Pictures Corp. from 1974 to 1984. From October 1984 to April 1992 he was the chairman and CEO of Fox, Inc., where he created the Fox Television Stations group and established Fox Broadcasting as the United States' fourth broadcast television network. From December 1992 to December 1994 Diller was the chairman and CEO of the cable shopping network QVC Inc. While at QVC Diller attempted to gain control of CBS, but the merger was blocked by Comcast Corp., which subsequently took control of QVC. In 1994 Diller attempted to gain control of Paramount Pictures but lost a $10 billion bidding war to Viacom.

In August 1995 Diller was named the chairman and CEO of Silver King Communications, Inc. Silver King was a subsidiary of the Home Shopping Network, which owned and operated 12 TV stations that carried primarily HSN programming. Eight of Silver King's stations served the top 12 markets in the United States. Diller gained control of Silver King with the help of investors such as billionaire David Geffen and John Malone, the head of the nation's then largest cable system, Tele-communications Inc., later known as TCI Inc.

Although Diller was interested in Silver King's television stations and their potential to reach an audience of nearly 30 million viewers, he was perhaps more interested in gaining control of Silver King's parent company, Home Shopping Network, Inc. (HSN). HSN had been founded in 1982 as the Home Shopping Club in St. Petersburg, Florida, by radio station owner Lowell "Bud" Paxson and attorney and real estate investor Roy Speer. In 1985 the Home Shopping Club went national as the Home Shopping Network, and in 1986 the company went public. Paxson resigned from HSN in 1990 and went on to establish the Pax TV network. From 1991 to 1995 HSN's annual sales leveled off to about $1 billion per year.

At the end of November 1995 Diller agreed to acquire the 41 percent controlling interest in HSN that was held by Liberty Media, a subsidiary of TCI, for a stock swap valued at nearly $1.3 billion. Liberty's stake in HSN represented 80 percent of HSN's voting stock, and Diller became HSN's chairman. At the same time he also acquired Savoy Pictures Entertainment Inc., a film and television production firm. After these acquisitions passed regulatory approval, Silver King, HSN (including the Internet Shopping Network), and Savoy Pictures merged in December 1996. Silver King Communications, Inc. was renamed HSN, Inc.

Key Dates:

1977: Madison Square Garden Network (MSGN) is founded.

1979: Cable network MSGN, now renamed USA, is sold to a joint venture of Time, MCA, and Paramount.

1982: Home Shopping Club is founded in St. Petersburg, Florida, by Lowell Paxson and Roy Speer.

1985: Home Shopping Club goes national as the Home Shopping Network (HSN).

1986: HSN becomes a public company, and Silver King Broadcasting is formed as a subsidiary.

1992: Silver King Communications, Inc. is spun off to HSN shareholders.

1995: Barry Diller, former head of Paramount Studios, Fox Broadcasting, and QVC Inc., is named chairman and CEO of Silver King.

1996: Diller acquires Silver King, which then acquires HSN for $1.2 billion; the company is renamed HSN, Inc.

1997: HSN acquires 50 percent of Ticketmaster Group, Inc. from Microsoft cofounder Paul Allen, in exchange for 17 percent of HSN.

1998: HSN completes its acquisition of cable networks USA and the Sci-Fi Channel, along with the domestic television interests of Universal Studios, from Seagram Co. for $4 billion; HSN is renamed USA Networks, Inc.; USA Networks acquires remaining interest in Ticketmaster; Ticketmaster Online merges with CitySearch; Ticketmaster Online-CitySearch, Inc. (TMCS) completes its initial public offering.

1999: USA Networks acquires Hotel Reservations Network, and TMCS acquires Sidewalk city guides from Microsoft.

2000: Acquisitions include Precision Response Corporation and North American Television.

2001: USA Networks completes the sale of its television station group to Univision and announces the contribution of its entertainment group to a joint venture with Vivendi Universal.

2002: USA Networks is renamed USA Interactive, Inc. upon completion of its deal with Vivendi Universal; acquisition of controlling interest in Expedia, Inc. is approved.

Following the merger, Liberty Media owned about 20 percent of HSN and about 36 percent of Silver King's stock.

In mid-1997 HSN, Inc. completed its acquisition of 50 percent of the Ticketmaster Group, Inc. from Microsoft cofounder Paul Allen in a stock-for-stock deal valued around $210 million. The acquisition of the ticket sales and fulfillment company gave HSN additional capabilities in interactive electronic commerce.

Acquisition Resulting in Creation of USA Networks, Inc.: 1998

Diller's next deal transformed HSN into USA Networks, Inc., a diversified company with interests in cable television, broadcasting, television programming and production, electronic retailing, ticketing, and full-service fulfillment. In October 1997 it was announced that HSN would acquire the majority of the television assets of Universal Studios, a subsidiary of the Seagram Co. Those assets included the cable networks USA Network and the Sci-Fi Channel as well as Universal Television's U.S. production and distribution operations. In exchange, HSN would give Universal 45 percent of its outstanding common equity, valued at $4.07 billion, plus $1.2 billion in cash. The new company would be renamed USA Networks, Inc.

One immediate benefit was an increased distribution of HSN to more cable homes. At the time the Home Shopping Network reached 45 million cable households, while USA Network was in 73.3 million households. By packaging USA Network, Sci-Fi, and Home Shopping Network together, HSN would reach a wider customer base.

Other aspects of the Universal deal, which closed in February 1998, included an exclusive 15-year license for the domestic distribution of Universal's large TV library. In addition, Universal and USA Networks, Inc. would be equal partners in international offshoots of the USA Network and Sci-Fi Channel as well as any other Universal-branded international channels. When the deal closed in February 1998, USA Networks had a market capitalization of approximately $8 billion. Liberty Media owned about 15 percent of the company, with an option to increase its ownership to 25 percent. In March 1998 Liberty Media paid $300 million to increase its stake in USA Networks to 20 percent.

USA Network: 1977–97

The USA Network that Barry Diller acquired from Seagram Co. was founded in 1977 as the Madison Square Garden Network (MSGN). UA/Columbia Cablevision's CEO Bob Rosencrans wanted to distribute cable broadcasts of Madison Square Garden sporting events to cable operators nationwide. He asked Kay Koplovitz, who had developed new franchises at UA/Columbia since 1973, to head the new network. In 1978 and 1979 Koplovitz persuaded the major franchises in Major League Baseball, the National Basketball Association, and the National Hockey League to sign up with MSGN for cable broadcasts, and MSGN soon had several million viewers. Koplovitz also added children's programming and changed the cable network's name to USA. When USA was sold to a joint venture of Time Inc., MCA, and Paramount in 1979, Koplovitz remained as CEO.

For nearly two decades Koplovitz expanded the programming at USA Network to include original movies, first-run theatricals, off-network series, and an original block of Sunday night dramatic series such as the hit *La Femme Nikita*. During much of the 1990s USA Networks and Turner Broadcasting's TNT competed as cable's highest rated ad-supported network. In 1992 USA Networks acquired the Sci-Fi Channel.

Koplovitz and several other executives resigned from USA Network shortly after it was acquired by Diller from Seagram Co. In April 1998 Diller created the position of co-president and hired Stephen Chao to head programming and USA Network veteran Stephen Brenner to handle operations and related matters. Chao had worked with Diller at Fox and was instrumental in developing popular Fox shows such as *Cops, America's Most Wanted,* and *Studs.*

Once the new USA Networks was formed, the company announced that it would acquire the remaining interest in Ticketmaster. Later in the year Ticketmaster Online merged with CitySearch. In December 1998 Ticketmaster Online-CitySearch, Inc.'s initial public offering raised $92 million, with USA Networks retaining a 69.5 percent ownership of the company. In other deals USA Networks paid $150 million to MGM for programming to air on the Sci-Fi Channel, including the 1960s series *The Outer Limits.*

Not all of Diller's proposed acquisitions were successful. In mid-1998 it was revealed that talks had taken place between Diller and Jack Welch at General Electric Co. about a proposed merger with General Electric subsidiary NBC. The merger was effectively opposed, however, by Edgar Bronfman, Jr., chairman of Universal Studios, which held some 45 percent of USA Networks. Bronfman had veto power over any proposed merger exceeding $2 billion.

USA Networks Pursuing Electronic Commerce: 1999

Another proposed merger that failed to materialize involved USA Networks, Ticketmaster Online-CitySearch, and Internet search engine company Lycos, Inc. In February 1999 it was announced that Diller planned to acquire Lycos to create USA/Lycos Interactive Networks Inc. in a deal valued at $22 billion. The takeover was opposed, however, by CMGI Inc., Lycos's largest shareholder. With Lycos's shares losing nearly one-third of their value when the proposed takeover was announced, the deal was declared officially dead in May 1999.

In May 1999 USA Networks acquired most of the assets of PolyGram Filmed Entertainment from Seagram Co., which had acquired PolyGram Holdings for $10.4 billion in December 1998. The assets acquired by USA Networks included the video division and specialty film distributor Gramercy Pictures as well as Seagram's October Films. The new combined entity was named USA Films, with PolyGram Video changing its name to USA Home Entertainment.

Two acquisitions in 1999 strengthened USA Networks' electronic commerce capabilities. In May the company acquired the Hotel Reservations Network, which booked discount hotel reservations over the Internet and by telephone. In September USA Networks' subsidiary Ticketmaster Online-CitySearch (TMCS) acquired the Sidewalk city guides from Microsoft in exchange for a 9 percent interest in TMCS.

Before the end of 1999 USA Networks formed a new subsidiary, USA Electronic Commerce Solutions, which would integrate business-to-business telemarketing and services, product fulfillment, database marketing, and customer service. The new unit offered turnkey e-commerce services drawing on the resources of Home Shopping Network, Ticketmaster, and TMCS.

Acquisitions and Divestitures Strengthening and Reshaping USA Networks: 2000

Two acquisitions in early 2000 added to the resources of the Home Shopping Network. One involved Ingenious Designs Inc.

(IDI), a manufacturer of direct response products such as the Miracle Mop, which had about 200 employees and $190 million in annual sales. IDI's products would be sold over HSN, with IDI head Joy Mangano to appear on the shopping channel.

The acquisition of Precision Response Corporation for $608 million in stock added to HSN's call-handling capabilities. Precision Response was merged with HSN and Ticketmaster to create a network of 10,000 workstations that could handle more than 160 million calls a year in 40 worldwide call centers.

USA Networks operated two e-commerce web sites, Firstauction.com and Firstjewelry.com, through its interactive business unit, USA Networks Interactive. In January 2000 the company announced that it would acquire e-commerce solutions provider Styleclick.com, Inc., which operated the web sites Fashiontrip.com and Styleclick.com and had its own e-commerce technology platform. The acquisition was completed in July 2000 when Styleclick.com merged with USA's Internet Shopping Network in a deal valued at $500 million.

Throughout 2000 Diller continued to shop for new cable networks. In May 2000 he acquired two niche cable networks from Canada-based North American Television Inc. for $100 million. They were Toronto-based Newsworld International, a 24-hour news channel, and Trio, an arts and entertainment channel. Although the two channels had satellite distribution over DirecTV, they had little cable distribution when acquired by Diller.

In mid-2000 USA Networks reorganized into three business units: USA Entertainment, USA Electronic Retailing, and USA Information and Services. USA Entertainment included the cable channels USA Network, the Sci-Fi Channel, Trio, and Newsworld International, as well as Studios USA, USA Films, USA Broadcasting, and Scifi.com. Stephen Chao, who was president of the recently formed USA Cable unit, became president of USA Entertainment. USA Electronic Retailing included the Home Shopping Network, HSN International, and HSN Interactive. Falling within the USA Information and Services unit were Ticketmaster, City Search, Match.com Inc., Hotel Reservations Network, Precision Response Corp., USA eSolutions, and Styleclick.com, Inc.

The reorganization at USA Networks came as Seagram Co. formally announced an agreement to merge with French media conglomerate Vivendi S.A. to form a new company, Vivendi Universal. Vivendi was the parent company of French pay-television company Canal Plus and was expected to support USA Networks' growth. Vivendi acquired Seagram for an estimated $34 billion in stock.

Before the end of 2000 USA Networks sold its group of 13 television stations to Spanish-language television network, Univision Communications, Inc., for $1.1 billion in cash. Univision planned to convert the stations, most of which were Home Shopping Network affiliates, to Spanish-language programming.

USA Networks reported mixed results for 2000. Its revenue increased to $4.6 billion from $3.36 billion in 1999 on a comparable basis. Although the firm's cash flow increased, its net loss widened from $27.6 million in 1999 to $148 million in 2000, with 1999's results restated to reflect recent acquisitions.

Vivendi's Acquisition of USA Networks' Entertainment Division: 2001–02

In a move to acquire more cable channels, Diller offered Rainbow Media and its parent company Cablevision Systems Corporation $4.2 billion to acquire Rainbow Media and its cable channels American Movie Classics, its WE spinoff for women (formerly Romance Classics), arts channel Bravo, and the Independent Film Channel. With companies such as Viacom and MGM also interested in acquiring Rainbow, Cablevision Systems decided to hold an auction for its networks. That caused Diller to lose interest and withdraw his offer for Rainbow Media.

In January 2001 Ticketmaster merged with TMCS, which changed its name to Ticketmaster. It was apparent that companies with both online and offline properties were doing better than pure-play dot-coms. USA Networks also formed new e-commerce partnerships with the PGA Tour, NASCAR.com, and Sportsline.com, while obtaining the domain name and other URLs from defunct sports e-tailer MVP.com. In March USA Networks acquired the web site Crime.com and announced plans to launch a digital network based on the web site in 2002.

In July 2001 USA Networks agreed to pay $1.5 billion for a controlling interest in Microsoft's online travel service, Expedia.com, which had been spun off as a separate company, Expedia, Inc., in 1999. USA Networks also wanted to acquire the National Leisure Group (NLG), which was known primarily as the largest seller of vacations and cruises through infomercials. The events of September 11 and their aftermath negatively affected the financial condition of NLG, however, and USA Networks backed away from acquiring the company. Instead, USA Networks agreed to invest $20 million in NLG for a minority interest and agreed to make NLG a preferred provider of cruises and tours on the new cable TV travel channel that it planned to launch.

The acquisition of Expedia was delayed while USA Networks and Vivendi Universal negotiated the sale of USA's entertainment assets. The launches of USA's planned crime and travel networks also were put on hold. It was around this time in November 2001 that Stephen Chao resigned from the company. USA Networks finally completed its purchase of Expedia in February 2002, acquiring 67 percent of the company's stock.

Meanwhile, Vivendi Universal's chairman Jean-Marie Messier was eager to change the relationship between Vivendi and USA Networks. Although Vivendi held a 40 percent interest in USA Networks, it was unable to consolidate USA's financial results into its own. As a result, USA's financial performance was not a factor in determining Vivendi's stock price and market value.

In December 2001 it was revealed that Messier and Diller were in discussions regarding the possible acquisition of USA Networks' entertainment assets. Under the terms of the agreement between Vivendi and USA Networks, Vivendi would pay $10.3 billion in cash and stock to USA Networks for its entertainment group, including cable channels USA Network, the Sci-Fi Channel, Trio, and other assets including its Studios USA movie studio. These assets would be contributed to a new joint venture to be called Vivendi Universal Entertainment, with Diller as its CEO. Vivendi would contribute the business of its Universal Studios Group and own 94.6 percent of the joint venture. Thus Vivendi Universal Entertainment would combine content provided by Universal Studios and Studios USA with the distribution afforded by USA Networks' cable channels. In the same month Vivendi further extended its distribution with a $1.5 billion investment in satellite TV provider EchoStar Communications Corp., which was in the process of acquiring DirecTV.

In addition, USA Networks was renamed USA Interactive, Inc., again with Diller in charge. USA Interactive's assets included all of the company's Internet assets, including Ticketmaster.com, Match.com, CitySearch.com, Hotel Reservations Network, Home Shopping Network and HSN.com, Precision Response Corp., USA's Electronic Commerce Solutions, Styleclick.com, Inc., and others. Once the proposed transactions passed regulatory approval, Expedia.com would also become part of USA Interactive.

While the deal between Vivendi and USA Networks was still being finalized, Diller announced a sweeping three-year plan for USA Interactive in February 2002. He told investment analysts that USA Interactive would become the number one interactive-commerce company by capturing 20 percent of the total market, primarily through acquisitions. As always, investors would be watching for reports of Diller's latest deal.

Principal Subsidiaries

Ticketmaster Group, Inc. (68%); Expedia, Inc. (64.6%); Hotel Reservations Network, Inc. (70%).

Principal Divisions

Entertainment Group; Interactive Group.

Principal Operating Units

USA Network; Sci-Fi Channel; Trio; Newsworld International; October Films; Gramercy Pictures; Home Shopping Network; Ticketmaster; Precision Response Corporation; Citysearch .com; Match.com; USA Electronic Commerce Solutions; Styleclick.com, Inc.

Further Reading

"Addenda: Liberty Media," *Mediaweek,* March 16, 1998, p. 3.

Ashman, Anastasia, "Ticketmaster: First of Many Reunions?," *Internet World,* December 1, 2000, p. 24.

Barnard, Bruce, "Vivendi Universal Continued Its Spectacular Transformation from a Dull French Water Utility to a Glamorous Global Entertainment Company," *Europe,* February 2002, p. Sup4.

Bowers, Katherine, "Sportsline and USA Purchase MVP Assets," *WWD,* January 30, 2001, p. 9.

"Bronfman and Diller: Together Forever?," *Business Week,* February 21, 2000, p. 48.

"Bronfman Breaks Up USA-NBC Dance," *Mediaweek,* July 20, 1998, p. 4.

Burgi, Michael, et al., "Piecing Together a TV Power," *Mediaweek,* October 27, 1997, p. 4.

Colman, Price, "Diller Consolidates Position with HSN Deal," *Broadcasting & Cable,* September 2, 1996, p. 48.

Dempsey, John, "Diller Ends Koplovitz Era at USA Web," *Variety,* April 13, 1998, p. 2.

"Diller Buy of Silver King OK'd," *Broadcasting & Cable,* June 10, 1996, p. 76.

"Diller to Buy Controlling Stake in Expedia.com," *United Press International,* July 16, 2001.

DiOrio, Carl, "Diller Backs Off Rainbow Battle," *Variety,* January 22, 2001, p. 40.

Donohue, Steve, "Diller, USA Gobble Up Trio, NWI," *Multichannel News,* May 22, 2000, p. 5.

——, "USA Splits into Three Units," *Multichannel News,* July 26, 2000, p. 5.

Edelson, Sharon, "Universal Sells Some Assets to HSN Inc.," *WWD,* October 21, 1997, p. 2.

Evans, Liz, "USA Networks Adds to Its Sports E-Tail Partners," *Sporting Goods Business,* March 9, 2001, p. 14.

"Expedia Sale Takes New Turn," *New Media Age,* December 20, 2001, p. 3.

"Expedia-USA Merger Gets Final Approval," *Travel Weekly,* February 11, 2002, p. 6.

Farrell, Mike, "Seagram Takeover Could Boost USA," *Multichannel News,* June 19, 2000, p. 63.

——, "USA Buys Database-Management Firm," *Multichannel News,* January 17, 2000, p. 36.

——, "USA Talks Up E-Commerce Deals," *Multichannel News,* February 4, 2002, p. 34.

——, "Vivendi's Toehold," *Multichannel News,* December 17, 2001, p. 1.

——, "Vivendi Wants More Credit for USA," *Multichannel News,* October 8, 2001, p. 31.

Freeman, Michael, and Michael Burgi, "What's Diller Up to Now?," *Mediaweek,* September 2, 1996, p. 4.

Goldsmith, Jill, "Barry Very Merry," *Variety,* June 19, 2000, p. 84.

Grillo, Jean Bergantini, "Trail Blazer," *CED,* December 2001, p. S20.

Grover, Ron, "Return of the Mogul," *Business Week,* January 25, 1999, p. 49.

Gunther, Marc, "Once Again, It's Diller Time," *Fortune,* November 24, 1997, p. 37.

Harris, Kathryn, "Is Diller Scheming or Just Dreaming?," *Fortune,* December 25, 1995, p. 164.

Hertzberg, Robert, "USA-Lycos, Reconsidered," *Internet World,* March 22, 1999, p. 9.

Higgins, John M., "Chao Reborn in USA," *Broadcasting & Cable,* April 27, 1998, p. 8.

——, "Diller Balks at Rainbow Auction," *Broadcasting & Cable,* January 15, 2001, p. 10.

——, "Diller Has His Way at USA," *Broadcasting & Cable,* June 15, 1998, p. 10.

——, "Diller Under the Rainbow," *Broadcasting & Cable,* January 1, 2001, p. 5.

——, "GE Seeks Perfect Partner for NBC," *Broadcasting & Cable,* July 20, 1998, p. 7.

——, "How Now, Down Chao?," *Broadcasting & Cable,* November 5, 2001, p. 9.

——, "HSN Gets a New Sibling," *Broadcasting & Cable,* January 17, 2000, p. 133.

——, "HSN Takeover Underwhelms Wall Street," *Broadcasting & Cable,* September 2, 1996, p. 3.

Hisey, Pete, "Changing the Channel on Low Quality," *Discount Store News,* September 4, 1995, p. 21.

"Hotel Reservation Network Bought by USA Networks," *Content Factory,* April 15, 1999.

"HSN, Ticketmaster Close Deal," *WWD,* July 21, 1997, p. 4.

Lacter, Mark, "Amazon Should Be So Prosperous," *Forbes,* September 4, 2000, p. 106.

Littleton, Cynthia, "Diller Redefines USA, Eyes New Day," *Variety,* February 16, 1998, p. 37.

McClellan, Steve, "Diller Ponders Newfound Independents," *Broadcasting & Cable,* September 4, 1995, p. 20.

——, "HSN, Savoy Deals May Put Diller Back on Dial," *Broadcasting & Cable,* December 4, 1995, p. 47.

McConville, Jim, "USA Turning to Crime," *Electronic Media,* March 19, 2001, p. 1.

McConville, Jim, and Chris Pursell, "Vivendi Deal May Boost USA," *Electronic Media,* June 26, 2000, p. 3.

"A Media Mogul's Career," *Electronic Media,* November 29, 1999, p. 52.

Mermigas, Diane, "Diller Forms E-Commerce Unit," *Electronic Media,* October 18, 1999, p. 2.

"Microsoft's Sidewalk Hits the Bricks," *Editor & Publisher,* July 24, 1999, p. 14.

Miller, Stuart, "Chao in Charge," *Cablevision,* November 29, 1999, p. 24.

Moss, Linda, "Network Launches Are Pushed Back," *Multichannel News,* October 15, 2001, p. 6.

——, "USA to Pitch Pair of Diginets," *Multichannel News,* July 23, 2001, p. 8.

"The New Barry Diller," *Business Week,* September 10, 2001, p. 77.

Oppelaar, Justin, "USA's Year Shows Mixed Results," *Variety,* February 5, 2001, p. 35.

Schaal, Dennis, "USA Networks Buys Stake in Cruise and Package Seller," *Travel Weekly,* November 1, 2001, p. 4.

Seckler, Valerie, "USA Networks Unit, Styleclick Set Merger," *WWD,* January 26, 2000, p. 4.

Sharkey, Betsy, "It's Chao Time at USA," *Mediaweek,* April 27, 1998, p. 8.

Stroud, Michael, and Joe Schlosser, "USA Paying $150M for MGM Shows," *Broadcasting & Cable,* March 30, 1998, p. 10.

"Tele-Communications Inc. Exercised Its Option to Buy Shares of USA Networks Inc. at a Reduced Rate," *Broadcasting & Cable,* July 6, 1998, p. 64.

"USA Networks, Inc. Has Agreed in Principle to Buy Ticketmaster Group," *Broadcasting & Cable,* March 16, 1998, p. 92.

"USA Networks, Lycos and Ticketmaster Form New Company," *United Press International,* February 9, 1999.

"USA Networks, Lycos Terminate Deal," *United Press International,* May 13, 1999.

"Vivendi Signs Deal," *Television Digest,* December 24, 2001.

"Vivendi to Buy Division of USA Networks," *Knight-Ridder/Tribune Business News,* December 18, 2001.

Waddell, Ray, "Ticketmaster Online-CitySearch Inc.," *Amusement Business,* October 19, 1998, p. 8.

"White Knight or Thorn in Barry's Side?," *Business Week,* September 10, 2001, p. 82.

Wilson, Wendy, "PolyGram Video to Become Part of Cable's USA Networks," *Video Business,* April 12, 1999, p. 4.

Young, Kristin, "Styleclick Merger OK'd," *WWD,* July 27, 2000, p. 2.

Zoltak, James, "Ticketmaster Online, CitySearch Unite," *Amusement Business,* August 24, 1998, p. 4.

—David P. Bianco

Vans, Inc.

15700 Shoemaker Avenue
Santa Fe Springs, California 90670
U.S.A.
Telephone: (562) 565-8267
Fax: (562) 565-8406
Web site: http://www.vans.com

Public Company
Incorporated: 1966 as Van Doren Rubber Co.
Employees: 1,688
Sales: $341.2 million (2001)
Stock Exchanges: NASDAQ
Ticker Symbol: VANS
NAIC: 316211 Rubber & Plastics Footwear
    Manufacturing; 448210 Shoe Stores

Vans, Inc. is a premier manufacturer of shoes and apparel for a target group of young and active consumers. Vans snowboarding boots and skateboarding sneakers are specifically designed for today's extreme sports culture, and are the footwear of choice among elite athletes worldwide. Through event sponsorships and a chain of skateboarding parks, Vans has forged a unique niche in the booming youth sportswear market. The company's unflagging commitment to tracking the latest trends has put it in an excellent position to grab an even larger market share as it heads into the 21st century.

Birth of a California Style: 1966

Paul Van Doren gained experience manufacturing shoes on the East Coast in the early 1960s. By 1965, Van Doren had developed the idea to start up his own plant. But instead of selling his shoes to retailers, Van Doren decided to take on retailing activities as well and to sell the shoes he manufactured directly to the public.

Van Doren, together with partners Serge D'Elia, an investor based in Japan, and Gordy Lee, who also had shoe manufacturing experience, moved to southern California, building a factory and opening a first 400-square-foot retail store in Anaheim in March 1966. The company was incorporated as the Van Doren

Rubber Company, and Van Doren's shoes came to be known simply as Vans. Later, Van Doren's younger brother, James Van Doren, joined the company. Paul Van Doren and D'Elia owned the majority of the company; James Van Doren and Gordy Lee each were given a 10 percent stake.

As the company itself tells it, the opening of its first store was inauspicious. Vans offered three styles, priced from $2.49 to $4.99, but on the day the store opened for business, the company had only made display models. The store racks were filled with empty boxes. Nevertheless, 12 customers came into the store and chose the colors and styles they wanted. The customers were asked to come back in the afternoon, while Van Doren and Lee rushed to the factory to make their shoes. When the customers returned to pick up the shoes, Van Doren and Lee realized that they had neglected to have money available to make change. The customers were given the shoes and asked to return the next day to pay for them. All 12 customers did.

Over the next year, the company opened a new retail store almost every week. A pattern developed in which Paul Van Doren scouted locations on Monday, signed a lease on Tuesday, remodeled on Wednesday, added shoe racks on Thursday and displays on Friday, hired a store manager on Saturday, and trained staff on Sunday. Retail operations would generate the bulk of Van Doren's early sales; the stores also enabled the company to get close to its public. Complaints over the early design of the company's rubber soles, which featured a diamond pattern that cracked too easily along the ball of the outsole, led to the addition of vertical lines to the ball area. The new design was patented as Vans' waffle sole.

A new type of customer boosted the company's fortunes in the early 1970s. The skateboarding craze, an outgrowth of California's surfing culture, provided an opportunity for Van Doren to prove its flexibility. When skateboarders began requesting new colors and patterns, the company responded by offering the Era, a red-and-blue shoe designed by professional skateboarders. Vans quickly became the skateboard shoe of choice, beginning the company's long, and devoted, association with the sport. Many more color combinations and patterns were added in the 1970s. A new style, the slip-on, was introduced in 1979, and it became the rage of southern California.

Company Perspectives:

VANS footwear, apparel and accessories are created to be comfortable, durable and stylish . . . traits demanded by our customers. VANS-sponsored athletes, who are some of the most talented and colorful personalities in Core Sports, endorse and help design our products, providing a bond with our consumers that is strengthened by the credibility of our athletes and the authenticity of our brand.

In 1976, ownership of the company was equalized among the four original partners, and James Van Doren was given control of the company's direction. The younger Van Doren set out to expand the company. He was helped by the latest sports craze sweeping California, the BMX bicycle: Vans became the shoe of choice among the young BMXers. But it was a movie that gave Vans a national market.

From Dude to Dud in the 1980s

The 1982 hit film *Fast Times at Ridgemont High* featured the California surfer dude Jeff Spicoli, played by Sean Penn, wearing a pair of Vans checkerboard slip-ons. The film made a star of Penn and launched Vans nationwide, bringing the company's shoes into department stores and independent retailers. With sales skyrocketing, James Van Doren boosted production capacity, moving the company to a new 175,000-square-foot plant in Orange, California, in 1984 and raising the number of employees to more than 1,000. The Vans slip-on craze spawned a variety of licensing agreements, including items such as sunglasses and notebooks. Van Doren also pushed the company deeper into specialty sports footwear, developing baseball, football, umpiring, basketball, soccer, wrestling, boxing, and skydiving shoes. Most companies had already begun to move manufacturing to Asia, where labor costs were lower and environmental regulations were less restrictive, but Vans remained dedicated to domestic production, while expanding product offerings to include widths from EEEE to AAAA.

Faced with high labor and expansion costs, and the expense of maintaining the breadth and depth of its line, Van Doren was soon hit by a flood of competitors selling cheap imitations and knockoffs. In response, Van Doren was forced to drop its prices below manufacturing costs. Adding to the company's troubles was a 1984 raid by federal immigration officials, which resulted in the arrest of nearly 150 suspected illegal workers. Then the bottom dropped out of the slip-on craze.

Over 21 months, Van Doren lost some $3.6 million, building up a total debt of $12 million. When the company's bank demanded payment on a $6.7 million note in 1984, the company was forced to declare bankruptcy. Conditions for its Chapter 11 bankruptcy reorganization called for the ouster of James Van Doren. Paul Van Doren returned to lead the company out of bankruptcy, which was accomplished in 1986.

From Leveraged Buyout to Initial Public Offering: 1987–92

Demand for Vans shoes continued to be strong and, by 1987, with two million pairs of shoes manufactured at its Orange plant

bringing in $50 million in sales, Van Doren returned to profitability. International sales, particularly to Mexico and Europe, were also growing strongly, accounting for 10 percent of company sales. A third of the company's business went to custom-designed shoes. In a time when almost all of the major sneaker makers had shifted production to South Korea, Vans clung to its tradition of domestic production, boasting order-to-delivery times of five days for its catalogue items, compared with an industry average of nine months.

In 1988, Paul Van Doren, explaining that he was tired of overseeing the company's day-to-day operations, agreed to sell the company in a leveraged buyout organized by the San Francisco-based venture banking firm McCown De Leeuw & Co. The leveraged buyout, worth $74.4 million including the assumption of existing liabilities, left Paul Van Doren in place as chairman and Gordy Lee as vice-chairman. Richard Leeuwenberg, formerly with Boise Cascade Corp., was brought in as president and CEO for the company, now renamed Vans, Inc.

In 1989, raids by U.S. and Mexican officials shut down several counterfeit operations that had flooded the market with cheap Vans imitations. Despite losses to counterfeits, Vans' sales topped $70 million in 1990, with international sales rising to 25 percent of sales, and special orders continuing to play a strong role in revenues. The following year, Vans went public, with an initial offering of 4.1 million shares, at $14 per share. Paul Van Doren, while retaining shares in the company, stepped down from the board.

By 1992, however, the recession of the early 1990s, and especially poor earnings performances among the major footwear producers, forced Vans' share price down to $7. Yet, revenues from the company's 70 retail stores and 4,500 independent outlets grew to $91 million, raising net income to $6.5 million in 1992. By then, more than 32 percent of sales came from international exports. But on the domestic front, Vans was losing ground.

Vans' production techniques had changed little in the past two decades. Although its catalogue offerings swelled to more than 200 different styles, its original canvas-and-rubber shoe continued to provide roughly half of its sales. But sport shoe fashions had changed in the 1990s, with new materials and styles eroding Vans' market. The other manufacturers were producing their shoes in Asia, where labor costs were as low as 14 cents an hour. Foreign production allowed manufacturers to use solvents and other materials that were closely controlled by California's environmental regulation.

Vans clung to domestic production, spending $5 million to build a state-of-the-art plant in Vista, California. But sales and earnings were slipping, down to $86.5 million and $2.7 million, respectively, in 1993, and to $80.5 million and $1.4 million in 1994. In 1993, the company again ran afoul of immigration laws; 300 employees were deported and the company was fined $400,000.

Enter Walter Schoenfeld: 1993

By 1993, Vans sought to replace Richard Leeuwenberg. Gary Schoenfeld, then a partner at McCown De Leeuw suggested his father, Walter Schoenfeld. In the late 1960s, the senior Schoenfeld had joined his father's company, a small

Key Dates:

1966: Paul Van Doren founds Van Doren Rubber Co.
1979: Vans slip-on shoe is introduced.
1984: Vans opens manufacturing plant in Orange, California.
1988: Paul Van Doren sells company to McCown De Leeuw & Co. in leveraged buyout.
1993: Gary Schoenfeld is named president and CEO.
1995: Vans shuts down manufacturing facilities in Orange.
1998: Vans skateboarding park opens in Orange, California.
1999: Vans joins with Pacific Sunwear to form VanPac, a joint venture to market skateboarding apparel.

maker of ties. In 1971, Schoenfeld launched a new division, to be called Brittania Sportswear, with $1.5 million raised equally among himself, two investors, and a bank. Brittania married the burgeoning blue jeans trend with coordinated jackets, sportshirts, and sweaters. Sales took off from $100,000 in 1973 to more than $50 million in 1975, and Schoenfeld Industries revenues increased to more than $300 million by 1981. In the early 1980s, Schoenfeld sold Brittania to Levi Strauss and retired.

Brought out of retirement to head Vans, Schoenfeld acted to expand the Vans product line, going overseas for the first time to manufacture a new line of shoes in step with the current fashion. Schoenfeld also addressed the company's troubled chain of retail stores, which had been hit hard by California's continued recession, closing some stores and converting others as factory outlets to siphon off misfired shoes and excess inventory. Schoenfeld sought to boost the company's marketing efforts, hiring new designers and marketing staff. In 1994, with revenues and profits on the rise again, Schoenfeld retired again, bringing in Christopher G. Staff, former president and CEO of the Speedo and Action Sports divisions of Authentic Fitness Corp.

Sales of Vans's foreign-made "international collection" took off and soon accounted for as much as 75 percent of the company's revenues. Domestic production, however, had become a drag on the company's profits. Sales were falling, inventory was climbing, and Vans stock dropped to a low of $3.125. To stem problems, the company laid off 300 workers, then idled their plants for two weeks in March 1995. In May 1995, Schoenfeld came out of retirement again, resuming leadership of the company.

In July 1995, the company closed its Orange plant, firing nearly all of the 1,000 workers there. Restructuring and write-off charges from the plant closing created most of the company's $37 million loss on its $88 million in 1995 revenues. The Vista plant continued operations, but most of Vans' production was now contracted through a dozen or so factories in South Korea.

Importantly, Schoenfeld worked to change the focus of the company. From a company rooted in manufacturing, Vans would become far more market-oriented, that is, producing what would sell, rather than selling what it produced. The

introduction of the Vans line of snowboarding boots in 1995 added $7 million to gross sales and within one year gained the company the number three position among the leaders in that market. Deeper expansion into women's and children's lines also produced strong successes. With analyst estimates of revenues climbing to $118 million, with earnings reaching to $4 million, and with its stock rebounding to $11 per share in early 1996, Vans appeared, finally, to be on a steady course for the future.

Sportswear Trends in the 21st Century

Vans snowboard boots played a vital role in the company's resurgence as a major contender in the youth sportswear market. Sales of the boots rose from 6,000 in 1995 to over 110,000 in 1996, and almost singlehandedly restored the company to profitability after the near disastrous losses suffered following the closing of the Orange plant. The growing popularity of snowboarding in Europe and Japan also provided the company's overseas business with a significant boost. Vans further strengthened its foothold in overseas markets in 1998, when it opened retail outlets in Liverpool, England, and Barcelona, Spain. Overall, international sales more than doubled between 1997 and 2001, from $46.4 million to $98.2 million.

A more diversified line of shoes, designed for a wider range of outdoor sports, also contributed to the company's rapid growth. In addition to launching new lines of skateboarding shoes named after world-class athletes such as Geoff Rowley and Cory Nastazio, the company also introduced a number of products aimed at women, including the distinctive Compel Tones line, white leather shoes that changed colors when exposed to ultraviolet light. The company also responded to the increasing popularity of women's sports by developing plans to introduce a complete line of women's outdoor shoes by the spring of 2002.

The primary impetus behind this expanded product line proved to be the shift from domestic to global manufacturing. Because plants overseas were able to produce shoes more cheaply and quickly than their American counterparts, Vans was able to respond to the latest trends with more immediacy than had previously been possible. The subsequent rise in the company's profitability made domestic down-sizing inevitable; the company shut down its Vista operations permanently in 1998, and began contracting out all of its manufacturing to factories in China and Korea.

In 1997 Vans took an even bolder step toward diversification when it introduced a line of young men's apparel. While sales of the Vans clothing line were initially insubstantial, they received a major boost in 1999, when the company joined forces with Pacific Sunwear to form VanPac, with the goal of becoming the dominant name in skateboarding apparel in the United States. The marriage of the Vans name and Pacific Sunwear's extensive retail network proved to be a fortuitous one for both companies, and the new venture was soon able to compete for market share with such established brands as Rusty and Quiksilver.

Vans further solidified its reputation as the brand of choice for skateboarders with the opening of its 46,000-square-foot indoor skateboarding park in Orange, California, in 1998. The venture quickly proved profitable, inspiring the company to launch a series of similar parks nationwide. By the end of 2001 Vans owned four skateboarding parks in California, along with parks in New Jersey, Virginia, Texas, and Colorado. At the same time, the company was generating a great deal of publicity through sponsorship of a range of Triple Crown sporting events, including skateboarding, snowboarding, motocross, and surfing. With its diversified product line, highly publicized event sponsorships, and popular skateboarding facilities, Vans was clearly right back in the thick of things.

Principal Subsidiaries

VanPac LLC (51%).

Principal Competitors

Converse Inc.; K2 Inc.; NIKE, Inc.

Further Reading

Apodaca, Patrice. "Vans Inc. to Build Skate Park at Mall in Orange," *Los Angeles Times*, May 8, 1998, p. D2.

Barron, Kelly. "Vans, Famous for Sneakers, Boosts Status with Snowboard Boots," *Orange County Register*, March 2, 1996.

Ferguson, Tim W., "Grandpa to the Grunges," *Forbes*, February 12, 1996, p. 88.

Granelli, James S., "Little Leverage in Shoemaker's Buyout," *Los Angeles Times*, April 4, 1989, Sec. 4, p. 9F.

Lee, Don, "Sneaker Maker Had—Till Now—Bounced Back," *Los Angeles Times*, June 1, 1995, p. D1.

Maio, Patrick J., "Kicking," *Investor's Daily*, January 31, 1996, p. A4.

McAllister, Robert, "Vans Optimistic with Schoenfeld at the Helm," *Footwear News*, August 9, 1993, p. 108.

Paris, Ellen, "As the Twig Is Bent," *Forbes*, April 27, 1981, p. 131.

—M.L. Cohen
—update: Steve Meyer

Venetian Casino Resort, LLC

3344 Las Vegas Boulevard South
Las Vegas, Nevada
U.S.A.
Telephone: (702) 414-1000
Toll Free: (877) 283-6423
Fax: (702) 414-1100
Web site: http://www.venetian.com

Limited Liability Company
Incorporated: 1997
Employees: 3,500
Sales: $186.0 million (2001)
NAIC: 721120 Casino Hotels

Venetian Casino Resort, LLC is a limited liability company serving as the operator of The Venetian Resort Hotel Casino, located in Las Vegas, Nevada, on the plot of land formerly occupied by the Sands Hotel. The hotel property is adjoined by the Sands Expo and Convention Center, from which the Venetian draws a substantial percentage of its business. The Venetian, situated along the Las Vegas Strip, is a $1.5 billion, 3,036-room, 35-story gaming and hotel facility featuring full-scale replications of several of Venice's famous landmarks, including the Doge's Palace, the Rialto Bridge, and the Campanile. The Venetian includes more than 100,000 square feet of gaming space, and the largest standard hotel rooms in the world.

The Career of Sheldon Adelson

The opening of the Venetian on the Las Vegas Strip in 1999 marked the beginning of a new chapter in the roller-coaster career of its creator, Sheldon G. Adelson. In many respects, the Venetian represented the denouement of Adelson's career, incorporating certain aspects from previous chapters in his personal history, which found expression in the surreal replication of an Adriatic city in the middle of a Nevada desert. Adelson's rise in the business world smacked of the classic entrepreneurial success story. "This could be a rags-to-riches story," Adelson was quoted as saying in the October 23, 2000 issue of *Business Week.* "But my family was too poor to own rags."

Adelson was born August 4, 1933, the son of a cab driver. Raised in the working-class Boston neighborhood of Dorchester—referred to as a slum by some—Adelson entered the entrepreneurial world at age 12. He borrowed $200 from his uncle's credit union to buy the rights to sell the *Boston Globe* on a corner near his home. The war in Europe was over, and Adelson had experienced his first taste of financial independence, however meager the proceeds from newspaper sales may have been. His dreams soon escalated beyond what newspaper sales on a Dorchester street corner could offer. Adelson, as a youth, pined to own a block of stores, a strip, presenting him with the opportunity to pick whatever he wanted without having to pay for it—everything from candy, pastry, pickles, a haircut, and a bicycle.

As a young adult, Adelson experimented with several career choices. He attended stenography school after high school, preparing to become a court reporter. He studied corporate finance at City College in New York City. By his early 20s, Adelson was operating his own business, selling amenities to motel operators. He sold small packages of shaving cream, shampoo, soap bars, and similar items to his clientele, items that, at the time, were rarely found in motel rooms. His exposure to corporate finance at City College led him into financial consulting and real estate, fields in which Adelson demonstrated considerable skill, registering his first genuine success in the business world. By the mid-1960s, when he was in his early 30s, Adelson had parlayed his efforts in financial consulting and real estate into a career as a venture capitalist. He held investments in as many as 75 companies, possessing stakes in everything from pet stores to nuclear energy firms. It was the fulfillment of his childhood fantasy on a grand corporate scale far removed from the streets of Dorchester.

Adelson had become a millionaire by age 35, but his rise to riches soon collapsed. The stock market plummeted in 1969, delivering a deadly blow to his far-flung investments. He lost his fortune—not for the last time—but wasted little time lamenting his loss. "I turned around," he reflected in an October 1984 interview with *Nation's Business,* "went right to work, and started again." He returned to real estate brokerage, "a field I found very easy," he remarked in his *Nation's Business* interview, and began rebuilding his fortune. By the early 1970s, Adelson was working in two directions. His attention to the real estate market led him into converting apartments into condominiums. He worked for a company that owned thousands of apartments, providing him with a steady stream of work, but when interest rates climbed during the early and mid-1970s, the company Adelson worked for declared bankruptcy. Adelson was unable to recover his investment and lost everything except for one apartment building he had purchased to convert into condominiums on his own.

Before Adelson's condominium-conversion business collapsed, he developed interests in a second direction. In 1971, he purchased controlling interest in a small publisher of trade magazines, which provided indirect entry into a business field that Adelson would exploit like no one before him. From his perusal of trade publications, Adelson learned of a real estate exposition that was scheduled to be held in Anaheim, California, in 1972. At the time, his condominium-conversion business showed no sign of slowing, prompting him to make plans to attend the exposition. Once in attendance, Adelson was struck by the operation of the exposition rather than the subject matter of the exposition. In a matter of days, he realized he wanted to be in the convention business, not in the real estate business.

Adelson's curiosity was piqued when he learned that the magazine that advertised the Anaheim exposition also owned it. In his October 1984 interview with *Nation's Business,* Adelson explained, "I saw that there was a synergism between the magazine and the show," his desires for profit sparked by the relationship among the magazine's readers, the exposition's attendees, and the magazine's advertisers who purchased exhibition space. According to Adelson's calculations, the Anaheim real estate exposition brought in $1 million, a total realized for three days of work. Adelson was hooked, convinced he could orchestrate the same type of shows and turn them into profit-generating events. His belief in himself proved justified. Adelson, in a few short years, developed into an organizer of meetings without parallel.

Less than a year after the Anaheim exposition, Adelson was ready for his debut as a convention organizer. Through his publishing company's magazine, *Data Communications User,* Adelson launched his first convention in March 1973, an event intended for users of sophisticated computer systems that was held in Dallas. Two years later, Adelson had a disagreement with the other investors in the publisher of *Data Communications User* that could not be resolved. Adelson sold his interest in the magazine, but he retained ownership of the expositions, which, along with the condominium building he owned, consti-

tuted his assets in the wake of the collapse of his condominium-conversion business.

The Creation of COMDEX in 1979

During the latter half of the 1970s, Adelson devoted himself to the promotion of conventions. He sold his condominium building and used the proceeds to found Interface Group, Inc., selecting Needham, Massachusetts, as the home for his convention and exposition business. The fortunes of Interface and Adelson were enriched exponentially after Adelson read an article about a new product in the computer industry. The year was 1979, and what Adelson read about was desktop computers. Before the year was through, Adelson had promoted and launched a trade show catering to manufacturers and retailers within the then obscure industry niche.

Manufacturers such as Tandy, Heathkit, and a small company called Apple Computer bought booths at Adelson's first Computer Dealers Exposition, more commonly known as COMDEX. The first event, staged in Las Vegas in 1979, was a success, quickly developing into the largest of its kind in the world. For those involved in the personal computer industry, which would record explosive growth for the next two decades, Adelson had provided a Mecca. As waves of attendees faithfully made their pilgrimages to Las Vegas and COMDEX, Adelson turned to the business of generating as much profit as possible from the annual, sometimes seasonal, gatherings.

Adelson's strength was demonstrated in his ability to create profit-producing opportunities from Interface's conventions and expositions, particularly from the largest of all, COMDEX. "I was criticized for squeezing every ounce of profit; I must admit I was good at that," Adelson confided in an October 23, 2000 interview with *Business Week.* At COMDEX, he sold advertising on banners draped throughout the meeting space, he published a daily newsletter for COMDEX attendees, creating additional advertising space, and he sold advertising on tote bags.

With the profits realized from the highly successful COMDEX, Adelson moved in yet another direction, as Interface's convention and exposition activities intensified. In 1981, through Interface, he purchased GWV Travel Co., a tour-operating firm with offices in Washington, New York, and Boston. Together, the two Adelson entities were generating roughly $175 million in revenues annually. By 1984, five years after the first COMDEX, Interface produced nearly 40 conferences and expositions a year for the computer industry, including COMDEX/Fall—a $20 million event—COMDEX/Winter, COMDEX/Spring, and COMDEX/Europe. COMDEX/Japan was slated for launch in the spring of 1985.

The business of conventions became the art of Adelson. He became a multimillionaire, collecting vast sums from creating venues for people to gather. As his fortune grew, he made other investments, including one transaction that set the stage for the creation of his biggest project, the Venetian Hotel.

1990s: The Sands Gives Way to the Venetian

In 1989, Adelson delved into the hotel business, roughly 30 years after his stint at selling soap and shaving cream to motel

Key Dates:

1990: The Sands Expo and Convention Center is built.
1996: The Sands Hotel is imploded, making room for the Venetian.
1997: Construction of the Venetian begins.
1999: The Venetian opens for business.

operators. He paid $128 million for the Sands Hotel, owned at the time by Kirk Kerkorian. To many observers, the Sands Hotel, once the haven of Frank Sinatra, Dean Martin, and Sammy Davis, Jr., was a run-down hotel property. The Sands Hotel's tarnished image was made glaringly apparent when Steve Wynn's $630 million Mirage property opened just across the Las Vegas Strip from the dilapidated property acquired by Adelson. "Their [the Mirage] front desk looked better than our whole hotel," mused Henri Lewin, the manager of the Sands Hotel under Adelson, in a December 1, 1997 *Forbes* article. Adelson's ownership of the Sands Hotel proved a disaster. He went through four management teams in seven years, failing to engineer a revival of the storied hotel. As Wynn's Mirage, located across the street, went on to pay for itself twice over, Adelson's Sands Hotel lost money for five consecutive years. His frustration was vented in a Las Vegas spectacle. In 1996, Adelson dynamited the Sands Hotel, imploding a failure to make room for a dream.

Before the Sands Hotel investment collapsed, literally and figuratively, Adelson built an adjacent facility whose presence spurred the development of the Venetian. In 1990, Adelson built the world's largest convention center, the 1.2 million-square-foot Sands Expo Center, designed to house the world's largest trade show, COMDEX. When Adelson razed the Sands Hotel, he left the Sands Expo Center standing. In the lot created by the demolition of the Sands Hotel, Adelson planned to build Las Vegas's premier hotel property, its rooms and concept designed to attract Adelson's prized customers: conventioneers.

Aside from proving to be a perennial money loser, the Sands Hotel in Adelson's eyes was not large enough to accommodate the volume of business enjoyed by the adjacent Sands Expo and Convention Center. During the latter half of the 1990s, more than one million conventioneers visited Adelson's showcase meeting complex annually, and he wanted a hotel that could attract and accommodate those business travelers. In 1995, he sold COMDEX and 16 other convention events to Japanese software distributor Softbank Corp. for a staggering $862 million. The following year, he imploded the Sands Hotel. In April 1997, construction of the new hotel-casino began, its completion scheduled for April 1999.

Adelson relished the opportunity to break with convention in the design of the Venetian. "I wasn't swaddled like the others in green felt," he remarked in an April 12, 1999 interview with *Business Week.* "I'm going to do things differently," he vowed.

The Venetian, like Las Vegas's other premier hotel properties, was designed as an elaborate, themed resort, featuring life-size replicas of some of Venice's famous landmarks, such as the Doge's Palace, the Rialto Bridge, and the Campanile. The six-million-square-foot Venetian—to be the largest hotel in the world once completed—was distinct because of the type of clientele Adelson was after. Typically, hotel rooms in Las Vegas were designed to keep guests in the casinos. The rooms were small and bereft of amenities. Adelson's Venetian, however, was designed to attract business travelers, the conventioneers who attended meetings and expositions at the adjoining Sands Expo and Convention Center. Accordingly, the Venetian's 3,036 suites were outfitted with fax machines, large televisions, telephones capable of handling conference calls, safes, refrigerators, and other amenities. At 700 square feet, the Venetian's rooms were the largest standard hotel rooms in the world, according to the *Guinness Book of World Records.*

When the $1.5 billion, 35-story Venetian opened in May 1999, Adelson's unique marketing approach was put to the test. After a troubled beginning stemming from construction delays, the property began to exhibit some of the potential Adelson had promised. By late 2001, the Venetian's casino was generating more than $2,600 in profits per square foot per day, ranking as the fourth best performer in Las Vegas. In early 2002, the hotel itself exuded encouraging strength, supported largely by conventioneers and their corporate travel allowances. With a daily room rate of $213 and 96 percent occupancy, the Venetian ranked as one of the premier revenue generators on the Las Vegas Strip. In the years ahead, Adelson planned to expand the Venetian, intending to make good on a promise he made in an October 23, 2000 interview with *Business Week.* Adelson declared, "This will be the highest-grossing hotel in the history of hotels."

Principal Competitors

MGM Mirage; Park Place Entertainment Corporation; Mandalay Resort Group; Harrah's Entertainment, Inc.

Further Reading

Edelhart, Mike, "Leaving the Flash Behind," *PC Week,* November 26, 1985, p. 3.

Gorham, John, "High Noon in Vegas," *Forbes,* December 1, 1997, p. 45.

Nelton, Sharon, "Making His Fortune Again and Again," *Nation's Business,* October 1984, p. 47.

Palmeri, Christopher, "His Venice Isn't Sinking," *Business Week,* October 23, 2000, p. 86.

Smith, Stephen, "A Corner of America That Is (for a While) Europe," *New Statesman,* August 9, 1999, p. 24.

Somerson, Paul, "Welcome to CALMDEX (COMDEX 1984)," *PC Magazine,* January 22, 1985, p. 33.

"Vegas' Latest Long Shot," *Business Week,* April 12, 1999, p. 40.

Weingarten, Tara, "Venice, Vegas, Vici?," *Newsweek,* May 3, 1999, p. 56.

—Jeffrey L. Covell

VeriSign, Inc.

**487 East Middlefield Road
Mountain View, California 94043
U.S.A.
Telephone: (650) 961-7500
Fax: (650) 961-7300
Web site: http://www.verisign.com**

Public Company
Incorporated: 1995
Employees: 3,400
Sales: $983.6 million (2001)
Stock Exchanges: NASDAQ
Ticker Symbol: VRSN
NAIC: 511210 Software Publishers; 541519 Other
   Computer Related Services

VeriSign, Inc. has grown and expanded into new markets through acquisitions since it was spun off from RSA Data Security Inc. in 1995. The company is known principally for its domain registration business, which was the result of acquiring Network Solutions, Inc. in 2000. However, VeriSign also offers a wide range of services through its Enterprise and Service Provider Division and its Mass Market Division. In addition to registry services, VeriSign offers managed security and network services to enterprises and service providers that facilitate secure transactions and communications in corporate infranets and virtual private networks as well as in Internet-based services. With the acquisition of Illuminet Holdings Inc. and H.O. Systems in 2001 and 2002, VeriSign now offers a wide range of specialized services to telecommunications providers. The company's Mass Markets Division provides three general types of services: Web Presence Services, including domain name registration services and related value-added services; Web Trust Services, including web site digital certificates; and Payment Services, which enable online merchants to process a range of payment types.

Birth Via Spinoff: 1995

VeriSign, Inc. was spun off from RSA Data Security Inc., a leader in encryption technology, in April 1995 and began devel-

oping Digital ID's for corporations and individuals in June 1995. Digital ID's utilized public- and private-key cryptography to authenticate a data sender's identity. Also known as certificates, the digital ID's ensured privacy and authenticated the content of electronic transmissions on public and private networks. The company recruited Stratton Sclavos, a Silicon Valley veteran, as president in August 1995.

The separation of the two companies allowed RSA to focus on encryption technology, while VeriSign focused on providing products and services that utilized encryption technology to ensure secure online transactions. VeriSign received financial backing from a group of companies and investors interested in addressing the problem of adequate security on the Internet, the lack of which was hindering the development of electronic commerce. In addition to RSA, companies providing financial backing for VeriSign included Visa International, Ameritech Corp., Bessemer Venture Partners, Fischer International Systems, Mitsubishi Corporation, and Security Dynamics Technologies Inc.

Widespread Support for Its Technology: 1996

After testing its digital ID system, VeriSign publicly demonstrated the first online digital certificate issuing system at the RSA Data Security Conference in San Francisco in January 1996. Since the system utilized proprietary technology from VeriSign, it was necessary that browsers and servers be equipped with that technology. By January 1996, VeriSign had signed up a dozen hardware makers, including Netscape Communications, IBM, Cybercash Inc., CompuServe Inc., and OpenMarket Inc.

Authentication was regarded as the missing technology link in secure electronic transactions, and VeriSign received widespread support throughout the computer industry for its technology. During 1996, several major computer companies entered into licensing agreements with VeriSign to incorporate its technology in their products and services. VeriSign announced it was working with Microsoft to develop an industry standard for secure transactions and a version of its digital identification systems for Microsoft Internet servers. Dun & Bradstreet Software Services signed a partnership agreement with VeriSign to

Company Perspectives:

VeriSign, Inc. is a leading provider of digital trust services that enable Web site owners, enterprises, communications service providers, electronic commerce ("e-commerce"), service providers, and individuals to engage in secure digital commerce and communications. Our digital trust services include three core offerings: managed security and network services, registry and telecommunications services, and Web presence and trust services. We market our products and services through our direct sales force, telesales operations, member organizations in our global affiliate network, value added resellers, service providers, and our Web sites.

develop an Internet-based electronic data interchange (EDI) for business-to-business transactions. Netscape Communications licensed the technology for use in the new version of its browser, Navigator 3.0.

In mid-1996, VeriSign and Visa International announced they would offer digital certification of credit cards to allow consumers to purchase products over the Internet without giving out their credit card numbers. VeriSign also announced a private label initiative to enable Visa's member banks to issue digital equivalents of plastic credit cards to their customers.

In another major deal, VeriSign and America Online reached an agreement for VeriSign to provide digital IDs to merchants on AOL's Primehost Storefront. The Merchant ID verified a business's authenticity to customers, hopefully making them more comfortable about making online purchases. At the time, personal digital IDs were available as options on both Netscape's and Microsoft's Internet browsers.

By the end of 1996, VeriSign had secured the backing of a broad cross-section of companies that hoped digital authentication would become more widely adopted. Additional companies supporting VeriSign included Cisco Systems, AT&T, and Merrill Lynch. Cisco planned to integrate VeriSign's technology into a total solution for enterprises working over the Internet. AT&T planned to use VeriSign technology with its Easy Commerce systems for deploying enterprise-scale electronic commerce initiatives. Merrill Lynch and Intuit Inc. were exploring the use of digital certificate systems with their online financial systems. These and other companies provided support for VeriSign by investing $30 million in the firm at the end of the year.

New Security Products: 1997

At the beginning of 1997, VeriSign was the dominant certificate authority and was hoping to make its authentication technology the industry standard. The company had issued 12,000 server ID's at $295 each as well as half a million user IDs that needed to be renewed for a low annual fee.

In January 1997, VeriSign rolled out its private label service for OEMs (original equipment manufacturers). In March the company introduced a major enhancement that increased the amount of personal information its digital certificates could carry.

VeriSign's new certificates, called Universal ID Cards, were able to contain demographic information, including gender, age, address, ZIP code, and other personal data. Its Private Label Digital ID Service allowed corporations to add customized data for specific users. These features would help companies automate their web-based interactions with customers or clients.

VeriSign also signed an agreement with Network Solutions, Inc. of Herndon, Virginia, to provide one-stop registration for Internet domains. New domain registrants would have the option of signing up for VeriSign's digital identification when they registered their domain name with Network Solutions. Network Solutions was the leading provider of registration services for domain names. VeriSign's digital identification served to authenticate companies doing business online to their potential customers.

Raising Cash for Acquisitions Through an IPO: 1998–99

When VeriSign went public on January 30, 1998, its filing with the Securities and Exchange Commission (SEC) indicated it had issued more than two million digital certificates. On the first day of trading, the company's stock rose 82 percent, from an initial price of $14 to close at $25.50. Intel, Microsoft, and Visa International each owned about 5 percent of VeriSign's equity, while RSA Data Security held about 25 percent.

Following its strategy of forming partnerships and alliances, VeriSign entered into a preferred provider agreement with Verifone, Inc., a subsidiary of Hewlett Packard Co. The non-exclusive partnership combined Verifone's expertise in online payments with VeriSign's authentication technology. Both companies agreed to bundle Verifone's vWallet, vGate, and vPOS virtual payment products with VeriSign's digital certificate technology. VeriSign characterized the deal as "the first end-to-end solution that we have done with a market leader."

VeriSign made its first acquisition in July 1998 when it bought privately held SecureIT, an Atlanta-based Internet security company, for $69.1 million in stock. The acquisition would help VeriSign compete in the enterprise market. Later in the year VeriSign redesigned its web site to reflect a growing emphasis on marketing to enterprises rather than to consumers. In October, the company released version 4.0 of OnSite, its suite of software and services for corporations that was first introduced in January 1998. OnSite was VeriSign's public key infrastructure (PKI) software that allowed corporations to control their digital certificates. New services offered in version 4.0 included centralized key management and distributed key recovery as well as back-end processing and verification services that VeriSign would handle for its customers.

During the first quarter of 1999, VeriSign entered into an extensive agreement with Netscape Communications to deliver digital certificate services through Netscape's Netcenter portal. Under the agreement Netscape granted "premier provider" status to VeriSign, which would develop a Security Center within Netcenter to provide information, products, and services relating to electronic authentication technology.

In mid-1999, VeriSign introduced OnSite for Microsoft Exchange, a PKI service that simplified the management of secure e-mail systems. The new product was the first in VeriSign's Go Secure family of implementation aids for enterprises. In other developments, VeriSign reported its first quarterly profit, both in terms of operating income and net income. Later in the year, the company entered into an alliance with Eccelerate.com, an online spinoff from Dun & Bradstreet, to provide transaction services for electronic commerce. Under the alliance, the two companies would prequalify the more than 57 million public and private companies in Dun & Bradstreet's database for digital certificates. VeriSign also reported that its technology was being used in more than 40 federal government pilot programs, including those of the Federal Bureau of Investigation (FBI) and the Internal Revenue Service (IRS).

VeriSign announced two major acquisitions in the last month of 1999. The company paid between $700 and $800 million to acquire privately held Signio Inc. by issuing 5.6 million common shares of stock. Signio specialized in online payment services, which it offered to a wide range of online merchants, business-to-business exchanges, payment processors, and financial institutions. The second acquisition involved Thawte Consulting of South Africa. Thawte was also a payment service provider with an established customer base. VeriSign acquired the company for $575 million in stock.

Acquisition of Network Solutions: 2000

With its stock price rising in value more than 1,000 percent in 1999, VeriSign announced in March 2000 that it would acquire the leading domain registration firm Network Solutions, Inc. for $21 billion in stock. The combined companies would have one of the largest subscriber bases on the Internet. As reported by United Press International, VeriSign President and CEO Stratton Sclavos stated, "With Network Solutions as the gateway to establishing online identity and Web presence, and VeriSign as the provider of Internet authentication, validation and payment services, our combined company will serve as the trust utility that will power the Internet economy."

Network Solutions was originally established in 1979 by black entrepreneur Emmitt McHenry and three partners as a network integration firm that developed and managed voice, data, and video communications networks. The company be-

came involved in Internet domain registration in 1993, when it began assigning domain names under contract from the National Science Foundation (NSF). The NSF was a federal agency charged with handling the administration of the Internet since 1991. Network Solutions was responsible for assigning top-level domain names ending in .com, .edu, .net, .org, and .gov. Registering a domain name was free until 1995, when Network Solutions began charging a $50 annual registration fee to cover its expenses. At the time, some 110,000 top-level Internet domain names were registered. In 1995, Network Solutions was acquired by Science Applications International Corp. (SAIC) for $4.8 million. Network Solutions had a successful IPO in 1997.

Network Solutions had a monopoly on domain name registration until 1999, when it was placed under the oversight of the semi-public Internet Corporation for Assigned Names and Numbers (ICANN) and opened up to competition. At the time it was acquired by VeriSign, Network Solutions had a 40 percent market share of the domain registration business. It had a database of 8.1 million domain registrations and 240 partners worldwide.

VeriSign paid a 40 percent premium for Network Solutions, based on the company's stock price, largely because of the opportunities available to the combined company. It could capture small and medium-size businesses when they registered their domain names, then offer them a suite of higher-priced trust services such as authentication and payment services. In addition to domain name registration, VeriSign planned to offer companies e-mail, web site creation, e-commerce capabilities, secure extranet services, virtual private networks (VPNs), and global trading.

When the transaction was completed in mid-2000, the acquisition of Network Solutions was valued at $15.5 billion, according to *Business Week.* SAIC, which had owned 23 percent of Network Solutions, gained a 9 percent interest in VeriSign. Network Solutions became a subsidiary of VeriSign and operated under its own name until it was integrated into VeriSign's domain registration. Later in 2000, VeriSign acquired a competing domain registration firm, GreatDomains.com, for $20 million in cash and 300,000 shares of stock in a deal valued at $100 million.

Preparing for increased acceptance of public key infrastructure (PKI)—a set of standards, technologies, and procedures for user authentication and the secure transfer of data—VeriSign released its new Trust Services platform suite in mid-2000. It was designed to let enterprises and their trading partners incorporate authentication, payment, and validation for high-volume transactions conducted over the Internet, extranets, and business-to-business exchanges.

Another new service introduced by VeriSign in mid-2000 was a fraud-screening service. The company's Payflow Fraud Screen was offered as an enhancement to its Payflow Pro program, which cost merchants $59.95 a month for up to 5,000 transactions a month. Payflow Fraud Screen cost an additional $39.95 a month for the same level of transactions.

It was around this time that the Electronic Signatures in Global and National Commerce Act (E-Sign) was signed into law by President Bill Clinton. The E-Sign law replaced a patchwork of state laws and went into effect in October 2000. It made signatures, contracts, and other records in electronic formats legally valid and binding. The law was expected to increase the market for digital certificates.

New Domain Registration Agreement: 2001

In the first half of 2001, VeriSign negotiated a new agreement with ICANN covering domain name registrations. The agreement was opposed by some in the Internet community as unfair, but it was reviewed and approved by the U.S. Department of Commerce in May 2001. The agreement with ICANN specified how much control VeriSign would have over the registration of top-level domain names. Under the agreement VeriSign retained control of the .com registry until November 2007, with the option to renew for an additional four years. VeriSign was given another year to operate the .org registry, but was required to turn it over to a nonprofit body in 2002. Its right to operate the .net registry would expire at the end of June 2005, when registration of .net domains would be opened to competitive bidding. Meanwhile, other registrars could register those top-level domain names, but VeriSign would collect $6 for each top-level domain name registered by another registrar. VeriSign was also required to invest $200 million in registration infrastructure research and development and contribute $5 million for operating expenses to the nonprofit organization that would oversee .org registration. At the time of the agreement with ICANN there were 21 million registered .com names, four million .net names, and three million .org names.

VeriSign also expanded its domain name registration to encompass more international languages. The company began offering multilingual domain names in November 2000. The first four languages offered were Japanese, Korean, traditional Chinese, and a simpler version of Chinese. The company soon added Western European languages, and by April 2001 VeriSign had added support for more than 350 languages. Through an agreement with Los Angeles-based .tv Corporation International, VeriSign began registering .tv domain names in January 2001.

In April 2001, VeriSign was part of a group that successfully bid for the operating assets of online payment services firm Cybercash Inc., which had declared bankruptcy. Although payment services represented a small portion of VeriSign's revenue compared to domain name registration, the company planned to invest more to support its payment services business. At the time VeriSign provided payment services to about 15,100 merchants and processed $1.3 billion worth of electronic commerce settlements in 2000. In 2001, that figure rose to $6 billion worth of e-commerce transactions.

VeriSign continued to expand through acquisitions in the second half of 2001. After acquiring Internet Domain Registrars from Network Commerce, VeriSign announced it would acquire Illuminet Holdings Inc. for $1.2 billion in stock. Illuminet was a provider of infrastructure services to telephone networks, including services that facilitated caller ID, cell phone roaming, and portable phone numbers. The acquisition strengthened VeriSign's ability to provide trust services in anticipation of the convergence of voice and data networks. Toward the end of 2001, VeriSign acquired two smaller domain name registration

companies, 1GlobalPlace Inc., which specialized in foreign domain names, and NameEngine, Inc., which managed intellectual property rights and corporate brands for its clients.

In early 2002 VeriSign acquired The .tv Corporation International, the exclusive registrar for .tv domain names, for $45 million. The company also announced it would acquire H.O. Systems Inc., a company that provided billing and customer care solutions to wireless carriers, for $340 million in cash and stock. Among the new initiatives VeriSign announced for 2002 was a Digital Trust Services framework that would take an open standards approach to automating business processes in a secure way across distributed applications. An interface for VeriSign's Digital Trust Services would be embedded in major platforms from OEMs such as BEA Systems, Hewlett-Packard, IBM, Microsoft, Oracle, and Sun Microsystems. Meanwhile, VeriSign would devote much of 2002 to integrating the acquisitions it made in 2001.

Principal Divisions

Enterprise and Service Provider Division; Mass Market Division.

Principal Competitors

Baltimore Technologies plc; Certicom Corp.; Digital Signature Trust Co.; Entrust Technologies Inc.; GeoTrust, Inc.; International Business Machines Corporation; Register.com; Tucows.com, Inc.

Further Reading

Balderston, Jim, "VeriSign Acts As an Online Notary Public," *Info-World,* July 29, 1996, p. 41.

Blankenhorn, Dana, "VeriSign's Key to Change," *Business Marketing,* October 1998, p. 31.

Brown, Eryn, "Are You Really You?," *Fortune,* March 30, 1998, p. 154.

"Control over Dot-Com and Dot-Org to Split," *United Press International,* March 1, 2001.

Daniels, Alex, "Ultimate Solutions," *Washington Techway,* October 9, 2000, p. 21.

"Domain Name Seller Sold," *Los Angeles Business Journal,* November 6, 2000, p. 53.

Doyle, Eric, "VeriSign Unveils Its Web Services Security Framework in San Jose," *Computer Weekly,* February 28, 2002, p. 33.

"E-Business Services Team," *InformationWeek,* November 8, 1999, p. 95.

Epper, Karen, "Microsoft, VeriSign to Work on Data Security Standard," *American Banker,* March 15, 1996, p. 13.

Fonseca, Brian, "Authentication Services Come to the Fore," *Info-World,* May 8, 2000, p. 36.

Gardner, Elizabeth, "Commerce, Congress Eye VeriSign Pact," *Internet World,* May 1, 2001, p. 16.

Gerwig, Kate, "Just Sign Here—E-Signature Bill Creates New Questions for Providers," *Tele.com,* July 31, 2000, p. 20.

Gruenwald, Juliana, "ICANN Critics Await Commerce Move," *Interactive Week,* April 9, 2001, p. 34.

Harrison, Ann, "VeriSign Launches Flat-Fee Fraud-Screening Service," *Computerworld,* August 14, 2000, p. 6.

"Internet Corporation for Assigned Names and Numbers (Icann)," *Computer Weekly,* March 22, 2001, p. 58.

Kerstetter, Jim, "VeriSign/Net Solutions Deal Speeds Domain Registration," *PC Week,* March 17, 1997, p. 46.

——, "VeriSign Raises Digital Certificate Bar," *PC Week,* October 19, 1998, p. 33.

Knowles, Anne, "RSA Spin-off Plans to Offer 'Digital Ids,' " *PC Week,* June 26, 1995, p. 16.

Koehler, Wallace, "Recent Trends Result in a New Status for VeriSign," *Information Today,* April 2001, p. 21.

Littman, Jonathan, "The Secret to Success," *PC Week,* January 27, 1997, p. A1.

Luhby, Tami, "E-Payment Firms in Expansion Mode," *American Banker,* July 13, 1998, p. 14.

Maclachlan, Malcolm, "VeriSign's AOL Deal Keeps It at Top of Digital ID Industry," *Business Journal,* October 21, 1996, p. 4.

"Mixed Signals at VeriSign," *Business Week Online,* March 12, 2002.

Moeller, Michael, and Jim Kerstetter. "Signings of the Times: Visa, VeriSign to Set up Digital Certificates," *PC Week,* July 22, 1996, p. 1.

"Network Commerce," *Washington Business Journal,* June 22, 2001, p. 27.

"Network Solutions Incorporated: Global Communicator," *Black Enterprise,* August 1994, p. 24.

Perrotta, Tom, "VeriSign Victory: A Closed-Door Deal," *Internet World,* June 15, 2001, p. 11.

Petersen, Scot, "D&B and VeriSign Partner for Transaction Services," *PC Week,* November 8, 1999, p. 30.

Power, Carol, "E-Sign Law Gives Equality to E-Signatures," *American Banker,* October 12, 2000, p. 14A.

Roth, Andrew, "VeriSign Sees Fortune in Rival CyberCash's Bankruptcy Woes," *American Banker,* March 12, 2001, p. 14.

Rupley, Sebastian, "Virtual Plastic: Banks to Issue Digital Visas," *PC Magazine,* September 24, 1996, p. 34.

Schaff, William, "VeriSign Seems a Secure Pick," *InformationWeek,* September 18, 2000, p. 160.

Scheier, Robert L., "Facing PKI's Big Guns," *Computerworld,* March 5, 2001, p. 50.

Serwer, Andrew, "VeriSign of the Times," *Fortune,* February 16, 1998, p. 193.

Siedsma, Andrea, "Network Solutions Sale Initiates New E-Biz Model," *San Diego Business Journal,* March 13, 2000, p. 6.

Snel, Ross, "On-Line Deals Put VeriSign in Thick of Payments Fray," *American Banker,* December 21, 1999, p. 1.

Spangler, Todd, "In Web We Trust," *Interactive Week,* September 24, 2001, p. 45.

Tucker, Tracey, "Start-up Offers 'Digital ID' for Security on the Internet," *American Banker,* June 28, 1995, p. 14.

——, "VeriSign to Test On-Line IDs for Electronic Commerce," *American Banker,* September 21, 1995, p. 15.

"VeriSign to Acquire H.O. Systems," *RCR Wireless News,* January 14, 2002, p. 13.

Vogelstein, Fred, "The Man Who Bought the Internet," *Fortune,* June 25, 2001, p. 126.

"Washington Approves VeriSign's '.com' Deal," *TechWeb,* May 22, 2001.

"The Web's Virtual Vault: VeriSign," *Business Week,* October 23, 2000, p. 74.

Weiss, Todd R., "Domain Name Registration Gets 64 More Languages," *Computerworld,* March 5, 2001, p. 20.

——, "Multilingual Domain Name Registrations Hit 700,000," *Computerworld,* January 1, 2001, p. 16.

Wingfield, Nick, "Digital IDs to Help Secure Internet," *InfoWorld,* October 23, 1995, p. 12.

——, "NSF Ends Internet Subsidy," *InfoWorld,* September 18, 1995, p. 8.

Yasin, Rutrell, "PKI Crosses Enterprise Boundaries," *InternetWeek,* May 1, 2000, p. 1.

—David P. Bianco

Wachtell, Lipton, Rosen & Katz

51 West 52nd Street
New York, New York 10019-6188
U.S.A.
Telephone: (212) 403–1000
Fax: (212) 403-2000
Web site: http://www.wlrk.com

Partnership
Founded: 1965
Employees: 400
Gross Billings: $317 million (2000 est.)
NAIC: 541110 Offices of Lawyers

Wachtell, Lipton, Rosen & Katz (Wachtell Lipton) is famous for serving companies involved in mergers and acquisitions. During the heyday of mergers in the 1980s, Wachtell Lipton made a major contribution by coming up with the "poison pill defense" that prevented hostile takeovers. The firm's banking practice is particularly noteworthy. It is the most profitable law firm in the world, based on its average profits per equity partner of $3.28 million in 2000. Unlike many other large law firms, Wachtell Lipton has only one office. Yet it serves clients in many nations and thus is a major force in globalization. Although it is a relatively young law firm, Wachtell Lipton has an outstanding track record of providing top-notch legal services to clients such as Amoco, BankBoston, and AT&T.

Origins and Early Accomplishments

Herbert Wachtell, Leonard Rosen, and George Katz graduated from New York University Law School in 1954, and Martin Lipton graduated the following year. Lipton, Katz, and Rosen began their legal careers at the bankruptcy law firm of Seligson, Morris & Neuberger. Meanwhile, Wachtell helped NYU law professor Bernard Schwartz in a congressional probe of federal regulatory agencies and later defended Schwartz, his first litigation client, before starting his own New York City litigation practice.

In 1965 the four NYU Law School graduates formed their own law firm of Wachtell, Lipton, Rosen & Katz, which origi-

nally included three other lawyers, two from the Seligson law firm and one of Wachtell's associates. The New York City partnership initially hired top graduates from their alma mater and continued to recruit a substantial number of NYU Law School graduates in the years ahead.

Although the new firm included relatively few lawyers, it soon gained a reputation for excellence. Wachtell headed its litigation team and also wrote a book called *New York Practice Under the CPLR* used often by both those preparing for the state bar exam and practicing lawyers. First published in 1963, its sixth edition came out in 1986.

Lipton became well known as an expert in corporate transactions, especially in mergers and acquisitions. Lipton and his wife Erica Steinberger, also a partner at the firm, wrote a two-volume M&A study called *Takeovers and Freezeouts,* which Erwin Cherovsky described, in *The Guide to New York Law Firms,* as the "the bible on takeovers and freezeouts."

In 1970 the firm described itself in the annual *Martindale-Hubbell Law Directory* as having a "general practice" with expertise in "corporation, securities, creditors' rights, antitrust, motion pictures, broadcasting, tax, municipal securities, real estate, labor and probate law," and "trials and appeals in all state and federal courts." At that point it had seven partners, ten associates, and one "of counsel" (emeritus) lawyer. In 1980 it included 23 partners, 27 associates, and one of counsel lawyer.

The public knew little about law firms like Wachtell Lipton until the late 1970s, even though they played important roles in business and government. As Kim Isaac Eisler wrote in *Shark Tank,* law firms' ". . . activities, their profits, their methods of operation were among the most secret in America, and everything about the so-called code of legal ethics [of the American Bar Association] was designed to insulate and protect them from public scrutiny. Many lawyers considered even answering a press call unethical."

That situation began to change when Steve Brill in 1978 began writing a law column for *Esquire* and the following year began the *American Lawyer.* The *National Law Review* about the same time also began examining the operations and finances of big law firms. This rise of legal journalism, combined with

1970s court decisions that said professional restrictions on advertising were unconstitutional, opened the floodgates. Soon many law firms sought publicity and even hired their own public relations managers.

In 1980 Wachtell Lipton, along with other major law firms, helped rescue Chrysler from financial ruin as it competed with more efficient foreign car makers. A group of 15 lending institutions chose Leonard Rosen as their special counsel as they set up complicated loans guaranteed by the federal government.

In *Lions of the Eighties,* Rosen told about the unusual challenge that he and others faced when trying to close the Chrysler deal after six months of intensive work. On the evening of June 24, 1980, a fire broke out in the Westvaco Building where Rosen was meeting with Debevoise & Plimpton lawyers in their office just below the Wachtell office. Everyone evacuated the building that became what Rosen called a "raging inferno." After the fire was under control, Rosen and others returned to the building to get the documents they needed. At about 1 a.m. they pushed eight carts of records up Park Avenue to the office of Shearman & Sterling, where work continued until the deal was closed in the morning. James B. Stewart in *The Partners* said this was "the largest corporate rescue mission ever attempted."

Wachtell Lipton in 1980 and 1981 represented Curtiss-Wright when it successfully fought a takeover bid by Kennecott. Fought out in the court system, this protracted struggle cost Kennecott so much that it soon agreed to being taken over.

Martin Lipton played a key role in the much publicized acquisition of Getty Oil Company, the firm founded by J. Paul Getty in the 1930s. In 1983 and 1984 Lipton represented the J. Paul Getty Museum, which owned 11.8 percent of the oil company's stock. The museum, the Sarah Getty Trust, which owned 40 percent of the stock, and the company were in the midst of an internal conflict when Lipton drew up an agreement that seemed to settle the dispute.

Soon, however, the quarrel resumed and Pennzoil bid to take over Getty Oil. A $10 billion handshake between Lipton and Pennzoil's lawyer Arthur Liman seemed to seal that deal, but it was blocked by lawsuits. Ultimately Texaco came in as a "white knight" and made a higher offer of $10.2 billion that was accepted. Robert Lenzer, in a 1985 book, called Texaco's purchase "the largest corporate acquisition in American history."

According to Cherovsky, Wachtell Lipton in the 1980s dealt "almost solely in transactional work" such as defending companies against hostile takeovers. One of its major contributions to recent business history was developing in the 1980s the "poison pill defense" against unwanted takeovers. Cherovsky said Wachtell Lipton was not interested in becoming a "full service" law firm representing corporate clients continually on a wide range of legal matters. In other words, its lawyers did not seek to become general counsel to corporations.

Although Wachtell Lipton had only about 90 lawyers at the time, in 1987 it led the nation's law firms with profits per partner of $1.4 million and in 1988 was number one with $1.09 million in revenue per lawyer. Cherovsky attributed the firm's financial success mainly to its "top-to-bottom, across-the-board strength" of both partners and associates. He also cited Wachtell Lipton's internal cohesiveness and "true firm identity." Unlike many large American law firms, Wachtell Lipton opened no domestic or international branch offices.

"In a relatively short time," concluded Cherovsky, "[Wachtell Lipton] has reached almost legendary status for its proficiency and achievements." That reputation for legal excellence continued into the next decade.

Law Practice in the 1990s and Beyond

In 1992 the New York law firm of Kaye, Scholer, Fierman, Hays & Handler hired Wachtell Lipton partner Bernard Nussbaum to help defend itself against a lawsuit filed by the federal Office of Thrift Supervision (OTS). The federal government charged that Kaye, Scholer had knowingly helped Lincoln Savings & Loan defraud its bondholders before it collapsed in 1989, in return for a total of $13 million in legal fees received between 1985 and 1989. The government eventually paid out about $3 billion in the biggest bailout in the history of savings and loan institutions. The OTS sought $275 million in fines from Kaye, Scholer, but the law firm, with Nussbaum's help, settled the lawsuit by paying the government $41 million and agreeing that two of its partners would no longer serve financial institutions insured by the government. Five other law firms also paid huge fines to the government because of their roles in the savings and loan scandal. None of these six law firms admitted to or were convicted of breaking any laws.

Based on Wachtell Lipton's 1994 gross revenue of $108 million, it was ranked as the United States' 62nd largest law firm in the *American Lawyer*'s July/August 1995 issue. It had just 109 lawyers, far less than most big law firms.

In the late 1990s Wachtell Lipton continued as one of the few large law firms that dominated the mergers and acquisitions field. Citing research firm Securities Data Company, the *Wall Street Journal*'s Richard B. Schmitt said in an April 22, 1998 article that Wachtell Lipton had done "more giant bank mergers during the past two years than any other law firm."

In April 1998 Wachtell Lipton's Edward Herlihy represented BankAmerica Corporation when it merged with NationsBank Corporation, a longtime client of the New York law firm. About the same time, Herlihy also represented both Banc One Corporation and First Chicago NBD Corporation when they merged, a controversial arrangement because of the possibility of a conflict

Key Dates:

1965: The firm is founded in New York City.
1980: As part of its growing banking practice, the firm serves 15 lending institutions that loaned money to save Chrysler.
1995: The firm ranks fourth in the nation for serving bidding companies in 16 acquisitions and second for representing targeted companies in 17 deals, typical of their leadership in mergers and acquisitions.

of interest. According to *Fortune* on May 25, 1998, Herlihy and H. Rodgin Cohen of Sullivan & Cromwell had represented principals in 18 of America's 25 major bank mergers.

Business Week on February 28, 2000, reported that Wachtell Lipton was ranked as the world's ninth largest mergers and acquisitions firm, based on total 1999 acquisitions worth $405.8 billion. That came from just 84 deals, far less than most of the top ten M&A law firms.

In 2000 Wachtell Lipton advised AT&T in its plans to organize four new companies: AT&T Wireless, AT&T Broadband, AT&T Consumer, and AT&T Business. AT&T intended that the four companies would become public entities by 2002 and would cooperate through intercompany agreements. The law firm also represented AT&T when it acquired Media One for $60.5 billion.

The firm in 2000 served as cocounsel, along with Greenberg Traurig, to Madrid's Terra Networks, S.A. when it acquired Lycos, Inc. This $12.5 billion deal resulted in one of the world's major Internet businesses. Wachtell Lipton's corporate division also advised VoiceStream Wireless Corporation when it was acquired by Deutsche Telekom AG for $50.7 billion, Motorola in its $17 billion acquisition of General Instrument, Warner-Lambert in its $93.4 billion transaction with Pfizer, and Vivendi when it acquired Seagram for $33.8 billion. According to Wachtell's web site, in 2000 it participated in announced acquisitions worth almost $425 billion.

Meanwhile, the firm's antitrust lawyers served Phillips Petroleum in its $6 billion joint venture with Chevron and Reynolds Metals in its $6 billion merger with Alcoa. Its real estate lawyers also were busy serving clients such as Security Capital, Lend Lease, Taubman, and Avalon Bay in various merger and acquisition transactions. Wachtell Lipton's creditors' rights lawyers advised Montgomery Ward's official creditors' committee, the senior lenders to Breed Technology, and Integrated Health's bondholders. According to its web site, the firm's litigation practice participated in several landmark corporate governance cases in Delaware, including those involving Household, Revlon, Macmillan, Time Warner, and Paramount. Other litigation clients were AT&T, Philip Morris, and National Semiconductor.

To help its 170 lawyers keep up with the rapid pace of legal developments, Wachtell Lipton in 2001 purchased access to Law.com. The web site provided 24-hour access to decisions, papers, and seminars in corporate law, intellectual property, employment law, litigation, and technology law.

Although Wachtell Lipton did not have offices in the World Trade Center when terrorists destroyed its twin towers on September 11, 2001, it provided office space for its longtime client Keefe, Bruyette & Woods Inc., a securities firm that reported losing 67 of its employees from its offices in the north tower. Back in 1993 Wachtell Lipton had given Keefe, Bruyette & Woods free use of a conference room and secretarial assistance for a month after the World Trade Center bombing.

In October 2001 the *American Lawyer* published an interesting article about the law firm's operations and finances. Writer Douglas McCollam said the firm's legal bills were an "amazing phenomenon" that were "the stuff of campfire legend, discussed around boardroom tables in hushed whispers by awestruck competitors." A Wachtell Lipton memo obtained by the magazine indicated to potential clients that the firm did not deal with routine legal concerns. It emphasized its quality service provided by partners working directly with clients. Instead of using lawyers' hours in its billing, Wachtell Lipton charged a percentage of overall transaction values. Its flat fees ranged from one-tenth of 1 percent on larger deals to a full 1 percent of deal value on smaller transactions worth only $100 million. These bills only applied to completed transactions.

According to the *American Lawyer*'s listing of "The Global 100" in its November 2001 issue, Wachtell Lipton was rated as number 46 with 2000–2001 gross revenue of $317 million. With just 72 equity partners, fewer than most firms on the list, its average profits per equity partner were $3.28 million, the highest in the world. Such profitability was part of the firm's heritage as it entered the new millennium.

Principal Operating Units

Corporate; Litigation; Creditors' Rights; Tax; Executive Compensation and Benefits; Antitrust; Real Estate.

Principal Competitors

Cleary, Gottlieb, Steen & Hamilton; Skadden, Arps, Slate, Meagher & Flom; Sullivan & Cromwell.

Further Reading

Cherovsky, Erwin, *The Guide to New York Law Firms,* New York: St. Martin's Press, 1991, pp. 205–08.

Eisler, Kim Isaac, *Shark Tank: Greed, Politics, and the Collapse of Finley Kumble, One of America's Largest Law Firms,* New York: St. Martin's Press, 1990, pp. 82–83, 117.

Hoffman, Paul, *Lions of the Eighties: The Inside Story of the Powerhouse Law Firms,* Garden City, N.Y.: Doubleday & Company, Inc., 1982, pp. 94–97, 280–81.

Lenzer, Robert, *The Great Getty: The Life and Loves of J. Paul Getty—Richest Man in the World,* New York: Crown Publishers, Inc., 1985.

Liman, Arthur L., with Peter Israel, *Lawyer: A Life of Counsel and Controversy,* New York: PublicAffairs, 1998.

McCollam, Douglas, "Wachtell's Secret Formula," *American Lawyer,* October 2001, pp. 20–21.

McNatt, Robert, "Top 10 M&A Law Firms," *Business Week,* February 28, 2000, p. 6.

Nader, Ralph, and Wesley J. Smith, *No Contest: Corporate Lawyers and the Perversion of Justice in America,* New York: Random House, 1996, pp. 41–48.

Sapsford, Jathon, and Paul Beckett, ''Keefe Bruyette Goes on Despite Awful Toll of Attack,'' *Wall Street Journal,* September 25, 2001, p. 11.

Seigel, Matt, ''The Bank Merger Masters,'' *Fortune,* May 25, 1998, p. 44.

Schmitt, Richard B., ''All the Way to the Bank: Wachtell Is an Omnipresent Mergers Firm,'' *Wall Street Journal,* April 22, 1998, p. B6.

Stewart, James B., *The Partners: Inside America's Most Powerful Law Firms,* New York: Simon and Schuster, 1983, pp. 201, 225–27, 267–82.

—David M. Walden

Wendy's International, Inc.

4288 West Dublin-Granville Road
Post Office Box 256
Dublin, Ohio 43017-0256
U.S.A.
Telephone: (614) 764-3100
Fax: (614) 764-3330
Web site: http://www.wendys.com

Public Company
Incorporated: 1975
Employees: 44,000
Sales: $2.39 billion (2001)
Stock Exchanges: New York
Ticker Symbol: WEN
NAIC: 722211 Limited-Service Restaurants; 533110
Lessors of Nonfinancial Intangible Assets (Except
Copyrighted Works)

Wendy's International, Inc. is the operator, developer, and franchiser of the Wendy's restaurant chain, which is the number three hamburger chain in the United States (with a market share of 12.7 percent in 2000), trailing McDonald's (43.1 percent) and Burger King (18.8 percent). At the end of 2001, there were more than 6,000 Wendy's restaurants around the world; about 5,300 of these were located in the United States with the balance located in 26 other countries and territories. About 1,200 of the units were company operated, while the remainder were run by franchisees. Systemwide sales for the Wendy's chain totaled $6.84 billion in 2001. Wendy's hallmark square hamburgers and homey atmosphere were introduced in Columbus, Ohio, in 1969, and since that time the company has enjoyed phenomenal growth.

Since December 1995 Wendy's International has also owned Tim Hortons, Canada's second largest restaurant chain. Tim Hortons outlets feature coffee and fresh-baked goods, and some units also sell sandwiches and soups. There were more than 2,000 Tim Hortons open in Canada at the end of 2001 and 140 in the United States, most of which were operated by franchisees; fewer than 100 of the Tim Hortons were company

operated. Systemwide sales for Tim Hortons amounted to $1.46 billion in 2001. Seeking new avenues for growth, Wendy's International in early 2002 acquired a 45 percent stake in Café Express, an "upscale bistro" that was part of the emerging fast-casual segment of the restaurant industry. There were 13 Café Express outlets in Houston, Dallas, and Phoenix at the time of the investment.

Dave Thomas Enters the Restaurant Business: 1956

The Wendy's chain was created by R. David "Dave" Thomas, who credited part of his success to his challenging youth. Thomas was born during the depths of the Great Depression in Atlantic City, New Jersey. His early life was punctuated by tragedy. Abandoned at birth, he was adopted by a Michigan couple, Rex and Auleva Thomas. Auleva died when Dave was five years old, and his father was forced to move from state to state seeking work as a handyman. Rex remarried three times and moved his family ten times over the next eight years.

Dave Thomas entered the world of work at the age of 12, delivering groceries in Knoxville, Tennessee. He lied about his age to circumvent child labor laws, and worked 12-hour shifts to keep his job. Thomas's adulthood began early. When he was 15, his family moved to Fort Wayne, Indiana, and he started work as a busboy at a local restaurant, the Hobby House. When his family announced another move, Thomas elected to set out on his own, taking a room at the local YMCA. As his work began to demand more time than his education, Thomas gave up on the latter, leaving school after the tenth grade and later enlisting in the army. (Decades later, Thomas would return to high school, receiving his GED in 1993.) Trained as a cook in the military, he returned to a job behind the grill of the Hobby House, where he met Lorraine, a waitress—and his future wife.

Thomas entered the restaurant business in earnest in 1956 in partnership with Phil Clauss. Just a few years later, Thomas and Clauss met Colonel Harland Sanders, who offered them Kentucky Fried Chicken (KFC) franchises. Clauss purchased one for Fort Wayne, and the pair broke into the chicken business.

By 1962 Clauss was deep into KFC—he owned four unprofitable franchises in Columbus, Ohio, and needed someone to

Company Perspectives:

Our guiding mission is to deliver superior quality products and services for our customers and communities through leadership, innovation and partnerships.

Our vision is to be the quality leader in everything we do.

Our organization has a strategic vision focused on these core values: Quality: Freshly-made products and superior service are our passion; consistent excellence is our goal. Integrity: We keep our promises. All actions are guided by absolute honesty, fairness and respect for every individual. Leadership: We lead by example and encourage leadership qualities at all levels. Everyone has a role to play. People Focus: We believe our people are key to our success. We value all members of our diverse family for their individual contributions and their team achievements. Customer Satisfaction: Satisfying internal and external customers is the focus of everything we do. Continuous Improvement: Continuous improvement is how we think; innovative change provides competitive opportunities. Community Involvement: Giving back is our heritage. We actively participate and invest in the communities where we do business. Commitment to Stakeholders: We serve all stakeholders and, through balancing our responsibilities to all, we maximize value to each of them.

turn them around. If Thomas could turn the stores' $200,000 deficit into a profit, Clauss promised him a 45 percent share of the Columbus franchises. Against the advice of Colonel Sanders, who had become a mentor, Thomas took the challenge. He cut the menu from 100 items down to just a few—Thomas urged the Colonel to concentrate on chicken alone—improved the chicken "bucket," bartered radio advertising with buckets of chicken, invented KFC's spinning bucket sign, and built four additional locations in less than six years. His earnest, imaginative work paid off; Thomas was promoted to regional operations director of KFC and sold his stake in the Columbus restaurants for $1.5 million in 1968, thereby reaching millionaire status by the age of 35.

Wendy's Born in 1969

Thomas parlayed his windfall into a new venture named after his eight-year-old daughter Melinda Lou, or Wendy, as her brothers and sisters nicknamed her. The first restaurant, which opened on November 15, 1969, was located on Broad Street in downtown Columbus, Ohio. Its menu featured made-to-order hamburgers, "secret recipe" chili, french fries, soft drinks, and the Frosty frozen dessert. Thomas kept the menu simple to save labor costs, remembering his KFC experience. The Wendy's Old Fashioned Hamburgers decor differed from other fast-food joints that abounded with easy-clean vinyl and tiled surfaces. Instead, Thomas put in tiffany-style lamps, bentwood chairs, carpeting, and tabletops embellished with vintage newspaper advertisements. Although his ideas were refreshingly original, some industry experts criticized Thomas's use of expensive fresh beef and noted that the fast-food industry seemed overcrowded. With all the criticism, Thomas hoped only for a local chain that would provide his children with summer jobs.

Against all predictions, the business took off immediately. Thomas opened a second location just one year later and began franchising his idea in 1972. Wendy's soon enlisted franchisees at the rate of ten per month. Thomas added a new wrinkle to the franchising concept, giving geographic licenses, rather than single-store rights. Wendy's also commenced its first advertising campaign that year with locally broadcast "C'mon to Wendy's" spots. The 30-second, animated ads stressed Wendy's superiority through the "Quality Is Our Recipe" slogan and featured a red-haired, pig-tailed "Wendy" with dancing hamburgers.

The 1970s heralded phenomenal, and somewhat reckless, growth at Wendy's. By the end of 1974 the chain's net income topped $1 million, and total sales reached almost $25 million. In mid-1975 the business celebrated the opening of its 100th restaurant, and that fall Wendy's opened its first international restaurant, located in Canada. Wendy's went public in 1976 with an offering of one million common shares valued at $28 per share. By the end of the year, shareholders understood that their money fueled growth; Wendy's opened its 500th shop.

The chain's rapid expansion was supported by Wendy's first national advertising campaign in 1977. The effort earned Wendy's another entry in the history books: it became the first chain with less than 1,000 restaurants to launch network television commercials. The "Hot 'n Juicy" campaign ran for three years and won a Clio Award for creativity, setting the pace for future Wendy's advertising.

Before the decade's end, the restaurant chain set even more records. In 1978, the 1,000th Wendy's opened, in Springfield, Tennessee, not far from the site of Thomas's first job. By the next year the number of shops had increased by half, and the first European Wendy's opened in Munich, West Germany. In November 1979 Wendy's celebrated its tenth birthday with many "firsts" to flaunt. Wendy's was the first in its industry to surpass $1 billion in annual sales within its initial ten years, in addition to reaching the 1,000th restaurant opening faster than any of its competitors. It boasted 1,767 sites in the United States, Canada, Puerto Rico, and Europe, and had opened more than 750 restaurants from February 1978 to November 1979, averaging nearly 1.5 each day.

In the early 1980s, growth slowed slightly from that hectic pace, but Wendy's was distinguished from its competitors through celebrated advertising and winning menu additions. "Wendy's Has the Taste," the first ad of the decade, depicted customers and employees singing a catchy jingle. The ad emphasized Wendy's new chicken sandwich and all-you-can-eat salad bar. The chain had introduced its "Garden Spot" in 1979 over Thomas's protestations, becoming the first national restaurant chain to offer salad bars nationwide.

Founder Dave Thomas made his first appearance as Wendy's spokesperson in 1981 in a controversial ad titled, "Ain't No Reason (to go anyplace else)." Customers' use of the idiomatic double negative "ain't no" in the ads generated national attention for the chain, though not all of it favorable. Thomas left his position as CEO in 1982, taking the title of senior chairman. After working for more than 30 years, Thomas

Key Dates:

1969: Dave Thomas opens the first Wendy's restaurant in downtown Columbus, Ohio.
1972: Wendy's franchising begins.
1975: First international restaurant opens in Canada.
1976: Wendy's International, Inc. goes public.
1977: Company begins national television advertising.
1978: The 1,000th Wendy's opens in Springfield, Tennessee.
1979: Salad bars are added to Wendy's restaurants.
1981: Thomas makes his first appearance as Wendy's advertising spokesperson.
1984: Famous and award-winning "Where's the Beef?" ad campaign is run.
1986: James W. Near becomes president and COO and launches a major reorganization.
1989: Thomas begins another stint as advertising spokesperson; the Super Value Menu debuts.
1995: Wendy's International acquires Tim Hortons, a Canadian coffee and baked goods chain.
1997: The 5,000th Wendy's restaurant opens in Columbus, Ohio.
2002: Dave Thomas dies; Wendy's International acquires a 45 percent stake in Café Express.

felt that he had earned a break, and was confident that he had hired capable managers to carry on his work.

Mixed Results in the 1980s

A recession in the early 1980s, combined with high beef prices and Wendy's explosive—as well as threatening—growth incited the "burger wars." Wendy's moved into the number three spot behind McDonald's and Burger King, fueled by its introduction of a chainwide salad bar, chicken breast sandwiches, and baked potatoes. Burger King and McDonald's responded with moderately successful menu extensions of their own, then moved to a hard-nosed ad campaign. Burger King fired the first shot, but Wendy's responded with a string of hard-hitting, well-known commercials.

In 1983 Wendy's ads depicted "victims" of other hamburger restaurants, humorously bemoaning the long waits endured in indoor and drive-up lines for frozen hamburger patties. In 1984 Wendy's agency, Dancer Fitzgerald Sample, teamed up with celebrated commercial director Joe Sedelmaier on a campaign that registered the highest consumer awareness levels in the advertising industry's history, in addition to captivating judges at the 1984 Clio Awards and winning three of the industry's highest honors. Moreover, the "Where's the Beef?" campaign consisted of four network television spots starring senior citizen Clara Peller. It was voted the most popular commercial in the United States in 1984. One of the ads, "Parts Is Parts," pointed out the difference between the competition's pressed chicken patties and Wendy's chicken breast filet sandwiches.

"Parts" focused on Wendy's true moneymakers at that point; hamburger sales actually accounted for only 40 percent of the chain's revenues. Much of Wendy's sales growth could be credited to such menu extensions as the grilled chicken sandwich, Garden Spot salad bar, and stuffed baked potatoes. These new products and the phenomenal success of the "Where's the Beef?" campaign catapulted Wendy's to a record $76.2 million in earnings in 1985.

As one unnamed Wendy's executive confessed in *Barron's,* management started to believe that everything they touched would "turn to gold." Unfortunately, 1985 marked a summit from which Wendy's quickly plummeted. In 1986 the chain introduced sit-down breakfasts featuring omelettes and French toast. The new breakfasts involved a huge investment of capital and labor, and could not be served quickly enough to fit in with the fast-food format. Eventually, the breakfast menu was scuttled. At the same time, McDonald's, Burger King, and Hardee's assaulted Wendy's on the hamburger front.

A kind of domino effect plunged the company toward a $4.9 million loss in 1986. Some of the chain's original franchisees sold their stores to new owners who flouted Wendy's high standards. Others became absentee managers, leaving the day-to-day supervision to employees. As standards of cleanliness, quality, and service slipped at some Wendy's locations, sales dropped. In response to the falling income, store labor was cut, the morale of those who remained plunged, and turnover rates began to explode. By the end of the year, 20 percent of Wendy's restaurants were nearing failure, and franchisees presented the chain's management a vote of no confidence.

The desperate situation brought Dave Thomas out of semiretirement and challenged one of Wendy's most successful franchisees to revive the failing business. James W. Near had been one of Dave Thomas's competitors in the late 1960s when they both operated restaurants in Columbus. Practically raised in his father's White Castle hamburger chain, Near built a 50-unit Burger Boy Food-A-Rama chain of his own by the end of the decade. Near had become a Wendy's franchisee in 1974, opening 39 successful restaurants in West Virginia and Florida within four years. In 1978 he sold the restaurants back to Wendy's and established Sisters Chicken & Biscuits as an expansion vehicle for the hamburger chain. Sisters became a subsidiary of Wendy's in 1981 and was sold to its largest franchise owner in 1987.

New Leadership Rejuvenates Wendy's in the Late 1980s

Near agreed to take the position of president and chief operating officer on the condition that Thomas would sustain an active role in the company as a spokesperson and traveling mentor. Thomas agreed. His new business card read "Founder and Jim's Right Hand Man." Near's turnaround strategy started with an internal reorganization. Weak stores were eliminated and a new building design lowered the initial franchise investment. Near fired four top managers, cut 700 administrative positions, and revamped field operations. New programs gave the remaining employees a vested interest in the chain's success: base pay, benefits, and bonuses were raised; an employee stock option called "We Share" made workers shareholders; and standardized training gave all employees a new perspective on their jobs. When Near took over, Wendy's was replacing employees at a rate of 55 percent a year; six years later, turnover stood at 20 percent.

With renewed chainwide standards for cleanliness and customer service, Near turned his attention to the menu. Changes were based on several industry trends, including discount pricing, consumer health concerns, and premium menu items. Spurred by the recession of the late 1980s and early 1990s, many fast-food chains established discount pricing to appeal to more frugal customers. Wendy's introduced its Super Value Menu in 1989. The daily feature included seven 99-cent items, allowing it to appeal to thrifty consumers without issuing profit-eating coupons. An expanded salad bar and skinless chicken breast sandwich catered to more health-conscious consumers, while the Big Classic, Dave's Deluxe, and Chicken Cordon Bleu specialty sandwiches appealed to Wendy's traditional hearty eaters.

As Near worked to cover all of the menu bases, Thomas returned to the television studio for the promotional push. In 1989 Thomas reappeared in commercials offering customers a special money-back guarantee if they did not concur that Wendy's had the best-tasting hamburgers in the industry. The ad was supported by one of the largest testimonial advertising campaigns in television history. Local residents in about 100 U.S. markets pronounced Wendy's burgers best.

"Old Fashioned Guy," the next series of TV spots, featured Thomas declaring, "Our hamburgers are the best in the business, or I wouldn't have named the place after my daughter." The hamburgers might have been the best, but Thomas's performances in these spots earned some poor ratings from some critics at *Advertising Age,* one of whom commented that he looked like "a steer in a half-sleeved shirt." Thomas himself admitted that he was not an ideal subject—he joked that it took two hours to get the expression "muchas gracias" right for one commercial. Unlike the critics, however, consumers gave Thomas an enthusiastic reception—his promotions earned Wendy's highest advertising awareness figures since the "Where's the Beef?" campaign and were credited with boosting the chain's turnaround. In fact, such campaigns even helped earn Thomas the designation, "the Colonel Sanders of Wendy's," in reference to the promotional efforts of Thomas's early mentor.

The success of Wendy's revitalization showed in sales, rejuvenated expansion, and widespread recognition of the accomplishment. Despite a lingering recession, in 1991 and 1992 Wendy's had outperformed the industry with 24 consecutive months of same-store sales gains. Earnings increased steadily in the early 1990s to $78 million in 1993, the fourth consecutive year of 20 percent earnings growth. Wendy's five-year average earnings-per-share growth hit 58 percent, more than four times that of McDonald's for the same period. Representing an irrefutable confirmation of Wendy's successful turnaround, 1995 earnings rose above the company's 1985 high of $.82 a share to reach $.94 per share.

Expanding Again in the Early 1990s

In the early 1990s expansion picked up once again. The company opened its 4,000th restaurant in 1992, and projected another 1,000 openings by mid-decade. Within the United States, the company planned to be opening approximately 400

stores a year by 1996. Wendy's plans, however, also targeted international growth, where opportunities for expansion were infinitely better than those in the saturated American market.

Near and Thomas accumulated numerous awards in recognition of the dramatic turnaround at Wendy's. In 1989 Near was given the title of CEO and was named chairman two years later. Moreover, he was honored by his colleagues in the restaurant industry when he was named Operator of the Year by *Nation's Restaurant News* and Executive of the Year by *Restaurants and Institutions. Restaurant Business* acknowledged both men's entrepreneurial efforts with its annual Leadership Awards. Thomas also received the Horatio Alger Award, named for the author who popularized the concept of the "self-made man."

As Wendy's "ambassador," Thomas began spending most of his time traveling to and from book promotions, public appearances, and franchise openings. His promotional work complemented Near's continuing efforts to "grow the company." A new corporate theme, "Do It Right! Performance Pays!," related customer-responsiveness to sales and profits for worker-shareholders.

Wendy's recovery seemed well-established in the mid-1990s, judged not just by the numbers but by public opinion as well. Consumer polls in 1994 judged Wendy's to have the best food in the fast-food burger business, the best menu variety, and the most pleasant atmosphere. *Restaurants and Institutions* gave Wendy's its overall top rating from 1988 to 1994, putting it ahead of eight other burger chains. Montgomery Securities analyst Michael Mueller told *Financial World* in 1995, "They're doing everything one should in the fast-food industry."

Having brought Wendy's to this high point, Near decided to step down from the CEO position in late 1994 (while remaining chairman). He was replaced by Gordon Teter, who had served Wendy's as senior vice-president for three years and chief operating officer for four. Before joining Wendy's, Teter had accumulated 25 years of experience at the restaurant chains Arthur Treacher's, Casa Lupita, and Red Robin. His strengths were regarded by many as exactly what Wendy's needed to go the next step, that of stealing market share from the big guys. A firm believer in sticking to the basics, Teter was expected to apply his talents for cost control and well-regulated operations. "Once you have success, as we have been having here, people can get distracted," Teter explained to *Financial World* in 1995. "The biggest thing we have to do is maintain a sense of discipline," he noted.

Teter had a tough act to follow. Wendy's phenomenal growth slowed somewhat in the mid-1990s. In 1994 same-store sales dropped to 2.7 percent in the first nine months of that year, compared to the quarter-to-quarter rate of 5 percent for the previous few years. Because fast-food profits were much higher overseas, Wendy's saw foreign expansion as a way to keep growth and profitability up.

In 1995, Wendy's aggressive foreign expansion plan called for the company to open at least 150 new restaurants a year around the world. Most store openings, however, were planned for Latin America, the Far East, and Canada. Wendy's previous attempt to expand overseas, in the early to mid-1980s, was a flop. Wendy's changed its decor and food to suit local tastes, but in less than a decade many of its foreign sites were floundering. Teter told *Financial World* in 1995 that after making every mistake you can make, Wendy's would stick to basics: "We just can't get diverted to things that sound sexy and look attractive."

Late 1990s and into the New Millennium: Growing Beyond the Wendy's Chain

As part of its expansion plan, Wendy's acquired the privately owned Canadian restaurant chain Tim Hortons. Canada's largest coffee and baked goods chain exchanged all outstanding shares of its stock for 16.2 million shares of Wendy's stock and the assumption of its $125 million in debt. The acquisition strengthened Wendy's presence in Canada, bringing the total number of its restaurants in that country to 1,186. Wendy's had been experimenting with sites that combined Wendy's and Tim Hortons restaurants since 1992. The logic behind such "combo" sites was that they enabled Wendy's outlets to add a breakfast menu, and indeed Tim Hortons units in Canada typically tallied 60 to 65 percent of their sales before 10 a.m. The success of the combo units led Wendy's to plan on opening 30 more such sites a year after the merger. In addition, in 1996, Wendy's bought out Hardee's restaurants in the northern tier of states, strengthening the company's position there as well.

Wendy's also continued to invest in its successful, homespun ads featuring Dave Thomas. The "Letters to Dave" campaign, focusing on the restaurant's Super Value Menu and featuring customers' letters to the restaurateur, paired Thomas with soap opera star Susan Lucci. In another series, Dave joined Olympic gold medalist Kristi Yamaguchi to participate in such winter sports as pairs figure skating and ski jumping. Although long-known for its popular ad campaigns, Wendy's spent only $80 million on advertising in 1994, one-fifth what McDonald's spent. Still, Wendy's brand recognition trailed that of McDonald's by only a few points.

As Wendy's moved into the late 1990s, management focused on maintaining the momentum the company had generated in the early 1990s, with an emphasis on street-level operations, marketing, and efficient administration. Continued expansion remained a priority as well. The 5,000th Wendy's restaurant opened in Columbus, Ohio, in March 1997. By the end of that year, there were more than 5,200 Wendy's units, up from 4,400 in 1994. Following Near's death in July 1997, president and CEO Teter became chairman of Wendy's International as well. Also in 1997 Wendy's introduced a line of pita sandwiches.

After net income fell in 1997, in part because of the effects of the Asian economic crisis and in part because of disappointing results at Tim Hortons outlets in the United States, Teter responded by closing more than 60 underperforming restaurants in 1998 and by slowing down the pace of expansion. The total number of units—including both Wendy's and Tim Hortons—increased by only 215 in 1998, reaching the 7,000 mark, while the unit gain in 1999 was 344. The Wendy's chain also continued to build on its reputation as having a more healthful and diverse menu than its rivals, and it concentrated on such improvements as cutting the time that a customer spent in the drive-through line by 25 percent. Another key initiative in the late 1990s was the extension of the hours of operation at Wendy's outlets to include late-night dining. First introduced in 1996, the late-night service helped the chain gain market share at the expense of its two main rivals. Backed by heavy advertis-

ing, after-10 p.m. sales grew to 10 percent of overall sales by 1999, and that year sales during that part of the day increased 30 percent. Overall, profits began increasing again in 1999, reaching $167 million on Wendy's International revenues of $2.07 billion. Systemwide sales for the Wendy's chain that year were just under $6 billion, while Tim Hortons saw its systemwide sales exceed $1 billion for the first time.

Overseas, the Wendy's chain continued to have difficulty getting established—it simply could not compete with the deeper-pocketed McDonald's and Burger King chains. Thus, Wendy's pulled out of South Korea in 1998, closed most of its outlets in the United Kingdom in 1999, and then exited from both Argentina and Hong Kong in 2000. With the closures of company-operated outlets in Argentina, Wendy's had eliminated nearly all of its international company-operated restaurants, with the exception of those in Canada. The focus overseas would now be almost exclusively on franchise possibilities. The announcement in 2000 of plans to open 100 (franchised) restaurants in Mexico over a ten-year period showed that the company had not completely given up on international growth—and highlighted the concentration on the Latin American market. (The 6,000th Wendy's restaurant, in fact, opened in Tijuana, Mexico, in October 2001.)

In December 1999 Teter died suddenly at age 56. John T. "Jack" Schuessler was named president and CEO of Wendy's International in early 2000. Schuessler had a long association with the company. He became a manager trainee for a Wendy's franchisee in Atlanta in 1974. He joined Wendy's International when the company bought the franchised outlet he worked at in 1976. He then worked his way up the ladder through regional and national posts, eventually becoming president and COO of the U.S. operations of the Wendy's chain in 1997. After Schuessler's appointment as president and CEO, Wendy's International operated for a time without a chairman, but Schuessler was named chairman as well in May 2001.

With its financial results improving again, Schuessler quickened the pace of expansion, and 535 new restaurants were opened systemwide in 2001. That year the company formed a joint venture with IAWS Group/Cuisine de France, an Irish baking conglomerate, to build a baking facility in Canada to supply the Tim Hortons chain with baguettes and breads. Always seeking to enhance the menu, the Wendy's chain tested a new Garden Sensations salad line, which featured a variety of prepackaged salads that customers could customize by selecting among various toppings and dressings. Following positive test results, the new line was rolled out nationally in early 2002 backed by the biggest ad campaign in company history.

Schuessler was also looking for new avenues for company growth as concerns increased about the limited growth prospects for the Wendy's chain in the core U.S. market. In addition to a new effort to expand the Tim Hortons chain in the United States, Schuessler announced in February 2001 that Wendy's International was looking to further diversify its restaurant lineup and had as much as $500 million at its disposal to pursue acquisitions, mergers, and joint ventures. The first such move came in February 2002, when the company announced that it had spent $10 million for a 45 percent stake in Café Express, a pioneer in the burgeoning fast-casual sector. Fast-casual restaurants combined the casual dining of a Chili's or Ruby Tuesday with the self-service, walk-up service of a typical fast-food outlet. Founded in Houston in 1984, Café Express was an "upscale bistro" featuring pastas, salads, sandwiches, roasted chicken, soups, side dishes, and an "Oasis Bar" where customers could customize their food with a variety of condiments. By early 2002 Café Express was a 13-unit chain operating in Houston, Dallas, and Phoenix. With the infusion of capital from Wendy's International, the chain hoped to expand to 50 units by 2005.

Early 2002 also brought an end to an era at Wendy's International with the death of Dave Thomas on January 8 as a result of complications from liver cancer. Thomas had become an American icon, having starred in more than 800 commercials from 1989 to 2002 in what had been the longest-running advertising campaign in history featuring a company founder. Would Wendy's continue to thrive without its famous pitchman? Company managers believed that the Wendy's brand had become established enough to overcome Thomas's absence, and in fact plans had already been made for a smooth advertising transition in the event of his death. It seemed certain, however, that the next Wendy's advertising campaign was going to be a particularly important one.

Principal Subsidiaries

Wendy's Old Fashioned Hamburgers of New York, Inc.; Wendy's Capital Corporation; Wendy Restaurant, Inc.; Wendy's of Denver, Inc.; The New Bakery Co. of Ohio, Inc.; Delavest, Inc.; Wentexas, Inc.; Restaurant Finance Corporation; Wendy's of N.E. Florida, Inc.; Wendcreek Venture; WendServe, Inc.; Wenark, Inc.; Delcan, Inc.; Alberta (Delaware) Inc.; Tim Donut U.S. Limited, Inc.; T.H.D. Donut (Delaware), Inc.; Markdel, Inc.; Findel Corp.; Domark Investments, Inc.; Wendy's Financing I; THD Nevada, Inc.; The THD Group; BDJ 71112, LLC; Scioto Insurance Co.; Oldemark LLC; Nattlan I (Argentina); Nautilus Land S.A. (Argentina); Wendy's Old Fashioned Hamburger Restaurants Pty. Ltd. (Australia); Ranew Development Ltd. (Bahamas); Barhav Developments Limited (Canada); Delcan Finance No. 1, Inc. (Canada); Delcan Finance No. 2, Inc. (Canada); Delcan Finance No. 3, Inc. (Canada); Delcan Finance No. 4, Inc. (Canada); The TDL Group Ltd. (Canada); The TDL Group (Canada); The TDL Group No. 2 (Canada); The TDL Group Co. (Canada); THD RE No. 1 Co. (Canada); TH N.S. Finance No. 1 Co. (Canada); TH N.S. Finance No. 2 Co. (Canada); TIMWEN Partnership (Canada); Wendy's Restaurants of Canada Inc.; WENTIM, LTD. (Canada); Wendy's Old Fashioned Hamburgers of Guam, L.L.C.; Wendy's Restaurants (Ireland) Limited; Wendy's Restaurants (NZ) Limited (New Zealand); Timeweald Limited (U.K.).

Principal Competitors

McDonald's Corporation; Burger King Corporation; CKE Restaurants, Inc.; Jack in the Box Inc.; Sonic Corp.; Checkers Drive-In Restaurants, Inc.; White Castle System, Inc.; Whataburger, Inc.; TRICON Global Restaurants, Inc.; Doctor's Associates Inc. (Subway).

Further Reading

Basralian, Joseph, "Ground Game," *Financial World,* January 17, 1995, pp. 40–42.

Blyskal, Jeff, "Hot Stuff," *Forbes,* June 4, 1984, pp. 169–71.
Breckenridge, Tom, and Sandy Theis, "Wendy's Founder Dave Thomas Dies," *Cleveland Plain Dealer,* January 9, 2002, p. A1.
Byrne, Harlan S., "Wendy's International: It Is Finally Learning How to Handle Success," *Barron's,* January 7, 1991, pp. 43–44.
Campanella, Frank W., "Beefed-Up Menu: At Wendy's International, It's More Now Than Just Meat and Potatoes," *Barron's,* November 16, 1981, pp. 41+.
Chaudhry, Rajan, "James Near Cleans Up Wendy's," *Restaurants and Institutions,* July 22, 1992, pp. 72–82.
"Dave's World," *Forbes,* January 3, 1994, p. 149.
Elliott, Stuart, "After Founder Dies, Wendy's Ponders New Ways to Pitch," *New York Times,* January 9, 2002, p. C1.
"From Peril to Profit: The Man Who Saved Wendy's," *Success,* February 1992, p. 10.
Galuszka, Peter, "Can Wendy's Sizzle Again?," *Business Week,* November 1, 1999, p. 100.
Gebolys, Debbie, "A Great, Big, Lovable Man," *Columbus (Ohio) Dispatch,* January 9, 2002, p. 1A.
Hamstra, Mark, "Wendy's Begins Rolling Tim Hortons into New Markets," *Nation's Restaurant News,* July 13, 1998, pp. 3, 105.
——, "Wendy's Restructuring Addresses Margins, Growth," *Nation's Restaurant News,* February 16, 1998, pp. 3, 73.
History of Wendy's Advertising, 1969–1993, Dublin, Ohio: Wendy's International, Inc., 1993.
Hume, Scott, "Thomas Shines As Wendy's Col. Sanders," *Advertising Age,* August 6, 1990, p. 3.
——, "Why Wendy's Is Losing Its Sizzle," *Advertising Age,* March 2, 1987, pp. 3+.
Killian, Linda, "Hamburger Helper," *Forbes,* August 5, 1991, pp. 106–07.
King, Michael L., "Its Vigor Lost, Wendy's Seeks a New Niche," *Wall Street Journal,* July 8, 1980.
——, "Wendy's New Management Cooks Up Plans for Growth and Diversification," *Wall Street Journal,* March 27, 1981.
Kramer, Louise, "Wendy's Importing Tim Hortons to U.S.," *Advertising Age,* November 29, 1997, p. 17.
Leung, Shirley, "Wendy's Sees Future Growth in Acquisitions and Ventures: Hamburger Chain Is Looking at Purchases of Other Food Concepts," *Wall Street Journal,* February 11, 2002, p. B4.
Near, James W., "Wendy's Successful 'Mop Bucket Attitude'," *Wall Street Journal,* April 27, 1992.
"A New Chef Lights a Flame Under Wendy's," *Business Week,* May 8, 1989, p. 70.
Papiernik, Richard L., "Wendy's Taps M&A Chief, Gears Up for Acquisitions," *Nation's Restaurant News,* September 17, 2001, pp. 1+.
Perlik, Allison, "Ever Forward," *Restaurants and Institutions,* October 15, 2001, pp. 59–60+.
Roth, Daniel, "Where's the Beef?," *Forbes,* August 11, 1997, p. 134.
Ruggless, Ron, "Café Express, Wendy's Take Fast-Casual Approach," *Nation's Restaurant News,* February 25, 2002, pp. 1+.
Sachdev, Ameet, "Wendy's Emerges As Rising Star Among Fast Food Companies," *Chicago Tribune,* March 9, 2002.
Scarpa, James, "RB Leadership Award: R. David Thomas, James W. Near," *Restaurant Business,* May 1, 1992.
Tatge, Mark, "Burgertory," *Forbes,* June 11, 2001, p. 76.
Thomas, R. David, *Dave's Way: A New Approach to Old-Fashioned Success,* New York: Putnam Publishing, 1991, 256 p.
Wolf, Barnet D., "Maintaining a Legacy," *Columbus (Ohio) Dispatch,* February 24, 2002, p. 1F.
Zuber, Amy, "Industry Mourns Wendy's Founder Thomas," *Nation's Restaurant News,* January 21, 2002, pp. 1, 41.
——, "Wendy's Reveals Acquisition War Chest," *Nation's Restaurant News,* February 26, 2001, pp. 1+.

—April S. Dougal
—updates: Susan Windisch Brown, David E. Salamie

Williams & Connolly LLP

> **725 Twelfth Street, N.W.**
> **Washington, D.C. 20005-5901**
> **U.S.A.**
> **Telephone: (202) 434-5000**
> **Fax: (202) 434-5029**
>
> *Partnership*
> *Founded:* 1951 as the Law Office of Edward Bennett
>   Williams
> *Employees:* 200
> *Gross Billings:* $126 million (2000 est.)
> *NAIC:* 541110 Offices of Lawyers

Williams & Connolly LLP is one of the United States' largest law firms. Although it describes itself in the *Martindale-Hubbell Law Directory* as having a "Practice in Federal Courts and before Federal Departments and Agencies," it does other work in a variety of legal specialties. The firm is well known for criminal defense, the expertise of firm founder Edward Bennett Williams. It is particularly famous for its long record of representing prominent individuals in politics, sports, business, and entertainment, but it also serves corporations, nonprofit organizations, and other law firms.

The Founder and His Early Law Practice

Born in Hartford, Connecticut, in 1920, Edward Bennett Williams graduated from Holy Cross College in 1941. After graduating from Georgetown Law School in 1944, Williams worked in the Washington, D.C. law firm of Hogan & Hartson. In 1949 he left Hogan & Hartson to become the junior name partner of Chase & Williams. After two years, Williams started his own law firm in the nation's capital.

In the 1950s Williams represented several individuals involved in the post-World War II Red Scare. His success as a young lawyer serving entertainment figures such as Martin Berkeley and Sidney Buchman helped build his reputation as an outstanding defense lawyer. His most famous client during this anticommunist hysteria was U.S. Senator Joseph McCarthy, the Republican from Wisconsin elected in 1950.

Williams in 1956 began representing four leaders of the Teamsters Union in Minneapolis who were later found guilty of violating the Taft-Hartley Labor Act. Later Williams defended Teamsters President Dave Beck at hearings of the Senate Rackets Committee. Beck later was convicted of embezzlement and tax evasion.

In 1957 Williams defended Jimmy Hoffa, who also was investigated by the Rackets Committee. Senator John F. Kennedy was a member of the committee and his brother Robert F. Kennedy was its chief counsel. Then Williams defended Hoffa against bribery charges in a trial. Hoffa was acquitted in July 1957 and soon became head of the Teamsters Union. Williams's biographer Robert Pack concluded, "Edward Bennett Williams won the battle on behalf of Jimmy Hoffa, but in the process the country lost the war. Thanks to the triumph of injustice, Hoffa graduated from being a totally corrupt individual on a relatively minor scale, becoming one of the country's most powerful figures and a blight on the national landscape."

By November 1957 Williams had become general counsel for the Teamsters Union, which paid him a $50,000 annual retainer. From that point on, his support for Hoffa declined, partially out of conflict of interest from representing both the union and its leader. In 1967 Hoffa was sent to prison for misusing Teamsters money and jury-tampering. Williams, who refused to help Hoffa in that case, said the Teamsters leader probably was murdered later by Teamsters with mob connections.

The Growing Williams Law Firm (1960–88)

In 1960 the Williams firm was still relatively small, with only about 12 lawyers, but its reputation was growing. Ed Williams was well known for his criminal defense work and also played a major role in racially integrating the legal profession in Washington, D.C. In the late 1950s he had become a board member of the American Civil Liberties Union (ACLU) and chairman of the District of Columbia Bar Association Committee on Civil Rights.

Beginning in 1956, Ed Williams represented Frank Costello, the alleged role model for the main character in *The Godfather* book and movie. Costello's problems over tax evasion and

---

Key Dates:

1949: Williams leaves Hogan & Hartson to form a practice with Nicholas Chase.

1951: The practice becomes known as the law offices of Edward Bennett Williams after a split with Nicholas Chase.

1954: Williams serves Senator Joseph McCarthy, one of many clients involved in the Red Scare.

1957: Williams represents Jimmy Hoffa and later becomes the Teamsters Union's general counsel (a position he held until 1973).

1962: The firm is renamed Williams & Stein.

1967: Williams suffers a major defeat as a criminal defense lawyer: client Bobby Baker is convicted.

1968: The firm's new name is Williams & Connolly.

1971: Joseph Califano joins the firm, which leads to its Watergate involvement.

1975: Williams defends John Connolly in a federal trial.

1987: The firm represents Oliver North in the Iran-Contra scandal.

1988: Ed Williams's death results in new firm leadership.

Late 1990s: The firm represents President Clinton.

---

denaturalization cases ended in 1964 when the U.S. Supreme Court ruled that the government could not deport him back to Italy.

Several years later attorney Sol M. Linowitz commented, "Good lawyers don't have to take bad clients. Edward Bennett Williams, the brilliant trial lawyer, once sought to explain his representation of people like Frank Costello by saying, 'Everyone is entitled to a lawyer.' 'Yes,' was the response, 'but they are not entitled to *you*.' "

In late 1963 Robert G. ("Bobby") Baker chose Ed Williams to defend him against several charges of political corruption. Baker resigned as secretary of the Senate Democrats in October 1963 over the corruption charges that implicated Lyndon Johnson, the Democratic Senate leader who became president in November 1963 following the assassination of President Kennedy. A grand jury in 1966 indicted Bobby Baker for tax evasion, fraud, and related charges. In January 1967 a jury convicted Baker of seven of nine charges, for which he eventually served 16 months in prison, while President Johnson avoided any legal charges. Baker was "Williams's only client in a major trial to serve time in prison," wrote Robert Pack in his biography of Williams.

The firm changed its name a few times in the 1960s. It became known in 1962 as Williams & Stein with name partner Colman Stein, then in 1963 changed to Williams, Wadden & Stein after the addition of Tom Wadden as a name partner. After Stein resigned in 1966, it was Williams & Wadden.

In 1968 the partnership changed to Williams & Connolly with the departure of Wadden and the addition of Paul Connolly, one of Williams's former students at the Georgetown Law School who worked at Hogan & Hartson 20 years before joining his former professor. Connolly helped the firm for the

first time make both criminal and civil law practice of equal importance.

In 1971 Joseph Califano, attorney for the Democratic National Committee (DNC), joined the Williams law firm, which gained the DNC as a new client. The law firm with the new name of Williams, Connolly & Califano had about 24 lawyers in 1971.

The following year the firm filed a civil lawsuit against the Republicans who had broken into the DNC headquarters at the Watergate Hotel. Both Ed Williams and Joseph Califano admitted years later that the lawsuit had been filed in part to hurt President Nixon's bid for reelection. Williams interviewed several Watergate players, including G. Gordon Liddy and John Mitchell, but the trial was postponed until after the November 1972 election.

President Nixon considered Ed Williams and the *Washington Post,* a client of the Williams firm since the early 1970s, his main enemies in the Watergate scandal, which lasted until 1974 when Nixon finally resigned before being impeached. Some speculated that Williams was Deep Throat, the informant who aided the *Post* in its investigation, but Williams's biographer Robert Pack discounted that possibility. A Nixon supporter actually asked Williams to defend the President, but Williams turned down the offer because of conflict of interest. Williams also stated publicly that Nixon should have destroyed the White House tape recordings before they were ordered as evidence in the case. That advice was criticized by several people, including Ralph Nader, who thought Williams would have advised what amounted to a major cover-up.

In 1974 John Connolly, former Texas governor and President Nixon's secretary of the Treasury Department, hired Ed Williams to defend him against corruption charges. Connally was accused of receiving illegal money from the dairy industry in return for influencing the Nixon Administration to raise milk price supports in 1971. A jury in 1975 acquitted Connally in the only courtroom loss of the Watergate Special Prosecutor's Office.

Williams, Connolly & Califano appeared quite prosperous in the 1970s. For example, Joseph Califano stated publicly that his 1976 income at the law firm was $505,490, a very high income for that time. All new cabinet members, including Califano as secretary of the Department of Health, Education, and Welfare, had been directed by newly elected President Jimmy Carter to reveal their income.

From 1977 to 1987 tax lawyer Robert Arnold Schulman was one of the prominent partners at Williams & Connolly. He represented many professional sports teams and their leaders, including the Washington Redskins, former Redskins President Edward Bennett Williams, and the owners of the Redskins, the New York Giants, the St. Louis Cardinals, the New England Patriots, the Oakland Raiders, and the San Diego Chargers. Schulman's clients also included the major television networks and several well-known individuals, including Merv Griffin, Howard Cosell, Frank Sinatra, Jackie Gleason, and Leslie Stahl.

A sensational case for Williams & Connolly came in 1981 when it successfully defended John W. Hinckley, Jr., after he tried to kill President Ronald Reagan. Partner Vincent J. Fuller persuaded the jury that Hinckley was insane. By the early 1980s the firm's growing list of business clients included Boeing Aircraft, the Motion Picture Association of America, and International Harvester.

In 1983 Robert Pack in his biography of Ed Williams made a good point "that someone who knew little or nothing about what had happened in America during the last thirty years could learn about the major developments of this era simply by studying the cases and causes that Williams has been associated with." In addition to the clients already mentioned, he or other members of his law firm represented leaders of the United Mine Workers; Frank Sinatra; Angie Dickinson; Joe DiMaggio; Hugh Hefner; Gerald Ford; Peter Yarrow of Peter, Paul, and Mary; cartoonist Al Capp; George Steinbrenner, owner of the New York Yankees; mobsters Vito Genovese and Sam Giancana; Occidental Petroleum owner Dr. Armand Hammer; Burt Lancaster; former U.S. Senator Thomas Dodd; William F. Buckley, Jr.; the *National Enquirer*; and former CIA director Richard Helms. No wonder Andy Rooney of "60 Minutes" called Ed Williams one of the ten most interesting Americans. Pack interviewed Williams and more than 100 others in his well-documented study of a man who was important in law, sports, politics, and journalism. The author reported that the law firm had about 80 lawyers when the book was published.

Attorneys from the Williams law firm in 1987 represented Oliver North in his much publicized testimony before the congressional committee examining the Iran-Contra scandal and again later served North when he was tried by independent counsel Lawrence E. Walsh. North was so pleased that he still used Williams & Connolly in the late 1990s.

The Partnership After Williams's Death in 1988

In August 1988 Ed Williams died after an 11-year fight against cancer. Marc Fisher in the *Los Angeles Times* described Williams as "the locomotive of the law who charmed thousands of jurors, set the pace for a generation of trial lawyers and, from a private position, became a powerhouse in the public arenas of politics and sports." Former partner Joseph Califano added that Williams "had absolute influence touching all facets of Washington without holding any position."

Williams's law firm continued under a five-man committee of partners groomed by Williams. They all emphasized the smooth transition planned by Williams. Part of that involved keeping long-term clients with the firm. For example, oilman Marvin Davis said he would continue to use Williams & Connolly, since he was pleased with its help when he sold the Twentieth Century-Fox Film Company in the early 1980s to Rupert Murdoch. The *Washington Post*'s publisher Donald Graham also remained committed to the law firm. Ed Williams had represented the newspaper since 1971. Other corporate or institutional clients at the time of Williams's death included the *National Enquirer,* Georgetown University, and Anheuser-Busch Companies.

Such clients were important, but at the time of Williams's death the firm's litigation practice still accounted for about 70 percent of its revenue. Some of the firm's leaders wanted to continue emphasizing litigation, but others thought more corporate work such as mergers and acquisitions was a better option.

Big law firms that focused on corporate clients rapidly increased in size and revenues during the 1980s when corporate mergers and acquisitions abounded. Several such firms declined, however, when the economy finally slowed. The *National Law Journal* reported that 44 percent of the United States' largest law firms in 1990 reported having fewer lawyers, an unprecedented decline during the publication's 14-year history.

On the other hand, Washington, D.C. firms like Williams & Connolly generally avoided the decline. "If you look at Washington firms, they had very consistent measured growth over the '80s . . . Now we're not experiencing the downturn," said Paul Wolff of Williams & Connolly in the *Washington Post* on September 24, 1991. The firm in 1990 expanded to have 129 lawyers, which for the first time earned it a ranking as number 250 on the *National Law Journal*'s annual survey.

In 1992 Williams & Connolly defended boxer Mike Tyson, but an Indiana judge rejected defense pleas for understanding and leniency. Tyson was sentenced to six years in prison for raping an 18-year-old woman.

In 1995 a judge in the U.S. Court of Appeals for the District of Columbia Circuit overturned a lower court ruling in *Shepherd v. ABC*. The broadcasting company, assisted by Williams & Connolly and other law firms, finally got what it wanted after ten years in this racial discrimination case. In a chapter called "The Obstructionists" in his book *No Contest,* Ralph Nader cited this case as an example of large corporations that use big law firms to wear down their accusers, who simply lacked comparable legal firepower.

In the late 1990s President Clinton used lawyers from many firms, including Williams & Connolly, in his numerous legal challenges. When he had to face questions about Monica Lewinsky from independent counsel Kenneth Starr, the president received advice from Williams & Connolly partner David E. Kendall and associate Nicole K. Seligman.

The *National Law Journal* on November 16, 1998, ranked Williams & Connolly as number 207 in its annual list of the nation's largest law firms. That was based on the firm's 172 lawyers. The firm in 1997 ranked as number 198 with 166 lawyers.

Williams & Connolly in the 1990s advised Juan Miguel Gonzalez, the father of Elian Gonzalez, the Cuban boy who eventually was forced by U.S. courts to return from Florida to Cuba to be with his father. Other clients in the late 1990s or the new millennium included Archer Daniels Midland, Lockheed Martin, Chairman Haley Barbour of the Republican National Committee, and MicroStrategy Inc. in a legal battle with its shareholders. George W. Bush used Williams & Connolly and several other law firms in the contested 2000 election in Florida. The Houston law firm of Vinson & Elkins selected Williams & Connolly to help it deal with the controversy over its representation of collapsed Houston oil company Enron Corporation.

In January 2001 Calvin Klein agreed to a settlement with Warnaco Group, the designer jeans manufacturer, that ended litigation filed by both parties. Warnaco was represented by Williams & Connolly. Also in 2001, Pacifica radio hired Williams & Connolly to defend itself against three lawsuits filed by former employees and listeners. Pacifica owned Washington, D.C.'s WPFW and four other stations in New York, Los Angeles, Houston, and Berkeley, California. A few months later state governments hired Williams & Connolly to help them in their antitrust lawsuits against Microsoft Corporation.

The *American Lawyer* ranked Williams & Connolly, with $126.0 million in gross revenue, as the nation's 117th largest law firm in 2000. Its revenue increased 7.2 percent from 1999. The firm reported no information on its pro bono activities. According to the *American Lawyer,* Williams & Connolly ranked number 70 based on its profits per partner of $645,000 in 2000. The *National Law Journal* ranked the firm as number 195 in 2001 based on its 199 lawyers, which was up from 187 lawyers the previous year.

In 2002 the law firm did not have any branch offices or a web site, both common practices at most of the nation's largest law firms. In any case, Williams & Connolly looked forward to continuing as one of the nation's top law firms.

Principal Competitors

Arnold & Porter; Hogan & Hartson; Akin, Gump, Strauss, Hauer & Feld.

Further Reading

Abramson, Jill, "Williams Took Steps to Ensure Law Firm He Set Up Would Thrive After His Death," *Wall Street Journal,* August 17, 1988, p. 1.

Ahrens, Frank, "In Image Battle, Pacifica Takes Aggressive Action," *Washington Post,* August 21, 2001, p. C1.

Broder, John M., "For Elian's Father, A Lawyer with Ties to Clinton," *New York Times,* April 4, 2000, p. A16.

Cummings, Jeanne, et al., "Law Firm Reassured Enron on Accounting—Vinson & Elkins Discounted Warnings by Employee About Dubious Dealings," *Wall Street Journal,* January 16, 2002, p. A18.

Fisher, Marc, "Obituaries Edward B. Williams: Famous and Powerful Lawyer, Sports Figure," *Los Angeles Times,* August 14, 1988, p. 39.

Goulden, Joseph C., *The Million Dollar Lawyers,* New York: G.P. Putnam's Sons, 1977, p. 323.

Hilzenrath, David S., and Cynthia L. Webb, "Settlement Cleared in Investor Lawsuit; MicroStrategy Deal May Affect Stock," *Washington Post,* April 3, 2001, p. E1.

Jackson, Robert L., "The Iran-Contra Hearings Sullivan Known As 'Pure Attorney' Lawyer's Feisty Style Gets Leeway for Client," *Los Angeles Times,* July 9, 1987, p. 22.

Kaufman, Leslie, "Calvin Klein Suit Against Warnaco Is Settled," *New York Times,* January 23, 2001, p. C1.

Lawrence, B.H., "The Passing of Power at Williams & Connolly," *Washington Post,* September 19, 1988, p. f01.

Lewis, Nancy, "Tax Lawyer Robert A. Schulman, 71, Dies," *Washington Post,* March 4, 1987, p. C05.

Linowitz, Sol M., with Martin Mayer, *The Betrayed Profession: Lawyering at the End of the Twentieth Century,* New York: Charles Scribner's Sons, 1994, p. 31.

Marcus, Ruth, "The Lawyer's Lawyer; Counsel Nicole Seligman, Williams & Connolly's Early Riser," *Washington Post,* August 17, 1998, p. B1.

——, "Price of Political Life Is Increasingly Tallied in Lawyers' Fees," *Washington Post,* August 11, 1997, p. A6.

Muscatine, Alison, "Tyson Gets 6 Years in Prison for Rape; Boxer Immediately Taken into Custody As Appeal Is Readied," *Washington Post,* March 27, 1992, p. A01.

Nader, Ralph, and Wesley J. Smith, *Corporate Lawyers and the Perversion of Justice in America,* New York: Random House, 1996, pp. 110–14, 134–36.

Pack, Robert, *Edward Bennett Williams for the Defense,* New York: Harper & Row, Publishers, 1983.

Schmidt, Susan, and John Mintz, "Florida's Instant Invasion; How Gore and Bush Rushed in Legal and Political Armies," *Washington Post,* November 26, 2000, p. A1.

Torry, Saundra, "Survey Finds U.S. Law Firms Shrinking; D.C. Bucks Trend," *Washington Post,* September 24, 1991, p. D01.

Wilke, John R., "States in Microsoft Case Retain Leading Trial Lawyer Sullivan," *Wall Street Journal,* October 25, 2001, p. A4.

—David M. Walden

World Fuel Services Corporation

700 S. Royal Poinciana Boulevard, Suite 800
Miami Springs, Florida 33166
U.S.A.
Telephone: (305) 884-2001
Fax: (305) 883-0186
Web site: http://www.wfscorp.com

Public Company
Incorporated: 1984 as International Recovery Corp.
Employees: 181
Sales: $1.53 billion (2001)
Stock Exchanges: New York Pacific
Ticker Symbol: INT
NAIC: 422720 Petroleum and Petroleum Products
    Wholesalers (Except Bulk Stations and Terminals)

World Fuel Services Corporation (WFSC) is a leading downstream marketer of aviation and marine fuel products. It markets fuel products, acquired from the world's major oil companies, at more than 1,100 airports and seaports for use in commercial and corporate vessels and aircraft. WFSC claims a 10 percent share of the global marine fuel market and less than 1 percent of the aviation fuel market.

WFSC's operating companies in the aviation division are Baseops, AirData Services, and World Fuel Services, Inc. In the marine division, they are Trans-Tec Services, Bunkerfuels, and Pacific Horizon Petroleum Services. Through these subsidiaries, WFSC brokers fueling of ships, resells fuel, and provides hedging. WFSC launched a new fuel management division in early 2001 aimed at helping airlines manage their exposure to variations in jet fuel prices. The corporation has 27 offices in 12 countries.

The Aviation Fuel Services division specializes in servicing small and mid-sized carriers. World Fuel provides them needed trade credit. The Marine Fuel Services division helps shipping companies obtain the vital fuel they need every day from the highly fragmented world oil market. Whereas even major oil companies have limited geographical reaches, World Fuel prides itself on getting fuel to customers "anytime, anywhere."

Origins

World Fuel began as a regional used oil recycling company with sales of $6 million a year. It was incorporated in Florida on July 20, 1984, as International Recovery Corp. Ralph Weiser and Jerrold Blair were cofounders of the company, which was based in Miami Springs. Blair became president and chief operating officer in January 1985. After trading over-the-counter under the symbol IRPC, International Recovery began listing on the American Stock Exchange in June 1987 under the symbol INT.

In 1986, International Recovery acquired a three-year-old aviation fuel company, Advance Petroleum, Inc. (later doing business as World Fuel Services of FL). Thus the company entered a promising new line of business, which was expanded into an international sales operation covering airports throughout the world. One of Advance Petroleum's founders, Philip S. Bradley, was made CEO of World Fuel's Aviation Fuel Services division.

International Recovery acquired another aviation fueling business, JCo Energy Partners, Ltd., in October 1989 and renamed it World Fuel Services, Inc. A new subsidiary, International Petroleum Corporation of Delaware, was formed in April 1993 upon the completion of an oil and water recycling plant in Wilmington. The business involved collecting waste oil, wastewater, and other petroleum-contaminated liquids from auto shops, utilities, and other generators. The recycled products were sold to industrial and commercial customers.

Making Waves in 1995

World Fuel entered the marine fuel business via the January 1995 acquisition of the Trans-Tec Services group of companies, based in New York, Costa Rica, the United Kingdom, and Singapore. Trans-Tec had been founded in 1985 by Paul H. Stebbins and Michael J. Kasbar; both became executives at World Fuel.

The company changed its name from International Recovery Corp. to World Fuel Services Corporation in August 1995.

World Fuel's revenues were about $500 million in fiscal 1996. The company had a presence at more than 1,100 airports and 1,000 seaports in more than 150 countries.

Late 1990s Acquisitions

World Fuel acquired Baseops, a Houston-based corporate aviation services company, in January 1998 for $3.5 million in cash and stock. Baseops had been formed seven years earlier by former employees of Air Routing International, which itself had been formed by former employees of Universal Weather and Aviation. According to the *Houston Chronicle*, these companies were the industry's top three players, although Baseop's annual sales ($15.3 million in 1997) were dwarfed by those of the other two (estimated at more than $150 million for Universal and $100 million for Air Routing). These companies provided weather information and flight plans for pilots and performed a variety of services for private jet owners.

The operations of the Bunkerfuels companies, a substantial marine fuel brokerage, were acquired in April 1999 in a deal worth $8.5 million. Bunkerfuels had 1998 earnings of $1.7 million on revenues of $84 million. Based in Cranbury, New Jersey, it had been founded in 1978 by Robert Fitzgerald, chairman, who was retiring. Bunkerfuels was credited as the first to establish a worldwide presence to serve international fleets. It was to operate independently from Trans-Tec Services. Combined with the other holdings, the acquisition made World Fuel the world's largest marine fuels brokerage.

Plans to form a subsidiary in Indonesia, PT World Fuel Services, were announced in April 1999. Trans-Tec, which had a 10 percent share of the world bunker market, was opening an office in Tokyo, its 11th.

In August 1999, company officials reported an unusual act of piracy. A shipment of fuel to the Nigerian offshore oil industry did not reach its intended customers. World Fuel recorded a $3.3 million charge as a result and filed a claim with its insurance company. This was settled for $1 million in 2001. Earlier in 1999, the company had taken a $2.2 million charge related to bad debts, particularly in Ecuador.

In spite of the growth, World Fuel executives perceived the company's stock to be undervalued. After hitting $22 per share earlier in the year, in April the stock was trading at slightly more than $11. One of the main difficulties was a lack of similar companies available for comparison by analysts. World Fuel weathered a stockholders' class-action lawsuit that was dismissed in December 2000.

Exiting Oil Recycling in 2000

In February 2000, World Fuel exited the used oil recycling business by divesting its International Petroleum Corporation subsidiaries to the EarthCare Company of Dallas. Net income fell by a third to $9.6 million in fiscal 2000 on sales of $1.2 billion, up from 1999's $720 million.

In December 2000, World Fuel entered an aviation fuel marketing joint venture called PAFCO (formerly Page Avjet Fuel Corporation) with Signature Flight Support Services Corporation. Signature, described as the world's largest flight support operator and distribution network for business and commercial aviation services, was a subsidiary of the BBA Group.

Company President Jerrold Blair was named chairman and CEO in August 2000 upon the retirement of fellow cofounder Ralph R. Weiser. In the following few months, the company cut its staff by nearly 40 percent as part of a bid to make its financial performance less unpredictable.

President and COO Paul Stebbins, a cofounder of Trans-Tec (along with Michael J. Kasbar, CEO of the Marine Fuel Services division since 1995), explained the business to John T. Fakler of the *South Florida Business Journal*. The world fuel market was highly fragmented and unpredictable. World Fuel provided volume buying power, and its specialized staff tracked the many variables of market dynamics.

Great Results in 2001

Total revenues increased 27 percent to $1.5 billion for the fiscal year ending March 31, 2001. Net income rose 10 percent to $10.6 million. A rise in world fuel prices in the winter of 2000–01 helped send belt-tightening customers to the firm. World Fuel also was emphasizing the logistics side of the business, rather than the credit side, as it had in the past.

In March 2001 WFSC acquired the software company TransportEdge as it worked to move its business online. Two marine fuel brokerage companies, Norway-based Norse Bunker A.S. and Marine Energy of Dubai, also were acquired during the fiscal year. Both were located in vitally important seafaring areas.

WFSC launched a new fuel management division in spring 2001 aimed at helping airlines manage their exposure to variations in jet fuel prices. This promised to broaden its customer base to include larger commercial and corporate accounts, said Chairman Jerrold Blair.

A decline in passenger airline traffic followed the terrorist attacks on the United States on September 11, 2001, yet cargo traffic, charters, and military support flights all posted an increase. One of World Fuel's largest customers was the U.S. government. Analysts expected the increasing trend toward fractional ownership of business jets to continue, to the benefit

Key Dates:

1986: The company enters the aviation fuel business with purchase of Advance Petroleum.
1989: JCo Energy Partners is acquired.
1998: World Fuel acquires Baseops International, provider of ancillary aviation services.
2001: PAFCO joint venture increases World Fuel's involvement in corporate aviation.

of World Fuel. An agreement to acquire Rotterdam's Oil Shipping Group was announced in December 2001.

Principal Subsidiaries

Advance Petroleum, Inc. d.b.a. World Fuel Services of FL; Baseops Europe Ltd. (U.K.); Baseops International, Inc.; Bunkerfuels (Del), Inc.; Bunkerfuels UK Limited; Casa Petro S.A. (Costa Rica); Pacific Horizon Petroleum Services, Inc.; PAFCO L.L.C. (50%); Trans-Tec International S.R.L. (Costa Rica); Trans-Tec Services, Inc.; Trans-Tec Services (U.K.) Ltd.; World Fuel ApS (Denmark); World Fuel International S.R.L. (Costa Rica); World Fuel Services, Inc.; World Fuel Services, Ltd. (U.K.); World Fuel Services (Singapore) PTE. Ltd.

Principal Divisions

Aviation Fuel Services; Fuel Management; Marine Fuel Services.

Principal Competitors

BP p.l.c.; Caltex Corporation; Exxon Mobil Corporation; Mercury Air Group, Inc.; Royal Dutch/Shell Group.

Further Reading

Alderstein, David, "World Fuel Services Names CEO," *South Florida Business Journal,* August 1, 2000.

Cordle, Ina Paiva, "Miami-Based Fuel Reseller Blames Fraud, Theft for $3.3 Million Charge," *Miami Herald,* August 27, 1999.

Fakler, John T., "World Fuel Stoked by Energy Pinch," *South Florida Business Journal,* February 23, 2001.

Flynn, Matthew, "Bunker Giant Bucks the Trend by Putting Down Tokyo Roots," *Lloyd's List,* July 17, 1999, p. 6.

Martinez, Matthew, "World Spans Globe for Options," *Mergers & Acquisitions Report,* May 10, 1999, p. 4.

McLaughlin, John, "World Fuel Looks to Realise Value," *Lloyd's List,* April 30, 1999, p. 1.

Moreno, Jenalia, "Success in the Air; Corporate Aviation Takes Flight; Industry Booms with Competition, Expanded Services," *Houston Chronicle,* March 7, 1998, p. 1.

Osler, David, "World Fuel in Major Bunker Buy," *Lloyd's List,* March 24, 1999, p. 1.

Velshi, Ali, interview with Paul Stebbins, President & COO of World Fuel Services, *Business Unusual,* CNNfn, November 28, 2001.

"World Fuel Acquires Norse Bunker," *South Florida Business Journal,* February 15, 2001.

"World Fuel Hails Dismissal of Lawsuit," *South Florida Business Journal,* December 15, 2000.

"World Fuel Services to Form Joint Venture with Signature Flight Support," *South Florida Business Journal,* December 26, 2000.

"World Fuel Settles Suit Over Loss of Oil Shipments," *Broward Daily Business Review,* July 11, 2001, p. A3.

—Frederick C. Ingram

Worldwide Restaurant Concepts, Inc.

15301 Ventura Boulevard, Suite 300
Sherman Oaks, California 91403
U.S.A.
Telephone: (818) 662-9800
Fax: (818) 662-9832
Web site: http://www.sizzler.com

Public Company
Incorporated: 1991 as Sizzler International, Inc.
Employees: 8,370
Sales: $245.30 million (2001)
Stock Exchanges: New York
Ticker Symbol: SZ
NAIC: 722110 Full-Service Restaurants; 533110 Lessors
of Nonfinancial Intangible Assets (Except Copyright
Works); 551112 Offices of Other Holding Companies

Worldwide Restaurant Concepts, Inc. is the operator of the Sizzler restaurant chain, the Pat & Oscar's restaurant chain, and the franchisee of Kentucky Fried Chicken outlets in Australia. Worldwide Restaurant operates and franchises roughly 350 Sizzler steak house restaurants in the United States and abroad, maintaining a substantial presence in Australia. The company's 107 Kentucky Fried Chicken franchises are located in Queensland, Australia. The Pat & Oscar's chain, added in 2000, comprises 13 restaurants located in California and Arizona.

The Birth of Sizzler

Worldwide Restaurant, the name adopted by Sizzler International Inc. in 2001, began its corporate life in the late 1950s. Specifically, the company started business on January 27, 1958, when the first "Sizzler Family Steak House" opened in Culver City, California. The first unit of what would become a chain of budget steak houses opened with $50 in the cash register and a menu featuring four steak items. The Sizzler concept, which came under the ownership of Collins Foods International—formed during the early 1960s—fared well as a chain operating in the budget steak house segment of the restaurant industry. The company expanded throughout the western United States and into the southwestern reaches of the country, growing through the establishment of company-operated units and through the licensing of the concept to franchisees. Roughly 20 years of expansion produced a chain of 450 Sizzler restaurants, the majority of which were operated by franchisees.

Despite the impressive growth, Sizzler was failing to impress at the end of its two-decade expansion period. Industry-wide, the budget steak house segment was experiencing a downturn in business, Sizzler included. Moreover, the Sizzler chain had expanded too aggressively between 1978 and 1980, increasing its exposure to anemic market conditions. Many of the company's restaurants were performing poorly, causing overall operating profit margins to shrink considerably. Industry observers noted the company's lackluster performance, criticizing what they perceived as a stale, sprawling chain occupying a market niche that suffered from diminishing attractiveness to the dining public. Thankfully for Sizzler, executives within the company reached the same discouraging assessment, and began to make needed changes. One executive in particular, Thomas L. Gregory, was frustrated by Sizzler's prospects as a budget steak house operator. In response, he spearheaded sweeping change, transforming the market orientation of the struggling chain and fashioning a company ripe for growth.

A Detroit native, Gregory earned a hospitality management degree at Michigan State University before joining Marriott Corporation. He spent seven years at Marriott, ultimately serving as executive assistant to then Senior Vice-President Woodrow Marriott. Next, Gregory entered the U.S. Army, serving in the Quartermaster Corps, before joining the New York firm of Cresap, McCormick and Paget, where he spent five years as a management consultant. Gregory kept on the move, joining A&W Food Services of Canada as a vice-president. After a three-year stay at A&W, Gregory briefly served as president of Red Barn Systems of Canada before joining Collins Foods in 1974 as vice-president.

1980s: A Decade of Change

In 1980, Gregory was named president and chief executive officer of the Sizzler chain, assuming the responsibilities of

452

Key Dates:

1958: First Sizzler Family Steak House opens in Culver City, California.

1980: Thomas Gregory is named president and chief executive officer of the Sizzler chain.

1983: Sizzler's parent company, Collins Foods, sells 34 percent of the chain to the public.

1985: Chain of Rustler Steak House restaurants is acquired.

1991: Collins Foods merges with Sizzler Restaurants, forming Sizzler International.

1996: Sizzler International files for Chapter 11 bankruptcy protection.

1997: Sizzler International emerges from bankruptcy.

2000: Eight-unit Oscar's restaurant chain is acquired.

2001: Sizzler International changes its name to Worldwide Restaurant Concepts, Inc.

his new leadership posts at a critical point in the history of the 22-year-old company. In an interview with *Restaurant Business* published on November 1, 1987, Gregory remembered the state of the company upon his promotion, noting that Sizzler "was in deep trouble and had seen better days." His reaction to the situation steered Sizzler in a new direction, the impetus for change stemming from dissatisfaction with the status quo. Gregory continued in the *Restaurant Business* interview: "Mike Minchin, our executive vice president, and I both knew that being a budget steak house was not a very profitable place to be, and neither of us was committed to being in a low-end business. We knew we were heading into a different world, but felt that the operational system in place was good and efficient, and that the chain could be molded into something profitable."

Gregory, by his own admission, did not have a detailed plan for the alterations to come when he set out in 1980. He decided to retain three of the fundamental characteristics that described Sizzler before 1980, opting for "an evolutionary development, rather than a revolutionary one," according to his interview with *Restaurant Business*. As they had before 1980, Sizzler units would continue to offer limited table service, thereby realizing savings in labor costs. The menu selection, as well, would continue to be limited, giving Gregory the third characteristic that would remain unchanged during his reign: the method of short-order cooking and food preparation only possible with a limited menu.

Having decided which aspects of the past to take into the future, Gregory next tried to determine what Sizzler's future might be. He had no clear idea, but the general feeling among executives at corporate headquarters was a need to move Sizzler slightly up-market, a few notches above the traditional budget steak house yet below the more expensive dining experience prevalent at full-service, white-tablecloth restaurants. Gregory and his management team took their cue from extensive customer surveys and came up with a concept that, once actualized, was trend setting. Gregory added fresh seafood, poultry, salads, tostadas, and new pasta bars, helping give birth to the "seafood-and-steak" restaurant concept that took root during the 1980s. Gregory's version of the concept, on display as the "new" Sizzler of the 1980s, featured the new additions to the menu in a buffet-style setting, enabling patrons to serve themselves.

The repositioning initiated by Gregory touched off an era of strident and profitable growth for the Sizzler's chain, much to the delight of James Collins, founder and chairman of Collins Foods, and his team of executives. Backed by its parent company, Sizzler expanded internationally as the company's new format scored success domestically. At roughly the same time Gregory began repositioning Sizzler in the United States, the chain debuted, in its original budget steak house format, in Japan. The overseas expansion program began with a five-year plan promising the establishment of 55 Sizzler franchised restaurants in Tokyo. The foray into Japan proved unprofitable, ending in 1989 with only three units in operation. Far more encouraging results were registered in Australia, where the company carved out a substantial and lasting presence.

Against the backdrop of strategic change and physical growth, Sizzler made strident progress throughout the 1980s, blossoming into a vibrant enterprise during the "Gregory Decade." Investors were able to share in the company's success after Collins Foods sold 34 percent of Sizzler to the public in 1983, a transaction that made Sizzler a majority-owned subsidiary of Collins Foods and forced Gregory to pay heed to the expectations of Wall Street. As the number of Sizzler units increased, both through franchising and the establishment of company-operated units, the chain bolstered its stature through acquisitions. The most significant purchase during the decade occurred in 1985, when Sizzler acquired Rockville, Maryland-based Tenly Enterprises, operator of roughly 100 Rustler Steak House restaurants and a six-unit auto-memorabilia theme concept called Curly's Garage. The Rustler Steak House restaurants, located primarily along the East Coast, stretching from Washington, D.C., to Long Island, New Jersey, added substantially to the company's presence in the Northeast. The Curly's Garage units, featuring a full-service, full-bar format specializing in barbecued ribs, were located in Virginia, Maryland, and New Jersey.

Although internal and external means of growth added appreciably to Sizzler's stature during the 1980s, Gregory's greatest gains were to be measured by the financial health of the chain and its popularity among the dining public. Between 1980 and 1987, the Sizzler chain expanded from 128 company-operated and 324 franchised units to 170 company-operated and 373 franchised units. The growth was substantial, to be sure, but more impressive was the 24 consecutive quarters of year-to-year growth in sales and earnings recorded during the seven-year period. By the end of the decade, the chain exuded a formidable presence, both domestically and abroad. There were 26 restaurants in Australia, one in Guam, and three in the Persian Gulf region, with units slated for development in Taiwan, Singapore, Thailand, and Malaysia. In the United States, the chain comprised 650 units, half of which were located on the West Coast, with the Northeast home to 30 percent of the chain's units. Systemwide, the company generated nearly $1 billion in annual sales by the beginning of the 1990s, marking an exponential leap from the $250 million in sales the company recorded at the beginning of the Gregory era.

1990s: Failure and Revival

As Gregory's tenure wound to a close, Sizzler prepared for a major restructuring, one intended to provide the company with additional strength. In September 1990, Sizzler announced it was merging into its parent company, Collins Foods. To complete the transaction, Collins Foods sold its largest wholly owned business, a chain of 209 Kentucky Fried Chicken (KFC) outlets to PepsiCo for approximately five million shares of PepsiCo stock. Concurrent with the PepsiCo deal, Collins Foods purchased the 34 percent of Sizzler that was publicly held. The reorganization, completed in January 1991, created Sizzler International, Inc., parent company of Sizzler Restaurants International, Inc., a company, excluding the sales generated by franchised units, with an annual revenue base of $492 million. As part of the reorganization, changes were made in the company's leadership. James Collins, chairman of the former Collins Foods, became chairman of Sizzler International. Dick Bermingham, who was president and chief executive officer of Collins Foods, became chief executive officer of Sizzler International. Gregory served as president, delaying his planned retirement until April 1992. The newly reorganized Sizzler planned to focus on the international expansion of its signature buffet-and-grill concept in the coming years, intending to develop 100 units in the Pacific Rim during the ensuing five years.

In the wake of the reorganization, the steps that Sizzler took were faltering steps. As during the late 1970s, Sizzler suffered from a number of unprofitable restaurants, and the company began to reel. By the mid-1990s, the company's domestic operations were losing an estimated $1 million per month, draining Sizzler of its former vitality. Its debts soared toward $100 million, forcing the company to take evasive action. On June 2, 1996, Sizzler International Inc. and its U.S. subsidiary, Sizzler Restaurant International, Inc., filed for bankruptcy-court protection, citing its debilitating leasehold obligations at many of its underperforming stores. Chapter 11 bankruptcy reorganization immediately followed, forcing Sizzler to scramble to find a way toward survival. During the year-long reorganization process, Sizzler shed 130 of its domestic, company-operated restaurants, sold six of its upscale Buffalo Ranch Steakhouses, and laid off more than 4,000 employees. The bankruptcy reorganization also engendered several significant changes in the company's leadership. Christopher Thomas, formerly the chief financial officer and chief operating officer, was promoted to president and chief executive officer of Sizzler Restaurants International, Inc. Chairman James Collins assumed the additional role of chief executive officer of Sizzler International, Inc. Kevin Perkins, formerly the president and chief executive officer of Sizzler International Inc., was named president and chief executive officer of the parent company's international restaurant division.

Under two separate plans approved by the bankruptcy court, Sizzler International paid an estimated $70 million in creditors claims, deriving the bulk of its payment from revenue generated by its international operations. The company emerged from bankruptcy in June 1997, possessing 69 company-operated units in the United States, 39 company-operated units overseas, 199 franchised units operating domestically, and 97 units operating overseas. Out from the gates, the restructured Sizzler enterprise pinned its recovery on an aggressive marketing campaign for a new nine-item line of hamburgers. Supported by a

$1 million advertising strategy, the new hamburger line was introduced immediately after the company received bankruptcy-court approval. The campaign represented one of several programs that were implemented by the company to help fuel sales and to regain lost customers. The emphasis was on menu changes and their support by new marketing programs. Said CEO Christopher Thomas, in a June 16, 1997 interview with *Nation's Restaurant News,* "We've increased the number of hamburger products from four to nine. . . . We've tried to modernize and contemporize the line, and we are still targeting the upper end of the midscale niche."

By the end of the 1990s, Sizzler had resolved the difficulties that plunged the company into bankruptcy. Smaller and leaner, the company entered the 21st century, marking the arrival of the new era with the completion of an acquisition. In August 2000, Sizzler acquired an eight-unit chain of restaurants operating under the name Oscar's, which was renamed Pat & Oscar's in April 2001. The chain of Pat & Oscar's, representing a third line of business for Sizzler, grew to 13 restaurants by the end of 2001, when company executives decided to acknowledge the diversity of their business by changing the company's corporate banner. In September 2001, Sizzler International changed its name to Worldwide Restaurant Concepts, Inc., the corporate umbrella under which Sizzler, Pat & Oscar's, and the Kentucky Fried Chicken franchises operated independently, each contributing to the success of their parent company.

Principal Subsidiaries

Collins Food Group Pty, Ltd. (Australia); CFI Insurers, Ltd.; Bermuda Collins Finance and Management Pty, Ltd. (Australia); Collins Foods Australia Pty, Ltd.; Collins Foods International, Pty, Ltd.; Collins International, Inc.; Collins Properties, Inc.; Collins Property Development Pty, Ltd. (Australia); Curly's of Springfield, P.A., Inc.; Affiliated Restaurant Corp.; Furnace Concepts Australia Corp.; Furnace Concepts International, Inc.; Collins Restaurants Queensland Pty, Ltd. (Australia); Josephina's, Inc.; Restaurant Concepts International, Inc. Nevada Restaurant Concepts of Australia Pty, Ltd.; Scott's & Sizzler Ltd. (Canada); Sizzler Australia Pty, Ltd.; Sizzler Family Steak Houses, Inc.; Sizzler Franchise Development, Ltd. (Bermuda); Sizzler Holdings of Canada, Inc.; Sizzler International Marks, Inc.; Sizzler New Zealand Limited; Sizzler of N.Y., Inc.; New York Sizzler Restaurants Group Pty, Ltd.; Australia Sizzler Restaurant Services, Inc.; Sizzler South Pacific Pty, Ltd.; Sizzler Southeast Asia, Inc.; Sizzler Steak Seafood Salad (S) Pte. Ltd. (Singapore); Sizzler USA Franchise, Inc.; Sizzler USA Real Property, Inc.; Sizzler USA Restaurants, Inc.; Delaware Sizzler USA, Inc.; Collins Restaurants Management Pty, Ltd. (Australia); Collins Restaurants NSW Pty, Ltd. (Australia); Sizzler Asia Holdings, Inc.

Principal Competitors

Investors Management Corp.; Metromedia Company; Ryan's Family Steak Houses, Inc.

Further Reading

Chaudhry, Rajan, "Collins' CEO Hints at Consolidation with Sizzler," *Nation's Restaurant News,* March 20, 1989, p. 2.

Henderson, Justin, "Steak Chain Sizzles with Pride," *Restaurant Business,* March 1, 1983, p. 94.

Howard, Theresa, "Sizzler Out of Ch. 11 with New Campaign," *Nation's Restaurant News,* June 16, 1997, p. 3.

Leibowitz, David S., "Getting Their Just Desserts?," *Financial World,* August 21, 1990, p. 73.

Liddle, Alan, "Thomas Gregory: Striving for Perfection," *Nation's Restaurant News,* June 25, 1990, p. 7.

Long, Dolores A., "Thomas L. Gregory, Sizzler Restaurants," *Restaurant Business,* November 1, 1987, p. 88.

Martin, Richard, "Sizzler Acquiring 100 Rustlers; Purchase Will Enhance Chain's Position in Northeast," *Nation's Restaurant News,* May 27, 1985, p. 1.

——, "Sizzler Lights Up Hot-Food Tests at Expanded Buffets," *Nation's Restaurant News,* January 29, 1990, p. 3.

——, "Sizzler Prexy Gregory Set to Retire in '92," *Nation's Restaurant News,* June 24, 1991, p. 7.

"Sizzler Parent's 1st-Q Profits Fall 42 Percent on Sales Rise," *Nation's Restaurant News,* September 10, 2001, p. 12.

"Sizzler Parent's 2nd-Q Net Up, but 6-Mo. Profits Decline," *Nation's Restaurant News,* December 10, 2001, p. 12.

Walsh, James, "A Simpler Sizzler," *California Business,* December 1990, p. 25.

Warren, Elaine, "Hamburger Hamlet, Sizzler Serve Up Declining Profits, Analysts Blame Changing Market, Outmoded Concepts," *Los Angeles Business Journal,* April 25, 1994, p. 8.

—Jeffrey L. Covell

YOCREAM International, Inc.

5858 NE 87th Avenue
Portland, Oregon 97220
U.S.A.
Telephone: (503) 256-3754
Fax: (503) 256-3976
Web site: http://www.yocream.com

Public Company
Incorporated: 1977 as Yogurt Stand, Inc.
Employees: 52
Sales: $15.9 million (2001)
Stock Exchanges: NASDAQ
Ticker Symbol: YOCM
NAIC: 311520 Ice Cream and Frozen Dessert
  Manufacturing

YOCREAM International, Inc., with corporate headquarters and manufacturing facilities in Portland, Oregon, makes, markets, and sells frozen yogurt, smoothies, ice cream, and frozen custard in both organic and non-organic formulations. Its products are available in supermarkets, grocery stores, convenience stores, restaurants, hospitals, school district foodservices, military installations, yogurt shops, fast-food chains, and discount club warehouses. Its customers are mostly foodservice suppliers throughout the United States and 11 other countries.

1977–86: The First Ten Years

The Hanna brothers came up with the idea for Yogurt Stand, Inc. in 1976, "one day when we sat around wondering what else to do," according to John Hanna, an accountant by training. All three—John, David, and James—had "[grown] up on yogurt and were entranced when we heard about them selling frozen yogurt in New York," he was quoted as saying in a 1986 *Oregonian* article. David, a real estate agent, James, a retired school principal, and John visited New York City for three weeks, "stopping in the shops and talking to the public" about the new hot food item. They returned home where their mother, Norma, and they developed their own recipe for the sweet concoction. The new company, which changed its name to International Yogurt Company, Inc. later that first year, contracted with Darigold and then with Alpenrose to produce the family recipe. The frozen yogurt sold in milk containers under the name 800 Yo Cream, which doubled as the company's toll free number.

In 1977, the brothers, whose father had had a food store in southeast Portland until his retirement in 1962, franchised a chain of specialty retail outlets, called Healthy Delis, through which they sold their yogurt. Frozen yogurt was in its heyday then, and the franchises did well, expanding to about 17 company-owned and franchised outlets by the early 1980s. But when their product then began to fade in popularity, the trio gradually shifted the company's focus to foodservice sales. In 1982, International Yogurt began selling Yo Cream to foodservice operations and restaurants. "We knew the fad interest was leveling off," said John Hanna, the company's president, in a 1985 *Portland Business Journal* article. Consequently, the company cut back its outlets to ten and began taking steps in 1981 to get its premium-priced product into grocery stores where 70 to 80 percent of all ice cream sales occurred.

By 1985, International Yogurt had 24 employees, about $727,000 in sales, and a solid customer base of hospitals, fast-food restaurants, and pizza parlors in 12 states—Hawaii, Alaska, California, Oregon, Washington, Idaho, Utah, Missouri, Arkansas, Oklahoma, Kansas, and Tennessee—as well as in British Columbia, Canada. The company also had the good fortune to have two financial backers—Orians Investment Co. of Portland, and Far West Federal Bank—each of which loaned International Yogurt $200,000.

The company positioned its frozen yogurt as a gourmet item, hoping to take on the premium ice cream market, an increasingly competitive market, which then pulled in $3 million in annual sales. International Yogurt perfected a hard-packed version of its gourmet dessert, which had none of the tanginess of its earlier product, but closely resembled ice cream in taste and consistency, then spent $10,000 to come up with a silver-colored tub designed by the local Jenson Display for its container. In early January 1986, the first hard-packed frozen Yo Cream, available in vanilla, chocolate, and strawberry, went on sale at several local supermarkets. Later that year, the company moved to new manufacturing headquarters, a 30,000-square-foot plant, complete with two laboratories and a staff biochemist, near Portland's International Airport. By year's end, International Yogurt had sales of $1.4 million, although expenses entailed in the move contributed to net operating losses that year of about $400,000.

In choosing the name Yo Cream for its hard-packed product, International Yogurt became embroiled in a federal trademark lawsuit with subsidiaries of General Mills. The lawsuit had its roots in 1979 when General Mills registered the name Yo Creme for an as-yet-undetermined product that would complement its Yoplait line. International Yogurt, although aware of this, decided to go forward with Yo Cream in 1982, reasoning that since there was still no Yo Creme product, there would be no problem. Then, in 1984, General Mills began the development of a rich, pudding-like yogurt, which it introduced in 1986 under the name Yo Creme, the same year International Yogurt began putting its Yo Cream in supermarkets.

The lawsuit cost International Yogurt some $350,000 by the end of 1986, or about 8 percent of the company's $5 million in revenue on sales of 500,000 gallons of frozen yogurt for that year. A district judge ruled in 1987 that the $5.3 billion General Mills had "improperly warehoused" a name, and that International Yogurt had established rights to its product name in 32 states and could market its products in all 50 states. General Mills had rights to its product name in 18 states. General Mills had to pay International Yogurt $225,000 in a cash settlement for the right not to take its products off supermarket shelves immediately in the 32 other states. Ironically, the company later dropped this retail venture because of the intense capital investment required, instead focusing on selling to the foodservice sector.

1987–97: The NORPAC Years

However, the lawsuit served International Yogurt well in other ways. It brought the company to the attention of the NORPAC Group, one of the nation's leading processors of frozen fruits and vegetables. NORPAC agreed to market and distribute the local International Yogurt's products on a national level. NORPAC also bought shares of the newly public company at its $2 million initial public offering held that year. It was an "exciting" time in the company's development, according to the Hanna Brothers, who retained slightly less than 50 percent control of the company: The lawsuit had given the company national clout; the plant was producing 10,000 gallons of frozen yogurt a week on one shift and could "easily . . . increase beyond that dramatically to the 100,000 (gallon range)," according to John Hanna in a 1987 *Oregonian* article. International Yogurt entered into a ten-year exclusive agree-

ment with the NORPAC Group in 1987 to expand its sales nationally. It also began selling its products in 14 PX's and military commissaries and at Dunkin' Donuts shops in 1987.

Sales took off in the spring of 1988. With 105 distributors (compared to 12 at the end of 1987), International Yogurt began selling Yo Cream to schools, colleges, hospitals, in-plant cafeterias, delis, commissaries, and other outlets. By the end of 1989, Yo Cream was available in 46 states—although only 12 to 15 percent of its sales occurred in retail stores. In 1989, the company sold its Healthy Deli trademark, and in 1991, it licensed a Swiss corporation to manufacture and distribute its products throughout Europe.

According to an article in *Dairy Field*, this period of growth was spurred by Americans' obsession with the health consequences of eating high-fat foods. However, when that obsession faded in the 1990s, so, too, did the market for frozen yogurt. As many manufacturers discontinued the bulk of their healthier offerings, International Yogurt's sales leveled off and its stock price declined. The company finished 1992 with earnings in the $160,000 range on revenues of $6.5 million. Then suddenly in 1993, investors took notice and the company's stock price quadrupled. More positive change occurred for the company in December when it began to package frozen desserts under the Weight Watchers label, catapulting the company overnight from 30 to 50 percent of production capacity. Shortly thereafter, the Hanna brothers each sold some of their own shares so that a New York bank holding company could accumulate about a 10 percent stake in International Yogurt.

Throughout the 1990s, International Yogurt introduced new products, capitalizing on its growth trend. In 1993, a decaffeinated coffee yogurt drink called Yo Caffe Latte debuted, followed, in 1995, by a sorbet line in response to requests from foodservice operators for fat-free products and overall growth in the sorbet segment. In 1997, the company introduced Yo Cream Pure, a 100 percent organic line of soft serve frozen yogurt mixes, directed at foodservice operators, and hard packed, low-fat ice cream. In 1999, as the popularity for smoothies grew, it debuted a bottled frozen smoothie product called Bountiful Harvest at Wal-Mart.

1997–2001: Focus on Expansion Through New Distribution Plan

Having focused its sights on expansion, International Yogurt ended its marketing agreement with NORPAC in 1997, going to a distribution plan that entailed direct brokerage relationships supported by trained product specialists. Earlier, in 1994, it had entered into a joint venture with Western Family Foods to distribute and market its products under both the Western Family Foods and Yo Cream labels to grocers. Another big break came in 1996 with an agreement with SYSCO Corporation, the nation's largest foodservice distributor, to supply frozen yogurt and sorbet under SYSCO's label. In 1997, International Yogurt entered into a marketing agreement with Pocohontas Foods USA, an association of 140 independent foodservice distributors nationwide, to market its products.

Although production of frozen yogurt nationally had been on the decline for several years, International Yogurt saw its

---

Key Dates:

1977: The company incorporates as the Yogurt Stand, Inc., and later changes its name to International Yogurt Company, Inc.

1986: The company moves into a new 30,000-square-foot factory in Portland; General Mills sues the company for trademark infringement.

1987: The company holds its initial public offering and begins national distribution through NORPAC.

1993: The company begins to package frozen desserts under the Weight Watchers label.

1997: The company exits its marketing agreement with NORPAC.

1999: The company changes its name to YOCREAM International, Inc.

2001: YOCREAM International expands production capability and partners with The Dannon Group to cobrand a product.

---

sales grow 90 percent during the second half of the 1990s. In 1997 it totaled revenues of about $8.7 million; in 1998, that number reached $10.2 million and in 1999 $14.6 million. By 2000, with revenue of $15 million, the yogurt maker had experienced seven consecutive quarters of increased sales and income and had had five years of profit.

The declining market forced the company to push harder for new products and a larger market share. After changing its name to YOCREAM International in 1999 in a move to reflect its broad line of frozen desserts, the company spent $443,000 in 2000 to come up with new products to boost revenue. It targeted new markets with new products, including soft serve frozen custard, a shake base, a soft serve ice cream, coffee smoothie for high volume dispensers, and margarita mix for blenders. In addition, it experimented with a premium line of hard-packed, low-fat frozen yogurt for the European market. In 2001, it finished expanding its production capacity by reconfiguring its plant space in Portland. The expanded plant, which cost more than $2 million, had mix tanks outside the facility, which were connected to production equipment via piping, and a bottling line as well as a bag-in-a-box machine to package bulk smoothies.

Increased capacity created new opportunities for YO-CREAM, which began looking for new business relationships in 2001. It partnered with Dannon to cobrand a line of soft serve frozen yogurt, "one of the most significant events historically" for the company, according to John Hanna in a 2001 *Portland Business Journal* article. Capitalizing on the growing market for smoothies, YOCREAM also inked a deal with Blimpie International to include a smoothie bar in its outlets and was poised to explore additional co-packing arrangements with other manufacturers. According to one major investor quoted in the *Portland Business Journal*, the company's earning potential was "outrageous." Hanna put it more modestly: "Frozen yogurt is entrenched in the American economy. When other [companies] get 'disenamored' with the market, we have the opportunity to grab the market share.' "

Further Reading

Anderson, Michael A., "I Scream, You Scream for Frozen Yo Cream," *Portland Business Journal*, August 26, 1985, p. 1.

Cook, Julie, "Smooth Sensation," *Dairy Field*, February 2001, p. 18.

Gauntt, Tom, "Lawsuit's Glare Softens Profits of Yogurt Maker," *Portland Business Journal*, June 8, 1987, p. 2.

Goranson, Eric, "Portland Brothers Find Hard Sell Not Needed for Frozen Yogurt," *Oregonian*, January 9, 1986, p. ME1.

——, "Yogurt Firm Savors Taste of Success," *Oregonian*, October 15, 1987, p. ME1.

Hamburg, Ken, "Yogurt Deal Spoons Up National Distribution Plans," *Oregonian*, September 17, 1987, p. D18.

Strom, Shelly, "Yo Cream Gets Aggressive As Its Core Market Shrinks," *Portland Business Journal*, June 15, 2001, p. 14.

—Carrie Rothburd

INDEX TO COMPANIES

Index to Companies

Listings in this index are arranged in alphabetical order under the company name. Company names beginning with a letter or proper name such as Eli Lilly & Co. will be found under the first letter of the company name. Definite articles (The, Le, La) are ignored for alphabetical purposes as are forms of incorporation that precede the company name (AB, NV). Company names printed in bold type have full, historical essays on the page numbers appearing in bold. Updates to entries that appeared in earlier volumes are signified by the notation (**upd.**). Company names in light type are references within an essay to that company, not full historical essays. This index is cumulative with volume numbers printed in bold type.

Rockwell International Corporation, I
71, **78–80**, 154–55, 186; **II** 3, 94, 379;
6 263; **7** 420; **8** 165; **9** 10; **10** 279–80;
11 268, 278, **427–30 (upd.)**, 473; **12**
135, 248, 506; **13** 228; **18** 369, 571; **22**
51, 53, 63–64; **32** 81, 84–85; **33** 27; **35**
91; **36** 121–22; **39** 30; **44** 357
Rocky Mountain Bankcard, **24** 393
Rocky Mountain Financial Corporation, **13**
348
Rocky Mountain Pipe Line Co., **IV** 400
Rocky River Power Co. *See* Connecticut
Light and Power Co.
Rocky Shoes & Boots, Inc., 26 415–18
Rod's Food Products, **36** 163
Rodale, Inc., 47 336–39 (upd.)
Rodale Press, Inc., 22 443; **23 415–17**
Rodamco N.V., IV 698; **26 419–21**
Rodel, Inc., **26** 425
Röder & Co., **34** 38, 40
Rodeway Inns of America, **II** 142; **III** 94;
11 242; **25** 309
Rodgers Instrument Corporation, **38** 391
Rodney Square Management Corp., **25** 542
Rodven Records, **23** 391
Roederstein GmbH, **21** 520
Roegelein Co., **13** 271
Roehr Products Co., **III** 443
Roermond, **IV** 276
Roessler & Hasslacher Chemical Co., **IV**
69
Roger Cleveland Golf Company, **15** 462;
43 375–76
Roger Williams Foods, **II** 682
Rogers & Oling, Inc., **17** 533
Rogers Bros., **I** 672
Rogers CanGuard, Inc., **32** 374
**Rogers Communications Inc., 30 388–92
(upd.).** *See also* Maclean Hunter
Publishing Limited.
Rohde & Schwarz GmbH & Co. KG, 39
350–53
Rohe Scientific Corp., **13** 398
Röhm and Haas Company, I 391–93; 14
182–83; **26 422–26 (upd.)**
ROHN Industries, Inc., 22 467–69
Rohölgewinnungs AG, **IV** 485
Rohr Gruppe, **20** 100
Rohr Incorporated, I 62; **9 458–60; 11**
165
Roja, **III** 47
The Rokke Group, **16** 546; **32** 100
Rokuosha, **III** 547
Rol Oil, **IV** 451
Rola Group, **II** 81
Roland Berger & Partner GmbH, 37
333–36
Roland Corporation, 38 389–91
Roland Murten A.G., 7 452–53
Roland NV, **41** 340
Rolex. *See* Montres Rolex S.A.
Roll International Corporation, 37
337–39
Rollalong, **III** 502; **7** 208
Rollerblade, Inc., 15 395–98; 22 202–03;
34 388–92 (upd.)
Rolling Stones Records, **23** 33
Rollins Burdick Hunter Company, **III** 204;
45 27
Rollins Communications, **II** 161
Rollins, Inc., 11 431–34
Rollins Specialty Group, **III** 204
Rollo's, **16** 95
Rolls-Royce Allison, 29 407–09 (upd.)

Rolls-Royce Motors Ltd., I 25–26,
81–82, 166, **194–96; III** 652; **9** 16–18,
417–18; **11** 138, 403; **21** 435
Rolls-Royce plc, I 41, 55, 65, **81–83**, 481;
III 507, 556; **7 454–57 (upd.); 9** 244;
11 268; **12** 190; **13** 414; **21 433–37**
(upd.); 24 85; **27** 495–96; **46** 358–59;
47 7, 9
Rolm Corp., **II** 99; **III** 149; **18** 344; **22** 51;
34 512
Rolodex Electronics, **23** 209, 212
Rolscreen. *See* Pella Corporation.
Rombas, **IV** 226
Rome Cable and Wire Co., **IV** 15
Rome Network, Inc., **24** 95
Romper Room Enterprises, Inc., **16** 267
Rompetrol, **IV** 454
Ron Nagle, **I** 247
Ronco, Inc., 15 399–401; 21 327
Rondel's, Inc., **8** 135
Ronel, **13** 274
Roni-Linda Productions, Inc., **27** 347
Ronnebyredds Trävaru, **25** 463
Ronningen-Petter, **III** 468
Ronzoni Foods Corp., **15** 221
Roombar S.A., **28** 241
Rooms To Go Inc., 28 389–92
Rooney Brothers Co., 25 402–04
Roots Canada Ltd., 27 194; **42 325–27**
Roots-Connersville Blower Corp., **III** 472
Roper Industries Inc., III 655; **12** 550; **15**
402–04; 25 89
Ropert Group, **18** 67
Ropes & Gray, 40 377–80
RoProperty Services BV. *See* Rodamco
N.V.
Rorer Group, I 666–68; 12 4; **16** 438; **24**
257
Rosaen Co., **23** 82
Rosarita Food Company, **25** 278
Rose & Co., **26** 65
Rose Exterminator Company, **25** 15
Rose Foundation, **9** 348
Rose's Stores, Inc., 13 261, **444–46; 23**
215
Rosebud Dolls Ltd., **25** 312
Rosefield Packing Co., **II** 497
Rosehaugh, **24** 269
RoseJohnson Incorporated, **14** 303
Rosemount Inc., II 20; **13** 226; **15**
405–08; 46 171
Rosen Enterprises, Ltd., **10** 482
Rosenblads Patenter, **III** 419
Rosenbluth International Inc., 14 407–09
Rosenfeld Hat Company. *See* Columbia
Hat Company.
Rosenmund-Guèdu, **31** 158
Rosenthal A.G., **I** 347; **18** 236; **34** 493,
496
Rosevear, **III** 690
Rosewood Financial, Inc., **24** 383
Roshco, Inc., **27** 288
Roslyn Bancorp, **46** 316
Ross Carrier Company, **8** 115
Ross Clouston, **13** 244
Ross Gear & Tool Co., **I** 539; **14** 510
Ross Hall Corp., **I** 417
Ross Stores, Inc., 17 408–10; 43 332–35
(upd.)
Rossendale Combining Company, **9** 92
Rossignol Ski Company, Inc. *See* Skis
Rossignol S.A.
Rössing Uranium Ltd., **IV** 191
Rossville Union Distillery, **I** 285

Rostocker Brauerei VEB, **9** 87
Roswell Public Service Company, **6** 579
Rota Bolt Ltd., **III** 581
Rotadisk, **16** 7
Rotan Mosle Financial Corporation, **II** 445;
22 406
Rotary International, 31 395–97
Rotary Lift, **III** 467–68
Rotax, **III** 555–56. *See also* Orbital Engine
Corporation Ltd.
Rote. *See* Avery Dennison Corporation.
Rotelcom Data Inc., **6** 334; **16** 222
Rotex, **IV** 253
Roth Co., **16** 493
Roth Freres SA, **26** 231
Rothmans International BV, **33** 82
Rothmans International p.l.c., I 438; **IV**
93; **V 411–13; 27** 488
Rothmans UK Holdings Limited, 19
367–70 (upd.)
Rothschild Financial Corporation, **13** 347
Rothschild Group, **6** 206
Rothschild Investment Trust, **I** 248; **III** 699
Roto-Rooter Corp., 13 149–50; **15**
409–11; 16 387
Rotodiesel, **III** 556
Rotor Tool Co., **II** 16
Rotork plc, 46 361–64
Rotterdam Bank, **II** 183–85
Rotterdam Beleggings (Investment)
Consortium. *See* Robeco.
Rotterdam Lloyd, **6** 403–04; **26** 241–42
The Rottlund Company, Inc., 28 393–95
Rouge et Or, **IV** 614
Rouge Steel Company, 8 448–50
Roughdales Brickworks, **14** 249
Rougier. *See* Groupe Rougier, SA.
Round Hill Foods, **21** 535
Round Table, **16** 447
Roundup Wholesale Grocery Company, **V**
55
Roundy's Inc., 14 410–12
The Rouse Company, II 445; **15 412–15;**
22 406
Roussel Uclaf, I 669–70; 8 451–53
(upd.); 18 236; **19** 51; **25** 285; **38** 379
Rousselot, **I** 677
Routh Robbins Companies, **21** 96
Roux Séguéla Cayzac & Goudard. *See*
Euro RSCG Worldwide S.A.
Rover Group Ltd., I 186; **7 458–60; 11**
31, 33; **14** 36; **21 441–44 (upd.); 24**
87–88; **38** 83, 85–86
Rowan Companies, Inc., 43 336–39
Rowe & Pitman, **14** 419
Rowe Bros. & Co., **III** 680
Rowe Price-Fleming International, Inc., **11**
495
Rowell Welding Works, **26** 433
Rowenta. *See* Groupe SEB.
Rowland Communications Worldwide, **42**
328, 331
Rowntree and Co., **27** 104
Rowntree Mackintosh PLC, II 476, 511,
521, 548, **568–70; 7** 383; **28** 311
Roxana Petroleum Co., **IV** 531, 540
Roxell, N.V., **43** 129
Roxoil Drilling, **7** 344
Roy and Charles Moore Crane Company,
18 319
Roy F. Weston, Inc., 33 369–72
Roy Farrell Import-Export Company, **6** 78
Roy Rogers, **III** 102
Royal Ahold. *See* Koninklijke Ahold N.V.

INDEX TO INDUSTRIES

Index to Industries

AEROSPACE

AIRLINES

AUTOMOTIVE

Adam Opel AG, 7; 21 (upd.)
Alfa Romeo, 13; 36 (upd.)
Alvis Plc, 47
American Motors Corporation, I
Applied Power Inc., 32 (upd.)
Arvin Industries, Inc., 8
Automobiles Citroen, 7
Automobili Lamborghini Holding S.p.A., 13; 34 (upd.)
Bajaj Auto Limited, 39
Bayerische Motoren Werke AG, I; 11 (upd.); 38 (upd.)
Bendix Corporation, I
Blue Bird Corporation, 35
Bombardier Inc., 42 (upd.)
Borg-Warner Automotive, Inc., 14; 32 (upd.)
The Budd Company, 8
CARQUEST Corporation, 29
Chrysler Corporation, I; 11 (upd.)
CNH Global N.V., 38 (upd.)
Consorcio G Grupo Dina, S.A. de C.V., 36
CSK Auto Corporation, 38
Cummins Engine Company, Inc., I; 12 (upd.); 40 (upd.)
Custom Chrome, Inc., 16
Daihatsu Motor Company, Ltd., 7; 21 (upd.)
Daimler-Benz A.G., I; 15 (upd.)
DaimlerChrysler AG, 34 (upd.)
Dana Corporation, I; 10 (upd.)
Deere & Company, 42 (upd.)
Delphi Automotive Systems Corporation, 45
Don Massey Cadillac, Inc., 37
Douglas & Lomason Company, 16
Ducati Motor Holding S.p.A., 30
Eaton Corporation, I; 10 (upd.)
Echlin Inc., I; 11 (upd.)
Edelbrock Corporation, 37
Federal-Mogul Corporation, I; 10 (upd.); 26 (upd.)
Ferrari S.p.A., 13; 36 (upd.)
Fiat S.p.A, I; 11 (upd.)
FinishMaster, Inc., 24
Ford Motor Company, I; 11 (upd.); 36 (upd.)
Ford Motor Company, S.A. de C.V., 20
Fruehauf Corporation, I
General Motors Corporation, I; 10 (upd.); 36 (upd.)
Gentex Corporation, 26
Genuine Parts Company, 9; 45 (upd.)
GKN plc, 38 (upd.)
Harley-Davidson Inc., 7; 25 (upd.)
Hayes Lemmerz International, Inc., 27
The Hertz Corporation, 33 (upd.)
Hino Motors, Ltd., 7; 21 (upd.)
Hometown Auto Retailers, Inc., 44
Honda Motor Company Limited (Honda Giken Kogyo Kabushiki Kaisha), I; 10 (upd.); 29 (upd.)
Insurance Auto Auctions, Inc., 23
Isuzu Motors, Ltd., 9; 23 (upd.)
Kelsey-Hayes Group of Companies, 7; 27 (upd.)
Kia Motors Corporation, 12; 29 (upd.)
Lear Seating Corporation, 16
Lithia Motors, Inc., 41
Lotus Cars Ltd., 14
Lund International Holdings, Inc., 40
Mack Trucks, Inc., I; 22 (upd.)
The Major Automotive Companies, Inc., 45
Masland Corporation, 17
Mazda Motor Corporation, 9; 23 (upd.)
Mel Farr Automotive Group, 20
Metso Corporation, 30 (upd.)
Midas International Corporation, 10

Mitsubishi Motors Corporation, 9; 23 (upd.)
Monaco Coach Corporation, 31
Monro Muffler Brake, Inc., 24
National R.V. Holdings, Inc., 32
Navistar International Corporation, I; 10 (upd.)
Nissan Motor Co., Ltd., I; 11 (upd.); 34 (upd.)
O'Reilly Automotive, Inc., 26
Officine Alfieri Maserati S.p.A., 13
Oshkosh Truck Corporation, 7
Paccar Inc., I
PACCAR Inc., 26 (upd.)
Pennzoil Company, 20 (upd.)
Penske Corporation, 19 (upd.)
The Pep Boys—Manny, Moe & Jack, 11; 36 (upd.)
Peugeot S.A., I
Piaggio & C. S.p.A., 20
Porsche AG, 13; 31 (upd.)
PSA Peugeot Citroen S.A., 28 (upd.)
Regie Nationale des Usines Renault, I
Renault S.A., 26 (upd.)
Republic Industries, Inc., 26
Robert Bosch GmbH., I; 16 (upd.); 43 (upd.)
RockShox, Inc., 26
Rockwell Automation, 43 (upd.)
Rolls-Royce plc, I; 21 (upd.)
Rover Group Ltd., 7; 21 (upd.)
Saab Automobile AB, 32 (upd.)
Saab-Scania A.B., I; 11 (upd.)
Safelite Glass Corp., 19
Saturn Corporation, 7; 21 (upd.)
Sealed Power Corporation, I
Sheller-Globe Corporation, I
Sixt AG, 39
Skoda Auto a.s., 39
Spartan Motors Inc., 14
SpeeDee Oil Change and Tune-Up, 25
SPX Corporation, 10; 47 (upd.)
Standard Motor Products, Inc., 40
Superior Industries International, Inc., 8
Suzuki Motor Corporation, 9; 23 (upd.)
Sytner Group plc, 45
Tower Automotive, Inc., 24
Toyota Motor Corporation, I; 11 (upd.); 38 (upd.)
TRW Inc., 14 (upd.)
Ugly Duckling Corporation, 22
United Auto Group, Inc., 26
United Technologies Automotive Inc., 15
Valeo, 23
Volkswagen Aktiengesellschaft, I; 11 (upd.); 32 (upd.)
Walker Manufacturing Company, 19
Winnebago Industries Inc., 7; 27 (upd.)
Ziebart International Corporation, 30

BEVERAGES

A & W Brands, Inc., 25
Adolph Coors Company, I; 13 (upd.); 36 (upd.)
Allied Domecq PLC, 29
Allied-Lyons PLC, I
Anchor Brewing Company, 47
Anheuser-Busch Companies, Inc., I; 10 (upd.); 34 (upd.)
Asahi Breweries, Ltd., I; 20 (upd.)
Bacardi Limited, 18
Banfi Products Corp., 36
Baron Philippe de Rothschild S.A., 39
Bass PLC, I; 15 (upd.); 38 (upd.)
BBAG Osterreichische Brau-Beteiligungs-AG, 38
Beringer Wine Estates Holdings, Inc., 22

Boston Beer Company, 18
Brauerei Beck & Co., 9; 33 (upd.)
Brown-Forman Corporation, I; 10 (upd.); 38 (upd.)
Canandaigua Brands, Inc., 34 (upd.)
Canandaigua Wine Company, Inc., 13
Carlsberg A/S, 9; 29 (upd.)
Carlton and United Breweries Ltd., I
Casa Cuervo, S.A. de C.V., 31
Cerveceria Polar, I
The Chalone Wine Group, Ltd., 36
Coca Cola Bottling Co. Consolidated, 10
The Coca-Cola Company, I; 10 (upd.); 32 (upd.)
Corby Distilleries Limited, 14
D.G. Yuengling & Son, Inc., 38
Dean Foods Company, 21 (upd.)
Distillers Company PLC, I
Dr Pepper/Seven Up, Inc., 9; 32 (upd.)
E. & J. Gallo Winery, I; 7 (upd.); 28 (upd.)
Ferolito, Vultaggio & Sons, 27
Florida's Natural Growers, 45
Foster's Brewing Group Ltd., 7; 21 (upd.)
Fuller Smith & Turner P.L.C., 38
G. Heileman Brewing Company Inc., I
The Gambrinus Company, 40
Geerlings & Wade, Inc., 45
General Cinema Corporation, I
Golden State Vintners, Inc., 33
Grand Metropolitan PLC, I
Green Mountain Coffee, Inc., 31
The Greenalls Group PLC, 21
Greene King plc, 31
Grupo Modelo, S.A. de C.V., 29
Guinness/UDV, I; 43 (upd.)
The Hain Celestial Group, Inc., 43 (upd.)
Hansen Natural Corporation, 31
Heineken N.V, I; 13 (upd.); 34 (upd.)
Heublein, Inc., I
Hiram Walker Resources, Ltd., I
Interbrew S.A., 17
Jacob Leinenkugel Brewing Company, 28
JD Wetherspoon plc, 30
Karlsberg Brauerei GmbH & Co KG, 41
Kendall-Jackson Winery, Ltd., 28
Kikkoman Corporation, 14
Kirin Brewery Company, Limited, I; 21 (upd.)
König Brauerei GmbH & Co. KG, 35 (upd.)
Labatt Brewing Company Limited, I; 25 (upd.)
Laurent-Perrier SA, 42
Maison Louis Jadot, 24
Marchesi Antinori SRL, 42
Marie Brizard & Roger International S.A., 22
MBC Holding Company, 40
Miller Brewing Company, I; 12 (upd.)
The Minute Maid Company, 28
Moët-Hennessy, I
The Molson Companies Limited, I, 26 (upd.)
National Beverage Corp., 26
National Grape Cooperative Association, Inc., 20
Nichols plc, 44
Ocean Spray Cranberries, Inc., 25 (upd.)
Odwalla, Inc., 31
Panamerican Beverages, Inc., 47
Paulaner Brauerei GmbH & Co. KG, 35
Peet's Coffee & Tea, Inc., 38
The Pepsi Bottling Group, Inc., 40
Pepsico, Inc., I; 10 (upd.); 38 (upd.)
Pernod Ricard S.A., I; 21 (upd.)
Pete's Brewing Company, 22
Philip Morris Companies Inc., 18 (upd.)
Pyramid Breweries Inc., 33

BIOTECHNOLOGY

CHEMICALS

CONGLOMERATES

CONSTRUCTION

FINANCIAL SERVICES: BANKS

FINANCIAL SERVICES: NON-BANKS

HEALTH & PERSONAL CARE PRODUCTS

HEALTH CARE SERVICES

INSURANCE

LEGAL SERVICES

MANUFACTURING

MATERIALS

MINING & METALS

PERSONAL SERVICES

PETROLEUM

PUBLISHING & PRINTING

REAL ESTATE

RETAIL & WHOLESALE

TEXTILES & APPAREL

UTILITIES

WASTE SERVICES

GEOGRAPHIC INDEX

Geographic Index

Germany

NOTES ON CONTRIBUTORS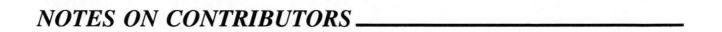

Notes on Contributors

BAXTER, Melissa Rigney. Indiana-based freelance writer.

BIANCO, David P. Freelance writer.

BROWN, Susan Windisch. Freelance writer and editor.

BRYNILDSSEN, Shawna. Freelance writer and editor based in Bloomington, Indiana.

COHEN, M. L. Novelist and freelance writer living in Paris.

COVELL, Jeffrey L. Freelance writer and corporate history contractor.

DINGER, Ed. Freelance writer and editor based in Brooklyn, New York.

HALASZ, Robert. Former editor in chief of *World Progress* and *Funk & Wagnalls New Encyclopedia Yearbook*; author, *The U.S. Marines* (Millbrook Press, 1993).

INGRAM, Frederick C. South Carolina-based business writer who has contributed to *GSA Business, Appalachian Trailway News,* the *Encyclopedia of Business,* the *Encyclopedia of Global Industries,* the *Encyclopedia of Consumer Brands,* and other regional and trade publications.

LORENZ, Sarah Ruth. Minnesota-based freelance writer.

MEYER, Steve. Freelance writer living in Missoula, Montana.

PEIPPO, Kathleen. Minneapolis-based freelance writer.

ROTHBURD, Carrie. Freelance writer and editor specializing in corporate profiles, academic texts, and academic journal articles.

SALAMIE, David E. Part-owner of InfoWorks Development Group, a reference publication development and editorial services company.

TRADII, Mary. Freelance writer based in Denver, Colorado.

UHLE, Frank. Ann Arbor-based freelance writer; movie projectionist, disc jockey, and staff member of *Psychotronic Video* magazine.

WALDEN, David M. Freelance writer and historian in Salt Lake City; adjunct history instructor at Salt Lake City Community College.

WOODWARD, A. Freelance writer.